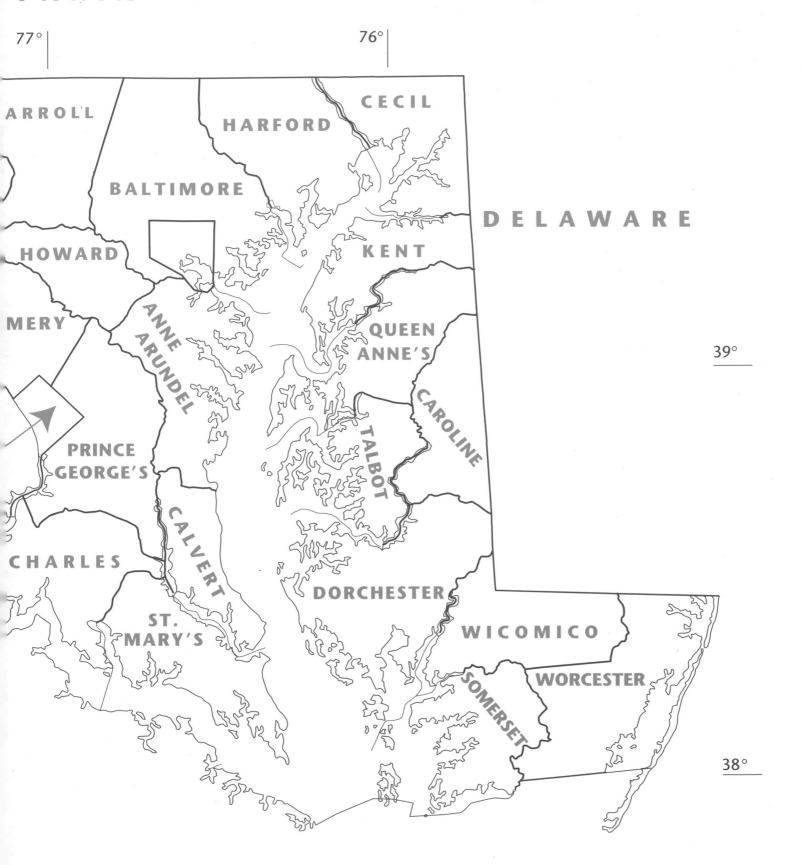

VANIA

77°   76°

ARROLL

HARFORD   CECIL

BALTIMORE

DELAWARE

HOWARD   KENT

MERY

ANNE ARUNDEL   QUEEN ANNE'S

39°

CAROLINE

PRINCE GEORGE'S   TALBOT

CHARLES   CALVERT

DORCHESTER

ST. MARY'S   WICOMICO

SOMERSET   WORCESTER

38°

Atlas of the Breeding Birds of Maryland and the District of Columbia

Pitt Series in Nature and Natural History

Atlas of the Breeding Birds of Maryland and the District of Columbia

Chandler S. Robbins, *Senior Editor*

Eirik A. T. Blom, *Project Coordinator*

University of Pittsburgh Press

Pittsburgh

Published by the University of Pittsburgh Press, Pittsburgh, Pa. 15260

Copyright © 1996, University of Pittsburgh Press

All rights reserved

Manufactured in the United States of America

Printed on acid-free paper

10 9 8 7 6 5 4 3 2 1

Library of Congress Cataloging-in-Publication Data

Atlas of the breeding birds of Maryland and the District of Columbia /

    Chandler S. Robbins, senior editor ; Eirik A. T. Blom, project coordinator.

      p.   cm.— (Pitt series in nature and natural history)

    "A project of the Maryland Ornithological Society and the Maryland

    Department of Natural Resources."

    Includes bibliographical references (p.   ) and index.

    ISBN 0-8229-3923-1 (cl : alk. paper)

    1. Birds—Maryland.   2. Birds—Washington (D.C.)   3. Bird popula-

tions—Maryland.   4. Bird populations—Washington (D.C.)   5. Birds—

Maryland—Geographical distribution—Maps.   6. Birds—Wash-

ington (D.C.)—Geographical distribution—Maps.   I. Robbins,

Chandler S.   II. Blom, Eirik A. T.   III. Maryland Ornithological

Society.   IV. Maryland. Dept. of Natural Resources.   V. Series.

QL684.M3A85   1996

598.29752—dc20   96-2425

A CIP catalog record for this book is available from the British Library.

Contents

List of Figures and Tables

Preface

More than any other creatures, birds are early indicators of the health of the environment. Small, fragile, and with rapid metabolism, they are susceptible to even minor changes in the surroundings. Miners knew this years ago when they kept canaries nearby while working underground. The birds respond more rapidly to changes in air quality than do humans, and if the canaries died the miners would know the air had become poisoned. A more recent warning was given when raptors declined dramatically in the 1950s for no apparent reason; in solving this riddle, scientists uncovered the pervasive effects of DDT. Birds were among the first victims of this new environmental peril, and early recognition of their plight gave humans time to ban this insecticide in North America before the environment was irreversibly damaged. Today, ecologists throughout the world study the robustness of bird populations for clues about the condition of the birds' environments because these are also our own environments.

This *Atlas* was created because the Maryland Ornithological Society (MOS) and the Maryland Department of Natural Resources (DNR) wanted to establish an accurate baseline of data for future studies. They believed it was important to determine the breeding distribution of birds throughout Maryland and the District of Columbia. They knew that those involved in conservation, land-use planning, education, science, and assessing the impact of the changing environment needed this essential information. They thought the material would be useful to government officials, concerned citizens, business executives, scientists, and amateur naturalists. Finally, they felt an urgent need to document Maryland's ornithological heritage because of the rapid changes that are occurring in land use (especially in the suburban counties) and leading to the disappearance of many birds from their former haunts.

The foundation of this *Atlas* is five years of intensive fieldwork undertaken by about eight hundred volunteers from 1983 through 1987. The fieldwork was carefully planned by professional wildlife biologists to meet standards and conventions for atlas projects. The field observers achieved over 99 percent coverage of the study area and generated over 100,000 records, each of which was reviewed before being added to the database or being used to update existing records. After duplicate data were removed and records were updated, the Atlas database contained 91,876 records. In addition to the field records, the *Atlas* includes historical distribution data collected since the mid-1800s, nest records collected over the past 100 years, data from Breeding Bird Censuses (BBC) conducted since 1942, trend data from Breeding Bird Surveys (BBS) conducted since 1966, and relative-abundance information from miniroute data collected since 1983. Every analysis, conclusion, or statement in this *Atlas* was reviewed for accuracy and clarity by nearly a dozen wildlife biologists or experienced birdwatchers. The result is an important scientific contribution that describes the status, distribution, and nesting habits of the 201 species of birds that were found breeding in Maryland and the District of Columbia from 1983 through 1987.

This *Atlas* is the result of tens of thousands of hours of work in the field, in libraries, in file rooms, at computer terminals, and at kitchen tables. Virtually all the effort was volunteered by dedicated birdwatchers seeking to create an exceptional document. They have succeeded. On behalf of everyone who will use this *Atlas,* I thank them.

John G. Malcolm
President, MOS

Coordinator's Message

Atlasing has been at the center of my professional life for more than a decade. It started in 1978 when Bob Ringler, Jim Stasz, and I organized and coordinated the breeding bird atlas of Baltimore County, and it continued with the formation and fieldwork of the Carroll and Garrett county atlas projects. The data from those efforts have been incorporated into this *Atlas*. I became the coordinator of the Maryland/DC Atlas project in 1983.

From 1978 through 1987, I spent every summer (except 1982) atlasing breeding birds in Maryland. I spent the fall and winter months editing data, and the springs traveling to regional meetings with volunteers. I enjoyed every minute of it, and along the way I learned a lot.

I learned that thousands of Maryland citizens who know little or nothing about birds care passionately about the environment. They were generous with their time and with permission to enter their land. They offered encouragement, introductions to other landowners, and, frequently, a glass of iced tea on a hot summer afternoon. They asked nothing in return, and most will never know how important this project was or what far-reaching effects it will have.

I learned that the overwhelming majority of owners and employees of private businesses, clubs, and organizations believe in preserving our natural heritage. The concern that an endangered species found breeding on their property would disrupt their lives may have entered their minds, but it did not stop them from granting permission to fieldworkers. Some even made financial contributions to the Atlas, without which we might have foundered. Most public debate does not permit us to see beyond a single issue or to understand how often people are willing to do what they think is right, even if it is difficult.

I learned that railing against the government and the bureaucracy is an American tradition, but that working with one can be a pleasure. The Maryland state government, through the Department of Natural Resources, adopted the Atlas project with a commitment that carried us through many uncertain times. They found the major portion of the necessary funding, but that was only part of the story. Scores of DNR employees contributed, from department heads to park managers. Routinely, they found solutions to problems: access to land, places to stay, use of boats and four-wheel drive vehicles, computer programs and programmers for handling and manipulating data, and much more. Over and over when we came to an Atlas board meeting with a problem, they would say, "Let us check into that and get back to you." They always came back with a solution. In addition, they supplied us with information from their own work, such as studies on colonial waterbirds, waterfowl, Bald Eagles, Osprey, Ruffed Grouse, Wild Turkey, American Woodcock, and raptors. Digging out data we needed took time and effort, and much of it was done after working hours and on weekends. Behind the rules and regulations are exceptionally dedicated people, and their contributions underpin every aspect of this project.

I learned a great deal about the dedication of the Maryland Ornithological Society and its members. It was from the MOS that we drew the bulk of the almost eight hundred volunteers who did the fieldwork. In every chapter we found individuals eager to take the responsibility of coordinating the atlasing in their counties. These local coordinators recruited fieldworkers, dispensed materials, collected data, checked discrepancies, spent days on the phone, and ran up postage bills. Their energy drove the Atlas with a force we could never have generated at the state level.

The coordinators provided the drive, but the heart of this project was the volunteers who did the fieldwork. The raw figures are impressive: over 100,000 records, 99 percent coverage, five years of fieldwork. Raw figures, however, do not tell how these feats were accomplished. People with careers, families, and a host of obligations committed weekend after precious summer weekend to the task. They did it with a determination to reach and exceed coverage goals we frankly thought were impossible when we set them. They did it without complaint—scouring fields and woodlots and scrub patches, wringing every last bird out of the block. And then they went back to try for one more. And one more after that. Not one demanded recognition for his or her efforts. They taught us a lot about selflessness. They were the Atlas project. We have worked hard to produce a book worthy of their effort, but the pride of accomplishment is theirs. There is no way to say how much I admire every one of them. You folks are the best.

There is also no way to thank all the people who sat on the board throughout this project. Month after month, year after year, they attended meetings. They took on a seemingly endless series of difficult and time-consuming jobs without hesitation or reward. They did all the things I failed to do. To name one would be unfair to the rest, but I am grateful to all of them.

I learned something about birds, too. I learned that atlasing begins where most birdwatching ends, with the identification of the species. I saw the courtship of Downy Woodpeckers, the home life of the Wood Thrush, the territorial battles of Grasshopper Sparrows. I learned to predict which woodlot would have an Acadian Flycatcher, which field would have an Eastern Meadowlark, which pond would have a Green Heron. I had the pleasure of sharing these discoveries with other people, trading stories and ideas, and sharing the excitement of observing birds in a new way. In the end I got a lot more than I gave. It was a great ten years, and I would not have missed it for anything.

Rick Blom
Project Coordinator

Acknowledgments

A project of this magnitude, with years of planning, field-work, and publication preparation, required the help and cooperation of many people and organizations. Without this support this Atlas project would not have been completed.

The **Planning and Advisory Board** (later the *Advisory Board*) laid the foundation for the project and directed the effort through publication. Original board members Danny Bystrak, John Cullom, M. Kathleen Klimkiewicz, Robert F. Ringler, Chandler S. Robbins, and Gary J. Taylor were later joined by additional members: Eirik A. T. Blom, Martha Chestem, Jane H. Farrell, Mark L. Hoffman, Emily D. Joyce, John G. Malcolm, D. Ann Rasberry, Joanne K. Solem, Glenn D. Therres, and Tony White.

Atlas committees were formed to assist in the execution of the Atlas project. The committees and their members follow. *Technical:* Danny Bystrak, M. Kathleen Klimkiewicz, John A. Gregoire, Robert Hilton, Paul F. Leifer, David W. Mehlman, Carol Swartz, Gary J. Taylor, Glenn D. Therres, and Charles R. Vaughn. *Training:* Chandler S. Robbins, Richard O. Bray, James W. Cheevers, William Ellis, Alex Hammer, Helene Hammer, Sue Ridd, and the original members of the Planning and Advisory Board. *Publicity and Newsletter:* Tony White, Jon E. Boone, Emily D. Joyce, Paul F. Leifer, Byron Swift, and Joy G. Wheeler. *Budget and Fund Raising:* John Cullom and Delos C. Dupree. *Editing:* Paul F. Leifer and Wayne Klockner. *Verification:* Robert F. Ringler, Eirik A. T. Blom, Danny Bystrak, M. Kathleen Klimkiewicz, and Chandler S. Robbins. *Blockbusting:* David W. Holmes and the original members of the Planning and Advisory Board. *Computer:* David W. Mehlman, John C. Barber, M. Kathleen Klimkiewicz, Randolph Stadler, Glenn D. Therres, Charles R. Vaughn, and Tony White. *Publication:* Chandler S. Robbins and M. Kathleen Klimkiewicz. *Miniroutes:* D. Daniel Boone and Danny Bystrak.

The **Maryland Ornithological Society** (MOS) was a driving force and an enthusiastic supporter of the Atlas project. During the planning stage and throughout the first year of fieldwork, it provided the bulk of the financial support. The MOS organized special fund-raising events at annual conferences and through matching grants. It provided housing at its tum Suden Sanctuary in Harford County for the project coordinator and allowed the Atlas project to use its mailing permit. Not only did the state organization provide assistance, but the local chapters made financial contributions and funded the activities of the local coordinators. The vast majority of fieldworkers were MOS members. The *MOS presidents* during the project focused this effort. From the beginning of the project through publication submission, the presidents were John Cullom, Martha K. Chestem, Tony White, Robert F. Ringler, and John G. Malcolm.

The **Department of Natural Resources** (DNR), State of Maryland, was the other driving force and the primary financial provider. This money was from the revenue generated from hunting licenses and from Federal Aid in Wildlife Restoration funds provided by an excise tax on guns and ammunition. The DNR provided not only computer services—with storage and retrieval capabilities and personnel to assist—but also boats, camping facilities, and free access to DNR lands. Especially important in the state involvement were Gary J. Taylor, who secured state participation and funding; Glenn D. Therres and Mark L. Hoffman, who developed and maintained the database; and D. Ann Rasberry, who did the mapping, maintained the personal computer database, and did the conversion routines. They were assisted by Mary A. Garner, who verified the database, and Carol R. Johnson, who keypunched the data. Additionally, state-funded research projects provided invaluable assistance. These include the Colonial Waterbird Project—an inventory of colonial nesting waterbirds by David F. Brinker and Joan McKearnan—and a distributional study of rails and other marsh birds by Harold L. Wierenga. The Maryland Natural Heritage Program generously allowed the Atlas to use 24 drawings done for them by Michael O'Brien.

County coordinators were invaluable in the fieldwork part of the Atlas project. They recruited fieldworkers, assured that records were accurate, and directed the fieldwork. Their counties and names follow. *Allegany:* Thomas P. Mathews and Robert Paterson. *Anne Arundel:* James W. Cheevers. *Baltimore:* Eirik A. T. Blom, Robert W. Dixon, Robert F. Ringler, James L. Stasz, and Joy G. Wheeler. *Calvert:* James L. Stasz and Dwight F. Williams. *Caroline:* Marvin W. Hewitt. *Carroll:* William Ellis and Robert F. Ringler. *Cecil:* Clark F. Jeschke. *Charles:* George B. Wilmot. *Dorchester:* Marvin W. Hewitt, Donald W. Meritt, and Sam Droege. *Frederick:* David H. Wallace. *Garrett:* Frances B.

Pope. *Harford:* William A. Russell, Jr. and Jamie Rapaport. *Howard:* Delos C. Dupree and Jane H. Farrell. *Kent:* Stephen B. Hitchner, Floyd L. Parks, and Ed Soutiere. *Montgomery:* Keith D. Van Ness, Jr. *Prince George's:* John A. Gregoire. *Queen Anne's:* Marvin W. Hewitt, Donald W. Meritt, and Eirik A. T. Blom. *St. Mary's:* Ernest J. Willoughby. *Somerset:* Charles R. Vaughn. *Talbot:* Donald W. Meritt. *Washington:* Theodore J. Banvard. *Wicomico:* Charles R. Vaughn. *Worcester:* Robert F. Ringler. *Washington, DC:* Dave Czaplak and Byron Swift.

The **U.S. Fish and Wildlife Service** (USFWS) provided trend graphs from the Breeding Bird Survey (BBS), miniroute maps, maps showing the 1958 distribution, and library assistance. Bruce Peterjohn provided the BBS data, John R. Sauer designed the analysis program, and Paul and Barbara Keywood prepared the graphs. Danny Bystrak designed and directed the miniroute project, Sam Droege generated the maps showing relative abundance, and Susan Liga and Kinard Boone prepared the final copies for publication. Chandler S. Robbins edited the 1958 maps and prepared final publication copies. Ralph Andrews, Sam Droege, R. Michael Erwin, M. Kathleen Klimkiewicz, Jerry Longcore, and Richard L. Jachowski reviewed portions of the manuscript. Two USFWS research projects conducted in Maryland during the Atlas period directly benefited the Atlas. One was a study of breeding bird populations in a random sample of isolated mature woodlots (Robbins et al. 1989a). The other was an intensive study of a 2 percent random sample of Maryland Atlas blocks designed to test the efficiency of atlasers in detecting the various breeding species (Robbins and Dowell 1989). Lynda J. Garrett and Wanda Manning assisted with locating references and completing and verifying literature citations.

Numerous **special projects** contributed to the completion of the Atlas. A. Blair Jones III, Virginia Department of Game and Inland Fisheries, provided computer programming for mapping. Kimberly Titus's study of the breeding ecology of birds of prey in western Maryland provided valuable data. D. Daniel Boone, Danny Bystrak, Sam Droege, and John R. Sauer wrote portions of the introduction to the *Atlas* dealing with the presettlement forest of Maryland, BBS trend graphs, and miniroutes. The following persons and institutions provided access to nest record files or compiled nest record data: Gregory S. Butcher and James D. Lowe, Cornell Library of Ornithology; Lloyd F. Kiff and Dawn Mautner, Western Foundation of Vertebrate Zoology; Kenneth C. Parkes, Carnegie Museum of Natural History; David M. Niles, Delaware Museum of Natural History; and Bonnie Farmer, National Museum of Natural History. Work on the newsletter was done by Tony White and Edward D. Fingerhood, with the World Wildlife Fund providing technical assistance. Lucy and Nancy MacClintock prepared the index. The following individuals assisted with other special projects: Joy A. Aso, Sam Atcherson, Clark Austin, Maud Banks, Marty Barron, Polly Batchelder, Lana Beers, Connie Bockstie, D. Daniel Boone, David F. Brinker, Joseph B. Byrnes, Danny Bystrak, Lois Carleton, Martha Chestem, Eileen Clegg, Dianne Cohan, Paul Connell, John Cullom, Deanna K. Dawson, Lonnie Dorgan, Sam Droege, Delos C. Dupree, Jane H. Farrell, Alfred T. Fitch, George L. Fortwengler, Jr., Anthony G. Futcher, Diane Gansauer, Kevin Gillen, Jennifer Gieg, Kim Gross, Terry Hallinger, Mark Johnson, Michael Kerwin, Barbara Keywood, Gerald S. Kleiman, M. Kathleen Klimkiewicz, David Kubitsky, Nancy Magnusson, John G. Malcolm, Elwood M. Martin, Helen Meleney, Marjorie Mountjoy, William L. Murphy, Jay T. Nelson, M. Suzanne Probst, Donald E. Randle, Janet Randle, D. Ann Rasberry, Chandler S. Robbins, John R. Sauer, Lynn Schoenholtz, Paula Schugam, Elise Seay, Scott A. Smith, Joanne K. Solem, Robert P. Solem, Thomas J. Solomon, Jeff Spendelow, James L. Stasz, Eva Sunell, Glenn D. Therres, Sandra A. Turner, Jan Westervelt, Guy W. Willey, Sr., Kurt Wollenberg, Michele Wright, Helen Zeichner, and Gregg Zuberbier.

Species account authors did research on each species, explained the history of the species in the state, and provided a narrative account. The account authors are Eirik A. T. Blom, D. Daniel Boone, David F. Brinker, James W. Cheevers, Martha Chestem, Mary F. Clarkson, Steve Clarkson, John Cullom, Dave Czaplak, Lynn M. Davidson, Barbara A. Dowell, Sam Droege, Delos C. Dupree, Frederick W. Fallon, Jane H. Farrell, Alfred J. Fletcher, John A. Gregoire, David A. Harvey, Robert Hilton, Stephen B. Hitchner, Ann S. Hobbs, Mark L. Hoffman, David W. Holmes, Clark F. Jeschke, Emily D. Joyce, M. Kathleen Klimkiewicz, Elwood M. Martin, Thomas P. Mathews, Joan McKearnon, Donald W. Meritt, Claire E. Miller, William L. Murphy, Michael O'Brien, D. Ann Rasberry, Jan G. Reese, Sue A. Ricciardi, Robert F. Ringler, Chandler S. Robbins, William A. Russell, Jr., John R. Sauer, Frances C. Saunders, Norman C. Saunders, David R. Smith, Scott A. Smith, Joanne K. Solem, James L. Stasz, Nancy J. Stewart, Byron Swift, Glenn D. Therres, Kimberly Titus, Keith D. Van Ness, Jr., Charles R. Vaughn, Jack Wennerstrom, Harold L. Wierenga, James R. Wilkinson, Ernest J. Willoughby, George B. Wilmot, Sue Yingling, Elizabeth E. Zucker.

Species account artists added visual beauty to accounts with an accurate drawing of each species. Michael O'Brien coordinated the artists. The artists are Roy H. Brown, Melinda Byrd, Patricia J. Moore, Gail Mundis, Michael O'Brien, M. Suzanne Probst, Andrea Robbins, Edith R. Thompson, and Marilu Tousignaut.

Sizable **grants** from the *Chesapeake Bay Trust* and from the *Maryland DNR Tidewater Administration* made publication of the *Atlas* possible.

Contributors of $100 or more supplied valuable support; many of these contributions were made in response to urgent appeals. These contributors are as follows:

Allegany County Chapter, MOS
Elting Arnold
Mrs. C. H. Asmis
Atlantic Seabirds
Audubon Naturalist Society
Addison and Patricia Ball
Baltimore Bird Club, MOS
Baltimore Gas & Electric Company
Henry Bielstein
Buchanon Estate
Lois Carleton
Chesapeake Bay Trust
Martha Chestem
Gerald Cotton
Mrs. Edwin Crocker
John and Lettie Cullom
Frances J. Ehlers
Robin English Advertising
William and Gladys Faherty
Jane H. Farrell
Henry Fleckenstein, Jr.
Frederick County Chapter, MOS
Dr. Mildred E. Gebhard
Shirley Geddes
Robert Hilton
Howard County Chapter, MOS
Heidi Hughes
George M. Jett
Kent County Chapter, MOS
M. Kathleen Klimkiewicz
C. Haven Kolb, Jr., and Mary Kolb
Bruce and Felicia Lovelett
Nancy MacClintock
John G. Malcolm
Maryland Ornithological Society
Montgomery County Chapter, MOS
Robert W. Moss
Commander and Mrs. E. R. Mumford
Oregon Ridge Nature Center Council
Patuxent Chapter, MOS

Frances B. Pope
Mrs. John W. Poteet, Jr.
Chandler S. Robbins
Lester Simon
Turbit H. C. and Edwardine G. Slaughter
Joanne Smale and John Smale, Jr.
Robert P. and Joanne K. Solem
Southern Maryland Audubon
Wallace and Joan Stephens
Janet Sundby
Byron Swift
Dave Thorndill
Eileen Train and the Honorable Russell Train
David H. Wallace
John Wanuga
Washington County Chapter, MOS
Mike Welch
Tony White
Erika M. Wilson

Other financial contributors also provided needed funds. They are as follows:

Jean B. Adamson
Don Allison
Anne Arundel Bird Club, MOS
Maryanne C. Bach
Harold F. Baker
Faye I. Barnes
L. Barnes
Allison Barrett
Mrs. Ralph W. Beach
Ben Oaks Garden Club
John A. Bjerke
Judith M. Blake
John and Martha Blaisdell
Jim Blanchard
John and Marjorie Blodgett
Liz Bobo
Cynthia A. Bocian
Marion W. Boggs
Peggy Bohanan
Michael Bowen
Edna Boyce

Hervey Brackbill
Marian L. Brennan
Winston T. Brundige
Eunice E. Burdette
Chris Burnett
Susan Buswell
John Canoles
Kate H. Carlson
Caroline Chapter, MOS
Mr. and Mrs. Robert Caswell
Norman H. Chamberlin
Cedarcroft Garden Club
James W. Cheevers
Patricia Chiles
Steve Clarkson
John and Eileen Clegg
Richard S. Cleveland
Mr. and Mrs. John W. Coffman
Dwight and Serene Collmos
Dianne Cohan
Don Conley
Robert and Ann Coren
Elizabeth Crayford
Irwin and Florence Cromwell
James S. Cromwell, Jr.
Mary Crosby
Richard Cummings
James W. Davison
Jane Decker
Dorothy DeCrette
William and Louise Dove
D. D. Dowling
Truman and Leontine Doyle
Sam Droege
Margaret L. Duncan
Robert B. DuVal
Wes and Susan Earp
Muriel Eastman
Rodger Eastman
Gerald E. Einem
Roswell Eldridge
Gene Evans
Dr. Virginia J. Evans
Else Fawcett
James and Eleanor Ferris
Linda Fields
Mrs. Ruth Finegan
Elwood L. Fisher

Lottie Fishpaw
Laddie Flyger
Robert B. Ford
Anna B. Forster
Judge Dulaney Foster
Robert and Alice Frandsen
Harvey E. Funkk
Pierre Gagne
Margo Garner
Lydia B. Geare
William and Sheila Gehrlein
Jane and Ralph Geuder
Ivan M. Gibbs
E. Fidelia Gilbert
Delores H. Grant
Mary B. Haas
J. Habert
Florence Haff
Margaret Haile
Harford Chapter, MOS
Al Haury
Mrs. William J. Hayden
Rosemary R. Hein
Dr. and Mrs. Thomas Herbert
Stephen B. Hitchner
Ann S. Hobbs
Lynn and Linda Holley
Mr. and Mrs. J. W. Hollis, Jr.
David W. Holmes
Pearl S. Hood
Ronnie Hooper
Charles A. Porter Hopkins
Thomas Horwath
Glory K. Houck
David R. Howell
Miriam B. Hubbert
Mary H. Humphreys
Dale and Nancy Huting
Cornelia Hyatt
Peter Jay
Peter Jayne
Helen Louise Johnson
Mark Johnson
Margaret Jones
Mary Alice Jost
Emily and Doug Joyce
Paul D. Jung
Cleo and Gus Karafas
Louis Kauffman
Mrs. Alexander Kauffman

Robert A. Keedy
Frederick H. Keer
Bill Keimig
Dr. James Kerr
Ruth C. Klein
Nell Koonce
Shepard Krech, Jr.
Howard Kulp
Chet and Margie Kupiec
Marcia Lakeman
Leo and Harriet Lathroum
Robert J. Lavell
Joyce Letaw
Lloyd and Dorothy Lewis
Paul and Marlee Lindon
Cynthia A. Lockley
Bernice Long
Hilton Long
Laura Sheridan Lyons
Gail B. MacKiernan
Mrs. Paul D. MacLean
Lt. Col. Charles R. Madary
Nancy Magnusson
Grace Mahanes
C. N. Mason
Diane Makuc
Jana McCallum
Minette McCullough
Mary W. McDavit
James C. McFalls, Jr.
Mr. and Mrs. John
    McKitterick
Irving Meade
Benjamin and Catherine
    Mehlman
Claire E. Miller
Patricia J. Moore
Susan D. Moran
Joanne Moroney
Georgia Morris
Mrs. Larry Morris, Jr.
Marjorie Mountjoy
Dorothy M. Mumford
Rosamond and C. G.
    Munro
Mrs. J. E. Murphy
Kenneth M. Nagler
Mrs. Orsen N. Nielsen
Capt. T. A. Nisewaner,
    USN (Ret)
Paul O'Brien
John D. Oetting

Llelanie S. Orcutt
Peter C. Osenton
Kenneth C. Otis
Jan Owings
Mary E. Paxton
David Perry
William and Dick Perry
Ella R. Pfeiffer
Marianne R. Phelps
Patricia Pidlaney
Marie H. Plante
Larry Pratt
Gilbert and Anne
    Pumphrey
Vivian E. Rall
Judy Ray
Kathrine Reed
Michael Reid
Erin Rosalie Reilly
Sue A. Ricciardi
William J. Richter
Susan E. Ridd
Rosamond Ridgley
Jon W. Robinson
Dr. R. C. and B. W. Rock
Leslie and Carolyn Roslund
Katherine Rowe
Bennett Y. Ryan, Jr.
Anthony J. Sacco
Florence Saito
Dr. Nancy L. Sasavage
Eugene J. Scarpulla
F. Schilling
Nicholas Schneider
Philip B. Schnering
R. Schoenhofer
Isobil Schum
Elise Seay
Winifred Sewell
Charles M. Shaneybrook
J. Shearer
William Showalter
Marjorie Skolnick
Michael L. Smith
Godwin Stevenson
H. G. Stevenson
Stoneleigh Garden Club
Thomas Strikwerda
Eva Sunell
Charles E. Swift
Thomas and Sallie Thayer
Helen Thompson

Mark Traversa
V. Edwin Unger
Charles R. Vaughn
Mary A. Vincett
Dr. Stewart H. Walker
Imogene Warden
Gayle Ware
William H. Weaver
Helen Webb
Betty Wells
Jack Wennerstrom
Dorothy K. Williams
John C. Williamson
George B. Wilmot
Michele M. Wright
William C. Young
Howard Youth
Mr. and Mrs. Alger Zapf, Jr.
Helen Zeichner
Lawrence Zeleny
Paul A. Zucker

Fieldworkers provided the extensive field data for each species; without these data the Atlas project would have failed. The fieldworkers are as follows:

Jackson M. Abbott
David Aborn
Larry Adams
Cary Adshead
Ms. Alden
Nancy Aldous
Burton J. Alexander
Donald T. Allen
W. Don Allison
Bob Altman
Jeff Anders
Samuel J. Anders, Jr.
Chet Anderson
Marianne Anderson
Paul Anecharico
Joyce Angleberger
Henry T. Armistead
Maralyn Ashcraft
Joy A. Aso
Stephen P. Atzert
Daniel Audet
Bob Augustine

Charles Baker
Margaret Baker
Marlene V. Ball
Maud Banks
Mary Bannister
Lawrence E. Banvard
Richard A. Banvard
Theodore J. Banvard
Cathrine Baptist
John C. Barber
Margaret M. Barber
Richard Barron
Edwin M. Barry
Pauline M. Batchelder
Chris Beaton
Genevieve S. Beck
Lana Beers
Edward A. Behr
Marcia W. Behr
Wayne H. Bell
Carol Belton
Alice Bender
Deborah Bennett
Melvin D. Bennett
Gilbert Berry
Susan Betterly
Lance Biechele
Warren Bielenberg
Anne Bishop
John A. Bjerke
Judith M. Blake
Ed Blazek
Bryan J. Blazie
Eirik A. T. Blom
Maria Bochicchio
Peggy Bohanan
David J. Bohaska
Paula W. Bohaska
Chip Bonde
D. Daniel Boone
Jon E. Boone
Jon K. Boone
Emmy Bortwick
Mark Bortwick
Joan Boudreau
Albert Bourgeois
Steven Boyce
Elsie I. Brady
David Brandes
Richard O. Bray
Steven W. Brennan
David F. Brinker

Carol Broderick
Donald H. Broderick
Marie Brooks-Demudd
Roy H. Brown
W. Hayes Brown
Chandra L. Bruce
Douglas A. Bruce
Walter M. Bryant
Margaret V. Bullock
Barbara Burg
Frederick Burggraf
Karen Burggraf
Daniel Burns
Renee Burns
Enid Busse
William Busse
Wade Butler
Joseph B. Byrnes
Danny Bystrak
Stephen P. Cardano
Skip Carlson
Linda A. Cashman
Anthony L. Casucci
Robert L. Caswell
Norman H. Chamberlin
Betty Chance
Robert C. Chance
James W. Cheevers
Martha Chestem
Patricia Chiles
Wanda T. Ciekot
Edward A. Clark
Eileen Clegg
John Clegg
George Cleland
Richard S. Cleveland
Lester Coble
Amelia Cochran
Roger M. Cole
Serene Q. Collmos
Cora Ann Condrey
Thomas J. Congersky
Mary C. Corderman
Roscoe D. Corderman
Scott Crabtree
Patricia A. Craig
Bonnie Craighead
Mildred Crewe
Anna Crowe
Jean Crump
James Cubie
John Cullom

David Cummings
Carol Cunningham
Dave Czaplak
Kathy Dale
Elizabeth A. Daniel
Sonia Dapper
Vivian Dauciunas
Lucy David
Lynn M. Davidson
Anneke Davis
Charles Davis
D. Maurice Davis
Mariam Davis
Robert H. Davis
Deanna K. Dawson
L. Edward DeMoll
Ruth Denit
Leland Devore
Joe DiDonato
Alverta Dillon
Louise Dillon
Robert W. Dixon
Richard J. Dolesh
Margaret T. Donnald
Morrill B. Donnald
Bradley D. Dorf
Lonnie Dorgan
Sue Dorney
Christina H. Dorset
Alexis Doster III
Barbara A. Dowell
Robert J. Doyle
Truman L. Doyle
Susan Drake
Lisa Drees
Sam Droege
Paul G. DuMont
Margaret L. Duncan
Betty Dunlop
Delos C. Dupree
Samuel H. Dyke
Julie Dzaack
Georgia Eacker
Leslie Ray Eastman
William Eckert
Diane Eckles
Nancy Edwards
Jeffrey Effinger
Graham Egerton
Frances J. Ehlers
Gerald E. Einem
Cathy Elliott

William Ellis
Clint Englander
Ethel Q. Engle
Josephine C. Engle
Wilber Engle
Jeanette Evans
C. Faanes
Gladys W. Faherty
William J. Faherty
John H. Fales
Frederick W. Fallon
Bonnie Farmer
Jane H. Farrell
Alice Fazekas
Barbara Feaga
Ilia Fehrer
George Fenwick
Christine R. Ferrand
Helen Ferrand
Herbert Ferrand
Edward Fingerhood
Linda L. Finn
Diane Finnel
Emily Fintel
William A. Fintel
Stan Fisher
Mildred Fitez
Kerry Fitzpatrick
Allen Flanigan
Alfred J. Fletcher
Roberta B. Fletcher
Harold Henry Fogleman, Jr.
Harold Henry Fogleman, Sr.
Charlotte L. Folk
Kristine Folker
Robert V. Folker
Bob Ford
Helen Ford
John C. Ford, Jr.
Stephen M. Ford
Gail Frantz
Laura French
Bonnie Friend
Jean L. Fry
Larry R. Fry
Marchal Fuller
Stan Fuller
William S. Fuller
Cora Fulton
Anthony G. Futcher
Carolyn Gamble
Mark S. Garland

D. Gauthey
Shirley Geddes
Sheila E. Gehrlein
William V. Gehrlein
Bill Geise
Jane Geuder
Ralph Geuder
Carol Ghebelian
Richard M. Giannola
Dick Gibbs
Rob Gibbs
Helen Gibson
William M. Giese, Jr.
Florence Giffin
E. Fidelia Gilbert
Jeanne Gilbert
Jeff Gilbert
Liz Rees Gilbert
Kevin Gillen
Ellen Gizzarelli
Inez G. Glime
Luther C. Goldman
Steven Goodbred, Jr.
Steven Goodbred, Sr.
Sandra Goolsby
Greg Gough
Virginia S. Graebert
Mildred Graham
Delores H. Grant
Susan Gray
Beulah Green
Jim Green
Morris M. Green, Jr.
Rosanell Green
Irene Greenfield
John A. Gregoire
Suzanne M. Gregoire
Mike Gregory
Sandi Gregory
Flo Griffin
Frank Griffin
Jeff Griffith
Liz Griffith
James G. Gruber
Patricia Gruber
Eilene Gruys
Robert H. Hahn
Deborah Hall
Alex Hammer
Helene Hammer
Pauline Hancock
Christopher D. Handley

Marvin L. Hann
Evan Hannay
Hugh K. Hanson
Sally Hanson
Dave Hansroth
Bollinger Hardiman
Willie Harris
Mike Harrison
Linda Harsey
Stephen Harsey
Anne Hart
Kenneth Hart
Elizabeth Hartline
David A. Harvey
Paul Hastings
John B. Hattrup
Margaret I. Hawk
Woody Hawkins
Anthony J. Heatwole
Kevin Heffernan
Richard Hegner
Scott J. Heim
John Hench
Inez Henley
Mr. Henline
Marvin W. Hewitt
Hazel Hignutt
Charles Hill
James P. Hill
Robert Hilton
Larry Hindman
Rev. George Hipkins
Stephen B. Hitchner
Ann S. Hobbs
Marge Hobdey
Kendrick Y. Hodgdon
Phyllis Hodge
Mark L. Hoffman
S. Todd Holden
Scott Hollingsworth
David W. Holmes
Harold Hooper
Mary Hope
John Horton
Marshall Howe
Thomas Howell
Susan Hudson
Jane Huff
Sheila Hughes
Carl Hull
Mary E. Humphreys
Miriam L. Hursey

Davis Hurt
Albert Iager
Elizabeth S. Iber
Pat Jackson
Ottavio Janni
Peter S. Jayne
Simone Jenion
Mert Jensen
Clark F. Jeschke
Craig Jeschke
George M. Jett
Mr. and Mrs. Sam G. Jewell
Barbara M. Johnson
Jeanne H. Johnson
Mildred Johnson
Richard A. Johnson
William Johnson
Alice F. Jones
Margaret H. Jones
Steve Jones
Emily D. Joyce
Paul D. Jung
Hank Kaestner
Peter Kaestner
Ronald Kagarise
Steve Kahn
Ramona Kasdan
Jack Kaspersky
Don Kauffman
Lois B. Kauffman
Helen Kavanagh
Gregory Kearns
Mary E. Keedy
Robert A. Keedy
Geraldine Keller
Gloria Keller
Linda D. Keller
Patrick Keyser
Ray Kiddy
Ross Kilpatric
Matthew Kineke
Kay R. King
Marjorie W. Kinsey
Dennis L. Kirkwood
Richard L. Kleen
M. Kathleen Klimkiewicz
Wayne Klockner
Peter Knight
Barbara Knox
William Koch
Marcia Krishnamoorthy
V. Krishnamoorthy

Bill Kulp
Jay Kunkle
Margie Kupiec
Dixie Kyle
Lawnie Kyle
Keith R. Langdon
Barbara Larraby
Harriet Lathroum
Leo Lathroum
Joseph P. Leahy
Paul R. Lee II
Paul F. Leifer
Henry Leskinen
Michael Leumas
A. Scott Lewis
Cam Lewis
Gregory Lewis
Norma Lewis
Ralph E. Lewis
Ralph H. Lewis
Letty A. Limbach
Roland Limpert
Kara Linthicum
David Litton
David R. Livengood
Bonnie Lizer
Robert Lizer
Alexis Loo
John C. Lorenz
Dennis Luck
Christopher Ludwig
Samuel Lyon
Lucy MacClintock
Nancy MacClintock
Stuart MacClintock
Debra E. Mackenna
Gail MacKiernan
Edward Macon
Hugh Mahanes
Carolyn C. Maize
Kennedy P. Maize
John G. Malcolm
Dorothea Malec
Alice B. Mallonee
Kitty Marconi
Elwood M. Martin
Griffin Martin
Mabel Martin
Bill Marx
Alice Mason
Mrs. Edwin R. Mathews
Thomas P. Mathews

Carolyn A. Matthews
Timothy M. Matthews
Karen Belle Mattingly
Donna Mattson
Roger Mattson
Mike L. Maughlin
Richard Maurer
James P. Mause
Marilyn Mause
Colin McAllister
Maureen McAllister
Michael McAllister
Joseph J. McCann
Grazina McClure
Michael McClure
Betty McCoy
Raymond McCoy
Minette McCullough
William B. McIntosh
Joan B. McKearnan
Janet McKegg
Richard McLean
Jack McMillan
Carol McNulty
David W. Mehlman
Donald Mehlman
Mieke Mehlman
Helen E. Meleney
Bob Melville
Patricia Melville
William G. Meredith
Donald W. Meritt
Donald H. Messersmith
Timothy Mihursky
Charles E. Miller
Claire E. Miller
Elinor Miller
Mr. and Mrs. Miller
Robert Miller
Stauffer Miller
Stephen A. Miller
Ann S. Mitchell
Eba Moore
Guy Moore
Lynn Moore
Neal Moore
Patricia J. Moore
Charles Morris
Dawn Morris
Don Morris
Dorothy Morris
Georgia Morris

Virginia F. Morris
Robert W. Moss
David H. Moulton
Marjorie Mountjoy
Elaine Mowry
David Mozurkewich
Harvey Mudd
Marion Mudd
Charles L. Mullican
Dorothy M. Mumford
Gail Mundis
Rosamond Munro
Gail D. Murphy
Mrs. J. E. Murphy
William L. Murphy
Diane Musick
Mike Musick
Paul J. Nazelrod
Jean Neely
Gary R. Nelson
Timothy Newberger
Bea Newkirk
William Newman
Paul E. Nistico
Susan Noble
John Norvell
Marianna E. Nuttle
John O'Brien
Michael O'Brien
Michael D. O'Brien
Mr. and Mrs. Paul J.
   O'Brien
Mr. and Mrs. Robert W.
   Oberfelder
J. William Oberman
Lola Oberman
Ted Oberman
Jane Offutt
Harold C. Olson
Bryan Olszewski
Joe Ondrejko
John Orange
James Orgain
Margo Osantowski
Peter C. Osenton
Jo Osterhouse
Dorothy P. Palmer
Earl H. Palmer
Hurlburt Palmer
Marie Palmer
Floyd L. Parks
Robert Paterson

Helen Patterson
Phyllis Peake
Richard Peake
C. Penland
Roger L. Penwell
Don R. Perkuchin
William P. Pfingsten
Carol Pickett
Paul A. Pisano
Elizabeth L. Pitney
Klara K. Pitts
Marie H. Plante
Bertie S. Plutschak
Bill Pope
Frances B. Pope
Calvert Posey
Gary Potter
John M. Price
Ann Pumphrey
Willard Rahn
Kyle Rambo
Donald E. Randle
Janet Randle
Robert Rasa
Douglas Redmund
Elizabeth Reeder
Jan G. Reese
Michael Reid
R. Elizabeth Remsberg
Judy Renkie
Michael E. Resch
Robert R. Reynolds
Nanine Rhinelander
Sue A. Ricciardi
Mark E. Richardson
Peggy Y. Rieke
Robert F. Ringler
Wilbur H. Rittenhouse
Julie Rizzello
Chandler S. Robbins
Eleanor C. Robbins
George C. Robbins
Jane S. Robbins
Stuart B. Robbins
Nancy C. Roberts
Randolph C. Robertson
Bruce Rodgers
John M. Roman
Willem Roosenburg
Les Roslund
Barbara Ross
Chester Ross

Dorothy Ross
Jean L. Rossen
Ronald R. Runkles
Margaret Rusk
Richard W. Russell
William A. Russell, Jr.
Doris Ruthrauf
William Ruxton
David Ryder
Len Sandler
Joshua L. Sandt
Stephen G. Sanford
Josephine Satloff
Leonard Satloff
Leslie Saulsbury
Paul Schmidt
Philip B. Schnering
Barbara E. Schrock
Robert M. Schutsky
Sharon Schwemmer
Carol Scudder
William H. Scudder
Bill Shafer
Joyce Shafer
Janet E. Shaffer
Harriet M. Sheetz
Jay Sheppard
Bill Shermer
William N. Shirey
L. T. Short
Nicholas M. Short
Peter Shumar
Teresa Simons
Martha Simpkins
Susan Sires
Connie S. Skipper
Karen Skuldt
James Slater
Edwardine G. Slaughter
Turbit H. C. Slaughter
Ann Smith
Bonita M. Smith
Donald B. Smith
Dot Smith
Frank O. Smith
Linda H. Smith
Marian Smith
Mike Smith
Oliver Smith
Paul Smith
Pearl Smith
Therese E. Smith

Joanne K. Solem
Robert P. Solem
Olive Sorzano
Edward Soutiere
Jackie Spangler
Wanda Spencer
Barbara Stadler
Randolph Stadler
Mark Staley
Margaret O. Stambaugh
Richard A. Stambaugh
Barbara Stamps
James L. Stasz
Barbara A. Stephens
James M. Stephens
Joan Stephens
Rose M. Stevens
H. Godwin Stevenson
M. P. Stevenson
Margaret C. Stevenson
Charles Stirrat
Donna Stone
Thomas E. Stone
Vernon D. Stotts
Susan B. Strange
Thomas Strikwerda
Anne Sturm
Rex Sturm
Joseph Suess
Alex Summers
Janet Sundby
Helen Sundergill
Ron Sundergill
Eva Sunell
Beverly Sutton
Mark E. Swick
Byron Swift
Charles E. Swift
Ellsworth R. Swift
John Symonds
John Tam
Calvin Taylor
Gary J. Taylor
Herb Taylor
John L. Taylor
V. Ray Taylor
John A. Thaw
Sallie Thayer
Glenn D. Therres
Vera Thoman
Ed Thompson
Linda Thompson

Patty V. Thornhill
Elise H. Thrasher
Jean Tierney
Kimberly Titus
Isabelle Todd
Mary Ann Todd
Michael Todd
Kathleen Trever
Edward Trice, Sr.
Hugh Trimble
John Trott
Roy Trudel
Gilbert M. Turner
Mary G. Twigg
Robert W. Twigg
Kenneth Tyson
V. Edwin Unger
Kermit L. Updegrove, Jr.
Thomas M. Valega
Holly Van Ness
Keith D. Van Ness, Jr.
Gary VanVelsir
Charles R. Vaughn
Gail C. Vaughn
June A. Vaughn

Neil Vigilante
Ms. Vogel
Kristin Vogt
Joseph Wagner
Paula Wagner
Christopher Wagnon
David E. Walbeck
Sally Ann Waldschmidt
David H. Wallace
Henry C. Wallace
Mark D. Wallace
Jane Ward
Gayle Ware
Doris C. Warfield
Frank H. Warfield
Frank Wastler
R. Watson
Virginia McC. Watson
Donald Waugh
Mark C. Weatherholt
Helen Webb
Peter A. Webb
Charles M. Webster
Dorothy S. Webster
Richard Webster

Michael J. Welch
Elizabeth Wells
Meme Wells
William Wells
Jack Wennerstrom
John S. Weske
Steve Westre
Joy G. Wheeler
Bob Whitcomb
Jan White
Tony White
Harold Wierenga
Harold L. Wierenga
Claudia P. Wilds
Martin Wiley
James R. Wilkinson
Guy Willey
Levin I. Willey
Morris Willey
Dwight F. Williams
Walter F. Williams
Phyllida M. Willis
Ernest J. Willoughby
George B. Wilmot
Barbara Wilson

Erika M. Wilson
Patricia Wilson
David Winner
Frank G. Witebsky
J. E. M. Wood
Libby Wood
Jeanne Woods
Richard Woods
Jean R. Worthley
William D. Worthley
John D. Wortman
Michele Wright
Gary Yoder
Irene Mae Yoder
Marvin Ray Yoder
Marilyn L. Yost
Howard Youth
Beulah Zander
Helen Zeichner
Bettie Zickrick
Karl Zickrick
Paul A. Zucker
Francis O. Zumbrun
John Zyla

Atlas of the Breeding Birds of Maryland and the District of Columbia

Introduction

The Maryland and District of Columbia (DC) Breeding Bird Atlas Project was undertaken in 1982 to address concerns that rapid changes in the landscape of these two jurisdictions were causing declines in populations of many of our native birds. The officers and directors of the Maryland Ornithological Society (MOS) believed it was important to document the distribution of breeding birds throughout Maryland and DC so that our avian resources would be known and future changes could be detected.

As of 1981, initial atlases of Montgomery and Howard counties had been completed and published (Klimkiewicz and Solem 1978), and other county atlases had been started in Baltimore, Garrett, Prince George's, Somerset, Washington, and Carroll counties. The MOS atlas planners were faced with a major decision: Should they continue to census several counties at a time over the next 10 to 15 years or launch a statewide atlas project? MOS planners held several meetings with personnel of the Maryland Department of Natural Resources (DNR) Wildlife Division, and the two organizations then drafted plans to census all of Maryland and DC from 1983 through 1987.

Purposes of the Atlas Project

Although the preparation of breeding bird distribution maps was the Atlas project's primary objective, several other goals were defined during the MOS-DNR meetings. The DNR needed more detailed information on the breeding distribution of rare species. Conservation organizations— such as The Nature Conservancy (TNC), which has a very active Maryland chapter—needed information on the occurrence of rare and declining species because they are given priority consideration in land purchases. Identifying sites with special wildlife values or with unusually high species diversity was identified as another goal of the Atlas project.

The planners realized that, beyond formal goals, Atlas data are a rich source of information that can be used in many ways. They can be compared with habitat and climatic data, thereby yielding new information on factors associated with breeding concentrations. These combined data can also contribute to an interpretation of the limits of the breeding range of individual species.

In numerous ways, Atlas data provide information on the effects of habitat fragmentation on breeding birds. For example, failure to find a species in a well-covered Atlas block with only fragments of appropriate habitat suggests that more extensive tracts are required. In the final years of the Maryland/DC Atlas project, fieldworkers made special efforts to search for area-sensitive species, such as warblers and tanagers, in the largest patch of woodland in each Atlas block; these searches were undertaken to confirm that the species was absent rather than overlooked. When presence and absence data from many blocks are combined, the habitat requirements of a species become more readily understandable. Comparisons will be possible with all adjacent states. During much or all of the same five-year period covered by the Maryland/DC Atlas, atlas fieldwork was also being conducted in Delaware, Pennsylvania, West Virginia, and Virginia, as well as in most states bordering those states.

In addition to distribution data, the miniroute data described in the species accounts add a new dimension to the Maryland/DC Atlas by providing information on breeding bird abundance. Miniroutes, consisting of 15 three-minute roadside stops in each Atlas block, can be rerun in subsequent years to obtain information about changes in breeding bird populations for any portion of the Atlas area.

The *Atlas of the Breeding Birds of Maryland and the District of Columbia* will serve educational as well as conservation and land-planning objectives. Most Maryland and DC residents still are unaware of the large number of bird species that breed in the area and near their homes. By increasing their awareness, the *Atlas* will also increase the chance that wildlife will be considered in land planning. Even in the early years of fieldwork, Atlas data were used to provide documentation of the presence or absence of species at specific sites within the Chesapeake Bay Critical Area for purposes of the Critical Area legislation. This use promises to continue well into the future and has expanded statewide for use in environmental assessment.

The planned publication of the *Atlas* provided the incentive for summarizing data from the Maryland Nest Record File (MNRF), to which MOS members have been contributing since 1950. To these have been added turn-of-the-century records collected by F. Kirkwood and his colleagues, records from the Patuxent Wildlife Research Center (PWRC), and Maryland records obtained from various museums and institutions around the country. The resulting data bank, containing information from more than 27,000 Maryland nests, may be the largest for any state in the country. This file provides information on nest locations, nesting habitats, dates, clutch size, and nesting success as well as on changing rates of cowbird parasitism.

Known changes in the breeding distribution of Maryland and DC birds are shown by comparing the Atlas maps with distribution spot maps compiled by R. Stewart and C. Robbins (1958) during the 1950s, when they were writing *Birds of Maryland and the District of Columbia*. Fifty-one of the maps were published in generalized form in that book; the others have not been published previously. Where appropriate, comparisons with the Howard and the Montgomery County atlases (Klimkiewicz and Solem 1978) from the 1970s are also made in the introduction and the species accounts in this *Atlas*.

The Atlas data file, entered into a computer by the DNR, will have many land-use planning and research applications, some of which are now in progress. Portions of the data have already been used to show possible increases and decreases in Howard County since its first atlas was conducted from 1973 through 1975; to compute similarity indexes among Atlas blocks in different parts of the state; to estimate efficiency of Atlas coverage for various species; to compare lists of expected and observed species; and, in conjunction with other data, to prepare lists of Maryland and DC's rarest breeding birds.

Another important aspect is the use of miniroute data as an independent source of population information for comparison with the Breeding Bird Survey (BBS) data obtained from the U.S. Fish and Wildlife Service (USFWS). Similarly, Atlas data also can be used for seasonal comparisons with the quantitative Midwinter Bird Survey (MBS) data that MOS members and other Maryland birdwatchers collected throughout Maryland and DC.

The Atlas project had many secondary but significant benefits. It introduced project participants to new ways of studying and appreciating birds and accumulating nesting data, and it increased their awareness of habitat loss. Many atlasers were pleasantly surprised when they recorded species they had not known were nesting locally. By showing breeding ranges, the Atlas will continue to alert birdwatchers to new local birding opportunities.

History of Grid-based Atlases

In grid-based atlases, the country, state, province, or county is divided into blocks of identical size and shape, and each block is searched for breeding bird evidence. The first grid-based avian atlas was Lord and Munn's (1970) *Atlas of Breeding Birds of the West Midlands,* based on the 1966 through 1968 study of three British counties; this atlas included only 77 squares, each 10 kilometers by 10 kilometers.

It was a trial run for the *Atlas of Breeding Birds in Great Britain and Ireland* (Sharrock 1976), which summarized more than 285,000 observations collected from 3,862 ten-kilometer squares from 1968 through 1972. This effort was stimulated by Perring and Walters's (1962) *Atlas of the British Flora.* Both of the latter atlases were based on topographic maps bounded by the British national grid.

The British breeding bird atlas stimulated almost all other Western European nations to initiate atlas projects, most of which were based on five years of fieldwork. Formation of the European Ornithological Atlas Committee provided some standardization of codes and procedures, but block sizes varied among countries. The first national atlases to follow the British lead were those of France (Yeatman 1976), Denmark (Dybbro 1976), West Germany (Rheinwald 1977), The Netherlands (Teixeira 1979), and Switzerland (Schifferli et al. 1980). In the meantime, the British began publishing county atlases with a 2-kilometer by 2-kilometer tetrad grid. The first of these were from London (Montier 1977), Bedfordshire (Harding 1979), and Hertfordshire (Mead and Smith 1982). Other regional atlases published at about the same time included those of West Berlin (Bruch et al. 1978); the Rioja (de Juana 1980) and Navarra (Elosegui 1985) in Spain; and Lower Saxony in West Germany (Heckenroth 1985).

Several atlas projects have been completed in Africa. Two of the first to be published were a month-by-month atlas for Natal (Cyrus and Robson 1980) and a year-round atlas of both historic and recent field observations for Sudan (Nikolaus 1987). A provisional loose-leaf atlas of New Zealand (Bull et al. 1978) was the first for the southwest Pacific. This was followed by the comprehensive *Atlas of Australian Birds* (Blakers et al. 1984).

In North America, the first atlas project was *The Breeding Bird Atlas of Montgomery and Howard Counties, Maryland* (Klimkiewicz and Solem 1978). The first of the North American state and provincial atlases was started in Massachusetts in 1974 (Veit and Petersen 1993). To date, projects have been started or completed in all Canadian provinces and, in the United States, in several western states and all states east of the Mississippi River except Mississippi, Alabama, and South Carolina. The following have been published: Vermont (Laughlin and Kibbe 1985), Ontario (Cadman et al. 1987), Maine (Adamus 1988), New York (Andrle and Carroll 1988), Ohio (Peterjohn and Rice 1991), Michigan (Brewer et al. 1991), Alberta (Semenchuk 1992), Maritime Provinces (Erskine 1992), Pennsylvania (Brauning 1992), Rhode Island (Enser 1992), Massachusetts (Veit and Petersen 1993), Connecticut (Bevier 1994), New Hampshire (Foss 1994), West Virginia (Buckelew and Hall 1994), Saskatchewan (Smith 1996), and South Dakota (Peterson 1955). The North American Ornithological Atlas Committee (1990) published (in

English and Spanish) a *Handbook for Atlasing American Breeding Birds,* to standardize atlas methodology and encourage other atlas projects throughout the Americas.

In several countries where breeding bird atlases have been published, new atlas projects have already been undertaken. Among them are *The Atlas of Wintering Birds in Britain and Ireland* (Lack 1986) and a Dutch atlas, showing distribution month by month over a five year period, the *Atlas van de Nederlandse Vogels* (Bekhuis et al. 1987).

The Maryland/DC Atlas in Relation to Other Bird Surveys

During the past several decades, MOS members have participated in many other bird surveys. The oldest of these is the Christmas Bird Count (CBC). The first Maryland/DC counts date from 1901, but coverage prior to 1948 was fragmentary. In the middle and late 1940s, R. Stewart and C. Robbins established standard 15-mile diameter (24-km) Christmas Count circles in various physiographic regions of the state. Most of these original circles continue to be surveyed each Christmas season, as do many newer ones. Continental Christmas Count maps summarizing 10 years of numerical data were published by Root (1988) and provide an interesting comparison with Maryland/DC Breeding Bird Atlas Data. An even better comparison is provided by the Midwinter Bird Survey maps for Maryland, 1988–1993 (Hatfield et al. 1994).

The Breeding Bird Survey (BBS), sponsored jointly by the U.S. Fish and Wildlife Service (USFWS) and the Canadian Wildlife Service, was initially field tested in Maryland and Delaware in 1965, and it became operational in all states and provinces east of the Mississippi River in 1966 (Robbins and Van Velzen 1967). The rest of the contiguous states and Canadian provinces were included within the next two years. Except for a few changes caused by road modifications, the Maryland routes are still being run exactly as they were in 1965, some by the original observers (S. Droege, pers. comm.). The main purpose of the BBS is to detect bird population changes or trends. Birds are counted at each of 50 stops, but no efforts are made to confirm nesting.

The Breeding Bird Census (BBC), sponsored from 1937 through 1983 by the National Audubon Society (NAS) and published in *Audubon Field Notes* and *American Birds,* has included some Maryland and DC study plots nearly every year since 1946. From 1984 through the present, the BBC has been sponsored by the Cornell Laboratory of Ornithology; the results are now published annually in the *Journal of Field Ornithology.* These censuses give bird population densities, expressed as the number of territorial males of each species per 100 acres (40.5 ha), in a specified habitat. Stewart and Robbins (1958) reviewed published and unpublished BBC densities and cited the highest for each species.

The Winter Bird-Population Study (WBPS), like the BBC, records bird populations by habitat. It, too, has been sponsored by the NAS and Cornell Laboratory of Ornithology and has been published in the same journals. A few Maryland and DC sites have been part of the WBPS for many years.

The Winter Bird Survey (WBS) was a five-year experimental study of winter bird populations in central Maryland from 1970 through 1974 (Robbins and Bystrak 1974). It was designed to test the adequacy of the Christmas Bird Counts for monitoring winter bird populations. The survey consisted of a 5-mile (8-km) walking transect at the center of each 7.5-minute U.S. Geological Survey topographic map. The 40 transects sampled all of Howard and Anne Arundel counties and parts of Baltimore and Prince George's counties.

A Midwinter Count was undertaken by the Howard County chapter of MOS in 1986 and by the Allegany chapter in 1987. It has been conducted annually since. The count is held within county boundaries on a single date between 10 January and 10 February to compare the results of annual Christmas Bird Counts with midwinter bird populations. The format is the same as that for the May Count. At least ten counties conducted Midwinter Counts in 1992.

The Midwinter Bird Survey (MBS) (Hatfield et al. 1994) was a program conducted in Maryland from 1988 to 1993. It involved four hours of foot coverage starting at 7:30 a.m., with one survey route in each of alternate Atlas blocks throughout the state. The count was made during the period 10 January through 10 February. Each block was covered only once during the six-year project.

The May Statewide Bird Count, which has been conducted annually since 1948, was traditionally held on the first Saturday in May until 1988, when the date was changed to the second Saturday in May. Results are summarized by counties and published, together with party-hours of coverage, in *Maryland Birdlife.*

This impressive list of projects provides multiple opportunities for comparisons of distribution, habitat requirements, trends, and techniques.

Historical Summary

Throughout this *Atlas* there are references to early accounts of the birdlife of Maryland and the District of Columbia. Most of the early publications are not readily available, so the majority of readers have not seen them and know very little about the authors. This brief review introduces these ornithologists so that their abbreviated names, such as F. Kirkwood and G. Eifrig, will mean more to the users of this *Atlas*. For a more comprehensive review of early ornithologists, see the historical sketch in *Birds of Maryland and the District of Columbia* (Stewart and Robbins 1958).

The earliest references to DC and Maryland birds were incidental observations or short lists in nonornithological publications; rarely was there any indication of abundance or any separation of nesting from nonnesting species. The first definitive list of the birds of DC appeared in 1862 in the annual report of the board of regents of the Smithsonian Institution. Elliott Coues (1842–99), a founder of the American Ornithologists' Union, and another enthusiastic young birder, D. Webster Prentiss (1843–99), authored this 33-page report that included common and scientific names, statuses, and migration dates for 226 species (Coues and Prentiss 1862). Twenty-one years later the same authors, both medical doctors and professors at the National Medical College, published *Avifauna Columbiana*, a 133-page follow-up volume (Coues and Prentiss 1883). This book included 248 species, and the authors anticipated that about 20 more would ultimately be discovered in DC.

Edward Alexander Preble (1871–1957) was a field naturalist for the U.S. Biological Survey from 1892 to 1935; he then served as associate editor of *Nature Magazine* until his death. He spent much of his life exploring Arctic Canada. His ornithological survey of western Maryland in 1899 was one of his few field assignments in the eastern United States and was the first survey for that part of Maryland (Preble 1900).

Frank Coates Kirkwood (1862–1945) was an Irish immigrant who came to Maryland at the age of eighteen. For 20 years he worked in his uncle's soap factory, then he bought a small farm. He spent most of his adult life birding and collecting in the Dulaney's Valley area of Baltimore County. In the mid 1920s he began a revision of his 144-page *List of the Birds of Maryland* (Kirkwood 1895), but the revision was never completed. Thus his 1895 book, reprinted from the

Transactions of the Maryland Academy of Sciences, served for more than half a century as the definitive treatise on Maryland's avifauna.

Charles William Gustave Eifrig (1871–1949) compiled the first comprehensive year-round observations of the birds of western Maryland. Eifrig, who emigrated to Pennsylvania from Saxony, Germany, at age seven, served as pastor of the Lutheran church in Cumberland, Maryland, from 1899 to 1903. He then moved to a pastorate in Ottawa, Canada, and subsequently he joined the faculty of Concordia Teachers College in Illinois, where he spent the rest of his professional life. He made several return trips to Maryland and published his observations on changing bird populations in Garrett County.

Wells W. Cooke (1858–1916) and his daughter, May Thacher Cooke (18——–1963), were biologists with the U.S. Biological Survey, which later became the U.S. Fish and Wildlife Service. Wells W. Cooke was called the "father of cooperative study of bird migration in America" by historian T. S. Palmer (1917). May Thacher Cooke expanded the Washington region to include a radius of about 20 miles (32.2 km) from the Capitol (Cooke 1921). Her 1921 list included 299 species and subspecies, and her 1929 list contained 301 (actually 287 full species) (Cooke 1929).

Alexander Kenrick Fisher (1856–1948), another founder of the AOU, left the medical profession to devote his life to ornithology. He worked with C. Hart Merriam to set up the Branch of Economic Ornithology, later to become the Biological Survey, predecessor of the USFWS. His most influential publication—*The Hawks and Owls of the United States in Their Relation to Agriculture*, published in 1893—greatly reduced hunting pressure on these birds. His principal Maryland publication was *Natural History of Plummers Island, Maryland. Part IV. Birds* (Fisher 1935); it was revised in 1968 by Alexander Wetmore (1886–1978), secretary of the Smithsonian Institution, and by Richard H. Manville (1910–74).

Then followed the present-day ornithologists. The late Maurice Brooks (1900–93), who did much ornithological exploration of Garrett County, was a retired professor of forestry at West Virginia University. The late Irving E. Hampe and C. Haven Kolb, who published the *Preliminary List of the Birds of Maryland and the District of Columbia* in

1947, were active in the Natural History Society of Maryland for more than 50 years and were founders of the MOS.

Wildlife biologists of the USFWS at Patuxent Wildlife Research Center (PWRC) have made many contributions to Maryland ornithology, beginning with the publication of *Birds of Maryland and the District of Columbia,* by Robert E. Stewart (1913–93) and Chandler S. Robbins in 1958. Of the 333 species that Stewart and Robbins (1958) included in their book, 192 were known to have bred in Maryland. Publica-tions by more than 60 other Patuxent biologists are cited in this *Atlas.*

The Maryland amateur ornithologist most frequently cited in the middle of the twentieth century is Hervey G. Brackbill, who published many papers on bird behavior. As early as 1940 he was honored with an elective membership in the AOU in recognition of his ornithological research. He spent his professional life writing and editing for the *Baltimore Sun.*

Procedures

Committees

Planning for the Maryland/DC Atlas began seriously in 1982. By January 1983, the Advisory and Planning Board (later to become the Advisory Board) was in operation, as were the Technical, Training, Publicity and Newsletter, Budget and Fund-Raising, Editing, Verification, Block-busting, Computer, Publication, and Miniroute committees. Some of these committees functioned throughout the entire project, and some on an as-needed basis. Others helped during the planning phase but not operationally.

Coordination

A statewide project coordinator was hired to oversee the day-to-day coordination and operation of the project. His responsibilities included stimulating and training observers, soliciting and editing field data from observers and county coordinators, reporting progress to the Advisory Board, and working with the various committees as needed.

Much of the responsibility for the successful completion of the Atlas project fell to the county coordinators and their assistants. The county coordinators participated in planning and training sessions arranged by the Advisory Board and helped with preparation of maps and other materials used by field observers. Their principal responsibilities were to stimulate and coordinate coverage in their counties and to screen incoming records. In some counties a quad captain was designated to help coordinate coverage of the six blocks in each 7.5-minute quadrangle.

Training sessions were held in nearly all Maryland counties at the beginning of the project, and more advanced training sessions were offered in the majority of counties in each subsequent year. The basic training included discussions of the purposes of the Atlas project, procedures, use of forms, map reading, explanation of codes, explanation of Atlas safe dates, importance of visiting all habitats, importance of obtaining permission from landowners, and hints on how to search for the rarer species.

Subsequent training sessions were held in most counties in late winter of each year, prior to the beginning of fieldwork. These sessions focused on achieving full coverage in local areas, presented new information about atlasing techniques, discussed methods for finding secretive and nocturnal species, and mentioned changes in Atlas codes and recording procedures. They also provided an opportunity to discuss local distribution of birds. In particular, the sessions served as a forum that gave observers in each county a chance to see the Atlas results to date and to be alerted to give special attention to species that appeared to be expanding into the area or species that were anticipated in an area but had not been recorded. In addition, these sessions served as an effective means of maintaining communication between local observers and the state organization. The statewide organization was able to hear and address firsthand the concerns of local observers, who were, in turn, kept informed on the progress of the project. These meetings contributed significantly to success of the project. The tremendous enthusiasm and commitment of fieldworkers was buttressed, and the state organization received dozens of suggestions that were implemented, adding significantly to our efforts and efficiency.

The Maryland & DC Breeding Bird Atlas Project Handbook was prepared for the use of all participants (Advisory and Planning Board 1982). The handbook included a brief history of atlas projects, the purposes and scope of the Maryland/DC Atlas Project, an explanation of the grid system, and definitions of the codes with examples of their use. In addition to recommendations on the best use of time, upgrading observations, and using the forms, the handbook discussed Atlas terminology and block busting. A centerfold map of Maryland and DC identified by name and number each of the 239 7.5-minute quadrangles used for the project, and it showed the numbering system for the six blocks in each quadrangle and for quarterblocks. Land access, atlasing ethics, permission and thank-you letters, training sessions, fund raising, sources of additional data, and income tax deductions were covered briefly. A table gave the status for each species in each of the six major regions of Maryland, its preferred habitat, and Atlas "safe dates"—the dates within which a species could reasonably be assumed to be a breeding bird rather than a transient. (See appendix A.) A brief list of references, along with the telephone numbers and addresses of the committee chairpersons and county coordinators, was included, as were samples of field cards, summary sheets, and verification forms.

Eight issues of the "Maryland/DC Breeding Bird Atlas

Newsletter" were published from summer 1983 through spring 1987, covering such topics as changes in county coordinators, common errors detected, confirmation of difficult species, city censusing, coverage maps, preliminary species maps, mystery maps to be identified, ethics, and the blocks with the most species detected and most confirmations reported to date.

Forms

Examples of the Atlas Field Card and Summary Sheet are shown as figures 1 and 2 on page 10. Because the safe dates were made available to each observer through the handbook, observers were not required to report the date of each observation, as is done in some atlas projects. Although this saved considerable data-entry time, some useful information on nesting dates was lost as a result. Nest record cards were made available to observers who wished to use them, but training sessions stressed that it was not necessary to find nests to be an effective Atlas participant. The strategy of the Advisory Board was to keep the data-gathering requirements simple so as not to discourage fieldworkers. For the same reason, participants were not asked to report elevations except when documenting unusual occurrences.

Maps

The Atlas project purchased two complete sets of 7.5-minute U.S. Geological Survey topographic maps. One set was divided among the county coordinators for planning purposes. The other was cut into sixths (Atlas blocks) for reference use by fieldworkers. A third partial set was later acquired for the project coordinator to use as needed. A black-and-white set was made available by the DNR for field use by atlasers.

Block Size

The traditional size of atlas blocks has been 10 kilometers by 10 kilometers (6.25 x 6.25 mi), and from the beginning of the atlasing movement, the European Ornithological Atlas Committee has recommended strongly that all atlas projects should use 10 kilometers or a multiple of that number (such as 5 km in Denmark and The Netherlands, or 50 km for the atlas of Europe). In actual practice, however, the boundaries have been determined on the basis of the most readily available suitable maps. Some projects have used the worldwide Universal Transverse Mercator (UTM) grid, others have used a national metric grid, and still others have used a grid based on latitude and longitude.

The Maryland/DC project used one-sixth of the 7.5-minute topographic map as an Atlas block. This decision was made for the following reasons:

• Standard topographic maps (scale of 1:24,000) were readily available.

• These maps carry tick marks in the left and right margins for dividing them into thirds, and a scale at the bottom for dividing them in half. Only the top margin needs to be measured to divide the map into six equal parts (2.5 minutes of latitude by 3.75 minutes of longitude).

• The resulting subdivisions at the latitude of DC measure about 2.83 miles (4.56 km) north-south by 3.37 miles (5.42 km) east-west, for an area of 9.54 square miles (24.7 sq km), which is within 1.2 percent of the area of a 5-kilometer by 5-kilometer block.

• All surrounding states—in fact, almost all states in the eastern United States—also used one-sixth of a 7.5-degree block, making them all comparable and compatible.

• Although the UTM grid is shown in the margin of recent Maryland topographic maps, its use would have necessitated extensive cutting and pasting to construct each Atlas map. Furthermore, being a rectangular grid superimposed on a spherical surface, the UTM grid has a column of odd-sized blocks every six degrees of longitude, so all blocks would not have been the same size.

Maryland/DC Atlas blocks are designated by the name of the quadrangle (see fig. 3 on page 11), followed by *NW, NE, CW, CE, SW,* or *SE.* Many states, including New York, Pennsylvania, and Delaware, atlased all blocks in the state. Others, such as Virginia and West Virginia, targeted for coverage only one block out of six (the one in the southeast corner of the quad). Vermont and New Hampshire randomly selected one block in each quad. Maryland/DC covered all blocks and, in addition, designated the northwest block in each quadrangle for quarterblock coverage.

Quarterblock Coverage

Among state atlases, quarterblocks are unique to the Maryland/DC Atlas. In the original atlas of Montgomery County from 1971 through 1973, 32 of the 135 breeding species were found in all 60 of the 5-kilometer blocks (Klimkiewicz and Solem 1978). This meant that if the Montgomery atlas were repeated in the future, it would be impossible to document any increase in these species and difficult to show changes in many other species found in a high percentage of the blocks. As long as any suitable habitat for a species remained anywhere within the 25 square kilometers of the block, a declining species could still be present and the decline would not be detected.

To eliminate this possibility, the Howard County atlas from 1973 through 1975 divided each of the 34 atlas blocks into quarters (Klimkiewicz and Solem 1978). A separate species list was kept for each quarterblock, but the highest atlas breeding category achieved in any quarterblock within a given block was applied to all other quarterblocks in which the species was recorded in that block. Because it was not necessary to look for "confirmed" or even "probable" status in each quarterblock, little additional time and effort were

COVERAGE

DATE	LOCATION	START	END	HOURS

RARE AND LOCAL SPECIES

The following 43 species breed in Maryland, but are expected in fewer than 20 blocks statewide. Reports of any of these species from outside of known nesting areas must be accompanied by completed verification forms.

Eastern Shore Specialties

Little Blue Heron	American Oystercatcher
Cattle Egret	Wilson's Plover
Great Egret	Piping Plover
Snowy Egret	Great Black-backed Gull
Louisiana Heron	Herring Gull
Black-crn. Night Heron	Laughing Gull
American Bittern	Gull-billed Tern
Glossy Ibis	Forster's Tern
Mute Swan	Common Tern
Gadwall	Royal Tern
Bald Eagle	Black Skimmer
Black Rail	Swainson's Warbler

Western Maryland Specialties

Sharp-shinned Hawk	Golden-crowned Kinglet
Upland Sandpiper	Nashville Warbler
Saw-whet Owl	Northern Waterthrush
Yellow-bell. Sapsucker	Mourning Warbler
Alder Flycatcher	Dark-eyed Junco
Bewick's Wren	

Rare Throughout Maryland

Pied-billed Grebe	Sedge Wren
Yellow-cr. Night Heron	Loggerhead Shrike
Hooded Merganser	Dickcissel
Northern Harrier	Henslow's Sparrow

The following 20 species have only been recorded breeding in Maryland a few times, or are anticipated breeders. Extensive details are required. Nesting attempts by any of these species, or any not on this card must be reported immediately.

Green-winged Teal	Long-eared Owl
Ruddy Duck	Red-cockaded Woodpecker
Northern Goshawk	Olive-sided Flycatcher
Peregrine Falcon	Red-breasted Nuthatch
Sora	Winter Wren
Purple Gallinule	Swainson's Thrush
American Coot	Pine Siskin
Roseate Tern	Lark Sparrow
Sandwich Tern	Bachman's Sparrow
Short-eared Owl	White-throated Sparrow

NOTES

FIELD CARD

MARYLAND & DC BREEDING BIRD ATLAS

QUADRANGLE

Quad name | Quad no.

BLOCK (circle one) | YEAR

NW NE CW CE SW SE
1   2   3   4   5   6

Observer's Name:

Address:

Phone:

BREEDING CRITERIA & CODES

POssible
O Species observed but not in breeding habitat
X Species heard or seen in breeding habitat

PRobable
A Agitated behavior or anxiety calls
P Pair seen
T Bird holding territory
C Courtship or copulation
N Visiting probable nest site
B Nest building by wrens or woodpeckers

COnfirmed
DD Distraction display
NB Nest building
UN Used nest
FL Recently fledged young
FS Parent with fecal sac
FY Parent with food for young
ON Adult leaving/entering nest site
NE Nest with eggs
NY Nest with young

Figure 1. Atlas Field Card

Quarter Block Numbering
1	2
3	4

SPECIES	PO	PR	CO	QB
Heron, Great Blue				
Green				
Bittern, Least				
Goose, Canada				
Mallard				
Duck, Black				
Teal, Blue-winged				
Duck, Wood				
Vulture, Turkey				
Black				
Hawk, Cooper's				
Red-tailed				
Red-shouldered				
Broad-winged				
Osprey				
Kestrel, American				
Grouse, Ruffed				
Bobwhite				
Pheasant, Ring-necked				
Turkey, Wild				
Rail, King				
Virginia				
Clapper				
Gallinule, Common				
Killdeer				
Willet				
Sandpiper, Spotted				
Woodcock, American				
Tern, Least				
Dove, Rock				
Mourning				
Cuckoo, Yellow-billed				
Black-billed				
Owl, Barn				
Eastern Screech				
Great Horned				

SPECIES	PO	PR	CO	QB
Owl, Barred				
Chuck-will's-widow				
Whip-poor-will				
Nighthawk, Common				
Swift, Chimney				
Hummingbird, Ruby-thr.				
Kingfisher, Belted				
Flicker, Common				
Woodpecker, Pileated				
Red-bellied				
Red-headed				
Hairy				
Downy				
Kingbird, Eastern				
Flycatcher, Great Crested				
Phoebe, Eastern				
Flycatcher, Acadian				
Willow				
Least				
Pewee, Eastern Wood				
Lark, Horned				
Swallow, Tree				
Bank				
Rough-winged				
Barn				
Cliff				
Martin, Purple				
Jay, Blue				
Raven, Common				
Crow, American				
Fish				
Chickadee, Black-capped				
Carolina				
Titmouse, Tufted				
Nuthatch, White-breasted				
Brown-headed				

SPECIES	PO	PR	CO	QB
Creeper, Brown				
Wren, House				
Carolina				
Marsh (long-billed)				
Mockingbird				
Catbird, Gray				
Thrasher, Brown				
Robin, American				
Thrush, Wood				
Hermit				
Veery				
Bluebird, Eastern				
Gnatcatcher, Blue-gray				
Waxwing, Cedar				
Starling				
Vireo, White-eyed				
Yellow-throated				
Solitary				
Red-eyed				
Warbling				
Warbler, Black-and-white				
Prothonotary				
Worm-eating				
Golden-winged				
Blue-winged				
Northern Parula				
Yellow				
Magnolia				
Black-throated Blue				
Black-throated Green				
Cerulean				
Blackburnian				
Yellow-throated				
Chestnut-sided				
Pine				
Prairie				

SPECIES	PO	PR	CO	QB
Ovenbird				
Waterthrush, Louisiana				
Warbler, Kentucky				
Yellowthroat, Common				
Chat, Yellow-breasted				
Warbler, Hooded				
Canada				
Redstart, American				
Sparrow, House				
Bobolink				
Meadowlark, Eastern				
Blackbird, Red-winged				
Oriole, Orchard				
Northern (Baltimore)				
Grackle, Boat-tailed				
Common				
Cowbird, Brown-headed				
Tanager, Scarlet				
Summer				
Cardinal, Northern				
Grosbeak, Rose-breasted				
Blue				
Bunting, Indigo				
Finch, Purple				
House				
Goldfinch, American				
Towhee, Rufous-sided				
Sparrow, Savannah				
Grasshopper				
Sharp-tailed				
Seaside				
Vesper				
Chipping				
Field				
Swamp				
Song				

Figure 2. Atlas Summary Sheet

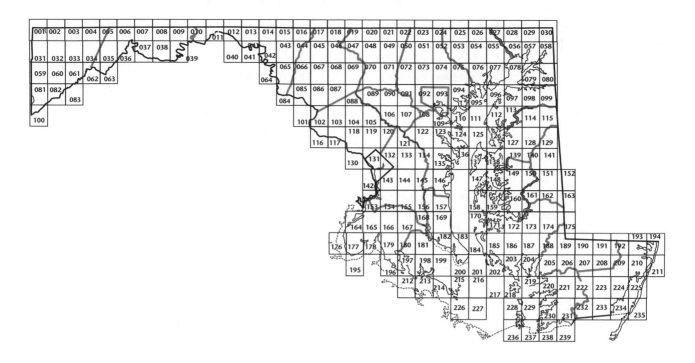

Figure 3. Names of Quadrangles

001 Friendsville	041 Hedgesville	081 Table Rock	121 Laurel	161 Preston	200 Solomons Island
002 Accident	042 Williamsport	082 Gorman	122 Odenton	162 Federalsburg	201 Barren Island
003 Grantsville	043 Funkstown	083 Mount Storm	123 Round Bay	163 Seaford West	202 Honga
004 Avilton	044 Myersvile	084 Harper's Ferry	124 Gibson Island	164 Indian Head	203 Wingate
005 Frostburg	045 Catoctin Furnace	085 Point of Rocks	125 Love Point	165 Port Tobacco	204 Nanticoke
006 Cumberland	046 Woodsboro	086 Buckeystown	126 Langford Creek	166 La Plata	205 Wetipquin
007 Evitts Creek	047 Union Bridge	087 Urbana	127 Centerville	167 Hughesville	206 Eden
008 Flintstone	048 New Windsor	088 Damascus	128 Price	168 Benedict	207 Salisbury
009 Artemas	049 Westminster	089 Woodbine	129 Goldsboro	169 Prince Frederick	208 Wango
010 Bellegrove	050 Hereford	090 Sykesville	130 Falls Church	170 Sharps Island	209 Ninepin
011 Hancock	051 Hamstead	091 Ellicott City	131 Washington West	171 Church Creek	210 Berlin
012 Cherry Run	052 Phoenix	092 Baltimore West	132 Washington East	172 Cambridge	211 Ocean City
013 Clear Spring	053 Jarrettsville	093 Baltimore East	133 Lanham	173 East New Market	212 Stratford Hall
014 Mason-Dixon	054 Bel Air	094 Middle River	134 Bowie	174 Rhodesdale	213 St. Clements Island
015 Hagerstown	055 Aberdeen	095 Gunpowder Neck	135 South River	175 Sharpstown	214 Piney Point
016 Smithsburg	056 Havre de Grace	096 Hanesville	136 Annapolis	176 Widewater	215 St. Marys City
017 Blue Ridge Summit	057 Northeast	097 Betterton	137 Kent Island	177 Nanjemoy	216 Point No Point
018 Emmitsburg	058 Elkton	098 Galena	138 Queenstown	178 Mathias Point	217 Richland Point
019 Taneytown	059 Oakland	099 Millington	139 Wye Mills	179 Popes Creek	218 Bloodsworth Island
020 Littlestown	060 Deer Park	100 Davis	140 Ridgely	180 Charlotte Hall	219 Deal Island
021 Manchester	061 Kitzmiller	101 Waterford	141 Denton	181 Mechanicsville	220 Monie
022 Lineboro	062 Westernport	102 Poolesville	142 Alexandria	182 Broomes Island	221 Princess Anne
023 New Freedom	063 Keyser	103 Germantown	143 Anacostia	183 Cove Point	222 Dividing Creek
024 Norrisville	064 Sheperdstown	104 Gaithersville	144 Upper Marlboro	184 Taylors Island	223 Snow Hill
025 Fawn Grove	065 Keedysville	105 Sandy Spring	145 Bristol	185 Golden Hill	224 Public Landing
026 Delta	066 Middletown	106 Clarksville	146 Deale	186 Blackwater River	225 Tingles Island
027 Conowingo Dam	067 Frederick	107 Savage	147 Claiborne	187 Chicamacomico	226 St. George Island
028 Rising Sun	068 Walkersville	108 Relay	148 St. Michaels	188 Mardela Springs	227 Point Lookout
029 Bayview	069 Libertytown	109 Curtis Bay	149 Easton	189 Hebron	228 Kedges Straits
030 Newark West	070 Winfield	110 Sparrows' Point	150 Fowling Creek	190 Delmar	229 Terrapin Sand Point
031 Sang Run	071 Finksburg	111 Swan Point	151 Hobbs	191 Pittsville	230 Marion
032 McHenry	072 Reisterstown	112 Rock Hall	152 Hickman	192 Whaleysville	231 Kingston
033 Bittinger	073 Cockeysville	113 Chestertown	153 Mount Vernon	193 Selbyville	232 Pocomoke City
034 Barton	074 Towson	114 Church Hill	154 Piscataway	194 Assawoman Bay	233 Girdletree
035 Lonaconing	075 White Marsh	115 Sudlersville	155 Brandywine	195 King George	234 Boxiron
036 Cresaptown	076 Edgewood	116 Sterling	156 Lower Marlboro	196 Colonial Beach North	235 Whittington Point
037 Patterson Creek	077 Perryman	117 Seneca	157 North Beach	197 Rock Point	236 Ewell
038 Oldtown	078 Spesutie	118 Rockville	158 Tilghman	198 Leonardstown	237 Great Fox island
039 Pawpaw	079 Earleville	119 Kensington	159 Oxford	199 Hollywood	238 Crisfield
040 Big Pool	080 Cecilton	120 Beltsville	160 Trappe		239 Saxis

required beyond normal good coverage of all sections of the block, although additional recordkeeping was necessary. The original quarterblock effort was highly successful. Of the 39 species found in all 34 blocks in Howard County, only 7 were found in all 136 quarterblocks.

After considerable discussion of the pros and cons of quarterblock coverage, we decided to atlas DC and the most rapidly changing portions of Maryland at the quarterblock level (fig. 4). This included all of Montgomery, Prince George's, Howard, and Baltimore counties, and the two southern quadrangles in Carroll County. Because a number of Maryland's breeding species are restricted to Garrett County in the far west, the blocks in that county were also divided into quarters. In addition, the northwest block in all other quadrangles was designated for quarterblock coverage.

Six county quarterblock atlases were begun at various times from the mid-1970s to 1980: Prince George's (Patterson 1978), Washington (Boone 1978), Somerset (Vaughn 1978), Baltimore, Carroll, and Garrett (unpub. data). The Somerset (1976 on), Baltimore (1978 on), Carroll (1980 on) and Garrett (1979 on) data were incorporated into the Maryland/DC Atlas. Prince George's and Washington counties started over again in 1983. Because some records prior to 1983 were admitted from counties that had already begun atlas fieldwork, it was decided that records dating back to 1978 would be accepted from other counties if observers wished to submit them. Few observers did.

Status Codes

The codes adopted for the Maryland/DC Atlas are essentially those of the European Ornithological Atlas Committee and are the same as those adopted at the Northeastern Breeding Bird Atlas Conference (Laughlin 1982), with three exceptions. We used separate codes of *FY* (food for young) and *FS* (fecal sac) instead of combining them under the code *AT* (attending young). We also considered carefully identified eggshells on the ground under a nest as a nest with eggs *(NE)* instead of used nest *(UN)*. And we restricted the code for physiological evidence *(PE)*—which includes incubation patch and egg in the oviduct—to use by bird banders who examine birds in the hand; we did not publish the *PE* code in the handbook for fear of its misuse by untrained observers.

The Maryland/DC definitions included more explanation than those published by the atlas conference. The only code that might be interpreted more loosely in the handbook is the code for territorial display *(T)*. The conference proceedings specify that the observations must be made at least a week apart to qualify for this code; in the handbook, the period between observations is not defined, in part because migrants were thought to be eliminated by the safe dates. Early training sessions stressed the importance of cau-

tion in using the *T* code and suggested that at least a week should pass between observations, especially for uncommon or rare species.

The three major categories, "possible," "probable," and "confirmed," have generally been accepted worldwide. Examples of the use of various codes were published in the handbook. The codes as used and refined during the 1983 through 1987 Maryland/DC Atlas project are shown in table 1.

Atlas Safe Dates

The safe dates given in the *Maryland & DC Breeding Bird Atlas Project Handbook* indicated the period between migration seasons when each species can be assumed to be on territory. (See appendix A.) Many species present in Maryland throughout the year are considered safe for only a few months, either because they wander or because additional birds from the north are present. Barn Owls, for example, nest here every month of the year, but birds from farther north also migrate into or through the state without nesting. Blue Jays begin nesting here in April, but migrants, especially one-year-old birds, are still passing northward through the state as late as 10 June. In one year, the migration continued to the extraordinary date of 2 July (Robbins 1967b). Although Blue Jays confirmed as nesting in April are acceptable for Atlas purposes, mere presence, even in pairs, is not acceptable evidence unless it is within safe dates. Problems developed for a few species—Blue-winged Teal, Spotted Sandpiper, Common Raven, and some of the swallows—for which the safe dates were not adequate.

Verification of Unusual Records

To exercise some control over reporting of rarities, we required observers to submit a verification form detailing the basic information of each unusual record. An example of the form was printed in the handbook, and a supply of forms was given to each county coordinator. The criteria for requiring documentation were also given in the handbook. Documentation was required for any region of the state in which a species was listed as rare, local, or formerly nested, or in which the status was uncertain or not given.

The verification form requested the species name; any available sketches or photos; the observer's name, address, and telephone number; the location of the observation (quad, block, exact locality) and its date and time; a full description of the area and habitat in which the bird was observed; full details of breeding evidence and behavior; the conditions under which the observation occurred (distance, length of time, light, weather, optical equipment, etc.); the means of identifying the species (full details regarding plumage, song, call notes, size comparison, behavior, etc.); and names, addresses, and telephone numbers of other observers.

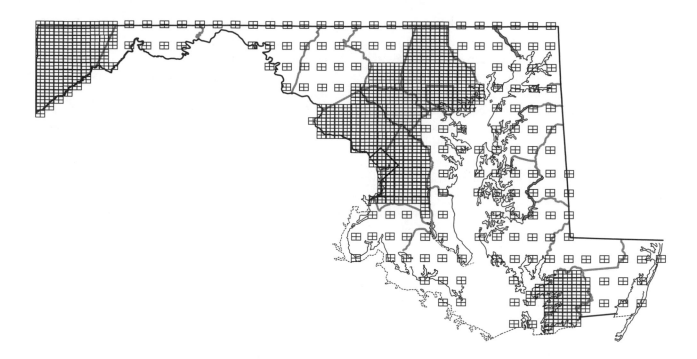

Figure 4. Areas Designated for Quarterblock Coverage

Table 1. Status Codes Used in the Maryland/DC Atlas Project

"OBSERVED"

O   Species observed in block but not in breeding habitat. This code was primarily for birds that do not breed in a block—for example, the thousands of Laughing Gulls in plowed fields on the lower Eastern Shore or the subadult Ring-billed Gulls that spend the summer in Maryland. Flyovers, such as soaring Turkey Vultures, were also in this category. Any species seen within Atlas safe dates with no further evidence of breeding were recorded as *O*.

"POSSIBLE"

X   Species heard or seen in breeding habitat within safe dates. For observations outside of safe dates, fieldworkers were urged to seek evidence of "probable" or "confirmed" breeding, the only categories that would be accepted during those times.

"PROBABLE" (Always a Single-letter Code)

A   Agitated behavior or anxiety calls from an adult. Parent birds respond to threats with distress calls or by attacking intruders. This did not include responses to "pishing" or tape playing.

P   Pair observed in suitable breeding habitat within safe dates. Caution was urged in using this code.

T   Territorial behavior or singing male present at the same location on at least two different days. Territoriality was presumed if an atlaser observed defensive encounters between individuals of the same species or a male singing from a variety of perches within a small area.

C   Courtship or copulation observed. This included displays, courtship feeding, and birds mating.

N   Visiting probable nest site; applied primarily to cavity nesters. This code was applied when a bird was observed visiting the site repeatedly, but no further evidence was seen.

B   Nest building by wrens or excavations by woodpeckers. Both groups build dummy nests or roosting cavities at the same time that they build one for nesting. However, because unmated males exhibit the same behavior, nest building by these groups is coded "probable."

"CONFIRMED" (Always a Two-letter Code)

NB   Nest building (except by wrens and woodpeckers) or adults carrying nest material. Carrying sticks is part of the courtship ritual (code *C*) of some species; caution was therefore urged in using this code.

DD   Distraction display. This included such behavior as feigning injury to distract an observer away from a nest. The Killdeer is well known for this behavior.

UN   Used nest found. Because nests are difficult to identify, extreme caution was applied in using this code. Nests were not collected for further identification because federal and state permits are required to do so. This code was particularly useful after the leaves had fallen.

FL   Recently fledged young or downy young. This code was used for dependent young only. Some species range widely soon after fledging, so caution was encouraged. Dead fledglings or nestlings on the road also confirmed breeding. Young Brown-headed Cowbirds begging for food confirmed both the cowbird and the host species.

FS   Adult bird seen carrying fecal sac. Feces of nestlings of many species are contained in a membranous sac, which parents carry away from the nest.

FY   Adult carrying food for young. The *FY* code was used with caution because a few species feed young long after wandering from nest sites, carry food a long distance, or engage in courtship feeding.

ON   Occupied nest presumed by activity of the parents: entering a nest hole and staying, parents exchanging incubation responsibilities, etc. This category was intended primarily for cavity nesters and for nests too high for the contents to be seen.

NE   Nest with eggs, or eggshells on the ground. Eggs and shells had to be carefully identified. Brown-headed Cowbird eggs in nests confirmed both the cowbird and the host species.

NY   Nest with young seen or heard. A Brown-headed Cowbird chick in a nest confirmed both the cowbird and the host species.

Because the breeding range and abundance of some species had been underestimated, so many verification reports—literally hundreds—were received the first year that it was impossible to verify them in person. (The Cedar Waxwing was the most notable example.) In addition, the use of verification forms proved to be inconsistent. Some observers used the forms for species that did not require them; other observers did not bother to submit forms. Local observers rarely verified reports. Instead, the Verification Committee was forced to make decisions based on the available information. They deleted all records of rarities not supported by verification forms. The Verification Committee also checked for typographical errors in data entry.

Data Processing

The Maryland Department of Natural Resources provided all data-entry services, computer storage, and data and retrieval functions for the Atlas project. An IBM mainframe was used for storage, retrieval, and analysis of Atlas data. The DNR's interactive minicomputer system provided direct-line access to the mainframe. SAS (Statistical Analysis System) and PL/1 were the primary software packages used. Therres (1986) summarized the initial data processing system, which was modified as necessary as the project progressed. The following paragraphs briefly summarize the process.

At the end of each field season, data were keyed directly from the summary sheets provided by the fieldworkers. The data included quadrangle name and number, block name and number, year, species identification number, breeding code, and quarterblock data. The data-entry program edited data as they were entered, checking for gross errors, such as incorrect breeding codes or invalid species numbers. This step saved time in the editing process. At this stage, the data were stored in batch files on the minicomputer.

A computer edit was then run to check for discrepancies between quadrangle name and number and invalid species numbers. Once the discrepancies were resolved, a paper copy of the block data was produced. It was manually edited for data-entry mistakes that could not be edited by computer, such as data for a species not reported on the summary sheet or data missed during entry. Corrections were then made to batch files on the minicomputer.

After all data for the year were edited and corrected, they were electronically transferred to the mainframe and merged into a master file. The merge program eliminated duplicate records and upgraded the breeding code for a given species within a block to the highest recorded category. From this master file a variety of data summary printouts were generated, including listings of species within blocks, listings of all blocks in which a given species was recorded, statistical summaries of block coverage, and summaries of species status by breeding code. For editing purposes, an interim map was generated for each species by a custom PL/1 program.

While data were being edited on the minicomputer, programs were written to handle the digitizing and plotting routines necessary to complete the mapping for the final publication. A microcomputer database management system, Advanced Revelation, was used to develop the mapping database. County boundaries were digitized into the database. A mathematical formula was used to generate 7.5-minute quadrangle map boundaries, based on the scale of the map being produced. The county and quadrangle map was then used as the base map for the Atlas data.

Four symbols were chosen, one to represent each of the four breeding categories "observed," "possible," "probable," and "confirmed." For each species, the mapping program read the database to determine the appropriate block in which to enter the symbol representing the Atlas code. Although the block boundaries were not plotted, the symbol was plotted in the block location within the quad.

The Atlas database is currently maintained on computer by the DNR. Requests for data should be directed to the Wildlife and Heritage Division, DNR, Tawes State Office Building, Annapolis, MD 21401.

Coverage

Goals

Most Maryland Atlas blocks were presumed by the Atlas Advisory Board to contain 90 to 100 breeding species; exceptions were blocks in urban areas and those containing a large percentage of open water. The Maryland/DC Atlas goal was the same one adopted by many other eastern states: to locate 75 percent of the number of species estimated to occur in the block. As a general rule, observers were encouraged to try for 70 species in rural blocks and 40 species in urban areas. Minimum time suggested for the coverage of a single block was 20 hours, but coordinators emphasized that thorough coverage of all habitats in the block was more important than the number of hours involved.

Some state atlas projects have put considerable emphasis on "confirmed" records and have attempted to "confirm" half the species detected in each block. Because many species require hours of effort to "confirm," Maryland chose instead to emphasize raising all common species to at least "probable" status, suggesting that a valid goal for each block was 25 percent "confirmed," 50 percent "probable," and a maximum of 25 percent "possible." Coordinators also requested special effort to "confirm" rare and locally unexpected species.

The Atlas board also believed that an understanding of the breeding status of widely distributed birds was not a function of the number of confirmations (see, for example, the Northern Cardinal). A high percentage of "confirmed" records for common species would occur in the normal course of fieldwork, and additional time and effort spent specifically attempting to produce such records for the European Starling, Mourning Dove, Carolina Chickadee, Tufted Titmouse, and other common birds could detract from the effort to find and establish the breeding status of rarer species.

Special Efforts

Special efforts were necessary in some areas of the state, especially in counties without MOS chapters. These efforts included block-busting trips (to record as many species as possible in a short period of time), all-night owl trips, special atlasing trips during MOS conventions, and participation with other states and provinces in the observance of a World Atlas Day at the height of the breeding season.

Special Studies

Graduate students, the DNR, and the Migratory Bird Research staff of the USFWS stationed at PWRC conducted several special field studies during the Atlas period. These included studies of breeding ecology of birds of prey in western Maryland, an inventory of colonial nesting waterbirds, a distributional study of rails and other marsh birds, and a study of the use of mature woodlots of various sizes by migratory birds (Robbins et al. 1989a).

Another study by PWRC biologists was directly related to the Maryland/DC Atlas project (Robbins and Dowell 1989). It focused on atlas methodology, with special reference to the ability of atlases to monitor changes in bird populations over a period of years. As part of this study, the Patuxent Migratory Bird Research staff intensively covered a random 2 percent sample of the Maryland Atlas blocks. Because Garrett County, the Atlas's only high elevation county, was not represented in the random sample of 25 blocks, a separate sample of 5 random blocks was covered in that county. The coverage of these 30 random blocks was in addition to any work done in these blocks prior to the beginning of the 1984 PWRC study. Regardless of who found them, all recorded birds were used in the block totals. For example, some blocks extended into Pennsylvania, and some species were detected only by Pennsylvania observers. Those records were nevertheless included.

The average effort in the 30 random blocks was about 30 hours. The average number of species detected in the 25 blocks exclusive of Garrett County was 88, and the average for the 5 Garrett County blocks was 101. The average number of species per Atlas block for Maryland and DC, including bayside blocks that contained very little dry land, was 73. Comparisons of the species lists for the 30 random blocks with Atlas records from the rest of the state showed that the common species were recorded equally well in both sets. In contrast, comparisons of records for rare and secretive species, or for those that are rare in portions of the state showed a difference in the species lists. Several of these differences are discussed in the species accounts, but a few examples are given here.

The Cedar Waxwing is an abundant breeding species in Garrett County, and it becomes progressively more scarce as one moves eastward across the state. This species was found in all 30 of the random blocks, including the block that included Assateague Island. Statewide, however, the Cedar Waxwing was found in only half of the Atlas blocks. Cooper's Hawk is a secretive species that requires special effort; it was found in 46 percent of the 30 random blocks, but in only 14 percent statewide. Another special-effort bird was the Eastern Screech-Owl, which was found in 90 percent of the random blocks but in only 53 percent statewide. Thus these special-effort blocks serve to calibrate the effectiveness of statewide coverage.

Within the area of the Chesapeake Bay and the tidal portions of its tributaries is one of the largest marsh ecosystems in the eastern United States. By the end of the fourth year of fieldwork, it was apparent that even experienced and highly motivated fieldworkers were having trouble with marsh species, especially nocturnal and secretive ones. Normal at-las techniques are largely ineffective in mapping the distribution of these birds (Blom 1986). The DNR therefore funded a summer of atlasing rails and other marsh birds; this effort was undertaken during the last year of fieldwork.

Another special study was the intensive effort devoted by Howard County participants during the final two years of the Atlas project. They launched a concerted effort to search every quarterblock in the county for each species that had not been detected up to that time. This effort even exceeded a similar effort during the previous Howard County quarterblock atlas from 1973 through 1975 (Klimkiewicz and Solem 1978); thus, it provided an unprecedented opportunity to detect changes that had occurred during the intervening decade (Robbins et al. 1989c). The major changes detected are discussed under the heading Population Changes.

The Environment

Location and Size of Maryland and the District of Columbia

Maryland is located midway along the Atlantic Coast of the United States between north latitudes 38° and 40° and west longitudes 75° and 79°30'. The total area of Maryland is only 10,577 square miles (27,394 sq km), of which the total land area is 9,837 square miles (25,478 sq km). DC lies near the geographic center of Maryland and is crossed by latitude 39° and longitude 77°. Despite its small size, Maryland occupies a strategic position. In addition to stretching from the Ohio River drainage west of the Allegheny Divide to the Atlantic Ocean (see fig. 5), Maryland boasts one of the world's great estuaries, the Chesapeake Bay, which has a longer tidal shoreline than that which borders the entire state of California.

The Mason-Dixon line separates Maryland from Pennsylvania on the north. The Potomac River, which lies entirely in Maryland, forms most of the southern boundary. Delaware forms the eastern boundary, except for the southernmost 31 miles (50 km), which are on the Atlantic Ocean. Garrett, Maryland's westernmost county, is bounded on its western and southern borders by West Virginia.

Soils

Soils, which have a strong influence on vegetation and thus on bird distribution, have been mapped in detail for each Maryland county, as shown in U.S. Department of Agriculture Soil Conservation Service soil survey publications. In addition to providing maps and descriptions of each soil type, these publications show the principal crops and forest trees typical of each soil type. At the Atlas block scale, one is more concerned with the major soil types than with the complex configuration of soils identified at the county level. The Atlas soil map is a simplified version of the General Soil Map of Maryland (Miller 1967) and shows three major soil types. (See fig. 6, page 18.)

Consolidated sedimentary rocks from acid shale and sandstone are the parent materials from which all soils in western Maryland were derived. This region includes all of Maryland from the western boundary east through the Hagerstown Valley in Washington County. It also includes the Monocacy Valley from the eastern base of Catoctin Mountain east to Union Bridge, Woodsboro, and Buckeystown in Frederick County, and the western tip of Montgomery County from Dickerson and Martinsburg east to Seneca Creek.

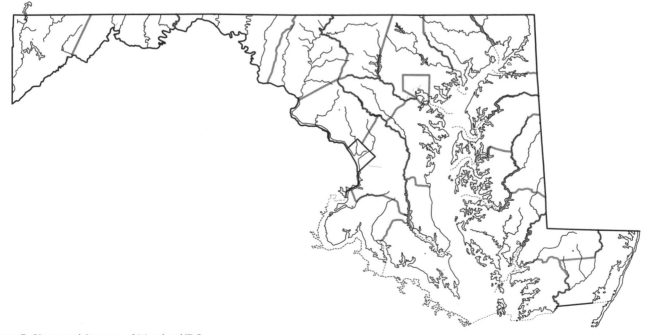

Figure 5. Rivers and Streams of Maryland/DC

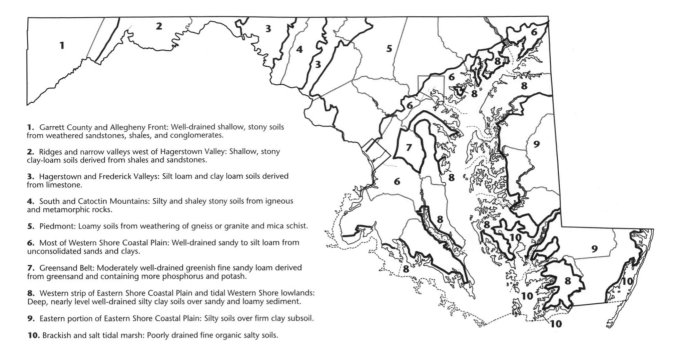

1. **Garrett County and Allegheny Front:** Well-drained shallow, stony soils from weathered sandstones, shales, and conglomerates.

2. **Ridges and narrow valleys west of Hagerstown Valley:** Shallow, stony clay-loam soils derived from shales and sandstones.

3. **Hagerstown and Frederick Valleys:** Silt loam and clay loam soils derived from limestone.

4. **South and Catoctin Mountains:** Silty and shaley stony soils from igneous and metamorphic rocks.

5. **Piedmont:** Loamy soils from weathering of gneiss or granite and mica schist.

6. **Most of Western Shore Coastal Plain:** Well-drained sandy to silt loam from unconsolidated sands and clays.

7. **Greensand Belt:** Moderately well-drained greenish fine sandy loam derived from greensand and containing more phosphorus and potash.

8. **Western strip of Eastern Shore Coastal Plain and tidal Western Shore lowlands:** Deep, nearly level well-drained silty clay soils over sandy and loamy sediment.

9. **Eastern portion of Eastern Shore Coastal Plain:** Silty soils over firm clay subsoil.

10. **Brackish and salt tidal marsh:** Poorly drained fine organic salty soils.

Figure 6. Generalized Soil Map of Maryland

By way of contrast, basic igneous and metamorphic rocks formed the chief parent material for soils of the Maryland Piedmont and also of Catoctin and South mountains, the Middletown Valley, Sugarloaf Mountain, and Maryland's small share of the Blue Ridge Mountains.

The entire Coastal Plain comprises soils formed from unconsolidated coastal plain sediments. Within the Coastal Plain, the most distinctive soil subdivisions are the tidal marshes, sand dunes, coastal beaches, and the Greensand Belt that extends from DC to Annapolis and Mayo in Anne Arundel County.

Physiographic Regions

The six physiographic regions are the same as those adopted by Stewart and Robbins (1958): They are the Allegheny Mountain, Ridge and Valley, Piedmont, Western Shore, Eastern Shore, and Upper Chesapeake sections. (See fig. 7.) These regions are a slight modification of Braun's proposed classification of the regions of the eastern deciduous forests of North America (Braun 1950).

The Allegheny Mountain Section, in the far west, extends westward from the base of the Allegheny Front in western Allegany County. It consists primarily of the Allegheny Plateau, which is crossed by several higher ridges. The western half of Garrett County lies in the Mississippi drainage basin. Deciduous trees now dominate the Allegheny Mountain Section.

The Ridge and Valley Section includes the Catoctin ridge, the Middletown Valley, the South Mountain ridge, the Hagerstown Valley, and the series of heavily wooded ridges between there and the base of the Allegheny Front to the west. The Piedmont and the Ridge and Valley sections are in

Braun's (1950) Oak-Chestnut Forest Region, from which the once-typical American chestnut has all but disappeared. Flowering dogwood was still an ever-present understory tree during this Atlas period, but because of disease problems it may not long remain an important indicator for this region.

The Piedmont Section extends eastward from the base of Catoctin Mountain, which is the northern extension of the Blue Ridge Mountains of Virginia, to the Fall Line. The Fall Line, which runs northeastward from DC through Baltimore to Wilmington, Delaware, separates the Piedmont from the Coastal Plain Province.

The southeastern half of Maryland lies on the Atlantic Coastal Plain, which is divided into three sections not recognized by Braun (1950): the Western Shore (west of the Chesapeake Bay), the Eastern Shore (east of the Chesapeake Bay and north to southern Kent County and central Caroline County), and the Upper Chesapeake (which includes the flat necks on the northwestern side of the Chesapeake Bay and the portion north of the Eastern Shore Section on the eastern side). The Coastal Plain lies in the Oak-Pine Forest Region and occupies slightly more than half of the state. Loblolly pines are characteristic of the Eastern Shore Section, whereas Virginia pines are prominent in much of the Western Shore Section. The Upper Chesapeake Section is characterized primarily by the absence of pines.

Elevations

Elevations in Maryland range from low flat terraces below 100 feet (30 m) to mountain ridges at 3,360 feet (1,024 m). (See fig. 8.) The Allegheny Mountain Section averages about 2,500 feet (760 m), with the ridges about 500 feet (152 m) above the rolling valleys. The highest point in Maryland

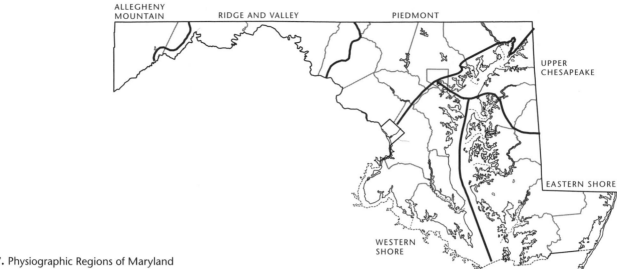

Figure 7. Physiographic Regions of Maryland

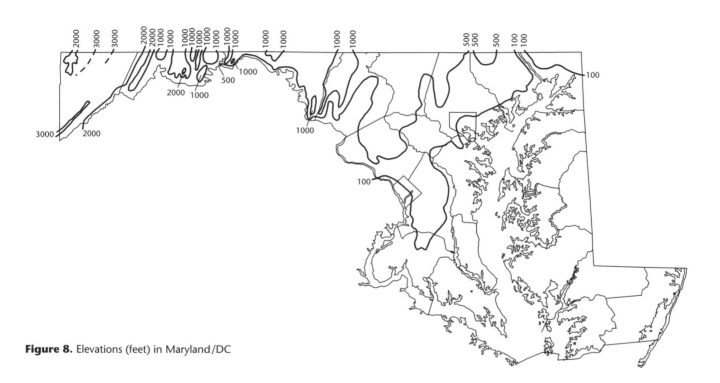

Figure 8. Elevations (feet) in Maryland/DC

is at 3,360 feet (1,024 m) on Backbone Mountain, within 2 miles (3 km) of the southern tip of Garrett County. The Ridge and Valley Section ranges from 500 to 800 feet (152–244 m) in the valleys to 2,000 feet (610 m) on the higher ridges. The Piedmont Section is largely between 300 and 800 feet (91–244 m), whereas most of the Coastal Plain west of the Chesapeake Bay ranges between 100 and 300 feet (30–91 m) in elevation. The Eastern Shore Section is low and flat and is composed of three terraces, all at elevations below 100 feet (30 m).

Land Use

The Presettlement Forest of Maryland

Before the arrival of Europeans, Maryland was part of a vast wilderness of forests and wetlands. The region was dynamic and the landscape was subject to many disturbances. The small population of Native Americans learned to harness long-established ecological processes to supply their needs. Their use of fire was legendary, but their likely strategy for game management was to maintain openings in areas naturally predisposed to fire (Pyne 1982). The Native American active manipulation of habitat was only one of many disturbances that created or maintained forest openings; however, fire and other destructive forces barely affected the prevalence of virgin forest over large tracts of the landscape.

Many species and processes worked against the old-growth forest. Several animals associated with early successional habitat were common. Beaver numbered in the hundreds of thousands, and elk and bison are recorded in the names of many landmarks, such as Elkton and Buffalo Marsh. The herbivorous feeding habits of these animals helped to arrest the natural succession of openings to forest. Wind and ice storms also strafed the old-growth forest canopy, toppling patches of trees of various ages and providing habitat for edge and open country species.

The presettlement forest of Maryland supported a rich diversity of early successional species and habitats embedded within its cloak of old-growth forest. Several large areas of open "barren" habitat, as well as numerous meadows, glades, and sapling woods were observed by the first European colonists (Mayre 1955; Pyne 1982). The original land patents are replete with descriptions of early successional habitat. One of the largest unforested tracts was in the Hagerstown Valley, which Charles Carroll discovered near his Carrollton Manor in the lower valley of the Monocacy Creek (Frederick County). Mayre (1955) cites his 1753 description:

about thirty miles from Navigable Water is a Range of barren dry Land without Timber about nine miles wide which keeps a Course about North East and South West parallel with the mountains thro this province Virginia & Pennsilvania but between that and the Mountains the lands mend and are Very good in Several parts.

Fire is probably the chief reason that large openings were maintained. Post oak and blackjack oak are representative of vegetation typically associated with fire, growing on dry soils (Lutz 1934; Christensen 1988; Greller 1988). Brush et al. (1980) identified and mapped several areas of this forest association still in evidence today, covering a large region of southern Maryland, in scattered locales on the Eastern Shore, on a broad expanse north and west of Baltimore (e.g., Soldiers Delight Serpentine Barrens), and at the base of one of the mountain ranges in the Hagerstown Valley. As in most areas of high fire frequency, the burn is often patchy and creates a mosaic of variable disturbance over time. The fact that the Greater Prairie Chicken (Heath Hen) once inhabited the tidewater region of Maryland (last reported in 1860 from southern Prince George's County) is further evidence for the presence and persistence of significant forest openings.

Many bird species were believed to have moved into Maryland from other regions of the country subsequent to extensive clearing of the state's forest. It is more likely, however, that most of these purported immigrants were native to the natural openings in the presettlement landscape. The Upland Sandpiper, Northern Harrier, Loggerhead Shrike, Savannah Sparrow, Lark Sparrow, Henslow's Sparrow, and Bachman's Sparrow probably shifted their nesting requirements to man-made fields after Europeans usurped the natural openings. Nevertheless, these species largely retained fidelity to their historic breeding grounds in the state. The Loggerhead Shrike, although an extremely rare breeding bird in Maryland today, still regularly attempts to nest in pastures in the Hagerstown Valley. Its breeding range is a strong indication that natural disturbances maintained continuous populations in the vicinity.

Old-growth forests were shaped by dynamic forces. The frequency of small-scale disturbances in the vast forest was much greater than today. The large crowns of old-growth trees predispose them to the forces of wind and gravity. Fire, beavers, streams and associated marshes and other wetlands, Native American agriculture, and environmental conditions all created gaps of various sizes in the forest canopy. As a consequence, sufficient edge habitat was continually developing to support populations of scrubland birds. The American Woodcock, Red-winged Blackbird, Northern Bobwhite ("small quail-sized partridge"), and Northern Cardinal ("redbird") were noticed by the early settlers (Hall 1910).

The matrix supporting these relatively small patches of early successional habitats, however, was contiguous old-growth forest (Brown et al. 1987). The primeval forest was heavily dominated by mast-producing species, particularly oak, hickory, chestnut, and walnut. Lord Baltimore stated that the abundance of nuts enabled the colonist to overwinter "cattel and Hoggs . . . in the woods, without fodder, or other helpe. . . . The Mast and the Chestnuts, and what rootes they find in the woods, doe feede the Swine very fat, and will breede great store" (Hall 1910).

The abundance of mast in the state's old-growth forest enabled many species to attain their optimal population size. George Alsop wrote an essay in 1666 titled "Character of the Province of Maryland," which describes the abundance of Wild Turkey in the original forest: "I have seen in whole hundreds in flights in the Woods of Mary-Land" (Hall 1910).

The primeval habitat supplied essential conditions for several species of birds. Maryland's old-growth forest ecosystem probably provided critical food and nesting sites for the Northern Goshawk, Carolina Parakeet, Passenger Pigeon, Red-cockaded Woodpecker, and possibly even the Ivory-billed Woodpecker (Kirkwood 1895; Wright 1912; Jackson 1988c; Boone, this volume). Old-growth forest conditions may be the optimal habitat for many other species, such as the Pileated Woodpecker, Hairy Woodpecker, Hooded Merganser, Wood Duck, Winter Wren, Cerulean Warbler, and Blackburnian Warbler (Conner 1978; DeGraaf and Rudis 1986; Adkisson 1988; Haramis 1991; Robbins et al. 1992).

Destruction of old growth curtailed the forest's great mast-producing capabilities, and it also caused a shift in forest dominants to trees with lighter seeds, such as red maple and pines. Brown et al. (1987) observed that red maple was not included among the more than six hundred kinds of trees and other plants collected by early naturalists in colonial Maryland. This omission is surprising because red maple is now the most numerous tree species in the state (Frieswyk and DiGiovanni 1988). "It is likely that pure stands of pine were rare in colonial Maryland, and even mixed pine-oak woodlands were scattered.... [T]he expansion of pine since colonial times has resulted from the cutting of native hardwood species" (Brown et al. 1987).

Although disturbances periodically created openings and set back succession in the extensive canopy of the old-growth deciduous forest, the dominant disturbance pattern in most forest types was the death of individual trees. Approximately 0.5 to 2 percent of the canopy trees die each year in an old-growth forest, allowing sunlight through the resultant gap to stimulate regeneration or facilitate the emergence of formerly suppressed trees (Runkle 1985).

The result of this extensive but low-intensity disturbance is a forest composed of trees of all ages, with many small and a few giant-sized individuals. An abundance of dead and downed trees is typical, accumulating coarse woody debris on the forest floor in the absence of frequent fires. Multiple although indistinct layers of foliage, from the forest floor to the spreading crowns of dominant trees, help to deflect the wind and preserve soil moisture and humidity. The great diversity of structures and high levels of biomass within the old-growth forest enable many birds that dwell in the forest interior to sustain their highest population density (Stewart and Robbins 1947a; Gauthreaux 1978; Shugart et al. 1978).

The forest-interior birds probably thrived in precolonial times. Although large disturbances did occur, the ratio of edge to forest interior habitat was vastly lower than it is today. Increasing forest fragmentation aggravates the problems associated with the edge effect. The Brown-headed Cowbird was probably fairly rare in Maryland prior to the introduction of cattle and intensive agriculture. This brood parasite is now potentially a major factor in the viability of breeding bird populations (Brittingham and Temple 1983). In comparison to their burgeoning populations today, crows, jays, and grackles were also relatively uncommon predators on forest birds. Our current highly fragmented forest has all of these problems and more.

The creation of more edge and the reduction of forest interior are radically altering the balance between interior-dwelling species and their predators and competitors. In precolonial times, edge species were not significant competitors with interior species for food and nesting space because edge habitat was comparatively scarce. Small populations were rarely isolated from nearby sources of recolonization. Larger predators, such as wolves and mountain lions, controlled the populations of raccoons and other nest predators, which probably did not attain high populations in forest-interior habitat. Although white-tailed deer were abundant in Maryland's primeval forest, their population probably failed to attain the density of today's edge-supported herds. Large predators and Native American hunters would check population imbalances long before browsing deer could eliminate the forest understory, as is happening in many of Maryland's woodlands today.

The abundance of edge compared with the scarcity of forest interior in Maryland's present landscape decreases the ability of many forest-nesting bird species to survive. They must cope with an environment drastically different from the comparatively stress-free condition in which they evolved. Although the Red-eyed Vireo and Eastern Wood-Pewee may continue to be abundant in Maryland's dwindling forest landscape, the prospects are growing dim for the Hooded Warbler and many other forest-interior dwellers as their habitat continues to be shredded and homogenized.

Fragmentation continues to eat away at Maryland's forests. Only about 40 percent of the acreage of presettlement forest still remains, and Maryland is rapidly losing its remaining trees—more than 70,000 acres (28,329 ha) of forest disappeared between 1985 and 1990 (Maryland Office of Planning 1991). Compared with the conditions in which most of our forest-nesting birds evolved, today's forest is not providing a good balance of habitat for Maryland's wildlife.

Of all the hardwood trees that comprise Maryland's present timberland, only 2 percent are hard, mast-producing species (i.e., oak, hickory, and beech) exceeding 13 inches (33 cm) in diameter. Fewer than 1 percent exceed 19 inches (48 cm) in diameter, and more than 82 percent are less than 7 inches (18 cm) in diameter (Frieswyk and DiGiovanni 1988). The time has come to reverse this trend and allow some forestland to continue to grow, eventually reestablishing old-growth conditions.

Large tracts of structurally diverse old-growth forest, containing trees of all ages (uneven-aged), are missing from Maryland's present landscape. A significant component of the state's birdlife would greatly benefit if some even-aged hardwood stands were allowed to undergo succession to develop a more diverse structure. Statewide plans for the conservation and restoration of key tracts of forestland throughout Maryland are urgently needed to safeguard forest-interior–nesting birds before they become endangered.

Forest Cover

When European settlers arrived 350 years ago, the percentage of Maryland's forest cover may have been as high as 95 percent, excluding only the tidal marshes, according to some estimates. That percentage would be a bit lower, but still at least 90 percent, if the Hagerstown Valley were unforested at that time. The maximum amount of cleared land occurred about 1860 (Besley 1910), followed by a trend toward abandoning farmland. Besley (1910) reported that 35 percent of Maryland was again forested in 1900. By the time

Figure 9. Forest Cover of Maryland

of the 1986 forest inventory, 39 percent of the state was commercial forest land and an additional 4 percent was noncommercial forest (Frieswyk and DiGiovanni 1988). (See fig. 9, page 22.) The proportion of commercial forest varied greatly by county, ranging from as little as 24 percent in Baltimore, Carroll, Montgomery, and Prince George's counties, to more than 50 percent in the eastern, southern, and western fringes of the state in Worcester (51%), St. Mary's (54%), Calvert (54%), Charles (61%), Garrett (71%), and Allegany (71%) counties. See figure 10 for map of county names. Total forested land in Maryland decreased by more than 10 percent from 1964 to 1975 (Powell and Kingsley 1980); all of this loss occurred on commercial forest land. The greatest loss (22%) occurred in the central block of counties, from Washington County east to the Delaware line and south through Prince George's, Anne Arundel, Talbot, and Caroline counties. Only in Garrett and Allegany counties in the far west did forest land increase (6%), as marginally productive farmland was allowed to revert to forest.

Forest Composition

The distribution of commercial forest land in 1986 by major forest type (Frieswyk and DiGiovanni 1988) was oak-hickory (60%), loblolly and shortleaf pine (12%), oak-pine (12%), oak-gum (5%), northern hardwoods (5%), elm-ash-red maple (3%), and red and white pine (2%). From west to east, the major forest communities are as follows:

• The Allegheny Mountain Section, including nearly all of Garrett County and the western edge of Allegany County, is in the Mixed Mesophytic Forest Region. The higher ridges are dominated by northern red oak and red maple, frequently with chestnut and black oaks, yellow birch, and other northern hardwoods. Deciduous trees also predominate in the valleys, where the principal species are sweet birch, sugar and red maples, black cherry, basswood, beech, shagbark hickory, and white and northern red oaks. Eastern hemlock and white pine also are frequent, especially on the north slopes and in the valleys. Characteristic trees of the bogs are red maple, yellow birch, eastern hemlock, and, locally, tamarack and red spruce. The evergreen plantings of the DNR, especially those that contain spruce, are an important new habitat that to some extent replaces the loss through logging of the native red spruce in the uplands. Most of Maryland's breeding Golden-crowned Kinglets now nest in planted spruce, and other northern birds may find the spruce plantations attractive in the future.

• The Blue Ridge and the Ridge and Valley described by Fenneman (1938) are combined into the Ridge and Valley Section of the Oak-Chestnut Forest Region. This includes most of Allegany County, all of Washington County, and the western, mountainous portion of Frederick County. Chestnut oak is dominant and, since the disappearance of American chestnut, occurs in nearly pure stands on some of the ridgetops and upper slopes. Scarlet oak predominates on some of the drier slopes, along with patches of Virginia, pitch, or Table Mountain pine. The Mixed Mesophytic Forest communities of the Allegheny Mountain Section are found on the steep northern slopes and in the ravines; on the valley floors, the white and black oaks and tuliptree are to be expected. The Hagerstown Valley is largely devoid of forest except in a narrow strip of floodplain along the Potomac River and in the limestone area west of Conococheague Creek, which support groves of eastern red cedar.

• The Piedmont Section also falls in the Oak-Chestnut Forest Region. Dominant Piedmont trees in the upland are white, chestnut, black, and scarlet oaks and tuliptree. On the steep north slopes, one also finds northern red oak, beech, hickories, basswood, and, locally, some white pine and eastern hemlock.

• The Upper Chesapeake, Western Shore, and Eastern Shore sections of the Atlantic Coastal Plain are in the Oak-Pine Forest Region. The Upper Chesapeake Section, however, is almost entirely deciduous and is dominated by white, black, Spanish, and willow oaks, mockernut and pignut hickories, and sweet gum, with American hornbeam and flowering dogwood as dominant understory trees. The upland swamps, which are at least seasonally wet in spring, have pin oak, red maple, and black and sweet gums. In the floodplain forest along the major streams one finds American elm, white ash, and sweet gum.

• On the Western Shore Coastal Plain, oak-hickory forests are dominant, whereas Virginia pine stands are common on poor dry soils. All the tree species of the Upper Chesapeake Section also occur here. In the southern part of this section, especially near the Potomac River, loblolly pine replaces Virginia and pitch pine.

• The Eastern Shore Section is characterized by widespread loblolly pine and by bald cypress in the extensive swamps typical of this flat country. The other Coastal Plain trees occur here as well.

These brief descriptions hardly do justice to the great variety of forest habitats and the huge variety of forest trees with which Maryland is blessed. For example, Brown and Brown (1972) included 19 oak species, 21 hawthorn species, 15 willow species, and 9 native pine species among the Maryland flora.

Recently passed state laws now require identification of the location of Maryland's existing forests. The DNR has forest vegetation maps for each county. For additional information on composition of forest habitats in Maryland, contact DNR Forest Service. For detailed forest statistics, refer to Frieswyk and DiGiovanni (1988). For habitat descriptions of BBC plots, see the various population study issues of *Audubon Field Notes* (1947–70), *American Birds* (1971–84), and *Journal of Field Ornithology* (1989–96 supplements).

Area Constraints

Just as important as the kind of forest are the size, shape, and isolation of the forest; these factors determine whether the forest can support various species of breeding birds, especially the neotropical migrants. These insectivorous species—primarily tanagers, warblers, vireos, thrushes, and some of the flycatchers—are especially susceptible to predation and Brown-headed Cowbird parasitism, factors that are concentrated along forest edges. The only woodlots likely to provide safe nesting for most of the area-sensitive long-distance migrants are woodlots large enough to contain several hectares of forest interior at a distance of more than 330 feet (100 m)—preferably twice that distance—from any edge. For more details on this problem, see Robbins (1979, 1980), Whitcomb et al. (1981), Lynch and Whigham (1984), and Robbins et al. (1989a).

Agriculture

At the beginning of this century there were 46,012 farms in Maryland with an average of 112.4 acres (45 ha) and a total of 5,170,075 acres (2.09 million ha) (Blodgett 1910). Calvert, Somerset, and Howard counties each had fewer than 150,000 acres (60,700 ha) in farms. Frederick had the highest number of acres, at 308,041 (124,662 ha), in farmland. Statewide, the greatest cropland acreage was in corn (658,010 acres), wheat (634,446 acres), and hay (357,224 acres). There were 147,284 dairy cows.

By 1987 the number of farms had decreased by more than 60 percent to 16,500 (Maryland Department of Agriculture 1988). The average farm size had increased to 148 acres, and the total land in farms had dropped to 2,450,000 acres (0.99 million ha), a 53% drop. The chief crops, in acres harvested, were corn for grain (460,000 acres), soybeans (410,000), hay (235,000), wheat (165,000), barley (89,000), and vegetables (43,700). The number of dairy cows had also decreased by 23 percent, to 114,000. Poultry, not mentioned in Blodgett's (1910) report, resulted in the marketing of 1.1 billion pounds (500 million kg) of broilers, 926 million eggs, and 2.6 million pounds (1.18 million kg) of turkeys in 1987.

During the short period from 1975 to 1987, the total Maryland farm acreage dropped 17 percent, from 2,950,000 to 2,450,000 (1,193,850 to 991,500 ha) (Maryland Department of Agriculture 1988).

Human Population

The human population of Maryland has been increasing at a very high rate, especially since 1940. This is having, and will continue to have, a major impact on wildlife resources. The more adaptable species can be expected to increase, but birds with special habitat requirements—such as those that rely on wetlands, beaches, abandoned fields, floodplain forest, and extensive undisturbed forest—will decline. In 1970, Maryland ranked fifth among the 50 states in population density, averaging 397 people per square mile (153 per sq km). By 1990, Maryland had 481 people per square mile (186 per sq km). A summary of population data for Maryland (Maryland Office of Planning 1991) is presented in table 2.

During the next one hundred to two hundred years, if not much sooner, Maryland residents will face many difficult decisions regarding priorities for land use. In most Maryland counties, the human population has been spiraling upward each decade since 1900. (See fig. 10 and table 3.) Only Baltimore City and Allegany County registered a decline from 1970 to 1980. From 1900 to 1990 the state population increased 298 percent from 1,188,044 to 4,732,934. If the population increases during the next century at the rate of the 1970s, Maryland will have about 10,000,000 residents by the year 2100. That figure would average more than 1,000 people per square mile (386 per sq km), or the equivalent of making the rural counties as populous as the suburban counties were in

Table 2. Human Population of Maryland, Showing Rate of Increase by Decades

Year	Population	Percentage of Increase
1900	1,190,050	—
1910	1,295,346	8.8%
1920	1,449,661	11.9%
1930	1,631,526	12.5%
1940	1,821,244	11.6%
1950	2,343,001	28.6%
1960	3,100,689	32.3%
1970	3,922,399	26.5%
1980	4,216,975	7.5%
1990	4,732,934	12.2%

Table 3. Human Population Growth by Counties
(Data from Maryland's Office of Planning)

| | 1980 Census | | Percentage Change | |
	Population	People per sq mile	1970–80	1980–90
Jurisdiction				
Baltimore City	786,775	9,793	-13.1	- 8.5
Baltimore suburbs				
Baltimore	655,615	1,097	+ 5.7	+ 4.9
Carroll	96,356	213	+39.6	+27.8
Harford	145,930	326	+26.5	+24.0
Howard	118,572	472	+90.0	+57.0
Washington suburbs				
Charles	72,751	161	+52.6	+27.5
Montgomery	579,053	1,169	+10.8	+29.7
Prince George's	665,071	1,366	+ 0.5	+ 8.2
Annapolis suburbs				
Anne Arundel	370,775	886	+24.4	+14.3
Calvert	34,638	162	+67.5	+46.3
Queen Anne's	25,508	69	+38.5	+32.1
Salisbury suburbs				
Wicomico	64,540	170	+19.0	+14.6
Western Maryland				
Allegany	80,548	188	- 4.3	- 7.5
Frederick	114,792	173	+35.2	+30.3
Garrett	26,498	40	+23.4	+ 1.2
Washington	113,086	249	+ 8.9	+ 7.7
Southern Maryland				
St. Mary's	59,895	161	+26.4	+25.3
Eastern Shore (except Queen Anne's and Wicomico)				
Caroline	23,143	72	+17.0	+15.7
Cecil (Newark, DE, suburbs)	60,430	168	+13.4	+17.4
Dorchester	30,623	52	+ 4.1	- 0.6
Kent	16,695	60	+ 3.4	+ 3.1
Talbot	25,604	99	+ 8.1	+18.5
Somerset	19,188	57	+ 1.4	+21.7
Worcester	30,889	65	+26.4	+11.7
STATE TOTAL	4,216,975	429	+ 7.5	+12.2

1980. How much land will be left for providing food, forest products, recreational opportunities, and wildlife habitat?

Climate

Maryland has a favorable climate with moderate temperatures, abundant sunshine, precipitation that is well distributed throughout the year, few prolonged periods of drought, and few severe storms. Climate has an enormous influence not only on the vegetation that birds need for food and cover, but also on the arthropods on which most birds depend. Among these influences are extreme temperatures, precipitation, high winds, and high tides. Birds have many periods of stress, especially when they are feeding young or migrating, and any one of many climatic factors can result in death or reproductive failure. If temperatures are too high, they can cause death by exposure to the sun; if they are too low, birds may become chilled or important plant or insect food may be destroyed by freezing. Too little rain can reduce plant or insect foods, and too heavy or prolonged rains may cause flooding or make flying insects unavailable. Heavy snow,

Figure 10. Names of Maryland Counties

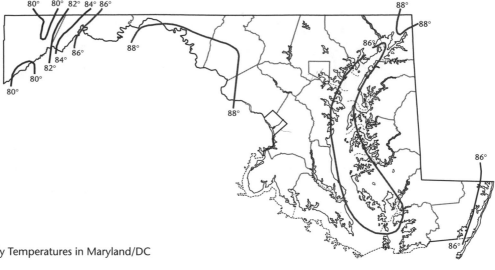

Figure 11. Mean Maximum July Temperatures in Maryland/DC

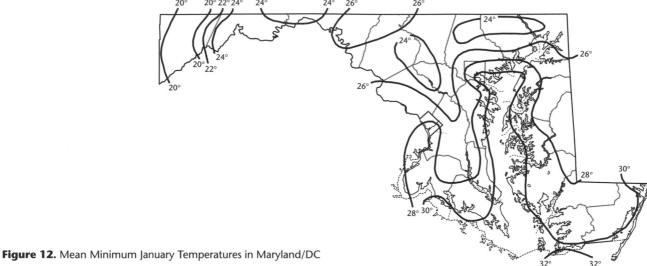

Figure 12. Mean Minimum January Temperatures in Maryland/DC

sleet, or prolonged icing in the winter or early spring can induce starvation among permanent residents or early migrants, and cold soaking rains during migration cause stress by making insect food unavailable when it is most needed. Finally, wind storms at any season can destroy nests, kill young and adults, and make food more difficult to obtain.

Climatic maps demonstrate some of the reasons for the distributional limits or abrupt changes in abundance of certain bird species. (See figs. 11–14.) For example, one might expect the breeding range of a half-hardy permanent resident species such as the Northern Bobwhite to be influenced by the amount of snowfall, and that of a northern species such as the Magnolia Warbler to be limited to Garrett County with its cooler summer temperatures. Although many limits still are not understood completely, we hope the maps will help readers understand some of the influences that climate exerts on the distribution and abundance of some of the state's breeding species. Those interested in exploring distributional limits in more detail may make acetate overlays from the climatological maps in this volume.

Temperature

Average July temperatures are near 76°F (24°C) except in the two western counties. As one ascends the Allegheny Front in western Allegany County, the average July temperature drops from 74°F (23°C) to 70°F (21°C), and in central Garrett County the average is 68°F (20°C). Temperatures of 100°F (38°C) or higher occur somewhere in Maryland every year; the highest on record is 109°F (43°C) in 1898. Mean maximum July temperatures throughout the state are shown in figure 11. Average January temperatures are 38°F (3°C) on the lower Eastern Shore, dropping gradually to 32°F (0°C) east of the mountains as one approaches the Pennsylvania state line, and to 28°F (-2°C) in central Garrett County. Minimum January temperatures (see fig. 12) probably have a more serious effect on winter survival of birds than do mean temperatures in that month. The length of the growing season ranges from 120 days at the southern tip of Garrett County to 210 days in southern St. Mary's County and western Somerset County. In the Frederick-Elkton-Laurel triangle in the center of the state, the growing season is about 180

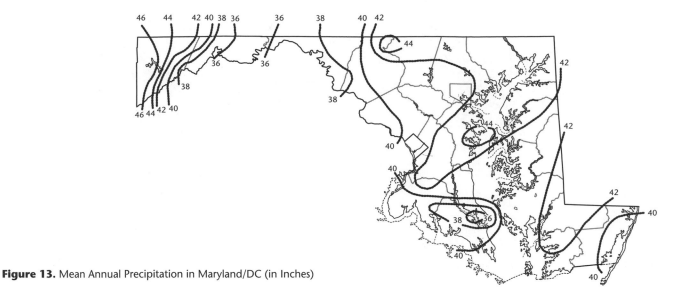

Figure 13. Mean Annual Precipitation in Maryland/DC (in Inches)

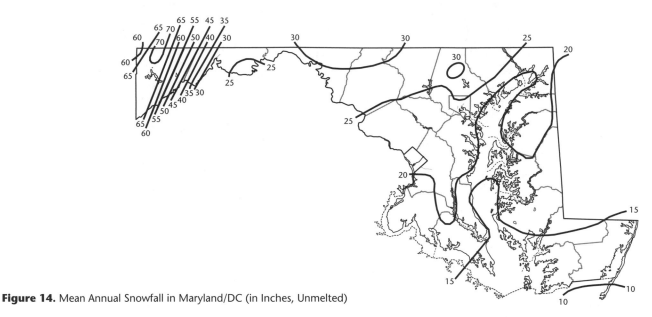

Figure 14. Mean Annual Snowfall in Maryland/DC (in Inches, Unmelted)

days; it rises rapidly to 200 days along the shore of the Chesapeake Bay.

Precipitation

Average annual precipitation is lowest in the Allegheny Mountain rain shadow in Allegany County at 36 inches (91 cm), and highest along the western border of Garrett County at 46 inches (117 cm). Most of Maryland averages between 40 and 44 inches (102–12 cm) of precipitation. (See fig. 13.) Precipitation tends to be a little higher during the growing season than it is in winter. Excessive rain, if it occurs, is most likely on the Coastal Plain. Some snow falls each winter in all parts of the state (see fig. 14), but on the Coastal Plain it usually does not remain on the ground more than a

week at a time. In contrast, the ground in Garrett County is usually covered with snow throughout most of January and February.

Wind

The average annual wind speed is 7.7 miles per hour (3.44 m/sec) at Baltimore and 7.3 (3.26 m/sec) at DC. The prevailing wind direction at Baltimore is from the southwest, and in DC it is from the south in summer and the northwest in winter. The highest recorded sustained winds for a five-minute period at both Baltimore and DC are 54 miles per hour (24 m/sec) in July 1902. Tornadoes are rare in Maryland, and most of the Atlantic coastal hurricanes veer eastward over the ocean before reaching the latitudes of Maryland.

Effects of Weather on Bird Populations

Weather affects the reproduction, survival, distribution, abundance, and migration of birds in many ways. Many of the weather effects are beyond the scope of this *Atlas*, but some that are closely tied to the distribution and abundance of breeding populations can be mentioned briefly here.

Flooding

Flash floods from summer thunderstorms frequently wipe out nesting attempts of ground-nesting birds. The timing of such floods can be critical to the successful reproduction of Kentucky Warblers, Louisiana Waterthrushes, Ovenbirds, and Veeries. The flooding of two successive nesting attempts in the same season can prevent these species from raising any young during the entire season.

June and July hurricanes have the potential to cause severe flooding even if the center of the storm passes offshore. Such a storm in 1973, the final year of the first Montgomery County atlas, caused swollen streams to rise over dozens of bridges at night, drowning a high percentage of the county's Eastern Phoebes. Observers who tried to find used nests after the storm could not even find the bridges, most of which had been washed away in the flood.

Flooding is also a problem with ground-nesting colonial waterbirds and other species that nest on beaches and in salt and brackish marshes. Storm tides, especially at the time of a new or a full moon, raise the water just enough to wash away nests of plovers, gulls, terns, Black Skimmers, American Oystercatchers, rails, Willets, Saltmarsh Sharp-tailed Sparrows, Seaside Sparrows, and some of the herons.

Prolonged Rain

During the nesting season, rain occasionally continues unabated for several days. This situation sometimes accompanies the inland passage of the remains of a summer tropical storm from the Gulf of Mexico, as happened in 1968 and 1972 (Robbins et al. 1986). In both of these years the rain coincided with the period when Purple Martins, which are single-brooded in Maryland, were trying to find flying insects to feed their young. Not only did the young birds starve but great numbers of adults also died because they were unable to find food for themselves and their young. Deaths also occurred among other swallows and flycatchers, but, unlike Purple Martins, most of the other species had the possibility of attempting a second brood if the adults survived.

Late Spring Freezes

About once each decade a hard freeze hits parts of Maryland after many trees have put out leaves. These late freezes reduce the supply of insects, often at a time when a flood of migrants is using the limited food supply. In addition to the immediate effect of restricting the food supply when the birds are under stress from the cold, the freeze also kills the new vegetation. The resulting loss of green vegetation makes nests more visible and more subject to predation. In many instances, flowers that would have produced berries or other food later in the season are also killed.

Wind Storms

Many nests are blown down by wind storms. The shallow, fragile nest of the Mourning Dove is a frequent victim, but even well-protected nests such as the cavity nests of woodpeckers are subject to destruction if the tree snaps off at the position of the nest. No nest is completely safe from a severe wind gust.

Results

Coverage

Maryland/DC atlasers achieved excellent coverage. Of the 1,262 5-kilometer Atlas blocks that contained at least 0.5 square kilometers (2%) land area, 1,256 (99.5%) were visited during the Atlas period. Blocks with less than 0.5 square kilometers of land area were not included in computations of percentage of blocks in which a species was found. We selected the 0.5 square kilometers of land area as the criterion for inclusion because that had been used in the Danish atlas (Dybbro 1976), which was the only published atlas that defined a minimum land area. Four of the six blocks that were not visited included a high percentage of Chesapeake Bay; only two of the missed blocks (Charlotte Hall CE and SW) were primarily land blocks that should have been included. Most of the blocks with fewer than 50 recorded species were tidewater blocks containing a high percentage of open water. The total species recorded in each block, including "observed" records, is given in appendix G.

Bird Populations

Of the 201 species recorded during the Atlas period, breeding was "confirmed" for 194. Species recorded but not "confirmed" during this period were the Double-crested Cormorant, American Bittern, Ringed Turtle-Dove, Monk Parakeet, Northern Saw-whet Owl, Yellow-bellied Sapsucker, Swainson's Warbler, and Pine Siskin. The Double-crested Cormorant, Northern Saw-whet Owl, and Pine Siskin were confirmed subsequent to the Atlas period. Several other species that formerly nested in Maryland were not found during the Atlas fieldwork. (See appendix C.) During that fieldwork, however, three new nesting species for Maryland were discovered: the Northern Shoveler at Blackwater National Wildlife Refuge (NWR) in 1985, the Brown Pelican on a spoil island off South Point in 1987, and the Black-necked Stilt at Deal Island Wildlife Management Area (WMA) in 1987. An additional 30 species that were recorded as summer vagrants appear in appendix D.

The number of species detected per 5-kilometer block varied from one in several Chesapeake Bay blocks that are mostly or entirely water to 115 in Bristol SE and 110 in Frostburg CW and 109 in Cumberland SE. There were 13 blocks in which 100 or more species were found. Six of these were in Garrett County, the others were Cumberland SE, Cherry

Run CW, Myersville SE, Laurel CW, Bristol SW, Brandywine SW, and Blackwater River CW. The average number of species recorded per block (73) is lowered by the dozens of tidewater blocks that contain very little land area.

The ten most widespread species were the Barn Swallow (1,221), Northern Cardinal (1,217), Common Grackle (1,211), European Starling (1,208), Common Yellowthroat (1,206), American Crow (1,207), Red-winged Blackbird (1,205), Mourning Dove (1,204), American Robin (1,202), and Gray Catbird (1,198). The number indicated in parentheses represents the number of blocks out of a possible 1,256.

The following species were rarities, confirmed in only one or two blocks: Brown Pelican, Northern Shoveler, Wilson's Plover, Black-necked Stilt, Gull-billed Tern, Ringed Turtle-Dove, and Bewick's Wren.

Composition of the Breeding Avifauna

The Atlas data provide the first opportunity to conduct numerical analyses of the composition of the breeding avifauna of Maryland and DC. This analysis can be accomplished at local, county, or state scale. One may compare the total number of species (or families or orders) among urban, residential, agricultural, forested, and marshland blocks. One may show, using miniroute data, which is the dominant (most common) species in various parts of a county or throughout the state, or one may map the number of species of warblers, block by block, to determine which factors combine to produce good warbler habitat.

It would be informative to show the number of rare, threatened, and endangered species in each Atlas block; to determine which species are missing from urban blocks or suburban blocks; to determine the characteristics of those Atlas blocks in which exceptional numbers of species were found; to compare results from blocks with nature preserves with a random sample of other blocks; and to compare blocks with different farming or timber management practices.

Continentally, no two bird species have the same distribution. Within Maryland, no species has a uniform numerical distribution. Thus no two miniroute maps are identical. There is much to be learned from these maps, and what we learn may help to provide, in a more constructive way, for the future of each species within the state.

Interested parties may undertake more sophisticated challenges and compute similarity indexes among different blocks. An atlas study in The Netherlands divided the entire country into 18 "bird districts" by analyzing the national atlas data with a computer program (TWINSPAN) developed at Cornell University (Kwak and Reyrink 1984).

Changes in the Breeding Bird Distribution

Long-term Changes

Bird populations are constantly changing as nature strives toward a new equilibrium in response to natural and human-induced changes in the environment. Many changes of the past three decades are depicted graphically in the pages of this *Atlas*. Other longer-term changes can be gleaned from the text. The main concern is that these changes are now taking place more rapidly than at any previous time in the history of our country. Species that Maryland birders had always taken for granted, such as the Loggerhead Shrike and Bewick's Wren, are no longer found at their traditional nesting places. Horned Larks and Eastern Meadowlarks have disappeared from many of the fields, and warblers no longer nest in the nearby woods. To appreciate the rapidity with which some of the changes are taking place, one need look no farther than Howard County in central Maryland.

Short-term Changes

Bird population changes during the past decade are best illustrated by comparing Howard County atlas results for the periods from 1973 through 1975 and 1983 through 1987. Montgomery and Howard County atlas maps for all breeding species were published by Klimkiewicz and Solem (1978). Although the Montgomery data were based on 5-kilometer blocks, the Howard County data were plotted by quarterblocks, which enable many more changes to be detected.

During both atlas time periods, all of Howard County's 136 quarterblocks (including those that overlap into surrounding counties) were thoroughly searched by field observers. In the final year of each survey, special attention was paid to searching the best habitat patches for each species. Most observers who participated in the final search for missing species in 1987 were the same people who had done so in 1975, and in both cases the coverage was excellent. In spite of the many species that decreased over the intervening decade, the results of the second survey revealed more than 80 species in every quarterblock in the county.

Our best estimate of population changes was made by first calculating an expected number of quarterblocks for each species for the 1983–87 period, assuming no population change. This was done by multiplying the number of quarterblocks for the species in 1973–75 by a correction factor of 1.413, the estimated difference in atlasing effort. Then, using

Table 4. Changes in Breeding Bird Distribution in Howard County from 1973–75 to 1983–87, Based on Number of Quarterblocks (out of 136) in Which Each Species Was Found. The expected values for 1983–87 were obtained by multiplying the 1973–75 figures by 1.413, which is the estimated difference in atlasing effort, based on the difference in total number of observations for all species except those expected in all quarterblocks.

Number of Quarterblocks

Species	1973–75 Observed	1983–87 Expected	1983–87 Observed	Percentage Change
House Finch	0	0	129	—
Canada Goose	8	11	46	+318%
Black Vulture	18	25	71	+184%
Cliff Swallow	6	8	20	+150%
Cedar Waxwing	17	24	56	+133%
Pileated Woodpecker	29	41	86	+110%
Fish Crow	50	71	114	+ 61%
Red-tailed Hawk	48	68	93	+ 37%
White-breasted Nuthatch	55	78	105	+ 35%
Yellow-breasted Chat	103	136	108	- 21%
Ring-necked Pheasant	94	133	102	- 23%
Eastern Meadowlark	126	136	103	- 24%
Blue-gray Gnatcatcher	104	136	100	- 26%
Yellow-billed Cuckoo	109	136	101	- 26%
Whip-poor-will	30	42	21	- 50%
Grasshopper Sparrow	103	136	78	- 57%
Vesper Sparrow	51	72	22	- 69%
Black-billed Cuckoo	19	27	8	- 70%
Prothonotary Warbler	9	13	3	- 72%
Horned Lark	47	66	18	- 73%
American Black Duck	10	14	3	- 79%

a chi-square test, we determined whether the actual number of quarterblocks in the 1983–87 period differed significantly ($p<0.05$) from the expected number. Significant changes were indicated for the species listed in table 4.

The method of calculating the correction factor of 1.413 is described here so it can be duplicated in the future. It is a modification of the method used previously (Robbins et al. 1989c; Robbins 1990b). There was no way to estimate the difference in effective time afield, so the numbers of bird records were used. There were 8,297 quarterblock records for Howard County in the 1973–75 period and 9,683 in the 1983–87 period, a ratio of 1 to 1.167. This is an average of 61 species per quarterblock for the first period and 71 for the second period. Multiplying each 1973–75 species quarterblock total by 1.167 would give an initial estimate of the expected number for 1983–87, but for 38 species (e.g., American Robin, which was found in all quarterblocks) the estimated number of quarterblocks would exceed the county total of 136 quarterblocks by a combined total of 672 records. That is, 9,683 - 8,297 = 1,386; but 167 of the 1,386 records represent the sum of records required to bring the 38 common species up to the county total of 136 quarterblocks. 1,386 - 167 = 1,219 records attributed to the other 89 Howard County species. For 1983–87, 9,683 - (38 x 136) =

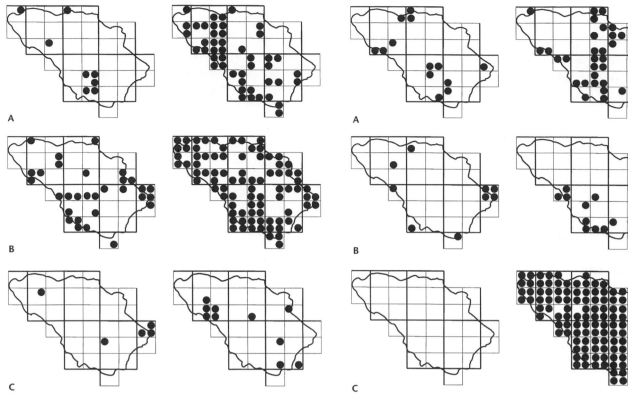

Figure 15. Changes in Distribution of Canada Geese (A), Pileated Woodpeckers (B), and Tree Swallows (C) in Howard County, 1973–75 to 1983–87

Figure 16. Changes in Distribution of Blue-winged Warblers (A), Pine Warblers (B), and House Finches (C) in Howard County, 1973–75 to 1983–87

4,515. For 1973–75, 8,291 - 5,001 = 3,296. And 4,515/3,296 = 1.370, which is a revised correction factor for the other 89 species. But using 1.370 causes estimates for 10 additional species to exceed 136 quarterblocks. By doing a second iteration to correct for these 10 species, the final factor of 1.413 was reached.

Range expansion was an important factor in several of the increases shown in table 4. The expansion of the Canada Goose is related to the spread of the offspring of released birds, together with construction of large numbers of ponds in Howard County. Black Vultures are expanding their range beyond any historic records in Maryland. Cliff Swallows have adapted to nesting on dams and under bridges. Many of the declines are linked to loss of extensive fields and pastures.

Representative changes in distribution in Howard County of 12 species of special interest are shown in figures 15 through 18. Canada Geese (fig. 15a), which were restricted to a few farm ponds from 1973 through 1975, were widespread from 1983 through 1987. Pileated Woodpeckers (fig. 15b), which were largely restricted to the extensive woodlands along the Patapsco, Patuxent, and Middle Patuxent valleys from 1973 through 1975, had spread into many other woodlands by 1983–87. Tree Swallows (fig. 15c), which had just started to nest in Howard County from 1973 through 1975, were found in twice as many quarterblocks a decade later, assisted by the large number of nest boxes provided for Eastern Bluebirds.

Blue-winged Warblers probably reached their peak of abundance in Howard County during the period from 1983 through 1987 when abandoned farmland purchased for construction of Columbia had been fallow long enough to produce excellent nesting habitat for this species. (See fig. 16a.) Pine Warblers, formerly rare in the county, are now nesting in the maturing pine plantations along the Triadelphia and T. Howard Duckett (Rocky Gorge) reservoirs (fig. 16b). House Finches had been found summering in four atlas blocks in neighboring Montgomery County by 1973 (Klimkiewicz and Solem 1978) but were not found in Howard County during the 1973 through 1975 period. From 1983 through 1987, however, they were recorded in all but seven of the 136 Howard County quarterblocks. (See fig. 16c.)

Black-billed Cuckoos are never common on the Maryland Piedmont during the breeding season. Numbers vary greatly from year to year, with local increases responding to some extent to heavy infestations of hairy caterpillars. Although tent caterpillars and gypsy moths were prevalent locally during both atlas periods, the influx of Black-billed Cuckoos from 1973 through 1975 was not repeated from 1983 through 1987. (See fig. 17a.) During the interval between the two atlas periods, Whip-poor-wills largely disappeared from the suburban areas of Laurel and Columbia as woodlands gave way to residential development. (See fig. 17b.) Horned Larks (fig. 17c) left this same area as the large agricultural fields disappeared.

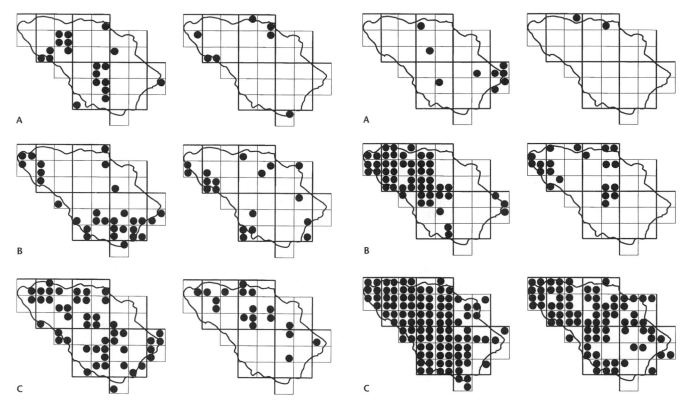

Figure 17. Changes in Distribution of Black-billed Cuckoos (A), Whip-poor-willls (B), and Horned Larks (C) in Howard County, 1973–75 to 1983–87

Figure 18. Changes in Distribution of Prothonotary Warblers (A), Vesper Sparrows (B), and Grasshopper Sparrows (C) in Howard County, 1973–75 to 1983–87

Wooded swamps with standing water are rare in Howard County, and Prothonotary Warblers (fig. 18a) are at the limit of their breeding range here. There was a substantial decline in this species prior to the 1983–87 survey. Vesper Sparrows (fig. 18b), which occurred in fields throughout most of the Piedmont portion of the county as recently as 1973–75, were no longer to be found in most of the county a decade later. Grasshopper Sparrows are following the same pattern. (See fig. 18c.) By 1987, they had disappeared from several quarterblocks in which they had been found in 1983 and 1984.

Conservation

Several recent government initiatives are responding to the public's demand for more effective protection of our natural resources. Two such initiatives are the Chesapeake Bay Critical Area Act (Natural Resources Article 8-1808, Annotated Code of Maryland) and a new policy of the U.S. Forest Service to plan for multiple use and for protection of biodiversity in the nation's forests (Szaro and Shapiro 1990). A third is the commitment on the part of the U.S. Fish and Wildlife Service: "A goal of the Service is to conserve avian diversity in North America. This includes maintaining populations of all native bird species and their essential habitats at reasonable levels, preventing any of these species from having to be listed as endangered or threatened, and ensuring continued opportunities for people to enjoy these birds" (Office of Migratory Bird Management 1990).

A recent study used satellite imagery to map habitat distribution in several western states (Scott et al. 1991). The purpose was to determine the extent to which species that most urgently need protection were receiving it. On the habitat maps the researchers outlined (1) all lands that had been committed for preservation of biotic diversity, and (2) the distribution of rare, threatened, and endangered species. The shocking results in Idaho showed that although huge acreages were committed to management for maintaining biotic diversity, most of the rare, threatened, and endangered species were outside the protected areas.

The *Atlas* provides an excellent resource for comparing breeding concentrations of each species with maps of protected areas. It is important to realize, however, that lands in public management are not necessarily managed for preservation of biotic diversity. Hopefully, as conservation needs are demonstrated, this *Atlas* will play a major role in obtaining the long-term commitments that will be needed. In addition to showing breeding ranges of each individual species, the *Atlas* can be used to show which areas are most important for retaining combinations of rare and declining species that depend on the same habitats. (See Robbins et al. (1989a: 27) for an example of the effect of forest area on the number of area-sensitive species that can be detected from a single random listening point.)

Conservation Areas

Maryland and the District of Columbia are blessed with a large number of public and private lands where wildlife habitats are protected or managed. Although many of these areas are designated for specific uses, ranging from human recreation and watershed protection to timber harvest, the present trend is to provide for multiple use, including maintenance of biotic diversity. These conservation areas will become increasingly important for maintaining viable populations of breeding birds as Maryland continues to lose its privately owned woods and agricultural fields to homesites, shopping centers, highways, and transmission lines. Federal and state properties are identified on Maryland's official highway map.

Federal Lands

As of January 1992, Maryland had 181,410 acres (73,416 ha) in federal lands containing wildlife habitat. These include, in order of decreasing size, Aberdeen Proving Ground, Blackwater National Wildlife Refuge, Patuxent Wildlife Research Center, Beltsville Agricultural Research Center, the Chesapeake & Ohio Canal National Monument, Fort George G. Meade, Patuxent River Naval Air Station, Assateague Island National Seashore, Catoctin Mountain Park, Indian Head Naval Proving Ground, Martin NWR, Andrews Air Force Base, Chesapeake and Delaware Canal, Eastern Neck Island NWR, and various small national monuments, military bases, and U.S. Army Corps of Engineers lands.

State Forests

The largest state holdings are the state forests, which total 163,231 acres (66,059 ha). These include Buckingham, Cedarville, Doncaster, Elk Neck, Garrett, Green Ridge, Pocomoke River, Potomac, Savage River, Seth Demonstration, Stoney Forest, and Wicomico. They are located in Allegany, Cecil, Charles, Garrett, Prince George's, Wicomico, and Worcester counties.

State Parks

Maryland's 48 state parks include parts of 22 counties and contain more than 100,367 acres (40,618 ha). The only counties without a state park are Kent and Wicomico.

Wildlife Management Areas

Wildlife Management Areas (WMA), covering 115,598 acres (46,782 ha), also are widely distributed throughout Maryland. The only counties without one of the 37 designated areas are Harford, Calvert, and Talbot.

In addition, six Natural Environmental Areas in five counties comprise a total of 16,734 acres (6,772 ha). There are seven Natural Resources Management Areas, consisting of 21,469 acres (8,688 ha) spread over parts of 11 counties. Fishing management areas cover a total of 1,375 acres (556 ha), and there are 979 acres (396 ha) in Heritage Conservation Fund purchases.

County and Municipal Parks

Numerous county and municipal parks are found throughout Maryland and DC. Local park departments can offer information on their use and location.

Preserves of the Nature Conservancy

The Maryland chapter of The Nature Conservancy has an active program of acquiring outstanding tracts of special ecological significance. Some of these are transferred to the state or to other conservation organizations; others are retained and managed by TNC. As of June 1992, the Maryland chapter of TNC owned 28 preserves totaling 8,493 acres (3,437 ha). Some of these preserves were established to protect certain rare plants; most are large enough to be important for nesting birds as well. Old-growth forest is promoted when possible.

Sanctuaries of the Maryland Ornithological Society

The Maryland Ornithological Society owns ten wildlife sanctuaries totaling about 2,085 acres (844 ha). All physiographic regions of Maryland are represented, as are many of the most important habitats in the state.

Other Preserves

Scattered throughout the state are other protected areas operated by organizations such as the Izaak Walton League, Smithsonian's Chesapeake Bay Center, Remington Farms, and Horsehead Sanctuary.

Using the Species Accounts

Original Drawing and Narrative

Each species account consists of an original drawing of the species and a narrative describing the bird's distribution, migratory status, habitat preference, nesting habits, history in Maryland/DC, present status, population trend, and conservation needs. The Atlas map accompanying each account shows the species' present distribution, based on the fieldwork; the accompanying tabular data summary relates to this map. For most species, a second and smaller map depicts breeding distribution as of 1958 for comparison, and a third map shows the present relative abundance as determined from miniroutes. The BBS Trend Graph presented for most species shows the population trend for Maryland from the Breeding Bird Survey data.

Much of the information presented in the species accounts is based on observations made in Maryland and the District of Columbia. For many of the rarer species, that information has been supplemented with data from other areas.

The nesting details in the accounts came primarily from the Maryland Nest Record File (MNRF), which includes thousands of records submitted by MOS members and many hundreds of nest records gathered by F. C. Kirkwood from ornithologists who were active in the late nineteenth and early twentieth centuries. In addition, nest records from the DNR, the Cornell Laboratory of Ornithology, the Delaware Museum of Natural History, the Carnegie Museum in Pittsburgh, the National Museum of Natural History, and the Western Foundation for Vertebrate Zoology were examined. Many of the nest records included information based on multiple visits, or contained comments on the age of the embryos, indicating that the clutch was complete. Observers who make single visits generally cannot determine whether a clutch is complete. Calculations of mean clutch size omitted all records in which clutches were suspected to be incomplete and those that contained Brown-headed Cowbird eggs. Nevertheless, some incomplete clutches undoubtedly were included in clutch-size data, and they tend to give a mean that is slightly lower than the true mean.

Breeding population densities from Maryland and DC study plots were obtained from a PWRC computer printout that includes the Breeding Bird Censuses published in the years 1937 through 1970. More recent densities were taken from various issues of *American Birds* and from supplements to the *Journal of Field Ornithology*, as well as from unpublished data on file at PWRC.

Data from Delaware and Virginia are from atlas work in those states, unpublished at the time of this writing.

Atlas Map: Breeding Distribution, 1983–87

The Atlas maps for the years 1983 through 1987 were generated by computer from the edited results of the present *Atlas*. The solid dots on the large Atlas maps represent "confirmed" breeding. The small dots surrounded by circles indicate "probable" breeding. The circles with an **X** stand for "possible" breeding. The open circles used for a few species indicate presence in the breeding season but not in the breeding habitat. The symbols show only the degree of certainty of actual nesting, not abundance.

Atlas Summary Table

The "Total" line at the top of the summary table accompanying each Atlas map shows the number and the percentage of blocks (of a possible 1,256) in which the species was recorded, including those in which the highest category was "observed." The remainder of the table breaks out the blocks by category, showing the number of blocks in which the highest category was "confirmed," "probable," "possible," and "observed." It also gives percentages of observations in each of the three major breeding categories (excluding "observed").

Map of Breeding Distribution, 1958

The 1958 maps are copies of field maps made by R. Stewart and C. Robbins when preparing their 1958 book *Birds of Maryland and the District of Columbia*. The Atlas effort was much more intense than the fieldwork in the 1940s and 1950s, but the comparison between the 1958 maps and the Atlas maps presents an opportunity to detect some of the many distributional changes that have taken place over three decades. More intensive land use has increased pressures not only on rare species but also on common ones. By identifying changes that have occurred during the past 30 years, we are in a better position to manage the Maryland landscape for the benefit of our native avifauna.

Stewart and Robbins (1958) published maps showing the Maryland breeding distribution of 65 species—about one-third of Maryland's breeding species. A few of these species were mapped using spots for individual records. For the majority of mapped species, however, the principal breeding range was extrapolated based on available records, and only outlying localities were identified with individual spots. The 1958 maps for the other two-thirds of Maryland's breeding species were not previously published. The great majority of records represent birds recorded by R. Stewart, C. Robbins, and their PWRC colleagues during their surveys of the state from 1943 through 1957. Records from other twentieth-century observers were also included.

To facilitate comparison with the present Atlas data, all of the 1958 maps are published in this volume, and all are presented in the form of spot maps rather than with extrapolated ranges. These maps are intended to show breeding distribution as of 1958 rather than to indicate relative abundance. To prevent overlapping, many of the spots for common species had to be omitted; furthermore, many of the original spots represented multiple sightings.

Miniroute Map: Relative Abundance, 1983–89

Miniroute maps are provided for 129 species. Breeding bird atlas projects give a remarkably good picture of bird distribution, but they provide only a crude indication of relative abundance. By noting the varying densities of blocks reporting a species and, to some extent, the percentage of "confirmed" records, one can infer that a species is more or less common. The wide variation in extent and quality of coverage in each block, however, renders these data inadequate for more precise measurements of abundance.

As an independent study, a statewide miniroute project was undertaken to coincide with the Atlas. This project consisted of a 15-stop roadside route in each Atlas block. At each stop, observers spent three minutes recording all bird species they saw or heard. Stops were at approximately 0.5-mile (0.8-km) intervals and were designed to sample habitats in the block in proportion to their occurrence. For example, if an Atlas block were 50 percent suburbs, 25 percent forest, and 25 percent open fields, the observer would make seven or eight stops in suburbs, three or four in forests, and three or four in fields. Whenever possible, routes were scouted to adjust placement of stops to compensate for habitat differences that could not be distinguished from topographic maps, such as pine versus deciduous forest, hayfields versus old fields, and recent changes in land use. Some routes were covered by bicycle or canoe or on foot to sample special habitats. Routes were not started until official sunrise; in most instances the same observer could run two adjacent routes in a morning. Routes were to be completed within 2.5 hours after sunrise. Each route was run once, achieving almost complete coverage in the urban corridor and at least 50 percent coverage in the more remote areas. A few miniroutes were not run until 1988; data from the 1988 coverage were included in the miniroute maps but were not added to the Atlas database.

Only presence or absence was recorded. Because no attempt was made to estimate individuals at each stop, relative frequency was measured, not relative abundance. This method was chosen for two reasons: It is easier for the observer, and the results are more comparable among observers (D. Bystrak, pers. comm.). Because frequency is closely correlated with abundance, it is safe to assume that regions of greatest frequency are those of greatest abundance, although it is not possible to define abundance in terms of numbers or ratios.

For the common species, miniroute data have an advantage over Atlas data: the consistency of effort and the sampling design of miniroutes permits counts to be used as a relative measure of abundance. Miniroutes were run throughout the state, and we therefore were able to use the relative abundance data to produce maps of bird distributions throughout Maryland. To produce these maps for each species, we first found the latitude and longitude for the center of each block in which a miniroute was run, and we used the percentage of total number of stops on which the species was recorded as the index of relative abundance for that location. We then used SURFER (Golden Software 1987), a computer program for contour mapping, to estimate the relative abundance for the species throughout Maryland. A procedure called *inverse distancing* was used to create a smooth map from the abundances estimated at the miniroute locations. To display regional patterns, 129 of the species accounts in this *Atlas* provide miniroute data maps. Shading in these maps represents the estimated regions in which 0.1 to 10 percent, 10 to 50 percent, and more than 50 percent of the stops of a miniroute detected the species. The miniroute map caption sometimes uses the terms *uncommon, common,* and *abundant* to distinguish these three categories, but these abundance terms should not be compared directly with those in the main text.

For most species, the miniroute maps present a realistic picture of relative abundance. Exceptions are the rare species seldom detected at random roadside stops and colonial nesting species, especially those that nest on islands not sampled by miniroutes. Most miniroutes were run in June, at the peak of the breeding season of most species. Thus some of the early nesting species were undersampled. Miniroutes also undersample soaring birds, such as vultures and hawks, as a result of miniroute coverage being conducted early in the morning before these birds take flight. Because the miniroutes are based only on presence or absence of the species at each stop rather than on a count of individuals detected, colonial species (e.g., the Cliff Swallow) that are locally distributed are never depicted as common. Their

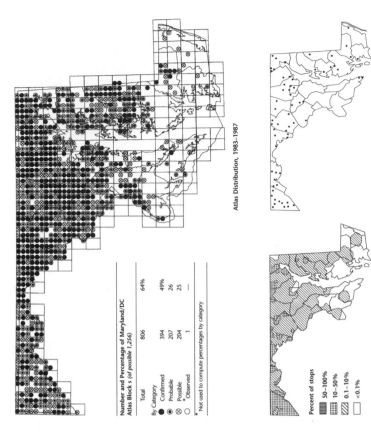

Atlas Distribution, 1983–1987

Number and Percentage of Maryland/DC
Atlas Block s *(of possible 1,256)*

Total	806	64%
By Category		
● Confirmed	394	49%
◉ Probable	207	26
⊗ Possible	204	25
○ *Observed	1	—

* Not used to compute percentages by category

Percent of stops

- ▦ 50–100%
- ▤ 10–50%
- ▨ 0.1–10%
- ☐ <0.1%

Relative Abundance, 1982–1989

The Baltimore Oriole is most common in the western and northern parts of the state. It decreases to the south and east and is uncommon to rare and local on most of the Coastal Plain.

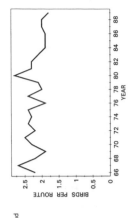

Breeding Distribution, 1958

Maryland BBS Trend Graph, 1966–1989

Baltimore Oriole

Icterus galbula

The AOU (1983) combined the eastern Baltimore Oriole and the western Bullock's Oriole into a single species, the Northern Oriole, then separated them thirteen years later (AOU 1995). Whatever its official name, this handsome bird will always be the Baltimore Oriole to birdwatchers and other Maryland residents. It is the state bird, and the Baltimore baseball team is named for it. Legend has it that George Calvert, the first Baron Baltimore, was cheered by its beauty and took its colors for his coat of arms. Later, when Linnaeus saw the skins of the Golden Robin or Fire-hangbird, he named it the Baltimore Oriole, as it wore the colors of Lord Baltimore (Forbush 1927). The appearance of the two males is so distinct that field observers had continued to use the names c and Bullock's (Robbins et al. 1986) during the brief time these two species were combined.

Coues and Prentiss (1862, 1883) considered the Baltimore Oriole chiefly a spring and autumn migrant, although they noted that many bred. Kirkwood (1895) called it a locally common summer resident. Stewart and Robbins (1958) listed it as a fairly common breeding bird in the Allegheny Mountain, Ridge and Valley, and Piedmont sections; uncommon in the Upper Chesapeake and Eastern Shore sections; and rare, or perhaps absent, in the Western Shore Sec-tion. During migration it is fairly common in all sections. Spring migration is from late April to late May, with a peak in mid-May; fall migration is from early August to late September, with a peak between 20 August and 15 September. The winter range extends from Mexico to northern South America (AOU 1983).

The Baltimore Oriole nests in shade trees in residential areas, on farms, and in open stands of floodplain and moist upland forests (Stewart and Robbins 1958). Baltimore County had a high nesting density of 10 territorial males per 100 acres (40.5 ha) in a mixed habitat of tall trees and shrubs at Lake Roland (Cooley 1947). The nest—deeply pendent, like a sock, with a side entrance near the top—hangs by its rim from the tip of a drooping forked branch,

usually high in a deciduous tree (Tyler 1958a). It is woven of long fibers, such as string, grapevine bark, and, when available, horsehair. Soft materials like hair, wool, and soft grass line the nest, which takes five to eight days to complete and is about 5 in. (13 cm) long and 2.5 in. (6 cm) wide. The female is the principal nest builder and builds a new nest each year. The Baltimore Oriole is single-brooded.

The nesting period of early May to early July peaks between mid-May and mid-June (MNRF). The earliest recorded nest-building date is 28 April (Ringler 1990b). Heights of 141 Maryland nests (MNRF) range from 5 to 100 ft (1.5–31 m), with a mean of 30 ft (9.1 m); 80 percent are 40 ft (12 m) or lower. Clutch sizes from 12 nests range from 2 to 6 (mean of 4.5). Although the earliest observed egg date is 18 May, an earlier date of about 4 May can be reached by subtracting the 14-day incubation period from the earliest date for young. The latest egg date is 16 June. The female incubates the eggs for 12 to 14 days (Forbush 1927). Brood sizes in 32 Maryland nests range from 1 to 5, with a mean of 2.4 (MNRF). The earliest date of a nest with young is 18 May; the latest is 27 August, with a peak in mid-June (MNRF). Both parents tend the nestlings for 12 to 14 days (Stokes and Stokes 1983). Friedmann (1929, 1963) considered the Baltimore Oriole an uncommon victim of the Brown-headed Cowbird. Peck and James (1987) reported a 6 percent parasitism rate (10 of 168 nests) in Ontario. This rate may be low because the Baltimore Oriole frequently rejects Brown-headed Cowbirds eggs (Rothstein 1975). No Maryland records exist.

Northern Orioles feed heavily on caterpillars, often destroying whole infestations of the forest tent caterpillar. They also eat larvae of the whitemarked tussock moth, gypsy moth, and browntail moth, and even the spiny caterpillar of the mourning cloak butterfly (McAtee 1926).

Atlas data show the Baltimore Oriole is widespread throughout the Allegheny Mountain, Ridge and Valley, and Piedmont sections; spottily distributed in the northern Coastal Plain; and decreasing south into southern Maryland and on the lower Eastern Shore. The major change since the 1950s is expansion into the Western Shore Section. Because of the difficulty of examining its highly placed pendent nests, only 48 "confirmed" records (12%) resulted from the examination of nest contents. Most of these were observations of fledged young (22%), occupied nests (19%), or nest building (16%).

BBS data from 1966 through 1989 show stable populations in the Eastern Region and Maryland; Maryland data from 1980 through 1989, however, indicate a decline. Continental data from 1966 through 1989 indicate an increase in Baltimore Oriole populations. Robbins et al. (1989b) concluded that forest destruction in both the breeding and wintering ranges is contributing to population declines of migratory forest birds, including the Baltimore Oriole. Protection of breeding and wintering habitat is required to maintain healthy Baltimore Oriole populations.

John Cullom

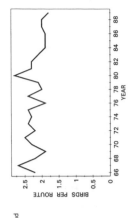

geographic range, like that of rare species, is exaggerated by the SURFER program.

Maryland BBS Trend Graph, 1966–89

Breeding Bird Survey (BBS) data were obtained from the USFWS, Office of Migratory Bird Management. BBS Trend Graphs for Maryland are given for 130 species accounts.

The BBS trend data given in the text of the species accounts are presented, depending on the context, for the state of Maryland, for the Eastern Region (states and provinces east of the Mississippi), or for the continent (United States and Canada). Average annual increases or declines were used for probability levels of 0.05 (significant) and 0.01 (highly significant). Trends at the probability level of 0.10 are used only as an indication of a possible increase or decrease, and an average annual percentage is not given. If the average annual index departed only 1 percent from zero, the population was considered stable. Data for species recorded on 10 or fewer Maryland routes were not used. It should be noted that average annual increases or decreases cannot be multiplied by the number of years to compute an overall change. To compute this figure, the following formula must be used:

$$\{[(\% \text{ annual change}/100) + 1]^{N} - 1\} \, (100),$$

where N is the last year minus the first year.

Although BBS data are consistently collected on routes over a period of time, several aspects of the survey complicate analyses. First, all analyses are unbalanced because not all routes are run each year. New routes are initiated, and old routes are dropped. In addition, the proportion of routes with changes in coverage varies from year to year. These complications can greatly bias the view of population changes if one simply averages counts by year on BBS routes. Geissler and Noon (1981) and Sauer and Droege (1990a) discuss these biases at greater length. This section explains how average population changes, or trends, and composite annual indexes of abundance were estimated from BBS data for Maryland. Geissler and Sauer (1990) and Sauer and Droege (1990a) explain the technical and nontechnical aspects of these methods.

Population trends are estimated from BBS route data using route-regression, a statistical procedure that was developed at PWRC (Geissler and Sauer 1990). In this procedure, average yearly rate of change for a species is estimated for each BBS route using linear regression on the natural logarithms of counts on year. Only data from routes with valid data are used. For example, routes with less skilled observers, late starts, and other problems are eliminated. Observer differences also are taken into account in the regression. State trends are estimated as a weighted average of route trends; this weighting accounts for factors influenced by the consistency of the route coverage, the average count of the species on the route, and the area of the physiographic stratum in which the route occurs. These weighting factors adjust the contribution of the route trend to the overall state trend with regard to the quality of the route data and the relative importance of the stratum in which the species occurs. The statistical significance of the trend must be estimated to determine the validity of the data. This is done by estimating a variance of the trend estimate, using a statistical procedure called *bootstrapping,* and using a Z-test to determine the probability that the observed trend differs from zero due to chance alone.

As stated earlier, simply averaging yearly counts from BBS routes can produce biased estimates of yearly counts. Further, a smooth trend line formed by multiplying or dividing the average counts for the state by the average trend provides little insight into short-term changes in the population. Consequently, a statistical procedure for estimating annual indexes of abundance which accommodates for missing data and observer changes is used. First, an average trend for a species is estimated, using the procedures described earlier. Then the data are examined for the species from each route, fitting the estimated average trend to the route data and determining the difference between the estimated count in each year and the actual count. These differences, called *residuals,* are averaged by year over all routes in the state. This average residual, which represents the average difference between the predicted trend and the real data for the year, is then added to the yearly predicted count from the state trend line to form the annual index for the species.

Metric conversions for the *Atlas* were done with a Shareware program called SCICALC. The following guidelines were used: feet to meters were converted to one decimal place, up to 33 feet, and were rounded to a whole meter for 33 feet and above; inches were rounded to whole centimeters; miles and acres were converted to kilometers and hectares and rounded to one decimal place.

A list of acronyms and abbreviations precedes the species accounts. Abundance definitions are given in appendix B. Scientific names for nonavian fauna mentioned in the species accounts are given in appendix E, and those for plants are in appendix F.

Acronyms and Abbreviations Used in the Text

AOU	American Ornithologists' Union
BBC	Breeding Bird Census (NAS; Cornell Laboratory of Ornithology)
BBS	Breeding Bird Survey (USFWS/NBS)
C	Celsius
CBC	Christmas Bird Count
DC	Washington, District of Columbia
DDT	Dichlorodiphenyltrichloroethane
DNR	Maryland Department of Natural Resources
F	Fahrenheit
ft	feet
ha	hectares
in.	inches
km	kilometer
MBS	Midwinter Bird Survey
MCWP	Maryland Colonial Waterbird Project
m	meters
mi	miles
MNRF	Maryland Nest Record File
MOS	Maryland Ornithological Society
mph	miles per hour
NAS	National Audubon Society
NBS	National Biological Service
NPS	National Park Service
NWR	National Wildlife Refuge
PWRC	Patuxent Wildlife Research Center
sq mi	square miles
TNC	The Nature Conservancy
USFWS	United States Fish and Wildlife Service
UTM	Universal Transverse Mercator
WBPS	Winter Bird Population Survey
WBS	Winter Bird Survey
WMA	Wildlife Management Area
yd	yards

Species Accounts

Pied-billed Grebe

Podilymbus podiceps

Quietly slipping between the stalks of tall grass in a shallow pond, the Pied-billed Grebe eased below the surface without a ripple as an observer approached. This was often the situation when Maryland's only nesting grebe was encountered during Atlas fieldwork. Although the Pied-billed Grebe is a rare semicolonial breeder in the state, it is most common in migration. It is uncommon in winter in the eastern half of Maryland. Spring migration spans late February to mid-May, and fall migrants pass through the state from mid-August to early December (Stewart and Robbins 1958).

Early authors knew the Pied-billed Grebe as an abundant to fairly common migrant and an uncommon wintering bird (Coues and Prentiss 1862, 1883; Kirkwood 1895; Cooke 1929). Court (1936) found the first Maryland nest on 3 June 1932 at Broadwater Marsh in Anne Arundel County. From that time until the Atlas fieldwork began, there were few nesting records, with reports from Anne Arundel, Baltimore, Prince George's, St. Mary's, and Worcester counties (Stewart and Robbins 1958) and, later, in Somerset (Armistead 1970) and Montgomery (Klimkiewicz and Solem 1978) counties. Nesting evidence was reported for only one year at some of these locations.

Ponds or streams with open water, some aquatic vegetation, and little wave action are the preferred habitat. The nest is a platform of reeds and grasses on or near the surface of shallow water, typically 1 to 3 ft (0.3–0.9 m) deep (Palmer 1962). Adults defend a territory within about 150 ft (46 m) of the nest but use an area twice that size. They sometimes nest on ponds as small as 0.5 acre (0.2 ha) (Glover 1953).

Egg dates in Maryland (MNRF) range from 17 May to 5 June. Clutch sizes in four Maryland nests are 3, 5, 6, and 7. Typical clutch sizes are 5 to 7; Charbeck (1963) found that clutch sizes are smaller as the season progresses. Only one brood is attempted, but renesting after nest failure is common (Sealey 1978). The most common causes of nest failure appear to be flooding and high winds (Charbeck 1963; Sealey 1978). Incubation is performed by both sexes

and lasts about 23 days (Palmer 1962). The young leave the nest shortly after hatching, and downy young have been observed in Maryland from 28 May to 11 August (MNRF). These dates seem to be slightly later than those expected for this latitude (Palmer 1962). In eight Maryland records (MNRF), brood sizes range from 3 to 5. About 50 percent of their diet consists of aquatic insects; the remainder consists of amphibians, crustaceans, and fish (Wetmore 1924).

Most of the "confirmed" Atlas records are from the Coastal Plain, but two are from the Piedmont. Man-made freshwater habitats were preferred. Nesting Pied-billed Grebes are most common in the impoundments of the Deal Island WMA in Somerset County, where counts of 100 or more birds have been made during the summer (Ringler 1980b). The nearby Fairmount WMA is also used for nesting. Other man-made sites used by nesting Pied-billed Grebes include Brandon Shores, a spoil disposal site in northern Anne Arundel County; a pond at Lilypons Water Gardens in Frederick County; a pond in an old sand pit in Worcester County; and a pond on a golf course in Baltimore County. Natural habitats include a cattail marsh at Huntley Meadows Park in Virginia (part of a Maryland Atlas block) and the Western Branch of the Patuxent River in Prince George's County. The other five sites were not described.

The safe dates for this species, mid-May to mid-July, were slightly liberal, and it became apparent that a few migrants might have been included. Spring migrants occasionally remain into late May, and fall migrants can occasionally appear by mid-July (Stewart and Robbins 1958). In addition, young birds arriving in fall may retain some juvenal plumage. As a result, all records were carefully edited, and reports believed to refer to migrants were deleted from the database. Those shown as "observed" on the Atlas map may include some migrants, but most refer to summering adults for which no breeding evidence was obtained.

All but two of the "confirmed" records are from the Coastal Plain. More acceptable habitat is found there than in the rest of the state, but Pied-billed Grebes will use any satisfactory habitat in an undisturbed area. Ten of the 13 "confirmed" records were either young in the nest or fledglings. The BBS data show stable populations in Maryland and the Eastern Region from 1966 through 1989. Managed impoundments, such as those at Deal Island and Fairmount WMAs, are especially important for this species.

Robert F. Ringler

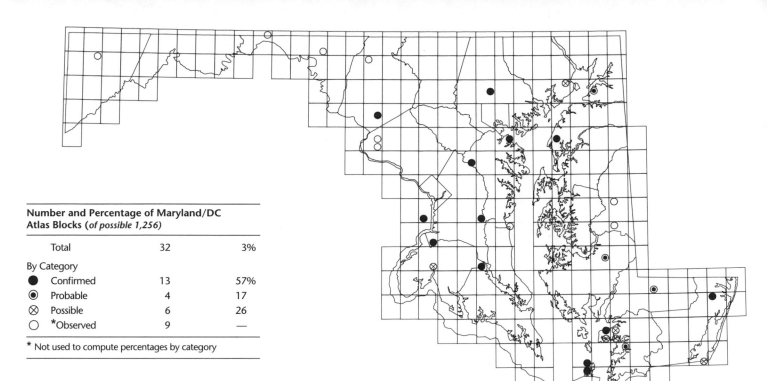

Number and Percentage of Maryland/DC Atlas Blocks (*of possible 1,256*)

Total	32	3%
By Category		
● Confirmed	13	57%
◉ Probable	4	17
⊗ Possible	6	26
○ *Observed	9	—

* Not used to compute percentages by category

Atlas Distribution, 1983–1987

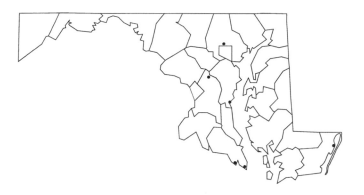

Breeding Distribution, 1958

Brown Pelican
Pelecanus occidentalis

The recovery of Brown Pelican populations from the pesticide-related declines of the twentieth century is an avian success story resulting from increased concern for the environment. The southeastern U.S. population was removed from the Endangered Species list in 1985 because it had flourished in response to the banning of some harmful pesticides (Mendenhall and Prouty 1978). Expansion of the Brown Pelican into Maryland as a breeding species is an excellent example of the positive results of the federal Endangered Species Act.

In Maryland, Brown Pelicans are now uncommon summer residents normally restricted to the beaches and bays of Worcester County. They feed by diving for menhaden and other fishes (Palmer 1962), primarily in the shallow waters along the outer edges of barrier islands and along sandbars in the coastal bays. Roosting and loafing sites are barren sandbars and quiet beaches.

The earliest record of a Brown Pelican in Maryland was of one collected in the late 1800s on the lower Potomac River (Kirkwood 1895). During the first half of the twentieth century, there were seven records of Brown Pelicans in Maryland (Stewart and Robbins 1958)—probably nonbreeders or juvenals dispersing after fledging. There were two Maryland records from 1950 through 1956 (Stewart and Robbins 1958) and from 1956 through 1979 only two more reports (Robbins 1965, 1977b). This period corresponded with the most severe reduction in Brown Pelican populations as a result of pesticide contamination (Blus et al. 1974). On 16 August 1980 two were observed on Assateague Island in Worcester County (Ringler 1981a); another was sighted near St. Martin on 16 January 1981 (Taylor and Dawson 1981). Observations have increased dramatically since 1981 and are now considered routine from mid-spring through late fall.

The first Brown Pelican nesting in Maryland occurred in 1987 (D. Brinker, unpub. data), the final year of the Atlas, making it one of the most recent additions to the state's list of breeding birds. Nesting in Maryland occurred at a single South Point spoil island in Worcester County, where a large heron and egret rookery is located on spoils from dredging of the original channel through Sinepuxent Bay in the late 1930s. Brown Pelicans were also observed in the Atlas blocks immediately surrounding the Ocean City Inlet. The Maryland colony is the northernmost on the Atlantic Coast (Spendelow and Patton 1988; Williams 1989).

The breeding population of Brown Pelicans in Maryland has prospered (MCWP). From 1987 through 1991, the population size ranged from a low of six breeding pairs in 1987 to a high of 26 pairs in 1989. Clutch sizes in 74 Maryland nests range from 1 to 3 eggs, with a mean of 2.3. Between 1987 and 1991, annual nest success varied from 45 percent to 95 percent. During the same years, the mean number of young produced per successful nest varied from a low of 1.0 in 1990 to a high of 2.2 in 1988 and 1989. The highest productivity occurred in 1991, with 2.0 young produced per breeding pair. Within six months of fledging, banded Maryland Brown Pelicans have been encountered as far away as New York and Florida (D. Brinker, unpub. data). In 1991, a banded breeding adult was encountered in the South Point colony; this individual was originally banded as a nestling near Cape Fear, North Carolina, on 11 July 1985.

Nesting is restricted to remote coastal estuarine islands where other colonial waterbirds nest. In Maryland, nests are most frequently placed 3.3 to 10 ft (1–3 m) high in young red cedar, cherry, mulberry, or hackberry trees, or on small brush piles. This contrasts with the ground-nesting colonies immediately to the south in Virginia (Williams 1989) and the Carolinas (Palmer 1962; Parnell and Shields 1990). Maryland nests are built primarily of small to medium-size sticks and are thickly lined with phragmites.

Brown Pelicans have an extremely long nesting period; they require a minimum of 4.5 months from courtship to fledging (Schreiber 1980). As they have only recently expanded into Maryland, the nesting season is still being defined (MCWP). Spring arrival time from the southeastern U.S. wintering grounds (AOU 1983) has not been firmly established but is probably during mid-April (Assateague NPS personnel, pers. comm.). Nest building begins in mid-May and the first eggs are laid in late May (D. Brinker, unpub. data). Peak egg laying occurs in mid-June, but it has continued into early September. The earliest Maryland egg date is 23 May; the latest is 14 September. Clutches initiated after mid-August are seldom successful. Chicks begin fledging in mid- to late August, with the last fledging as late as early November.

Since 1982 the number of summering Brown Pelicans has increased annually, from no summer records during the 1960s and 1970s to over 400 summering individuals in the late 1980s (Ringler 1982, 1983b, 1984b, 1985b, 1986a and c; D. Brinker, unpub. data). During 1987 about 125 nonbreeding Brown Pelicans were associated with the six breeding pairs at the South Point spoils colony (MCWP).

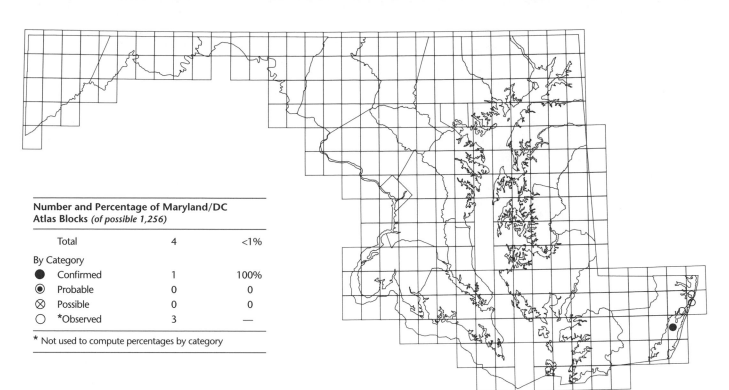

Number and Percentage of Maryland/DC Atlas Blocks *(of possible 1,256)*

Total	4	<1%
By Category		
● Confirmed	1	100%
◉ Probable	0	0
⊗ Possible	0	0
○ *Observed	3	—

* Not used to compute percentages by category

Atlas Distribution, 1983–1987

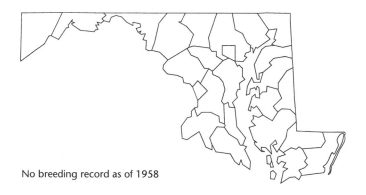

No breeding record as of 1958

Breeding Distribution, 1958

The BBS data from 1966 through 1989 show stable populations in the Eastern Region; there are too few data to estimate a trend for Maryland.

Continuation of breeding by Brown Pelicans in Maryland depends on the availability of suitable sites for nesting colonies. Erosion from the combined effect of storms and the gradually rising sea level threatens many of the isolated islands used by colonial nesting waterbirds. The South Point spoil island used by this species lost approximately 25 percent of its land mass to erosion between 1985 and 1989 (D. Brinker, unpub. data). Secure sites for nesting Brown Pelicans are extremely rare within Maryland, and protection of these sites is an absolute necessity.

David F. Brinker

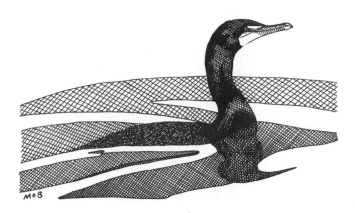

Double-crested Cormorant

Phalacrocorax auritus

The Double-crested Cormorant, familiar as a spring and fall migrant, was not found nesting in Maryland until 1990, three years after Atlas fieldwork was completed. Spring migration in Maryland occurs from late March to mid-May; fall migration occurs from August to November (Robbins and Bystrak 1977). The Double-crested Cormorant is found throughout North America (AOU 1983). Banded birds encountered in Maryland during migration had been tagged as nestlings in Maine, Ontario, and Quebec (Stewart and Robbins 1958).

Early in the twentieth century, the Double-crested Cormorant abandoned many of its former breeding sites in the eastern United States (Palmer 1962), and by the mid-1920s, the population had reached a low. During the 1930s it began to recover, and breeding colonies appeared along the St. Lawrence River, on the Great Lakes, in the Maritime Provinces, and southward into New York (Arbib 1988a). It also breeds along the Atlantic Coast from North Carolina south, and on the Gulf Coast through Texas (Clapp et al. 1982). Breeding was first observed in Virginia at Hopewell in Charles City County in 1978 (Blem et al. 1980), and small numbers have bred there since (S. Ridd, pers. comm.).

Kirkwood (1895) knew the Double-crested Cormorant as a not-common migrant and winter visitor. Stewart and Robbins (1958) described it as an uncommon to common migrant in tidewater areas and in the Allegheny Mountain Section, and as rare elsewhere. They wrote that it was uncommon in winter in the tidewater areas of the Eastern and Western Shore sections. In recent years the Double-crested Cormorant has become increasingly common during the summer in some areas of the Chesapeake Bay (R. Ringler, pers. comm.), and many Atlas field observers predicted its first Maryland breeding record would come during the Atlas period.

The Double-crested Cormorant nests in a variety of sites, from tall deciduous and coniferous trees to low brush, and even on the ground (Pearson 1926; Palmer 1962; Arbib 1988a). It is a colonial nester and prefers to nest away from areas disturbed by man (Palmer 1962; Arbib 1988a). Both sexes assist with nest construction, which usually takes

about four days (Palmer 1962). Both parents share incubation, which begins before all the eggs are laid (Palmer 1962). Incubation lasts 24 to 29 days, and the hatching of a clutch may be spread over a week. Clutch sizes generally vary from 2 to 7, with 3 to 6 most common (Palmer 1962; Godfrey 1979). Renesting has been observed when the first clutch is destroyed. Young are capable of flight at five to six weeks (Palmer 1962).

The Double-crested Cormorant was first observed breeding in Maryland in the summer of 1990 (D. Meritt, pers. obs.). A colony of 55 pairs nested on Poplar Island in Talbot County in a small grove of loblolly pines. These trees had previously been used by Snowy and Cattle Egrets. The island has been used by a mixed colony of egrets for years, with over 1,300 total nests recorded during the 1990 season (D. Brinker, pers. comm.). Double-crested Cormorants took over some of these nests and, after some modification, successfully reared over 80 young. It is not known whether they displaced the egrets or took advantage of abandoned nests.

Nesting Double-crested Cormorants were first seen on Poplar Island on 5 July 1990, apparently incubating. Early and late Maryland egg dates were subsequently recorded as 12 May and 1 August (MNRF). The nests were 40 to 60 ft (12–18 m) above the ground. Young, which were only a few days old, were first seen on 1 August, when egg shells were noted under the nests. According to published incubation periods, the eggs were probably laid during the first week in July. On 31 August, D. Meritt climbed one of the trees and determined that the nests contained from 1 to 4 young, with 2 or 3 most common. No eggs were present, and most young were able to clamber about the trees. By 12 September most of the young had fledged. On the final visit, on 27 September, only three nests contained young, which appeared ready to fledge. This nesting was considerably later than in most other colonies on the Atlantic Coast, where egg laying occurs principally in April and May (Palmer 1962). The onset of breeding may be considerably later than average in new colonies. Timing can be affected by weather or the age of the adults. The adults returned to nest again at Poplar Island in 1991, and they established a new colony on the South Point spoil islands in Worcester County (D. Brinker, pers. comm.). Atlas data show nonbreeding Double-crested Cormorants scattered throughout tidewater Maryland. The diet of this bird consists almost entirely of fish (Palmer 1962).

BBS data from 1966 through 1989 show a highly significant average annual increase of 9.1 percent in the Eastern Region. Although the Maryland sample is small, the population appears to be stable. It remains to be seen what will become of this addition to Maryland's breeding avifauna. Poplar Island is rapidly eroding and the nest sites are in serious danger of being washed away, but nearby islands offer other suitable sites to which the birds may move.

Donald W. Meritt

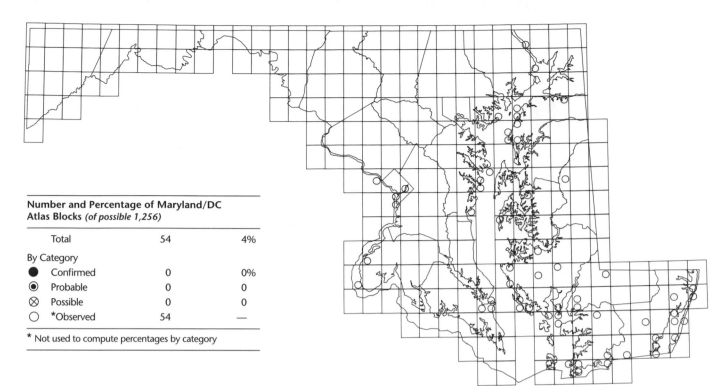

Number and Percentage of Maryland/DC Atlas Blocks *(of possible 1,256)*

Total	54	4%
By Category		
● Confirmed	0	0%
◉ Probable	0	0
⊗ Possible	0	0
○ *Observed	54	—

* Not used to compute percentages by category

Atlas Distribution, 1983–1987

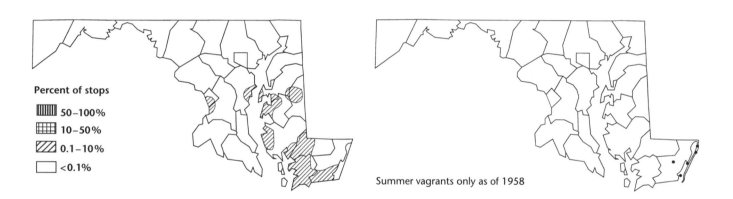

Percent of stops

▥ 50–100%
▦ 10–50%
▨ 0.1–10%
☐ <0.1%

Relative Abundance, 1982–1989

Summer vagrants only as of 1958

Breeding Distribution, 1958

Double-crested Cormorants were recorded at scattered locations around the Chesapeake Bay and its tributaries. Miniroutes do not sample colonial breeding birds effectively; most records represent nonbreeding wanderers or birds foraging away from nest sites.

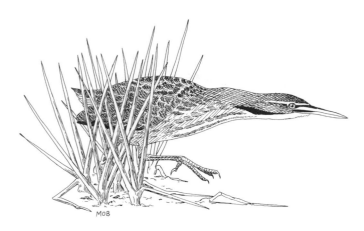

American Bittern

Botaurus lentiginosus

The American Bittern is one of the most solitary, secretive, and cryptically patterned members of the heron family. Its streaked plumage and habit of freezing with its bill pointed skyward enable it to blend with the surrounding vegetation. In Maryland, it occurs principally in brackish and salt marshes and is less common in fresh marshes (Stewart and Robbins 1958). While the reclusive nature of this species makes it difficult to observe, its distinctive, deep, resonant call of *plum-puddin'* or *pump-er-lunk* readily reveals its presence during the breeding season (Bent 1926). The American Bittern is found in Maryland throughout the year, but it is at least partially migratory, with spring records from late March through May and fall records from September through November (Robbins and Bystrak 1977). This species is thought to be declining throughout its range and was included on the NAS Blue List from 1976 through 1986 (Tate 1986). The USFWS (1987) considered the species to be one of management concern, and the DNR currently lists it as in need of conservation.

Coues and Prentiss (1862, 1883) thought the American Bittern was rather common in riverine marshes around DC; Kirkwood (1895) considered it fairly common in migration in Maryland, with only a few summering birds that may have bred. Summer records included a late August 1891 specimen collected near Easton in Talbot County and one seen 14 July 1894 at Hog Creek on the Gunpowder River in Baltimore County (Kirkwood 1895). Except for an undated record of Maryland eggs in the British Museum (Oates 1902), the first documented breeding was by Court (1921), who found two nests with young and one with eggs on 3 June 1917 in the Potomac River marshes in or near DC. Stewart and Robbins (1958) considered the American Bittern a fairly common breeder in the tidal marshes of Dorchester, Wicomico, and Somerset Counties; uncommon in the remaining tidewater areas; and rare in the Allegheny Mountain Section.

During courtship, males extend a pair of white fanlike ruffs on the upper back and shoulders (Bent 1926). Females gather dead reeds, sticks, cattails, tall grasses, and other vegetation to build a platform nest either on dry ground or several inches above water among tall vegetation. Clutch sizes average 4 to 5 eggs. The female incubates the eggs for 24 to 28 days, and the nestlings typically fledge about 14 days after hatching. American Bitterns probably rear only one brood per year (Terres 1980). Their strictly animal diet consists mainly of frogs, fish, crayfish, and small mammals (Martin et al. 1951).

The nesting season in Maryland extends from at least mid-April to mid-July. A female with developing eggs was collected by W. Wholey on 10 April 1893 in the Gunpowder River marsh in Baltimore County (Kirkwood 1895). Nests with eggs have been recorded in Prince George's County from 11 May to 30 May (MNRF). Young in the nest were found in early July 1953 at Blackwater NWR in Dorchester County and on 18 June 1948 in Somerset County (Stewart and Robbins 1958). Fledged young were recorded on 30 June 1902 in Allegany County (Eifrig 1904), on 18 July 1936 in Baltimore County, and on 28 August 1937 in Anne Arundel County (Stewart and Robbins 1958).

There were no "confirmed" records during the Atlas period. Five of the eight "probable" records were for birds on territory. The remaining three included one each of courtship, adults visiting an apparent nest site, and a pair of adults. Twelve records were reported as "possible." Breeding distribution was similar to that of the Least Bittern; however, the American Bittern appears to be much less abundant. Most records were from the marshes along the Patuxent River and on the lower Eastern Shore, including those at Blackwater NWR in Dorchester County and Deal Island WMA in Somerset County. Very few inland records were reported. The Garrett County "possible" record was for a single bird seen in Cranesville Swamp in June.

The low number of reports and lack of breeding confirmation are not surprising, considering the habitat requirements, secretive nature, and rarity of the American Bittern. Most marsh habitats were surveyed from roadsides and, as a result, only a fraction of the total available habitat was covered. In addition, this bittern's behavior and coloration make detection difficult, even when birds are near roads. An accurate estimate of this species' abundance in Maryland could be achieved only by intensive survey efforts. Although the American Bittern was considered a fairly common breeder on the lower Eastern Shore only 30 years ago (Stewart and Robbins 1958), it appears to have declined in Maryland. BBS data from 1966 through 1989 for the Eastern Region show a stable population; the Maryland sample is too small to detect a trend. This species is afforded some protection under Maryland's Nongame and Endangered Species Conservation Act. Conservation efforts aimed at protecting this species are best accomplished through the protection of wetlands.

Lynn M. Davidson

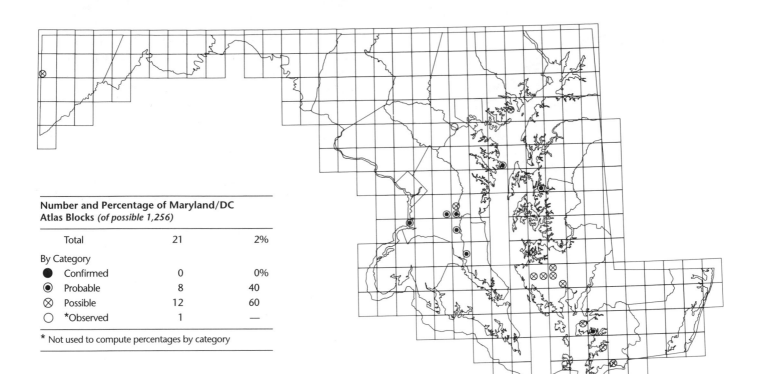

Number and Percentage of Maryland/DC Atlas Blocks *(of possible 1,256)*

Total	21	2%
By Category		
● Confirmed	0	0%
◉ Probable	8	40
⊗ Possible	12	60
○ *Observed	1	—

* Not used to compute percentages by category

Atlas Distribution, 1983–1987

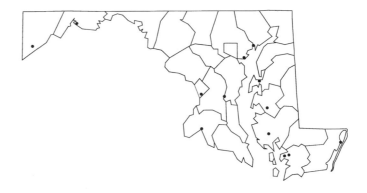

Breeding Distribution, 1958

MOB

Least Bittern

Ixobrychus exilis

The Least Bittern is the smallest North American member of the heron family. It flashes buffy inner wing patches as it takes flight from dense cover. Freezing, reedlike, with bill pointed upward is a habit characteristic of bitterns, allowing them to hide in the fresh, brackish, and salt-marsh vegetation they inhabit. Although the Least Bittern is primarily a solitary nester, it may be found in greater densities in suitable habitat, possibly becoming loosely colonial (Kushlan 1973). In Maryland it is most commonly found in narrow-leaved cattail marshes (Stewart and Robbins 1958). This species is thought to have declined as its breeding habitat disappeared. The Least Bittern was on the NAS Blue List from 1979 through 1986 (Tate 1986), and the DNR lists it as in need of conservation.

The first DC specimen was collected in June 1843 (Baird et al. 1858), but the earliest Maryland specimen is an undated skin from the Patuxent River in the collection of the British Museum (Sharpe 1898). Early accounts called the Least Bittern rather uncommon (Coues and Prentiss 1883), rare (Richmond 1888), and common during summer (Kirkwood 1895). The inconsistency in these descriptions probably resulted from the bird's secretive nature rather than from actual changes in abundance. Kirkwood (1895) also thought it occurred fairly regularly in inland swamps. Eifrig (1904) was aware of only two western Maryland records and considered it rare in Allegany and Garrett counties. Cooke (1929) included it as a locally common summer resident within a 20-mile (32-km) radius of DC. Although Hampe and Kolb (1947) agreed that the Least Bittern was possibly common on the Western Shore, they had no records for the Eastern Shore. Stewart and Robbins (1958) described its breeding status as common in the Chesapeake Bay tidewater areas and occasional in all other sections, yet they lacked breeding evidence from any inland location except PWRC.

Least Bitterns arrive in Maryland from their West Indian and Central American wintering grounds (AOU 1983) during April (Robbins and Bystrak 1977). The male chooses the nest site and the female joins in nest building by collecting material (Palmer 1962). Nests are platforms of dead vegetation interwoven among live plants. They are constructed on or near the ground, typically over water (Bent 1926). Maryland egg dates range from 10 May to 12 July, with the peak in mid June (MNRF). Of 23 records with nest heights, the lowest nest was on the ground and the highest was 4 ft (1.2 m) above standing water. Mean height for these nests is 1.4 ft (0.4 m). Clutch sizes in 18 Maryland nests (MNRF) range from 1 to 5, with a mean of 3.2; two-thirds of the nests contained 3 or 4 eggs. Incubation, performed mostly by the female, lasts 17 to 19 days (Weller 1961). There are seven records of nests with young, all between 8 June and 10 July. Brood sizes ranged from 2 to 5 in these nests. The nestlings can assume the hiding position of adults within a few days of hatching (Palmer 1962); they leave the nest in 10 to 14 days. Least Bitterns may have two broods per season. Their food consists mainly of insects, amphibians, small fish, and crustaceans (Bent 1926). Fall migration in Maryland occurs from early August into October (Robbins and Bystrak 1977).

Most Atlas records are from the Coastal Plain, with a few records in the Piedmont and Ridge and Valley sections. There were no reports from the Allegheny Mountain Section. Coastal Plain records are concentrated in two main geographic areas: the marshes along the Patuxent River and the Nanticoke and Blackwater River marshes. The large concentration of "confirmed" records along the Patuxent River can probably be attributed to the use of boats to explore river marshes. The scattering of records elsewhere in tidewater areas indicates that the breeding distribution remains similar to that described by Stewart and Robbins (1958). The low density of records, however, suggests that Least Bitterns may be less abundant than previously believed. They may be nearly absent from the marshes along the Potomac River and the coastal bays. As with most marsh-dwelling species, the number of reports is low, in part due to the relative inaccessibility of the habitat. An accurate assessment of the Least Bittern's status would require specialized surveys. BBS data from 1966 through 1989 show stable populations in the Eastern Region; however, data are too few to estimate a trend for Maryland.

Over the past 30 years, Chesapeake Bay marshes have been altered, degraded, and destroyed, with about 1,000 acres (405 ha) lost annually (Tiner 1984). Conservation measures designed to maintain and increase Least Bittern populations must begin with protection of wetland habitats, which must then be managed to promote a healthy ecosystem. As long as wetlands continue to be ditched, drained, filled, or otherwise degraded, the birds that depend on them will continue to disappear.

Lynn M. Davidson

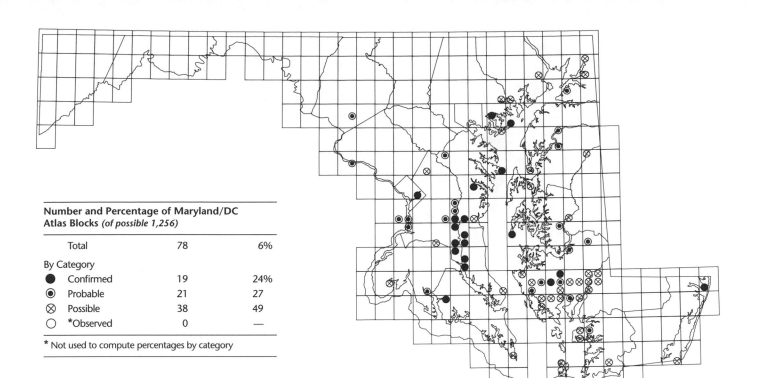

Number and Percentage of Maryland/DC Atlas Blocks *(of possible 1,256)*

Total	78	6%
By Category		
● Confirmed	19	24%
◉ Probable	21	27
⊗ Possible	38	49
○ *Observed	0	—

* Not used to compute percentages by category

Atlas Distribution, 1983–1987

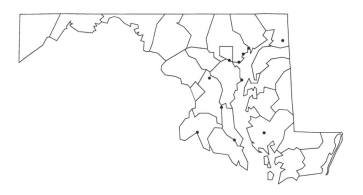

Breeding Distribution, 1958

Great Blue Heron

Ardea herodias

The large, graceful Great Blue Heron is the most widely distributed heron in North America. They usually nest in colonies ranging in size from a few pairs to several hundred (Hancock and Kushlan 1984), but a few nest as single pairs (Walbeck 1988). Although some individuals remain in Maryland year-round, most winter in the southeastern states (AOU 1983). In Maryland, they are most common in the fresh and brackish marshes on the Coastal Plain; farther west they are more frequently seen during migration. Great Blue Herons are usually seen foraging along shorelines and in marshy areas. Their principal prey is fish, but crustaceans, frogs, snakes, and, occasionally, small mammals are taken (Bent 1926; Hancock and Kushlan 1984).

Great Blue Herons have probably always nested in Maryland. Kirkwood (1895) reported seeing them "with more or less regularity, but so far I have been unable to find a 'heronry' in Maryland." Stewart and Robbins (1958) reported 18 colonies: 11 on the Western Shore, four on the upper Eastern Shore, and three on the lower Eastern Shore. Aerial surveys conducted from 1975 through 1977 located 24 colonies: three on the Western Shore, three on the upper Eastern Shore, and 18 on the lower Eastern Shore (Osborn and Custer 1978; Erwin and Korschgen 1979). During these studies, the mean annual breeding population was estimated at 1,800 pairs, approximately 33 percent of the Atlantic Coast population (Spendelow and Patton 1988). However, these surveys did not search farther inland and did not record colonies such as the large one at Nanjemoy Creek in Charles County.

The Great Blue Heron prefers to nest in mature deciduous trees; in Maryland, however, it frequently nests in loblolly pines (MCWP). Nest sites are usually located in a floodplain, swamp, or upland shoreline, but some have been found as far as 2 mi (3.2 km) from open water or marshlands. Colonies also have been located in scrubby salt marsh,

where nests were placed as low as 3 ft (0.9 m) on snags or cedar shrubs (MCWP). Nest heights in Maryland range from 3 to 116 ft (0.9–35 m) (MNRF); the mean height for 287 nests (MCWP) is 46 ft (14 m).

In Maryland, Great Blue Herons return to their colonies in mid- to late February and begin laying eggs in mid-March (MCWP). The early egg date for the state is 15 March (Bridge and Riedel 1962). Clutch sizes are difficult to obtain because of the great height of most nests. Twelve Maryland nests had clutch sizes ranging from 2 to 4 eggs, with a mean of 3.0 (MNRF). The incubation period is 25 to 29 days (Harrison 1975). Chicks begin to hatch in mid-April, with Maryland's earliest chick recorded on 14 April (MCWP). Both parents tend the young (Bent 1926), which fledge in approximately 60 days (Palmer 1962). As a result of banding programs, more is known about brood size (MNRF) than about clutch size. Broods in 347 Maryland nests ranged from 1 to 5, with a mean of 2.1; only 13 nests had 5 chicks. The latest Maryland egg date is 14 June (Bridge 1963) and for young in the nest, 8 August (MNRF). These herons raise one brood per season.

During the Atlas period, ground surveys located 38 colonies and estimated the mean annual population at 3,000 pairs (MCWP). Most Maryland colonies were found in tidal areas along the Chesapeake Bay. With the exception of Calvert County, all counties along the Chesapeake Bay had at least one colony; Charles and Prince George's counties also had colonies. Solitary nests were located on the Monocacy River in Carroll County and near Cumberland in Allegany County (Walbeck 1988). Great Blue Heron colonies along the Atlantic Coast are uncommon (Erwin and Korschgen 1979), and no colonies were found in Worcester County. Because Great Blue Herons can travel several miles to reach feeding sites, many birds sighted in areas without known breeding colonies may be from Maryland colonies or colonies in adjacent states, such as the one in Bedford County, Pennsylvania (Brauning 1992). Other unconfirmed sightings may represent transients or nonbreeding wanderers.

BBS data from 1966 through 1989 show a highly significant average annual increase of 3.4 percent in the Eastern Region; Maryland BBS data show a highly significant average annual increase of 3.5 percent. Although the population has increased, monitoring of colonies should continue, and colony sites should be reported to the DNR. These sites should not be entered unnecessarily during the breeding season because human activity can disturb nesting birds. Activities such as logging and the creation of artificial impoundments, which occasionally destroy Great Blue Heron habitat (Parnell et al. 1988), should be restricted to areas without colonies. The Patuxent River Naval Air Station has been managing the Bloodsworth Island colony in Dorchester County by providing nesting platforms. Researchers at the station are also seeking a long-term solution by planting salt-tolerant trees that may provide nest sites in marshes (K. Rambo, pers. comm.).

Joan McKearnan

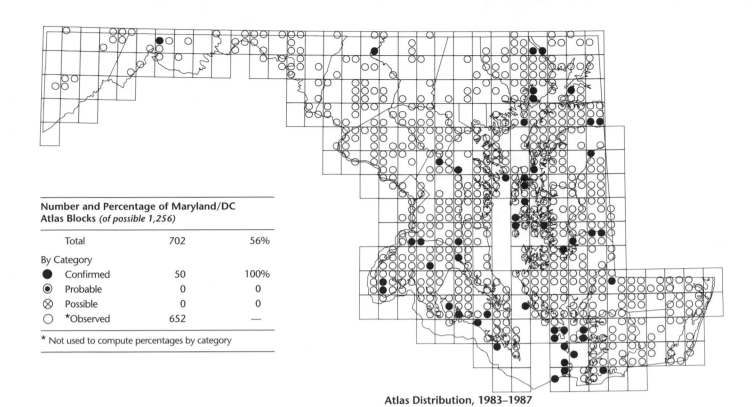

Number and Percentage of Maryland/DC Atlas Blocks *(of possible 1,256)*		
Total	702	56%
By Category		
● Confirmed	50	100%
◉ Probable	0	0
⊗ Possible	0	0
○ *Observed	652	—

* Not used to compute percentages by category

Atlas Distribution, 1983–1987

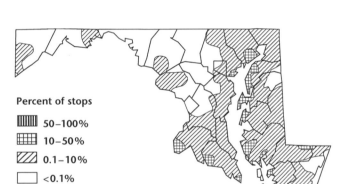

Percent of stops

▥ 50–100%
▦ 10–50%
▨ 0.1–10%
☐ <0.1%

Relative Abundance, 1982–1989

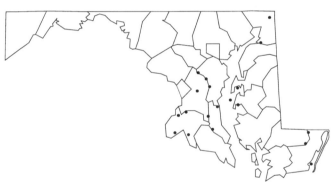

Breeding Distribution, 1958

The Great Blue Heron was recorded throughout tidewater Maryland, most frequently near breeding colonies. Miniroutes do not sample colonial breeding birds effectively; most records represent nonbreeding wanderers or birds foraging away from nest sites.

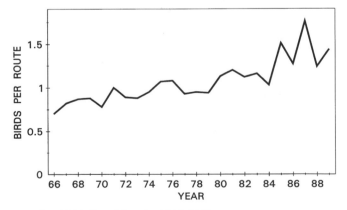

Maryland BBS Trend Graph, 1966–1989

Great Egret

Ardea alba

The Great Egret is a common sight as it forages for aquatic vertebrates, crayfish, and insects (Palmer 1962) in Maryland's salt marshes. This large white heron, formerly known as the American or Common Egret, typically nests in mixed-species heronries. Adults return from their Gulf Coast and Latin American wintering areas (AOU 1983) in mid-April. The 10-year (1977–86) median early arrival date is 8 April (Ringler 1986b); the 10-year median late departure date is 14 October (Ringler 1986a). They are rare in Maryland during the winter.

Long white plumes on the adult's head were the cause of its near demise near the end of the nineteenth century, when egrets were killed by the thousands to obtain feathers for fashionable ladies' hats (Bent 1926). Cooke (1929) reported that "in the early days these herons were tolerably common in summer, but by the time Coues and Prentiss were writing [1883] they had become rare." In 1905, federal legislation was enacted to protect them, and populations have slowly recovered (Erwin 1985). Stewart and Robbins (1958) reported breeding birds in coastal Worcester County and on the Pocomoke River along the Worcester–Wicomico County boundary. They were considered rare in the Chesapeake Bay with only two known colonies: one each in Charles and Queen Anne's counties.

Osborn and Custer (1978) and Erwin and Korschgen (1979) located 22 colonies in five counties from 1975 through 1977: eight each in Dorchester and Somerset, one in Talbot, two in St. Mary's, and three in Worcester. The estimated mean annual population during these surveys was 664 pairs, approximately 14 percent of the Atlantic Coast population (Spendelow and Patton 1988).

Great Egrets nest in evergreen or deciduous shrubs surrounded by salt marsh or in shrubs and phragmites on dredge spoil islands (MCWP). Eastern red cedar and hackberry are commonly used, probably because of their availability in high salinity habitats. Nests in Maryland have been found as low as 1 ft (0.3 m) in phragmites stands (MNRF)

and as high as 92 ft (28 m), in Great Blue Heron colonies (MCWP). Both adults build the platform nest of twigs, sticks, or reeds (Bent 1926). The nest, averaging 10 to 12 in. (25–30 cm) in diameter, is smaller than that of the Great Blue Heron (Harrison 1978). Egg laying begins in mid-April, with an early egg date of 9 April (Robbins and Bystrak 1977) and a late date of 23 June (MNRF). Incubation, performed by both adults, takes 25 or 26 days (Bent 1926). Eggs hatch in mid-May and chicks fledge in five to six weeks. The earliest Maryland date for a nest with young is 4 May; unfledged young have been observed as late as 22 August (MCWP). Bent (1926) reported that the single clutch per season usually consists of 4 or 5 eggs, but data for 32 Maryland nests examined during the MCWP show clutch sizes ranging from 1 to 4, with a mean of 2.8. Mean brood size from 130 Maryland nest records in the MNRF is 2.6. Palmer (1962) noted that Great Egrets will attempt to renest after nest failure.

In a study conducted from 1985 through 1988 (MCWP), 20 colonies (in 14 Atlas blocks) were occupied by Great Egrets: seven in Somerset, six in Dorchester, five in Worcester, and one each in Talbot and St. Mary's counties. Population estimates fluctuate annually and may be biased by the sampling techniques. Estimates ranged between 500 and 800 pairs, with a mean of 714 pairs, and have not increased significantly since the mid-1970s (MCWP).

During the Atlas period, most Great Egret colonies were located in Worcester County or on the Bloodsworth–Smith Island archipelago in Dorchester and Somerset counties. The colonies in St. Mary's County and on Barren Island in Dorchester County were associated with Great Blue Herons. The northernmost colony, in Talbot County, was a mixed-species heronry of Snowy Egrets, Cattle Egrets, and three to six pairs of Little Blue Herons. Reports other than Atlas confirmations were widespread, especially in the Eastern Shore marshes, and probably were of foraging breeders, postbreeding wanderers, or stragglers.

Aerial surveys are fairly successful in locating egret colonies and could be used to monitor populations. Colonies can be located by watching adults fly to and from potential nest sites, especially when carrying nesting material, but ground censuses of nests are more accurate than aerial counts (MCWP). Colonies should be posted and protected during the breeding season, and nesting habitat should be protected. If necessary, habitat could be created on dredge spoil islands, but natural succession takes 30 to 40 years before the area becomes suitable for heron use (Soots and Parnell 1975).

BBS data from 1966 through 1989 show an indication of a decline in the Eastern Region and an increase in Maryland; the continental population is stable. The Maryland population appears stable at present, but colony sites are vulnerable to rises in sea level and other forms of disturbance. Long-term management plans, including the possible creation of colony sites on dredge spoil islands, will play an important part in determining the future of the Great Egret in Maryland.

Joan McKearnan

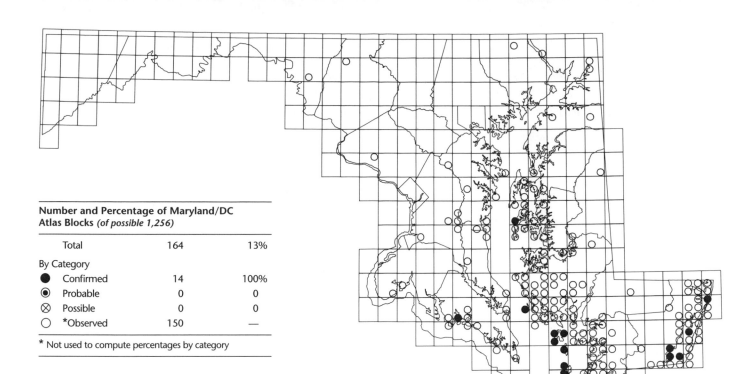

Number and Percentage of Maryland/DC Atlas Blocks *(of possible 1,256)*

Total	164	13%
By Category		
● Confirmed	14	100%
◉ Probable	0	0
⊗ Possible	0	0
○ *Observed	150	—

* Not used to compute percentages by category

Atlas Distribution, 1983–1987

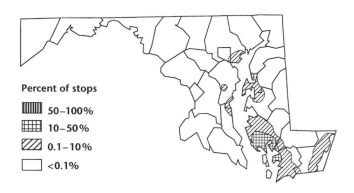

Percent of stops

▥ 50–100%
▦ 10–50%
▨ 0.1–10%
☐ <0.1%

Relative Abundance, 1982–1989

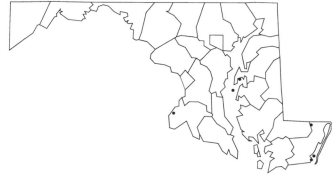

Breeding Distribution, 1958

The Great Egret is a colonial breeder. The highest densities were recorded near colonies in the marshes on the lower Eastern Shore. Miniroutes do not sample colonial breeding birds effectively; most records represent nonbreeding wanderers or birds foraging away from nest sites.

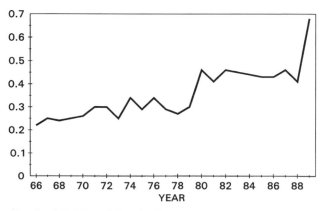

Maryland BBS Trend Graph, 1966–1989

Snowy Egret

Egretta thula

The Snowy Egret, a slender member of the heron family, breeds locally in lower portions of the Chesapeake Bay and in coastal Worcester County. It is a fairly common post-breeding wanderer on the Western Shore, uncommon on the Piedmont in late summer, and rare in winter on the lower Eastern Shore (Stewart and Robbins 1958). The first spring migrants return to Maryland from their wintering grounds in the southeastern states (AOU 1983) in mid-April (Ringler 1985b), and the last fall migrants leave during early October (Ringler 1985a).

Like many colonial waterbirds, Snowy Egrets were victims of the feather trade in the 19th century (Bent 1926). Recovery was apparently slower for this species than for some others. Hampe and Kolb (1947) described it as occurring in Maryland only in late summer during postbreeding dispersal, but Stewart and Robbins (1947a) found the first two Maryland colonies in Worcester County in 1946. Snowy Egrets were considered fairly common in the coastal areas of Worcester County and on Smith Island in Somerset County (Stewart and Robbins 1958); they were possible breeders in tidewater areas of Somerset, Wicomico, and southern Dorchester counties. Surveys conducted from 1975 through 1977 located five colonies in coastal Worcester County and seven on islands in the lower Chesapeake Bay: five in Dorchester County and two in Somerset County (Osborn and Custer 1978; Erwin and Korschgen 1979). The estimated mean annual population in Maryland was 1,100 pairs, about 10 percent of the Atlantic Coast population (Spendelow and Patton 1988).

Snowy Egrets nest in mixed-species colonies. Most colonies are located on hammocks in salt marshes or on dredge spoil sites with stands of phragmites (MCWP). They also were found nesting on marsh elder in salt marshes and on cherry saplings in a second-growth forest. Heights of Mary-land nests (MNRF) range from 0.6 to 50 ft (0.2–15 m) above the ground, but the great majority are placed at 5 ft (1.5 m) or lower. Nests are small, round platforms 8 to 17 in. (20–43 cm) in diameter (Burger 1978b) and are constructed of fine twigs and reeds. Nests and eggs are indistinguishable from those of Little Blue and Tricolored Herons. Both adults participate in nest building, incubation, and care of the young (Palmer 1962). The clutch of 3 or 4 eggs is laid in mid- to late April (MNRF). Clutch sizes in 153 Maryland nests range from 1 to 5, with a mean of 2.8. The earliest Maryland egg date is 4 May; the latest is 7 August (Robbins and Bystrak 1977). The incubation period is listed as 18 days, but this is probably a little short (Hancock and Kushlan 1984). The earliest Maryland date for nests with young is 14 May; the latest is 22 August (MCWP). Young begin leaving the nest three to four weeks after hatching (Palmer 1962), but they are not fully fledged for another week, usually at the end of June or beginning of July in Maryland (MCWP). Snowy Egrets are more active foragers than Little Blue Herons but less active than Tricolored Herons (Kent 1986). Their diet consists mainly of small fish and crustaceans.

Atlas fieldworkers located twelve colonies containing Snowy Egrets: four in coastal Worcester County; six at Smith Island, Somerset County; one on Poplar Island, Talbot County; and one in a Great Blue Heron colony on Bloodsworth Island, Dorchester County. Two single nesting attempts also occurred on or near Tilghman Island in Talbot County. The total breeding population during the Atlas period was estimated between 1,000 and 1,650 pairs, with an annual mean of 1,290 pairs (MCWP). Reports of nonbreeding individuals from throughout the state probably refer to postbreeding wanderers, transients, and foraging birds some distance from the colonies. A few pairs of Snowy Egrets nested near the Maryland line on the Susquehanna River and in a colony along the Delaware River; both are in Pennsylvania (Brauning 1992). Another colony was reported along the Delaware River in Delaware. Although they can be found in freshwater habitats, Snowy Egrets are primarily associated with salt and brackish habitats along the Atlantic Coast; few colonies are found inland (Spendelow and Patton 1988).

Snowy Egret populations are stable in Maryland, according to BBS data from 1966 through 1989; the Eastern Region data indicate a possible increase and the continental population is stable. Monitoring should continue in Maryland, and known colony sites should be protected from disturbance. New sites should be reported to the DNR. In addition, potential nesting sites should be identified and protected from development and environmental contamination. Cattle Egrets may pose a threat to other herons and egrets. Burger (1978b) reported the Snowy Egret to be the heron species most commonly affected by Cattle Egret competition and aggression. Snowy Egret populations in Maryland do not seem to have been significantly affected by Cattle Egrets when the data from the mid-1970s and the mid-1980s are compared, but additional studies may be needed.

Joan McKearnan

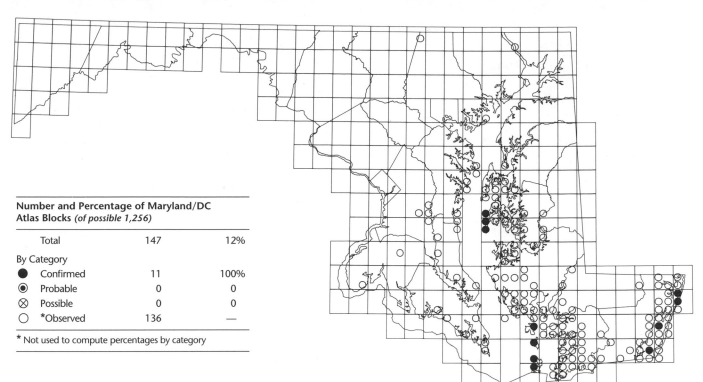

Number and Percentage of Maryland/DC Atlas Blocks *(of possible 1,256)*

Total	147	12%
By Category		
● Confirmed	11	100%
◉ Probable	0	0
⊗ Possible	0	0
○ *Observed	136	—

* Not used to compute percentages by category

Atlas Distribution, 1983–1987

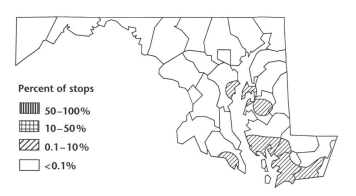

Percent of stops

▥	50–100%
▦	10–50%
▨	0.1–10%
☐	<0.1%

Relative Abundance, 1982–1989

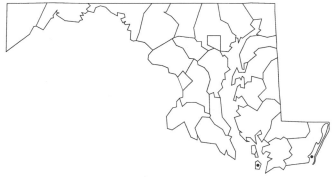

Breeding Distribution, 1958

The Snowy Egret is a colonial species. Miniroutes do not sample colonial breeding birds effectively; most records represent non-breeding wanderers or birds foraging away from nest sites.

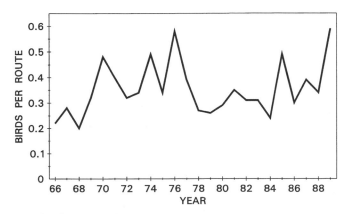

Maryland BBS Trend Graph, 1966–1989

MOB

Little Blue Heron

Egretta caerulea

This attractive colonial heron is less common in Maryland than its close relatives, the Snowy Egret and the Tricolored Heron. The Little Blue Heron was formerly placed in the monotypic genus *Florida* (AOU 1983). It is a summer resident, often found foraging along tidal guts and ponds in salt marshes. The first spring migrants arrive from their wintering grounds in the Caribbean basin (AOU 1983) in early April (Ringler 1986b), and most birds depart by late September (Ringler 1986a). It is rare in winter in the tidewater areas of the Eastern Shore and Western Shore sections (Stewart and Robbins 1958).

Little Blue Herons have always been most common in late summer when breeding adults and young are joined by postbreeding wanderers from the south (Kirkwood 1895; Hampe and Kolb 1947). Some writers have described this species as rare (Coues and Prentiss 1883; Kirkwood 1895), but because immature birds are white, they may have been misidentified as Snowy Egrets. Stewart and Robbins (1958) reported three colonies in Worcester County, one each in Dorchester and St. Mary's counties, and possible nesting along the Pocomoke River and in Charles County. Osborn and Custer (1978) found ten colonies in their aerial censuses of 1975 and 1976: four each in Dorchester and Somerset counties and two in Worcester County. Maryland population estimates during those censuses ranged from 100 to 325 pairs, with an annual mean of 231 pairs (Osborn and Custer 1978; Erwin and Korschgen 1979). This is approximately 3 percent of the Atlantic Coast population (Spendelow and Patton 1988). During the Atlas period, eight colonies were located and censused. The state population ranged between 300 and 400 pairs, with an annual mean of 343 pairs (MCWP).

Little Blue Herons walk slowly as they forage in tidal pools and along shorelines (Kent 1986). Their diet consists of a variety of invertebrates, including grasshoppers, cutworms, crustaceans, and, occasionally, frogs and lizards.

Maryland Little Blue Herons nest exclusively in mixed-species heronries which may be located in hammocks on salt-marsh islands, in phragmites on dredge spoil islands, or in secondary scrub growth on estuarine islands (MCWP). The nests and eggs are indistinguishable from those of Snowy Egrets and Tricolored Herons (Harrison 1978), which makes recording of egg dates difficult. The MNRF has no nest records for this species. The earliest Maryland egg date is 23 May and the latest is 4 June (Robbins and Bystrak 1977). However, since chicks have been found in Maryland in mid-May and incubation lasts 22 to 24 days (Palmer 1962), egg laying must begin in late April. Incubation is performed by both parents. Chicks start to leave the nest at two to four weeks of age but are flightless until they are 35 to 40 days old (Werschkul 1979). Little Blue Herons usually fledge in late July (MCWP).

During the Atlas period, all but one of the Little Blue Heron colonies were found on Smith Island in Somerset County or on islands in Sinepuxent and Assawoman bays in Worcester County. The other colony, on Poplar Island in Talbot County, contained from 2 to 6 pairs each year. Little Blue Herons recorded in Atlas blocks without known colonies probably represented foraging breeders, wandering nonbreeders, and postbreeding wanderers. Little Blue Herons can be found in fresh, estuarine, and marine waters. They seem to prefer fresh water and are more numerous inland than on the coast (Bent 1926; Spendelow and Patton 1988). This may explain low populations in Maryland relative to other herons and egrets. Potential nesting and foraging sites are less numerous away from tidal waters in Maryland. Although BBS data from 1966 through 1989 indicate an increase in the Eastern Region, Maryland and continental populations are stable.

The Little Blue Heron population in Maryland seems to have increased slightly since the mid-1970s, but monitoring should continue because the large annual fluctuations tend to obscure population trends (MCWP). Human disturbance of mixed-species heronries during the breeding season can be disastrous, especially in areas where Fish Crows can prey on eggs and nestlings if the adults are flushed. Entrance into colonies should be avoided and colony sites should be posted. New colony sites should be reported to the DNR. Conservation efforts should focus on protecting both nesting and foraging habitat. Although herons typically use sites for several years in succession, overfertilization resulting from defecation can destroy the habitat (Custer et al. 1980). A rise in sea level may flood salt-marsh and dredge spoil islands now in use. Nest sites can be created using dredge spoil material, but because the natural succession of plants required for nest sites can take several years (Soots and Parnell 1975), this should be done before the sites are needed.

Joan McKearnan

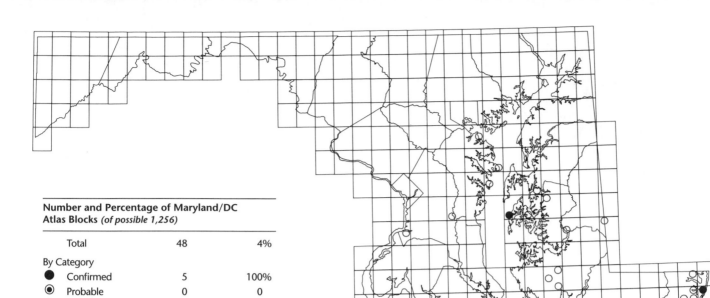

Number and Percentage of Maryland/DC Atlas Blocks *(of possible 1,256)*

Total	48	4%
By Category		
● Confirmed	5	100%
◉ Probable	0	0
⊗ Possible	0	0
○ *Observed	43	—

* Not used to compute percentages by category

Atlas Distribution, 1983–1987

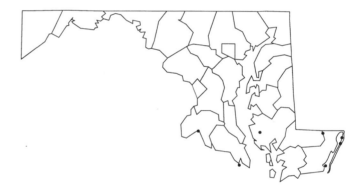

Breeding Distribution, 1958

Tricolored Heron

Egretta tricolor

The colonial-nesting Tricolored Heron is locally common during the summer in the tidal marshes of the lower Chesapeake Bay and in coastal Worcester County. It is rare in Maryland in winter, as most birds winter farther south along the Atlantic Coast (AOU 1983). Breeding birds return in mid- to late April and leave in late September and early October (Stewart and Robbins 1958). This species was formerly known as the Louisiana Heron *(Hydranassa tricolor)* (AOU 1983).

Kirkwood (1895) knew of only one report for Maryland, and Cooke (1929) considered this species accidental in DC. Stewart and Robbins (1958) regarded the Tricolored Heron as uncommon and local in the Chincoteague Bay area of Worcester County. They cited only one breeding location for Maryland, Mills Island in southeastern Worcester County. In 1958, a pair raising young was recorded on a South Point spoil island, also in Worcester County (MNRF); 92 young were banded there in 1963 and 117 in 1965, and about 210 pairs were present in 1971. Surveys from 1975 through 1977 (Osborn and Custer 1978, Erwin and Korschgen 1979) found 13 colonies: five on Smith Island in Somerset County, four in Worcester County, and four in Dorchester County. They estimated that the breeding population fluctuated between 125 and 470 pairs during this period, with an annual mean of 286 pairs. This was approximately 3 percent of the Atlantic Coast population, excluding Florida (Spendelow and Patton 1988). The northernmost nesting record in the Chesapeake Bay occurred in 1972 when J. Reese (pers. comm.) found one pair nesting on Long Marsh Island in Queen Anne's County. Since that time, this island has disappeared through erosion.

The Tricolored Heron breeds in mixed-species colonies

and places its nest in shrubs or phragmites stands near salt marshes. No records of Maryland nest heights exist for this species. Because the nests and eggs are indistinguishable from those of the Snowy Egret and Little Blue Heron, determining egg dates is difficult. The earliest Maryland egg date is 15 May, which coincides with the earliest date a chick has been found in a Maryland nest (MCWP); the latest egg date is 5 June (MNRF). With an incubation period of 21 days (Palmer 1962), the earliest Maryland eggs are estimated to be laid in late April (MCWP). Both adults incubate the single clutch of 3 to 5 eggs, and both feed and care for the young (Palmer 1962). In 46 Maryland nests, brood sizes range from 1 to 4, with a mean of 2.3 (MNRF). No Maryland nests had 5 eggs (MCWP). Young leave the nest three to four weeks after hatching; they begin to fly one to two weeks later (Hancock and Kushlan 1984). The last date young have been observed in a Maryland nest is 15 July (MNRF). Fledglings, which are distinguished from adults by the reddish wash on their necks, are first observed outside the colonies in early July. Tricolored Herons are relatively active feeders, foraging most often on salt-marsh shorelines and in tidal pools. Their prey consists mostly of fish, but also includes some crustaceans, insects, and amphibians (Bent 1926; Kent 1986).

During the Atlas period, censuses conducted by the MCWP estimated a population range of 365 to 1,100 pairs, with an annual mean of 901 pairs, a possible increase of about 215 percent in a decade (MCWP). Methodologies differed between the two groups of censuses, however, so the counts cannot be directly compared. Colonies with Tricolored Herons were located on two dredge spoil islands in Worcester County (one in Sinepuxent Bay and one in Assawoman Bay) and in five mixed-species heronries on Smith Island in Somerset County. In addition, approximately three pairs were found in a Great Blue Heron colony on Bloodsworth Island in Dorchester County. Despite their greater number, Tricolored Herons were reported away from the breeding areas less frequently than were Little Blue Herons, possibly because Tricolored Herons do not breed as far north in the Chesapeake Bay and are more strictly confined to saltwater habitats (Bent 1926; Spendelow and Patton 1988). It is also interesting that, although the population more than doubled between the mid-1970s and the mid-1980s, the number of active colony sites declined from 13 to 8, and the breeding range in Maryland contracted. Causes for the colony site decline and range contraction are not known. BBS data show a stable continental population from 1966 through 1989; data for Maryland are insufficient to estimate a trend.

Monitoring of Tricolored Heron populations should continue, and any possible nest sites should be reported to the DNR. Known colony sites should be protected from disturbance by posting the sites and development should be prohibited in the vicinity of colonies. It is also important to determine whether it is feasible to try to control the erosion of islands containing heron colonies.

Joan McKearnan

Number and Percentage of Maryland/DC Atlas Blocks *(of possible 1,256)*

Total	45	4%
By Category		
● Confirmed	5	100%
◉ Probable	0	0
⊗ Possible	0	0
○ *Observed	40	—

* Not used to compute percentages by category

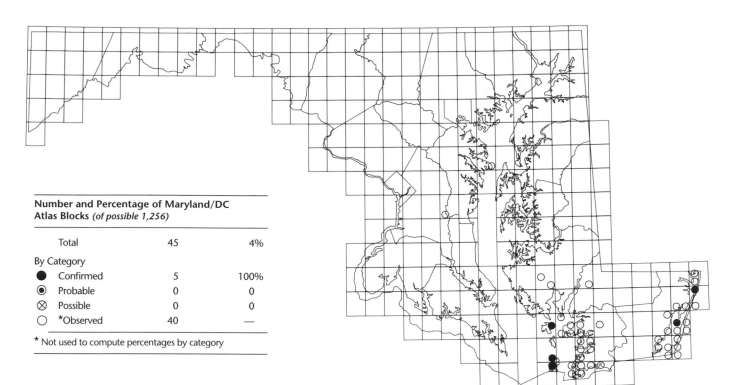

Atlas Distribution, 1983–1987

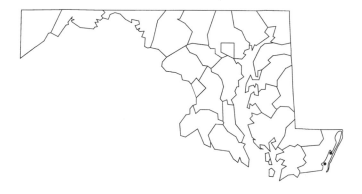

Breeding Distribution, 1958

Cattle Egret

Bubulcus ibis

The Cattle Egret is the only heron in Maryland that eats primarily nonaquatic animals. Flocks of these highly social egrets are most often observed foraging in roadside ditches and fields for insects, reptiles, amphibians, and small mammals (Arendt 1988). In Maryland this species is locally abundant in summer and nests in large mixed-species colonies. The 10-year median spring arrival date is 12 April (Ringler 1988b), and the median fall departure date is 12 October (Ringler 1988a). It winters from the southeastern United States to South America (AOU 1983). Nonbreeding observations are usually coastal or along the edge of the Chesapeake Bay, although the Cattle Egret has been recorded as far inland as Allegany County (Paulus 1975).

Native to Africa, southern Spain, northern Australia, and tropical Asia (Arendt 1988), Cattle Egrets have expanded to every continent except Antarctica within the twentieth century. They apparently invaded the southeastern United States from the Guianas by way of the West Indies, and they currently nest locally across North America north to Idaho, southern Canada, and Maine (AOU 1983; Peck and James 1983).

The first Cattle Egret was reported in Maryland on 25 April 1953 (Stewart and Robbins 1958). N. Hotchkiss and G. Miller confirmed breeding four years later, on 1 June 1957, when they found a nest with 3 eggs on Mills Island in Worcester County (Miller 1959). During the following summer, on 15 June 1958, Valentine (1958) observed 12 Cattle Egret nests in the Mills Island colony. Since then, the number of colonies and the number of pairs have increased substantially. Osborn and Custer (1978) and Erwin and Korschgen (1979) located nine mixed-species heronries with Cattle Egrets from 1975 through 1977 on the Eastern Shore of the Chesapeake Bay: two in Somerset, four in Dorchester, one in

Talbot, and two in Worcester counties. Using aerial censuses they estimated an annual average breeding population of 930 pairs, with extremes of 730 and 1,325 pairs, representing approximately 14 percent of the Atlantic Coast population (Spendelow and Patton 1988). From 1985 through 1988, ground censuses conducted by the MCWP estimated a mean population of 1,560 pairs with extremes of 700 and 2,200 pairs (MCWP). BBS data from 1966 through 1989 show a significant average annual increase of 2.6 percent in the Eastern Region; the Maryland population is showing some sign of stabilizing.

Cattle Egrets often nest in the same dense scrub habitats and phragmites stands as Snowy Egrets, Little Blue Herons, and Tricolored Herons. Their nests are typically placed lower in the vegetation than those of Little Blue Herons but higher than those of Snowy Egrets and Tricolored Herons (Burger 1978b, 1979b). Nests are similar to those of the other three but are slightly smaller; their bluish eggs are also smaller and paler. Laying begins only a few days after arrival (Burger 1978b). The female lays one clutch of 4 or 5 eggs a season; both adults tend the nest (Harrison 1975).

The earliest Maryland egg date is 9 April (Robbins and Bystrak 1977) and the latest is 30 August (MNRF). Clutch sizes in 202 Maryland nests (MNRF) range from 1 to 5, with a mean of 3.1. The incubation period lasts 21 to 26 days (Weber 1975). The earliest record of young in the nest is 15 May (MCWP). The laying season may not be as synchronized in Cattle Egrets as in other herons; 57 nests with eggs were found as late as 15 August (Bystrak 1970). Brood sizes in 210 Maryland nests (MNRF) range from 1 to 6, with a mean of 2.8. Chicks fledge after about 30 days (Skead 1956), and flying young may be observed by late June and early July. Young have been found hatching off South Point, Worcester County, as late as 30 August (Ringler 1983a).

During the Atlas period, Cattle Egrets were found in two colonies on Smith Island in Somerset County, two in Worcester County, and one in Talbot County. Because Cattle Egrets will forage farther inland than most herons, they were recorded as nonbreeders in more blocks than any heron except the Great Blue Heron. Some of the sightings from the upper Chesapeake Bay may have been foraging birds from the large heronry on the Susquehanna River in Lancaster County, Pennsylvania (Brauning 1992). This site, which had 1,500 pairs of herons in the early 1980s, including 1,200 pairs of Cattle Egrets, was abandoned during the 1988 season (Witmer 1988).

Because this species is still in a period of expansion and may compete with native herons for nest sites, its population should be carefully monitored. In Maryland, waterbird censuses have documented no adverse impact on other herons by Cattle Egrets (MCWP). Competition for nest sites has been recorded in New Jersey (Burger 1978b) and Louisiana, although not in Texas (Spendelow and Patton 1988). Similar studies need to be conducted on Cattle Egrets in Maryland to determine if there is competition. New breeding sites should be reported to the DNR.

Joan McKearnan

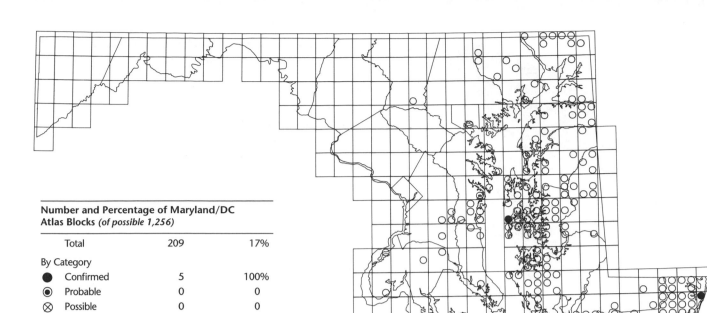

Number and Percentage of Maryland/DC Atlas Blocks *(of possible 1,256)*		
Total	209	17%
By Category		
● Confirmed	5	100%
◉ Probable	0	0
⊗ Possible	0	0
○ *Observed	204	—

* Not used to compute percentages by category

Atlas Distribution, 1983–1987

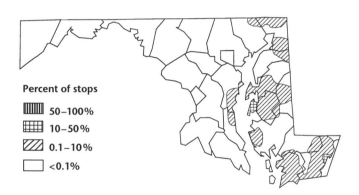

Percent of stops

▥ 50–100%
▦ 10–50%
▨ 0.1–10%
☐ <0.1%

Relative Abundance, 1982–1989

Breeding Distribution, 1958

Cattle Egrets are colonial nesters. Miniroutes do not sample colonial breeding birds effectively; most records represent non-breeding wanderers or birds foraging away from nest sites. The records from northeastern Maryland probably represent birds from colonies in Pennsylvania and Delaware.

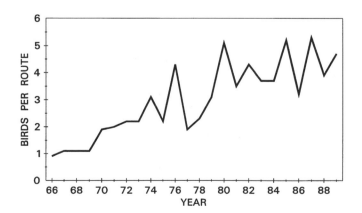

Maryland BBS Trend Graph, 1966–1989

Green Heron

Butorides virescens

The small, dark Green Heron is one of the most widespread of Maryland's wading birds. It may be found in nearly any freshwater or saltwater woody habitat and is an adaptable nester (Stewart and Robbins 1958). When the AOU (Eisenmann 1976) classified the Green Heron of North America as conspecific with the Striated Heron *(Butorides striatus)* of South America and the Old World, they selected the name Green Heron to represent the entire population, then later (AOU 1983) changed it to Green-backed Heron. The AOU (1993) again split this complex into two species, Striated Heron and Green Heron. Green Herons arrive in Maryland from their wintering grounds in Florida, the Caribbean basin, and South America (AOU 1983) in April, and most depart by October (Stewart and Robbins 1958). A very few overwinter on the Coastal Plain in some years (Robbins and Bystrak 1977).

All early writers considered the Green Heron a common summer resident and breeding bird in Maryland and DC (Coues and Prentiss 1862, 1883; Kirkwood 1895; Cooke 1929; Hampe and Kolb 1947). Although distributed statewide, it is most common in the tidal areas of the Coastal Plain (Stewart and Robbins 1958). In Maryland, they nest in scattered pairs or in small colonies. Stewart and Robbins (1958) reported occasional colonies of 6 to 20 pairs. From surveys conducted in 1976 and 1977, Erwin (1979) identified Maryland colonies with 3 to 15 pairs and reported a decline in numbers in coastal locations from Maine to Virginia. From 1968 through 1989, BBS data show a stable population in the Eastern Region and Maryland. Surveys in Dorchester, Somerset, Talbot, and Worcester counties found 14 to 15 colonies with a combined population of from 60 to 79 pairs from 1985 through 1987 (MCWP).

The male selects territory and initially defends it (Palmer 1962). After pair formation, both birds defend the territory, which is restricted to an area within a few feet of the nest. Occasionally, two broods are raised. Nest sites vary widely; nests have been found on top of a small rise in a marsh, in trees, located generally in swampy woods, in dry woodlands and orchards, and in conifers near water. In Maryland, nests also have been found in the camouflage on the sides of duck blinds (G. Therres, pers. comm.). Green Herons primarily use twigs for their nest platforms (DeGraaf and Rudis 1986).

There are 427 Maryland nest records citing height above the ground or water (MNRF). They range from 0 to 40 ft (0.0–12 m), with a mean of 5.0 ft (1.5 m). In 752 Maryland nests with eggs, dates range from 21 April to 26 July, with a peak in mid-June. Clutch sizes in 471 Maryland nests (MNRF) range from 1 to 7, with a mean of 3.2. Of 347 Maryland nests with young, the earliest was recorded on 11 May and the latest on 5 August, with a peak in early July. Brood sizes in 156 Maryland nests (MNRF) range from 1 to 7, with a mean of 2.9. Incubation typically takes 20 days, and the young make their first flight at 21 to 23 days (Palmer 1962).

The principal foods of Green Herons are fish and aquatic invertebrates, although they occasionally take insects and terrestrial invertebrates (Meyerriecks 1960). They hunt mainly by hunkering at the shoreline of a stream or pond waiting for prey to approach or by wading slowly; they sometimes feed by gently stirring the bottom of creeks and ponds with their feet (Meyerriecks 1971). Green Herons are patient and sometimes creative foragers. They have been known to use feathers (Palmer 1962) and fish-food pellets (Sisson 1974) as bait to attract small fish.

Maryland Atlas field observers confirmed nesting in all counties. There were a few clusters of "confirmed" blocks, most notably in the larger marshes on the Patuxent River and around Blackwater NWR in Dorchester County. Even though Green Herons are known to nest away from waterways (Palmer 1962), nearly all of the "confirmed" records were near larger rivers, reservoirs, marshes, and swamps.

In spite of being widespread and adaptable, the Green Heron populations should continue to be monitored in Maryland. Although marshy areas are protected by law within buffer areas around the Chesapeake Bay, that protection does not extend to all wetlands and wooded areas statewide. Shoreline tracts are prime development sites, as are unprotected tidal wetlands. Protection to ensure successful Green Heron breeding in Maryland should include, at a minimum, controlling human disturbance around nest sites during the breeding season and preserving wetlands statewide (Landin 1978).

D. Ann Rasberry

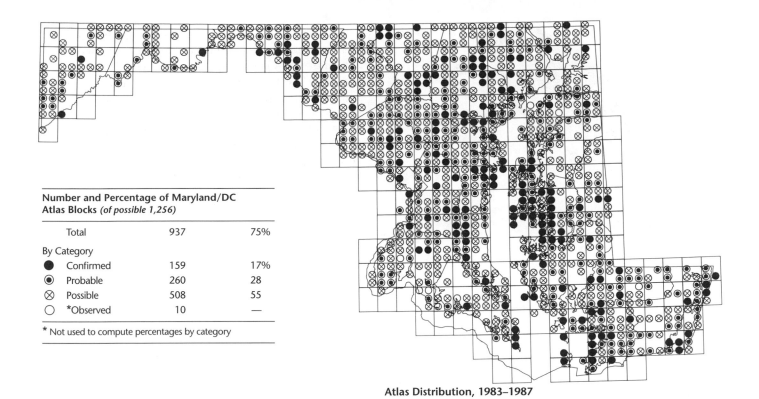

Number and Percentage of Maryland/DC Atlas Blocks *(of possible 1,256)*

Total	937	75%
By Category		
● Confirmed	159	17%
◉ Probable	260	28
⊗ Possible	508	55
○ *Observed	10	—

* Not used to compute percentages by category

Atlas Distribution, 1983–1987

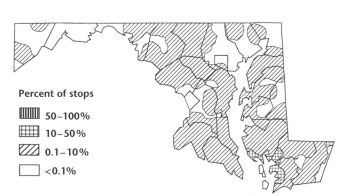

Percent of stops

▥	50–100%
▦	10–50%
▨	0.1–10%
☐	<0.1%

Relative Abundance, 1982–1989

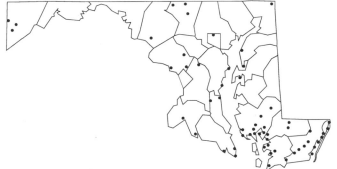

Breeding Distribution, 1958

The Green Heron is widely and evenly distributed. Higher numbers were found in the marshes of Dorchester, Wicomico, and Somerset counties and in the northeastern corner of Worcester County. Few were recorded in western Maryland, which is extensively wooded, or in heavily urbanized and suburbanized areas.

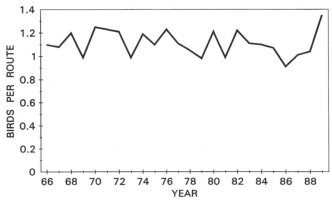

Maryland BBS Trend Graph, 1966–1989

Black-crowned Night-Heron

Nycticorax nycticorax

The short, stocky Black-crowned Night-Heron is seldom seen during the day. These night foragers are seen mainly at dawn and dusk, except during the nesting season when they spend more time searching for food for their young (Fasola 1984). They feed primarily in tidal ponds or guts and at the edges of streams. Black-crowned Night-Herons are opportunistic feeders, preying primarily on fish or aquatic invertebrates (Collins 1970). They also take eggs and chicks—especially those of other colonial waterbirds—and, less commonly, small mammals. Black-crowned Night-Herons are colonial nesters, both in small colonies of conspecifics and in larger mixed-species groups (Spendelow and Patton 1988). Although some individuals occur year-round in Maryland, many spend the winter in the southern United States (AOU 1983). In summer they are locally common (Stewart and Robbins 1958).

Black-crowned Night-Herons have long been known to nest in Maryland and DC. Kirkwood (1895) described in detail two colonies near Baltimore City. Cooke (1929) reported a small breeding colony near the outside aviary at the National Zoological Park in DC, where captive Black-crowned Night-Herons are kept. This colony is still active. Stewart and Robbins (1958) reported 14 colonies in Maryland: one each in St. Mary's and Cecil counties, two each in Anne Arundel, Dorchester, and Somerset counties, and three each in Charles and Worcester counties. They also reported three colonies in DC. By the mid-1970s the distribution was more restricted. The only known Western Shore colony was in St. Mary's County (Osborn and Custer 1978; Erwin and Korschgen 1979), but DC and the Potomac tributaries were not surveyed. Seven colonies were located in Dorchester County, and five each in Somerset and Worcester counties. These censuses, conducted from 1975 through 1977, showed wide fluctuations in annual numbers, ranging from 400 to 960 pairs, with an annual mean of 745 pairs. This represented approximately 10 percent of the Atlantic Coast population (Spendelow and Patton 1988).

Black-crowned Night-Herons nest in a variety of habitats. Nests have been found in tall shrubs in dense scrubby areas near water, in phragmites stands on dredge spoil islands, in low marsh elder bushes in salt marshes, and in small deciduous trees in a second-growth woodlot on a river shoreline near Baltimore City (MCWP). The heights of Maryland nests (MNRF) range from 0 to approximately 50 ft (0–15 m). In many cases the number of nests was not specified and therefore a mean cannot be calculated. Clutch size is usually 3 to 5 (Bent 1926) and, although typically only one brood is raised per year, double-brooding has been reported (Gross 1923; Nickell 1966). Data collected from 116 Maryland nests from 1985 through 1988 found clutch sizes ranging from 1 to 5, with a mean of 2.7 (MCWP). Egg laying starts in late April with early dates of 14 April in Maryland (MNRF) and 3 February in DC (Davis 1945); the latest Maryland egg date is 5 July (Robbins and Bystrak 1977). The incubation period is 24 to 26 days (Gross 1923); eggs start to hatch in Maryland in mid-May (MCWP). Chicks fledge in about six weeks (Palmer 1962). Stewart and Robbins (1958) reported nestlings as early as 22 February in DC and as late as 15 July in Worcester County. On Smith Island in Somerset County, chicks have been observed as late as 5 October (MCWP). Backdating indicates that the onset of incubation for these birds would have been about 29 July.

Atlas observers recorded colonies in the following Maryland counties: one colony in Baltimore, four in Dorchester, seven in Somerset, and nine in Worcester. They also recorded one in DC. Records other than "confirmed" nesting were probably for birds foraging near colony sites. Breeding birds from large colonies along the lower Susquehanna River in Lancaster County, Pennsylvania, are seen throughout the year around Conowingo Dam in Cecil and Harford counties. During the MCWP surveys from 1985 through 1988, population estimates ranged from 196 to 1,072 pairs per year, with a mean of 660 pairs (MCWP). The slight decrease from the estimates of the 1970s may be the result of sampling variability. BBS data from 1966 through 1989 show stable populations in the Eastern Region, but the Maryland sample is too small to estimate a state trend.

Development and habitat changes may have restricted foraging opportunities in the upper Chesapeake Bay, limiting the birds to southern portions of the bay. Birds from the large colony near Baltimore City, however, foraged more frequently in industrialized areas than in streams (Erwin et al. 1990). Organochlorine contamination has been associated with egg-shell thinning and lowered hatching success in the Black-crowned Night-Heron (Custer et al. 1983), suggesting that ongoing studies of the Baltimore colony should be continued. Known colony sites and key foraging areas should be protected from disturbance and habitat destruction. Potential colony sites can be created on dredge spoil islands, and the introduction of salt-tolerant plants could be a long-term approach to habitat maintenance. Colony sites should be reported to the DNR.

Joan McKearnan

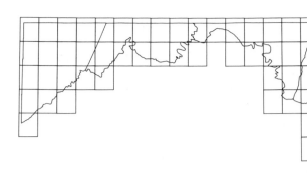

Number and Percentage of Maryland/DC Atlas Blocks *(of possible 1,256)*

	Total	74	6%
By Category			
●	Confirmed	16	100%
◉	Probable	0	0
⊗	Possible	0	0
○	*Observed	58	—

* Not used to compute percentages by category

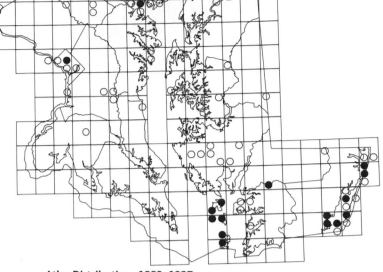

Atlas Distribution, 1983–1987

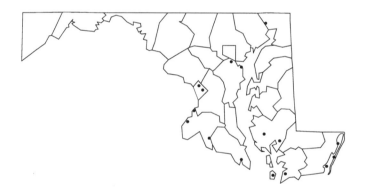

Breeding Distribution, 1958

Yellow-crowned Night-Heron

Nyctanassa violacea

The Yellow-crowned Night-Heron is the rarest colonial nesting heron in Maryland. It is locally common in the lower part of the Chesapeake Bay and rare in the rest of the state. Pairs nest in a variety of situations: alone, in single-species colonies, or in mixed-species colonies. Although principally nocturnal, these herons are occasionally observed during the day as they forage along tidal guts, ponds, stream edges, and other water margins. The diet of the Yellow-crowned Night-Heron consists primarily of crustaceans (Hancock and Kushlan 1984). Birds feeding in estuaries take mostly fiddler crabs, whereas those feeding at inland ponds and streams eat crayfish (E. Blom, pers. comm.). Two species of fiddler crabs and one species of mud crab were found to comprise 94 percent of the diet of birds breeding in the Virginia portion of the Chesapeake Bay (Watts 1988). This species is accidental in Maryland in winter and usually returns from its southeastern U.S. wintering grounds (AOU 1983) in late March and leaves by late October (Robbins and Bystrak 1977).

The Yellow-crowned Night-Heron was first recorded in DC in August 1901 when W. Palmer collected one on the Smithsonian Institution grounds (Cooke 1929). It was not until 30 June 1927, however, that B. Overington shot the first two Maryland specimens in Laurel, Prince George's County (Ball 1932). Cooke (1929) listed the Yellow-crowned Night-Heron as an accidental visitor from the south in DC, and Hampe and Kolb (1947) considered it rare in summer in Maryland. Nesting was first confirmed on 21 April 1921 when E. Court collected a clutch of five fresh eggs (Delaware Museum of Natural History Collection) near Seneca in Montgomery County; E. Stoehr found seven nests at this site in 1939 (USFWS Distribution and Migration File). There was at least one pair in the Mills Island heronry in Worcester County in 1946 and 1947 (Stewart and Robbins 1947a).

Stewart and Robbins (1958) considered this species a rare and local breeder around the Chesapeake Bay and in the Piedmont Section. They knew of only a single nest in DC. Aerial censuses conducted from 1975 through 1977 found four colonies in Dorchester County and eight in Somerset; none, however, were found on the ocean side of the Delmarva Peninsula (Osborn and Custer 1978; Erwin and Korschgen 1979). The mean annual population was 77 pairs, approximately 15 percent of the Atlantic Coast population (Spendelow and Patton 1988). Ground censuses in the mid-1980s showed a population ranging from 83 to 252 pairs, with an annual mean of 197 (MCWP). This would represent an increase of 156 percent, but, because the census techniques were different, the numbers cannot be directly compared. BBS data from 1966 through 1989 show an indication of an increase in the Eastern Region; Maryland data are too few to estimate a trend. Nevertheless, Yellow-crowned Night-Herons have probably increased in Maryland over the past 15 years.

Solitary pairs often nest as high as 50 ft (15 m) in tall trees in floodplain forests or swamps (MNRF). All large Maryland colonies, however, were situated in tall shrubs, saplings, and deciduous trees on islands surrounded by salt marsh (MCWP). The nests and eggs, which are indistinguishable from those of the Black-crowned Night-Heron, have been found in Maryland as low as 3.2 ft (1 m) (MCWP) to as high as 60 ft (18 m) (MNRF) above the ground. Adults arrive in the colony in early April and start laying eggs in late April and early May.

Maryland records of Yellow-crowned Night-Heron nests with eggs are rare; the earliest Maryland egg date is 21 April and the latest is 18 July (MNRF). Data from 25 Maryland nests (MNRF; MCWP) show clutch sizes ranging from 1 to 5, with a mean of 2.8. Incubation is shared by both adults (Palmer 1962) and lasts 21 to 25 days. Chicks fledge about 24 days later (Hancock and Kushlan 1984). Maryland dates for young in the nest range from 4 June to 14 July (MNRF). Adults have been observed on nests from 17 April in DC and 18 April in Maryland to 18 July in Maryland. Brood sizes in 37 Maryland nests (MNRF) range from 1 to 8, with a mean of 3.0. A single brood is attempted each season (Hancock and Kushlan 1984), but they may renest after nest failure (Palmer 1962).

During the Atlas period, ten colonies were located on Smith Island in Somerset County and two on Holland Island in Dorchester County. Single nests were observed in three blocks in Baltimore County, and a pair was observed in one block in Montgomery County. Many of the unconfirmed observations of adults may have been foraging birds from these locations, and some may represent stragglers or postbreeding transients. Because nests are difficult to locate, some single observations could represent solitary pairs in areas where nests were not located.

Very little is known about the breeding biology of Yellow-crowned Night-Herons, and further studies would enhance our knowledge and aid in conservation efforts. Because Smith and Holland Islands are major breeding sites, these areas should be protected from erosion and habitat destruction. Some of the colonies are within the boundaries of

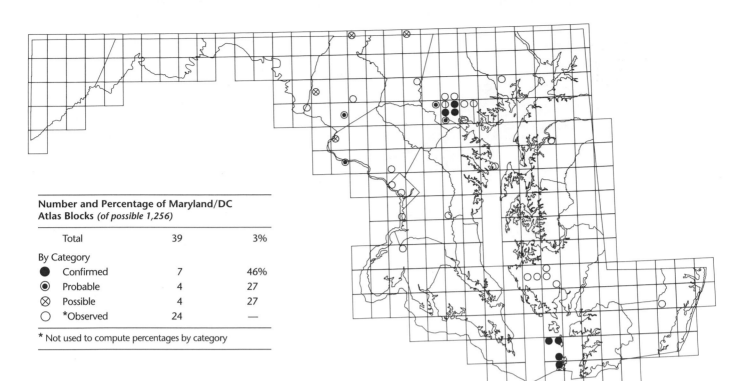

**Number and Percentage of Maryland/DC
Atlas Blocks** *(of possible 1,256)*

Total	39	3%
By Category		
● Confirmed	7	46%
◉ Probable	4	27
⊗ Possible	4	27
○ *Observed	24	—

* Not used to compute percentages by category

Atlas Distribution, 1983–1987

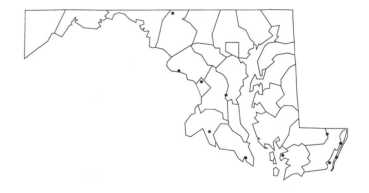

Breeding Distribution, 1958

Glenn L. Martin NWR and are protected, but the others are on private land. Holland Island is eroding quickly, and what was once one island is now two. Other colony sites may deteriorate if the sea level rises as predicted. Observers should refrain from entering colonies, and all new breeding locations should be reported to the DNR.

Joan McKearnan

Glossy Ibis

Plegadis falcinellus

The Glossy Ibis is the only ibis breeding in Maryland. It nests in large mixed-species colonies; flocks often are observed flying over salt marshes or feeding on mud flats and along marsh edges. Glossy Ibis are fairly common but local in summer and rare in winter in Maryland. They are locally common residents in most of the southeastern United States (Spendelow and Patton 1988). The 10-year median arrival date for Maryland is 15 April (Ringler 1989a), and the median fall departure date is 23 September (Ringler 1985a). Glossy Ibis prey mainly on crayfish, insects, and worms, though they occasionally take aquatic snakes (Palmer 1962). They typically forage in groups, including mixed-species assemblages, probing the mud with their long bills. Often they scare up prey beyond their reach and it is grabbed by a nearby bird. This feeding behavior is referred to as a *commensalistic* or *beater-attendant* relationship, with the ibis acting as the beater and the heron or egret acting as attendant (Kushlan 1978). Erwin (1983) found the Snowy Egret to be the most common attendant in North Carolina.

The Glossy Ibis was considered a rare straggler in Maryland and DC prior to the 1950s (Kirkwood 1895; Hampe and Kolb 1947). Early in this century, this species was known to breed only in southern Florida (Bent 1926). By the 1940s, it had begun to spread northward (Miller and Burger 1978). The first documented nesting in Maryland was on Mills Island in Worcester County on 25 June 1956 (Stewart 1957). The only Maryland nesting record west of the Chesapeake Bay was a single nest containing two half-grown young in a mixed-species heronry on St. Catherine's Island, St. Mary's County, on 12 June 1962 (Weske and Fessenden 1963). Censuses, conducted mostly by air from 1975 through 1977, located 13 mixed-species colonies containing Glossy Ibis (Osborn and Custer 1978; Erwin and Korschgen 1979). Somerset, Dorchester, and Worcester counties each had four colonies, and Talbot County had one colony with four pairs. The breeding population was estimated to range from

slightly fewer than 150 to 360 pairs, with an annual mean of 314 pairs. Maryland birds were estimated to comprise less than 5 percent of the entire Atlantic Coast population (Spendelow and Patton 1988).

In Maryland, Glossy Ibis nest in dense scrub surrounded by salt marsh and on dredge islands in phragmites stands. The nest platforms are built of reeds or twigs, typically less than 3 ft (0.9 m) above the ground (MCWP). The highest Maryland nest reported is 15 ft (4.6 m) up (MNRF). Clutch sizes from 68 Maryland nests range from 1 to 4, with a mean of 2.7. The earliest Maryland egg date is 21 April (MCWP) and the latest is 15 July (MNRF). Incubation lasts 21 days and both adults participate (Baynard 1913). Chicks hatch in mid-May and fledge in late June or early July (MCWP). Extreme Maryland dates for chicks in nests are 13 May (MCWP) and 15 July (MNRF). Brood sizes in 50 Maryland nests (MNRF) range from 1 to 3, with a mean of 2.0. Chicks have dark down, a short yellow bill with black bands, and yellow legs. Bill length and curvature increase with growth. Only one brood is raised per season (Miller and Burger 1978).

During the Atlas period, nesting in Maryland was restricted to six Smith Island sites and two dredge spoil islands in Worcester County. Most single observations probably represented either foraging breeders from known colonies or nonbreeding stragglers and transients. In the 1970s Glossy Ibis nested in a mixed-species colony on the lower Susquehanna River in Pennsylvania, but they have not been found there since (R. Schutsky, pers. comm.). While the number of active Glossy Ibis colonies has decreased from 13 to 8 since the mid-1970s and the range has contracted from four counties to two, the Maryland breeding population estimate has shown a 332 percent increase. Ground censuses conducted from 1986 through 1988 estimated a population ranging from 800 to 1,700 pairs, with an annual mean of 1,355 pairs (MCWP). The censuses of the mid-1970s may not be directly comparable to these figures because aerial censuses usually underestimate the populations of dark birds nesting below the canopy (MCWP). Even allowing for differences in censusing techniques, Glossy Ibis breeding populations have undoubtedly increased during the period. BBS data from 1966 through 1989 show an indication of an increase in the Eastern Region and in Maryland; however, the Maryland data are based on only 10 routes.

Conservation measures are similar to those for herons. Colonies should be protected from human disturbance and habitat deterioration. In particular, colony sites on Smith Island should not be entered during the nesting season because Fish Crows take eggs and chicks from nests when the adults are flushed (MCWP). Populations should be monitored on a regular basis, and nesting and foraging habitat should be protected. Colony sites should be reported to the DNR.

Joan McKearnan

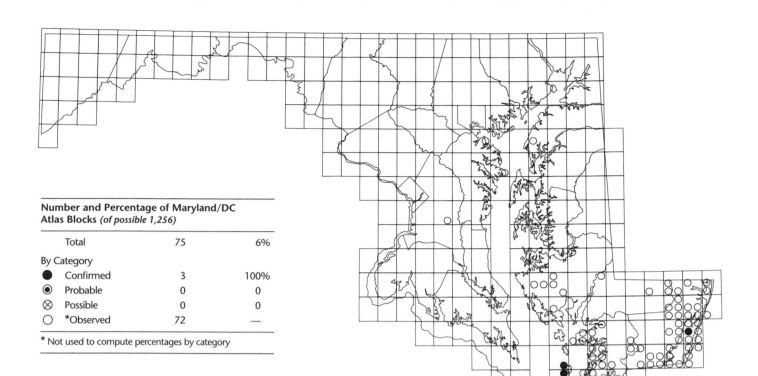

Number and Percentage of Maryland/DC Atlas Blocks *(of possible 1,256)*

Total	75	6%

By Category

●	Confirmed	3	100%
◉	Probable	0	0
⊗	Possible	0	0
○	*Observed	72	—

* Not used to compute percentages by category

Atlas Distribution, 1983–1987

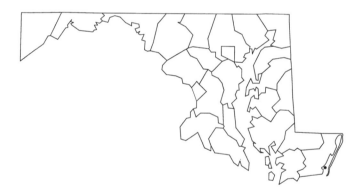

Breeding Distribution, 1958

Mute Swan

Cygnus olor

Mute Swans have been cherished as symbols of purity and elegance for centuries. European immigrants transported them to North America in the late nineteenth century (Bump 1941). Some swans eventually escaped or were deliberately released into the wild and subsequently established breeding populations. Several thousand birds are now resident in coastal and estuarine habitats along the Atlantic Coast from New Hampshire to Virginia, in Lake Michigan, and on southeastern Vancouver Island in British Columbia (AOU 1983).

The present population of Mute Swans in the Chesapeake Bay originated when three males and two females escaped into Eastern Bay from waterfront estates along the Miles River in Talbot County during a storm on 7 March 1962 (Reese 1969a). A pair of these pinioned birds bred successfully that summer, and the flock increased to 18 by 1968, 151 by 1974, and more than 400 by 1980 (Reese 1969a, 1975b, 1984, unpub. data).

From 1965 through 1980, Reese (1975b, 1980, 1984, unpub. data) conducted studies of Mute Swans in the Chesapeake Bay and its tributaries, providing the following data on nesting chronology and reproductive success. Two-thirds of the females paired as two-year-olds and first nested as three-year-olds. Two-thirds of the males paired as four-year-olds and first nested as five-year-olds. Pairs select and establish a territory, averaging 13 acres (5.3 ha) in size, where they stay for life. Territories include small, shallow-water, grass-lined coves, bays, or inlets that provide food and nesting cover. Courtship and aggressive territorial defense begin in late February. Mute Swans typically use the previous year's nest after making repairs. The earliest observed construction of a new nest was on 15 March. The female builds the nest of coarse marsh grasses piled in a mound about 4 ft (1.2 m) in diameter and 1.5 ft (0.5 m) above the high-tide mark, in marshland just back from the shoreline. Extreme egg dates for Maryland are 13 March and 23 June; 61 percent of the nests contained eggs from 9 through 16 April. Incubation, principally by the female, commences after the clutch is complete and lasts 35 days. Clutch sizes in 151 Maryland nests range from 4 to 10, with a mean of 6.2. An average of 49 percent of the eggs hatched. Disappearance and high tides accounted for over 50 percent of egg failures. A second clutch may be laid if the first is lost before mid-May. The earliest observation of hatchlings was 4 May, and 51 percent of the pairs had young from 11 through 25 May. Brood sizes for 137 nests range from 2 to 9, with a mean of 3.9. The young become independent when 125 to 132 days old. Survival of young to fledging averaged 82 percent, with most mortality occurring among young fewer than 40 days old. People who observe Mute Swans near their homes report many young are preyed on by marine turtles. The average annual number of fledglings per nest with eggs ranged from 1.2 to 4.1 annually, with a mean of 2.2. The survival rate of fledglings less than one year old was 83 percent. The cause of death could not be ascertained for many fledglings, but collision with overhead utility cables is a known and important factor.

Mute Swans are locally common in a few areas of the east-central Chesapeake Bay and rare elsewhere in the state. Adolescent swans from the Chesapeake population have been seen in all Maryland tidewater areas, but rarely outside the area between Rock Hall in Kent County and Hooper's Island in Dorchester County. The nesting portion of the population has enlarged its distribution slowly from its 1962 Eastern Bay origin. Atlas results show birds centered in the Chester River, Eastern Bay, and Choptank River tributaries. There was one "confirmed" record from the Piedmont, but no Atlas sightings were reported in the Ridge and Valley and Allegheny Mountain sections.

Mute Swans nest in eastern Delaware and at Chincoteague in Virginia, and swans from these populations may expand into coastal Maryland. Mute Swans were reported in many inland sections of the state in the 1980s, and a few nested during the Atlas period. These occurrences appear to be escaped or released birds separate from the tidewater nesting population. BBS data from 1966 through 1989 show a highly significant average annual increase of 13.7 percent in the Eastern Region; Maryland data are too few to compute a trend.

The Chesapeake Bay Mute Swan population increased at an annual mean rate of 36 percent from 1963 through 1979 (Reese 1980, 1984). This rate of increase may be sustained until the environmental carrying capacity is reached. Shallow-water habitats are much more limited in inland and Atlantic Coast areas and, though feral populations in these areas are just becoming established, carrying capacity may be reached quickly. Submerged aquatic plants, such as pondweed, milfoil, and widgeon-grass, comprise most of the diet. Although insects, crustaceans, and fish may be important for young and molting birds in other areas (Wilmore 1974; Bellrose 1976), Chesapeake Bay Mute Swans have never been observed feeding on fish. Insects are taken only rarely, incidental to their association with this swan's plant diet (Reese 1980, 1984, unpub. data). A large sedentary population of Mute Swans could jeopardize aquatic vegetation, lessening its availability to native nesting or wintering waterfowl. Mute Swans are highly visible, live in close association with humans, and, if warranted, could be easily managed in the future. A continued slow expansion can be expected.

Jan G. Reese

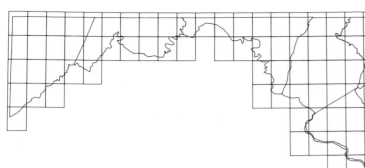

**Number and Percentage of Maryland/DC
Atlas Blocks** *(of possible 1,256)*

Total	60	5%
By Category		
● Confirmed	45	79%
◉ Probable	3	5
⊗ Possible	9	16
○ *Observed	3	—

* Not used to compute percentages by category

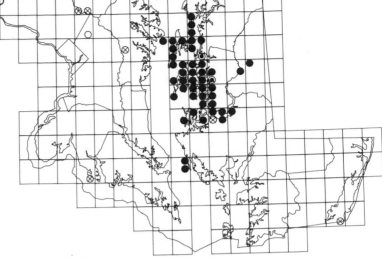

Atlas Distribution, 1983–1987

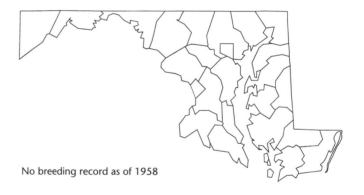

No breeding record as of 1958

Breeding Distribution, 1958

Canada Goose

Branta canadensis

For many people, the calls of Canada Geese passing high overhead herald the arrival of autumn. Historically, Canada Geese did not breed in Maryland. They were known as wintering birds, primarily in the upper Chesapeake Bay and on the Eastern Shore. Early records indicate they were most common in migration (Kirkwood 1895; Eifrig 1904; Cooke 1929; Fisher 1935; Stewart et al. 1952). Most of Maryland's wintering population nests in the upper reaches of the Hudson Bay and on the Ungava Peninsula in Canada (Bellrose 1976). Winter populations of Canada Geese along the Atlantic Flyway experienced a 139 percent increase from 1955 to 1974 (Bellrose 1976), but Maryland's wintering populations have been declining during the past decade (Hindman and Ferrigno 1990). Hunting mortality and reproductive failure have been cited as major causes (L. Hindman, pers. comm.).

Canada Geese of wild ancestry nested for the first time in Maryland at PWRC in the summer of 1946 (Stewart et al. 1952). These geese were part of a flock of 17 wild birds captured in winter at Blackwater NWR, Dorchester County, and pinioned and released at PWRC in 1945 and 1946. Their offspring remained in the area and ultimately bred at PWRC, establishing a flock that spread to farm ponds in nearby counties. Since then, breeding pairs have been found in every county in the state. Releases at wildlife refuges and by waterfowl propagators contributed to the expansion of the breeding range. Canada Geese have strong pair bonds (Bellrose 1976). If one partner is injured during the hunting season and is unable to migrate, the pair often remain to nest in their wintering area. Maryland BBS data from 1966 through 1989 show a significant average annual increase of 8.2 percent; the Eastern Region showed a highly significant average annual increase of 10.2 percent.

Canada Geese use the greatest variety of nest sites of any native waterfowl (Bellrose 1976). Most nests are on the ground, usually on a slightly elevated site, on small islands and gravel bars, in marshes and fields, and on muskrat or beaver lodges (Palmer 1976a). Canada Geese use old crow, heron, egret, and hawk nests and also cliff ledges and talus slopes. They readily use artificial structures, including nest baskets. Nest sites are almost always within 150 ft (46 m) of water (Bellrose 1976). The age of the birds and spring weather conditions have been cited as factors affecting clutch size (Brakhage 1965; MacInnes et al. 1974). Incubation, by the female, lasts from 26 to 28 days; nesting success varies between populations but averages about 70 percent (Bellrose 1976). Both parents assist in the protection of the young. The female remains close to the brood, while the male defends a larger territory from intrusion by other geese. Goslings are capable of flight at about 63 days (Sherwood 1965; Mickelson 1973). Net production of young averages about 2.8 per breeding pair (Bellrose 1976). In summer, Canada Geese browse on the leaves of clover and grass and also consume some cultivated grains.

Maryland nest sites are usually on the ground in or near marsh vegetation, but also include artificial structures, such as duck blinds and nesting baskets. Thirty-five Maryland nest records (MNRF) show nests with eggs from 22 March to 21 May. Clutch sizes in 83 PWRC nests range from 1 to 9, with a mean of 5.0 (Rummel 1979; PWRC, unpub. data). Dates for 106 broods of downy young range from 15 April to 18 July. Brood sizes in 43 PWRC broods at hatching range from 1 to 8, with a mean of 5.1; 75 percent of these goslings survived to flight age (Rummel 1979). In a sample of older PWRC goslings, the mean number of young in 96 broods was 4.3 (PWRC, unpub. data). Although the MNRF has no nest records from western Maryland, breeding there must occur later. Many nests at PWRC are in man-made baskets positioned over water (C. Robbins, pers. comm.).

Atlas data show Canada Geese breeding throughout Maryland. Concentrations occur in central Maryland in the vicinity of DC and PWRC, in the upper Chesapeake Bay near Aberdeen Proving Ground in Harford County, and in the marshes of the lower Eastern Shore, especially near Blackwater NWR in Dorchester County. Data from the Pennsylvania, Virginia, and Delaware atlases show the Canada Goose becoming a widespread breeder in those states also. Wildlife management agencies in Maryland and surrounding states report that a substantial resident population of Canada Geese developed over the past two to three decades, although the AOU (1983) reported Canada Geese nesting no farther south than Ohio and Maine.

Canada Geese, like Mallards, commonly exploit nesting habitat in close proximity to people, often using parks, golf courses, and other high-disturbance areas. Their large size and propensity for nesting where they are easily visible undoubtedly explain the high percentage of "confirmed" nestings during the Atlas fieldwork. Fledged young accounted for 76 percent of the "confirmed" records and 41 percent of all observations. The continued presence of breeding Canada Geese throughout Maryland seems assured.

Donald W. Meritt

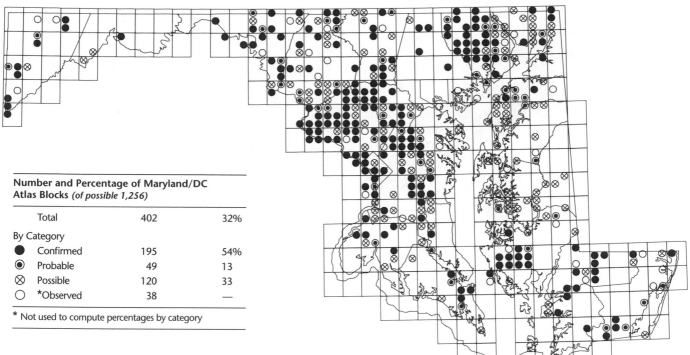

Atlas Distribution, 1983–1987

Number and Percentage of Maryland/DC Atlas Blocks *(of possible 1,256)*		
Total	402	32%
By Category		
● Confirmed	195	54%
◉ Probable	49	13
⊗ Possible	120	33
○ *Observed	38	—

* Not used to compute percentages by category

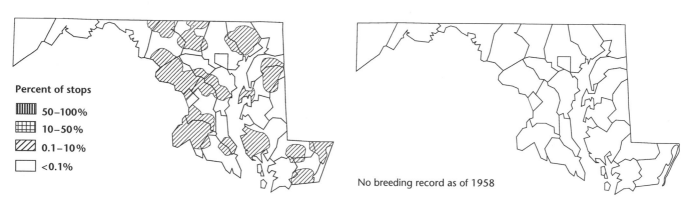

Percent of stops

▥	50–100%
▦	10–50%
▨	0.1–10%
☐	<0.1%

No breeding record as of 1958

Relative Abundance, 1982–1989

Breeding Distribution, 1958

The Canada Goose is most common in central Maryland, the origin of the expanding breeding population. It was most frequently detected around farm and golf course ponds and reservoirs in the central part of the state. It was not recorded on miniroutes in western Maryland.

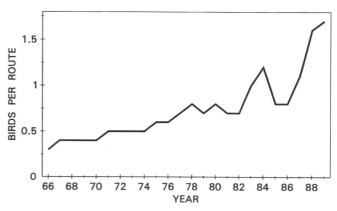

Maryland BBS Trend Graph, 1966–1989

Wood Duck

Aix sponsa

The male Wood Duck, the most colorful of North American waterfowl, is often the highlight of spring birding trips. In recent decades, the Wood Duck has become a common breeding bird along the Atlantic Coast, in the Mississippi drainage, and in some sections along the Pacific Coast (Bellrose 1976). It is more abundant in Maryland during the breeding season than during the winter, and it occurs in greatest numbers during migration (Cooke 1929; Stewart and Robbins 1958).

During the nineteenth century, the Wood Duck was nearly extirpated from parts of its range by uncontrolled hunting (Bellrose 1976). By the 1880s, Coues and Prentiss (1883) reported it was seldom seen except in winter around DC, and Richmond (1888) did not mention it as a breeding bird. Grinnell (1901) feared it might become extinct. Implementation of strict hunting regulations and nest box programs contributed to a population resurgence (Phillips and Lincoln 1930); by the 1970s, the Wood Duck was one of the most commonly hunted ducks in the eastern and central states (Bellrose 1976). Stewart and Robbins (1958) considered it uncommon in the Allegheny Mountain Section and fairly common elsewhere.

Wood Ducks are the only dabbling ducks that typically nest in cavities. They inhabit wet bottomland and flooded hardwood forests, lakes, ponds, and freshwater marshes (Stewart and Robbins 1958). The nesting season begins in early March and lasts until birds begin leaving in September (Stewart and Robbins 1958) for their southeastern U.S. wintering grounds (AOU 1983).

Nest heights in 17 Maryland nest boxes (MNRF) range from 2 to 8 ft (0.6–2.4 m), with a mean of 4.7 ft (1.4 m); heights from five nests in natural cavities range from 20 to 45 ft (13.7–11.4 m). Nest heights in 115 nest boxes (MNRF) were not given. Natural cavities as high as 65 ft (20 m) above the ground may be used (Bellrose 1976). Wood Ducks prefer sites above 30 ft (9.1 m) (Bellrose et al. 1964). Extreme Maryland egg dates are 1 March and 15 August (Robbins and Bystrak 1977). Clutch sizes in 125 Maryland nests (MNRF)

range from 1 (incomplete) to 32 (a dump nest), with a mean of 11.0. Dump nesting, in which multiple females lay eggs in one nest, is common in some Wood Duck populations. Up to five females have used one nest (Grice and Rogers 1965), and as many as 48 eggs have been found in a single nest (Morse and Wight 1969). Any nest containing more than 15 eggs is probably a dump nest (Jones and Leopold 1967; Morse and Wight 1969). Most dump nests are never incubated, but, in rare instances, two females will incubate side by side on the same nest (Bellrose 1943, 1976; Fuller and Bolen 1963).

Incubation, performed almost exclusively by the female, lasts from 28 to 37 days, with an average of 30 days (Bellrose 1976). Raccoons and squirrels are major nest predators (Bellrose et al. 1964). European Starlings are major nest box competitors (J. Kelley, pers. comm.) and are known to puncture eggs in attempts to displace Wood Ducks. On the Eastern Shore of Virginia, 17 of 36 nest boxes were usurped by European Starlings (Armistead 1991). Snapping turtles and bass take Wood Duck chicks in this area and undoubtedly also affect nesting success in Maryland. Sizes of 162 Maryland broods (MNRF) range from 1 to 20, with a mean of 8.0. The earliest date for downy young is 8 April; the latest is 2 September. Young leave the nest about 24 hours after hatching, often jumping more than 60 ft (18 m) to ground or water (Bellrose 1976); yet, they are rarely injured. Ducklings can fly at eight to ten weeks (Bellrose 1976). About half (22%–66%) of all ducklings survive to fledging (Grice and Rogers 1965; McGilvrey 1969; Brown 1973), with earlier broods showing a higher survival rate than later ones (Bellrose 1976). Ducklings hatched from dump nests show similar survival rates (Heusmann 1972). The principal food items of adults are the fruits and seeds of various plants, especially acorns (Bellrose 1976). Birds younger than six weeks feed predominantly on aquatic and flying insects, shifting to plant matter as they grow older. Renesting is common; some pairs may attempt three broods. Even when the first brood has been successful, Wood Ducks occasionally produce a second brood.

Atlas data show that the Wood Duck is still one of Maryland's most common breeding ducks and that it nests in all sections of the state. Records are concentrated along the major rivers, especially the Potomac and Patuxent. As with other waterfowl, the majority of "confirmed" records were observations of young out of the nest. BBS data from 1966 through 1989 show the Maryland population to be stable or increasing; the entire Eastern Region has experienced a significant average annual increase of 3.4 percent. Increased awareness and an active nest-box campaign have allowed this species to again become a common breeding bird in Maryland. Only habitat destruction or overliberalization of hunting regulations would stand in the way of permanent recovery.

Donald W. Meritt

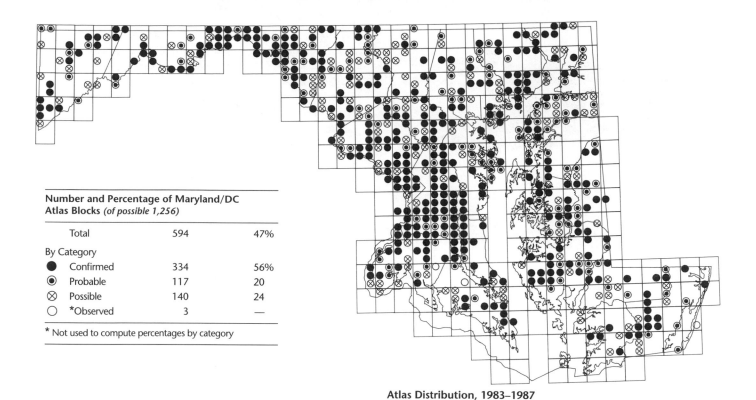

Number and Percentage of Maryland/DC Atlas Blocks *(of possible 1,256)*		
Total	594	47%
By Category		
● Confirmed	334	56%
◉ Probable	117	20
⊗ Possible	140	24
○ *Observed	3	—

* Not used to compute percentages by category

Atlas Distribution, 1983–1987

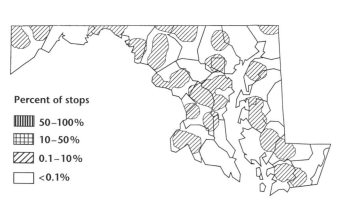

Percent of stops

▥ 50–100%
▦ 10–50%
▨ 0.1–10%
☐ <0.1%

Relative Abundance, 1982–1989

Breeding Distribution, 1958

Wood Duck records are distributed fairly evenly throughout the state. The early courtship period and generally small numbers resulted in birds being missed in many extensively agricultural areas and in the drier woodlands of Allegany County.

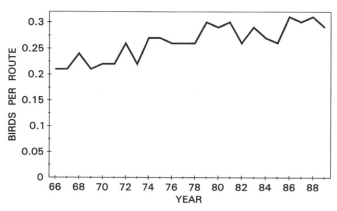

Maryland BBS Trend Graph, 1966–1989

American Black Duck

Anas rubripes

The American Black Duck has long been considered one of the most wary of North American waterfowl. It is Maryland's only breeding duck that is not sexually dimorphic. It is more common and widespread here in winter and during migration than in summer (Stewart and Robbins 1958). Principal foods in Maryland are the seeds of various aquatic plants and, to a lesser extent, small invertebrates (Stewart 1962).

In the middle of the twentieth century, the American Black Duck was a common breeder in the tidewater areas of Maryland (Stewart and Robbins 1958); earlier reports of nesting activity for western Maryland are limited (Kirkwood 1895; Brooks 1938). It did not nest regularly in DC until 1935 (Petrides 1942) and at PWRC until 1949 (C. Robbins, pers. comm.)

Continental populations of American Black Ducks have been declining for the past few decades because of habitat loss and the increase in Mallard numbers (Johnsgard 1961, 1967; Heusmann 1974; Morgan et al. 1984). Maryland BBS data from 1966 through 1989 indicate a decline, but the population was stable from 1980 through 1989. Eastern Region data show stable populations from 1966 through 1989. Hybridization between Mallards and American Black Ducks is a major concern and poses a severe problem for American Black Duck populations (Johnsgard 1967; Heusmann 1974; Morgan et al. 1984). Owing to the comparatively small range of the American Black Duck and the small gene pool, the species is becoming genetically swamped by the Mallard (Johnsgard 1967). Present-day observers cannot hope to match the 40,240 American Black Ducks that H. Jackson reported on the Potomac River in and near DC on an 11 February 1928 waterfowl census for the U.S. Biological Survey (USFWS Distribution and Migration files).

In Maryland, the American Black Duck typically nests in tidal marshes, along the margins of the Chesapeake Bay and its estuaries, and occasionally in upland areas (Stotts and Davis 1960). In many of the more northern areas of its range, it typically nests in totally freshwater habitats like ponds, lakes, and rivers. Offshore structures such as duck blinds are commonly used, and nest sites among fallen logs and stumps are not uncommon (Stewart 1962; Bellrose 1976). The American Black Duck tends to avoid areas of human activity for nesting, and many nests are abandoned because of human disturbance. Tidal flooding and predation by raccoons and by birds such as crows and gulls also contribute to nest failure (Bellrose 1976).

Like Mallards, American Black Ducks begin to breed at the end of their first year of life (Bellrose 1976). In Maryland, the nesting season begins in mid-March and lasts through August, with a peak from early April through late June (Stewart and Robbins 1958). The MNRF contains 114 reports of nests with eggs. The dates range from 4 March to 24 August. The peak period for nests with eggs is mid-May. Clutch sizes range from 1 to 20 (probably a dump nest used by multiple females), with a mean of 7.9. If the first nest is destroyed the ducks will renest, usually in the vicinity of the old one, but the second clutch averages one fewer egg (Stotts and Davis 1960). The incubation period for the American Black Duck in Maryland lasts from 23 to 33 days and averages 26 days (Stotts and Davis 1960). There are 88 reports of Maryland nests (MNRF) with young or broods, the earliest on 8 April and the next to last on 13 August, with a peak in mid-June. On the extraordinarily late date of 13 October 1937, W. McAtee saw an adult with two half-grown young on the Potomac River at East Potomac Park, DC (USFWS files). Maryland brood sizes range from 2 to 12, with a mean of 5.5 (MNRF). Bellrose (1976) reported that nesting success averaged 42 percent over the entire range, but Stotts and Davis (1960) reported success was 38 percent in Maryland. Young are capable of flight after 58 to 63 days (Bellrose 1976). Mortality during the preflight period is high.

Atlas data indicate that the American Black Duck still breeds in its traditional range in Maryland, although probably in reduced numbers. There were "confirmed" nesting reports from as far west as the Allegheny Mountain Section. Most confirmations came from the observation of broods. Data collected by atlas observers in surrounding states show that the American Black Duck still nests in areas far removed from tidal brackish or salt water in those states as well. At least for now, Maryland still has a viable breeding population. Habitat loss and the ongoing annual release of tens of thousands of Mallards threaten the American Black Duck's continued success throughout much of its range.

Donald W. Meritt

Number and Percentage of Maryland/DC Atlas Blocks (of possible 1,256)

Total	243	19%
By Category		
● Confirmed	98	42%
◉ Probable	48	20
⊗ Possible	89	38
○ *Observed	8	—

* Not used to compute percentages by category

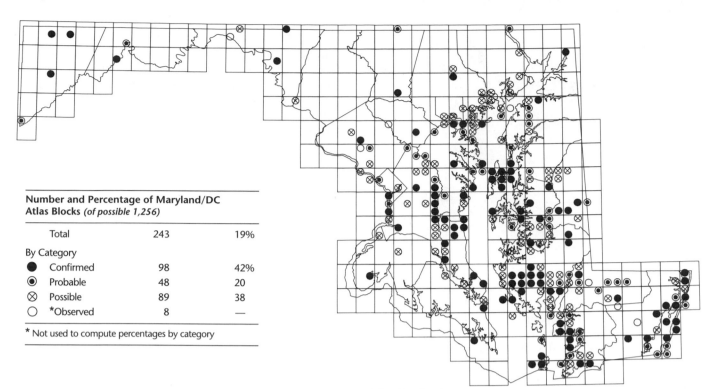

Atlas Distribution, 1983–1987

Percent of stops

▥ 50–100%
▦ 10–50%
▨ 0.1–10%
☐ <0.1%

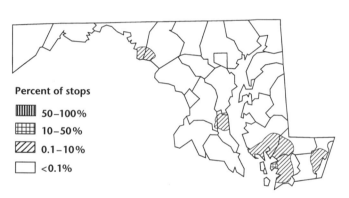

Relative Abundance, 1982–1989

Breeding Distribution, 1958

The American Black Duck is found primarily in marshes on the lower Eastern Shore, with the highest concentration in the Dames Quarter Marsh of Deal Island WMA in Somerset County. Miniroutes provide incomplete sampling of marsh habitats; consequently, birds in many breeding areas not close to roads were missed.

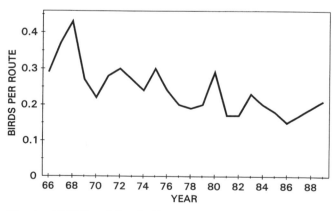

Maryland BBS Trend Graph, 1966–1989

Mallard

Anas platyrhynchos

The Mallard is easily the most widespread and best known of Maryland's ducks. Anderson and Henny (1972) believed it was the most abundant wild duck in North America and probably in the world. It is common throughout the year in Maryland, although some locally raised birds leave in the winter and are replaced by individuals from farther north (Bird Banding Laboratory, unpub. data). Birds banded in Maryland have been recovered in Alberta, Idaho, Manitoba, North Dakota, Minnesota, Wisconsin, Michigan, Ontario, Illinois, Indiana, Ohio, Quebec, Massachusetts, New York, New Jersey, Pennsylvania, Delaware, Virginia, South Carolina, Tennessee, Georgia, and Alabama. Birds banded in many of those states and provinces have also been recovered in Maryland. In Maryland, the Mallard's diet is composed largely of aquatic vegetation but varies greatly with the habitat used (Stewart 1962).

Few people realize that Mallards have become breeding birds in Maryland and much of the East only during the past 50 years. Early authors considered the Mallard a rare breeder (Coues and Prentiss 1862, 1883; Eifrig 1904). Kirkwood (1895), Cooke (1929), and Hampe and Kolb (1947) were not able to cite a single breeding record for Maryland. In 1944 Mallards first nested at PWRC (Stewart et al. 1952), and in 1945 a wild drake was found paired with a domestic hen on Plummers Island, Montgomery County (Wetmore and Manville 1968). By 1958 Mallards were known to have nested in eight Maryland counties and DC (Stewart and Robbins 1958). Scattered pairs of apparently feral birds were found in all tidewater areas and on inland lakes, ponds, and streams in all sections. As recently as 1962, the Mallard was described as only a scattered breeder in the state (Stewart 1962). Maryland BBS data for 1966 through 1989 show a highly significant average annual increase of 8.5 percent; the Eastern Region had a significant average annual increase of 4.4 percent.

The Mallard's rapid colonization in the East probably has two causes. The first is a natural range expansion from its midcontinent stronghold southward and eastward along the Gulf Coast and then northward along the Atlantic Coast (Johnsgard 1961). The second is the widespread practice by state wildlife agencies and private sporting groups of releasing farm-raised Mallards. These releases introduced millions of semiwild birds into the Atlantic Flyway, and birds that survived the fall hunting season joined the breeding population. Fletcher et al. (1956) were among the first to comment on this in Maryland; they reported numerous domesticated Mallards nesting in Caroline County.

The Mallard breeds in ponds or streams fringed with marsh vegetation (Stewart and Robbins 1958). In addition, it is the most easily domesticated of the waterfowl and readily adapts to life in parks and around public and private waterfronts. The dramatic increase in Mallard populations in the East has resulted in the decline of the American Black Duck (Johnsgard 1961; Heusmann 1974). Hybridization between the two species poses a severe problem for the remaining American Black Duck populations (Johnsgard 1967; Heusmann 1974; Morgan et al. 1984).

Most Mallards begin courtship in late winter (Bellrose 1976); by the time migrating Mallards reach their breeding territories, pair bonding has already occurred (Barclay 1970). They usually lay one egg per day until the clutch is complete. Incubation lasts from 26 to 30 days, but hens often continue to incubate infertile eggs for longer periods (Bellrose 1976). Mallard renesting is not uncommon but is most common among older hens. Ducklings remain in the downy stage for about 18 days and are capable of flight at 49 to 60 days (Hochbaum 1944; Gollop and Marshall 1954). Survival is poor; by fall only about one young per adult is still alive (Bellrose 1976).

The typical Maryland nesting season is mid-March through late July. Extreme egg dates are 12 March and 31 July, with a peak in mid-May (MNRF). Clutch sizes in 177 Maryland nests ranged from 1 to 40 (almost certainly a dump nest used by multiple females); the mean clutch size in 175 nests (excluding obvious dump nests) is 9.0. Although almost all nests were on the ground, a few were on man-made structures, primarily offshore duck blinds. Broods were found from 25 March to 7 August (MNRF); brood sizes from 53 records range from 1 to 12, with a mean of 6.8.

Atlas results show Mallards as common breeding birds throughout most of Maryland. They are more scattered and local in the Ridge and Valley and Allegheny Mountain sections, where there are fewer lakes and ponds. There was a high percentage of confirmations because of the Mallard's habit of nesting close to human activity, making observations of broods easy (77% of "confirmed" records). Most Mallards can best be described as semidomesticated, and many, if not most, Atlas records involved these birds. They are firmly established as part of Maryland's avifauna, and their habits indicate that they will be part of our birdlife for the foreseeable future.

Donald W. Meritt

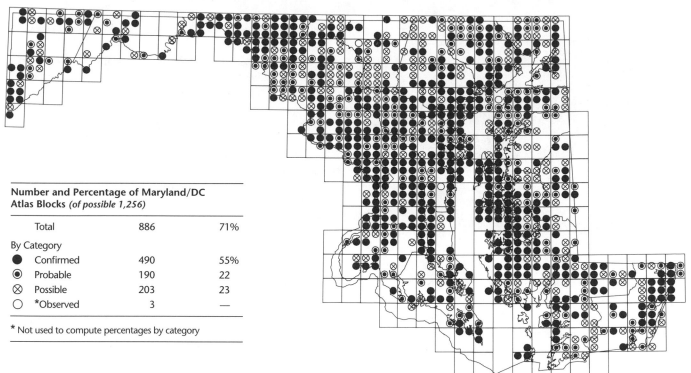

Number and Percentage of Maryland/DC Atlas Blocks *(of possible 1,256)*

Total	886	71%
By Category		
● Confirmed	490	55%
◉ Probable	190	22
⊗ Possible	203	23
○ *Observed	3	—

* Not used to compute percentages by category

Atlas Distribution, 1983–1987

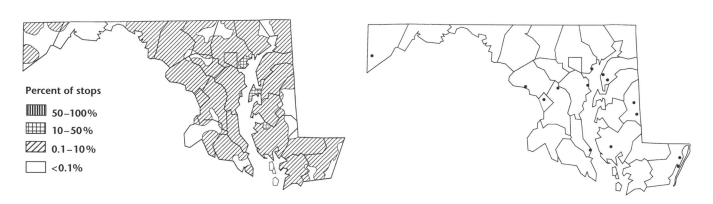

Percent of stops

⦀	50–100%
▦	10–50%
▨	0.1–10%
☐	<0.1%

Relative Abundance, 1982–1989

Breeding Distribution, 1958

The Mallard is uncommon and widely distributed in the eastern three-fourths of the state. Small numbers in the forested areas of western Maryland resulted in low detection. Small concentrations result from the large number of semidomesticated birds found throughout tidewater areas and from ongoing release programs.

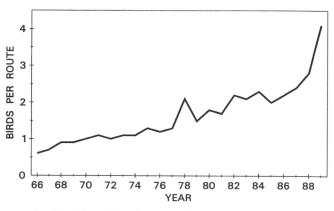

Maryland BBS Trend Graph, 1966–1989

Mallard 79

Blue-winged Teal

Anas discors

The striking white face crescent and large blue wing patches of the drake Blue-winged Teal make it one of Maryland's most distinctive nesting ducks. This species breeds over a wide range in North America, from Alaska to the Maritime Provinces of Canada and south to Texas, Louisiana, and North Carolina (Gooders 1986). The Blue-winged Teal has long been recognized as common to abundant during migration in many areas of the state (Coues and Prentiss 1862, 1883; Cooke 1929; Stewart and Robbins 1958). The greatest numbers are found in spring and fall in the tidewater areas of the Eastern Shore, Western Shore, and Upper Chesapeake sections (Stewart and Robbins 1958). Spring migration spans mid-March to late May, and fall migration lasts from late July through November. Stragglers remain into early winter on the lower Eastern Shore (Stewart and Robbins 1958). Cold weather pushes this species south to Florida, Louisiana, Central and South America, and the West Indies (Bent 1923).

Austin (1932) recorded the first Maryland nest of the Blue-winged Teal on 17 May 1931 at Shorter's Landing in Dorchester County. On 6 May he flushed 37 pairs along 5 mi (8 km) of the Blackwater River; local residents claimed they had nested there in "goodly" numbers for as long as they could remember. Stewart and Robbins (1958) listed the Blue-winged Teal as a fairly common breeder in the tidewater areas of Dorchester County, uncommon in the remaining tidewater areas of the Eastern Shore Section, and rare in tidewater areas of the Western Shore and Upper Chesapeake sections. They also cited breeding records from St. Mary's, Anne Arundel, and Baltimore counties.

Bellrose (1976) stated that the Blue-winged Teal prefers to nest in grass, hayfields, and sedge meadows. Breeding habitat in Maryland is primarily short-growth tidal marsh meadows (Stewart and Robbins 1958). The maximum breeding density recorded in Maryland is 6.2 territorial males per 100 acres (40.5 ha) in a brackish bay marsh in Dorchester County in 1956 (Stewart and Robbins 1958). Nests have been found close to water and as far away as 1 mi (1.6 km), with the average being about 125 ft (38 m). The nest is usually started as a simple depression in the ground into which the eggs are laid. Grass and other nearby vegetation are added during the

laying period, and feathers are added as the clutch grows (Bellrose 1976).

Nests with eggs have been found in Maryland from 25 April to 12 July, with a peak in mid-June (MNRF). Clutch sizes in 1,735 Blue-winged Teal nests ranged from 6 to 15, with a mean of 9.8 (Bellrose 1976). In seven Maryland records (MNRF), clutch sizes range from 5 to 12. One egg is laid each day until the clutch is complete (Bent 1923). Broods have been seen in Maryland from 25 May to 11 August (MNRF), but with too few records to indicate a peak. Brood sizes in eight records range from 2 to 9 in Maryland. Incubation, performed by the female, takes about 23 or 24 days, and ducklings are capable of flight at 35 to 44 days (Bellrose 1976; Palmer 1976a). Renesting may occur if the first clutch is destroyed early in the incubation period, but the Blue-winged Teal is less likely to renest than other waterfowl (Sowls 1955). Late-season clutches are generally smaller than first clutches (Bellrose 1976). Nest failure is common and success rates vary from 13 percent to 60 percent (Glover 1956; Bellrose 1976). Predation by mammals accounts for almost half of the nest failures; skunks are the major culprits (Bellrose 1976). Raccoons, foxes, other mammals, birds (especially crows), and farming activity have also been linked to nest failure. In spring and summer, the Blue-winged Teal consumes mostly animal foods, especially small mollusks, minute crustaceans, and beetles (Stewart 1962). The seeds of Olney's bulrush and widgeon-grass are major fall foods in the Chesapeake Bay marshes.

Atlas data show that the extensive tidal marshes of Dorchester and Somerset counties are still the breeding strongholds for the Blue-winged Teal in Maryland. Observations in coastal Worcester County indicate that the species probably still nests in the marshes there. This is consistent with Delaware atlas results, which recorded nesting along the coast. It is interesting that both the Virginia and Pennsylvania atlases recorded Blue-winged Teal nesting in the mountains. Given this species' history of nesting in any suitable habitat, it is likely that an occasional pair may nest in far-western Maryland. Atlas distribution shows a large number of "observed" records. When the original Maryland Atlas safe dates were found to be too liberal, undated records without breeding evidence were treated as "observed" records.

BBS data from 1966 through 1989 show stable populations in the Eastern Region. The Blue-winged Teal seems to be a very adaptable duck, taking advantage of small potholes, marshes, and even farm ponds (Linduska 1964). Nesting along the East Coast is scattered; nowhere are they common breeders there (Bellrose 1976). Loss of marsh habitat is the greatest threat facing this species.

Donald W. Meritt

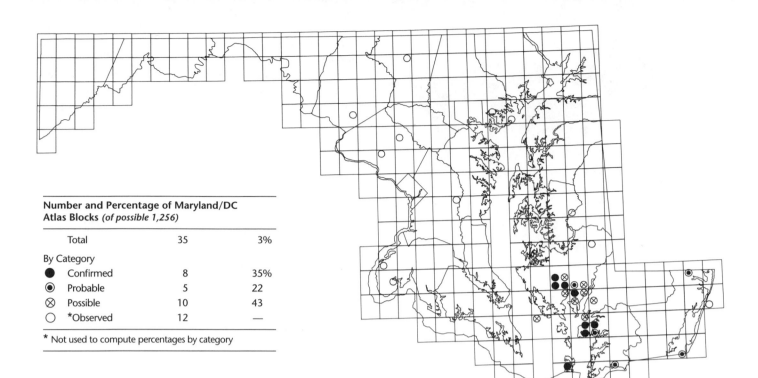

Number and Percentage of Maryland/DC Atlas Blocks *(of possible 1,256)*

	Total	35	3%
By Category			
●	Confirmed	8	35%
◉	Probable	5	22
⊗	Possible	10	43
○	*Observed	12	—

* Not used to compute percentages by category

Atlas Distribution, 1983–1987

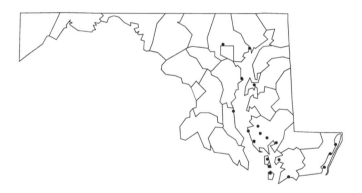

Breeding Distribution, 1958

Northern Shoveler

Anas clypeata

Breeding by the Northern Shoveler had long been anticipated in Maryland, and the first "confirmed" record for the state occurred during the Atlas period. In appearance and diet, the Northern Shoveler is one of the area's most unusual dabbling ducks. Its broad, spatulate bill distinguishes it from all other ducks in North America. It eats more animal matter than any other dabbling duck (Palmer 1976a), as much as 90 percent in the spring, consisting especially of gastropods and crustaceans (Ankney and Afton 1988). In winter, vegetable matter, especially Olney's bulrush and widgeon-grass, dominates the diet in Maryland (Stewart 1962).

Early authors described the Northern Shoveler as a winter resident (Coues and Prentiss 1883); rare winter visitant, more frequently recorded in fall migration (Cooke 1929); winter visitant (Hampe and Kolb 1947); and very rare spring and fall transient (Stewart et al. 1952). Concerning its state-wide status, Stewart and Robbins (1958) described the Northern Shoveler as fairly common in the tidewater areas during migration, being most common in the marshes of lower Dorchester and Somerset counties. Peaks of migration in Maryland occur in March and from early September through October. They called it uncommon in winter in Dorchester County and rare elsewhere. The discrepancies with earlier reports may represent a change in the status of this duck or may simply reflect the availability of better information.

The Northern Shoveler breeds primarily in the prairies of north-central North America north into Alaska and the Yukon and Northwest territories of Canada; it also breeds in the northern Rocky Mountains (Palmer 1976a). The greatest breeding densities have been recorded in Saskatchewan and Alberta provinces in Canada, with over six nesting pairs per sq mi (2.3 per sq km) (Bellrose 1976).

Northern Shovelers prefer to nest in dry meadows, usually within 75 to 200 ft (23–61 m) of water but rarely close to the water's edge (Bent 1923; Bellrose 1976; Palmer 1976a). They prefer grasses both for nest sites and nest material (Bellrose 1976). Nests are usually started as a scrape in the ground and are lined with grass and feathers (Girard 1939). Unlike Mallards and Gadwalls, Northern Shovelers do not build their nests near clumps of vegetation or other landmarks (Bellrose 1976). They nest near many wetland habitats and are frequently found in heavily sedimented rivers, coves, and ponds, many of which are polluted (Palmer 1976a). The Northern Shoveler male, unlike the area's other dabbling ducks, remains with the female, at least through the incubation period and actively establishes and defends a territory (Afton 1979). The male's behavior is thought to have evolved because of the high energy requirements of the female during the nesting period and may be required because of the high percentage of animal matter in the diet.

Courtship begins on the wintering grounds. Hepp and Hair (1983) reported that in North Carolina 95 percent of the females were paired in February, prior to their migration. There are no data on clutch sizes from Maryland, but in other states and Canadian provinces they range from 5 to 14, with 10 to 12 being typical (Bent 1923; Bellrose 1976; Palmer 1976a). One egg is typically laid each day until the clutch is complete, although occasionally a day is skipped (Bellrose 1976). Dates for 40 clutches from Minnesota and North Dakota ranged from 9 May to 3 July, with a peak in the first half of June (Bent 1923). Smaller samples from states closer to Maryland fall within the same range, except that Palmer (1976a) gave early April to early May for first clutches at Bombay Hook NWR in Delaware. Incubation is by the female only and lasts 23 days (Ankney and Afton 1988).

Nest success of the Northern Shoveler is fairly high compared with that of other ducks, ranging from 42 percent to 90 percent (Girard 1939; Bellrose 1976; Palmer 1976a). Mammals, most notably skunks, are responsible for most nest failures, but avian predators, especially crows, also destroy many nests (Bellrose 1976). If the first nest is destroyed, renesting is common, with a generally smaller second clutch (Sowls 1955). After hatching, the ducklings are led to water by the hen and are capable of flight in 36 to 66 days (Hochbaum 1944; Hooper 1951).

The first and only confirmed Maryland nesting of the Northern Shoveler was recorded at Blackwater NWR in Dorchester County during the atlas period. A female was found with seven young on 12 June 1985 (Ringler 1985b). Northern Shoveler nesting records are scattered along the Atlantic Coast from Long Island, New York, to Delaware (Eaton 1988a). There were several records in southeastern Pennsylvania (Brauning 1992).

The future of the Northern Shoveler in Maryland is uncertain. BBS data from 1966 through 1989 show stable continental populations and a highly significant average annual increase of 1.7 percent in the Eastern Region; data are too few to estimate a Maryland trend. Expansion along the East Coast in recent decades suggests that Maryland can anticipate additional records. Preservation of the marsh habitats favored by this and other nesting waterfowl is needed.

Donald W. Meritt

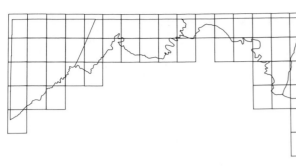

Number and Percentage of Maryland/DC Atlas Blocks *(of possible 1,256)*

	Total	2	<1%
By Category			
●	Confirmed	1	100%
◉	Probable	0	0
⊗	Possible	0	0
○	*Observed	1	—

* Not used to compute percentages by category

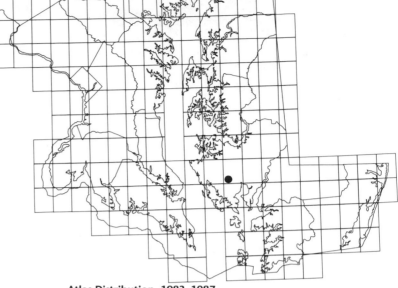

Atlas Distribution, 1983–1987

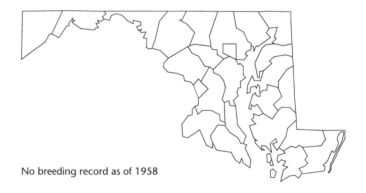

No breeding record as of 1958

Breeding Distribution, 1958

Gadwall

Anas strepera

The Gadwall is one of the few ducks to have experienced a long-term population increase. From the late 1950s to the mid-1970s, Gadwall populations on both the wintering and breeding grounds showed a marked increase (Bellrose 1976). BBS data for 1966 through 1989 show a highly significant average annual increase of 3.2 percent in the continental population; the Eastern population is stable. Data for Maryland are too few to estimate a trend. This species is traditionally associated with the pothole regions of the northern plains, where it has reached breeding concentrations of over four birds per sq mi (1.6 per sq km) (Bellrose 1976). The first East Coast breeding records are from Bombay Hook NWR in Delaware and Pea Island NWR in North Carolina (Henny and Holgersen 1974). The Gadwall now breeds at sites along the Atlantic Coast from the St. Lawrence region of Canada to South Carolina (Gooders 1986). Some of these sites are the result of introductions (Borden and Hochbaum 1966; Palmer 1976a), but others are undoubtedly the result of natural range expansion (Gooders 1986).

In Maryland, Gadwalls are primarily wintering and migrant birds, arriving in mid-October and leaving in late April (Robbins and Bystrak 1977). In the DC region, Cooke (1929) noted an increase in migrating and wintering Gadwalls a decade before breeding was detected in the Atlantic coastal states. In Maryland, the first reported nesting was in 1948 when Springer and Stewart (1950) found seven pairs and a nest with eggs in the tidal marshes of Somerset County near Dames Quarter, and F. Uhler sighted a brood of 10 young in the same area. During the next few years, nests were recorded in other Somerset County marshes as well as in the tidal marshes in southern Dorchester County (Stewart and Robbins 1958).

Gadwalls nest in a variety of situations, usually within 100 yd (91 m) of water, with most being much closer (Bellrose 1976). They do not readily nest in heavy vegetation over water as is common among other ducks; instead, they prefer islands, dikes, or meadows as nesting sites. The type of vegetation does not seem to be a factor in site selection, but Gadwalls prefer higher, more dense cover than do other dabbling ducks (Martz 1967; Bellrose 1976). Nests, con-

structed only by the female, are typically scooped-out depressions on the ground lined with vegetation and feathers (Bent 1923; Palmer 1976a).

There are only four nest records from Maryland in the MNRF. Gadwall nests with eggs have been observed in Maryland as early as 4 May and as late as 19 July (Stewart and Robbins 1958), but downy young were observed only from 13 June to 3 July (MNRF). No brood counts were available in the MNRF. Because so little nesting information is available for Maryland, breeding biology is summarized from continentwide sources. Clutch sizes in 2,545 nests were typically 5 to 13, with a mean of 10 (Bellrose 1976). Dump nesting is fairly common and, in such instances, up to 20 eggs have been reported. In North America, Redheads, Mallards, Lesser Scaups, and Northern Pintails have been observed depositing their eggs in Gadwall nests (Palmer 1976a). Apparently, the Gadwall rarely takes advantage of other species in this manner. These multiple-species broods are sometimes successful, with the hen Gadwall accepting and being accepted by the nestlings of other species. Renesting is common if the first nest is destroyed and conditions are favorable (Keith 1961; Gates 1962), but the clutch sizes are usually smaller (Sowls 1955). Incubation, performed by the female only, lasts 22 to 29 days, depending on the weather (Palmer 1976a).

Gadwall nesting success is among the highest for all puddle ducks, ranging from 39 percent to 90 percent with an average of 67 percent (Bellrose 1976; Palmer 1976a). Reasons cited for this high degree of success include late nesting, upland nest sites, a preference for nesting in heavy vegetation, and the fact that females frequently leave the nest unattended but covered. After the young hatch, the female leads them to water and is responsible for their protection until they can fly (Palmer 1976a). Ducklings are capable of flight after 48 to 62 days, with late broods reaching flight stage earlier (Oring 1968; Bellrose 1976). The Gadwall's diet in Maryland consists almost entirely of the leaves, stems, and stalks of submerged vegetation, particularly widgeon-grass, eelgrass, and muskgrass (Stewart 1962).

The artificial impoundment at Deal Island WMA, the marshes that surround it, and Blackwater NWR are the strongholds for nesting Gadwalls in Maryland. Atlas data confirm that although Gadwalls still nest in these areas, they have expanded into tidal portions of Worcester County. Data from the Delaware atlas show that Gadwalls now breed along its central coast as well. In addition to these Eastern Shore nesting areas, Gadwalls were observed at several Western Shore locations. If these trends continue, Gadwalls may become increasingly common breeding members of Maryland's waterfowl community.

Donald W. Meritt

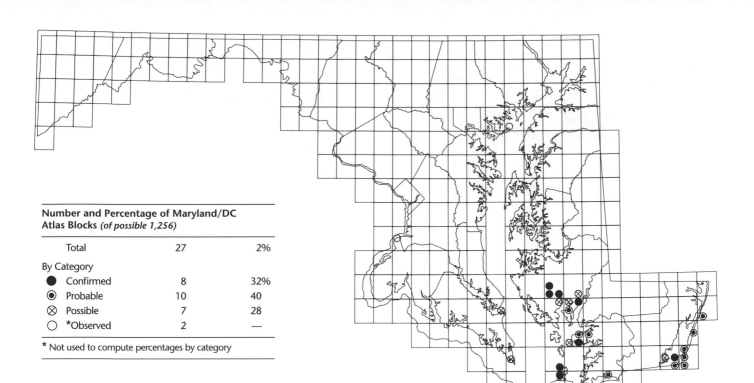

Number and Percentage of Maryland/DC Atlas Blocks *(of possible 1,256)*		
Total	27	2%
By Category		
● Confirmed	8	32%
◉ Probable	10	40
⊗ Possible	7	28
○ *Observed	2	—

* Not used to compute percentages by category

Atlas Distribution, 1983–1987

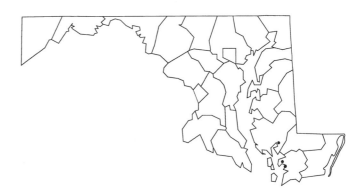

Breeding Distribution, 1958

Hooded Merganser

Lophodytes cucullatus

The elegant Hooded Merganser, familiar to Maryland birdwatchers during migration and in winter, is a rare breeding bird in the state. Its eastern breeding range is confined primarily to Canada and the northern United States, with Maryland near its southern periphery (AOU 1983). It winters throughout the southeastern United States, north to the limit of open water. Fall migrants arrive in Maryland from late September through November, and substantial numbers winter on inland ponds and streams as long as there is open water (Stewart and Robbins 1958). Northbound migrants arrive in Maryland during February and March, and all except breeding birds depart by the end of April (Robbins and Bystrak 1977). Hooded Mergansers can be seen in all sections of Maryland during migration.

Coues and Prentiss (1883) considered the Hooded Merganser rare around DC. On the basis of summer reports, Kirkwood (1895) thought it probably bred in Maryland, although he lacked specific evidence. The first breeding record for Maryland was a female with a brood of eight young near McHenry in Garrett County on 21 June 1946 (Stewart and Robbins 1947a). The second record was for an adult and young found near Seneca in Montgomery County on 1 May 1954 (Stewart and Robbins 1958). Hooded Mergansers began nesting in Wood Duck boxes at PWRC impoundments in 1961 (MNRF). The first breeding report on the Eastern Shore was for a female incubating 11 Hooded Merganser eggs and one Wood Duck egg in a Wood Duck box at Millington WMA in Kent County on 3 May 1977 (Loughry and Wheatley 1977).

The breeding habitat of Hooded Mergansers consists of wooded swamps, streams, ponds, and lakes (Palmer 1976b). They prefer a natural tree cavity but also use hollow logs, cavities in banks, hollow tops of stumps, and Wood Duck boxes. The height of the cavity above the ground does not appear to be important. Hooded Mergansers may use the same cavity in successive years.

Because specific data for Maryland are sparse, most information about the timing of breeding must be extrap-

olated from the reports from PWRC and from other scattered records. East of the Allegheny Mountain Section most Hooded Merganser nests probably are initiated from mid-March to early April. In the mountains, nesting probably begins in May or early June. Maryland egg dates range from 14 March to 15 May (MNRF). In seven Maryland nests, all but one from PWRC, clutch sizes range from 4 to 12. Typical clutch sizes are 10 to 12, but as few as 6 and as many as 18 have been found (Bent 1923). Only one Maryland nest contained a Wood Duck egg, although Wood Ducks are known to lay their eggs in Hooded Merganser nests elsewhere in their range (Zicus 1990). Hooded Mergansers have also been reported to lay their eggs in other ducks' nests (Morse et al. 1969), and the female has even been known to share incubation with a female Wood Duck (Harrison 1975). Incubation is by the female only and takes about 31 days (Bent 1923). Because the male leaves the female shortly after the eggs are laid, renesting and second nesting attempts are unlikely. The young leave the nest immediately after hatching. The MNRF contains only five records of brood counts: 2, 3, 6, 8, and 9 young. Maryland dates for small young range from 30 April to 21 June. Small fish are the predominant food of the Hooded Merganser in Maryland (Stewart 1962). It also eats black-fingered mud crabs, crayfish, dragonfly nymphs, and caddisfly larvae.

Atlas fieldwork produced only eight scattered records. The only report from the Eastern Shore was of a "possible" breeder. The confirmations were from Garrett County, PWRC, and Charles County. After the Atlas period, Ringler (1989a) found a female with young at Meyers Station in Anne Arundel County on 30 April 1989. All records, except for confirmations, should be viewed with caution; in the absence of specific nesting evidence, it is not easy to separate summering, nonbreeding waterfowl from nesting birds. In Pennsylvania, Hooded Mergansers nest predominantly in the northern and western parts of the state; Delaware had no records and Virginia had only one.

Although BBS data from 1966 through 1989 show stable populations in the Eastern Region, Root (1988) found the Hooded Merganser to be declining in North America, probably because of the loss of wetlands. Atlas results suggest that the breeding status in Maryland is tenuous, although the Hooded Merganser may be gradually expanding into the eastern and southern parts of the state. Perhaps the increase in Wood Duck boxes will benefit this species as it has the Wood Duck. Certainly the Hooded Merganser's status should be carefully monitored, and wooded swamps should be protected. An active program of nest box construction and maintenance could help sustain this bird as a breeder in Maryland.

George B. Wilmot

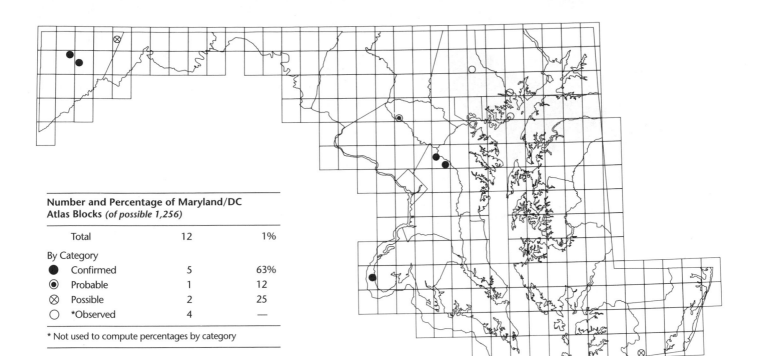

Number and Percentage of Maryland/DC Atlas Blocks *(of possible 1,256)*

	Total	12	1%
By Category			
●	Confirmed	5	63%
◉	Probable	1	12
⊗	Possible	2	25
○	*Observed	4	—

* Not used to compute percentages by category

Atlas Distribution, 1983–1987

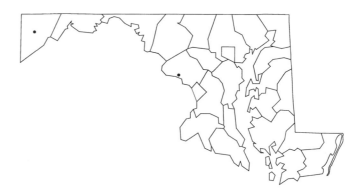

Breeding Distribution, 1958

Black Vulture

Coragyps atratus

The Black Vulture, with its contrasting black body and white wing patches, is less graceful in the air than its larger relative, the Turkey Vulture. Because it has shorter wings, it must flap them more frequently to maintain flight (Jackson 1988a). It is also more gregarious than the Turkey Vulture and soars, feeds, and roosts in groups (Jackson 1988a).

The Black Vulture is a permanent resident that has expanded its breeding range in Maryland during the twentieth century. The first Maryland record was of four birds at Kensington, Montgomery County, on 30 March 1895 (Kirkwood 1895). The first nest record was from St. Mary's County on 29 April 1922 (Court 1924). Cooke (1929) listed all ten known sightings in the DC area and reported breeding near La Plata, Charles County. First records for Montgomery County were a bird seen on Plummers Island in 1920 (Fisher 1935) and a pair nesting at Seneca in 1938 (Wimsatt 1939). By the late 1940s, Hampe and Kolb (1947) considered it a permanent resident in southern Maryland, and Dorsey (1947) considered it common in the Annapolis area of Anne Arundel County. In Caroline County, the Black Vulture was first observed near Denton in 1951 (Fletcher et al. 1956). Stewart and Robbins (1947a) described it as rare in central and western Maryland and, surprisingly, absent from most of the Eastern Shore. They reported local populations around Wye Mills, Queen Anne's County, and around Pocomoke City and Snow Hill, Worcester County. They noted that the breeding range included the southern part of the Western Shore, north to Baltimore, west through the Piedmont of Montgomery County, and along the Potomac River to Williamsport in Washington County. The range remained much the same a decade later, with the addition of the Susquehanna River Valley (Stewart and Robbins 1958).

As the Black Vulture population increased, so did its competition with the Turkey Vulture for carrion. Based on studies of the foraging habits of both species in Maryland and Pennsylvania, Coleman and Fraser (1987) concluded that a form of coexistence had emerged between the two. Black Vultures feed earlier in the day, on larger carrion, closer to roost sites, and remain longer at fewer locations while feeding. The Black Vulture's preference for fresh meat has led to numerous records of attacks on livestock, especially newborn animals (Jackson 1988a). Instances of this behavior occur each spring in Maryland (L. Terry, pers. comm.).

Black Vultures occur in agricultural and other open habitats and in adjacent forested areas (Stewart and Robbins 1958). Nest sites are primarily in long-abandoned houses, barns, or other outbuildings that are completely overgrown by vegetation, but sites include woodlands, dense thickets, and hollow logs (Townsend 1937; Jackson 1983). Dorsey (1947) reported the area surrounding a nest in Anne Arundel County was clean, with no remnants of food seen throughout the nesting period. This vulture does not construct a nest; it lays its eggs on the ground or floor of a building (MNRF). Seven of the eight Maryland nest records that specified height above the ground reported it as 0 ft; the exception was 10 ft (3 m), on the second floor of a deserted building.

The earliest Maryland egg date is 14 March; the latest is 22 May (MNRF). In 13 Maryland nests clutch sizes were either 1 or 2, with a mean of 1.8. The usual clutch size is 2 eggs, but occasionally 3 have been found in other states (Jackson 1988a). Both sexes participate in incubation, which requires 37 to 41 days. Extreme Maryland nestling dates are 29 April and 19 July (MNRF). Brood sizes in six Maryland nests were either 1 or 2. Fledging occurs 75 to 80 days after hatching (Jackson 1988a).

Atlas results show "confirmed" observations in all sections of Maryland except the Allegheny Mountain Section. Black Vultures are most common in the Western Shore and Piedmont sections, although they are largely absent from the suburbs of Baltimore, Annapolis, and Washington. They are less common on the Eastern Shore and are local in the Ridge and Valley Section. The breeding range has expanded since the 1950s. Maryland BBS data from 1966 through 1989 show a highly significant average annual increase of 6.6 percent; the Eastern Region populations are stable. Maryland has the highest breeding season density in the northeastern states from Maryland north (Coleman and Fraser 1989).

Black Vulture nests are difficult to locate. The large numbers of "observed" records were the result of birds soaring overhead. Black Vultures probably nested in many blocks in which they were listed as "observed," but no further evidence was obtained. If Black Vultures were observed departing from a wooded area or an old building early in the day, they were classified as "possible" or "probable." Unless other evidence was found, they were classified as "observed."

The Black Vulture appears to be secure in Maryland, and expansion will probably continue on the Eastern Shore and elsewhere in the state.

John A. Gregoire and Glenn D. Therres

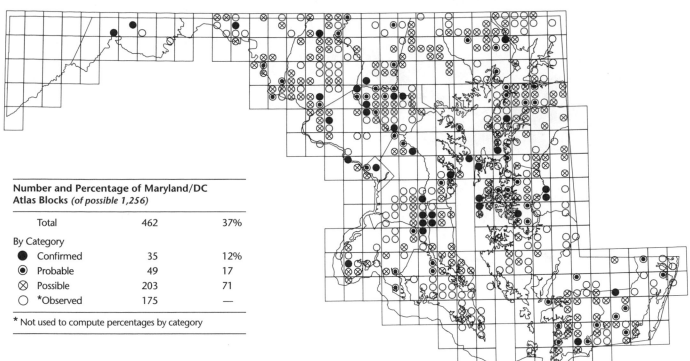

Number and Percentage of Maryland/DC Atlas Blocks *(of possible 1,256)*

Total	462	37%
By Category		
● Confirmed	35	12%
◉ Probable	49	17
⊗ Possible	203	71
○ *Observed	175	—

* Not used to compute percentages by category

Atlas Distribution, 1983–1987

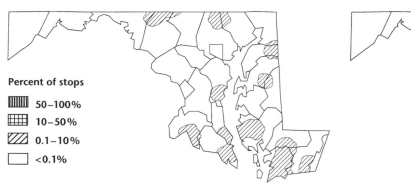

Percent of stops

▥	50–100%
▦	10–50%
▨	0.1–10%
☐	<0.1%

Relative Abundance, 1982–1989

Breeding Distribution, 1958

The Black Vulture was detected at scattered locations, primarily on the Coastal Plain. The early morning sampling period of mini-routes typically results in poor sampling of vultures.

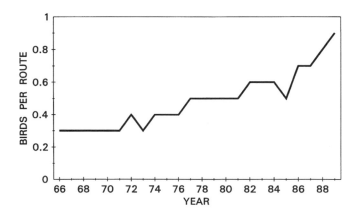

Maryland BBS Trend Graph, 1966–1989

Turkey Vulture

Cathartes aura

Often referred to as a buzzard (the common British *Buteo*), the Turkey Vulture is the major avian scavenger in North America. While soaring over field and forest, the bird has a characteristic V-shaped wing silhouette that makes it recognizable at a great distance. Its naked reddish head, which resembles the head of the Wild Turkey, probably led to this species' common name.

The Turkey Vulture is a permanent resident throughout Maryland except in the mountainous western counties. Migratory birds from the north also winter here (Stewart and Robbins 1958). The migration peaks are poorly defined, but on the average they can be expected in February and November (Robbins and Bystrak 1977). Coues and Prentiss (1883) reported it as common in DC, although less abundant than when arrangements for the disposition of dead horses and other animals were more primitive. Kirkwood (1895) considered it a common resident, except in western Maryland, where he wrote that it was casual near Cumberland in Allegany County. Eifrig (1904) stated that the Turkey Vulture could not be called common or rare in Allegany and Garrett counties. Hampe and Kolb (1947) reported that western Maryland was the only major section of the state that lacked definite breeding records. Stewart and Robbins (1958) described its breeding status as common in the Coastal Plain and the Piedmont, fairly common in the Ridge and Valley Section, and uncommon in the Allegheny Mountain Section. The BBS data from 1966 through 1989 show a highly significant average annual increase of 1.7 percent in the Eastern Region and a similar but greater increase of 3.5 percent in Maryland.

The Turkey Vulture is a wide-ranging edge species that occurs regularly in agricultural, marsh, and other open areas as well as in adjacent forested tracts (Stewart and Robbins 1958). It seems to be more numerous in lowland areas, perhaps because of a greater abundance of thickets and hollow trees (Jackson 1988b). In addition to dense thickets and hollow bases of trees, its nest sites include hollow logs, caves, and old buildings (Tyler 1937; Jackson 1988b). Wetmore and Manville (1968) reported a pair nesting in a cavity among the rocks on the bluffs opposite Plummers Island along the Potomac River in Virginia. Most nest sites found in North Carolina were in abandoned houses, barns, and other outbuildings (Rabenold and Decker 1989). The nest is no more than a place on the ground (Tyler 1937). All but two Maryland nest records (MNRF) give the height as 0 ft, although one was found at 20 ft (6.1 m), in the attic of an abandoned farmhouse.

Maryland egg dates range from 3 April to 10 June (Stewart and Robbins 1958), with half the records from 21 April to 2 May (MNRF). Clutch sizes range from 1 to 3, with a mean of 2.0, in 67 Maryland nests. Incubation, conducted by both sexes, lasts 34 or 35 days (Buhnerkempe and Westemeier 1984). The adults brood the young for about five days until they are thermally independent; parental duties then primarily involve feeding the young. Extreme nestling dates in Maryland are 5 May and 29 August (Stewart and Robbins 1958), with a peak in early to mid-June (MNRF). Brood sizes in 11 Maryland nests were all either 1 or 2, with a mean of 1.4. The young fledge when nine weeks old (Jackson 1988b).

Atlas data show that the Turkey Vulture breeds throughout Maryland. It is widely distributed over most of the state, although slightly less so in Allegany and Garrett counties. It is missing from the major urban centers and the Chesapeake Bay islands. This is consistent with the 1950s distribution (Stewart and Robbins 1958), although more of these birds are found today in western Maryland. The preponderance of "possible" and "observed" records are mostly observations of foraging and wandering individuals rather than of locally nesting birds. Turkey Vultures are known to average 4.8-mi (7.7-km) foraging distances from the nest site (Coleman and Fraser 1987). The high number of "observed" records resulted from the fieldworkers' inability to find any breeding evidence. If Turkey Vultures were observed departing from a wooded area or an old building early in the day, they were classified as "possible" or "probable." Unless other evidence was found, they were classified as "observed." Turkey Vultures surely nested in many of the Atlas blocks where they were recorded as only "observed."

There currently seems to be a good balance between Turkey Vulture numbers and the availability of carrion, which is nearly their sole food (Jackson 1988b). The expansion of suburbia will probably cause the species to decline or to range farther in search of an adequate food supply. By and large, the Turkey Vulture is secure in Maryland for the foreseeable future.

John A. Gregoire and Glenn D. Therres

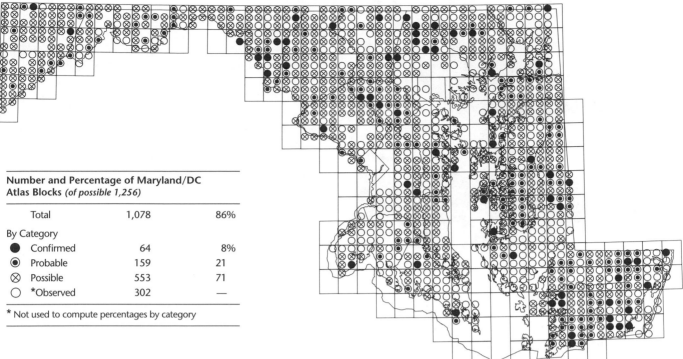

Number and Percentage of Maryland/DC Atlas Blocks *(of possible 1,256)*		
Total	1,078	86%
By Category		
● Confirmed	64	8%
◉ Probable	159	21
⊗ Possible	553	71
○ *Observed	302	—

* Not used to compute percentages by category

Atlas Distribution, 1983–1987

Percent of stops

▥	50–100%
▦	10–50%
▨	0.1–10%
☐	<0.1%

Relative Abundance, 1982–1989

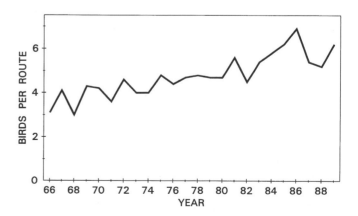

Breeding Distribution, 1958

Turkey Vultures were not detected in the developed Baltimore-Washington corridor, in most of southern Maryland, or in parts of the wooded highlands of western Maryland. Scattered areas of higher abundance were on the Eastern Shore. The early morning sampling period of miniroutes typically results in poor sampling of vultures.

Maryland BBS Trend Graph, 1966–1989

Osprey

Pandion haliaetus

The Osprey is the only North American hawk that feeds almost exclusively on live fish. It hovers, then plunges feet first into surface water to impale its prey with tonglike talons. Although the Osprey is found throughout the world except in the polar regions, the largest known nesting concentration is in the Chesapeake Bay (Henny et al. 1974). It is a common nesting bird along most Chesapeake Bay tributaries but is uncommon on nontidal and inland waters.

Historically, Ospreys were common nesters along shorelines of the Chesapeake Bay and its tributaries (Coues and Prentiss 1883; Kirkwood 1895). Stewart and Robbins (1958) considered Ospreys common in tidewater areas on the Eastern Shore and Western Shore and in the Upper Chesapeake Section; summer vagrants were found in the Piedmont Section. Subsequent human encroachment and contamination of estuarine habitats resulted in poor reproductive success. Declining populations brought nationwide attention to the plight of Ospreys by the 1960s (Ames and Mersereau 1964; Hickey and Anderson 1968; Peterson et al. 1969). Studies during the 1960s and 1970s suggested that adverse effects were less severe in the Chesapeake Bay than in other areas (Wiemeyer et al. 1975; Reese 1977). Henny et al. (1974) surveyed the Chesapeake Bay nesting population in 1973 and determined it to be about 1,450 pairs, of which 742 were in Maryland. Nationwide banning of DDT and other persistent environmental contaminants in the 1970s resulted in more successful reproduction. From 1966 through 1968, Reese (1969b) found 31 active nests distributed along shorelines in an area of rural Eastern Bay and the Chester River where F. Kirkwood (unpub. data) had found 32 in 1892. Henny et al. (1974) located 17 active nests in Virginia along the Little Wicomico River in 1973, where Tyrrell (1936) had recorded 56 in 1934. These surveys suggest that the present population in tidewater Maryland is fairly similar to that in historic times. Maryland BBS data from 1966 through 1989 show a highly significant average annual increase of 6.0 percent; the Eastern population shows a similar increase of 4.0 percent.

Most subadult Ospreys remain in the Caribbean basin and South America until the third spring after hatching (Henny and Van Velzen 1972). They then return in March to nest near their natal area. Pairing is for life, and birds return to nest at the same site each year (Spitzer 1980). Both birds gather sticks and construct the nest in a tree or on top of a man-made structure, such as a marine navigational aid, utility pole, or duck blind. Nest construction takes place from late March to mid-April (J. Reese, unpub. data). Nests, bulky stick structures about 2.3 ft (0.7 m) in diameter, may be located as low as 3 ft (0.9 m) (G. Therres, pers. comm.) on offshore structures, but they are generally above 40 ft (12.2 m) in tree sites (J. Reese, unpub. data).

Eggs are laid soon after nest construction is finished, one each day until the normal clutch of three is completed. Incubation is primarily by the female and lasts 38 to 42 days (Garber and Koplin 1972; J. Reese, unpub. data). Hatching is asynchronous and peaks in mid to late May. Egg dates in Maryland range from 26 March to 23 May, with a peak in mid-April (Reese 1970, 1977). Clutch sizes in 992 Maryland nests range from 1 to 4, with a mean of 2.9. Brood sizes in the same nests range from 1 to 4, with a mean of 1.3. Nestlings are brooded almost exclusively by the female for 48 to 59 days (Stotts and Henny 1975), while the male provides a steady diet of fresh fish. One brood is raised annually. Adults migrate south in early August shortly after the last nestlings have fledged, and the young migrate a few weeks later (J. Reese, unpub. data).

Atlas results confirm nesting in all tidewater blocks except those in densely populated areas. Ospreys are reasonably tolerant of normal human activities and can be lured to artificial nest structures offshore in broad tributaries, but this management technique is not a panacea. Birds also need privacy and an ample fish supply to sustain themselves and raise young, and these must coincide with site availability each year during the nesting period.

Development, human disturbance, and environmental pollution all operate to the detriment of Ospreys. An increasing human population has created disturbances for fishing and nesting Ospreys (Reese 1975a, 1977), and many Chesapeake waterways are now crowded with boats. In addition, environmental pollutants seriously impeded Osprey reproductive success from 1950 to the 1970s, and they sharply diminished or eliminated many Chesapeake fish species (Hall et al. 1985) on which Ospreys depend. At least for now, Ospreys have adapted to nesting on artificial terrestrial and offshore structures (Reese 1970, 1977) and to feeding on a few remaining abundant fish species. How much longer this opportunistic behavior, environmental quality, and food supply will last is uncertain. Development, human disturbance, and environmental pollution sharply reduced or extirpated Osprey populations from the New England states, Long Island Sound, and northern New Jersey within the past 40 years (Ames and Mersereau 1964; Spitzer et al. 1978; Wiemeyer et al. 1975, 1978). Maryland Ospreys may suffer a similar fate unless these detrimental factors can be controlled.

Jan G. Reese

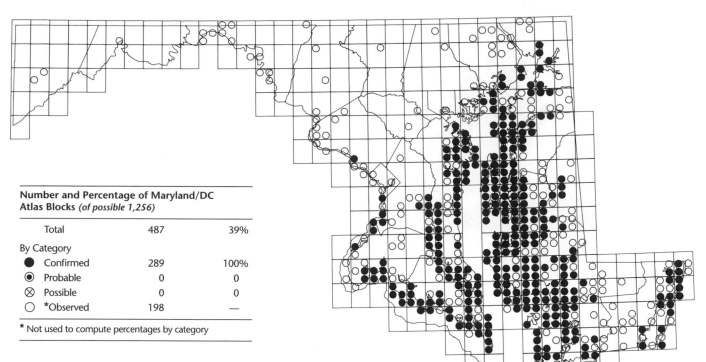

Number and Percentage of Maryland/DC Atlas Blocks *(of possible 1,256)*

Total	487	39%
By Category		
● Confirmed	289	100%
◉ Probable	0	0
⊗ Possible	0	0
○ *Observed	198	—

* Not used to compute percentages by category

Atlas Distribution, 1983–1987

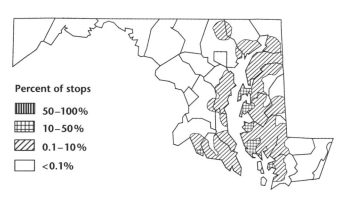

Percent of stops

▦	50–100%
▦	10–50%
▨	0.1–10%
☐	<0.1%

Relative Abundance, 1982–1989

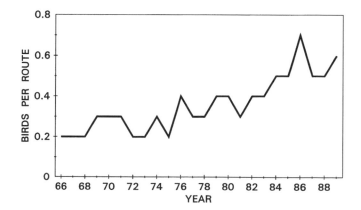

Breeding Distribution, 1958

Ospreys were detected most frequently on Eastern Shore peninsulas where observers had views of open water. They were detected less frequently along the rest of the Chesapeake Bay shoreline and its broader tributaries. Some inland reports probably refer to nonbreeding birds.

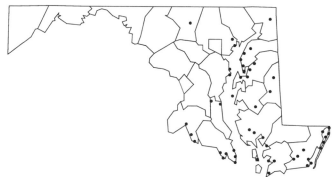

Maryland BBS Trend Graph, 1966–1989

Bald Eagle

Haliaeetus leucocephalus

The Bald Eagle, our national symbol, calls Maryland home year-round. The Chesapeake Bay supports a healthy resident population and accommodates visitors from both the North and the South. During the cold months, Bald Eagles from Canada and New England, primarily Maine, winter here (Buehler et al. 1991). In summer, Florida Bald Eagles move north to feed and loaf in Maryland.

The major attraction in Maryland is the Chesapeake Bay and its tributaries. This highly productive estuary provides all the life requirements needed by Bald Eagles. Shallow water areas with an abundance of fish and other prey are the key element followed by wooded shorelines and extensive marshes. Bald Eagles can be found elsewhere in Maryland, but they are most abundant in association with tidal waters.

Historically, Bald Eagles nested throughout tidewater Maryland (Stewart and Robbins 1958). They were reported to have nested along the Potomac River near Great Falls in Montgomery County (Cooke 1929) and as far west as Hancock in Washington County (Kirkwood 1895). Around 1855, a pair was reported nesting regularly near Glenarm in Baltimore County (Kirkwood 1895). Fisher (1899) believed eight to ten pairs were nesting within a 15-mi (24.1-km) radius of Baltimore during the 1890s. Based on an NAS survey conducted by W. Tyrrell in 1936, 600 pairs of Bald Eagles were estimated to nest in the Chesapeake Bay area (USFWS 1982). As Maryland currently supports approximately 50 percent of the Chesapeake Bay's breeding population, 300 pairs may have nested annually in Maryland in the 1930s. It is believed that by 1962 the breeding population had declined to only 25 percent of the population of the 1930s and that productivity was less than 15 percent of the 1930s level (USFWS 1982). The USFWS listed the fish-eating Bald Eagle as an endangered species in 1968. The persistence of organochlorine pesticides, such as DDT, had caused reproductive failure, resulting in significant population declines by the late 1960s

(Stickel et al. 1966). In 1977, only 39 active nests were found by state aerial surveys (DNR unpub. data).

Nests are usually located in the uppermost crotch of a tall coniferous or deciduous tree in or on the edge of a wooded area. Loblolly pine is the most commonly used tree in Maryland (Andrew and Mosher 1982). The vast majority of Maryland nest sites are within 1 mi (1.6 km) of tidal water (Andrew and Mosher 1982), many of them located along the shoreline. The nest, which is made of large sticks and branches, is typically 5 to 6 ft (1.5–1.8 m) in diameter (Stalmaster 1987). Bald Eagles add new material to the nest each year, and as a result it can get much larger over time. Smith (1936) reported that a Maryland nest occupied for over 30 years weighed 1.5 tons (1,361 kg).

Bald Eagles have a very long breeding season. In Maryland it begins in December when the pair establishes or reoccupies a territory. Bald Eagles are thought to mate for life (Stalmaster 1987), and they use the same nesting territory year after year. During December and January, the pair builds a nest or adds to the previous year's nest, performs courtship rituals, and copulates. Egg laying normally occurs in February, and most eggs are laid by mid-March. Extreme egg dates in Maryland are 5 February in Charles County (Oological Collection Western Foundation Vertebrate Zoology) and 29 April in Baltimore County (Stewart and Robbins 1958). One to 3 eggs are laid, with 2 being most common in Maryland (DNR, unpub. data). Brood sizes in 744 Maryland nests averaged 1.7 young per successful nest during 15 years of nest monitoring by the DNR. In 1986, a brood of 4 was successfully raised in Kent County (Cline 1986). The incubation period averages 35 days (Stalmaster 1987). Most young hatch between mid-March and late April. The DNR (unpub. data) reported nestlings as early as 5 February in Dorchester, Somerset, and Worcester counties, and J. Taylor, Jr., found young still in a DC nest as late as 9 July (Stewart and Robbins 1958). Young fledge at approximately 12 weeks of age (Stalmaster 1987).

Atlas data for the Bald Eagle were treated differently from those of most other species. Because of the extreme mobility of nesting Bald Eagles and the presence of adults from northern and southern populations in Maryland during the breeding season, only "confirmed" sightings were used. All other sightings were classified as "observed." Most Bald Eagle nest records were provided by the DNR as a result of their annual aerial monitoring of Maryland nests. The Atlas breeding distribution is similar to the historic range, except that no nesting now occurs above Great Falls on the Potomac River in Montgomery County. With the exception of the Great Falls nest and Susquehanna River nest in Harford County, all nesting is associated with tidal waters. Subsequent to the Atlas period, Bald Eagles nested at Triadelphia Reservoir, Montgomery County in 1990 and 1991 and on Fort George G. Meade property at PWRC, Anne Arundel County, in 1991. The BBS data from 1966 through 1989 show a highly significant average annual increase of 2.8 percent in Eastern Region populations; Maryland shows a similar increase of 3.0 percent.

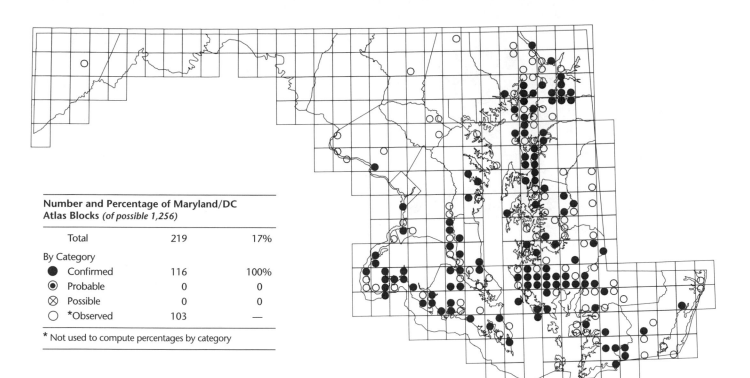

Number and Percentage of Maryland/DC Atlas Blocks *(of possible 1,256)*

Total	219	17%
By Category		
● Confirmed	116	100%
◉ Probable	0	0
⊗ Possible	0	0
○ *Observed	103	—

* Not used to compute percentages by category

Atlas Distribution, 1983–1987

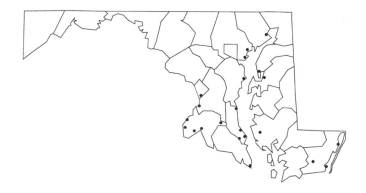

Breeding Distribution, 1958

During the Atlas project, the breeding population of Bald Eagles in Maryland increased steadily from 59 pairs in 1983 to 86 in 1987, and the proportion of successful nests increased from 68 percent to 79 percent (DNR, unpub. data). By protecting existing nest sites and maintaining suitable habitat throughout tidewater Maryland, the Bald Eagle should continue to increase in numbers in our state.

Glenn D. Therres

Northern Harrier

Circus cyaneus

The white-rumped, owl-faced Northern Harrier is commonly observed quartering over grassland and marsh in search of prey. Until recently, this raptor was known as the Marsh Hawk in North America and it is known as the Hen Harrier in Europe (Brown and Amadon 1989).

Coues and Prentiss (1883) considered the Northern Harrier abundant in Maryland, calling it "one of the commonest Hawks" and noting it was "one of the species most frequently exposed for sale in the markets." Eifrig (1904), however, did not find this species in western Maryland. Stewart and Robbins (1958) considered it a fairly common breeder in sedge meadows of the Allegheny Mountain Section and in tidewater marshes on the lower Eastern Shore. It is more common in migration and in winter, although in the Allegheny Mountain Section it is rare in winter. Peaks of migration in Maryland extend from mid-March to mid-April and from mid-October to mid-November (Robbins and Bystrak 1977).

The first reported Northern Harrier nest in Maryland was in a salt marsh adjacent to the Blackwater River in Dorchester County on 2 June 1895 (Kirkwood 1895). The first nest records for western Maryland were two nests found by J. Sommer on 11 June 1925 in Garrett County (MNRF). The Northern Harrier nests in a variety of open habitats, including abandoned fields, wet meadows, coastal and inland marshes, old dune communities, shrub wetlands, grasslands, upland heaths (Serrentino and England 1989), fallow fields, willow-grass swales (Follen 1986), undisturbed grass-legume fields (Duebbert and Lokemoen 1977), and bogs (Harrison 1975). In Maryland, nests have been found in tidal marshes, marsh meadows, and upland sedge meadows (Stewart and Robbins 1958).

Northern Harriers nest singly or in loose colonies of one polygynous male with a harem of two or more females (Hamerstrom 1969; Clark 1972). They build two types of nests, depending on moisture conditions at the site. On dry uplands, the nest is little more than a ground scrape lined with grasses; on wet sites the nest is a raft of herbaceous vegetation (Clark 1972). The female builds the nest, although the male may help gather materials (Harrison 1975). Nests, which are well concealed from all sides and open from above, are typically placed in stands of dense vegetation, usually more than 1 ft (0.3 m) high. Dead vegetation from the previous growing season is an important component of nesting cover. On upland sites, Northern Harriers prefer cover that is not mowed, grazed, or burned annually (Duebbert and Lokemoen 1977).

The 3- to 9-egg clutch (typically 4 or 5) is laid at intervals of two to three days. Incubation, by the female only, begins soon after the first egg is laid (Clark 1972; Harrison 1975; Duebbert and Lokemoen 1977). Five Maryland clutches (MNRF) contain 3 to 6 eggs; dates range from 28 April to 23 June. Maryland nestling dates range from 11 June to 1 July. The male feeds the female during the 30 to 31 days of incubation (Hamerstrom 1969; Hamerstrom et al. 1985). Young remain near the nest for several weeks after fledging. Only one brood is raised per year, but replacement clutches are laid if the original clutch fails early in the nesting season (Simmons 1984). A pair of breeding Northern Harriers requires large tracts of open country. Various studies have reported breeding densities of 0.5 to 5.1 nesting females per sq mi (1.3–13.1 per sq km) (Serrentino 1987). The Northern Harrier is an opportunist with an extremely varied diet. On the average, rodents and birds head the list, but reptiles, amphibians, large insects, spiders, fish, and carrion are eaten in large quantities (Palmer 1988a).

Atlas results suggest that the Northern Harrier range has contracted in Garrett County, an area Stewart and Robbins (1958) considered part of their principal breeding range in Maryland. There appears to be little change elsewhere, with the marshes on the lower Eastern Shore still retaining good numbers of breeding Northern Harriers. Scattered sightings were recorded from other areas in the Eastern and Western Shore sections. Of the 12 "confirmed" records, 4 were of adults carrying food for young, 3 were observations of fledglings, and 2 were of adults on nests. There was one instance each of nest with eggs, nest with young, and distraction display.

The Northern Harrier's current status in Maryland is unclear. Robbins and Boone (1984) reported a general decline. BBS data from 1966 through 1989 show an indication of an increase in the Eastern Region, but data are too few to estimate a Maryland trend. The USFWS (1987) listed the Northern Harrier as a nongame bird of management concern in the Northeast, and it has been on the NAS's Blue List in this region since 1972 (Tate 1986). The primary factors believed responsible for this species' decline are the loss of habitat resulting from wetland destruction and from reforestation of agricultural habitats (Serrentino and England 1989). Human disturbance and environmental contaminants have also been implicated (USFWS 1987).

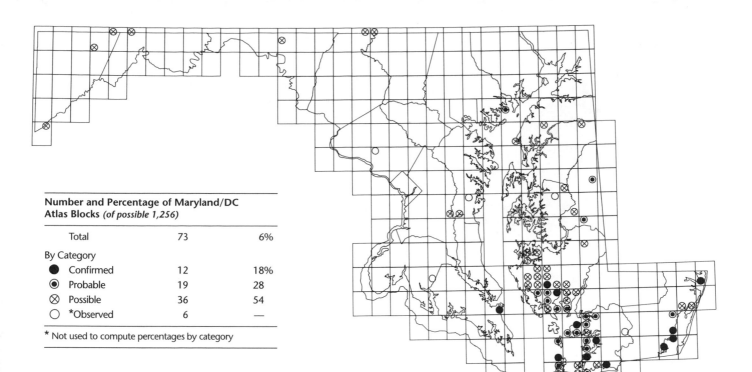

Number and Percentage of Maryland/DC Atlas Blocks *(of possible 1,256)*

Total	73	6%
By Category		
● Confirmed	12	18%
◉ Probable	19	28
⊗ Possible	36	54
○ *Observed	6	—

* Not used to compute percentages by category

Atlas Distribution, 1983–1987

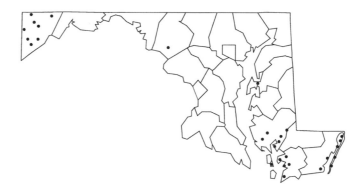

Breeding Distribution, 1958

Although Northern Harriers appear secure in the extensive marshlands on the lower Eastern Shore, populations elsewhere in the state are vulnerable to environmental disturbances. As is the case with other grassland birds, protection of large tracts of undisturbed nesting cover is critical for the promotion and maintenance of healthy populations of this species.

Scott A. Smith

Sharp-shinned Hawk

Accipiter striatus

The Sharp-shinned Hawk is a true bird hawk. The proportion of birds in its diet (90%) is greater than in the diet of any other North American raptor (May 1935). It is the most sexually dimorphic in size of any North American bird (Palmer 1988a). Although it is frequently seen during migration and is bold at winter feeders, the Sharp-shinned Hawk is a secretive, elusive, uncommon summer resident in Maryland. It breeds throughout much of North America (Palmer 1988a), particularly in the boreal forests of southern Canada. In the East, it is a common breeder in the forested portions of eastern Canada and becomes increasingly less common south to North Carolina (Meyer and Mueller 1982) and Alabama (Summerour 1986), where it occurs principally in the Appalachian Mountains. In Maryland, the Sharp-shinned Hawk nests primarily in Garrett County. Its migration peaks are from early April to early May and from mid-September to late October (Stewart and Robbins 1958).

Historic accounts present a mixed picture of this species' nesting status. Some authors referred to it as common or abundant (Coues and Prentiss 1883; Eifrig 1904), but others claimed it was numerous only during migration (Cooke 1929; Hampe and Kolb 1947). The earliest accounts of Sharp-shinned Hawks breeding in Maryland are from the late 1800s, when nests were found in Montgomery County (Stabler 1891) and DC (Stewart and Robbins 1958). Stewart and Robbins (1958) described the Maryland breeding distribution as fairly common in the Allegheny Mountain Section, uncommon in the Ridge and Valley Section, and rare (formerly more numerous) in the Piedmont Section. Present-day Maryland Sharp-shinned Hawk populations have been much reduced by the combined effects of land-use changes, persecution by humans, and the effects of DDT (Bednarz et al. 1990). Analyses of long-term trends in migrants observed

at fall concentration areas, however, showed that continental populations are stable or slowly increasing (Bednarz et al. 1990; Titus and Fuller 1990).

Few Sharp-shinned Hawk nests have been reported in Maryland, and little is known of its breeding biology in the state. From 1980 through 1990, only three nests were found, two in Garrett County and one in Allegany County (K. Titus, unpub. data); these nests were in pines, both red and Virginia. Five of six earlier Maryland nests were about 30 ft (9.1 m) high in pines (MNRF). Sharp-shinned Hawks prefer large forested tracts inhabited by an abundance of small birds. Such tracts are usually mixed forests of evergreen and deciduous trees, although observers have reported use of a wide variety of forest types (Palmer 1988a). This hawk frequently uses much younger forests than Cooper's Hawks and Northern Goshawks. In the East, Sharp-shinned Hawks nest almost exclusively in conifers (Palmer 1988a).

Compared with other breeding raptors in Maryland, Sharp-shinned Hawks nest late (Palmer 1988a), beginning in late April or early May (K. Titus, pers. obs.). Nests are approximately 18 to 25 in. (46–64 cm) in outside diameter, are composed of small sticks, and are placed on horizontal branches near the trunk (Peck and James 1983). Bent (1937) summarized 29 egg dates from New Jersey to Georgia; half the records were from 18 to 29 May, but extreme dates ranged from 5 May to 30 July. Extreme Maryland egg dates are 12 May and 30 June (MNRF). Clutch sizes are normally 4 or 5 eggs (Palmer 1988a), with an extreme of 8 (Bent 1937). Of five Maryland nests (MNRF), two contained 4 eggs and three contained 5 eggs. Maryland's nestling dates extend from 31 May (Kirkwood 1895) to 11 July (Stewart and Robbins 1958).

Breeding by Sharp-shinned Hawks was confirmed during the Atlas period in seven blocks, six in Garrett County (three nests with young, two adults with food for young, and one distraction display) and one (a nest with young) in Allegany County. Fifteen additional records were in the Allegheny Mountain Section. This distribution differs considerably from that of the nineteenth century, but is consistent with atlas data from neighboring states. Sharp-shinned Hawks are now uncommon breeders in Pennsylvania (Brauning 1992), West Virginia, and Virginia, and they are rare in Delaware. Because Sharp-shinned Hawks are late nesters, prefer dense coniferous habitats, and are relatively secretive, confirmation is much more difficult than for most raptors. Adult Sharp-shinned Hawks at the two Maryland nests visited by K. Titus (unpub. data), for example, were neither aggressive nor vocal. Furthermore, the area near the nests was clear of whitewash, prey remains, and plucking perches, which added to the difficulty of detection.

Both Atlas work and detailed searches by raptor specialists often fail to locate nesting Sharp-shinned Hawks. They may nest in large mixed forests at several locations outside Garrett County, such as the Green Ridge State Forest in Allegany County, other mountain forests in the Ridge and Valley Section, or large conifer plantations in or near other forested areas. BBS data from 1966 through 1989 show stable popu-

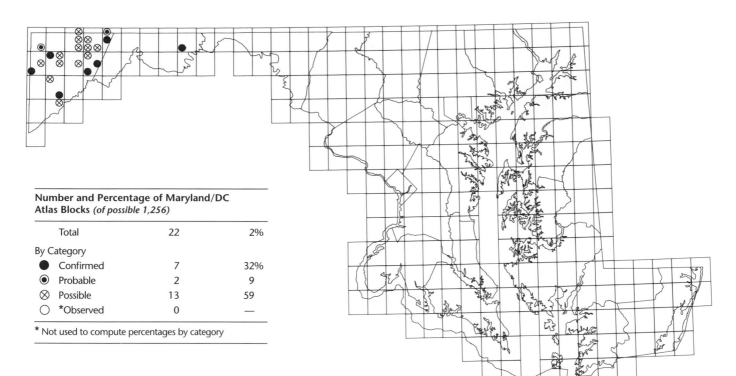

Number and Percentage of Maryland/DC Atlas Blocks *(of possible 1,256)*

	Total	22	2%
By Category			
●	Confirmed	7	32%
◉	Probable	2	9
⊗	Possible	13	59
○	*Observed	0	—

*Not used to compute percentages by category

Atlas Distribution, 1983–1987

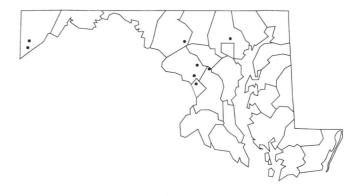

Breeding Distribution, 1958

lations in the Eastern Region; there are too few data to estimate a trend for Maryland.

To maintain Sharp-shinned Hawk populations in Maryland, both public and private timber management policies should include provisions to discourage forest fragmentation and to maintain tracts of timber containing conifers.

Kimberly Titus and David F. Brinker

Cooper's Hawk

Accipiter cooperii

The medium-size, long-tailed, short-winged Cooper's Hawk is not uncommon as a nesting bird in Maryland, although it is seldom encountered because it is secretive during the nesting season. It nests throughout most of Maryland; its breeding range includes most of the United States and extreme southern Canada (AOU 1983). Nesting Cooper's Hawks are probably resident, although some northern birds migrate through the state or winter here.

The Cooper's Hawk may have been one of the more common nesting raptors in Maryland in the nineteenth century. Early breeding records include a Howard County nest found in 1888, one discovered in 1891 at Sandy Spring in Montgomery County (Kirkwood 1895), and another from Montgomery County in 1892 (Stewart and Robbins 1958). By the early part of the twentieth century, the Cooper's Hawk was thought to be less abundant in many eastern states. Human impact, principally shooting and environmental contaminants, may have led to the decline (Bednarz et al. 1990). Some traditional Maryland sites have lost the Cooper's Hawk as a nesting species. In 1944, for example, three pairs nested at PWRC (Stewart et al. 1952), but during the 1980s no evidence of nesting was found there (C. Robbins, pers. comm.). BBS data from 1966 through 1989, however, show stable populations in Maryland and in the Eastern Region.

Cooper's Hawks nest in a wide variety of habitats. These include loblolly pine forests on the Eastern Shore, oak-hickory forests in the Ridge and Valley Section, and northern hardwood forests in the Allegheny Mountain Section (K. Titus, unpub. data). Based on visits to more than 50 active nests in Garrett and Allegany counties, nest trees include northern red, white, chestnut, and scarlet oaks; red and sugar maples; various hickories; black locust; white pine; and hemlock (K. Titus, pers. obs.). One common feature was that the nests were usually placed within, not below, the canopy. As a result, Cooper's Hawk nests in western Maryland were usually 46 to 56 ft (14–17 m) above the ground,

which is higher than most Red-shouldered and Broad-winged Hawk nests (Titus and Mosher 1981; K. Titus, unpub. data). Although Cooper's Hawks prefer to nest within the canopy, it is not unusual for them to use nest structures built by the two other species. The nests were constructed of small twigs, and western Maryland nests were seldom decorated with green sprigs except during the nest-building period, when a sprig of pine or hemlock might be present. In the western part of the state, nests often were in close proximity to Red-shouldered and Broad-winged nests.

Janik and Mosher (1982) found a mean clutch size of 3.6 for Maryland nests in research conducted from 1978 through 1980. In western Maryland, eggs are usually laid in early May, although the timing can vary considerably. The mean hatching date for seven nests was 19 June. There are 36 records of nesting Cooper's Hawks in the MNRF; most are from Baltimore, Dorchester, and Montgomery counties. Heights for 25 nests range from 25 to 75 ft (7.6–23 m), with a mean of 50.6 ft (15.4 m). Egg dates range from 22 April (21 April in DC) to 5 June, with a peak in early May. Clutch sizes for 34 nests range from 2 to 5, with a mean of 3.8. Young in the nest were found from 5 June to 23 July. Cooper's Hawks in western Maryland consume a variety of thrush-size birds; however, one of their most common prey items during the nesting season is the eastern chipmunk (K. Titus, pers. obs.).

Atlas data show that Cooper's Hawks seldom nest in major urban areas; there are few "probable" or "confirmed" records in the Baltimore-Washington corridor, where most records were obtained from 1871 through 1945. They do still nest on the Eastern Shore, although only one "confirmed" observation was recorded there. East of Allegany County, "confirmed" nesting was reported in only 16 percent of the blocks in which these hawks were detected. Cooper's Hawks were "confirmed" in 54 percent of the blocks in which they were found in Allegany and Garrett counties. This much higher rate of confirmation may be partly the result of greater abundance, but the principal reason was the research into nesting raptors in those two counties.

All blocks in western Maryland almost certainly contain this species, so atlas results probably underestimate their abundance and distribution. For example, Robbins and Dowell (1989) found Cooper's Hawks in 52 percent of the random sample (2%) of Maryland Atlas blocks that they covered intensively. Cooper's Hawks are probably second only to Broad-winged Hawks in nesting density in western Maryland, nesting even within the city limits of Frostburg. The extremely secretive nature of breeding Cooper's Hawks makes nests difficult to locate. Most birds slip away long before an observer approaches, and females often remain hidden on a nest while researchers stand directly beneath it. More species-specific surveys are required to assess the true population level as well as Maryland population trends.

Specific locations of Cooper's Hawk nests should not be revealed. This will help ensure that eggs and young will be protected from falconers and incubating birds will not be driven from their nests by well-meaning visitors.

Kimberly Titus

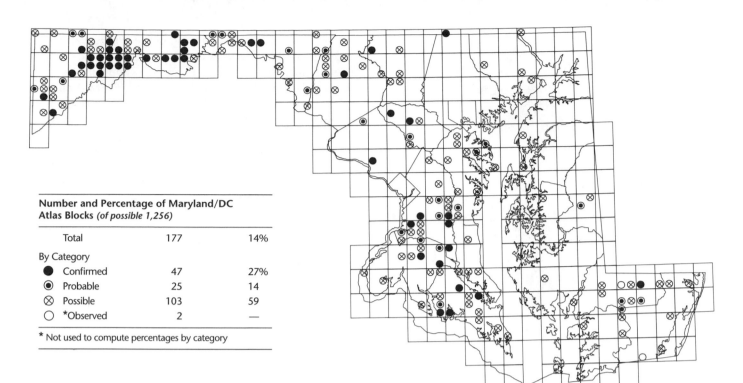

Number and Percentage of Maryland/DC Atlas Blocks *(of possible 1,256)*

Total	177	14%
By Category		
● Confirmed	47	27%
◉ Probable	25	14
⊗ Possible	103	59
○ *Observed	2	—

* Not used to compute percentages by category

Atlas Distribution, 1983–1987

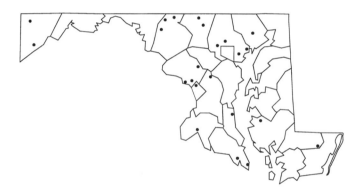

Breeding Distribution, 1958

Northern Goshawk

Accipiter gentilis

Little is known about the historical status and distribution of the Northern Goshawk in Maryland; however, it once nested throughout the southern Appalachian highlands from western Pennsylvania to North Carolina and Tennessee (AOU 1983). Although normally a permanent resident wherever found, it has staged impressive southward incursions in two consecutive winters in each of the last two decades when its winter prey populations crashed in the north (Speiser and Bosakowski 1987; Kimmel and Yahner 1990).

Early accounts of nesting Northern Goshawks in the central Appalachians connect them with old-growth or virgin forest (Warren 1890; Simpson 1909; Todd 1940). Although large-scale timber removal did not begin in Garrett County until the 1880s (Kline 1976), less than 5 percent (25,000 acres or 10,125 ha) of its extensive forests remained uncut by 1902 (Curran 1902). The state's Northern Goshawk nesting was recorded in 1901 near Jennings, Garrett County (Behr 1914); Stewart and Robbins (1958) called this species formerly rare, with this breeding attempt the only one known for Maryland.

Destruction of eastern forests late in the nineteenth century may have contributed to the disappearance of breeding Northern Goshawks in the Appalachians. Loss of mast-producing trees may have been a factor in the population collapse and extinction of the Passenger Pigeon, perhaps a significant component of the Northern Goshawk diet. When Passenger Pigeons were abundant in Pennsylvania, Northern Goshawks bred there commonly (Bent 1937). By the 1930s, they were rare and bred only in some of the mountainous counties with extensive mixed forests. Kimmel and Yahner (1990) estimated from 144 to 348 Northern Goshawk nests in Pennsylvania in the late 1980s.

Probably more critical in the loss of the Northern Goshawk as a breeding species was the clearing of the old-growth timber from most mountain slopes and hollows. Successful nesting depends on a large block of contiguous and relatively undisturbed forest to minimize increased predator and competitor populations associated with forest fragmentation. At more northern latitudes, however, Northern Goshawks also use stands of second-growth aspen or white birch forests (McGowan 1975; T. Erdman and D. Brinker, unpub. data). Crocker-Bedford (1990) found that, despite undisturbed buffers of 3 to 500 acres (1.2–200 ha) around nests, partial timber cutting in the nesting territory resulted in a high rate of nest abandonment (75–80%) and loss of nestling production (94%) in the southwestern United States. This decrease in productivity was attributed to increased competition with open-forest raptors, such as Red-tailed Hawks and Great Horned Owls, and from changes in foraging habitat and prey abundance.

In the eastern United States, Northern Goshawks prefer deciduous nest trees, such as maple, beech, and birch (Palmer 1988a). Maturing forests with nest trees averaging 15 in. (38 cm) diameter at breast height are frequently selected (Speiser and Bosakowski 1987). Nests are located near the trunk at the base of the canopy, usually 30 to 40 ft (9.1–12 m) above ground (Palmer 1988a).

Nesting activities begin in March, so that by late April most pairs are incubating (Palmer 1988a). The female builds the nest of twigs and limbs from both dead and live trees and lines it with dry bark or other similar material. Greenery, usually deciduous (Schnell 1958), is frequently added to the nest from egg laying through fledging of the young (Palmer 1988a). Nests are fairly easy to locate before the trees leaf out. The male feeds the female from two weeks prior to egg laying to fledging of the young. Speiser and Bosakowski (1991) found the mean onset of incubation of 20 nests in New York and New Jersey was 23 April. Simpson (1909) found eggs as early as 2 April in western Pennsylvania. Clutch sizes range from 1 to 4, but 2 to 4 eggs are usual (Bent 1937); however, clutch size and reproductive success are strongly influenced by prey availability (Palmer 1988a). Incubation, principally by the female, requires 32 to 34 days. The Northern Goshawk diet consists of birds as large as grouse or Barred Owls and a variety of mammals as large as rabbits (Bent 1937).

Speiser and Bosakowski (1987) suggested that maturation of the eastern forests is a major factor in the recent recolonization of the southern portions of the Northern Goshawk's former range. On 24 June 1980 a nest containing two small young was found 26 ft (7.9 m) up in a large red oak in an extensively forested area in western Garrett County (Boone 1984), but it was later destroyed by predators. The pair could not be found the next year (K. Titus, pers. comm.). This nesting was very late compared with dates in northern states. By late June most Northern Goshawks in Wisconsin are fledging young (T. Erdman and D. Brinker, unpub. data). Three other sightings, all during the Atlas period, suggest that Northern Goshawks are rare

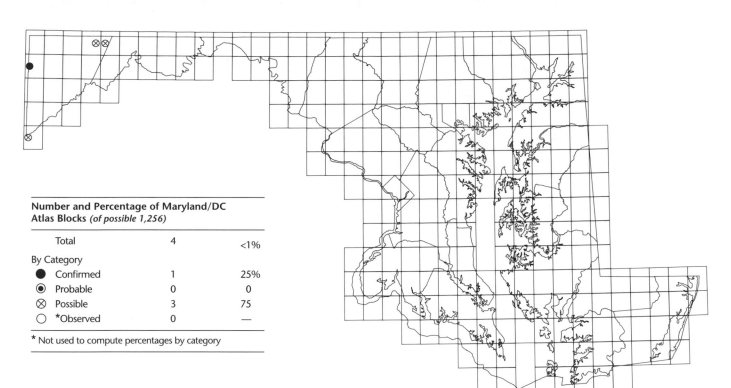

Number and Percentage of Maryland/DC Atlas Blocks *(of possible 1,256)*

Total		4	<1%
By Category			
●	Confirmed	1	25%
◉	Probable	0	0
⊗	Possible	3	75
○	*Observed	0	—

* Not used to compute percentages by category

Atlas Distribution, 1983–1987

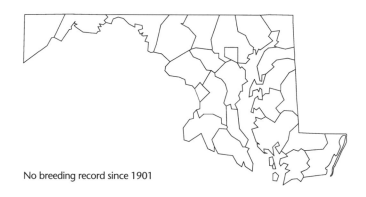

No breeding record since 1901

Breeding Distribution, 1958

and irregular breeders in the remaining unfragmented, mature forests in Garrett County. The DNR listed this raptor as endangered in 1990.

Maintenance of extensive mature forest in large enough blocks to inhibit open-forest and edge-benefited competitors and predators is critical (Crocker-Bedford 1990). Ideally these blocks should contain or be near a swamp or bog to provide habitat diversity and a greater density and variety of prey (Speiser and Bosakowski 1987). Only about 20 percent

of Garrett County is publicly owned, and even this land is highly fragmented by private inholdings, roads, and utility rights of way. Because economic incentives to cut timber and develop private lands are increasing, successful maintenance of Northern Goshawk habitat is possible only in state-owned forests. Protecting large tracts of unfragmented old forest is imperative if Maryland is to sustain a breeding population of Northern Goshawks.

D. Daniel Boone

Red-shouldered Hawk

Buteo lineatus

The Red-shouldered Hawk is one of Maryland's most widespread and common large raptors. Those in the western counties are migratory (K. Titus, pers. comm.), but those in the eastern counties, where the winter climate is less severe, are permanent residents (E. Martin, unpub. data). With young birds, movements that do occur may be as much dispersal as migration; with adults, movements are usually a population shift and may involve one sex more than the other. Red-shouldered Hawks migrate through Maryland from mid-February to late April and from mid-September to mid-November (Stewart and Robbins 1958).

According to Coues and Prentiss (1883), the Red-shouldered Hawk was common and doubtless resident in DC but was seen chiefly in winter. Kirkwood (1895) wrote that it was the most common hawk in Baltimore City at any season, but that the Red-tailed Hawk outnumbered it in Baltimore County. Eifrig (1904) found it throughout western Maryland in both winter and summer. Cooke (1929) called it rare but formerly common around DC. Stewart and Robbins (1958) described its breeding status as locally common in the Eastern and Western Shore sections, fairly common in the Piedmont and Upper Chesapeake sections, and uncommon in the Ridge and Valley and Allegheny Mountain sections.

A comparison of the period 1924 through 1945 with the period 1946 through 1968 indicates a decrease of 7 percent in the number of young per successful nest in Maryland and vicinity (Henny 1972). Using central Maryland data from the 1940s (Stewart 1949) and from 1956 through 1971, Henny et al. (1973) found that deterioration and loss of habitat were significant factors in this decrease. Data collected annually since 1972 in the same area show a continuing slow population decline as destruction of habitat in the Baltimore-Washington corridor continues (E. Martin, unpub. data). In contrast, BBS data from 1966 through 1989 show a significant average annual increase of 2.0 percent in Maryland;

data from 1980 through 1989 show a similar but greater increase of 5.7 percent. Eastern Region populations are stable. Intensive studies in Garrett and Allegany counties from 1979 through 1984 indicated relatively high, stable populations there (K. Titus, unpub. data). Although most common in mature bottomland woods along streams, Red-shouldered Hawks nest in many other habitats. In western Maryland, they use beaver flowages, swamps, and moist seeps, even at high elevations, and narrow streams with little bottomland (K. Titus, pers. comm.). The highest breeding density for Maryland is 1.5 territorial males per 100 acres (40.5 ha) in lowland forest at PWRC (Robbins 1991).

Nests are usually in a main crotch or at a fork of a large branch in large trees (E. Martin, pers. obs). In Maryland, there is little species preference in nest trees; in western Maryland, 69 percent were in the most common old-growth species, red or white oaks (Titus and Mosher 1987); in central Maryland, preferred nest trees are American beech, tulip tree, and sweet gum (MNRF). Heights of 238 Maryland nests (MNRF) range from 20 to 90 ft (6.1–27 m), with a mean of 51.9 ft (16 m). Nests are constructed with a base of sturdy sticks lined with various plant fibers (E. Martin, pers. obs.). Some green leaves or pine needles in the nest and bits of down on the nest structure assist in identifying active nests.

Nesting chronology depends on weather conditions (E. Martin, pers. obs.). On the Coastal Plain, nesting often begins in February, and most egg laying occurs from mid-March to late April. In western Maryland, these events are delayed a few weeks to a month (Janik and Mosher 1982). Extreme Maryland egg dates are 4 March and 31 May (MNRF). Clutch sizes in 66 nests range from 1 to 5, with a mean of 2.7. Young hatch from mid-April to late May on the Coastal Plain, with an average hatching date of 27 April (E. Martin, unpub. data). Extreme brood dates in Maryland are 5 April (E. Martin, unpub. data) and 6 July (MNRF), with a peak in late May. Brood sizes in 182 nests (MNRF) range from 1 to 5, with a mean of 2.6. The incubation period is about 28 days (Bent 1937). Red-shouldered Hawks are single-brooded and rarely renest. Mice, frogs, and snakes comprise the bulk of their diet (May 1935).

Atlas observers found Red-shouldered Hawks in almost every block within 25 mi (40.2 km) of DC. Other concentrations were in the Pocomoke and Blackwater river drainages on the lower Eastern Shore, in woodlands along the Fall Line, on Catoctin and South Mountains, and in the extensive forests of western Maryland.

Although habitat loss is the main threat to this species, over a dozen nests were found virtually in backyards in central Maryland (E. Martin, unpub. data). This is strong evidence that, with sufficient woodland for nesting and habitat for feeding, the Red-shouldered Hawk can adapt to living close to humans. Maryland's population appears healthy, but it shows signs of decline from habitat loss in the heavily populated areas. Preservation of extensive wooded stream valleys and floodplain forest with tall trees is needed.

Elwood M. Martin

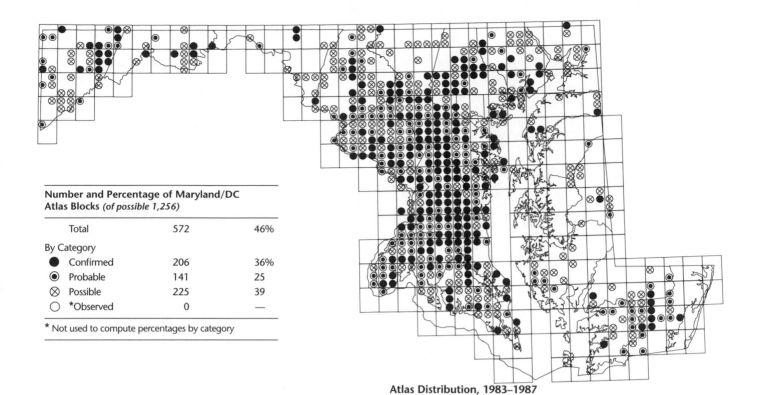

Number and Percentage of Maryland/DC Atlas Blocks *(of possible 1,256)*

Total	572	46%
By Category		
● Confirmed	206	36%
◉ Probable	141	25
⊗ Possible	225	39
○ *Observed	0	—

* Not used to compute percentages by category

Atlas Distribution, 1983–1987

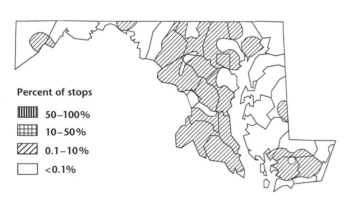

Percent of stops

ⅢⅢ	50–100%
▦	10–50%
▨	0.1–10%
☐	<0.1%

Relative Abundance, 1982–1989

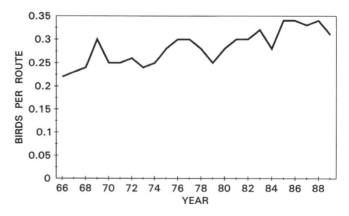

Breeding Distribution, 1958

The Red-shouldered Hawk is uncommon but widely distributed in the Piedmont and Western Shore sections and in the Pocomoke River drainage on the lower Eastern Shore. It was absent or very rarely found on the rest of the Eastern Shore or in western Maryland.

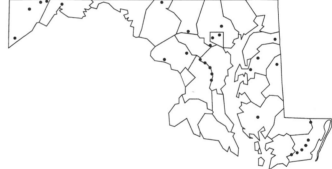

Maryland BBS Trend Graph, 1966–1989

MOB

Broad-winged Hawk

Buteo platypterus

The Broad-winged Hawk is best known for its spectacular autumn migration, when kettles in the latter half of
September occasionally exceed 1,000 individuals. This hawk
breeds throughout eastern North America from the southern United States north to southern Canada (Palmer 1988b).
It is most abundant in the mesic forests of the northern
United States and southern Canada. Maryland's smallest
nesting buteo is a common summer resident in extensive
forested areas west of the Chesapeake Bay, particularly in the
Ridge and Valley and Allegheny Mountain sections. Its dependence on extensive woodlands is reflected in spottier distribution east of Washington County, especially on the Eastern Shore.

The first published Maryland nesting records for Broad-
winged Hawks are from late in the nineteenth century (Bendire 1892; Kirkwood 1895). During the early 1900s, their
breeding status ranged from rare, to "tolerably" common, to
fairly frequent, which probably reflected local rather than
statewide status (Coues and Prentiss 1883; Cooke 1929;
Hampe and Kolb 1947). Stewart and Robbins (1958) described the breeding status as common in the Allegheny
Mountain and Ridge and Valley sections, fairly common in
the Piedmont and Western Shore sections, and uncommon
in the Upper Chesapeake and Eastern Shore sections. During the past 50 years continental populations have remained
relatively stable (Bednarz et al. 1990; Titus and Fuller 1990),
and this is probably the situation in Maryland. Reforestation
of cutover lands and abandoned farms has certainly benefited this species.

Broad-winged Hawks return to Maryland from their
South American wintering grounds (AOU 1983) in April and
May, and most depart before mid-October (Stewart and
Robbins 1958). Nest construction begins shortly after pairs
are formed. For breeding, Broad-winged Hawks prefer large

contiguous woodlands over fragmented forests, but studies
have shown that nests are usually close to forest openings
and edges, such as fields and roads, typically near ponds,
streams, and other wet areas (Matray 1974; Keran 1978; Fuller
1979; Titus and Mosher 1981). Although these hawks seem to
prefer deciduous trees, nests have been recorded in over 40
tree species, including evergreens (Palmer 1988b). Titus and
Mosher (1987) found that 71 percent of 112 western Maryland nests were in oak trees; the mean height of these nests
was 48.6 ft (15 m) and the mean diameter of the nest trees at
breast height was 17 in. (43 cm). The nest is lined with flakes
of bark and usually contains one or more branches with
green leaves (Riley 1902).

Maryland egg dates span 23 April through 16 June, with
the peak in mid-May (MNRF). Maryland clutch sizes are
normally 2 or 3 eggs, but occasionally 1 or 4. The mean
Maryland clutch size for 25 nests (MNRF) is 2.6; in a separate sample from western Maryland (Janik and Mosher
1982), the mean for 15 nests is 2.7. Incubation is by the female and requires about 31 days (Bush and Gehlbach 1978).
Maryland brood sizes in six nests (MNRF) range from 1 to
4. In western Maryland, 31 (86%) of 36 active nests fledged
59 young, a mean of 1.7 young per successful nest (Janik and
Mosher 1982). Nestlings fledge at about 5 weeks and remain
in the vicinity of the nest for another 2 to 3 weeks while being fed by the adults (Palmer 1988b). Lyons and Mosher
(1987) reported that in western Maryland young left the nest
after 29 to 31 days. Chipmunks and small birds comprise
much of their food (Palmer 1988b).

The Broad-winged Hawk is the most common breeding
hawk in the Allegheny Mountain Section and in the western
and eastern portions of the Ridge and Valley Section, where
it was found in 63, 52, and 70 percent of all Atlas blocks respectively. Because extensive woods are less frequent east
of Washington County, the occurrence of Broad-winged
Hawks decreases, and the proportion of blocks where they
were confirmed declines to 31 percent in the Piedmont Section and 25 percent in the Western Shore Section. They are
uncommon to rare east of the Chesapeake Bay. These hawks
are common breeders in forested areas of Pennsylvania
(Brauning 1992), West Virginia, and Virginia but are rare
and local in Delaware. Nest building coincides with the
period of rapid leaf emergence, which makes nests difficult to locate and breeding difficult to confirm. Although
Broad-winged Hawks are frequently heard calling, either
while perched or soaring, they generally sit very tight while
incubating and tolerate fairly close approach by humans
(D. Brinker, pers. obs.).

BBS data from 1966 through 1989 show stable populations in both the Eastern Region and Maryland; however,
these hawks are moderately sensitive to forest fragmentation
(Robbins et al. 1989a). Because they are not selective about
the type of forest habitat used for nesting, any efforts to
conserve forest lands, particularly large contiguous tracts,
will help conserve populations of Broad-winged Hawks in
Maryland.

John A. Gregoire and David F. Brinker

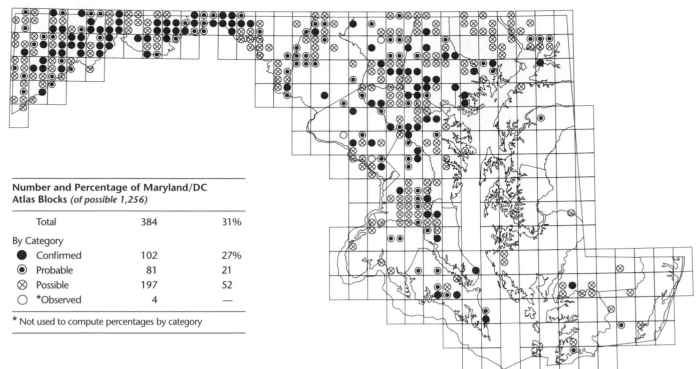

Number and Percentage of Maryland/DC Atlas Blocks *(of possible 1,256)*

Total	384	31%
By Category		
● Confirmed	102	27%
◉ Probable	81	21
⊗ Possible	197	52
○ *Observed	4	—

* Not used to compute percentages by category

Atlas Distribution, 1983–1987

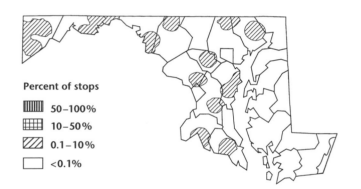

Percent of stops

▦	50–100%
▦	10–50%
▨	0.1–10%
☐	<0.1%

Relative Abundance, 1982–1989

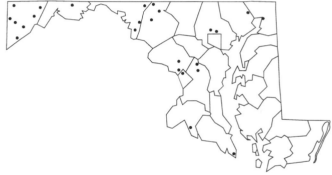

Breeding Distribution, 1958

The Broad-winged Hawk is most widespread in the extensive woodlands of western Maryland. It was detected in such small numbers on miniroutes that differences in abundance are not evident. It was recorded at scattered locations west of the Chesapeake Bay but not on the Eastern Shore.

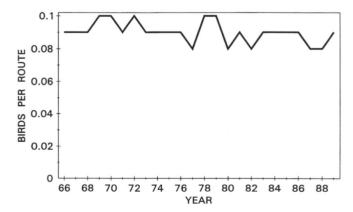

Maryland BBS Trend Graph, 1966–1989

Red-tailed Hawk

Buteo jamaicensis

The Red-tailed Hawk, keen of vision, muscular, and alert, is one of Maryland's most widespread nesting raptors. Although this hawk is found year-round throughout the state, considerable numbers of migrants pass through Maryland, and winter populations are supplemented by birds from the north (Stewart and Robbins 1958). The principal migration periods are late February to early April, and early October to late November.

Coues and Prentiss (1883) called the Red-tailed Hawk an abundant resident in DC; Kirkwood (1895) labeled it common but rarely seen in summer. Cooke (1929) called it rare in summer and doubted that it bred around DC. Red-tailed Hawk populations suffered when hawk shooting was a sport and bounties were paid. Because of its high visibility, this species was wrongly blamed for many barnyard abductions and was often the easiest target for gunners (Sprunt 1955). Eifrig (1904) noted that many were also caught in traps set by farmers. Years of shooting, trapping, habitat transformation, and pesticide ingestion brought populations to an all-time low in the late 1940s (Broun 1949). Stewart and Robbins (1958) called it a fairly common breeder in the Eastern and Western Shore sections and uncommon throughout the rest of the state. BBS data from 1966 through 1989 show a stable population in Maryland; however, the Eastern Region had a highly significant average annual increase of 2.1 percent. When Titus and Fuller (1990) used two methods for analyzing raptor trends from migration counts in the northeastern states, they found no evidence of changes in Red-tailed Hawk populations from 1972 through 1987.

In Maryland, breeding Red-tailed Hawks occupy a variety of edge habitats, especially in agricultural and marsh areas; they also use extensive forest tracts (Stewart and Robbins 1958). The highest breeding density reported for Mary-land is 0.05 territorial males per 100 acres (40.5 ha) in mixed woodland and open habitats on the border of Prince George's and Anne Arundel counties in 1951 (Stewart and Robbins 1958). Courtship, often accompanied by spectacular aerobatics, begins in February (Bent 1937). In courtship flights occurring several times during the day, pairs climb high and stoop at each other while calling. The male occasionally assumes a position just above the female and drops his talons. The female flips, locks talons with the male, and together they plummet several hundred feet. They then sometimes head for a common perch and copulate.

Nests, which are constructed of sticks placed in the upper branches of mature trees, are often lined with bark and decorated with fresh evergreen sprigs (Bent 1937). Titus and Mosher (1981) discovered that Red-tailed Hawk nests in western Maryland were placed higher than those of other hawks and were farther from water. Nests were most often on east-facing slopes and on slopes steeper than those used by other hawks. Speiser and Bosakowski (1988) reported that in New Jersey, 82 percent of nests were in oak trees, usually placed close to the canopy. Most nests were in secondary rather than primary tree crotches.

Heights of 52 Maryland nests (MNRF) range from 30 to 100 ft (9.1–31 m), with a mean of 55.9 ft (17 m). Maryland egg dates range from 8 March to 28 June. In 48 nests (MNRF), clutch sizes range from 1 to 4 (mean of 2.2). Nests with young have been found in Maryland from 25 April to 16 July. In 14 Maryland nests, brood sizes were either 1 or 2 (mean of 1.7). Janik and Mosher (1982) reported that in western Maryland the mean clutch size in 15 nests was 2.0; 67 percent of nests were successful, and the average number of young fledged per successful nest was 1.4. They noted that nestling mortality was greatest in the second and third weeks after hatching, and they attributed most failures to inclement weather and to predation by Great Horned Owls.

The diet of the Red-tailed Hawk is extremely varied, including almost any small or medium-size mammal, as well as some reptiles, amphibians, and birds (May 1935). Janik and Mosher (1982) found that juvenile fox squirrels dominated the diet in western Maryland.

Atlas observers found the Red-tailed Hawk throughout Maryland. It was absent from the most heavily urbanized and suburbanized blocks and from a few heavily forested areas without nearby open lands for hunting. Its habit of high soaring made it fairly easy to locate but not easy to upgrade. Hence, 47 percent of the reports were for "possible" breeding.

Both changes in land use and forest fragmentation may have benefited the Red-tailed Hawk by providing additional open nesting habitat and access to areas previously more suited to forest-dwelling raptors (Bednarz and Dinsmore 1982). Although the future of this large, soaring hawk seems assured in Maryland, observers should not approach or disturb active nests.

John A. Gregoire

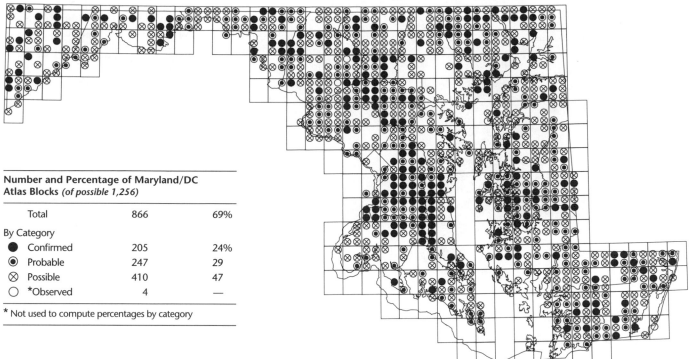

Number and Percentage of Maryland/DC Atlas Blocks (of possible 1,256)

Total	866	69%
By Category		
● Confirmed	205	24%
◉ Probable	247	29
⊗ Possible	410	47
○ *Observed	4	—

* Not used to compute percentages by category

Atlas Distribution, 1983–1987

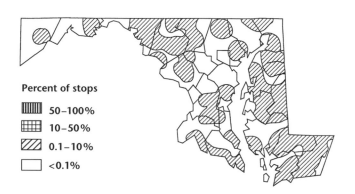

Percent of stops

▥ 50–100%
▦ 10–50%
▧ 0.1–10%
▢ <0.1%

Relative Abundance, 1982–1989

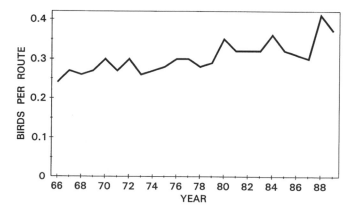

Breeding Distribution, 1958

The Red-tailed Hawk was widely and evenly recorded. It was generally not found in the wooded expanses of western Maryland or in most of the urbanized Baltimore-Washington corridor. Other absences may be the result of low numbers and the early hours of miniroute coverage.

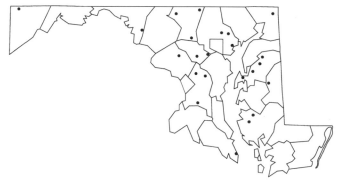

Maryland BBS Trend Graph, 1966–1989

American Kestrel

Falco sparverius

The American Kestrel is one of the smallest and most widespread birds of prey in North America and is Maryland's most common falcon. It is frequently observed hunting along roadsides from an exposed perch or while hovering. Unlike other Maryland falcons, American Kestrels nest in cavities and feed primarily on insects—especially grasshoppers, beetles, and crickets—and on small mammals (May 1935).

Formerly known as the Sparrow Hawk (AOU 1957), the American Kestrel has long been considered a fairly common year-round resident throughout Maryland and DC (Coues and Prentiss 1862, 1883; Kirkwood 1895; Cooke 1908, 1929; Stewart and Robbins 1958). Some regional differences in abundance have been noted, however. Eifrig (1904) found it more common at higher than at lower elevations in Garrett and Allegany counties, and Hampe and Kolb (1947) reported a lack of breeding records from the Eastern Shore and southern Maryland.

American Kestrels use a variety of open to partly wooded habitats. Stewart and Robbins (1958) stated that they use predominantly open agricultural areas in Maryland. Although American Kestrels are found throughout the year, there are strong spring and fall migrations. Spring migration extends from early March through early May (Stewart and Robbins 1958). Fall migration begins in early September and is virtually complete by November (Robbins and Bystrak 1977). In several wintering localities across North America, the sexes use different habitats, with males occurring more frequently in wooded sites and females in more open areas (Koplin 1973; Mills 1976; Smallwood 1987). In Maryland, however, males and females appear to use similar open and edge habitats (D. Smith, unpub. data).

The nesting season in Maryland extends from late March through late August (Stewart and Robbins 1958). Males generally establish the breeding territory, often by engaging in elaborate roller coaster flight displays and frequent calling (Willoughby and Cade 1964). After a female arrives and pairs with the male, they select a nest site. American Kestrels do not construct a nest (Palmer 1988b); they deposit their eggs directly on the floor of the cavity. Preferred sites are old woodpecker cavities, particularly those of Northern Flickers, or natural cavities from 10 to 35 ft (3.0–11 m) above the ground (Roest 1957). Artificial structures, such as nest boxes, are also readily accepted; of 29 Maryland nests, 16 were in nest boxes or other artificial structures (MNRF). Other structures include silos, building ledges, and the eaves and gutters of houses (D. Smith, unpub. data). The high percentage of nests in artificial structures probably reflects the relative ease with which such nests are found and reported rather than their true frequency as compared with natural sites. Heights of 29 Maryland nests (MNRF) range from 14 to 55 ft (4.3–17 m), with a mean of 29 ft (8.8 m). European Starlings and gray squirrels compete with American Kestrels for nest sites; squirrels and snakes may prey on kestrel eggs.

Extreme egg dates for Maryland are 23 March and 4 August, with the peak period in May and early June (MNRF). Completed clutches usually contain 3 to 5 eggs, and the mean for 23 Maryland clutches is 4.5 (MNRF). Incubation, performed primarily by the female, lasts about 30 days (Palmer 1988b). The female does little hunting during incubation, relying instead on the male to supply food early in the nesting cycle. The female begins hunting early in the nestling stage when the demands of the young increase (Palmer 1988b). Young have been found in Maryland and DC nests from 15 May through 5 August (MNRF). Brood sizes in 14 Maryland nests range from 1 to 5, with a mean of 3.1. The young fledge after about 30 days (Palmer 1988b). Only one brood is raised per year, but renesting following nest failure has been reported.

Atlas results indicate that American Kestrels still nest throughout Maryland. However, consistent with the findings of Hampe and Kolb (1947), the numbers of records and "confirmed" nestings were low in Garrett County, on the central Eastern Shore, and especially in the tidewater areas of the lower Eastern Shore and southern Maryland. Sightings of fledged young provided nearly half of the "confirmed" records.

Prospects for American Kestrels in Maryland are generally good because of their preference for edge habitats and their ready use of nest boxes and other man-made structures. BBS data show that the Maryland and Eastern Region populations have been stable from 1966 through 1989. Local and state governments, however, should protect cavity trees and allow only necessary cutting of trees during development or should require reforestation on portions of developed land. These practices will ensure that suitable habitat will remain available for Maryland's smallest falcon.

David R. Smith

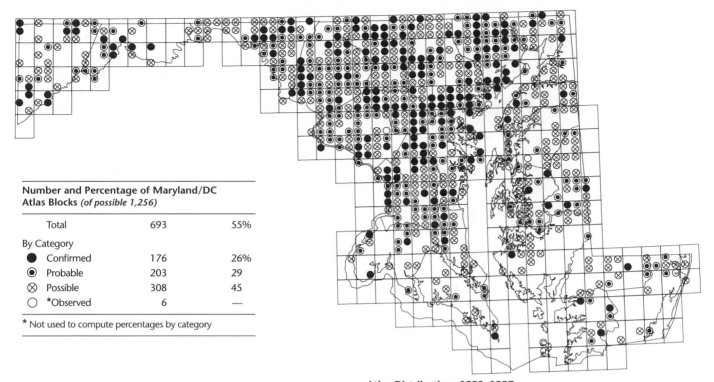

Number and Percentage of Maryland/DC Atlas Blocks *(of possible 1,256)*		
Total	693	55%
By Category		
● Confirmed	176	26%
◉ Probable	203	29
⊗ Possible	308	45
○ *Observed	6	—

* Not used to compute percentages by category

Atlas Distribution, 1983–1987

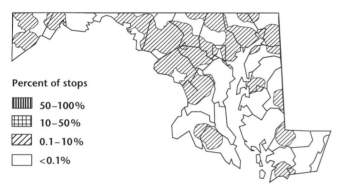

Percent of stops

▦	50–100%
▦	10–50%
▨	0.1–10%
☐	<0.1%

Relative Abundance, 1982–1989

Breeding Distribution, 1958

The American Kestrel was found in small numbers throughout the state, primarily in agricultural areas. It was less frequently recorded on the Coastal Plain and in the extensive woodlands of the western Ridge and Valley Section.

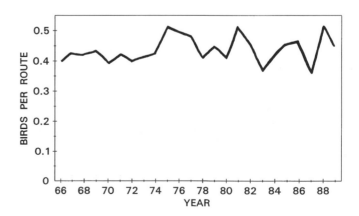

Maryland BBS Trend Graph, 1966–1989

Peregrine Falcon

Falco peregrinus

Once extirpated from the state as a breeding species, the Peregrine Falcon has returned. This endangered species now breeds in Maryland because of the success of a reintroduction program and because DDT and other organochlorine pesticides, which caused reproductive failure, no longer occur in such high concentrations in our environment.

Formerly known as the Duck Hawk, the Peregrine Falcon was never a common breeder. Coues and Prentiss (1883) reported breeding near Harper's Ferry along the Potomac River in West Virginia, and Kirkwood (1895) reported breeding on the Susquehanna River in Pennsylvania. Wimsatt (1939, 1940) observed nesting on Maryland cliffs opposite Harper's Ferry from 1936 through 1939. Stewart and Robbins (1958) reported ten nest sites in Harford, Montgomery, Frederick, Washington, and Allegany counties between 1932 and 1952. The Peregrine Falcon probably disappeared as a breeding bird in Maryland in the early 1950s (Robbins and Boone 1984). In 1970, the species was listed as endangered nationwide by the USFWS. Too few BBS routes sample Peregrine Falcon populations to estimate trends for either the Eastern Region or Maryland.

Reintroduction was accomplished through the cooperative efforts of the Maryland DNR, the USFWS, and the Peregrine Fund. Captive-produced Peregrine Falcon chicks, called *eyases,* were released into the wild through a technique called *hacking.* Two- to three-week-old chicks were substituted for infertile eggs or placed in structures specifically designed for this reintroduction technique.

The first hacking attempt in Maryland was in 1975 on Carroll Island in Baltimore County (Therres et al. 1993). Additional attempts were made at Aberdeen Proving Ground in Harford County and along the Patuxent River in Prince George's County. Because of problems with Great Horned Owls at these sites, hacking efforts between 1980 and 1985 were shifted to special towers erected on salt marshes on the lower Eastern Shore (G. Taylor, pers. comm.). Another 18 young were fostered by Scarlet, the female Peregrine Falcon on the United States Fidelity and Guaranty (USF&G) building in Baltimore City between 1979 and 1983 (J. Barber, pers. comm.).

The reintroduction efforts proved fruitful in 1983 when two pairs attempted nesting (Therres et al. 1993). One pair produced two young on a tower on the lower Eastern Shore. The second pair, which nested on the Chesapeake Bay Bridge in Anne Arundel County, was unsuccessful that year. These birds are thought to be products of the reintroduction program, although their origins are unknown. Peregrine Falcons have nested successfully in Maryland each year since 1983.

Historically, nest sites were on cliff ledges along major rivers. Peregrine Falcons now nest on artificial structures, including salt-marsh towers, large bridges, and tall buildings. This species does not build a nest; boxes or nesting scrapes lined with pea gravel are placed on the artificial structures as nest sites. The eggs are simply laid on the gravel substrate.

Nesting in Maryland occurs between mid-February and early July (Therres 1996). Usually 2 to 4 eggs are laid in March or April. The earliest egg dates in Maryland were reported as around 12 February by Wimsatt (1940); 16 June is the latest recorded egg date (Therres 1996). Over an 11-year period, the average first date for egg laying at the USF&G building in Baltimore City was 19 March (J. Barber, pers. comm.). Eggs hatch after an incubation period of 33 to 35 days (Bent 1938); both adults tend the young for the next several weeks. The female attends young more frequently, while the male does most of the hunting. The eyases fledge after five to seven weeks.

During the Atlas period, six nest sites were documented. Only two were used during all five years, two were occupied for four years, another was used the last two years, and one was occupied only during the last year. All were "confirmed" as either nest with eggs or nest with young. The six sites were the USF&G building and the Francis Scott Key Bridge in Baltimore City, the Chesapeake Bay Bridge in Anne Arundel County, and three Eastern Shore hack towers in Somerset and Dorchester counties. Unconfirmed reports were considered "observations" only because Peregrine Falcons range over large areas when foraging.

Although breeding records were widely scattered, the Peregrine Falcon's breeding range has changed. Historically, this species did not nest on the Coastal Plain of Maryland, and it has not been documented on cliffs in its historic breeding range since its reintroduction. This shift in range is in part a result of the reintroduction methodology. It is hoped that once the limited available nesting sites on the Coastal Plain are occupied, a movement up the Potomac and Susquehanna rivers will return this species to natural cliff ledges.

Protection of suitable nest sites and occupied man-made structures is essential for the continued recovery of this endangered species. Minimizing human disturbance at nest sites during the breeding season will help ensure increases in the Peregrine Falcon population.

Glenn D. Therres

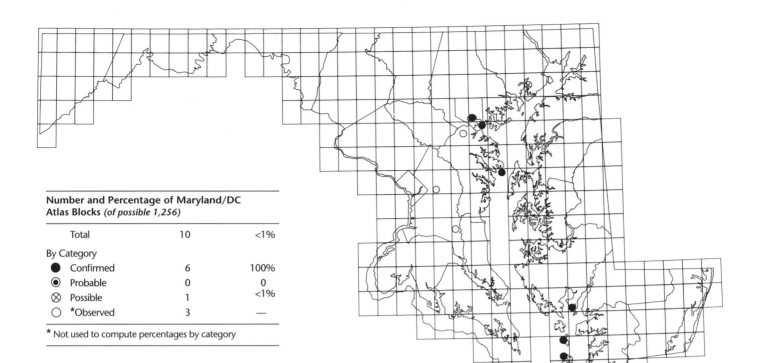

Number and Percentage of Maryland/DC Atlas Blocks *(of possible 1,256)*

Total	10	<1%
By Category		
● Confirmed	6	100%
◉ Probable	0	0
⊗ Possible	1	<1%
○ *Observed	3	—

* Not used to compute percentages by category

Atlas Distribution, 1983–1987

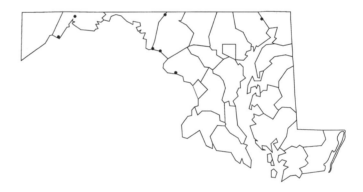

Breeding Distribution, 1958

Ring-necked Pheasant

Phasianus colchicus

The Ring-necked Pheasant, an exotic from Asia, is a popular game bird in Maryland. Although a permanent resident, it is uncommon to rare throughout much of its range. It occurs on agricultural lands, particularly abandoned fields, croplands, hedgerows, and brushy or weedy field margins (Stewart and Robbins 1958), and it can also be found in woodland edges and open woodlands near cultivated areas (AOU 1983). Corn, ragweed, and blackberries rate highest in its diet, which is 90 percent vegetable matter (Martin et al. 1951).

In the early 1800s, European settlers introduced the English Black-necked Pheasant *(P. c. colchicus)* along the East Coast of the United States, but with little success (H. Palmer, pers. comm.). Several species and subspecies of pheasant were introduced in Maryland after 1900, including Japanese Green *(P. versicolor);* Korean Ring-necked *(P. c. karpowi);* Iranian Black-necked *(P. c. talischensis);* Chinese Ring-necked *(P. c. torquatus);* English Ring-necked (a hybrid); melanistic mutants *(P. c.* mut. *tenebrosus);* Silver, Fancy, Reeve's *(Syrmaticus reevesi);* Golden *(Chrysolophus* sp.); Lady Amherst *(Chrysolophus* sp.); Chinese-melanistic mutant crosses; and English-melanistic mutant crosses (DNR Archives). From this genetically mixed ancestry came *Phasianus colchicus,* the Ring-necked Pheasant we have today (Trautman 1982).

The Ring-necked Pheasant's existence in Maryland has been tenuous. In 1847 the Maryland legislature prohibited the hunting of this species between 1 February and 1 September, presumably to protect nesting birds (DNR Archives). In 1870 it was protected in Baltimore County. Kirkwood (1895) made the first mention of an established population in Maryland, reporting a population in Washington County originating from birds released some years earlier. Three birds were recorded by Fisher (1935) on Plummers Island in the Potomac River in Montgomery County. This species was first noted at Loch Raven Reservoir in Baltimore County in 1939; males established breeding territories there in 1951 (Stewart and Robbins 1958). Fletcher et al. (1956) described them as rare permanent residents in the northern half of Caroline County.

The first documented Maryland nest record is from Parson's Island in Queen Anne's County in 1946 by A. Stokes (MNRF). The Maryland Game and Inland Fish Commission's (now DNR) 1946 Annual Report noted that Ring-necked Pheasants were established in only a few isolated pockets along the Pennsylvania line, and Hampe and Kolb (1947) concluded a viable Maryland population could not be maintained. Stewart and Robbins (1958) stated that the Ring-necked Pheasant was unable to maintain itself in numbers, except locally in the Piedmont, Ridge and Valley, and Allegheny Mountain sections. At that time, it occurred most commonly along the Pennsylvania border in Cecil, Harford, Baltimore, Carroll, Frederick, and Washington counties.

Maryland's Ring-necked Pheasant population began declining in the early 1970s (DNR 1983) after the state's release program ceased. The population is now at its lowest level in recent years (P. Jayne, pers. comm.). BBS data from 1966 through 1989 show a highly significant average annual decline of 4.1 percent in the Eastern Region but stable Maryland populations. Maryland data from 1980 through 1989, however, show a highly significant decline of 15.5 percent. Loss of habitat through increased urbanization and changing agricultural practices has been implicated in the decline (Therres 1989).

Nancy Stewart and S. Smith (unpub. data) found that, in Maryland, wintering birds concentrate in shrub wetlands, wooded stream corridors, and wooded swamps adjacent to fields of waste grain or spread manure. Primary wintering areas usually contain some sort of wetland cover (Gates and Hale 1974). Stewart and Smith (unpub. data) found early-season Maryland nests in old fields, shrublands, field margins, hedgerows, and small grain fields; later nests were in hayfields, vineyards, and grassy drainage ditches. The height of herbaceous vegetation at onset of laying was greater than 10 in. (25 cm). The nest is a grass-lined depression on the ground. Ring-necked Pheasants are polygynous (Harrison 1975).

Clutch sizes in nine Maryland nests range from 7 to 17 eggs (MNRF; N. Stewart and S. Smith, unpub. data) The earliest egg date is 1 April (N. Stewart and S. Smith, unpub. data); the latest is 18 July (MNRF). Peak nesting is from mid-April to mid-June. Young out of the nest have been recorded from 13 May to 22 July, but the DNR (unpub. data) estimates that 90 percent of the clutches hatch by mid-June.

Atlas results indicate that the Ring-necked Pheasant occurs at least sparingly throughout the state; it is, however, most common in the Piedmont and Ridge and Valley sections. Of interest is an isolated population on the Eastern Shore in Dorchester County. Historically, the Eastern Shore has been considered to have too warm a climate and not enough soil calcium for the Ring-necked Pheasant to become successfully established (DNR Archives). The extent to which any of these populations is maintained by private releases is unknown. In any case, continuing habitat loss should be a concern.

Scott A. Smith

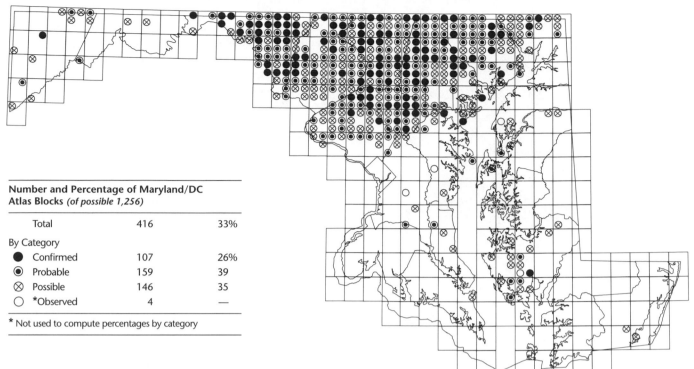

Number and Percentage of Maryland/DC Atlas Blocks *(of possible 1,256)*		
Total	416	33%
By Category		
● Confirmed	107	26%
◉ Probable	159	39
⊗ Possible	146	35
○ *Observed	4	—

* Not used to compute percentages by category

Atlas Distribution, 1983–1987

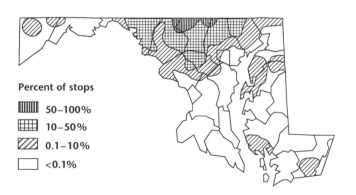

Percent of stops

▥	50–100%
▦	10–50%
▨	0.1–10%
▢	<0.1%

Relative Abundance, 1982–1989

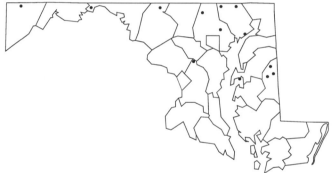

Breeding Distribution, 1958

The Ring-necked Pheasant is most abundant in the northern Piedmont and northeastern Ridge and Valley sections; numbers decline rapidly to the south. The small numbers found in Dorchester and southern Worcester counties, on the central Eastern Shore, and in Garrett County were the result of ongoing releases.

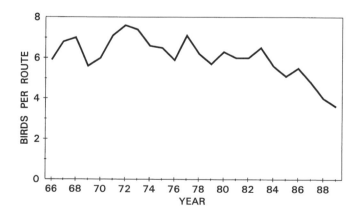

Maryland BBS Trend Graph, 1966–1989

Ruffed Grouse

Bonasa umbellus

The Ruffed Grouse, a popular game bird, is best known for its habit of "drumming" to attract mates and defend territory. The male drums by standing on a log and beating his wings rapidly, creating a deep pulsing noise. It is one of the few birds that communicates primarily by producing sound with its wings rather than its voice.

Coues and Prentiss (1862) considered the Ruffed Grouse not uncommon in the impenetrable laurel brakes in and around DC. Two decades later (Coues and Prentiss 1883), most of the grouse sold in the Washington market came from beyond the limits of DC. Kirkwood (1895) listed the Ruffed Grouse as a common resident and reported young near Ellicott City in Howard County in 1894 and at Vale Summit in Allegany County in 1895. Wetmore and Manville (1968) reported that the last Ruffed Grouse was recorded on Plummers Island in the Potomac River, Montgomery County, in 1913. Cooke (1929) mentioned one below Great Falls in Montgomery County in 1916 and one near Bowie in Prince George's County in 1917. By the 1920s, Ruffed Grouse had disappeared from much of the Piedmont and Coastal Plain (Stewart and Robbins 1958). In Carroll County, Perkins and Allen (1931) found a Ruffed Grouse in 1931, and D. Jones saw one near Westminster in 1953 (Stewart and Robbins 1958). Hampe and Kolb (1947) reported there were no records on the Eastern Shore; however, in 1953 and 1954, a few were reported in the Pocomoke River swamp in Worcester County (Stewart and Robbins 1958). The Ruffed Grouse is still a permanent resident in western Maryland, where it occurs throughout the forested areas.

The Ruffed Grouse is a resident of early successional forests. Throughout much of its North American range, it is closely associated with aspens (Gullion 1977). Aspens are not a dominant forest type in Maryland (Frieswyk and DiGiovanni 1988); thus, Ruffed Grouse are found primarily in second-growth oak forests here, similar to forested habitats used in Pennsylvania (Therres 1982). Stewart and Robbins (1958) characterized the Ruffed Grouse as an edge species in extensive forest tracts, being most common near forest openings or in young stands of cutover second-growth timber. They are often found in association with clearcuts. In Pennsylvania, Sharp (1963) reported that broods use clearcut areas up to eight years after cutting. Therres (1982) found drumming males in clearcuts as early as four years after timber removal, although most of the occupied drumming sites occurred in older second growth. Males usually drum atop a fallen log on the forest floor. Drumming logs are usually located in second-growth forests with dense woody vegetation and are frequently covered by vegetation (Stoll et al. 1979).

In Maryland, the nesting season extends from mid-April to early July (Stewart and Robbins 1958). Nests are on the ground, usually at the base of a tree (Bent 1932). Extreme egg dates are 8 April in Allegany County (DNR, unpub. data) and 20 June in Garrett County (MNRF). Twelve Maryland nests show a range in clutch size from 3 to 19 eggs (mean of 11.0). The larger clutch sizes (12–19 eggs) were found in May; smaller clutches (3–8 eggs) found in June may have been renesting attempts. Only one brood is attempted each year (Bent 1932). The incubation period is 23 days (Bump et al. 1947), and the young are precocial. Most (86%) of the "confirmed" Atlas records were of downy young.

Atlas results show that Ruffed Grouse are still found throughout the forested areas of western Maryland. Their absence in the Hagerstown and Frederick valleys is probably due to lack of forest rather than inadequate Atlas coverage. In Pennsylvania, Ruffed Grouse were found along the Susquehanna River near the Maryland border (Brauning 1992). Although breeding was not documented along the Susquehanna River in Maryland, a flock of six was reported in Harford County on the Rock Run CBC in 1986 (Ringler 1987a). As this species is basically nonmigratory, a small population probably exists there but was undetected by Atlas observers. BBS data from 1966 through 1989 show stable populations in the Eastern Region; data are too few to detect a trend for Maryland.

The Ruffed Grouse's future in Maryland looks good, provided western Maryland remains heavily forested. Grouse depend on second growth, so there is no conflict with timber management in that region. In the future, Ruffed Grouse may become established in other areas of their former range. In 1990 and 1991, the DNR (unpub. data) released wild-trapped Ruffed Grouse in Charles County in an attempt to reestablish a Coastal Plain population. Some young were raised and a few birds were still there in 1995.

Glenn D. Therres

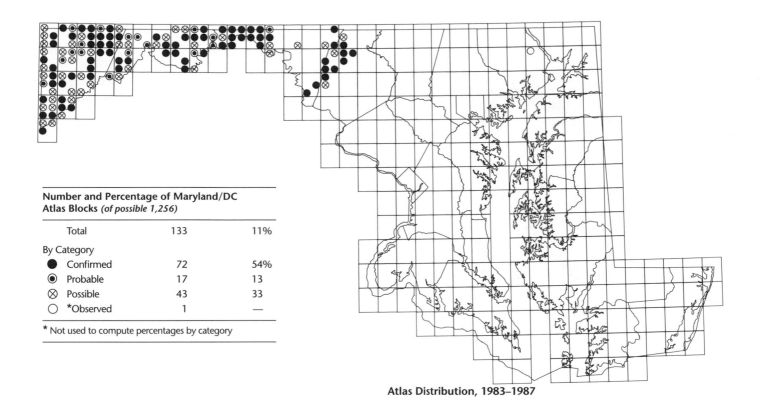

Number and Percentage of Maryland/DC Atlas Blocks *(of possible 1,256)*

Total	133	11%
By Category		
● Confirmed	72	54%
◉ Probable	17	13
⊗ Possible	43	33
○ *Observed	1	—

* Not used to compute percentages by category

Atlas Distribution, 1983–1987

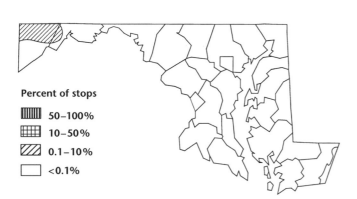

Percent of stops

▦	50–100%
▦	10–50%
▨	0.1–10%
☐	<0.1%

Relative Abundance, 1982–1989

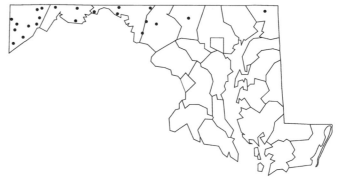

Breeding Distribution, 1958

Ruffed Grouse drumming and courtship typically occur early in the season before miniroutes are run. Grouse were missed on miniroutes in most of their range in Maryland. Roadside surveys do not adequately sample grouse habitat.

Wild Turkey

Meleagris gallopavo

The Wild Turkey is the largest and most colorful upland game bird in Maryland. It is a common permanent resident throughout the forests of Garrett, Allegany, and Washington counties and is locally common in 13 other counties (DNR, unpub. data). During precolonial and colonial times, Wild Turkeys were abundant and widely distributed in Maryland, but they began to decline as land was cleared by early settlers (Shugars 1978). Although market hunting contributed to this decline, the major cause was habitat loss from land clearing. By the last half of the nineteenth century, the Wild Turkey was largely extirpated from most of its original range and was found in only a few areas in the western counties. It disappeared from Montgomery County in 1894 and Frederick County in 1900 (Stewart and Robbins 1958).

The first management effort was a closed hunting season in Garrett County from 1920 through 1933 (Shugars 1978). In 1925 a program of importation and release of game farm birds was begun, and in 1930, it was converted to a program of game farm propagation and release. Between 1930 and 1971, pen-reared birds were released in Garrett, Allegany, Washington, Frederick, Anne Arundel, Harford, Dorchester, Somerset, and Worcester counties. The number released annually varied from 15 to 3,610. The program was terminated in 1971 after these birds failed to establish self-sustaining populations.

Other eastern states, suffering similar declines, also tried reintroduction programs that failed. It was not until wild, live-trapped Wild Turkeys were relocated that reintroduction programs began to show positive results. This effort began in Maryland in 1966 (Shugars 1978). In 1979 an intensive effort to reintroduce wild birds into the former range in Maryland began (DNR, unpub. data). Since that time, releases appear to have successfully established populations in all of the Eastern Shore counties except Talbot. Release programs continue in Baltimore, Carroll, Charles, and Howard counties (J. Shugars, pers. comm.). Some of these releases were too recent to be detected by Atlas fieldwork.

Wild Turkey habitat is not easily defined or quantified because this species is adapting to areas formerly considered unsuitable. Its primary need seems to be sufficient forest for foraging and cover, but the adaptability of the bird has exceeded all expectations (T. Mathews, pers. obs.). The early view that Wild Turkeys were wilderness birds that avoided human encroachment has given way to the realization that, provided appropriate habitat, they readily accept the proximity of people.

Wild Turkeys have a varied diet consisting mainly of seeds and wild fruits, including acorns, nuts, leaves, and buds, but also insects, snails, and spiders (Martin et al. 1951). Wild Turkeys nest on the ground, usually in fairly dense brush, vines, tangles, deep grass, or fallen tree tops (Bent 1932). Where concealing vegetation is unavailable, they will nest on the bare forest floor, usually against a tree trunk or beside a bush.

Extreme egg dates for Maryland are 28 April and 15 July (DNR, unpub. data). Clutch sizes range from 8 to 20, but 10 to 15 eggs are more typical (Bent 1932; Bull 1974). Occasionally, more than one female may lay eggs in the same nest, resulting in much larger clutches (Bent 1932). No clutch-size data are available for Maryland. The hen scratches a shallow depression on the ground and lays her first egg while standing. She then places a few dry leaves over the egg and departs (Bent 1932). A new egg is laid every day until the clutch is complete; the nest is built by a gradual accumulation of debris, rather than by a deliberate effort (Hewitt 1967). Incubation, by the female only (Bent 1932), begins after the last egg is laid and lasts an average of 28 days (Williams 1981). In Maryland, the peak hatching period is about the third week of May (J. Shugars, pers. comm.). The earliest record of young in Maryland is 19 May (DNR, unpub. data). If the first nest fails, second and even third attempts are usually made (Hewitt 1967). The young are precocial and capable of traveling considerable distances after a few days (Bent 1932). No data on brood sizes are available.

Wild Turkey populations in Maryland continue to expand. Maryland is approximately 43 percent forested (Frieswyk and DiGiovanni 1988), and the DNR (unpub. data) estimates that there are 3,261 sq mi (8,446 sq km) of Wild Turkey habitat in Maryland. About 1,398 sq mi (3,621 sq km) of that habitat are at present occupied. The rest of the potential range will be filled by expansion of more recently introduced populations or by continued transplants.

Population estimates for Garrett, Allegany, and western Washington counties are 5 to 8 birds per sq mi (1.9–3.1 per sq km) of suitable habitat (DNR, unpub. data). In the Blue Ridge Mountains and the Piedmont Section, the populations vary from 12 to 15 birds per sq mi (4.6–5.8 per sq km) of suitable habitat. In the introduced population in Calvert

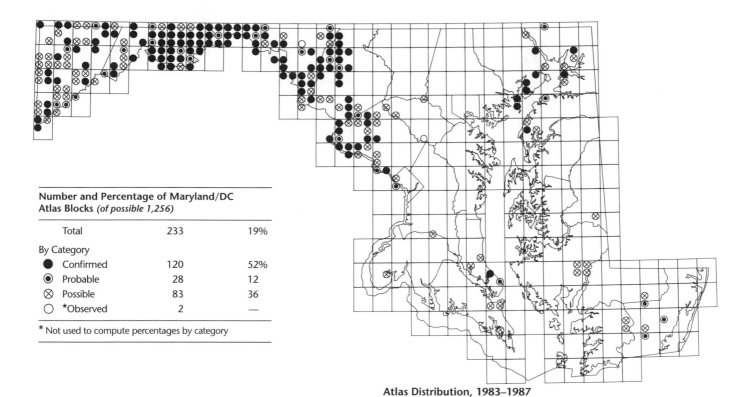

Number and Percentage of Maryland/DC Atlas Blocks *(of possible 1,256)*

	Total	233	19%
	By Category		
●	Confirmed	120	52%
◉	Probable	28	12
⊗	Possible	83	36
○	*Observed	2	—

* Not used to compute percentages by category

Atlas Distribution, 1983–1987

Breeding Distribution, 1958

County, the density has reached 8 to 10 birds per sq mi (3.1–3.9 per sq km). Most introduced Coastal Plain populations are continuing to expand. It is anticipated that Wild Turkeys will inhabit all Maryland counties by 1993 (DNR, unpub. data). BBS data from 1966 through 1989 show an indication of an increase in the Eastern Region; Maryland data are too few to estimate a state trend.

Atlas fieldworkers found Wild Turkeys in nearly every block in Allegany and western Washington counties and in at least half the blocks in Garrett County and the Catoctin

Mountains of Frederick County. In the Piedmont, they were most frequently found near the Potomac River. On the Coastal Plain, most observations were near the Chesapeake Bay or in the Nanticoke and Pocomoke watersheds. Observations of fledged broods comprised 88 percent of "confirmed" records. The future of Wild Turkeys in Maryland seems bright.

Thomas P. Mathews

Northern Bobwhite

Colinus virginianus

The Northern Bobwhite, named for its well-known, clearly whistled *bob-white* call, is a relatively common but declining permanent resident throughout most of Maryland. It is a popular upland game bird and is most abundant in southern Maryland and on the Eastern Shore. Smaller populations occur in the Piedmont and Ridge and Valley sections. It is uncommon in the mountains of western Maryland (Stewart and Robbins 1958). Maximum numbers are found in areas where field abandonment has resulted in grassy, weedy, and brushy overgrowth and before woodland stages of plant succession predominate (DNR, unpub. data). Ragweed, lespedeza, corn, and smartweed are among the most frequent foods, but many insects, spiders, snails, and other invertebrates are eaten in summer (Martin et al. 1951).

The first reported Maryland sighting of a Northern Bobwhite was in 1634 by A. White, a member of the Leonard Calvert party aboard the ships the *Ark* and the *Dove* (DNR 1983). One of the earliest nest records was reported by Farnham (1891) in DC. Numerous historical accounts report this species as common in early times (Coues and Prentiss 1862, 1883; Kirkwood 1895; Cooke 1929). Eifrig (1904) reported that the western Maryland population had been severely affected by adverse winter conditions some years earlier but had been supplemented by released birds.

Since the mid-1800s, Northern Bobwhites have been managed as upland game birds in Maryland. In 1847, legislation was enacted to limit the hunting season; season length and bag limits have periodically been changed since then (DNR 1983). The first propagation farm was built in 1919 at Gwynnbrook, Baltimore County. Birds raised there were released in an attempt to establish new populations for hunting. Game refuges were established as unhunted reservoirs. The DNR stocking was discontinued in 1971.

Northern Bobwhites prefer areas where approximately half of the ground is exposed and half contains upright vegetation (Rosene 1969), such as agricultural areas, fallow fields, upland brush areas, weedy pastures, recently cutover forests, and woodland edges. Roseberry and Klimstra (1984) reported that areas of intensive agriculture were less desir-

able but farms with hedgerows or unmowed grassy roadsides were heavily used. The highest breeding density reported from Maryland is 5 territorial males per 100 acres (40.5 ha) in field and edge habitat in Baltimore County (Hampe et al. 1947). Burger and Linduska (1967) demonstrated the value of hedgerows in a study at Remington Farms, Kent County. During the past 30 years, the quantity and quality of Northern Bobwhite habitat in Maryland has decreased. The direct impact of habitat loss due to development and urbanization, along with indirect effects of clean farming and widespread use of pesticides, have probably contributed to decreased populations in many parts of the state (P. Jayne, pers. comm.).

The breeding season in Maryland extends from late April to mid-October (Robbins and Bystrak 1977). Northern Bobwhites construct well-concealed grass nests on the ground in grassy or weedy areas, usually within 50 ft (15 m) of brushy cover (DNR 1983). Both sexes build the nest (Stokes 1967), which is typically placed in a tussock of dead or living grass (Harrison 1975), frequently along an edge between grass and bare soil (Rosene 1969).

Maryland egg dates range from 21 April to 14 October, with peaks in early June and early August (MNRF). Clutch sizes from 48 nests (MNRF) range from 6 to 25 (mean of 14.0). Incubation, performed primarily by the female, lasts 23 days (Bent 1932). Downy young have been reported in Maryland from 7 June to 25 September (MNRF). Brood sizes in 49 nests range from 4 to 19 (mean of 9.7). The precocial young leave the nest immediately after hatching. Family groups remain together until early fall, when they form winter coveys. Predators, agricultural activities, and wet weather cause the loss of 60 to 70 percent of nests (DNR 1983). Renesting after a clutch is lost is typical (Stoddard 1931). Northern Bobwhites are prolific, except in years when an unusually wet spring and early summer interfere with nesting. Under normal conditions, only 20 to 30 percent of the birds need to survive the winter to maintain a healthy population (DNR 1983). The severe winter of 1977–78 caused a major decline, from which this species has not recovered. BBS data from 1966 through 1989 show a highly significant average annual decline of 3.4 percent in the Eastern Region. Maryland data show a highly significant average annual decline of 3.5 percent from 1966 through 1989; the sharp decline since 1986 cannot be explained by winter weather conditions.

Atlas data show the Northern Bobwhite's continued presence over most of Maryland, although it is absent from much of Garrett and Allegany counties. Low winter food supplies and insufficient cover are limiting factors (Schroeder 1985). This species still breeds in most of its original range, but populations are greatly reduced. The causes seem to be occasional severe weather and loss of habitat. Between 1969 and 1978, 168,329 acres (68,173 ha) of farmland were taken out of production in Maryland (DNR, unpub. data). Most of Maryland's upland agricultural areas are privately owned; therefore, reversal of this decline lies primarily in the hands of landowners.

Thomas P. Mathews

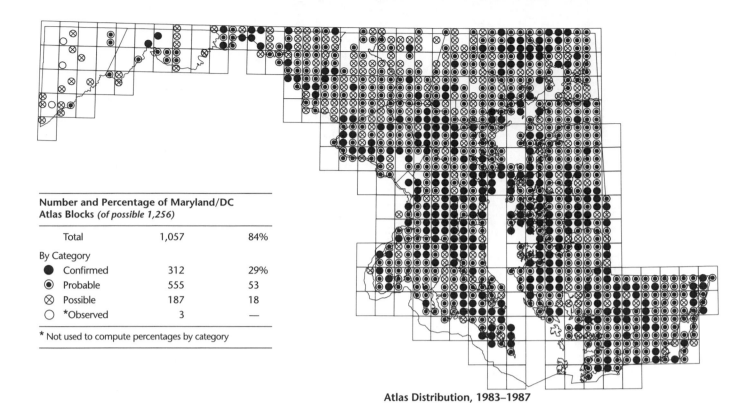

Atlas Distribution, 1983–1987

Number and Percentage of Maryland/DC Atlas Blocks *(of possible 1,256)*

Total	1,057	84%
By Category		
● Confirmed	312	29%
◉ Probable	555	53
⊗ Possible	187	18
○ *Observed	3	—

* Not used to compute percentages by category

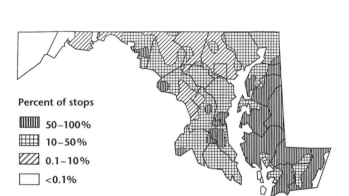

Percent of stops

▥	50–100%
▦	10–50%
▨	0.1–10%
☐	<0.1%

Relative Abundance, 1982–1989

Breeding Distribution, 1958

The concentration of Northern Bobwhites generally decreases from southeast to west, with the highest concentrations found in the agricultural areas on the Eastern Shore. West of the Chesapeake Bay, numbers are lowest in Garrett County, in the Ridge and Valley and northern Piedmont sections, and in urban and suburban areas.

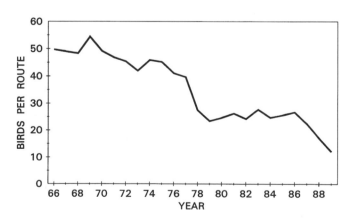

Maryland BBS Trend Graph, 1966–1989

Black Rail

Laterallus jamaicensis

The Black Rail's small size, secretive nature, and nocturnal habits make it one of the most enigmatic and poorly known species in North America. On the rare occasions when seen, it is most often darting through the grass like a mouse. In Maryland, Black Rails breed most commonly in the extensive tidal marshes of Dorchester, Somerset, and Worcester counties. There are also scattered summer records for eight other Maryland Coastal Plain counties and for DC (H. Wierenga, unpub. data). Currently, the DNR lists Black Rail as a species in need of conservation.

The Black Rail, discovered on the island of Jamaica in 1760, was probably a wintering bird (Ripley 1977). It was not found in the United States until 1836. The first DC record was for a September 1861 sighting by Coues and Prentiss (1862); the first Maryland specimen was taken at Glymount, Charles County, in October 1868 (Cooke 1929). A male collected near Washington, DC, on 6 June 1879 furnished the first area breeding-season record (Cooke 1929). The first Maryland nest, with two eggs, was recorded by A. Nelson and F. Uhler on 16 June 1931 in the Elliott Island marshes in Dorchester County (Stewart and Robbins 1958). The Black Rail is considered to be a fairly common but local breeder and transient in tidewater Dorchester County; it is rare and local elsewhere in tidewater areas of the Eastern and Western Shore sections. The highest one-night count in Maryland is of more than 100 birds calling in the Elliott Island marshes on 2 June 1954.

The first spring migrants return from their Gulf Coast wintering grounds (AOU 1983) in early April (Robbins and Bystrak 1977), and many birds apparently depart by mid-October. Palmer (1909) reported that more were shot by hunters in the Patuxent River marshes in October than in September. A DNR (unpub. data) study in winter 1992, however, discovered several Black Rails lingering through at least February on the lower Eastern Shore. This discovery, and two earlier winter reports from Dorchester County (Robbins 1974; Reese 1975c), raise the possibility that a few Black Rails may be permanent residents in Maryland. They are known to winter regularly in small numbers as far north as coastal North Carolina (J. Fussell, pers. comm.).

Black Rail nesting habitats include wet meadows, grassy fields, and a wide variety of fresh, brackish, and salt marshes (Ripley 1977). In Maryland, the preferred habitat appears to be extensive marshes dominated by saltmeadow cordgrass, smooth cordgrass, and seashore saltgrass dotted with scattered clumps of taller vegetation such as cattail, needlerush, or Olney's bulrush (H. Wierenga, pers. obs.). In 1990, Black Rails used wet, grassy fields at Carroll Island in Baltimore County and wet, grassy sewage treatment impoundments at Easton in Talbot County (DNR, unpub. data).

The nest, a tightly woven cup, is buried deep in the dense vegetation and is typically covered with a wispy canopy of grasses (Ripley 1977). Egg dates from eight Maryland nests, all from Elliott Island, range from 20 May (Stewart and Robbins 1958) to 8 August (W. Burt, unpub. data). Clutches average 6 to 10 eggs (Terres 1980), although one complete clutch from Elliott Island contained only 5 eggs (W. Burt, unpub. data). Three other Maryland nests contained clutch sizes of 7, 8 (W. Burt, unpub. data), and 8 (R. Edwards, unpub. data). Both sexes assist with incubation, which for two Maryland nests lasted no more than 13 days (R. Edwards, pers. comm., W. Burt, unpub. data). The tiny, black, downy chicks leave the nest almost immediately after hatching (Burt 1987). How long the broods remain intact or are dependent on their parents is not known. Their diet is not well known but includes aquatic insects, isopods, and the seeds of aquatic plants (Weske 1969; Ripley 1977).

There were only 18 records for Black Rails during the Atlas period. Of the 5 "confirmed" records, 1 was of fledged young at Sandy Point State Park in Anne Arundel County, 1 was of distraction display and peeping chicks at Black Marsh in Baltimore County, and 3 were of nests with eggs or young at Elliott Island. Because Black Rails are seldom seen, vocalize mostly late at night, and have several calls that are largely unknown to observers, they were undoubtedly underrecorded by the standard atlas techniques. A study conducted by the DNR (unpub. data) in 1990 and 1991 used taped calls to elicit responses and found greater numbers of Black Rails ranging over a wider area than during the Atlas project. The DNR survey found Black Rails in 40 Atlas blocks, all but 3 on the lower Eastern Shore, where the study was concentrated. This is more than double those recorded during the Atlas fieldwork, and it clearly shows that alternative techniques should be used to survey and assess populations of secretive marsh species. Too few BBS routes sample Black Rail populations to estimate a trend for either the Eastern Region or Maryland.

Conservation efforts for Black Rails should concentrate on protecting the marsh habitat necessary for their existence. Questionable marsh-management techniques, such as ditching, spraying, draining, burning, and impounding, certainly must exact a toll on Black Rails and other marsh species.

Harold L. Wierenga

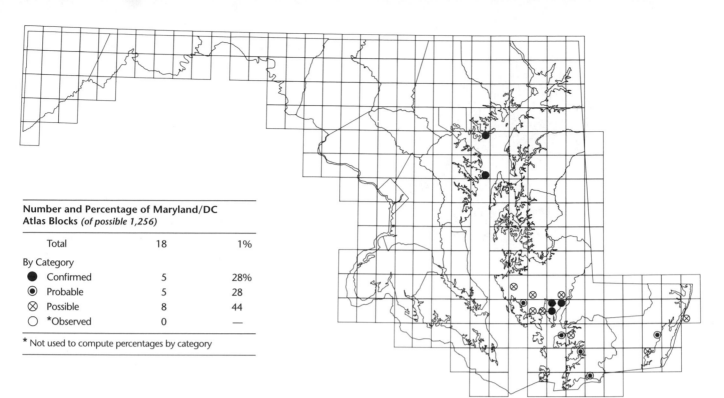

Number and Percentage of Maryland/DC Atlas Blocks (of possible 1,256)

	Total	18	1%
By Category			
●	Confirmed	5	28%
◉	Probable	5	28
⊗	Possible	8	44
○	*Observed	0	—

* Not used to compute percentages by category

Atlas Distribution, 1983–1987

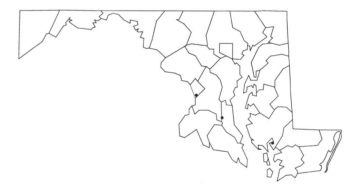

Breeding Distribution, 1958

Clapper Rail

Rallus longirostris

The Clapper Rail is the salt-marsh counterpart of the closely related King Rail. The two are treated as a single species by some ornithologists (Ripley 1977) and are known to hybridize (Meanley 1985). Clapper Rails are common summer and uncommon winter residents in the coastal marshes of Worcester County and in the saltier marshes of the lower Chesapeake Bay. Questions persist concerning their distribution and breeding status on the western shore of the Chesapeake Bay.

The Maryland distribution of Clapper Rails seems largely unchanged over the past century, although numbers have undoubtedly been reduced by habitat loss; no quantitative data exist for comparison, however. Kirkwood (1895) described them as fairly common in Maryland salt marshes and reported three individuals shot in the Patapsco River marsh near Baltimore on 17 May 1893. Although there have been a few reports north of the normal breeding range in the Chesapeake Bay, including a spring bird at Fort Smallwood in northern Anne Arundel County (H. Wierenga, pers. comm.), the 1893 Patapsco River record cited by Kirkwood (1895) is extraordinary. Confusion between Clapper Rails and King Rails persists to the present time, and even birds in the hand may be misidentified. Stewart and Robbins (1958) described the Clapper Rail as common in coastal Worcester County and uncommon and local in the tidewater areas of Somerset County and the fringe marshes of the lower Chesapeake Bay, including southern St. Mary's County on the Western Shore.

Along the Atlantic Coast, including Maryland, Clapper Rails strongly favor marshes dominated by smooth cordgrass, especially in those areas where stands taller than 3 ft (0.9 m) meet stands less than 6 in. (15 cm) (Meanley 1985). This juxtaposition is most often found along tidal guts. Clapper Rails are also found in marshes dominated by saltmeadow cordgrass, rush, seashore saltgrass, and glasswort (Stewart 1951; Meanley 1985). Their diet consists of fish,

crabs, toads, crayfish, aquatic insects, and seeds (Ripley 1977; Meanley 1985).

Nests are usually placed in taller vegetation (Ripley 1977); heights above the ground or water for 37 Maryland nests (MNRF) range from 0 to 36 in. (0–91 cm), with a mean of 8.2 in. (21 cm). Maryland egg dates range from 14 May to 20 July, but almost all reports came from two observers whose efforts were concentrated in late May and early June (MNRF). Normal clutch sizes range from 5 to 12, with 7 to 11 being most common (Meanley 1985). Clutch sizes for 36 nests range from 3 to 13, with a mean of 7.6 (MNRF). Half the nests had 8 or more eggs. At nearby Chincoteague, Virginia, Stewart and Meanley (1960) found that complete first clutches averaged 9.0 eggs and second clutches 5.6 eggs. Because young leave the nest almost immediately after hatching (Meanley 1985), few nests with chicks are reported. There are scattered reports of adults with small young, with extreme dates of 6 June and 13 August (MNRF). The incubation period lasts about 20 days, and young remain dependent on adults for an additional 9 to 10 weeks (Meanley 1985). The breeding season in Maryland must stretch from early May through at least late August. Although Clapper Rails are at least partly migratory, some remain in the salt marshes of Maryland throughout the winter. Little is known about the timing and the extent of the migration. Winter populations may be augmented by birds from farther north.

Atlas data show the distribution to be similar to that shown by Stewart and Robbins (1958), although no birds were found during the Atlas period in southern St. Mary's County, where the King Rail was recorded. A DNR survey in 1991 found Clapper Rails to be fairly numerous at Point Lookout and St. George Island, both in southern St. Mary's County (DNR, unpub. data). The only reports from the Western Shore during the Atlas period are from Sandy Point State Park in Anne Arundel County, where a mixed Clapper–King Rail pair attempted to breed, and from Patuxent River Naval Air Station at the mouth of the Patuxent River in northern St. Mary's County, although no evidence of breeding was obtained (K. Rambo, pers. comm.). The northern limit on the Eastern Shore is in southeastern Talbot County. Clapper Rails are common to abundant in the marshes of southern Dorchester and Somerset counties and in coastal Worcester County. Recent DNR (unpub. data) marsh-bird surveys support the Atlas results, although birds were found at more locations. The overlap zone between King Rails and Clapper Rails in Maryland seems to be on the lower Eastern Shore but has not yet been adequately defined. BBS data from 1966 through 1989 show a stable population in the Eastern Region; Maryland data are too few to estimate a state trend.

The greatest threats to Clapper Rails in Maryland are the loss of the brackish and salt-marsh habitat they require and the degradation of marshes by ditching and draining for mosquito control. Preservation of salt-marsh habitat is crucial if this species is to remain a part of the state's breeding avifauna.

Eirik A. T. Blom

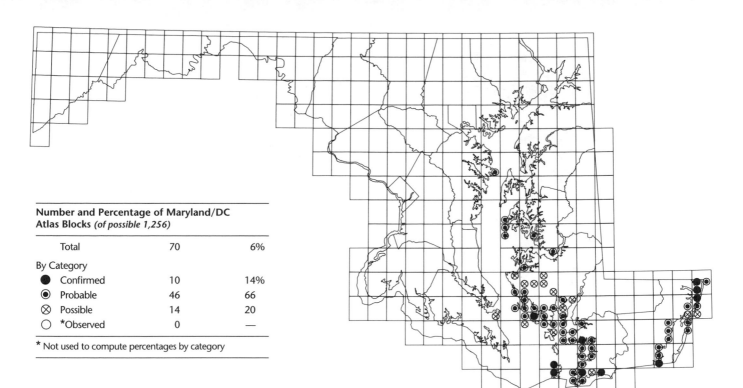

**Number and Percentage of Maryland/DC
Atlas Blocks** *(of possible 1,256)*

Total	70	6%
By Category		
● Confirmed	10	14%
◉ Probable	46	66
⊗ Possible	14	20
○ *Observed	0	—

* Not used to compute percentages by category

Atlas Distribution, 1983–1987

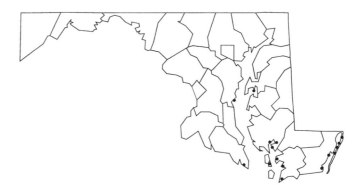

Breeding Distribution, 1958

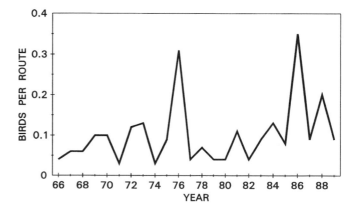

Maryland BBS Trend Graph, 1966–1989

Clapper Rail 125

King Rail

Rallus elegans

The King Rail is the freshwater counterpart of the salt-marsh dwelling Clapper Rail; some authorities consider them a single species (AOU 1983). Although information is sketchy, this resident of fresh and brackish marshes has probably declined as a breeding bird during the twentieth century, and its range in Maryland appears to have contracted.

Most early writers knew the King Rail from only one or two local records, but Kirkwood (1895) referred to it as a fairly common summer resident of fresh and brackish marshes. He cited breeding season records from only two locations: the Patapsco River marsh in Baltimore County and Tolchester in Kent County. Stewart and Robbins (1958) called the King Rail fairly common in the tidewater areas of the Eastern Shore, Western Shore, and Upper Chesapeake sections, and uncommon and local in the Piedmont and interior of the Eastern Shore. They mapped it as occurring in freshwater streams and ponds around the Chesapeake Bay, along the Pocomoke River, and at West Ocean City in coastal Worcester County. Meanley (1969) recorded a high breeding density of 40 territorial males per 100 acres (40.5 ha) in a mixture of shrub swamp and marsh in PWRC impoundments in 1965.

Confusion with the Clapper Rail has always clouded the question of the King Rail's status and distribution in Maryland. Few, if any, of the vocalizations of the two species are reliably diagnostic (H. Wierenga, pers. comm.), and plumage differences in the range of overlap are subtle (Ripley 1977). Hybridization between the two has been documented (Ripley 1977) and has been observed in Maryland (H. Wierenga, pers. comm.).

The following information is from Meanley's (1969) study of the King Rail. The habitat in Maryland is primarily fresh and brackish marshes dominated by narrow-leaved cattail, Olney's bulrush, switchgrass, arrow arum, and especially big cordgrass. King Rails prefer to breed in areas of high marsh with scattered shrubs and small trees. Spring migrants are thought to return from the southeastern United States in early April, but some portion of the population probably overwinters. Fall migration patterns are poorly known, but summering birds left PWRC in September. King Rails in the tidal marshes of the Patuxent River feed on killifish, crayfish, dragonfly nymphs, snails, grasshoppers, crickets, and seeds of marsh plants.

Nest heights were recorded for only two nests in the MNRF: one was 5 in. (13 cm) up in common rush, and one was 3 ft (0.9 m) up in a swamp rosemallow. Meanley (1969) reported that nest height above water was related to water depth, with heights ranging up to 1 ft (0.3 m) above the high-tide mark in coastal areas and as low as 2 in. (5 cm) above water in nontidal areas. The earliest of 17 Maryland egg dates is 18 May and the latest is 5 July. Clutch sizes in 14 nest records (MNRF) range from 6 to 12 (mean of 7.9). Seven broods, ranging in size from 1 to 8, have been reported in Maryland from 26 May to 20 July (MNRF). Meanley (1969) reported that the most common clutch sizes are 10 to 12, although he has seen complete clutches of 6 eggs in Maryland. Incubation, by both sexes, lasts 21 or 22 days (Meanley 1969).

Atlas results show three King Rail concentration areas: the extensive marshes of the upper Choptank and upper Nanticoke rivers on the Eastern Shore and the Patuxent River marshes in southern Maryland. These areas received special attention during Atlas fieldwork. Coverage of the marshes of the upper Chesapeake Bay was fairly good, but few birds were found. Although coverage was less intense in southern Maryland, only one bird was found in the marshes of the Potomac River. King Rails are known to breed in the freshwater impoundments of Deal Island and Fairmount WMAs in Somerset County (H. Wierenga, pers. comm.). Inland nesting is apparently very rare and irregular. In addition to the nests from PWRC (Meanley 1969), there are older reports from Hughes Hollow in Montgomery County and from the Lilypons Water Gardens in Frederick County (MNRF), as well as scattered summer reports without evidence of breeding.

Until more intensive studies are conducted, the true status of the King Rail in Maryland cannot be determined. DNR studies (unpub. data) conducted in 1990 and 1991 confirmed the King Rail's occurrence in inland marshes on the Eastern Shore but failed to find them in the Upper Chesapeake, in southern Maryland, or in Worcester County. BBS data from 1966 through 1989 show a highly significant average annual decline of 3.1 percent in the Eastern Region; however, continental populations are stable. Data are too few to estimate a trend for Maryland. Preserving tidal and nontidal fresh and brackish marshes is crucial if the King Rail is to maintain a breeding population in Maryland.

Eirik A. T. Blom

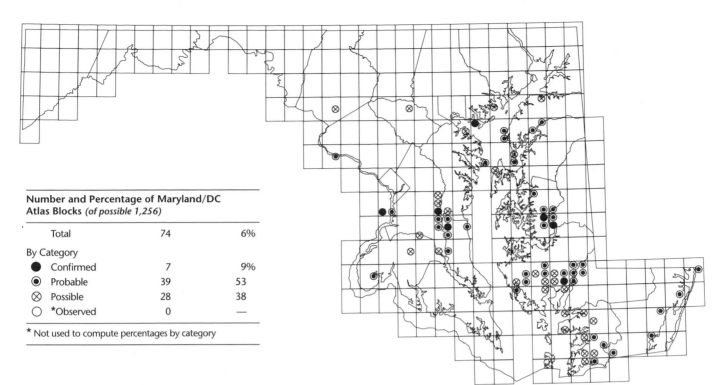

Number and Percentage of Maryland/DC Atlas Blocks *(of possible 1,256)*

Total		74	6%
By Category			
●	Confirmed	7	9%
◉	Probable	39	53
⊗	Possible	28	38
○	*Observed	0	—

* Not used to compute percentages by category

Atlas Distribution, 1983–1987

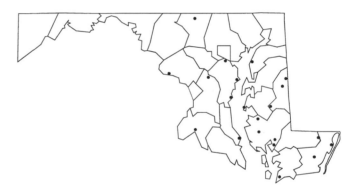

Breeding Distribution, 1958

Virginia Rail

Rallus limicola

Although the Virginia Rail is the most widespread and common rail breeding in Maryland, it is as secretive and difficult to observe as other rails and is far more often heard than seen. Selections from its large repertoire of songs and calls are most frequently heard late in the day or at night (H. Wierenga, pers. obs.). The Virginia Rail uses a wider variety of breeding habitats than Maryland's other rails and occurs in most salt, brackish, and fresh marshes on the Coastal Plain and in scattered fresh marshes and wet meadows throughout the rest of Maryland.

Virginia Rails breed across North America from southern Canada south through most of the United States, except in the southeastern states. In fall, they migrate out of the northern portions of their breeding range to the warmer marshes of the Atlantic, Pacific, and Gulf coasts (Ripley 1977). In Maryland, which is near the southeastern edge of their breeding range (AOU 1983), many may be permanent residents. The first recorded Virginia Rail for Maryland was one shot near Baltimore in late December 1879 (Kirkwood 1895). Coues and Prentiss (1862, 1883) described it as a migrant around DC. Although it was reported by Richmond (1888) in DC during the breeding season and was undoubtedly breeding there, the first nest (with eggs) was not recorded until 3 June 1917 (Cooke 1929). Stewart and Robbins (1958) described the Virginia Rail as a common breeder and transient in the tidewater areas of the Eastern Shore and Upper Chesapeake sections, fairly common and local in the Allegheny Mountain Section and in tidewater areas of the Western Shore Section, and rare in all other sections. They described its winter status as common in the tidewater areas of the Eastern Shore and uncommon in all other tidewater areas on the Coastal Plain. The migration periods are less well known but may extend through April and early May in spring and from late August to early November in the fall (Stewart and Robbins 1958).

The breeding season in Maryland is thought to extend from late April to late August (Stewart and Robbins 1958), but a few individuals probably start sooner and continue later in some years (H. Wierenga, pers. obs.). Virginia Rails usually nest in the wetter portions of tidal marshes, often characterized by three-square, needlerush, narrow-leaved cattail, and other marsh grasses (Stewart and Robbins 1958;

Ripley 1977). Away from tidewater areas, they often choose wet sedge meadows or stands of broad-leaved cattail. Their nest is a loosely woven, well-concealed cup of rather coarse vegetation and is sometimes covered with a grassy canopy (Ripley 1977). It is fastened in a clump of plants from a few inches to 1 ft (0.3 m) above the mud or water (Terres 1980). The eggs, which are buff-colored and irregularly spotted with brown or gray, range from 5 to 12 per clutch.

Extreme egg dates for Maryland are 14 May and 16 August (Stewart and Robbins 1958). In six Maryland nests (MNRF), clutch sizes range from 4 to 9. Incubation lasts 18 to 20 days and is performed by both sexes (Pospichal and Marshall 1954). The black downy chicks leave the nest almost immediately (Townsend 1926), but they are dependent on the adults for food for two to three weeks (Johnson and Dinsmore 1985). Extreme dates for downy young in Maryland are 11 May (MNRF) and 24 July (N. Magnusson and J. Solem, pers. obs.); in seven records, brood sizes range from 1 to 4 (MNRF). Brood sizes are probably underestimated; since many young birds were seen away from nests, it is doubtful that observers saw all the young in any group. Two broods may be attempted each year (Pospichal and Marshall 1954). The diet of Virginia Rails consists largely of larval insects (especially flies) but also includes numerous other items: snails, small fishes, beetles, crayfish, and aquatic plants such as duckweed (Horak 1970).

Atlas results show the Virginia Rail in most of the extensive tidal marshes in the Coastal Plain, with concentrations in Dorchester and Somerset counties and along tidal portions of the Patuxent and Choptank rivers. The few upland records are widely scattered. Only 14 percent of the Atlas records were for "confirmed" breeding. This is understandable because much of the Virginia Rail's habitat is unaccessible, and observation of secretive, largely nocturnal, marsh birds is difficult. An intensive survey of breeding marsh birds, initiated in 1990 by the DNR (unpub. data), found Virginia Rails to be extremely common in many of the lower Eastern Shore marshes and provided evidence that they may be more common and widespread than the Atlas results suggest. The same study found only a few birds in the marshes of the upper Chesapeake Bay, where Stewart and Robbins (1958) listed them as common. Habitat loss and degradation and other human disturbances are the probable causes for the decline.

BBS data from 1966 through 1989 show stable Virginia Rail populations in the Eastern Region; too few data for Maryland exist to estimate a population trend. Only by protecting wetlands can we ensure that the Virginia Rail and other marsh birds will not disappear as breeding species in Maryland.

Harold L. Wierenga

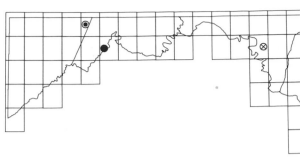

Number and Percentage of Maryland/DC Atlas Blocks *(of possible 1,256)*

	Total	125	10%
By Category			
●	Confirmed	17	14%
◉	Probable	69	55
⊗	Possible	39	31
○	*Observed	0	—

* Not used to compute percentages by category

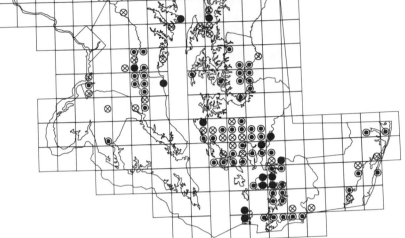

Atlas Distribution, 1983–1987

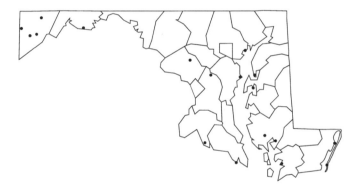

Breeding Distribution, 1958

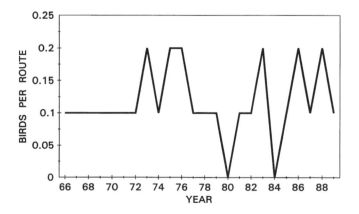

Maryland BBS Trend Graph, 1966–1989

Sora

Porzana carolina

The Sora is one of the most widely distributed and best known of all North American rails and one of the few birds with a common name of native American origin (Choate 1973). A regular migrant, primarily in fresh marshes, it is recorded more frequently in Maryland in fall than spring. Soras are still hunted in Maryland, most commonly in the marshes along the Patuxent River.

The Sora was well known to hunters in the middle of the nineteenth century (Coues and Prentiss 1862). The first breeding season record in Maryland was on 25 July 1893 at North Point, Baltimore County (Kirkwood 1895). The first documented nest with eggs was photographed by W. Fisher on 25 May 1899 in the Bush River marshes, Harford County (Bent 1926). Eifrig (1902b) found many at the "swamp ponds" in Allegany County on 23 and 30 May 1901 but found none during the summer. Stewart and Robbins (1958) considered the Sora a rare and local breeder in the tidewater areas of the Western Shore and Upper Chesapeake sections.

Soras are thought to arrive in Maryland from their wintering grounds in the Caribbean Basin (AOU 1983) as early as late March, and the peak of migration occurs between mid-April and mid-May (Robbins and Bystrak 1977). Nesting habitat includes freshwater marshes, bogs, and swamps with dense stands of cattails, reeds, bulrushes, or sedges. This species is a rare breeder in saltwater habitats (Ripley 1977). Inland, Soras occupy many of the same locations as Virginia Rails; however, Soras typically nest in wetter areas or in areas with deeper water. In Iowa, Johnson and Dinsmore (1985) found that radio-tagged males maintained home ranges of 0.4 acre (0.2 ha), whereas females ranged over 0.5 acre (0.2 ha).

Both adults assist in building the basket nest. They construct it of dead cattails and other vegetation, which is woven around and attached to live plants up to 6 in. (15 cm) above standing water (Bent 1926; Ripley 1977). Clutches av-

erage 10 to 12 eggs (Bent 1926). Incubation is performed by both adults and lasts 18 to 20 days (Walkinshaw 1957). The young are fed invertebrates and aquatic plant seeds for up to 21 days. For adults, animal food, such as beetles, spiders, snails, and crustaceans, predominates in summer; seeds of aquatic plants such as wild rice and bulrush predominate in fall and winter (Martin et al. 1951). Horak (1970) found that the Sora eats much more plant material than the Virginia Rail, with seeds of sedges, grasses, and smartweed ranking highest.

The nesting season in Maryland probably begins in early May. A female with an egg in the oviduct was killed by a dog on 5 May 1899 in the Gunpowder River marsh (Stewart and Robbins 1958). There are only two MNRF nest records: a nest with 7 eggs (plate 84 in Bent 1926) in Harford County on 25 May 1899, and a nest with 3 eggs and 1 young found by B. Meanley on 3 June 1965 at PWRC. The Meanley nest was 3 in. (8 cm) above standing water in a freshwater rush marsh. Fledging occurs 21 to 25 days after hatching (Ehrlich et al. 1988). Fall migration in Maryland is from early August to late October and peaks in September; small numbers overwinter (Robbins and Bystrak 1977).

Atlas records are distributed across most of the state with two each on the Eastern Shore and Western Shore and one each in the Piedmont and Ridge and Valley sections. Prior to the Atlas fieldwork, most summer records in Maryland came from the freshwater impoundment at Deal Island WMA in Somerset County. Several factors help explain the paucity of Sora records. Maryland is near the southern limit of the breeding range in the East (AOU 1983). The Pennsylvania atlas reported about 65 Sora records scattered across that state (Brauning 1992). This relatively large number just north of Maryland may indicate a significant change in either the available food supply or the breeding habitat. A more likely possibility is that the low number of Maryland records reflects inadequate coverage by field observers. Most nocturnal species were underreported during the Atlas period, and this may be particularly true for wetland species (Blom 1986). Survey efforts designed specifically for nocturnal marsh birds need to be undertaken before an estimate of Sora breeding abundance and distribution can be made. Such fieldwork was conducted by the DNR (unpub. data) in 1990 and 1991; Soras were found in greater abundance, especially on the lower Eastern Shore, than was determined during the Atlas period. BBS data from 1966 through 1989 show a significant average annual decline of 2.4 percent in the continental population; the Eastern Region populations are stable. Too few data exist to estimate a Maryland trend.

Like other wetland dependent species, Soras may be at risk in Maryland because of the loss and degradation of wetlands (Tiner 1984). Conservation measures aimed at maintaining and increasing the Sora population in Maryland must primarily emphasize the protection and management of wetlands for rails. As long as wetlands are ditched, drained, filled, or otherwise degraded, the birds that depend on them will continue to decline.

Lynn M. Davidson

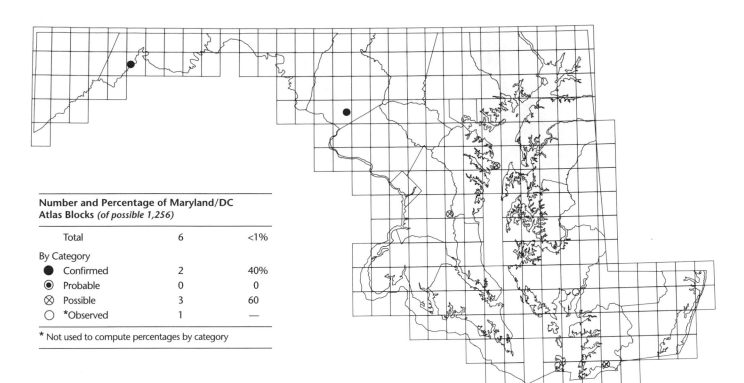

**Number and Percentage of Maryland/DC
Atlas Blocks** *(of possible 1,256)*

		Total	6	<1%
		By Category		
●	Confirmed		2	40%
◉	Probable		0	0
⊗	Possible		3	60
○	*Observed		1	—

* Not used to compute percentages by category

Atlas Distribution, 1983–1987

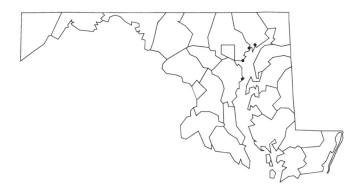

Breeding Distribution, 1958

MOB

Common Moorhen

Gallinula chloropus

The Common Moorhen, a skittish and secretive summer resident of fresh and brackish water habitats, is more commonly located by its loud, discordant calls than by sight. The American population was known as the Florida Gallinule until 1957, when the name was changed to Common Gallinule (AOU 1957). The current name, Common Moorhen, has been in use since 1983 (AOU 1983).

This regular, although rare (Kirkwood 1895) to uncommon, bird was considered, as recently as 1947, to be only a spring and fall migrant in Maryland (Hampe and Kolb 1947). The first DC-area specimen was obtained in a Washington market in the autumn of 1863 (Coues and Prentiss 1883). Jackson (1941) established the first Maryland nesting record on 10 May 1916 in Dorchester County. Stewart and Robbins (1958) described it as a common breeder along the Gunpowder River estuary and uncommon and local in other tidewater areas of Maryland. All breeding season sightings except two—one in Frederick County and one in Montgomery County—have occurred on the Coastal Plain.

Its winter range extends from South Carolina southward (AOU 1983). The migration periods are poorly known, but the spring peak is probably in April and early May and most fall records are in September and early October (Stewart and Robbins 1958).

Because the Common Moorhen is secretive and inhabits thick vegetation, little is known about its status in Maryland. Much more information is needed concerning its distribution and population trends in Maryland. It is listed as a species in need of conservation by the DNR and does not appear to be common anywhere within the North American part of its range (Strohmeyer 1977). In the Upper Midwest and the Great Lakes region, where populations are large enough for differences to be noticed, Strohmeyer (1977) reported that it is declining. Loss of habitat through the filling or draining of wetlands probably poses the greatest threat to this species.

The Common Moorhen's preferred habitats contain emergent vegetation growing in water 1 ft (0.3 m) or more in depth (Strohmeyer 1977). Its diet includes leaves and seeds of aquatic plants as well as snails, insects, and spiders (USFWS Food Habits File). It places its nest on a hummock or other clump of emergent vegetation woven into surrounding vegetation and partially floating, or, occasionally, in a willow or alder shrub (Reilly 1968; DeGraaf and Rudis 1986). The nest, a shallow cup constructed primarily of stems of dead emergent vegetation, is normally well concealed in vegetation 1 to 3 ft (0.3-0.9 m) above the water and usually has an entrance ramp and a canopy (Reilly 1968; Strohmeyer 1977). Common Moorhens sometimes nest in small colonies, and one pair may build several nests (Reilly 1968; Rue 1973). Harrison (1975) reported measurements of one nest with an outside diameter of 15 in. (38 cm), an inside diameter of 8 in. (20 cm), a depth of 3 in. (8 cm), and a height of 8 in. (20 cm). Clutch sizes range from 2 to 17 eggs, with an average of 8 to 10, although clutches may be larger in the northern portion of the range (Strohmeyer 1977).

The nesting season in Maryland is typically from early May to mid-July. Although extreme egg dates are 10 May and 21 June (Stewart and Robbins 1958), nest building was observed at Tanyard in Caroline County as late as 16 July (Ringler 1987b). Both sexes assist in nest construction, incubation, brooding, and feeding of the young. Incubation lasts 18 to 21 days per egg and begins after the first egg is laid (Reilly 1968). Adults with downy young were noted at Tilghman Island in Talbot County on 11 June and at Sparrows Point in Baltimore County on 10 August (Ringler 1987b). The young are precocial and capable of leaving the nest within hours of hatching (Rue 1973); they attain flight in 6 to 7 weeks (Reilly 1968; Frederickson 1971). Common Moorhens may raise two broods a year (Frost and Siegfried 1977).

Atlas results show the Common Moorhen to be locally distributed. Small concentrations of records occur in the Patuxent, Choptank, and Blackwater river marshes and near Deal Island WMA in Somerset County. The few records near Baltimore were generally in disturbed habitats, especially dredge-spoil impoundments with standing water and extensive phragmites growth. Fieldwork by the DNR (unpub. data) in 1990 revealed good numbers of Common Moorhens nesting in dredge-spoil impoundments in the Upper Chesapeake Section. The Virginia atlas project also had few sightings, but Delaware had several "confirmed" records along the coast. Pennsylvania had several "confirmed" records near the Delaware border (Brauning 1992). The majority of Maryland Atlas "confirmations" were for adults with downy young.

BBS data from 1966 through 1989 show stable Common Moorhen populations in the Eastern Region; too few Maryland data exist to estimate a trend for the state. What was once considered a locally common species is now not considered common anywhere in Maryland. The outlook for this species largely depends on maintaining the integrity of wetlands and discouraging human encroachment.

Nancy J. Stewart

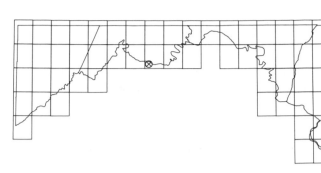

Number and Percentage of Maryland/DC Atlas Blocks *(of possible 1,256)*

Total	42	3%
By Category		
● Confirmed	16	40%
◉ Probable	10	25
⊗ Possible	14	35
○ *Observed	2	—

* Not used to compute percentages by category

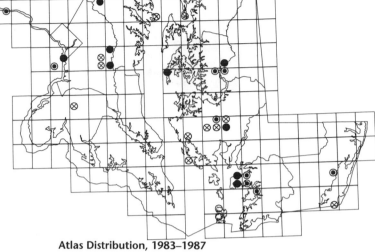

Atlas Distribution, 1983–1987

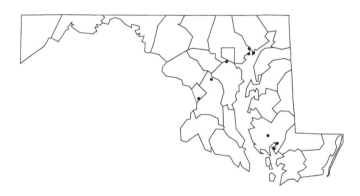

Breeding Distribution, 1958

American Coot

Fulica americana

Although the American Coot is often mistaken for a duck, it is actually a member of the rail family. It is common in migration and in winter, frequenting all the tidewater sections of Maryland and also inland reservoirs, ponds, and lakes (Stewart and Robbins 1958). In spring, migrants move through the state from early March to mid-May and, in fall, from mid-September to early December. Often found in large flocks, American Coots are highly animated birds (Ripley 1977). The largest reported flock in Maryland is 11,500 on the Susquehanna Flats at the head of the Chesapeake Bay on 31 March 1955 (Stewart and Robbins 1958). Since the massive decline in submerged aquatic vegetation in the Chesapeake Bay and its tributaries during the early 1970s, the largest flock reported has been 1,300 in the hydrilla of the Potomac River and its tributaries in Prince George's County on 1 November 1987 (Ringler 1988a).

Kirkwood (1895) called the American Coot a common migrant in Maryland, but Eifrig (1904) knew of only a single record for western Maryland. Stewart and Robbins (1958) considered it a local transient and winter resident but only casual as a summer vagrant in Queen Anne's and Prince George's counties and DC. The American Coot is a relatively new breeding species in Maryland. The first breeding evidence was obtained on 16 August 1970 when Armistead (1970) discovered broods of six and five downy young among 68 American Coots in the marshes of the Deal Island WMA in Somerset County. He also observed adults with young on 14 June 1973 in the Fairmount and Deal Island WMAs in Somerset County in mixed smooth cordgrass–narrow-leaved cattail marshes (Robbins 1973a).

Nesting habitat includes ponds in brackish marshes that contain a plentiful growth of aquatic plants such as wild celery, red-head pondweed, and sago pondweed (Stewart and Robbins 1958). In upland situations, American Coots prefer wetlands with cattail, bulrush, bur reed, and phragmites, but they will also use waterlily and pickerelweed marshes (Faanes 1981).

American Coots nest over much of North America (Low and Mansell 1983), with the greatest breeding concentrations in the prairie pothole region, where densities of over 430 pairs per sq mi (166 per sq km) have been recorded (Stewart and Kantrud 1972). Their floating nests are usually constructed in thick stands of emergent vegetation, especially bulrush and cattail (Frederickson 1977) and are tightly woven into the stalks for support (Eckert 1981). Both sexes participate in the nest building (Frederickson 1977).

From 4 to 17 eggs are laid, but the normal clutch is 9 to 11 (Low and Mansell 1983). Dump nesting occurs but is not common (Frederickson 1977). Although renesting is not common, second broods have been recorded in some populations (Gullion 1954). One egg is laid per day, and incubation, which lasts 21 or 22 days, begins with the laying of the first egg (Bent 1926). Both sexes participate in incubation, but it is primarily performed by the female (Frederickson 1977). Some studies have indicated the male is more likely to attend the nest during the night (Gullion 1954). Both parents care for the newly hatched chicks (Frederickson 1977). Nesting success for the American Coot is higher than for most species of waterfowl, ranging from 87 to 97 percent (Frederickson 1977). The relative inaccessibility of its nest certainly contributes to this high success rate, as does the aggressiveness of the parents (Linduska 1964). Young are capable of flight in about 75 days (Gullion 1954).

Throughout much of the year, the diet of the American Coot consists almost entirely of the plants and seeds of submerged aquatic vegetation, especially pondweed, duckweed, wild rice, and bulrush (Martin et al. 1951). In summer, about 45 percent of its diet consists of insects and bivalves.

During the Atlas period, American Coots were confirmed at only one location, Deal Island WMA in Somerset County. There were scattered reports from other localities, primarily sewage ponds and other artificial impoundments. American Coots occasionally summer at such locations in Maryland (R. Ringler, pers. comm.); occurrences do not necessarily indicate breeding. This secretive species can easily be overlooked in its dense nesting habitat. Based on the presence of breeding populations both north and south of Maryland (Frederickson 1977), the American Coot can probably be assumed to be a regular but very rare breeder on Maryland's lower Eastern Shore.

BBS data from 1966 though 1989 show a highly significant average annual decline of 2.4 percent in the Eastern Region; however, the continental population is stable. Data are too few to estimate a trend for Maryland. At present, Deal Island WMA is the only known regular breeding locality in Maryland. A more intense survey of similar impoundments is needed to determine the real status of this bird in Maryland. For the foreseeable future, we can expect it to remain a rare breeding bird, entirely dependent on the management and water levels at Deal Island.

Donald W. Meritt

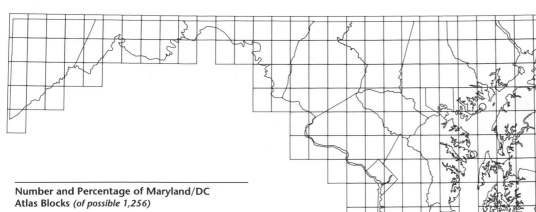

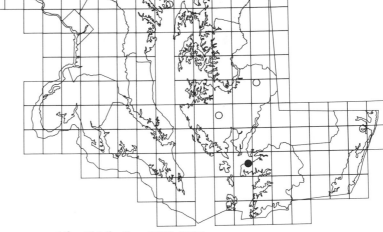

Atlas Distribution, 1983–1987

Number and Percentage of Maryland/DC Atlas Blocks *(of possible 1,256)*

Total		6	<1%
By Category			
● Confirmed		1	100%
◉ Probable		0	0
⊗ Possible		0	0
○ *Observed		5	—

* Not used to compute percentages by category

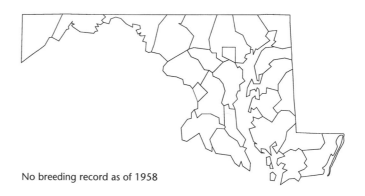

No breeding record as of 1958

Breeding Distribution, 1958

MOB

Wilson's Plover

Charadrius wilsonia

The Wilson's Plover, formerly known as the Thick-billed Plover (Pough 1951), is one of Maryland's rarest breeding birds. It is confined to the beaches and sand mounds of Assateague Island in Worcester County. The Wilson's Plover breeds along the Atlantic and Gulf coasts, and Maryland has been the northern limit of its breeding range in recent years (AOU 1983). The Wilson's Plover arrives in Maryland as early as 16 April and has lingered as late as 6 September (Robbins and Bystrak 1977). It winters from the coasts of Florida, Louisiana, and Texas south through the West Indies to northern South America (AOU 1983).

The Wilson's Plover has probably always been a rare species in Maryland. Bailey (1913) stated it was becoming less common along the Virginia coast. The first Maryland sighting was not until 17 August 1925 by F. Kirkwood (Stewart and Robbins 1958). Historical summer records include downy young banded on Assateague Island on 10 July 1947; a nest with two young and one egg, 1.5 mi (2.4 km) north of Ocean City on 26 June 1948; and a pair courting at West Ocean City on 16 April 1949 (Stewart and Robbins 1958). The 1948 nest was found by S. Low in a large patch of bulldozed sand in an area being prepared for development near what is now the Ocean City Convention Center (C. Robbins, pers. comm.). More recently, a nest with three eggs was found on Assateague Island on 15 May 1976 (Robbins 1976). As many as 12 birds were seen during the summer of 1976, but no recent breeding locations, other than the large dredge-spoil mound opposite the Ocean City Airport, have been reported. Foraging birds have been seen occasionally on the bayside shoreline of Assateague Island and on some of the large sand flats in Sinepuxent Bay. This species, which feeds by night as well as by day, does not show a preference for feeding in the intertidal zone of the ocean beach (M. Hoffman, pers. obs.), which is a major foraging zone for other shorebirds. Its diet consists primarily of small crabs, shrimps, sand worms, small mollusks, and flies (Bent 1929; Tomkins 1944).

The breeding habitat of the Wilson's Plover in Maryland is slightly different from that of its close relative, the Piping Plover. The Piping Plover nests near the ocean on relatively flat open washes or beach. In contrast, the one recent Wilson's Plover breeding site is a very large dredge-spoil mound on the bay side of Assateague Island. This mound was created when the Sinepuxent Bay channel was last dredged in 1976. Vegetation has begun to colonize the mound and may become too dense to permit breeding by Wilson's Plovers; habitat manipulation may be needed to maintain this spoil mound as a bare area appropriate for nesting.

Development apparently was not responsible for the disappearance of the Wilson's Plover from New Jersey, the northern limit of its historical breeding range (J. Stasz, pers. comm.). No specific information about the breeding habits of Wilson's Plover in Maryland is available. The following data are from Georgia (Tomkins 1944). The nest site is a simple scrape in the sand. The normal clutch size is 3, with a range of 2 to 4. Incubation lasts 24 or 25 days, and the young leave the nest shortly after hatching. They are able to fly when they are about 21 days old. Bergstrom (1986) found that males do most of the incubation at night and females incubate during the day. This species is single-brooded but will renest if a nest is destroyed. In Maryland, nests with eggs have been found from 15 May to 26 June, and downy young have been found from 26 June to 10 July (MNRF). Bent (1929) cited 22 egg dates for Virginia, extending from 4 May to 20 June, with the peak from 27 May to 6 June.

During the Atlas period, the Wilson's Plover was found nesting in only a single block. On 15 May 1985, a nest lined with shell fragments, surrounded on three sides by low beach vegetation, and containing three eggs was located on a large dredge-spoil mound on the bay side of Assateague Island opposite the Ocean City Airport. On 26 May, this nest was empty. Observations during the summer of 1985 indicated that, at most, one additional nonbreeding individual was present on the north end of Assateague Island (M. Hoffman, unpub. data). On 4 June 1986, an adult was seen on Assateague within 300 ft (91 m) of the jetty at the north end. On 17 June of the same year, two adults were seen about 1 mi (1.6 km) north of the entrance road to Assateague Island, and four days later a single bird was observed at the same location (M. Patterson, pers. comm.). The only report since then was of one bird seen on northern Assateague Island on 29 May 1989 (Ringler 1989a). The eight BBS routes in the continent and six in the Eastern Region are too few to estimate a trend for the Wilson's Plover.

Maryland's Wilson's Plover population is in extreme peril, if not already extirpated, and it needs complete protection. The DNR currently lists this species as endangered. Management by the NPS, the managing agency of Assateague Island National Seashore, to reduce or eliminate vegetative growth on dredge spoils is urgently needed. Sightings should be reported to the DNR, and birds should not be disturbed.

Mark L. Hoffman

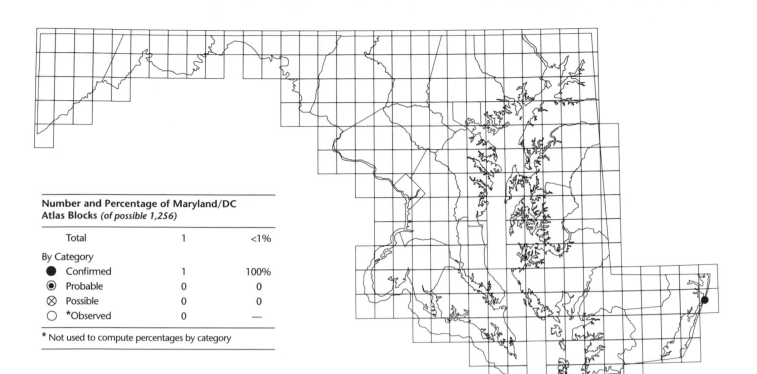

Number and Percentage of Maryland/DC Atlas Blocks *(of possible 1,256)*

Total	1	<1%
By Category		
● Confirmed	1	100%
◉ Probable	0	0
⊗ Possible	0	0
○ *Observed	0	—

* Not used to compute percentages by category

Atlas Distribution, 1983–1987

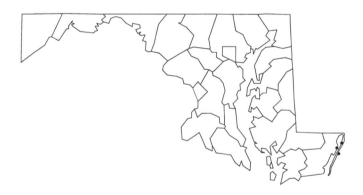

Breeding Distribution, 1958

Piping Plover

Charadrius melodus

The Piping Plover has a limited breeding distribution in Maryland, where it is confined to the relatively undisturbed ocean beaches and dunes of Assateague Island in Worcester County. This plover's need for ocean frontage in close proximity to bayside mudflats for brood rearing—a combination of conditions that is extremely limited along Maryland's coastline—has placed it in direct conflict with humans. For similar reasons there has been a reduction in Piping Plover numbers along the entire Atlantic Coast (Haig and Oring 1985). This species is listed as endangered in Maryland by the DNR; the Atlantic Coast population is officially listed as threatened by the USFWS (Sidle 1984, 1985).

Information on the historical distribution and abundance of the Piping Plover as a breeding species in Maryland is limited. Even though the entire Maryland breeding population has always been confined to a strip of ocean frontage between the Delaware and Virginia state lines, no surveys or counts were conducted prior to the Atlas. Kirkwood (1895) noted evidence of Piping Plovers nesting near Ocean City in June 1894. Hampe and Kolb (1947) described them as summer residents on the barrier beaches along the ocean and cited three records of confirmed breeding from 1904 through 1939. Stewart and Robbins (1958) considered the Piping Plover an uncommon breeding species in coastal Worcester County and listed a spring high count of 7 on 14 April 1951 and a summer high count of 22 on 23 July 1949, both on Assateague Island. At one time Piping Plovers nested in the Ocean City–Fenwick Island area, but the intense development of this area led to their extirpation there about 40 years ago (C. Robbins, pers. comm.).

Piping Plovers arrive in Maryland from their wintering grounds in the southeastern United States and the Caribbean Basin (AOU 1983) during late March and early April (Stewart and Robbins 1958). Males establish breeding territories and perform courtship flights over their shell- and pebble-strewn nesting grounds (Cairns 1982). Nests are no more than a scrape in the sand. The normal clutch size is 3 or 4 eggs (Tyler 1929). Downy young dates in Maryland nests range from 21 May (DNR, unpub. data) to 23 July (MNRF). Although only one brood is attempted each year, the destruction of a clutch of eggs results in one to five re-nesting attempts (MacIvor 1990). Their diet consists largely of marine worms, fly larvae, beetles, crustaceans, and mollusks (Tyler 1929).

During the Atlas period Piping Plovers were confirmed in four blocks. Nesting was confined to two areas on Assateague Island: from the northern boundary of Assateague Island State Park to the Ocean City Inlet, and in an overwash area approximately 0.6 mi (1 km) north of the Virginia line. Approximately 20 pairs of plovers nested in Maryland during 1985 (M. Hoffman, unpub. data), 17 pairs in 1986 (Patterson et al. 1991), and 23 pairs in 1987. Data from the 1986 and 1987 surveys show the following results (DNR, unpub. data). The earliest nest with eggs was found on 12 April and the latest on 10 July, with a peak in early and mid-May. Sixteen nests with eggs were monitored, and 76 percent of the eggs in these nests hatched. A total of 33 nests with young were found; 48 percent were successful. Forty-six chicks fledged for a rate of 1.4 per nest (Patterson et al. 1991). In 1990 the breeding population dropped to only 14 pairs (DNR, unpub. data). The Atlantic Coast population is estimated at 634 to 662 pairs (Haig and Oring 1985), so Maryland harbors approximately 3 percent of that population. BBS data are insufficient for estimating trends, even at the continental level.

The survival of the population in Maryland depends on the maintenance of habitat on Assateague Island National Seashore, which is under the management of the NPS. In 1986, NPS initiated a series of Piping Plover studies, in part to determine how to protect them from the human use of the northern end of Assateague Island. Although no access is available by road, many people boat or walk to the area, especially during the nesting season. These studies found no nest failures attributable to human disturbance; 91 percent of nest failures were the result of predation, primarily by red foxes and raccoons (Patterson et al. 1991).

The ongoing migration of the northern end of Assateague Island toward the mainland of Worcester County is especially significant. Construction of jetties at the Ocean City Inlet has prevented sand flow from the north and has resulted in erosion of the northern tip of the island. NPS and other agencies are evaluating possible management actions to stabilize Assateague Island. Stabilization, however, would eliminate the mudflats and perhaps the nesting plovers as well. It has been predicted that, without stabilization, a large portion of the northern end of Assateague Island could be washed away by a major storm (Leatherman 1984). This would eliminate the area with the largest Maryland population of Piping Plovers. This presents a quandary for resource managers. Their inclination to let natural processes take their course could result in the extirpation of one segment of the breeding population of a threatened species.

Mark L. Hoffman

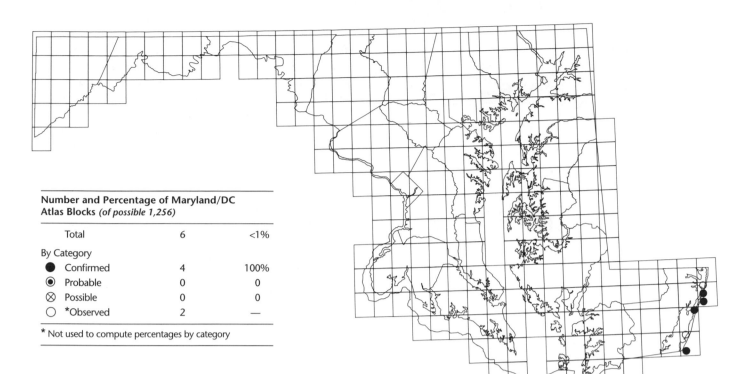

Number and Percentage of Maryland/DC Atlas Blocks *(of possible 1,256)*

Total	6	<1%
By Category		
● Confirmed	4	100%
◉ Probable	0	0
⊗ Possible	0	0
○ *Observed	2	—

* Not used to compute percentages by category

Atlas Distribution, 1983–1987

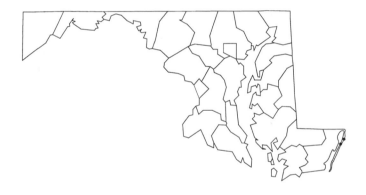

Breeding Distribution, 1958

Killdeer

Charadrius vociferus

The conspicuous Killdeer "makes its presence known by loud calls and cries, to which it owes both its common and scientific names—killdeer and vociferus" (Townsend 1929). Unlike most other shorebirds, the Killdeer can commonly be found miles from water. It nests in pastures, meadows, cultivated fields, on bare gravel-strewn ground, and even on graveled roofs. The normal spring migration in Maryland extends from mid-February to mid-April and normal fall migration from mid-July to mid-December (Robbins and Bystrak 1977). In winter, it is fairly common in the Eastern Shore Section, uncommon in the Western Shore and Upper Chesapeake sections, and rare in the Piedmont Section (Stewart and Robbins 1958). At least some Maryland birds winter in the southeastern United States.

The Killdeer has long been recorded as a common summer resident in Maryland's farmlands (Coues and Prentiss 1862, 1883; Kirkwood 1895; Cooke 1929). Stewart and Robbins (1958) listed its breeding status as fairly common in all sections. The highest breeding densities reported in Maryland are 3.9 territorial males per 100 acres (40.5 ha) in recently plowed and sprout-wheat fields in Prince George's County in 1949 and 1.4 territorial males per 100 acres in mixed agricultural habitats (including residential areas) in Prince George's County in 1943 and 1947 (Stewart and Robbins 1958). BBS data from 1966 through 1989 show a significant average annual increase of 1.1 percent in the Eastern Region; the Maryland population was variable but stable. The Maryland population, however, shows a significant average annual increase of 5.4 percent from 1980 through 1989 reflecting a partial recovery from the severe winter of 1976–77 in the state.

A study conducted in Minnesota (Lenington and Mace 1975) showed that Killdeer tend to nest in the same territory year after year, with males returning to previous nest sites more often than females. This study reported that the Killdeer, a monogamous species, tended to retain the same mate for more than one breeding season. Some females are sequentially polyandrous, however, and mate with a second male after the first brood hatches (Brunton 1988). Nests are situated in a slight depression on the ground in the open, so that the bird on the nest has an extended view (Townsend 1929). Killdeer make these hollowed depressions or scrapes both as part of the courtship display and as a nest (Phillips 1972). They strongly favor pale or white pebbles, weeds, or sticks for nest construction (Kull 1977). Incubation ranges from 24 to 26 days (Townsend 1929). Both sexes incubate the eggs and care for the young, and they are fearless in defense of their young. Both male and female Killdeer perform distraction displays, including the well-known broken-wing display, to lure possible predators away from their nests and young. Of all of Maryland's breeding species, this species had the highest number "confirmed" by distraction display—148 of the 424 "confirmed" blocks (35%).

The earliest egg date for Maryland is 16 March (Stewart and Robbins 1958) and the latest is 23 July (MNRF). The earliest date for downy young is 8 April and the latest is 3 August (MNRF). Of the 91 Maryland nests with height reported, all but two were located on the ground; one of the other two was on a church roof. In 101 Maryland nest records, clutch sizes range from 1 (probably incomplete) to 6 (mean of 3.7); 75 contained 4 eggs. This is consistent with Townsend's (1929) statement that Killdeer almost always lay 4 eggs. Brood sizes in 56 Maryland nests range from 1 to 5 (mean of 3.3); 30 of the 56 nests contained 4 young. Occasionally two broods are raised, and renesting after egg loss is common (Nol and Lambert 1984). The Killdeer diet consists primarily of insects, with 37 percent beetles, 40 percent other insects, and 21 percent other invertebrates, such as centipedes, spiders, ticks, worms, snails, and crustaceans (McAtee and Beal 1912).

This species may be more widespread and common in much of the East than it was before European settlement. Prior to the clearing of the forests, most Killdeer probably nested along the shores of large bodies of water. In an Ontario study, Nol and Lambert (1984) showed that Killdeer in inland disturbed and artificial habitats began nesting earlier and had larger clutches than those nesting on natural shorelines. Birds nesting earlier had greater success renesting and raising second broods. This is explained by the Killdeer diet and the delayed appearance of insect prey near large bodies of water where the average temperature remains lower.

Atlas data show that the Killdeer still nests in all sections of Maryland. It was absent only from a few heavily urbanized blocks, the extensive marshlands of the lower Eastern Shore, and an area on the Kent and Cecil county border on the upper Eastern Shore. No explanation for this latter gap has been proposed. The needs of the Killdeer are being met in Maryland.

Alfred J. Fletcher and Jane H. Farrell

Number and Percentage of Maryland/DC Atlas Blocks *(of possible 1,256)*

Total	1,035	82%
By Category		
● Confirmed	424	41%
◉ Probable	243	23
⊗ Possible	368	36
○ *Observed	0	—

* Not used to compute percentages by category

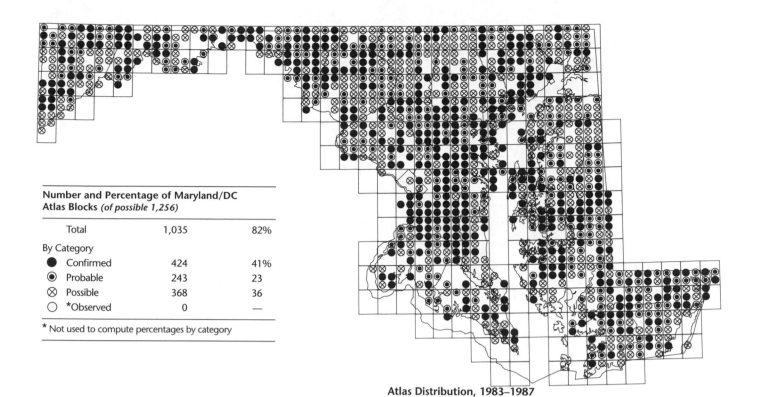

Atlas Distribution, 1983–1987

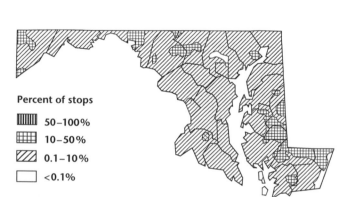

Percent of stops

▥	50–100%
▦	10–50%
▨	0.1–10%
☐	<0.1%

Relative Abundance, 1982–1989

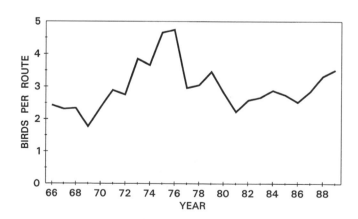

Breeding Distribution, 1958

The Killdeer, although generally uncommon, is widely and evenly distributed. Slightly higher concentrations were found in the heavily agricultural areas of the interior Eastern Shore and in scattered agricultural lands throughout the rest of the state.

Maryland BBS Trend Graph, 1966–1989

MOB

American Oystercatcher

Haematopus palliatus

American Oystercatchers are large, vociferous, coastal shorebirds. They frequent salt-marsh edges, estuarine islands, and tidal mudflats where they feed on Atlantic ribbed mussels, other bivalves, and marine worms (Bent 1929). Less frequently they forage for mole crabs along ocean beaches (D. Brinker, pers. obs.). Coastal Worcester County is the stronghold of their Maryland range. Although formerly considered only migrants and summer residents (Robbins and Bystrak 1977), American Oystercatchers are now uncommon permanent residents, with many individuals present in Worcester County every January and February (D. Brinker, unpub. data; Ringler 1990a). They also nest in the lower Chesapeake Bay, but their winter status in that location has not been determined; there has been only one January sighting.

In the 1600s, American Oystercatchers were common as far north as Massachusetts (Forbush 1912). Subsequently, they were extirpated by hunting and egg collecting (Melvin 1984). Recovery has been recent: nesting resumed in New Jersey in 1947, New York in 1957, Massachusetts in 1967 or 1968, Rhode Island in 1978, and Connecticut in 1981 (Zeranski and Baptist 1990). Until recently, they were considered rare in Maryland. Kirkwood (1895) had only a single observation, in the vicinity of Ocean City on 5 June 1891. Brooke Meanley established the first Maryland nesting record on 6 June 1939 when he photographed downy young on Assateague Island (Stewart and Robbins 1958). Referring to occurrence rather than breeding, Hampe and Kolb (1947) took a different view: "Records are few only because of lack of observers at the right time and place." Stewart and Robbins (1958) listed them as rare summer residents. In 1972, H. Armistead reported the first breeding record in the Maryland section of the Chesapeake Bay, in the Adam and Holland Island area in Dorchester County (Robbins 1972). He also documented the first nesting in Dorchester County (Armistead 1977). As recently as the early 1980s, American Oystercatchers were still considered rare (Robbins and

Boone 1984), with "probably fewer than 20 pairs breed[ing] annually in Maryland."

Maryland seems to offer sufficient nesting habitat for American Oystercatchers. Basic nest site characteristics include isolation from mammalian predators, close proximity to food sources, and minimum exposure to high tides. Nest scrapes have been found in a variety of situations, from typical sand or shell beach sites to open areas on wrack lines along the edges of salt marshes. Over half of Maryland nests are found on microbeaches, tiny patches of sand or shell deposited on the edge of salt-marsh islands by storm wave action (D. Brinker, pers. obs.). These nests are often partly concealed in vegetation, but nests located in open situations atop wrack lines are also fairly common.

Small islands in coastal Worcester County frequently contain multiple pairs (D. Brinker, pers. obs.). In these instances each pair defends a small nest territory while foraging at disjunct locations where food is abundant. Nesting territories are traditional and once established are typically active for several years (D. Brinker, pers. obs.). Adults aggressively defend the nest territories and young, often flying broad circles around intruders while calling loudly. The intensity of an adult's response increases as the intruder moves closer to the nest or young; this served as a useful clue to Atlas workers trying to find nests or young.

The earliest Maryland egg date for American Oystercatchers is 9 April, and viable eggs have been found as late as 5 July (Robbins and Bystrak 1977). Breeding chronology along the Maryland coast should parallel that of the extensively studied population nesting in Virginia near the Chincoteague Inlet. First clutches were initiated there between 6 April and 13 May, with the peak occurring between 14 and 22 April (Nol et al. 1984). Maryland clutch sizes varied from 1 to 4 eggs, with 2 or 3 being most common (D. Brinker, unpub. data). Replacement clutches were found through mid-June (Nol et al. 1984). Dates for flightless young in Maryland range from 18 May to 14 July (D. Brinker, unpub. data).

During the Atlas project, nesting American Oystercatchers were found in Dorchester, Somerset, and Worcester counties. The high number of "confirmed" records was the result of fieldwork associated with the MCWP. Nests with eggs or young represent 60 percent of the confirmations. The Maryland breeding population is estimated to be at least 50 and probably closer to 75 pairs (D. Brinker, unpub. data).

Although it is unlikely that American Oystercatchers will spread much farther north in the Chesapeake Bay, wetland and mudflat habitat in Dorchester and Somerset counties is sufficient to support a larger population. Many successful nests in the Ocean City area have been close to human activity and development (D. Brinker, unpub. data). One nest was found in a recently created salt marsh that was part of mitigation for wetland filling associated with a condominium development; another was located on a small island occupied by a substantial home (D. Brinker, unpub. data). Several successful pairs also annually contend with considerable disturbance from Ocean City area recreationists.

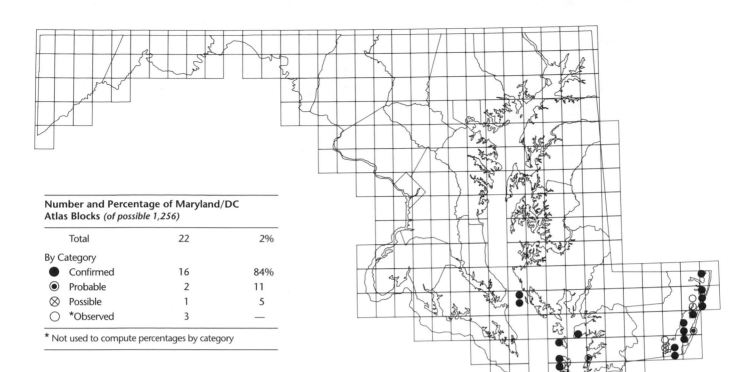

Number and Percentage of Maryland/DC Atlas Blocks (of possible 1,256)

	Total	22	2%
By Category			
●	Confirmed	16	84%
◉	Probable	2	11
⊗	Possible	1	5
○	*Observed	3	—

* Not used to compute percentages by category

Atlas Distribution, 1983–1987

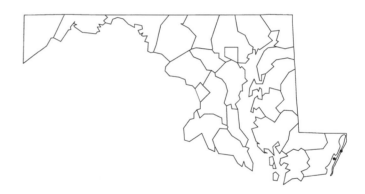

Breeding Distribution, 1958

Most American Oystercatchers in Maryland nest in remote areas where human influence is minimal. Given the habitat protection provided most of these areas by wetland laws and regulations, there is little threat to American Oystercatchers from habitat modification. BBS routes that sample American Oystercatcher populations are too few to estimate a trend for the Eastern Region or Maryland, but no evidence indicates that the American Oystercatcher is in jeopardy in Maryland. In fact, populations appear to be increasing.

David F. Brinker

Black-necked Stilt

Himantopus mexicanus

The Black-necked Stilt is a large shorebird with black and white plumage strikingly offset by long, pinkish-red legs. Other than flamingos, stilts have the longest legs proportional to their body size of any bird (Terres 1980). Considered by some authorities to be a race of the Black-winged Stilt *(H. himantopus)* of the Old World (Hayman et al. 1986), the Black-necked Stilt is a rare migrant to Maryland's coastal wetlands. Spring records range from 7 April to 1 June (Ringler 1977, 1986b). Fall migration in Maryland apparently occurs in late August; the only later sighting was probably a hurricane-blown bird (Ringler 1980a, 1984a). The winter range includes the U.S. Gulf Coast and the wetlands of Latin America (AOU 1983). Although the Black-necked Stilt had been suspected of nesting in Maryland for several years, breeding was not confirmed until 1987 (Armistead 1987). It is one of three species added to Maryland's list of breeding birds during the Atlas period; the other two are Brown Pelican and Northern Shoveler.

The only historical suggestion that Black-necked Stilts might have occurred in Maryland came from Kirkwood (1895), who wrote that they were once uncommon on the Atlantic Coast from Maine to Florida. Although they had become rare by then, he suspected they still might occur on the Maryland coast. Wilson (1810) reported that they nested regularly in Cape May County, New Jersey, and W. Baird secured a specimen there in July 1843 (Stone 1937). Turnbull (1869) mentioned finding a nest on Egg Island, New Jersey, in Delaware Bay. Black-necked Stilts have bred in small numbers in coastal Delaware since 1964. They have also attempted to nest in southeastern Pennsylvania (B. Haas, pers. comm.). In 1989, one pair bred in a marsh near Philadelphia, Pennsylvania, but their chicks disappeared after a rainstorm in early July (Brauning 1992). This was the first breeding for that state. The adults returned for two weeks in May 1990 but did not remain. BBS data from 1966 through 1989 show a stable population in the Eastern Region; data are too few to estimate a Maryland trend.

Black-necked Stilts have been found in Maryland nearly every year since the first documented state record in 1967 at Blackwater NWR in Dorchester County (Armistead and Russell 1967). This shorebird has been most commonly reported from Deal Island WMA, and observers suspected that it may have bred there in 1983 when up to six birds were seen (Ringler 1983b). At least one pair has been seen annually at Blackwater NWR, and nesting may have occurred there. Observations of Black-necked Stilts during the breeding season have been reported to *Maryland Birdlife* from at least seven counties and eleven wetland areas, including Sandy Point in Anne Arundel County; Hart–Miller Island in Baltimore County; Cove Point in Calvert County; Piney Run in Carroll County; Blackwater NWR, Elliott Island, and Hills Point in Dorchester County; Deal Island WMA and Smith Island in Somerset County; and Assateague National Seashore and Big Bay Marsh in Worcester County.

In the East, Black-necked Stilts favor brackish ponds in salt marshes and fresh to brackish ponds behind coastal beaches, where they breed in colonies of six to 10 pairs (Terres 1980). Hamilton (1975) has provided the following information about nesting activities in California. Both adults assist in nest construction. Nests vary from a hollowed-out mound of sticks, mud, shells, and debris built up over shallow water, to a sparsely lined scrape on dry ground, to no nest at all. The average clutch size is 4 eggs, and both adults participate in the incubation, which lasts 22 to 26 days. Black-necked Stilts defend nesting territories and young from intruders by circling low overhead and persistently giving harsh yelping notes. The young fly approximately 28 to 32 days after hatching. During the breeding season, their diet consists principally of insects and invertebrates, especially aquatic bugs and beetles (Wetmore 1925). Black-necked Stilts are believed to rear only one brood per season (Hamilton 1975).

Black-necked Stilts were recorded in three Atlas blocks centered around the marshes of Deal Island WMA in Somerset County. Two reports were considered only "possible," but the third was the first "confirmed" Maryland record. Although adults with immatures were seen at Deal Island WMA from 21 June to 6 August in 1985 (Ringler 1985b), breeding was not confirmed until 1987 when a nest was found in May and downy young were observed in June (Armistead 1987).

Black-necked Stilts may be gradually increasing in Maryland and expanding their breeding range from coastal marshes to more inland locations. It is unknown, however, whether Maryland breeding birds have come from Delaware or from locations farther south. As long as conditions remain favorable at Deal Island WMA, Black-necked Stilts should continue to breed in Maryland.

Lynn M. Davidson

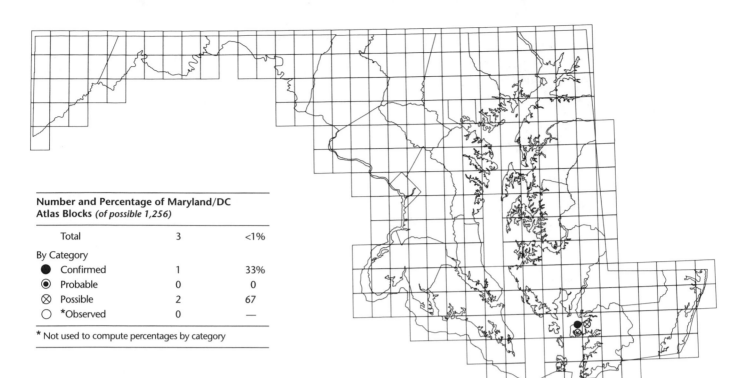

Number and Percentage of Maryland/DC Atlas Blocks *(of possible 1,256)*		
Total	3	<1%
By Category		
● Confirmed	1	33%
◉ Probable	0	0
⊗ Possible	2	67
○ *Observed	0	—

* Not used to compute percentages by category

Atlas Distribution, 1983–1987

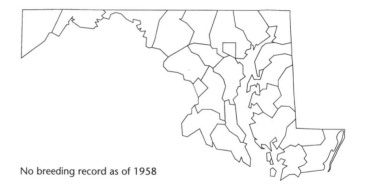

No breeding record as of 1958

Breeding Distribution, 1958

Willet

Catoptrophorus semipalmatus

The noisiest sentinel of the salt marsh, the Willet vigorously defends its nest site by flying through the air, flashing its bold black-and-white wing pattern, and voicing the loud alarm call from which its name is derived. Even after an intruder has moved far from the nest area, the Willet's raucous calls may persist for several minutes.

The Willet is a common inhabitant of salt marshes on the lower Eastern Shore. The breeding birds arrive from their wintering grounds in the South Atlantic states and Latin America (AOU 1983) in April and depart by August (Robbins and Bystrak 1977). Birds thought to represent western populations are found in late summer and sometimes linger into winter (Tomkins 1955, 1965).

In 1832, A. Wilson noted that the Willet bred "in great numbers" along the shores of New York, New Jersey, Delaware, and Maryland (Bent 1929); however, the first definite nest record for Maryland was by E. Court on 10 May 1904 near Ocean City in Worcester County (Hampe and Kolb 1947). Kirkwood (1895) wrote that the Willet was "not as numerous as it used to be," although it still bred in limited numbers on the Maryland ocean front. Bent (1929) noted that at the beginning of the twentieth century this species appeared "destined to disappear from at least the northern portion of its range on the Atlantic coast." Hunting and the harvesting of eggs for food were largely to blame for this decline (Bent 1929).

Now that it is no longer a game bird, the Willet has slowly recovered. Stewart and Robbins (1958) called it locally common in tidewater areas of Somerset and Wicomico Counties and southern Dorchester County but uncommon in the coastal area of Worcester County. BBS data from 1966 through 1989 show a stable population for the Eastern Region. Data are too few to estimate a Maryland trend.

Nesting Willets choose salt marshes (especially those dominated by salt-meadow cordgrass), small sandy or marshy islands, or sandy areas with beach grass (Bent 1929; Stewart and Robbins 1958). In a study on Wallops Island, Virginia, Howe (1982) noted that most vegetated areas above the normal intertidal zone were potential nesting sites, including upland areas with a mixture of grasses and shrubs such as marsh elder and wax myrtle. The nest, which is on the ground and lined with bits of dry grass, sedge, and small sticks, is usually well hidden in the grass but occasionally may be on bare sand (Bent 1929). In addition to the actual nest site, a family of Willets requires a feeding area for the adults, typically a patch of cordgrass along a tidal creek. The family also needs a brood-rearing site, such as a large shallow pond (Howe 1982).

Egg dates for 67 Maryland Willet nests (MNRF) range from 23 April to 12 July. Thirty-six of these records were from 1 to 15 June. Howe (1982) noted that the first eggs are usually laid 1.5 to 2 weeks after arrival on the breeding grounds. Clutch sizes for 56 Maryland nests range from 1 (presumably incomplete) to 5 (MNRF). Eleven nests had 3 eggs and 44 had 4 eggs, but only 1 had 5 eggs. Howe (1982) reported that, although the females incubate during the day, the male incubates at night and sometimes relieves the female in the middle of the day. He determined the incubation period to be 25.2 ± 1.2 days from the laying of the last egg to the hatching of the last egg. Downy young leave the nest the day they hatch (Bent 1929) or, if hatching takes place late in the day, the next day (Howe 1982). Downy young dates for Maryland range from 5 June to 11 July (MNRF). As with most shorebirds, there is only one brood per year (H. H. Harrison 1975; C. Harrison, 1978). Willet diet is strictly aquatic, consisting mainly of aquatic insects, marine worms, crabs, small mollusks, and fish, with some tender roots and seeds (Bent 1929).

Atlas results show that the Willet is now a common summer resident in coastal Worcester County and in the tidewater areas of Somerset, Wicomico, and Dorchester counties. The northernmost report, near Rock Hall in Kent County, probably does not refer to a breeding bird. Confirmations came easily, and nearly half the "confirmed" records were of nests with eggs. It was also fairly easy to observe distraction displays and dependent young. The northernmost nesting in the Chesapeake Bay was recorded in 1991 when a nest with eggs was found on the north side of Kent Island, Queen Anne's County (M. Iliff, pers. comm.). A half-grown young was seen later in the company of two adults (J. Reese, pers. comm.).

To ensure that this species continues to be a common breeding bird in Maryland, the salt-marsh habitat of the lower Eastern Shore must be protected, particularly in the vicinity of ponds, tidal creeks, and tidal flats.

Michael O'Brien

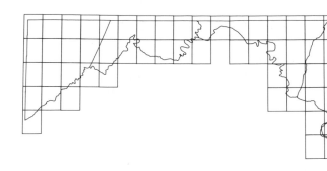

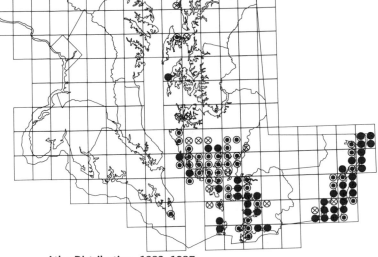

Number and Percentage of Maryland/DC Atlas Blocks *(of possible 1,256)*		
Total	100	8%
By Category		
● Confirmed	41	41%
◉ Probable	45	45
⊗ Possible	14	14
○ *Observed	0	—

* Not used to compute percentages by category

Atlas Distribution, 1983–1987

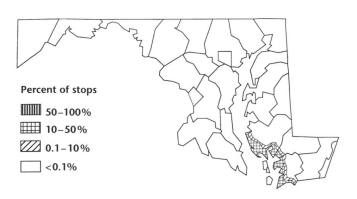

Percent of stops

▥ 50–100%
▦ 10–50%
▨ 0.1–10%
☐ <0.1%

Relative Abundance, 1982–1989

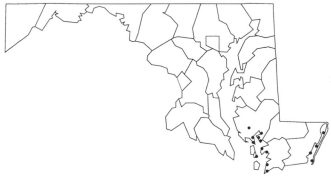

Breeding Distribution, 1958

The Willet was found only where roads penetrate the extensive brackish marshes on the southern Eastern Shore. Miniroutes provide incomplete sampling of marsh habitats; consequently, birds in many breeding areas not close to roads were missed.

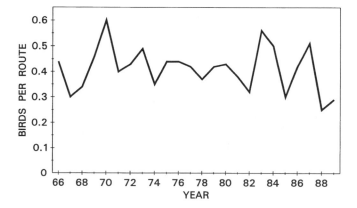

Maryland BBS Trend Graph, 1966–1989

Spotted Sandpiper

Actitis macularia

Teetering its way along the edge of a stream or pond, the Spotted Sandpiper is probably the most frequently seen sandpiper that migrates through Maryland, where it is a rare and local breeder. It returns from its Central and South American wintering grounds (AOU 1983) by early April; a few are still moving through the state during early June (Robbins and Bystrak 1977). The first fall migrants arrive by early July, and the last usually leave by mid-October.

Many early writers failed to distinguish accurately between breeding birds and migrants. Coues and Prentiss (1883) called the Spotted Sandpiper a very abundant summer resident around DC, but Richmond (1888) thought it a rather uncommon breeder there. Kirkwood (1895) classified it as a common summer resident throughout Maryland; Eifrig (1904) wrote that this species was abundant in western Maryland in summer. Hampe and Kolb (1947) noted that evidence of breeding was rather scarce. Stewart and Robbins (1958) called it a fairly common breeding bird in the tidewater areas of the Eastern Shore Section and uncommon elsewhere.

Spotted Sandpipers prefer shoreline habitats along inland ponds and streams, tidal bays, and estuaries for nesting (Stewart and Robbins 1958). They also use field and meadow habitats with short or sparse vegetation near permanent water. Their diet consists primarily of winged insects, although crustaceans, mollusks, and small fish are also taken (Oring et al. 1983).

Nests usually are placed in semi-open vegetation near the water's edge, but suitable nest sites vary from year to year, depending on flooding, vegetative succession, and the presence of predators (Oring et al. 1983). The nest, a depression in the soil, is often constructed with hay and moss. It is gen-

erally in the shelter of high weeds or grass (Davie 1898). All Maryland nests are on the ground (MNRF). The earliest and latest egg dates are 10 May (MNRF) and 15 July (Stewart and Robbins 1958). The average date of 23 clutches in Dorchester County was 15 May (Jackson 1941). Of 28 Maryland clutches (MNRF), 26 contained four eggs and two contained three. Downy young have been seen in Maryland from 4 June (Stewart and Robbins 1958) to 19 July (Ringler 1987b).

Studies in New York (Hays 1972) and Minnesota (Oring and Knudson 1972) established that Spotted Sandpipers are sequentially polyandrous. Females arrive on the breeding grounds first, establish and defend territories, and choose nest sites (Oring et al. 1983). They mate, lay eggs, and terminate the relationship with the male, which incubates the eggs. The female then repeats the sequence with another male (Hays 1972). Females leave males as soon as clutches are complete, except for the final clutch, for which they share incubation. Even then, however, the female does not help the male care for the young. They mate with an average of 1.4 to 2.1 males per year (Oring et al. 1983). Experienced females had significantly more mates, eggs, chicks, and fledglings than did inexperienced females. The Spotted Sandpiper is a pioneering species that quickly and frequently colonizes new areas. It leaves in response to reproductive failure, breeds at an early age, lives a short time, and lays many eggs per female per year with low nest success. Small mammals, such as mice, were responsible for most nest predation.

Most breeding Spotted Sandpipers located during the Atlas period were found in disturbed habitats, such as sewage lagoons and dredge spoil areas. Others were found along rivers in the uplands and tidal guts on the coast. Historically, most Maryland nests were found in Dorchester County more than 70 years ago (Jackson 1941), but no Spotted Sandpipers were found there during the Atlas period. Based in part on Jackson's 1941 report, Stewart and Robbins (1958) described this species as a fairly common breeder in the tidewater areas of the Eastern Shore Section. During the Atlas period, fewer Spotted Sandpipers were found on the Eastern Shore than in any other section. Clearly, something has changed during the past 70 years. Changes in agricultural practices probably have made nesting habitat less available. Most "confirmed" Atlas records were in the Baltimore area, possibly because of the abundance of disturbed habitats there. Most confirmations were by observations of downy young.

Determining whether unconfirmed reports are of migrants or nesting birds is difficult because the migration in both spring and fall overlaps the breeding season. Spotted Sandpipers are extremely vocal and often appear agitated, even in migration; such behavior could easily be misinterpreted as representing breeding. The only way to prove breeding is by finding a nest or downy young. No nests were found during the Atlas period.

The BBS data from 1966 through 1989 show a stable population in the Eastern Region; data are too few for estimating a Maryland trend. As demands on Maryland's open

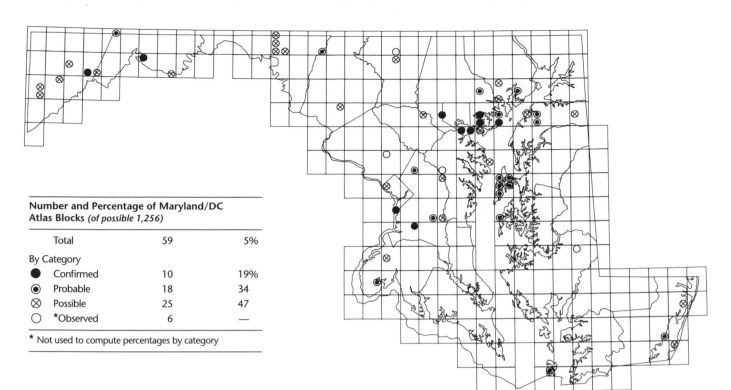

Number and Percentage of Maryland/DC Atlas Blocks *(of possible 1,256)*

Total	59	5%
By Category		
● Confirmed	10	19%
◉ Probable	18	34
⊗ Possible	25	47
○ *Observed	6	—

* Not used to compute percentages by category

Atlas Distribution, 1983–1987

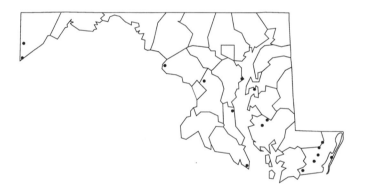

Breeding Distribution, 1958

spaces increase, nesting habitat for these sandpipers will continue to disappear. For the next several decades, Spotted Sandpipers may continue to find nesting sites in a variety of disturbed habitats. Creation of dredge spoil islands could provide additional sites.

Robert F. Ringler

Upland Sandpiper

Bartramia longicauda

The Upland Sandpiper is a bird of hayfields and pastures. It is most commonly seen fluttering over a meadow or alighting on a fence post while emitting short, rapid whistles. This migratory species often nests in loosely spaced colonies (Harrison 1975). The Upland Sandpiper has borne many names through the years, including Upland Plover, Bartramian Sandpiper, Grass Plover, Field Plover (Coues and Prentiss 1883; AOU 1957), and Prairie Pigeon (Buss and Hawkins 1939). It was listed as endangered by the DNR in 1990.

Upland Sandpipers return to Maryland from their South American wintering grounds (AOU 1983) in April and early May (Robbins and Bystrak 1977). Southbound migrants are on the move as early as late July, and the last birds depart by mid-September. The first confirmed breeding in Maryland was in 1895, when Kirkwood (1895) reported two pairs nesting in the north end of Dulaney Valley, Baltimore County. Meanley (1943b) monitored a stable population in Baltimore County from 1935 through 1942. It was considered a fairly common breeder from 1895 through 1958 but by 1984 was considered rare by Robbins and Boone (1984). They estimated a population of fewer than 20 pairs statewide, concentrated primarily in a few areas in Garrett County, with a few pairs in the Frederick Valley. By that time, it had disappeared from Baltimore and Washington counties, possibly because of a loss of extensive upland hayfields, an increase in row crop agriculture, and urbanization (Robbins and Boone 1984). BBS data from 1966 through 1989, however, show a stable population in the Eastern Region, although results indicate a possible slight increase. Continental data show a highly significant average annual increase of 3.7 percent for the same time period; data are too few to estimate a trend for Maryland.

Nesting Upland Sandpipers were fairly common in the Frederick Valley and uncommon locally in the larger fertile valleys of northern and western Maryland, particularly the Allegheny Mountain, Ridge and Valley, and Piedmont sections (Stewart and Robbins 1958). However, there have been no records in the Ridge and Valley and Piedmont sections since 1983. In Maryland, this species is now confined to Garrett County. It has been observed in all sections during migration (Meanley 1943b; Fletcher et al. 1956; Robbins and Bystrak 1977).

Upland Sandpipers' preferred nesting habitats include ungrazed hay meadows (Meanley 1943b), agricultural areas with extensive hayfields and pastures (Stewart and Robbins 1958), standing stubble, moderately grazed fields, mowed areas with heavy regrowth, brush clumps with some understory vegetation, airport grasslands, undisturbed vegetation on poor soils (Kirsch and Higgins 1976), and nontilled uplands (Higgins 1975). Annually tilled croplands, such as summer fallow fields, mulched stubble, and growing grain fields, are used but not preferred (Higgins 1975). Their food is primarily insects, with grasshoppers, crickets, and beetles taken in large numbers (USFWS Food Habits File).

The ground nest, which consists of a cup of grasses twisted in a circle, is hidden in a depression among thick clumps of vegetation usually arching over the top of the nest (Harrison 1975). Short and sparse, thin and uniform, or scattered clumps of fairly dense nesting cover are preferred; most nesting cover is residual vegetation less than 25 in. (64 cm) high from the previous growing season (Lindmeier 1960; Kirsch and Higgins 1976). Meanley (1943b) noted that Upland Sandpipers in Maryland appear to choose their nest sites randomly within an ungrazed meadow; the nest is often only an exposed depression in the grass.

Nesting in Maryland occurs from early May to late June (Stewart and Robbins 1958; Robbins and Bystrak 1977). The normal clutch size is 4 eggs, though 3 and 5 have been reported (Lindmeier 1960; Harrison 1975). Meanley (1943b) found nine nests in Baltimore County, each with 4 eggs. He reported extreme egg dates of 10 May and 10 June and extreme downy young dates of 25 May and 21 June. Incubation, by both parents, lasts for 21 days and one brood is raised per nesting season (Harrison 1975). The precocial young are fully grown and feathered 30 days after hatching (Buss and Hawkins 1939). Nesting is usually confirmed by observing young flying with adults in areas where breeding activity was previously noted.

During the Atlas period, "confirmed" records of Upland Sandpipers were reported only in southern Garrett County. The absence of birds in the Frederick Valley, noted as the principal range by Stewart and Robbins (1958), is disappointing. Despite fairly intensive searching by birdwatchers, no summer birds have been reported from the traditional nesting field in the Oland Road area of Frederick County

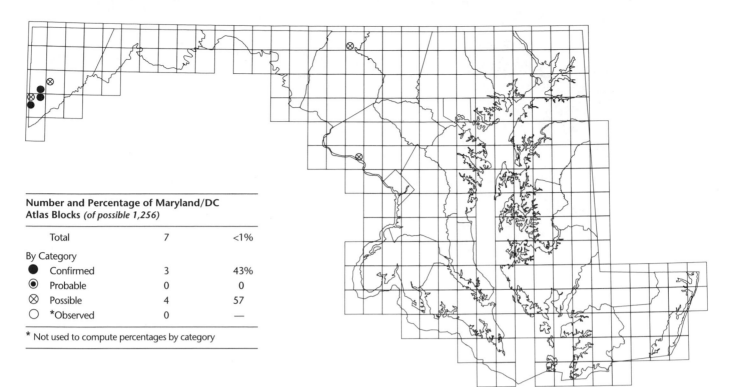

Number and Percentage of Maryland/DC Atlas Blocks *(of possible 1,256)*

	Total	7	<1%
By Category			
●	Confirmed	3	43%
◉	Probable	0	0
⊗	Possible	4	57
○	*Observed	0	—

* Not used to compute percentages by category

Atlas Distribution, 1983–1987

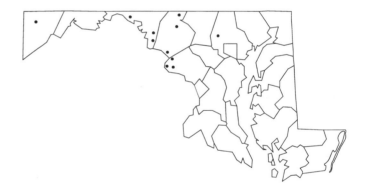

Breeding Distribution, 1958

since 1982. Scott Smith and N. Stewart (unpub. data) observed characteristic breeding behavior of a lone bird on Hoover Mill Road near Thurmont in Frederick County on 27 June 1988, suggesting that a few Upland Sandpipers continue to nest in the area. Birds breed in areas of both Pennsylvania (Brauning 1992) and Virginia adjacent to the Frederick Valley in Maryland.

Maryland is at the southeastern edge of the breeding range (AOU 1983) of the Upland Sandpiper and its status in the state is tenuous. Its continued presence within our borders depends on the availability of large upland areas of undisturbed grasslands.

Scott A. Smith

American Woodcock

Scolopax minor

The American Woodcock's unique aerial courtship display has made it a favorite of birdwatchers, while its erratic flight and tendency to hold tight in thick cover have made it a favorite of hunters. It is a migratory game bird, wintering in the southeastern United States and breeding primarily in the northeastern Midwest and the Northeast (Owen 1977). Maryland is near the southern limit of its breeding range along the Atlantic Coast (AOU 1983). During mild winters some birds remain, especially on the lower Eastern Shore (Stewart and Robbins 1958).

Although classified as a shorebird, the American Woodcock is physically and behaviorally adapted to damp woodlands (Sepik et al. 1981). Its habitat in Maryland is typically early stages of forest succession, such as thickets and open stands of shrubs and small trees adjacent to wet or damp areas (DNR 1983). This crepuscular bird prefers areas where little or no vegetation covers the ground, including pine and sweet gum fields, alder swamps, young second-growth hardwood stands, and cutover areas. It also uses abandoned agricultural areas and fields too wet for farming or timber growing. A breeding density of 6 territorial males per 100 acres (40.5 ha) was recorded in brushy, poorly drained, abandoned farmland at PWRC in 1943 (Stewart and Robbins 1958).

Early authors noted a decline in American Woodcock populations in this area and attributed it largely to hunting (Coues and Prentiss 1883; Richmond 1888; Kirkwood 1895). Hampe and Kolb (1947) wrote that most experienced observers believed American Woodcock were much less common than 40 years earlier. Stewart and Robbins (1958) described them as fairly common locally in the Eastern Shore, Western Shore, Upper Chesapeake, Ridge and Valley, and Allegheny Mountain sections, and uncommon and local in the Piedmont Section.

The first American Woodcock legislation, passed in Maryland in 1847, prohibited hunting from 20 February to 1 June (DNR 1983). In 1919, the first formal season and bag limits were imposed. Since the 1950s the Maryland DNR has cooperated with the USFWS to conduct censuses of singing woodcock to index the breeding population. From 1968 through 1990, the Maryland breeding population index fell 79 percent from 2.9 to 0.6 (Bortner 1990). A similar trend has been noted in most eastern states. BBS data from 1966 through 1989 show stable populations in Maryland and the Eastern Region; however, this survey does not adequately sample crepuscular species.

Spring migrants begin returning to Maryland from the southern United States (AOU 1983) in late January and early February (Stewart and Robbins 1958). The male performs his courtship display at dusk and dawn on singing areas ranging in size from 0.2 to 100 acres (0.1–40.5 ha) and consisting of open areas in early successional stages (Liscinsky 1972). In Maryland, this display can be observed from late January to early May. Nests are placed on the ground, most within a few yards of brushy field edges (Sheldon 1967; Owen 1977) and often within 300 ft (91 m) of the singing ground. Nests are shallow depressions lined with a few leaves; occasionally a few twigs or stems are placed around the edge (Sheldon 1967).

The MNRF contains 19 reports of nests with eggs, with clutches of either 3 or 4 (mean of 3.7). The earliest egg date is 25 February, in Baltimore County, and the latest is 25 May, with most reported before late April (MNRF). Incubation, by both sexes, requires 20 or 21 days (Bent 1927). Broods were reported in Maryland from 9 April to 16 June (MNRF). In 15 reports, brood sizes range from 2 to 4 (mean of 3.5). Renesting often occurs if the initial effort fails (McAuley et al. 1990), but one brood is typical (Owen 1977). Nesting habitat and habitat used by very young broods appear to be similar. Alder swales and pockets of second-growth hardwoods are favorite daytime haunts. One of the major requirements is fertile, moist soil, which enables the American Woodcock to probe for the earthworms that constitute 50 to 90 percent of its diet (Owen 1977).

Atlas results show concentrations of records on the central Eastern Shore, central Western Shore, and in the Upper Chesapeake sections. This distribution is similar to that reported by Stewart and Robbins (1958), except that the Atlas data suggest a scarcity in the southern counties. The secretive nature of the American Woodcock, as well as its crepuscular courtship, probably resulted in underdetection by Atlas workers. Although it still nests throughout the state, wildlife agencies believe the population has declined, and they have attempted to reduce the number taken by hunters. The American Woodcock needs special consideration in management plans because of its low reproductive rate and need for early successional habitats (Liscinsky 1972).

Forest management and land-use trends may be the most important factors affecting future population levels. The American Woodcock requires young, diverse, vigorously growing forests. As more habitat is lost to urbanization and large-scale agriculture, management of the remaining habitat becomes more crucial.

Thomas P. Mathews

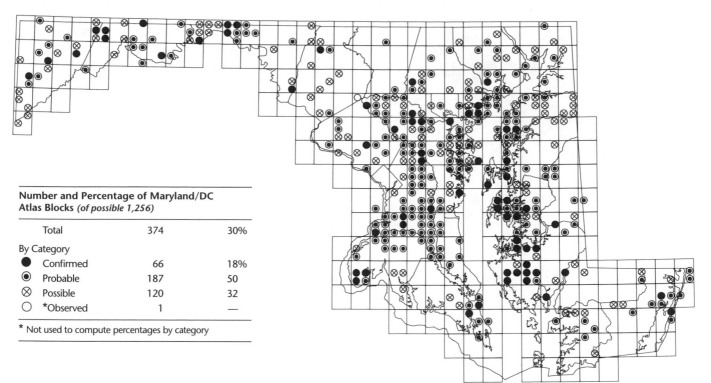

Number and Percentage of Maryland/DC Atlas Blocks *(of possible 1,256)*

Total	374	30%
By Category		
● Confirmed	66	18%
◉ Probable	187	50
⊗ Possible	120	32
○ *Observed	1	—

* Not used to compute percentages by category

Atlas Distribution, 1983–1987

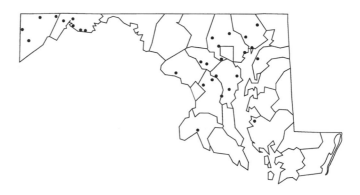

Breeding Distribution, 1958

Laughing Gull

Larus atricilla

Laughing Gulls are commonly seen foraging for earthworms and other invertebrates in agricultural fields on the Delmarva peninsula during summer. They occur on the Coastal Plain of Maryland from April through November (Stewart and Robbins 1958); in winter some Maryland birds occur as far south as Panama (Stewart and Robbins 1958). Despite their abundance, Laughing Gulls are rare breeders in Maryland.

Kirkwood (1895) assumed that Laughing Gulls bred in Worcester County and possibly in the lower Chesapeake Bay during the late 1800s, but he was unable to locate a colony. The first reported Maryland colony, approximately 100 pairs, was found by H. Bailey in 1915 at Striking Marsh in Worcester County (Stewart and Robbins 1958). Other breeding sites, now unused or eroded away, included Robins Marsh (1951 through 1977), South Point spoil islands (1953 through 1955), Oyster Island (1975 through 1976), Outward Tump (1976), and the Cedar Islands (1976) in Worcester County; Cornfield Harbor (1935 through 1946) in St. Mary's County; and Sharps Island (1954 through 1956) in Talbot County (Kleen 1956; Stewart and Robbins 1958; Osborn and Custer 1978; Erwin and Korschgen 1979). Other than a single attempt by several pairs at South Sand Point during 1989, Laughing Gulls have not bred in the Maryland portion of the Chesapeake Bay since the late 1950s. At present, their breeding is restricted to tidal salt-marsh islands in coastal Worcester County.

Historically, nests were built on the ground in open salt marshes (Burger and Shisler 1978). Nests consist of vegetation piles constructed primarily of smooth cordgrass, built to a sufficient height to protect the eggs from normal high tides (D. Brinker, pers. obs.). With the expansion of breeding Herring Gulls into Maryland, Laughing Gulls have modified their nest placement. Most Maryland nests now are located on the ground in dense patches of marsh elder in higher portions of the salt marsh (MCWP); nest building begins in late April.

The first eggs are laid during mid-May, with 10 May the earliest Maryland egg date (MCWP). Data from 243 Maryland nests with eggs show early and late egg dates of 17 May and 18 July (MNRF). Clutch sizes range from 1 to 3 (mean of 2.3). Peak egg laying occurs in late May, and chicks begin hatching in early June (MCWP) after an incubation period of about 20 days (Bent 1921). Nests with young were found from 1 June (MCWP) to 26 July (MNRF). Maryland brood sizes in 36 nests (MNRF) range from 1 to 4 (mean of 2.0).

During the Atlas period, Laughing Gull breeding was restricted to three blocks in Worcester County. Within two of these blocks, colonial nesting occurred at the Snug Harbor, Gray's Cove, and Bridge islands; solitary nesting occurred in other waterbird colonies on Horsehead Tump and Big Bay Marsh (MCWP). From a high of approximately 2,500 pairs in the mid-1970s (Erwin 1979), Laughing Gull populations in Maryland had fallen to their lowest recorded levels by 1987, with fewer than 50 pairs in most years and only 25 pairs in 1991 (MCWP). Production was very poor, with few young fledged in any year after 1985 (MCWP). A substantial decline in Laughing Gull breeding populations has also been noted from Maine through Massachusetts (Clapp et al. 1983); increased populations of Herring Gulls and Great Black-backed Gulls seem responsible for this decline (Nisbet 1971; Burger and Schisler 1978; Burger 1979a). In spite of declines in parts of this gull's range, BBS data indicate significant increases in Maryland and the Eastern Region from 1966 through 1989. New Jersey and Virginia still have large, stable breeding populations (Spendelow and Patton 1988), which are probably the source of the non-breeding Laughing Gulls that are so common on the Eastern Shore each summer.

In Maryland, a lack of secure nesting habitat appears to be a critical factor in the decline of breeding populations. During the past 20 years, erosion, geomorphological changes along the coast, disturbance by feral horses, and, especially, competition with expanding Herring Gull populations have combined to remove six locations from the list of Maryland sites available to Laughing Gulls. Another, Bridge Island, was mysteriously abandoned in 1987 (MCWP). Islands previously used by Laughing Gulls, such as Robins Marsh and Outward Tump, now support substantial colonies of Herring Gulls that are excluding Laughing Gulls. BBS data from 1966 through 1989 show a highly significant average annual increases of 6.8 percent for the Eastern Region and 9.5 percent for Maryland.

There is little evidence to implicate direct human influence in the recent decline of breeding Laughing Gulls within

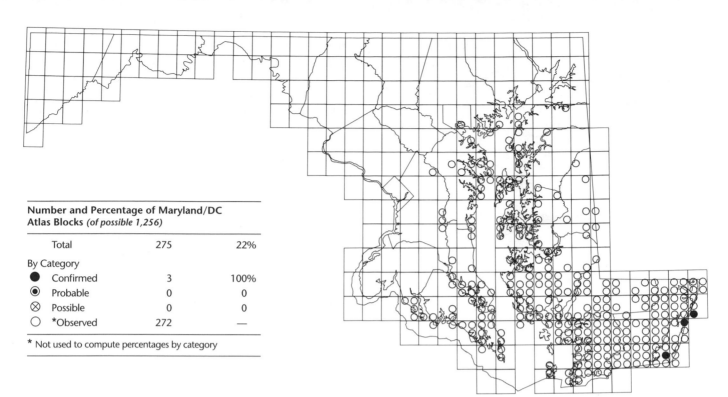

Number and Percentage of Maryland/DC Atlas Blocks *(of possible 1,256)*

Total		275	22%
By Category			
●	Confirmed	3	100%
◉	Probable	0	0
⊗	Possible	0	0
○	*Observed	272	—

* Not used to compute percentages by category

Atlas Distribution, 1983–1987

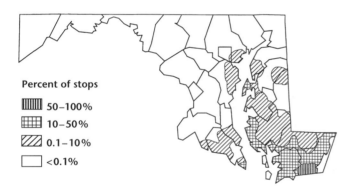

Percent of stops

▥ 50–100%
▦ 10–50%
▨ 0.1–10%
☐ <0.1%

Relative Abundance, 1982–1989

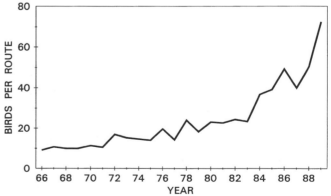

Breeding Distribution, 1958

The Laughing Gull is a colonial nester; its offshore breeding sites are not sampled by miniroutes. The high densities in southern Worcester County may represent foragers from colonies in Virginia. Most other records represent nonbreeding birds feeding in agricultural areas or roosting along the Chesapeake Bay.

Maryland. Their concentrated foraging in agricultural fields, however, creates a potential danger in that agricultural chemicals could depress egg viability and reproductive success. A better understanding of the relationship between agricultural chemical usage and Laughing Gull reproductive success is needed. Present information indicates that breeding Laughing Gulls are in serious danger of disappearing from Maryland.

David F. Brinker

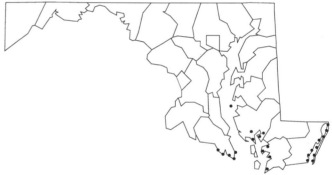

Maryland BBS Trend Graph, 1966–1989

Herring Gull

Larus argentatus

Prior to 1940, Herring Gulls were primarily winter residents in Maryland; now they are the most abundant breeding gulls in the state. They are encountered year-round throughout the Chesapeake Bay but are most abundant in the lower Bay and in coastal Worcester County. Although adept at locating natural food sources, such as small fish, crustaceans, and mollusks (Martin et al. 1951), these gulls often forage behind the boats of watermen and at landfills.

Kirkwood (1895) considered Herring Gulls common winter residents. By the 1940s, substantial numbers remained in coastal Worcester County throughout the summer (Hampe and Kolb 1947). The first Maryland breeding record was of three nests found on Sharps Island, Talbot County, in 1955 (Kleen 1956). This tiny island had seven nests in 1956 and eight in 1958 (Miller 1958). The first coastal nesting occurred in 1958, when three pairs used a South Point spoil island (Miller 1958). This colony had eight pairs in 1960 and 1961 (Bridge and Weske 1961; Bridge and Riedel 1962). In 1962, a colony of at least 50 pairs was discovered on Smith Island, Somerset County (Robbins 1962). The first three pairs nested in Robins Marsh, Worcester County, in 1963, where there were eight pairs in 1964 and about the same number through 1969 (MNRF). The colony increased to about 40 pairs in 1971.

Little information is available on the rapid expansion of breeding Herring Gulls in Maryland between 1971 and 1976. By 1976 Herring Gulls had established 10 Maryland colonies; the population was estimated at 4,500 pairs (Erwin 1979) in Dorchester, Somerset, and Worcester counties combined (Erwin and Korschgen 1979). Colonies are restricted to islands where mammalian predators are absent or rare. In Maryland, two site types are commonly used: dredge spoil disposal areas and tidal salt marshes (MCWP). Colonies on dredge spoil are most frequent in the Chesapeake Bay, while salt-marsh use predominates in Worcester County.

Nest building begins in late March and the first eggs are laid in mid-April (MCWP). Herring Gull eggs are only slightly smaller than those of Great Black-backed Gulls, and in mixed colonies they cannot be reliably distinguished (R. Clapp, pers. comm.). The earliest Maryland egg date is 12

April (F. Rohwer, pers. comm.); the latest is 26 July (MNRF). Peak egg laying occurs in mid-May (F. Rohwer, pers. comm). A sample of 2,212 Maryland clutch sizes ranged from 1 to 5, with 2 and 3 eggs most frequent (Armistead 1978); the mean was 2.6. The first chicks hatch in mid-May (MCWP) after an incubation period of 24 to 28 days (Townsend 1921); they begin fledging by late June (MCWP). The latest Maryland date for downy young is 11 August (F. Rohwer, pers. comm.).

Nests are always built on the ground, but their placement with respect to vegetation varies considerably (MCWP). In Worcester County salt marshes, nests are in open situations or are scattered throughout low (3 ft [0.9 m]) stands of marsh elder. At Chesapeake Bay dredge spoil sites, nests are often deep in dense vegetation, such as phragmites stands, or in the open on bare dry mudflats. In Baltimore County, at Hart–Miller Island, nests were scattered over a large rock pile, and at Bethlehem Steel's Sparrow's Point foundry, they were scattered over a much larger slag pile. Nests are constructed primarily of fine vegetation and grass. Nests in salt marshes are typically tall enough to protect eggs from normal high tides. At more upland dredge spoil sites, there is no relation between nest height and placement.

In a special study during the Atlas period (MCWP), Herring Gulls were "confirmed" in 13 blocks: five in the Chesapeake Bay and eight in Worcester County. In these blocks, nesting occurred at 20 locations (MCWP); this is twice the number found during the mid-1970s. The largest colony was at Easter Point, a dredge spoil disposal area near Ewell on Smith Island. The most unusual record was nesting attempted by 506 pairs at Hart–Miller Island in 1986 (MCWP). This was the first nesting attempt north of the Chesapeake Bay Bridge. All the nests failed because of severe red fox predation, and nesting has not been attempted there again. The colony moved to a very large waste slag pile at Sparrow's Point (MCWP).

The Maryland breeding population represents approximately 5 percent of the Atlantic Coast population (Spendelow and Patton 1988). The southward expansion of Herring Gulls appears to have slowed, with little recent (1977 through 1983) expansion southward in North Carolina (Clapp and Buckley 1984).

The BBS does not sample gulls on the nesting islands, but it monitors the future nesters that have not yet reached breeding age. Data from 1966 through 1989 show stable populations in the Eastern Region. Maryland data from a small sample of 12 routes show a significant average annual increase of 21.6 percent. Although this increase may be high because of the small sample size, it is still cause for concern. Herring Gulls benefit from their ability to coexist with people. The largest Maryland colony probably owes its success to the combination of a relatively secure dredge spoil disposal site for nesting and easily obtainable food from the crabbing industry of Smith Island (D. Brinker, pers. obs.). The Maryland Herring Gull population is relatively healthy, possibly too healthy. The recent increase in breeding Herring Gulls may have seriously affected Maryland Laughing Gull populations.

David F. Brinker

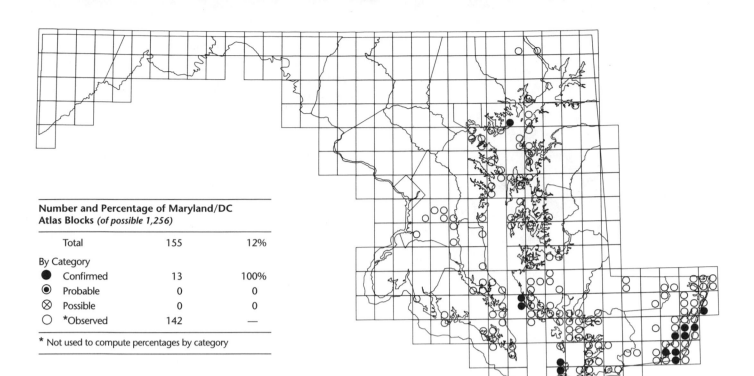

Number and Percentage of Maryland/DC Atlas Blocks *(of possible 1,256)*

	Total	155	12%
By Category			
●	Confirmed	13	100%
◉	Probable	0	0
⊗	Possible	0	0
○	*Observed	142	—

* Not used to compute percentages by category

Atlas Distribution, 1983–1987

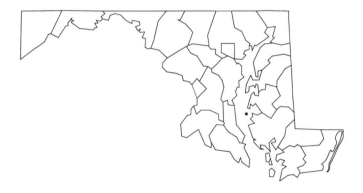

Breeding Distribution, 1958

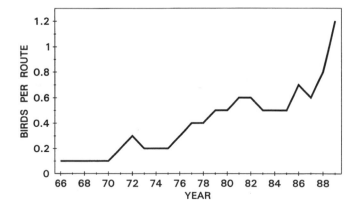

Maryland BBS Trend Graph, 1966–1989

Great Black-backed Gull

Larus marinus

Great Black-backed Gulls are the largest and most aggressive gulls along the Atlantic Coast. They have taken prey as large as Glossy Ibis (D. Brinker, pers. obs.). Prior to 1950, they were uncommon to rare winter residents and summer vagrants in Maryland; they are now uncommon breeders and common winter residents. Although found throughout the Chesapeake Bay, they are primarily coastal birds and reach their highest breeding density in Worcester County.

Kirkwood (1895) considered Great Black-backed Gulls rare winter visitors. By the 1940s, the frequency of winter observations had increased to the point where Hampe and Kolb (1947) considered them uncommon, with most observations in the lower Chesapeake Bay and the Ocean City area in Worcester County. Expansion of their breeding range brought nesting birds south to Maine in 1928, Massachusetts in 1931, and New York in 1942 (Zeranski and Baptist 1990). Stewart and Robbins (1958) recorded five summer vagrants in Worcester, Talbot, and Dorchester Counties in 1951 through 1955. The first Maryland breeding record was of a chick found in 1972 on a South Point spoil island in Worcester County (Boone 1975). Armistead (1975) documented the first breeding record for the Maryland portion of the Chesapeake Bay at Smith Island in Somerset County in 1975. This species may have bred in Maryland several years earlier than the published records indicate, since the first recorded nesting for Virginia was in 1970 at Fishermans Island (Scott and Cutler 1970) and for North Carolina was in 1972 at Oregon Inlet (Parnell and Soots 1975).

A USFWS survey of colonial waterbirds during 1976 and 1977 found Great Black-backed Gulls nesting in four Maryland colonies (Erwin 1979). These colonies were at Easter Point near Ewell on Smith Island in Somerset County and at Outward Tump, Robins Marsh, and Striking Marsh in Worcester County (Erwin and Korschgen 1979). In 1977, Maryland's breeding population was approximately 33 pairs. Dur-

ing the next summer, Armistead (1978) counted a total of 46 nesting pairs in four Somerset County colonies. Although found mostly in association with Herring Gull colonies, Great Black-backed Gulls also nest as solitary pairs. No solitary nests were found during the Atlas period, but nesting away from known colonies is possible. The Maryland Great Black-backed Gull breeding population represents approximately 0.5 percent of the Atlantic Coast population (Spendelow and Patton 1988) and has been increasing since the 1970s. BBS data from 1966 through 1989 show stable populations in the Eastern Region; there are too few data to estimate a trend for Maryland.

Great Black-backed Gulls are the earliest nesting gulls in Maryland. Nests are placed on the ground and are essentially indistinguishable from those of Herring Gulls. As with Herring Gulls, nest placement with respect to vegetation varies considerably. The tendency to place nests on the highest portions of salt-marsh islands has been noted elsewhere (Burger 1978a; McGill-Harelstad 1981; Spendelow et al. 1983) but has not been found in Maryland. In Maryland, nest building begins in mid-March and the first eggs are laid during mid-April (F. Rohwer, pers. comm.). Most egg laying occurs during a short period from mid- to late April. The earliest Maryland egg date is 11 April, and the latest newly initiated nest is 15 May (F. Rohwer, pers. comm.). The latest egg date is 20 June (MNRF). Clutch sizes for Maryland nests vary from 1 to 3, with most being 2 or 3 eggs (MCWP). The incubation period is 26 to 30 days (Godfrey 1986). Chicks begin hatching in early May and fledge during late June (MCWP). The earliest hatching date is 11 May (MCWP); the latest is 5 July. Although eggs of Great Black-backed Gulls are slightly larger than those of Herring Gulls, the overlap in egg size in Maryland makes field separation unreliable (R. Clapp and D. Brinker, unpub. data). Because downy chicks are also essentially indistinguishable from those of Herring Gulls, the only certain way to confirm breeding is to observe incubating adults or to see large, feathered young. The diet is similar to that of the Herring Gull. Fish is the staple food, but it is supplemented by eggs and chicks of other species during the nesting season (Bent 1921).

During the Atlas period, breeding was restricted to nine blocks: four in the Chesapeake Bay and five in Worcester County. Within these blocks, nesting occurred at 12 locations from 1985 through 1991 (MCWP), nearly twice the number of locations found during surveys conducted in the mid-1970s. The largest colony was at Easter Point in Somerset County, where Great Black-backed Gulls were mixed with the large Herring Gull colony. The most unusual record, a single pair in a Herring Gull colony in 1986 far up the Bay at Hart–Miller Island near Baltimore (MCWP), was unexpected. This attempt failed when all nests in the colony were destroyed by red foxes (D. Brinker, pers. obs.). Since this initial failure, nesting Great Black-backed Gulls were found in 1990 and 1991 in the large Herring Gull colony that has formed at Sparrow's Point, also in Baltimore County.

Great Black-backed Gulls appear to be continuing their expansion in Maryland. They are now firmly established at

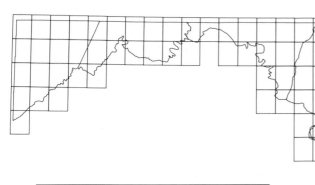

Number and Percentage of Maryland/DC Atlas Blocks *(of possible 1,256)*

Total	81	6%
By Category		
● Confirmed	9	100%
◉ Probable	0	0
⊗ Possible	0	0
○ *Observed	72	—

* Not used to compute percentages by category

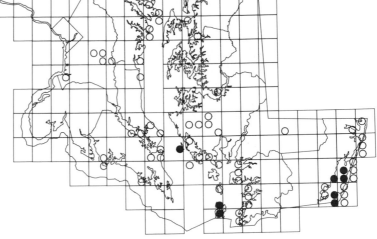

Atlas Distribution, 1983–1987

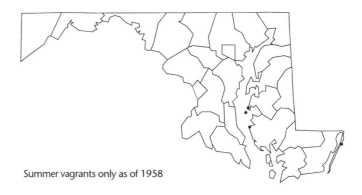

Summer vagrants only as of 1958

Breeding Distribution, 1958

over ten Maryland colonies; recent statewide breeding estimates are approximately 175 pairs (MCWP), several times greater than those of the mid-1970s. If this rate of expansion continues, it may adversely affect other species and necessitate management initiatives directed toward controlling the Great Black-backed Gull population.

David F. Brinker

MOB

Gull-billed Tern

Sterna nilotica

Gull-billed Terns, the rarest regularly breeding terns in Maryland, nest on all continents except Antarctica. Despite their wide distribution, they are uncommon in most places. Although worldwide census data are incomplete, available information indicates that the Texas coast has one of the largest breeding concentrations of Gull-billed Terns in the world (Spendelow and Patton 1988). Other places with nesting populations in excess of 1,000 pairs are Virginia (Buckley and Buckley 1984), Mauritania (Urban et al. 1986), Australia (Blakers et al. 1984), Spain, and the Soviet Union (Cramp 1985). In Maryland, Gull-billed Terns are rare summer residents, with few records outside the Worcester County breeding colonies. They winter from the Gulf of Mexico south to South America (AOU 1983). They begin returning to Maryland in late April and depart in September (Stewart and Robbins 1958).

The first recorded nesting of Gull-billed Terns in Maryland was in 1945 at the South Point spoil islands in Worcester County (Stewart and Robbins 1947a). They may have begun using the South Point spoil islands a few years after their creation in the mid-1930s and continued until vegetative growth resulted in unfavorable nesting habitat in the early 1960s. Gull-billed Terns have been found breeding at four other Worcester County locations: Clam Harbor Tumps in 1946 (Stewart and Robbins 1947a), Oyster Island from 1974 through 1976 (Robbins 1975a, 1976), Big Bay Marsh from 1984 through 1986 (Ringler 1984c; MCWP), and Ocean City spoils in 1987 (MCWP). The first two of these five locations have eroded to below mean sea level.

Nests are usually located on barren areas of sand or shell fragments in association with nests of other colonial waterbirds, especially the Common Tern, Forster's Tern, and Black Skimmer (MCWP). Maryland nesting information is based on a very small set of observations. The earliest reported egg date is 15 May and the latest is 18 July (Robbins and Bystrak 1977). Clutches are usually 2 or 3 eggs, with 3 more common (MCWP). Both parents participate in incubation, which requires 22 or 23 days (Cramp 1985). Chicks begin hatching in early June and fledging occurs as early as the beginning of July (MCWP). Downy young have been found in Maryland from 6 June to 18 July (Stewart and Robbins 1958).

During the Atlas period, Gull-billed Terns bred at only two sites, Big Bay Marsh and Ocean City spoils (MCWP). Prior to 1985, the highest population recorded in Maryland was 25 to 30 breeding pairs from 1950 through 1955 (Stewart and Robbins 1958). Populations have been considerably lower in many other years. From 1977 through 1983, for example, no nestings were recorded in Maryland. During the 1970s, the highest recorded number breeding in Maryland was three pairs on Oyster Island in 1975 (Therres et al. 1978). Since 1985, Maryland Gull-billed Tern breeding populations have fluctuated between 0 and 33 pairs (MCWP). The breeding population from 1985 through 1988 was 9, 33, 1, and 0 pairs respectively, and was limited to a single site in any one year (MCWP).

Within Maryland, the limiting factor appears to be the availability of suitable nesting habitat in reasonable proximity to foraging areas in open salt marshes, fields, and beaches. Unlike most other terns, the Gull-billed Tern eats large numbers of dragonflies, grasshoppers, ghost crabs, and fiddler crabs and consumes relatively small numbers of fish (USFWS Food Habits File).

Gull-billed Terns are now most frequently found nesting on dredge spoil areas or other artificial sites (Clapp et al. 1983). The lack of suitable nesting areas is well illustrated by marginal sites used by Maryland birds during recent years. The nest found on Ocean City spoils during 1987 was in a small disjunct sand beach of only a few square meters, and it failed when destroyed by a high spring tide (MCWP). The Big Bay Marsh site consists of a very narrow 6.6 to 9.8 ft (2–3 m) long shell beach that is barely above wind-blown storm tides.

Clapp et al. (1983) noted that "because the species nests in areas highly susceptible to environmental perturbations and because it may be easily affected by human disturbance, development of coastal areas may seriously affect the well-being of this little-studied species." This statement certainly applies to the present situation in Maryland. The Gull-billed Tern took advantage of habitat made available by dredging activities of the 1930s, and varying numbers bred within Maryland over the next 50 years on both artificial and natural sites. BBS data from 1966 through 1989 show stable populations in the Eastern Region; too few data exist to estimate a trend for Maryland.

The Gull-billed Tern is listed by the DNR as a threatened species and its future in Maryland is uncertain. Development of a new spoil island in a remote area of Worcester County would be very beneficial to this tern and other beach-nesting colonial waterbirds.

David F. Brinker

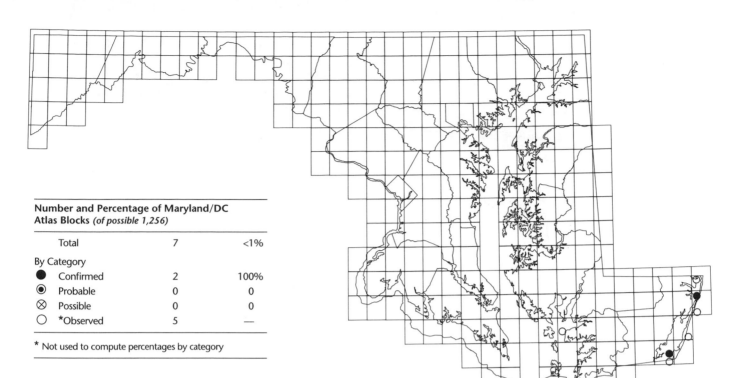

Number and Percentage of Maryland/DC Atlas Blocks *(of possible 1,256)*

	Total	7	<1%
By Category			
●	Confirmed	2	100%
◉	Probable	0	0
⊗	Possible	0	0
○	*Observed	5	—

* Not used to compute percentages by category

Atlas Distribution, 1983–1987

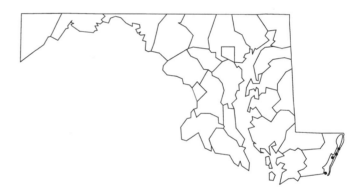

Breeding Distribution, 1958

Royal Tern

Sterna maxima

Royal Terns, Maryland's largest breeding terns, are rare summer residents. Maryland is at the northern edge of their breeding range (AOU 1983). Their population may be gradually expanding, as the first successful nesting in New Jersey occurred in 1988 (Gochfeld et al. 1989).

The first Royal Tern record for Maryland is from one collected on 27 August 1945 at Ocean City, Worcester County. The first breeding record was in 1950, when two pairs nested on a South Point spoil island (Stewart and Robbins 1958), one of approximately ten small islands created in Sinepuxent Bay by dredging operations during 1936 and 1937 (Poole 1942). Royal Terns used these islands, with varying success, from 1953 until the early 1960s, when vegetative growth made the islands unsuitable for nesting (Therres et al. 1978). There were 115 nests in 1953, 500 adults in 1954, 76 young in 1955, and 31 young in 1956 (Stewart and Robbins 1958). In the 1960s, Maryland's average breeding population of Royal Terns was probably several hundred pairs. During the 1970s, the Maryland breeding population varied between 100 and 1,160 pairs (Therres et al. 1978), and the Virginia breeding population was estimated at 4,500 to 6,750 pairs (Buckley and Buckley 1972; Erwin 1979). BBS data from 1966 through 1989 show stable populations in the Eastern Region; data are too few to estimate a trend for Maryland.

Royal Terns have never been known to occupy more than three Maryland sites in any one year. In addition to the South Point spoil islands, during the last 20 years these terns have used six other sites in Worcester County and one in Dorchester County: the Cedar Islands in several years (Bystrak 1971; Therres et al. 1978; Colonial Bird Register), Oyster Island in the mid-1970s (Therres et al. 1978; J. Weske, pers. comm.), Horsehead Tump in 1982 (Ringler 1982), Bridge Island in the early 1980s (Colonial Bird Register), South Sand Point in 1989 (Armistead 1990), Big Bay Marsh in 1990 (MCWP), and the newly accreted sandbars near the U.S. Route 50 bridge outside of Ocean City in 1990 and 1991 (MCWP). Since the Sinepuxent Bay dredge spoil islands have eroded away or have been gradually rendered unsuit-

able by vegetative changes, sites for Royal Tern breeding have become rare and are restricted to small beaches, usually on the edges of salt-marsh islands. At best, all post-1980 locations have been marginal sites for Royal Tern colonies.

Royal Terns return to Maryland from West Indian waters (AOU 1983) as early as late March and begin searching for potential colony sites (MCWP). Frequently, habitat conditions are unsuitable and Royal Terns do not breed in Maryland. The earliest date for their single-egg clutch is 15 May (Robbins and Bystrak 1977), and the latest is 1 August (MCWP). After an incubation period of 22 or 23 days (Cramp 1985), the chick hatches in mid-June and fledging occurs about four weeks later (MCWP). Extreme Maryland dates for downy chicks are 7 June (Robbins and Bystrak 1977) and 6 August (MCWP). Royal Terns feed largely on fish and crabs (Bent 1921).

In Maryland, the breeding population of Royal Terns appears to be limited by the availability of suitable nesting habitat. These terns nest in dense colonies, usually on open sandy beaches, preferably on islands inaccessible to mammalian predators. They also require large expanses of shallow water and a location at or near an inlet for foraging (Buckley and Buckley 1980). In Sinepuxent Bay, dredge spoil islands provided excellent nesting sites from the late 1930s through the early 1970s. One of the salt-marsh islands used during this period had relatively little sand or shell, and the Royal Terns nested on trampled mats of dried eelgrass over hard mud and scattered shells (Therres et al. 1978).

During the Atlas period, no "confirmed" breeding was reported for Royal Terns in Maryland. Subsequent to the Atlas, they have attempted to breed at four Maryland sites. Although a colony frequently nests on Shank's Island, just south of the Maryland-Virginia line in the Smith Island archipelago, there were no nesting records for the Maryland portion of the Chesapeake Bay until an unsuccessful attempt at South Sand Point in Dorchester County in 1989 (Armistead 1990). The best of the recent sites were the sand bars near Ocean City; unfortunately, the substantial development and high recreational use of the Ocean City Inlet area will be a deterrent to Royal Tern use of this sand bar.

Compared with other colonial species, Royal Terns tend to nest in large numbers but at few sites (Clapp et al. 1983). As a result, they are particularly vulnerable to human disturbance. Although colonies close to Ocean City were at least occasionally disturbed by recreational boaters in the past (J. Weske, pers. comm.), this probably was not the major factor that led to the loss of the Royal Tern from Maryland's regularly nesting avifauna and its subsequent listing as an endangered species by the DNR. Rather, the leading cause was probably the disappearance of suitable nesting habitat. Creation and maintenance of a new spoil island as bare nesting habitat in an area of Worcester County removed from the intense and growing recreational pressure near Ocean City would greatly improve the future of the Royal Tern as a Maryland breeding species.

David F. Brinker

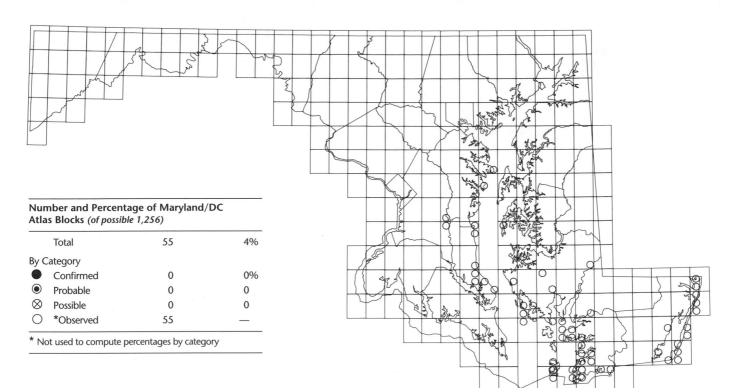

Number and Percentage of Maryland/DC Atlas Blocks (of possible 1,256)

Total	55	4%

By Category

●	Confirmed	0	0%
◉	Probable	0	0
⊗	Possible	0	0
○	*Observed	55	—

* Not used to compute percentages by category

Atlas Distribution, 1983–1987

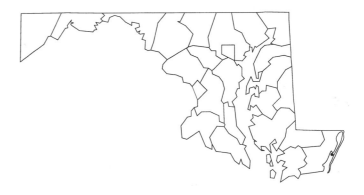

Breeding Distribution, 1958

Common Tern

Sterna hirundo

The Common Tern fits its name well: it nests throughout most of the northern hemisphere and is Maryland's most abundant breeding tern. It is a common summer resident in coastal Worcester County and the lower Chesapeake Bay. Spring migrants return from their wintering grounds in the Caribbean (AOU 1983) in early April, and most depart by late September (Robbins and Bystrak 1977). During post-breeding dispersal and migration, they occur throughout the Chesapeake Bay.

The earliest reports of Common Terns breeding in Maryland are from Dutcher (1901), who reported nesting along the coast in 1900, and Jackson (1941), who reported 30 pairs breeding in 1919 at Long Island in Dorchester County. Since 1900 there have been records of over 25 colony sites in Maryland. Although populations were thought to have been reduced by the plume trade during the late 1800s, they had already begun to recover by the early 1900s (Cooke 1929). Stewart and Robbins (1958) listed Common Terns as common in the coastal area of Worcester County, fairly common locally in tidewater areas of Somerset County, and rare and local in tidewater areas of Dorchester, Talbot, and St. Mary's counties. The St. Mary's colony at Point Lookout on the Western Shore was found in 1937; however, there are no recent records of breeding on the lower Western Shore. A 1976 USFWS survey found 11 Maryland colonies with an estimated breeding population of approximately 1,700 pairs (Erwin 1979).

Although Common Terns return to Maryland in April, nest initiation is delayed until May. The earliest reported egg date is 9 May (MCWP) and the latest is 5 August (Webster 1951). Clutches are usually 2 or 3 eggs, with 3 more common (MCWP). The incubation period lasts 21 days (Bent 1921). The first chicks hatch at the time of peak incubation in late May and begin to fledge in mid- to late June (MCWP). Maryland dates for downy young extend from 29 May (MCWP) to 22 August (MNRF).

Common Terns prefer nesting on open sand and broken shell beaches on predator-free islands. As relatively undisturbed beaches have gradually disappeared in Maryland and other states, Common Terns have begun nesting on mats of wrack deposited by winter storms on salt-marsh islands. When found on wrack, Common Tern nests and eggs are virtually indistinguishable from those of the Forster's Tern if both breed in the area. In the larger Chesapeake Bay colonies, Common and Forster's Terns are found in mixed groups.

From 1980 through 1988, Common Terns were found breeding at 17 locations in 14 Atlas blocks: eight in the Chesapeake Bay and six in coastal Worcester County (MCWP). A solitary pair nested on Dickinson Island in the Choptank River in Talbot County near Cambridge. The northernmost record came from Hart–Miller Island in Baltimore County in 1986. This colony initially failed because of red fox and Herring Gull predation (D. Brinker, pers. obs.), but it was finally successful in 1990 and 1991 when the birds found a predator-free location within the Hart–Miller Island impoundment (R. Ringler, pers. comm). Most Common Tern breeding was restricted to Dorchester, Somerset, and Worcester counties. The Smith Island archipelago record in Somerset County is from the early 1980s; there have been no breeding attempts by Common Terns in the Smith Island area since 1985.

The two largest colonies were in the Chesapeake Bay: South Sand Point near Barren Island and a small island near Spring Island, both in Dorchester County. The colonies in Worcester County were much smaller; they were generally located close to the Ocean City Inlet or immediately behind the barrier islands, where distances to foraging areas in the ocean surf are minimized. Their food consists almost entirely of small fish not over 3 or 4 in. (8–10 cm), including the American sand lance and the northern pipefish, which are supplemented by some shrimp and aquatic insects (Bent 1921). During the mid-1980s, the Maryland breeding population averaged approximately 2,050 pairs (MCWP) or about 6 percent of the Atlantic Coast population (Spendelow and Patton 1988). Compared with the USFWS survey, this represents a 20 percent increase since the mid-1970s.

Common Tern breeding in Maryland is limited primarily by the availability of suitable colony sites, as demonstrated by the opportunistic nesting at Hart–Miller Island. The scarcity of traditional sites in Maryland is illustrated by the fact that 50 percent of all colonies here are marsh sites rather than typical beach locations. Many of the colony sites used in Maryland during the early 1900s have been lost to disturbance or erosion. The coastal barrier beaches are now unsuitable because of competing human use and increased red fox populations. The St. Mary's County colony of the 1930s probably was abandoned for similar reasons. Several colony sites, such as Long Island, Sharps Island, and Piney Island, have been lost to erosion.

BBS data for 1966 through 1989 show a highly significant average annual decline of 4.5 percent in the Eastern Region; although there are too few data to estimate a Maryland

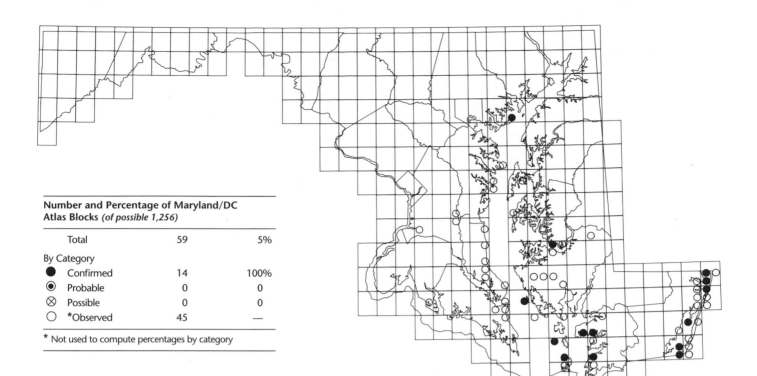

Number and Percentage of Maryland/DC Atlas Blocks *(of possible 1,256)*

Total	59	5%
By Category		
● Confirmed	14	100%
◉ Probable	0	0
⊗ Possible	0	0
○ *Observed	45	—

* Not used to compute percentages by category

Atlas Distribution, 1983–1987

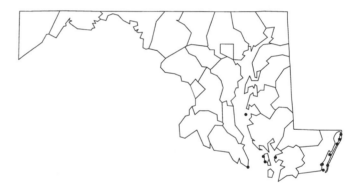

Breeding Distribution, 1958

trend, the population appears to be stable. Long-term survival depends, however, on continued use of salt-marsh nesting sites and the availability of undisturbed, predator-free islands. Management and protective efforts should be aimed at maintenance of such habitats.

David F. Brinker

Forster's Tern

Sterna forsteri

Forster's Terns are truly wetland birds. Although they breed in three widely disjunct areas in North America—the Atlantic Coast, the interior, and the Gulf Coast (AOU 1983)—all three areas have extensive marshes. In Maryland, Forster's Terns are fairly common summer residents in coastal Worcester County and the lower Chesapeake Bay. They arrive from nearby wintering areas in the southeastern United States (AOU 1983) in late March and April and normally depart by mid-December (Robbins and Bystrak 1977). During postbreeding dispersal and migration they can be seen throughout the Chesapeake Bay.

The earliest report of breeding Forster's Terns in Maryland is from Kirkwood (1895), who in June 1894 visited three colonies at North Beach, about 10 mi (16 km) south of Ocean City in Worcester County. The first Chesapeake Bay breeding was reported by Stewart and Robbins (1958) from the tidewater areas in Somerset County. In 1973, Armistead (1974) found a mixed colony of Common Terns and Forster's Terns on a small salt-marsh island in the Manokin River in Dorchester County. In subsequent years he located other colonies in the lower Bay (Armistead 1978). Since 1900, over 20 Forster's Tern colony sites have been reported in Maryland. The largest known colony in the state was reported by Kirkwood (1895), who estimated 1,000 pairs on 6 June 1894 on a marsh island near North Beach (now part of Assateague Island). Stewart and Robbins (1958) reported approximately 700 pairs breeding on Robins Marsh, Worcester County, in 1951. In 1976 the USFWS surveyed colonial waterbirds from Maine to Virginia and estimated the Maryland population at 520 pairs in seven colonies (Erwin 1979); this was 18 percent of the Atlantic Coast population (Spendelow and Patton 1988).

The Forster's Tern's almost exclusive dependence on marshes for nesting distinguishes it from most other North American terns. In Maryland, it seems to prefer small, predator-free, salt-marsh islands. In recent years, Maryland's largest colonies have been on the lower Chesapeake Bay islands with shallowly flooded interiors (MCWP). There, Forster's Terns build characteristic floating nests anchored to smooth cordgrass; however, they also frequently nest on wrack in a manner indistinguishable from that of Common Terns. In the largest colonies, the two species are intermixed, and identification of individual nests is virtually impossible.

The earliest reported egg date for Maryland is 7 May (Stewart and Robbins 1958) and the latest is 28 July (MCWP). Clutches usually consist of 2 or 3 eggs, with 3 most typical (MCWP). Mean clutch size, estimated from 697 Maryland clutches of 2 to 4 eggs, is 2.6 (MNRF). The first chicks hatch during the peak of incubation in late May, and fledging begins in mid- to late June (MCWP). Downy young dates for Maryland extend from 2 June to 20 July (MNRF). There is no information on brood sizes in Maryland.

During the Atlas period, Forster's Terns were found breeding in 14 blocks: four in the lower Chesapeake Bay (Dorchester and Somerset Counties) and 10 in coastal Worcester County. In these blocks, nesting occurred at 18 locations (MCWP). As with Common Terns, the two largest colonies were both in the Chesapeake Bay: South Sand Point near Barren Island and a small island near Spring Island, both in Dorchester County. This contrasts with the known distribution in the late 1800s when the largest known colonies were in Worcester County (Kirkwood 1895). In Worcester County, atlasers found Forster's Tern colonies farther from the Ocean City inlet and in more remote locations than those of Common Terns. This contrast with Common Tern preferences has been noted elsewhere (Buckley and McCaffrey 1978; Storey 1978; Erwin et al. 1981). The more inland distribution (marsh rather than beach nesting) may be correlated with feeding habits. The Forster's Tern takes fewer fish than the Common Tern and eats many more flying and floating insects, such as dragonflies and caddisflies (Bent 1921).

In the mid-1980s, the average breeding population of Forster's Terns in Maryland was 1,700 pairs (MCWP). Although it is difficult to compare the 1976 USFWS survey (Erwin 1979) to the mid-1980s MCWP survey, this may represent as much as three times as many pairs as were recorded in 1977. If the number and distribution of colonies—but not their sizes—were roughly similar in the 1890s to those of the 1990s, a considerable decline may have taken place over the past 100 years. If so, this decline may be fairly recent, since Stewart and Robbins (1958) reported a large colony in Worcester County in 1951. Even though complete censuses are available only for recent years (1976 and 1985 through 1989), the long-term decline may be real. From 1985 through 1988 the colony at Robins Marsh averaged 250 pairs (MCWP), compared with Stewart and Robbins' (1958) estimate of 700 pairs for 1951. The Robins Marsh colony had 327 pairs in 1985, 165 in 1988, and had been abandoned by 1990 (MCWP). Although BBS data from 1966 through 1989 show a highly significant average annual increase of 17.2 percent in Eastern Region populations, there are too few data to estimate a trend for Maryland.

The availability of suitable colony sites is a limiting factor for breeding Forster's Terns in Maryland, but it may not be the only one. Although the apparent decline of the Forster's Tern population from historical levels remains to be verified by continued monitoring, efforts should be initiated immediately to determine any possible causes for the decline.

David F. Brinker

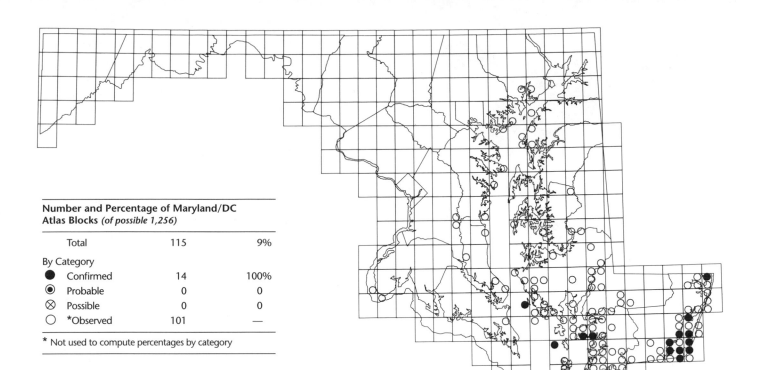

Number and Percentage of Maryland/DC Atlas Blocks *(of possible 1,256)*

Total	115	9%
By Category		
● Confirmed	14	100%
◉ Probable	0	0
⊗ Possible	0	0
○ *Observed	101	—

* Not used to compute percentages by category

Atlas Distribution, 1983–1987

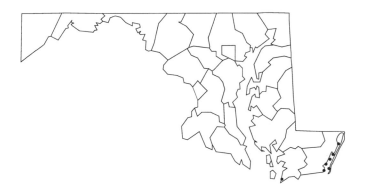

Breeding Distribution, 1958

Least Tern

Sterna antillarum

The Least Tern is the smallest nesting tern in Maryland. This colonial species is often observed foraging in shallow ponds and bays or loafing on mainland beaches, sandspits, or sandbars. It is locally distributed in Maryland's tidal waters from late April until September (Stewart and Robbins 1958) and migrates to South America for the winter (AOU 1983).

Kirkwood (1895) was the first to confirm nesting of Least Terns in Maryland. He found 24 nests with eggs at the mouth of the Miles River in Talbot County on 13 June 1894. In the 1940s and 1950s colonies were located on both shores of the Chesapeake Bay north to Baltimore and Kent Counties and in Worcester County (Stewart and Robbins 1958). Most colonies were on natural beaches along the shoreline.

Today, more than 50 percent of the nesting colonies occur on artificial sites such as dredge spoils, tar and gravel rooftops, parking lots (MCWP), and the jet pad at Patuxent River Naval Air Station in St. Mary's County (Altman and Gano 1984). This habitat shift is related to the increased use of beaches for recreation and development and the erosion of natural beach sites (Buckley and Buckley 1976). Nesting sites have at least three factors in common: light-colored unconsolidated substrate, proximity to water, and sparse vegetation. The substrate is usually a sand and shell mix or white stone less than 0.4 in. (1 cm) in diameter. Most sites are adjacent to estuarine or marine waters, but artificial sites in Maryland have been found as far as 1.7 miles (2.7 km) from open water (MCWP). Least Tern nests are usually located on beaches with little or no vegetation; they will abandon colonies when vegetation becomes too dense (J. McKearnan and D. Brinker, pers. obs.). Least Terns frequently move their colonies between and within seasons for two reasons: many sites are located on mainland shorelines where mammalian predators have easy access, and colonies adjacent to water are exposed to flooding (Carreker 1985). If nests are destroyed, adults will move to other sites to renest.

Least Terns begin the breeding cycle in mid-May with the onset of courtship (MCWP). Nests are constructed by digging a shallow scrape in the sand or gravel. Sand nests are often lined with light-colored shells. Laying begins in late May, with the earliest recorded egg date being 16 May (MCWP). During the MCWP from 1985 through 1988, the contents of 1,002 Least Tern nests were recorded. Mean clutch size was 1.8; 759 nests (76%) contained 2 eggs, 196 nests (20%) contained 1 egg, 46 nests (5%) contained 3 eggs, and one nest had 4 eggs (MCWP). Incubation lasts 19 to 22 days (Harrison 1978), and eggs usually start to hatch in mid-June. The early date for chicks is 8 June (MCWP). Chicks begin to fly at 15 to 17 days of age, but they continue to accept food from adults until migration begins (Tomkins 1959; Akers 1975). Least Terns are single-brooded but will renest if the first attempt fails early in the breeding cycle (Akers 1975). The period between loss of nest and initiation of a second clutch has been estimated at three weeks. A second and generally less successful (MCWP) wave of nesting often occurs when inexperienced subadult birds breed for the first time or older birds renest (Massey and Atwood 1981), usually beginning in late June or early July.

Reproductive success varies from colony to colony. Estimates from some Maryland colonies in 1987 ranged from 0 to 0.4 fledglings per nest (MCWP). The extreme late egg date for Maryland is 10 August (Robbins and Bystrak 1977), and the latest date a chick has been observed is also 10 August (MCWP). Small fish constitute most of the diet, but sand lances, shrimps, and prawns are also taken (Bent 1921).

During the Atlas project, Least Tern colonies were found in St. Mary's and Baltimore counties on the Western Shore and in Queen Anne's, Dorchester, Somerset, and Worcester counties on the Eastern Shore. There were also "confirmed" records for Anne Arundel and Talbot counties, as well as for DC. Scattered small groups bred on the north end of Assateague Island in Worcester County. Reports other than "confirmed" records probably represented foraging adults, but a few, especially the one from Deep Creek Lake in Garrett County, represent nonbreeding stragglers. Currently, the Maryland population appears to be stable at about 500 pairs (MCWP). BBS data from 1966 through 1989 show stable populations in the continent and the Eastern Region; there is, however, a slight indication that populations may be declining.

The Least Tern is currently listed by the DNR as a species in need of conservation. Efforts should be directed toward protecting existing nesting sites and possibly creating unvegetated sand and shell beaches on islands. Frequent colony relocations demonstrate the need to protect as much available nesting habitat as possible, not just currently protected sites. Colonies should be posted against intruders. If colonies are discovered or birds are observed flying around and landing in potential nesting areas, the locations should be reported to the DNR.

Joan McKearnan

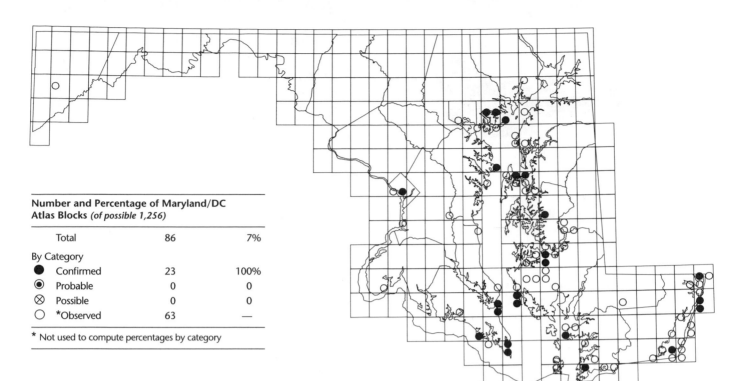

Number and Percentage of Maryland/DC Atlas Blocks *(of possible 1,256)*

Total	86	7%
By Category		
● Confirmed	23	100%
◉ Probable	0	0
⊗ Possible	0	0
○ *Observed	63	—

* Not used to compute percentages by category

Atlas Distribution, 1983–1987

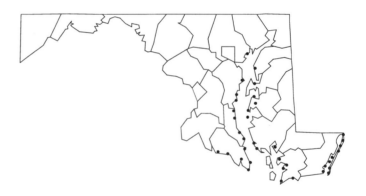

Breeding Distribution, 1958

Black Skimmer

Rynchops niger

The Black Skimmer's long, slender lower mandible and slit iris, combined with its unique foraging strategy, make it one of Maryland's most unusual breeding birds. The Black Skimmer, which feeds by skimming the water with its open bill, has an all-animal diet consisting mainly of fish, shrimp, and other small crustaceans (Martin et al. 1951). It is a summer resident in Maryland, arriving from its wintering grounds along the southeastern coast of the United States (AOU 1983) in mid-April and departing by late November (Stewart and Robbins 1958).

This species has gradually been reexpanding its breeding range northward. In the early 1600s, Black Skimmers nested north to Massachusetts (Forbush 1925), but by the late 1800s they were not known to breed north of Virginia. Nesting was reestablished in New Jersey in 1921 (Stone 1937), Long Island in New York in 1934, Massachusetts in 1946, and Connecticut in 1982 (Zeranski and Baptist 1990). The first reported Maryland nesting was a 1936 observation of as many as ten colonies on a series of dredge spoil islands south of the newly formed Ocean City inlet (Poole 1942). From the time they were created until the 1970s, these islands were the stronghold of breeding Black Skimmers in Maryland.

The breeding population of Black Skimmers in Maryland from 1945 through 1960 was approximately 250 to 300 pairs (Stewart and Robbins 1958; Erwin 1979). If Poole's (1942) estimate is valid, however, the population in the late 1930s may have been 500 or more pairs. During the 1970s, the highest recorded number of Black Skimmers breeding in Maryland was 218 pairs in 1977 (Erwin 1979). From 1980 through 1991, populations have fluctuated between approximately 150 and 325 pairs (MCWP). The establishment of the Heron Harbor colony in 1986 substantially increased Maryland's breeding population. BBS data from 1966 through 1989 show a significant average annual decline of 12.1 percent in the Eastern Region; continental data show a highly significant decline of 13.3 percent. Data are too few to estimate a Maryland trend.

Fourteen breeding sites have been recorded for the Black Skimmer in 5 Maryland blocks, with 12 from Worcester County. Four of the 12 are dredge spoil sites: the South Point spoil islands were important during the 1950s (Stewart and Robbins 1947a, 1958); Ocean City Spoils has been occupied in various years (Erwin 1979); Oyster Island was used during the mid-1970s (Therres et al. 1978); and Bridge Island was used in 1981 and 1982 (B. Rogers, pers. obs.). Use of natural sites in Worcester County has been limited to seven loca-

tions: Big Bay Marsh, Cape Windsor Island, Cedar Islands, Horsehead Tump, North Assateague Island, Outward Tump, and Reedy Island. Most of the known use of natural sites occurred during the past 15 years and probably represented an effort to locate new sites as the dredge spoil islands were gradually rendered unsuitable by vegetative changes and erosion. Poole (1942) originally referred to these small dredge spoil islands as "about ten in number"; in 1985 only four remained. Only two nesting sites are in the Chesapeake Bay: South Sand Point and Oyster Bar, both natural sites near Barren Island in Dorchester County (Ringler 1983b, 1984c; MCWP). Nesting at these sites probably represents recent (post-1980) expansion by Black Skimmers from colonies in the Virginia portion of the Chesapeake Bay.

Nests are located on barren areas of sand or shell fragments, usually in association with other colonial waterbirds, especially Common Terns. Nest sites in marshes have been reported from New Jersey, where Black Skimmers often nest on wrack washed onto salt marshes by winter storms (Frohling 1965; Gochfeld 1978; Buckley and Buckley 1980). This behavior is rare in Maryland, with only a single wrack-nesting attempt recorded from 1985 through 1991 (D. Brinker, pers. obs.).

Nesting does not usually begin until late May. The earliest reported egg date for Maryland is 15 May and the latest is 3 August (Robbins and Bystrak 1977). The earliest clutches often contain 4 eggs, but 7 to 10 days after laying has begun in a colony, new clutches seldom exceed 3 eggs (Erwin 1977; D. Brinker, unpub. data). Clutch sizes vary from 1 to 4, with 2 or 3 most commonly observed (MCWP). Chicks begin hatching in mid-June and fledge during late July or early August. Maryland dates for chicks range from 18 June to 12 August (Stewart and Robbins 1958).

During the Atlas period, Black Skimmers were found breeding at eight sites in five blocks: Big Bay Marsh, Cape Windsor Island, Heron Harbor, Horsehead Tump, Ocean City spoils, and Reedy Island in Worcester County; and Oyster Bar and South Sand Point in Dorchester County (MCWP). The largest colony was at Heron Harbor, where 108 pairs bred in 1986. At Heron Harbor, a condominium development, Black Skimmers initially used barren mainland areas filled for future construction, but in 1988 they moved to an island constructed specifically for waterbird nesting.

The primary limiting factor for breeding Black Skimmers in Maryland is lack of suitable nesting habitat, which has become acute as erosion has gradually claimed the dredge spoil islands. This species generally requires open beaches of sand or shell for colony sites (Clapp et al. 1983). Competition with humans has also caused severe reductions in populations: The potential for human impact to reduce the Maryland Black Skimmer breeding population by 50 percent within one or two summers is serious. Listed as a threatened species by the DNR, Black Skimmers deserve all protection efforts that can be directed toward them.

David F. Brinker

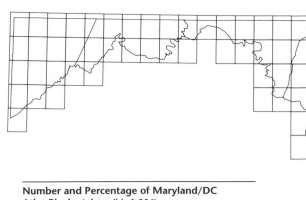

Number and Percentage of Maryland/DC
Atlas Blocks *(of possible 1,256)*

	Total	25	2%
By Category			
●	Confirmed	5	100%
◉	Probable	0	0
⊗	Possible	0	0
○	*Observed	20	—

* Not used to compute percentages by category

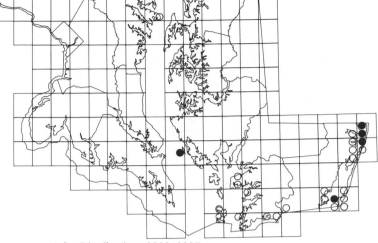

Atlas Distribution, 1983–1987

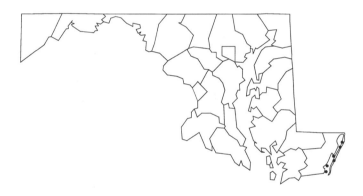

Breeding Distribution, 1958

Rock Dove

Columba livia

The Rock Dove, or feral pigeon, is the ubiquitous street pigeon of cities all over the world. It nimbly dodges vehicles and bustling crowds, cadging handouts in parks and on street corners. Although no other bird has adapted so successfully to life in urban areas, the Rock Dove has also found a niche around the barns and silos associated with intensive agriculture and animal husbandry. In addition, it is raised for food and sport and is bred for speed and homing ability.

Considering this bird's close association with people, it is remarkable that almost nothing is known about its breeding biology in Maryland. As far as ornithologists and birdwatchers are concerned, the Rock Dove barely exists, despite its large numbers. That we know so little about such a common bird reveals our prejudice against an introduced species commonly bred in captivity and released into the wild. This prejudice may be unfounded because, unlike most other introduced species, there is no proof that Rock Doves have had a negative impact on native wildlife.

Early ornithologists did not include the Rock Dove in their lists of birds of Maryland and DC. It was not mentioned in Kirkwood (1895) or Eifrig (1904). In an appendix, Stewart and Robbins (1958) described its status this way: "The great majority of observations refer to privately owned or escaped birds. No truly wild population is recognized in this area." The Rock Dove was first introduced into North America in Nova Scotia, Canada, in 1606 and 1607 (Long 1981). Undoubtedly, many additional introductions were made, and the first birds probably were brought into the United States around 1621. Because they have been introduced in many parts of the world, reconstructing the original native range of this species is nearly impossible. Although introduced birds have been interbred with domestic

varieties, the birds have established feral populations in many parts of their new range (Long 1981). Goodwin (1967) suggested that almost all introduced populations probably arose from carefully bred dovecote pigeons, racing pigeons, and homing pigeons that escaped or were released.

The Rock Dove places its nest on building ledges, on girders under bridges, under eaves, and in barns, silos, and other farm buildings (Forbush 1927; Goodwin 1970). Tree nesting has been reported in parklike habitat in towns, although it is rare in North America (Peterson 1986). Nest heights for 22 Maryland nests (MNRF) range from 0 to 40 ft (12 m), with a mean of 19.4 ft (5.9 m).

Throughout much of their range Rock Doves nest year-round (Goodwin 1970), except during their postbreeding molt in mid- to late fall. They lay 1 or 2 eggs and attempt four or five broods a year (Cramp 1985). Maryland egg dates range from 2 January (Robbins and Bystrak 1977) to 27 October (MNRF). Clutch sizes in 13 Maryland nests are either 1 or 2, with a mean of 1.5 (MNRF). Both parents assist in incubation, which requires 16 to 19 days (Cramp 1985). The few broods reported in Maryland were found from 13 March to 21 June (MNRF), but egg dates indicate the season is obviously longer. Brood sizes in five Maryland nests are either 1 or 2. Nestlings are fed crop milk until they leave the nest after about 26 days (Cramp 1985). Free-flying birds feed primarily on grains, seeds, some insects, and, in urban areas, human handouts and scavenged items (Goodwin 1970). In rural areas where they nest in barns, they feed almost entirely on agricultural grains.

Atlas results show that Rock Doves are widely distributed except in southern Maryland, the marshes of the lower Eastern Shore, and western Maryland, where they are more widely scattered. Western Maryland's extensive forested blocks offer little habitat for Rock Doves, and their relative absence from the wetlands of the lower Eastern Shore is not surprising. The scarcity of records from southern Maryland is not so easily explained, however. The area has extensive agricultural fields, although many of them are planted in tobacco rather than grain crops. Atlas workers found Rock Doves common and widespread in towns and cities, but in locations away from the denser pockets of human habitation they were restricted almost exclusively to the vicinity of farmyards.

BBS data from 1966 through 1989 show a highly significant average annual decline of 1.8 percent in the continental population, but the Eastern Region shows a significant average annual increase of 1.7 percent. Maryland data show a stable population for the same period; however, data from 1980 through 1989 indicate a decline for the state.

Although Rock Doves have become agricultural pests in some areas (Goodwin 1970), little evidence of serious crop destruction has been demonstrated. They may have been nonbirds to many ornithologists and birdwatchers, but they are a significant part—and one of the few avian components—of the urban environment. Rock Doves are certainly here to stay.

Eirik A. T. Blom

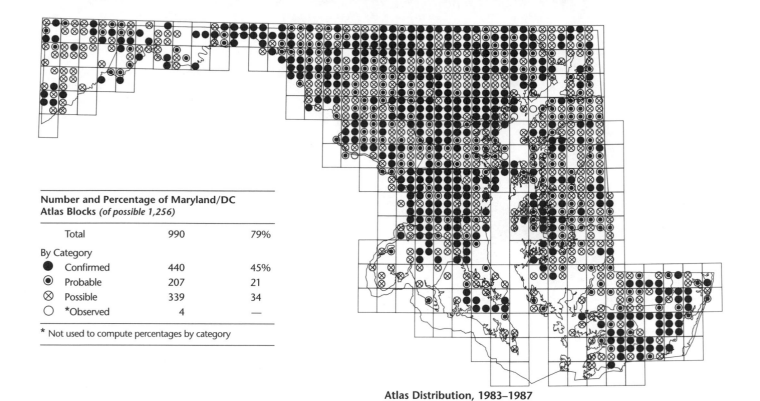

Number and Percentage of Maryland/DC Atlas Blocks *(of possible 1,256)*

Total	990	79%
By Category		
● Confirmed	440	45%
◉ Probable	207	21
⊗ Possible	339	34
○ *Observed	4	—

* Not used to compute percentages by category

Atlas Distribution, 1983–1987

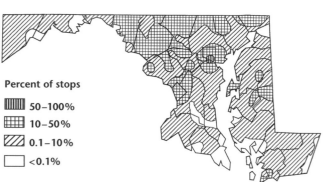

Percent of stops

▦	50–100%
▦	10–50%
▨	0.1–10%
☐	<0.1%

Relative Abundance, 1982–1989

No data recorded for 1958 map

Breeding Distribution, 1958

The centers of Rock Dove abundance are in the urban and agricultural areas of the Piedmont and eastern Ridge and Valley sections. Numbers decrease to the south and west. The species was not detected in southern St. Mary's County, the marshes on the lower Eastern Shore, or eastern Allegany County.

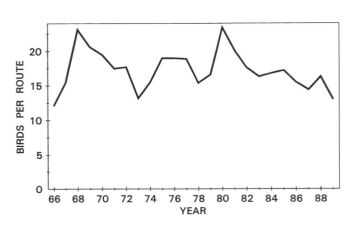

Maryland BBS Trend Graph, 1966–1989

PJM

Mourning Dove

Zenaida macroura

Mourning Doves, the most widespread and abundant North American columbids, are year-round residents throughout Maryland. They gather in large winter flocks at feeders and in agricultural fields, making migration patterns difficult to discern. Migrants move through Maryland in the spring from mid-February to late April and in the fall from late July to early November (Stewart and Robbins 1958). They are popular game birds throughout the Southeast, including Maryland. Their diet consists almost entirely of seeds and grains. The young are fed crop milk for the first week of their lives, but seeds quickly become a significant part of their diet (Tyler 1932; Westmoreland et al. 1986).

Kirkwood (1895) called Mourning Doves common residents in central Maryland. Eifrig (1904) was unsure of their winter status in western Maryland but called them common in summer. Stewart and Robbins (1958) described their breeding status as common in the Piedmont, Upper Chesapeake, and Western Shore sections and fairly common elsewhere throughout the state. The USFWS Mourning Dove Call-Count Survey (Dolton 1991) data from 1966 through 1991 show a stable population in the East and a significant average annual decline of 2.6 percent in Maryland. BBS data from 1966 through 1989 for the Eastern Region and Maryland show stable populations.

The Mourning Dove is an adaptable bird and nests in a variety of circumstances. Its primary habitats in Maryland are agricultural land and adjacent hedgerows, wood margins, woodlots, and residential areas (Stewart and Robbins 1958). The highest reported Maryland breeding density is 41 territorial males per 100 acres (40.5 ha) in a selectively logged mature tulip tree–oak forest in Prince George's County in 1988 (Robbins 1989).

Nests are placed in coniferous and deciduous trees, shrubs, and ornamental bushes (Goodwin 1967), as well as occasionally on the ground (Cooley 1982). The nest, loosely composed of twigs and weed stems, is constructed by the female in fewer than four days (Tyler 1932; Goodwin 1967). The male participates by bringing materials to the female. Heights of 240 Maryland nests (MNRF) range from 0 to 60 ft (0–18 m), with a mean of 10.4 ft (3.2 m). Only six nests found were above 25 ft (7.6 m).

The breeding season is very long in Maryland. Nests with eggs have been found from 17 February (Van Velzen 1966) to 27 October (Robbins and Bystrak 1977), with a peak in late April. The February date is very unusual as the season appears to begin in earnest in late March (MNRF). Two or three broods are commonly attempted, but as many as six in a single season were observed in a study of marked birds in Texas (Swank 1955). The time period between initiation of successful clutches in Illinois was 30 days (Hanson and Kossack 1963). Clutch size is almost always 2 eggs (Goodwin 1967). Westmoreland and Best (1987) investigated the two-egg clutch in Mourning Doves and discovered that when a third egg was added to existing clutches, the young were smaller and hatching success dropped. They hypothesized that feeding the young with crop milk limits clutch size because adults can produce only a fixed amount of milk. Of 132 Maryland nests (MNRF), 130 had 2 eggs and two contained 3 eggs.

Both parents participate in the incubation, which requires 13 or 14 days; the male is generally on the nest from 10 a.m. to 6 p.m., and the female replaces him for the remaining hours (Bergtold 1917; Westmoreland et al. 1986). The young fledge about 14 or 15 days after hatching. Young in the nest have been found in Maryland from 26 February (Meanley 1973) to 4 October (Stewart and Robbins 1958), with a peak in early May (MNRF). All but two of 82 Maryland nests had 2 young. One nest contained 1 young bird, and the other had 3 young. The earliest reported fledging date for Maryland is 1 March (Meanley 1973).

The Mourning Dove is one of the most widely distributed and common birds in Maryland. Atlas data show it in nearly every block but absent from islands in the lower Chesapeake Bay. Its mournful cooing song is a constant background to spring and summer mornings, and its gliding courtship flights are easy to observe. The high percentage of "confirmed" records resulted from the ease of finding nests and the frequent observation of young birds feeding on the ground in the open. The large number of broods also increased the probability that observers would confirm nesting.

The Mourning Dove seems to be in no trouble in Maryland; in fact, it may be more common than in previous years in some sections of the state. No management recommendations are necessary at this time.

Eirik A. T. Blom

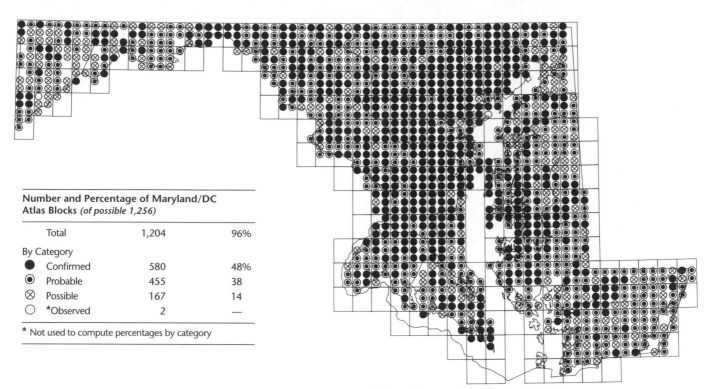

Number and Percentage of Maryland/DC Atlas Blocks *(of possible 1,256)*		
Total	1,204	96%
By Category		
● Confirmed	580	48%
◉ Probable	455	38
⊗ Possible	167	14
○ *Observed	2	—

* Not used to compute percentages by category

Atlas Distribution, 1983–1987

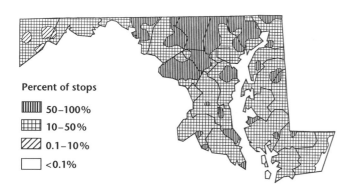

Percent of stops

▥ 50–100%

▦ 10–50%

▨ 0.1–10%

☐ <0.1%

Relative Abundance, 1982–1989

Breeding Distribution, 1958

The Mourning Dove is common to abundant throughout Maryland. The highest concentrations are in the agricultural and suburban areas of the Piedmont Section and in the Frederick and Hagerstown valleys. The lowest numbers were recorded in the heavily forested portions of the Allegheny Mountain Section.

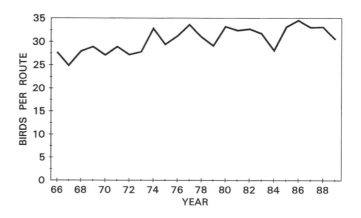

Maryland BBS Trend Graph, 1966–1989

Black-billed Cuckoo

Coccyzus erythropthalmus

The Black-billed Cuckoo shares many traits with the closely related Yellow-billed Cuckoo. Both species arrive in and depart from Maryland at the same time, have similar food habits, prefer open woodlands for breeding, and have similar vocalizations. This last factor must be considered in evaluating the distribution, as identification is usually determined by ear. The problem of determining distribution is further compounded by two factors: migration that continues well into June and a habit of wandering in search of food concentrations. These problems were avoided in the Atlas fieldwork; the proportion of Black-billed Cuckoos to Yellow-billed Cuckoos is similar to the 1 to 10 ratio reported by Robbins et al. (1989c) using skilled observers. Most spring migration through Maryland occurs from early May to mid-June; fall migration reaches its peak in August (Stewart and Robbins 1958; Robbins and Bystrak 1977). The winter range extends from Colombia to Bolivia (AOU 1983).

Although this species breeds from Oklahoma and the southern Appalachians to the tree line in northern Canada (AOU 1983), BBS results from 1966 through 1979 (Robbins et al. 1986) show its core range to be a belt stretching from the Maritime Provinces to southern Alberta; Maryland ranked 31 among the 41 states and provinces in which the Black-billed Cuckoo was recorded. From 1966 through 1989, BBS data show stable populations in the Eastern Region and an indication of an increase in Maryland. Although no breeding densities are available for Maryland, Hall (1983) reported 7 territorial males per 100 acres (40.5 ha) in six mountain sites in West Virginia.

Coues and Prentiss (1883) knew the Black-billed Cuckoo as a not rare summer resident that was less abundant than the Yellow-billed Cuckoo. Kirkwood (1895) and Cooke (1929) described it as a fairly common migrant and rare summer resident. In western Maryland, Eifrig (1904) found it more common at lower elevations in migration but noted that it bred in the higher areas. Fletcher et al. (1956) called it a rare transient in Caroline County, echoing Hampe and

Kolb (1947): "Records of it in migration are common except from the Eastern Shore." Stewart and Robbins (1958) called it a fairly common breeder in the Allegheny Mountain Section; uncommon in the Ridge and Valley, Piedmont, and Upper Chesapeake sections; and rare in the Western Shore and Eastern Shore sections.

There is little nesting information for Black-billed Cuckoos in Maryland. Heights of five Maryland nests (MNRF) range from 2 to 10 ft (0.6–3.1 m), which is typical (Bent 1940). Four of the nests were in small trees or shrubs with dense grapevine or honeysuckle. The nest is a loose structure of twigs with many protruding ends, lined with finer material. Extreme Maryland egg dates are 18 May and 19 July (MNRF). Clutch sizes in four nests range from 2 to 5. Clutches of 2 or 3 eggs are typical; only a single brood is attempted (Harrison 1978). Incubation, by both parents (Bent 1940), lasts 10 or 11 days (Spencer 1943). Nests with young have been found in Maryland from 23 May to 26 July (MNRF). Broods of 2 and 3 young have been recorded in Maryland. Both parents tend the nestlings, which fledge in seven to nine days (Bent 1940).

Both the Black-billed and Yellow-billed Cuckoos occasionally nest parasitize—most commonly each other but on rare occasions other host species, such as the Wood Thrush, American Robin, and Northern Cardinal (Bent 1940). One of the six known instances of parasitism of Black-billed Cuckoos by Brown-headed Cowbirds is from Maryland (Friedmann 1963, 1971; Friedmann et al. 1977; Peck and James 1983).

Atlas results show the same distribution reported by Stewart and Robbins (1958). No "confirmed" records were reported from southern Maryland or the Eastern Shore. Usually heard rather than seen, 65 percent of the 196 records were "possible" and 23 percent were "probable." This contrasts with the much more abundant Yellow-billed Cuckoo, for which 36 percent of the 1,117 records were "possible" and 51 percent were "probable." In the "confirmed" category, the two species did not differ significantly.

Management poses special problems. The relatively large, maturing, open woodland required for production of the food supply during breeding can easily be established and maintained by techniques such as selective harvest. The Black-billed Cuckoo's principal foods—hairy caterpillars such as gypsy moths, tent caterpillars, and sawfly larvae (Bent 1940)—are often controlled by pesticide spraying. Major outbreaks of these forest pests create an opportunity for this species. Long-term infestations may create localized damage to the woodland with an effective woodland loss similar to selective harvest but without the economic benefits that may be required to maintain a large area in forest use. The question, therefore, is not a simple one of managing this species rather than the forest, but rather of managing for the entire ecosystem. Another crucial factor affecting many neotropical migrants is destruction of their winter habitat in the tropical rain forests. Coupled with maintenance of breeding habitat, protection of winter habitat is needed.

James L. Stasz

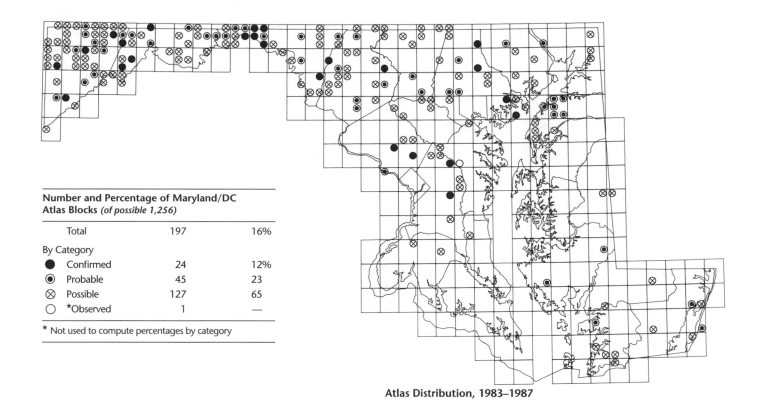

Number and Percentage of Maryland/DC Atlas Blocks (of possible 1,256)

Total	197	16%
By Category		
● Confirmed	24	12%
◉ Probable	45	23
⊗ Possible	127	65
○ *Observed	1	—

* Not used to compute percentages by category

Atlas Distribution, 1983–1987

Percent of stops

▥	50–100%
▤	10–50%
▧	0.1–10%
☐	<0.1%

Relative Abundance, 1982–1989

Breeding Distribution, 1958

The Black-billed Cuckoo is widespread and uncommon in the western part of the state and is rare and irregularly distributed elsewhere. Some birds are still migrating through Maryland when miniroutes are run; these late migrants may have biased the results.

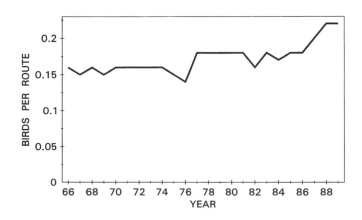

Maryland BBS Trend Graph, 1966–1989

Yellow-billed Cuckoo

Coccyzus americanus

The Yellow-billed Cuckoo, which is much easier to hear than to see, is a fairly common, widely distributed summer resident in Maryland. It prefers open forests or swamps at low to medium elevations. Although this species generally arrives from its South American wintering grounds (AOU 1983) in early May, migration continues through mid-June (Robbins and Bystrak 1977). Yellow-billed Cuckoos are noted for erratic migrations; in 1951, for example, few birds were in the state before 10 June and most arrived in July (Stewart and Robbins 1958). Fall migration begins in August, and most birds have left by late September (Robbins and Bystrak 1977).

Early Maryland ornithologists considered the Yellow-billed Cuckoo common to abundant (Coues and Prentiss 1862, 1883; Kirkwood 1895; Eifrig 1904). Stewart and Robbins (1958) described its breeding status as uncommon in the Allegheny Mountain Section and fairly common in all other sections. BBS data from 1966 through 1989 show a highly significant average annual decline of 1.7 percent in the Eastern Region. Maryland data show a stable population for that period but a highly significant average annual decline of 6.0 percent from 1980 through 1989.

Breeding habitat in Maryland consists of high, open woods (Coues and Prentiss 1883); thick, dark woods with abundant overgrowth (Richmond 1888); and residential areas, orchards, and swamps (Cooke 1929; Stewart and Robbins 1958). As farms were abandoned and grew up into forest in the first half of the twentieth century, potential habitat increased. Robbins et al. (1989a) found Yellow-billed Cuckoos in Maryland nesting in both small isolated woodlands and extensive forest. They prefer deciduous woods with many tree species. Maryland's high population density of 15 territorial males per 100 acres (40.5 ha) was found in selectively logged mature tulip tree–oak forest in Prince George's County (Robbins 1989). This figure is low, compared with densities reported from surrounding states.

Maryland nests (MNRF) are constructed in the forks of tree or shrub branches that are overgrown with vines, al-though one nest was in a honeysuckle-covered fence post. Four nests are described as thin stick platforms, one as deeply cupped and open, and one as closely made of short fine twigs lined with bark and grass tops. Heights for 42 Maryland nests range from 2.8 to 45 ft (0.9–14 m) above the ground, with a mean of 11.6 ft (3.5 m). Egg dates range from 13 May to 28 August, with no evident peak. Clutch sizes in 30 Maryland nests range from 2 to 4, with a mean of 2.4; 19 nests contained 2 eggs. Young in the nest are found from 24 May to 16 September. In 11 nests, brood sizes vary from 1 to 3, with a mean of 2.0.

The Yellow-billed Cuckoo is single-brooded in the north but is sometimes double-brooded in the south (Forbush 1927). Although the incubation period was thought to be about 14 days (Bent 1940), more recent research showed it to be nine to 11 days (Nolan and Thompson 1975; Potter 1980). Young leave the nest at seven to nine days of age (Preble 1957; Potter 1980). The Yellow-billed Cuckoo is a rare victim of Brown-headed Cowbird parasitism (Friedmann 1963, 1971); only five instances are recorded, none in Maryland. Although hairy caterpillars, which are eaten by few other birds, are the main component of its diet, it also eats locusts, grasshoppers, crickets, beetles, and, occasionally, birds' eggs (Bent 1940).

Studies of Yellow-billed Cuckoos in Indiana (Nolan and Thompson 1975) and North Carolina (Potter 1980) noted several peculiarities in its reproductive biology. There appears to be a postmigration prebreeding period when individuals wander and appraise local food resources. Periods of abnormally abundant food have been correlated with year-to-year changes in populations as well as shifts within the nesting season. Caterpillar outbreaks are correlated with interspecific brood parasitism; Yellow-billed Cuckoo eggs have been found in nests of the Black-billed Cuckoo and in those of several robin- or catbird-size songbirds. Caterpillar outbreaks also are correlated with advanced laying dates (two to three weeks) and irregular timing of egg laying (four-or five-day rather than one-day intervals).

Atlas work shows the Yellow-billed Cuckoo as widespread in Maryland, although less so in the Allegheny Mountain Section. It is absent from urban and other areas that lack forests. In Pennsylvania, this southern species is most widespread in the southern part of the state (Brauning 1992).

Although the Yellow-billed Cuckoo is flexible in its choice of nest sites, it still must have dense vegetation. The current practice of building virtually treeless housing developments and shopping malls reduces available habitat. And, because this species is a neotropical migrant that winters in South American forests (AOU 1983), its winter habitat is also disappearing (Terborgh 1989). Maryland needs to preserve extensive woodlands and to retain thickets and wooded corridors in suburban areas to provide habitat for Yellow-billed Cuckoos and other woodland birds.

Robert Hilton

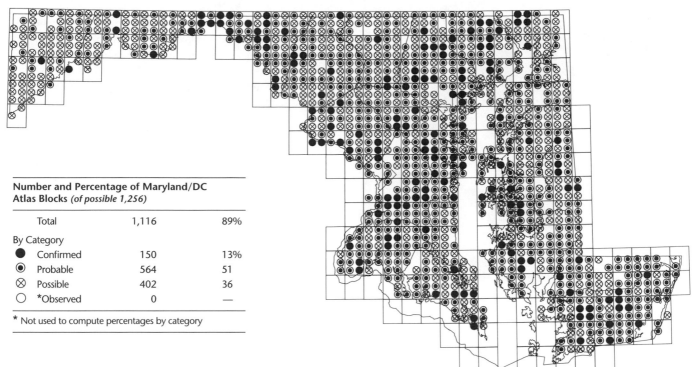

Number and Percentage of Maryland/DC Atlas Blocks *(of possible 1,256)*

Total	1,116	89%
By Category		
● Confirmed	150	13%
◉ Probable	564	51
⊗ Possible	402	36
○ *Observed	0	—

* Not used to compute percentages by category

Atlas Distribution, 1983–1987

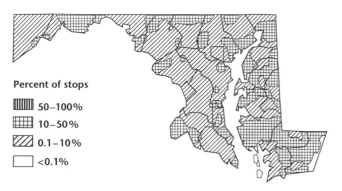

Percent of stops

▦ 50–100%
▤ 10–50%
▨ 0.1–10%
□ <0.1%

Relative Abundance, 1982–1989

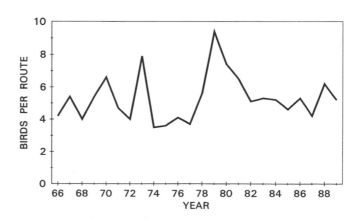

Breeding Distribution, 1958

The Yellow-billed Cuckoo is widespread and generally uncommon, but it tends to be slightly more common on the Eastern Shore. Some birds are still migrating through Maryland when miniroutes are run; these late migrants may have biased the results.

Maryland BBS Trend Graph, 1966–1989

Barn Owl

Tyto alba

The Barn Owl posed a challenge to Atlas workers. It is generally uncommon, highly nocturnal, and rarely seen or heard. Populations have decreased significantly in parts of the United States (Stewart 1980). It is on the NAS Blue List (Tate 1986) and is listed as a species of management concern by the USFWS (1987).

True to its name, the Barn Owl often nests in barns as well as in silos, attics, duck blinds, and other artificial structures. It is associated with agriculture, hunting over fields and pastures, but it is also a bird of coastal marshes (Therres and Bendel 1990). It feeds almost exclusively on meadow voles and other small rodents. The Barn Owl can be found year-round in Maryland, although banding records suggest some birds leave the state in winter, when the population is supplemented by birds from farther north (Stewart and Robbins 1958). Spring migration spans late February to mid-May and peaks from mid-March to early April.

The Barn Owl has probably never been common in Maryland. It was first recorded in DC in 1877 (Jouy 1877). Bendire (1895b) reported that, as early as 1861, it nested in one tower of the Smithsonian Institution. Kirkwood (1895) noted that it was seen only occasionally in the tidewater areas of Maryland. In the nineteenth century, numbers probably increased as a result of clearing of woodlands and creation of pasture lands. Cooke (1929) called it a fairly common resident within 20 mi (32 km) of DC. Hampe and Kolb (1947) noted that it was found in all sections of the state. Stewart and Robbins (1958) listed it as fairly common in the Eastern Shore Section and uncommon locally elsewhere, except in the Allegheny Mountain Section, where it was rare. Certainly the status of such a secretive and nocturnal bird was poorly known at those times, and the true status remains uncertain even now.

Barn Owls nest in both natural cavities and artificial

structures. Colvin (1984) reported that 50 percent of all nests found on his study area in New Jersey were in tree cavities. He also found nests in barns, silos, chimneys, buildings, bridges, and nest boxes. Reese (1972) and Klaas et al. (1978) documented the Barn Owl's use of off-shore duck blinds in Maryland. Other examples of Maryland nest sites include a hollow sycamore tree on the bank of the Potomac River (Wetmore and Manville 1968), an old cistern and a barrel atop a 20-ft (6.1-m) tower (Reese 1972), and an empty 55-gallon drum embedded in the face of a sand cliff along the Patuxent River (G. Kearns, pers. comm.). Heights of 134 Maryland nests range from 1 ft (0.3 m) over water in a duck blind to 210 ft (64 m) in an observation tower (MNRF). The mean height above water of the 117 duck blind nests is 3.5 ft (1.1 m). Nineteen nests in towers and buildings range from 18 (5.5 m) to 210 ft (64 m), with a mean of 42.4 ft (13 m). The two nests reported in tree cavities are 20 ft (6.1 m) and 23 ft (7.0 m) above ground.

Barn Owls nest throughout the year in Maryland, with peaks in early March and late July (Stewart and Robbins 1958). Extreme egg dates are 2 January (Stewart and Robbins 1958) and 20 September (S. Smith, pers. comm.). Clutch sizes are extremely variable and may be related to the availability of food. Clutch sizes of 153 Maryland nests range from 1 to 10, with a mean of 4.8 (MNRF). Incubation begins with the laying of the first egg and lasts 30 to 35 days (Bent 1938); thus, the young hatch asynchronously, resulting in young of various ages in the same nest. Extreme nestling dates are 12 March (Bendel and Therres 1990) and 29 December (E. Blom, pers. comm.). Brood sizes of 132 Maryland nests range from 1 to 7, with a mean of 3.7 (MNRF). Bendel and Therres (1990) found a higher mean of 4.2 young from 15 nests in Eastern Shore marshes.

Atlas results suggest that the range of the Barn Owl is fragmented. The farmlands of Washington, Frederick, and Howard counties and parts of southern Maryland and the Eastern Shore appear to be the strongholds for this species. These differences may result in part from differences in Atlas coverage. Barn Owls are not easy to find, although they frequently nest close to human habitation. They are not especially vocal and thus were seldom recorded on nocturnal Atlas forays. Some were found with the help of local farmers. As a result, the percentage of "confirmed" reports (43%) is very high for a nocturnal species. Nests with young comprise more than one-third of the "confirmed" records. The assumption of earlier writers that Barn Owls are rare in the mountains of Garrett County appears to be supported by the Atlas results; only two pairs were found there. A large gap in the Pennsylvania range (Brauning 1992), just north of Garrett County, also supports the rarity of Barn Owls at high elevations.

The difficulty in finding Barn Owls makes it nearly impossible to say if they are increasing or decreasing in Maryland. The BBS does not adequately sample nocturnal species, and there are not enough data to estimate trends. Analysis of CBC results suggests that the Maryland population has declined (S. Smith and G. Therres, unpub. data).

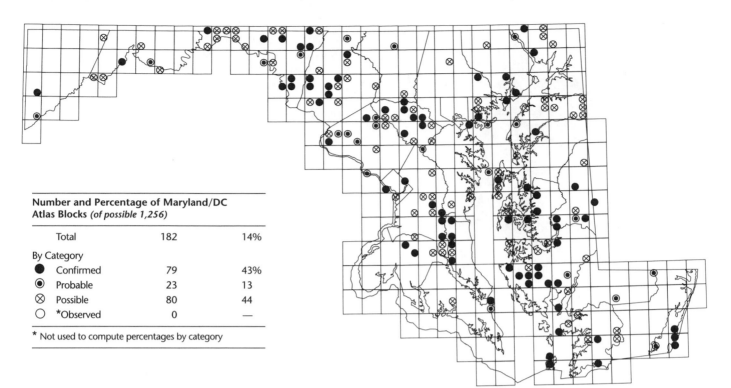

Number and Percentage of Maryland/DC Atlas Blocks *(of possible 1,256)*

Total	182	14%
By Category		
● Confirmed	79	43%
◉ Probable	23	13
⊗ Possible	80	44
○ *Observed	0	—

* Not used to compute percentages by category

Atlas Distribution, 1983–1987

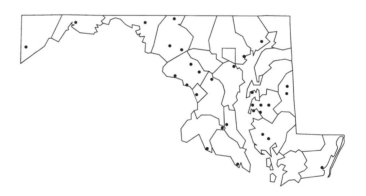

Breeding Distribution, 1958

Public education and erection of nest boxes may help. Just as important as nest sites, however, is prey availability. Agricultural practices, such as grain farming, that reduce or eliminate small mammals have a negative effect on Barn Owl populations (Colvin 1985).

Clark F. Jeschke and Glenn D. Therres

Eastern Screech-Owl

Otus asio

The Eastern Screech-Owl is the smallest of Maryland's common breeding owls; only the Northern Saw-whet Owl is smaller. The Eastern Screech-Owl's quavering whistle, either in a descending scale or on one pitch, is a familiar sound to nocturnal birders. As one listens to the call of this nocturnal raptor, it is easy to understand why Native Americans thought of owls as creatures of mystery.

The Eastern Screech-Owl is a permanent resident throughout Maryland. It can be found in a variety of habitats, from pine woods on the Eastern Sh e to the suburban and urban areas of Baltimore and DC, and from woodlots in agricultural areas to the forest edges of Garrett County (Stewart and Robbins 1958). It tends to shun the depths of large tracts of woodland and prefers to remain on the fringes of such habitat. This may, at least partially, explain why the bird is less common and less widespread in the heavily wooded areas of Garrett County. The Eastern and Western Screech-Owls were formally considered as one species, Screech Owl (AOU 1957), until the AOU (1983) recognized that they were specifically distinct.

Determining the historical distribution and abundance of the Eastern Screech-Owl is difficult. Descriptions such as "most abundant of the owls" (Coues and Prentiss 1883), "common resident . . . around Baltimore" (Kirkwood 1895), and "uncommon in all sections" (Stewart and Robbins 1958) do not give an accurate picture of its status. Because of its nocturnal habits, this cavity-nesting species is generally difficult to census. Prior to the Atlas fieldwork, owls had not been systematically sampled throughout most of their Maryland breeding range using a taped playback of their calls to determine their distribution.

Courtship begins in February (Bent 1938). Most nests are in natural cavities, but Eastern Screech-Owls readily nest in Wood Duck boxes. The female incubates the eggs, and the male feeds her as she sits (Sherman 1911). The range in heights of 16 Maryland nests (MNRF) is 5 to 85 ft (1.5–26 m), with a mean of 24.6 ft (7.5 m). The earliest egg date for Maryland is 8 March and the latest is 9 May, with a peak in mid-April. Incubation lasts about 26 days, and the young remain in the nest about 31 days after hatching (Sherman 1911). Clutch sizes in 11 Maryland nests range from 3 to 6, with a mean of 3.9 (MNRF). VanCamp and Henny (1975) reported mean clutch sizes ranging from 3.0 in Florida to 4.4 in northern Ohio. Of 18 Maryland nests (MNRF) with young, the earliest was found on 24 April and the latest on 22 June, with the records fairly evenly scattered throughout that period. In DC, however, a fledgling was seen on the remarkably early date of 19 March (Ringler 1990b). Brood sizes in 18 Maryland nests range from 1 to 5, with a mean of 3.1.

The Eastern Screech-Owl has an immensely varied diet, consisting of small birds, mammals, insects, fish, amphibians, and crustaceans (Bent 1938). In an Ohio study, Van-Camp and Henny (1975) found the percentage of birds in the owl's diet rose to slightly more than 60 percent during the breeding season after being about 40 percent the rest of the year.

Atlas data show Eastern Screech-Owls are generally distributed throughout Maryland and DC but less widespread in the higher elevations of Garrett County. It is unclear from the data whether this is a function of temperature, elevation, or the fact that these higher elevations have larger tracts of forests and, therefore, less suitable habitat. Still other explanations, such as variable observer coverage, cannot be ruled out. Several field observers with experience throughout Maryland reported, however, that it was more difficult to record Eastern Screech-Owls in the western third of the state than in the central and eastern portions. Uneven distribution of Eastern Screech-Owls in the central and eastern parts of the state is generally attributable to coverage differences. Areas of heavy coverage, such as Talbot County and the northeastern corner of the state, are clearly visible on the map, as is the relatively light coverage in the southern counties along the Chesapeake Bay and the Potomac River. Eastern Screech-Owls are not easily confirmed. Indeed, the vast majority of records were of birds heard, not seen. Detection of fledged young provided 69 percent of the "confirmed" records. BBS data from 1966 through 1989 for both Maryland and the Eastern Region show stable populations.

In parts of Maryland, the Eastern Screech-Owl may be as common as it ever has been but in other areas, such as the DC suburbs, it has become difficult to find. The greatest threats to its existence are loss of woodlands and the indiscriminate felling of dead trees which it uses for nest sites.

Clark F. Jeschke

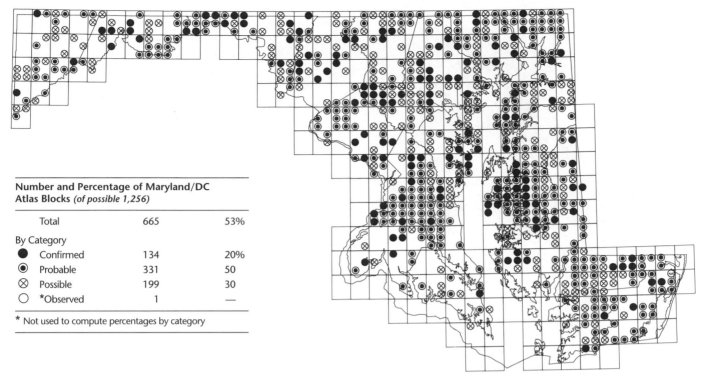

Number and Percentage of Maryland/DC Atlas Blocks *(of possible 1,256)*

Total	665	53%
By Category		
● Confirmed	134	20%
◉ Probable	331	50
⊗ Possible	199	30
○ *Observed	1	—

* Not used to compute percentages by category

Atlas Distribution, 1983–1987

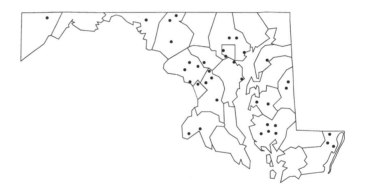

Breeding Distribution, 1958

Great Horned Owl

Bubo virginianus

The Great Horned Owl is the largest and most powerful owl breeding in Maryland. It is primarily nocturnal and is a permanent resident throughout the state (Stewart and Robbins 1958). It uses medium to extensive stands of upland forest with fields and edges nearby for hunting. In Maryland it inhabits deciduous, pine, and mixed woodlands. This fierce predator is large, fast, and strong enough to take prey such as skunks, rabbits, and grouse (Austing and Holt 1966).

In the late 1950s, the Great Horned Owl was common in the tidewater areas of Dorchester County, fairly common in the other sections of the Eastern Shore and in the Allegheny Mountain Section, and uncommon in all other sections of the state (Stewart and Robbins 1958). Earlier, it was more common in central Maryland, but by the mid-1940s it was "no longer as common" (Hampe and Kolb 1947), probably because of persecution and habitat alteration. Great Horned Owls were shot and trapped for decades before receiving federal protection. Even now, their habitat is disappearing as the state continues to lose woodlands to agriculture and development, and as a result the population remains low in the central and southeastern parts of the state.

Great Horned Owls nest in abandoned nests of other large birds, in old squirrel nests, in natural tree cavities, and on cliff ledges. The MNRF cites instances of these owls using abandoned nests of the Red-tailed Hawk, Bald Eagle, Osprey,

and Great Blue Heron. Kim Titus (pers. comm.) found four Great Horned Owl nests on cliff ledges along the Potomac River in Allegany County, a type of nesting site not previously reported in Maryland.

This is one of the earliest nesting birds in the state, with courtship beginning in December. Heights above ground of 15 Maryland nests (MNRF) range from 25 to 85 ft (7.6–26 m), with a mean of 48 ft (15 m). The nesting season is from late January to late May, peaking from February through late April. Maryland records for 46 nests show extreme egg dates of 8 January and 15 May. All nests recorded in the MNRF contained 1 or 2 eggs. Incubation is performed almost exclusively by the female (Austing and Holt 1966) and lasts approximately 35 days. Dates for 32 nests with young range from 24 February to 14 May (Stewart and Robbins 1958; MNRF), with the peak from late March through mid-April. Nests contained 1 or, rarely, 2 or 3 young (MNRF). The young remain in the nest five to six weeks before fledging (Austing and Holt 1966).

Atlas results, as with other nocturnal species, reflect uneven coverage by Atlas observers and may underrepresent actual distribution in some counties, especially Allegany, Calvert, Caroline, Charles, Dorchester, St. Mary's, and Worcester. Nevertheless, low densities in some areas are apparently accurate. In the north-central part of the state much of the forest has been cleared for agriculture, leaving only small woodlots along streams and rivers; Great Horned Owls are absent from many of these blocks. The cause of low densities in Garrett County is uncertain. The limiting factor may be relative scarcity of extensive open areas and edges for hunting, or possibly it is the harsher winter climate of the mountains. The Pennsylvania atlas shows a similar gap in the area just north of Garrett County.

Like other nocturnal birds, the Great Horned Owl was difficult to confirm. Most Atlas "confirmed" reports, which accounted for only 23 percent of the records, were of active nests or the observation of dependent young. Most records were "probable," usually birds recorded calling on multiple nights during the breeding season. Some fieldworkers used taped calls to locate this species, which seemed to be most vocal and responsive in January and February. Observers noted that Great Horned Owls were slightly less responsive to taped calls than either Barred Owls or Eastern Screech-Owls and that they were more likely to vocalize spontaneously.

BBS data from 1966 through 1989 show a stable population in the Eastern Region. Maryland data for the same time period show a highly significant average annual increase of 5.4 percent. The future seems fairly bright for the Great Horned Owl. In many areas it is probably as common as it was in the past. Although protected by law, it still occasionally suffers from human disturbance. Public education is important, as is the preservation of extensive woodlands.

Clark F. Jeschke

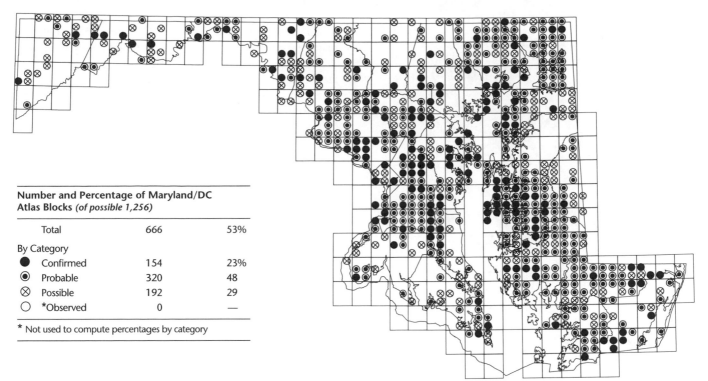

Number and Percentage of Maryland/DC Atlas Blocks *(of possible 1,256)*

Total	666	53%
By Category		
● Confirmed	154	23%
◉ Probable	320	48
⊗ Possible	192	29
○ *Observed	0	—

* Not used to compute percentages by category

Atlas Distribution, 1983–1987

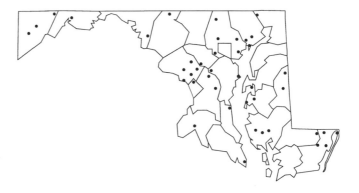

Breeding Distribution, 1958

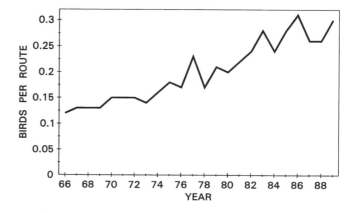

Maryland BBS Trend Graph, 1966–1989

Great Horned Owl 185

PJM

Barred Owl

Strix varia

The Barred Owl is the common "hoot owl" of moist forests, river bottoms, and swamps in eastern and central North America. It may also be found in drier upland woods. Although primarily nocturnal, this owl frequently calls during daylight hours, especially when the sky is overcast. The typical call is eight hoots with a characteristic drawn-out descending note at the end: *who-cooks-for-you, who-cooks-for-you-allll.*

Coues and Prentiss (1883) and Richmond (1888) considered the Barred Owl rare around DC. Kirkwood (1895), discussing its status around Baltimore, called this species fairly common, noting that it was more common on the "necks on the eastern side of the city." Stewart and Robbins (1958) described the Barred Owl as a common permanent resident in the Eastern and Western Shore sections and fairly common elsewhere in the state.

In Maryland, Barred Owls inhabit deciduous and mixed woods as well as wooded swamps (Bushman and Therres 1988). Atlas observers also found them in relatively small woodlots containing streams. This species is primarily confined to relatively mature woods; this habitat provides large trees with a sufficient number of cavities for nesting, and an open understory conducive to its perch-and-drop style of hunting (Nicholls and Warner 1972). Courtship, which starts in late winter and early spring, consists of loud vocal displays of hoots, squawks, and whistles that are given by both sexes. Barred Owls typically raise only one brood per year (Bent 1938).

The MNRF provides the following information. Heights of 39 Maryland nests range from 8 to 60 ft (2.4–18 m); 21 of these nests were at 20 to 30 ft (6.1-9.1 m). Every nest was in a large tree cavity. Clutches from 18 Maryland nests ranged from 1 to 3 eggs, with a mean of 1.9. Thirteen of the 18 nests were found between 28 March and 24 April. Egg dates extended from 28 February to a very late 26 May, which may represent a renesting attempt, as it is more than two weeks later than the next-latest date. Twenty-two Maryland nests had young, ranging from 1 to 5, with a mean of 2.0.

From a study of eight nests in mature upland forests in the Green Ridge State Forest in Allegany County, Devereux and Mosher (1984) reported that six were in the tops of hollow tree stubs, one in a tree cavity, and one in an old stick nest. The mean height of the nests was 30 ft (9.1 m). The mean size of seven clutches was 2.3. The mean hatching date for six clutches was 10 April. The female does most of the incubating, which requires about four weeks (Bent 1938). In addition to mice, which form the bulk of the diet, Barred Owls eat other mammals, birds, fish, crayfish, insects, spiders, lizards, small snakes, and snails (Bent 1938).

Although Atlas data show Barred Owls occurring in all sections of the state, they are concentrated along wooded rivers and streams and in the more heavily forested sections. The gap in north-central Maryland represents an extensive agricultural area with little appropriate habitat. Gaps in the range on the lower Eastern Shore also reflect unsuitable habitat. Barred Owls are not found on the barrier islands, in the vast Chesapeake Bay marshes, or in most of the extensive pine woods. Competition with the large population of Great Horned Owls apparently creates an inhospitable environment in the pine woods (C. Jeschke, pers. obs.). Many pine woods are dry woods and are more suitable for Great Horned Owls than for Barred Owls (K. Klimkiewicz, pers. obs.). Where the two species occur together, the Barred Owl is relegated to the wettest parts of the woods, which are seldom used by the Great Horned Owl. Barred Owls also appear to be uncommon in the mountains of Garrett County. The majority of "confirmed" records were for recently fledged young.

Barred Owls are very vocal and were fairly easily recorded in most blocks, but their nocturnal habits made confirmation difficult (only 20 percent of the Atlas records). Some fieldworkers used taped calls to find Barred Owls. The birds seemed most vocal and responsive in March and early April, and after young were out of the nest from mid-June through August. This species was fairly common over most of its range in Maryland. The BBS data from 1966 through 1989 show an indication of an increase in the Eastern Region and a significant average annual increase of 2.3 percent in Maryland. The major factor limiting Barred Owl populations is availability of mature woods with large dead trees for nesting. Protecting mature forest stands and larger dead trees in extensive forests will ensure a continuing population in Maryland.

Clark F. Jeschke

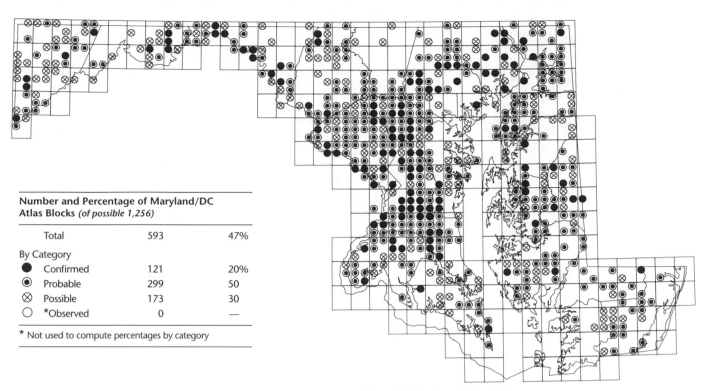

Number and Percentage of Maryland/DC Atlas Blocks (of possible 1,256)

Total	593	47%
By Category		
● Confirmed	121	20%
◉ Probable	299	50
⊗ Possible	173	30
○ *Observed	0	—

* Not used to compute percentages by category

Atlas Distribution, 1983–1987

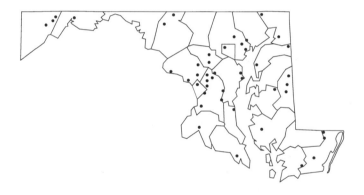

Breeding Distribution, 1958

Northern Saw-whet Owl

Aegolius acadicus

The Northern Saw-whet Owl is Maryland's smallest owl. Although often considered rare, it is relatively common and widespread across southern Canada (Godfrey 1986) and much of the United States (Clark et al. 1987). In the East, breeding has been recorded as far south as the mountains of North Carolina (Simpson and Range 1974). There are breeding records from Pennsylvania (Brauning 1992), New Jersey (Stiles 1978), West Virginia (Hall 1983), and Virginia (atlas data). Northern populations are highly migratory, and wintering birds move into the Piedmont and Coastal Plain of Maryland in late October and early November (D. Brinker, unpub. data).

A juvenile bird captured near Cumberland in Allegany County in 1903 (Eifrig 1904) provided the first evidence of possible breeding in Maryland. Hampe and Kolb (1947) wrote only that this owl was supposed to breed in Maryland. Stewart and Robbins (1958) mentioned summer records at Cranesville, Finzel, and Wolf swamps in Garrett County but had no other breeding evidence. Since 1958 there have been other summer records, but as of 1991 no nest had been located in Maryland.

The breeding biology of the Northern Saw-whet Owl is not well known. It uses a variety of habitats, primarily mixed forests, bogs, shrub swamps, and riparian woods (Bent 1938; Cannings 1987; Swengel and Swengel 1987). It is a cavity nester, primarily using natural holes in trees or abandoned cavities of larger woodpeckers (Levine 1988a). In the Pine Barrens of New Jersey, nests are often found in abandoned Northern Flicker and other large woodpecker cavities in dead pitch pines in beaver ponds (J. Stasz, pers. comm.).

It also uses artificial structures, such as nest boxes erected for Wood Ducks (Follen and Haug 1981) and American Kestrels (E. Jacobs, pers. comm.) and cavities in utility poles (L. MacIvor, pers. comm.). Cannings (1987) erected nest boxes for Northern Saw-whet Owls in British Columbia with considerable success.

Northern Saw-whet Owls begin courtship and territorial calling early, generally during late February or early March (Bent 1938). In Maryland, calling birds have been heard in Finzel Swamp as early as late February (J. McKearnan, pers. comm.). In Wisconsin, they are incubating by early April and typically fledge young by the first of June (E. Jacobs, pers. comm.). Maryland birds are probably on a similar or even earlier schedule. In a sample of 25 clutches from the Atlantic Coastal Plain, the average clutch size was 5.0, with a range of 1 to 7 (Murray 1976). Egg dates from New York and New England range from as early as 19 March to 3 July, peaking in mid-April (Bent 1938). Their principal food is mice, but they also eat some birds and young squirrels.

There were three records of Northern Saw-whet Owls during the Atlas period. The two Garrett County records were along the Casselman River, where one was heard calling repeatedly during the spring of 1985, and from Wolf Swamp, where another calling bird was heard. A single bird was also heard calling in June 1987 in Green Ridge State Forest, Allegany County.

Determining the breeding status of the Northern Saw-whet Owl during the Atlas period was complicated by the early safe date of 5 May, chosen to ensure that calling birds did not include tardy migrants. Migrant Northern Saw-whet Owls are now believed to leave Maryland by early April (M. Hoffman and D. Brinker, pers. obs.). This timing is supported by evidence that migrants depart New Jersey by mid-April (Holroyd and Woods 1975) and central New York by late April (Slack and Slack 1987). Because most calling by Maryland breeding birds probably occurred before 5 May, only late breeders would have been encountered after that date.

Judging from recent observations, an earlier safe date would have resulted in more records. Calling and probably breeding Northern Saw-whet Owls have occurred in Garrett County at Finzel Swamp in 1990 (J. McKearnan, pers. obs.), at Cranesville Swamp from 1987 through 1991 (D. Brinker, J. McKearnan, D. Walbeck, and K. Dodge, pers. obs.), at Wolf Swamp in 1986 (D. Brinker and J. McKearnan, pers. obs.), near Meadow Mountain in 1990 (Ringler 1990b), and near Cherry Creek in 1989 and 1990 (R. Teets, pers. obs.). A juvenile bird was found on the ground in a yard in Frederick, Frederick County, by F. Backham (pers. obs.) on 15 July 1986. The uninjured bird was hand-reared, banded, and released when it was capable of caring for itself, but its origin was never discovered. George Durner (pers. obs.) found a road-killed juvenile near Frostburg, Allegany County, in 1990, and D. Williams (pers. obs.) found a dead female near Battle Creek Cypress Swamp in Calvert County in May 1981. Additional records might have been generated with tape playbacks. Experiments during April and May 1991 with tape

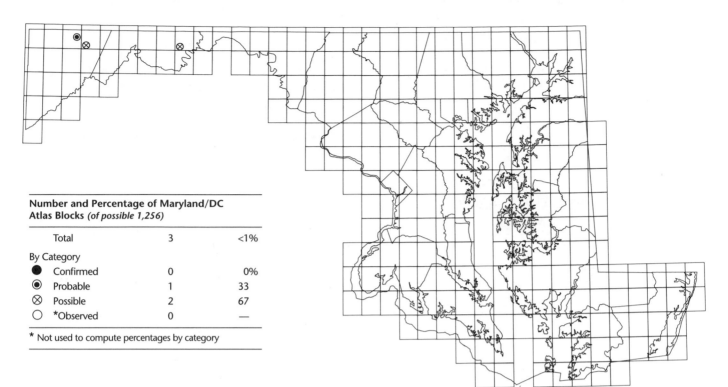

Number and Percentage of Maryland/DC Atlas Blocks *(of possible 1,256)*

Total	3	<1%
By Category		
● Confirmed	0	0%
◉ Probable	1	33
⊗ Possible	2	67
○ *Observed	0	—

* Not used to compute percentages by category

Atlas Distribution, 1983–1987

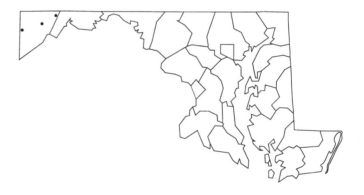

Breeding Distribution, 1958

playback in Garrett County resulted in the discovery of nine locations where frequent calling over a five-week period suggested breeding (K. Dodge and D. Brinker, unpub. data).

Although this is a nocturnal species and is not well sampled by the BBS, data from 1966 through 1989 for 27 routes show an indication of an increase in the continental population. There are too few data to estimate a trend for the Eastern Region.

Breeding by the Northern Saw-whet Owl in Maryland was not confirmed until after the close of the Atlas period. On 24 April 1993, Brinker and Dodge (1993) found a nest with 4 eggs in the Maryland portion of Cranesville Swamp. Additional fieldwork is clearly needed to define its habitat requirements and status in Maryland.

Clark F. Jeschke and David F. Brinker

M. Byrd

Common Nighthawk

Chordeiles minor

Common Nighthawks are often seen at dusk, foraging batlike for insects. Their courtship dives, which end with an upward turn and a musical whir of wind between the primary feathers, are highly visible and entertaining. In early May, the first migrants return to Maryland from their wintering grounds in South America (AOU 1983), and most birds leave in the fall by the end of September (Robbins and Bystrak 1977). Common Nighthawks are most common in Maryland and DC during fall migration; they are much less frequently observed in spring (Stewart and Robbins 1958). Their diet consists almost entirely of flying insects taken on the wing; these include flying ants, May beetles, flies, leaf chafers, mosquitoes, moths, and grasshoppers (Martin et al. 1951).

As early as the mid-1800s a few Bull-bats, as they were called, were known to nest in DC; in fact, the commons at Iowa Circle was a popular place where gunners gathered to shoot them (Coues and Prentiss 1862, 1883). Kirkwood (1895) called the Common Nighthawk locally common, although he cited records only from Baltimore City and DC. Stewart and Robbins (1958) described the breeding status as uncommon and local in all sections.

Although the Common Nighthawk is a bird of open country, it frequently occurs in cities, where it uses flat roofs for nesting. Flat roofs were first constructed in the mid-1800s (Gross 1940), and shortly thereafter the Common Nighthawk was observed roof-nesting in Baltimore (Kirkwood 1895). The species does not construct a nest, but lays its eggs in open areas. Another nickname, Burnt-land Bird, came from its use of recently burned land for nesting and foraging (Gross 1940). Walbeck (1989) found that Common Nighthawks in Frostburg, Allegany County, tended to select larger, dark-colored roofs for nesting.

Of 11 Maryland nests (MNRF) found on the ground, nine were on the beach at Point Lookout State Park in St. Mary's County. Thirteen other nests were on buildings. These 24 nests were distributed among the following counties: St. Mary's (9), Caroline (6), Allegany (5), Talbot (2), Baltimore (1), and Frederick (1). The 24 Maryland nests range in height above ground from 0 to 61 ft (0–19 m). All nests were either on the ground or on roofs; the mean height is therefore irrelevant.

The earliest Maryland egg date is 23 May and the latest is 13 July, with the majority in late May and early June (MNRF). Clutch sizes in 13 Maryland nests range from 2 to 4, with a mean of 2.2. Nests with young have been reported from 1 June to 27 July, with no evident peak. Brood sizes recorded in six Maryland nests range from 1 to 3 (MNRF). Incubation lasts 17 days, and young fledge in 21 to 23 days (Walbeck 1989). A single brood is raised (Forbush 1927).

Atlas results show clusters of sightings near DC, Baltimore City, Hagerstown and Hancock in Washington County, the Cumberland-Frostburg area in Allegany County, and other towns. "Confirmed" nest sites were scattered throughout the state, generally in association with buildings. Similar widespread distributions with relatively few "confirmed" breeding sites are evident in the Pennsylvania (Brauning 1992), Virginia, and Delaware atlases. Generalizations from such a small sample size are difficult, but it is interesting that recent nest records and most "confirmed" Atlas records were associated with buildings, possibly indicating a decline in natural nesting sites. It is tempting to conclude that the Common Nighthawk has changed to urban nesting. Open habitats, however, such as construction sites and burned areas, are poorly sampled in Maryland nest records, and nesting Common Nighthawks are very visible in cities. Nevertheless, Brigham (1989) found that in British Columbia, nesting Common Nighthawks preferred natural ground sites to rooftops.

Unfortunately, monitoring the population status of crepuscular species is difficult. The BBS routes are not begun until a half hour before sunrise, after Common Nighthawks have gone to roost. BBS data from 1966 through 1989 show a significant average annual decline of 2.3 percent for the Eastern Region; Maryland data are too few to estimate a trend for the state. BBS data for the same time period show stable continental populations. Some authorities have suggested that western populations have been declining (Tate 1981), but solid evidence and possible causes remain elusive.

More studies are needed on the habitat requirements of Common Nighthawks in Maryland. It is not known whether they still use natural ground sites, or what effect moving to man-made sites has had on productivity or nesting success. Any species totally dependent on artificial structures may be vulnerable to changes in human behavior, so continued attention to the status of the Common Nighthawk is necessary if we are to keep this species as a breeding bird in Maryland.

John R. Sauer

Number and Percentage of Maryland/DC Atlas Blocks *(of possible 1,256)*

	Total	149	12%
By Category			
●	Confirmed	10	8%
◉	Probable	34	25
⊗	Possible	90	67
○	*Observed	15	—

* Not used to compute percentages by category

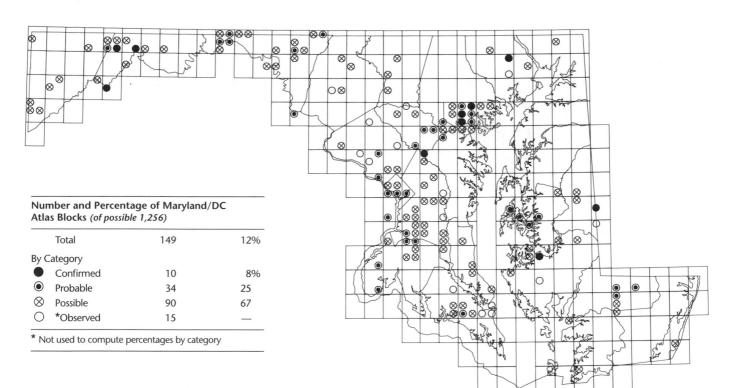

Atlas Distribution, 1983–1987

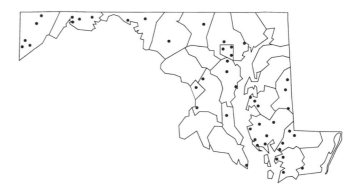

Breeding Distribution, 1958

Chuck-will's-widow

Caprimulgus carolinensis

The Chuck-will's-widow, North America's largest caprimulgid, is close to the northern limit of its range in Maryland (AOU 1983). It uses its large funnellike mouth—fully 2 in. (5.1 cm) wide (Bent 1940)—to catch flying insects rather than to suckle milk from goats, as the myth and the colloquial family name *goatsucker* imply. Its diet consists almost entirely of insects, especially May beetles, although small birds have been taken (Bent 1940). Its plumage, patterned like flaky bark and dead leaves, camouflages it during the daylight hours spent on the forest floor or nestled lengthwise on a tree limb. The Chuck-will's-widow is an uncommon nesting bird in coniferous and mixed woodlands that adjoin open clearings, brushy areas, agricultural grassland, and fallow land near tidewater. Spring migrants return to Maryland from their Caribbean, Mexican, and Central American wintering grounds (AOU 1983) in mid-April; the last birds leave by late September (Robbins and Bystrak 1977).

Kirkwood (1895) included the Chuck-will's-widow among Maryland birds based on two July observations at Odenton, Anne Arundel County. Cooke (1921) included it on the list of DC area birds, based on birds R. Ridgway heard singing at Brookland in DC on 22 July 1895, and those C. Richmond heard in the summer of 1896 near Laurel, Prince George's County. Court (1921) collected a clutch of two eggs in St. Mary's County on 10 May 1921, and F. Kirkwood reported finding a nest in St. Mary's County on 27 May 1930. Wetmore (1936) reported birds heard at North Beach, Calvert County, on 28 June 1930; at Clements, St. Mary's County, on 14 August 1932; and near Laurel, Prince George's County, on 12 May 1935. Perkins (1933) reported a mounted specimen in a collection taken before 1933 near Cambridge, Dorchester County. By the 1940s, the Chuck-will's-widow was generally accepted as a summer resident north to Leonardtown, St. Mary's County; Holland Point, Anne Arundel County; Nanticoke, Wicomico County; and the Delaware state line (Stewart and Robbins 1947a; Hampe and Kolb 1947). On the evening of 20 May 1945, R. Stewart and C. Robbins heard them at six of ten roadside stops between Point Lookout and Leonardtown in St. Mary's County (USFWS Field Report). A decade later, Stewart and

Robbins (1958) described the breeding status as common near tidewater in the Eastern Shore Section north to Kent Island in Queen Anne's County; common in the Western Shore Section north to the Shadyside Peninsula in Anne Arundel County; and uncommon elsewhere in the state.

Breeding activity starts in late April. Nesting occurs in well-drained portions of coniferous and mixed coniferous-deciduous woodlands with little underbrush. The two eggs are deposited on fallen leaves on the ground in an area clear of underbrush (Bent 1940). Extreme egg dates for Maryland are 10 May and 8 July, with a peak in early June (MNRF). In all eight Maryland nests, the clutch size is 2; the only Maryland brood had 2 chicks on 18 June (MNRF). Renesting may occur if the first clutch is lost (Bent 1940). Females brood young on the ground at or near the site of egg laying.

Atlas results indicate that the Chuck-will's-widow is scattered throughout the Eastern and Western Shore sections, with the largest concentrations along the Pocomoke River and on the Talbot County necks. The population centers are mature coniferous forests near Chesapeake Bay tributaries south of the Patapsco and Chester rivers, in coastal Worcester County, and in the Potomac watershed south of DC. The pattern of distribution is very similar to that given by Stewart and Robbins (1958) but shows additional records in the northern portions of the Eastern and Western Shore sections, in the interior of the Western Shore, and to the boundary of the Western Shore along the Potomac River. The few occurrences in the extreme eastern and southern Piedmont are exceptional. A bird heard near Hancock, Washington County, is near a small population reported in nearby West Virginia (Hall 1983). Atlas results suggest that the Chuck-will's-widow has slightly expanded its range to the north and west, while also increasing in the interior woodlands on the lower Eastern Shore. Intensive Atlas efforts, however, may have discovered birds that previous fieldwork had overlooked. BBS data from 1966 through 1989 show a significant average annual decline of 1.7 percent in the Eastern Region; data are too few to estimate a Maryland trend.

Residential waterfront development, ditching to drain land, indiscriminate use of biocides, human disturbance, and land clearing for commercial or development purposes have reduced the habitat and food supply of the Chuck-will's-widow in recent decades. Numbers decreased substantially in the 1970s and 1980s in the rapidly developing tidewater areas of Queen Anne's and Talbot counties (J. Reese, pers. obs.); this change is probably ongoing in other developing areas within the Chuck-will's-widow's range. Disappearance from areas where forest clearing and increasing urbanization are occurring should be anticipated.

Jan G. Reese

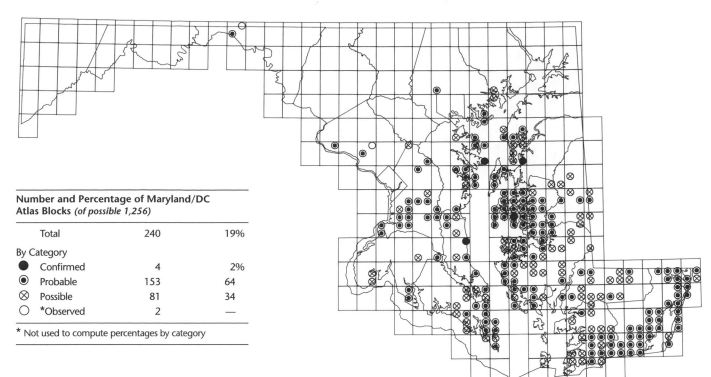

Number and Percentage of Maryland/DC Atlas Blocks *(of possible 1,256)*

Total	240	19%
By Category		
● Confirmed	4	2%
◉ Probable	153	64
⊗ Possible	81	34
○ *Observed	2	—

* Not used to compute percentages by category

Atlas Distribution, 1983–1987

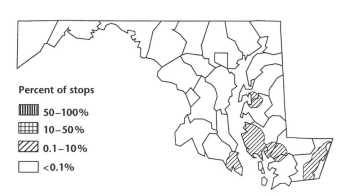

Percent of stops

▥ 50–100%
▦ 10–50%
▨ 0.1–10%
▢ <0.1%

Relative Abundance, 1982–1989

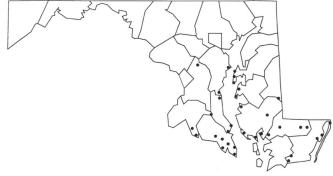

Breeding Distribution, 1958

The Chuck-will's-widow is found in small numbers in woodlands bordering marshes on the lower Eastern Shore and in southern St. Mary's County on the Western Shore. Miniroutes generally provide poor coverage for nocturnal and crepuscular species.

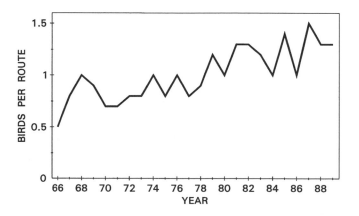

Maryland BBS Trend Graph, 1966–1989

M. Byrd

Whip-poor-will

Caprimulgus vociferus

This denizen of twilight is rarely seen, but the resounding, often repeated, three-note song reveals its presence even on the darkest nights. The song of the Whip-poor-will has been immortalized in stories, songs, and poems, making it the best known and most popular of the North American goatsuckers. It uses its large, bugle-shaped mouth to capture flying insects, not to suckle milk from goats, as the family name suggests. Moths, grasshoppers, crickets, mosquitoes, beetles, and caddisflies are among the insects taken (Bent 1940). Its plumage is patterned like flaked bark or dead leaves, and the bird spends the day on the forest floor or nestled parallel on a wide tree limb. The Whip-poor-will is a migrant and uncommon nester in all parts of the state, being found primarily in upland, mature woods with adjoining clearings, brushy areas, fallow ground, or agricultural grasslands (Stewart and Robbins 1958).

Coues and Prentiss (1883) reported Whip-poor-wills as rare summer residents in DC, but common in "more primitive country.... In former years we saw them in places, now built up, between Le Droit Park and the city limits." This suggests localized changes in distribution were occurring prior to the turn of the century. Kirkwood (1895) described them as locally common in Maryland and cited two nesting records. Hampe and Kolb (1947) and Stewart and Robbins (1958) considered Whip-poor-wills common in all sections of the state except the Upper Chesapeake, Piedmont, and Allegheny Mountain sections, where they were fairly common.

Whip-poor-wills begin returning to Maryland from the Gulf Coast states and Central America (AOU 1983) in early April (Robbins and Bystrak 1977), and the last fall migrants leave by mid-October. Breeding activity commences in late April in eastern and southern Maryland. Detailed information on the timing of breeding is lacking for the Piedmont, Ridge and Valley, and Allegheny Mountain sections. Nesting occurs in well-drained deciduous woodlands with little or no underbrush, most frequently near small openings or margins where tiny gaps in the canopy create a bold pattern of shade and light on the forest floor (Bent 1940). The eggs, which are white with gray, brown, and lilac spotting, are deposited directly on fallen leaves on the ground in the fragmented light. Incubation, principally by the female, requires about 20 days.

Extreme egg dates for Maryland are 24 April and 7 July (Robbins and Bystrak 1977), with most clutches observed in May (Stewart and Robbins 1958). A second attempt may occur if the first clutch is lost. Clutch sizes in 11 Maryland nests are 1 or 2 eggs, with a mean of 1.8. Brood sizes in six Maryland nests are 1 and 2; extreme dates are 31 May and 17 July. Young are brooded by the female on the ground at or near the site of egg laying for at least 20 days (Bent 1940). The female will sometimes feign injury to lure intruders away from the eggs or young.

Atlas results show that the Whip-poor-will occurs largely in the nontidal portions of the Eastern and Western Shore sections and in the western part of the Ridge and Valley Section. It occurs less frequently in the Upper Chesapeake, Piedmont, and Allegheny Mountain sections and is most scarce in the central and northern Piedmont. This distribution is identical to that reported by Stewart and Robbins (1958). The paucity of records in the tidewater areas of the Eastern and Western Shore sections may be attributable to the predominance of coniferous woodland in those areas. Whip-poor-wills were recorded in pine woods, however, at Soldiers Delight in Baltimore County and in Green Ridge State Forest in Allegany County. This species may be further limited on the lower Eastern Shore by competition with Chuck-will's-widows, which have substantially increased their range in Maryland during the past 20 years. Comparison of the two Atlas maps shows Chuck-will's-widows strongly entrenched along the edges of the Chesapeake Bay, while Whip-poor-wills are confined more generally to the center of the Eastern Shore and to the inland portions of the lower Western Shore. Pine woods are widespread in the Upper Chesapeake and Piedmont sections; scarcity of Whip-poor-will records in these sections may also be attributable, in part, to lack of extensive nocturnal coverage. Additionally, large areas of the north-central part of the state are agricultural, with only small isolated woodlots remaining, resulting in poor Whip-poor-will habitat. The exceptional effort by fieldworkers in Montgomery and Howard counties may account for the large number of records there. BBS data from 1966 through 1989 show stable populations in the Eastern Region; Maryland data show a highly significant average annual decline of 2.9 percent. The Maryland population was stable from 1980 through 1989.

The clearing of forests for development, agriculture, and transportation; the indiscriminate use of biocides; and human disturbance will undoubtedly exert increasing pressure on Whip-poor-will populations. Withdrawal from increasingly urbanized and suburbanized habitats should be anticipated. General land development will depress populations in other parts of the state.

Jan G. Reese

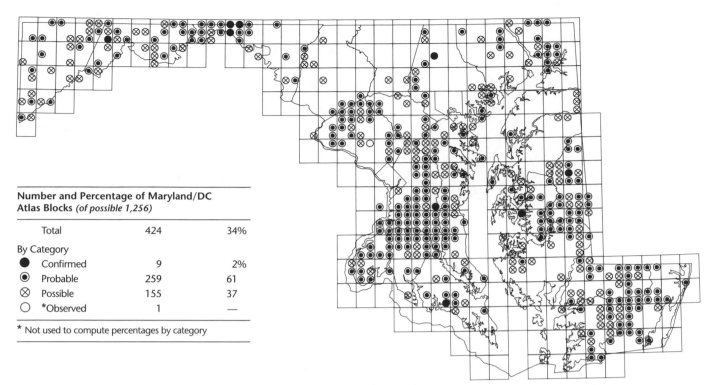

Atlas Distribution, 1983–1987

Number and Percentage of Maryland/DC Atlas Blocks *(of possible 1,256)*

Total	424	34%
By Category		
● Confirmed	9	2%
◉ Probable	259	61
⊗ Possible	155	37
○ *Observed	1	—

* Not used to compute percentages by category

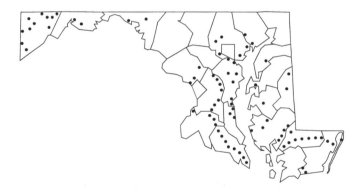

Breeding Distribution, 1958

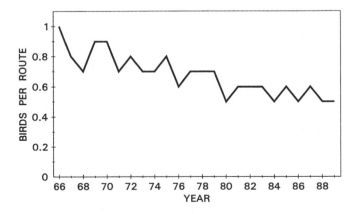

Maryland BBS Trend Graph, 1966–1989

m.Byrd

Chimney Swift

Chaetura pelagica

The aerial acrobatics of the Chimney Swift as it darts and glides over rooftops are a familiar summer sight over Maryland's cities and towns. This species, which now nests almost exclusively in chimneys, has benefited greatly from the increased availability of nest sites created by the construction of buildings. The first spring migrants return to Maryland from South America (AOU 1983) in early April; the bulk of the migration occurs in the second half of the month (Stewart and Robbins 1958). Fall migration begins in the middle of August and the last birds linger until late October.

Since the mid-1800s the Chimney Swift has been a common summer resident and an abundant migrant throughout Maryland and DC (Coues and Prentiss 1862; Richmond 1888; Kirkwood 1895). Coues and Prentiss (1883) mentioned that they always bred in the chimneys of the Smithsonian Institution, the White House, and other public buildings in DC. Stewart and Robbins (1958) described them as common in all sections. The highest breeding density reported for Maryland is a low 0.6 territorial males per 100 acres (40.5 ha) in 1943 on the border between Anne Arundel and Prince George's counties in an area of mixed forest, brush, and field that included 12 buildings with chimneys (Stewart and Robbins 1958).

Chimney Swifts spend their daylight hours in flight, so courtship and collection of nest material occurs on the wing (Fischer 1958). A half-saucer nest of short, straight twigs is glued together with a saliva-like secretion and fastened to a vertical wall, usually in a dark, protected area of a building. Chimneys, and formerly the eaves of barns, are the most typical nest sites. The two main nest site requirements are darkness and shelter from the weather. Before the arrival of Europeans, Chimney Swifts nested in hollow trees and under loose bark (Tyler 1940a). Although such nests are still reported on occasion, they are far less frequent in modern times (Tyler 1940a). The MNRF includes no reports of nests in natural sites. Blodgett and Zammuto (1979) reported a nest in a hollow tree in Illinois in 1977, and they found fewer than ten reports of nesting in natural sites in the previous 100 years.

Nest building takes 18 to 30 days, but the first eggs may be laid before the nest is complete (Fischer 1958). Height of the nest above the ground is determined by the height of the chimney. Heights of 20 Maryland nests (MNRF) range from 4 to 60 ft (1.2–18 m), with a mean of 21.7 ft (6.6 m). More relevant is the placement of the nest in relation to the top of the chimney. In 16 Maryland reports (MNRF), the nests were placed from 4 to 18 ft (1.2–5.5 m) below the top of the chimney, with a mean of 11.0 ft (3.4 m).

Extreme Maryland egg dates are 9 May and 12 August, with the records evenly distributed (MNRF). Clutch sizes in 30 Maryland nest records range from 3 to 5, with a mean of 3.9. Although only one brood is raised per season (Forbush 1927), R. Jackson reported three attempts in one chimney in Dorchester County in 1918 (MNRF). Nests with young have been found in Maryland from 30 May through 1 September. Reports of nests outside those dates are of "young heard" in a chimney and may not represent nestlings. In 14 Maryland reports of nests with young, brood sizes range from 2 to 4, with a mean of 3.2 (MNRF). Both parents incubate and take turns brooding the nestlings (Dexter 1981). Breeding pairs are sometimes assisted by male or female helpers that feed the young and occasionally incubate. Incubation lasts 19 to 21 days, and the young fledge in about four weeks (Fischer 1958). There are no records of Brown-headed Cowbird parasitism (Friedmann 1963).

Postbreeding Chimney Swifts gather in flocks of hundreds or even thousands. At night these large flocks roost communally in chimneys, steeples, and other structures. The largest fall flock reported numbered 4,000 to 5,000 in mid-September 1924 in DC (Stewart and Robbins 1958).

Atlas results show that Chimney Swifts breed in all sections of Maryland; they are absent from only a few heavily forested blocks in western Maryland and from the extensive marshes of the lower Eastern Shore. Most confirmations (58%) were sightings of adults entering chimneys.

The availability of artificial structures for nest sites has undoubtedly aided Chimney Swifts, but because most modern chimneys are used for venting noxious fumes, nesting swifts cannot use them. Chimney Swifts rely on a diet of flying insects, especially beetles, flies, and ants (Tyler 1940a), so they are vulnerable if significant reductions in their prey occur from the use of pesticides. BBS data from 1966 through 1989 show a significant average annual decline of 1.1 percent in Chimney Swift populations in the Eastern Region. Maryland data for the same time period also show a significant average annual decline (1.9%); however, data from 1980 through 1989 show stable populations in the state. Continued monitoring of this species is recommended.

Elizabeth E. Zucker

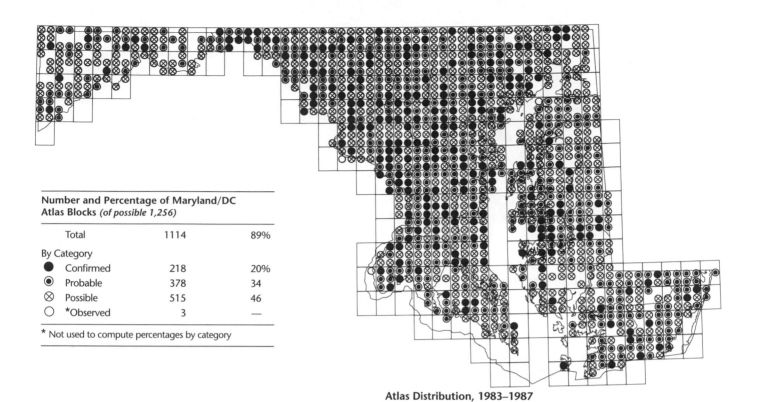

Atlas Distribution, 1983–1987

Number and Percentage of Maryland/DC Atlas Blocks *(of possible 1,256)*

Total	1114	89%
By Category		
● Confirmed	218	20%
◉ Probable	378	34
⊗ Possible	515	46
○ *Observed	3	—

* Not used to compute percentages by category

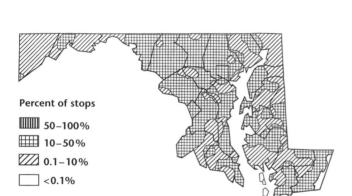

Percent of stops

▥	50–100%
▦	10–50%
▧	0.1–10%
☐	<0.1%

Relative Abundance, 1982–1989

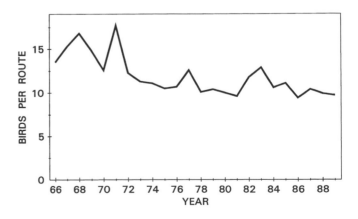

Breeding Distribution, 1958

The Chimney Swift is most common in urban, suburban, and agricultural areas in the eastern two-thirds of Maryland and around Cumberland in Allegany County. It is less common in the forested highlands of western Maryland, in the marshes and wooded areas on the Eastern Shore, and in southern Maryland.

Maryland BBS Trend Graph, 1966–1989

Ruby-throated Hummingbird

Archilochus colubris

The Ruby-throated Hummingbird is Maryland's smallest bird. It nests throughout the eastern half of the United States and southern Canada (AOU 1983). Spring migrants return to Maryland from their Central American wintering grounds (AOU 1983) in late April and early May; the last fall birds depart by early October (Stewart and Robbins 1958).

Most early writers considered the Ruby-throated Hummingbird a common or fairly common summer resident in Maryland and DC (Coues and Prentiss 1862, 1883; Kirkwood 1895; Eifrig 1904). Cooke (1929) cited a record of 100 individuals seen in a single horsechestnut tree in DC in mid-May 1895, a sight no modern birdwatcher is likely to experience. Stewart and Robbins (1958) reported it to be a fairly common breeder and migrant in all sections. Some local populations have been reported as declining in recent years, so this species was on the NAS Blue List from 1978 through 1986 (Tate 1986). BBS data from 1966 through 1989 show that the Maryland and Eastern Region populations of Ruby-throated Hummingbirds have remained stable; however, Maryland data from 1980 through 1989 show a significant average annual decline of 3.8 percent.

This species breeds in moist forests, often near streams and wooded swamps, and in hedgerows, wood margins, and other edge habitats that contain brush or small trees (Terres 1980). The highest breeding density reported in Maryland is 15 territorial males per 100 acres (40.5 ha) in well-drained floodplain forest on the Anne Arundel-Prince George's County border in 1945 (Stewart et al. 1946). The female builds the nest, incubates the eggs, and tends the young without assistance from the male (Allen 1930). The nest usually is constructed on a fork of a downward sloping twig of a tree or shrub, often in the vicinity of water (Harrison 1978). Banding records show that the female frequently returns to the same locality each year (R. C. Leberman, pers. comm.).

Of 57 MNRF records, 42 nests (74%) were in oak, maple, sycamore, or American beech trees, with oak and maple trees preferred. Nest heights range from 3 to 40 ft (0.9–12.2 m), with a mean of 13.9 ft (4.2 m). The tiny cup-shaped nest is composed of plant material, bound compactly with spider webs. It is thickly lined with plant down, covered on the outside with lichens, and averages 1.5 in. (3.8 cm) across (Harrison 1978). Incubation lasts 11 to 16 days and the young remain in the nest for 14 to 28 days (Tyler 1940b; Harrison 1978). The only reported instance of Brown-headed Cowbird parasitism was from Massachusetts; the Brown-headed Cowbird egg completely filled the tiny nest (Friedmann 1963).

The earliest egg date for Maryland is 14 May and the latest is 20 August; records are fairly evenly distributed from mid-May to early August (MNRF). Clutch sizes in 59 Maryland nests range from 1 (11 nests) to 3 (1 nest), with a mean of 1.8. One brood per season is normal, but two are possible (Tyler 1940b; DeGraaf et al. 1980). Of 23 Maryland records for nests with young, the earliest date is 25 May and the latest is 2 September, with records evenly distributed from early June to mid-August (MNRF). Brood sizes in these nests were either 1 or 2, with a mean of 1.6.

The Ruby-throated Hummingbird's small size and inconspicuous nest made confirmation difficult. Nevertheless, it was widely recorded during the Atlas and was found to be fairly evenly distributed throughout the state. The most frequent "confirmed" records were of adults on nests (30%), fledged young (22%), and nest building (15%). There were 19 records of used nests (11%), but only 12 (7%) each for nests with eggs and nests with young. Most "probable" records were observations of pairs or of birds on territory (38% each). Only 29 (8%) "probable" reports were based on the characteristic pendulum display flight. The Ruby-throated Hummingbird's quick flight and virtually inaudible vocalizations made it difficult to find in some blocks. A few records came from feeders, although hummingbird feeding is not especially common in the East. One field observer had considerable success locating these birds by spending at least 15 minutes observing every flowering mimosa tree he encountered. He detected hummingbirds at over 75 percent of the trees he watched (C. Jeschke, pers. comm.). The Ruby-throated Hummingbirds' summer diet consists almost entirely of nectar, especially from red or orange tubular flowers such as trumpet creeper, American bee balm, and jewelweed (Terres 1980). Insects are taken in small numbers except in the winter, when they constitute the bulk of their diet. These birds commonly frequent specialized feeders that contain a sugar solution.

At present there is no major threat of habitat loss for the Ruby-throated Hummingbird. Although BBS data show stable populations in Maryland and for the Eastern Region of the continent, the local declines reported in other states emphasize the need to continue monitoring the Maryland population.

Sue A. Ricciardi

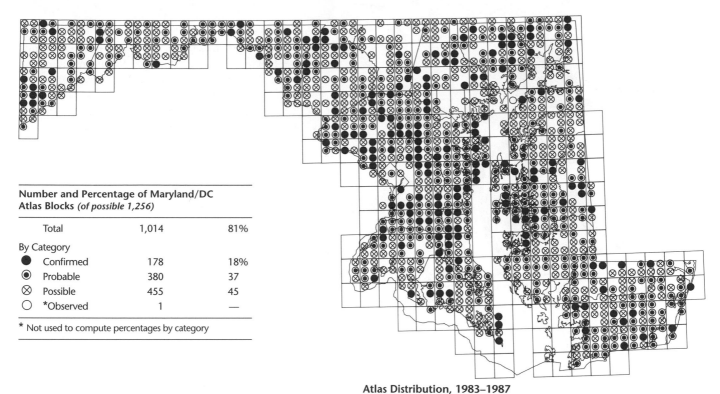

Number and Percentage of Maryland/DC Atlas Blocks *(of possible 1,256)*

Total	1,014	81%
By Category		
● Confirmed	178	18%
◉ Probable	380	37
⊗ Possible	455	45
○ *Observed	1	—

* Not used to compute percentages by category

Atlas Distribution, 1983–1987

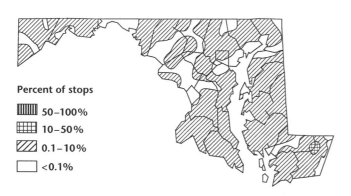

Percent of stops

▦	50–100%
▦	10–50%
▨	0.1–10%
☐	<0.1%

Relative Abundance, 1982–1989

Breeding Distribution, 1958

The Ruby-throated Hummingbird is uncommon but widely distributed. Because of the smaller numbers, it was not detected in many areas, especially in the most developed and agricultural areas in the center of the state and in the dry woodlands of the Ridge and Valley Section.

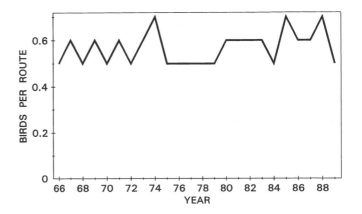

Maryland BBS Trend Graph, 1966–1989

Belted Kingfisher

Ceryle alcyon

The loud, rattling call of the Belted Kingfisher is a familiar sound along streams, rivers, and pond edges. In Maryland, this species nests commonly throughout upland areas and less commonly in the tidal waters of the Chesapeake Bay and along the coast. Common in suitable habitat in spring, summer, and fall, many Belted Kingfishers migrate only when frozen water prevents them from fishing. Their diet is varied (Terres 1980); they take small fish, tadpoles, crabs, crayfish, lizards, frogs, toads, small snakes, turtles, grasshoppers, butterflies, beetles, young birds, mice, shellfish, and, occasionally, berries.

The status of the Belted Kingfisher has not changed in this century. Earlier authors considered it a common summer resident and migrant and irregular in winter (Coues and Prentiss 1862, 1883; Kirkwood 1895; Cooke 1929; Hampe and Kolb 1947). Stewart and Robbins (1958) were more specific, reporting it as fairly common in the tidewater areas of the Eastern Shore, Western Shore, and Upper Chesapeake sections but uncommon elsewhere. Distribution is restricted to streams, reservoirs, bay shores, and other aquatic edge habitats.

Belted Kingfishers are generally solitary except during the nesting season (Bent 1940). Within a territory, individual birds have regular perches, usually on a branch over water, from which they can seek prey. They build their nests in suitable sandbanks, river bluffs, road and railroad cuts, sand and gravel pits, and, more rarely, in hollow stumps and tree cavities. Although nests are usually close to the water's edge, a few have been found up to 1 mi (1.6 km) from water (Cornwell 1963). Most nests are burrows in river or stream banks, generally placed 1 to 3 ft (0.3–0.9 m) below the top of the bank (MNRF) and extending inward and slightly up-

ward, most often to a depth of 3 to 7 ft (0.9–2.1 m). Both sexes excavate the burrows (Bent 1940), a process that sometimes takes two to three weeks, though, depending on the nature of the soil, it may be much less. A pair may use the same burrow in succeeding years. The nest cavity is an enlarged, circular, dome-shaped chamber at the end of the tunnel. The diameter of the chamber ranges from 7 to 12 in. (18–31 cm) (Bent 1940; MNRF). The male may excavate a second burrow near the nest site and use it for roosting while the female incubates at night (Bent 1940).

Belted Kingfishers nest in Maryland from late March to mid-July (Stewart and Robbins 1958). Heights above the ground or water of 18 Maryland nests (MNRF) range from 2 to 18 ft (0.6 m–5.5 m), with a mean of 8.0 ft (2.4 m). There are 18 records of Maryland nests with eggs, with dates from 11 April to 5 June and clutch sizes ranging from 2 to 7 (mean of 6.6). Bent (1940) reported that clutch sizes ordinarily range from 5 to 8. The eggs are laid on the bare dirt of the newly dug burrow, but in subsequent years they are deposited on the residue of fish scales from previous nestings. Incubation, performed by both sexes, lasts 23 or 24 days. There are 12 records of Maryland nests with young, ranging from 7 May to 7 July (MNRF). Brood sizes range from 1 to 7 (mean of 4). Young fledge after 30 to 35 days, and only one brood is raised (Bent 1940). There are no known instances of Brown-headed Cowbird parasitism of the Belted Kingfisher (Friedmann 1963; Peck and James 1983).

During the Atlas project, most "confirmed" records were observations of fledglings or of adults entering nest burrows or carrying food for young, with about equal numbers in each of these categories. It is often difficult to determine whether a bird is carrying food to nestlings or intends to eat it. Several atlas observers in other states reported that when adults carried small fish lengthwise in their bills, they entered a burrow; otherwise, the birds carried the fish crosswise (E. Blom, pers. comm.). This technique was discussed in Atlas training sessions and was used by some observers in Maryland.

Atlas observers found these birds throughout Maryland, although they were less common in southern Maryland and on the lower Eastern Shore, where most river banks are too low for nest sites. The stability of Belted Kingfisher populations may be illustrated by comparing data collected on the Howard County atlas from 1973 through 1975 (Klimkiewicz and Solem 1978) with present information. Belted Kingfishers were found in 31 of 34 blocks (91%) and in 79 of 136 quarterblocks (58%) in the first atlas (Klimkiewicz and Solem 1978). During the Maryland/DC Atlas, they were found in all 34 blocks and in 78 of 136 quarterblocks (57%). BBS data from 1966 through 1989 for Maryland and the Eastern Region show stable Belted Kingfisher populations; Maryland data from 1980 through 1989 show an indication of a slight increase.

Protecting steep banks that serve as nesting sites and maintaining waterways free of fish-killing pollutants and siltation will help sustain Belted Kingfisher populations.

Delos C. Dupree

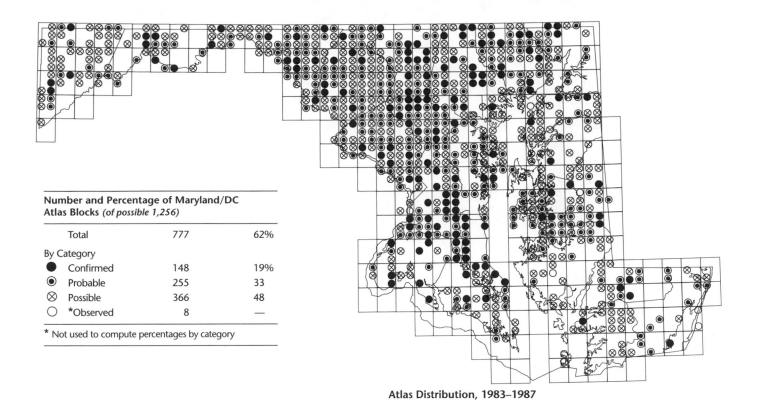

Number and Percentage of Maryland/DC Atlas Blocks *(of possible 1,256)*		
Total	777	62%
By Category		
● Confirmed	148	19%
◉ Probable	255	33
⊗ Possible	366	48
○ *Observed	8	—
* Not used to compute percentages by category		

Atlas Distribution, 1983–1987

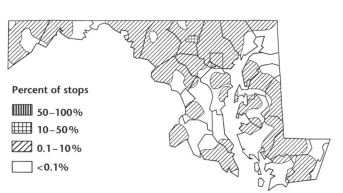

Percent of stops

▦ 50–100%
▦ 10–50%
▨ 0.1–10%
☐ <0.1%

Relative Abundance, 1982–1989

Breeding Distribution, 1958

The Belted Kingfisher is most widely distributed west of the Fall Line. It is more local on the Coastal Plain, where it occurs primarily along the broader rivers of the interior of the central and southern Eastern Shore and near bluffs along the Chesapeake Bay.

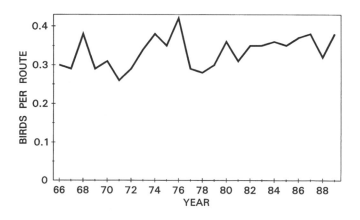

Maryland BBS Trend Graph, 1966–1989

Red-headed Woodpecker

Melanerpes erythrocephalus

The colorful Red-headed Woodpecker can be found, at least sparingly, in every Maryland county. An uncommon and local breeder, it is more common in some parts of the state during migration and in winter. Migration peaks occur from late April to late May and during the latter two-thirds of October (Stewart and Robbins 1958). Winter numbers fluctuate considerably, depending on the food crop locally and to the north. The Red-headed Woodpecker is more of a vegetarian than other members of the woodpecker family; its diet is two-thirds vegetable matter (Beal 1911), with insects, especially beetles, predominating only during summer. It eats various grains and berries throughout the year, but mast, especially acorns, dominates its winter diet.

The Red-headed Woodpecker was clearly more common a century ago. Coues and Prentiss (1883) referred to it as the most abundant member of the woodpecker family in the DC area, and Richmond (1888) also called it common there. Kirkwood (1895) described it as very erratic in Maryland, common one year and largely absent the next. Eifrig (1904) wrote that in western Maryland it had declined at lower elevations but was still very abundant in the higher parts, a status that has changed.

Cooke (1929) thought it was still "tolerably" common in summer around DC. Stewart and Robbins (1958) called the Red-headed Woodpecker fairly common locally in the Allegheny Mountain Section but rare or uncommon and local in the rest of the state, except for Dorchester, Talbot, and Caroline counties, where it no longer bred.

The Red-headed Woodpecker nests in open woodlands, forest edges, and especially in areas with numerous large dead trees (Kahl et al. 1985). Nests are almost always in dead trees or snags (Graber et al. 1977). Heights of 32 Maryland nests (MNRF) range from 15 to 82 ft (4.6–25 m), with a mean of 43 ft (13 m). Both sexes excavate the cavity, which has an entrance diameter of about 1.8 in. (5 cm), a depth of 8 to 24 in. (20–61 cm), and a cavity diameter of 3 to 4.3 in. (8–11 cm) (Jackson 1976). No nest material is used, but wood chips from the excavation may cover the cavity floor. Nest sites other than dead trees include utility poles, fence posts, and man-made nest boxes (Bent 1939). Rumsey (1970) found that all nests in utility poles treated with creosote failed because of its toxicity to eggs and chicks.

The earliest Maryland egg date is 25 April and the latest is 20 June (23 June in DC), with a peak in late May (MNRF). Clutch sizes in 11 Maryland nests range from 3 to 5, with a mean of 3.8. One egg is laid per day, and incubation begins before the last egg is laid (Bent 1939). Both parents incubate and hatching occurs in about 14 days. Young fledge in about 27 days and in Maryland have been found in the nest from 8 May through 26 August, with a peak from early to mid-July (MNRF). Information on brood size is not available for Maryland. Two broods are sometimes attempted, and renesting after a failed attempt is common (Bent 1939). Friedmann (1929, 1963) listed the Red-headed Woodpecker as a rare victim of Brown-headed Cowbird parasitism. There are no Maryland records.

The Atlas map shows that the greatest concentrations of Red-headed Woodpeckers occur in the northern portions of Washington, Frederick, and Carroll counties, where they are found in sparsely wooded pastureland and along sycamore-dominated creeks. There is also a concentration on the lower Eastern Shore, primarily in cutover woodlots in pine forests. The species is less common but fairly evenly distributed throughout the rest of the state, except in the western portion of the Ridge and Valley Section and the northern part of the Allegheny Mountain Section. The explosion of the beaver population in the Western Shore Section during the past 15 years may be partly responsible for the population increase there, since beavers created flooded woods with abundant dead snags.

BBS data from 1966 through 1989 show a highly significant average annual decline of 1.9% in the Eastern Region. Maryland data for 1980 through 1989 show a highly significant average annual increase of 9.2 percent, suggesting that this bird is rebounding from the low levels of the 1950s. Competition with other woodpeckers for nest sites and the cutting of dead trees may reduce breeding success of the Red-headed Woodpecker (Graber et al. 1977). European Starlings have also had an impact when nest sites were in short supply. A study by Ingold (1989) in Mississippi however, showed that European Starlings usurped 52 percent of Red-bellied Woodpecker nest cavities but only 7 percent of Red-headed Woodpecker cavities because the Red-headed Woodpecker nests later than the Red-bellied Woodpecker and the European Starling. Protection of the Red-headed Woodpecker can best be achieved by maintaining large tracts of suitable habitat, and by active management to conserve dead and dying trees.

George B. Wilmot

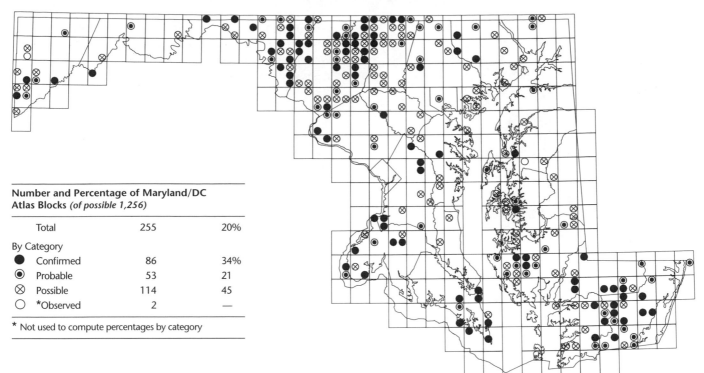

Number and Percentage of Maryland/DC Atlas Blocks *(of possible 1,256)*

Total	255	20%
By Category		
● Confirmed	86	34%
◉ Probable	53	21
⊗ Possible	114	45
○ *Observed	2	—

* Not used to compute percentages by category

Atlas Distribution, 1983–1987

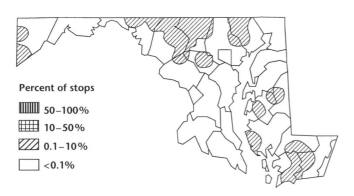

Percent of stops

▥	50–100%
▦	10–50%
▨	0.1–10%
☐	<0.1%

Relative Abundance, 1982–1989

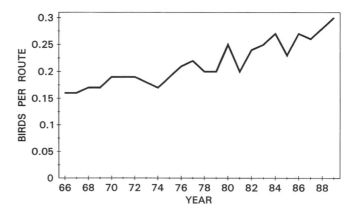

Breeding Distribution, 1958

The Red-headed Woodpecker is uncommon and local; it is most widespread in the northeast Ridge and Valley and northern Piedmont sections. Low numbers in other parts of the state resulted in irregular detection in some areas.

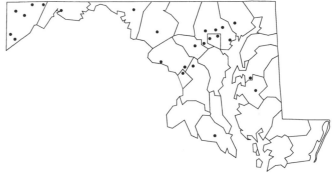

Maryland BBS Trend Graph, 1966–1989

Red-bellied Woodpecker

Melanerpes carolinus

The Red-bellied Woodpecker is better recognized by the highly visible red blaze on its crown and nape than by the faint red blush on its belly. It is a permanent resident throughout Maryland and is found in moist upland wooded habitats as well as in floodplain and swamp forests (Stewart and Robbins 1958). The low-pitched *churr, churr, churr* (Borror 1970; Walton and Lawson 1989) call of this woodpecker is typically repeated two to five times.

The historical record documents a gradual population increase in Maryland. Coues and Prentiss (1883) found the Red-bellied Woodpecker to be a rare permanent resident in the DC area. Kirkwood (1895) described it as an uncommon permanent resident in the Baltimore-Washington area. Fisher (1903) saw his first Harford County Red-bellied Woodpecker on 21 April 1891, and after 12 years of searching, he discovered the first nest there in 1902. Eifrig (1904) considered it accidental and knew of only one record for Allegany County and none for Garrett County. By the 1950s it was a common, permanent resident in Caroline County (Fletcher et al. 1956). Stewart and Robbins (1958) described it as common in the Western Shore Section, locally common in the Eastern Shore Section (most numerous along the Pocomoke River and its tributaries), fairly common in the Upper Chesapeake and Piedmont sections, and rare in the Ridge and Valley and Allegheny Mountain sections.

The Red-bellied Woodpecker is most likely to be found in extensive, thinly stocked, species-rich deciduous forests with tall trees (Robbins et al. 1989a). The highest breeding density reported for Maryland is 35 territorial males per 100 acres (40.5 ha) in mature tulip tree–oak forest in Prince George's County in 1977 (MacClintock 1978).

Both the male and the female excavate the nest cavity (Terres 1980). In an Illinois study, Graber et al. (1977) re-

ported that Red-bellied Woodpeckers often excavated nest cavities in the dead limbs of live trees, whereas Red-headed Woodpeckers selected dead trees. The entrance hole is slightly elliptical and usually 1.7 to 2.2 in. (4–6 cm) in diameter (Fisher 1903; Bent 1939). The cavity is usually 10 to 12 in. (25–31 cm) deep and 5 to 5.5 in. (13–14 cm) wide. A cavity of this size requires a tree with a diameter of at least 10 in. (25 cm) at breast height. Kilham (1961) has observed nest excavation in Maryland as early as 22 February. Heights of 69 Maryland nests (MNRF) range from 9 to 60 ft (2.7–18 m), with a mean of 29.5 ft (9 m).

The Red-bellied Woodpecker is single-brooded in Maryland (Kilham 1961) but will renest if a clutch is lost. Clutches usually contain 4 or 5 eggs, and incubation is shared by both sexes for 12 or 13 days (Harrison 1978). The earliest Maryland egg date is 18 April and the latest is 1 June, with a peak in early May (MNRF). The three Maryland clutches examined contained 4, 3, and 4 eggs (Fisher 1903; Jackson 1941; Kilham 1961). The young are altricial and naked when hatched. Both parents tend the nestlings until they fledge at 26 days (Kilham 1961). Young have been found in Maryland nests from 24 April to 20 August, with the peak in early June (MNRF). Brood sizes in ten Maryland records are for 2 or 3 young, with a mean of 2.5. The average annual survival rate of a population on PWRC was 66 percent (Karr et al. 1990). The Red-bellied Woodpecker feeds largely on the larvae of woodboring insects but also frequently feeds on the ground, taking a variety of insects, acorns, seeds, and nuts (Bent 1939). It also eats a wide variety of fruits and berries. On rare occasions it has been known to take eggs of House Sparrows (Brackbill 1969a). There are no records of Brown-headed Cowbird parasitism of the Red-bellied Woodpecker (Friedmann 1929, 1963).

The Red-bellied Woodpecker was found in almost every Atlas block except those on the barrier islands of Worcester County, the marshes of the lower Eastern Shore, and the high elevations of the Allegheny Plateau in Garrett County. Its range is now slightly more extensive than described by Stewart and Robbins (1958); it is no longer rare in the Ridge and Valley Section. Most "confirmed" records (40%) were observations of recently fledged young. BBS data from 1966 through 1989 show stable populations in the Eastern Region and an indication of an increase in Maryland; data from 1980 through 1989 show a significant average annual increase of 2.9 percent in Maryland.

In a three-year study of 96 pairs of Red-bellied Woodpeckers in Mississippi, Ingold (1989) found that 52 percent of nest cavities were usurped by European Starlings. In urban and suburban areas in Maryland, European Starlings frequently displace Red-bellied Woodpeckers as well as Northern Flickers (K. Klimkiewicz, pers. obs.). Nevertheless, the Red-bellied Woodpecker in Maryland does not appear to be threatened or currently in need of special conservation measures. Large snags and dead trees should be preserved to provide nesting habitat for this and other cavity-nesting species.

Keith D. Van Ness, Jr.

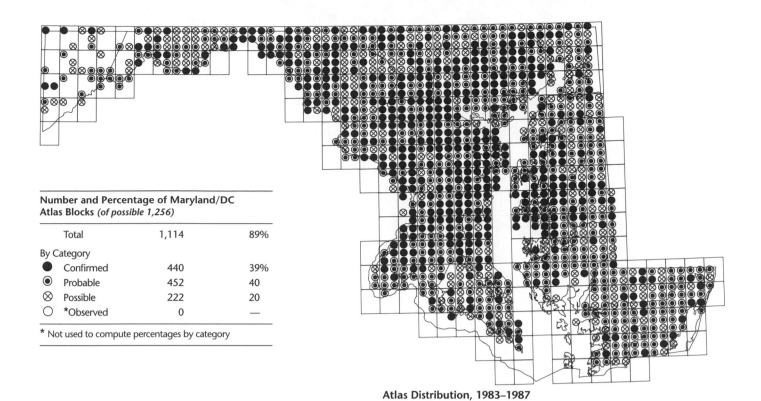

Atlas Distribution, 1983–1987

Number and Percentage of Maryland/DC Atlas Blocks (of possible 1,256)

Total	1,114	89%
By Category		
● Confirmed	440	39%
◉ Probable	452	40
⊗ Possible	222	20
○ *Observed	0	—

* Not used to compute percentages by category

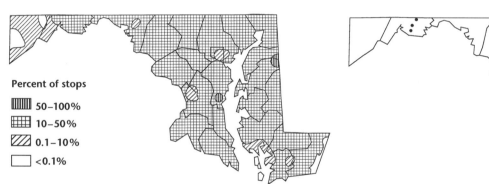

Percent of stops

▦	50–100%
▦	10–50%
▨	0.1–10%
☐	<0.1%

Relative Abundance, 1982–1989

The Red-bellied Woodpecker is widely and evenly distributed. It is least common in the high elevations of the Allegheny Mountain Section, in the urban areas of Baltimore and Washington, and in extensive marsh blocks in southern Dorchester, southwestern Wicomico, and western Somerset counties.

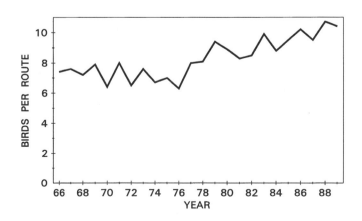

Maryland BBS Trend Graph, 1966–1989

Yellow-bellied Sapsucker

Sphyrapicus varius

Although it was considered a locally common bird in Garrett County as recently as the mid-1950s, the Yellow-bellied Sapsucker has virtually disappeared as a Maryland nesting species. It bred only in Garrett County, where it was found in moist forests or swamps in or near bogs at elevations above 2,400 ft (730 m) or in dry forests on ridges above 3,000 ft (915 m) (Stewart and Robbins 1958). Its spring migration extends from late March to early May, and the fall migration spans mid-September to late October. In winter, Yellow-bellied Sapsuckers are uncommon to rare (Stewart and Robbins 1958). They winter from the central portion of the eastern United States south through the Caribbean into Central America (AOU 1983); on the average, males winter farther north than females (Howell 1953).

The first Maryland nesting record was of an adult feeding fledged young at Deer Park on 6 July 1895 (Kirkwood 1895). In 1899, Preble (1900) saw dependent young in late June at Bittinger, where he described Yellow-bellied Sapsuckers as common in the "heavy" woods. He collected specimens there and in early July at Mountain Lake Park. He also found adults at Finzel and Grantsville in June and both adults and young at Swanton in July. Coues and Prentiss (1883) mistakenly considered Yellow-bellied Sapsuckers permanent residents in the vicinity of DC. Eifrig (1904, 1920a, 1933) wrote that they were not uncommon in western Maryland, especially at higher elevations. He saw a few at Accident in 1918 and 1928. Stewart and Robbins (1958) cited four additional records: a nest with eggs in June 1925, nests with young in May 1929 and July 1945, and a report of adults feeding fledged young in June 1949. Between 1958 and the beginning of the Atlas fieldwork, there was only one summer report: June 1978 from Garrett County (E. Blom, pers. comm.). Robbins and Boone (1984) considered this species

extirpated in Maryland because there had been no confirmed breeding record since 1949.

Runde and Capen (1987), who studied nest tree characteristics in Vermont, found that 68 percent of 38 nests were in quaking aspen and 25 percent were in American beech, red maple, or sugar maple. Eighty percent of the nests were in trees infested with the heartwood decay fungus. The infested trees were taller and larger than trees that were not used. Runde and Capen (1987) reported that the mean height of 38 nests was 28.0 ft (8.5 m). The range of heights was not given. Maryland cavity heights for two nests (MNRF) are 19 and 60 ft (5.8–18 m). Kilham (1962) reported that half the pairs he studied in New Hampshire began three or four excavations before completing the nest. Both males and females excavated, and they used fresh nest holes each year.

Normal Yellow-bellied Sapsucker clutch sizes are 5 or 6, although 4 or 7 eggs are sometimes laid (Kilham 1977). Both sexes incubate. Very few egg dates are available from neighboring states. Illinois egg dates range from 20 April to 3 June (Tyler 1939). Maryland's only egg date is 5 June 1925 in Garrett County by J. Sommer and F. Kirkwood (Stewart and Robbins 1958). This species is single-brooded, with an incubation period of 12 or 13 days; young fledge in 25 to 29 days (Lawrence 1967). Maryland nestlings were found only on 29 May 1949 and 7 July 1945 (Stewart and Robbins 1958). Both parents care for the young (Kilham 1977). The Yellow-bellied Sapsucker has a varied diet consisting of insects, especially ants, wasps, beetles, and moths during the summer months; tree sap and fruits are important in the winter (Beal 1911). There are no records of Brown-headed Cowbird parasitism in this species (Friedmann 1929, 1963; Peck and James 1983).

During the Atlas period there were only three reports of Yellow-bellied Sapsuckers. An adult was seen twice near Carey Run Sanctuary in northeastern Garrett County, and one bird was reported in the central part of the county. A single bird at a feeder in Allegany County was considered to be a nonbreeder. Breeding was not confirmed during the Atlas period.

It is unlikely that many Yellow-bellied Sapsuckers were overlooked in Garrett County during the Atlas period. New York atlas observers referred to nest sites as "talking trees" because of the noise the young make (Levine 1988b). Given the decline noted in surrounding states and the cold winters of 1976–77 and 1977–78, it is probable that the Yellow-bellied Sapsucker is, at best, a sporadic breeder in Maryland. Its true status is hard to determine because nonbreeding subadult birds are occasional in summer in Maryland.

BBS data from 1966 through 1989 show a significant average annual decline of 2.4 percent in Eastern Region populations of this species. There are too few data for Maryland to estimate a trend. Robbins et al. (1986) attributed the regional decline to the cold winters of 1976–77 and 1977–78. Pennsylvania (Gill 1985) and West Virginia (Hall 1983) have reported declines in recent years, but in New York (Levine 1988b) Yellow-bellied Sapsuckers have expanded portions of their range.

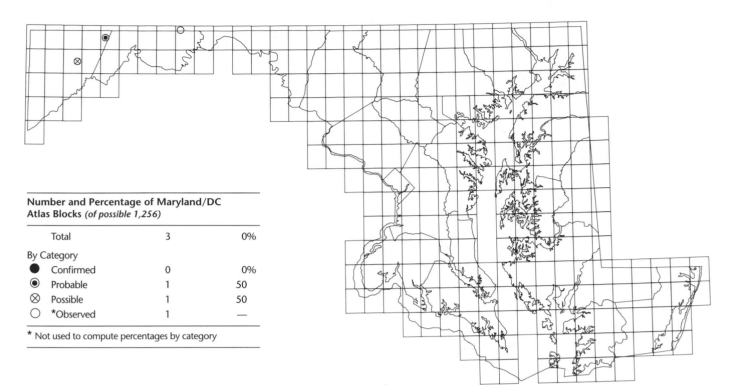

Number and Percentage of Maryland/DC Atlas Blocks *(of possible 1,256)*

Total	3	0%

By Category

●	Confirmed	0	0%
◉	Probable	1	50
⊗	Possible	1	50
○	*Observed	1	—

* Not used to compute percentages by category

Atlas Distribution, 1983–1987

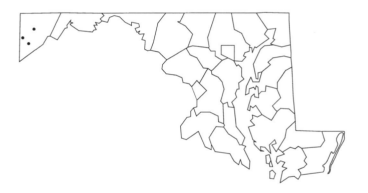

Breeding Distribution, 1958

Preservation of mature forests on ridgetops and in bogs will be necessary for the Yellow-bellied Sapsucker if it returns to Maryland as a breeding bird. Searches should be conducted periodically in Garrett County to locate breeding Yellow-bellied Sapsuckers. Runde and Capen (1987) noted that routine forest-management plans that result in even-aged stands of trees would eliminate most nest sites.

Robert Hilton

Downy Woodpecker

Picoides pubescens

The Downy Woodpecker is the smallest member of its family in Maryland. Despite its size, it is neither shy nor secretive and is one of the most common woodpeckers in the state. It is often found foraging with chickadees and titmice and is a frequent visitor to bird feeders. Its diet consists of a wide variety of insects and their larvae, including beetles, ants, moths, and caterpillars, which are most often gleaned from tree bark (Terres 1980). It also eats a wide variety of fruits, berries, and seeds, especially during the winter. Males are reported to forage on smaller limbs and tree trunks than those used by females (Jackson 1970).

The Downy Woodpecker has long been considered a common permanent resident of Maryland and DC. This designation appears consistently in the literature from the mid-1800s through the first half of this century (Coues and Prentiss 1862, 1883; Kirkwood 1895; Cooke 1929; Stewart et al. 1952; Stewart and Robbins 1958). According to BBS data, the Downy Woodpecker may be more common in Maryland than in most other states. During the period from 1966 through 1979, Maryland ranked third in the United States in mean density of Downy Woodpeckers (Robbins et al. 1986). Relative abundance in western Maryland has been variably described as uncommon (Preble 1900; Eifrig 1904), common (Hampe and Kolb 1947), or fairly common (Stewart and Robbins 1958). Klimkiewicz and Solem (1978) considered it the second most conspicuous woodpecker (after the Red-bellied Woodpecker) in both Howard and Montgomery counties. BBS data from 1966 through 1989 show stable populations in the Eastern Region and Maryland; however, data from 1980 through 1989 show a significant average annual decline of 2.8 percent in the Maryland population.

Wherever there is woodland, Downy Woodpeckers are likely to reside. They prefer wood margins, open woodland, orchards, and other forest edge habitats (Stewart and Robbins 1958). In a study of 469 woodlands, Robbins et al. (1989a) found that Downy Woodpeckers occurred most frequently in tall, fragmented deciduous forest with sparse ground cover in flat terrain. In Montgomery and Howard counties during the early 1970s, Klimkiewicz and Solem (1978) found the Downy Woodpecker to be an edge species that is very adaptable to a variety of habitats. The highest reported breeding density of Downy Woodpeckers in Maryland is 25 territorial males per 100 acres (40.5 ha) in mixed hardwood forest in Calvert County (Fales 1972).

This cavity nester most often chooses a dead stump or tree stub for its nest site. An examination of 47 records in which nest trees were identified showed that red maple, oaks, and sweet gum accounted for more than half of the nest trees (MNRF). Cavity heights in 59 Maryland records (MNRF) were found 8 to 92 ft (2.4–28 m) above the ground, with 50 percent of the cavities in the 20- to 40-ft (6.1- to 12-m) range. Both parents share in the excavation of the cavity, although the female does most of the work (Harrison 1975).

The early and late egg dates for Maryland are 5 April and 5 June, with the peak in mid-May (MNRF). Only 4 of 41 reports in the MNRF were prior to 8 May. Clutch sizes of 24 nests range from 2 to 6, with a mean of 4.6. The eggs are incubated for 12 days (Lawrence 1967) by both sexes; the male incubates at night (Harrison 1978). Although double broods occasionally occur in the southern United States, the Downy Woodpecker is single-brooded in Maryland and DC (Stokes and Stokes 1983). Nestling dates in Maryland range from 7 May to 7 July, with the peak in early June. Brood sizes in 13 nests (MNRF) range from 2 to 5, with a mean of 3.6. The young fledge in 20 to 25 days (Stokes and Stokes 1983). The average annual survival rate in a population of Downy Woodpeckers at PWRC was 64 percent (Karr et al. 1990). There are no records of Brown-headed Cowbird parasitism in Downy Woodpecker nests (Friedmann 1929, 1963; Peck and James 1983).

Atlas results document the widespread occurrence of the this species throughout Maryland and DC. The only areas in which it was not consistently found were the tidewater islands and the bayside blocks of Somerset and Dorchester counties where woodlands yield to marsh and water. The "confirmed" rate was fairly high, primarily because of the species' habit of traveling about in noisy family groups (60% of "confirmed" records). The Downy Woodpecker population in Maryland is currently healthy. Because of this woodpecker's dependence on dead wood for nest excavation, the removal of dead or dying trees from woodlots or forested areas should be discouraged.

Sue A. Ricciardi

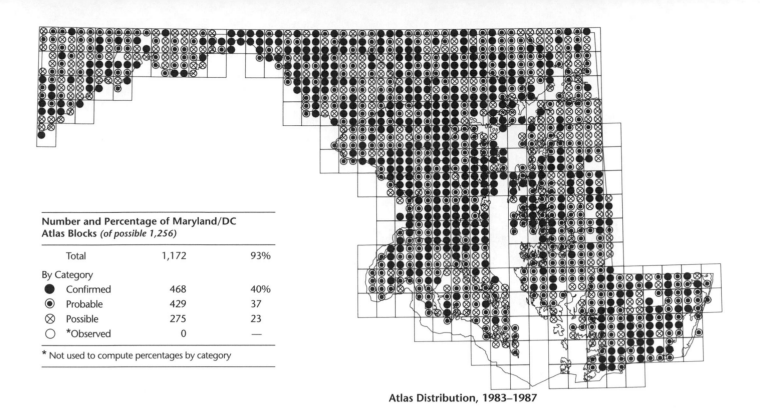

Number and Percentage of Maryland/DC Atlas Blocks *(of possible 1,256)*

Total	1,172	93%
By Category		
● Confirmed	468	40%
◉ Probable	429	37
⊗ Possible	275	23
○ *Observed	0	—

* Not used to compute percentages by category

Atlas Distribution, 1983–1987

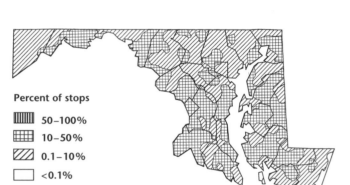

Percent of stops

▮▮▮ 50–100%
▦▦▦ 10–50%
▨▨▨ 0.1–10%
☐ <0.1%

Relative Abundance, 1982–1989

Breeding Distribution, 1958

Highest densities of the Downy Woodpecker are in southern Maryland, on the Eastern Shore, in Allegany County, and in the Catoctin Mountain area. Lowest densities are in the Allegheny Mountain Section, the residential and agricultural areas of the northern Piedmont, and the lower Eastern Shore marshes.

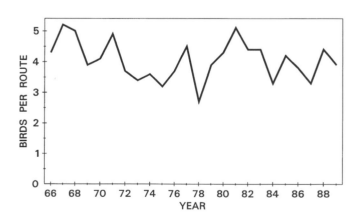

Maryland BBS Trend Graph, 1966–1989

Hairy Woodpecker

Picoides villosus

Although it is widespread throughout Maryland, the Hairy Woodpecker is less common than the similar but smaller Downy Woodpecker. A fairly common permanent resident, the Hairy Woodpecker breeds primarily in extensive tracts of mature deciduous forest, especially those over 17 acres (7 ha) (Robbins et al. 1989a). The highest breeding density recorded in Maryland is 6 territorial males per 100 acres (40.5 ha) in mature floodplain forest at PWRC in 1969 (C. Robbins, unpub. data).

The Hairy Woodpecker reportedly is more common than it was a century ago, despite the loss of large wooded tracts to development. In the 1800s and early 1900s it was described as rare (Coues and Prentiss 1862, 1883; Eifrig 1904), very rare (Richmond 1888), or not common (Kirkwood 1895). In later accounts, however, it was described as fairly common or locally fairly common (Cooke 1929; Stewart and Robbins 1958; Klimkiewicz and Solem 1978). It may be that nineteenth-century observers mistook Hairy Woodpeckers for Downy Woodpeckers because optical equipment was poor at that time. The Maryland population of Hairy Woodpeckers has remained stable from 1966 through 1989, as shown by BBS data.

Eifrig (1904) stated that the Hairy Woodpecker was abundant in migration but otherwise rare, although we now know that very few Hairy Woodpeckers migrate. Lawrence (1967) called the adult a highly sedentary individual that tends to remain for life in its territory. Reported seasonal movements may be the result of postbreeding dispersal of young, or possibly of changes in food availability (Stokes 1979). Bull (1974) reported that fall flights were rare in New York but definitely occurred.

While various sources (e.g., Harrison 1978; Stokes 1979) have reported that the Hairy Woodpecker prefers to excavate its nest cavity in live wood, only two of 24 nests in the MNRF were described as such. The remainder were in dead trees or in dead limbs of living trees. Both sexes excavate the hole, which is 10 to 15 in. (25–38 cm) deep; this takes one to three weeks, depending on the hardness of the wood (Bent 1939). In Virginia, Conner (1975) found that nest holes were always on the side of the branch or tree that faced downward; he suggested that this reduced the risk of rain entering the cavity. Of 23 Maryland nests with heights recorded (MNRF), the range was 9.5 to 85 ft (2.9–30 m), with half the nests from 12 to 20 ft (3.7–6.1 m). Deciduous trees are chosen almost exclusively, with oaks and maples preferred (MNRF). The Hairy Woodpecker is single-brooded but will renest, sometimes twice, after nest failure (Bent 1939). The female lays from 3 to 6 eggs, typically 4, on a bed of fresh wood chips (Harrison 1978).

The Maryland nesting season of the Hairy Woodpecker extends from early April to mid-July. Nests with eggs in Maryland have been observed from 19 April to 29 April, but these dates are based on only five reports (MNRF). Maryland clutch sizes are 2 (probably incomplete), 3, 4, 4, and 4 (MNRF). Incubation is shared and lasts 11 or 12 days (Bent 1939), with the parents alternating during the day and the male incubating at night. Extreme nestling dates of 25 April and 4 July (MNRF), along with an extremely early record of newly hatched young on 9 April in DC (Daniel 1901), indicate that nests with eggs occur during a longer period. Ten Maryland brood sizes range from 1 to 4, with a mean of 2.5 (MNRF). The young remain in the nest about 28 to 30 days and fledge a few days later (Stokes 1979). There are no records of Brown-headed Cowbird parasitism of Hairy Woodpeckers. Their diet is about 75 percent insects, primarily wood borers, and various beetles (Bent 1939). They also eat a variety of wild fruits, berries, and seeds.

Although the Hairy Woodpecker breeds across Maryland, it is predictably absent in some locations, owing to its preference for large forested areas. It will use large standing trees in clearcuts, however (Conner and Adkisson 1977). Gaps in Atlas data occur in urban areas, marshland, and extensive agricultural lands with only narrow wooded strips and small woodlots. Hall (1983) reported that Hairy Woodpeckers were more common than Downy Woodpeckers at high elevations in West Virginia, whereas the relationship was reversed at lower elevations. Fledged young (45%) and adults with food for young (29%) accounted for the great majority of "confirmed" records. BBS data from 1966 through 1989 show a significant average annual increase of 1.3 percent in the Eastern Region; the Maryland population is stable.

The Hairy Woodpecker is one of the species designated as a forest-interior breeding bird by the DNR (Bushman and Therres 1988). Maryland's Chesapeake Bay Critical Area regulations, adopted in 1986, require protection and conservation of forested properties that contain forest-interior-dwelling species within the Critical Area. Priority should be given to preserving extensive forested tracts to maintain habitat for Hairy Woodpeckers and other forest-interior species.

Sue A. Ricciardi

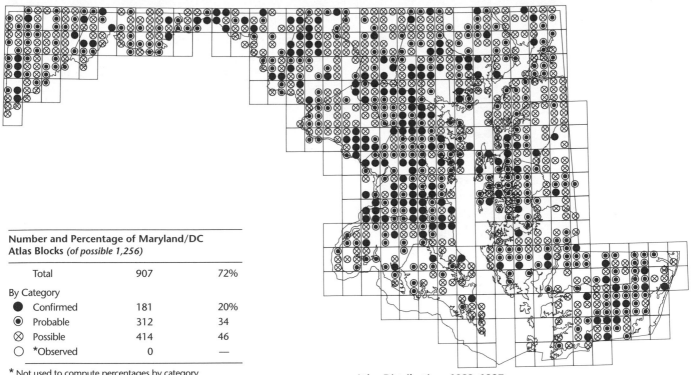

Number and Percentage of Maryland/DC Atlas Blocks *(of possible 1,256)*

	Total	907	72%
By Category			
●	Confirmed	181	20%
◉	Probable	312	34
⊗	Possible	414	46
○	*Observed	0	—

* Not used to compute percentages by category

Atlas Distribution, 1983–1987

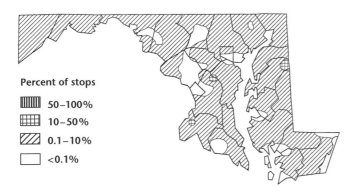

Percent of stops

▦	50–100%
▦	10–50%
▨	0.1–10%
☐	<0.1%

Relative Abundance, 1982–1989

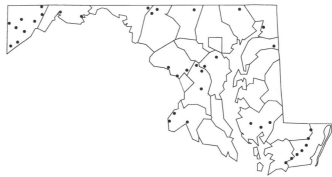

Breeding Distribution, 1958

The Hairy Woodpecker is fairly evenly distributed throughout the state. It was less frequently recorded in urban and suburban areas and in the most extensive marsh blocks on the lower Eastern Shore.

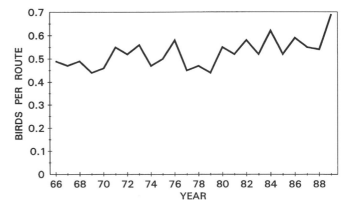

Maryland BBS Trend Graph, 1966–1989

Northern Flicker

Colaptes auratus

Until recently, the Yellow-shafted Flicker in the East and the Red-shafted Flicker throughout most of the West were considered separate species (Eisenmann 1973; AOU 1983, 1995). The flicker that nests in Maryland is one of the Yellow-shafted races, and many birdwatchers still refer to it as the Yellow-shafted Flicker. Although found year-round in Maryland, it is less common in winter, especially in the Allegheny Mountain and Ridge and Valley sections. Spring migrants begin arriving from the wintering grounds in the southeastern United States (AOU 1983) in early March, and migration is over by early May (Stewart and Robbins 1958). In fall, birds move through Maryland from early September to mid-November. The Northern Flicker is the most terrestrial of the area's woodpeckers and feeds primarily on the ground. Its summer diet consists of about 75 percent animal matter, of which almost 50 percent is ants (Martin et al. 1951). It also eats other insects and some fruits and berries, especially in winter.

The Northern Flicker has been considered common throughout Maryland since at least the mid-1800s. Coues and Prentiss (1862, 1883) and Cooke (1929) called it common to very abundant in DC. Kirkwood (1895) considered it a common breeding bird in Maryland, although more numerous during migration. Eifrig (1904) described it as common to abundant in western Maryland, especially at higher elevations. Stewart and Robbins (1958) detailed the Maryland breeding status as common in the Allegheny Mountain Section and uncommon (formerly common) in all other sections.

Northern Flickers favor more open areas than do the other woodpeckers. They are found in sparse woodlands, edge habitats, areas with isolated standing trees, parklands, and orchards (Bent 1939; Graber et al. 1977). The highest breeding density recorded in Maryland is 9 territorial males per 100 acres (40.5 ha) in selectively logged mature tulip tree–oak forest in Prince George's County in 1976 (Whitcomb et al. 1977). Northern Flickers occasionally use nest boxes, especially in urban and suburban areas. They are weak excavators so they select weathered, dead softwood trees for their nest cavities (Graber et al. 1977). Northern Flickers mate for life (Stokes 1979), and a pair often uses the same territory for several years. They sometimes use the same tree, excavating a new cavity each year. Nest cavities are typically 10 to 30 ft (3.0–9.1 m) above the ground and 7 to 18 in. (18–46 cm) deep (Bent 1939). The round entrance hole is about 2 in. (5 cm) in diameter. Heights of 154 Maryland nests (MNRF) range from 0 to 73 ft (0–22 m), with a mean of 21.2 ft (6.5 m). The single nest below 2 ft (0.6 m) was found by H. Brackbill, who noted that the entrance was 12.5 in. (32 cm) above the ground but, because of the depth of the cavity, the eggs were actually at ground level (MNRF).

Nests with eggs have been found in Maryland from 12 April to 26 June, with a peak in mid-May (MNRF). Clutch sizes in 34 Maryland nests range from 5 to 10, with a mean of 6.7. The Northern Flicker has an extraordinary ability to replace lost eggs. One female laid 71 eggs in 73 days when Phillips (1887) removed from its nest every egg except the first. Incubation, by both sexes, lasts 11 or 12 days; the young fledge at 25 to 28 days (Bent 1939). Nests with young have been reported in Maryland from 15 May to 8 August (MNRF). In 12 Maryland records, brood sizes range from 2 to 7, with a mean of 3.8. One brood is typical, but two are sometimes attempted (Forbush 1927). The nest with young in August suggests that two broods may be attempted in Maryland on occasion. There are no known instances of Brown-headed Cowbird parasitism in Northern Flicker nests (Friedmann 1963; Peck and James 1983).

This woodpecker was found in every part of Maryland during the Atlas period. It was absent from only a few of the most urbanized blocks and from those that are almost exclusively water or marshland. BBS data from 1966 through 1989 for the Eastern Region show a highly significant average annual decline of 3.3 percent in Yellow-shafted Flicker (the eastern race of the Northern Flicker) populations, attributed in part to competition for nest cavities with European Starlings (Robbins et al. 1986). Maryland's long-term decline is similar although not statistically significant. The Northern Flicker's habit of foraging extensively on the ground may make it vulnerable to loss of prey or to direct poisoning by pesticides. That, along with predation from domestic cats and competition from European Starlings for nest sites, suggests that continued monitoring of the population is warranted.

Keith D. Van Ness, Jr.

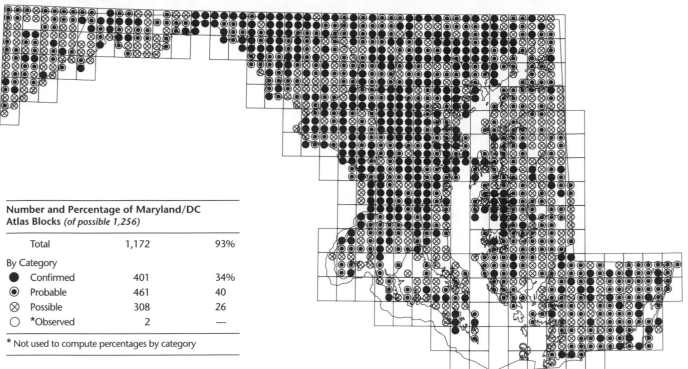

Number and Percentage of Maryland/DC Atlas Blocks *(of possible 1,256)*

Total	1,172	93%
By Category		
● Confirmed	401	34%
◉ Probable	461	40
⊗ Possible	308	26
○ *Observed	2	—

* Not used to compute percentages by category

Atlas Distribution, 1983–1987

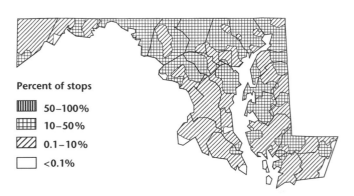

Percent of stops

⦀	50–100%
⊞	10–50%
⧄	0.1–10%
☐	<0.1%

Relative Abundance, 1982–1989

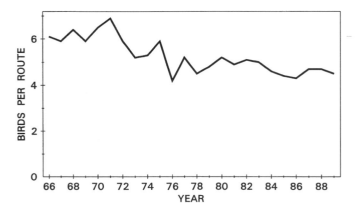

Breeding Distribution, 1958

The Northern Flicker is generally most common in extensive agricultural lands and is slightly less common in heavily forested, urban, and suburban areas.

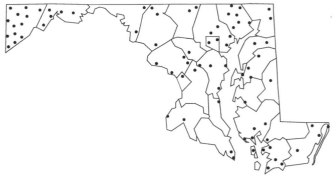

Maryland BBS Trend Graph, 1966–1989

Pileated Woodpecker

Dryocopus pileatus

Hearing the ringing call of a Pileated Woodpecker early in the morning never fails to momentarily conjure up a vision of the primeval forest. The Pileated Woodpecker is a permanent resident in Maryland and is found primarily in old deciduous woodlands.

This woodpecker was considered rare at the turn of the century in DC (Coues and Prentiss 1883) and in Allegany and Garrett counties (Eifrig 1904). Kirkwood (1895), however, reported it as fairly common in the heavily wooded parts of Maryland. Hampe and Kolb (1947) had records from all sections of the state except central Maryland. Stewart and Robbins (1958) described it as fairly common in the Allegheny Mountain Section and in the western part of the Ridge and Valley Section; fairly common locally in the Eastern Shore Section (particularly in the Pocomoke River drainage), in the Western Shore Section (especially along the Patuxent River and in Zekiah Swamp in Charles County), and in the Piedmont Section (especially the Potomac River drainage of Montgomery County); and uncommon locally in the eastern part of the Ridge and Valley Section.

Pileated Woodpeckers, formerly thought to require large areas of mature forest, may be found in woodland edges as well, although in smaller numbers. They could be adapting to habitat changes in Maryland, particularly to the fragmentation of large forested tracts. Pileated Woodpeckers now occur sparingly in narrow, forested stream valleys and are fairly common wherever mature floodplain forest occurs.

Mated pairs remain on territory all year (Christy 1939). Preferred nesting habitat is mature swamp forest, mature floodplain forest, and mature moist upland forest (Stewart

and Robbins 1958). The highest breeding density reported for Maryland is 2 territorial males per 100 acres (40.5 ha) in extensive floodplain forest on the Anne Arundel–Prince George's County border in 1990 (Robbins 1991). Pileated Woodpeckers feed primarily on carpenter ants (Christy 1939) and actively forage by bark gleaning in territories as large as 150 to 200 acres (60.8–81.0 ha) (Stokes and Stokes 1989). Renken and Wiggers (1989) found that territory size was correlated with the density of stumps and rotting logs in the forest. Pileated Woodpeckers forage primarily on rotting wood; therefore, the greater the abundance of foraging sites, the smaller the territories.

Unmated males advertise for a mate in late winter or early spring. Mated pairs excavate their nest cavities in dead wood (Christy 1939). Heights above the ground in 22 Maryland records in the MNRF range from 12 to 60 ft (3.7–18 m), with a mean of 36 ft (11 m). The hole is about 3.5 in. (9 cm) in diameter, with a cavity 10 to 24 in. (25–61 cm) deep. No nest materials are added (Christy 1939). The earliest Maryland egg date is 18 April, and the latest is 2 June, with a peak in early May (MNRF). Clutch sizes in two Maryland nests are 1 egg and 4 eggs. In other areas, clutch size is typically 4 eggs (Christy 1939). Incubation, by both parents, lasts about 18 days (Bendire 1895a). Both the male and female brood and feed the young. The earliest Maryland record of a nest with young is 2 May, and the latest is 7 July, with a peak in late May (MNRF). Brood sizes in five Maryland nests range from 1 to 4. When the young are about 15 days old, they can climb to the nest hole and stick their heads out (Christy 1939). They fledge in three to four weeks. Pileated Woodpeckers spend the night in roost holes, each in its own cavity; mated pairs rejoin in the morning and forage together (Stokes and Stokes 1989). There are no known instances of Brown-headed Cowbird parasitism of Pileated Woodpeckers (Friedmann 1963; Peck and James 1983).

Atlas results show the Pileated Woodpecker to be widespread in the Allegheny Mountain, Ridge and Valley, and Piedmont sections and the southern part of the Eastern Shore Section; slightly less so in the Western Shore Section; and local in the northern part of the Eastern Shore Section and in the Upper Chesapeake Section. The breeding range on the Eastern Shore is limited only by the distribution of mature floodplain or swamp forest. The Pileated Woodpecker's nesting range has expanded greatly since 1958. "Confirmed" records were most frequently of adults entering active nests. BBS data from 1966 through 1989 show a highly significant average annual increase in the Eastern Region of 2.3 percent; Maryland data show a highly significant average annual increase of 4.4 percent. The increase in Maryland, however, may have stabilized since 1983.

Preservation of extensive areas of mature, floodplain swamp and moist, upland forest should ensure the continued success of the Pileated Woodpecker in Maryland.

Keith D. Van Ness, Jr.

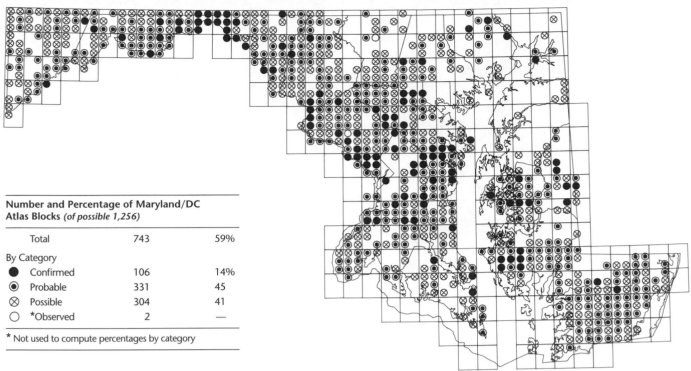

Atlas Distribution, 1983–1987

Number and Percentage of Maryland/DC Atlas Blocks (of possible 1,256)		
Total	743	59%
By Category		
● Confirmed	106	14%
◉ Probable	331	45
⊗ Possible	304	41
○ *Observed	2	—
* Not used to compute percentages by category		

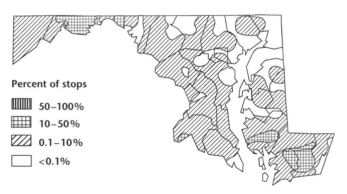

Percent of stops

▦	50–100%
▦	10–50%
▨	0.1–10%
□	<0.1%

Relative Abundance, 1982–1989

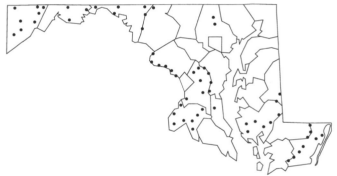

Breeding Distribution, 1958

The highest densities of the Pileated Woodpecker are in the extensive mixed woodlands of Allegany County, Dorchester County, and the Pocomoke River drainage on the lower Eastern Shore. It is largely absent from the agricultural areas of northeastern Maryland and the Hagerstown and northern Frederick Valleys.

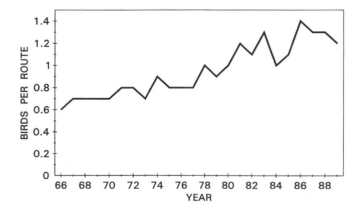

Maryland BBS Trend Graph, 1966–1989

MOB

Eastern Wood-Pewee

Contopus virens

The Eastern Wood-Pewee's distinctive *pee-o-weee* song is instantly recognizable, but the European Starling's nearly perfect imitation can fool observers. The Eastern Wood-Pewee is an active singer through most of the long summer, even in the heat of a mid-July afternoon when most birds and birdwatchers are resting quietly in the shade. Smith (1988) reported that in the Philadelphia area of Pennsylvania, singing reaches its peak in mid-June. Most Eastern Wood-Pewees return to Maryland from their South and Central American wintering grounds (AOU 1983) in late April and May, and most depart by late September (Robbins and Bystrak 1977).

The status of the Eastern Wood-Pewee does not appear to have changed significantly in Maryland over the past 100 years. Early writers (Coues and Prentiss 1883; Kirkwood 1895; Cooke 1929) called it common to abundant in Maryland and DC. Stewart and Robbins (1958) described it as fairly common throughout the state. BBC data from 1971 through 1975 show that the Eastern Wood-Pewee was the second most abundant flycatcher at that time in mature hardwood forests in central Maryland, outnumbered only by the Acadian Flycatcher.

The Eastern Wood-Pewee nests in mature deciduous and mixed forests, woodland edges, woodlots, and mature orchards and is common wherever there are large trees (Stewart and Robbins 1958). Robbins et al. (1989a) found that Eastern Wood-Pewees are not affected by the size of the forest; they favor tall, rather dry deciduous woods with openings in the canopy. Breeding densities ranged from 19 territorial males per 100 acres (40.5 ha) in an old-growth central hardwood deciduous forest (Stewart and Robbins 1947a) to 5 territorial males per 100 acres in damp deciduous scrub with standing dead trees (Stewart et al. 1947), both in Prince George's County in 1947. On the lower Eastern Shore, Springer and Stewart (1948b,c) reported densities of 17 territorial males per 100 acres in immature loblolly–shortleaf pine and 7 territorial males per 100 acres in an unsprayed apple orchard with infrequently mowed ground cover, both in Worcester County in 1948.

The lichen-covered nests are placed well out on a horizontal limb of a tall tree (Tyler 1942c). Heights of 148 Maryland nests (MNRF) range from 5 to 70 ft (1.5–21 m), with a mean of 22.5 ft (6.9 m). Nests with eggs have been reported in Maryland from 21 May to 15 August (Stewart and Robbins 1958). Maryland clutch sizes (MNRF) are typically 2 or 3; the mean of 72 clutches is 2.7. Incubation, performed by the female only, lasts about 13 days (Tyler 1942c). Nests with young have been reported in Maryland from 13 June to 13 September (Stewart and Robbins 1958). Brood sizes in 41 Maryland nests range from 1 to 4, with a mean of 2.4 (MNRF). The young leave the nest in 15 to 18 days (Tyler 1942c). Despite the long breeding season, most Eastern Wood-Pewees are believed to raise only a single brood. They are uncommon victims of the Brown-headed Cowbird (Friedmann 1963). Only 1 of 110 Maryland nests (0.9%) contained Brown-headed Cowbird eggs or young (MNRF), but 6 of 117 Ontario nests (5.1%) were parasitized (Peck and James 1987). The diet of the Eastern Wood-Pewee consists almost entirely of insects, primarily flies, bees, wasps, ants, and beetles, and a few berries (Beal 1912).

Eastern Wood-Pewees were found in virtually every Atlas block. They were absent only from intensely urban areas, the marshy areas of the lower Eastern Shore, and portions of coastal Worcester County. Almost 60 percent of all atlas records were of territorial birds, evidence of the pervasiveness and recognizability of the song. The majority of "confirmed" records were of fledged young (31%) or of an occupied nest (20%). Most nests were too high for fieldworkers to examine the contents.

BBS data from 1966 through 1989 show a significant average annual decline of 1.2 percent in the Eastern Region, and a similar but not significant decline in Maryland. For the past decade, the population has been stable in Maryland.

Charles Vaughn

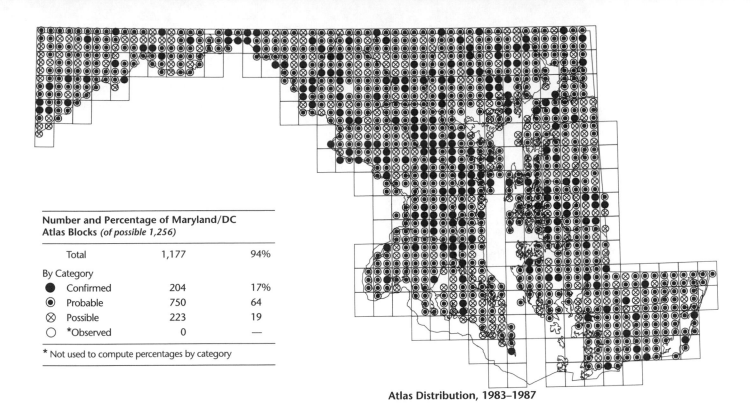

Number and Percentage of Maryland/DC Atlas Blocks *(of possible 1,256)*		
Total	1,177	94%
By Category		
● Confirmed	204	17%
◉ Probable	750	64
⊗ Possible	223	19
○ *Observed	0	—

* Not used to compute percentages by category

Atlas Distribution, 1983–1987

Percent of stops

▥ 50–100%
▦ 10–50%
▧ 0.1–10%
☐ <0.1%

Relative Abundance, 1982–1989

Breeding Distribution, 1958

The Eastern Wood-Pewee is most abundant in the extensive dry woodlands of eastern Allegany County. It is least common in the urban and suburban areas of Baltimore and Washington and the more developed sections of Talbot County on the Eastern Shore.

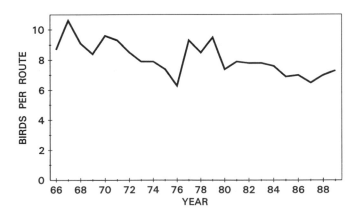

Maryland BBS Trend Graph, 1966–1989

Acadian Flycatcher

Empidonax virescens

The Acadian Flycatcher is the most widespread and common *Empidonax* breeding in Maryland. It has expanded its range into higher elevations since the beginning of this century and has established itself firmly throughout the state. Spring migrants begin returning from Central and South American wintering grounds (AOU 1983) in late April or early May, and the last southbound birds depart by the end of September (Robbins and Bystrak 1977).

Early writers described the Acadian Flycatcher as a common to fairly common breeding bird in the Washington-Baltimore area (Coues and Prentiss 1862, 1883; Kirkwood 1895). Eifrig (1904) called it a rare migrant in western Maryland, citing only one fall report and one summer report, near Oldtown in Allegany County. Hampe and Kolb (1947) called it locally common in western Maryland. Stewart and Robbins (1958) described it as common east of the Fall Line, fairly common in the Piedmont and Ridge and Valley sections, and uncommon and local in the Allegheny Mountain Section, noting only one locality there.

Acadian Flycatchers breed in the interior of lowland swamps, riparian woodlands, and tall, moist, upland deciduous forests (Stewart and Robbins 1958; Robbins et al. 1989a). They need a lush understory and are most common in the presence of water, preferably a stream (Christy 1942). Many nests are placed directly over water. The greatest breeding density recorded in Maryland is 75 territorial males per 100 acres (40.5 ha) in mixed hardwood forest in Calvert County (Fales 1969).

The nest is suspended from a small crotch near the tip of a drooping branch (Christy 1942). Records of 145 Maryland nests (MNRF) show heights ranging from 3 to 30 ft (0.9–9.1

m), with a mean of 10.2 ft (3.1 m). Only 16 nests were above 15 ft (4.6 m). Beech (43%) is by far the preferred tree for nesting, followed by dogwood (15%), American hornbeam (9%), and maple (8%). One Maryland nest was in a pine. In West Virginia, they are not found in pine or pine-oak forests (Hall 1983).

The nesting season in Maryland is long, lasting from late May to mid-August. Maryland egg dates range from 19 May to 3 August, with the peak in early to mid-June (MNRF). In 91 nests, clutch sizes range from 2 to 4 (mean of 2.9). A clutch of 3 contained 2 Brown-headed Cowbird eggs, and a clutch of 2 contained 1. The female incubates for 13 to 15 days and occasionally is fed by the male (Mumford 1964). Both parents feed the young, which fledge in 12 to 14 days. Young in the nest have been recorded in Maryland from 4 June to 16 August, with a peak in late June (MNRF). Brood sizes in 48 nests range from 1 to 4 (mean of 2.7), and two broods are usually attempted. Only 3 of 108 Maryland nests (2.7%) with 2 or more eggs contained Brown-headed Cowbird eggs. This is in marked contrast to an Illinois sample, in which as many as 50 percent of the nests were parasitized (Graber et al. 1974). In Ontario, 3 of 15 nests (15%) were parasitized (Peck and James 1987). The diet of the Acadian Flycatcher consists almost entirely (97%) of flying insects, especially wasps, bees, and ants (40%); moths and caterpillars (19%); and beetles (14%) (Beal 1912).

Acadian Flycatchers were found throughout Maryland during the Atlas period. They were largely absent from the most heavily suburbanized and urbanized areas, the extensive marshes and pine woods on the lower Eastern Shore, and coastal Worcester County. Few were found in the agricultural areas of the Frederick and Hagerstown valleys, where woodlots are small and riparian woodlands are narrow. This species was widespread but uncommon in Garrett County. Its expansion into that county during the twentieth century may be related to extensive logging there during the nineteenth century, which resulted in the replacement of native spruce forests with hardwoods.

The majority of records were of birds defending territory (55%), almost always detected by the presence of a singing male. Most observers are familiar with the males' explosive *pizz-zza* call, and males sing persistently into the afternoon, increasing the probability of observations. Unlike most other passerines, female Acadian Flycatchers sing on occasion (Kellner and Ritchison 1988). Fledged young (27%) and adults on nests (23%) comprised most of the "confirmed" records, but 25 (16%) records in this category were of nests with eggs or young.

BBS data from 1966 through 1989 show stable populations in the Eastern Region and in Maryland. Preservation of the Acadian Flycatcher in Maryland requires the protection of extensive moist and riparian woodlands with brushy understories.

Eirik A. T. Blom

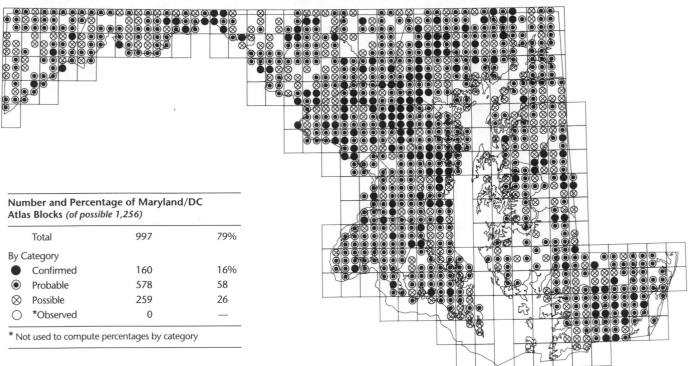

Number and Percentage of Maryland/DC Atlas Blocks *(of possible 1,256)*

Total	997	79%
By Category		
● Confirmed	160	16%
◉ Probable	578	58
⊗ Possible	259	26
○ *Observed	0	—

* Not used to compute percentages by category

Atlas Distribution, 1983–1987

Percent of stops

▥	50–100%
▦	10–50%
▧	0.1–10%
☐	<0.1%

Relative Abundance, 1982–1989

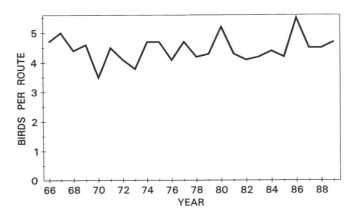

Breeding Distribution, 1958

The Acadian Flycatcher is most common in the larger woodlands of the Piedmont, southern Maryland, the lower Eastern Shore, the Catoctin Mountains, and Allegany and southeast Garrett counties, particularly along the major river systems. It is less common in agricultural areas with small woodlots.

Maryland BBS Trend Graph, 1966–1989

Alder Flycatcher

Empidonax alnorum

The Alder Flycatcher, one of the most difficult *Empidonax* flycatchers to identify, is easily confused with its closest relative, the Willow Flycatcher. Song and nest construction are the best ways to separate the two species in the field. Historical records treated them as one under the name Alder Flycatcher, and then briefly (1957 through 1973) as Traill's Flycatcher (AOU 1957; Stein 1963). The species now known as the Alder Flycatcher is the more northern and eastern in its distribution (AOU 1983). The Willow Flycatcher has only recently invaded Maryland from the west. Stewart and Robbins (1958) considered Traill's Flycatchers to be rare migrants in all sections. Breeding Alder Flycatchers return to Maryland in mid- to late May and a few migrants linger into June. Fall migrants arrive from the north in mid-August, and most leave by the end of September (Stewart and Robbins 1958). The wintering ground is not known in detail but is presumed to be restricted to South America (AOU 1983). Their diet consists almost entirely of insects, especially wasps, bees, ants, flies, and bugs (Beal 1912).

Preble (1900) was the first to record the Alder Flycatcher summering in Maryland, when he collected two males on 3 and 4 July 1899 in an alder swamp at Mountain Lake Park in Garrett County. Brooks (1936) found them summering both at Cranesville Swamp in Garrett County and at Mountain Lake in Mountain Lake Park. Stewart and Robbins (1958) reported the Traill's Flycatcher was uncommon in the Allegheny Mountain Section and uncommon and local in the Piedmont Section. Their Allegheny Mountain birds were all Alder Flycatchers; their Piedmont birds were Willow Flycatchers (C. Robbins, pers. comm.). Alder Flycatchers were found, however, in two atlas blocks each in Montgomery

and Howard counties in the 1970s (Klimkiewicz and Solem 1978).

This species is known to nest in alder thickets located along streams or in swamps and occasionally in other types of brushy thickets in damp situations (Stein 1958). It places its nest, a compact cup, in the fork of a small upright or slanting alder bush, typically lower than those of the Willow Flycatcher. In New York, Stein (1958) found 17 nests that were between 1 and 3 ft (0.3–0.9 m) above the ground, with a mean height of 23 in. (58 cm). Of 39 Ontario nests (Peck and James 1987), extremes of height were 1 and 6 ft (0.3 and 1.8 m), and half of the nests were from 2 to 3 ft (0.6–0.9 m). Clutch sizes are most commonly 3 or 4, the incubation period is usually 12 days, and the number of broods is unknown (Stein 1958). A late nest containing young was found on 24 August 1938 near Bittinger in Garrett County, and another nest, containing three dead young, was found at Mountain Lake in Garrett County on 11 June 1939 (Stewart and Robbins 1958). The Alder Flycatcher is known to be victimized by the Brown-headed Cowbird (Friedmann 1963); Peck and James (1987) reported that 7 of 47 Ontario nests (14.9%) were parasitized. There are no known cases for Maryland.

In Ontario, Prescott (1987) reported that Alder Flycatchers sing less frequently when sharing habitats with Willow Flycatchers than when nesting solitarily. Less vocal birds would have been easy for fieldworkers to overlook; therefore, this species may be underrepresented in the Atlas results. Atlas workers found it, however, in most Garrett County bogs that contained alder bushes. During the Atlas period, the only report outside of Garrett County was of a pair present for at least two summers in a small alder thicket near Monkton in Baltimore County. Breeding was not confirmed, however. A pair of Willow Flycatchers shared the same site. There was only one "confirmed" record of the Alder Flycatcher during the Atlas period, which is indicative of the scarcity of the species, the relative inaccessibility of its habitat, and its reputation for remaining secretive in the vicinity of the nest. The 14 "probable" records were of birds holding territory. In Pennsylvania, atlas fieldworkers reported Alder Flycatchers at scattered locations directly north of Garrett County and through the northern half of the state (Brauning 1992).

BBS data are too few to estimate a trend for Maryland, but the western Maryland population appears to be stable. Hall (1983), however, suggested that Willow Flycatchers have replaced Alder Flycatchers at some locations in West Virginia. He wrote that if the trend is legitimate and continues, the Alder Flycatcher may be driven from that state. The preservation of the Alder Flycatcher as a breeding bird in Maryland will require the conservation of alder bogs in Garrett County. Collection of additional information about the status, timing, and habitat requirements of this species is needed.

William L. Murphy

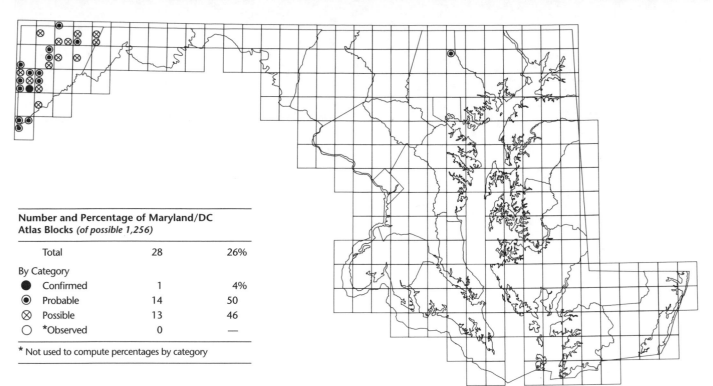

Number and Percentage of Maryland/DC Atlas Blocks *(of possible 1,256)*

Total	28	26%
By Category		
● Confirmed	1	4%
◉ Probable	14	50
⊗ Possible	13	46
○ *Observed	0	—

* Not used to compute percentages by category

Atlas Distribution, 1983–1987

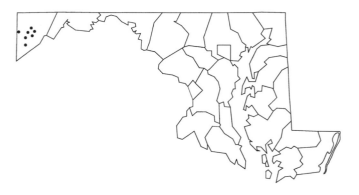

Breeding Distribution, 1958

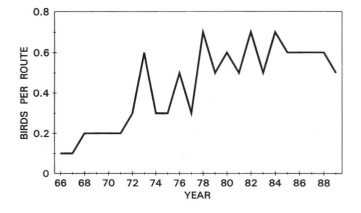

Maryland BBS Trend Graph, 1966–1989

MOB

Willow Flycatcher

Empidonax traillii

The Willow Flycatcher is nearly impossible to identify until its buzzy, two-note song is learned. Then, in a shrubby old field, willow thicket, or boggy area, it will be found, head back, sounding a distinctive *fitz-bew* or *frit fitz-bew*. Willow and Alder Flycatchers were previously treated as a single species, Traill's Flycatcher (Stein 1963). As the two species were not officially separated until 1973 (Eisenmann 1973), determining which species some of the early authors observed is impossible. Early migrants return from Central and South American wintering grounds (AOU 1983) in mid-May, and birds are still moving through Maryland in early June (Robbins and Bystrak 1977).

All breeding birds heard in Maryland in the 1940s and 1950s by C. Robbins (pers. comm.) were of the Alder Flycatcher song type. The few birds he found in midsummer, and most if not all those reported by other observers in DC in 1950 and 1951 and in Baltimore County in 1954 (Robbins 1952; Stewart and Robbins 1958), however, were Willow Flycatchers; Alder Flycatchers were not known to nest in these areas prior to the 1970s. The main invasion of Willow Flycatchers into Maryland occurred primarily in the 1960s (Robbins 1961). On 26 June 1961, B. Newman found a nest with three eggs near Bladensburg in Prince George's County, and on 29 June he found a nest with young in nearby DC (Bridge and Riedel 1962). By the summer of 1966, Willow Flycatchers had been found on territory in Frederick, Carroll, Baltimore, Howard, Prince George's, and Cecil counties (Robbins 1966).

The Willow Flycatcher establishes its territory in moist old-field habitats, and it builds its nest 1.5 to 8.9 ft (0.5–2.7 m) high (mean of 38 nests, 4.6 ft [1.4 m]) in a bush, shrub, or small tree, often in an upright fork (Stein 1958). Heights of four Maryland nests (MNRF) are 4, 4, 6, and 9 ft (1.2, 1.2,

1.8, 2.7 m). The compact cup-shaped nest is made of grass, weeds, and, often, shredded bark from milkweed and is lined with finer grasses and weeds (Stein 1958). The height at which the nest is built and its compact structure and grayish color help distinguish it from an Alder Flycatcher nest. A normal clutch is 3 or 4 eggs (Stein 1958). In the four Maryland nests with eggs (MNRF), the earliest on 4 June and the latest on 28 July, clutches were 2, 2, 3, and 4. The young hatch after a 12- to 14-day incubation by the female (Stein 1958). Two Maryland broods, on 23 June and 21 July, contained 3 and 4 nestlings (MNRF); recently fledged young were seen on 4 July and 21 July. The young fledge 12 to 15 days after hatching (Harrison 1978).

The Willow Flycatcher is a common victim of the Brown-headed Cowbird (Friedmann 1963); Peck and James (1987) reported that 19 of 71 Ontario nests (26.8%) were parasitized. No cases of parasitism have been reported for Maryland. Wasps and bees are the most frequently recorded food items, but beetles, flies, and caterpillars are also eaten in large numbers (Bent 1942).

Atlas results show that the Willow Flycatcher's eastern limit in Maryland coincides almost exactly with the Fall Line, with only scattered records on the Coastal Plain. Birds were found breeding at Chesapeake Beach in Calvert County in willows lining a river channel in marshland. Others found near Ocean City in Worcester County probably represent an extension of the central Delaware coastal population. The primary Maryland range is in the Piedmont, extending into the eastern half of the Ridge and Valley Section. The western half of the Ridge and Valley Section is probably too dry to support Willow Flycatchers. The range resumes in the Allegheny Mountain Section. In Garrett County, Willow and Alder Flycatchers have been found sympatrically in some spruce bogs, and Willow Flycatchers now appear to be more common. Hall (1983) noted that they invaded West Virginia beginning in the 1930s, spread throughout that state, and replaced Alder Flycatchers in some areas.

As with other *Empidonax* flycatchers, fieldworkers most often located breeding sites by means of the bird's distinctive song. The low number of "confirmed" records reflects both the Willow Flycatcher's retiring nature around the nest and the wet conditions in which many pairs establish territory. Almost all "probable" records were of birds holding territory, usually with singing for an extended period at one location.

Maryland BBS data from 1966 through 1989 show a highly significant average annual increase of 7.2 percent. The cause of the range extension in the East is unknown. To ensure the Willow Flycatcher's continued nesting success in Maryland, moist scrub and shrubby old-field habitats should be preserved. Some sites may need management to maintain an early successional stage.

Keith D. Van Ness, Jr.

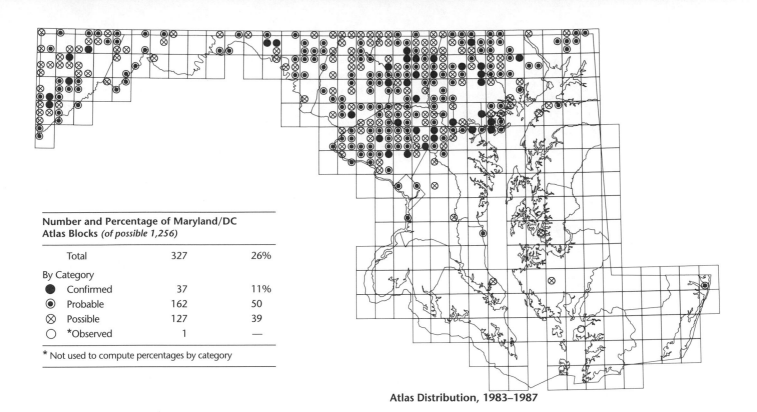

Number and Percentage of Maryland/DC Atlas Blocks (*of possible 1,256*)

Total	327	26%
By Category		
● Confirmed	37	11%
◉ Probable	162	50
⊗ Possible	127	39
○ *Observed	1	—

* Not used to compute percentages by category

Atlas Distribution, 1983–1987

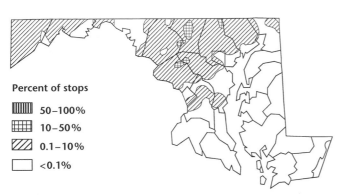

Percent of stops

▥	50–100%
▦	10–50%
▨	0.1–10%
☐	<0.1%

Relative Abundance, 1982–1989

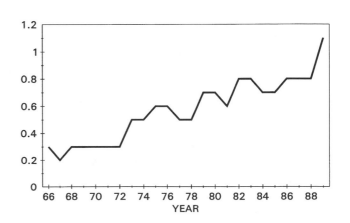

Breeding Distribution, 1958

The Willow Flycatcher is uncommon but widespread in the Piedmont and eastern Ridge and Valley sections and in western Maryland. It is largely absent from the driest portions of the western Ridge and Valley Section.

Maryland BBS Trend Graph, 1966–1989

MOB

Least Flycatcher

Empidonax minimus

The Least Flycatcher is the smallest, grayest, and perhaps least conspicuous of the eastern *Empidonax* flycatchers. It seldom reveals its presence except when defending and defining its territory with a rapid series of dry *che-béc* notes. Although Least Flycatchers are fairly numerous on the breeding grounds and during migration, few birdwatchers in Maryland are lucky enough to identify more than one or two a year. Spring migrants begin returning from their southern Mexican and Central American wintering grounds (AOU 1983) in late April (Stewart and Robbins 1958). In the fall a few birds linger into the first days of October, but the bulk of the migration occurs between mid-August and mid-September. The Least Flycatcher has a remarkably varied insect diet (Bent 1942). It sallies out from its perch on the end of a little branch to catch almost anything small that flies, especially ants, beetles, flies, bugs, and moths. Its diet also includes a small amount of fruit and berries.

Kirkwood (1895) knew the Least Flycatcher only as a rare migrant, but he noted that Richmond (1888) had called it common in passage in DC. Eifrig (1904) thought it common as a migrant and rare as a breeding bird in western Maryland, suggesting he was more familiar with it than was Kirkwood. It is also possible that the population increased subsequent to the logging of the extensive spruce forests in Garrett County around the close of the nineteenth century. Stewart and Robbins (1958) called it fairly common in the breeding season in the Allegheny Mountain Section, uncommon in the western part of the Ridge and Valley Section, and rare and local in the Piedmont and Western Shore sections.

The Least Flycatcher is a bird of open deciduous and mixed woodlands, scrublands, orchards, and parks (Norse and Kibbe 1985). It shuns woods where there is too much understory or too many low branches (Breckenridge 1956). It usually places its small cup nest in the crotch of a horizontal limb in a small hardwood tree, occasionally in a crotch of the trunk, sometimes in shrubs, and occasionally in conifers (Bent 1942). The female builds the nest (Bent 1942), but the male may help select the site (Mumford 1962). They occasionally reuse old nests in subsequent years or, if the initial nesting attempt fails, even in the same year (Briskie and Sealey 1988). Nest heights range from 2 to 60 ft (0.6–18 m) (Bent 1942). Heights of 11 Maryland nests (MNRF) range from 10 to 45 ft (3.7–14 m), with an mean of 28.3 (8.6 m).

The breeding season of the Least Flycatcher is short. Adults begin moving south by mid-July, two weeks before their offspring (Sealey and Bierman 1983). The six MNRF nests with eggs were found between 19 May and 17 June. Clutches range from 2 (possibly incomplete) to 4. In a Canadian study, 192 clutches varied in size from 2 to 5 eggs, and 78 percent had 4 eggs (Briskie and Sealey 1989). Incubation is by the female and lasts 13 or 14 days. The young fledge 12 to 16 days after hatching and are attended by both parents during the fledgling period (Holmes et al. 1979). The few Maryland nestling dates are confined to the brief period 2 to 10 June, but an occupied nest with unknown contents was found in Garrett County as late as about 15 August (Stewart and Robbins 1958). In New York, nestlings have been found from 22 June to 6 August (Bull 1974). Polygyny and double-brooding, although rare, have been documented for this species (Briskie and Sealey 1987). The Least Flycatcher is a rare host of the Brown-headed Cowbird (Friedmann 1963); 5 of 99 Ontario nests (5%) were parasitized (Peck and James 1987). There are no reports of parasitism from Maryland.

During the Atlas period Least Flycatchers were widespread in Garrett County, scattered in Allegany County and western Washington County, and very rare in the Piedmont. An occasional pair will attempt to breed east of the regular range, but this is probably accidental.

BBS data from 1966 through 1989 show a highly significant average annual decline in the Eastern Region; there are too few data to estimate a trend for Maryland. A management plan that preserves extensive open deciduous woodlands in Maryland's western mountains would provide protection for the Least Flycatcher.

Eirik A. T. Blom

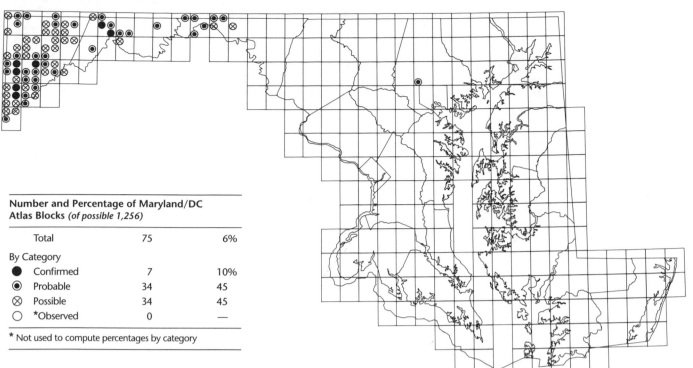

Number and Percentage of Maryland/DC Atlas Blocks *(of possible 1,256)*

Total		75	6%
By Category			
●	Confirmed	7	10%
◉	Probable	34	45
⊗	Possible	34	45
○	*Observed	0	—

* Not used to compute percentages by category

Atlas Distribution, 1983–1987

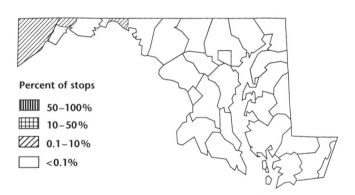

Percent of stops

▯ 50–100%
▤ 10–50%
▨ 0.1–10%
▯ <0.1%

Relative Abundance, 1982–1989

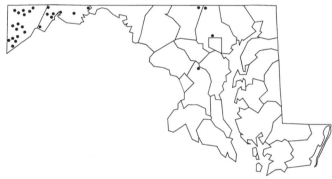

Breeding Distribution, 1958

The Least Flycatcher was found in small numbers throughout the Allegheny Mountain Section in Garrett County and in the Ridge and Valley Section in northwestern Allegany County and western Washington County. Because of the very low numbers, it was not detected in the rest of its Maryland range.

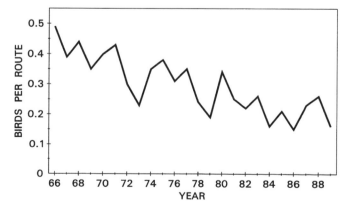

Maryland BBS Trend Graph, 1966–1989

Eastern Phoebe

Sayornis phoebe

The Eastern Phoebe is the tail-wagging attendant of many small bridges in Maryland. It frequently nests at conspicuous sites under these structures and on buildings. It is by far the earliest flycatcher to reach Maryland in spring, with the first birds arriving in late February (Stewart and Robbins 1958) from the wintering grounds in the southeastern United States (AOU 1983). Most depart by mid-November, but it is uncommon to rare in winter, especially on the lower Eastern Shore and in southern Maryland (Stewart and Robbins 1958).

All of the early students of Maryland birdlife described the Eastern Phoebe as a common summer bird (Coues and Prentiss 1862, 1883; Eifrig 1904; Cooke 1929; Hampe and Kolb 1947), although Kirkwood (1895) wrote that it was absent from the Baltimore area from mid-May to mid-September. Stewart and Robbins (1958) described its breeding status as fairly common in all sections.

The Eastern Phoebe favors a variety of edge habitats in Maryland, including woodland margins and field borders (Stewart and Robbins 1958). Although the nest may be placed on a rock ledge or in a cave, most are on, in, or under man-made structures, such as barn rafters, sheds, eaves, windowsills, doorsills, porch rafters, and, especially, girders under bridges (Tyler 1942b). Despite this association with humans, the Eastern Phoebe is seldom found nesting in urban areas, where there are many available nest sites. It favors the vicinity of water or farm buildings for nest sites (Ridgway 1889); Graber et al. (1974) found that it also required nearby woody cover and was not found in open situations. The highest breeding density reported for Maryland is 7 territorial males per 100 acres (40.5 ha) in mixed agricultural habitats in Prince George's County in 1949 (Stewart and Robbins 1958).

The Eastern Phoebe often uses the same site from year to year, repairing the old nest; it has also been known to build on old Barn Swallow nests (Graber et al. 1974). Faanes (1980) found that 70 of 71 nests placed under bridges were within 6 ft (1.8 m) of the upstream side of the bridge, near the deepest water. Weeks (1978) found that nests attached to the sides of walls were, on average, twice the weight of nests placed on top of girders; he found that mean clutch size was reduced by 0.2 and suggested this was caused by the extra energy required to build adherent nests. Hill (1987) reported an exceptionally tall Eastern Phoebe nest, 29 in. (74 cm) from base to rim, in a shed in Ohio; he speculated that the reason may have been the desire to have the rim as close as possible to the overhanging structure above the nest.

Heights of 84 Maryland nests (MNRF) range from 1 to 20 ft (0.3–6.1 m), with a mean of 7.2 ft (2.2 m). Nests with eggs have been found in Maryland from 25 March (Stewart and Robbins 1958) to 22 July (MNRF), with a small peak in early May. In 276 Maryland nests (MNRF), clutch sizes range from 3 to 6, with a mean of 4.7. Incubation, by the female only, takes 14 to 17 days (Tyler 1942b). Young in the nest have been found in Maryland from 27 April to 25 July, with a small peak in late May (MNRF). In 195 Maryland nests (MNRF), brood sizes range from 3 to 5, with a mean of 4.4. Both parents feed the young, and fledging occurs in 15 to 17 days (Graber et al. 1974). Two broods, sometimes three, are attempted. Weeks (1978) found that clutch sizes diminished as the summer progressed. He also reported that birds that had raised two successful broods in one season did not attempt a third. The Eastern Phoebe can be a fairly common victim of Brown-headed Cowbird parasitism. Only 14 of 578 Maryland nests (2.4%) were parasitized (MNRF), but Graber et al. (1974) reported Illinois parasitism rates as high as 33 percent. Peck and James (1987) reported 162 of 1,389 Ontario nests (12%) were parasitized.

The Eastern Phoebe's diet is 90 percent insects, especially ants, bees, wasps, beetles, grasshoppers, crickets, and bugs (Beal 1912). The vegetable component is primarily small berries and seeds.

Atlas results show that Eastern Phoebes are still well distributed throughout Maryland, except in the Eastern Shore marshes, in urban centers like Baltimore and DC, and in the southern counties. There are fewer birds in and along the salt marshes because of the scarcity of man-made structures. The ease of finding nests (75% of "confirmed" records), especially under bridges, accounted for the very high rate of "confirmed" records (58%).

In 1980, after several severe winters in the East and Midwest, the Eastern Phoebe was put on the NAS Blue List of threatened species (Tate 1981). BBS data from 1966 through 1989, however, show stable populations in Maryland and the Eastern Region. Although the future of the Eastern Phoebe in Maryland appears secure, fastening small brackets in large highway culverts would provide additional nesting sites.

James W. Cheevers

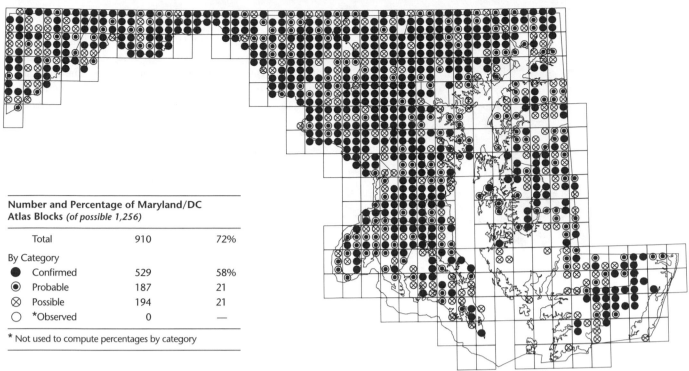

Atlas Distribution, 1983–1987

Number and Percentage of Maryland/DC Atlas Blocks *(of possible 1,256)*		
Total	910	72%
By Category		
● Confirmed	529	58%
◉ Probable	187	21
⊗ Possible	194	21
○ *Observed	0	—

* Not used to compute percentages by category

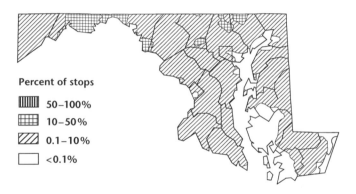

Percent of stops

- ▥ 50–100%
- ▦ 10–50%
- ▨ 0.1–10%
- ☐ <0.1%

Relative Abundance, 1982–1989

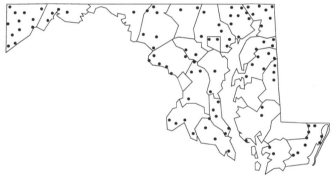

Breeding Distribution, 1958

The Eastern Phoebe was found in greatest abundance in the extensive mixed woodlands of the western Ridge and Valley Section and northern Piedmont Section. It was not detected in the tidewater portion of the lower Eastern Shore, where marshes and flat land may limit nest sites.

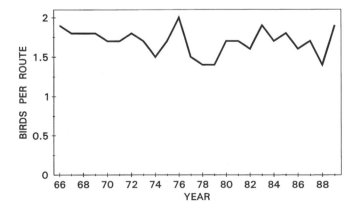

Maryland BBS Trend Graph, 1966–1989

Great Crested Flycatcher

Myiarchus crinitus

Unlike other eastern flycatchers, the Great Crested Flycatcher nests in cavities. Cavity choice is influenced by size rather than shape, situation, or height, as it must be large enough to hold the bulky nest (Forbush and May 1939). Spring migrants arrive in Maryland from their Cuban and Central and South American wintering grounds (AOU 1983) in late April and early May; most return south by October (Robbins and Bystrak 1977).

The Great Crested Flycatcher is a common summer resident throughout Maryland and DC and was described that way by early writers (Coues and Prentiss 1862, 1883; Kirkwood 1895; Cooke 1929). Stewart and Robbins (1958) noted regional differences in abundance: common in the Eastern and Western Shore sections; fairly common in the Upper Chesapeake, Piedmont, and Ridge and Valley sections; and uncommon in the Allegheny Mountain Section. The large number of Garrett County records on the 1958 map reflects the extra effort they apportioned to that county. BBS data from 1966 through 1989 show stable populations in the Eastern Region, although there is an indication of a long-term decline in Maryland.

The Great Crested Flycatcher inhabits wood margins and open stands of pine or deciduous forest (Stewart and Robbins 1958). It prefers forests with mature trees (DeGraaf et al. 1980). Bent (1942) surmised that, although it originally preferred forest interiors, the Great Crested Flycatcher adapted to more open habitats, especially old orchards and open woodlots, when extensive logging resulted in the loss of many large, old trees with hollow trunks or branches. The highest breeding density reported in Maryland is 8 territorial males per 100 acres (40.5 ha) in old-growth central hardwood deciduous forest in Prince George's County (Stewart and Robbins 1947b) and in mixed oak forest in Baltimore County (Kolb 1950).

An examination of the MNRF reveals that this species uses a variety of nest cavities. Of 71 nests, only 14 were in natural tree cavities. The other 57 nests were all in artificial structures: 27 in mailboxes or newspaper tubes; 25 in nest boxes; and one each in a fence post, a water trough, under the gable of a garage, on top of a natural gas tank, and in the cover of a liquid petroleum gas tank. The proportion of artificial sites is probably exaggerated, because observers may be more likely to submit a card for an unusual site or for an easily accessible nest. Heights of the 14 nests in natural cavities ranged from 5 to 40 ft (1.5–12 m), with a mean of 19 ft (5.8 m). Including all nests for which heights were recorded, the mean is 9.8 ft (3.0 m). Inside the cavity, the small cup is lined with hair, fur, feathers, and fine material and is surrounded by a bulky assortment of debris, including plant material, feathers, hair, and often a cast-off snakeskin (Bendire 1895a), smooth paper (Bent 1942), or bits of aluminum foil (Wetmore 1964). It was once thought the snakeskin was used to repel predators, but a more recent theory contends that it reflects a preference for something shiny (Bent 1942). European Starlings compete with Great Crested Flycatchers for nest sites (Bull 1974).

Extreme egg dates for Maryland are 13 May and 15 July (Stewart and Robbins 1958), with a peak in the second and third weeks of June (MNRF). A single brood is raised per season (Bendire 1895a). In 37 Maryland nests (MNRF), clutch sizes range from 3 to 6, with a mean of 4.7. The female incubates unassisted for 13 to 15 days. Both parents tend the young, which leave the nest 13 to 15 days after hatching (Bent 1942). Nests with young have been found in Maryland from 24 May to 4 August, with a peak in early July (MNRF). In 28 records, brood sizes range from 2 to 6, with a mean of 3.5. The Great Crested Flycatcher is a rare victim of the Brown-headed Cowbird. Stewart and Robbins (1958) reported two cases from Maryland, and Friedmann (1963) knew of only three others in the United States In Ontario, 6 of 218 nests (2.8%) were parasitized (Peck and James 1987).

Beal (1912) reported that the Great Crested Flycatcher is unique among our flycatchers in consuming a high percentage (21%) of moths and their larvae but very few (3%) flies. On average, beetles comprise 17 percent of the diet, grasshoppers and crickets 16 percent, and bugs, bees, wasps, and ants 14 percent each.

Atlas data show a fairly even and widespread distribution for this species. It was absent only from some of the most extensive marsh blocks in the lower Chesapeake Bay and from the very highest elevations in Garrett County. The scattered gaps in southern Maryland may reflect the less intense coverage. The Great Crested Flycatcher's ability to use nest boxes and other artificial structures, and the fact that it breeds in edge habitats bodes well for its future. Still, mature woodlands and dead or dying trees should be conserved to maintain habitat for this species.

Sue A. Ricciardi

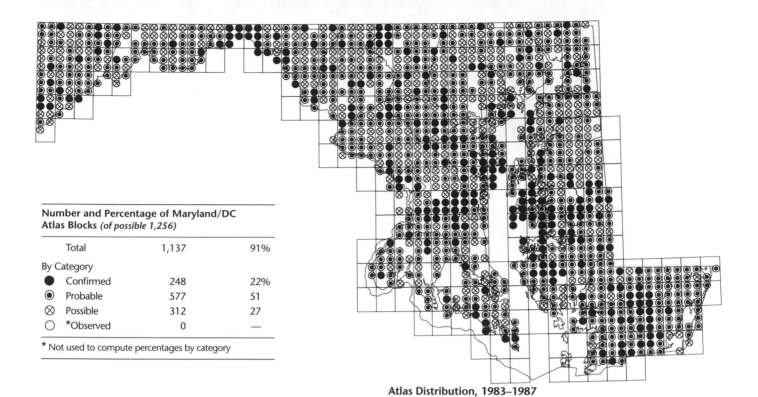

Number and Percentage of Maryland/DC
Atlas Blocks *(of possible 1,256)*

	Total	1,137	91%
By Category			
●	Confirmed	248	22%
◉	Probable	577	51
⊗	Possible	312	27
○	*Observed	0	—

* Not used to compute percentages by category

Atlas Distribution, 1983–1987

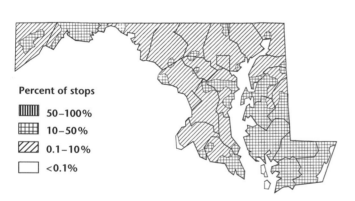

Percent of stops

▦ 50–100%
▦ 10–50%
▨ 0.1–10%
☐ <0.1%

Relative Abundance, 1982–1989

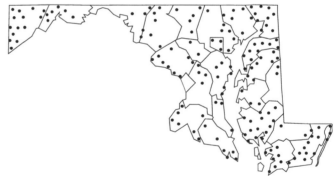

Breeding Distribution, 1958

The Great Crested Flycatcher was most common on the southern Eastern Shore, at scattered sites on the Coastal Plain of the Western Shore, in the extensive woodlands of the western Ridge and Valley Section, and in central Garrett County.

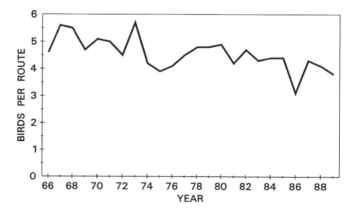

Maryland BBS Trend Graph, 1966–1989

Eastern Kingbird

Tyrannus tyrannus

The Eastern Kingbird is a diurnal migrant that arrives in Maryland from its South American wintering grounds (AOU 1983) in late April and departs by late September (Stewart and Robbins 1958). In migration, it is frequently seen perched on telephone wires, fences, trees, and, in cooler weather, on the ground (Graber et al. 1974). Although flocks of 30 or more may still be encountered (Ringler 1988a), groups in the hundreds and even thousands in fall migration, such as were reported in the past (Stewart and Robbins 1958), are no longer seen in Maryland.

Coues and Prentiss (1862, 1883) and Kirkwood (1895) called the Eastern Kingbird a common summer bird in Maryland and DC. Hampe and Kolb (1947) reported it as rather common statewide. Stewart and Robbins (1958) considered it a fairly common breeder in all sections. Eastern Kingbirds typically breed in edge or parklike habitats such as orchards, farms, old fields, and streamsides (Stewart and Robbins 1958; Graber et al. 1974). They have been found in densities as high as 10 territorial males per 100 acres (40.5 ha) in a suburban residential area in Prince George's County in 1942 (Stewart and Robbins 1958).

Eastern Kingbirds are well known for their aggressive defense of their territories against hawks, owls, crows, and Atlas observers, but they are tolerant of other birds, such as Orchard Orioles, even when they nest in the same tree (Graber et al. 1974). A pair of nesting Eastern Kingbirds in Maryland shared a large sycamore tree with nesting Orchard and Northern Orioles and Warbling Vireos (J. Wilkinson, pers. obs.).

The Eastern Kingbird's nest is a rather loose mass of sticks, straw, and other material, lined with a well-constructed inner cup of fine grass, roots, and hair (Tyler 1942a). It is frequently placed near the end of a tree branch (MNRF). In 146 Maryland nests (MNRF), heights range from 2 to 80 ft (0.6–24 m), with a mean of 27 ft (8.2 m). The very low nests are usually over water (Tyler 1942a). The earliest Maryland egg date is 12 May and the latest is 22 July, with a peak in early June. In 42 Maryland nests (MNRF), clutch sizes range from 1 to 4 (mean of 2.9). The eggs take 14 to 16 days to hatch and the female does all the incubating (Graber et al. 1974). Brood sizes in 48 nests (MNRF) range from 1 to 4 (mean of 2.7). Dates for nestlings range from 29 May to 24 August, with a peak at the end of June.

The young spend about two weeks in the nest (Tyler 1942a), during which time they are fed a diet of large insects such as beetles, wasps, cicadas, and grasshoppers. A prolonged period of rainy, cool weather at this time may result in the nestlings' starvation from lack of insect prey (Murphey 1987). After leaving the nest, the young may spend as long as five weeks with their parents before becoming independent. This unusually long postfledging period may be the reason Eastern Kingbirds raise only one brood (Stokes 1979; Murphey 1983, 1987, 1988). Only once has the Eastern Kingbird been reported as a host of the Brown-headed Cowbird in Maryland (MNRF). Peck and James (1987) reported 12 of 989 Ontario nests (1.2%) parasitized. Murphey (1986) found an average parasitism rate of 9 percent in Kansas and New York.

Maryland Atlas records show a fairly even distribution of this species across the state, except in Garrett and Allegany counties, where much of the countryside is dominated by forested mountains, resulting in a lack of suitable habitat. Atlas results include a high number of "confirmed" reports because Eastern Kingbirds nest in open areas, approach their nests directly when bringing food to their young, and are vocal and visible around their nests. Fledged young and occupied nests that were too high to be examined accounted for more than half (52%) of the "confirmed" records. Nests on transmission line towers were easy to find but impossible to examine.

BBS data from 1966 through 1989 show stable populations in the Eastern Region and an indication of a decline in Maryland; Maryland data from 1980 through 1989, however, show a stable population. Eastern Kingbirds are still common in Maryland but are losing breeding habitat to development and current agricultural practices, which remove large trees and mature hedgerows. Some evidence also indicates insect populations are declining as a result of the widespread use of pesticides (Graber et al. 1974). Insects, especially large ones, provide the protein needed to nourish rapidly growing young; fruit and small insects are not adequate. To aid the Eastern Kingbird as a breeding species, use of persistent pesticides should be further reduced, and open, parklike areas with large trees should be preserved.

James R. Wilkinson

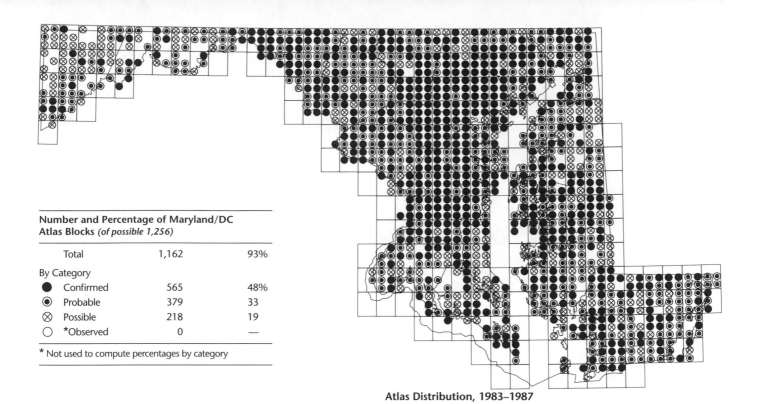

Number and Percentage of Maryland/DC Atlas Blocks *(of possible 1,256)*

Total	1,162	93%
By Category		
● Confirmed	565	48%
⊙ Probable	379	33
⊗ Possible	218	19
○ *Observed	0	—

* Not used to compute percentages by category

Atlas Distribution, 1983–1987

Percent of stops

▥	50–100%
▦	10–50%
▨	0.1–10%
☐	<0.1%

Relative Abundance, 1982–1989

Breeding Distribution, 1958

The Eastern Kingbird is most common in open areas of the Piedmont and Ridge and Valley sections, as well as around lower Eastern Shore marshes. It is less common in western Maryland woodlands, southern Maryland, the interior Eastern Shore, and urban areas.

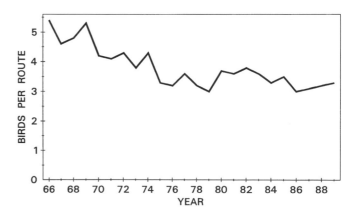

Maryland BBS Trend Graph, 1966–1989

Horned Lark

Eremophila alpestris

The Horned Lark is the only native New World representative of a large Old World family. It may not have bred in Maryland or much of eastern North America prior to clearing of the forests by European settlers. Horned Larks are present in Maryland throughout the year; in winter, the population is supplemented by birds from the north and west. Spring migrants pass through from mid-January to late March, and fall migration occurs from late September to mid-December (Stewart and Robbins 1958).

There is evidence that the Horned Lark has greatly expanded its breeding range in eastern North America in the past 150 years. It was not known to breed in Ontario away from the Arctic Coast prior to the 1860s (Hussell 1987), and the first nest record for New York was in 1875 (Bull 1974). The first Maryland breeding record was from Garrett County in 1904, although the Horned Lark had been seen there for several years prior to that time (Eifrig 1923). The first breeding record east of Garrett County was on 23 June 1922 near Laurel, Prince George's County (Swales 1922). Yet by 1958, Stewart and Robbins (1958) described its breeding status as fairly common in the Allegheny Mountain, Ridge and Valley, and Piedmont sections and in the coastal areas of Worcester County, and uncommon elsewhere. It now breeds throughout most of the agricultural areas of Maryland.

Horned Larks are birds of open spaces and prefer sparsely vegetated fields, beaches, and waste areas (Bent 1942). During the breeding season they can be found wherever the ground is flat and areas of soil are exposed, especially in agricultural fields but also at airports, beaches, pastures, golf courses, and other open habitats with sparse or short vegetation (Stewart and Robbins 1958).

The nest, made of fine grasses and lined with feathers (Davie 1898), is a small cup in a shallow depression on the ground. This depression often is excavated by the female; she selects the site and builds the nest (Beason and Franks

1974). The male selects and defends the territory, either by singing from a clump of dirt or a small hillock or by its towering flight display (Terres 1980). The flight song is reminiscent of the tinkling sound of glass wind chimes.

The Horned Lark is one of the earliest nesting passerines. Bent (1942) speculated that early nesting increased the probability that vegetation would be low enough and sparse enough to meet the Horned Lark's requirements. He noted that although Horned Larks did not commence nesting until the mean temperature had risen above 40°F (4.4°C) for at least two consecutive days, there were many weather-related nest failures. The earliest recorded Maryland egg date is 3 March and the latest is 6 July (MNRF); 12 of 21 egg dates fall in the brief period from 30 March to 23 April. Clutch sizes in 20 Maryland nests range from 3 to 5, with a mean of 3.6. Incubation, by the female, lasts about 11 days (Beason and Franks 1974). Young have been seen in the nest in Maryland from 10 March to 30 August (MNRF); the 30 August date supports the possibility of two broods. Maryland brood sizes in 10 nests range from 2 to 5 (mean of 3.4). Young fledge in about 10 days (Verbeek 1967). Horned Larks are uncommon hosts of Brown-headed Cowbirds (Friedmann 1963). There are no records of parasitism in Maryland, and only 4 of 161 Ontario nests (2.5%) were parasitized (Peck and James 1987). During the spring and summer months, weed seeds, especially those of bristle grass and ragweed, make up two-thirds of their diet (Martin et al. 1951). Beetles, caterpillars, and grasshoppers comprise the bulk of the insect food.

Atlas results show that the Horned Lark is expanding its breeding range on the Eastern Shore, where it is now common throughout the agricultural areas. It is also numerous in Garrett County but is uncommon and scattered over most of the rest of the state. It has declined sharply in central Maryland as suburban sprawl has replaced agricultural fields. In Howard County, for example, the number of quarter-blocks with Horned Larks declined 67 percent in the decade between the Howard County atlas of 1973 through 1975 (Klimkiewicz and Solem 1978) and 1983 through 1987 (Robbins et al. 1989c).

BBS data from 1966 though 1989 show stable Horned Lark populations in Maryland and the Eastern Region. The greatest threats to nesting birds continue to be loss of extensive fields and changes in agricultural practices (Beason and Franks 1974). It is inevitable that many nests are destroyed and that bare soil areas chosen in March and April are too heavily vegetated later in the season to permit high nesting success.

Where expansive areas of open, short-grass habitat persist, this species will remain a significant member of Maryland's breeding avifauna. In the suburban areas, however, where agricultural fields are replaced by lawns and homes, the Horned Lark has disappeared.

Alfred J. Fletcher

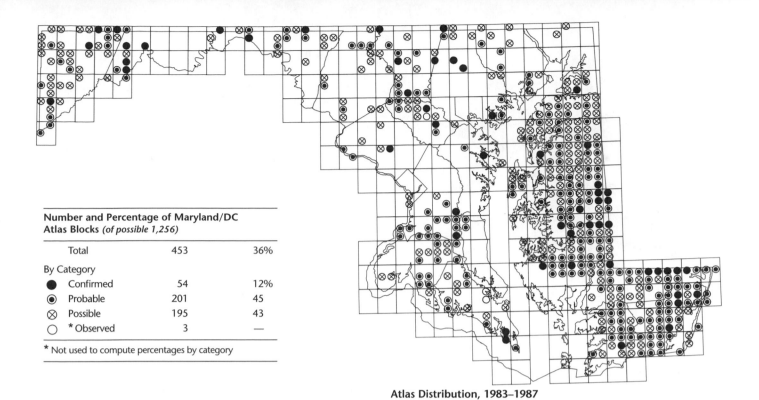

Number and Percentage of Maryland/DC Atlas Blocks *(of possible 1,256)*

Total	453	36%
By Category		
● Confirmed	54	12%
◉ Probable	201	45
⊗ Possible	195	43
○ * Observed	3	—

* Not used to compute percentages by category

Atlas Distribution, 1983–1987

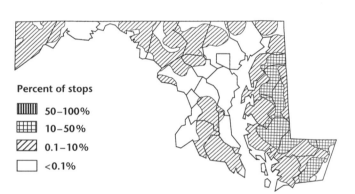

Percent of stops

▥	50–100%
▦	10–50%
▨	0.1–10%
☐	<0.1%

Relative Abundance, 1982–1989

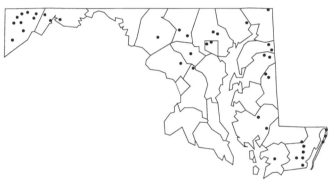

Breeding Distribution, 1958

The Horned Lark is most common in agricultural areas on the central Eastern Shore and in coastal Worcester County. It is less common but widely distributed in other agricultural areas and is rare or absent in most developed areas and in the woodlands of the western Ridge and Valley Section.

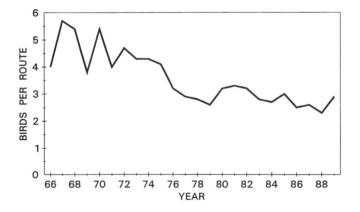

Maryland BBS Trend Graph, 1966–1989

Purple Martin

Progne subis

Purple Martins, North America's largest swallows, have long fascinated humans. Native Americans hung gourds for them, recognizing their potential to control insects (Sprunt 1942). They return from their wintering grounds in the Amazon Basin and Sao Paulo regions of Brazil (AOU 1983) from mid-March to early June (K. Klimkiewicz, pers. obs.). From late July through August, they gather in large staging roosts of several thousand or more and depart from mid-July through early September.

Kirkwood (1895) considered Purple Martins common summer residents. Hampe and Kolb (1947) called them widespread but local, and more common in the tidewater areas. Stewart and Robbins (1958) described them as common in the tidewater sections, fairly common in the Piedmont, and uncommon elsewhere. Prior to 1972, they were locally common in the Allegheny Mountain Section, but these colonies were destroyed during Hurricane Agnes in June 1972 (K. Klimkiewicz, pers. obs.). Because Purple Martins feed only on flying insects—especially bees, wasps, and ants (23%); flies (16%); dragonflies (15%); and bugs (15%) (Beal 1918)—they cannot feed during prolonged heavy rains, and many adults and most young perished from starvation.

Unless otherwise stated, the following information on Maryland breeding demography is from unpublished data gathered by the author from 1972 through 1991. Purple Martins breed in open areas, usually near human habitation, and often near water. Although they use gourds and historically have used cavities in trees or buildings (Kirkwood 1895), the eastern population is colonial and requires multicompartment artificial houses or cavities for nesting. The last observed Maryland natural cavity nesting was in a dead tree in Montgomery County in the early 1970s.

Nests consist of mud bases with small twigs, grass, leaves, stems, and straw, with bark shreds on top. They frequently contain items such as paper, metal, glass, pebbles, or mollusk shells. All MNRF nests were in nest boxes, including those of Wood Ducks. Nest heights for 86 nests range from 1 to 25 ft (0.3–7.6 m). These records fell into three groups: 5 ft (1.5 m) or less, 10 to 12 ft (3.0–3.7 m), and 25 ft (7.6 m); a mean height therefore would be misleading. Nest-box height does not seem to be a limiting factor, but the box must be in an open area large enough to allow the birds easy access.

The clutch consists of 1 to 8 eggs, usually 4 to 6; older pairs lay larger clutches than first-year birds. Extreme egg dates are 9 May (R. Smith, pers. comm.) and 10 August (E. Morton, pers. comm.), although most clutches are laid from mid-May to early July. Clutch sizes, brood sizes, and fledging success were derived from a sample of 300 Maryland nests with complete data. Clutch sizes range from 1 to 8, with a mean of 4.0. The female incubates for 15 to 21 days, depending on the ambient temperature; the warmer the temperature, the shorter the incubation time. Brood sizes range from 1 to 7, with a mean of 2.6. Young hatch as early as 30 May and fledge at 24 to 30 days; mean fledging success was 2.4 young per nest. The latest date for nestlings is 24 August (MNRF). After fledging, the parents assist the young for several days, and family groups may roost together up to two weeks. Most adults return to the same colony; 5 percent or fewer young return to the natal colony. Purple Martins are single-brooded in Maryland, but they may renest if the nest is destroyed; late nests are often unsuccessful. There are no confirmed records of Brown-headed Cowbird parasitism (Friedmann 1963; Peck and James 1987).

Purple Martins have several natural predators. House Sparrows pose the greatest threat by displacing adults and destroying eggs and young. European Starlings are staunch competitors in wooden boxes but seldom use aluminum ones. Fish Crows and American Crows can quickly destroy a colony by eating eggs and young. Other avian predators include Great Horned Owls, Eastern Screech-Owls, and American Kestrels. Nonavian predators include raccoons, snakes, and Virginia opossums. Weather also influences breeding success. Cool, wet springs cause adult mortality and affect egg fertility and viability. DDT had been suspected of affecting egg viability, but eggs from Prince George's and Montgomery counties that were tested at PWRC had extremely low residues (C. Grue, pers. comm.).

Although Purple Martins were found throughout Maryland during the Atlas period, they were scattered in the Allegheny Mountain and western Ridge and Valley sections. The rate of "confirmed" records was high (65%) because martins are highly visible. Most "confirmed" records were observations of active nests (77%) or fledglings (14%).

BBS data from 1966 through 1989 show stable populations in the Eastern Region and an indication of an increase in Maryland. Purple Martins have recovered well from Hurricane Agnes in most sections of Maryland, and the population now appears stable. Their future success depends on weather conditions, availability of nest sites, and proper colony management. House Sparrows and European Starlings must be controlled, boxes should be cleaned and closed for the winter, and predator guards should be added as needed.

M. Kathleen Klimkiewicz

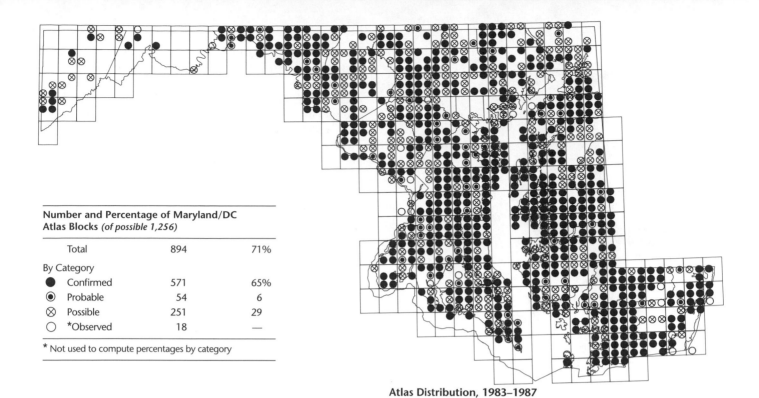

Atlas Distribution, 1983–1987

Number and Percentage of Maryland/DC Atlas Blocks *(of possible 1,256)*

Total	894	71%
By Category		
● Confirmed	571	65%
◉ Probable	54	6
⊗ Possible	251	29
○ *Observed	18	—

* Not used to compute percentages by category

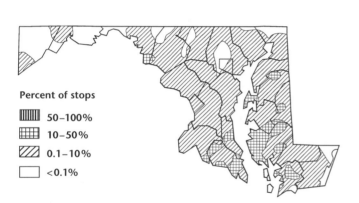

Percent of stops

▦	50–100%
▦	10–50%
▨	0.1–10%
▢	<0.1%

Relative Abundance, 1982–1989

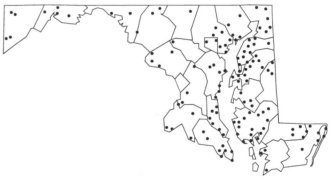

Breeding Distribution, 1958

The Purple Martin is localized around nest boxes. Highest concentrations are in scattered tidewater areas along the lower Chesapeake Bay. It is widespread throughout the rest of the state but very local in western Maryland.

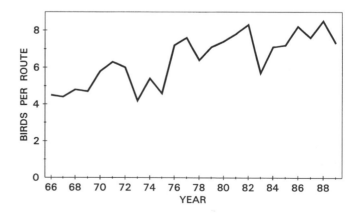

Maryland BBS Trend Graph, 1966–1989

PJM

Tree Swallow

Tachycineta bicolor

Tree Swallows, the first swallows to arrive in spring, are perhaps best known for the huge flocks that gather along the coast in the fall. Tree Swallows that breed in the East spend the winter from Florida to Cuba and Honduras (Butler 1988). Migrants begin returning to Maryland in mid-March, and most depart by mid-November, although small numbers occasionally winter in coastal Worcester County (Stewart and Robbins 1958).

Kirkwood (1895) described the Tree Swallow as largely confined to tidewater areas on the Eastern Shore in summer. Eifrig (1920b) did not observe this species in western Maryland until 1919, when he found it nesting at Crellin in Garrett County. Stewart and Robbins (1958) described its breeding status as fairly common in the tidewater areas of Somerset, Wicomico, and Dorchester counties and uncommon to rare elsewhere in the Eastern Shore, Western Shore, and Upper Chesapeake sections. They also noted that it was still uncommon or rare in the Allegheny Mountain Section.

Stewart and Robbins (1958) described the breeding habitat in Maryland as being near water in areas with standing dead trees. Although Maryland Tree Swallows formerly nested almost exclusively in dead snags, they now frequently use nest boxes and other artificial cavities. Erskine (1979) estimated that as high as 81 percent of the population in Canada used nest boxes, although the number of birds using natural cavities may have been underestimated (Turner and Rose 1989). Tree Swallows nest in individual pairs or loose colonies and are aggressive in their territorial defense. Even in loose colonies, Tree Swallows prefer to space their nests as far apart as possible (Muldal et al. 1985). Although nests in both natural cavities and bird boxes vary considerably in size and height, Rendell and Robertson (1989) found that females laid larger clutches in cavities with the greatest floor size, and that nests closest to the ground or water were more frequently victims of predation. In 133 Maryland nests (MNRF), heights range from 3 to 10 ft (0.9–3.0 m), with a mean of 5.2 ft (1.6 m). Of those nests, 115 were in boxes.

Nests with eggs have been found in Maryland from 24 April to 3 July, peaking during the last two weeks of May (MNRF). Cold weather or prolonged rains can delay the onset of breeding by as much as a week (Bittner 1990). Clutch sizes in 359 Maryland nests (MNRF) range from 2 to 7, with a mean of 5.1. Incubation is only by the female and lasts about 14 days (Turner and Rose 1989). The young are fed by both parents and fledge in 19 or 20 days. Nests with young have been found in Maryland from 20 May to 27 July, with a peak in mid-June (MNRF). Brood sizes in 320 nests range from 1 to 7 (mean of 4.7). One brood is typical, but renesting after failure is fairly common (Kuerzi 1941). Although attendants have been reported at Tree Swallow nests, Lombardo (1986) determined they do not aid in feeding or raising the young. Tree Swallows are extremely rare victims of Brown-headed Cowbird parasitism (Friedmann 1963), and none has been reported in Maryland. In Ontario, Peck and James (1987) reported that 1 of 4,149 nests (0.02%) were parasitized. The Tree Swallow's diet consists almost entirely of flying insects—overwhelmingly flies, aphids, and leafhoppers (Quinney and Ankney 1985).

Atlas results show a significant range expansion from that described by Stewart and Robbins (1958). Tree Swallows are now widely distributed on the Eastern Shore, especially along the river systems. West of the Chesapeake Bay they are found in large numbers everywhere except in the northern Piedmont. They are particularly widespread along the Patuxent and Potomac rivers and in western Maryland, where they seem to have solidified their range over the past 40 years. Although most of the expansion seems to be along river systems, Tree Swallows were also found away from the major river drainages. There is little doubt that the availability of nest boxes has greatly facilitated population increases and range expansion. BBS data from 1966 through 1989 show a significant increase of 1.7 percent in the Eastern Region and a stable Maryland population. Maryland populations, however, declined at a highly significant average annual rate of 8.9 percent from 1980 through 1989.

The expansion of the Tree Swallow's range in Maryland and the availability of nest boxes suggest that this species has a fairly bright future in this state. The recent decline is a cause for concern, however, and continued monitoring is needed. If the decline continues, efforts must be made to determine its cause.

Steve Clarkson

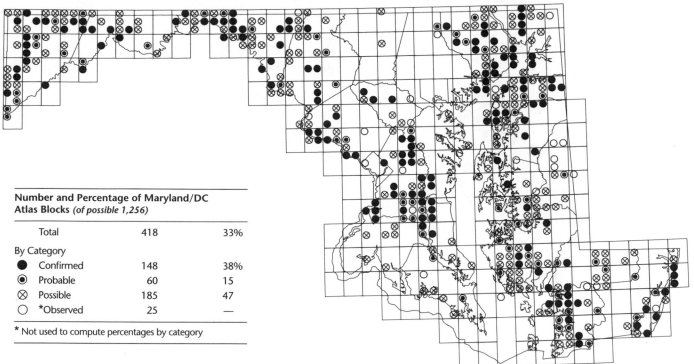

Number and Percentage of Maryland/DC Atlas Blocks *(of possible 1,256)*		
Total	418	33%
By Category		
● Confirmed	148	38%
◉ Probable	60	15
⊗ Possible	185	47
○ *Observed	25	—

* Not used to compute percentages by category

Atlas Distribution, 1983–1987

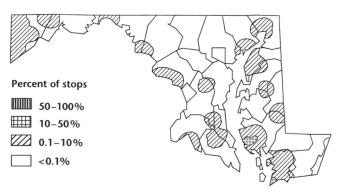

Percent of stops

▥	50–100%
▦	10–50%
▨	0.1–10%
☐	<0.1%

Relative Abundance, 1982–1989

Breeding Distribution, 1958

The highest Tree Swallow densities are in marsh blocks in Dorchester and Somerset counties. Small numbers were found in the Allegheny Mountain Section, along stretches of the Potomac and Patuxent rivers, and at scattered locations on the Coastal Plain, especially around the Chesapeake Bay and its tributaries.

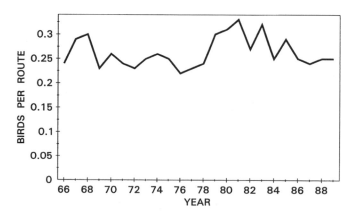

Maryland BBS Trend Graph, 1966–1989

Northern Rough-winged Swallow

Stelgidopteryx serripennis

The Northern Rough-winged Swallow's name was derived from the serrations on its outer primaries. It was formerly known as simply the Rough-winged Swallow. The earliest spring migrants return from their Mexican and Central American wintering grounds (AOU 1983) in late March, but the bulk of the migration occurs in April. Fall migrants are on the move in late June, and the last birds depart in October (Robbins and Bystrak 1977). This burrow-nesting swallow breeds uncommonly throughout Maryland, usually near waterways.

The earliest Maryland accounts listed the Northern Rough-winged Swallow as rather rare (Coues and Prentiss 1862) or not common (Coues and Prentiss 1883; Kirkwood 1895). Eifrig (1904) wrote that in western Maryland it was less common than the Barn Swallow but outnumbered the Bank Swallow. Cooke (1929) claimed, however, that it was the most widely distributed swallow in the DC area. Stewart and Robbins (1958) reported it to be fairly common along the Potomac River and uncommon and local throughout the rest of Maryland.

Although similar in appearance to its close cousin the Bank Swallow, the Northern Rough-winged Swallow is generally a solitary nester. Unlike the Bank Swallow, it does not always excavate its own burrows, often using those of other species or artificial substitutes (Dingle 1942). Nests are frequently constructed in burrows abandoned by Bank Swallows, Belted Kingfishers, or rodents. An adaptable bird, the Northern Rough-winged Swallow has also nested in drain pipes, culverts, quarries, crevices in cliffs and buildings, niches under bridges, the interior of a lime kiln, and crevices

in locks in the Chesapeake and Ohio Canal (MNRF). When Northern Rough-winged Swallows nest in a Bank Swallow colony, their larger and more elliptical entrance holes can often be identified from a distance (Dingle 1942). Hill (1988) reported that the mean depth of 44 nests built in drain pipes was 32.4 in. (82 cm).

Northern Rough-winged Swallows are single-brooded (Lunk 1962), and nest building in Maryland begins in early April (MNRF). Heights of 50 Maryland nest records range from 0.5 to 75 ft (0.2–23 m), with a mean of 10 ft (3 m). The earliest egg date is 19 April and the latest 24 June, with the peak in late May and early June (MNRF). Clutch sizes in 39 nests range from 3 to 7, with a mean of 5.3. The female incubates for about 11 days (Dingle 1942). Because the burrows are long and narrow, observers rarely can count the nestlings. In about 70 Maryland reports of nests with young, only four reported the actual number of young: 3, 5, 5, and 6 (MNRF). The earliest record for nestlings is 15 May, the latest is 7 July, and the peak is in mid-June (MNRF). Both parents tend the young, which fledge after 20 or 21 days (Dingle 1942). Their diet consists almost entirely of flying insects, especially flies, bugs, beetles, and ants (Beal 1918). There is no record of Brown-headed Cowbird parasitism of this species (Friedmann 1963; Peck and James 1987).

The Northern Rough-winged Swallow seems to be faring well in the eastern third of the continent; BBS data for 1966 through 1989 show a significant increase throughout the Eastern Region. In Maryland this species has maintained a stable population and distribution since the accounts of the early naturalists. Atlas results show it concentrated along the Potomac and Patuxent rivers and locally distributed throughout the rest of the state. Distribution is clustered not only along rivers but also near large reservoirs, such as Deep Creek Lake in Garrett County, Rocky Gap in Allegany County, and Liberty Reservoir in Carroll and Baltimore counties. This pattern is consistent with this bird's tendency to breed near water. Northern Rough-winged Swallows appear to be more widespread in the Piedmont and Ridge and Valley sections than elsewhere. The Eastern Shore has slow-moving rivers without the high banks that are preferred for nest sites, and the mountainous western edge of the state has mostly small, fast-moving streams in heavily wooded areas; neither offer as many good nest sites as the central part of the state.

The future of the Northern Rough-winged Swallow appears good. Like Barn and Cliff Swallows, it is able to adapt its nest preferences to include man-made objects and structures. Because it needs unpolluted stream valleys, river corridors, and watersheds, these habitats need to be protected if this species is to continue to do well.

Lynn M. Davidson

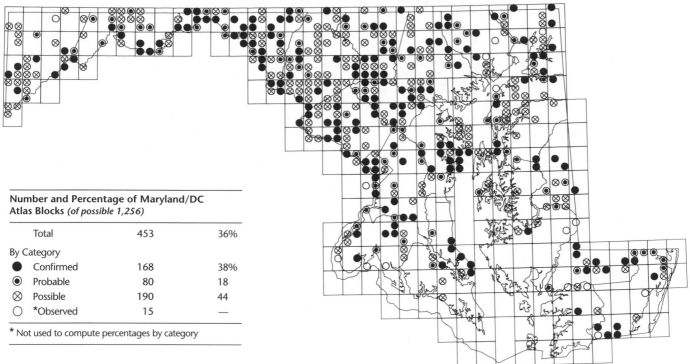

Atlas Distribution, 1983–1987

Number and Percentage of Maryland/DC Atlas Blocks *(of possible 1,256)*		
Total	453	36%
By Category		
● Confirmed	168	38%
◉ Probable	80	18
⊗ Possible	190	44
○ *Observed	15	—
* Not used to compute percentages by category		

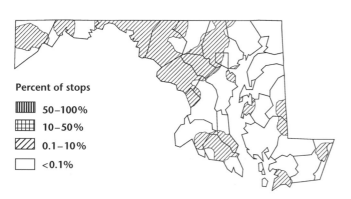

Percent of stops

▥	50–100%
▦	10–50%
▨	0.1–10%
☐	<0.1%

Relative Abundance, 1982–1989

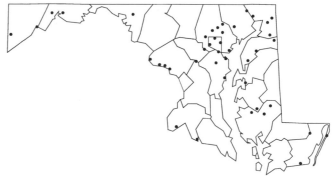

Breeding Distribution, 1958

The Northern Rough-winged Swallow is uncommon and local, and it was found primarily in the Piedmont and eastern Ridge and Valley sections. On the Coastal Plain it is largely limited to areas where high river banks provided nest sites. It is local in western Maryland.

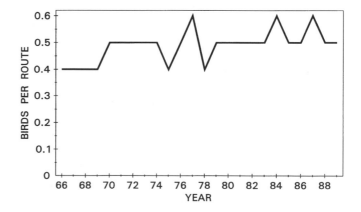

Maryland BBS Trend Graph, 1966–1989

Bank Swallow

Riparia riparia

Thirty years ago the graceful Bank Swallow, known in Eurasia as the Sand Martin, nested along both shores of the Chesapeake Bay (Stewart and Robbins 1958). Since then it appears to have undergone a major relocation to stream valleys in Maryland. The first spring migrants return to Maryland from their South American wintering grounds (AOU 1983) in mid-April, and postbreeding dispersal begins by late June. All birds have left by the end of September (Robbins and Bystrak 1977).

The earliest recorded Bank Swallow colonies in Maryland were found in May 1891 in Baltimore and Kent counties (MNRF). Historically this species was abundant in migration and common in summer, but little was known about nest sites (Coues and Prentiss 1862, 1883; Kirkwood 1895; Eifrig 1904; Cooke 1929). Hampe and Kolb (1947) reported that nesting was limited to tidewater areas; Stewart and Robbins (1958) added two colonies on the Potomac River in Washington County, two on the Susquehanna River in Harford County, and one on the Gunpowder River in Baltimore County. Currently, breeding colonies are few and limited mainly to gravel pits and the tidal portions of major rivers leading to the Chesapeake Bay. Bank Swallows have not adapted as well to human presence and development as have the other swallow species.

Bank Swallows always nest in colonies, placing their burrows in sandy banks of rivers and in transient habitats such as road cuts, gravel pits, and quarries (Gross 1942a). Nest excavation begins shortly after arrival at the breeding site and is interspersed with territorial disputes and courtship displays, including aerial acrobatics in which a feather is passed from bird to bird (Turner and Rose 1989). Tunnels are exca-

vated in the soft soil of a sand bank (Gross 1942a), typically in the portion most inaccessible to predators. Tunnels range from 12 to 67 in. (31–170 cm) deep, with an average of about 33 in. (84 cm); they are shorter when the soil is hard. Nest heights above ground or water vary considerably. Blem and Blem (1990) studied a Bank Swallow colony in the bank of a shipping channel near Hopewell, Virginia; as slumping and erosion of the bank left a harder and more compact soil, the colony declined from 435 burrows in 1975 to none in 1988. John (1991), studying nest-site requirements in Ontario, found that the soil must be hard enough to support a vertical face of at least 10 ft (3.0 m), yet soft enough to permit excavation. Heights of 21 Maryland nests (MNRF) range from 4 to 50 ft (1.2–15 m). Calculating a mean height is not possible because many reports cited multiple nests without providing exact heights. Topmost burrows were found within 2 ft (0.6 m) of the bank top (MNRF).

The nesting season extends from early May to mid-July in Maryland; nests were constructed of grass, straw, bark, and twigs and often included feathers. The earliest Maryland egg date is 5 May, the latest 23 June, with a peak in late May. Clutch sizes in 28 Maryland nests (MNRF) range from 4 to 7, with a mean of 5.1. Incubation, by both parents, lasts 14 to 16 days (Gross 1942a). Young have been found in the nest in Maryland from 30 May (Stewart and Robbins 1958) to 19 July (MNRF). Three of the four Maryland nests with young had 4 and one had 6. The Bank Swallow's diet consists almost entirely of flying insects, with mayflies, other flies, ants, bees, wasps, and beetles comprising the bulk of its summer food (Beal 1918). There are three records of Brown-headed Cowbirds parasitizing the Bank Swallow (Friedmann 1929, 1963); none are from Maryland.

Atlas results show that Bank Swallows have abandoned or been driven from some traditional shoreline sites as developments, roads, and bulkheading of shorelines destroyed much of the habitat. No colonies were recorded along the Chesapeake Bay shoreline during the Atlas period. Breeding activity has shifted to gravel pits and major river systems, especially the Patuxent, Susquehanna, Sassafras, Chester, and Choptank. In addition, colonies were reported as far west as central Allegany County. All "possible" and "probable" records are shown as "observed" because Bank Swallows forage great distances from the colonies and are early migrants. Thus, traditional colonies such as those along the upper Choptank River in Caroline County, where Bank Swallows still nest regularly and were seen repeatedly during all five summers, are shown only as "observed."

BBS data from 1966 through 1989 show stable populations for the Eastern Region. Maryland data are too variable to detect a clear trend. The past 30 years have seen extensive development on both shores of the Chesapeake Bay. The Bank Swallow will remain a breeding bird in Maryland only as long as traditional gravel pits and major segments of river shorelines, to which they have retreated, can be protected from similar development.

Norman C. Saunders and Frances C. Saunders

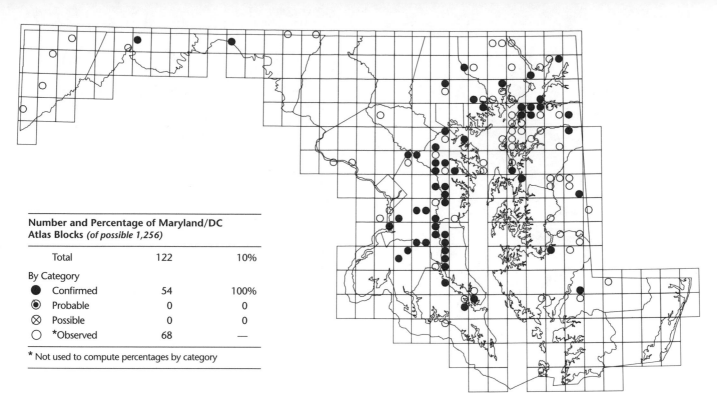

Number and Percentage of Maryland/DC Atlas Blocks *(of possible 1,256)*

Total	122	10%
By Category		
● Confirmed	54	100%
◉ Probable	0	0
⊗ Possible	0	0
○ *Observed	68	—

* Not used to compute percentages by category

Atlas Distribution, 1983–1987

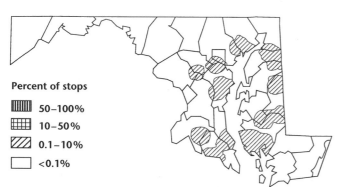

Percent of stops

▦	50–100%
▦	10–50%
▨	0.1–10%
☐	<0.1%

Relative Abundance, 1982–1989

Breeding Distribution, 1958

The Bank Swallow breeds at scattered locations on the Coastal Plain; it is rare west of the Fall Line and is absent from much of the flat country of the lower Eastern Shore. Miniroutes do not sample colonial breeding birds effectively; some records represent birds foraging away from nest sites.

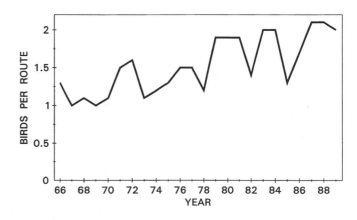

Maryland BBS Trend Graph, 1966–1989

Cliff Swallow

Hirundo pyrrhonota

Cliff Swallow populations have ebbed and flowed considerably since the arrival of the first Europeans; they are rarely reported today using the natural nest sites from which the common name is derived. Spring migrants return from their wintering grounds in South and Central America (AOU 1983) in mid-April, and most birds leave Maryland by mid-September (Robbins and Bystrak 1977).

Before land was cleared for agriculture, the Cliff Swallow nested only on cliffs and bluffs (Gross 1942b). From the arrival of Europeans until the late 1880s, it expanded its range and population and used barns and other outbuildings for nest sites. By the early twentieth century, populations had declined. Two factors seem most important in this decline: the growing tendency to paint barns, which reduces the birds' ability to attach their nests, and the explosive spread of the House Sparrow, which usurps their nests (Gross 1942b). During the past several decades, however, the Cliff Swallow has expanded its breeding range southward in the eastern United States by taking advantage of concrete bridges and culverts for nest sites (Alsop 1981).

Kirkwood (1895) called Cliff Swallows extremely local and not common in central Maryland, while Eifrig (1904) said they were common in western Maryland. Stewart and Robbins (1958) considered them common in the Allegheny Mountain Section and fairly common in the western Ridge and Valley Section. They also cited a few old records from the Piedmont of Baltimore County. Cliff Swallows had expanded into the Piedmont by 1958 (Booth 1958). Patterson (1981) documented the first Coastal Plain breeding records when he found a nest under a bridge over Western Branch in Prince George's County in 1976 and a nest in a Bank Swallow burrow near Crofton in Anne Arundel County in 1980.

Prerequisites for successful nesting are an open foraging area, a vertical substrate with an overhang for nest attachment, a supply of mud suitable for nest construction (Emlen 1954), and smooth-surfaced fresh water for drinking (Grinnell and Miller 1944). Cliff Swallows are colonial during the breeding season, with colonies as large as 3,000 pairs reported (Brown 1985); they have also been found in groups as small as five or six pairs (Alsop 1981). Their diet consists almost entirely of flying insects, with beetles and bugs comprising more than 50 percent of the content of 375 stomachs (Beal 1918).

These swallows usually place their gourd-shaped nest on a vertical surface, but they also use burrows and modify nests of other birds (Carpenter 1918; Mayhew 1958). A typical nest, containing 900 to 1,200 mud pellets, takes one to two weeks to complete (Emlen 1954). Heights of 20 Maryland nests (MNRF) range from 10 to 50 ft (3.0–15 m), with a mean of 13.7 ft (4.2 m). The male generally begins the nest construction and then is joined by the female (Turner and Rose 1989). Egg laying usually begins before the nest is complete.

Extreme egg dates for Maryland are 22 May (Stewart and Robbins 1958) and 9 July (MNRF). The late date can be extended because there are observations of young in nests into late August. In 10 Maryland nests, clutch sizes range from 3 to 5, with a mean of 3.7 (MNRF). Incubation is by both sexes and lasts 12 to 14 days (Turner and Rose 1989). Young have been found in Maryland nests from 7 June to 24 August (Bridge 1959). There are only four records of brood sizes for Maryland: one each with 1 and 2 young, and two with 4 young (MNRF). Single broods are typical, but second broods have been reported (Turner and Rose 1989). Brown and Brown (1988) showed that Cliff Swallows parasitize the nests of neighbors and destroy the eggs of other pairs; males will mate with neighboring females. Brown-headed Cowbird parasitism is very rare (Friedmann 1963) and has not been detected in Maryland.

Atlas data show Cliff Swallows are still widespread in Garrett and western Washington counties, where most nests are located in barns (Robbins 1963, 1975b). These adaptable birds have become solidly established along the Baltimore-Washington corridor, where they use bridges and reservoir dams for nest sites (Booth 1958; Robbins 1969, 1970, 1973a). For example, the courses of the Patuxent and Gunpowder rivers are clearly visible on the Atlas map.

BBS data from 1966 through 1989 for Maryland and the Eastern Region show stable or slightly increasing populations; continental populations indicate an increase. The limiting factor in the East seems now, as always, to be the availability of nest sites; populations fluctuate as new sites become available or disappear. Although these swallows undoubtedly still use natural sites occasionally, none was reported during the Atlas period.

The greatest risk to Cliff Swallows still appears to be competition from House Sparrows, even though House Sparrows have been declining in the eastern United States during the past 70 years (Robbins et al. 1986). At present, Cliff Swallows seem to be doing well in Maryland; there is no reason to believe they will not continue to flourish.

Barbara A. Dowell

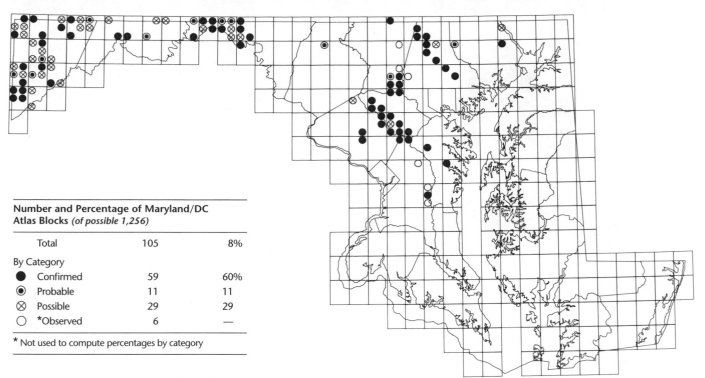

Number and Percentage of Maryland/DC Atlas Blocks *(of possible 1,256)*

Total	105	8%
By Category		
● Confirmed	59	60%
◉ Probable	11	11
⊗ Possible	29	29
○ *Observed	6	—

*Not used to compute percentages by category

Atlas Distribution, 1983–1987

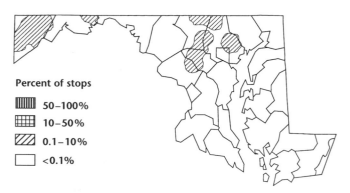

Percent of stops

▥	50–100%
▦	10–50%
▨	0.1–10%
☐	<0.1%

Relative Abundance, 1982–1989

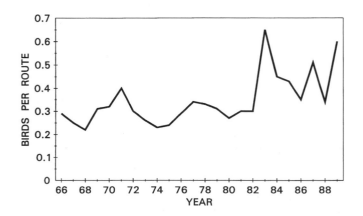

Breeding Distribution, 1958

The Cliff Swallow is found mainly in two areas. It is most widespread, primarily on barns, in the Allegheny Mountain Section; colonies also were recorded on bridges and dams in the Piedmont. Miniroutes do not sample colonial breeding birds effectively; some records represent birds foraging away from nest sites.

Maryland BBS Trend Graph, 1966–1989

Barn Swallow

Hirundo rustica

The Barn Swallow is the most widespread and recognized member of its family in Maryland. It breeds throughout continental North America as far north as northern Canada, Alaska, and the Beaufort Sea, and it winters from Costa Rica to Argentina, and from Puerto Rico south through the Lesser Antilles (AOU 1983). Spring migrants begin returning to Maryland in late March or early April, with the peak movement from late April to early May (Stewart and Robbins 1958). The first fall migrants are moving in early July; most have left by early October.

The Barn Swallow has been considered common to abundant in Maryland and DC since at least the mid-1800s (Coues and Prentiss 1862, 1883; Kirkwood 1895; Eifrig 1904; Cooke 1929). Stewart and Robbins (1958) described its breeding status as common in all sections. Its preferred foraging habitat is open fields, especially shrub areas or alfalfa and clover fields; it is usually most numerous near water. The highest breeding density reported for Maryland is 11 territorial males per 100 acres (40.5 ha) in mixed residential and agricultural habitat in Prince George's County in 1943 (Stewart and Robbins 1958). Much higher concentrations could be recorded in the immediate vicinity of dams and highway bridges.

Barn Swallows construct nests of mud and hay lined with feathers and, frequently, soft plant material (Bent 1942). They prefer to have their nests supported from beneath and sheltered from above. Nest sites in the wild include cave and cliff ledges, and, rarely, tree forks with a sheltering canopy of leaves. Most nests are built on artificial structures, including rafters and ledges in barns and sheds, bridges, and culverts in or near human habitation (Bent 1942). This species shows a decided preference for nesting in the vicinity of domesticated animals (Moeller 1983), presumably to ensure a good supply of flying insects on which to feed. Although the reported range of nest heights in Maryland (MNRF) is great, few were above 10 ft (3.0 m). This may reflect observer bias; nests under high bridges and on dams are less frequently examined. Heights of 169 Maryland nests range from 2 to 50 ft (0.6–15 m), with a mean of 8.3 ft (2.5 m).

Nests with eggs have been found in Maryland from 28 April to 4 August, with peaks in early to mid-May and in early June (MNRF). Two broods are regularly attempted each year, and, occasionally, a third is tried (Turner and Rose 1989). Clutch sizes in 133 Maryland nests (MNRF) range from 2 to 6, with a mean of 4.8. The incubation period is 9 to 17 days, averaging 13 or 14 days (Bent 1942); both parents participate, although the female assumes most of the burden. Nests with young have been found in Maryland from 18 May through 21 August, with peaks in early June and mid-to late July. Brood sizes in 109 Maryland nests range from 2 to 6, with a mean of 4.2 (MNRF). Young fledge in 18 to 23 days (Bent 1942). Fledglings stay in family groups for about a week after leaving the nest (Turner and Rose 1989), and young from first nests may help to feed second broods (Cramp 1988). Brown-headed Cowbird parasitism is very infrequent (Friedmann 1963); only 1 of 1,325 Maryland nests (0.07%) was parasitized (MNRF). Peck and James (1987) reported that 4 of 3,205 Ontario nests (0.1%) were parasitized. Their diet consists almost entirely of flying insects, with large flies the specialty of both Barn and Tree Swallows (Beal 1918).

Barn Swallows were found in more Atlas blocks (97%) than was any other species. They were absent from some of the extensive marsh blocks on the lower Eastern Shore that provided no nesting sites. In a few blocks where they were unrecorded, they may have been missed. Because Barn Swallows are abundant and highly visible and nest on artificial structures such as buildings, 80 percent of Atlas records were for "confirmed" breeding, with 44 percent of all records for observations of active nests.

BBS data from 1966 through 1989 show stable populations in Maryland and the East; continental data show a significant average annual increase of 1.2 percent. Commenting on the increase, Robbins et al. (1986) noted that the breeding range has expanded southward through the southeastern states, and that the Barn Swallow has definitely benefited from human activities. Although early twentieth-century efforts to make farms and outbuildings more sanitary may have reduced its numbers, the construction of dams and superhighway bridges has provided protected nesting sites so that populations of this species have greatly increased. There appears to be no present threat to the population of Barn Swallows in Maryland. Barring any unforeseen event, we can look forward to many more summers enhanced by these graceful, useful, and beautiful birds.

Steve Clarkson

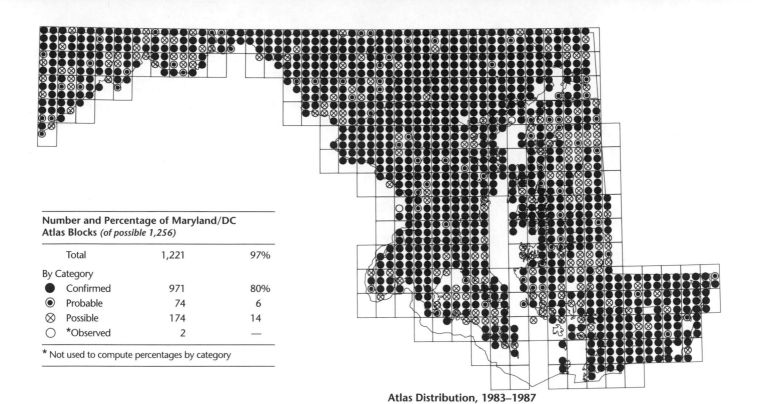

Atlas Distribution, 1983–1987

Number and Percentage of Maryland/DC Atlas Blocks *(of possible 1,256)*		
Total	1,221	97%
By Category		
● Confirmed	971	80%
◉ Probable	74	6
⊗ Possible	174	14
○ *Observed	2	—

* Not used to compute percentages by category

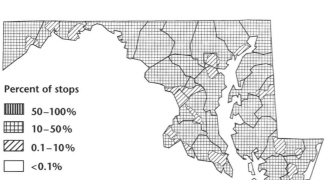

Percent of stops

- ||||| 50–100%
- ⊞ 10–50%
- ▨ 0.1–10%
- ☐ <0.1%

Relative Abundance, 1982–1989

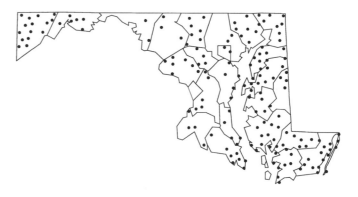

Breeding Distribution, 1958

The Barn Swallow is common and evenly distributed throughout the state. Small scattered areas of lower density occur primarily in urban areas.

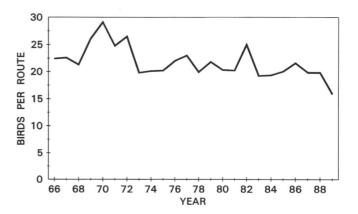

Maryland BBS Trend Graph, 1966–1989

Blue Jay

Cyanocitta cristata

The Blue Jay is the only jay found throughout most of the eastern United States. It is closely related to its western counterpart, the Steller's Jay, and occasional hybrids have been reported (AOU 1983). Although it is a permanent resident in Maryland and throughout the East, large numbers migrate through the state (Stewart 1982) and local populations may vary considerably. Spring migrants move through Maryland from mid-April through May, long after some resident birds have begun nesting; fall migrants can be found from late September to late October (Robbins and Bystrak 1977). Although Blue Jay populations fluctuate considerably from year to year (apparently in response to food availability), CBCs show they are scarce in Garrett County during the colder months.

The Blue Jay's status has not changed significantly in Maryland over the past century. Kirkwood (1895) called it a common resident throughout Maryland. Eifrig (1904) described it as common year-round at the higher elevations in western Maryland, a designation that seems inappropriate today. The discrepancy may reflect different perceptions of the bird's abundance or may be a different interpretation of the word *common*. Stewart and Robbins (1958) called the Blue Jay fairly common in summer throughout Maryland, except for the Eastern Shore Section, where it was described as uncommon. BBS data from 1966 through 1989 show a highly significant average annual decline of 2 percent in the Eastern Region. Maryland data show a highly significant average annual decline of 2.8 percent for the same period; however, data from 1980 through 1989 show a stable population in the state.

The Blue Jay is principally a woodland bird, favoring deciduous forests with beech and oak trees, although it generally builds its nest in a conifer (Bendire 1895a). In Maryland, 68 of 159 nests (43%) were in conifers (MNRF). It is also found in parks, suburban areas, small towns, and gardens (Tyler 1946a). Although Blue Jays are widely distributed and

fairly common, nesting densities are not high. In Maryland, the highest reported density is 17 territorial males per 100 acres (40.5 ha) in oak-gum mixed-hardwood forest in Charles County (Klimkiewicz 1974b). Blue Jays are noisy and gregarious most of the year, but pairs are typically solitary and skulking when nesting (Tyler 1946a).

Blue Jays commonly build a false nest prior to constructing the one used for breeding (Stokes 1979). The nest is placed in a crotch or on a branch in a variety of trees and shrubs or in vines. Several Maryland nests were located in unusual sites, such as behind a transformer on a utility pole, on the crossarm of a utility pole, in a bend of a rainspout on a porch roof, and in ivy on the side of a stone house (MNRF). Heights of 161 Maryland nests range from 3 to 86 ft (0.9–26 m), with a mean of 21.5 ft (6.6 m); only three were higher than 50 ft (15 m). Nests with eggs have been found in the state from 8 April to 30 July, with peaks in late April and mid-May (MNRF). The nesting season is a long one at this latitude, and two broods may be raised (Forbush 1927). Clutch sizes in 50 Maryland nests (MNRF) range from 3 to 6 (mean of 4.4). Incubation lasts about 17 days, with both sexes participating and aggressively defending the nest, and later the nestlings, by dive-bombing intruders, including humans (Tyler 1946a). Young in the nest have been found in Maryland from 28 April to 22 August, with a peak in late May (MNRF). Brood sizes from 67 Maryland nests (MNRF) range from 1 to 5 (mean of 3.6). The young fledge 17 to 21 days after hatching and are tended by both adults (Tyler 1946a). The Blue Jay diet is highly varied, consisting of about 75 percent plant matter, primarily acorns, beech nuts, and weed seeds; this omnivorous forager also consumes insects, small birds, eggs, grains, and fruits (Goodwin 1976).

None of the four reported instances (Friedmann 1929, 1963) of Brown-headed Cowbird parasitism is from Maryland. Peck and James (1987) did not report parasitism in Ontario. In a Connecticut experiment (Friedmann et al. 1977) in which S. Rothstein placed real or artificial Brown-headed Cowbird eggs in 24 Blue Jay nests, the jays ejected the intruder eggs from 22 nests and deserted the other two.

Atlas results show Blue Jays occurring in every section of Maryland, even in the most heavily urbanized blocks. The only areas in which they were regularly absent were on Assateague Island in coastal Worcester County and in a few of the most extensive marsh blocks on the lower Eastern Shore. The great majority (58%) of "confirmed" records were observations of fledged young. The noisy and gregarious family groups made this species fairly easy to locate.

The Blue Jay seems well established as a breeding bird in Maryland. As long as older deciduous woodlands are preserved, its raucous calls should continue to echo throughout Maryland.

William A. Russell, Jr.

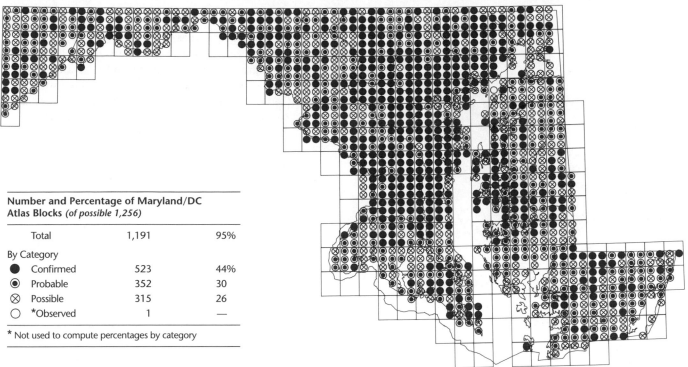

Atlas Distribution, 1983–1987

**Number and Percentage of Maryland/DC
Atlas Blocks** *(of possible 1,256)*

Total	1,191	95%
By Category		
● Confirmed	523	44%
◉ Probable	352	30
⊗ Possible	315	26
○ *Observed	1	—

* Not used to compute percentages by category

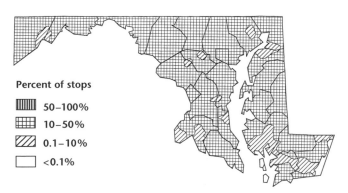

Percent of stops

▥	50–100%
▦	10–50%
▨	0.1–10%
☐	<0.1%

Relative Abundance, 1982–1989

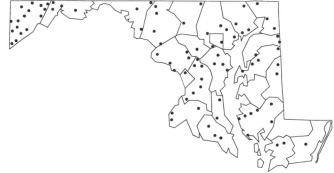

Breeding Distribution, 1958

The Blue Jay is common throughout the state. Smaller numbers occur in blocks in or near tidal marshes on the lower Eastern Shore.

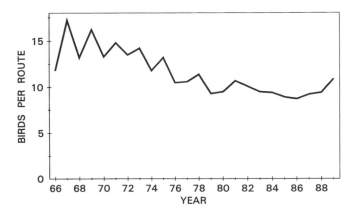

Maryland BBS Trend Graph, 1966–1989

American Crow

Corvus brachyrhynchos

Few birds are as well known to the general public as the American Crow, a large, gregarious, noisy inhabitant of every part of the state. Winter roosts numbering in the tens and even hundreds of thousands have been reported and discussed in the popular media. Migratory movements peak in early March and early November (Stewart and Robbins 1958) but are seldom noticed because of the heavy daily flights from and to the roosts at dawn and in late afternoon. Previously known as the Common Crow, which it is still frequently called (AOU 1983), it is common to abundant throughout Maryland at all seasons.

The American Crow has always been abundant throughout Maryland (Coues and Prentiss 1862, 1883; Kirkwood 1895; Cooke 1929; Hampe and Kolb 1947). In 1888, C. Edwards (in Barrows and Schwarz 1895) described a winter roost of 200,000 birds about seven mi (11.3 km) southeast of Baltimore. Oberholser (1920) recorded a roost of similar size in Brookland in DC. Eifrig (1904) called this crow abundant in western Maryland in all seasons. Stewart and Robbins (1958) described it as common in all sections. American Crows were killed in the past, and it is probable that populations have fluctuated as a result of control operations and hunting pressure. Gross (1946) described numerous instances in which tens of thousands were systematically killed by dynamite in a single night at winter roosts. American Crows are considered game birds in Maryland and there is a legal hunting season for them. BBS data from 1966 through 1989 show an indication of an increase in the Eastern Region and a highly significant average annual increase of 2.6 percent in Maryland. Maryland data from 1980 through 1989 show a stable population.

The American Crow is omnivorous, taking grain, small mammals, birds, eggs, insects, reptiles, amphibians, garbage, road kills, and almost anything else it can forage (Gross 1946). The percentage of animal food in its diet increases substantially in spring and early summer (Barrows and Schwarz 1895). Its primary habitat comprises woodlands bordered by agricultural areas, open woodlands, and suburban environments (Goodwin 1976). It is generally a solitary nester (Goodwin 1976), but more recently, Kilham (1985) described cooperative breeding in Florida birds. It is very adaptable to the presence of humans, and young removed from the nest at an early age will imprint on their captors (Gross 1946). Birds nesting in urban and suburban environments are less aggressive around the nest than are rural birds and will tolerate a much closer approach by humans (Knight et al. 1987). The nest is typically placed in a crotch of a deciduous or coniferous tree or on a limb near the trunk (Gross 1946). Heights of 72 Maryland nests (MNRF) range from 15 to 95 ft (4.6–29 m), with a mean of 41.0 ft (13 m). Twenty-nine nests (45%) were in pine trees, mostly Virginia pine, and 17 (27%) were in oaks. Although crows are noisy and conspicuous most of the year, they are extremely quiet during the nest building, egg laying, and incubation periods (Stokes 1979).

American Crows are early breeders. Nests with eggs have been found in Maryland from 13 March to 21 May, with a peak in mid-April (MNRF). Records of clutch sizes in 29 Maryland nests (MNRF) range from 3 to 7, with a mean of 4.5. Clutches as large as 9 and 10 eggs have been reported elsewhere, but they may have been laid by two females (Gross 1946). Although Harrison (1975) stated that both sexes incubate the eggs, Goodwin (1976) believed it was typically done only by the female. Incubation lasts 18 days, and the young fledge four to five weeks after hatching (Gross 1946). Brood sizes in 21 Maryland nests (MNRF) range from 1 to 6, with a mean of 3.4. Young in the nest have been reported in Maryland from 7 April to 16 June, with a peak in mid-May. Although two broods have been reported in South Carolina (Forbush 1927), there is no evidence of more than one brood each year in Maryland. There are no verified reports of parasitism by the Brown-headed Cowbird (Friedmann 1963; Peck and James 1987).

Atlas results show the American Crow to be a widespread breeder throughout Maryland, even in the most urbanized blocks. The only areas where it was not found were the coastal strip of Worcester County and some of the extensive marshes and offshore islands of the lower Chesapeake Bay. More than half (52%) the Atlas records were "confirmed"; 63 percent of those were observations of fledged young. Only three Atlas records were of nests with eggs and only one was a sighting of an adult carrying a fecal sac. The American Crow is well established in Maryland and will continue to be with us for the foreseeable future.

William A. Russell, Jr.

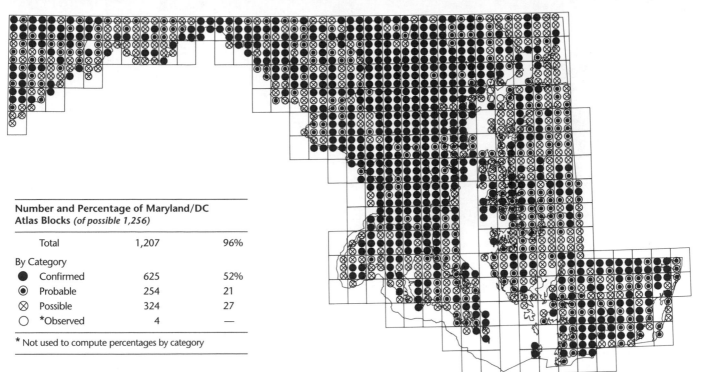

Number and Percentage of Maryland/DC Atlas Blocks *(of possible 1,256)*

		Total	1,207	96%
		By Category		
●	Confirmed	625	52%
◉	Probable	254	21
⊗	Possible	324	27
○	*Observed	4	—

* Not used to compute percentages by category

Atlas Distribution, 1983–1987

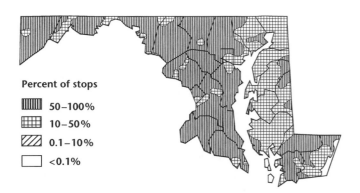

Percent of stops

▥	50–100%
▦	10–50%
▨	0.1–10%
▢	<0.1%

Relative Abundance, 1982–1989

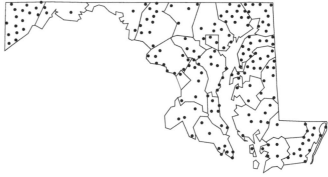

Breeding Distribution, 1958

The American Crow is abundant almost everywhere west of the Chesapeake Bay and over most of the lower Eastern Shore. It is less common throughout the remainder of the Eastern Shore and in the rest of the Upper Chesapeake Section.

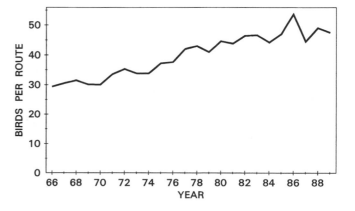

Maryland BBS Trend Graph, 1966–1989

Fish Crow

Corvus ossifragus

Few birds have expanded their Maryland breeding range so dramatically in the past few decades as has the Fish Crow. It is now well established over most of the state, except in the mountainous regions of western Maryland. A few authors consider Fish and American Crows conspecific, but recent investigations suggest they are not so closely related as once believed (AOU 1983).

The original range of Fish Crows in Maryland was limited. Kirkwood (1895) considered them confined to tidewater areas. In western Maryland, Eifrig (1904) was able to cite only two uncertain sight records for Allegany County, although he recognized them as common in the parks around DC. Stewart and Robbins (1958) described their breeding status as fairly common in the tidewater areas of the Eastern Shore, Western Shore, and Upper Chesapeake sections, and as uncommon and local in the Piedmont and Ridge and Valley sections, occurring primarily in the Hagerstown and Frederick valleys. In winter, they were considered uncommon in tidewater areas and rare in the interior. The maximum winter count was cited as 200 in DC (Stewart and Robbins 1958), but recent counts of winter roosts in Somerset County and on offshore Chesapeake Bay islands approach 20,000 (E. Blom and M. O'Brien, pers. comm.). This increase is illustrated by the CBCs from southern Dorchester County, where coverage has been comparable for more than 40 years. From 1947 through 1956, only three Fish Crows were recorded, all in 1954; now the counts average about 1,000 per year. In Maryland, they concentrate at landfills during the winter.

Little has been written about the habitat requirements of Fish Crows. In coastal and tidewater areas, they favor marshes, marsh edges, beaches, and offshore islands. In the interior, they most often are found along major river systems, using small and large woodlots in agricultural areas (Bent 1946; Goodwin 1976). Fish Crows feed on the ground like other crows but also forage in small trees and shrubs

(Goodwin 1976). They are omnivorous, taking many crustaceans, small fish, and aquatic invertebrates, as well as grain, fruits, small birds and mammals, and many eggs; they can be very damaging to the eggs and nestlings of herons and egrets (Bent 1946; Goodwin 1976). They often nest in loose colonies, although the nests are rarely placed in close proximity to each other (Goodwin 1976). They are typically less solitary during the breeding season than are other crows.

Fish Crows build their nest in the crotch of a tree or on a large limb close to the trunk (Bent 1946). They use many species of trees, such as beech, elm, oak, cherry, groundsel tree, and sycamore, but they prefer conifers and hollies. Heights above the ground of 22 Maryland nests (MNRF) range from 6 to 75 ft (1.8–23 m), with a mean of 33.0 ft (10 m). The breeding season in Maryland is slightly later than that of the American Crow. Nests with eggs have been found from 30 March to 8 June (MNRF). Nest heights preclude significant amounts of data on eggs and nestlings. Clutch sizes from eight Maryland nests (MNRF) are 3, 4, 4, 5, 5, 5, 5, and 5. Incubation lasts 16 to 18 days; young fledge about three weeks after hatching (Potter et al. 1980). Incubation by both sexes has been reported, but Goodwin (1976) and Meanley (1981) have expressed doubts that the male was involved. Nestlings have been found in Maryland from 14 May (Stewart and Robbins 1958) to 26 July (MNRF). Brood counts from six Maryland nests (MNRF) are 1, 2, 2, 2, 4, and 4. Probably only a single brood is raised (Goodwin 1976). There is no record of parasitism by the Brown-headed Cowbird (Friedmann 1963; 1971).

Atlas results show the Fish Crow to be well established in all parts of Maryland except for Garrett and Allegany counties. This is a major change since the 1950s, when this species was restricted to the tidewater zone, the Potomac Valley of Montgomery County, and the farmland of the Frederick and Hagerstown valleys (Stewart and Robbins 1958). In Howard County, where the Fish Crow was unknown as a nesting species in the 1950s, it was found in 50 (37%) of the 136 quarterblocks from 1973 through 1975 (Klimkiewicz and Solem 1978) and in 114 (84%) from 1983 through 1987. The Fish Crow is fairly widespread in the southeastern quarter of Pennsylvania. In Virginia, it has moved into the Shenandoah Valley along the rivers; breeding was first confirmed in 1981 (Meanley 1981). BBS data from 1966 through 1989 show a highly significant average annual increase of 3.7 percent in the Eastern Region; the Maryland population shows a highly significant average annual increases more than double that of the Eastern Region (8.6%). The dramatic increase in Maryland has continued through 1989. No explanation has been offered for the expansion of this species.

There seems to be little concern about the immediate future of the Fish Crow in Maryland, but the effect that the expanding population might have on breeding herons and egrets and the possible depredation of commercial grains need to be monitored.

William A. Russell, Jr.

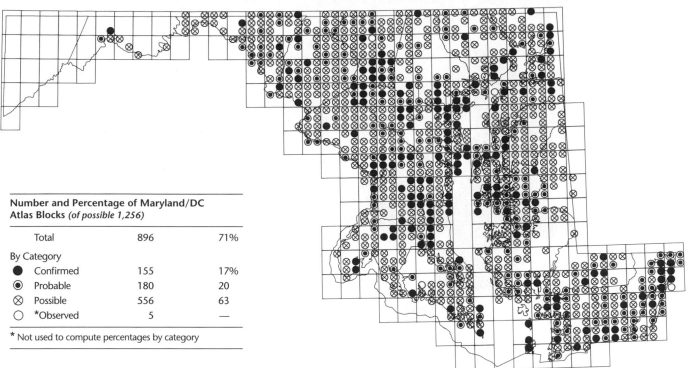

Atlas Distribution, 1983–1987

Number and Percentage of Maryland/DC Atlas Blocks *(of possible 1,256)*		
Total	896	71%
By Category		
● Confirmed	155	17%
◉ Probable	180	20
⊗ Possible	556	63
○ *Observed	5	—

* Not used to compute percentages by category

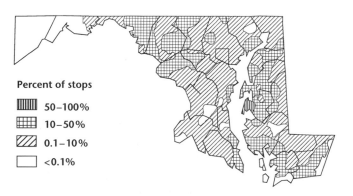

Percent of stops

▥	50–100%
▦	10–50%
▨	0.1–10%
▢	<0.1%

Relative Abundance, 1982–1989

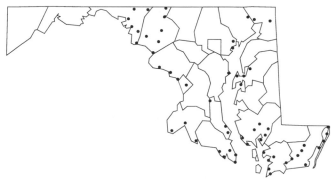

Breeding Distribution, 1958

The Fish Crow is most common in tidewater areas and in the Frederick and Hagerstown valleys. It is less common in the agricultural and forested interiors of the Eastern and Western shores; it is absent from the highlands of Western Maryland.

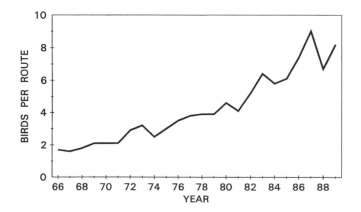

Maryland BBS Trend Graph, 1966–1989

Common Raven

Corvus corax

Thanks to Edgar Allen Poe, the Common Raven has been immortalized in American literature. He referred to it simply as Raven, as did ornithologists for many years. It is an uncommon permanent resident of western Maryland, usually nesting on cliffs. It is omnivorous, eating carrion, small mammals, lizards, snakes, poultry, eggs, fish, frogs, berries, and garbage (Bent 1946).

Maryland's earliest breeding records, all from Allegany and Garrett counties, date from 1899 to 1904 (Eifrig 1904). Common Ravens declined shortly after the beginning of the twentieth century; there were no further published reports from the two western counties until 1936 (Brooks 1936). This hiatus, during which they may have been present in small numbers, coincides with a decline of this species in Pennsylvania (Todd 1940). Stewart and Robbins (1958) described them as uncommon and local in the Allegheny Mountain and Ridge and Valley sections. Since the 1950s Common Ravens have spread eastward in Maryland and now nest in the mountains of Washington and Frederick counties. Fledged young found in Allegany County in 1981 represent the first Maryland nesting reported since 1950 (Ringler 1981c).

Virginia studies (Hooper et al. 1975; Hooper 1977) suggested that availability of food is the chief factor limiting breeding distribution. In Pennsylvania (Brauning 1992), West Virginia (Hall 1983), and Virginia, Common Ravens are now widely distributed along mountain ridges, with scattered records in Virginia and West Virginia at lower elevations. In Pennsylvania, where Harlow (1922) and Todd (1940) expressed fears about the Common Raven's possible extinction, it is now widespread in the central portion of the state. Kain (1987) reported a recent increase in the Virginia Piedmont. Hall (1983) stated that breeding populations in West Virginia have remained steady or are slightly increasing.

Studies in Pennsylvania (Harlow 1922; Todd 1940) and Virginia (Murray 1949; Hooper et al. 1975; Hooper 1977) revealed much about the breeding biology of eastern Common Ravens. Their favored nest site is a ledge on a cliff face sheltered by an overhang with a steep rock face below. The nest, a mass of sticks and twigs with a smaller cup, can either be symmetrical or take the shape of the cliff. When Common Ravens nest in trees, they frequently select the tallest available conifer that has good cover at the top. From year to year some pairs alternate between nest sites as far as 1.8 mi (3 km) apart. They are early nesters; beginning nest building in late January or early February and egg laying by the first week of March. The clutch is completed within a week; clutch sizes range from 2 to 7, with 4 or 5 eggs most common. There is only one brood per year, but replacement clutches may be laid. Incubation, normally by the female only, requires 20 days. Fledging starts at 41 days (Stiehl 1985). Mean fledging success in Virginia was 2.5 birds per nest (Hooper et al. 1975). The only nesting data available for Maryland are eggs on 10 and 23 March and large nestlings from 28 March to 7 May (MNRF). There are no records of Brown-headed Cowbird parasitism of Common Ravens (Friedmann 1929, 1963; Peck and James 1987).

Atlas results show that the current Maryland range of the Common Raven is in the Ridge and Valley and Allegheny Mountain sections, with an outlying pair in southeastern Frederick County. This range is more extensive than any previously recorded. Observers reported nests in five blocks and fledged young in seven. Most "confirmed" records were of recently fledged young. Halfway through the fieldwork, the beginning safe date was moved back about two months, from 1 May to mid-March, to reflect the early nesting of this species; therefore, a few "possible" and "probable" records may represent postbreeding wanderers from nearby nests. Additionally, nonbreeding Common Ravens form roosts during at least the early part of the breeding season (Hooper and Dachelet 1976), and a few lone birds dispersing from roosts may have been included as "possible" and "probable" records.

BBS data from 1966 through 1989 show a highly significant average annual increase of 4.4 percent in Eastern Region populations. Data are too few to estimate a trend for Maryland. The outlook for this species in the state is good if nesting sites are protected. The following suggestions, modified from Hooper (1977), should ensure minimum disturbance to nesting birds: pedestrians (such as hikers) should not approach nests closer than 1,000 ft (305 m); vehicular traffic should be allowed no closer than 650 ft (198 m); road construction should occur no closer than 1,000 ft; there should be no scenic overlooks on top of nesting cliffs; and rock climbing on active nesting cliffs should be prohibited from January to 15 May. Further studies are needed to ascertain the status of the Common Raven in Maryland and to investigate its breeding biology here.

Robert Hilton

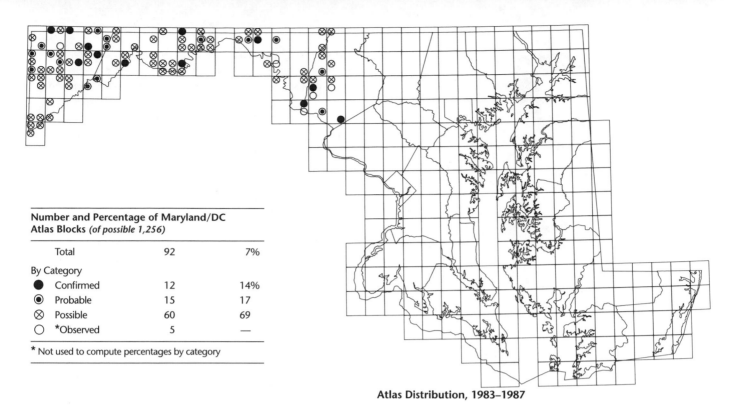

Atlas Distribution, 1983–1987

Number and Percentage of Maryland/DC Atlas Blocks (of possible 1,256)		
Total	92	7%
By Category		
● Confirmed	12	14%
◉ Probable	15	17
⊗ Possible	60	69
○ *Observed	5	—

* Not used to compute percentages by category

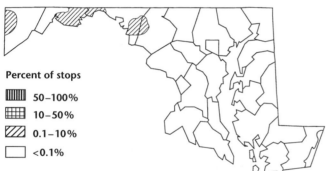

Percent of stops

▦	50–100%
▦	10–50%
▨	0.1–10%
☐	<0.1%

Relative Abundance, 1982–1989

Breeding Distribution, 1958

    The Common Raven was detected in small numbers in northwest Garrett County, in Allegany and western Washington counties, and around South Mountain on the Frederick-Washington county border. Although widespread in western Maryland, it is rare to uncommon and was not detected in parts of its range.

Black-capped Chickadee

Parus atricapillus

Black-capped Chickadees, the northern counterparts of the closely related Carolina Chickadees, have long been considered one of our most congenial permanent residents. In some winters, migrants from farther north invade our northern counties, rarely reaching southern Maryland and the lower Eastern Shore. In Maryland, their breeding range is limited to the western counties.

Kirkwood (1895) was not aware that Black-capped Chickadees nested in Maryland, presumably because he lacked specimens from the western counties. Preble (1900) first documented that they bred commonly in Garrett County. Eifrig (1904) also showed they were abundant residents in Allegany County. Stewart and Robbins (1958) found them summering on the higher ridges in Washington and Frederick counties and in north-central Carroll County.

Identification of Black-capped and Carolina Chickadees is difficult and complicated in the contact zone and created problems for Atlas workers. Parkes (1987) summarized the problem in nearby southwestern Pennsylvania. There is a north-south clinal variation in all field characteristics of both species, with the two species becoming more similar as their ranges converge. Identification by differences in vocalizations, long thought to be the most reliable field characteristic, has been questioned because abnormal songs have been heard in the contact zone. Although the safest way to identify birds is by the ratio of wing and tail measurements in combination with plumage characteristics, organizing a banding effort to establish an exact dividing line between the two species was not possible. Also clouding the issue is the possibility that hybrids occur in Maryland, as they do in adjacent states (Johnston 1971).

Black-capped Chickadees nest in both isolated and extensive deciduous and coniferous woods (Robbins et al. 1989a). They favor a low canopy and open shrub layer. Little is known about their nesting habits in Maryland. Nest sites include nest boxes and cavities in fence posts and tree stumps. They prefer dead deciduous stumps; nests are commonly 3 to 12 ft (0.9–3.7 m) above ground level (Peck and James 1987). The only reported egg dates for Maryland are 22 May and 2 June (MNRF). In West Virginia, egg dates extend from mid-April to late May (Tyler 1946b). Clutches usually have 6 to 8 eggs. Incubation, by the female only, takes 12 or 13 days; young remain in the nest about 16 days (Tyler 1946b). Nestlings have been noted in Maryland from 27 May to 24 June, but nest building has been observed as late as 26 June (Stewart and Robbins 1958). None of the seven published records of Brown-headed Cowbird parasitism (Friedmann et al. 1977) occurred in Maryland. In Ontario, 2 of 193 nests (1%) were parasitized (Peck and James 1987). Finding food for its large brood should not be a problem for this hardy chickadee. Although seeds and insect eggs comprise the bulk of its winter diet, the summer menu includes moths, caterpillars, spiders, flies, wasps, bugs, and many other insects (Martin et al. 1951).

Atlas results show that Black-capped Chickadees still nest throughout Garrett and Allegany counties, at the highest elevations in western Washington County, on South Mountain in Frederick and Washington counties, and on Catoctin Mountain in Frederick County. On both mountain ridges they seem to be adjacent to resident Carolina Chickadees. No Black-capped Chickadees were reported in northern Carroll County. An anomaly exists between the ranges in Allegany County and adjacent West Virginia. Hall (1983) stated that Black-capped Chickadees are absent from the three eastern counties of West Virginia, including the area directly across the Potomac River from eastern Allegany County, Maryland. It is unlikely that the river would serve as a boundary between the two species; this problem remains to be resolved. There was a high percentage of "probable" and "confirmed" reports (69%), with 48 percent of the "confirmed" based on the presence of fledged young and 56 percent of the "probable" based on birds holding territory. Black-capped Chickadees are common and conspicuous throughout most of their Maryland breeding range but are less conspicuous in the disjunct populations in the eastern portion of the Ridge and Valley Section.

Additional work is required to better define the eastern and low elevation limits of its breeding range and determine the status of the Black-capped Chickadee in the higher elevations of Washington and Frederick counties. Specifically, measurements from banded birds and specimens will be needed to establish whether Black-capped and Carolina Chickadees are breeding in adjacent territories or whether there are definite lines of demarcation between their breeding ranges, as there are in some states (Merritt 1981).

BBS data from 1966 through 1989 show a highly significant increase of 3.3 percent in the Eastern Region; there are too few data to estimate a Maryland trend. The status of the Black-capped Chickadee is likely to remain unchanged, as it seems to have adapted well to living in wooded areas near human habitation.

Robert F. Ringler

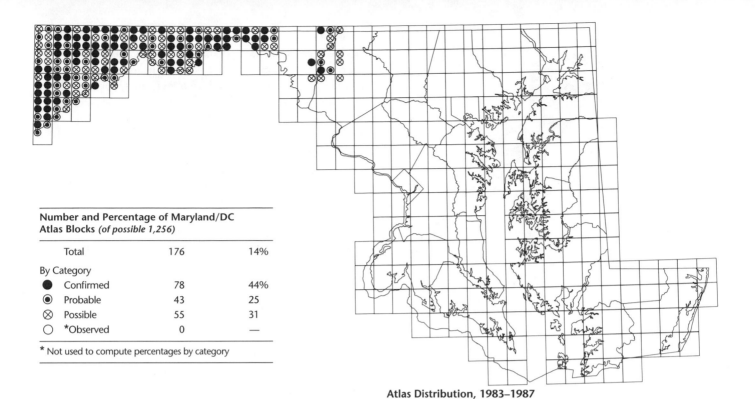

Number and Percentage of Maryland/DC Atlas Blocks *(of possible 1,256)*		
Total	176	14%
By Category		
● Confirmed	78	44%
◉ Probable	43	25
⊗ Possible	55	31
○ *Observed	0	—

* Not used to compute percentages by category

Atlas Distribution, 1983–1987

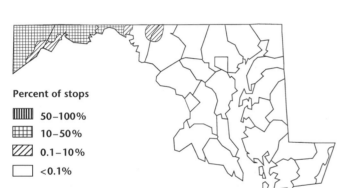

Percent of stops

▥	50–100%
▦	10–50%
▨	0.1–10%
☐	<0.1%

Relative Abundance, 1982–1989

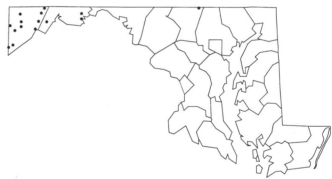

Breeding Distribution, 1958

The Black-capped Chickadee is common and fairly evenly distributed west of central Washington County. There are lower numbers along the Potomac River in western Allegany and southeastern Garrett counties, at the edge of the range in central Washington County, and in the disjunct population in the Catoctin Mountains.

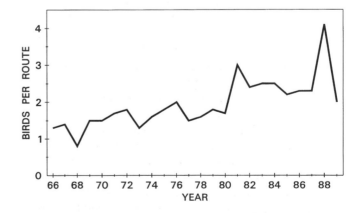

Maryland BBS Trend Graph, 1966–1989

Carolina Chickadee

Parus carolinensis

The Carolina Chickadee is one of Maryland's better known permanent residents. Its range stretches from the ocean to the foothills in western Washington County, and its vocalizations are frequently heard during all seasons and in all woodland habitats. This species is sedentary, with adults remaining close to the nest area even after summer dispersal of young. It is common throughout most of its Maryland range, although less so on Assateague Island, Worcester County, and in the contact zone with Black-capped Chickadees in western Washington County.

The Carolina Chickadee was once thought to be the only breeding chickadee in Maryland, a belief that persisted until western Maryland was explored by ornithologists early in the twentieth century. Kirkwood (1895) assumed a nest he found on Dan's Mountain in 1895 in western Allegany County was that of a Carolina Chickadee. Eifrig (1904) cited this report as the only evidence of Carolina Chickadees in western Maryland, stating that all specimens from that area were Black-capped Chickadees. On the basis of a few records in the lowlands, Stewart and Robbins (1958) included the eastern two-thirds of Allegany County in the Carolina Chickadee's range and showed it in contact with the Black-capped Chickadee there. Atlas results, however, show the contact zone is in western Washington County.

The Carolina Chickadee nests in many wooded habitats, with a slight preference for moist coniferous woods (Robbins et al. 1989a). It does not require extensive forest and readily uses isolated woods and wood margins. The highest breeding density reported for Maryland is 39 territorial males per 100 acres (40.5 ha) in mixed-hardwood forest in Calvert County (Fales 1973). Nests are commonly built in Eastern Bluebird and wren houses as well as in natural cavi-

ties (MNRF). Despite their small bills, chickadees are primary cavity nesters, excavating cavities in rotted limbs and tree trunks of both live and dead trees (Dingle 1946), and also using old woodpecker holes. Both sexes excavate, but the female constructs most of the nest, building a thick foundation of moss, bark strips, grass, thistle or milkweed down, and feathers, such as those of sparrows, bluebirds, or their own. The cup is well padded with silvery milkweed or thistle down and animal hair from cows, rabbits, deer, mice, and other mammals. The nest is built up on one side to create a flap that is used to cover the eggs.

Heights above ground of 164 Maryland nests (MNRF) range from 0 to 36 ft (0–11 m), with a mean of 5.5 ft (1.7 m). Eighty-eight of the 164 nests were in nest boxes or other artificial structures, resulting in a mean height lower than that for nests in natural cavities. Nest building has been observed as early as 18 March (MNRF).

The earliest recorded Maryland egg date is 12 April, but a nest with 8 eggs and another with 6 eggs were found on 14 April, indicating that laying can begin in early April (MNRF). The latest egg date is 6 June; the peak extends from early to mid-May. Clutch sizes in 80 Maryland nests (MNRF) range from 1 to 9, with a mean of 5.2. Incubation, performed by both sexes, lasts approximately 11 days (Dingle 1946). The earliest nestling date is 26 April and the latest 30 June (MNRF); the peak period is from mid-May to mid-June. Brood sizes in 59 Maryland nests range from 2 to 7 (mean of 4.4). Young fledge in approximately 17 days (Dingle 1946), and the earliest Maryland fledging date is 10 May (MNRF). The average annual survival rate of a population at PWRC was 60 percent (Karr et al. 1990). The Carolina Chickadee is a very rare victim of Brown-headed Cowbird parasitism (Friedmann 1963); there are only two Maryland records (Stewart and Robbins 1958; Friedmann 1963). The summer diet is primarily insects, especially moths and caterpillars. In winter, the Carolina Chickadee's diet includes plant seeds; it is a regular visitor at bird feeders (Terres 1980).

During the Atlas period, Carolina Chickadees were found in all counties except Garrett, with a lone report from eastern Allegany County. This bird had the appearance and vocalization of a Carolina Chickadee, but this mid-July report is difficult to interpret because it occurred in the hybrid zone. Interestingly, Hall (1983) stated that the Carolina Chickadee is the only chickadee known to breed in Morgan County, West Virginia, directly across the Potomac River from eastern Allegany County. The possibility of hybrids in areas where Carolina and Black-capped Chickadees come into contact makes it difficult to define the ranges of these two species accurately.

Although Eastern populations appear stable, Maryland BBS data from 1980 through 1989 show a highly significant average annual decline of 4.9 percent. The future of the Carolina Chickadee, however, seems assured in Maryland. It can be found in even the smallest woodlots and has adapted well to suburbanization.

Robert F. Ringler

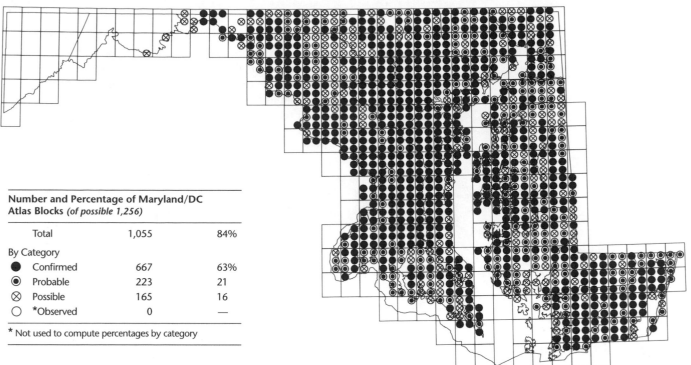

Number and Percentage of Maryland/DC Atlas Blocks (of possible 1,256)

Total	1,055	84%
By Category		
● Confirmed	667	63%
◉ Probable	223	21
⊗ Possible	165	16
○ *Observed	0	—

* Not used to compute percentages by category

Atlas Distribution, 1983–1987

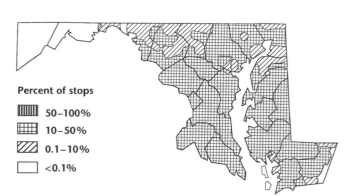

Percent of stops

▦	50–100%
▦	10–50%
▨	0.1–10%
☐	<0.1%

Relative Abundance, 1982–1989

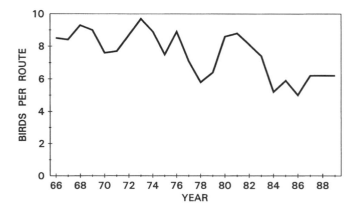

Breeding Distribution, 1958

The Carolina Chickadee is common throughout the eastern half of Maryland. Fewer were found in marsh blocks and in part of the Upper Chesapeake Section, including the urban areas of east Baltimore. Numbers decrease rapidly toward the edge of its range in the west.

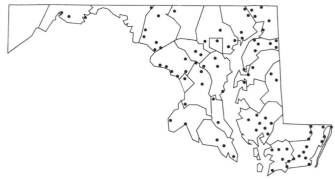

Maryland BBS Trend Graph, 1966–1989

Tufted Titmouse

Parus bicolor

The Tufted Titmouse is a permanent resident throughout Maryland but is most easily found in the central part of the state. Robbins et al. (1989a) reported that it is most frequently encountered in extensive, tall, upland deciduous forest with a closed canopy. The highest breeding density in Maryland, 42 territorial males per 100 acres (40.5 ha), was recorded in oak-beech mixed-hardwood forest in Charles County (Klimkiewicz 1974a).

Primarily a southern species, the Tufted Titmouse has gradually expanded its range northward. Although rare in Massachusetts in the nineteenth and early twentieth centuries (Forbush 1929), it now breeds well into Vermont (Nichols 1985) and southern Maine (Adamus 1988). Historically the Tufted Titmouse was extremely abundant (Coues and Prentiss 1862, 1883), to very common (Richmond 1888) in DC, and common in Maryland (Kirkwood 1895). Hampe and Kolb (1947) and Fletcher et al. (1956) noted a scarcity of breeding records. The disparity between its perceived abundance and the number of older nest records may be attributable to its nesting in high cavities and its secretiveness during nest building. Preble (1900) did not find it in Garrett County, but Brooks (1936) considered it a common permanent resident there. Stewart and Robbins (1958) described it as uncommon in the Allegheny Mountain Section, fairly common in the Ridge and Valley Section, and common elsewhere. BBS data from 1966 through 1989 show stable populations in the Eastern Region and an indication of an increase in Maryland.

Breeding activity begins in early spring with courtship feeding of the female by the male; this continues during nest building and incubation (Brackbill 1949). The male defends a limited territory in the immediate vicinity of the nest, which is in a decayed or woodpecker-excavated cavity or, occasionally, in a nest box. The nest is composed of moss, dead leaves, dry grass, and bark strips, lined with hair, fur, and bits of cloth (Bent 1946). According to Wayne (1910), nests in South Carolina invariably include a snakeskin, in the manner of the Great Crested Flycatcher. Pieces of snakeskin have been found in approximately 50 percent of 65 nests in nest boxes (D. Dupree, pers. comm.). Mark Wallace (pers. comm.) found pieces in 3 of 10 nests, but L. Zeleny (pers. comm.) did not find snakeskins in the dozen nests he examined. The hair used in the nest is a virtual necessity, however, and is often taken from a variety of live mammals, including humans (Bent 1946). Heights of 31 Maryland nests in natural cavities (MNRF) range from 3 to 75 ft (0.9–23 m), with a mean of 17.7 ft (5.4 m). Heights for 35 nests in artificial structures range from 3.5 to 30 ft (1.1–9.1 m), with a mean of 6.6 ft (2.0 m).

During the egg-laying period, the female covers the incomplete clutch with the nest lining when she leaves the nest (Brackbill 1970). Extreme egg dates in Maryland are 14 April and 7 July, with the peak period in mid-May (MNRF). Clutch sizes in 23 Maryland nests range from 3 to 7, with a mean of 5.7. Incubation is solely by the female and averages 13 days (Brackbill 1970). The incubating female is a close sitter, often refusing to leave a nest box even after it has been opened. When disturbed during incubation, she produces a snakelike hiss intended to frighten predators (Laskey 1957). In 44 nests with young (MNRF), dates range from 26 April to 17 July, with the peak in mid- to late May. Brood sizes in 38 Maryland nests range from 1 to 7, with a mean of 4.7. Both adults feed the nestlings, and fledging takes place in 17 or 18 days (Brackbill 1970). Cooke (1929) recorded recently fledged young on 3 August, as did Kirkwood on 4 August (1895), which led Cooke to conclude that more than one brood is raised. This seems to be the exception rather than the rule. Brackbill (1970) reported the Tufted Titmouse produces a single brood in the Baltimore area: two broods, although rare, may be attempted. The average annual survival rate in a PWRC population was 54 percent (Karr et al. 1990). In spring and summer, Tufted Titmice feed primarily on insects, with caterpillars forming more than half the diet (Martin et al. 1951). Acorns, beech nuts, and wild fruits are the staples in fall and winter. This species is a rare victim of the Brown-headed Cowbird (Friedmann 1929, 1963). There are no records in Maryland.

Tufted Titmice were widespread throughout Maryland and DC during the Atlas period. They frequently feed at woodland edges, where courtship feeding and begging young were easily observed. The majority of "confirmed" records were of fledged young. Despite widespread destruction of woodland habitat in the eastern half of the state, the Tufted Titmouse has adapted to wooded urban and suburban settings. As a cavity-nesting species, it shares the threat of nest-site loss with at least a dozen other species. Managers, planners, and owners of public and private lands must become aware of the value of dead and dying trees in the forest ecosystem, and of the absolute necessity for protecting them.

Joanne K. Solem

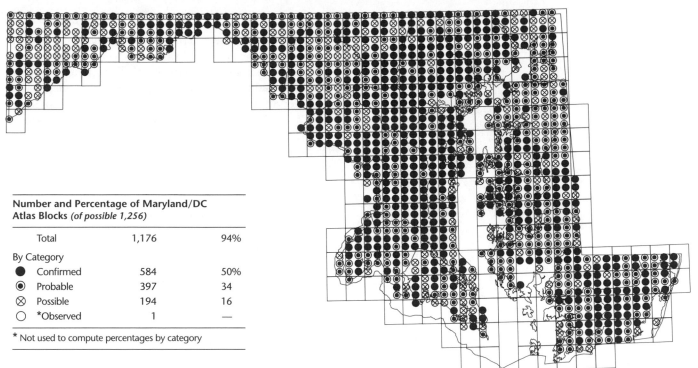

Atlas Distribution, 1983–1987

Number and Percentage of Maryland/DC Atlas Blocks *(of possible 1,256)*		
Total	1,176	94%
By Category		
● Confirmed	584	50%
◉ Probable	397	34
⊗ Possible	194	16
○ *Observed	1	—

* Not used to compute percentages by category

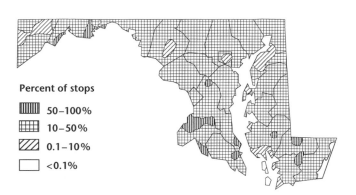

Percent of stops

▥	50–100%
▦	10–50%
▨	0.1–10%
☐	<0.1%

Relative Abundance, 1982–1989

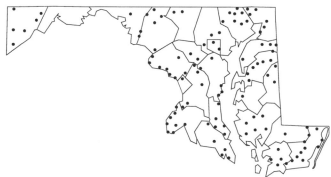

Breeding Distribution, 1958

The Tufted Titmouse is common throughout Maryland with scattered pockets of low density in some marsh and urban areas. There are a few small random areas of higher numbers.

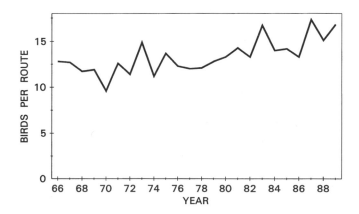

Maryland BBS Trend Graph, 1966–1989

Red-breasted Nuthatch

Sitta canadensis

The Red-breasted Nuthatch has long been assumed to breed in the mountains of Garrett County, but without definite evidence. It inhabits coniferous forests, especially spruce, but is also found in hemlocks and pines. Early authors recognized the irregular nature of its occurrence, noting that it was common in some winters and nearly absent in others (Kirkwood 1895). The normal spring migration period is from mid-March to early May, and the normal fall migration is from early September to early November (Stewart and Robbins 1958).

The first summer record for the state came from Preble (1900), who observed a family group near Bittinger in Garrett County in late June 1899. The next report was on 4 June 1919, when J. Sommer found a singing male along the Youghiogheny River in Garrett County (Stewart and Robbins 1958). Brooks (1937) reported Red-breasted Nuthatches nesting in the same locality but cited no details. He also reported seeing one in the Cranesville Swamp, also in Garrett County, in June 1932. More remarkable is the report of one to three birds seen from 27 June to 22 July 1961 at Camp Shadowbrook in Cecil County (Robbins 1961). This area is largely a serpentine pine barren, and, despite the low elevation, nesting may have occurred. A single bird was found on 22 July 1943 in Prince George's County (Stewart et al. 1952). In the 1960s and 1970s there were scattered reports of summer birds in Garrett County (R. Ringler, pers. comm.), but with no evidence of nesting. In the mid-1970s, a pair of Red-breasted Nuthatches summered near Laurel, Prince George's County, visiting the feeders of J. Sheppard (K. Klimkiewicz, pers. comm.). BBS data from 1966 through 1989 for the Eastern Region show a highly significant average annual increase of 2.2 percent; this species has not been recorded on Maryland BBS routes.

Although Red-breasted Nuthatches feed primarily in conifers, they nest in cavities in both dead and living coniferous or deciduous trees (Tyler 1948b). The great majority of Ontario nests were in mixed woods, with poplars and birches selected much more frequently than conifers for nest sites (Peck and James 1987). Most nests were near the tops of dead tree stubs, and cavity entrances invariably had conifer pitch applied around them. The nest cavity is typically 5 to 40 ft (1.5–12 m) above ground, although heights up to 120 ft (37 m) have been reported (Tyler 1948b). The female incubates the clutch of 4 to 7 eggs for 12 days, and the young fledge 14 to 21 days after hatching. The male feeds the incubating female (Kilham 1973). The number of broods raised is not known, nor is the breeding season in Maryland. In New York, egg dates range from late April to mid-June, and nestling dates from mid-May to mid-July (Bull 1974). This species' diet is varied, consisting almost entirely of insects such as beetles, ants, bees, wasps, and sawflies during the breeding season; seeds of conifers are added in winter (Knight 1908; McAtee 1926). The only known instance of Brown-headed Cowbird parasitism was human assisted: After the entrance hole to a nest cavity had been enlarged to permit inspection of a nest in Saskatchewan, a Brown-headed Cowbird egg was laid in the nest (Houston and Street 1959).

In the 1950s and 1960s, Golden-crowned Kinglets and Red-breasted Nuthatches began expanding southward from their breeding stronghold in the Adirondack Mountains of New York, taking advantage of maturing spruce plantations planted during the 1930s (Andrle 1971). They spread through southern New York; by the early 1980s they had spread through southern Pennsylvania (Brauning 1992). At Maryland's latitude, the Red-breasted Nuthatch is normally considered a bird of high elevations. Maryland's records indicate it is restricted more by the absence of northern conifers than by the elevation.

During the Atlas period, Red-breasted Nuthatches were found at four locations in Garrett County, in a single block in Allegany County, in two blocks in Carroll County along the border with Pennsylvania, and in a Virginia pine stand in Prince George's County. In the summer of 1983, Atlas fieldworkers in Carroll County found several pairs in spruce trees at the Hanover Watershed, which straddles the Maryland-Pennsylvania line. In July of that year a juvenile was observed, but only in the Pennsylvania portion of the block. Nesting was not confirmed for Maryland until after completion of Atlas fieldwork. On 28 April 1990, D. and M. Harvey (pers. comm.) observed a pair excavating in a dead tree near Finzel in Garrett County, the first definitive evidence of nesting in this state.

The precise status of Red-breasted Nuthatches in Maryland is unknown. They almost certainly have bred more frequently in Garrett County than records indicate and may nest regularly in small numbers. Reports from lower elevations suggest that breeding may occur, at least rarely, in other parts of the state. It is important to preserve existing stands of spruce as well as dead and dying trees to provide nest sites.

Eirik A. T. Blom

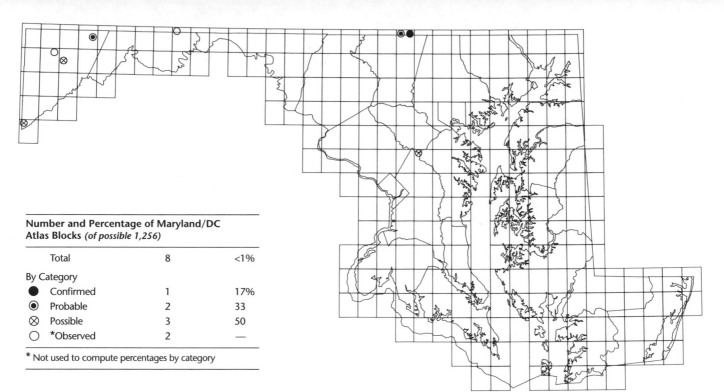

Number and Percentage of Maryland/DC Atlas Blocks (of possible 1,256)

	Total	8	<1%
By Category			
●	Confirmed	1	17%
◉	Probable	2	33
⊗	Possible	3	50
○	*Observed	2	—

* Not used to compute percentages by category

Atlas Distribution, 1983–1987

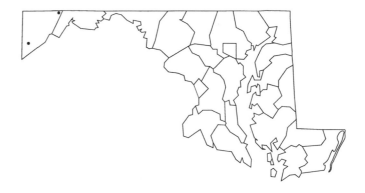

Breeding Distribution, 1958

White-breasted Nuthatch

Sitta carolinensis

The White-breasted Nuthatch moves head first down tree trunks with the air of a bird that marches to its own drumbeat. Its name comes from its habit of using its beak to hack or *hatch* soft-shelled nuts to open them (Allen 1929). Acorns, beechnuts, sunflower seeds, and grain comprise much of its winter diet; insects, especially beetles, ants, and caterpillars, are eaten in the summer (Martin et al. 1951).

Maryland has both wintering and resident populations of White-breasted Nuthatches (Stewart and Robbins 1958). Although the transient and wintering populations vary considerably from year to year, White-breasted Nuthatches are usually fairly common, at least locally, in all sections during the nonbreeding seasons. Spring migrants are seen from early March to mid-April, and fall migrants from early October to early November (Stewart and Robbins 1958).

The historical status of the White-breasted Nuthatch in Maryland is uncertain. Coues and Prentiss (1862, 1883) called it an abundant permanent resident in DC, but Richmond (1888) referred to it as rare five years later. Hampe and Kolb (1947) noted that numbers in the Baltimore area fluctuated considerably from year to year. Stewart and Robbins (1958) described its breeding status as fairly common in the Allegheny Mountain and Piedmont sections; uncommon in the Ridge and Valley Section; rare or absent in the Upper Chesapeake Section; and fairly common locally in the Eastern and Western Shore sections, most common along the Pocomoke River and in east-central Prince George's County.

Extensive tall deciduous forest is its preferred habitat (Robbins et al. 1989a). The highest breeding density for Maryland is 9 territorial males per 100 acres (40.5 ha) in moist tulip tree–red maple upland forest in Howard County in 1989 (Robbins 1990a). In Maryland, the nesting territory for one pair in a residential area was approximately 32 acres (12.9 ha) (Brackbill 1969b). A study in New York by Butts (1931) defined territory sizes ranging from 25 to 48 acres (10.1–19.4 ha).

Although White-breasted Nuthatches may appear virtually identical in plumage, Kilham (1972) was able to track individual females by subtle differences in head pattern. He noted that the species' close pair bond and varied courtship are unusual for birds of the northern hemisphere; the pair bond may be permanent (Brackbill 1969b).

The nest is typically in a natural cavity, in either deciduous or coniferous woodland (Tyler 1948a). Heights above the ground for 23 Maryland nests (MNRF) range from 4 to 40 ft (1.2–12 m), with a mean of 21 ft (6.4 m); two nests were in nest boxes. White-breasted Nuthatches often choose relatively large cavities for nesting and roosting, with entrances double or triple the size of their bodies (Kilham 1971). The nest cavity is lined with feathers, hair, fur, bark strips, and leaves (Allen 1929).

Nest excavation has been observed in Maryland as early as 25 March (MNRF). Nests with eggs have been found from 7 April to 20 May, with a peak in mid-April. Clutch sizes of five nests (MNRF) range from 5 to 8. Incubation, performed by the female, lasts 12 days (Stokes and Stokes 1983). Nests with young have been reported in Maryland from 30 April to 17 June, with a peak in mid-May (MNRF). Kirkwood (1895) saw young just out of the nest in Baltimore County as late as 26 July. Brood sizes for five nests (MNRF) range from 2 to 8. Young fledge about 14 days after hatching and are tended by both parents for another two weeks (Tyler 1948a). One brood is attempted per year (Forbush 1929). The average annual survival rate in a PWRC population was 35 percent (Karr et al. 1990). White-breasted Nuthatches are rarely victimized by Brown-headed Cowbirds. Friedmann (1929, 1963) listed only five instances; 1 of 25 Ontario nests (4%) was parasitized (Peck and James 1983). There are no records of parasitism in Maryland.

Atlas results show the White-breasted Nuthatch is widely distributed west of the Fall Line, where it was found in almost every block. On the Western Shore the distribution thins toward the south, except for the concentration of records in the Greensand District of Prince George's County, and in the deciduous woodlands along the Patuxent and Potomac rivers. On the Eastern Shore, records are scattered except for the concentration in the Pocomoke River drainage. This distribution is very close to that mapped by Stewart and Robbins (1958), although they had no summer records for Kent, Queen Anne's, Caroline, or Talbot counties. "Confirmed" records were not easily obtained, with fledged young and food for young most frequently reported in this category.

BBS data from 1966 through 1989 show highly significant average annual increases in the Eastern Region (1.7%) and Maryland (2.7%). The White-breasted Nuthatch shows a marked preference for natural cavities in old-growth trees (Brewster 1906), although it will use nest boxes on occasion. To maintain this species in Maryland, large dead and dying trees must be preserved wherever possible, especially in mature forests in stream valleys.

Joanne K. Solem

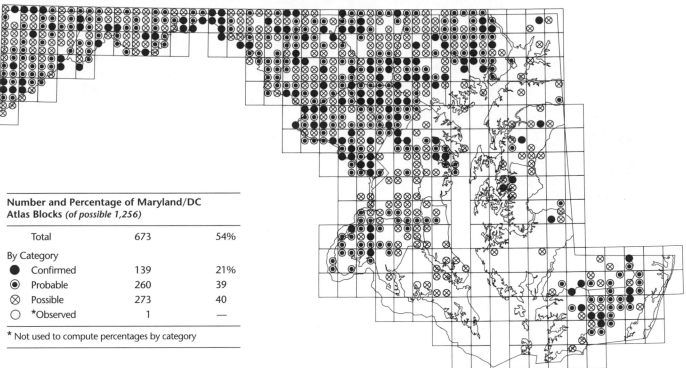

Atlas Distribution, 1983–1987

Number and Percentage of Maryland/DC Atlas Blocks *(of possible 1,256)*		
Total	673	54%
By Category		
● Confirmed	139	21%
◉ Probable	260	39
⊗ Possible	273	40
○ *Observed	1	—

* Not used to compute percentages by category

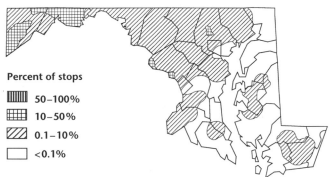

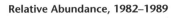

Percent of stops

▦	50–100%
▦	10–50%
▨	0.1–10%
☐	<0.1%

Relative Abundance, 1982–1989

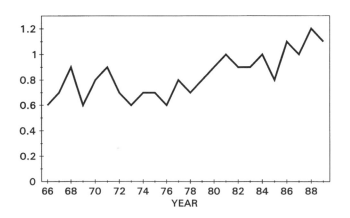

Breeding Distribution, 1958

The White-breasted Nuthatch is most common in the woodlands of Allegany and southern Garrett counties. On the Coastal Plain it occurs in woodlands along rivers, especially the Potomac, Patuxent, and Pocomoke, and in the mature deciduous woodlots of Talbot County.

Maryland BBS Trend Graph, 1966–1989

Brown-headed Nuthatch

Sitta pusilla

The gregarious little Brown-headed Nuthatch is a characteristic inhabitant of loblolly pine forests in the southern portion of Maryland's Coastal Plain. Its dependence on loblolly pine is readily apparent when one compares the bird's distribution with a map of forest types (e.g., Brown and Brown 1972), for its range coincides with that of the loblolly–Virginia pine forest type. The Brown-headed Nuthatch is a permanent resident, with bands of 6 to 20 birds wandering over a large area all year, except during the breeding season, when pairs establish smaller individual territories (Pough 1946).

Kirkwood (1895) first recorded Brown-headed Nuthatches nesting in Maryland, a pair building a nest on the rather late date of 28 May 1892 in Queen Anne's County. Jackson (1941) reported them in small numbers in pine woods along the rivers in the Cambridge area in Dorchester County. Stewart and Robbins (1958) described them as common in tidewater areas of the lower Eastern Shore, fairly common in southern St. Mary's County, and uncommon and local in tidewater areas of Queen Anne's County and southern Calvert County.

The Brown-headed Nuthatch nests in open stands of loblolly or other long-leaved pines, especially in clearings or burned areas that contain rotting stumps suitable for nest holes (Bent 1948). The pair excavates the nest cavity, with the male doing most of the work. Over 50 percent of the nest consists of pine seed wings; the rest is composed of various materials such as cotton, feathers, wool, caterpillar silk, pine needles, and strips of bark. Nest heights range from 0.5 to 90 ft (0.2–27 m); most reported heights are under 10 ft (3.0 m). The nest is usually placed in a rotting stump or post (Bent 1948; Norris 1958). The cavity averages 7 in. (18 cm) deep with an entrance hole 1.5 to 2 in. (4–5 cm) in diameter.

Most Maryland nests were in loblolly pine, but one was in a bird box (MNRF). Heights of 15 Maryland nests range from 10 to 40 ft (3.0–12 m), with a mean of 16.5 ft (5.0 m). One nest was in a nest box at 6 ft (1.8 m). Eggs have been recorded in Maryland from 15 April (Stewart and Robbins 1958) to 7 May (Jackson 1941). There are only four Maryland nests (MNRF) with clutch sizes: one with 6, two with 5, and one with 4 eggs. Nestlings have been reported in Maryland from 2 May to 9 July. Brood size in the two Maryland nests was 4. Fledged young have been observed with adults from 4 June through 10 August. Friedmann (1929, 1963) listed the Brown-headed Nuthatch as free from Brown-headed Cowbird parasitism because it nests in cavities with small entrance holes; there are no Maryland records of parasitism.

The following information is from Georgia (Norris 1958). The area immediately around the nest site is defended primarily by the male, who sings and chases away other males. A larger territory, occupied by both adults and their offspring throughout the year, includes both nesting and feeding areas. Territory sizes range from 5 to 10 acres (2.0–4.0 ha). Clutch sizes range from 3 to 9, most commonly 5. One brood per year is typical. Incubation, primarily by the female, lasts 14 days. The male joins her in the cavity at night. Both parents feed the nestlings, although only the female broods them. Fledging occurs 18 or 19 days after hatching, and both parents feed the fledglings for another 24 days. Of the nesting pairs studied, 17 percent were accompanied by a young male, who helped feed the nestlings and fledglings. In summer, Brown-headed Nuthatches eat mostly insects and spiders collected from the trunks, branches, and leafy twigs of pines (Norris 1958). Occasionally they pick food from the ground or even obtain it by flycatching. In winter they feed mostly on pine seeds.

Atlas results show that the Brown-headed Nuthatch has lost some ground in Calvert and St. Mary's counties since Stewart and Robbins (1958) mapped its range north to Piney Point on the Potomac River and to the southern tip of Calvert County on the Chesapeake Bay. During the Atlas period, it was recorded on the Western Shore only at the southern tip of St. Mary's County at Point Lookout State Park, Ridge and Kitts Point, and Piney Point. This retreat may be the result of housing developments and logging that have eliminated or fragmented what were once extensive stands of loblolly pine. Since August 1989, however, B. Millsap (pers. comm.) has seen them throughout the year at his feeder near Drum Point, Calvert County. On the Eastern Shore the range has remained stable and may have expanded slightly into the interior of Somerset, Worcester, and Wicomico counties. Maryland BBS data show a stable population from 1966 through 1989; however, there is a significant average annual decline of 2.2 percent in the Eastern Region.

As long as there are extensive stands of loblolly pine containing suitable nesting cavities, we can expect this species to remain in Maryland.

Ernest J. Willoughby

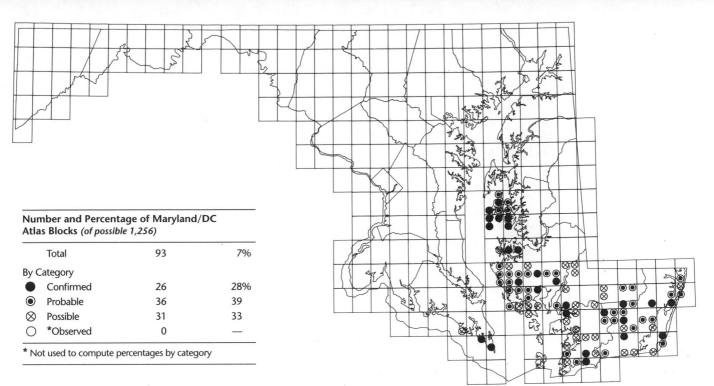

Number and Percentage of Maryland/DC Atlas Blocks *(of possible 1,256)*

Total	93	7%
By Category		
● Confirmed	26	28%
◉ Probable	36	39
⊗ Possible	31	33
○ *Observed	0	—

* Not used to compute percentages by category

Atlas Distribution, 1983–1987

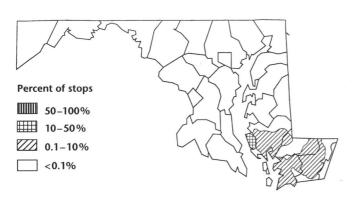

Percent of stops

▦ 50–100%
▦ 10–50%
▨ 0.1–10%
☐ <0.1%

Relative Abundance, 1982–1989

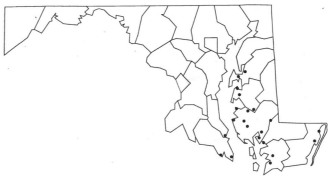

Breeding Distribution, 1958

The Brown-headed Nuthatch was found throughout most of the lower Eastern Shore, with a small pocket of higher abundance in western Dorchester County. It was not detected on miniroutes in the other parts of its breeding range, where it is locally distributed.

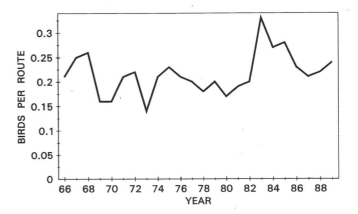

Maryland BBS Trend Graph, 1966–1989

Brown Creeper

Certhia americana

The familiar tree-climbing Brown Creeper is one of America's most inconspicuous songbirds. Its song is faint and its single high-pitched call note may escape detection. It is easily recognized, however, by its diagnostic behavior of propping itself with its relatively long, stiff tail as it climbs ever upward, probing bark crevices in search of insects and spiders.

Until recent decades the Brown Creeper was considered only a migrant and winter resident in Maryland, occurring from late September to late April (Stewart and Robbins 1958). The first summer record for the state was of a female that Preble (1900) collected at Bittinger in Garrett County on 28 June 1899, but he failed to observe whether the bird was in breeding condition. Brooks (1936) recorded a Brown Creeper during the nesting season in the West Virginia portion of Cranesville Swamp, leading Stewart and Robbins (1958) to list it as a possible breeder in Maryland's Allegheny Mountain Section. They considered three summer records farther east to be vagrants: 2 June 1944 at PWRC; 22 July 1949 at Pikesville, Baltimore County; and 3 August 1953 at Gibson Island, Anne Arundel County. In the light of recent breeding records, these probably were nesting birds occupying previously unrecognized low-elevation nest sites. The AOU (1957) listed the southern breeding limit as "through the mountains to south-central Pennsylvania (Crumb, Somerset County, Harrisburg) and western Maryland (Bittinger)."

The first confirmed breeding for Maryland was from Meadow Mountain in the Bittinger area of Garrett County on 14 June 1958, when participants on an MOS field trip saw a pair of Brown Creepers with two young (Fletcher and Fletcher 1959). Since 1961, one or more pairs have been found each summer at PWRC, where Van Velzen (1967) discovered the first Maryland nest on 8 June 1964, at an elevation of only 65 ft (20 m) above sea level. In the next two summers, P. and D. Bystrak found Brown Creepers at sea level in June and July in the Pocomoke Swamp at Shad Landing State Park, Worcester County (Van Velzen 1967), and on 17 June 1966, D. Simonson recorded the first summer observation for DC (Scott and Cutler 1966). Hall (1969) described the expansion of the breeding range in the Middle Atlantic states during the 1960s. BBS data from 1966 through 1989 show stable populations in the Eastern Region; there are too few data to estimate a trend for Maryland.

This species' critical habitat requirement for nesting is dead trees with loosely attached bark, under which it can conceal its nest. Such habitat is created when water is backed up by road crossings, dikes, or beaver dams, or when trees are killed by forest fires, gypsy moths, or disease. The nesting season in Maryland is still poorly defined. Nest building has been noted as early as 29 March at Seneca in Montgomery County (MNRF), but no Maryland egg dates have been reported. Egg data can be summarized from New York records, where 33 egg dates were from 5 May to 18 July, with 17 records from 19 May to 11 June (Tyler 1948c). Young in Maryland nests have been noted from 8 to 15 June at PWRC; the earliest date for fledged young remains 14 June on Meadow Mountain (Van Velzen 1967).

Davis (1978) summarized nesting habits from 20 Michigan nests. Heights above the ground or water range from 5.2 to 23 ft (1.6–7.0 m), with a mean of 10.2 ft (3.1 m). Diameter at breast height for 20 nest trees range from 6 to 22 in. (15–56 cm), with a mean of 9.9 in. (25 cm). The nest is placed under loose bark and is attached to the rough inner surface by binding twigs, bark, and bark scale with spider egg cases and insect cocoons. Nest construction, incubation, and brooding were exclusively by the female; the male feeds the incubating female. Nesting territories ranged from 5.7 to 15.8 acres (2.3–6.4 ha). The most frequent clutch size was 6, with a range of 4 to 7; incubation averaged 15 days. Fecal sacs were not dropped but were slapped on the trunk of another tree. Both parents feed the nestlings, and fledging occurs in 15 or 16 days. There were no renesting attempts after a successful effort. The Brown Creeper is a rare victim of the Brown-headed Cowbird; Davis (1978) reported that 1 of 20 Michigan nests (5.0%) was parasitized. There are no other confirmed records of parasitism (Friedmann 1929, 1963, 1971; Terrill 1961; Peck and James 1987).

It is for specialized, secretive species such as the Brown Creeper that the Atlas project sometimes yielded dramatic results. Brown Creepers were found in DC and in 19 of the 23 Maryland counties. Observations range from sea level along the Pocomoke River and its tributaries to 2,625 ft (800 m) in Garrett County. The largest numbers of Atlas records are from the western half of Garrett County and the central Pocomoke and Nassawango Creek area. Most other records are from the valleys of the Potomac, Patuxent, and Pocomoke rivers and their tributaries. There is a scattering of

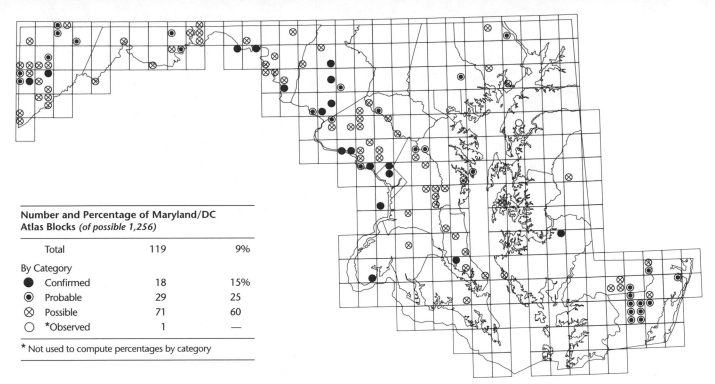

**Number and Percentage of Maryland/DC
Atlas Blocks** *(of possible 1,256)*

Total	119	9%
By Category		
● Confirmed	18	15%
◉ Probable	29	25
⊗ Possible	71	60
○ *Observed	1	—

* Not used to compute percentages by category

Atlas Distribution, 1983–1987

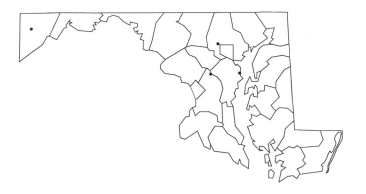

Breeding Distribution, 1958

sightings from elsewhere on the Eastern Shore, and only one or two records each from Howard and Baltimore counties.

Dead trees that still retain much of their bark are essential for nesting Brown Creepers. Probably no other nesting bird in Maryland is so dependent on dead trees. Large dead trees in forested habitat should be allowed to stand at least until most of the bark is gone.

Chandler S. Robbins

Carolina Wren

Thryothorus ludovicianus

With its tail tilted at a jaunty angle, the Carolina Wren moves busily through the brush and brambles, merrily singing one of the 27 to 41 songs in its repertoire (Morton 1982). Its ringing song is familiar in suburban areas throughout most of Maryland, and its ready tolerance of humans makes this species one of the state's better known birds.

The Carolina Wren was historically a permanent resident in DC and Maryland (Coues and Prentiss 1862, 1883; Kirkwood 1895). It is found throughout Maryland at all elevations, although 90 years ago Eifrig (1904) found it common only in the lower elevations of western Maryland. Stewart and Robbins (1958) described it as common in the Eastern and Western Shore sections; fairly common in the Upper Chesapeake, Piedmont, and Ridge and Valley sections; and rare in the Allegheny Mountain Section. This wren is very susceptible to widespread winter mortality (Stewart and Robbins 1958) during periods when the ground is covered by snow and the vegetation is covered with ice for long periods. Snow cover precludes foraging in leaf litter, and ice and deep snow cover berries. Following the severe winter of 1976–77 (Robbins 1977a), seasonal reports in *Maryland Birdlife* reflected a severe drop in Carolina Wren populations (Ringler 1977, 1978a, 1979a), especially in Garrett County where it completely disappeared until the mid-1980s. Periodic winter mortality has been documented as long ago as 1918 (Cooke 1929). This winter mortality, especially in the northern part of the Carolina Wren range and at high elevations in the south, can be extreme (Bent 1948). Several mild winters may be necessary before the population recovers. BBS data from 1966 through 1989 show dramatic increases before and after the sudden decline in 1977 in Maryland and the Eastern Region. Maryland data from 1980 through 1989 show a highly significant increase of 9.9 percent per year.

Although its preferred habitats are undergrowth near water, fallen treetops, or brushy hedges, Carolina Wrens are of-

ten found in suburban areas (Bent 1948). The highest breeding density reported from Maryland is 72 territorial males per 100 acres (40.5 ha) in mixed-hardwood forest in Calvert County (Fales 1974). Carolina Wrens sometimes use manmade nest boxes as well as old hornet nests, mailboxes, hats, pockets of clothes left hanging outside, and many other unlikely places (Bent 1948). The bulky nest, built by both sexes, is usually dome-shaped unless it is built in a cavity. It is made of plant material and lined with fine grasses, rootlets, hair, and feathers.

The mean height of 170 Maryland nests (MNRF) is 5.4 ft (1.6 m), with a range of 0 to 30 ft (0.0–9.1 m). Nest building has been recorded as early as 22 March in Baltimore County (Stewart and Robbins 1958). The earliest of 100 Maryland egg dates is 4 April and the latest 13 September, with peaks in late April, May, and mid-July (MNRF). A pair of Carolina Wrens usually has at least two broods a year, sometimes three (Bent 1948). Clutch sizes range from 1 to 7, with a mean of 4.3 (MNRF). The eggs are white to pale pink, often with heavy brown spots concentrated at the large end. The female incubates the eggs for 12 to 14 days (Bent 1948).

In 115 records of nests with young (MNRF), brood sizes range from 1 to 6, with a mean of 3.9. Nests with young were found as early as 15 April and as late as 26 September, with peaks in mid-May and late July (MNRF). Both parents tend the young while they are in the nest and may do so after the brood fledges at 12 to 14 days of age (Bent 1948). The female may leave the care of one set of fledglings to the male while she starts the next nest (Lansdowne and Livingston 1970). Their diet consists largely of insects, mostly ants, bees, and wasps, supplemented in winter by berries of poison ivy and bayberry (Martin et al. 1951). The Carolina Wren is a very rare victim of Brown-headed Cowbird parasitism (Friedmann 1929, 1963). There are no records from Maryland and few known instances of Carolina Wrens successfully fledging young cowbirds (Luther 1974).

Carolina Wrens were found in almost all Atlas blocks, but they were recorded less frequently in the Allegheny Mountain Section. Pennsylvania (Brauning 1992) showed similar patterns of occurrence with few, if any, sightings in mountainous areas or in the northern part of the state. The Virginia distribution was similar to that of Maryland, both reflecting this species' vulnerability to harsh winter weather. More than 40 percent of the "confirmed" reports were of fledged young; nests with young, and adults carrying food for young, comprised most of the additional records in this category. Because Carolina Wrens are so vocal, it is not surprising that most "probable" records were of territorial behavior.

Preservation of the Carolina Wren in Maryland seems assured, although we can expect periodic changes in the population after severe winters with prolonged periods of deep snow or ice cover.

Emily D. Joyce

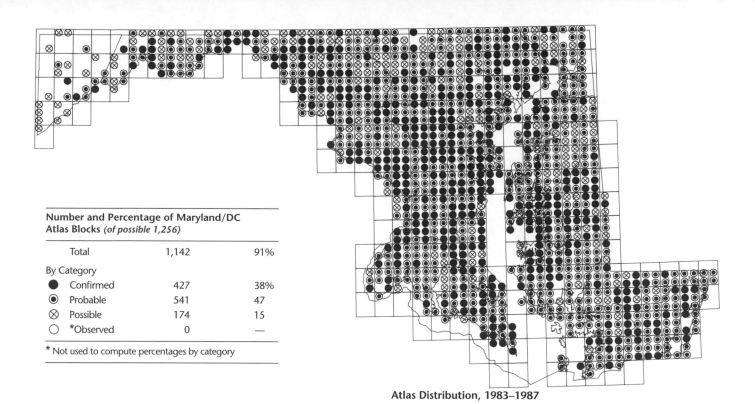

Number and Percentage of Maryland/DC Atlas Blocks *(of possible 1,256)*

Total	1,142	91%
By Category		
● Confirmed	427	38%
◉ Probable	541	47
⊗ Possible	174	15
○ *Observed	0	—

* Not used to compute percentages by category

Atlas Distribution, 1983–1987

Percent of stops

▥	50–100%
▦	10–50%
▨	0.1–10%
☐	<0.1%

Relative Abundance, 1982–1989

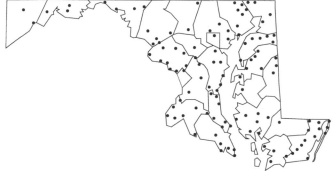

Breeding Distribution, 1958

The greatest abundance of Carolina Wrens is on the lower Eastern Shore, with numbers decreasing to the north and west. They were not detected in northern Garrett County in the Allegheny Mountain Section.

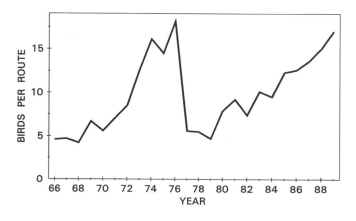

Maryland BBS Trend Graph, 1966–1989

Carolina Wren   269

Bewick's Wren

Thryomanes bewickii

The Bewick's Wren, once a common breeding bird in western Maryland, may no longer nest in the state. This species has declined dramatically throughout the eastern portion of its range. It is now considered threatened or endangered in most states east of the Mississippi River, including Maryland, where the DNR classifies it as endangered. Causes for the decline are not known, but there is considerable speculation. There is also evidence of a rapid decline in recent years; cold winters may have been a contributing factor (Robbins et al. 1986). Birds of the Appalachian race, *T. b. altus,* historically wintered from Ohio and Pennsylvania south to northeastern Texas, the Gulf Coast, and northern Florida (Aldrich 1944). Recent records for Maryland are scarce. The normal migration period for Maryland was from late March to early May in the spring, and from early September to mid-November in the fall (Stewart and Robbins 1958).

According to Eifrig (1904), the Bewick's Wren was a common breeding bird throughout Garrett and Allegany counties at the beginning of the twentieth century. Elsewhere in the state it was a rare and irregular breeder and migrant (Kirkwood 1895). Stewart and Robbins (1958) called it fairly common in the western portion of the Ridge and Valley Section, uncommon in the Allegheny Mountain Section and the eastern part of the Ridge and Valley Section, and casual in the Piedmont Section. It was considered rare or casual in migration and in winter east of the Ridge and Valley Section. Declines were suspected by the 1960s; yet R. Rowlett found 25 birds in eastern Allegany and western Washington counties from 4 to 11 June 1972, including a nest with young on 8 June (Robbins 1972).

The only "confirmed" Atlas record was acquired prior to the start of the statewide Atlas but during the county atlas efforts that were incorporated into the database. Daniel Boone (pers. comm.) found a nesting pair in Blair's Valley in Washington County in May 1976, and the birds were present at least through 1979. At Dan's Rock in Allegany County, where Bewick's Wrens have been more consistent than at any other location in recent decades, M. Hoffman observed two fledglings on 6 June 1980 (Ringler 1980b). There has been no evidence of breeding in Maryland since then, although a bird was photographed by R. Johnson (pers. obs.) at Dan's Rock in May 1988. This is the last known report for Maryland. Hall (1983) noted that, although the Bewick's Wren was once the common dooryard wren throughout West Virginia, it can be relied on only just east of the Allegheny Divide and only in very small numbers. He noted that the decline coincided with the explosive invasion of the House Wren into West Virginia; he commented that some authors have argued that the two events may be related. Gill (1985) wrote that the Bewick's Wren was once common in southwestern Pennsylvania but had apparently disappeared by 1985. Bewick's Wrens are unsuccessful competitors with House Wrens (Gill 1985). Alsop (1980) and Hall (1983) stated, however, that Bewick's Wrens have also declined in places where House Wrens are not numerous and that they began to disappear from some areas before House Wrens were well established. BBS data from 1966 through 1989 show a highly significant average annual decline of 7.7 percent in the Eastern Region. The Bewick's Wren has not been recorded on a Maryland BBS route since 1976.

Specific information about the breeding biology of the Bewick's Wren in Maryland is scarce. Its favorite breeding habitat in the east is wooded edges and thickets, especially around houses, barns, and other buildings. Hall (1983) noted that "the more junk in the form of old rusting farm machinery, old automobile bodies, piles of fence wire, etc., there is in the farmyard the more likely there will be a Bewick's Wren nesting there." The nest is placed in natural cavities, in brush piles, and in a startling variety of abandoned artificial objects (Terres 1980). Nest heights range from 0 to 25 ft (0–7.6 m) (Simmons 1925; Bent 1948). In Maryland, nests with eggs have been found from 30 April to 26 June and nests with young from 12 May to 13 July (Stewart and Robbins 1958). Clutch sizes vary from 4 to 11 eggs, with 5 to 7 most common (Bent 1948). The female incubates for 12 to 14 days, and the young fledge 14 days after hatching. Bewick's Wrens, like other cavity-nesting species, are rare hosts to the Brown-headed Cowbird (Friedmann 1963), and there is no record of parasitism in Maryland. Their diet consists of about 97 percent insects and spiders (Terres 1980).

A few Bewick's Wrens may still breed in Maryland, especially in eastern Allegany County where, according to Atlas data, House Wrens are scarce. While searching for Bachman's Sparrows in clearcuts in Tennessee during 1987, observers found numerous Bewick's Wrens (Robinson 1989); this is an area from which Bewick's Wrens were thought to have largely disappeared. Similar searches in Maryland should be undertaken immediately, especially within the historic range, to determine if this species still breeds in Maryland. Suspected breeding sites should be reported to the DNR and protected from intrusion.

Eirik A. T. Blom

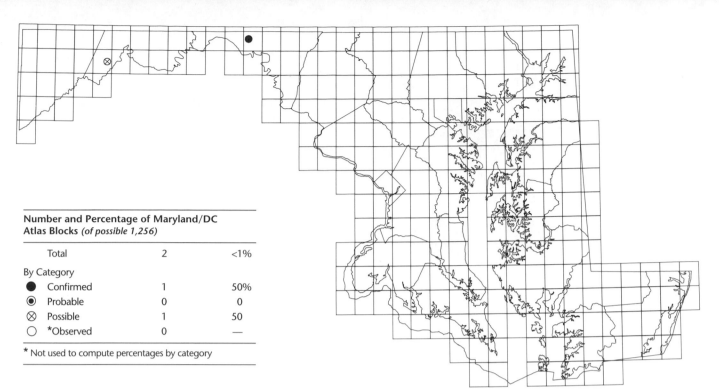

Number and Percentage of Maryland/DC Atlas Blocks (of possible 1,256)

Total	2	<1%

By Category

●	Confirmed	1	50%
◉	Probable	0	0
⊗	Possible	1	50
○	*Observed	0	—

* Not used to compute percentages by category

Atlas Distribution, 1983–1987

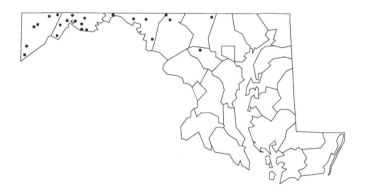

Breeding Distribution, 1958

House Wren

Troglodytes aedon

An avian dynamo with an incessant and effervescent song, the House Wren has long been a favorite of backyard bird enthusiasts. It nests throughout Maryland but is least common on the Eastern Shore and in southern Maryland. Spring migrants return from their wintering grounds in the southeastern United States and Mexico (AOU 1983) in mid-April; most birds depart by mid-October (Robbins and Bystrak 1977). A few overwinter on the lower Eastern Shore (Stewart and Robbins 1958).

Although there have probably been population changes over the past 100 years, most early authors considered the House Wren a very common to abundant summer resident in DC and Maryland (Coues and Prentiss 1862, 1883; Kirkwood 1895; Eifrig 1904; Cooke 1929; Hampe and Kolb 1947). Stewart and Robbins (1958) gave its breeding status as common in all sections.

Although it originally preferred open woodland and edge habitats, this wren adapted remarkably well to human alteration of the environment (Gross 1948a). It commonly nests in buildings, fence posts, gourds, and nest boxes and frequently attacks the nests of other birds living nearby, pecking the eggs and removing nest material (Belle-Isles and Picman 1986a). This behavior has led to speculation that the House Wren may be involved in the decline of Bewick's Wrens in the East (Monroe 1955; Hall 1983).

The breeding season in Maryland is from late April to late August (MNRF). The nest, placed in a cavity, is constructed of fine grasses, hair, and twigs (Gross 1948a); House Wrens also build dummy nests in addition to the one used for nesting. Heights above ground of 362 Maryland nests (MNRF) range from 1 to 35 ft (0.3–11 m), with a mean of 6.5 ft (2.0 m). Most nests were in nest boxes or other artificial structures. In 19 nests in natural cavities, heights range from 3 to 20 ft (0.9–6.1 m), with a mean of 8.8 ft (2.7 m). Heights of 278 nests in nest boxes and gourds range from 2 to 25 ft (0.6–7.6 m), with a mean of 6.3 ft (1.9 m). The remaining 65 nests were in a wide variety of artificial structures, such as pipes, sheds, and porches; the heights range from 1 to 25 ft (3.0–7.6 m), with a mean of 6.6 ft (2.0 m).

The earliest Maryland egg date is 18 April (a nest from which two young fledged on 7 May); the next earliest date is 3 May, and the latest 16 August (MNRF). Typically two broods are raised, with breeding peaks in late May and mid-July. Clutch sizes in 200 Maryland nests (MNRF) range from 2 to 8, with a mean of 5.4. Incubation, performed principally by the female, lasts about 13 days (Gross 1948a). Brood dates in Maryland range from 30 April to 2 September (MNRF), with peak periods in mid-June and late July. In 162 Maryland nests, brood sizes range from 1 to 8 (mean of 4.9). Friedmann (1963) knew of only six instances of Brown-headed Cowbird parasitism, none from Maryland. In Ontario, 4 of 1,120 nests (0.4%) were parasitized (Peck and James 1987). Beal et al. (1916) found that bugs were the most important food (29%), followed by grasshoppers, crickets, and locusts (18%); moths and caterpillars (14%); and beetles (14%).

Atlas results show House Wrens breeding throughout Maryland, although less widespread on the Eastern Shore and in southern part of the state. Nesting in Somerset and Worcester counties is confined largely to marsh edges, where natural cavities abound; a few birds use nest boxes in residential areas. More than 25 percent of "confirmed" records were of eggs or young in the nest, reflecting this wren's habit of using nest boxes and gourds, which are easily seen. Kendeigh (1963) demonstrated a relationship between daily temperature and photoperiod for the development of breeding condition in House Wrens. He showed that, in southern parts of the range, smaller and less successful clutches were laid. House Wrens, which in Maryland are near the southeastern edge of their breeding range (AOU 1983), may be limited by the high average daily temperatures in May in the eastern and southern parts of the state.

BBS data from 1966 through 1989 show stable populations in Maryland. Continental data show a highly significant average annual increase of 1.4 percent, which may be attributable to the number of nest boxes erected during the past 30 years. Not only are more cavities available, but a study in Ontario (Belles-Isles and Picman 1986b) showed that nests placed in areas of sparse vegetation were about ten times as likely to be successful as nests placed in heavily vegetated areas. In this study, the principal cause of nest failure was predation; the authors speculated that predation risk is reduced for nests in open areas because predators are not able to sneak up on nests. Most nest boxes are placed in open, lightly vegetated areas.

The success of the House Wren as a breeding species in Maryland seems assured.

Delos C. Dupree

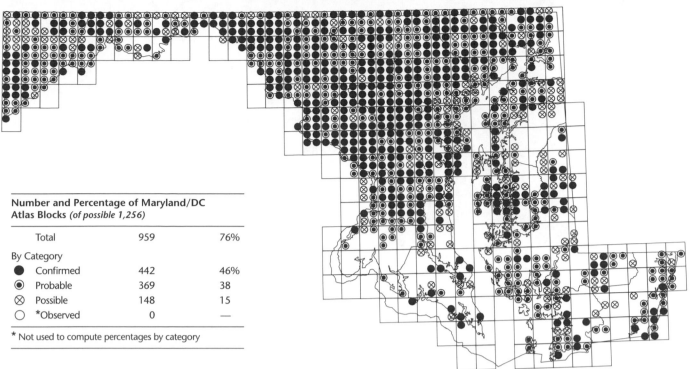

Number and Percentage of Maryland/DC Atlas Blocks *(of possible 1,256)*

Total	959	76%
By Category		
● Confirmed	442	46%
◉ Probable	369	38
⊗ Possible	148	15
○ *Observed	0	—

* Not used to compute percentages by category

Atlas Distribution, 1983–1987

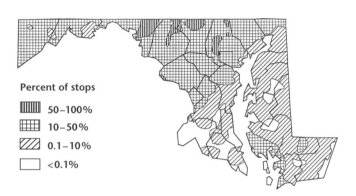

Percent of stops

||||| 50–100%

⊞ 10–50%

▨ 0.1–10%

☐ <0.1%

Relative Abundance, 1982–1989

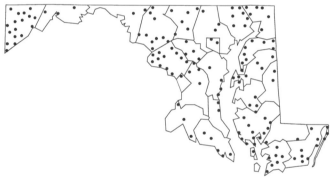

Breeding Distribution, 1958

The House Wren is common in western Maryland and decreases to the east. It is abundant in parts of the eastern Ridge and Valley and northern Piedmont sections. It is generally scarce on the Coastal Plain except at marsh edges and in Salisbury on the lower Eastern Shore.

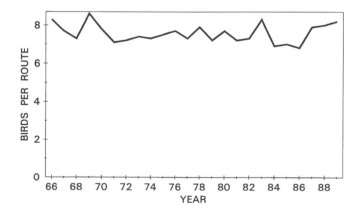

Maryland BBS Trend Graph, 1966–1989

Winter Wren

Troglodytes troglodytes

A certain element of mystery and paradox attends the tiny Winter Wren. In the United States, it is uncommon and secretive, and, until quite recently, its breeding status in Maryland was uncertain. Of the state's 201 breeding species, it is, next to the Northern Raven and Horned Lark, the most cosmopolitan native passerine. It nests on four continents in a range that spans North America from the Aleutians to Newfoundland; Iceland, the British Isles, and the rest of Europe; parts of northern Africa and the Middle East; and Asia as far south as Korea, Taiwan, and southern Japan (Heinzel et al. 1972; Terres 1980; Cramp 1988). Although mouselike in dimensions and movements, it has a mighty voice and is easily the state's loudest singer for its size.

Most Maryland birders know the Winter Wren as a migrant and occasional winter resident. It occurs in all sections of the state from mid-September to mid-May (Robbins and Bystrak 1977). As a wintering species it favors swamp and floodplain forests or moist, wooded uplands; it is locally common on the Eastern Shore, especially along the Pocomoke River and its tributaries, and becomes progressively less common to the west (Stewart and Robbins 1958). Its diet consists largely of insects and spiders, including ants, beetles, bugs, dragonflies, and caterpillars (Forbush 1929).

Winter Wrens have long been confirmed as breeders in both Pennsylvania (Brauning 1992) and Virginia, where large sections of suitable habitat exist. In Maryland, the Winter Wren's only viable breeding habitat occurs in Garrett County. Since statewide bird records first appeared in the late 1800s, confirmation of the Winter Wren as a breeding species has been thwarted by lack of suitable evidence. Eifrig's (1915) summer encounter with a "small colony" of Winter Wrens in a spruce, hemlock, and rhododendron habitat between Bittinger and Accident was, although interesting in light of scarce prior data, merely a brush with singing males. Behr's (1914) report simply stated, without

documentation, that the Winter Wren bred in Garrett County. From that date until the completion of Atlas fieldwork in 1987, breeding evidence consisted either of sightings in suitable habitat within safe dates or the presence of singing males.

The expected Winter Wren breeding season in Maryland would be at least one to two weeks earlier than in New York, where Bull (1974) reported egg dates from 22 May to 7 July and nestlings from 3 June to 4 August. Brown-headed Cowbird parasitism has not been recorded in this species (Friedmann 1963; Peck and James 1987). Specific knowledge of the species' breeding habits in Maryland was regrettably meager until the summer of 1990, when the breeding of Winter Wrens in Maryland was finally confirmed. Edward Thompson (pers. comm.), a biologist with the Maryland Natural Heritage Program, found and photographed a nest with two eggs on 7 June, in a region of sandstone outcroppings near Loch Lynn, southeast of Oakland. The eggs rested in a moss-covered cup along a recessed sandstone ledge, well inside a sizable rock overhang. The clutch was probably incomplete, as 4 to 7 eggs is usual (Bent 1948). Nearby vegetation consisted mainly of red maple, white oak, and black cherry. Six weeks later, on 19 July, at an elevation of about 3,000 ft (914 m) on Backbone Mountain, he also heard two singing males and observed one very close to a nest built in the narrow opening of a rock crevice, again on a sandstone outcropping. No eggs were found, but the nest was worked with fresh moss; two more nests were found, in similar locations, within 150 ft (46 m) of the first. Although male Winter Wrens often build one to four dummy nests (Terres 1980), the proximity of two singing males to these three nests seems significant. This site was at a higher elevation than the first; however, the vegetation was also largely northern hardwoods, with yellow birch and American mountain ash predominating.

Discovery of these nests will facilitate further data collection in the seasons ahead, which may confirm the Winter Wren's fondness for overhangs, narrow ledges, and rock crevices in Maryland sandstone outcroppings; at one time such sites as tree roots and stumps in coniferous forests (Harrison 1975) might have been considered more worthy of scrutiny.

Atlas fieldworkers reported 15 Winter Wren records: 6 "probable" and 9 "possible." There was also an odd incident in which a singing male was observed on 9 June 1979 in Gwynn Falls Park in Baltimore City, far from the normal breeding range (Ringler 1979b). BBS data from 1966 through 1989 show sharp declines in Winter Wren numbers following severe winters, but the Eastern Region populations have recovered from the severe winters of 1976–77 and 1977–78 and are stable. Maryland's breeding population is too low to estimate a state trend. Additional study is needed to determine the habitat requirements and population status of Winter Wrens in Maryland.

Jack Wennerstrom

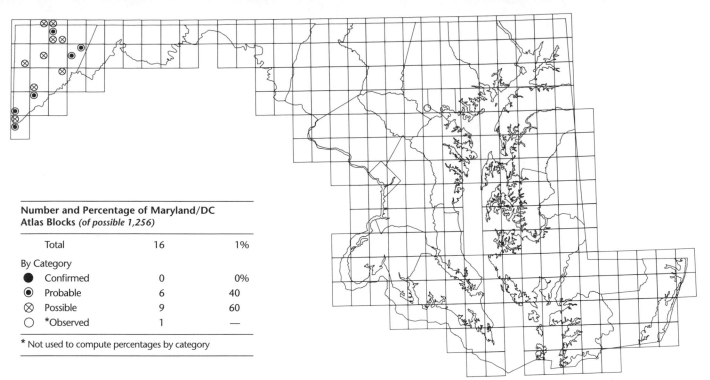

Number and Percentage of Maryland/DC Atlas Blocks (of possible 1,256)

Total		16	1%
By Category			
●	Confirmed	0	0%
◉	Probable	6	40
⊗	Possible	9	60
○	*Observed	1	—

* Not used to compute percentages by category

Atlas Distribution, 1983–1987

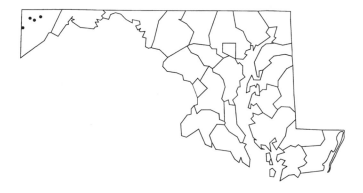

Breeding Distribution, 1958

Sedge Wren
Cistothorus platensis

The Sedge Wren's highly opportunistic breeding behavior makes determination of the exact breeding status at any particular site difficult. These wrens show little site fidelity and often shift locations from year to year, sometimes even within years (Stewart et al. 1952). Sedge Wrens, formerly known as Short-billed Marsh Wrens, winter in the southeastern United States (AOU 1983). Birds may arrive on the breeding grounds any time between mid-May and mid-July, so the presence of singing males is not evidence that nesting is being attempted. Migration in Maryland occurs throughout May and from late September to mid-November (Stewart and Robbins 1958).

Maryland is at the southeastern edge of the Sedge Wren's breeding range (AOU 1983). Kirkwood (1895) thought the Sedge Wren was very rare. This sentiment was echoed by Cooke (1929) and by Hampe and Kolb (1947), who thought it bred only in the DC area and southern Maryland. Up to that time, little fieldwork had been done in the Eastern Shore marshes. Stewart and Robbins (1947a) reported it as a fairly common breeding bird in the Chesapeake Bay marshes on the Eastern Shore. They also cited records from Anne Arundel, St. Mary's, and Garrett counties. A decade later, Stewart and Robbins (1958) described its breeding status as common in the tidal areas of Somerset, Wicomico, and Dorchester counties, uncommon in tidewater areas elsewhere in the Eastern Shore and Western Shore sections and in the Allegheny Mountain Section, and rare and irregular elsewhere in the state.

Compared with the closely related Marsh Wren, the Sedge Wren prefers the drier portions of marshes, damp meadows, and sedge meadows (Burns 1982). It is occasionally found in wetter marshes dominated by Olney's bulrush and saltmeadow cordgrass (Stewart and Robbins 1958; Burns 1982). The highest reported Maryland breeding density is 10 territorial males per 100 acres (40.5 ha) in a switchgrass marshmeadow in Somerset County (Springer and Stewart 1948a).

The first confirmed breeding record for Maryland was at Point Lookout in St. Mary's County on 25 June 1935, when Wetmore (1935) collected a nest with eggs; he estimated that half a dozen pairs were present. Nests without eggs were found in DC on 26 May, 15 June (Ball and Wallace 1936), and 25 June 1935 (Ulke 1935) and in Somerset County on 20 June 1952 (Stewart and Robbins 1958). There are Maryland clutches of 6, 7, and 7 eggs and brood sizes of 5 and 6 (MNRF). A late nest found at Elliott Island, Dorchester County, on 12 July 1958 by A. and B. Meanley contained 6 eggs (MNRF). On 13 September 1896, F. Kirkwood saw a young bird begging food from an adult in Baltimore County (Stewart and Robbins 1958).

The following breeding information is taken from Burns's (1982) study of nesting birds in Minnesota. Like Marsh Wrens, male Sedge Wrens build an average of at least seven dummy nests per bird. The nest is a ball of grass woven to standing vegetation, usually with a well-hidden side entrance. Nests are normally close to the ground but occasionally are found as high as 2 ft (0.6 m) (Bent 1948). Burns (1982) showed that territory size varies dramatically and depends on habitat, breeding density, and timing within the breeding cycle. Nest building was observed from mid-May to mid-August. Double-brooding and polygynous breeding are both fairly common. Some males had two mates; polygyny in Sedge Wrens can be as high as 19 percent (Crawford 1977). Burns (1982) discovered that primary females and first nests had significantly larger clutch sizes and a higher fledging success than did secondary females and second clutches. For monogamous females, clutch sizes averaged 7.0 for 5 first clutches and 5.7 for 8 later clutches. Polygynous males, however, produced more young per season than did monogamous males. Incubation, by the female, lasts 12 to 14 days; young fledge 12 to 14 days after hatching and are fed by both adults (Bent 1948). There are no reported cases of Brown-headed Cowbird parasitism of the Sedge Wren (Friedmann 1929, 1963, 1971). Its diet consists almost entirely of insects and spiders. Howell (1932) examined the stomachs of 34 Sedge Wrens and found ants, bugs, weevils, ladybug beetles, moths, caterpillars, locusts, crickets, and grasshoppers.

The true status of the Sedge Wren in Maryland remains unknown. Early observers may simply have overlooked them or failed to visit the nesting range within the state. At the middle of the twentieth century, the Sedge Wren was a locally common breeding bird in tidewater Maryland (Stewart and Robbins 1958). Atlas fieldwork resulted in only 12 records, none "confirmed." It appears certain that many of those birds failed to breed, because almost all reports involved singing males that could not be relocated subsequently. Safe dates may be meaningless for a species that is so irregular in its time of arrival at a nesting site.

Although BBS data from 1966 through 1989 show stable populations in the Eastern Region, the Sedge Wren may be on the verge of disappearing from Maryland as a breeding bird. It is listed by the DNR as a species in need of conser-

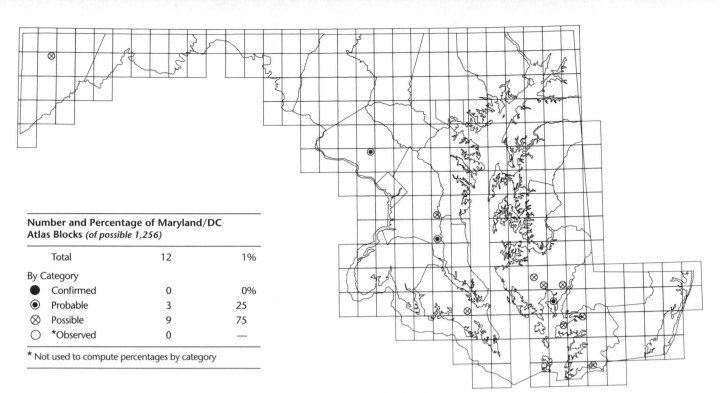

Number and Percentage of Maryland/DC Atlas Blocks *(of possible 1,256)*

Total	12	1%
By Category		
● Confirmed	0	0%
◉ Probable	3	25
⊗ Possible	9	75
○ *Observed	0	—

* Not used to compute percentages by category

Atlas Distribution, 1983–1987

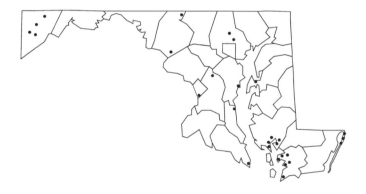

Breeding Distribution, 1958

vation. No explanation for the decline has been suggested. An immediate survey is needed to determine the status of the Sedge Wren in Maryland. Until then, the preservation of large wet meadows and extensive areas of switchgrass is required.

Eirik A. T. Blom

Marsh Wren

Cistothorus palustris

The dry, rattling, sewing-machine-like song of the Marsh Wren signals its presence in the tall marsh vegetation. This busy little denizen of the tidewater marshes returns to Maryland in mid-April (Robbins and Bystrak 1977) from its wintering grounds in the southern United States and central Mexico (AOU 1983). Fall migrants usually depart by late October, but a few winter in the marshes of the lower Chesapeake Bay (Stewart and Robbins 1958). Although it was formerly known as the Long-billed Marsh Wren (AOU 1983), the shorter name better befits the size of the bird.

Although the Marsh Wren's habitat is locally distributed in Maryland, this wren was historically considered abundant where marshes occurred. Kirkwood (1895) found it to be a common summer resident in the marshes of tidewater Maryland. Coues and Prentiss (1862, 1883) considered it abundant in the marshes along the Potomac River. Later authors agreed (Cooke 1929; Fletcher et al. 1956). Stewart and Robbins (1958) described it as abundant in the tidewater areas of the Eastern Shore, Western Shore, and Upper Chesapeake sections. BBS data from 1966 through 1989 show stable populations in the Eastern Region; there are too few data to estimate a reliable trend for Maryland, although the population appears to be declining.

Prime breeding habitat is needlerush marsh, as shown by a density of 104 territorial males per 100 acres (40.5 ha) in this vegetation in Somerset County in 1948 (Springer and Stewart 1948a). Other nesting habitats include saltmeadow cordgrass, smooth cordgrass, cattail, and big cordgrass (Stewart and Robbins 1958). Beetles and flies rank highest in the Marsh Wren diet, which consists almost entirely of insects (Bent 1948).

The song of the Marsh Wren echoes across the marshes not only during the day but also at night, making it the mockingbird of the marshes (Bent 1948). The night song continues throughout the breeding season regardless of environmental conditions or moon phases (Barclay et al. 1985). One reason suggested for night singing was that blackbirds chase the wrens low into the vegetation during the day, thereby suppressing daytime territorial activity. Marsh Wrens and marsh-nesting blackbirds have an adversarial relationship, often destroying each other's eggs and nestlings (Ehrlich et al. 1988). Marsh Wrens also attack eggs and nestlings of other Marsh Wrens (Picman 1984).

The male builds about four or five courting nests in the center of his territory (Verner 1965). He tries to attract a mate by flying up about 15 ft (4.6 m) and then fluttering down as he sings (Stokes and Stokes 1983). The female inspects his nests and may choose one as a breeding site or may start a new nest. Her role in building the dome-shaped nest of wet cattails, reeds, and grasses is to line it with cattail down, feathers, and fine plant material after the male has completed the exterior. The other nests are often used by adults for roosting, by fledglings for shelter after the breeding nest has been abandoned, and, occasionally, by wintering birds (Verner 1965).

Heights of 149 Maryland nests (MNRF) range from 1 to 6 ft (0.3–1.8 m) above water, with a mean of 2.9 ft (0.9 m). The earliest Maryland egg date is 3 May, the latest 17 August; peaks in mid-June and in mid- to late July (MNRF) indicate two broods. Clutch sizes in 190 Maryland nests range from 1 to 6, with a mean of 4.1. The female incubates the eggs, which hatch in about 13 days (MNRF). In 1951, E. Willis studied 42 nests at Strawberry Point near Middle River in Baltimore County; he estimated that 13 of these 42 nests (30.9%) fledged young. Nests with young have been found in Maryland from 5 June to 26 August, with a peak in early July. Brood sizes in 13 Maryland nests (MNRF) range from 1 to 5, with a mean of 3.3. Both parents feed the young, which fledge at 14 to 16 days. Marsh Wrens are often polygynous (Verner 1962, 1965). Verner showed that the male, after acquiring a mate and at about the time laying begins, will shift to another part of his territory, build new courting nests, and try to attract another mate. This timing allows him to assist with feeding the first brood before he is needed to help with the second, since he does not incubate. There is no record of Brown-headed Cowbird parasitism of Marsh Wrens (Friedmann 1963, 1971; Peck and James 1987).

Atlas results show Marsh Wrens clustered in the tidal marshes of the Eastern Shore, Western Shore, and Upper Chesapeake sections. They are especially widespread in the extensive marshes of Dorchester and Somerset counties and along tidal portions of the Patuxent and Choptank rivers. Owing to the highly vocal nature of this wren and the relative inaccessibility of its nests, almost 54 percent of the Atlas records are "probable," based primarily on territorial behavior.

Preservation of marsh habitat is the key to the well-being of the Marsh Wren. Support of strong wetlands legislation and the enforcement of this legislation is essential.

Emily D. Joyce

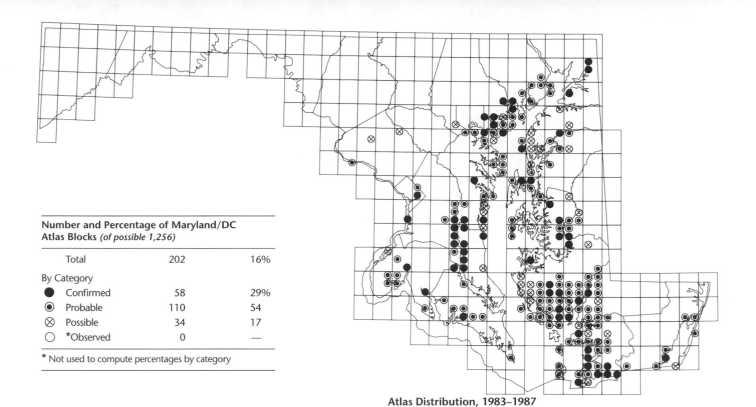

Number and Percentage of Maryland/DC Atlas Blocks (of possible 1,256)

Total	202	16%
By Category		
● Confirmed	58	29%
◉ Probable	110	54
⊗ Possible	34	17
○ *Observed	0	—

* Not used to compute percentages by category

Atlas Distribution, 1983–1987

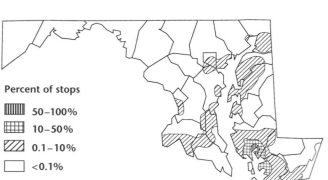

Percent of stops

▥	50–100%
▦	10–50%
▨	0.1–10%
☐	<0.1%

Relative Abundance, 1982–1989

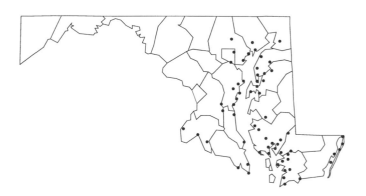

Breeding Distribution, 1958

The Marsh Wren is uncommon in Coastal Plain marshes, with a small area of higher abundance in the extensive tidal marshes of Dorchester, Somerset, and Wicomico counties. Miniroutes provide incomplete sampling of marsh habitats; consequently, birds in many breeding areas not close to roads were missed.

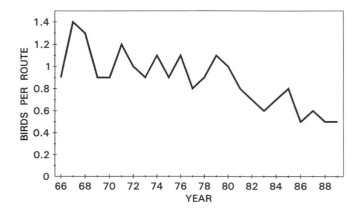

Maryland BBS Trend Graph, 1966–1989

PJM

Golden-crowned Kinglet

Regulus satrapa

The Golden-crowned Kinglet, one of the smallest passerines in North America, is an active, engaging inhabitant of northern coniferous, usually spruce, forests. It is an uncommon and local breeding bird in Maryland and a fairly common to common wintering bird over much of the state (Stewart and Robbins 1958). Migrants from the north begin arriving in early October and leave by mid-April (Stewart and Robbins 1958).

Kirkwood (1895), who knew the Golden-crowned Kinglet only as a migrant, noted its irregular occurrence in Maryland, reporting that it was common in some winters and nearly absent in others. In western Maryland, where the bird may have bred before much of the state's native spruce forest was logged, Eifrig (1904) had several summer records but no evidence of breeding. Behr (1914) reported that it bred near Jennings in Garrett County around the beginning of the twentieth century, but he provided no evidence. Stewart and Robbins (1958) described the breeding range as confined to several localities in Garrett County, although the only confirmation they had was their sighting of fledglings on 6 July 1945. Boone (1982) described the first observation of a Maryland nest. On 13 May 1982, D. Boone discovered a nest near Rock Lodge in central Garrett County. A month later, on 23 June 1982, J. E. and J. K. Boone watched a nest under construction in nearby New Germany State Park. It was 10 ft (3.0 m) up in a 60-ft (18 m) Norway spruce. The female was incubating seven eggs on 1 July, and on 29 July there were seven young. The nest was empty on 6 August, but the young were feeding actively nearby. Reports in *Maryland Birdlife* reflect that, in subsequent years, Golden-crowned Kinglets have been heard regularly during the summer at Garrett County locations.

The nesting cycle of the Golden-crowned Kinglet typically occurs in the high reaches of tall spruce trees. The small, globular nests most often are found 30 to 50 ft (9.1–15

m) above the ground, although some have been found as low as 4 ft (1.2 m) and as high as 64 ft (20 m) (Terres 1980; Galati and Galati 1985). Given the smallness of this species and its nest, the altitude of its home life, and the inconspicuousness of its song, it is not surprising that we know little of its breeding biology. Bull (1974) reported that the breeding season in New York extends from 28 May (eggs) to 25 July (nestlings). As two broods are regularly attempted (Galati and Galati 1985), the breeding season in Maryland probably starts slightly earlier. Clutch sizes range from 5 to 11 and are most commonly 8 or 9; incubation, performed by the female, lasts 14 to 15 days. The young fledge 14 to 19 days after hatching and are fed by both parents (Galati and Galati 1985). The Golden-crowned Kinglet diet consists almost entirely of insects and their eggs, which are gleaned from clumps of pine needles, picked from tree bark, and captured by active flycatching (Terres 1980). They consume some sap. The Golden-crowned Kinglet is a rare host of the Brown-headed Cowbird, with only six records, none from Maryland (Friedmann et al. 1977).

Although this species has apparently bred in western Maryland for over 100 years, it has increased in recent decades. Andrle (1971) showed how it spread into lowland areas of New York during the 1960s as spruce plantations established during the 1930s matured. He speculated that altitude is not a limiting factor as long as old spruce trees are available for breeding. The Pennsylvania atlas results show that the southward expansion at low altitudes has continued (Brauning 1992).

Two birds were heard singing in spruces in Carroll County, Maryland, adjacent to the Pennsylvania border on 28 June 1981 (Ringler 1981c). That area, part of the Hanover Watershed, has extensive stands of planted spruce. No other birds were reported that year. In July 1983, fledged young were found in both Maryland and Pennsylvania in the Hanover Watershed in an Atlas block that straddles the border. By the summer of 1985, at least 40 birds were present in the block. Although the population has varied considerably since then, Golden-crowned Kinglets bred annually. Continued expansion of the breeding range at low elevations should be anticipated. BBS data from 1966 through 1989 show a significant average annual increase of 3.3 percent for the Eastern Region; there are too few data to estimate a trend for Maryland. The thinness of this bird's song makes detection difficult. Also, the ability to detect a trend is hampered by drastic population changes, such as occurred following the particularly bitter winter of 1976–77 (Robbins et al. 1986).

Golden-crowned Kinglets seem to be expanding their breeding range and numbers in Maryland. Protection of existing spruce forests and plantations, as well as continued efforts to reestablish native red spruce in Garrett County, should provide adequate habitat for years to come.

Eirik A. T. Blom

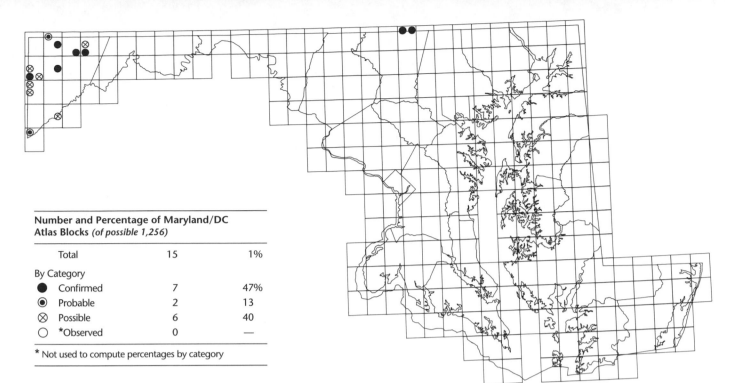

Atlas Distribution, 1983–1987

Number and Percentage of Maryland/DC Atlas Blocks *(of possible 1,256)*

		Total	15	1%
By Category				
●	Confirmed		7	47%
◉	Probable		2	13
⊗	Possible		6	40
○	*Observed		0	—

* Not used to compute percentages by category

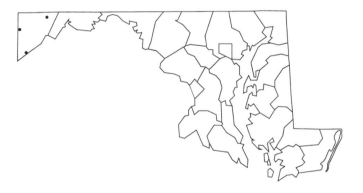

Breeding Distribution, 1958

Blue-gray Gnatcatcher

Polioptila caerulea

The Blue-gray Gnatcatcher is a tiny, active, tail-twitching sprite. Its high, thin, wheezy call is given repeatedly as it flits through treetops or brush. Spring migrants return from their southeastern U.S. and Caribbean wintering grounds (AOU 1983) in early April, and most depart by late September (Stewart and Robbins 1958).

Coues and Prentiss (1883) wrote that the Blue-gray Gnatcatcher was a common summer resident in DC, although it seemed to be less so than in previous years, indicating a decline since their 1862 publication. Kirkwood (1895) called it fairly common in restricted localities, but Eifrig (1904) wrote that it was very rare in western Maryland, where he had only two spring records. Brooks (1936) called it surprisingly common at some places in Garrett County, suggesting an increase since the beginning of the twentieth century. Hampe and Kolb (1947) considered it most common in tidewater areas. Stewart and Robbins (1958) described its breeding status in Maryland as common in the Eastern Shore, Western Shore, and Upper Chesapeake sections; fairly common in the Ridge and Valley Section and along the Potomac River in the Piedmont Section; uncommon elsewhere in the Piedmont; and rare in the Allegheny Mountain Section.

The Blue-gray Gnatcatcher is a bird of open deciduous woodland, floodplain forest, brushy areas, and orchards (Stewart and Robbins 1958). It is most common in extensive forests with a high canopy (Robbins et al. 1989a). The highest breeding density reported for Maryland is 18 territorial males per 100 acres (40.5 ha) in hickory-oak-ash floodplain forest in Howard County (Robbins 1973b). Males normally arrive on the breeding grounds a few days before females and establish territories averaging 4.6 acres (1.9 ha) (Root

1969). The nest is usually built on a horizontal branch but is sometimes in the vertical crotch of a tree. In 93 Maryland records (MNRF), nest heights range from 2 to 65 ft (0.6–20 m), with a mean of 26.8 ft (8.2 m).

The nesting season in Maryland is short. Nests with eggs have been reported from 11 April to 10 June, with a peak in early May (MNRF). Two broods are typical in southern California (Root 1969), but there is no evidence of a second brood being attempted in Maryland. Clutch sizes in 22 Maryland nests (MNRF) are 4 or 5 eggs, with a mean of 4.5. Incubation, performed by both parents, lasts 13 to 15 days (Weston 1949; Root 1969). Nests with young have been reported in Maryland from 6 May to 24 June with no evident peak (MNRF). Typically, the female broods the young, but sometimes the male assists; the young fledge in 12 or 13 days (Root 1969). Brood sizes in eight Maryland nests (MNRF) range from 2 to 5. The Blue-gray Gnatcatcher is a common victim of Brown-headed Cowbird parasitism (Friedmann 1963); 4 of 22 Ontario nests (18.2%) were parasitized (Peck and James 1987), but only 2 of 32 Maryland nests (6.3%) were victimized (MNRF). Watching the frantic efforts of a pair of Blue-gray Gnatcatchers attempting to satisfy the hunger of a young Brown-headed Cowbird, it is hard to imagine they could provide enough food for a young bird many times their own size (Blom, pers. obs.). The diet of the Blue-gray Gnatcatcher consists almost entirely of insects, such as flies, gnats, ants, and beetles (Weston 1949).

During the Atlas period, Blue-gray Gnatcatchers were found throughout Maryland. Apparently, the population has expanded considerably along the Piedmont river systems and in Garrett County, where they were found in the majority of the blocks. This is a significant change from the status described by Stewart and Robbins (1958) and earlier by Eifrig (1904), although it seems to support Brooks (1936), who stated that they were locally common in the mountains. Blue-gray Gnatcatchers were slightly less widespread on the central Eastern Shore and in the broad agricultural areas of the Hagerstown and Frederick valleys in Washington, Frederick, and Carroll counties. They were absent from the more extensive marsh blocks on the lower Eastern Shore and from coastal Worcester County. The majority of "confirmed" records were of fledged young (38%) or of adults with food for young (20%). Although most "probable" records were of territorial behavior (58%), many also were the result of detecting pairs or observing agitated behavior. Blue-gray Gnatcatchers are aggressive and conspicuous defenders of their territory.

BBS data from 1966 through 1989 show stable populations in the Eastern Region and Maryland. There appears to be no immediate threat to the Blue-gray Gnatcatcher in Maryland. Protection of floodplain forests should assure a bright future for this species.

Eirik A. T. Blom

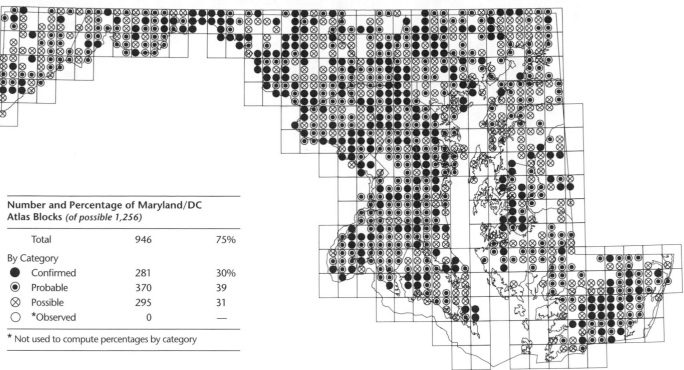

Number and Percentage of Maryland/DC Atlas Blocks *(of possible 1,256)*		
Total	946	75%
By Category		
● Confirmed	281	30%
◉ Probable	370	39
⊗ Possible	295	31
○ *Observed	0	—

* Not used to compute percentages by category

Atlas Distribution, 1983–1987

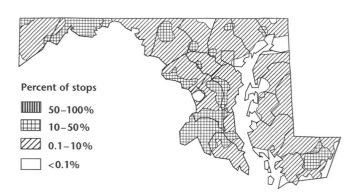

Percent of stops

▥	50–100%
▦	10–50%
▨	0.1–10%
☐	<0.1%

Relative Abundance, 1982–1989

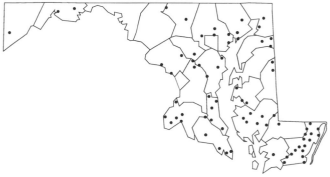

Breeding Distribution, 1958

The Blue-gray Gnatcatcher is most common and widespread in the moist woodlands of the Coastal Plain and the dry woods of the western Ridge and Valley Section. Small concentrations occur at scattered locations along rivers throughout the Piedmont. It is absent from a few urbanized and marsh blocks.

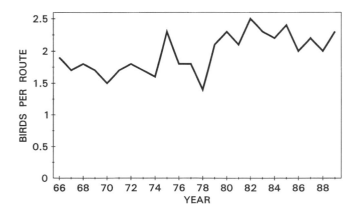

Maryland BBS Trend Graph, 1966–1989

MT

Eastern Bluebird

Sialia sialis

Since colonial times, the brilliant plumage and soft warbling song of the Eastern Bluebird have made it a favorite of both urban and rural dwellers. Once described as a very abundant permanent resident (Coues and Prentiss 1862, 1883), it has suffered severe population declines, variously attributed to diminishing winter food supply, adverse weather, insecticides, nest site and habitat loss, and competition from introduced species (Zeleny 1976). Its diet is 67 percent insects, with grasshoppers, crickets, katydids, and beetles comprising the great majority of animal food taken (Martin et al. 1951). Fleshy fruits such as berries of dogwood, Virginia creeper, blackberry, bayberry, blueberry, American holly, and poison ivy are the preferred plant items. Perched on a tree branch, telephone wire, or other vantage point, it locates its insect prey and then drops to the ground to secure it. Pastures, fallow fields, golf courses, lawns, cemeteries, newly burned areas, and other similar habitats with low vegetation provide ideal foraging habitat.

Maryland's highest breeding density is 23 territorial males per 100 acres (40.5 ha) recorded in an abandoned field saturated with nest boxes at PWRC in 1949 and 1950 (Stewart and Robbins 1958). Although Eastern Bluebirds may be found in all sections of Maryland during the breeding season, banding data indicate they may migrate farther south for the winter (Stewart and Robbins 1958). They become more local during winter and concentrate in sheltered stream valleys. Large numbers perish when snow and ice cover the berries on which they feed. As early as 1895 and again in 1912, winter storms greatly reduced their numbers (Cooke 1929). The most recent storms affecting the Maryland population occurred in the winter of 1977–78 (Sauer and Droege 1990b).

Spring migration occurs from early February to mid-April, with the peak from early March to early April (Stewart and Robbins 1958). Fall migration occurs from mid-September to mid-November; most have left by early December (Stewart and Robbins 1958). BBS data from 1966 through 1989 show a stable population in the Eastern Region and indicate an increase in Maryland; however, Maryland data from 1980 through 1989 show a highly significant average annual increase of 12.1 percent, reflecting a recovery from the harsh winters of 1976–77 and 1977–78.

Old woodpecker holes, hollows of decayed trees, and rock crevices are Eastern Bluebirds' preferred natural nest sites (Pearson 1936). In the absence of natural cavities, they readily accept artificial structures such as nest boxes, hollow gourds, fence post crevices, and flower pots. The female constructs the nest, generally of dry grass, although she may use other plant materials such as dry pine needles (Zeleny 1976).

Maryland nest heights in 62 artificial structures (MNRF) range from 3 to 9 ft (0.9–2.7 m), with a mean of 4.8 ft (1.5 m); heights in 35 natural cavities range from 2 to 30 ft (0.6–9.1 m), with a mean of 10.7 ft (3.3 m). Extreme egg dates are 12 March to 5 September (MNRF). Clutch sizes in 99 Maryland nests range from 3 to 5, with a mean of 4.3. Rarely are clutches as large as 6 or 7 (Zeleny 1976). Incubation, by the female, lasts 12 to 21 days (Pinkowski 1974). Nestling dates range from 17 April to 23 September (MNRF). Brood sizes in 55 Maryland nests range from 2 to 5 (mean of 3.8). The female broods the nestlings night and day until they are old enough to generate their own body heat. During the rest of the 17 or 18 days before fledging, she broods sporadically, depending on the weather, and stops several days before fledging (Zeleny 1976). Two broods, sometimes three, are usually attempted in Maryland. Although the Eastern Bluebird is not a common victim of the Brown-headed Cowbird, it is one of the more frequently parasitized cavity nesters (Friedmann 1929, 1963). Terrill (1961) recorded 1 of 54 Quebec nests (1.9%) parasitized; Peck and James (1987) had 4 of 3,167 Ontario nests (0.1%) affected. Although there were no instances of parasitism in 1,456 Maryland nests (MNRF), M. Wallace (pers. comm.) reported one instance in Howard County.

Atlas results emphasize the scarcity of Eastern Bluebirds in metropolitan areas, in the extensive marshes on the lower Eastern Shore, and on Assateague Island. As a result of nest box programs, Eastern Bluebirds were easy to confirm; for example, 117 of 136 quarterblocks (86%) in Howard County were confirmed. The importance of quarterblock data in rapidly developing areas is demonstrated by comparing data from Howard County ten years ago (Klimkiewicz and Solem 1978) with the present data. During this period, large tracts of farmland were subdivided into mostly 2- to 5-acre (0.8–2.0 ha) building lots, except in the Columbia area, where the lots were mostly less than 0.25 acres (0.1 ha). The transition from cropland to lawns generally proved beneficial to Eastern Bluebirds, increasing the number of blocks in which they occurred from 29 of 34 (85%) to all 34 (100%). Quarterblock coverage, however, pinpointed the absence of Eastern Bluebirds from the highly developed areas of Columbia, Elkridge, Ellicott City, and Laurel.

To maintain healthy populations of Eastern Bluebirds, we need to continue nest box programs, plant berry-producing trees and shrubs, and leave dead trees standing.

Delos C. Dupree

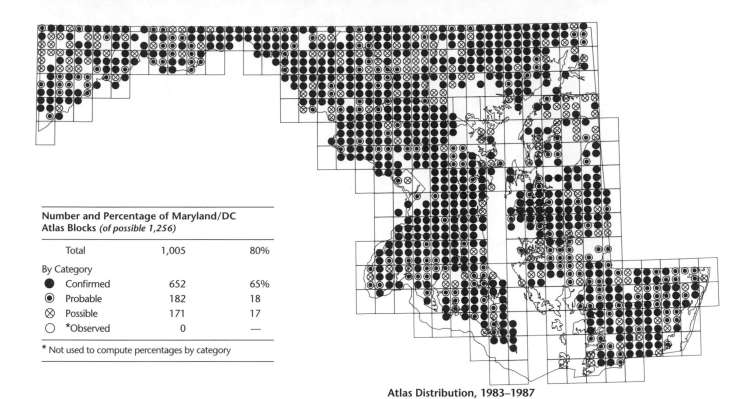

Number and Percentage of Maryland/DC Atlas Blocks *(of possible 1,256)*		
Total	1,005	80%
By Category		
● Confirmed	652	65%
◉ Probable	182	18
⊗ Possible	171	17
○ *Observed	0	—

* Not used to compute percentages by category

Atlas Distribution, 1983–1987

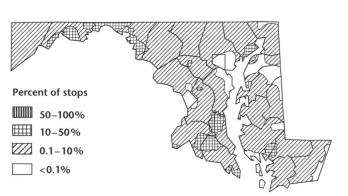

Percent of stops

▦ 50–100%
▦ 10–50%
▨ 0.1–10%
☐ <0.1%

Relative Abundance, 1982–1989

Breeding Distribution, 1958

The Eastern Bluebird is fairly evenly distributed. High densities are in southern Maryland, southern and western Washington County, and southern Allegany County. It was not recorded in the urban areas of Baltimore, Annapolis, and Washington; in southern Dorchester County marshes; or in a band across the upper Eastern Shore.

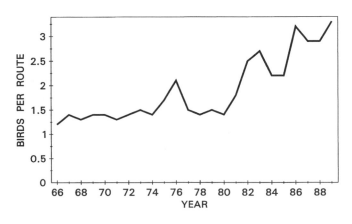

Maryland BBS Trend Graph, 1966–1989

Veery

Catharus fuscescens

The Veery is one of the few forest species that has significantly expanded its breeding range in Maryland during this century. A fairly common migrant throughout the state, the Veery formerly bred only in the Allegheny Mountain Section (Stewart and Robbins 1958). It began colonizing the eastern edge of the Piedmont in the 1940s. Today its beautiful song is heard in suitable forests from Cecil County to DC. Criswell and Briggs (1965) have plotted the arrival and increase in abundance of the Veery in three study sites in the DC area.

The first Maryland breeding record was reported in 1895 in Garrett County (Kirkwood 1895). Cooke (1929) listed the Veery as a transient in DC; the first breeding was recorded in 1942 (Halle 1948). The first breeding record for Montgomery County was in 1945. Stewart and Robbins (1958) listed records for Baltimore, Harford, and Frederick counties (Stewart and Robbins 1958). They gave its status as common in the Allegheny Mountain Section, rare in the Ridge and Valley Section, and rare and local in the Piedmont Section. The atlas project from 1971 through 1975 found the Veery widespread in eastern Montgomery and Howard counties (Klimkiewicz and Solem 1978). Thus, in less than 30 years, it colonized an extensive area of Maryland and DC along the Fall Line.

Veeries select extensive moist forests with a dense shrub layer; trees may be coniferous, deciduous, or mixed, but they must be mature and create a relatively low canopy (Robbins et al. 1989a). On the Allegheny Plateau of Garrett County, Veeries are common on the wetter slopes and in humid valleys as well as bog alder thickets, pine plantations, and hemlock groves along streams (D. Czaplak, pers. obs.). In the Piedmont, Veeries breed most abundantly in deep wet ravines but have also spread to upland forests. They arrive from their South American wintering grounds (AOU 1983) in late April; spring migration peaks in early May (Robbins and Bystrak 1977). Fall migration begins in late August and peaks by mid-September.

Veeries place their nest on or near the ground in a tangle of vines, roots, or fallen branches (Tyler 1949b). Heights from ten nests (MNRF) range from 0 to 11 ft (0–3.4 m), with a mean of 2 ft (0.6 m). Extreme egg dates are 5 May and 26 June; clutch sizes of eight nests (MNRF) range from 2 to 4. Incubation, by the female, requires 10 to 12 days (Tyler 1949b). The young fledge at ten days and are cared for by both sexes. Nestling dates are 19 May to 11 July (MNRF). The Veery has a single brood in the north (Peck and James 1987) but may have two broods in the south (Ehrlich et al. 1988). It is a fairly common victim of Brown-headed Cowbird parasitism (Friedmann 1963). In Ontario, 70 of 368 nests (19%) were parasitized (Peck and James 1987); there are no Maryland records. In spring and summer the Veery forages on the ground, feeding primarily on beetles, ants, caterpillars, grasshoppers, and spiders (McAtee 1926).

Atlas results show four disjunct Veery breeding areas: the Allegheny Plateau in Garrett County, South Mountain in Washington and Frederick counties, the eastern edge of the Piedmont from DC to western Cecil County, and the northern Eastern Shore in Cecil and Kent counties, contiguous with Delaware populations. The absence of Veeries from most of Allegany and Washington counties is probably related to the drier forests and relatively steep ridges. Along the Fall Line, it reaches its southern limit at the Potomac River. No Veery records were reported for adjacent areas in northern Virginia.

Although Garrett County contains more suitable habitat and is the center of abundance, the range is widespread in the Piedmont. The highest breeding densities per 100 acres (40.5 ha) for the Piedmont are 80 territorial males in Glover–Archbold Park in DC in 1971 and 1975 and 21 territorial males on Cabin John Island, Montgomery County, in 1965 (Briggs and Criswell 1979). Criswell and Briggs (1965) showed that the Veery's expansion into DC was accompanied by a local decline in Wood Thrush populations.

Despite the Veery's expansion southward through the Piedmont, there is cause for concern about its future. On two long-term local BBC plots, Veeries peaked in the 1960s and have now declined to less than 20 percent of their maximum numbers (Terborgh 1989). Probable causes for this decline are nest predation, Brown-headed Cowbird parasitism, and tropical deforestation.

Veeries are still very common on the Allegheny Plateau, and BBS data from 1966 through 1989 show stable populations in Maryland and the Eastern Region. As the Washington–Baltimore corridor becomes increasingly urbanized, Veeries face loss of their specialized nesting habitat as it is increasingly cleared for roads, picnic facilities, and biking or jogging paths. Federal and state forests should be managed to encourage growth of dense shrub layers. The presence of Brown-headed Cowbirds in even the largest forest tracts and our incomplete knowledge about the Veery's wintering range and habitat requirements (Ridgely and Tudor 1989) indicate that careful monitoring of populations across the state is important.

Dave Czaplak

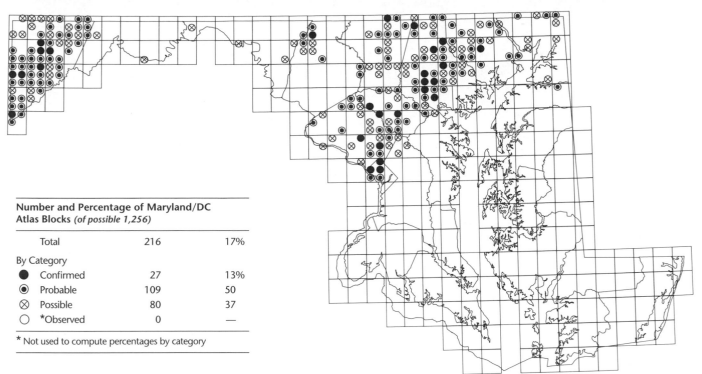

Atlas Distribution, 1983–1987

Number and Percentage of Maryland/DC Atlas Blocks (of possible 1,256)

Total	216	17%
By Category		
● Confirmed	27	13%
◉ Probable	109	50
⊗ Possible	80	37
○ *Observed	0	—

* Not used to compute percentages by category

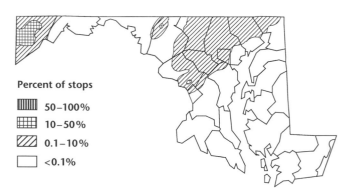

Percent of stops

▥ 50–100%
▦ 10–50%
▧ 0.1–10%
☐ <0.1%

Relative Abundance, 1982–1989

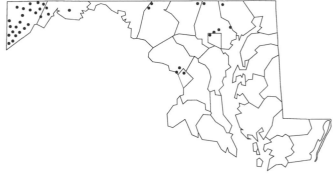

Breeding Distribution, 1958

The Veery occurs only along and west of the Fall Line. The highest densities are in the Allegheny Mountain Section in Garrett County. Lower numbers are found throughout the Piedmont and in the Catoctin Mountains and on South Mountain in the eastern Ridge and Valley Section.

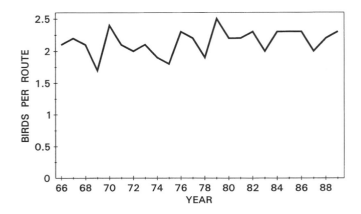

Maryland BBS Trend Graph, 1966–1989

Hermit Thrush

Catharus guttatus

Most Maryland birdwatchers know the Hermit Thrush only as an uncommon migrant and sporadic winter resident. It is the earliest of the *Catharus* thrushes to arrive in spring, with birds returning from their southeastern U.S. wintering grounds (AOU 1983) in early April (Robbins and Bystrak 1977). Migration continues through the first days of May. The first southbound fall migrants usually arrive in early October, and migration continues into mid-November. In winter, this species is fairly common to common in the Eastern and Western Shore sections and uncommon to rare and sporadic elsewhere (Stewart and Robbins 1958).

Kirkwood (1895) knew the Hermit Thrush only as an uncommon migrant and scarce winter visitor, although he noted that Resler (1890) had collected one on 9 June 1890 in Howard County. This is the only summer record for the state other than those from the western Maryland breeding grounds. Eifrig (1904), writing about western Maryland, called the Hermit Thrush common in summer on "the higher ground," presumably meaning Garrett County, but he cited no summer records or evidence of breeding. Stewart and Robbins (1958) called it uncommon and local in the Allegheny Mountain Section at elevations above 2,500 ft (762 m). They described the breeding habitat as open spruce-hemlock bogs, pine plantations in the vicinity of bogs, and oak and pine barrens on ridgetops. No population estimates have been made for Maryland, but Hall (1983) cited highs for West Virginia of 10 territorial males per 100 acres (40.5 ha) in a young spruce plantation and a young spruce forest.

The Hermit Thrush uses dense coniferous, mixed coniferous-deciduous, and pure deciduous woodlands during its breeding season (Dilger 1956). Few data are available for nest site selection or timing of breeding in Maryland. In eastern populations, it normally places its nest on the ground or, less commonly, a few feet high in a small sapling (Terres

1980). Nesting on rock faces has been observed in Ontario (Armstrong and Euler 1983). Clutch sizes vary from 3 to 6, most commonly 3 or 4 (Gross 1949). The only Maryland nest, with 3 eggs, was found on 30 May 1922 by J. Jacobs (MNRF) on the ground under a rhododendron. Bull (1974) noted that 40 of 55 New York clutches contained 3 eggs. Nests with eggs have been found in New York from 12 May to 24 August, the length of the season reflecting two broods attempted there. As many as three broods may be raised in southern populations (Gross 1949).

The female incubates the eggs for 12 or 13 days. The young fledge 12 days after hatching and are fed by both parents (Gross 1949). Young in the nest have been found in New York from 30 May to 31 August; fledglings have been observed as late as 23 September (Bull 1974). The breeding season in Maryland is probably similar to that in New York, although it may begin slightly earlier. Hermit Thrushes are infrequent victims of Brown-headed Cowbird parasitism (Friedmann 1963). No instances are known from Maryland, but 6 of 120 Quebec nests (5%) and 11 of 154 Ontario nests (7.1%) were parasitized (Terrill 1961; Peck and James 1987).

Hall (1983) noted that Hermit Thrushes, Swainson's Thrushes, and Veeries use the same habitat during the breeding season; however, the two larger species dominate the Hermit Thrush in habitat selection. Although Swainson's Thrushes have not been known to breed in Maryland since early in the twentieth century (Stewart and Robbins 1958), Veeries are common breeders in Garrett County and may limit the population of Hermit Thrushes. Populations may fluctuate in response to severe weather conditions during the colder months. BBS data from 1966 through 1989 for the Eastern Region indicate an increase in Hermit Thrush populations; data are too few to estimate a trend for Maryland.

The Hermit Thrush's diet consists of approximately 65 percent animal matter, largely beetles and ants, and 35 percent vegetable matter, mainly wild fruits and berries (Beal 1915). Insects predominate in spring and summer but are far less important during the colder months.

During the Atlas period, the Hermit Thrush was widespread in Garrett County, especially in the higher elevations at the southern end of the county. Only one "confirmed" report, a nest with eggs, was received for this shy, forest-dwelling bird. Perhaps this is not surprising, since much of the fieldwork in Garrett County was done by block busters from other parts of the state.

Protection of spruce forests and bogs seems to be the key to retaining the Hermit Thrush as a breeding bird in Maryland. Until more is known about the population, its habitat preference, and its relationship with other species, we can recommend little else specific that will aid in retaining what many authors refer to as America's finest singer.

Eirik A. T. Blom

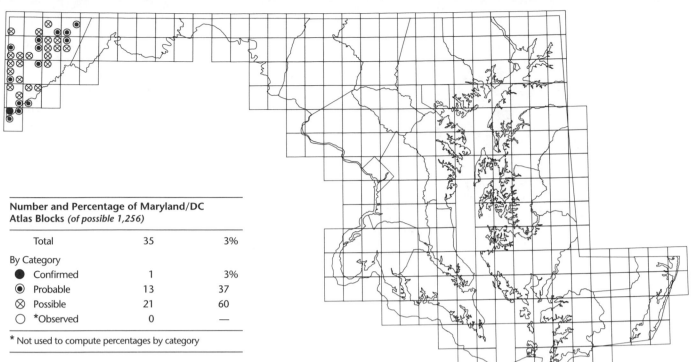

Number and Percentage of Maryland/DC Atlas Blocks *(of possible 1,256)*

Total	35	3%
By Category		
● Confirmed	1	3%
◉ Probable	13	37
⊗ Possible	21	60
○ *Observed	0	—

* Not used to compute percentages by category

Atlas Distribution, 1983–1987

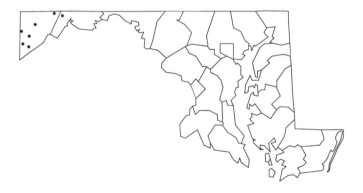

Breeding Distribution, 1958

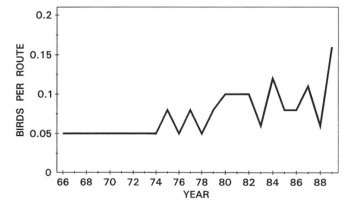

Maryland BBS Trend Graph, 1966–1989

Wood Thrush

Hylocichla mustelina

The large, handsome Wood Thrush, with its clear bell-like song, is a common breeder throughout Maryland. It establishes residence soon after its late April arrival (Brackbill 1943, 1958) from its wintering grounds in southern Mexico and Central America (AOU 1983). By late August, it begins to leave its breeding areas, and most migrants have left Maryland by early October (Stewart and Robbins 1958). During the nesting season, it forages in leaf litter for insects, spiders, snails, and worms (Martin et al. 1951).

Although the Wood Thrush is most often found in floodplain forests and moist deciduous woods with an ample understory, it also nests on dry wooded hillsides (Stewart and Robbins 1958), near woodland edges (Forbush 1929), and, in recent decades, in suburban situations (Brackbill 1958). Choice habitat is extensive, tall, deciduous forest with a relatively low density of trees but a large number of tree species (Robbins et al. 1989a). The highest Maryland breeding density of 125 territorial males per 100 acres (40.5 ha) was recorded in mixed-hardwood forest in Calvert County (Fales 1973). Although Kibbe (1985) stated that coniferous stands support few, if any, breeding Wood Thrushes in Vermont, the one high-elevation sample of old-growth hemlock forest surveyed in Garrett County held a substantial 20 territorial males per 100 acres (Robbins 1949a).

More than a century ago, Coues and Prentiss (1883) noted that the Wood Thrush was a summer resident with shy and retiring habits. Kirkwood (1895), Eifrig (1904), and Stewart and Robbins (1958) described it as a common summer resident. Cooke (1929) said it was more abundant than in previous years and nested freely about lawns in the suburbs as well as in woods. Brackbill (1958) studied nesting Wood Thrushes in suburban Baltimore and substantiated Cooke's (1929) observation regarding their adaptation to people during this century.

Male Wood Thrushes return before their mates and secure breeding territories by means of displays, but mostly by loud, intense song periods, reaching peaks at dawn and dusk (Brackbill 1943; Weaver 1949). The nest is usually located in a sapling or shrub, most commonly between 5 and 8 ft (1.5–2.4 m) but occasionally 2.5 to 42 ft (0.8–13 m) up in a fork or on a horizontal limb. This thrush slightly favors flowering dogwood as a nest site (MNRF). The nest, constructed over a period of five to seven days (Brackbill 1958), is a substantial cup of plant material with a middle layer of mud and dead leaves. Weaver (1949) noted that 18 of 20 nests examined contained paper, cellophane, or white cloth hanging from the base; a few nests also contained pieces of plastic during the past two decades (J. Solem, pers. obs.). Dead beech leaves hung from the majority of 80 nests found in Maryland in 1988 and 1989 (C. Robbins, pers. comm.). The use of these objects may help to break up the nest contour to foil predators (Weaver 1949).

The usual Maryland clutch is 3 or 4 eggs (MNRF). Only six of a sample of 175 complete clutches had as few as 1 egg or as many as 5; however, 12 percent of C. Robbins' (pers. comm.) first-brood nests in 1989 had 5 eggs. The extreme Maryland egg dates are 7 May and 6 August, with a peak from mid-May to mid-June (MNRF). Incubation, performed by the female, lasts 12 to 14 days (Brackbill 1958). The young are tended by both adults, fledge in 12 or 13 days after hatching, and reach total independence after 24 to 27 days. In central Maryland, the Wood Thrush raises two broods (Brackbill 1958). Roth et al. (1991) recorded one case of polygyny in an intensely studied population in Delaware.

Although the Wood Thrush is larger than the Brown-headed Cowbird, it is a regular host (Friedmann 1929). In Ontario, 53 of 195 nests (27.2%) were parasitized (Peck and James 1987); 20 of 215 Maryland nests (9.3%) were parasitized (MNRF). Brown-headed Cowbirds are more common at woodland edges than in the interior, and predation rates are higher in small woodlots in central Maryland than in more extensive woodlands or more remote areas (Wilcove 1985).

Atlas results show that the Wood Thrush was missing only from the barrier islands along the Atlantic Coast, islands in the Chesapeake Bay, narrow necks extending into the Bay, and the inner city of Baltimore.

Although the Wood Thrush is more flexible in the size of its territory and more tolerant of man's presence than most of the state's breeding neotropical migrants, Robbins et al. (1989a) found that the probability of maximum breeding density is reached in woodlands of 1,235 acres (500 ha). BBS data from 1966 through 1989 show highly significant average annual declines in Maryland (2.0%) and the Eastern Region (2.2%). Maryland data from 1980 through 1989 show a highly significant decline of 3.9 percent. Terborgh (1989) lists it among the North American species in peril because of tropical rain forest destruction on its wintering grounds. Efforts to preserve rain forests in Latin America and large contiguous wooded tracts throughout Maryland should have a positive effect, not only for Wood Thrushes but for numerous other area-sensitive species.

Joanne K. Solem

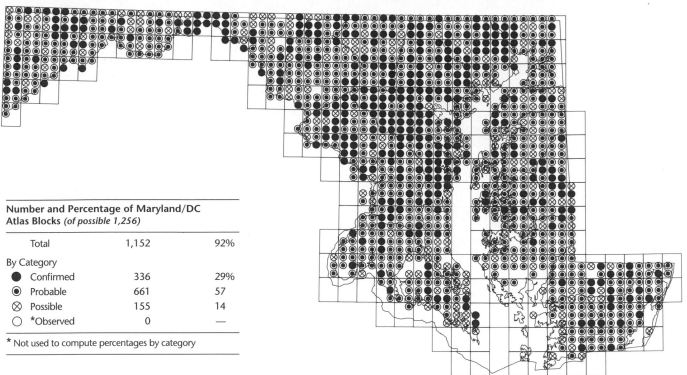

Number and Percentage of Maryland/DC Atlas Blocks *(of possible 1,256)*

Total		1,152	92%
By Category			
●	Confirmed	336	29%
◉	Probable	661	57
⊗	Possible	155	14
○	*Observed	0	—

* Not used to compute percentages by category

Atlas Distribution, 1983–1987

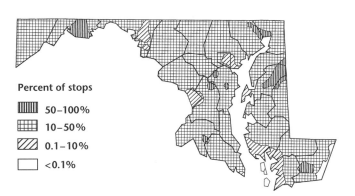

Percent of stops

▥	50–100%
▦	10–50%
▨	0.1–10%
☐	<0.1%

Relative Abundance, 1982–1989

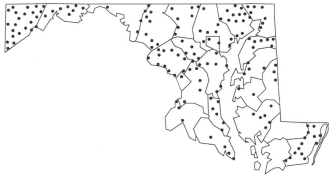

Breeding Distribution, 1958

The Wood Thrush is common, widespread, and evenly distributed. It is slightly less common in urban and extensive marsh habitats with randomly scattered pockets of high abundance.

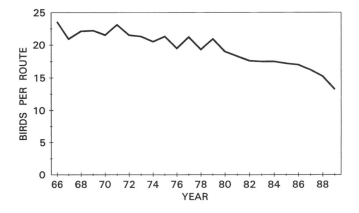

Maryland BBS Trend Graph, 1966–1989

American Robin

Turdus migratorius

The American Robin is almost certainly the best-known songbird in Maryland. It is abundant and widespread, frequenting suburban lawns, woodlots, forests, cutover areas, farmland, and many other habitats. An early spring migrant, the first birds arrive from mid- to late February (Robbins and Bystrak 1977). The spring migration peak is between early March and mid-April. Fall migrants move through Maryland from mid-September to late November (Stewart and Robbins 1958).

Southern Maryland may have been near the southern edge of the American Robin's breeding range 150 years ago. Coues and Prentiss (1862, 1883) wrote that a few bred in DC; Richmond (1888) called it common but did not specify the time of year. At the turn of the century, it was common during summer in central Maryland (Kirkwood 1895). By 1929, the American Robin was an abundant summer resident in DC (Cooke 1929). It has benefited from the settlement of North America, adapting readily to land cleared for agriculture, and especially well to urban and suburban habitats. Trimmed lawns, gardens, shrubbery, and fruit trees provide both food and nest sites. Stewart and Robbins (1958) considered it common in all sections. They reported the highest Maryland breeding density of 45 territorial males per 100 acres (40.5 ha) in an orchard-residential area at PWRC in 1942. The proliferation of suburban lawns has contributed greatly to the expanded range and population of the American Robin since much of the pre-Columbian forest was removed (Eiserer 1976). Its diet includes earthworms, insects, and a wide variety of fruits and seeds, but parents feed the young American Robins insects and earthworms almost exclusively (Tyler 1949a).

Males arrive before females in spring and establish nesting territories (Stokes 1979). The female builds the sturdy nest of mud and fine grasses. Because the mud base is nonporous, young have drowned after heavy rainstorms. Nest building has been recorded as early as 21 March in Maryland (Stewart and Robbins 1958). Heights of a sample of 258 nests (MNRF) range from 1 to 60 ft (0.3–18 m), with a mean of 13 ft (3.9 m). Nests were in a wide variety of plant species and artificial structures, including open sheds and under the eaves of houses (MNRF). Nest sites early in the season were often in conifers, which offer greater concealment and protection before deciduous trees are in leaf. Later in the season, deciduous trees and shrubs were used more often.

Extreme egg dates in Maryland are 4 April (MNRF) and 29 August (Robbins and Bystrak 1977), with peaks in late April and late May. Clutch sizes in a sample of 200 nests (MNRF) range from 2 to 6, with a mean of 3.7. Only four nests had 2 eggs, five had 5 eggs, and one had 6 eggs. As is typical among songbirds, clutch sizes declined as the season progressed. Forty-two percent of 3- and 4-egg clutches were found between 1 and 15 May and another 20 percent were found in the subsequent week. Although 19 clutches of 3 or 4 eggs were found in June, only 3 were found in July and none thereafter.

Only the female incubates the eggs for 12 to 14 days, but both parents feed the young in the nest and for a few days after fledging (Stokes 1979). Feeding then becomes the male's responsibility while the female begins another nest. In this manner, two to three broods a year are raised. Nests with young have been reported in Maryland from 23 April to 16 August, with a peak in mid-May (MNRF). Brood sizes of 117 Maryland nests range from 1 to 5, with a mean of 3.2. The American Robin is a rare host to the Brown-headed Cowbird and ejects their eggs (Friedmann 1963). Stewart and Robbins (1958) reported four instances of Brown-headed Cowbird parasitism in Maryland, but only one of a random sample of 1,000 Maryland nests (0.1%) was parasitized (MNRF). In Ontario, 17 of 4,446 nests (0.3%) were affected (Peck and James 1987).

Atlas data show that American Robins were found in almost every block; they were absent from only a few barrier islands and marsh blocks. The very high number of "confirmed" records reflects this species' abundance, its habit of nesting near humans, and the distinctive appearance of the young. Nests often are poorly concealed; thus, reports of nests with young or eggs were submitted from 150 blocks (15% of "confirmed" records). Adults with food for young (34%) and fledged young (32%) accounted for 66 percent of all "confirmed" records.

BBS data from 1966 through 1989 show a significant average annual increase of 1.2 percent in the Eastern Region and 1.4 percent in Maryland; Maryland data from 1980 through 1989 show a highly significant increase of 2.3 percent. Although American Robins have benefited from suburbanization, they have become increasingly susceptible to predation by domesticated pets. The widespread use of pesticides and herbicides on lawns and shrubs also presents a potential threat. Chemicals that leach into the soil may be absorbed by earthworms, a staple in the summer diet of the American Robin (Tyler 1949a). Despite these threats, the future of this species in Maryland seems assured.

Martha Chestem

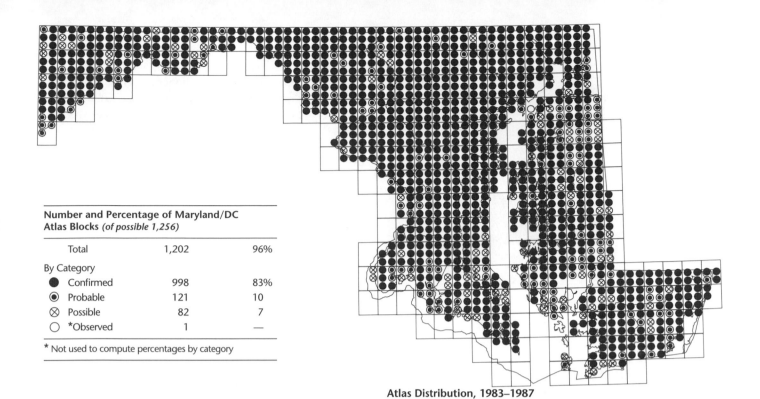

Number and Percentage of Maryland/DC Atlas Blocks (of possible 1,256)		
Total	1,202	96%
By Category		
● Confirmed	998	83%
◉ Probable	121	10
⊗ Possible	82	7
○ *Observed	1	—

* Not used to compute percentages by category

Atlas Distribution, 1983–1987

Percent of stops

▦ 50–100%
▦ 10–50%
▨ 0.1–10%
☐ <0.1%

Relative Abundance, 1982–1989

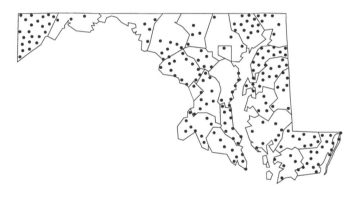

Breeding Distribution, 1958

The American Robin is most common along and west of the Fall Line, less so in the extensively forested areas of Garrett and eastern Allegany counties and in the Catoctin Mountains in Frederick County. On the Coastal Plain it is most common in suburban areas and least common in marshes.

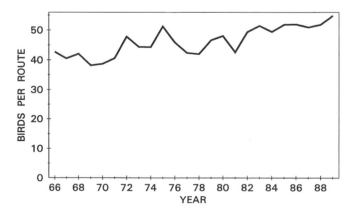

Maryland BBS Trend Graph, 1966–1989

Gray Catbird

Dumetella carolinensis

Hidden among the shrubbery of the forest's edge or in swamp land, the Gray Catbird is more readily detected by its mewing call than by its visibility. It is a common summer resident throughout the state. Spring migrants return from their southeastern U.S., Caribbean, and Central American wintering grounds (AOU 1983) in late April (Stewart and Robbins 1958). Although most individuals depart in the fall by mid-October, the Gray Catbird winters uncommonly on the lower Eastern Shore, and rarely on the rest of the Eastern Shore, on the Western Shore, and in the Piedmont.

Kirkwood (1895) described the Gray Catbird as common, and Eifrig (1904) reported it as abundant at all elevations in western Maryland. Stewart and Robbins (1958) called it common in all sections. They cited a maximum density of 80 territorial males per 100 acres (40.5 ha) in a shrub swamp in Prince George's County in 1945. Robbins (1949c) found 74 territorial males per 100 acres in an open hemlock-spruce bog in Garrett County in 1949. BBS data from 1966 through 1989 show a slight but significant increase in the northeastern states but no change on the continental level or in Maryland.

The Gray Catbird establishes its summer territory in the shrubs found in swamps, along stream beds, and along woodland margins. It is also found in hedgerows or even in residential areas and parks, provided thick brush is present for cover. It is an edge species that is not as tolerant of open spaces as the Brown Thrasher, and it is less likely to use hedgerows extending into open agricultural areas (Graber et al. 1970). Nest construction is primarily by the female, although the male may assist on occasion (Gross 1948b). Nests are usually constructed in shrubbery along forest edges and, secondarily, in hedges, orchards, and swampy woodlands. Nesting materials include grape bark, sticks, weed stems, horsehair, grasses, leaves, pine needles, rootlets, and twigs (Gross 1948b). Although the Gray Catbird will use thorny plants for nesting, it does so less frequently than does the Brown Thrasher, showing a strong preference for wild grape

plants (Graber et al. 1970). Heights of 235 Maryland nests (MNRF) range from 2 to 30 ft (0.6–9.1 m), with a mean of 7.3 ft (2.2 m). Only 10 nests were higher than 15 ft (4.6 m).

Maryland egg dates range from 1 May (MNRF) to 19 August (Robbins and Bystrak 1977), with a peak in late May and early June (MNRF). Two broods, rarely three, may be raised (Forbush 1929). Clutch sizes in 155 Maryland nests (MNRF) range from 2 to 5 (mean of 3.4). Clutch sizes decline as the season progresses. Scott et al. (1988) reported a mean clutch size in Ontario of 3.9 before 2 June and 3.1 after 23 June. Incubation takes 12 or 13 days (Gross 1948b); the young fledge in about 11 days (DeGraaf and Rudis 1986). Young in the nest have been found in Maryland from 20 May to 27 August, with a peak in mid-June and a smaller one in mid-July (MNRF). Brood sizes in 184 nests (MNRF) range from 1 to 5 (mean of 2.2). Gray Catbirds are rare hosts to the Brown-headed Cowbird (Friedmann 1963) and eject their eggs from the nest (Rothstein 1975); Maryland has no records of parasitism. In Ontario, 18 of 1,193 nests (1.5%) were parasitized (Peck and James 1987). Belles-Isles and Picman (1986c) reported that Gray Catbirds commonly destroy the eggs of other birds nesting nearby. During the nesting period, intrusion into the nest site results in scolding and mewing and, sometimes, desertion by the parents (P. Woodward, pers. comm.). Males show significantly more site fidelity from year to year than do females, and birds that nest successfully are more likely to return to the same site in subsequent years (Darley et al. 1977). Almost half of their diet consists of insects, especially crickets, grasshoppers, beetles, ants, and caterpillars (Martin et al. 1951). Principal plant foods are fruits, berries, and grapes.

During the Atlas period, Gray Catbirds were found throughout the state, including the most heavily urbanized blocks. They were recorded in every block in central and western Maryland. Their highly recognizable call and song and high tolerance for human activity made them easily detectable. The majority of "confirmed" records were of adults with food for young (40%) or of fledged young (27%). BBS data from 1966 through 1989 show stable populations in Maryland and the Eastern Region.

To maintain viable populations of the Gray Catbird, preservation of thickets and forest understory should be encouraged. The Gray Catbird's future in Maryland seems secure.

Stephen B. Hitchner

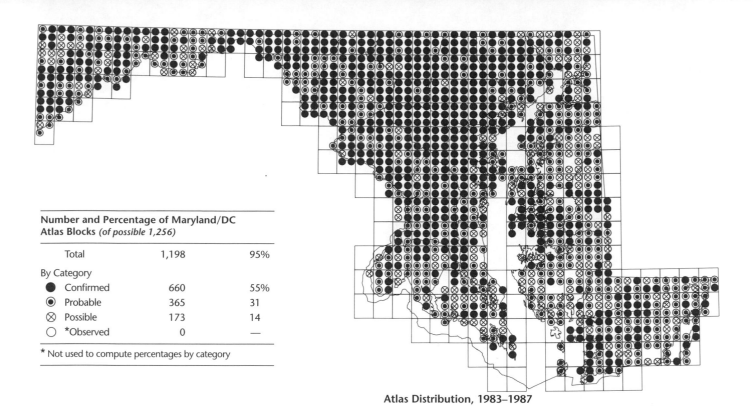

Number and Percentage of Maryland/DC Atlas Blocks *(of possible 1,256)*

Total	1,198	95%
By Category		
● Confirmed	660	55%
◉ Probable	365	31
⊗ Possible	173	14
○ *Observed	0	—

* Not used to compute percentages by category

Atlas Distribution, 1983–1987

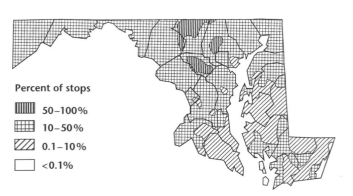

Percent of stops

▥	50–100%
▦	10–50%
▨	0.1–10%
□	<0.1%

Relative Abundance, 1982–1989

Breeding Distribution, 1958

The Gray Catbird is most abundant in the northern Piedmont Section and least common in the southern portions of the Coastal Plain, where it occurs most frequently around water, especially at the edges of marshes.

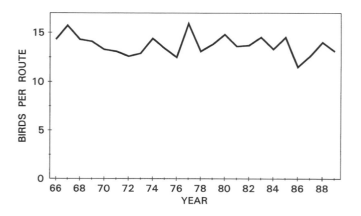

Maryland BBS Trend Graph, 1966–1989

Northern Mockingbird

Mimus polyglottos

A century ago, the Northern Mockingbird was rare in Maryland except in the southern counties. Coues and Prentiss (1862, 1883) called it a rare summer resident in DC, arriving in late April and departing in mid-September. A dozen years later, Kirkwood (1895) declared it a year-round resident in the southern counties and regular in summer as far north as Kent and Anne Arundel counties. He reported summer stragglers at four Baltimore County sites and mentioned two nests found in Towson in 1882.

Judd (1902) recorded the first nesting at Marshall Hall in Prince George's County; in about 1905 this species began to increase in DC (Cooke 1929). Eifrig (1909) reported the first nest for western Maryland, at Oldtown in Allegany County, in 1909. One pair apparently nested along the Chesapeake and Ohio Canal at Plummers Island, Montgomery County in May 1914, but the next record there was not until 1943 (Wetmore and Manville 1968). Stewart and Robbins (1958) called it common in the Eastern Shore and Western Shore sections, fairly common in the Upper Chesapeake Section and the southern Piedmont, uncommon elsewhere in the Piedmont Section and the eastern portion of the Ridge and Valley Section, and rare in the Allegheny Mountain Section.

The Northern Mockingbird benefits from close association with people. It favors suburban shrubbery and multiflora rose thickets for nesting and television antennas and chimneys for song perches. It also welcomes the winter shelter and food provided by the multiflora rose hedges that were widely established in the 1950s (Robbins et al. 1986). These hedges undoubtedly assisted in the winter survival and spread of this primarily sedentary, nonmigratory bird. Although berries comprise more than half its diet in fall and winter, insects such as beetles, ants, bees, wasps, and grasshoppers dominate the summer menu (Martin et al. 1951). The highest Maryland breeding density, 15 territorial males per 100 acres (40.5 ha) in the headquarters area of PWRC in 1942 (Stewart and Robbins 1958), would probably be exceeded if a census were conducted in a well-planted subdivision today.

Courtship takes place on open ground; the birds face each other about a foot apart and hop up and down with their heads held high and tails cocked up (Forbush 1929). Nest building in Maryland generally begins in April, although in warm years there are a few nests as early as March (MNRF). Early in the season, the birds select evergreens for nest sites, but as summer progresses they use deciduous trees more often, slightly increasing the average height of the nest above the ground. Heights of 329 Maryland nests range from 5 in. (13 cm) to 49 ft (15 m), with 199 (60%) between 3.3 and 6.6 ft (1–2 m). March, April, and May nests average 5.7 ft (1.7 m), compared with 5.8 ft (1.8 m) in June, 6.4 ft (2.0 m) in July, and 9.0 ft (2.7 m) in August. The bulky twig nest, which is built by the female, is lined with rootlets and dried grass (Sprunt 1948).

Maryland egg dates for full clutches range from 30 March to 21 August (MNRF). Egg laying reaches a peak in the middle third of May, then gradually declines into early August. Half of 320 Maryland clutches were completed between 1 May and 10 June (MNRF). The peak of nesting in Maryland is about a month later than in Tennessee, where Laskey (1962) did an intensive study of this species. Of 235 Tennessee clutches, 40 percent were laid in April, whereas 40 percent of Maryland clutches were laid in May (MNRF). Normal clutch size in Maryland is 3 or 4, with 3 being most common (54%). Only 4 percent of 253 Maryland clutches (10) contained 5 eggs (MNRF), compared with 14 percent of Tennessee nests (Laskey 1962). Incubation requires 11 to 13 days. Extreme dates for Maryland nestlings are 19 April and 1 September (MNRF). Northern Mockingbirds are aggressive around the nest, increasingly so as the young approach fledging age. The average annual survival rate of a PWRC population was 49 percent (Karr et al. 1990). They are rarely parasitized by Brown-headed Cowbirds (Friedmann 1929, 1963). Stewart and Robbins (1958) listed only two Maryland instances.

Atlas data show that the Northern Mockingbird now breeds throughout Maryland except for isolated islands in the lower Chesapeake Bay, the southern hálf of Assateague Island, the highlands of Garrett County, and the solid blocks of forest covering large portions of the Ridge and Valley Section. Because nests and fledged young are easily found, the rate of "confirmed" records was high (59%).

BBS data from 1966 through 1989 show a highly significant average annual decline of 0.4 percent in the Eastern Region. The Maryland population was stable during that time; however, data from 1980 through 1989 show a highly significant average annual increase of 2 percent in Maryland. The Northern Mockingbird requires no special help from people other than protection from cats and dogs and offerings of suet or fruit during severe winter weather.

Chandler S. Robbins

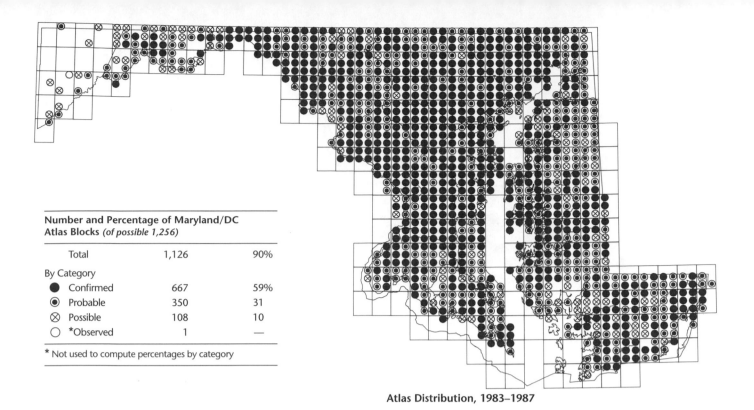

Number and Percentage of Maryland/DC Atlas Blocks *(of possible 1,256)*

Total	1,126	90%
By Category		
● Confirmed	667	59%
◉ Probable	350	31
⊗ Possible	108	10
○ *Observed	1	—

* Not used to compute percentages by category

Atlas Distribution, 1983–1987

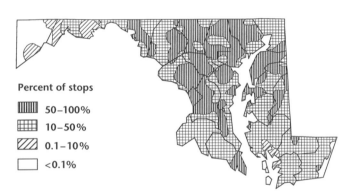

Percent of stops

▥	50–100%
▦	10–50%
▨	0.1–10%
☐	<0.1%

Relative Abundance, 1982–1989

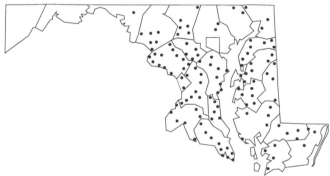

Breeding Distribution, 1958

The Northern Mockingbird is most abundant in the urbanized Baltimore-Washington corridor and in the more developed areas of the central Eastern Shore. It is virtually absent from the highlands of the Allegheny Mountain Section in Garrett County, where it is found only at lower elevations near the Potomac River.

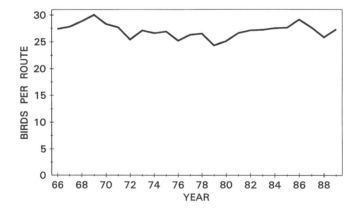

Maryland BBS Trend Graph, 1966–1989

Brown Thrasher

Toxostoma rufum

Slipping quietly through the low underbrush, Brown Thrashers may easily go undetected unless one is familiar with its variable song of whistles, chuck notes, and warbled phrases. Although a few remain in Maryland during the winter, primarily on the lower Eastern Shore (Stewart and Robbins 1958), most retire to the more hospitable climate of the southeastern United States (AOU 1983). Spring migrants begin returning in late March and early April, and most leave in the fall by mid-October (Robbins and Bystrak 1977).

The Brown Thrasher has been widespread in Maryland for at least 130 years. Coues and Prentiss (1862, 1883) recorded it as an abundant summer resident. Kirkwood (1895) called it common, as did Eifrig (1904) for western Maryland, although noting that it was not quite as numerous as the Gray Catbird. Stewart and Robbins (1958) described its breeding status as fairly common in all sections.

The Brown Thrasher's preferred habitats are hedgerows, dense shrubbery, berry thickets, and undergrowth along the forest's edge (Graber et al. 1970). It is more of an edge species and more likely to be found in hedgerows extending well into agricultural fields than is the Gray Catbird. The highest breeding density recorded for Maryland is 15 territorial males per 100 acres (40.5 ha) in a suburban residential area in Prince George's County in 1951 and 1952 (Stewart and Robbins 1958). Because Brown Thrashers are so prominent in suburban areas and nest close to the ground, considerable data on Maryland nests are available. Nest building has been recorded from 9 April to 18 July (Van Velzen 1968). Heights of 279 nests (MNRF) range from 0 to 25 ft (0–7.6 m), with a mean of 4.2 ft (1.3 m). Only 21 nests were above 7 ft (2.1 m), and 14 were on the ground. Both sexes participate in building nests, which are constructed of layers of twigs, dead leaves, paper, thin bark, grasses, and rootlets (Bent 1948).

Maryland egg dates range from 18 April to 30 July, with peaks in mid- and late May (MNRF). Maryland Brown Thrashers raise one or two broods per season (Van Velzen 1968). Clutch sizes in 168 Maryland nests (MNRF) range from 2 to 5 (mean of 3.7). Incubation, by both sexes, lasts 12 or 13 days (9 Maryland nests) (Van Velzen 1968). Young have been found in nests from 8 May through 13 August, with a peak in late May (MNRF). Brood sizes in 139 nests range from 1 to 5, with a mean of 3.1 (MNRF). Van Velzen (1968) reported that the young in 8 Maryland nests fledged after 11 to 14 days and that the success rate of Maryland nests increased steadily from 4 percent in April to 72 percent in July. Except for unusual incidents, the Brown Thrasher is the largest passerine victim of Brown-headed Cowbird parasitism; however, it is an uncommon host (Friedmann 1963) and a known rejector of Brown-headed Cowbird eggs (Rothstein 1975). Van Velzen (1968) found only 3 of 396 Maryland nests (0.8%) parasitized; in Ontario, 18 of 742 (2.4%) were parasitized (Peck and James 1987).

Brown Thrashers have one of the widest vocal repertoires of any North American songbird and occasionally mimic the songs and calls of other birds (Bent 1948). Unfortunately, they are actively vocal only early in the breeding season (Bent 1948). This vocal reticence made them harder to detect during the peak time of Atlas fieldwork. Although Brown Thrashers were found in 91 percent as many blocks as Gray Catbirds, the number of "confirmed" records was only 63 percent as high for Brown Thrashers; the number of records for birds holding territory was only 70 percent as high. They were absent from a few of the most heavily urbanized blocks and from some of the extensive marshlands and offshore islands of the lower Chesapeake Bay. Scattered absences in Dorchester and Worcester counties may be attributable to coverage at irregular intervals by observers residing in distant counties.

Maryland BBS data from 1966 through 1989 show a highly significant average annual decline of 4 percent; the Eastern Region also shows a highly significant decline (1.5%). Maryland data from 1980 through 1989 show only an indication of a decline. Many birdwatchers have expressed the opinion that Brown Thrashers have become increasingly difficult to find in recent years. Habitat loss, through the removal of hedgerows, may contribute to the decline. An additional potential threat may be a decline in insects during the spring and summer months. These birds forage primarily for beetles, grasshoppers, ants, and other insects (Martin et al. 1951), feeding largely on the ground in open and semi-open areas, especially in suburban and agricultural habitats. This may make them more vulnerable to the use of pesticides than are Gray Catbirds, which tend to use less-open areas. Both continued monitoring of the population and efforts to determine the reasons for the downward trend are needed.

Stephen B. Hitchner

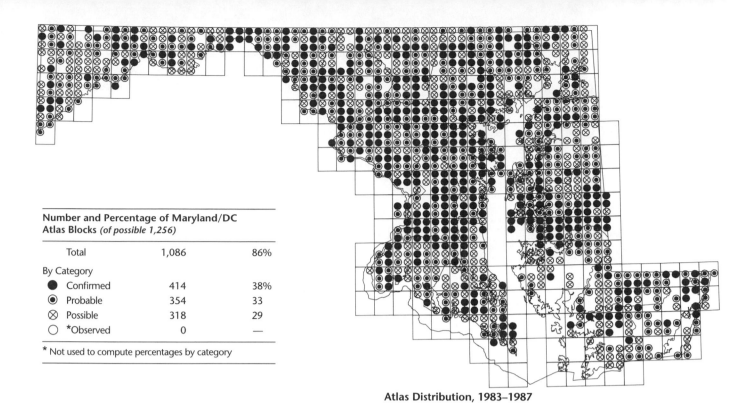

Number and Percentage of Maryland/DC Atlas Blocks *(of possible 1,256)*

Total	1,086	86%
By Category		
● Confirmed	414	38%
◉ Probable	354	33
⊗ Possible	318	29
○ *Observed	0	—

* Not used to compute percentages by category

Atlas Distribution, 1983–1987

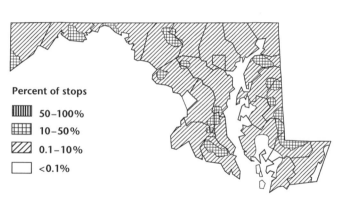

Percent of stops

▥	50–100%
▦	10–50%
▨	0.1–10%
☐	<0.1%

Relative Abundance, 1982–1989

Breeding Distribution, 1958

The Brown Thrasher is fairly evenly distributed, with scattered areas of higher abundance, mostly around agricultural areas on the Eastern Shore. It was not recorded in the extensive marsh blocks of southern Dorchester and adjacent counties.

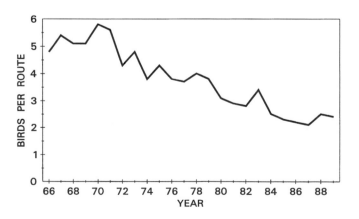

Maryland BBS Trend Graph, 1966–1989

E. THOMPSON

Cedar Waxwing

Bombycilla cedrorum

Cedar Waxwings are seldom seen alone; even during the breeding season there is evidence for semicolonial nesting (Bull 1974). Although they are present in Maryland year-round and flocks may be seen during migration, their wanderings are irregular, populations are variable, and patterns are hard to discern (Stewart and Robbins 1958). Migratory peaks typically occur from mid-May to early June and from mid-August to mid-November (Robbins and Bystrak 1977).

Kirkwood (1895) called Cedar Waxwings common throughout the year in central Maryland, and Eifrig (1904) termed them abundant summer residents in western Maryland. Stewart and Robbins (1958) described their breeding status as common in the Allegheny Mountain Section; uncommon in the Ridge and Valley, Piedmont, and Upper Chesapeake sections; and rare in the Western and Eastern Shore sections. Hall (1983) wrote that they were erratic breeders in West Virginia at the local level, being abundant in some years and absent in others, but present in good numbers across the state every year. BBS data from 1966 through 1989 show a highly significant average annual increase of 3.3 percent in the Eastern Region. Maryland data for that period show a highly significant average annual increase of 6 percent; however, data from 1980 through 1989 show an even higher increase of 8.6 percent.

The breeding season is long and starts late, reflecting this species' dependence on emerging fall fruits and their abundance (Tyler 1950a). Its diet consists largely of wild fruits, berries, and tree sap, but 20 percent of the summer food is insects (Martin et al. 1951). Nestlings are fed insects for a few days after hatching, then berries are added (Tyler 1950a). The Cedar Waxwing's breeding habitat is varied; it favors open deciduous and coniferous woodland, along with parkland, wooded swamps, residential areas, and plantings, especially orchards (Tyler 1950a; Stewart and Robbins 1958). High breeding densities recorded for Maryland per 100 acres

(40.5 ha) were 16 territorial males in a hemlock-spruce bog (Robbins 1949c) and 15 territorial males in a red pine plantation in Garrett County in 1949 (Robbins and Barnes 1949) and in a residential area in Prince George's County in 1946 (Stewart and Robbins 1958).

The nest usually is built in the crotch of a tree or shrub or on a horizonal limb. Heights of 37 Maryland nests (MNRF) range from 7 to 50 ft (2.1–15 m), with a mean of 19.7 ft (6.0 m). Nests with eggs have been found in Maryland from 7 June to 21 August. Eggs have been found into mid-October in New York (Bull 1974). Clutch sizes in 12 Maryland nests (MNRF) range from 3 to 5, with a mean of 4.4. Incubation, primarily by the female, lasts 12 to 14 days (Lea 1942); the male's role is not known with certainty. Nestlings have been found in Maryland from 18 June to 13 September, with one record on 17 October (MNRF). Brood sizes in seven nests range from 2 to 4. Young fledge about 16 days after hatching, are fed by both parents, but are brooded only by the female (Tyler 1950a).

Cedar Waxwings are common victims of the Brown-headed Cowbird in some places (Rothstein 1976a), but only 1 of 19 Maryland nests (5%) was parasitized (MNRF). Peck and James (1987) reported that 67 of 890 Ontario nests (7.5%) held Brown-headed Cowbird eggs or young. Cedar Waxwings usually eject Brown-headed Cowbird eggs (Rothstein 1975) or desert the nest and make a second nesting attempt (Rothstein 1976b). This response has caused debate about how many broods are raised. Leck and Cantor (1979) examined North American nest cards and found that when the data were divided into pre- and post-1970 records, the peak of the Cedar Waxwing breeding season shifted from late June to July and August. This may be in response to parasitism, which is more likely early in the nesting season. Brown-headed Cowbirds begin searching for nests in mid-April to early May and parasitism decreases as the nesting season progresses (C. Hahn, pers. comm.). Scott (1963) reported that in Ontario, the rate of parasitism dropped rapidly after early June.

This species expanded its Maryland breeding range during the Atlas period. Because the Cedar Waxwing was long considered a rare breeder on Maryland's Coastal Plain, fieldworkers were required to provide documentation for birds found breeding there during the first two Atlas seasons; this requirement was withdrawn in view of an overwhelming number of reports. As the Atlas map shows, Cedar Waxwings were widespread on the Coastal Plain; this continued throughout the Atlas period and was also evident during Virginia's atlas. Given the irregular and erratic nature of this species, this range extension may be temporary.

The Cedar Waxwing is doing well in Maryland, possibly expanding its range and population. By managing the habitat to provide an abundant supply of the its favorite berries, such as red cedar, cherry, dogwood, blackberry, viburnum, and grape (Martin et al. 1951), we can attract this species to our gardens and aid in its continued success.

Mary F. Clarkson

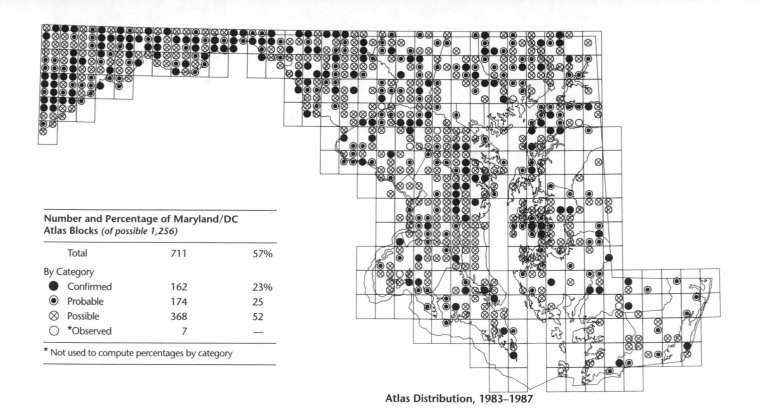

Atlas Distribution, 1983–1987

Number and Percentage of Maryland/DC Atlas Blocks *(of possible 1,256)*		
Total	711	57%
By Category		
● Confirmed	162	23%
◉ Probable	174	25
⊗ Possible	368	52
○ *Observed	7	—
* Not used to compute percentages by category		

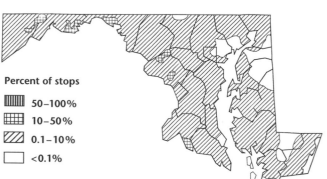

Percent of stops

▦	50–100%
▦	10–50%
▨	0.1–10%
☐	<0.1%

Relative Abundance, 1982–1989

Breeding Distribution, 1958

The Cedar Waxwing is uncommon and widespread. It is more common in scattered areas of western Maryland and is absent from some parts of the Eastern Shore.

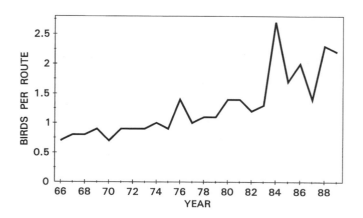

Maryland BBS Trend Graph, 1966–1989

MOB

Loggerhead Shrike

Lanius ludovicianus

The Loggerhead Shrike, a predatory songbird, feeds mostly on large insects such as grasshoppers, beetles, caterpillars, and wasps; it also takes small mammals and birds (Martin et al. 1951). It possesses a heavy, sharp-tipped bill for tearing flesh but lacks the powerful talons of raptors. It impales its prey on barbed wire, thorns, or sharp twigs, both for storage and to aid in feeding. This behavior has earned it the nickname *butcherbird.*

The Loggerhead Shrike is a bird of open habitats such as pastures, fields, and croplands; it frequently hunts from roadside fences and telephone wires. Although this general habitat type is abundant in Maryland, this species is now one of the rarest breeding birds in the state. It is listed by the USFWS (1987) as a nongame species of management concern, and *migrans,* Maryland's subspecies, is a candidate for federal listing as threatened or endangered and is listed by the DNR as an endangered species in Maryland.

The first breeding season report in Maryland was for an individual at Hagerstown, Washington County, in May of about 1880 (Kirkwood 1895). The first confirmed nesting was recorded by R. True on 20 May 1910 in Prince George's County (Stewart and Robbins 1958). In the 1880s, Loggerhead Shrikes were only suspected of being permanent residents around DC (Coues and Prentiss 1883). Nearly 50 years later they were considered uncommon permanent residents (Cooke 1929). Stewart and Robbins (1958) considered breeding uncommon in part of Prince George's County and rare and local elsewhere in Maryland, except for the Allegheny Plateau, where it was absent.

Breeding territories occur most frequently in areas of pastureland with a large number of perches, such as fence posts and telephone wires (Luukkonen and Fraser 1987). Loggerhead Shrikes hunt from perches; perch heights and the height of the ground vegetation affect prey detectability and may ultimately affect reproductive success. Short-grass pasture provides the best habitat for prey detection.

Because so little nesting information is available from

Maryland, the following is taken from a Virginia study by Luukkonen and Fraser (1987). Loggerhead Shrikes nest from early April to late June and typically attempt two broods, the first in early April and the second in late May. They build nests primarily in eastern red cedars and hawthorns that are often covered with grape or honeysuckle vines. Nest placement generally ranges from 5.5 to 18 ft (1.7–5.5 m) above the ground; the second nest is usually placed higher than the first. Both adults incubate the clutch of 4 to 6 eggs, and incubation takes 16 to 18 days. The young fledge in 17 to 20 days and are tended by the parents for at least four additional weeks.

Egg dates in Maryland and DC range from 19 April (MNRF) to 11 July (L. MacIvor, unpub. data); nestling dates in Maryland range from 9 May to 19 July (L. MacIvor, unpub. data). In six Maryland nests, clutch sizes were 4, 5, 5, 5, 6, and 6; brood sizes in nine nests range from 1 to 6 (MNRF; L. MacIvor, pers. comm.). Two broods are usually attempted in Maryland (Davidson 1988; L. MacIvor and W. Hershberger, unpub. data). A 1991 Loggerhead Shrike survey recorded eight breeding pairs in Maryland (L. MacIvor, unpub. data). Parasitism by Brown-headed Cowbirds is rare but has been recently documented (DeGeus 1991). Three of 261 Iowa nests (1.1%) were parasitized.

Atlas results show that breeding Loggerhead Shrikes in Maryland are now limited almost exclusively to Washington, Frederick, and Montgomery counties. "Confirmed" reports include adults on a nest, two nests with young, and fledged young. Because the Atlas project spanned five years, the reports may include some birds found at different locations in different years. Thus, the 13 reports probably represent fewer than 13 pairs. Reports from Calvert, Charles, and Prince George's counties on the Coastal Plain may have been nonbreeding individuals.

BBS data from 1966 through 1989 show a highly significant average annual decline of 4.8 percent in the Eastern Region; there are too few Maryland records to estimate a state trend. Although the main reason for the decline of Loggerhead Shrikes in Maryland and throughout the East is unknown, several causes are suspected. Both adults and young feed on roadways and typically fly low over the ground, remaining low when flying across roads. Collisions with automobiles have been documented as a major cause of mortality, including 29 percent of the observed fall and winter mortalities in Virginia (Blumton et al. 1989). It is also the most common cause of mortality known in Maryland. Three individuals, both adult and juvenal birds, were struck by cars during the summer of 1991 (L. MacIvor, unpub. data). Loggerhead Shrikes and their prey also are at risk from pesticide poisoning because they occupy agricultural and roadside habitats and are high on the food chain. Traces of pesticide contamination have been documented in several states, but none of the studies has directly linked contamination to reduced reproductive success or increased mortality (Luukkonen and Fraser 1987; Blumton et al. 1989). Loss of habitat is frequently a cause of population declines. Farmland occupied by Loggerhead Shrikes around DC in

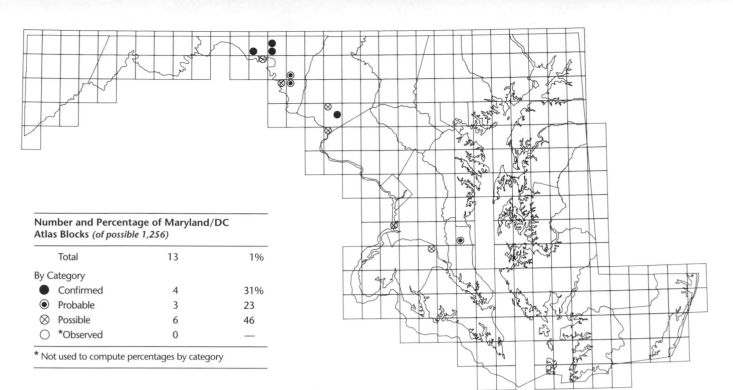

Number and Percentage of Maryland/DC Atlas Blocks *(of possible 1,256)*

Total	13	1%
By Category		
● Confirmed	4	31%
◉ Probable	3	23
⊗ Possible	6	46
○ *Observed	0	—

* Not used to compute percentages by category

Atlas Distribution, 1983–1987

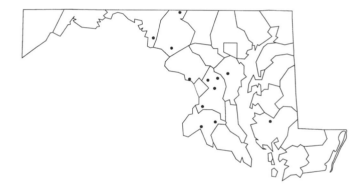

Breeding Distribution, 1958

the early 1900s has been almost completely lost to development, and total acreage in active pasture is continuing to decline. However, many areas of seemingly suitable habitat, especially in Washington and Frederick counties, remain unoccupied.

Conservation measures aimed at maintaining or increasing the Loggerhead Shrike population in Maryland will need to address all possible limiting factors, including consideration of reducing roadside spraying in areas known to be occupied by nesting Loggerhead Shrikes.

Lynn M. Davidson

European Starling

Sturnus vulgaris

The European Starling will never win a popularity contest among birdwatchers. It has become so widespread and abundant during this century that it is widely viewed as a pest. This adaptable bird makes itself at home in open fields, woodlands, cities, and suburbs and is abundant wherever found. Some individuals that winter in Maryland and DC migrate northward to breed, although the majority probably do not move far (Stewart and Robbins 1958).

Except during the breeding season, European Starlings roost in huge flocks in woodlots and on large buildings (Bent 1950). Flock sizes vary from a few hundred to hundreds of thousands. These birds are often found in mixed flocks, primarily with Red-winged Blackbirds, Common Grackles, and Brown-headed Cowbirds. In such large numbers, European Starlings are a nuisance to humans and native wildlife.

A native of the Old World, the European Starling was not known in North America until 1890. In March of that year, Eugene Schieffelin, a man consumed by the notion of introducing into North America every bird species mentioned in the works of William Shakespeare, released 80 starlings into Central Park, New York City (Page 1990). In less than 60 years, this bold, adaptive species had spread to the Pacific Coast (Garrett and Dunn 1981).

The bird's first appearance in Maryland was reported in the fall of 1906 in Baltimore City (Chapman 1907b). The following account of its spread in Maryland is condensed from Stewart and Robbins (1958). By 1917 the species was fairly common (flock of 10,000) in the Baltimore area. On 25 April 1917, a nest with young was found in Montgomery County, and on 27 May 1917 the first nest with young was found in Baltimore. By 1922 the European Starling was quite common around DC. Meanwhile, a flock of more than 75 was seen at Cambridge in Dorchester County in February 1916, and nesting was recorded there in 1920. Evidence of the westward spread was first noted in June 1918 when a nest was found in Frederick, Frederick County. By 1920 a flock of 100 was found in Cumberland, Allegany County. The European Starling was first recorded in the Allegheny Mountain Section in 1928. By 1947 it was a common to abundant permanent resident in all parts of the state (Hampe and Kolb 1947), a designation repeated by Stewart and Robbins (1958) a decade later.

The European Starling is generally a colonial breeder, requiring very little territory around its nest site. It competes successfully with native cavity-nesting birds, especially Eastern Bluebirds, woodpeckers, Great Crested Flycatchers, and Purple Martins (Bent 1950). In 217 Maryland nests (MNRF), heights range from 0 to 60 ft (0–18 m), with a mean of 14.9 ft (4.5 m). Only one nest—found at ground level in a hollow cedar stump—was below 3 ft (0.9 m); only seven nests were above 37 ft (11.0 m) (MNRF). The male locates the nest cavity and the female constructs the nest (Feare 1984). Maryland egg dates range from 22 March to 25 June, with peaks in early and late May (MNRF). Clutch sizes of 571 Maryland nests range from 3 to 8, with a mean of 5.1 (MNRF). Incubation, by both sexes (Stokes 1979), lasts about 12 days and begins before the final egg is laid; two broods are common. Nests with young have been reported in Maryland from 1 April to 24 July, peaking in the second week of May (MNRF). In 387 Maryland nests, brood sizes range from 1 to 6 (mean of 4). Young birds stay in the nest about 23 days, and the parents continue to tend them for about a week after they fledge (Stokes 1979). After fledging, the young birds join other juveniles to form large flocks. One of the two known instances of Brown-headed Cowbird parasitism occurred in Maryland, near Beltsville, Prince George's County (Friedmann 1963).

BBS data from 1966 through 1989 show a highly significant average annual decline in the Eastern Region, but the European Starling is anything but threatened. Maryland BBS data for the same period show a stable population. During the Atlas period, it was recorded in 96 percent of all blocks. It was absent only from the extensive marsh areas of the lower Eastern Shore, some tidewater blocks that are mostly open water, and five heavily wooded blocks in western Maryland.

Even though European Starlings have some redeeming qualities, such as eating clover leaf weevils, Japanese beetle grubs, and other insect pests (Bent 1950), they wreak havoc on agricultural fields and native cavity nesters. Waste from huge roosts also despoils many buildings. The North American population has grown from 80 birds in 1890 to over 200 million by 1990—one-third of the world's European Starling population (Page 1990). Programs designed to control this species have been implemented, but without significant success.

Sue Yingling

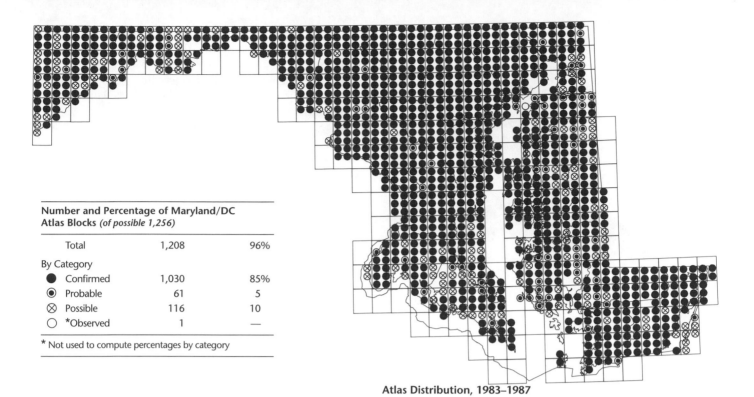

Number and Percentage of Maryland/DC Atlas Blocks *(of possible 1,256)*

Total	1,208	96%
By Category		
● Confirmed	1,030	85%
◉ Probable	61	5
⊗ Possible	116	10
○ *Observed	1	—

* Not used to compute percentages by category

Atlas Distribution, 1983–1987

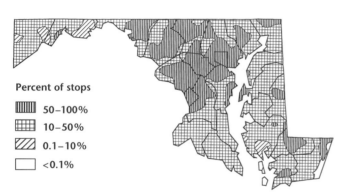

Percent of stops

▥	50–100%
▦	10–50%
▨	0.1–10%
☐	<0.1%

Relative Abundance, 1982–1989

Breeding Distribution, 1958

The European Starling is abundant in urban, suburban, and agricultural areas in central Maryland and in scattered developed areas on the Eastern Shore. It is common throughout the rest of the state. Lowest concentrations are in southern Dorchester County marshes and in Green Ridge State Forest in eastern Allegany County.

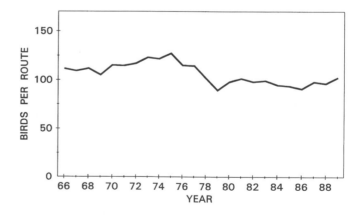

Maryland BBS Trend Graph, 1966–1989

White-eyed Vireo

Vireo griseus

The White-eyed Vireo is the elusive wide-eyed songster of swampy thickets, brushy hillsides, and hedgerows. Its distinctive song, *chick-per-weo-chick,* is easily learned, which is fortunate because this bird is more often heard than seen. Its song has been studied extensively because of the large number of variations, lack of duplication among individuals, and possible imitations of other species (Adkisson and Conner 1978; Bradley 1980; Borror 1987). Spring migrants return to Maryland from their wintering grounds in the southeastern United States and eastern Mexico (AOU 1983) in mid-April and remain until mid-September (Stewart and Robbins 1958).

Coues and Prentiss (1883) and Cooke (1929) called the White-eyed Vireo common around DC, as did Kirkwood (1895) when discussing Maryland as a whole. However, neither Kirkwood nor Eifrig (1904) had any record for western Maryland. Hampe and Kolb (1947) had no record for the Ridge and Valley Section, but they noted that Brooks (1936) called it uncommon in Garrett County. Stewart and Robbins (1958) described it as common in the Eastern and Western Shore sections, fairly common in the Upper Chesapeake Section and along the Potomac River in the Piedmont Section, uncommon in the rest of the Piedmont and Ridge and Valley sections, and rare in the Allegheny Mountain Section.

The White-eyed Vireo's preferred habitat consists of thickets, usually including blackberry, greenbrier, multiflora rose, witch hazel, and willow (Bent 1950). They also frequent abandoned pastures with young maple, elm, dogwood, and plum trees, as well as brushy woodlands and hedgerows, all with nearby streams or swamps. The highest breeding density recorded in Maryland is 40 territorial males per 100 acres (40.5 ha) in a shrub swamp in Prince George's County in 1945 (Stewart and Robbins 1958).

White-eyed Vireos suspend their nests from a fork of a branch, as is typical of the vireo family. Unlike other vireos nesting in Maryland, they usually nest near the ground;

heights of 29 Maryland nests (MNRF) range from 1 to 6 ft (0.3–1.8 m), with a mean of 3 ft (0.9 m). The nest, which is more cone-shaped than that of other vireos (Bent 1950), is placed in young trees or bushes. It is constructed by both adults and is woven from bark shreds, leaves, grasses, rootlets, other soft plant fibers and down, and spider webs. It is lined with fine grasses and decorated on the outside with moss, lichens, and material from paper wasp nests. The overall diameter and depth are each about 2 in. (5 cm) (Bent 1950). The earliest Maryland egg date is 22 April, and the latest is 26 July, with a peak in late May and early June (MNRF). Although there are no Maryland nest records from west of the Baltimore-Washington area, breeding is probably slightly later in Garrett County.

Typically, these vireos lay 4 dull white eggs with dark brown or black spots (Bent 1950). Clutch sizes in 20 Maryland nests are equally divided between 3 and 4 (MNRF). Both parents incubate, which requires 12 to 16 days (Bent 1950). They are fearless defenders of their nests. Usually only one brood is raised, although second broods are known in warmer climates (Bent 1950). Maryland nestling dates extend from 1 June to 19 August (MNRF). Brood sizes in nine Maryland nests range from 2 to 4. Both parents feed the young, which fledge in about two weeks (Bent 1950). The White-eyed Vireo's diet is almost exclusively insects during the breeding season but contains as much as 30 percent fruits and berries in the autumn (Martin et al. 1951). The White-eyed Vireo is a common host to the Brown-headed Cowbird (Friedmann 1963). Two of 29 Maryland nests (6.8%) were parasitized (MNRF). In Ontario, 2 of 4 nests (50%) were parasitized (Peck and James 1987).

Atlas fieldworkers penetrated the wet and thick nesting habitat of the White-eyed Vireo only infrequently. Fewer than 25 percent of the records were of "confirmed" breeding, while more than 50 percent were for birds holding territory. Atlas results show that the White-eyed Vireo has been expanding westward in Maryland during this century. It has moved solidly into the Piedmont Section and was found in about half the Atlas blocks in western Maryland. During the Atlas period it was found as high as 3,000 ft (914 m) on Backbone Mountain in Garrett County.

BBS data show a recent decline in White-eyed Vireo populations. Although data from 1966 through 1989 show stable populations in the Eastern Region and Maryland, Maryland data from 1980 through 1989 show a significant average annual decline of 2.9 percent. In view of this recent decline, continued monitoring of the population is needed, as is investigation into the causes of the decline. Preservation of riparian thickets, brushy areas, and hedgerows will help ensure that the White-eyed Vireo remains a fairly common breeding bird in Maryland.

James W. Cheevers

Number and Percentage of Maryland/DC Atlas Blocks (of possible 1,256)

Total	1,038	83%
By Category		
● Confirmed	239	23%
◉ Probable	542	52
⊗ Possible	257	25
○ *Observed	0	—

* Not used to compute percentages by category

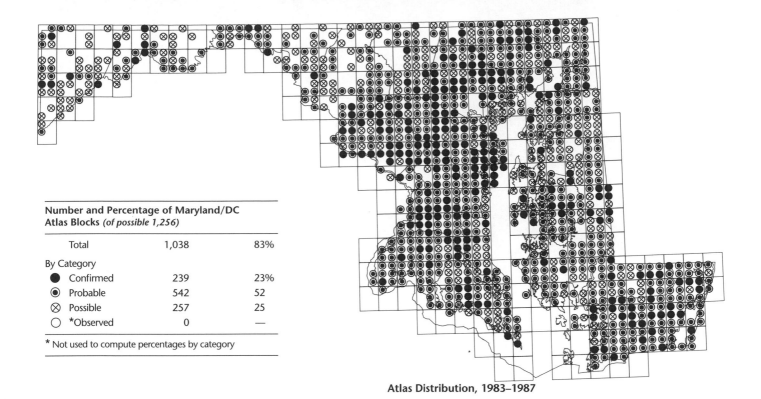

Atlas Distribution, 1983–1987

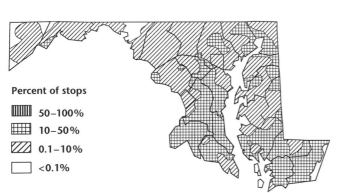

Percent of stops

▥	50–100%
▦	10–50%
▨	0.1–10%
☐	<0.1%

Relative Abundance, 1982–1989

Breeding Distribution, 1958

The White-eyed Vireo is most common on the Coastal Plain and declines to the west. It was not recorded in the agricultural expanse of the Hagerstown Valley or in the more open areas of Garrett County in the Allegheny Mountain Section.

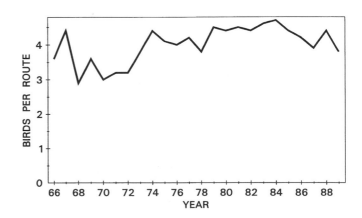

Maryland BBS Trend Graph, 1966–1989

White-eyed Vireo 307

Solitary Vireo

Vireo solitarius

The Solitary Vireo is the first vireo to arrive in the spring. It migrates through most of the state, primarily from mid-April to early May and from mid-September to mid-October (Stewart and Robbins 1958). It is a common nester only in the Allegheny Mountain Section. It winters from the southeastern United States to Costa Rica (AOU 1983).

Preble (1900) described the Solitary Vireo, at that time called the Blue-headed Vireo, as fairly common in the summer at Finzel, Grantsville, Bittinger, Kearney, Swanton, and Dan's Mountain. From these observations, he concluded that it must breed in the higher parts of Allegany and Garrett counties. John Sommer reported the first Maryland record of nest building, 27 May 1919, and also the first nest with eggs, 1 June 1925 (Stewart and Robbins 1958). Hampe and Kolb (1947) reported it as a fairly common breeding bird in western Maryland. Stewart and Robbins (1958) listed it as fairly common in the Allegheny Mountain Section at elevations above 2,000 ft (610 m).

The Solitary Vireo breeds in hemlock, white pine, and mixed mesophytic forests (Stewart and Robbins 1958). Robbins (1949a) reported the highest Maryland breeding density of 27 territorial males per 100 acres (40.5 ha) in an old-growth hemlock forest in Garrett County. Robbins and Stewart (1951a) found a density of 17 territorial males per 100 acres (40 ha) in a very different habitat, mature northern hardwood forest, also in Garrett County. Robbins et al. (1989a) found that in Maryland, nesting territories of the Solitary Vireo are highly correlated with extensive moist forest. Sabo (1980) noted that in New Hampshire the male sings infrequently in its large territory, averaging 12.4 acres (5.0 ha), where a stream is a key component. Maryland territories in prime habitat are smaller (Robbins 1949a; Robbins and Stewart 1951a).

James (1978) described the Solitary Vireo's ritualized nest-building display. He reported that unmated males search for nest sites and begin building before females arrive. After pairing, the pair takes eight days to construct the first nest of the season. Both sexes participate initially, but as the building continues, the male's role decreases. The female finishes and lines the nest, while the male accompanies her. Although Solitary Vireos sing high in the trees, they nest low in the forest.

Of 18 Maryland nests, 10 were built in hemlocks, 3 in maples, 2 in white oaks, 2 in witch hazels, and 1 in a red pine (MNRF). Heights of 16 Maryland nests range from 5.1 to 17 ft (1.5–5.2 m), with a mean of 9.6 ft (2.9 m). The female lays 3 to 5 (usually 4) eggs in the hanging-cup nest (Bent 1953). Incubation requires 13 or 14 days (Peck and James 1987). Egg and nestling data for Maryland show clutches ranging from 2 to 5. Maryland egg dates extend from 30 May to 22 July, and nestling dates range from 15 June to 1 July (MNRF). In 1976, W. Devlin reported nest building on the late date of 13 July and observed the adult feeding fledged young near that nest on 14 August (MNRF). Although most authorities state that the Solitary Vireo nests from late May to mid-July, Devlin's data extend this period to mid-August. Caterpillars and moths are their major food items (Chapin 1925). Friedmann (1963) considered the Solitary Vireo an uncommon victim of the Brown-headed Cowbird; however, 5 of 8 Maryland nests (62.5%) were parasitized (MNRF). This contrasts sharply with Ontario, where 2 of 44 nests (4.5%) were parasitized (Peck and James 1987).

Stewart and Robbins (1958) reported the Solitary Vireo as breeding only in the Allegheny Mountain Section of Maryland, and this is generally still true. Indeed, 56 of the 74 Atlas blocks in which some level of breeding category was reported were located in this section. Atlas data, however, show an extension of the Solitary Vireo's range into the Ridge and Valley Section, including a "confirmed" record of a nest with an egg in the Oldtown CE block. In the Bellegrove quadrangle, there were two blocks with males on territory, and in nine other blocks in the Ridge and Valley Section "possible" breeding was recorded. Even in the Piedmont, singing birds were reported in three blocks: "probable" breeding status in Manchester NW and Clarksville SW, and "possible" breeding in Woodbine CW. No breeding evidence was recorded from 1971 through 1973 or from 1973 through 1975 during the Atlas projects in Montgomery and Howard counties (Klimkiewicz and Solem 1978). However, the breeding-status reports for the Ridge and Valley and Piedmont sections are consistent with the presence of Solitary Vireos during the breeding seasons before and after the Atlas period (Ringler 1979b, 1981b, 1982, 1988c, 1989b).

BBS data from 1966 through 1989 show a highly significant average annual increase of 4.4 percent in the Eastern Region; there are too few data to estimate a trend for Maryland. The needs of the Solitary Vireo are being met in Maryland. In fact, the bird seems to be increasing as a nesting species. This situation should continue if extensive moist forests are maintained.

Jane H. Farrell

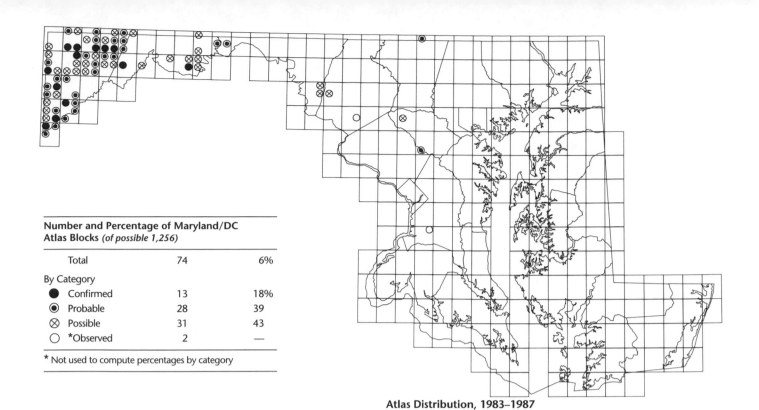

Number and Percentage of Maryland/DC Atlas Blocks *(of possible 1,256)*

	Total	74	6%
By Category			
●	Confirmed	13	18%
◉	Probable	28	39
⊗	Possible	31	43
○	*Observed	2	—

* Not used to compute percentages by category

Atlas Distribution, 1983–1987

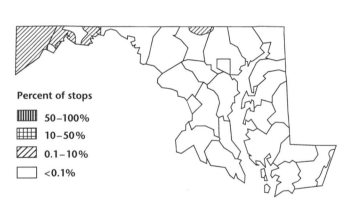

Percent of stops

▦	50–100%
▦	10–50%
▨	0.1–10%
▢	<0.1%

Relative Abundance, 1982–1989

Breeding Distribution, 1958

The Solitary Vireo is fairly common and evenly distributed throughout the Allegheny Mountain Section in Garrett County and in western and eastern Allegany County in the Ridge and Valley Section. The Carroll County record represents a single bird that was detected in the Pennsylvania portion of the block.

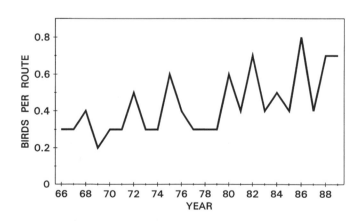

Maryland BBS Trend Graph, 1966–1989

Yellow-throated Vireo

Vireo flavifrons

The Yellow-throated Vireo is a fairly common summer resident in floodplain and lowland swamp forests, as well as in rich, moist upland forests in Maryland (Stewart and Robbins 1958). The DNR lists it as a forest interior–dwelling species, typically requiring large tracts of moist floodplain forest for breeding (Bushman and Therres 1988). Spring migrants return from their wintering grounds in the Caribbean Basin and Central America (AOU 1983) in late April, and the last fall migrants depart by early October (Robbins and Bystrak 1977).

Coues and Prentiss (1862, 1883) listed the Yellow-throated Vireo as an abundant or common summer resident in DC in the nineteenth century. Kirkwood (1895), however, wrote that it was not very common in summer in Maryland, as did Cooke (1929) early in the twentieth century. Eifrig (1904) described it as an uncommon nesting bird in Allegany and Garrett counties. Stewart and Robbins (1958) reported it as a fairly common breeding bird in the Eastern Shore, Western Shore, and Upper Chesapeake sections and in the Potomac River Valley of the Piedmont Section. They considered it uncommon to rare elsewhere.

Harrison (1978) described its nesting habitat as deciduous or mixed forest near clearings or water. The highest breeding densities reported in Maryland are 25 territorial males per 100 acres (40.5 ha) in mixed-hardwood forest in Calvert County (Fales 1973) and 19 territorial males per 100 acres in old-growth central hardwood deciduous forest in Prince George's County (Stewart and Robbins 1947a). The nest, a deep rounded cup made of plant fibers, covered with lichens and spider webs, and lined with fine grass or pine needles, is usually located on the end of a horizontal forked branch more than 20 ft (6.1 m) high (Bent 1950). The heights of 18 Maryland nests (MNRF) range from 10 to 50 ft (3.0–15 m), with a mean of 27.4 ft (8.4 m).

The earliest recorded Maryland egg date is 9 May (Stewart and Robbins 1958) and the latest is 21 July (MNRF); the latest date for DC is 21 July (Stewart and Robbins 1958). The Yellow-throated Vireo usually lays 4 oval, smooth white eggs that are sometimes blotched with brown, pale gray, or purple (Harrison 1978). There are only five Maryland records of nests with eggs: one with 2, two with 3, and two with 4 (MNRF). Incubation, by the female, lasts 14 days (Harrison 1978). There are only two Maryland nests records with brood size reported: one with 1 and one with 3 (MNRF). Young in the nest have been reported in Maryland from 4 June to 2 August. The height and placement of the nest make specific information hard to acquire. The Yellow-throated Vireo is a common victim of Brown-headed Cowbird parasitism (Friedmann 1963). Although no parasitized nests have been reported in Maryland, 22 of 44 Ontario nests (50.0%) contained Brown-headed Cowbird eggs or young (Peck and James 1987). Its diet consists almost entirely of insects, especially moths and caterpillars, bugs, and beetles; some berries, such as sassafras and grapes, are eaten in the fall (Chapin 1925).

Atlas results show the Yellow-throated Vireo widely distributed in the Pocomoke River basin in Wicomico, Somerset, and Worcester counties; in the forested portions of the Western Shore Section; in the eastern part of the Piedmont Section; and in the extensive forests of the Ridge and Valley Section, although it is generally absent from the agricultural valleys. It also is well distributed in the Upper Chesapeake Section. It is less frequent elsewhere in the Eastern Shore Section, occurring mostly along the Maryland-Delaware border. In Garrett County its distribution is spotty; it occurs mostly in the lower elevations along the Potomac River and in the northwestern part of the county. The scarcity of records in eastern Frederick County, western Carroll County, and parts of St. Mary's County may be because these areas are primarily agricultural without much floodplain forest. Yellow-throated Vireos are also missing from the extensive marshlands on the lower Eastern Shore and from coastal Worcester County. Their Maryland range appears to have expanded slightly from that described by Stewart and Robbins (1958). Almost half (47%) of all Atlas records are for singing males on territory. Adults with food for young, adults on nests, and fledged young account for 79 percent of "confirmed" records.

BBS data for 1966 through 1979 show stable populations for the Eastern Region and Maryland. Giving priority to preservation of extensive tracts of mature upland forest adjacent to floodplain forest is a step that local governments, developers, and private agencies should take to aid this species.

Keith D. Van Ness, Jr.

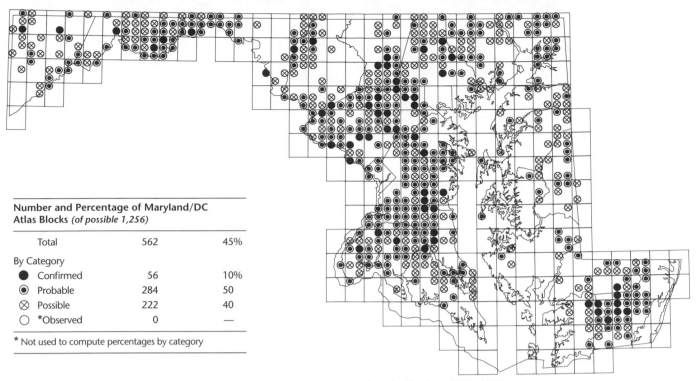

Number and Percentage of Maryland/DC Atlas Blocks *(of possible 1,256)*

Total	562	45%
By Category		
● Confirmed	56	10%
◉ Probable	284	50
⊗ Possible	222	40
○ *Observed	0	—

* Not used to compute percentages by category

Atlas Distribution, 1983–1987

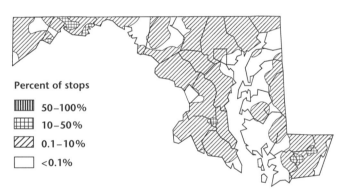

Percent of stops

▤	50–100%
▦	10–50%
▨	0.1–10%
☐	<0.1%

Relative Abundance, 1982–1989

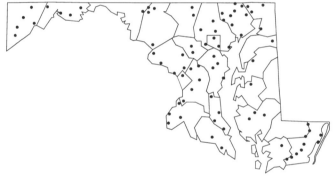

Breeding Distribution, 1958

The Yellow-throated Vireo is uncommon but widespread. It is absent from most of the extensive agricultural lands of the Eastern Shore, from the Frederick and Hagerstown valleys in the Ridge and Valley Section, and from urban areas.

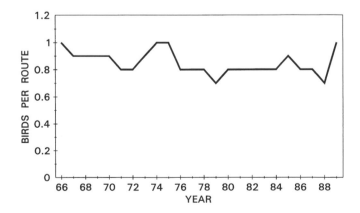

Maryland BBS Trend Graph, 1966–1989

Warbling Vireo

Vireo gilvus

The Warbling Vireo, a nondescript bird of tall trees, is more often heard than seen. Its family name, *Vireo*, of Latin derivation, means *I am green*. This is descriptive of many vireos, which were often referred to as greenlets in early literature (Coues and Prentiss 1883). The Warbling Vireo is grayer than many of the other vireos. Its rich, warbling song is atypical of vireos, and males may sing as frequently as 4,000 times per day (Pearson 1917). The opening seven notes of the song have been likened to the opening notes of Chopin's "Impromptu Fantasia." Spring migrants return to Maryland from their Mexican and Central American wintering grounds (AOU 1983) in late April, and most fall migrants depart by the end of September (Robbins and Bystrak 1977). Males typically arrive on the breeding grounds one day earlier than females (Howes-Jones 1985b).

Although the Warbling Vireo was formerly a common breeder in DC (Coues and Prentiss 1862, 1883), which is near the southeastern edge of its range (AOU 1983), it became uncommon before the end of the nineteenth century (Richmond 1888) and was very rare a few decades later (Cooke 1929). Historical data from Maryland are scanty; Kirkwood (1895) knew of no nesting records in the Baltimore area. He mentioned one mid-June observation from St. Michaels in Talbot County and quoted E. Small as saying they were common at Hagerstown in Washington County. Eifrig (1904) thought them uncommon in western Maryland. Jackson (1941) and colleagues collected nine sets of eggs from 1910 to 1926 in the Cambridge area of Dorchester County, where they are no longer known to nest. Stewart and Robbins (1958) described their breeding status as fairly common in the Ridge and Valley and Upper Chesapeake sections, uncommon in the Piedmont and the northern part of the Eastern Shore Section, uncommon and local in the southern part of the Eastern Shore, and rare in the Allegheny Mountain and Western Shore sections. BBS data from

1966 through 1989 show stable populations in Maryland and the Eastern Region; however, continental data show a highly significant average annual increase of 1.4 percent.

The principal habitat of the Warbling Vireo in Maryland consists of tall scattered trees in pastures, parklands, and along streams and rivers (Stewart and Robbins 1958). It can be found in open deciduous and mixed woodlands as well. Cooley (1947) recorded a high breeding density of 10 territorial males per 100 acres (40.5 ha) in a streamside habitat of tall trees and shrubs in Baltimore County. Because nests are high (MNRF), little is known about the breeding biology. The nest is usually placed on a long limb, well away from the trunk (Tyler 1950c). The heights of 15 Maryland nests (MNRF) range from 15 to 70 ft (4.6–21 m), with a mean of 39.4 ft (12 m). The female builds the nest while the male defends the territory with persistent song bouts; the male participates in incubation and frequently sings from the nest, a behavior often associated with this species (Howes-Jones 1985a,b).

Nests with eggs or nests with males incubating and singing have been reported in Maryland as early as 28 April, although most records are from 16 May to 22 June (MNRF). Clutch sizes in Maryland nests range from 3 to 5, most often 4 (MNRF). Incubation requires 12 days (Audubon 1842). Nests with young have been reported for Maryland only from 30 May to 8 June, although, based on egg dates, young may be in the nest into July (MNRF). There is no information on brood sizes in Maryland, and the number of broods per season is unknown. Young fledge 16 days after hatching (Howes-Jones 1985a) and are fed by both parents during this period. The Warbling Vireo's diet consists almost entirely of insects, especially caterpillars, beetles, and bugs (Martin et al. 1951). This species is thought to be a frequent victim of the Brown-headed Cowbird (Friedmann 1963), although Howes-Jones (1985b) reported that females abandoned nests that contained only Brown-headed Cowbird eggs. In Ontario, 6 of 55 nests (10.9%) were parasitized (Peck and James 1987); there was no parasitism in the 11 Maryland nests (MNRF).

During the Atlas period, Warbling Vireos were widespread in the Upper Chesapeake, Piedmont, and Ridge and Valley sections, especially along the Potomac River and near larger streams and rivers in the interior of the state. In the Western Shore Section, they were scattered along the Patuxent River, an area where they were not found in the 1950s. Atlas fieldwork revealed only one record from the Talbot-Caroline-Wicomico county area, demonstrating a sharp reduction in the breeding range described by Stewart and Robbins (1958). Spraying of pesticides on shade trees, which this vireo depends on for its insect food, may have contributed to this decline (Bull 1974).

Warbling Vireos need tall shade trees or tracts of tall deciduous or mixed open woodland, especially riparian habitat, in which to breed. These habitats must be maintained if this bird is to remain a breeding species in Maryland.

Steve Clarkson

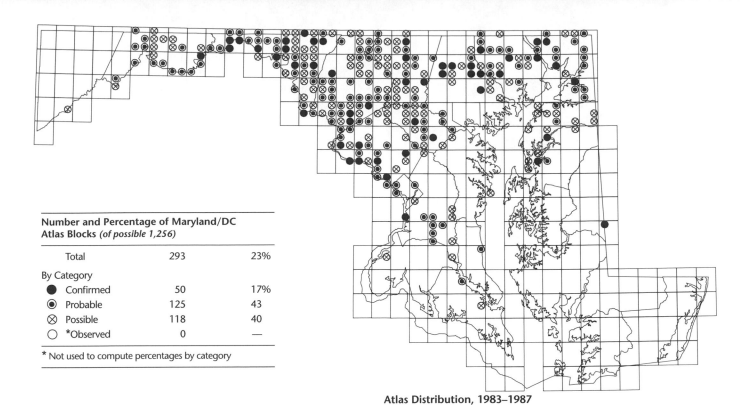

Number and Percentage of Maryland/DC Atlas Blocks *(of possible 1,256)*

Total	293	23%
By Category		
● Confirmed	50	17%
◉ Probable	125	43
⊗ Possible	118	40
○ *Observed	0	—

* Not used to compute percentages by category

Atlas Distribution, 1983–1987

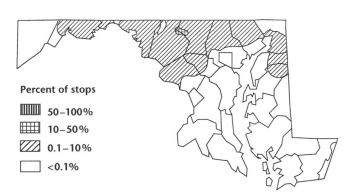

Percent of stops

▥	50–100%
▦	10–50%
▨	0.1–10%
☐	<0.1%

Relative Abundance, 1982–1989

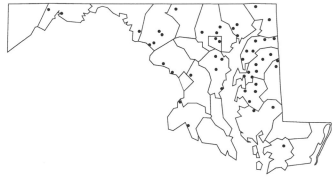

Breeding Distribution, 1958

The Warbling Vireo is uncommon and widespread in the Piedmont and Ridge and Valley sections, and in eastern portions of Cecil, Kent, and Queen Anne's counties on the upper Eastern Shore. It was not detected elsewhere within its breeding range.

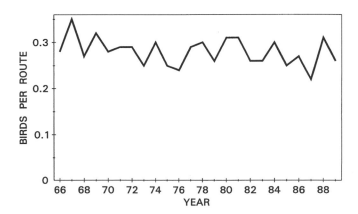

Maryland BBS Trend Graph, 1966–1989

Red-eyed Vireo

Vireo olivaceus

The Red-eyed Vireo, one of the most abundant songbirds in North America, can be found in almost every deciduous woodlot in Maryland. The male is a tireless singer, capable of delivering 20,000 songs daily (Lawrence 1953). It is a summer resident, with birds returning from their South American wintering grounds (AOU 1983) in late April (Robbins and Bystrak 1977). The last fall migrants linger into mid-October.

This vireo was apparently always common in Maryland and DC. Kirkwood (1895) called it very common in central Maryland, and Eifrig (1904) reported it as one of the most common summer birds in western Maryland. Hampe and Kolb (1947) thought it abundant in all sections. Stewart and Robbins (1958) described its breeding status as abundant in all sections except the Eastern Shore, where it was only common (because of less deciduous forest). The two highest breeding densities reported for Maryland are 138 territorial males per 100 acres (40.5 ha) in mixed-hardwood forest in Calvert County (Fales 1973) and 103 territorial males per 100 acres in a selectively logged mature tulip tree–oak forest in Prince George's County in 1988 (Robbins 1989). Robbins et al. (1989a) found that prime habitat for Red-eyed Vireos in Maryland is extensive, tall, deciduous forest with closed canopy, and that this species is more tolerant of forest fragmentation than are most neotropical migrants. An isolated woodlot would need to be, on average, only 6.2 acres (2.5 ha) to have a 50 percent probability of attracting Red-eyed Vireos.

When males arrive in spring, they establish territories of about 5 acres (2 ha); as they negotiate boundaries with adjacent males over the next few days, territories generally shrink to about 3 acres (1.2 ha) (Stokes 1979). The females arrive several days later, select the nest site, and build the nest. The nest is usually suspended from a horizontal fork of a small deciduous branch (Harrison 1975). Heights of 206 Maryland nests (MNRF) range from 2 to 50 ft (0.6–15 m), with a mean of 12 ft (3.7 m). Egg dates for Maryland span 9 May to 11 August, with a peak in mid-June. Clutch sizes in 115 Maryland nests range from 1 (probably incomplete) to 6, with a mean of 3.2 (MNRF). Two broods probably are attempted in Maryland. Incubation, by both sexes, lasts 11 to 14 days (Tyler 1950b). The young are tended by both parents and fledge in about 12 days. Nests with young have been found in Maryland from 1 June to 18 August, with a peak in late June (MNRF). Brood sizes in 54 Maryland nests range from 1 to 4 (mean of 2.4). The Red-eyed Vireo's diet is about 85 percent insects, with the remaining 15 percent being wild fruits and berries, which are usually taken in the fall (Chapin 1925). The bulk of the insect food consists of caterpillars and beetles.

The Red-eyed Vireo is one of the most frequent victims of the Brown-headed Cowbird. In Michigan, Southern (1958) found that 74 of 104 nests (72.0%) were parasitized, as were 136 of 354 Ontario nests (38.4%) (Peck and James 1987). In Maryland, only 37 of 162 nests (22.8%) with eggs were parasitized (MNRF). Red-eyed Vireo defenses against parasitism should be further investigated; some Brown-headed Cowbird eggs have been found buried under a second nest floor (Friedmann 1929).

With the continued clearing of woodlands, one would expect Red-eyed Vireos to be declining over eastern North America. The clearing apparently is balanced in some states by the reversion of abandoned land to second-growth woods. Maryland, however, is losing timberland 4 percent faster than it is being replaced (Frieswyk and DiGiovanni 1988). BBS data from 1966 through 1989 show a highly significant average annual increase of 1.6 percent in the Eastern Region. Maryland data show a stable population for the whole period, but there was an increase for 1966 through 1980 followed by a decline from 1980 through 1989.

Red-eyed Vireos were found throughout Maryland during the Atlas period. They were absent from only a few blocks on Assateague Island and from some treeless blocks dominated by extensive marshlands. The persistent singing of the males resulted in a large number of "probable" records, mostly (88%) of birds holding territory. Most "confirmed" records were of fledglings (36%) or adults carrying food for young (28%).

Although the Red-eyed Vireo was found in 94 percent of the Atlas blocks, it was missing or very hard to find in many quarterblocks, especially in urban, suburban, and highly agricultural areas. Unless the loss and fragmentation of Maryland's woodlands is stopped, the Red-eyed Vireo will disappear from many of our local birding areas.

William A. Russell, Jr.

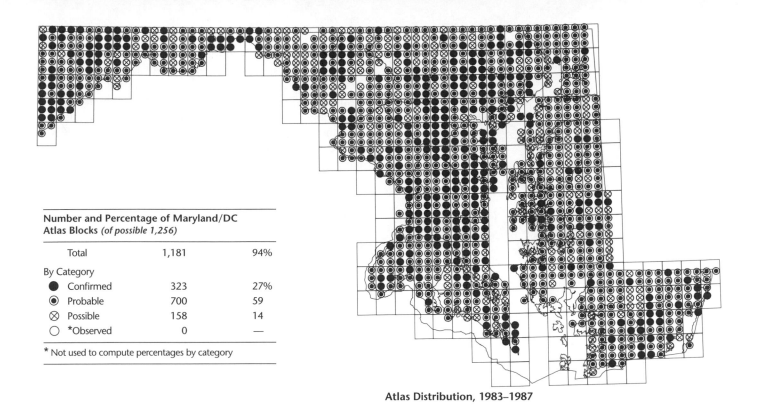

Atlas Distribution, 1983–1987

Number and Percentage of Maryland/DC Atlas Blocks *(of possible 1,256)*		
Total	1,181	94%
By Category		
● Confirmed	323	27%
◉ Probable	700	59
⊗ Possible	158	14
○ *Observed	0	—

* Not used to compute percentages by category

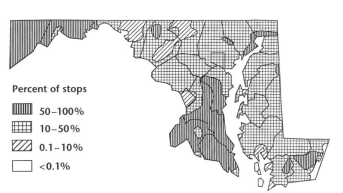

Percent of stops

▥	50–100%
▦	10–50%
▧	0.1–10%
☐	<0.1%

Relative Abundance, 1982–1989

Breeding Distribution, 1958

The Red-eyed Vireo is abundant in the extensive woodlands of Garrett and Allegany counties in western Maryland, in southern Maryland, the upper Bay, and Pocomoke State Forest in Worcester County. It is least common in agricultural areas of the Frederick and Hagerstown valleys and in marsh and urban areas.

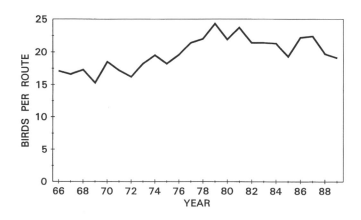

Maryland BBS Trend Graph, 1966–1989

Blue-winged Warbler

Vermivora pinus

The trim, colorful Blue-winged Warbler surprised Atlas fieldworkers by appearing on territory in many places where it previously had been undetected. Spring migrants begin returning from their Mexican and Central American wintering grounds (AOU 1983) in late April, and most depart by mid-September (Stewart and Robbins 1958).

Blue-winged Warblers are known to have nested in the Baltimore area for at least 100 years, but all early authors considered them rare and local during the breeding season (Kirkwood 1895; Cooke 1929; Hampe and Kolb 1947). Kirkwood (1895) reported eight nest records from 1892 to 1897 along Gwynn Falls in Baltimore County, but Eifrig (1904) did not have even a migration record from the two western counties. Coues and Prentiss (1883) recorded nesting near Laurel (no county given) in 1872. Summer records from other areas were almost nonexistent until fair numbers were reported within 5 mi. (8 km) of the Susquehanna River north of Rowlandsville, Cecil County, in 1946 (Stewart and Robbins 1947a). Stewart and Robbins (1958) described its breeding status as fairly common and local in the eastern part of the Ridge and Valley Section and the northeastern part of the Piedmont Section.

In Maryland, Blue-winged Warblers use moist, brushy, cutover forests (Stewart and Robbins 1958); Bent (1953) included areas of open grass in his description of moist scrubby habitat. These are the habitats that the closely related Golden-winged Warblers also use, although one source (Robbins 1950) suggests Blue-winged Warblers may prefer wetter areas. No Maryland breeding densities have been reported for Blue-winged Warblers. In West Virginia, Hall (1983) reported a high density of 49 territorial males per 100 acres (40.5) in mixed-hardwood forest.

Males arrive first in the spring and soon establish territories. Most nest building starts after 20 May (MNRF). Nests are typically built on the ground; all five well-described

Maryland nests were in clumps of sticks or grass, or in blackberry or poison ivy thickets within 6 in. (15 cm) of ground level. Nests with eggs have been reported in Maryland from 17 May to 18 June (MNRF). Clutch sizes in eight nests range from 3 to 5. Incubation, by the female only, lasts about 10 or 11 days (Bent 1953). Nests with young have been reported in Maryland from 13 June to 12 July; in all four reports, brood sizes are either 3 or 4 (MNRF). Young fledge in about 8 to 10 days, and both parents care for them (Bent 1953). The earliest Maryland date for fledged young is 11 June (MNRF). Two late Maryland nests contained young birds on 1 July and 12 July, and Kirkwood (1895) reported young just fledged on 5 July. These late dates suggest either two broods or renesting after an earlier failure.

The Blue-winged Warbler is a common victim of Brown-headed Cowbird parasitism; Friedmann (1929, 1963) reported 61 cases. There is only one record for Maryland (Stewart and Robbins 1958), but Bull (1974) reported 16 instances in New York (no sample size was given), and Peck and James (1987) stated that 2 of 6 Ontario nests (33.3%) were parasitized. Small beetles, ants, spiders, and caterpillars are the chief food items (Broun 1957).

Probably the most intriguing feature of Blue-winged Warbler behavior is its expansion into the traditional Golden-winged Warbler range and the hybridizations that sometimes result. Historically, the Blue-winged Warbler was extremely rare east of the Appalachians (Cooke 1904), and the precise timing of its spread into our area is not known. Although hybridization occurs in Maryland, no proof of Blue-winged X Golden-winged Warbler mating was obtained during the Atlas period.

The Blue-winged Warbler has expanded its range considerably in Maryland from that given by Stewart and Robbins (1958). Atlas data show it has reoccupied the area of the Piedmont along the Fall Line where it was found late in the nineteenth century. It has spread west through the Ridge and Valley Section, with a few reports from Garrett County in the Allegheny Mountain Section, the stronghold of the Golden-winged Warbler in Maryland. The two records on the lower Eastern Shore appear out of place but are consistent with the distribution shown by Delaware atlas data. The real surprise is the number of reports in Maryland compared with this species' near-absence in nearby Virginia. Blue-winged Warbler populations probably peaked in central Maryland in the late 1970s and the 1980s during the development of Columbia in Howard County, when great expanses of abandoned farmland were regenerating (C. Robbins, pers. comm.). They were detected in twice as many Howard County quarterblocks during this Atlas as in the county atlas of 1973 through 1975 (Robbins et al. 1989c).

BBS data from 1966 through 1989 show stable populations of Blue-winged Warblers in the Eastern Region and Maryland. As long as suitable habitat is available in both nesting and wintering areas, Maryland and DC should continue to enjoy their presence.

David W. Holmes

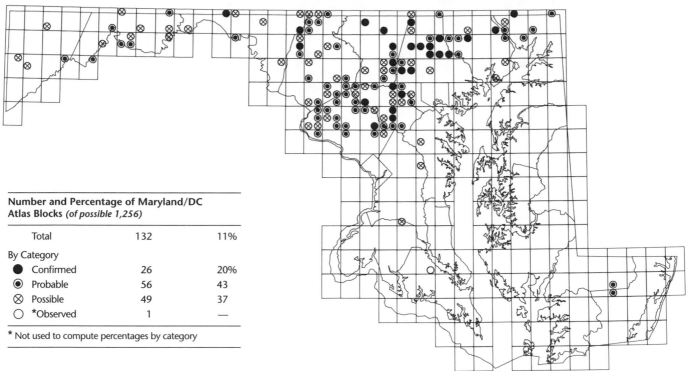

Atlas Distribution, 1983–1987

Number and Percentage of Maryland/DC Atlas Blocks *(of possible 1,256)*

	Total	132	11%
By Category			
●	Confirmed	26	20%
◉	Probable	56	43
⊗	Possible	49	37
○	*Observed	1	—

* Not used to compute percentages by category

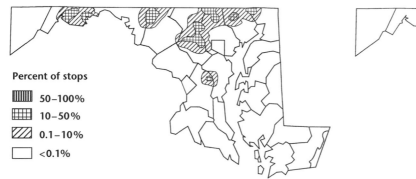

Percent of stops

▥	50–100%
▦	10–50%
▨	0.1–10%
☐	<0.1%

Relative Abundance, 1982–1989

Breeding Distribution, 1958

The Blue-winged Warbler is locally common in the northern Piedmont Section, in the Catoctin Mountains, and in eastern Allegany County in the Ridge and Valley Section. In this area there are small pockets of abundance surrounded by smaller numbers.

Golden-winged Warbler

Vermivora chrysoptera

The Golden-winged Warbler is not common, but it is fairly easy to find in early summer within its breeding range in the Maryland mountains. Migrants return to Maryland from their wintering grounds in Mexico and Central America (AOU 1983) in late April, stop singing by early June, and depart by mid-September (Stewart and Robbins 1958).

One of the most fascinating aspects of this species is its interaction, including hybridization, with the closely related Blue-winged Warbler. Confer and Knapp (1981) reported that the two species originally had completely disjunct ranges, with the Blue-winged Warbler staying almost totally west of the Appalachians. Although the Golden-winged Warbler has been expanding north and east since about 1800, the Blue-winged Warbler has been expanding more quickly into northern and eastern states for the past 100 years.

The first Maryland records of summering Golden-winged Warblers were in Allegany County in 1895 (Kirkwood 1895) and Garrett County in 1899 (Preble 1900). Eifrig (1904) described them as abundant migrants and increasingly common breeding birds in western Maryland. East of there, they were known only as uncommon to rare migrants (Coues and Prentiss 1862, 1883; Kirkwood 1895; Cooke 1929). Stewart and Robbins (1958) described their breeding status as fairly common in the Allegheny Mountain and western Ridge and Valley sections and uncommon in western Washington County.

In Maryland, Golden-winged Warblers breed in brushy, cut-over, oak-hickory and mixed-mesophytic habitats and bog forests (Stewart and Robbins 1958). They prefer to nest in loose colonies in suitable habitats of 50 acres (20.3 ha) or more, although individual territories are normally between 1 and 2 acres (0.4–0.8 ha) in size (Ficken and Ficken 1968b). The highest breeding density recorded in Maryland is 17 territorial males per 100 acres (40.5 ha) in dense second growth on top of Negro Mountain in Garrett County (Robbins 1949b).

The four recorded Maryland nests were on or very near the ground in clearings or bushy fields with woods not far away (MNRF). Three were near water: at a spring head, near a river, and near a lake. All four were in Garrett County. The only egg date reported for Maryland is 2 June in Garrett County (MNRF), but the span is probably similar to that of New York, where nests with eggs have been found from 18 May to 16 June (Bull 1974). Standard clutch sizes are 4 or 5 eggs, although 6 and 7 have been reported (Tyler 1953). Incubation, by the female, takes about 10 days. Ficken and Ficken (1968a) watched one male give food to a female on the nest several times within an hour. Nests with young have been found in Maryland only from 13 to 17 June, certainly not a true indication of the nestling period; each of the three recorded nests contained 4 young (MNRF). In New York, nestlings have been found from 8 June to 6 July (Bull 1974). The young fledge in about 10 days (Tyler 1953). Both parents feed the young, both in and out of the nest. Golden-winged Warblers are single-brooded (Forbush 1929).

Friedmann (1963) considered this species as only an occasional victim of Brown-headed Cowbird parasitism. Maryland observers have not yet detected parasitism but remain apprehensive because Peck and James (1987) reported parasitism in 13 of 32 Ontario nests (40.6%). Food habits of this warbler are poorly known, but Nelson (1933) described a Golden-winged Warbler in Maryland taking tiny leaf-roller caterpillars from pawpaw flowers, the only plant on which these moth larvae are known to feed.

Few species have been as exhaustively studied as have Blue-winged and Golden-winged Warblers and their hybrids. Literature exists on habitat preferences, vocalizations, pairing mechanisms, and hybrid plumages; however, the reasons Blue-winged Warblers are often replacing Golden-winged Warblers where their ranges overlap remain unclear. Some fascinating reading awaits those interested in these two species and their hybridization. (See Parkes 1951; Short 1963; Gill and Lanyon 1964; Ficken and Ficken 1967, 1968a,b, 1969; Gill and Murray 1972b; Murray and Gill 1976; Gill 1980, 1987; Confer and Knapp 1981.)

Atlas results show that the range of the Golden-winged Warbler has not changed significantly in Maryland since the publication of Stewart and Robbins (1958). Atlas observers found it is still widely distributed in western Maryland and in Washington County west of the Hagerstown Valley. The latter area has an increasing number of Blue-winged Warblers, so there is concern that Golden-winged Warblers will be driven from some of their traditional range here, as they have in other states. The only hybrid found during the Atlas period was a "possible" record of a Brewster's Warbler at Gray Hill in Garrett County in 1983.

BBS data from 1966 through 1989 show a highly significant average annual decline of 2 percent in Golden-winged Warbler populations in the Eastern Region; there are too few data to estimate a trend for Maryland. In light of this decline, monitoring of the Golden-winged Warbler in Maryland is warranted.

David W. Holmes

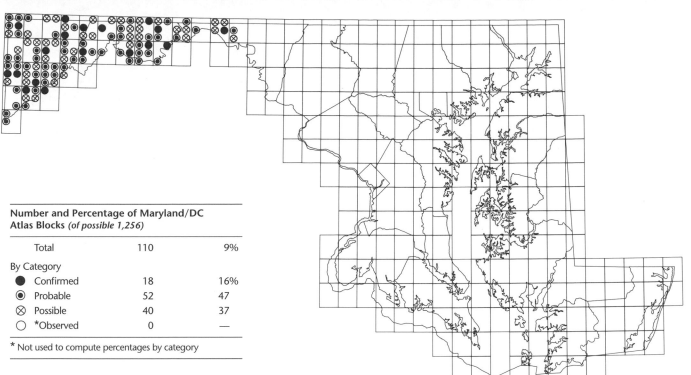

Number and Percentage of Maryland/DC Atlas Blocks *(of possible 1,256)*

	Total	110	9%
By Category			
●	Confirmed	18	16%
◉	Probable	52	47
⊗	Possible	40	37
○	*Observed	0	—

* Not used to compute percentages by category

Atlas Distribution, 1983–1987

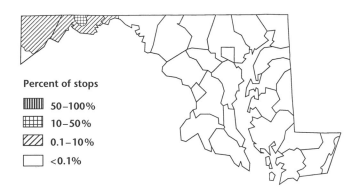

Percent of stops

- ▥ 50–100%
- ▦ 10–50%
- ▨ 0.1–10%
- ☐ <0.1%

Relative Abundance, 1982–1989

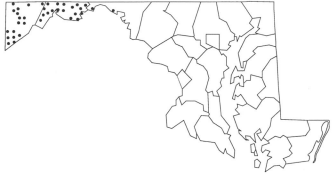

Breeding Distribution, 1958

The Golden-winged Warbler is uncommon but widely distributed in Garrett County in the Allegheny Mountain Section and throughout the western half of the Ridge and Valley Section.

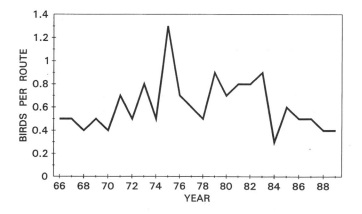

Maryland BBS Trend Graph, 1966–1989

Nashville Warbler

Vermivora ruficapilla

Contrary to its name, the Nashville Warbler is a bird of northern habitats. Maryland is near the southeastern edge of its breeding range, which extends south in the Allegheny Mountains to Cranberry Glades in central West Virginia (Hall 1983) and possibly to the adjacent highlands of Virginia. They arrive in Maryland from their wintering grounds in Mexico, Central America, and the Caribbean (AOU 1983) in late April and early May and depart by mid-October (Robbins and Bystrak 1977).

Eifrig (1904) knew the Nashville Warbler only as a spring migrant in western Maryland. Stewart and Robbins (1958) described its breeding status as uncommon and local in Maryland, limited to the Allegheny Mountain Section. Chandler Robbins found the first Maryland nest (MNRF) on 30 May 1951 in Wolf Swamp, Garrett County. Only five nesting localities were known in 1958, all in Garrett County in brushy cutover red spruce bogs (Stewart and Robbins 1958). The highest breeding density reported in Maryland is 39 territorial males per 100 acres (40.5 ha) in a scrub spruce bog in Garrett County (Robbins and Stewart 1951b).

Robbins and Boone (1984) suggested that the population might be increasing but, owing to the scarcity of and threats to its wetland habitat, recommended that it be considered for protection in Maryland. The Nashville Warbler is currently listed by the DNR as in need of conservation.

On 15 June 1980, Boone (1981) discovered a nest with 5 eggs near Sang Run in Garrett County and described the surrounding boggy habitat. He has since located several other nesting pairs in Garrett County in similar peatland habitat of large wetland areas comprising moss–sedge meadow, shrub, and conifer patches. On two occasions this species was located holding territory along brushy, open, wet meadows that apparently were former pastures adjoining small, low-gradient streams. In the northern portion of its range, the Nashville Warbler also nests in early successional uplands, usually in cutover areas or in fields reverting to forest (Pough 1946). In the southern portion of its range, however, it is more restricted to wetland habitats and openings in spruce forests (Hall 1983). Its diet consists almost entirely of insects, such as flies, young grasshoppers, leafhoppers, aphids, young caterpillars, and beetles (Forbush 1929).

Nashville Warblers nest on the ground, typically in a depression in moss that is hidden by herbaceous cover or low shrubs (Harrison 1975). A clutch typically contains 4 or 5 eggs (Bent 1953); the egg-laying period in Maryland probably ranges from mid-May through June. The only egg dates for Maryland are 30 May and 15 June (MNRF). In New York, egg dates range from 30 May to 22 June, and nests with young have been found from 30 May to 22 June (Bull 1974). The incubation period is 11 or 12 days (Burns 1915). The only Maryland nest with young was found on 16 June (Stewart and Robbins 1958). Young leave the nest at about 11 days (Bent 1953). The Nashville Warbler is a fairly common victim of Brown-headed Cowbird parasitism (Friedmann 1963); 9 of 86 Ontario nests (10.5%) were parasitized (Peck and James 1987).

The Nashville Warbler was detected in over a dozen blocks in Garrett County during the Atlas period. "Probable" records were also reported from western and central Allegany County in the Ridge and Valley Section. Although further investigation is needed to determine if a breeding population actually exists at this low an elevation, there are summer records from four Ridge and Valley counties in Virginia (Larner 1979). Two "confirmed" records were of a nest with eggs and an adult with a fecal sac.

Historically, Garrett County contained numerous large, boggy wetlands or glades (Browning 1859; Schlosnagle et al. 1989). (*Glade* is a colloquial term denoting a large grassy opening or meadow.) These extensive wetlands were scattered throughout the county. Today, only a few wetland complexes provide the early successional habitat required by nesting Nashville Warblers. We shall never know how common this bird once was in our state.

The spruce forests in Maryland were all cut at the turn of the century, and severe fires usually ensued in this disturbed habitat (Curran 1902). Consequently, the upland spruce habitats succeeded to other forest types, primarily hardwoods. Red spruce survived mainly in and around the colder wetlands in Garrett County (Fenwick and Boone 1984). Thus, protection of this warbler in Maryland requires preservation of wetland habitats, primarily spruce bogs. BBS data from 1966 through 1989 show stable populations of the Nashville Warbler in the Eastern Region, but too few are detected on Maryland routes for a state trend to be estimated.

Unfortunately, nearly half of the estimated 3,000 acres of bog habitat that once occurred in Garrett County has been destroyed, largely as a result of coal extraction (Fenwick and Boone 1984). Therefore, to ensure that the Nashville Warbler continues to nest in Maryland, an ecosystem-based management strategy is needed to protect wetland hydrology and maintain bogs in their natural condition.

D. Daniel Boone

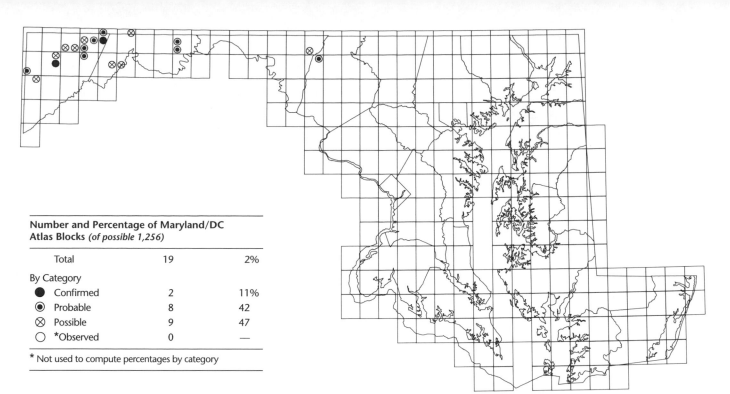

**Number and Percentage of Maryland/DC
Atlas Blocks** *(of possible 1,256)*

Total		19	2%
By Category			
● Confirmed		2	11%
◉ Probable		8	42
⊗ Possible		9	47
○ *Observed		0	—

* Not used to compute percentages by category

Atlas Distribution, 1983–1987

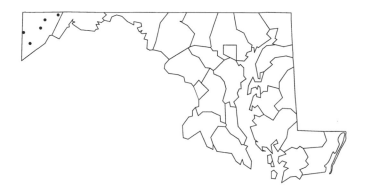

Breeding Distribution, 1958

Northern Parula

Parula americana

The Northern Parula was called the Blue Yellow-backed Warbler by Wilson, Audubon, and Coues and Prentiss. The genus name is derived from the diminutive for titmouse (Griscom and Sprunt 1957). The Northern Parula winters in southern Florida, the Caribbean, Mexico, and Central America as far south as Nicaragua (Bull and Farrand 1977). It returns to the Maryland breeding grounds beginning in mid-April; most leave by early October (Robbins and Bystrak 1977).

Coues and Prentiss (1883) thought a few Northern Parulas bred in the high open woods around DC and said that they could be seen in treetops or on the tips of branches "scrambling, skipping and fluttering with incessant activity on tufts of leaves and blossoms." Kirkwood (1895) found a pair feeding four recently fledged young on the Isle of Wight in Worcester County on 8 June 1894. Four days later he noted "at least 50 pairs of adults with young" there, "each brood keeping separate." Eifrig (1904) considered them rare breeders in Allegany County; in 1920 he obtained the first summer record for Garrett County (Eifrig 1920b). Hampe and Kolb (1947) reported that Northern Parulas were summer residents in the eastern part of Maryland. Stewart and Robbins (1958) considered them common on the Western Shore, locally common on the Eastern Shore, fairly common in the Piedmont, uncommon in the Ridge and Valley and Allegheny Mountain sections, and rare in the Upper Chesapeake Section.

This species needs mature, extensive floodplain and swamp forests and rich, moist upland forests for breeding (Robbins et al. 1989a); trees may be deciduous, coniferous, or mixed. The Northern Parula is one of many neotropical migrants that have been adversely affected by forest fragmentation (Robbins et al. 1989a). The highest breeding density for Maryland is 47 territorial males per 100 acres (40.5 ha) in well-drained, floodplain forest in Anne Arundel and Prince George's counties (Stewart et al. 1946).

The Northern Parula is frequently associated with beard lichen or Spanish moss (Bull and Farrand 1977). It is very adaptable and, in the absence of these plants, uses two good substitutes for nest sites: the tendrils of poison ivy vines and flood debris that has accumulated in the lower branches of trees over water (Robbins 1950). Nesting begins in late April and continues through late June (Stewart and Robbins 1958). While the male defends the territory, the female builds the nest (Bent 1953), which is composed of fine dry grass, very thin bark shreds, bits of plant down, and hair (Graber and Graber 1951). It is often pendent and pear-shaped, with an opening at the side or top (Harrison 1975, 1984).

Heights for 22 Maryland nests (MNRF) range from 1 to 50 ft (0.3–15 m), with a mean of 22 ft (6.7 m). The nest recorded at a height of 1 ft was in flood debris over deep water. Eleven Maryland nest records (MNRF) have clutches ranging from 2 to 5 eggs (mean of 3.1). The earliest egg date for Maryland is 7 April (MNRF) and the latest is 14 June (Stewart and Robbins 1958). There is little information on brood size in the MNRF. Extreme nestling dates for nine nests are 28 May and 25 June (Stewart and Robbins 1958). Incubation, by the female only, lasts 12 to 14 days; both parents tend the young (Harrison 1978). Fledging time is unknown, and there is no evidence of double brooding. Friedmann (1929, 1963) lists the Northern Parula as an uncommon host of the Brown-headed Cowbird. Maryland nest records (MNRF) show 3 (27.3%) of 11 nests with eggs contained Brown-headed Cowbird eggs. Roaming the tree limbs in a deliberate, methodical manner reminiscent of titmice and nuthatches (Griscom and Sprunt 1957), Northern Parulas feed on insects, spiders, and their eggs and larvae.

Atlas results show this species to be widespread along the major watersheds in Maryland. It is largely absent from the agricultural areas of the Ridge and Valley, Piedmont, and Eastern Shore sections and from the marshlands of the lower Chesapeake Bay. Because Northern Parulas typically nest very high and their nests are well concealed, confirming breeding is difficult. Thus, only 12 percent of records were "confirmed." The great majority (89%) of "probable" records were of birds holding territory.

BBS data from 1966 through 1989 show a significant average annual increase in the Eastern Region and a stable Maryland population. Data from 1980 through 1989, however, show a highly significant average annual increase of 5.5 percent in the Maryland population. Robbins et al. (1989c) compared the 1973 through 1975 atlas results for Howard County (Klimkiewicz and Solem 1978) with those of the current Atlas. The data show a 40 percent increase in Howard County.

Although the Northern Parula population is now stable or increasing in Maryland, floodplain and swamp forests still need protection from development, from excessive clearing for sewer lines, and from draining for farmland. Many of Maryland's streams and floodplain forests are protected, but we must remain vigilant to ensure that this habitat remains protected in the future.

M. Kathleen Klimkiewicz

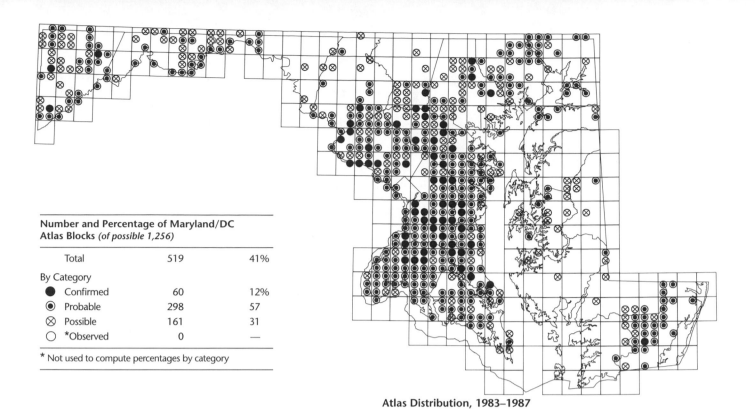

Number and Percentage of Maryland/DC Atlas Blocks *(of possible 1,256)*

Total	519	41%
By Category		
● Confirmed	60	12%
◉ Probable	298	57
⊗ Possible	161	31
○ *Observed	0	—

* Not used to compute percentages by category

Atlas Distribution, 1983–1987

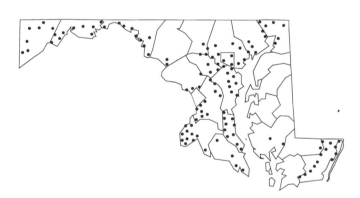

Percent of stops

▥	50–100%
▦	10–50%
▨	0.1–10%
▢	<0.1%

Relative Abundance, 1982–1989

Breeding Distribution, 1958

The Northern Parula is most common in the moist woodlands of southern Maryland. On the Eastern Shore it is found only in the wooded swamps of the south. It is absent from most of the eastern Ridge and Valley Section, where it was found only along the Potomac and Monocacy rivers.

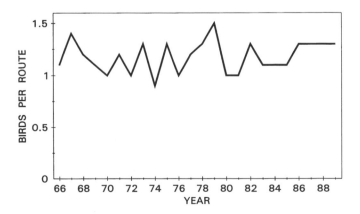

Maryland BBS Trend Graph, 1966–1989

Yellow Warbler

Dendroica petechia

The Yellow Warbler breeds over a larger area of North America than does any other wood warbler (AOU 1983). This sweet singer generally haunts water edges where willows and other short to medium-sized shrubbery form thickets. Spring migrants return to Maryland from their Caribbean, Mexican, and Central and South American wintering grounds (AOU 1983) in late April, and fall migrants depart by the end of September (Robbins and Bystrak 1977).

Historically, the Yellow Warbler has always been considered a common bird in Maryland and DC (Coues and Prentiss 1862, 1883; Kirkwood 1895; Cooke 1929; Hampe and Kolb 1947). Stewart and Robbins (1958) described it as fairly common in the Allegheny Mountain, Ridge and Valley, and Upper Chesapeake sections and in the tidewater areas of the Eastern and Western Shore sections and as uncommon elsewhere.

An open growth of willows and other trees and shrubs on wet ground provides nesting habitat for Yellow Warblers (Stewart and Robbins 1958). They also nest in thickets on dry hillsides, in orchards, and, rarely, in pine forests (Schrantz 1943). The highest breeding density reported in Maryland is 63 territorial males per 100 acres (40.5 ha) in a shrubby field bordering a stream in Baltimore County in 1946 and 1947 (Cooley 1947).

The Yellow Warbler's nest is usually placed in the fork of a shrub or small tree, but may be as high as 60 ft (18 m) above the ground (Bent 1953). The nest, which is constructed by the female, takes about four days to complete. Heights of 51 Maryland nests (MNRF) range from 3 to 32 ft (0.9–9.7 m), with a mean of 8.5 ft (2.6 m). A clutch contains 3 to 6 eggs, usually laid at one-day intervals (Schrantz 1943). Maryland egg dates range from 6 May to 23 June, with a peak in the third week of May (MNRF). Clutch sizes in 58 Maryland nests range from 2 to 5, with a mean of 4.1. Incubation, performed by the female, lasts about 11 days (Schrantz 1943). Nestlings have been found in Maryland from 23 May to 10 July, with a peak in early to mid-June. Brood sizes in 15 Maryland records range from 1 to 5, with a mean of 3.1 (MNRF). Young fledge in 9 to 12 days, and both parents care for them (Bent 1953). One brood is typical (Forbush 1929). Yellow Warblers have a varied insectivorous diet including cankerworms, tent caterpillars, gypsy moths, and beetles (Bent 1953).

The relationship between Yellow Warblers and Brown-headed Cowbirds has been the subject of considerable investigation. The Yellow Warbler is one of the three most common victims of the Brown-headed Cowbird in North America (Friedmann 1963), the others being the Red-eyed Vireo and the Song Sparrow. In Maryland only 8 of 67 Yellow Warbler nests (11.9%) contained Brown-headed Cowbird eggs (MNRF), but 399 of 1,350 Ontario nests (29.6%) were parasitized (Peck and James 1987). Yellow Warblers have evolved an elaborate defense mechanism for dealing with Brown-headed Cowbird eggs, one that is familiar to many bird-watchers. They frequently construct a new floor to the nest, burying the Brown-headed Cowbird egg and any of their eggs (Bent 1953). They may also abandon the nest and construct a new one nearby. Clark and Robertson (1981) found that Yellow Warblers buried Brown-headed Cowbird eggs about 50 percent of the time if there were 2 or fewer of their own eggs in the nest, but less than 20 percent of the time if 3 or more of their eggs were present. They found that unparasitized nests were nearly twice as successful as parasitized nests. Bent (1953) speculated that when Yellow Warblers nest near Red-winged Blackbirds, an aggressive enemy of Brown-headed Cowbirds, parasitism may be reduced.

Atlas results are similar to the distribution described by Stewart and Robbins (1958), although the population in the Piedmont has expanded, especially around farm ponds with willow borders. These warblers were difficult to locate in the Eastern Shore interior and were common on the lower Eastern Shore only along the dense groundsel tree and marsh elder shrub edges of tidal marshes. Although interior portions of Worcester, Wicomico, Somerset, Dorchester, Talbot, and Queen Anne's counties have extensive drainage ditches in agricultural areas, often with heavy shrub and willow edges, Yellow Warblers were absent from these areas, as they also were from adjacent inland portions of Delaware.

BBS data from 1966 through 1989 show a highly significant average annual increase of 1.7 percent in the Eastern Region; the apparent increase in the Maryland population is not significant. At present, Yellow Warblers are not threatened in Maryland. The preservation of willow-dominated riparian habitat and the planting of willows along farm ponds should ensure that they remain so for the foreseeable future.

Charles R. Vaughn

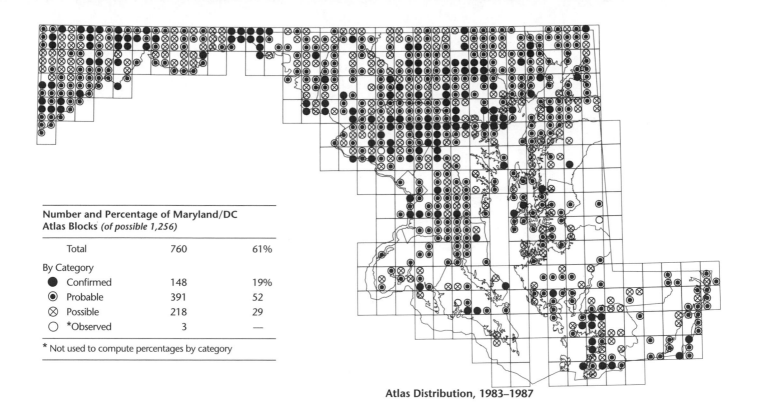

Number and Percentage of Maryland/DC Atlas Blocks *(of possible 1,256)*

Total	760	61%
By Category		
● Confirmed	148	19%
◉ Probable	391	52
⊗ Possible	218	29
○ *Observed	3	—

* Not used to compute percentages by category

Atlas Distribution, 1983–1987

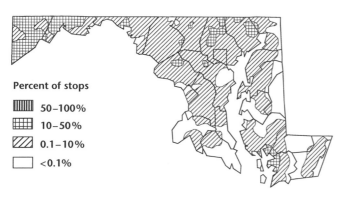

Percent of stops

▥	50–100%
▦	10–50%
▨	0.1–10%
☐	<0.1%

Relative Abundance, 1982–1989

Breeding Distribution, 1958

The Yellow Warbler is most common in the highlands of Garrett and Allegany counties in western Maryland and generally declines to the east. It is absent from the lower Western Shore and from the interior of the Eastern Shore but is common around tidal marshes there.

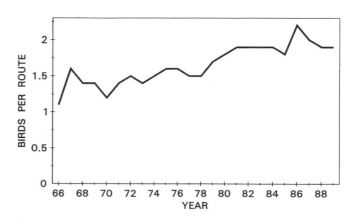

Maryland BBS Trend Graph, 1966–1989

Chestnut-sided Warbler

Dendroica pensylvanica

The Chestnut-sided Warbler is the characteristic breeding warbler of deciduous slash and early second growth in Maryland's mountain forests. Its required habitat must have been extraordinarily scarce in the seventeenth century, when Maryland's mountains were still cloaked in virgin forest. Only once in his life did Audubon lay eyes on one of these conspicuous, brightly colored birds (Forbush 1929). By the time of Coues and Prentiss (1883), the vast forests had succumbed to the ax, and the abundance of regenerating forest was great. The Chestnut-sided Warbler was recognized as an abundant spring and autumn migrant in DC at that time.

Kirkwood (1895) collected Maryland's first recorded nest with eggs on 9 June 1895 on Dan's Mountain in Allegany County. He had no information, however, from Garrett County, which is the current stronghold for this species in Maryland. Preble (1900) was the first to report the Chestnut-sided Warbler as a common breeding bird throughout the higher portions of Garrett and Allegany counties. In 1899 he found a newly built nest at Finzel and collected young birds on Dan's Mountain. Kirkwood (1895) reported summer records on Catoctin Mountain in Frederick County in July 1893. In Maryland's Piedmont, 10 specimens were taken in summer near Laurel in Prince George's County and DC during the period 1888 through 1891 (Stewart and Robbins 1958); there were also summer records from Reisterstown in Baltimore County (Brumbaugh 1915; Meanley 1938) and Fulton in Howard County (Robbins 1952).

Chestnut-sided Warblers arrive from their Central American wintering grounds (AOU 1983) in late April and early May (Robbins and Bystrak 1977). Late migrants are seen into early October. Breeding habitat is characterized by high shrub density within 1 to 3 ft (0.3–0.9 m) of the ground and trees with a small basal area (Robbins et al. 1989a). Breeding populations can be dense in prime habitat. For example, Robbins (1949b) found a density of 79 territorial males per 100 acres (40.5 ha) in dense oak-maple second growth on top of Negro Mountain in Garrett County and 67 per 100 acres in an adjacent open slash area, the two highest densities recorded in Maryland.

The following data are from the MNRF. The mean height of 22 nests is 2.8 ft (0.9 m). The lowest are six nests at 2 ft (0.6 m); the highest, four nests at 4 ft (1.2 m). Clutch sizes of 14 nests vary from 2 to 5, with a mean of 3.6. Egg dates range from 28 May to 26 June, but W. Van Velzen watched a female building a new nest on 24 June 1967 at Whites Knob in Garrett County. The three Maryland records of nests with young are in the short period of 14 to 19 June. This correlates with the peak dates for building and laying; half of those 34 dates are from 31 May to 10 June. Dates for dependent fledged young range from 24 June to 24 July. Although most nests were in small unidentified bushes, 6 were in blackberries, 3 in maple suckers, 3 in other small saplings, 1 in an arrowwood bush, 1 in a clump of weeds, and 1 in bracken fern. Bent (1953) reported that incubation is by the female alone and lasts 12 or 13 days; the young remain in the nest for 10 to 12 days.

None of the 15 nests with eggs found by Kirkwood and Sommer between 1895 and 1925 contained Brown-headed Cowbird eggs (MNRF); however, of 14 nests with eggs or young found from 1954 through 1972, five (35.7%) held Brown-headed Cowbird eggs or young (MNRF). Peck and James (1987) reported that 45 of 211 nests (21.3%) in Ontario were parasitized. Beetles and caterpillars make up the majority of the diet, which is almost entirely insectivorous (US-FWS Food Habits File).

Atlas data show essentially the same breeding distribution reported by Stewart and Robbins (1958): throughout the Allegheny Plateau, locally through the Ridge and Valley Section, at the higher elevations in the Catoctin–South Mountain range, and locally in the Piedmont near the Pennsylvania border. None, however, was found during the Atlas period in the portion of northern Carroll County where the elevation exceeds 1,000 ft (305 m). The disappearance of this species from northern Carroll County may be related to loss of early successional habitat to more intensive land use. No active nests were observed during the Atlas fieldwork. Adults carrying food for young accounted for 12 of the 16 "confirmed" records. BBS data from 1966 through 1989 show stable populations in the Eastern Region; there are too few data to estimate a Maryland trend.

The future of nesting Chestnut-sided Warblers in Maryland is linked directly to forest management practices. They should continue to prosper in Garrett County using the heavy brush that invades clearcuts and selective cuts. This species declined in the Catoctin–South Mountain area when habitat succession on the ridgetops crowded out the heavy brush between 1950 and 1970 (C. Robbins, pers. obs.). This species could disappear entirely from the northern Piedmont unless suitable habitat is provided periodically. If transmission corridors at elevations above 1,000 ft (305 m) were managed to maintain brushy habitat, the Chestnut-sided Warbler would benefit.

Chandler S. Robbins

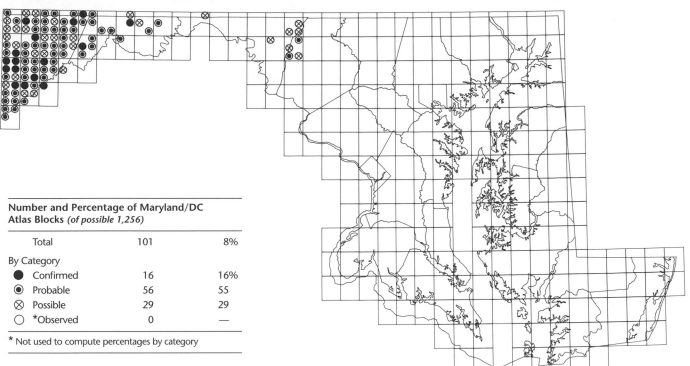

Atlas Distribution, 1983–1987

Number and Percentage of Maryland/DC Atlas Blocks *(of possible 1,256)*

Total		101	8%
By Category			
●	Confirmed	16	16%
◉	Probable	56	55
⊗	Possible	29	29
○	*Observed	0	—

* Not used to compute percentages by category

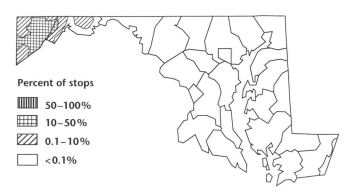

Percent of stops

▥	50–100%
▦	10–50%
▨	0.1–10%
☐	<0.1%

Relative Abundance, 1982–1989

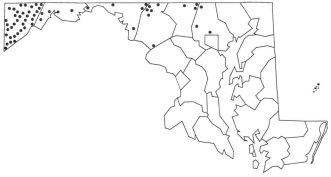

Breeding Distribution, 1958

The Chestnut-sided Warbler is fairly common in the more wooded sections of Garrett County in the Allegheny Mountain Section. It was less frequently detected in the more open north-west and southwest corners of Garrett County and in Allegany County in the western Ridge and Valley Section.

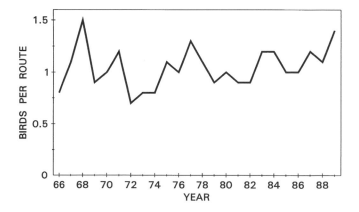

Maryland BBS Trend Graph, 1966–1989

Magnolia Warbler

Dendroica magnolia

The conspicuous flash of white in the tail of the brightly colored, very active Magnolia Warbler makes it easy to spot as it gleans insects from the foliage of evergreens. It is closely associated with northern conifers. Robbins (1950) wrote that he had not seen a Magnolia Warbler in summer in Maryland more than 100 yd (91 m) from eastern hemlock, spruce, red pine, or white pine trees. In West Virginia, however, Brooks (1944) found them in northern mixed forests, northern hardwoods, oak-pine, oak-chestnut, and even in the chestnut sprout association. Most of the Maryland nesting localities are at elevations of 2,200 to 2,700 ft (671–823 m), but Robbins (1950) cited extremes of 2,130 ft (649 m) along the Casselman River at Grantsville and 3,000 ft (914 m) on Backbone Mountain southeast of Swanton.

Although Kirkwood (1895) knew the Magnolia Warbler only as a migrant in Maryland, Eifrig (1904) called it a fairly numerous breeder in Garrett County. Preble (1900) reported the first Maryland nest near Bittinger on 27 June 1889. Before the removal of Garrett County spruce forests late in the nineteenth century, this species undoubtedly was more common and widespread there. Stewart and Robbins (1958) described its breeding status as common in the Allegheny Mountain Section at elevations above 2,500 ft (762 m) and local down to 2,100 ft (640 m).

Breeding Magnolia Warblers in Garrett County are associated with conifers, dense ground vegetation, and a high percentage of forest cover within 1.2 mi (2 km) of the nest site (Robbins et al. 1989a). Populations are fairly dense where suitable habitat is available. DeGarmo (1948) reported a record density of 127 territorial males per 100 acres (40.5 ha) in a young red spruce forest at 4,440 ft (1,350 m) in West Virginia. High Maryland breeding densities per 100 acres (40.5 ha), both from Garrett County, are 80 territorial males in an old-growth hemlock stand at Swallow Falls and 63 territorial males in an open spruce–eastern hemlock bog (Robbins 1949a,c).

Magnolia Warblers winter in eastern Mexico and throughout Central America (AOU 1983), returning to their Maryland breeding grounds in early to mid-May (Stewart and Robbins 1958); most depart by late October (Robbins and Bystrak 1977). Roberts (1936) reported that Minnesota nests were usually at heights of 4 to 6 ft (1.2–1.8 m); Peck and James (1987) wrote that 49 of 99 Ontario nests were at heights of 2.5 to 4.8 ft (0.8–1.5 m) and the highest was 20 ft (6.1 m). Heights of 14 Maryland (MNRF) nests range from 4 to 22 ft (1.2–6.7 m), with a mean of 12.4 ft (3.8 m); 10 of 15 nests were in eastern hemlocks.

Clutch sizes in 10 Maryland nests range from 2 to 5, with a mean of 3.9; egg dates range from 31 May to 28 June (MNRF). Eggs were found in New Hampshire as early as 24 May (Forbush 1929), so they probably occur in Maryland by at least the middle of May. The female incubates for 11 to 13 days; young fledge in about 10 days (Bent 1953). Singing continues into early July, so it is likely that two broods are regularly attempted in Maryland. There is only one record of Brown-headed Cowbird parasitism in Maryland; a Magnolia Warbler was observed feeding a young Brown-headed Cowbird on the late date of 2 August 1964 (MNRF). Only 11 of 111 Ontario nests (9.9%) and 6 of 147 southern Quebec nests (4.1%) were parasitized (Peck and James 1987; Terrill 1961). These are low rates for a warbler (Friedmann 1963). Insects, especially beetles, grubs, flies, caterpillars, and aphids, form the bulk of the summer diet, but spiders and daddy-long-legs are also eaten (Bent 1953).

Although the Atlas fieldwork produced no surprises regarding Magnolia Warbler distribution, it affirmed that this species remains widely distributed in Garrett County and that the presence of eastern hemlocks is not enough by itself to attract it during the breeding season. In addition to the presence of northern conifers, the elevation must be at least 2,100 ft (640 m) to attract breeding Magnolia Warblers in Maryland. Atlas coverage was sufficient to show the breeding distribution, but not intensive enough to produce a large number of "confirmed" records. There were only four records of birds carrying food for young, one of fledged young, and one of distraction display. Although the Magnolia Warbler is found in almost the same number of Atlas blocks as the Black-throated Blue Warbler, it is more restricted by habitat.

Robbins (1950) reported one-day counts for Garrett County of 35 birds on 7 July 1945 and 31 on 22 June 1946. There is no reason to believe any important change in the population has occurred since then. BBS data from 1966 through 1989 show a highly significant average annual increase of 2.8 percent in the Eastern Region; there are too few data to estimate a Maryland trend. Magnolia Warblers are taking advantage of the numerous plantations of mixed conifers in Garrett County. Because the Magnolia Warbler is highly adaptable on its wintering grounds, the future of this species is Maryland should be secure as long as extensive mixed-conifer plantations remain available.

Chandler S. Robbins

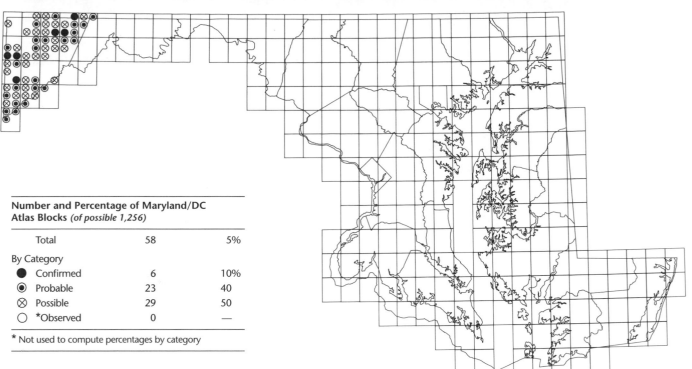

Number and Percentage of Maryland/DC Atlas Blocks *(of possible 1,256)*

Total		58	5%
By Category			
●	Confirmed	6	10%
◉	Probable	23	40
⊗	Possible	29	50
○	*Observed	0	—

* Not used to compute percentages by category

Atlas Distribution, 1983–1987

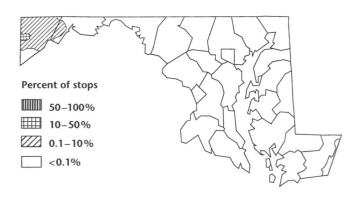

Percent of stops

- ▥ 50–100%
- ▦ 10–50%
- ▨ 0.1–10%
- ☐ <0.1%

Relative Abundance, 1982–1989

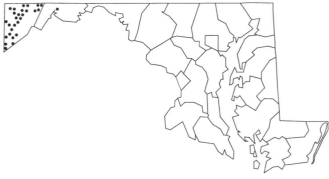

Breeding Distribution, 1958

The Magnolia Warbler was found only in the mountains of Garrett County in the Allegheny Mountain Section. A small pocket of abundance was detected in the hemlocks in and near Swallow Falls State Park.

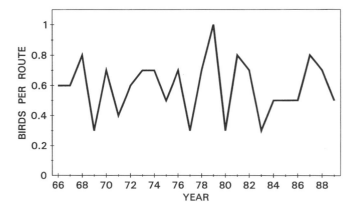

Maryland BBS Trend Graph, 1966–1989

Black-throated Blue Warbler

Dendroica caerulescens

The Black-throated Blue Warbler is one of the most common northern warblers in Garrett County, occurring in dense undergrowth in both deciduous and coniferous woodland above 2,100 ft (640 m) (Robbins 1950). It requires extensive forest and occurs most frequently when foliage is dense near ground level at 1 to 3.3 ft (0.3–1.0 m). It prefers a closed canopy but also nests in open bog habitats (Robbins et al. 1989a).

The Black-throated Blue Warbler arrives on its Maryland breeding grounds from its West Indian wintering grounds (AOU 1983) in late April and returns from late August to mid-October (Stewart and Robbins 1958). It was known as a migrant through DC in 1862 (Coues and Prentiss 1862), but not until June 1900 were abandoned nests found and specimens taken in Maryland (Preble 1900). John Sommer found the first occupied Maryland nest, with young, on 11 June 1918 near Grantsville (Robbins 1950). Stewart and Robbins (1958) stated it was a common breeding species in the Allegheny Mountain Section at elevations above 2,000 ft (610 m).

High breeding densities per 100 acres (40.5 ha) in Maryland are 58 territorial males in old-growth eastern hemlock forest at Swallow Falls (Robbins 1949a), 52 territorial males in old-growth red spruce–eastern hemlock bog forest in Wolf Swamp (Stewart and Robbins 1951a), and 48 territorial males in young second-growth resulting from the clearcutting of an oak-maple ridge forest at the summit of Negro Mountain (Robbins 1949b).

The 12 Maryland nests (MNRF) range in height above the ground from 0.8 to 2 ft (0.2–0.6 m), which is comparable to nest heights in other states (Robbins 1950). Six nests were in big laurel, but the majority reported from other states were in mountain laurel (Bent 1953). Extreme nest heights in other states are 4 in. (10.2 cm) and 20 ft (6.1 m), but the majority are under 4 ft (1.2 m) (Bent 1953; Bull 1974). The bulky nests are placed in upright forks and are con-

structed of dry grapevine bark, twigs, and roots, partially covered with wool from cocoons and lined with fine black roots and hair (Davie 1898).

The earliest Maryland egg date is 3 June 1925, when F. Kirkwood found four nests, three with eggs, at Boiling Spring on Big Backbone Mountain (Robbins 1950); the latest is 10 July for a nest found by J. McKearnan (MNRF). Egg dates from elsewhere extend from 5 May in North Carolina (Bent 1953) to 24 July in Ontario (Peck and James 1987). Extreme dates for young in the nest are 11 June and 22 July (MNRF). Late Maryland dates for fledged young being fed by adults are 15 and 24 July at Swallow Falls. The young are fed caterpillars, grubs, moths, dragonflies, crane flies, and ants (Bent 1953). It is probable that two broods are frequently attempted in Maryland (Robbins 1950). Friedmann (1963) knew of only ten instances of Brown-headed Cowbird parasitism of Black-throated Blue Warbler nests; none were south of New York. However, P. Bystrak and D. Bystrak found a male feeding a young Brown-headed Cowbird in Garrett County on 2 August 1964, and J. McKearnan found Brown-headed Cowbird eggs in 2 of 3 Garrett County nests in 1990 (MNRF). In Ontario, 3 of 23 nests (13.0%) were parasitized (Peck and James 1987).

During the Atlas period, this species was found in most Garrett County blocks, except at low elevations in the northwest corner and in the Potomac River Valley. Records at the quarterblock scale reveal that it is restricted to the bogs and mountain ridges and is largely absent from the intervening farmland. Robbins et al. (1989a) did not find Black-throated Blue Warblers in any isolated woodlots they studied. Adults carrying food for young accounted for 6 of the 10 "confirmed" Atlas records. One bird was observed on a nest, but the contents were not identified. "Confirmed" records in two blocks were of distraction display. Fledglings were found in one block.

Robbins (1950) believed that the population in Garrett County was similar to that of 50 years earlier because the Black-throated Blue Warbler does not rely on conifers. Although the Atlas project did not record any Black-throated Blue Warblers east of the Allegheny Plateau, Hall (1983) reported West Virginia sites as low as 1,475 ft (450 m). This species should be watched for in the western portion of the Ridge and Valley Section.

BBS data from 1966 through 1989 show stable Black-throated Blue Warbler populations in the Eastern Region; there are too few data to estimate a trend for Maryland. Breeding populations in Maryland will most likely decline as highways, transmission lines, ski trails, shopping centers, and housing developments continue to fragment the extensive forests of Garrett County. Nevertheless, the Black-throated Blue Warbler, being more adaptable than most warblers, should continue to nest here within the foreseeable future.

Chandler S. Robbins

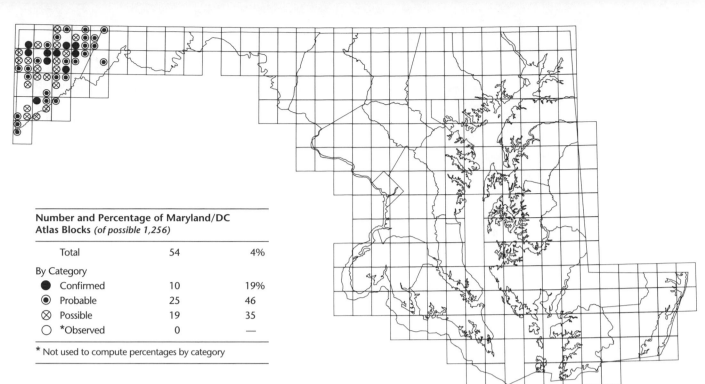

Number and Percentage of Maryland/DC Atlas Blocks *(of possible 1,256)*

	Total	54	4%
By Category			
●	Confirmed	10	19%
◉	Probable	25	46
⊗	Possible	19	35
○	*Observed	0	—

* Not used to compute percentages by category

Atlas Distribution, 1983–1987

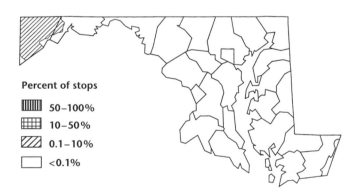

Percent of stops

▥	50–100%
▦	10–50%
▨	0.1–10%
▢	<0.1%

Relative Abundance, 1982–1989

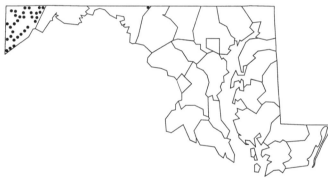

Breeding Distribution, 1958

The Black-throated Blue Warbler was found in small numbers throughout the Allegheny Mountain Section that includes Garrett County and the adjacent highlands of Allegany County. A few were detected in the Ridge and Valley Section of western Allegany County.

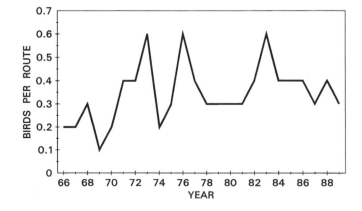

Maryland BBS Trend Graph, 1966–1989

Yellow-rumped Warbler

Dendroica coronata

The Myrtle Warbler, the eastern subspecies of the Yellow-rumped Warbler, was once treated as a separate species. It was recently merged with its western counterpart, the Audubon's Warbler (Eisenmann 1973). The Yellow-rumped Warbler is still commonly referred to as Myrtle Warbler throughout the East, as well as by its nickname *butter butt*. An abundant spring and fall migrant throughout Maryland, it is also common to abundant in winter on the lower Eastern Shore (Stewart and Robbins 1958). Winter populations in other parts of the state vary considerably from year to year, generally decreasing toward the west, where it is very rare in most years. Local winter populations may fluctuate considerably over the course of the season in response to changes in weather or food availability (Terrill and Ohmart 1984). The Yellow-rumped Warbler is one of the earliest spring and latest fall migrant warblers in Maryland. When it returns from its southeastern U.S. wintering grounds (AOU 1983), large numbers can be found in Maryland from mid-April into early May, with stragglers lingering until late May (Robbins and Bystrak 1977). The first fall migrants typically arrive around the end of September, but the bulk of the migration spans all of October and half of November.

Perhaps no bird has a more extraordinary breeding history in Maryland than the Yellow-rumped Warbler. Coues and Prentiss (1862, 1883), Kirkwood (1895), Cooke (1929), Hampe and Kolb (1947), and Stewart and Robbins (1958) knew it only as an abundant migrant and irregularly common wintering resident. There is one remarkable exception. In June 1879 a male and an injured female were found feeding three half-grown young near Havre de Grace in Harford County (Kumlien 1880). This record, certainly an aberration, is still the Yellow-rumped Warbler's only definitive claim to a place on the list of Maryland's breeding birds. Even as recently as 1957, regular breeding was unknown south of northeastern Pennsylvania (AOU 1957). Breeding in West Virginia was first suspected at Gaudineer Knob in 1978

(Hall 1983). The population in West Virginia has continued to expand, and in 1982 Hall (1983) noted a density of 41 territorial males per 247 acres (100 ha) on Spruce Knob in Pendleton County. The first confirmed breeding record for West Virginia was not recorded until 1987 when recently fledged young were found on Spruce Knob (Eddy 1988). BBS data for 1966 through 1989 show a steady upward trend in Yellow-rumped Warblers in the Eastern Region, in parallel with their expansion southward in the Appalachian Mountains.

Yellow-rumped Warblers favor a variety of coniferous and mixed coniferous-deciduous woodlands for breeding sites (Ellison 1985a). Although most abundant in stunted spruce–fir woodlands, they are also found in pure spruce stands, spruce bogs, white pines, and hemlocks. Their nests are usually in the thicker clumps of a horizontal conifer branch from 2 to 65 ft (0.6–20 m) above the ground (Peck and James 1987). Half of 149 Ontario nests were 6.5 to 19.7 ft (2–6 m) high, nearly all in open woodland or woodland margins; only one was reported in the forest interior. In New York, eggs have been found from 19 May to 10 July, and nestlings from 2 June to 22 July (Bull 1974). Clutch sizes in eastern birds are usually 3 or 4 (Peck and James 1987). One brood is typical (Forbush 1929). Incubation, by the female only, lasts 11 to 13 days (Bent 1953). The young fledge 10 to 12 days after hatching. The male assists in feeding the young and in nest sanitation. Their diet consists chiefly of insects in spring and summer, with a large number of berries and wild fruits taken in late fall and winter (Forbush 1929). Prior to the Brown-headed Cowbird's expansion, Yellow-rumped Warblers were apparently rarely parasitized (Bent 1953); Friedmann (1929) knew of only three records. In Ontario, however, parasitism is high. According to Peck and James (1987), Brown-headed Cowbirds parasitized 38 of 122 Ontario nests (31.1%). Bent (1953) noted that 65 percent of nests around Toronto, Ontario, were parasitized but that Yellow-rumped Warblers deserted nests containing only Brown-headed Cowbird eggs.

The possibility that the expanding Appalachian population had reached Maryland surfaced when D. Boone found a singing male on 12 June 1983 in a bog near Rock Lodge (McHenry CE) in central Garrett County (Robbins and Boone 1984). The bird was later observed carrying food but, because of the species' uncertain status in Maryland, this was recorded as only "probable" breeding. Another bird was observed in McHenry CE. The possibility that the Yellow-rumped Warbler will nest in the mountains of western Maryland, if it has not already done so, is high. BBS data from 1966 through 1989 show a highly significant average annual increase of 2.7 percent in the Eastern Region.

It remains to be seen if the Yellow-rumped Warbler will become established as a regularly breeding bird in Maryland. Searches of possible breeding localities should be undertaken, especially in the spruce bogs of Garrett County. There are compelling reasons for the preservation of the remaining bogs, with or without the presence of this species.

Eirik A. T. Blom

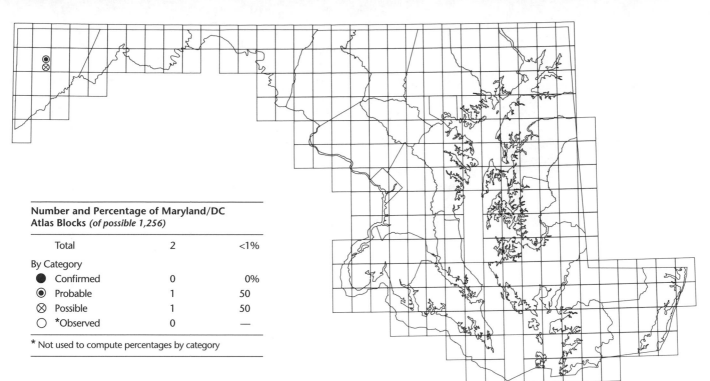

Number and Percentage of Maryland/DC Atlas Blocks (of possible 1,256)

Total	2	<1%

By Category

●	Confirmed	0	0%
◉	Probable	1	50
⊗	Possible	1	50
○	*Observed	0	—

* Not used to compute percentages by category

Atlas Distribution, 1983–1987

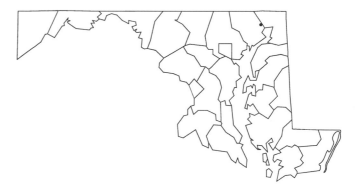

Breeding Distribution, 1958

Black-throated Green Warbler

Dendroica virens

From May through July, the lazy, wheezy song of the Black-throated Green Warbler is heard from within the uppermost branches of tall white pines and eastern hemlocks throughout Garrett County and locally elsewhere in the Allegheny ridges. This is one of the most widely distributed northern warblers in Maryland. In Garrett County it occurs locally both in moist deciduous woodlands and in evergreens. Black-throated Green Warblers typically arrive from their Mexican and Central American wintering grounds (AOU 1983) in the closing days of April and depart by mid-October (Robbins and Bystrak 1977).

Kirkwood (1895) provided the first breeding evidence for Maryland, when a pair of excited birds came within 3 ft (0.9 m) of him on Dan's Mountain, Allegany County, on 14 June 1895. He stated in his book that the pair was feeding flying young, but his field notes state that they probably had young. No young birds were actually observed until C. Eifrig (MNRF) saw a female with fledged young near Accident in Garrett County on 31 July 1901. Stewart and Robbins (1947a) were the first to record the Black-throated Green Warbler summering in dense hemlock stands on Catoctin Mountain at elevations as low as 800 ft (244 m) at Cunningham Falls in Frederick County. They later (1958) described its breeding status as common in the Allegheny Mountain Section, fairly common in the western part of the Ridge and Valley Section (Allegany County), and uncommon in the eastern part of the Ridge and Valley Section (Washington and western Frederick County south to Myersville).

In the absence of Maryland nest records, we must rely on nesting data from other sources. Both sexes participate in nest building, at least on the first day, but the female does most of the nest building and incubation (Stanwood 1910; Pitelka 1940). Heights of 41 Ontario nests (Peck and James 1987) range from 1.6 to 49 ft (0.5–15 m), with half of them at 9 to 25 ft (2.7–7.5 m). The majority were about two-thirds of the way out on horizontal branches of conifers. The mean height of nine nests at Hubbard Brook Forest in New

Hampshire was even higher at 37 ft (11 m), and the mean height of 270 foraging sightings was still higher at 50 ft (15 m) (Holmes 1986). Nests are generally well made and have relatively deep cups. Of 30 Ontario nests, 23 contained 3 or 4 eggs; 5 was the maximum (Peck and James 1987). Half the reported Ontario nests were found from 13 to 29 June, but the extremes of 5 June and 9 August suggest that some birds attempt second broods. Friedmann (1963) considered this species an infrequent victim of the Brown-headed Cowbird. In Ontario, however, 11 of 32 nests (34.4%) were parasitized (Peck and James 1987). The young normally remain in the nest 8 to 10 days (Bent 1953). Maryland dates for recently fledged young range from 12 June to 11 August (MNRF).

Habitat preferences in Maryland were indicated by the following highest breeding densities per 100 acres (40.5 ha) in Garrett County in 1949: 36 territorial males in mature oak-maple ridge forest on Negro Mountain (Robbins 1949b), 30 territorial males in old-growth eastern hemlock forest at Swallow Falls (Robbins 1949a), and 21 territorial males in an open hemlock-spruce bog at Cranesville (Robbins 1949c). In Maryland, the highest densities have come from deciduous rather than coniferous or mixed forest, as is typical farther north. Caterpillars, locusts, and beetles are the favorite food items, but poison ivy berries are added to the insect diet in autumn (Bent 1953).

Atlas results show the Black-throated Green Warbler nests throughout the Allegheny Plateau and locally in the western portion of the Ridge and Valley Section and on Catoctin and South mountains. This portion of the range is similar to that described by Stewart and Robbins (1958). The one observation of a bird on territory in Atlantic white cedar in the Wango quadrangle on the lower Eastern Shore is of special interest. Forty years ago Robbins (1950) suggested that "further search may show that small numbers [of the southern race of the Black-throated Green Warbler, *D. v. waynei*], breed locally in some years" in the Pocomoke Swamp. There is a gap of 100 mi (161 km) without suitable habitat between the Pocomoke Swamp and the Dismal Swamp of Virginia, where this subspecies breeds regularly (AOU 1983). Of 13 "confirmed" records, 5 were of fledged young, 5 were of adults carrying food for young, and 1 each was of nest building, fecal sac, and distraction display. The Black-throated Green Warbler remains the most widespread breeding species for which no Maryland nest has been found.

BBS data from 1966 through 1989 show stable populations in the Eastern Region; there are too few data to estimate a Maryland trend. If a population of the *waynei* race becomes established in the Pocomoke Swamp, the site would deserve special protection. The main threat to the mountain population is additional fragmentation of the forest habitat.

Chandler S. Robbins

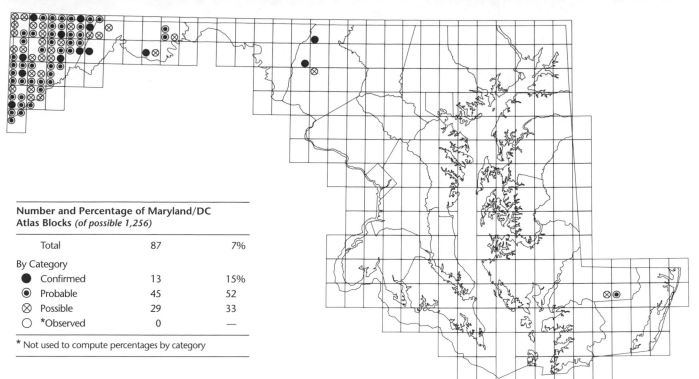

Number and Percentage of Maryland/DC Atlas Blocks *(of possible 1,256)*

Total	87	7%
By Category		
● Confirmed	13	15%
◉ Probable	45	52
⊗ Possible	29	33
○ *Observed	0	—

* Not used to compute percentages by category

Atlas Distribution, 1983–1987

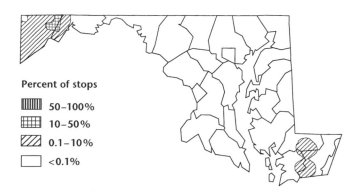

Percent of stops

▥	50–100%
▦	10–50%
▨	0.1–10%
☐	<0.1%

Relative Abundance, 1982–1989

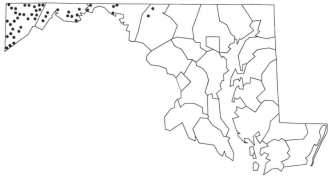

Breeding Distribution, 1958

The Black-throated Green Warbler was found throughout the Allegheny Mountain Section and in the western Ridge and Valley Section. Numbers in the rest of western Maryland were too small to be detected. Single individuals were recorded on two mini-routes on the lower Eastern Shore.

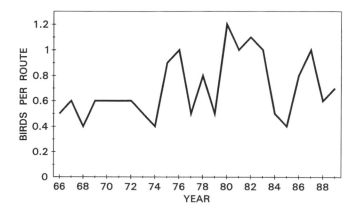

Maryland BBS Trend Graph, 1966–1989

Blackburnian Warbler

Dendroica fusca

Few North American birds match the male Blackburnian Warbler's brilliant plumage. In the western Maryland mountains, he whispers his high thin song from the uppermost branches of the eastern hemlocks in which he and his mate rear their young. Breeding birds are locally common in extensive stands of mature hemlock at elevations above 2,200 ft (671 m). After singing ceases in late June, the Blackburnian Warbler is hard to find. Spring migrants arrive in Maryland breeding areas from their South American wintering grounds (AOU 1983) in late April and early May, and fall migrants return from mid-August to early October (Stewart and Robbins 1958).

Although this northern species was recognized as a common migrant in DC as early as 1862 (Coues and Prentiss 1862), not until 10 June 1895 did Kirkwood (1895) record the first breeding for Maryland at Dan's Mountain in western Allegany County. It was undoubtedly common in the mature spruce forest that covered many Garrett County bogs before the close of the nineteenth century, but today so few mature spruces remain that the Blackburnian Warbler is confined largely to hemlock stands. A few occur in mature mixed and oak-hickory forests in Garrett County (Robbins 1950); in West Virginia (Hall 1983) they also breed in upland black cherry forests at 3,600 ft (1,097 m).

The old-growth hemlock stand along the Youghiogheny River in Swallow Falls State Park in Garrett County is one of the best places for finding Blackburnian Warblers (C. Robbins, pers. obs.). Breeding densities recorded in Maryland are 110 territorial males per 100 acres (40.5 ha), the highest on record anywhere for this species, in the old-growth eastern hemlock stand at Swallow Falls (Robbins 1949a); 96 territorial males per 100 acres in an old-growth spruce-hemlock bog forest in Wolf Swamp in 1951 (Stewart and Robbins 1951a); and 39 territorial males per 100 acres in a nearby scrub spruce bog with scattered mature spruces (Stewart and Robbins 1951b). Stewart and Robbins (1958) showed that the Maryland breeding range included all of Garrett County and all of Allegany County except the floodplain along the Potomac River. The Blackburnian Warbler was especially widespread in Garrett County, being found at 21 locations (C. Robbins, unpub. data). Most of these sites were at elevations of 2,200 to 2,600 ft (671 to 793 m). The easternmost summer localities were at 500 ft (152 m) along Licking Creek in western Washington County and at 1,300 ft (396 m) at Cunningham Falls in Catoctin Mountain Park in north-central Frederick County.

The first confirmed nesting in Maryland was recorded by Eifrig (1920b), who watched a bird building a nest about 35 ft (11 m) up in a hemlock near Accident, in Garrett County, on 15 June 1918. Fifteen years earlier, on 23 July 1903, he had observed fledged young on Negro Mountain in Garrett County. The only other reported Maryland nests (MNRF) are one under construction 55 ft (17 m) high in a red spruce at Wolf Swamp on 31 May 1951, one with one egg at Gormania in Garrett County on 31 May 1948, and one 25 ft (7.6 m) high in a black locust at Catoctin Mountain Park on 11 May 1969.

The earliest and latest published egg dates for the species are 23 May in New Hampshire (Bent 1953) and 8 July in Minnesota (Roberts 1936). The female incubates for 12 or 13 days (Godfrey 1986). Probably only one brood is raised; however, J. Taylor, Jr., watched an adult feeding its young and a Brown-headed Cowbird at Swallow Falls State Park on the late date of 19 July (MNRF). This was undoubtedly a second brood or a renesting. Friedmann (1929, 1963) considered the Blackburnian Warbler a very uncommon victim of the Brown-headed Cowbird because he knew of only 10 such instances. However, this warbler nests very high, and few nests had been examined. Peck and James (1987) reported 4 of 12 Ontario nests (33.3%) were parasitized. The Blackburnian Warbler gleans insects, mostly caterpillars, beetles, ants, and flies (Bent 1953), from foliage and branches.

This species was difficult to confirm; most records (57%) were of "possible" nesting. Too few Blackburnian Warblers are recorded on BBS routes in Maryland to estimate a trend for the state; however, data from 1966 through 1989 show stable populations in the Eastern Region. Breeding distribution in Maryland has not changed much in the past 30 years, but numbers have almost certainly declined as mature spruce trees have been cut and fragmentation of mature eastern hemlock groves has continued. Unlike the Northern Parula, the Blackburnian Warbler does not defend territories with only one or two spruce trees; it requires extensive old-growth forest (Chapman 1907a). Another major reason for the decline is Brown-headed Cowbird parasitism.

The best strategy for maintaining the Blackburnian Warbler as part of Maryland's breeding avifauna is to protect old-growth forest, especially old hemlocks on slopes greater than 40 percent (D. Boone, pers. comm.), to permit spruce to become reestablished in Garrett County bogs, and to plant extensive tracts of native red spruce in the uplands. When mature, and if undamaged by acid rain, red spruce plantations should provide ideal nesting cover.

Chandler S. Robbins

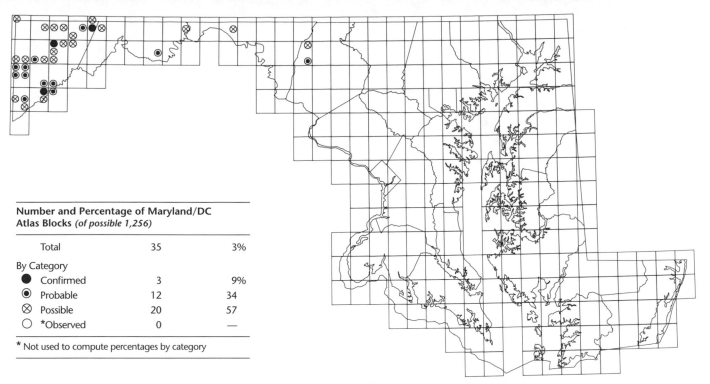

Atlas Distribution, 1983–1987

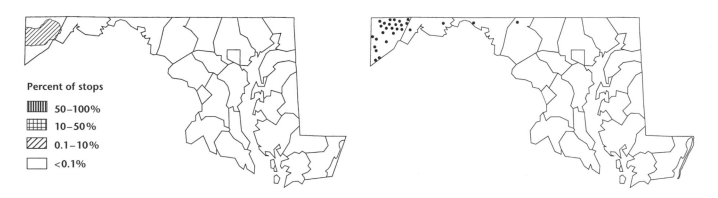

Percent of stops

▦	50–100%
▦	10–50%
▨	0.1–10%
☐	<0.1%

Relative Abundance, 1982–1989

Breeding Distribution, 1958

Small numbers of Blackburnian Warblers were recorded in the central two-thirds of Garrett County. It is rarer and more local in the rest of Garrett County and in the Ridge and Valley Section; it was not detected on miniroutes in those areas.

Yellow-throated Warbler

Dendroica dominica

The Yellow-throated Warbler is one of the most handsome members of the wood warbler family. Although migratory, it is hardier than many warblers and winters from the Carolinas south through Florida, Texas, the Caribbean, Mexico, and Central America (Griscom and Sprunt 1957). It returns to Maryland early, with the first migrants found in early April (Robbins and Bystrak 1977). Most birds leave by mid-September.

The Yellow-throated Warbler is found in swamps and pine woods, especially loblolly pines more than 25 ft (7.6 m) tall (Robbins 1950) in the southern and eastern part of the state, and locally in tall sycamores along rivers in the northern and western parts of Maryland. High breeding densities for Maryland are 29 territorial males per 100 acres (40.5 ha) in an immature loblolly-shortleaf pine stand and 12 territorial males per 100 acres in a second-growth river swamp, both in Worcester County (Springer and Stewart 1948c,d).

The Yellow-throated Warbler has expanded its range in Maryland during the past 100 years. Coues and Prentiss (1862, 1883) called it a southern bird of rare and casual appearance in the DC area. They knew of only two specimens, one collected in 1842, the other from Arlington, Virginia, in September 1883. Kirkwood (1895) considered this species regular only along the coast, but he cited a few reports from southern Maryland. Cooke (1929) called it "tolerably" common around DC. Hampe and Kolb (1947) and Stewart and Robbins (1947a) described it as regular on the lower Eastern Shore and in southern Maryland north to Anne Arundel County and DC. Robbins (1950) put the northern limits at Dalecarlia Reservoir in DC, Oxon Hill in Prince George's County, the Potomac River shore of Charles County, the Chesapeake Bay shore north to Gibson Island in Anne Arundel County, Kent Island in Queen Anne's County, Denton in Caroline County, and the Delaware line along the Pocomoke River. Stewart and Robbins (1958) mapped the range extension along the Potomac River into Montgomery County in the Piedmont Section but called it a vagrant north and west of there.

Nest data for the Yellow-throated Warbler in Maryland are scanty because of the heights of the nests. Nests are 3.5 to 120 ft (1.1–37 m) above the ground, usually 15 to 60 ft (4.6–19 m), and often are halfway out a horizontal limb (Sprunt 1953; Oberholser 1974). There are only five Maryland reports (MNRF) of nest heights, ranging from 40 to 55 ft (12–17 m). In the southern states the Yellow-throated Warbler nests in clumps of Spanish moss; in more northern parts of its range it often uses clumps of leaves (Sprunt 1953).

Typical clutch size is four (Griscom and Sprunt 1957). Nests with eggs have been found in Maryland as early as 16 May (Jackson 1941), and a nest with young was found on 9 June (Stewart and Robbins 1958). The incubation period is thought to be about 12 days (Ehrlich et al. 1988). This warbler may be double-brooded (Sprunt 1953) but precise evidence is lacking. An occupied nest was found in Anne Arundel County as late as 10 July in 1954 (Stewart and Robbins 1958).

The Yellow-throated Warbler is believed to be a rare host of the Brown-headed Cowbird; there are only two records, one for Oklahoma (Friedmann 1963) and one for Maryland (MNRF). Considering the difficulty of examining nests, however, parasitism may be more frequent than has been reported. The diet of the Yellow-throated Warbler is composed almost entirely of insects, including beetles, caterpillars, moths and their larvae, flies, bugs, and grasshoppers (Sprunt 1953).

The Yellow-throated Warbler appears to be expanding its range in Maryland, as it is in Ohio (Peterjohn and Rice 1991). Atlas results show that it has moved up the Potomac River Valley into Allegany County and into sycamore-lined river valleys in the Upper Chesapeake and Piedmont sections. The greatest concentration of records occurs in the Pocomoke River drainage on the lower Eastern Shore. There is also a cluster of records along the lower Patuxent River. A single bird singing from the steeple of Sang Run Church at an elevation of 2,015 ft (614 m) in Garrett County was probably a vagrant. BBS data from 1966 through 1989 show stable populations in Maryland and the Eastern Region.

The greatest threat to the Yellow-throated Warbler is probably destruction of its breeding habitat, but this warbler has proven to be fairly adaptable in Maryland. Many of the sycamore-lined streams it inhabits have a very narrow wooded edge, while in the pine woods of southern Maryland and the lower Eastern Shore it has been found in tall loblolly pines around housing developments. The future of this bird in Maryland appears to be secure.

Clark F. Jeschke

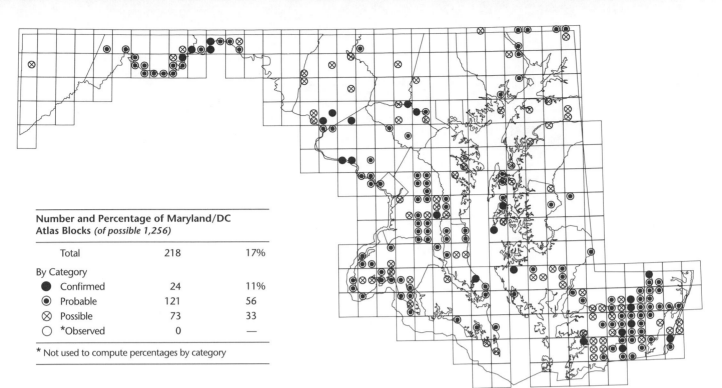

Number and Percentage of Maryland/DC Atlas Blocks *(of possible 1,256)*

Total	218	17%
By Category		
● Confirmed	24	11%
◉ Probable	121	56
⊗ Possible	73	33
○ *Observed	0	—

* Not used to compute percentages by category

Atlas Distribution, 1983–1987

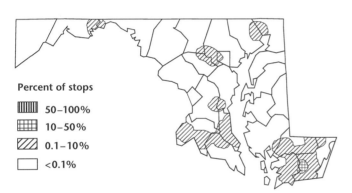

Percent of stops

▥	50–100%
▦	10–50%
▨	0.1–10%
▢	<0.1%

Relative Abundance, 1982–1989

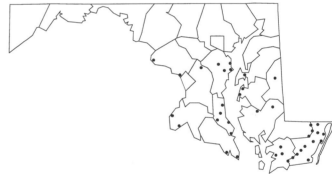

Breeding Distribution, 1958

The Yellow-throated Warbler is most widely distributed on the lower Eastern Shore and in southern Maryland, with a concentration in southern Pocomoke State Forest. A few were found west of the Bay along the Susquehanna, Patapsco, Patuxent, and Potomac rivers, but it was missed in much of its range.

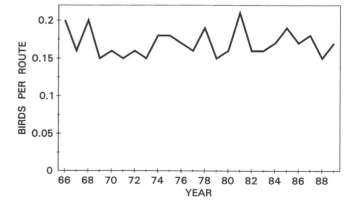

Maryland BBS Trend Graph, 1966–1989

Pine Warbler

Dendroica pinus

The Pine Warbler is the only primarily yellow bird that lives most of its life in stands of pine trees. The common name is appropriate; although the Pine Warbler may be found in deciduous forests or orchards during migration, it breeds exclusively in association with pine trees of various species (Stewart and Robbins 1958). In Maryland, it nests most frequently in loblolly pine, but mature stands of Virginia pine, pitch pine, and white pine also provide suitable habitat. The highest Maryland breeding densities are 76 territorial males per 100 acres (40.5 ha) in immature loblolly-shortleaf pine in Worcester County (Springer and Stewart 1948c) and 20 territorial males per 100 acres in Virginia pine–pitch pine–oak forest in Prince George's County in 1944 (Stewart and Robbins 1958). Spring migration comes early for this warbler, with the first birds returning from their southeastern U.S. wintering grounds (AOU 1983) in early March (Stewart and Robbins 1958). Fall migrants depart from Maryland by the end of October.

Coues and Prentiss (1862, 1883) called the Pine Warbler a sparse summer bird near DC, where nearly 50 years later Cooke (1929) called it "tolerably" common. Kirkwood (1895) wrote that it was numerous in migration but local in the summer. Eifrig (1904) called it a very common migrant in western Maryland but said it nested very sparingly. Stewart and Robbins (1958) described its Maryland breeding status as abundant in the Eastern Shore and southern Western Shore sections, fairly common in the rest of the Western Shore Section, uncommon and local in the Allegheny Mountain and western Ridge and Valley sections, and rare elsewhere. In winter, a few can be found on the Coastal Plain.

Nest building has been observed in Maryland as early as 23 March in Worcester County (J. Stasz, pers. comm.). Nesting is difficult to confirm; nests usually are well concealed among clusters of cones or needles and often are placed high in trees (Bent 1953; Weston et al. 1957; Stone 1937). Nest heights are governed by the height of available pines and

vary from 8 to 135 ft (2.4–41 m) (Bent 1953). Heights of 10 Maryland nests (MNRF) range from 14 to 55 ft (4.3–17 m), with a mean of 34.3 ft (11 m).

Egg dates for 17 Maryland nests are all in the brief period from 16 April to 20 May (MNRF). Clutch sizes range from 3 to 5, with 4 most common (Bent 1953). Seven Maryland nests contained 4 eggs each (MNRF). Although the incubation period is unknown, the male is reported to share in this duty; both parents feed the young (Bent 1953; Weston et al. 1957). Nests with young have been reported in Maryland from 28 April to 18 June (MNRF). Brood size was reported in only two instances: 3 young and 4 young (MNRF). Dependent fledged young have been observed in Maryland from 12 May through 12 August (MNRF). Pine Warblers incubating or tending fledglings have occasionally surprised observers by plummeting straight to the ground and performing a crippled-bird distraction display (Stone 1937). Friedmann (1929, 1963) considered the Pine Warbler to be a rare victim of the Brown-headed Cowbird with only 10 known records; however, Peck and James (1987) listed 4 of 8 Ontario nests (50%) as parasitized. Only 2 of 17 Maryland nests (12%) were parasitized (MNRF): One contained 3 Pine Warbler eggs and 1 Brown-headed Cowbird egg; the other, with 3 Brown-headed Cowbird eggs and 1 Pine Warbler egg, was abandoned.

This species feeds at all levels and in various styles within its pine habitat. In summer, it primarily eats insects gleaned from bark of the trunk and branches or from leaf and cone clusters at any level within the tree. It also secures prey by aerial flycatching. In winter it adds seeds and berries to its diet, often foraging on the ground in the style of, and sometimes accompanied by, Palm Warblers, Eastern Bluebirds, and sparrows (Stone 1937; Bent 1953; Weston et al. 1957; M. O'Brien, pers. comm.).

The status of the Pine Warbler has not changed appreciably during the twentieth century, and certainly not in the past 30 years. The Atlas map is similar to that of Stewart and Robbins (1958), although there are slightly more reports from the Upper Chesapeake, Piedmont, and eastern Ridge and Valley sections. Some reports from the latter areas were found in pine plantations that matured during the past quarter century. There are Atlas records from every county.

BBS data from 1966 through 1989 show a highly significant average annual increase of 2.3% in the Eastern Region and a stable population in Maryland. Although the Pine Warbler depends on stands of pine and is most abundant in areas of extensive pure pine forest, it is not restricted to pure stands or to very extensive stands. Thus, it is widely but locally distributed in Maryland outside of the extensive pine forests of the Coastal Plain. The Pine Warbler appears secure in Maryland for the foreseeable future.

Ernest J. Willoughby

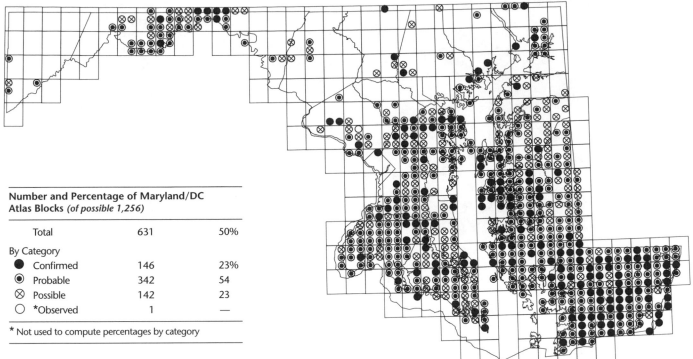

Number and Percentage of Maryland/DC Atlas Blocks *(of possible 1,256)*

Total	631	50%
By Category		
● Confirmed	146	23%
◉ Probable	342	54
⊗ Possible	142	23
○ *Observed	1	—

* Not used to compute percentages by category

Atlas Distribution, 1983–1987

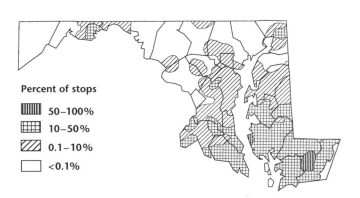

Percent of stops

▥	50–100%
▦	10–50%
▨	0.1–10%
☐	<0.1%

Relative Abundance, 1982–1989

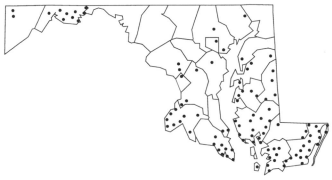

Breeding Distribution, 1958

The Pine Warbler is most abundant in the mixed woodlands along the Pocomoke River; its numbers decline to the north and west, as do pine trees. In western Maryland it was found in good numbers in the dry pine forests of eastern Allegany and western Washington counties.

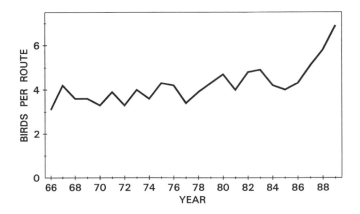

Maryland BBS Trend Graph, 1966–1989

Prairie Warbler

Dendroica discolor

The Prairie Warbler would often go undetected in summer if it were not for its distinctive song. This quiet, methodical feeder lacks the more animated behavior of most warblers. It is a summer resident throughout Maryland, although its habitat requirements make it localized in some areas. Spring migrants arrive from their Caribbean wintering grounds (AOU 1983) in mid-April, and most return south by mid-October (Robbins and Bystrak 1977).

Historically, Prairie Warblers probably occurred in stands of young or small pines and not in heavily forested areas. Early authors (Coues and Prentiss 1883; Kirkwood 1895; Cooke 1929) considered them very common to common but local in Maryland and the DC area. Eifrig (1904) described them as common at low elevations in western Maryland but noted they were absent from the highlands. Not until 1925 did F. Kirkwood obtain the first summer record for Garrett County (Robbins 1950). Stewart and Robbins (1958) described the Prairie Warbler as common in the Eastern Shore, Western Shore, and Ridge and Valley sections, fairly common locally in the Piedmont Section, and rare in the Upper Chesapeake and Allegheny Mountain sections.

Nesting habitats in Maryland include open stands of young pine or sweet gum, brushy cutover or burned upland forests, and weedy or abandoned orchards (Stewart and Robbins 1958). The highest breeding density reported for Maryland is 85 territorial males per 100 acres (40.5 ha) in burned-over upland oak forest in Prince George's County (Robbins et al. 1947). Nests are typically built in small trees and shrubs within 10 ft (3.0 m) of the ground (Nolan 1978). Heights of 41 Maryland nests (MNRF) range from 1 to 10 ft (0.3–3 m), with a mean of 3.9 ft (1.2 m). Nest building in Maryland has been observed as early as 5 May and as late as 9 June (Stewart and Robbins 1958). The latter date probably refers to a renesting attempt.

Extreme egg dates are 12 May and 11 July in Maryland and 19 July in DC (MNRF). Clutch sizes from 29 Maryland nests range from 2 to 5 (mean of 3.7). Late nesting attempts produce 3 eggs more frequently than 4 (Nolan 1978). Extreme Maryland nestling dates are 25 May (Stewart and Robbins 1958) and 25 July (MNRF). Brood sizes in 16 Maryland nests (MNRF) range from 1 to 4 (mean of 3.1). Dependent fledged young have been observed from 7 June through 8 August (Stewart and Robbins 1958). Nolan (1978) reported an average incubation period of 12 days and a nestling period of 9 or 10 days. The Prairie Warbler is a common victim of Brown-headed Cowbird parasitism (Friedmann 1963). Six of 29 Maryland nests (20.6%) had Brown-headed Cowbird eggs (MNRF); 5 of these 6 were deserted and the sixth was not revisited by the observer. In Ontario, 8 of 24 nests (33.3%) were parasitized (Peck and James 1987). The diet of the Prairie Warbler consists almost entirely of insects, including beetles and caterpillars (Nolan 1978). Spiders are also taken.

Atlas results show that the distribution of Prairie Warblers has changed slightly since 1958. They are no longer rare in the Allegheny Mountain Section; many breeding sites have been created by the planting of small pines and by strip-mine reclamation. In the Ridge and Valley Section, they are still common west of the Hagerstown Valley in Washington County but are absent from the valley itself. They are also absent from the Frederick Valley. In the Piedmont Section, they are fairly common outside of urbanized areas; on the Western Shore they are very common except in the southern portion. They are absent from much of the central Eastern Shore but are common on the lower Eastern Shore, partly in ancestral habitats and partly in cutover woodlots, which are proliferating there. Prairie Warblers are found even in the open pine woods on Assateague Island in coastal Worcester County.

BBS data from 1966 through 1989 show a highly significant average annual decline of 2.4 percent in the Eastern Region; Maryland data show a similar but greater decline of 5.1 percent. The Maryland decline lessened slightly to 4.4 percent from 1980 to 1989. Loss of habitat in suburban counties is one reason for this decline; suitable habitat is also lost as the process of natural succession progresses in cutover and brushy fields.

Human disturbance—strip mining, the planting of orchards and ornamental pines, and the extensive cutting of pine forests—has created new shrubby habitats suitable for this species. The population of Prairie Warblers will always vary in these transient habitats. In ancestral habitats on the lower Eastern Shore and in the mountainous areas dominated by small pines, the population should remain stable. As most of these areas are currently protected, advancing urbanization and natural habitat succession seem to be the only real threats to the Prairie Warbler in Maryland. However, in light of the recent decline, continued monitoring of the population is important. If the decline continues, studies will be needed to determine its causes.

Robert F. Ringler

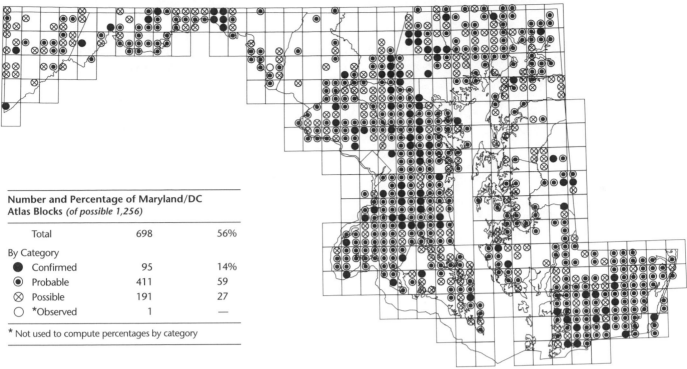

Atlas Distribution, 1983–1987

Number and Percentage of Maryland/DC Atlas Blocks *(of possible 1,256)*

Total		698	56%
By Category			
●	Confirmed	95	14%
◉	Probable	411	59
⊗	Possible	191	27
○	*Observed	1	—

* Not used to compute percentages by category

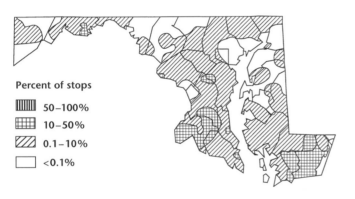

Percent of stops

▥	50–100%
▦	10–50%
▨	0.1–10%
☐	<0.1%

Relative Abundance, 1982–1989

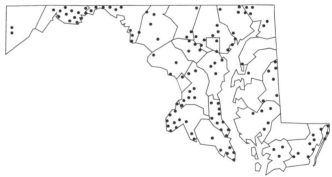

Breeding Distribution, 1958

The Prairie Warbler is most common on the southern Coastal Plain of the Eastern and Western shores. It is generally absent from urban and agricultural areas and is local in the Allegheny Mountain Section. Its numbers generally decrease to the north and west.

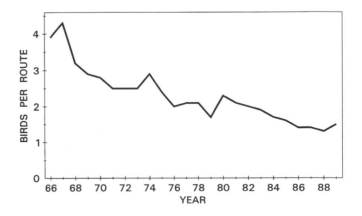

Maryland BBS Trend Graph, 1966–1989

Prairie Warbler 343

Cerulean Warbler

Dendroica cerulea

The Cerulean Warbler was named by ornithologist Alexander Wilson in 1810 (AOU 1983); he could scarcely have used a more appropriate name, given the bird's color. A locally common species, it favors extensive rich, moist, mature deciduous woods along rivers and streams (Robbins et al. 1989a). Although hard to see, the Cerulean Warbler is an incessant singer and can occasionally be spotted as it makes short flycatcherlike flights in pursuit of insects. It feeds primarily on bees, wasps, beetles, and caterpillars (Howell 1924). Spring migrants begin returning to Maryland from South American wintering grounds (AOU 1983) in late April and are rarely seen after August (Robbins and Bystrak 1977).

The original breeding range of the Cerulean Warbler was in the Ohio Valley. It was considered rare and irregular east of the Appalachian Mountains until early in the twentieth century (Cooke 1904); it has been expanding eastward since then. There was a period of nearly 50 years after Wilson named this species before the first nest was found along the Susquehanna River in Pennsylvania (Bent 1953). Coues and Prentiss (1862, 1883) reported that it had not been seen in DC, but they believed it would ultimately be found. Pleasants (1893) reported the first probable nesting for Maryland when he shot a singing male and two young in Baltimore on 14 July 1893. Kirkwood (1895) stated that the Cerulean Warbler was a transient at Hagerstown in Washington County and questioned whether it was a summer resident. Cooke (1929) listed it as very rare or accidental in migration in the DC area. Kirkwood (1901) located the first Maryland nest on 10 June 1900 in Baltimore County. In Allegany and Garrett counties in 1901 and 1902, Eifrig (1904) found this species breeding as low as Cumberland and believed it to be expanding its range. Kolb (1943) called it distinctly rare in the Baltimore and DC area. Stewart and Robbins (1958) wrote that it was fairly common in the western part of the Ridge and Valley Section and locally in the Piedmont Section, uncommon in the Savage River Valley in Garrett County, and rare elsewhere in the Allegheny Mountain Section.

Nest trees are principally oak, hickory, tulip tree, and sycamore, and, formerly, American chestnut (MNRF). The highest breeding density in Maryland, nine territorial males per 100 acres (40.5 ha), was recorded in hickory-oak-ash floodplain forest along the Middle Patuxent River in Howard County (Robbins 1973b). The nest is placed on a fork of a horizontal branch 20 to 75 ft (6.1–23 m) high (Chapman 1907a) and generally 5 to 8 ft (1.5–2.4 m) out from the trunk (Peck and James 1987). Usually there is an open area below the nest, and occasionally the branch extends out over a stream (Bent 1953). Clutch sizes range from 3 to 5, usually 4. The female incubates the eggs for 12 or 13 days. Both parents feed and care for the young (Ehrlich et al. 1988).

The nine reports in the MNRF are incomplete, owing to the difficulty of monitoring treetop nests. Maryland eggs were reported only once: 4 in a nest in a tulip tree on 10 June 1900 by F. Kirkwood. Five reports specified the species of nest tree: tulip tree (2), scarlet oak (1), white oak (1), and elm (1). The heights range from 30 to 50 ft (9.1–15 m) above ground. Two reports stated that the nests were 8.9 ft (2.7 m) and 7.2 ft (2.2 m) from the trunk. A nest found in Baltimore County by F. Kirkwood on 9 June 1901 contained 3 young, 1 newly hatched (MNRF). Reports of Brown-headed Cowbird eggs in Cerulean Warbler nests are few, perhaps because the nests are hard to find and harder to examine. In Ontario, 7 of 39 nests (17.9%) were parasitized (Peck and James 1987). Parasitism has not been reported in Maryland.

Atlas data show little change in the Maryland breeding range of the Cerulean Warbler over the years. Breeding is most evident along rivers and streams in the Ridge and Valley Section of Allegany, Washington, and Frederick counties, including the Catoctin Mountains. There are scattered local concentrations in the Piedmont Section in Montgomery, Howard, Carroll, Baltimore, Harford, and Cecil counties. Although the distribution has changed little, there has been a major change in abundance. BBS data from 1966 through 1989 show a highly significant average annual population decline of 3 percent in the Eastern Region; the Maryland population is stable.

Continued loss of habitat seems to be the greatest threat to the Cerulean Warbler, which is so dependent on extensive, tall hardwoods in heavily wooded areas (Robbins et al. 1989a, 1992). If breeding and wintering habitats can be protected, the population should remain stable, but one should not expect an increase in numbers. The USFWS (1987) considers the Cerulean Warbler a nongame bird of management concern in the Northeast. Further study of this warbler's life cycle is needed. This will be a challenge to even the most persistent researcher because of the bird's propensity for staying high in the canopies of the tallest trees.

Martha Chestem

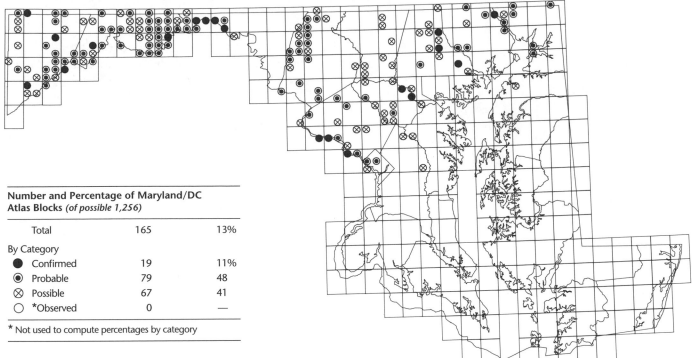

Number and Percentage of Maryland/DC Atlas Blocks *(of possible 1,256)*

Total	165	13%
By Category		
● Confirmed	19	11%
◉ Probable	79	48
⊗ Possible	67	41
○ *Observed	0	—

* Not used to compute percentages by category

Atlas Distribution, 1983–1987

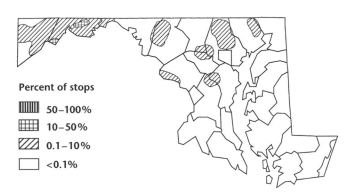

Percent of stops

▤	50–100%
▦	10–50%
▨	0.1–10%
☐	<0.1%

Relative Abundance, 1982–1989

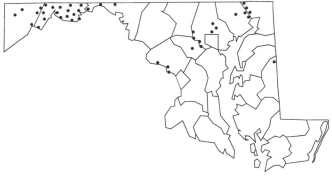

Breeding Distribution, 1958

The Cerulean Warbler is most widely distributed in western Maryland. There are concentrations in the Catoctin Mountains in Frederick County and along five major rivers—the Potomac, Patuxent, Patapsco, Gunpowder Falls, and Susquehanna—in the Piedmont.

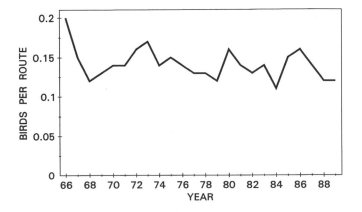

Maryland BBS Trend Graph, 1966–1989

Black-and-white Warbler

Mniotilta varia

More striking than the bold pattern of its plumage is the behavior of the Black-and-white Warbler. With a dexterity that exceeds that of the Brown Creeper and the nuthatches, the Black-and-white Warbler searches trunks and major branches of trees, gleaning food from the surface or fissures in the bark. Called the Creeping Warbler or Pied Warbler by early naturalists, it exploits a feeding niche only cursorily used by other wood warblers, consuming aphids, the larvae of various beetles, scale insects, cankerworms, caterpillars, and other still dormant or newly emerged insects (Hausman 1938). The Black-and-white Warbler returns from its Caribbean and Central and South American wintering grounds (AOU 1983) in early April (Robbins and Bystrak 1977) before the leaves have fully emerged on most deciduous trees; most depart by mid-October (Stewart and Robbins 1958).

Kirkwood (1895) called this warbler a common migrant but wrote that it thinned out in the breeding season. Eifrig (1904) reported that it was common in summer in Garrett and Allegany counties. Stewart and Robbins (1958) described its breeding status as common in the Allegheny Mountain and Ridge and Valley sections, fairly common in the Piedmont and Western Shore sections, fairly common and local in the Eastern Shore Section, and rare in the Upper Chesapeake Section. Robbins (1950) recorded one-day breeding season tallies ranging from 38 birds in the northern Catoctin Mountains, to 33 birds in Garrett and Allegany counties, to seldom more than 5 birds on the Eastern Shore.

Black-and-white Warblers nest in second-growth and mature deciduous or mixed woodlands (DeGraaf and Rudis 1986). Some of the trees need to be at least 30 ft (9 m) tall (Robbins 1950). A maximum of 21 territorial males per 100 acres (40.5 ha) was recorded in dense second-growth oak-maple ridge forest in Garrett County (Robbins 1949b). Several studies of Maryland populations (Robbins 1980; Lynch and Whigham 1984; Robbins et al. 1989a) show that this species is sensitive to forest fragmentation.

Field notes and local banding records indicate that locally breeding males arrive first in the spring and begin establishing territories before the larger waves of migrants pass through in May (J. Stasz, unpub. data). Nest building has been reported as early as 24 April in Worcester County and as late as 1 June in Caroline County (MNRF). All but one of the Maryland nests were placed on the ground. Kirkwood (1895) found the exception on 5 June 1895 in Allegany County in a crevice about 4 feet up the perpendicular face of Dan's Rock, on the summit of the mountain.

Extreme Maryland egg dates are 12 May and 19 June (MNRF). Clutch sizes for 14 Maryland nests range from 3 to 5 (mean of 4.1). Nestlings have been found from 24 May (Cooke 1929) to 7 July (MNRF). Brood sizes in eight Maryland nests (MNRF) range from 3 to 5. Incubation, by the female, lasts 13 days; only one brood is raised per year (Forbush 1929). Recently fledged young have been reported in Maryland from 3 June to 28 July (Robbins 1950). Friedmann (1963) considered the Black-and-white Warbler to be an uncommon victim of the Brown-headed Cowbird. Only one of 16 Maryland nests (6%) contained a Brown-headed Cowbird egg or young, but there are two records of fledged Brown-headed Cowbirds being fed. In Ontario, however, 9 of 43 Black-and-white Warbler nests (20.9%) were parasitized (Peck and James 1983).

Atlas results show the Black-and-white Warbler well distributed throughout Maryland, although with some obvious gaps. They are missing from areas dominated by marsh, field, small woodlots, and suburban and urban areas. In the western part of the Ridge and Valley Section, occurrence is spotty compared with that on the Allegheny Plateau. This species is apparently less widely distributed in the western Ridge and Valley Section than was described by Stewart and Robbins (1958), and perhaps occurs more widely in the Upper Chesapeake and Eastern Shore sections. The five nest categories *(NB, NE, NY, ON, UN)* yielded fewer than 12 percent of "confirmed" records; hatched-young categories *(FL, FS, FY)* constituted the rest. More than 85 percent of the "probable" records were of birds holding territory.

BBS data from 1966 through 1989 show stable populations in the Eastern Region and Maryland; the greatest densities are in central New England, the Blue Ridge Mountains, and the spruce-hardwood forest extending from Maine to Minnesota. Although the Maryland population is stable, preservation of extensive forests at least 500 acres (202.5 ha) in size (Robbins et al. 1989a) with a heavy understory will be necessary to maintain the Black-and-white Warbler population at a healthy level.

James L. Stasz

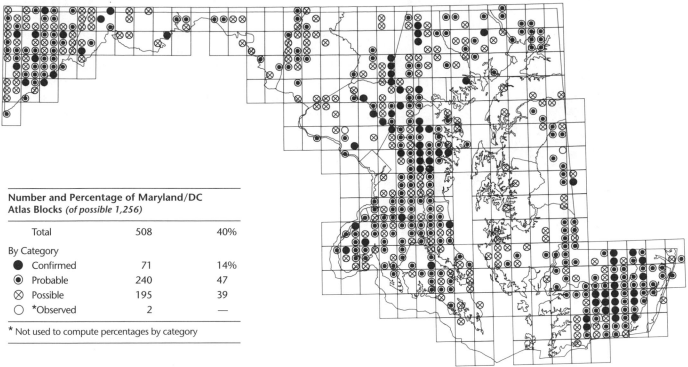

Number and Percentage of Maryland/DC Atlas Blocks *(of possible 1,256)*

Total	508	40%
By Category		
● Confirmed	71	14%
⊙ Probable	240	47
⊗ Possible	195	39
○ *Observed	2	—

* Not used to compute percentages by category

Atlas Distribution, 1983–1987

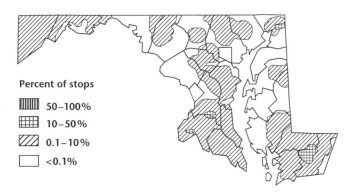

Percent of stops

▥	50–100%
▦	10–50%
▨	0.1–10%
☐	<0.1%

Relative Abundance, 1982–1989

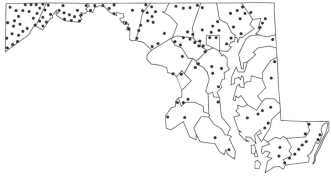

Breeding Distribution, 1958

The Black-and-white Warbler reaches its greatest abundance in Pocomoke State Forest on the lower Eastern Shore. It is fairly common in extensive forest but is absent from urban areas, marshlands, and agricultural areas with small woodlots, including the Hagerstown and Frederick valleys and the central Eastern Shore.

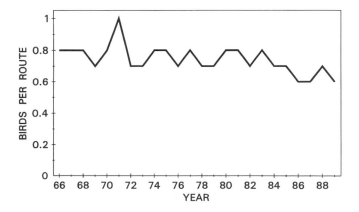

Maryland BBS Trend Graph, 1966–1989

American Redstart

Setophaga ruticilla

The colorful American Redstart is easily seen as it forages actively in the midstory canopy layer. It must have quickly caught the attention of the early colonists, who likened it to the red-tailed European Redstart—*start* being an old English word for tail. Both birds fan their tails as they flit about pursuing insects. Spring migrants return to Maryland from their Caribbean, Mexican, and Central and South American wintering grounds (AOU 1983) from mid-April to early June (Robbins and Bystrak 1977). In fall most birds depart by mid-October.

The American Redstart was formerly one of the most common warblers in Maryland and DC. Kirkwood (1895) called it a common migrant and locally common breeder in central Maryland, and he noted that in June at Dan's Rock in Allegany County its numbers equaled those of all other species combined. Eifrig (1904) considered it common to locally abundant in summer in western Maryland. Stewart et al. (1952) reported an almost incredible 275 breeding pairs at PWRC in 1943, mostly in the Patuxent River floodplain. Stewart and Robbins (1958) described its breeding status as common in the Allegheny Mountain, Ridge and Valley, Piedmont, and Western Shore sections; locally common in the Eastern Shore Section; and uncommon and local in the Upper Chesapeake Section.

The American Redstart nests in a wide variety of deciduous woods, from recently overgrown clearings, to stands of young trees within old forests, to mature floodplain forests. One requirement seems to be extensive understory. Robbins (1979) reported that this species requires extensive contiguous forest for breeding. It is considered a forest-interior-dwelling bird in the Chesapeake Bay Critical Area (Bushman and Therres 1988). High breeding densities for Maryland are 91 territorial males per 100 acres (40.5 ha) in a second-growth river swamp with dense understory in Worcester County (Springer and Stewart 1948d) and 51 per 100 acres in

well-drained floodplain forest at PWRC in 1945 (Stewart et al. 1946). Territory size apparently varies with breeding density. In New York, Sturm (1945) found territories in a Bass Island population averaged 0.23 acres (0.09 ha), whereas Ficken (1962) reported territories in an Ithaca population ranging from 0.5 to 1 acre (0.2–0.4 per ha). Territory size may shrink as the season progresses (Root 1970).

The female builds the nest (Gross 1953c), placing it in a tree or shrub, often an American hornbeam (Robbins 1950), and typically supporting it in a three- or four-way crotch (Ficken 1964). In 53 Maryland nests (MNRF), heights range from 4 to 40 ft (1.2–12 m), with a mean of 18 ft (5.5 m). Maryland egg dates range from 25 April to 20 June (30 June in DC) with a peak in early to mid-June (MNRF), suggesting that only one brood is attempted. In 26 Maryland nests all clutches contained 3 or 4 eggs (mean of 3.6).

Incubation, by the female, lasts 12 days (Gross 1953c). Nestlings have been found in Maryland from 17 May to 9 July (MNRF). Brood sizes in 16 Maryland nests range from 2 to 4 (mean of 3.2). The young fledge about nine days after hatching (Gross 1953c); both parents may tend the young in the postfledging period (Boxall 1983). The American Redstart is one of the commonest victims of Brown-headed Cowbird parasitism (Friedmann 1963); for example, 57 of 285 Ontario nests (20%) were parasitized (Peck and James 1987). Although there are three reports of American Redstarts feeding fledgling Brown-headed Cowbirds in Maryland, only 1 of 42 nests (2.3%) examined contained Brown-headed Cowbird eggs or young (MNRF). The American Redstart feeds almost entirely on insects, especially flying ones, and caterpillars (Gross 1953c).

Atlas results show a breeding range almost identical to that described by Stewart and Robbins (1958). American Redstarts were absent from the extensive agricultural areas of the Frederick and Hagerstown valleys and from most of the Eastern Shore, except for the Pocomoke River drainage. Fewer birds were found in the northern Piedmont than in 1958, perhaps reflecting continuing loss of forest in that area. The present breeding population is concentrated in the two western counties and along the Potomac, Patuxent, Patapsco, and Pocomoke river valleys.

BBS data from 1966 through 1989 show stable populations in the Eastern Region and Maryland. Despite stable populations at the state level, some local populations have declined alarmingly. In a 104-acre (42-ha) study site in the Patuxent River floodplain at PWRC, undisturbed except by browsing white-tailed deer, the number of territorial male American Redstarts dropped from 18 in 1964 to none in 1990 (Robbins 1991).

The American Redstart is vulnerable to any increase in Brown-headed Cowbird parasitism, to habitat fragmentation, and to habitat disturbance along stream valleys. Its decline at PWRC over the past few decades indicates a need for careful monitoring of local breeding population levels.

Frederick W. Fallon

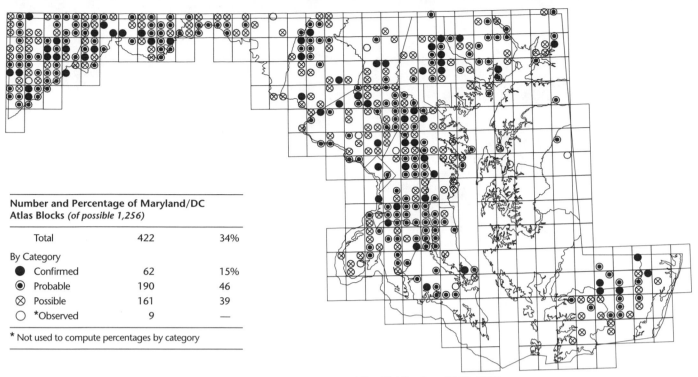

Number and Percentage of Maryland/DC Atlas Blocks *(of possible 1,256)*

Total	422	34%
By Category		
● Confirmed	62	15%
◉ Probable	190	46
⊗ Possible	161	39
○ *Observed	9	—

* Not used to compute percentages by category

Atlas Distribution, 1983–1987

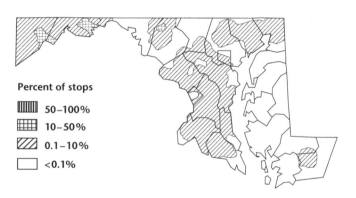

Percent of stops

▥	50–100%
▦	10–50%
▨	0.1–10%
☐	<0.1%

Relative Abundance, 1982–1989

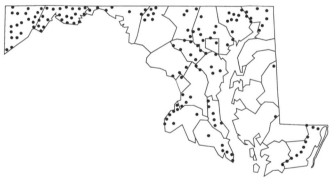

Breeding Distribution, 1958

The American Redstart is most widely distributed in the extensive woodlands of southern Maryland, the Allegheny Mountain Section, and the western Ridge and Valley Section. It is absent from the agricultural expanses of the Hagerstown and Frederick valleys and most of the Eastern Shore.

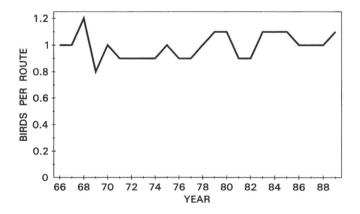

Maryland BBS Trend Graph, 1966–1989

Prothonotary Warbler

Protonotaria citrea

The handsome Prothonotary Warbler was once rare along the Atlantic Coast north of Virginia (Cooke 1904). Now it nests regularly as far north as Ontario (McCracken 1987) and New York (Eaton 1988b). Spring birds return from Central and northern South America (AOU 1983) to their Maryland breeding grounds in mid-April (Robbins and Bystrak 1977). Fall migrants are moving by mid-August; most leave by late September.

The first sight record for the Prothonotary Warbler in the DC area was on 2 May 1861 (Coues and Prentiss 1883); the first for Maryland was on 17 May 1888 near Laurel, Prince George's County (Kirkwood 1895). The only other nineteenth-century report was on 25 August 1895 at Dulaney Valley, Baltimore County. By 1920 this species appeared to be breeding in the DC area, but the first confirmed nesting was at Dyke Marsh on the Virginia side of the Potomac River on 9 June 1928 (Cooke 1929). In the 1940s it was a common breeder along the Pocomoke River and uncommon to fairly common in most of the Coastal Plain and up the Potomac River to Seneca in Montgomery County (Stewart and Robbins 1947a). A decade later, Stewart and Robbins (1958) described its breeding range as all of the Coastal Plain, along the Susquehanna River into the Piedmont Section, and along the Potomac River to Allegany County.

The Prothonotary Warbler is the only cavity-nesting warbler in the eastern United States. Its preferred habitat is mature swamp forests with standing water, but it also uses well-drained floodplain forests (Stewart and Robbins 1958). Nests are typically located over fresh water but have been found several hundred feet from water (Bent 1953). Favored nest sites are old woodpecker or chickadee cavities (Bent 1953), although it will use nest boxes and other artificial objects (Petit et al. 1987). The highest breeding density reported for Maryland is 40 territorial males per 100 acres (40.5 ha) in a second-growth river swamp in Worcester County (Springer and Stewart 1948d). Nest construction is by the female, but males may build dummy nests to attract females. Both sexes gather twigs, leaves, rootlets, and animal hair used in nest construction (Harrison 1975). The nest's interior is about 2 in. (5 cm) in diameter and about 1.5 in. (4 cm) deep.

Heights above water of 44 Maryland nests (MNRF) range from 1 to 20 ft (0.3–6.1 m), with a mean of 4.7 ft (1.4 m). Maryland egg dates range from 28 April to 3 July, with a peak in early June. Clutch sizes in 22 Maryland nests (MNRF) range from 3 to 5 (mean of 4.1). One egg is laid daily and incubation, by the female, starts the day before the last egg is laid (Bent 1953). Eggs hatch after 12 to 14 days, and the young fledge 10 to 12 days later. Dates of Maryland nests with young range from 11 May to 25 July, with no evident peak (MNRF). Brood sizes in 12 Maryland nests range from 2 to 5 (mean of 3.5). Both parents feed the nestlings and fledglings; two broods are commonly attempted (Bent 1953). Typically the first brood is fledged by the first week in June, and the second clutch is laid by the end of that month. The male sings from his arrival in the spring until the young have fledged.

Although Brown-headed Cowbird parasitism is rare among cavity-nesting species, Prothonotary Warblers are frequent victims (Friedmann 1963). Only 5 of 35 Maryland nests (14.3%) were parasitized (MNRF), but Peck and James (1987) reported that 12 of 34 Ontario nests (35.5%) were parasitized and Petit and others (1987) found Brown-headed Cowbird eggs in 27 of 117 Tennessee nests (23.1%).

The Prothonotary Warbler feeds low over water. It differs from other warblers in that it eats a significant number of land snails and small crustaceans in addition to beetles, moths, caterpillars, flies, and ants (Bent 1953; USFWS Food Habits File).

Atlas data show the Prothonotary Warbler's distribution to be nearly identical to that described by Stewart and Robbins (1958). It shows a strong preference for wooded swamps along freshwater rivers on the Coastal Plain. On the Eastern Shore the largest concentrations occur along the upper Choptank and Chester rivers, along the Nanticoke and Pocomoke rivers, and in the forested swamps of central Dorchester County. On the Western Shore, the center of occurrence is in the upper tidal reaches of the Patuxent River and along the lower Potomac. In the Piedmont and west, this warbler is found primarily in swampy parts of the Chesapeake and Ohio Canal. During the Howard County Atlas from 1973 through 1975 (Klimkiewicz and Solem 1978), it was found in nearly four times as many quarterblocks as during the present Atlas fieldwork (Robbins et al. 1989c), suggesting a decline during the intervening decade.

BBS data from 1966 through 1989 show stable populations in the Eastern Region and Maryland. In areas of declining populations, nest box programs might provide some assistance. The Prothonotary Warbler is considered a forest-interior-dwelling bird and thus receives special habitat protection in the Chesapeake Bay Critical Area (Bushman and Therres 1988).

George Wilmot

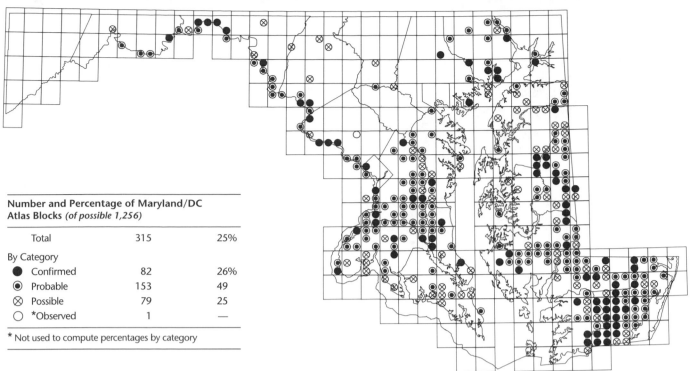

Number and Percentage of Maryland/DC Atlas Blocks (of possible 1,256)

	Total	315	25%
By Category			
●	Confirmed	82	26%
◉	Probable	153	49
⊗	Possible	79	25
○	*Observed	1	—

* Not used to compute percentages by category

Atlas Distribution, 1983–1987

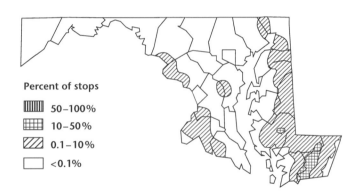

Percent of stops

▥	50–100%
▦	10–50%
▨	0.1–10%
☐	<0.1%

Relative Abundance, 1982–1989

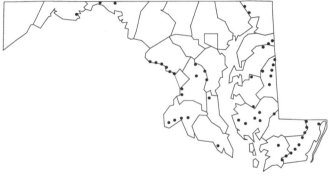

Breeding Distribution, 1958

The Prothonotary Warbler is most abundant in the wooded swamps along the Pocomoke River. Smaller numbers occur in wooded swamps and along slow-moving rivers throughout the interior on the rest of the Eastern Shore and along the Potomac, Susquehanna, and upper tidal Patuxent rivers west of the Chesapeake Bay.

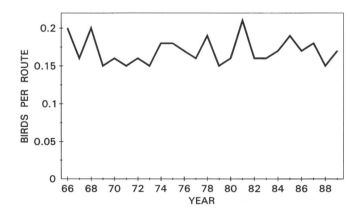

Maryland BBS Trend Graph, 1966–1989

Worm-eating Warbler

Helmitheros vermivorus

The shy, retiring Worm-eating Warbler is misnamed, as it is not known to eat worms. It feeds primarily above ground and is quite acrobatic as it seeks insect prey on the leaves of taller trees early in the summer and on the curled leaves of shrubs and saplings as the season progresses (Greenberg 1987). Among the many types of insects it eats are weevils, other beetles, bugs, caterpillars, wasps, and grasshoppers; spiders are also an important component of its diet (Imhof 1962). Spring migrants return to Maryland from their Caribbean, eastern Mexican, and Central American wintering grounds (AOU 1983) in late April; fall migrants depart by late September (Robbins and Bystrak 1977).

It is difficult to determine if the status of the Worm-eating Warbler has changed in Maryland during the past 100 years. Kirkwood (1895) called it sparingly resident but provided information only for the Baltimore-Washington area. Eifrig (1904) said it could be found in proper locations in western Maryland. Stewart and Robbins (1958) called it fairly common in the Ridge and Valley Section, locally common in the Piedmont Section, uncommon in the Western Shore Section and along the Pocomoke River drainage on the lower Eastern Shore, and rare elsewhere. Greenberg (1987) reported high densities of 100 to 150 singing males per 247 acres (100 ha) at Sugarloaf Mountain, Frederick County. BBS data from 1966 through 1989 show stable populations in both the Eastern Region and Maryland; data from 1980 through 1989 indicate a decline in Maryland.

The Worm-eating Warbler is strongly associated with large contiguous woodlands during the breeding season (Robbins et al. 1989a). It favors steep hillsides in the Piedmont and farther west and ravines and well-drained oak and oak-hickory forests on the inner Coastal Plain (Stewart and Robbins 1958; J. Stasz, pers. obs.). On the lower Eastern Shore, it is found in flatland white oak forests in association with mountain laurel understory along river terraces and in drier islands of extensive nontidal forested wetlands where American holly is the dominant shrub layer. Robbins et al.

(1989a) estimated the minimum forested habitat needed to support a viable population at 371 acres (150 ha); they did not find the Worm-eating Warbler in forested tracts of less than 52 acres (21 ha).

Nests invariably show the "characteristic reddish-brown lining of the flower stem of the hair [hair-cap] moss" (Bent 1953). All 14 nests in the MNRF were on the ground. Maryland egg dates range from 29 May to 4 July in DC (MNRF). The scarcity of records makes it difficult to define the breeding season. It is probably similar to Pennsylvania's, where eggs have been found from 15 May to 30 June, with 45 of 75 records in the brief period from 24 May to 5 June (Bent 1953). The three Maryland clutches (MNRF) contained 4, 5, and 6 eggs. Incubation, performed by the female, lasts 13 days (Forbush 1929), and the young fledge 10 days after hatching (Griscom and Sprunt 1957). Nests with young have been found in Maryland from 28 May to 4 July (MNRF). Only one brood is reported (Forbush 1929), so late dates may represent renesting attempts.

Friedmann (1963) considered the Worm-eating Warbler an uncommon victim of the Brown-headed Cowbird. The MNRF shows that only 2 of 13 nests (15.1%) reported from 1885 through 1968 were parasitized; however, R. Greenberg (pers. obs.) found Brown-headed Cowbird eggs in 12 of 17 nests (70.6%) examined in the mid-1980s at Sugarloaf Mountain, Frederick County. The mean number of Brown-headed Cowbird eggs in these nests was greater than the mean number of Worm-eating Warbler eggs.

Atlas results show this warbler to be widely distributed throughout Maryland, although in most parts of the state it is uncommon and local. The strength of its occurrence in Garrett County contrasts strongly with what Stewart and Robbins (1958) reported but agrees with what Eifrig (1904) found, suggesting that continuing changes may have been under way. In addition, it is distributed much more widely on the lower Eastern Shore, as well as locally in the Upper Chesapeake Section, than was previously reported.

Much remains to be learned about the biology of the Worm-eating Warbler in Maryland. Its fondness for well-drained woods is shared by the Black-and-white Warbler, but comparison of the Atlas maps shows the distribution of the Worm-eating Warbler to be more closely associated with Pine, Prairie, and Yellow-throated Warblers. The Black-and-white Warbler is more closely associated with the Hooded Warbler, American Redstart, and Northern Parula. And it is clear from Robbins et al. (1989a) that the Worm-eating Warbler needs extensive forests for breeding. Nevertheless, the microhabitat requirements behind these associations are unknown. Although the population is apparently stable, we are still uncertain about some of the habitat requirements, the timing of breeding, the number of broods attempted, and the length of the fledgling period. Until these questions are answered, formulating management plans for the Worm-eating Warbler will be difficult.

James L. Stasz

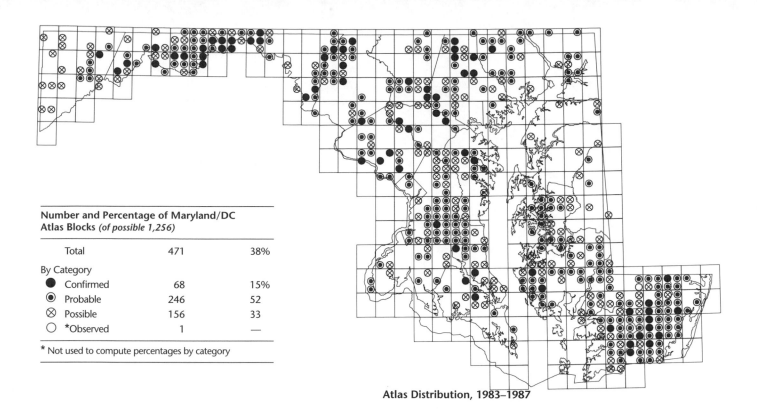

Number and Percentage of Maryland/DC Atlas Blocks *(of possible 1,256)*		
Total	471	38%
By Category		
● Confirmed	68	15%
◉ Probable	246	52
⊗ Possible	156	33
○ *Observed	1	—
* Not used to compute percentages by category		

Atlas Distribution, 1983–1987

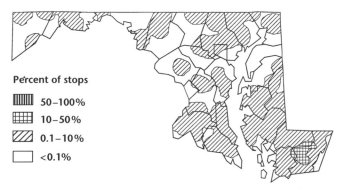

Percent of stops

▥ 50–100%

▦ 10–50%

▨ 0.1–10%

□ <0.1%

Relative Abundance, 1982–1989

Breeding Distribution, 1958

The Worm-eating Warbler is most common in the extensive forest along the Pocomoke River and its tributaries. It was found infrequently in developed and agricultural areas where woodlands are fragmented. It is scarce and local in the Allegheny Mountain Section.

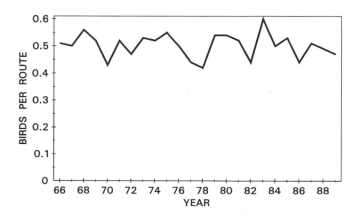

Maryland BBS Trend Graph, 1966–1989

Swainson's Warbler

Limnothlypis swainsonii

The much-sought Swainson's Warbler is an explosive but melodic singer. Although rare in Maryland, it still breeds locally on the lower Eastern Shore along the Pocomoke River and its tributaries in Worcester, Wicomico, and Somerset counties—the extreme northern breeding limit for this species on the Coastal Plain (AOU 1983). There is no evidence that it has ever been more than rare in Maryland. Swainson's Warblers begin to arrive in Maryland from their Central American wintering grounds (AOU 1983) in late April (Robbins and Bystrak 1977), but in Virginia's Great Dismal Swamp, Meanley (1971) found that many did not arrive until early May.

Joseph Cadbury first discovered the Swainson's Warbler in Maryland, a single bird near Willards in Wicomico County on 12 May 1942 (Robbins 1950). It was assumed this was a spring migrant that had overshot the breeding range until Stewart and Robbins (1947a) found two pairs in a bald cypress swamp, 5 mi (8 km) southwest of Pocomoke City in Somerset County on 2 May 1946. The next year, on 13 July 1947, R. Stewart found four singing males just south of the Delaware line in Worcester County (Robbins 1950), a location where singing males were subsequently heard for many years. Stewart and Robbins (1958) called this species uncommon in swamps along the Pocomoke River and its tributaries and rare in other stream swamps in Worcester County. Recently, there have been sporadic reports from locations near the Delaware line on the Worcester County side of the Pocomoke River and from the vicinity of Shad Landing State Park, also in Worcester County. Although reports during the breeding season have been restricted to swamps along the Pocomoke River, the birds are not found along the old river bed or the dredged channel, but only in the nearby swamps where there is standing water (Robbins 1950).

Meanley (1971), who studied this species in Maryland and Virginia, found that the Swainson's Warbler forages almost exclusively on dry ground, scratching under leaves for bee-

tles, spiders, ants, and crickets and for their eggs, larvae, and pupae. He reported that "the deep shade of the Swainson's Warbler environment is the result of the dense upper canopy, layer of lower trees, and shrub strata. Herbaceous ground cover is absent in most of the warbler's habitats, and where it occurs it is usually of little consequence as a shade producer." He added, "Swainson's Warbler foraged mostly in openings between clumps of sweet pepperbush and greenbrier and in the small pure stands of sweet pepperbush. It nested mostly in the greenbrier tangles."

In Illinois, Eddleman et al. (1980) found that the smallest forest tract where a male established a territory was about 875 acres (351 ha). The only population density available for Maryland is 11 territorial males per 100 acres (40.5 ha) in the second-growth river swamp at the traditional Pocomoke site near the Delaware line (Springer and Stewart 1948d).

The bulky nests are typically placed 2 to 6 ft (0.6–1.8 m) high in a tangle of vines (Meanley 1971). Clutch sizes range from 2 to 5, most often 3 (no sample size was given). Incubation, by the female, requires 13 to 15 days. Both parents feed the young, which fledge in 10 to 12 days. Although single broods may be most common, Meanley (1971) noted that renesting or second nestings occur throughout June and into July. The only egg date for Maryland is 15 May 1955, when a banded female laid an egg in a holding cage (Fletcher and Fletcher 1956). Meanley (1950) found newly hatched young in a nest in the Pocomoke Swamp on 13 June 1948, and E. Fleisher and L. Worley saw fledged young near Pocomoke City as early as 20 June 1953 (Stewart and Robbins 1958). In Virginia, however, 6 of 11 nests had active clutches after 1 June (Meanley 1971). Farther south, the peak of the nesting season extends from 12 May to 12 June in South Carolina and from 29 May to 17 June in Georgia (Dingle 1953). Swainson's Warblers are locally common hosts of the Brown-headed Cowbird. Sims and DeGarmo (1948) found that 17 percent of 18 nests at Charleston, West Virginia, were parasitized, but there has been no report of parasitism in Maryland.

The three Atlas records were for birds holding territory at widely scattered locations along the Pocomoke River drainage. In the past, birds near the Delaware line have been harassed by birdwatchers using tape recordings of the song to lure the birds into view (C. Robbins, pers. obs.). Because the Swainson's Warbler is so rare in Maryland, Atlas workers did not search for nests or other evidence of breeding behavior, and the specific locations of the singing birds were not revealed.

BBS data from 1966 through 1989 indicate an increase in the Eastern Region; continental data show a significant average annual increase of 2.2 percent. There are too few data to estimate a trend in Maryland.

The DNR lists the Swainson's Warbler as a species in need of conservation. Although TNC protection of the Nassawango Creek tributary has provided some potential habitat, the Swainson's Warbler has not been confirmed as breeding in that part of the watershed. Large tracts of the Pocomoke Swamp are still unexplored and may harbor ad-

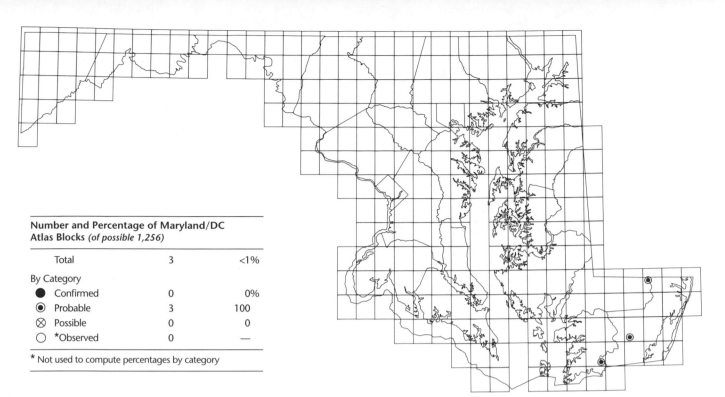

Number and Percentage of Maryland/DC Atlas Blocks (of possible 1,256)

Total	3	<1%
By Category		
● Confirmed	0	0%
◉ Probable	3	100
⊗ Possible	0	0
○ *Observed	0	—

* Not used to compute percentages by category

Atlas Distribution, 1983–1987

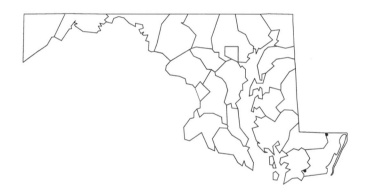

Breeding Distribution, 1958

ditional birds; however, extensive channelization of the Pocomoke River and its tributaries has greatly reduced the habitat available to this species. Efforts should be made to locate and protect the Swainson's Warbler and its habitat. The Maryland population is so isolated from the nearest nesting colony, 100 mi (160 km) to the south in the Great Dismal Swamp of Virginia, that recolonization is unlikely if the local birds become extirpated.

Charles R. Vaughn and Chandler S. Robbins

Ovenbird

Seiurus aurocapillus

The Ovenbird is a ground-dwelling, thrushlike warbler that is a typical summer inhabitant of woodlands throughout Maryland. Its common name is derived from its oven-shaped nest. The Ovenbird's ringing song of *teacher, teacher, teacher* is an unmistakable part of summer mornings. They arrive in Maryland from Central and South American wintering grounds (AOU 1983) in late April; most fall migrants leave by early October (Robbins and Bystrak 1977).

Coues and Prentiss (1862, 1883) called the Ovenbird an extremely abundant summer resident around DC; Kirkwood (1895) considered it common throughout Maryland. In western Maryland, Eifrig (1904) believed it was common at low elevations, less so at higher ones. Stewart and Robbins (1958) described it as an abundant breeding bird in the Ridge and Valley Section; common in the Allegheny Mountain, Piedmont, and Western Shore sections; fairly common locally in the Eastern Shore Section; and uncommon and local in the Upper Chesapeake Section.

Robbins et al. (1989a) found that Maryland Ovenbirds nest most commonly in extensive tall deciduous or pine forests with a high density of trees and a deciduous understory, especially in well-drained, flat terrain. The probability of detecting an Ovenbird at a single random point declined from 65 percent in a 247-acre (100-ha) forest, to 50 percent in 49 acres (19.8 ha), to 10 percent in 2.5 acres (1 ha). Ovenbirds are less common above 3,000 ft (914 m) and in spruce forests, where few dead leaves from deciduous trees are available for nest construction. Maryland's highest breeding density is 114 territorial males per 100 acres (40.5 ha) in an upland mixed forest with a small creek in Prince George's County (Whitcomb 1975).

Males arrive first on the breeding grounds and establish territories, often the same ones as in the previous year (Hann 1937). The female selects the nest site and the male defends the territory. The nest, usually built in a slight depression on the forest floor, is an arched, ovenlike structure with an opening on one side and is constructed of dead leaves, grasses, twigs, rootlets, bark, and moss. The roof of dead leaves protects the nest from rain and discovery. The only record of an Ovenbird nest built more than a few inches above ground level was a nest in a hollow log (Harrison 1975). The highest Maryland nests were 4 and 5 in. (10–13 cm) above ground (MNRF).

The earliest Maryland egg date is 2 May; the latest is 17 July, with a peak in early to mid-June (MNRF). Clutch sizes in 49 Maryland nests range from 3 to 6 (mean of 4.4). Incubation, by the female, lasts 11 to 14 days (Hann 1937). When flushed, the female performs a distraction display similar to that of the Killdeer (Hann 1937). Brood sizes in 23 Maryland nests (MNRF) range from 2 to 6 (mean of 3.8). Young in the nest have been found in Maryland from 22 May to 18 July. Both parents tend the young, which fledge in 8 to 11 days; the parents continue to feed them for up to three weeks before abandoning the territory (Hann 1937). Occasionally there are two broods and, rarely, three. Males frequently have more than one mate. Ovenbirds are common victims of the Brown-headed Cowbird (Friedmann 1963). Peck and James (1987) reported that 31 of 260 Ontario nests (11.9%) were parasitized. Six of 70 Maryland nests (8.5%) were parasitized, including one with 3 Brown-headed Cowbird eggs (MNRF).

The Ovenbird's diet consists principally of earthworms, beetles, crickets, ants, and other insects gleaned from the forest floor (Gross 1953a). Zach and Falls (1975) reported that spruce budworm outbreaks can increase clutch sizes and the number of broods.

Ovenbirds were widespread during the Atlas period but were largely absent from the intensely agricultural areas of the Frederick and Hagerstown valleys, parts of the central Eastern Shore and southern St. Mary's County, and the marshy areas along the coast and on the lower Eastern Shore. Elsewhere they were found in most nonurban blocks. Because of their well-camouflaged nests, barely 20 percent of the records were "confirmed." Most records (53%) were of singing males holding territory.

BBS data from 1966 through 1989 show stable populations in the Eastern Region and Maryland; however, data from 1980 through 1989 show a significant average annual decline of 3.5 percent in Maryland. Because Ovenbird nests are placed on the ground, predation by snakes, squirrels, skunks, and other mammals is common. There is a high death rate among Ovenbirds, particularly during fall migration, from collisions with tall, man-made structures (Taylor 1972). For example, over 6,500 were killed at the Eau Claire, Wisconsin, television tower from 1960 through 1969 (S. Robbins 1991). The worst threat, however, as with other species that require extensive forest, is the elimination of habitat through forest fragmentation due to continuing development as well as urban and suburban sprawl. Conservation of forest-interior habitat is a requisite to maintaining the Ovenbird in Maryland (Bushman and Therres 1988).

James W. Cheevers

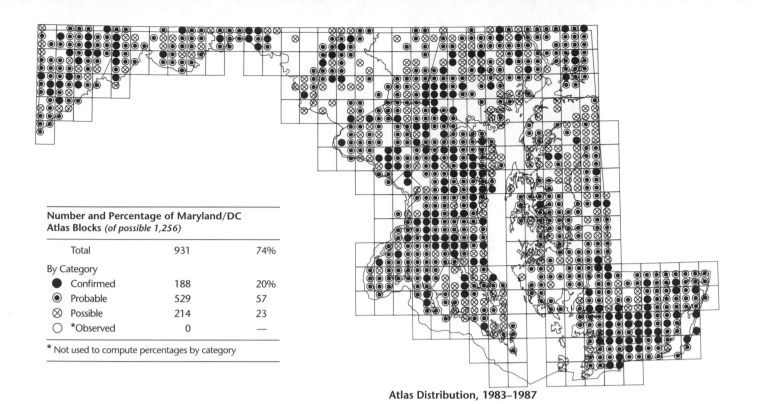

Number and Percentage of Maryland/DC Atlas Blocks *(of possible 1,256)*

Total	931	74%
By Category		
● Confirmed	188	20%
◉ Probable	529	57
⊗ Possible	214	23
○ *Observed	0	—

* Not used to compute percentages by category

Atlas Distribution, 1983–1987

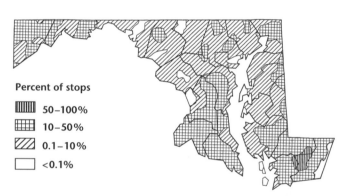

Percent of stops

▥	50–100%
▦	10–50%
▨	0.1–10%
☐	<0.1%

Relative Abundance, 1982–1989

Breeding Distribution, 1958

The Ovenbird is abundant only in the wet woodlands of Pocomoke State Forest on the lower Eastern Shore. It is least common, and occasionally undetected, in the most agricultural and developed sections of the state.

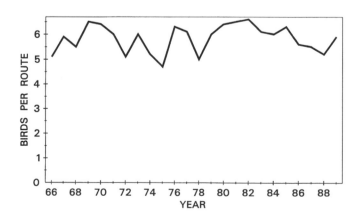

Maryland BBS Trend Graph, 1966–1989

Ovenbird 357

Northern Waterthrush

Seiurus noveboracensis

Although similar in appearance to its southern relative the Louisiana Waterthrush, the Northern Waterthrush is easily distinguished by the more even cadence of its song of slurred notes, gradually descending in pitch. This northern species is partial to boreal bogs in the Maryland portion of its range, rather than to the more rapidly moving streams favored by the Louisiana Waterthrush. The Maryland breeding ranges of the two species overlap only on the Allegheny Plateau in Garrett County, the only place the Northern Waterthrush breeds in Maryland.

The Northern Waterthrush arrives in Maryland from its Caribbean wintering grounds (AOU 1983) during the final days of April, and a few late migrants remain into early June (Robbins and Bystrak 1977). They spend only about three months on the breeding grounds. The first south-bound transients reach Maryland in the first week of August or even in late July in some years. Few remain after the opening days of October.

Preble (1900) recorded the first breeding activity in Maryland when he found the Northern Waterthrush to be fairly common in the Finzel region of northeastern Garrett County. Eifrig (1920a), however, had only one summer observation for the state until he found it at a second locality in 1918. It was not until the summer of 1945 that J. Cope and C. Robbins, during a systematic survey of Garrett County bogs, found this species in nearly every bog (Robbins 1950; Stewart and Robbins 1958). During the summers of 1945 through 1949, J. Cope, R. Stewart, and C. Robbins found territorial birds in Garrett County at elevations from 2,220 ft (677 m) at Swallow Falls to 2,720 ft (829 m) near Finzel. Their highest one-day count was 22 individuals on 22 June 1946 (Robbins 1950). Eaton (1957) found that territory size in New York ranged from 2.0 to 2.3 acres (0.8–0.9 ha) and that forested wetlands had to be at least 19.8 acres (8.0 ha) to attract this species in the breeding season.

The Northern Waterthrush differs from most warblers because it specializes on a diet of aquatic insects; it also eats tiny mollusks, crustaceans, small worms, and small fishes (Bent 1953). It is very habitat-specific on its breeding grounds. In Maryland, it is never found far from standing or slow-moving water. Garrett County's bogs attract it in high densities. A density of 84 pairs per 100 acres (40.5 ha) in an open eastern hemlock–spruce bog in the Maryland part of Cranesville Swamp is the highest on record anywhere for this species (Robbins 1950). This is remarkable because Cranesville is only about 50 miles (80.5 km) from the southern limit of the breeding range at Cranberry Glades in West Virginia (AOU 1983; Hall 1983).

In spite of the high breeding density, only two nests have been found in Maryland. One, with 1 egg and 3 newly hatched young, was found under a fallen log at Cranesville Swamp on 29 May 1949 (Robbins 1950). It was empty when next visited on 11 June, but persistent scolding by the adults indicated the presence of fledged young nearby. The other nest contained 5 eggs on 10 June 1990 (MNRF); all eggs had hatched on 16 June and the young were still in the nest on 25 June. Nests are typically among tree roots, in moss-covered hummocks and logs, or in depressions in the banks of streams (Davie 1898; Peck and James 1987). Nests are often over water and occasionally are placed as high as 3 ft (0.9 m). They generally contain 4 or 5 creamy-white eggs, heavily speckled and spotted at the larger end with hazel, lilac, and cinnamon-rufous. In Ontario, 52 egg dates ranged from 15 May to 3 July, with half of them in the brief period 27 May to 4 June (Peck and James 1987). The breeding season in Maryland is probably slightly earlier. The usual clutch size was 4. Friedmann (1963) considered the Northern Waterthrush to be rarely victimized by the Brown-headed Cowbird; however, 11 of 83 Ontario nests (13.3%) were parasitized (Peck and James 1987).

Atlas fieldwork yielded only four "confirmed" records: two instances of fledged young, one of a distraction display, and one of an adult with a fecal sac. The chief means of determining the breeding status was finding an adult holding territory. The breeding distribution shown by the Atlas is very similar to that found by Robbins (1950), except for additional sites south of Oakland, extending to the southernmost block in Garrett County. The complete absence of records outside the Allegheny Plateau shows the dependence of this species on mountain bogs, primarily at elevations above 1,900 ft (579 m).

BBS data from 1966 through 1989 show stable populations in the Eastern Region and an indication of an increase in the continental population. There are too few Maryland data to estimate a state trend. The southern wedge of its nesting range is very narrow, and few breeding sites are known south of Maryland's boundary with West Virginia. The future of breeding Northern Waterthrushes in Maryland depends on preserving the boreal bogs in which this species breeds.

Chandler S. Robbins

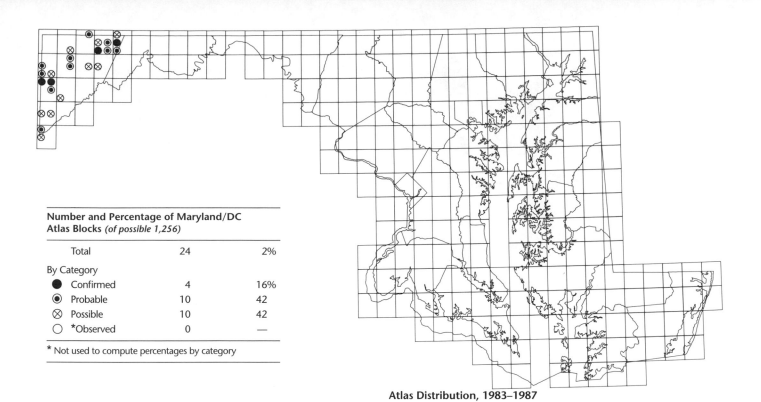

Number and Percentage of Maryland/DC Atlas Blocks *(of possible 1,256)*

Total		24	2%
By Category			
●	Confirmed	4	16%
◉	Probable	10	42
⊗	Possible	10	42
○	*Observed	0	—

* Not used to compute percentages by category

Atlas Distribution, 1983–1987

Breeding Distribution, 1958

Louisiana Waterthrush

Seiurus motacilla

The loud, ringing song of the Louisiana Waterthrush can be heard throughout Maryland in the spring and early summer, although the ventriloquial quality of its notes often makes finding the bird difficult. It breeds and forages at the water's edge, from fast-moving streams in the steep ravines of Garrett County to the sluggish swamps of the lower Eastern Shore. In fact, almost any Maryland wooded stream or swamp can support Louisiana Waterthrushes as long as there are ferns and tree roots lining the banks (C. Robbins, pers. obs.). Louisiana Waterthrushes return to Maryland from their Caribbean, Mexican, and Central American wintering grounds (AOU 1983) in late March and early April, and most birds depart in the fall by early September (Robbins and Bystrak 1977).

Until the mid-1800s, the Louisiana Waterthrush was confused with its close relative, the Northern Waterthrush, creating uncertainty about the status of both species (Bent 1953). Even after the two species were recognized, information about the breeding range of the Louisiana Waterthrush accumulated slowly. Coues and Prentiss (1883) reported that although "generally considered rare, we have found [it] to be not at all uncommon." Kirkwood (1895), noting that it was common in migration, added that it "probably spends the summer with us in greater numbers than is generally supposed." Stewart and Robbins (1958) reported it breeding throughout the state and considered it common in the Eastern and Western Shore sections; fairly common in the Upper Chesapeake, Piedmont, and Ridge and Valley sections; and locally fairly common in the Allegheny Mountain Section, generally preferring elevations below 2,300 ft (701 m).

BBS data from 1966 through 1989 show stable populations for the Louisiana Waterthrush both in Maryland and throughout its range in the southeastern United States. Atlas data from Howard and Montgomery counties in the early 1970s showed it to be present in more than 55 percent of the blocks and concentrated along the rocky portions of unpolluted and free-flowing streams (Klimkiewicz and Solem 1978). The present Atlas shows no change for this species.

This species prefers nesting in stream sites characterized by deciduous or mixed woods where oaks, maples, and hemlocks predominate (Eaton 1958). In most of Maryland, river birch replaces hemlock. The nest itself is never far from water and is most often tucked into a steep stream bank, usually under overhanging tree roots (MNRF). Eaton (1958) estimated the linear territory along a stream as 1,300 ft (396 m). Maryland's highest published breeding density is 16 territorial males per 100 acres (40.5 ha) in a second-growth river swamp in Worcester County (Springer and Stewart 1948d). Both sexes construct the nest, lining a shallow cup with decaying leaves and fortifying it with plant stems, pine needles, or small hemlock twigs (Eaton 1958). Some of the leaves form a pathway to the nest. All 15 Maryland nests (MNRF) were found on the ground or in a stream bank.

The earliest Maryland egg date is 17 April, the latest is 14 June; the peak is in mid- to late May (MNRF). In 10 nests, clutch sizes range from 4 to 7 (mean of 5.3). The female incubates the eggs for 12 to 14 days, beginning just before the last one is laid (Harrison 1978). Brood sizes from six Maryland nest records (MNRF) range from 3 to 6. Young in the nest in Maryland have been found from 6 May to 19 June. Both parents tend the young, which leave the nest after approximately 10 days; the adults continue to feed the fledglings for another week (Harrison 1978). Friedmann (1963) considered the Louisiana Waterthrush to be a frequent victim of the Brown-headed Cowbird. Although Peck and James (1987) reported parasitism in two of eight Ontario nests (25%) and two Maryland instances were recorded by Stewart and Robbins (1958), there are none among 15 nest records in the MNRF. The diet of the Louisiana Waterthrush consists primarily of aquatic and terrestrial insects, spiders, small snails, and other invertebrates (Bent 1953).

Atlas results suggest that the Louisiana Waterthrush is less widespread in the Eastern Shore and Upper Chesapeake sections than described by Stewart and Robbins (1958). At the same time, it appears to be slightly more widespread in the Piedmont, Ridge and Valley, and Allegheny Mountain sections. The decrease on the Eastern Shore may be a result of the loss of habitat to agriculture. It was absent from the tidewater blocks, the major urban areas, and the Frederick and Hagerstown valleys. The Louisiana Waterthrush needs continuous forest cover for breeding (DeGraaf et al. 1980), but ribbons of narrow woodland are more common on the Eastern Shore at present. The reason for the possible increase in the western part of the state is not obvious.

While the Louisiana Waterthrush is not declining at the present time, the amount of wooded habitat on which it depends is clearly decreasing. It is important to safeguard large tracts of mixed woodland containing streams if continued success of the Louisiana Waterthrush is to be guaranteed in Maryland.

Sue A. Ricciardi

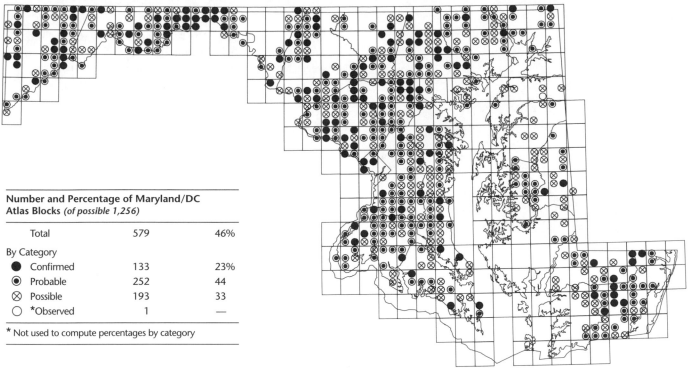

Number and Percentage of Maryland/DC Atlas Blocks *(of possible 1,256)*		
Total	579	46%
By Category		
● Confirmed	133	23%
◉ Probable	252	44
⊗ Possible	193	33
○ *Observed	1	—

* Not used to compute percentages by category

Atlas Distribution, 1983–1987

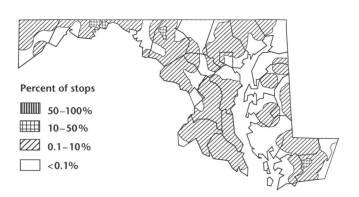

Percent of stops

▥ 50–100%

▦ 10–50%

▧ 0.1–10%

☐ <0.1%

Relative Abundance, 1982–1989

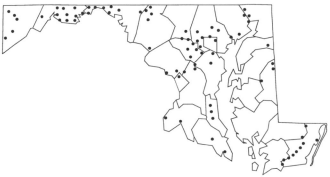

Breeding Distribution, 1958

The Louisiana Waterthrush is widespread and uncommon along wooded rivers and swamps. There are small concentrations in Green Ridge State Forest, the Catoctin Mountains, and southern Pocomoke State Forest. It is absent from urban areas and extensive agricultural areas in the Hagerstown and Frederick valleys and the central Eastern Shore.

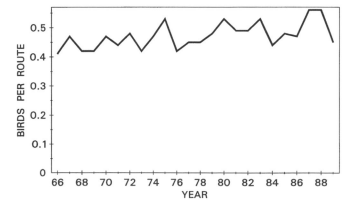

Maryland BBS Trend Graph, 1966–1989

Kentucky Warbler

Oporornis formosus

Alexander Wilson named this bird after the state in which he collected the first specimen known to science (Cantwell 1961). The Kentucky Warbler is a summer resident throughout much of the eastern United States and in all regions of Maryland. The first spring migrants can be found in Maryland in late April, but most arrive in May (Robbins and Bystrak 1977) from their Mexican and Central American wintering grounds (AOU 1983). Kentucky Warblers normally depart Maryland between early August and early September, and almost all have gone by mid-September (Robbins and Bystrak 1977).

For breeding, this warbler selects extensive tracts of tall, moist, deciduous forest with a heavy shrub layer and high tree species diversity (Robbins et al. 1989a). The highest breeding density reported from Maryland is 36 territorial males per 100 acres (40.5 ha) in mixed-hardwood forest in Calvert County (Fales 1973). The Kentucky Warbler is particularly vulnerable to the effects of forest fragmentation (Bushman and Therres 1988). Although the minimum acceptable forest size is 22 to 27 acres (8.9–10.9 ha), the optimum size is 740 acres (300 ha) or more (Robbins et al. 1989a).

Lists of DC birds from the late 1880s identified the Kentucky Warbler as a rare breeder. The first reported nest contained four eggs on 15 June 1879 along Rock Creek in DC (Oology Collection British Museum; MNRF). The earliest accounts for Maryland stated that the Kentucky Warbler was not rare in the Baltimore area (Kirkwood 1895) but was very rare in the mountains of Garrett and Allegany counties (Eifrig 1904). Stewart and Robbins (1958) considered it abundant in the Upper Chesapeake Section, common in the remainder of the Coastal Plain, fairly common in the Piedmont and easternmost Ridge and Valley Section, and local in the extreme northwest corner of Garrett County.

This ground-dwelling songbird seldom forages more than 3 ft (0.9 m) above the forest floor; it feeds on insects found primarily in leaves and debris or under roots and logs (Griscom and Sprunt 1957). It frequently nests under ferns,

in a dense tangle, or at the base of a tree or bush. Both the male and female help in constructing the cup nest of grass, weed stems, rootlets, and occasional threads and animal hairs (Bent 1953). Of 42 Maryland nests, 39 were on the ground and 3 were up to 1 ft (0.3 m) above the ground (MNRF).

The earliest date in 50 Maryland records (MNRF) of nests with eggs is 16 May and the latest is 31 July, with a peak in the first week of June. Clutch sizes in these nests range from 3 to 6 (mean of 4.4). Robbins (1950) found that clutch sizes in Maryland nests declined from a mean of 4.7 prior to 11 June to 3.8 after 20 June. The female incubates for 12 or 13 days (Harrison 1975). Dates for 39 records of nests with young (MNRF) range from 1 June to 11 August, with a peak around 10 June. Brood sizes in these nests range from 2 to 6 (mean of 3.8). The young fledge 8 to 10 days after hatching, but both parents continue to feed them for another 17 or 18 days (Bent 1953). Maryland birds raise two broods (Robbins 1950). The eggs or young of Brown-headed Cowbirds were found in 7 of 83 (8%) Maryland nests (MNRF).

Atlas results show that the Kentucky Warbler breeds in all Maryland counties, but some gaps are evident. Most of these reflect a lack of suitable breeding habitat. Few birds are found in the extensive agricultural areas and marshes of the Coastal Plain, in the urbanized Baltimore-Washington corridor, or in the agricultural and urban areas of the Frederick and Hagerstown valleys. There were scattered reports from most areas in the Ridge and Valley Section, where this species may be limited by the dryness of the woodlands. The present range in Garrett County is notable, as Kentucky Warblers were quite rare there in the late 1950s. BBS data from 1966 through 1989 show a stable population for Maryland and the Eastern Region.

Robert Leberman (pers. obs.) has suggested that white-tailed deer's grazing damage to the understory is the greatest threat to forest-understory birds in western Pennsylvania. Studies are needed to assess this threat and to review its implications for deer management. Extensive forests are crucial to sustaining Kentucky Warbler populations (Whitcomb et al. 1981; Robbins et al. 1989a). Land management plans designed to promote the survival of this species must include the preservation and maintenance of large blocks of mature, moist deciduous forest. The DNR has recognized the need for appropriate habitat conservation (Bushman and Therres 1988).

Lynn M. Davidson

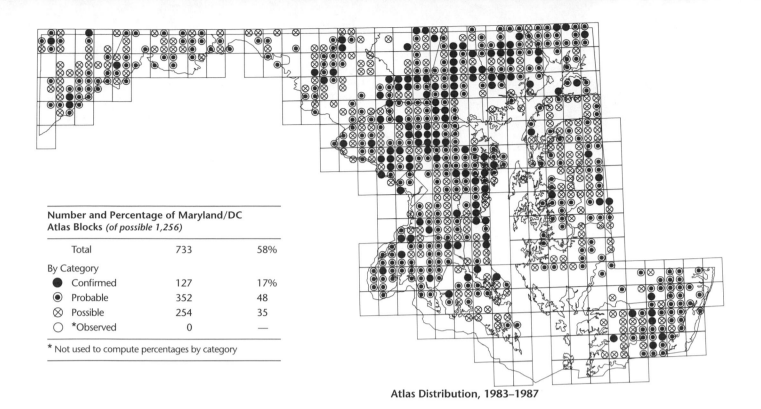

Number and Percentage of Maryland/DC Atlas Blocks *(of possible 1,256)*

Total	733	58%
By Category		
● Confirmed	127	17%
◉ Probable	352	48
⊗ Possible	254	35
○ *Observed	0	—

* Not used to compute percentages by category

Atlas Distribution, 1983–1987

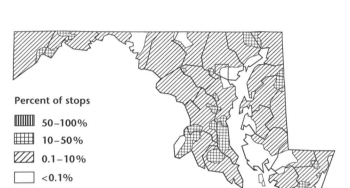

Percent of stops

▥	50–100%
▦	10–50%
▨	0.1–10%
☐	<0.1%

Relative Abundance, 1982–1989

Breeding Distribution, 1958

The Kentucky Warbler is locally common in woodlands on the lower Western and Eastern shores, the Upper Chesapeake Section, and in western Maryland. It is absent from the extensive marsh areas of the southern Eastern Shore, some urban areas, and the most open areas of the Hagerstown and Frederick valleys.

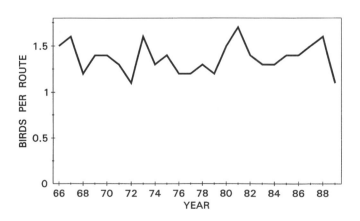

Maryland BBS Trend Graph, 1966–1989

MOB

Mourning Warbler

Oporornis philadelphia

The Mourning Warbler is one of the rarest breeding birds in Maryland, nesting only in the high country of Garrett County. There, in the dense underbrush of the Allegheny Plateau, scattered males sing loudly in late spring, enabling birders to locate this otherwise inconspicuous bird. Except on the Garrett County ridges, the Mourning Warbler is only an uncommon migrant in Maryland (Stewart and Robbins 1958). It is listed as an endangered species in Maryland by the DNR. The last warbler to return in the spring from its Central American wintering grounds (AOU 1983), the Mourning Warbler usually is not seen in Maryland until mid-May, and transients are still moving through the state during the first week of June (Robbins and Bystrak 1977). Most fall migrants pass through Maryland in September.

The Mourning Warbler was first detected as a summering species in Maryland by Brooks (1936) in the 1930s. It was not until 26 June 1949, at Roth Rock fire tower, that Robbins (1950) obtained the first nesting evidence; he watched adults carrying food into a blackberry thicket at an elevation of 3,240 ft (988 m) but was unable to find the nest. Stewart and Robbins (1958) stated that this species occurred regularly in summer on Backbone Mountain at elevations above 3,000 ft (914 m) and was rare and local on the east slope of Backbone Mountain down to 2,640 ft (805 m). They described its habitat preference as brushy, cutover oak-chestnut and northern hardwood forests, especially those containing blackberry thickets. Brooks (1936), however, believed it also bred away from the mountain ridges at Cranesville Bog. The only estimate of breeding density in Maryland came from the Roth Rock fire tower area, where Robbins (1949b) recorded a breeding density of 10 territorial males per 100 acres (40.5 ha) in dense second-growth maple-oak-hickory woods that had been cut about 12 years earlier. Robbins (1950) wrote that the population there declined from 1945 to 1949 as the blackberry thickets were crowded out by young trees. The highest one-day counts, of six birds each, were made on 23 June 1946 and 28 June 1946 on two different areas of Backbone Mountain (Robbins 1950). Hall (1983) described the Mourning Warbler as an abundant breeder along some U.S. Forest Service roads in the West Virginia mountains.

Cox (1960) described the male's flight song as chipping notes followed by a rapid version of the territorial song as he flies upward over his territory. The song stops when the male is about 20 ft (6.1 m) above ground (Bent 1953). This flight song has not yet been reported in Maryland. Cox (1960) described four Mourning Warbler territories in northern Minnesota: two in primarily deciduous woods and two in conifer stands. Average tree diameters at breast height were 6.3 to 8.4 in. (16–21 cm), canopy cover was 48 to 77 percent, and ground cover was 96 to 100 percent. Territory sizes were 1.6 to 2.2 acres (0.6–0.9 ha).

Because no nests have been found in Maryland, nesting data from Ontario (Peck and James 1987) are summarized. The cup nests have loosely built exteriors and typically are lined with black rootlets. Nineteen nests were on or within 6 in. (15 cm) of the ground, the other five within 1 to 3 ft (0.3–0.9 m). Normal clutch size is 3 or 4 eggs, but 4 of 29 nests contained 5 eggs. Ontario egg dates range from 25 May to 20 July, with half of 22 nests in the period 14 to 24 June. Hofslund (1954) reported the incubation period as 12 days, and Cox (1960) found that the young may leave the nest as early as 7 days after hatching, which is before they can fly. Friedmann (1963) considered the Mourning Warbler to be a fairly frequent victim of the Brown-headed Cowbird. Of 30 Ontario nests, 3 (10%) were parasitized (Peck and James 1987), as were 8 of 25 (32%) Quebec nests (Terrill 1961). As is the case with other warblers, the Mourning Warbler's food during the nesting season is composed almost entirely of insects and other arthropods (Cox 1960). Spiders, beetles, and the larvae of butterflies and moths constituted half the diet of eight Ontario birds.

During the Atlas period, fieldworkers found Mourning Warblers in only seven blocks, and in four of these it was only a "possible" breeder. The one "confirmed" (fledged young) and the two "probable" records were all in the southern part of Garrett County. More intensive fieldwork is needed to determine whether this species has disappeared from the highest elevations of the northern and central portions of Backbone Mountain as the Atlas map suggests. The Pennsylvania Atlas data (Brauning 1992) show only two blocks with this warbler in the southern half of that state. This suggests a possible gap in the breeding range between the main population in the St. Lawrence watershed (AOU 1983) and the birds in the central Appalachians.

BBS data from 1966 through 1989 show stable populations in the Eastern Region; data are too few to estimate a trend for Maryland. To maintain breeding Mourning Warblers in Maryland, it may be necessary to manage portions of the higher ridges of Garrett County to maintain the dense undergrowth that develops after timbering or fire. Transmission line corridors could potentially provide this habitat, but, to date, Mourning Warblers have not been found in these corridors in Maryland during the breeding season.

William L. Murphy and Chandler S. Robbins

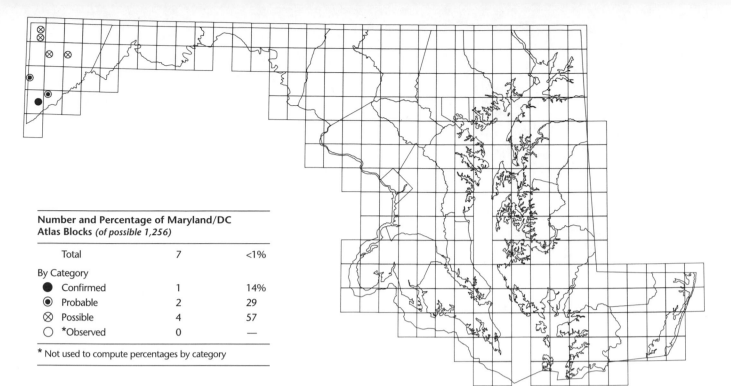

Number and Percentage of Maryland/DC Atlas Blocks *(of possible 1,256)*

	Total	7	<1%
By Category			
● Confirmed		1	14%
◉ Probable		2	29
⊗ Possible		4	57
○ *Observed		0	—

* Not used to compute percentages by category

Atlas Distribution, 1983–1987

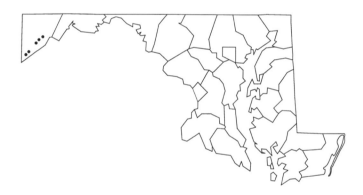

Breeding Distribution, 1958

Common Yellowthroat

Geothlypis trichas

Formerly known as the Maryland Yellow-throat, this bright little warbler with its black mask and contrasting yellow face and underparts is an abundant breeding bird throughout Maryland. Hampe and Kolb (1947) suggested it as the state bird because of its wide distribution and because it was the only bird with Maryland in its name. Birds arrive in Maryland from their wintering grounds in the Gulf Coast states, West Indies, Mexico, and Central America (AOU 1983) in mid-April (Stewart and Robbins 1958). Females usually arrive about 10 days after the males (Hofslund 1959). Most birds depart by late October (Stewart and Robbins 1958). A few winter on the Coastal Plain, especially in milder winters.

The Common Yellowthroat is found at all elevations in Maryland. Eifrig (1904) called it perhaps the most common warbler in western Maryland, even at high elevations. Kirkwood (1895) considered it Maryland's most abundant breeding warbler, as did Cooke (1929). Stewart and Robbins (1958) gave its breeding status as abundant in the Eastern Shore, Western Shore, and Upper Chesapeake sections; common in the Allegheny Mountain Section; and fairly common in the Piedmont and Ridge and Valley sections.

The Common Yellowthroat nests in wet meadows, salt and freshwater marshes, shrubby thickets, swamps, hedgerows, overgrown fields, and on brushy hillsides, with a preference for wet areas (Gross 1953b). The highest breeding densities recorded in Maryland are 111 territorial males per 100 acres (40.5 ha) in hedgerows bordering agricultural fields in 1948, and 108 territorial males per 100 acres in a shrub swamp in 1945, both at PWRC (Stewart and Robbins 1958). Territory size is variable, depending on the nature of the vegetation and the density of nesting birds. In one study it ranged from 0.5 to 7.1 acres (0.2–2.9 ha) (Hofslund 1959).

The female constructs the nest in two to five days (Stewart 1953) in dense vegetation on or near the ground (Gross 1953b). The male may accompany her on trips to gather nesting material. Nest heights of 46 Maryland nests (MNRF) range from 0 to 4 ft (0–1.2 m), with a mean of 0.6

ft (0.2 m). Average nest height increases as the summer progresses, probably because the surrounding vegetation is taller (Hofslund 1959). Coarse grasses, reed shreds, leaves, and moss comprise the exterior of the bulky nest; the outside dimensions average 3.2 in. (8.1 cm) in diameter and about 3.5 in. in height (8.9 cm) (Gross 1953b). It is lined with fine grasses, bark fibers, and hair.

Extreme Maryland egg dates are 4 May and 4 August (MNRF), with a peak in mid-June. Clutch sizes in 48 Maryland nests range from 1 to 5 (mean of 3.7). The female incubates for 12 days (Stewart 1953). Brood sizes in 29 Maryland nests range from 1 to 4, with a mean of 2.8 (MNRF). Nests contained young as early as 17 May and as late as 22 August, with a peak in mid-June.

Young leave the nest in 8 or 9 days, even though they are still unable to fly (Stewart 1953). They hop into nearby brush, where they are fed by the parents for about three days until they can fly. The young birds remain in a family group for about 20 days after fledging, although the adult female may leave the group earlier than that to start a second nest. When a second nesting occurs, a new nest is built and the boundaries of the territory may change slightly. Common Yellowthroats are occasionally polygynous (Powell and Jones 1978). Moths, various larvae, and spiders comprised 75 percent of 1,226 insects that Shaver (1918) classified as they were fed to nestling Common Yellowthroats in Iowa. Other insects delivered, in sequence of declining quantity, were mayflies, flies, caterpillars, and damselflies.

Atlas workers found Common Yellowthroats in nearly every Maryland block (96%). They remain Maryland's most abundant nesting warbler, primarily because they use a wide variety of habitats. This is the only warbler in Maryland that nests on treeless Chesapeake Bay islands and in extensive tidal marshes. It was missing only from the most urbanized blocks and from a very few entirely wooded blocks in western Maryland. That fewer than 1 percent of "confirmed" records were of nests with eggs or young can be attributed, in part, to the secretive nature of the female. She rarely flies directly to or from the nest, preferring to skulk some distance away, and she does not perform distraction displays when intruders are near (Hofslund 1959).

Although BBS data from 1966 through 1989 show stable populations in the Eastern Region, Maryland data indicate a highly significant average annual decline of 3.2 percent. The greatest threat to the Common Yellowthroat appears to be Brown-headed Cowbird parasitism. Friedmann (1963) considered them common victims; a Michigan study found that 10 of 22 nests (45%) contained Brown-headed Cowbird eggs (Stewart 1953). In Ontario, Peck and James (1987) reported that 32 of 168 Ontario nests (19%) were parasitized, as were 5 of 42 nests (12%) in Maryland (MNRF). The Common Yellowthroat faces a bright future in Maryland's extensive wetland areas, but populations will decline in the urban and suburban areas and in farmlands as natural wetlands diminish.

Emily D. Joyce

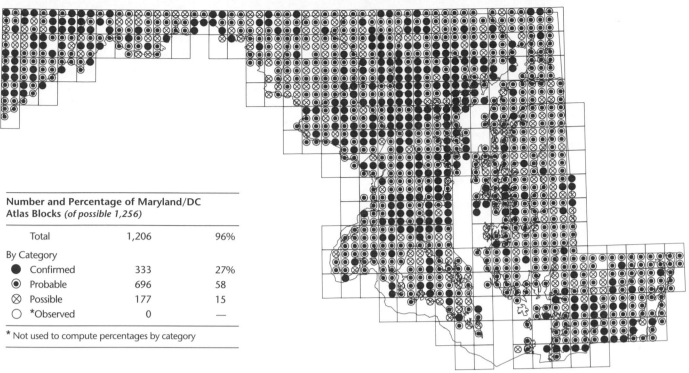

Number and Percentage of Maryland/DC Atlas Blocks *(of possible 1,256)*		
Total	1,206	96%
By Category		
● Confirmed	333	27%
◉ Probable	696	58
⊗ Possible	177	15
○ *Observed	0	—

* Not used to compute percentages by category

Atlas Distribution, 1983–1987

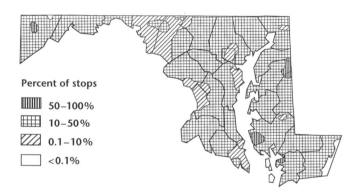

Percent of stops

▥	50–100%
▦	10–50%
▨	0.1–10%
☐	<0.1%

Relative Abundance, 1982–1989

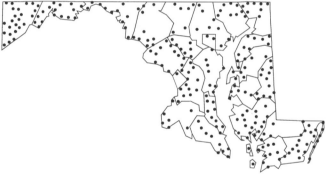

Breeding Distribution, 1958

The Common Yellowthroat is locally abundant at the edge of tidal marshes on the Eastern Shore. Low numbers were recorded in the agricultural areas of the Hagerstown and Frederick valleys; around the urban areas of Baltimore, Washington, and Annapolis; and in southern St. Mary's County on the Western Shore.

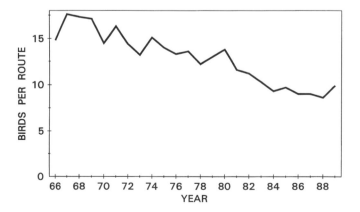

Maryland BBS Trend Graph, 1966–1989

Hooded Warbler

Wilsonia citrina

The Hooded Warbler was once known as the Mitered Warbler because of the male's black head and yellow face. Its song has been rendered as *come to the woods or you won't see me* (Chapman 1907a). Not any woods will do, for the Hooded Warbler requires extensive woodland with mature deciduous trees and dense shrub layers, often on the floodplain of a large stream (Robbins et al. 1989a). Breeding birds return from their wintering grounds in Mexico and Central America (AOU 1983) in late April (Robbins and Bystrak 1977). They concentrate in four distinct areas: the Pocomoke River drainage on the lower Eastern Shore; the wooded ravines of the stream-dissected Piedmont Section and inner Coastal Plain of the Western Shore; the Catoctin Mountains; and the Allegheny Mountain and western Ridge and Valley sections (Stewart and Robbins 1958). Most birds depart by mid-September (Robbins and Bystrak 1977).

Eifrig (1904) described the Hooded Warbler as rather common in western Maryland; Cooke (1929) thought it common in the DC vicinity, while noting that Coues and Prentiss (1883) had earlier known it only as a straggler. Kirkwood's (1895) account suggests the species was a rare breeding bird in the Baltimore-Washington area, but Hampe and Kolb (1947) clarified its status by noting that it was fairly common in southern Maryland while decreasing northward. Stewart and Robbins (1958) reported that it was common in the Western Shore and Ridge and Valley sections, locally common in the Eastern Shore Section, fairly common in the Piedmont Section, locally common in the Allegheny Mountain Section, and rare in the Upper Chesapeake Section.

The prime breeding habitats of the Hooded Warbler have a dense brushy understory with sweetbay, winterberry, southern arrowwood, sweet pepperbush, American holly, and swamp azalea (Stewart and Robbins 1958). It may be locally abundant. In Prince George's County, breeding population densities have reached 63 territorial males per 100 acres (40.5 ha) in a lowland seepage swamp forest in 1946, and 48 territorial males per 100 acres in a river terrace forest in 1944 (Stewart and Robbins 1958). Robbins (1979) estimated the minimum acreage needed to sustain a breeding population at 80 acres (30 ha).

The nest is a compact cup of grasses on a base of dead leaves in a small shrub or tangle (Bent 1953). Typically low, the average height of 21 Maryland nests is 3 ft (0.9 m), with a range of 1 to 10 ft (0.3–3.0 m) (MNRF). Five were in greenbrier, three in sweet pepperbush, and most others were in small deciduous trees. The extreme Maryland egg dates are 21 May and 30 July (MNRF). Hooded Warblers are becoming frequent victims of Brown-headed Cowbird parasitism. Of 19 Maryland nests found from 1932 through 1968, 11 percent were parasitized; however, 22 of 40 (55%) nests found from 1973 through 1991 contained Brown-headed Cowbird eggs. Clutch sizes in 10 Maryland nests (MNRF) without Brown-headed Cowbird eggs range from 2 to 5 (mean of 3.7). Incubation, by the female, lasts about 12 days (Bent 1953). Nests with young have been found in Maryland from 31 May to 11 July (MNRF). Brood sizes in six nests range from 1 to 4. Fledged young have been reported as early as 4 June and as late as 27 August (Stewart and Robbins 1958). Almost all the MNRF records are from PWRC. More information is needed from the lower Eastern Shore, where the nesting season probably begins earlier, and the Allegheny Mountain Section, where the season may be later. Most of the food is obtained on or near the ground in the forest undergrowth and is frequently caught on the wing (Bent 1953). Flies, ants, wasps, beetles, moths and their larvae, and grasshoppers comprise most of the diet.

Atlas results show a distribution similar to that reported by Stewart and Robbins (1958). The range in the Piedmont and eastern Ridge and Valley sections seems somewhat reduced; however, the distribution in Garrett County is probably more widespread than 30 years ago. The behavior of the Hooded Warbler is reflected in the Atlas data. Nearly half (49%) of the records were of birds on territory. Finding the general area of a Hooded Warbler's territory is reasonably easy because of its distinctive and relatively loud song. The male usually sings from an open perch and occasionally postures with his tail fully spread to reveal the extensive white in the outer feathers. The inconspicuous nest is tucked away in a leafy shrub in the dense undergrowth (Bent 1953), which explains the low (2%) number of records of occupied nests.

BBS data from 1966 through 1989 show a highly significant average annual increase of 3.2 percent in the Eastern Region and a stable population in Maryland. Conservation of extensive forested stream valleys should result in the continued existence of the Hooded Warbler as part of Maryland's avifauna.

James L. Stasz

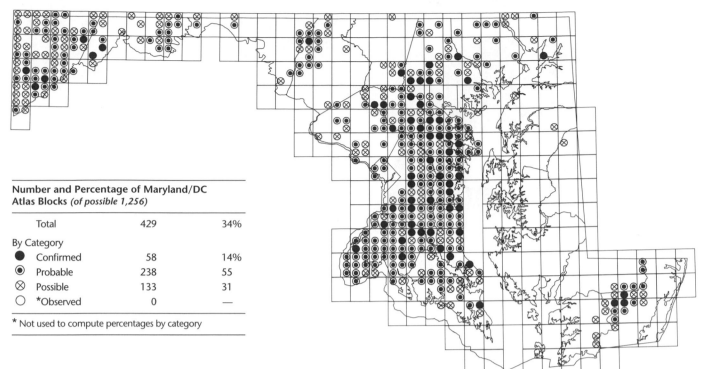

Atlas Distribution, 1983–1987

Number and Percentage of Maryland/DC Atlas Blocks *(of possible 1,256)*

Total	429	34%
By Category		
● Confirmed	58	14%
◉ Probable	238	55
⊗ Possible	133	31
○ *Observed	0	—

* Not used to compute percentages by category

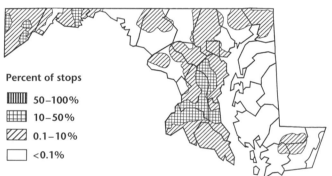

Percent of stops

⊞	50–100%
⊞	10–50%
⊘	0.1–10%
☐	<0.1%

Relative Abundance, 1982–1989

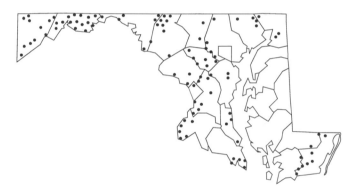

Breeding Distribution, 1958

The Hooded Warbler is most common in extensively wooded areas in southern Maryland, especially along the Patuxent River, and in scattered locations in Garrett County and in Green Ridge State Forest. It is absent from most of the Eastern Shore and agricultural habitats in the Piedmont and Ridge and Valley.

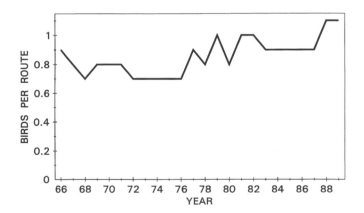

Maryland BBS Trend Graph, 1966–1989

GM

Canada Warbler

Wilsonia canadensis

A neat black necklace contrasting with bright yellow underparts is the trademark of this flycatching warbler of the north woods. In Maryland, extensive forest at moderate to high elevations seems to meet this bird's main nesting requirement. It is one of the most common boreal warblers breeding in Maryland; 83 were recorded at Cranesville Bog, Garrett County, on 20 June 1946 (Robbins 1950). Canada Warblers arrive from their South American wintering areas (AOU 1983) in early May and leave by the end of September (Stewart and Robbins 1958).

Kirkwood (1895) was the first to document breeding Canada Warblers in Maryland. The nest with young he discovered on Dan's Mountain, Allegany County, on 10 June 1895 is one of only two confirmed Maryland nest records outside Garrett County. Robbins (1950) and Stewart and Robbins (1958) gave Maryland elevation limits as 2,100 ft (640 m) near Grantsville and 3,240 ft (988 m) on Backbone Mountain at Roth Rock fire tower. On 2 and 3 July 1966, however, Bridge (1966) found four Canada Warblers as low as 1,530 ft (466 m) along Big Run, Garrett County.

Canada Warblers frequent a wide variety of habitats: young boreal hardwoods, mixed deciduous and coniferous forests, and almost pure coniferous forest. They nest commonly in Garrett County bogs and also on dry hillsides, as long as there is a heavy understory. The most important habitat factors associated with breeding Canada Warblers in Garrett County are high foliage density at 1 to 3.3 ft (0.3–1 m) from the ground, high soil moisture, large basal area of trees, and extensive woodland (Robbins et al. 1989a).

In Maryland, the two habitats with the highest breeding densities of Canada Warblers per 100 acres (40.5 ha) were 45 territorial males in dense second-growth oak-maple forest along the ridge of Negro Mountain (Robbins 1949b) and 44 territorial males in an old-growth spruce–eastern hemlock bog forest in Wolf Swamp (Stewart and Robbins 1951a). Al-

though Robbins (1950) found them in old-growth eastern hemlock forest, he noted they occurred only along the edge or where a fallen tree had allowed enough light penetration to permit development of a dense understory. Canada Warblers usually were associated with big laurel thickets.

Nests are placed on or near the ground, often in a hollow in a stream bank (Saunders 1938) or in a clump of grass at the base of a stump, beside a fallen log, or in a brush pile (Peck and James 1987). An Ontario nest 3 ft (0.9 m) above ground seems to be the highest recorded (Peck and James 1987). The earliest Maryland egg date is 28 May 1935 in Allegany County (MNRF). The only other Maryland egg dates are 2 June 1919, when a nest with 5 fresh eggs was found 5 in. (12.7 cm) up at the base of an upturned root of a fallen tree in eastern hemlock woods on Big Backbone Mountain near Deer Park, Garrett County, and 18 June 1959, when a nest with 2 eggs was found on the ground in a patch of club moss at Pleasant Valley near Bittinger, Garrett County. Egg dates elsewhere range from 26 May in Ontario (Peck and James 1987) to 4 July in New York (Saunders 1938). The normal clutch consists of 3 to 5 eggs, typically 4 (Bent 1953). Apparently only one brood is attempted even though males continue singing well into July (C. Robbins, pers. obs.).

Preble (1900) found adults feeding young just out of the nest on 20 June 1899 at Finzel, Garrett County. On 24 June 1967, in deciduous woods 4 mi (6.4 km) north of Oakland, Garrett County, a female was observed feeding a young bird that was unable to fly (MNRF). The only other record of fledged young involved a Brown-headed Cowbird. On 19 June 1969, at Cranesville bog, Garrett County, a male Canada Warbler was observed taking food to a fledged Brown-headed Cowbird that was barely able to fly. Peck and James (1987) reported that 5 of 25 Ontario nests (20%) were parasitized. The Canada Warbler catches much of its food on the wing, but it also feeds in the foliage and on the ground. Its chief prey items are flies, moths, beetles, locusts, and spiders (Bent 1953).

Atlas data show a distribution similar to that in Robbins (1950). Atlas coverage in the center of Garrett County was probably better; but, conversely, the absence of Atlas records in blocks along the Potomac River, in the vicinity of Oakland, and at the northeast corner of the county may have been the result of insufficient Atlas coverage. Food for young and fledged young accounted for all "confirmed" Atlas records.

BBS data from 1966 through 1989 show stable populations in the Eastern Region; there are too few data to estimate a Maryland trend. The Nature Conservancy's recent purchase of several of Maryland's best bogs ensures the protection of some prime Canada Warbler habitat. If Garrett County forests come under more intensive management for timber production, however, a reduction in big laurel and other dense shrubs could cause a sharp decline in Canada Warbler populations.

Chandler S. Robbins

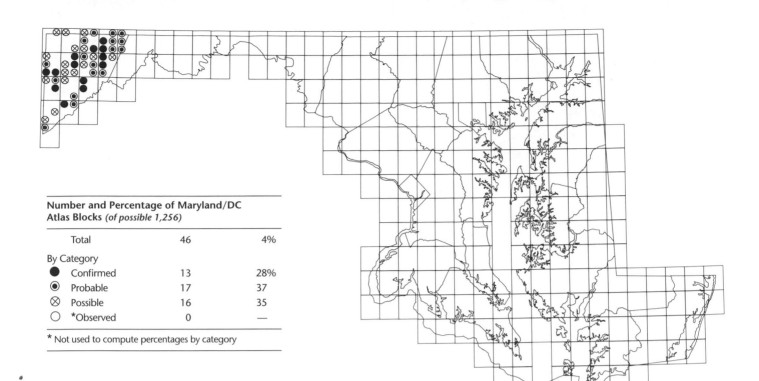

Number and Percentage of Maryland/DC Atlas Blocks *(of possible 1,256)*

Total	46	4%
By Category		
● Confirmed	13	28%
◉ Probable	17	37
⊗ Possible	16	35
○ *Observed	0	—

* Not used to compute percentages by category

Atlas Distribution, 1983–1987

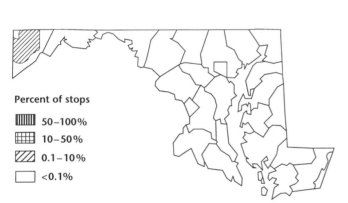

Percent of stops

⬚ (vertical lines)	50–100%
⬚ (grid)	10–50%
⬚ (diagonal)	0.1–10%
⬚ (blank)	<0.1%

Relative Abundance, 1982–1989

Breeding Distribution, 1958

In Maryland the Canada Warbler nests only in the Allegheny Mountain Section in Garrett County. It was detected on mini-routes only west of Backbone and Big Savage mountains; this verifies the Atlas distribution.

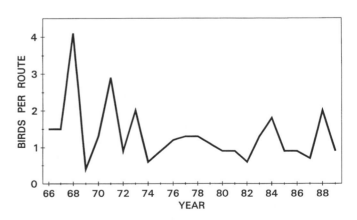

Maryland BBS Trend Graph, 1966–1989

Yellow-breasted Chat

Icteria virens

The Yellow-breasted Chat is by far the largest North American wood warbler and is so different from other warblers that some authorities have questioned its relationship to the warbler subfamily (AOU 1983). It is colorful and highly vocal, but secretive and elusive as well, and is heard far more often than seen. Its vocal repertoire is large; some writers believe it mimics the songs or calls of other birds (Bent 1953), although others question that conclusion (Ritchison 1988). Spring migrants begin arriving in Maryland from their Mexican and Central American wintering grounds (AOU 1983) in late April; the last fall migrants linger into October (Robbins and Bystrak 1977).

The Yellow-breasted Chat has been a common summer resident throughout Maryland for at least 130 years (Coues and Prentiss 1862, 1883; Kirkwood 1895; Eifrig 1904; Cooke 1929). Stewart and Robbins (1958) called it common or fairly common in all sections except the Allegheny Mountain Section, where it was uncommon. Many observers reported a decline in Yellow-breasted Chat populations during the late 1980s. BBS data from 1966 through 1989 show stable continental populations but an indication of a decline in the Eastern Region. Maryland data show a significant average annual decline of 1.9 percent, which stabilized from 1980 through 1989 with only an indication of a decline during that time. Hall (1983) noted a drastic decline throughout much of northern West Virginia beginning in the late 1970s.

More common at lower elevations and in less urbanized areas, the Yellow-breasted Chat prefers dense thickets with thorny shrubs, woodland edges, low wet areas near streams or ponds, swamps, abandoned pastures with thick second growth, and hedgerows (Petrides 1938; Dennis 1958). High breeding densities recorded in Maryland are 36 territorial males per 100 acres (40.5 ha) in a shrubby field bordering a stream in Baltimore County (Cooley 1947) and 28 per 100 acres in damp deciduous scrub with standing dead trees in Prince George's County (Oresman et al. 1948).

Yellow-breasted Chats occasionally nest in loose groups or colonies, but each male maintains a discrete territory (Dennis 1958). The territorial display of the male is spectacular (Petrides 1938). Gradually ascending from the depths of a thicket to a high perch, he utters a suite of unbirdlike calls: wolf whistles and notes that sound like cats, treefrogs, and crows. Continuing the cacophony, he springs into the air, fluttering his wings rapidly and dangling his feet as he descends to the perch again. The nest is usually constructed in a dense thicket of blackberries, small trees, and bushes (Dennis 1958). In Maryland, greenbrier and multiflora rose are popular nest sites (MNRF). The nest is rarely more than 5 ft (1.5 m) above the ground (Dennis 1958). Heights of 63 Maryland nests (MNRF) range from 1.5 to 7 ft (0.5–2.1 m), with a mean of 3.2 ft (1.0 m).

The breeding season in Maryland extends from mid-May through late July. Nests with eggs have been found from 22 May to 16 July, with a peak in early June (MNRF). Clutch sizes in 97 Maryland nests range from 2 to 5 eggs, with a mean of 3.5 (MNRF). The female incubates the eggs for 11 days (Petrides 1938). Young have been found in Maryland nests from 1 June to 26 July, with a peak in late June (MNRF). Brood sizes in 28 Maryland nests range from 1 to 4 (mean of 3.1). The young fledge nine days after hatching (Forbush 1929). A single brood is normal. The Yellow-breasted Chat diet is composed largely of insects, principally ants, wasps, beetles, caterpillars, and grasshoppers, but it also contains many fleshy fruits in summer and autumn (Martin et al. 1951).

This species is one of the most common victims of the Brown-headed Cowbird, but it destroys their eggs, along with its own at times (Friedmann 1963). Only 5 of 104 Maryland nests (4.8%) were parasitized (MNRF), but in Ontario (Peck and James 1987), 4 of 16 nests (25.0%) were affected.

Yellow-breasted Chats were found throughout Maryland during the Atlas period, although they were less common in the mountains of Garrett County and were absent from the major urban areas. Many fieldworkers found them among the most difficult birds to confirm; only two nests with eggs and five nests with young were reported.

The recent population decline of Yellow-breasted Chats, shown by the BBS, is cause for concern. The loss of scrub land to agriculture and housing and the maturing of second growth into woodland may be contributing factors. The population should be monitored to determine whether the downward trend is continuing. At the same time, studies aimed at determining the causes are needed. For the present, we can actively try to protect the thickets Yellow-breasted Chats prefer and to encourage management for shrub habitats in transmission line corridors.

James W. Cheevers

Number and Percentage of Maryland/DC Atlas Blocks *(of possible 1,256)*

Total	990	79%

By Category

●	Confirmed	119	12%
◉	Probable	569	57
⊗	Possible	302	31
○	*Observed	0	—

*Not used to compute percentages by category

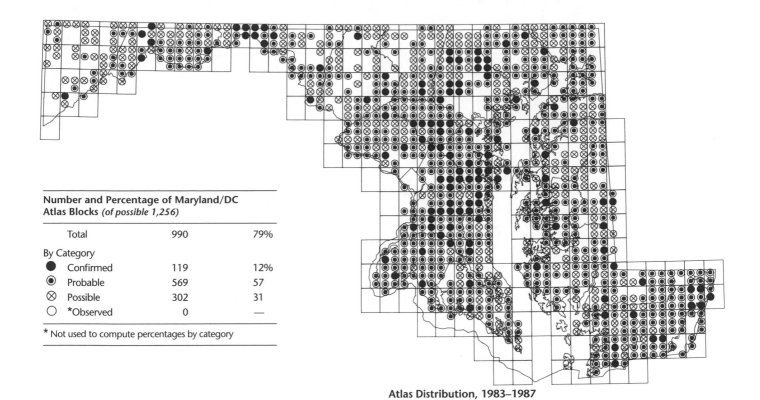

Atlas Distribution, 1983–1987

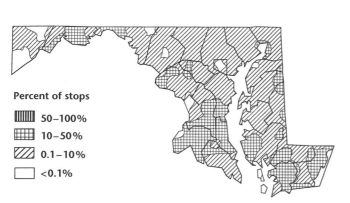

Percent of stops

▥	50–100%
▦	10–50%
▨	0.1–10%
☐	<0.1%

Relative Abundance, 1982–1989

Breeding Distribution, 1958

The Yellow-breasted Chat is most common on the southern Coastal Plain and in the western Ridge and Valley Section in mixed agricultural-woodlot habitats. It declines to the west and is absent from most forested highlands of Garrett County and from urban areas.

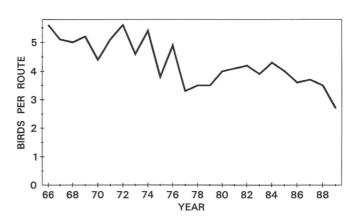

Maryland BBS Trend Graph, 1966–1989

Summer Tanager

Piranga rubra

The Summer Tanager, unlike the striking and widespread Scarlet Tanager, breeds primarily on Maryland's Coastal Plain and is rare in other parts of the state. Spring migrants return from their wintering grounds in Mexico and Central and South America (AOU 1983) in early May; most birds leave by the end of September (Stewart and Robbins 1958).

Over the past century, the distribution of the Summer Tanager has fluctuated in Maryland, which is at the northern edge of its breeding range (AOU 1983). Richmond (1888) found the first DC nest, with three eggs, on 4 July 1885. Kirkwood (1895) wrote that four or five pairs nested near his home in Baltimore County in 1895. Hampe and Kolb (1947) described the Summer Tanager as a very rare breeding bird anywhere in the state except near tidewater. Fletcher et al. (1956) called it a very rare breeder in Caroline County, with only two known records. Stewart and Robbins (1958) wrote that it was fairly common only in southern Worcester County and near tidewater in the Western Shore Section, and rare elsewhere, although it had formerly been more numerous.

The Summer Tanager's preferred habitats in Maryland are dry open pine, oak, and pine-oak woods (Stewart and Robbins 1958). Maryland's highest recorded breeding density, 10 territorial males per 100 acres (40.5 ha), was recorded in an immature loblolly–shortleaf pine stand in Worcester County (Springer and Stewart 1948c). The female builds the flimsy-appearing nest from weed stems, leaves, grasses, and pieces of bark, lining it with fine grasses. She carefully conceals it, usually well out on a lower horizontal branch of either a pine or a deciduous tree (Terres 1980). Heights of 29 Maryland nests (MNRF) range from 7 to 60 ft (2.1–18 m), with a mean of 15 ft (4.6 m).

The earliest egg date for Maryland is 2 May (Stewart and Robbins 1958) and the latest is 13 July (MNRF). In 17 Maryland nests (MNRF) clutch sizes range from 2 to 4 (mean of

3.1). Incubation, by the female, lasts about 12 days (Potter et al. 1980). The male feeds the incubating female and helps tend the young. Only one brood is attempted (Forbush 1927). Nests with young have been found in Maryland from 5 June to 27 July (MNRF). In six Maryland records, brood sizes range from 1 to 3. The Summer Tanager's diet consists largely of flying insects, especially bees and wasps, with some fruits and berries (Bent 1958).

The Summer Tanager was believed to be an infrequent victim of Brown-headed Cowbird parasitism (Friedmann et al. 1977), but five of the 19 records known at that time were from Maryland. Seven (16%) of 45 Maryland nests were parasitized (MNRF), indicating that this tanager is really a frequent victim.

Atlas results show that this species is confined almost entirely to the Eastern and Western Shore sections, with scattered reports from the Upper Chesapeake Section. There were fewer than 10 records for the Piedmont, and it was very rare west of there. In Allegany County there were two reports from the extensive pine forests of Green Ridge State Forest, and it may be a rare breeder there. The highest densities appear to be in Worcester and Wicomico counties, where Summer Tanagers were found in a large majority of the mainland blocks. This species avoids the coastal and Chesapeake Bay marshes; on the Eastern Shore they are confined largely to the interior of the Delmarva Peninsula. Although found in many fewer Western Shore blocks, they were no less common where they were found. Miniroute data show no major difference in the number of birds per route between the Eastern and Western Shore sections. The Atlas distribution in Delaware parallels that of Maryland, as does that of Virginia, although there were numerous records in the Piedmont of southern Virginia. In Pennsylvania, it was very rare except in the southwestern corner of the state (Brauning 1992).

BBS data from 1966 through 1989 show stable populations of Summer Tanagers in the Eastern Region and Maryland. However, the atlas of Montgomery and Howard counties from 1971 through 1975 recorded Summer Tanagers in seven blocks (Klimkiewicz and Solem 1978), compared with a single "observed" report in the present Atlas. Stewart and Robbins (1958) wrote that this species was formerly more common on the Piedmont. Thus, although it seems to be increasing on the Coastal Plain, it has declined in the Piedmont since the beginning of the twentieth century. The reasons for the historical decline in the Piedmont are unclear.

The Summer Tanager population appears to be stable now, but may be increasing slightly in some sections. Pine-oak forests are common within its Maryland range, so there is no immediate concern for its future habitat needs.

George B. Wilmot

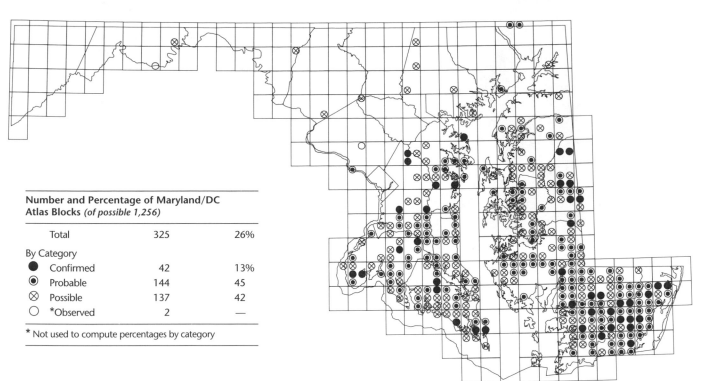

Number and Percentage of Maryland/DC Atlas Blocks (of possible 1,256)

Total	325	26%
By Category		
● Confirmed	42	13%
◉ Probable	144	45
⊗ Possible	137	42
○ *Observed	2	—

* Not used to compute percentages by category

Atlas Distribution, 1983–1987

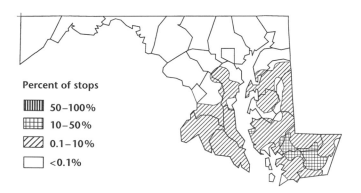

Percent of stops

▥ 50–100%
▦ 10–50%
▨ 0.1–10%
☐ <0.1%

Relative Abundance, 1982–1989

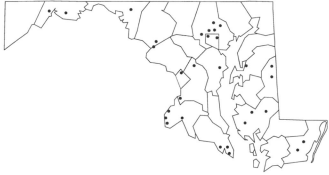

Breeding Distribution, 1958

The Summer Tanager is most common in the extensive mixed pine-oak woodlands on the lower Eastern Shore, especially around the Pocomoke River and its tributaries. It declines rapidly to the north and west.

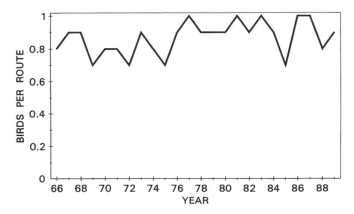

Maryland BBS Trend Graph, 1966–1989

Scarlet Tanager

Piranga olivacea

The vivid red and black male Scarlet Tanager is among the most colorful and striking birds in Maryland. It returns from its South American wintering grounds (AOU 1983) in late April and leaves by early October (Stewart and Robbins 1958).

Coues and Prentiss (1883) called it chiefly a migrant near DC, although they noted that a few bred in the area. Kirkwood (1895) reported that it bred widely but was local and not very common. Eifrig (1904) called it a common summer resident in western Maryland, especially on the forested mountain tops. Hampe and Kolb (1947) wrote that it was a common summer resident in the Baltimore-Washington area and west, but the only records on the Eastern Shore were of migrants. Stewart and Robbins (1958) described its breeding status as common in the Ridge and Valley, Piedmont, and Western Shore sections and fairly common in all other sections.

Robbins (1980) estimated the minimum forest area needed to sustain a viable Scarlet Tanager population at 25 acres (10 ha). Within such a forest the nesting territory defended may be 2 to 6 acres (0.8–2.4 ha) or greater. This species prefers deciduous trees of considerable height, particularly oaks; it nests less frequently in mixed deciduous and coniferous forests. Prescott (1965) found that 68 percent of a sample of New Jersey nests were in trees with diameters at breast height of at least 9 in. (23 cm). The highest breeding density reported for Maryland is 29 territorial males per 100 acres (40.5 ha) in mixed-hardwood forest in Calvert County (Fales 1974).

The female constructs a shallow, saucer-shaped nest (Tyler 1958b), placing it well out on a horizontal branch of a large tree—preferably an oak, though nests have been observed in maple, hemlock, elm, tulip tree, ash, American beech, apple, and others. Heights of 38 Maryland nests (MNRF) range from 8 to 70 ft (2.4–21 m), with a mean of 25.7 ft (7.8 m). The nest is a loose construction of twigs, rootlets, grass, plant stems, bark, and occasionally string; it is lined with fine grass and sometimes pine needles (Tyler 1958b). The female concentrates on nest building early in the morning and sings a short, fast song while building. Construction takes from three to seven days. The male often accompanies her when she is gathering materials (Tyler 1958b).

Maryland egg dates range from 12 May to 1 August (Stewart and Robbins 1958), with a peak in early June (MNRF). In 15 Maryland nests, clutch sizes range from 2 to 4 (mean of 3.1). The female incubates the eggs for 12 to 15 days, during which time the male occasionally brings food (Tyler 1958b). Both parents feed the young, which fledge in 9 to 11 days. Nests with young have been reported in Maryland from 4 June to 8 August, with a peak in late June (MNRF). Brood sizes in 10 Maryland nests range from 2 to 5, with a mean of 3.1. The young remain within the territory for about two weeks, being fed by both parents before dispersing (Tyler 1958b). Scarlet Tanagers usually produce only one brood per season.

Friedmann (1963) considered the Scarlet Tanager an uncommon victim of the Brown-headed Cowbird. Only 2 of 21 Maryland nests (9.5%) were parasitized by the Brown-headed Cowbird, but 7 of 36 Ontario nests (19.4%) were parasitized (Peck and James 1987). The worst enemy during nesting is high, gusty wind associated with spring thunderstorms, which can blow down the fragile nests (Tyler 1958b). Wasps, bees, ants, beetles, bugs, caterpillars, and moths are the primary foods (Martin et al. 1951).

Atlas data show that the Scarlet Tanager is distributed throughout Maryland and DC, except in urban areas, open farmland in the Piedmont, and open farmland and marshes on the Eastern Shore. Because of its distinctive singing, more than half the records (59%) were "probable" for birds holding territory. Singing decreases as nesting progresses, so despite the male's bright color, locating it later in the season is difficult. Because of these factors, only 16 percent of the records for this species were "confirmed"; 80 percent of the "confirmed" records were either of adults carrying food (43%) or of noisy fledglings (37%). Because nest building is done by the less colorful female and the nest's location high in the canopy makes it difficult to observe contents, few "confirmed" records were based on nest observations.

BBS data from 1966 through 1989 show stable populations in the Eastern Region. Maryland data from 1966 through 1989 indicate a significant average annual decline of 1.9 percent; data from 1980 through 1989 show a significant decline of 3.7 percent. The Scarlet Tanager is dependent on extensive woodlands for feeding and for nesting (Robbins et al. 1989a); the loss or fragmentation of forest is the greatest threat to this species. Outbreaks of gypsy moths throughout the northeastern United States, which extended into Maryland in the 1980s, initially were a boon in food resources for the Scarlet Tanager (Holmes and Sherry 1986). It remains to be seen what effect man's combating this pest with aerial spraying will have on the Scarlet Tanager.

James W. Cheevers

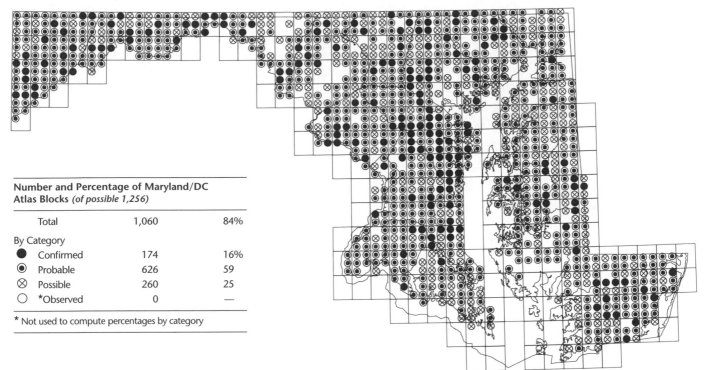

Number and Percentage of Maryland/DC Atlas Blocks *(of possible 1,256)*

Total	1,060	84%
By Category		
● Confirmed	174	16%
◉ Probable	626	59
⊗ Possible	260	25
○ *Observed	0	—

* Not used to compute percentages by category

Atlas Distribution, 1983–1987

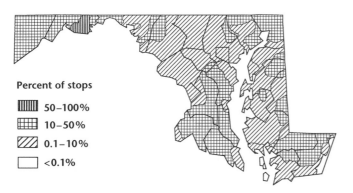

Percent of stops

⊞	50–100%
▦	10–50%
▨	0.1–10%
▢	<0.1%

Relative Abundance, 1982–1989

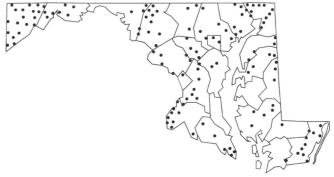

Breeding Distribution, 1958

The Scarlet Tanager is most abundant in the woodlands of eastern Allegany County. It is common in the rest of western Maryland, the Upper Chesapeake Section, southern Maryland, and the lower Eastern Shore. The lowest numbers are in the urban and agricultural areas of central Maryland and the Eastern Shore.

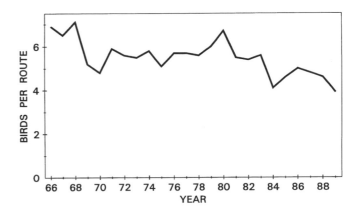

Maryland BBS Trend Graph, 1966–1989

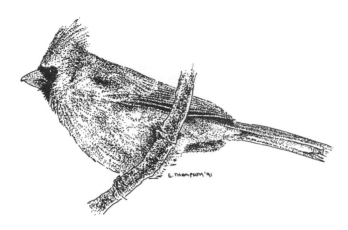

Northern Cardinal

Cardinalis cardinalis

The Northern Cardinal, or "redbird," is probably the most striking and visible backyard bird in Maryland. In Maryland, it is the only red bird with a prominent crest. The male's bright red color and the vocal ability of both sexes make this bird a favorite, even among nonbirdwatchers. Its popularity led seven states—Illinois, Indiana, Kentucky, North Carolina, Ohio, Virginia, and West Virginia—to choose the Northern Cardinal as their state bird. Years ago, when it was legal, collectors eagerly sought it as a cage bird, and one house pet lived 28.5 years (Terres 1980). Maximum longevity recorded in the wild is 15 years, 9 months, according to banding records (Klimkiewicz and Futcher 1987). This nonmigratory species spends its entire life within a few square miles (Laskey 1944).

Once considered southern, the Northern Cardinal has steadily extended its range northward during this century. Coues and Prentiss (1862) considered it an abundant permanent resident in DC; but Preble (1900) found only one Northern Cardinal in Garrett County on a pioneering trip to western Maryland in the summer of 1899. Eifrig (1904) found it very abundant in Cumberland, Allegany County, and noted a few in higher country, presumably referring to the ridgetops and to Garrett County. Brooks (1936) classed it as fairly common in summer in Garrett County. Stewart and Robbins (1958) considered it a common bird everywhere in Maryland except in the Allegheny Mountain Section, where they described it as uncommon and local. It now occurs throughout Maryland and north to northwestern Vermont (Pilcher 1985) and central Maine (Adamus 1988).

Northern Cardinals nest everywhere from swamps to residential yards, but they prefer edges of tall forests with a dense shrub layer (Robbins et al. 1989a). They often build in urban and suburban locations, such as backyards, parks, and gardens (Wetmore 1964). Maryland's record-high nesting density of 75 territorial males per 100 acres (40.5 ha) was in mixed-hardwood forest at Plum Point in Calvert County (Fales 1974).

The cup-shaped nest, which is constructed of twigs, vines, fibers, grasses, leaves, rags, and other debris, is placed in a vine tangle or shrub. Soft grasses, and sometimes hair, line the cup (Bent 1968a). The male does not help with nest building or incubation, although he defends the territory and feeds the female while she incubates.

Heights of 164 Maryland nests range from 1 to 20 ft (0.3–6.1 m), with a mean of 6 ft (1.8 m) (MNRF). The vast majority (96%) are at 8 ft (2.4 m) or lower. The earliest Maryland egg date is 8 April (5 April in DC); the latest is 23 August, with a peak in mid-May (MNRF). Clutch sizes in 122 Maryland nests range from 1 to 4 (mean of 2.7). In Kentucky, early clutches (1 April to 10 June) averaged 3.0 eggs; late clutches (20 June to 21 August) averaged 2.3 (Mengel 1965). Brood sizes in 93 Maryland nests range from 1 to 5, with a mean of 2.4 (MNRF). The earliest date for a nest with young is 12 April; the latest is 5 September, with a peak in mid-May. Brackbill (1955) has seen dependent young in Baltimore as late as 27 September. He found that in Maryland, Northern Cardinals can raise at least three broods in a season. The average annual survival rate of a PWRC population was 60 percent (Karr et al. 1990). Northern Cardinals are common victims of the Brown-headed Cowbird in parts of their range. Parasitism ranged from less than 1 percent at Nashville, Tennessee, to 45 percent in Michigan (Friedmann 1963). Of 525 Maryland nests, 21 (4.0%) were parasitized (MNRF). In Ontario, 63 of 299 nests (21.1%) were parasitized (Peck and James 1987).

Brackbill, whose observations were made in Baltimore, noted that the male helps tend the nestlings, which remain in the nest 9 to 11 days (Brackbill 1944). The young fly well at 19 days, are independent at 38 to 45 days, and sever all family ties at 56 to 59 days. The following information comes from Bent (1968a). The male sometimes feeds the first fledglings while the female starts a second clutch. The young may sing at three to four weeks of age. Young birds are fed grubs and other insects. Adults eat many insects in the warmer months, but their winter diet is about 90 percent vegetable matter, mostly seeds. They forage primarily on the ground. At feeding stations they prefer sunflower seeds.

Atlas results show "confirmed" or "probable" breeding over the entire state. Atlas records indicate the breeding range in the Allegheny Mountain Section has expanded from that shown by Stewart and Robbins (1958). Most "confirmed" records (56%) came from observations of fledged young; young birds are very visible, vocal, and easy to identify. BBS data from 1966 through 1989 indicate a decrease in the Eastern Region and show a stable population in Maryland. Range expansion from Pennsylvania and New Jersey north into New York and New England offsets a decrease in the southeastern United States (Robbins et al. 1986).

The outlook for the Northern Cardinal in Maryland seems secure. Its adaptability and tolerance of human disturbance should guarantee stable populations for the foreseeable future.

John Cullom

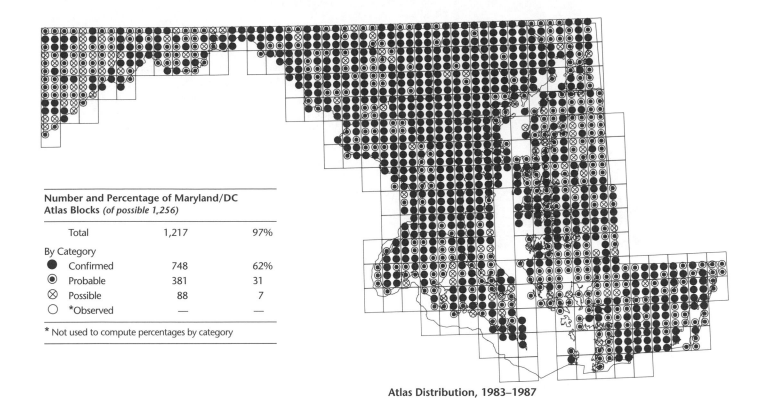

Number and Percentage of Maryland/DC Atlas Blocks *(of possible 1,256)*

Total	1,217	97%
By Category		
● Confirmed	748	62%
◉ Probable	381	31
⊗ Possible	88	7
○ *Observed	—	—

* Not used to compute percentages by category

Atlas Distribution, 1983–1987

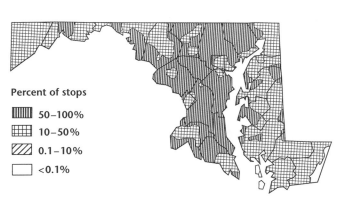

Percent of stops

▥	50–100%
▦	10–50%
▨	0.1–10%
☐	<0.1%

Relative Abundance, 1982–1989

Breeding Distribution, 1958

The Northern Cardinal is abundant in the suburban and lightly developed areas of central Maryland, where it benefits from ornamental plantings. Pockets of abundance occur around Cumberland and Hagerstown in western Maryland and in some developed areas on the Eastern Shore.

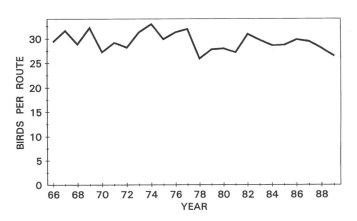

Maryland BBS Trend Graph, 1966–1989

Rose-breasted Grosbeak

Pheucticus ludovicianus

The male Rose-breasted Grosbeak is a striking black and white, robin-sized bird with a rosy bib. The duller female resembles the much smaller female Purple Finch. Learning to recognize its distinctive *chink* call note will alert birders to the presence of this uncommon breeding species in Maryland. The Rose-breasted Grosbeak hybridizes with its western counterpart, the Black-headed Grosbeak, where their ranges overlap in the Great Plains (AOU 1983). Some authorities treat the two as a single species. Rose-breasted Grosbeaks return to Maryland from their Mexican and Central and South American wintering grounds (AOU 1983) in early May; most depart by early October (Robbins and Bystrak 1977).

Kirkwood (1895) referred to the Rose-breasted Grosbeak as an irregular migrant through the Baltimore and DC area. Eifrig (1904) said it was rare in the lower parts of western Maryland, even in migration, but a rather common breeding bird at elevations above 2,000 ft (610 m). Stewart and Robbins (1958) called it a fairly common breeding bird in the Allegheny Mountain Section and rare in other sections west of the Chesapeake Bay. They cited several pairs nesting on Sugarloaf Mountain in Frederick County, and Ball (1930) reported a breeding record from Calvert County in 1925. Maryland is at the southeastern edge of its breeding range (AOU 1983).

The Rose-breasted Grosbeak's preferred habitat is the interface of two types of vegetation, including edges, cutover woods, bogs, second-growth woodlands, brushy and disturbed areas, and mixed mesophytic forests (Bent 1968b). Its nest, like that of the Mourning Dove, is a loosely woven, flimsy affair with the eggs often visible through the bottom. It is most commonly located in a bush or small tree and is built from 4 to 30 ft (1.2–9.1 m) above ground. The male often participates in the nest site selection, nest construction, and incubation. Heights of six Maryland nests (MNRF)

range from 6 to 12 ft (1.8–3.7 m); three were in crabapple trees.

Robbins and Bystrak (1977) listed extreme egg dates for Maryland as 22 May and 13 June, surely too narrow a range. For New York, Bull (1974) gave egg dates ranging from 6 May to 19 July and nestling dates from 30 May to 26 July. Stewart and Robbins (1958) gave nestling dates for Maryland as 8 to 14 June, also short of the full nesting period. Typical clutch sizes are 3 to 5 eggs, and incubation lasts 14 days (Bent 1968b). Clutch sizes in six Maryland nests (MNRF) are equally divided between 3 and 4 eggs. The male frequently sings while sitting on the nest in the manner of many vireos; it has also been known to sing at night (Bent 1968b). Batts (1958) reported that leaf beetle larvae are favored foods for nestlings. Beetles, locusts, moths, caterpillars, and other insects comprise half the food of the adults; wild fruits and tree seeds make up much of the rest (Bent 1968b).

Friedmann (1929, 1963) listed the Rose-breasted Grosbeak as a fairly common victim of Brown-headed Cowbird parasitism. There are no records for Maryland, but in Ontario, 18 of 275 nests (7.5%) were parasitized (Peck and James 1987).

Atlas results show that the Rose-breasted Grosbeak is still widely distributed in Garrett County, with scattered records eastward through the Ridge and Valley Section. It is one of the northern species that occasionally breeds at lower-than-normal elevations. In at least two instances, birds on the Piedmont were not found at the same sites in subsequent years, indicating that such breeding attempts are irregular at best. BBS data from 1966 through 1989 show stable populations in the Eastern Region; there are too few data to estimate a Maryland trend.

Rose-breasted Grosbeaks may prove to be excellent indicators of the effects of spraying forests with Dimilin to control gypsy moths. As early as 1908, McAtee (1908) listed gypsy moths as prey in the stomach analysis of Rose-breasted Grosbeaks. Forest fragmentation will increase the amount of preferred habitat for nesting Rose-breasted Grosbeaks, but it will also lead to increased parasitism by Brown-headed Cowbirds and degradation of the habitat for forest-interior nesting birds. We should continue to monitor population levels.

Barbara A. Dowell

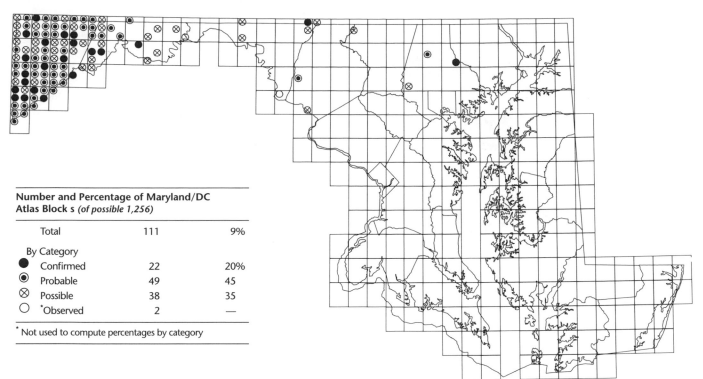

Number and Percentage of Maryland/DC
Atlas Block s *(of possible 1,256)*

Total	111	9%
By Category		
● Confirmed	22	20%
◉ Probable	49	45
⊗ Possible	38	35
○ *Observed	2	—

* Not used to compute percentages by category

Atlas Distribution, 1983–1987

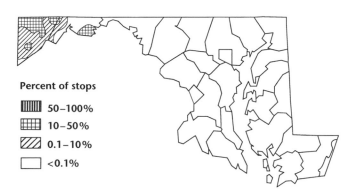

Percent of stops

▥	50–100%
▦	10–50%
▨	0.1–10%
☐	<0.1%

Relative Abundance, 1982–1989

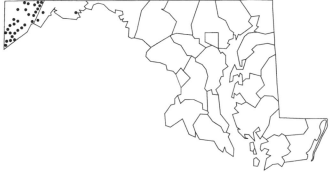

Breeding Distribution, 1958

The Rose-breasted Grosbeak is most common in the northern half of Garrett County in the Allegheny Mountain Section and was found locally in southeastern Allegany County in the Ridge and Valley Section. Because of its low numbers, it was not detected in some parts of its range.

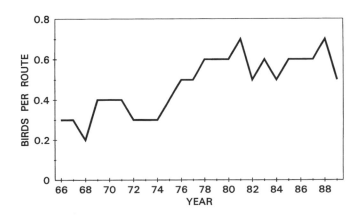

Maryland BBS Trend Graph, 1966–1989

Blue Grosbeak

Guiraca caerulea

The Blue Grosbeak resembles an overgrown Indigo Bunting with rust-colored wingbars. Although they are found in many of the same habitats, the Blue Grosbeak is more secretive and less abundant than the Indigo Bunting. It arrives from its wintering grounds in Mexico, Central America, and the Caribbean (AOU 1983) in late April and early May, and most fall migrants depart by the middle of October (Stewart and Robbins 1958). It can be found breeding throughout eastern Maryland, but it becomes increasingly rare to the north and west.

The first record of Blue Grosbeaks breeding in DC was a set of eggs collected on 28 May 1863 (Cooke 1929); the first in Maryland was a set collected 0.5 mi (0.8 km) east of DC on 24 June 1887 (Farnham 1891). Coues and Prentiss (1862, 1883) considered this species rather rare in DC. Kirkwood (1895) thought it was regular in southern Maryland, with DC at the northern limit of the breeding range. Stewart and Robbins (1947a) called it fairly common in Talbot and Queen Anne's counties but very rare or absent from the rest of the Eastern Shore. Ten years later its range had not expanded significantly on the Eastern Shore, but on the Western Shore it had extended up the Potomac River and inland as far as central Allegany County (Stewart and Robbins 1958). As Eifrig (1904) mentions no occurrence of the Blue Grosbeak in western Maryland, this suggests an expansion into western Maryland during the twentieth century.

The Blue Grosbeak inhabits shrubby thickets, hedgerows, orchards, and woodland edges (Stewart and Robbins 1958). Its nest is typically placed between the upright stems of a great variety of shrubs, briers, and small trees, especially red maple, multiflora rose, Japanese honeysuckle, sweet gum, and persimmon (MNRF). Heights of 34 Maryland nests (MNRF) range from 1 to 10 ft (0.3–3.0 m), with a mean of 4.3 ft (1.3 m).

This double-brooded bird (Bent 1968c) has a long nesting season. Maryland egg dates span the period from 5 May to 3 September (MNRF). Clutch sizes in 17 Maryland nests (MNRF) range from 2 to 4 (mean of 3.3). Incubation, by the female, lasts about 11 days; the young fledge about 13 days after hatching (Bent 1968c). Nests with young have been found in Maryland from 1 June to 11 September (MNRF). Brood sizes in 36 nests range from 1 to 4 (mean of 3). Blue Grosbeaks are reported to be common victims of Brown-headed Cowbird parasitism (Friedmann 1963), but only 1 of 104 Maryland nests (1%) was parasitized (MNRF).

The diet of the Blue Grosbeak consists primarily of insects, especially grasshoppers, weevils, May beetles, squash bugs, and caterpillars. A few snails, spiders, weed seeds, and wild fruits are also taken (Terres 1980). Alsop (1979) reported that the young in two Tennessee nests were fed mantids almost exclusively and that the female made three to five times as many feeding trips as the male.

Atlas results show that the Blue Grosbeak is well established throughout central and southern Maryland but less widely distributed in the northern Piedmont and the eastern Ridge and Valley sections. Several records in Garrett County in the Allegheny Mountain Section suggest that this species is in the process of colonizing even the higher elevations of Maryland. Since 1958 it has solidified its hold on the Eastern Shore and is now found in every part of the Coastal Plain. No explanation for this expansion has been put forward, but the Blue Grosbeak is also spreading at the southern edge of its breeding range. Taylor et al. (1989) related the expansion in Florida to the availability of frost-damaged citrus groves and an increase in abandoned fields. Most "confirmed" Atlas records (72%) were of fledged young or adults carrying food for young.

BBS data from 1966 through 1989 show a highly significant average annual increase of 2.6 percent in the Eastern Region; Maryland data show a highly significant average annual increase of 4.9 percent. The Maryland increase stabilized from 1980 to 1989.

During the twentieth century, the Blue Grosbeak has successfully expanded into and throughout Maryland. It is now a common, although never abundant, breeding bird on the Coastal Plain and occurs less frequently in the Piedmont and eastern Ridge and Valley sections. Although we do not know why it has increased and what factors might trigger a decline, the future of this species appears bright at present.

Ernest J. Willoughby

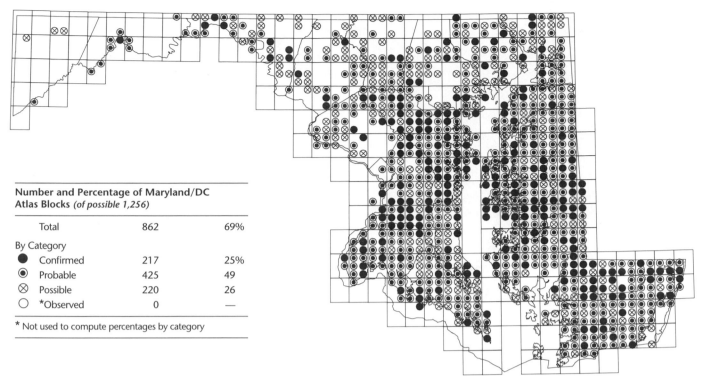

Atlas Distribution, 1983–1987

Number and Percentage of Maryland/DC Atlas Blocks *(of possible 1,256)*

Total	862	69%
By Category		
● Confirmed	217	25%
◉ Probable	425	49
⊗ Possible	220	26
○ *Observed	0	—

* Not used to compute percentages by category

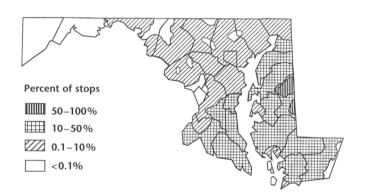

Percent of stops

▦	50–100%
▦	10–50%
▨	0.1–10%
☐	<0.1%

Relative Abundance, 1982–1989

Breeding Distribution, 1958

The Blue Grosbeak is most common on the southern and eastern Coastal Plain, with the highest concentrations in Caroline County on the central Eastern Shore. Abundance decreases to the north and west. It is largely absent from the DC urban area, the Catoctin Mountains, and Allegany and Garrett counties.

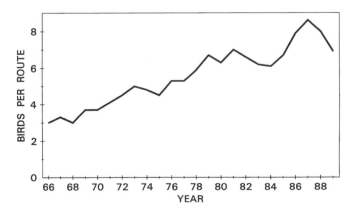

Maryland BBS Trend Graph, 1966–1989

MOB

Indigo Bunting

Passerina cyanea

The male Indigo Bunting appears uniformly dark blue, even black, when seen perched on a telephone wire or singing from a treetop. Up close, however, its brilliant deep blue plumage is striking, making it one of Maryland's most attractive breeding birds. The dull brown female can easily be mistaken for a sparrow. The Indigo Bunting is closely related to its western counterpart, the Lazuli Bunting, and some authors regard them as conspecific (AOU 1983). The two have hybridized in several contact zones in the Great Plains (Kroodsma 1975). Indigo Buntings begin returning to Maryland from their Mexican, Central American, and Caribbean wintering grounds (AOU 1983) in late April. The last fall migrants linger into mid-October (Robbins and Bystrak 1977).

Kirkwood (1895) described the Indigo Bunting as common in Maryland and DC. Eifrig (1904) found it common in western Maryland, noting that it was more common at low elevations. Stewart and Robbins (1958) called it abundant in the Ridge and Valley and Piedmont sections; common in the Allegheny Mountain, Upper Chesapeake, and Western Shore sections; and fairly common in the Eastern Shore Section. Johnston (1965) noted that its population and range has probably increased in North America since the arrival of European settlers. Clearing of the eastern forest created an abundance of the edge habitat it favors. Population increases were noted in several eastern states, including Florida (Sprunt 1954), Ohio (Trautman 1940), and Maryland (Warbach 1958). Recently the trend appears to have been reversed. BBS data from 1966 through 1989 show stable populations in the Eastern Region and Maryland, but data from

1980 through 1989 show a highly significant average annual decline of 2.5 percent in Maryland.

Indigo Buntings establish territories in a wide variety of open and semi-open situations with brushy vegetation, such as forest edges, overgrown old fields, roadside brush, and hedgerows, but they avoid deep forest (Kahl et al. 1985). The greatest breeding density reported from Maryland is 52 territorial males per 100 acres (40.5 ha) in an unsprayed apple orchard with unmowed grass cover in Allegany County (Springer and Stewart 1948b). Their summer diet consists primarily of caterpillars, beetles, and grasshoppers, supplemented with fleshy fruits and grains (Martin et al. 1951).

The nest is placed in the crotch of a small tree, shrub, or bush, or in a blackberry patch or weedy field (MNRF). It is usually close to the ground. Heights of 80 Maryland nest records range from 0 to 14 ft (0–4.3 m), with a mean of 2.8 ft (0.9 m). Only one nest was higher than 8 ft (2.4 m). Two broods are attempted (Taber and Johnston 1968), and the breeding season is long in Maryland. Males are frequently heard singing truncated versions of their primary song well into August, even in the middle of the hottest days.

Nests with eggs have been found in Maryland from 24 May to 18 August, with peaks in mid-June and early August. Clutch sizes in 55 nest records range from 1 (probably incomplete) to 4, with a mean of 2.9 (MNRF). Clutches of 3 and 4 are typical in Maryland. The female incubates for 12 or 13 days (Taber and Johnston 1968). Brood sizes in 51 Maryland nests range from 1 to 5, with a mean of 2.5 (MNRF). Young in the nest have been found in Maryland from 24 May to 13 September with no evident peaks. The young fledge 9 or 10 days after hatching (Taber and Johnston 1968). Males, which are occasionally polygynous, rarely feed the nestlings, but they are more active in the care of the fledglings (Westneat 1988).

Indigo Buntings are frequent victims of the Brown-headed Cowbird in some parts of their range. Peck and James (1987) reported that 40 of 165 Ontario nests (24.2%) were parasitized; Terrill (1961) listed 6 of 30 Quebec nests (20.0%) as parasitized. In contrast, only 4 of 55 Maryland nests (7.3%) contained Brown-headed Cowbird eggs.

The Indigo Bunting was one of the most widespread and abundant birds found by Atlas observers. It was present in 95 percent of all Atlas blocks and absent only from a few marsh and island blocks in coastal Worcester County and the lower Chesapeake Bay. Two-thirds of the "confirmed" records were of fledged young or adults carrying food for young.

Although at present there is little reason to be concerned about the future of this species in Maryland, the recent decline shown by BBS data is of concern. The decline may indicate that the creation of edge habitat by clearing of forests has been overtaken by loss of edge habitat to suburban development.

Stephen B. Hitchner

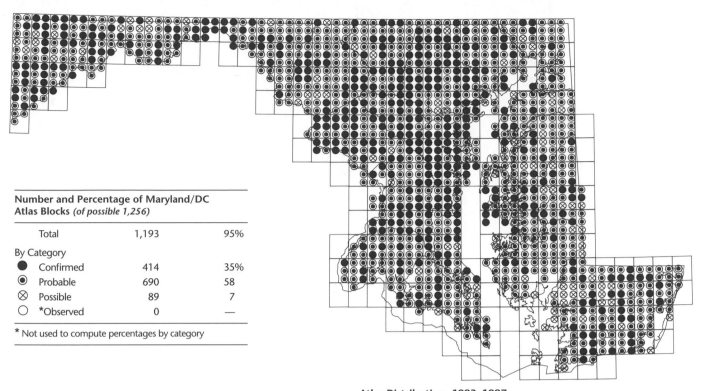

Number and Percentage of Maryland/DC Atlas Blocks *(of possible 1,256)*		
Total	1,193	95%
By Category		
● Confirmed	414	35%
◉ Probable	690	58
⊗ Possible	89	7
○ *Observed	0	—

* Not used to compute percentages by category

Atlas Distribution, 1983–1987

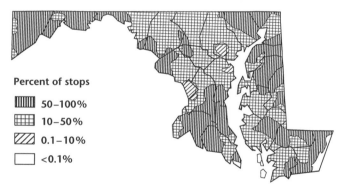

Percent of stops

▤ 50–100%
▦ 10–50%
▨ 0.1–10%
☐ <0.1%

Relative Abundance, 1982–1989

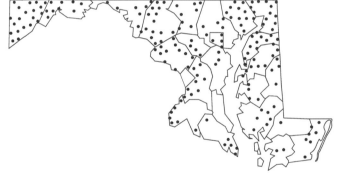

Breeding Distribution, 1958

The Indigo Bunting is most abundant in western Maryland, southern Maryland, and over much of the Eastern Shore. The lowest numbers are found in the urban centers in the Baltimore-Washington vicinity.

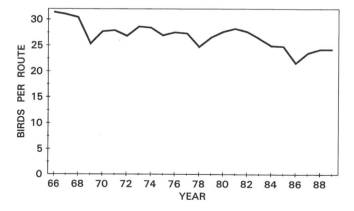

Maryland BBS Trend Graph, 1966–1989

Dickcissel

Spiza americana

The Dickcissel is a bird of hay and weedy fields. The male is recognized by his black-bibbed yellow breast and his habit of singing from conspicuous perches. The Dickcissel was formerly known as the Black-throated Bunting (Coues and Prentiss 1883). Migrants arrive from their Central and South American wintering grounds (AOU 1983) in late April and most depart by the end of September (Robbins and Bystrak 1977). Occasionally the Dickcissel winters in Maryland. It feeds primarily on insects, including grasshoppers, katydids, crickets, beetles, ants, and caterpillars (USFWS Food Habits File).

In the mid-nineteenth century, the Dickcissel was a summer resident and abundant spring migrant in DC (Coues and Prentiss 1862). Its disappearance during the next two decades was described as one of the most notable changes in the avifauna of the DC area (Coues and Prentiss 1883). Although specimens were collected in the Baltimore area in the 1870s by A. Resler, no nests were reported; Dickcissels "were quite common, and no special attention was paid to them" (Kirkwood 1895). The first confirmed nesting for Maryland was on 22 July 1928 when a young bird was observed near Dickerson in Montgomery County (Wetmore and Lincoln 1928). In the 1950s the Dickcissel bred regularly in variable numbers in the western Piedmont and eastern Ridge and Valley sections of Maryland (Stewart and Robbins 1958).

Preferred habitats of the Dickcissel include old fields in which tall and dense grasses and forbs predominate; weedy strips, such as roadsides, field edges, and wetland borders; and timothy, clover, and alfalfa fields with adjacent song perches (Zimmerman 1966, 1971, 1982; Harmeson 1974). Open cropland, orchards, graveyards, pastures, no-till corn

sod residue (Basore et al. 1986), and eastern red cedar woodlands with abundant grasses are also used. Elevated song perches are a habitat requirement.

The structure of the vegetation is the primary factor affecting nest site selection. Within the male's territory, females choose nest sites where vegetation is sufficiently tall and dense (Zimmerman 1971). Old fields are generally more suitable for nesting than are other habitats because the vegetation is taller and more heterogeneous and forb coverage is greater (Zimmerman 1982). Heights above ground of 149 nests from central states, summarized by Kahl et al. (1985), were 0 to 167 in. (0–424 cm) in tall forbs or low weedy vegetation. In Kansas, Zimmerman (1966) reported the mean height of nest rims and the vegetation directly above nests in grass, forb, and woody cover (sample size was not given). Nest rims were 9.5 to 13.5 in. (24–34 cm) above ground level. Vegetation heights above nests were 25 to 50 in. (64–127 cm). The nest is usually in a clump or tussock of residual or woody vegetation, although nests in green clover or hay are not uncommon (Fretwell 1977). In Illinois, Harmeson (1974) reported 20 of 33 nests (61%) were in aster, although the 7 nests in residual grasses were more successful (86% versus 45%). The nest, a cup built by the female, is made of weeds, grasses, and leaves lined with rootlets, fine grass, and hair (Harrison 1975). She places it on or near the ground, concealing it deep within the vegetation (Zimmerman 1966).

The male Dickcissel is polygynous, mating with as many as eight females in one season (Zimmerman 1966; Fretwell 1977). Clutch sizes in 149 Kansas nests range from 2 to 6 eggs, with a mean of 4 (Zimmerman 1982). The MNRF has only three records of Dickcissel nests, all found between 4 and 22 June; two of these had 4 eggs each. The female incubates for 11 to 12 days (Harrison 1975). The only reported Maryland nest with young was found on 26 June (MNRF). The young are fed primarily by the female, although the male sometimes assists (Zimmerman 1966). Nestlings fledge an average of 26 days after hatching. Females feed the fledglings for about two more weeks in the vicinity of the nest. One or two broods are attempted per year (Harrison 1975; Zimmerman 1982).

Friedmann (1971) lists the Dickcissel as a frequent victim of the Brown-headed Cowbird. In a Kansas study (Zimmerman 1966), 43 of 55 nests (78.2%) were parasitized; 26 nests (86%) of polygynous females were parasitized more heavily than the 29 nests (72%) of monogamous females. There are no records of parasitism in Maryland.

BBS data from 1966 through 1989 show a highly significant average annual decline of 1.9 percent in continental Dickcissel populations; Eastern Region populations are stable. There are too few records for Maryland to estimate a state trend. Fretwell (1977) suggested the decline was related to low female survival on the wintering grounds, resulting from replacement of natural grasslands by sorghum and rice. Seeds from these crops are too big to be eaten by the females, although the larger males are not similarly affected. Loss of grassland habitat to agriculture and urbanization in

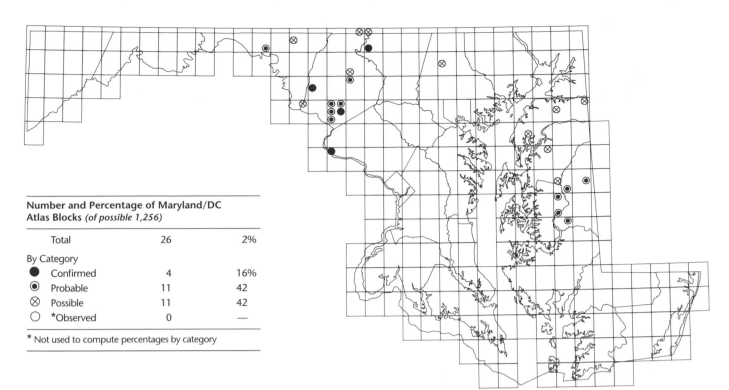

Number and Percentage of Maryland/DC Atlas Blocks *(of possible 1,256)*		
Total	26	2%
By Category		
● Confirmed	4	16%
◉ Probable	11	42
⊗ Possible	11	42
○ *Observed	0	—

* Not used to compute percentages by category

Atlas Distribution, 1983–1987

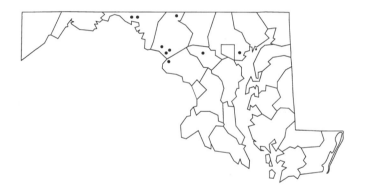

Breeding Distribution, 1958

the eastern United States is certainly a contributing factor in the decline.

Atlas results show the Dickcissel's breeding range in central Maryland to be nearly identical to that described by Stewart and Robbins (1958), but they also show a new population widely but thinly distributed through agricultural fields of the central Eastern Shore. There, where it was considered only a casual breeder in the 1950s (Stewart and Robbins 1958), it was recorded as "possible" or "probable" in 10

blocks. Although the records were spread over several years, no site was known to be used in more than one year. Dickcissels have also been observed in Prince George's County during the breeding season in recent years (Ringler 1988c). These results support the presumed stability of the Dickcissel population in Maryland. Managing for more old field habitat would increase nesting opportunities for this species.

Scott A. Smith

Eastern Towhee

Pipilo erythrophthalmus

The elegantly garbed male Eastern Towhee returns to Maryland from its southeastern U.S. wintering grounds (AOU 1983) in mid-March, and fall migrants leave by late October (Stewart and Robbins 1958). In spring the state rings with the *towhee* or *chewink* call from which the common name is derived. These introductory calls alert listeners to receive the complex, rapid trill that is the message component of the song (Richards 1981). Only in the most eastern birds can this trill be translated into the cheerful *drink-your-tea*.

The towhees of Maryland and the northeastern states have had their names changed every few decades. Initially described as Towhe-bird (*Passer niger oculis rubris*) by Catesby in 1758, this species was called Towhee Bunting by Coues and Prentiss (1883), and simply Towhee in the first three editions of the AOU Checklist. In the fourth edition (1931), the AOU changed the name of the northeastern subspecies to Red-eyed Towhee. In the fifth edition (1957) they combined the Red-eyed and the Spotted Towhee under the name Rufous-sided Towhee, and in the fortieth supplement to the Checklist (1995) they separated them again and called the northeastern bird the Eastern Towhee.

The breeding range of the Eastern Towhee in Maryland has not changed in 100 years. Early authors (Richmond 1888; Kirkwood 1895; Eifrig 1904; Cooke 1929) considered it common to abundant in summer and migration. Stewart and Robbins (1958) called it common to locally abundant as a breeding bird and migrant in all parts of the state, but they noted that Worcester County is the only place in Maryland where it regularly winters in large numbers. It is an uncommon to rare wintering bird throughout the rest of the state. The Eastern Towhee nests in dense brushy cover. The highest recorded breeding density in Maryland is 66 territorial males per 100 acres (40.5 ha) in oak-gum mixed-hardwood forest in Charles County (Klimkiewicz 1974b).

Nest building begins in late April. Barbour (1951) reported that the female alone constructs the nest and incubates the eggs; incubation requires 12 or 13 days (Dickinson 1968). The male remains in the territory and often accompanies the female while she forages. Early in the season, many nests are placed in small depressions on the ground, its upper surface flush with the ground or projecting only slightly above it (Barbour 1951; Davis 1960; Greenlaw 1978). Nests are overhung by vegetation or are sometimes roofed over. Heights of 79 Maryland nests (MNRF) range from ground level to 9 ft (2.7 m), with a mean of 1 ft (0.3 m); 58 nests were on the ground.

Maryland egg dates range from 22 April to 28 August, with peaks in mid-June and early to mid-July (MNRF). Eastern Towhees typically attempt two broods (Barbour 1951). Clutch sizes in 61 Maryland nests (MNRF) range from 2 to 5 (mean of 3.5). Young in the nest have been reported in Maryland from 30 April to 22 August, with no peaks evident. Brood sizes in 13 nests range from 2 to 4 (mean of 3.1). Greenlaw (1978) reported that birds in rich habitats in New Jersey nested earlier and had larger average clutch sizes than did birds in less rich habitats, which also were unlikely to be double-brooded. In some areas Eastern Towhees are frequent victims of Brown-headed Cowbird parasitism; only 6 of 111 Maryland nests (5%) were parasitized (MNRF), but 23 of 122 Ontario nests (18.9%) contained Brown-headed Cowbird eggs or young (Peck and James 1987).

The Eastern Towhee forages by scratching at dead leaves in search of the wide variety of insects, such as the beetles, moths, caterpillars, grasshoppers, crickets, ants, and bees, that constitute the bulk of its diet (Martin et al. 1951). It also consumes many ragweed seeds and some berries.

During the Atlas period, Eastern Towhees were found in all sections of Maryland; they were absent from only a few heavily urbanized and suburbanized blocks. Absences from other blocks may relate to coverage. The majority (61%) of "confirmed" records were of fledged young.

Although Eastern Towhees are widely distributed in Maryland, there is cause for concern. BBS data from 1966 through 1989 show a highly significant average annual decline of 2.9 percent in the Eastern Region. Maryland data show a similar but greater decline of 5.3 percent, most of which occurred prior to 1980. Maryland data from 1980 through 1989 show only an indication of a continuing decline. Although the decrease in the East is evident in all states from Ohio and New England south through Georgia, its causes have not been determined. Possible causes include the increasing loss of old-field habitat to succession and to more intensive land use, but there may be others. Although the rate of decline is leveling off, monitoring should continue until populations stabilize or appropriate management practices are developed and implemented.

Jane H. Farrell

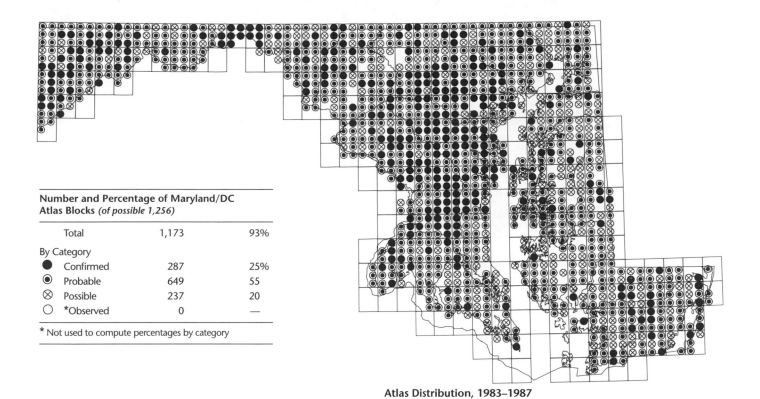

Number and Percentage of Maryland/DC Atlas Blocks *(of possible 1,256)*

Total		1,173	93%
By Category			
●	Confirmed	287	25%
◉	Probable	649	55
⊗	Possible	237	20
○	*Observed	0	—

* Not used to compute percentages by category

Atlas Distribution, 1983–1987

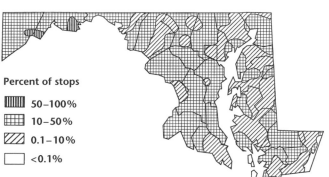

Percent of stops

▥	50–100%
▦	10–50%
▨	0.1–10%
☐	<0.1%

Relative Abundance, 1982–1989

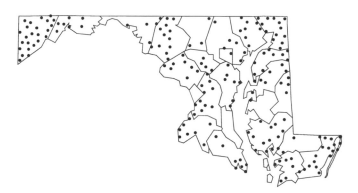

Breeding Distribution, 1958

The Eastern Towhee is abundant in small pockets in the western Ridge and Valley Section. It is least common over much of the central Eastern Shore, the Upper Chesapeake Section, urban areas, and the Frederick and Hagerstown valleys.

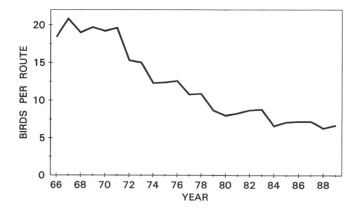

Maryland BBS Trend Graph, 1966–1989

MOB

Chipping Sparrow

Spizella passerina

The Chipping Sparrow, one of the best known and most widely distributed of Maryland sparrows, is a common breeder throughout the state. Although most birds migrate to the southeastern United States in the fall (AOU 1983), a few winter on the lower Eastern Shore and in the Piedmont in mild winters (Robbins and Bystrak 1977). Birds returning in spring typically arrive in late March and early April, and most fall migrants leave by late October.

The Chipping Sparrow has been described as very common to abundant in all parts of Maryland and DC since at least the middle of the nineteenth century (Coues and Prentiss 1862, 1883; Kirkwood 1895; Eifrig 1904; Cooke 1929). Stewart and Robbins (1958) wrote that it was common in all sections. For nesting it favors orchards, residential areas, and similar open, short-grass habitats (Stewart and Robbins 1958). Maximum densities reported in Maryland are 90 territorial males per 100 acres (40.5 ha) in a suburban residential area in Prince George's County in 1942 (Stewart and Robbins 1958) and between 42 and 51 territorial males per 100 acres in unsprayed and lightly sprayed apple orchards throughout the state (Springer and Stewart 1948b). Walkinshaw (1944) determined that territory sizes in Michigan were 1 and 1.5 acres (0.4–0.6 ha) in a residential area.

Nests are found in a variety of sites, especially coniferous trees and ornamental shrubs, but also in tangles, hedges, and, occasionally, on the ground (Stull 1968). Heights of 108 Maryland nests (MNRF) range from 1 to 30 ft (0.3–9.1 m), with a mean of 6.9 ft (2.1 m). Nest height increases as the season progresses (Walkinshaw 1944). The nest is a compact cup of grass, rootlets, and stems, lined with fur or hair. The female incubates the eggs for about 12 days; the male feeds her at the nest (Stull 1968). The earliest Maryland egg date is

22 April and the latest is 1 September, with a peak in late May (MNRF). Two broods are typically attempted (DeGraaf and Rudis 1986).

In 100 Maryland nests (MNRF), clutch sizes range from 2 to 5 (mean of 3.3). The young fledge 8 to 12 days after hatching (Stull 1968). Young in the nest have been found in Maryland from 7 May to 4 September, peaking in mid-June (MNRF). As only ten of 500 Maryland nests had eggs prior to 1 May, it is not surprising that young have not been seen earlier. Brood sizes in 100 Maryland nests range from 1 to 4 (mean of 3) (MNRF). Chipping Sparrows are usually monogamous, but some sources (Stull 1968; Middleton and Prescott 1989) have reported polygyny.

This sparrow is a common victim of Brown-headed Cowbird parasitism (Friedmann 1963). Peck and James (1987) reported that 451 of 1,412 Ontario nests (32.0%) were parasitized, as were 60 of 115 nests (52%) in Ohio (Hicks 1934). One study reported that nest failure was very high when Brown-headed Cowbird eggs were present (Buech 1982). Only 1 of 90 Maryland nests (1.1%) prior to 1950 contained Brown-headed Cowbird eggs, but 18 of 151 nests (11.9%) from 1950 to 1990 were parasitized (MNRF).

Insects, such as grasshoppers, caterpillars, beetles, leafhoppers, bugs, and ants, comprise more than half the diet in spring and summer (Martin et al. 1951). They are largely replaced by seeds of grasses and other herbs in fall and winter.

During the Atlas fieldwork, Chipping Sparrows were found in almost every block in Maryland, even in some of the most heavily urbanized areas. They were missing only from extensive marsh blocks on the lower Eastern Shore and from Assateague Island in coastal Worcester County. Common and often found in residential neighborhoods, these sparrows were easy to confirm. Two-thirds of the "confirmed" records were of fledged young or adults carrying food for young. Most "probable" records (83%) were of birds holding territory.

BBS data from 1966 through 1989 show stable Chipping Sparrow populations in the Eastern Region. Although Maryland data from 1966 through 1989 show a statistically significant average annual decline of 2.2 percent, this decline occurred prior to 1980; a highly significant average annual increase of 2.6 percent followed in the period 1980 through 1989. There appears to be no reason for concern about the future of this species in Maryland. Not only was it one of the most widely distributed and abundant birds found during the Atlas project, but it has adapted well to many aspects of human alteration of the habitat. The Chipping Sparrow should remain one of the most visible breeding sparrows in Maryland.

Alfred J. Fletcher

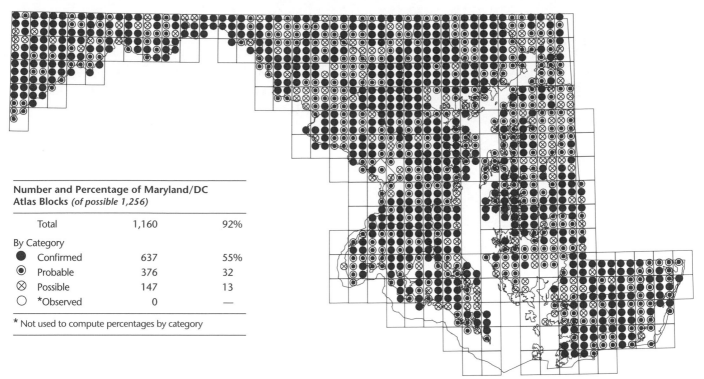

Atlas Distribution, 1983–1987

Number and Percentage of Maryland/DC Atlas Blocks *(of possible 1,256)*		
Total	1,160	92%
By Category		
● Confirmed	637	55%
◉ Probable	376	32
⊗ Possible	147	13
○ *Observed	0	—

* Not used to compute percentages by category

Percent of stops

▥ 50–100%
▦ 10–50%
▧ 0.1–10%
▢ <0.1%

Relative Abundance, 1982–1989

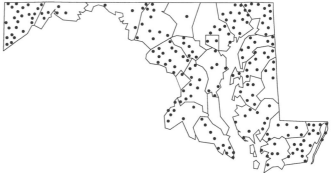

Breeding Distribution, 1958

The Chipping Sparrow is most common in the dry woodlands of the western Ridge and Valley Section, in pockets in the Allegheny Mountain Section, and along the Patuxent River in southern Maryland. It is least common in urban areas and in marshlands in southern Dorchester County.

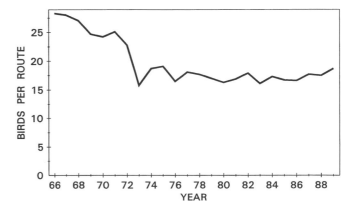

Maryland BBS Trend Graph, 1966–1989

MOB

Field Sparrow

Spizella pusilla

A series of sweet whistled notes, accelerating to a trill and emanating from the brushy edge of a weedy field, usually gives the first clue that Field Sparrows breed nearby. A diligent search may be rewarded by a glimpse of a small, pink-billed bird with rufous and gray-tinged plumage and an innocent wide-eyed look. Although Field Sparrows occur year-round throughout most of Maryland, numbers increase during spring migration, which extends from early March to late April, and fall migration from late September to early December (Stewart and Robbins 1958). During the summer, Field Sparrows are fairly common wherever suitable old-field habitat exists. In winter, flocks of a few to several dozen congregate with other sparrow species along the edges of grassy, weedy fields.

Kirkwood (1895) considered the Field Sparrow to be the most common breeding sparrow in Maryland, and other early authors also thought it common to abundant (Coues and Prentiss 1862, 1883; Eifrig 1904; Cooke 1929; Hampe and Kolb 1947). Stewart and Robbins (1958) described it as common in all sections.

Pairs establish nesting territories in weedy fields with scattered shrubs or small trees, in weedy orchards, or along brushy borders of farm fields (Stewart and Robbins 1958). Springer and Stewart (1948b) reported a maximum breeding density of 80 territorial males per 100 acres (40.5 ha) in an unsprayed apple orchard with unmowed ground cover in Allegany County, and J. Aldrich and A. Duvall recorded a high density of 79 per 100 acres in a field of Virginia pine in Montgomery County in 1943 (Stewart and Robbins 1958).

Its nest, constructed of dry grasses, weeds, rootlets, and hairs and usually lined with the thinnest fibers, is a simple cup with an inner diameter of about 2 in. (5 cm) and a depth of about 1.5 in. (4 cm); it is not attached or woven to supporting stems and branches and may tip over during nesting (Walkinshaw 1939b). Evans (1978) found that the

percentage of nests placed on the ground decreased as the season progressed.

Nest heights of 145 Maryland records (MNRF) range from 0 to 10 ft (0–3.0 m), with a mean of 1.3 ft (0.4 m). The earliest egg date in Maryland is 21 April and the latest is 25 August, with a peak in mid-May (MNRF). Clutch sizes in 115 Maryland nests range from 1 to 5 (mean of 3.7). Dates for Maryland nests with young range from 10 May to 1 September, peaking in late May (MNRF). Brood sizes in 104 Maryland nests range from 1 to 5 (mean of 2.9). During this long breeding season two, and sometimes three, broods are raised (Richmond 1888; Cooke 1929).

The female incubates about 11 days, and fledging normally occurs 7 or 8 days after hatching (Walkinshaw 1939b, 1968). Both parents feed the nestlings. The male cares for the fledglings, enabling the female to start another brood before the young are independent. Friedmann (1963) reported the Field Sparrow to be a frequent victim of the Brown-headed Cowbird. In Maryland, 19 of 115 nests (16.5%) were parasitized (MNRF), compared with 51 of 159 Ohio nests (32.0%) reported by Hicks (1934) and 62 of 334 Ontario nests (18.6%) reported by Peck and James (1987). Reporting rates are probably too low, however, because Field Sparrows often abandon parasitized nests (Walkinshaw 1968; Best 1978). Best (1978) found that nests more than 85 ft (26 m) from a woodland or scrub edge were not parasitized. Half the food eaten in spring and summer is insects, especially beetles, grasshoppers, and caterpillars; grass seeds are the principal plant foods (Martin et al. 1951).

During the Atlas period, Field Sparrows were found throughout Maryland, even in heavily wooded blocks in Garrett County. They were missing from only a few heavily urbanized blocks and from some of the extensive salt-marsh blocks on the lower Eastern Shore. Most (78%) "confirmed" reports were of fledged young or adults with food for young.

Field Sparrow populations in the eastern U.S. have declined significantly. BBS data from 1966 through 1989 show a highly significant average annual decline of 3.6 percent in the Eastern Region and 5 percent in Maryland. Observations in St. Mary's County indicate a continued decline that was especially notable around St. Mary's City in 1985 (E. Willoughby, pers. obs.); however, according to BBS data from 1980 through 1989, Maryland populations during that decade were stable. Although BBS data from 1966 through 1979 showed declines in some other sparrow populations in the Eastern Region, including the White-throated, Song, and Chipping Sparrows, these declines probably resulted from the severe winters of 1976–77 and 1977–78 (Robbins et al. 1986). Data from 1966 through 1989 for the Eastern Region show that the White-throated Sparrow has recovered and its population is stable. Although the Field Sparrow is still a common breeding species in the state, it may become less common if more intensive agricultural practices and the spread of urban development continue to restrict its nesting habitat of old weedy fields with shrubs or small trees.

Ernest J. Willoughby

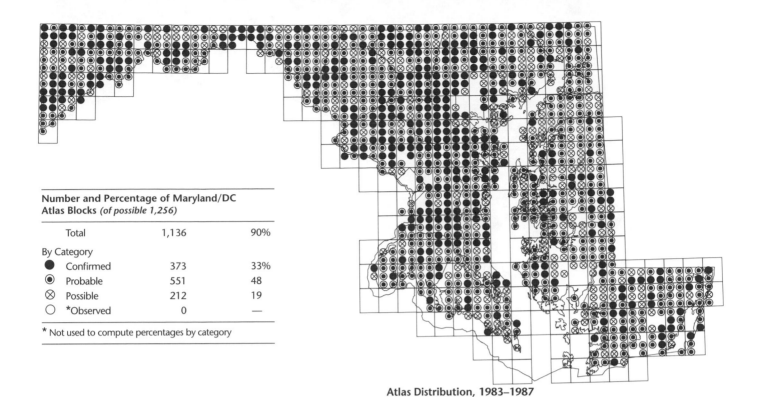

Atlas Distribution, 1983–1987

Number and Percentage of Maryland/DC Atlas Blocks *(of possible 1,256)*		
Total	1,136	90%
By Category		
● Confirmed	373	33%
◉ Probable	551	48
⊗ Possible	212	19
○ *Observed	0	—

* Not used to compute percentages by category

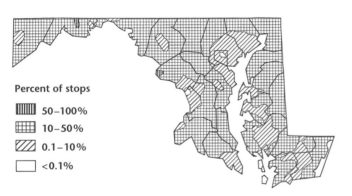

Percent of stops

⬛ (vertical lines)	50–100%
⬛ (grid)	10–50%
⬛ (diagonal)	0.1–10%
⬜	<0.1%

Relative Abundance, 1982–1989

Breeding Distribution, 1958

The Field Sparrow is widespread and common. It is uncommon only in urban and suburban areas, in extreme southern Maryland, and in the more wooded areas of the southern Eastern Shore in central Dorchester County and along the Pocomoke River and its tributaries.

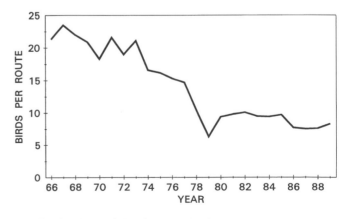

Maryland BBS Trend Graph, 1966–1989

Vesper Sparrow

Pooecetes gramineus

Formerly known as the Bay-winged Bunting (Coues and Prentiss 1862, 1883), the Vesper Sparrow is a melodious songster of dry, sparse grasslands. Its present name reflects its habit of singing at sunset (Coues and Prentiss 1883). The first spring migrants arrive in Maryland in late March, and the last leave by early May (Stewart and Robbins 1958). Fall migrants pass through from mid-September to mid-November en route to their southeastern U.S. wintering grounds (AOU 1983).

The Vesper Sparrow was common in Maryland in the late 1800s (Richmond 1888), although more so during migration than in summer or winter (Kirkwood 1895). At Roland Park, in Baltimore County, W. Fisher reported a flock of several hundred on 10 April 1897 (F. Kirkwood Card File). Eifrig (1904) stated it was a very common breeder at elevations above 2,000 ft (610 m) in western Maryland. The state's first nest was found by J. Fisher, Jr., on 19 June 1890 (Kirkwood 1895). Stewart and Robbins (1958) described its breeding status as common in the Allegheny Mountain, Ridge and Valley, and Piedmont sections, fairly common in the Upper Chesapeake Section, uncommon in the Eastern Shore and northern part of the Western Shore Section, and rare in the southern part of the Western Shore Section.

This sparrow prefers large, short-growth or sparsely vegetated pastures, hayfields, and fallow fields. It also uses field borders (Fletcher et al. 1956; Stewart and Robbins 1958), reclaimed surface mines (Wray and Whitmore 1979; Reed 1986), and agricultural areas dominated by corn and soybean crops (Rodenhouse and Best 1983; Best and Rodenhouse 1984). Wray et al. (1982) found, however, that reproduction on reclaimed surface mines was slightly below replacement levels because of the sites' high concentration of predators. The nest, a cup at the base of a forb or thin grass clump (Wiens 1969), is constructed of dry grasses, weed stalks, and rootlets, lined with finer grasses, rootlets, and, occasionally, hair (Harrison 1975).

Vesper Sparrows need conspicuous song perches but do not use grasslands that have succeeded to shrubland (Evans 1978). In Maryland, large fields with adjoining telephone wires for singing perches are commonly used (C. Robbins, pers. obs.). In agricultural habitats, early season nests are in clumps of crop residue, whereas later nests are at the bases of growing crop plants (Rodenhouse and Best 1983; Best and Rodenhouse 1984). Cropfield nests are typically within 260 ft (79 m) of hedgerows. Cropfields are unsuitable for nesting once the crop canopy closes. Rodenhouse and Best (1983) reported reproduction below replacement levels in fields with row crops.

This double-brooded sparrow builds its nest in Maryland as early as 14 April; extreme egg dates are 5 May and 1 August (Stewart and Robbins 1958). Clutch sizes in eight Maryland nests (MNRF) range from 3 to 5. The female incubates for 12 or 13 days (Berger 1968); young fledge in 10 to 12 days. Nests with young have been found in Maryland from 14 May to 23 July (MNRF). Brood sizes in 4 Maryland nests are equally divided between 2 and 4.

The Vesper Sparrow is a fairly frequent victim of Brown-headed Cowbird parasitism (Friedmann 1963), and the incidence may be increasing. Peck and James (1987) reported that 47 of 442 Ontario nests (10.6%) were parasitized. They noted that parasitism had increased in the second half of the twentieth century: 3 of 46 nests (6.5%) from 1877 through 1966, versus 15 of 44 nests (34.1%) from 1966 through 1984. Of 13 Maryland nests (MNRF) and 70 West Virginia nests found on reclaimed surface mines, none was parasitized (Wray et al. 1982).

During the warm months, half the Vesper Sparrow's diet is insects, especially beetles, grasshoppers, caterpillars, bugs, and ants (Judd 1901). Seeds of ragweed, bristlegrass, and smartweed are high on the list of plant material consumed.

Since 1958, this species' breeding range in Maryland has contracted. During the Atlas period it was not found on the lower Eastern Shore. It was rare on the central Eastern Shore except along the Delaware border and was largely absent from the Upper Chesapeake Section. Only scattered records were reported in southern Maryland. In Howard County, the number of quarterblocks with Vesper Sparrow records declined 69 percent between the original county Atlas (1973–75) and the present Atlas (1983–87) (Robbins et al. 1989c). Nesting was most frequently "confirmed" by seeing recently fledged young (41%) or by observing adults feeding young (39%).

BBS data from 1966 through 1989 show a disturbing highly significant average annual decline of 3.3 percent in the Eastern Region and 7.7 percent in Maryland; Maryland data from 1980 through 1989 show an even higher decline of 10.2 percent. These declines may reflect conversion of pastureland to row crop agriculture and suburban sprawl. Loss of hedgerows (Ryan 1986), Brown-headed Cowbird parasitism, and pesticide use may also be factors. In addition, more frequent mowing destroys nests before the young can

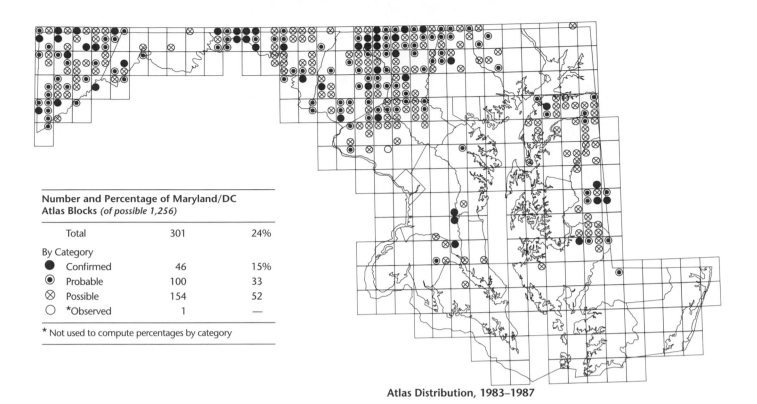

Number and Percentage of Maryland/DC Atlas Blocks *(of possible 1,256)*

Total	301	24%
By Category		
● Confirmed	46	15%
◉ Probable	100	33
⊗ Possible	154	52
○ *Observed	1	—

* Not used to compute percentages by category

Atlas Distribution, 1983–1987

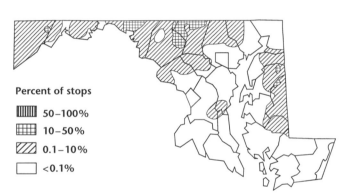

Percent of stops

▥	50–100%
▦	10–50%
▨	0.1–10%
▢	<0.1%

Relative Abundance, 1982–1989

Breeding Distribution, 1958

The Vesper Sparrow is most common in the Hagerstown and northern Frederick valleys and is uncommon elsewhere west of the Fall Line. It is uncommon but widespread in the agricultural fields of the interior of the central and northern Eastern Shore.

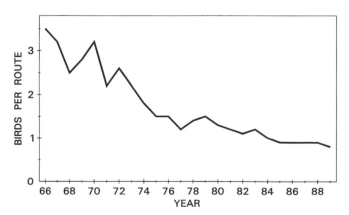

Maryland BBS Trend Graph, 1966–1989

fly. The serious and continuing decline in Vesper Sparrows parallels that of other grassland birds in Maryland. Management of public open land is urgently needed to protect all grassland nesting species.

Scott A. Smith

Savannah Sparrow

Passerculus sandwichensis

The Savannah Sparrow, a pink-legged bird of field, marsh, and grassy dune, is best known for its high-pitched buzzy song and its habit of skulking mouselike through the vegetation. It occurs over a wide geographic and ecological range, including both wet and dry grassland habitats from Maryland to California and north into the arctic (Wiens 1969). It winters primarily from Maryland to Central America (AOU 1983). Migrants arrive in Maryland in the latter half of March and leave in early November (Stewart and Robbins 1958). The various subspecies, now united into a single species, were at one time separated into four species (Dickerman and Parkes 1960). Among these was the large, pale Ipswich Sparrow (*P. s. princeps*), which breeds only on Sable Island, Nova Scotia (AOU 1983), but is regular in small numbers in migration and in winter on grass-covered sand dunes along the barrier beaches of Worcester County (Stewart and Robbins 1958).

The Savannah Sparrow was not known to breed in Maryland in the late 1800s (Coues and Prentiss 1883; Kirkwood 1895); Eifrig (1909) first reported it as a summer resident in Garrett County. The first confirmed breeding occurred in a lightly grazed pasture in Garrett County in 1951 (Stewart and Robbins 1951c). It was not confirmed in Virginia until 1973 (Ake et al. 1976).

Prior to the Atlas, Savannah Sparrows were considered locally common at elevations above 2,500 ft (762 m) in Garrett County (Stewart and Robbins 1958) and uncommon and local at elevations above 500 ft (152 m) in Howard County, 315 ft (96 m) in Montgomery County, and 620 ft (189 m) in Washington County (Robbins 1978). Elsewhere, they were rare and local, nesting at elevations down to sea level (Stewart and Robbins 1958). BBS data from 1966 through 1989 show a highly significant decline of 1.8 percent in the Eastern Region but a stable Maryland population.

Savannah Sparrows occupy open grassland habitats such as wet meadows, coastal marshes and grassy dunes, dry hayfields, overgrown or lightly grazed pastures, fallow fields, re-

claimed surface mines, and tundra (Stewart and Robbins 1958; Wiens 1969; Potter 1972; Whitmore and Hall 1978). Preferred nesting habitats are characterized by low, dense herbaceous vegetation; deep and variable litter; and shorter, denser, and uniformly distributed forbs (Wiens 1969, 1973; Whitmore and Hall 1978). Fields with shrubs or small trees are not used, but perches for singing and displays are important (Wiens 1969, 1973). Stewart and Robbins (1951c) found a breeding density of 50 territorial males per 100 acres (40.5 ha) in a lightly grazed pasture in Garrett County.

Usually a solitary nester, the Savannah Sparrow may nest colonially if suitable sites are scarce (Baird 1968). It constructs its nest in a hollow in the ground, filling it with coarse grasses and lining it with finer grasses, rootlets, and hair (Baird 1968). Nests are often partially domed or placed under overhanging litter (Wiens 1969), well concealed in fairly dense grass clumps or hummocks of litter. Grass cover is 10 to 12 in. (25–31 cm) at the nest (Potter 1972; Ake et al. 1976; Alsop 1978), compared with 3 in. (8 cm) in the rest of the territory (Wiens 1973).

Savannah Sparrows are monogamous. The female incubates the eggs for 11 to 13 days; the male assists only in feeding the young (Wiens 1969; Dixon 1978). Clutch sizes in Ontario (364 nests) ranged from 1 to 6, with a mean of 3.9 (Peck and James 1987); in Wisconsin (23 nests) from 2 to 5, with a mean of 4.1 (Wiens 1969); and in Manitoba (80 nests) from 3 to 6, with a mean of 4.7 (Weatherhead and Robertson 1978). Dixon (1978) reported clutch sizes in New Brunswick (284 nests) ranging from 2 to 5 (mean of 4); 60 percent of these nests contained 4 eggs. Young stay in the nest for 7 to 10 days and are fed by the adults for two weeks after fledging. Second broods are common (Wiens 1969; Dixon 1978; Rogers 1985).

There are only four Savannah Sparrow records in the MNRF. A nest with 4 eggs was observed between 24 June and 2 July. Dates for three nests with young (brood sizes of 1, 2, and 3) range from 30 May to 5 June. In the three instances where height was recorded, the nest was on the ground. The Savannah Sparrow is an infrequent victim of the Brown-headed Cowbird (Friedmann 1929, 1963). Terrill (1961) reported 5 of 140 nests (3.6%) parasitized, and Peck and James (1987) reported that 39 of 531 Ontario nests (7.3%) were parasitized.

During the nesting season, Savannah Sparrows mainly eat insects, such as beetles, caterpillars, grasshoppers, ants, bugs, and flies, but they also take spiders and snails (Martin et al. 1951). Seeds, especially of bristlegrass, crabgrass, ragweed, and panic grass, dominate the fall and winter diet.

Most "confirmed" records were of fledged young. Atlas results closely follow the range shown by Stewart and Robbins (1958). Garrett County is still the stronghold of Savannah Sparrows in Maryland. Differences include an apparent expansion into central Maryland and the lack of reports for Worcester County. Maintenance of grassland habitats in the state is crucial to ensure the continued well-being of this interesting species.

Scott A. Smith

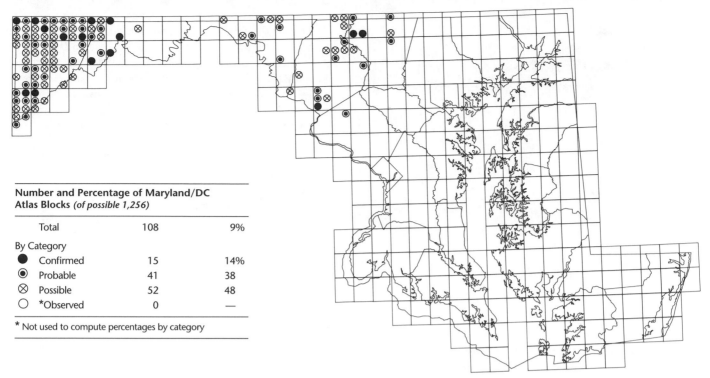

Atlas Distribution, 1983–1987

Number and Percentage of Maryland/DC Atlas Blocks *(of possible 1,256)*

	Total	108	9%
By Category			
●	Confirmed	15	14%
◉	Probable	41	38
⊗	Possible	52	48
○	*Observed	0	—

* Not used to compute percentages by category

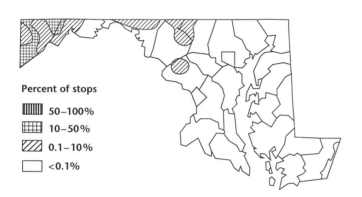

Percent of stops

▥	50–100%
▦	10–50%
▨	0.1–10%
☐	<0.1%

Relative Abundance, 1982–1989

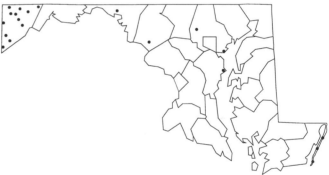

Breeding Distribution, 1958

The Savannah Sparrow is most common in the more agricultural areas of the Allegheny Mountain Section in Garrett County. It is uncommon and local in grasslands in the Ridge and Valley Section.

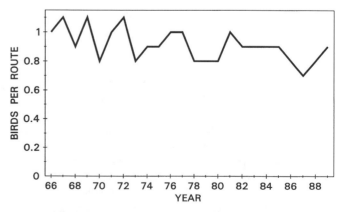

Maryland BBS Trend Graph, 1966–1989

Grasshopper Sparrow

Ammodramus savannarum

Tsc tsc a-bzzzzzzzzz! Hard to miss when you know it, easy to overlook when you don't; the Grasshopper Sparrow's song enlivens grasslands all over Maryland. In suitable habitat, it is common from the time spring migrants return from their southeastern U.S. wintering grounds (AOU 1983) in late April until fall migrants leave in September (Stewart and Robbins 1958).

Grasshopper Sparrows were certainly less common in Maryland before the European settlers cleared the forests in the 1600s and 1700s (Smith 1968); their abundance has depended on human disturbance for at least 300 years. Early authors (Coues and Prentiss 1862, 1883; Kirkwood 1895; Eifrig 1904) listed the Grasshopper Sparrow as a common to abundant summer resident. Stewart and Robbins (1958) reported it as common in all sections. BBS data from 1966 through 1989 show a highly significant average annual decline of 5 percent in the Eastern Region and 6.7 percent for Maryland, but the Maryland population was stable from 1980 through 1989. This decline resulted, at least in part, from loss of habitat, especially the conversion of grassland to row-crop agriculture and suburbs, and from the harvesting of winter wheat at the height of the breeding season. In recent decades, declines have also been noted in West Virginia (Hall 1983) and Pennsylvania (Gill 1985). The Grasshopper Sparrow was added to the NAS Blue List in 1974 (Arbib 1973).

Breeding Grasshopper Sparrows need a combination of living vegetation, grasses, or forbs averaging 1 ft (0.3 m) or less in height, with at least 24 percent bare, litterfree ground (Whitmore 1979). Within a grassy field, they always breed in areas with the appropriate ratio of cover to open ground, so the population at any site may vary considerably from year to year as vegetation patterns change. They defend territories of 1 to 3 acres (0.4–1.2 ha) (Smith 1968). The highest breeding density reported for Maryland is 77 territorial males per 100 acres (40.5 ha) in a weedy fallow field in Prince George's County in 1945 (Stewart and Robbins 1958). They often nest in loose colonies that may move from year to year, even though the habitat appears adequate in the old location (Smith 1968). Males arrive first and begin claiming territory as soon as the grass is high enough to hide them. They sing from the highest perch. They often claim new territories for renesting or second nestings, because mowing or lush growth may make the first territory unusable (Smith 1968). Grasshopper Sparrows often use reclaimed surface mines as breeding sites; Wray et al. (1982) found that increased predation at these sites limited productivity to below replacement levels.

The female builds a shallow cup-shaped nest of dried grasses lined with finer grasses, rootlets, or hair (Smith 1968; Harrison 1975). Nests, well hidden by a canopy of live or dead vegetation, are sometimes domed at the back. Jackson (1941) found many nests by randomly placing small bunches of hay for the birds to nest under after hay had been removed from a field. All 59 Maryland nests (MNRF) are on or within 2 in. (5 cm) of the ground.

Clutch sizes in 50 Maryland nests (MNRF) range from 3 to 5 (mean of 4). Extreme egg dates are 15 May (Smith 1968) and 19 August (Stewart and Robbins 1958). The mean date of 38 nests with eggs in Dorchester County was 5 June (Jackson 1941). Nonflying young, however, were reported from Baltimore County on 10 September (Stewart and Robbins 1958). The September fledglings suggest that three broods may be attempted in Maryland in some years. The female incubates the eggs for about 12 days (Smith 1968). Both parents care for the young, which grow quickly and usually leave the nest on their ninth day. Nests with young have been reported in Maryland from 25 May to 15 August, and in DC as late as 2 September (MNRF). Brood sizes in 10 nests range from 3 to 5 (mean of 3.8).

Friedmann (1963) considered the Grasshopper Sparrow a rare victim of Brown-headed Cowbird parasitism. No parasitism has been reported in Maryland; in Ontario, however, 6 of 74 nests (8.1%) were parasitized (Peck and James 1987). Their summer diet consists of about 60 percent insects, especially grasshoppers (Martin et al. 1951). Seeds of bristlegrass and panic grass are also taken in large quantities.

During the Atlas period, the Grasshopper Sparrow was "confirmed" in 15 percent of the blocks in which it was found; most "confirmed" records were of newly fledged young or of adults carrying food. It was widely distributed throughout the state, except in major metropolitan areas and large areas of Dorchester, Somerset, and Worcester counties on the lower Eastern Shore. Records were scattered in the primarily forested areas of Allegany and Garrett counties and the Catoctin Mountains.

The key to continued Grasshopper Sparrow presence as a breeding bird in Maryland is management of grasslands to maintain woody vegetation at less than 3 ft (0.9 m) tall (Kahl et al. 1985). Suitable oldfields and grasslands should not be cut until after the peak of the breeding season.

David W. Holmes

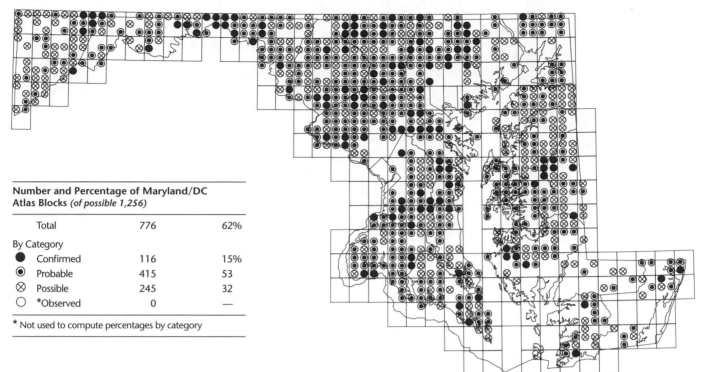

Number and Percentage of Maryland/DC Atlas Blocks *(of possible 1,256)*

	Total	776	62%
By Category			
●	Confirmed	116	15%
◉	Probable	415	53
⊗	Possible	245	32
○	*Observed	0	—

* Not used to compute percentages by category

Atlas Distribution, 1983–1987

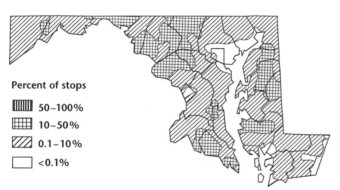

Percent of stops

▥ 50–100%
▦ 10–50%
▧ 0.1–10%
▢ <0.1%

Relative Abundance, 1982–1989

Breeding Distribution, 1958

The Grasshopper Sparrow is most common in grasslands in the Ridge and Valley, Piedmont, Western Shore, and Eastern Shore sections. It is absent from some marsh blocks and from urban centers around Baltimore and Washington.

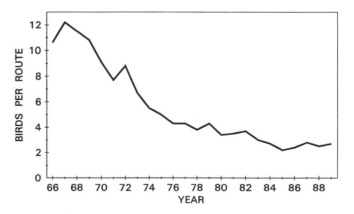

Maryland BBS Trend Graph, 1966–1989

MOB

Henslow's Sparrow

Ammodramus henslowii

An enigma to many birdwatchers, the Henslow's Sparrow is unpredictable in its year-to-year selection of fallow fields and other grassland habitats. Specialized breeding requirements and near total dependence on human-managed habitat are factors in the ongoing population collapse of this reclusive "fieldmouse-with-wings."

Its breeding range extends from Minnesota, Ontario, and New York south to Missouri and North Carolina (AOU 1983). The winter range is centered in northern Florida and reaches to Texas and South Carolina (Hyde 1939). Spring migrants arrive in Maryland in mid-April and fall migrants leave by early November (Stewart and Robbins 1958).

Although nothing is known about the distribution and abundance of this species before Audubon named it in 1829, there is evidence for the historical existence of suitable grassland habitat in the East. Numerous accounts describe widespread prairies, barrens, glades, meadows, and marshes that once interrupted the primeval forests (Kercheval 1833; Williams 1906; Maxwell 1910–11; Mayre 1955; Schlosnagle et al. 1989). The Henslow's Sparrow population probably increased when settlers cleared the eastern forest (Hyde 1939). With the passing of time and continuing development, this species became more dependent on managed habitats for its nesting.

As the human population continues to increase, development and increasingly intensive agricultural use are eliminating even marginal habitat for Henslow's Sparrows (USFWS 1987). The species was one of two birds of management concern in the United States "in the most danger of extinction" (Butcher 1989). Every Atlas project and National Heritage Program in the East reports that Henslow's Sparrows are rare and declining. BBS data from 1966 through 1989 show a highly significant average annual decline of 4.4 percent in the Eastern Region; data are too few to estimate a Maryland trend. Federal listing under the Endangered Species Act appears overdue.

Audubon (1839) considered the Henslow's Sparrow an abundant breeder in Maryland, but Kirkwood (1895) believed it to be one of the rarest sparrows, known to occur at only a few places near DC. Fifty years ago it was fairly widespread and bred at PWRC, but the last mention of breeding there was in 1950 (Stewart and Robbins 1958). They counted 48 individuals in Worcester County from 16 to 19 June 1945 (Field Report USFWS Files). Stewart and Robbins (1958) described it as fairly common on the Coastal Plain, uncommon in the Piedmont and Allegheny Mountain sections, and rare in the Ridge and Valley Section. Since 1958 the Maryland population has declined steadily.

The Henslow's Sparrow is a bird of wet meadows, weedy fallow fields, and, occasionally, hayfields. A density of 16 territorial males per 100 acres (40.5 ha) was recorded in a weedy unimproved pasture at PWRC in 1950 (Stewart and Robbins 1958), and a density of 7 territorial males per 100 acres was recorded in a switchgrass marsh meadow in Somerset County (Springer and Stewart 1948a). The well-concealed nest is placed about 1 to 3 in. (3–8 cm) above ground, often at or near the base of, but not attached to, a thick clump of overarching grass (Hyde 1939; Robins 1971). Maryland egg dates range from 10 May to 2 July (MNRF), but nesting probably continues through August. Clutch sizes in 22 Maryland nests range from 3 to 5 (mean of 4.1). The 11-day incubation appears to be solely by the female (Graber 1968).

Young have been found in Maryland nests only on 1 June of 1894 and 1930 (MNRF). Young leave the nest 9 or 10 days after hatching (Hyde 1939). Two broods are typical (Harrison 1975). Friedmann (1929, 1963) considered the Henslow's Sparrow a fairly uncommon victim of Brown-headed Cowbirds. Peck and James (1987) reported that only 1 of 12 Ontario nests (8.4%) was parasitized; in Maryland, 3 of 21 nests (14.3%) were affected (MNRF).

Ragweed seeds are the principal food in the Northeast (Martin et al. 1951). These sparrows also eat beetles, grasshoppers, bugs, leafhoppers, caterpillars, and ants.

The Atlas documented the Henslow's Sparrow in only three blocks on the Coastal Plain, all on the lower Eastern Shore; none of those sites has been occupied since 1989 (H. Wierenga, pers. comm.). It was not found in the Piedmont or the eastern part of the Ridge and Valley Section. Only a few hayfields, abandoned strip mines, and meadows in Garrett and Allegany counties harbored small colonies or single pairs. Many locations were used for only one year, a few were used erratically, but none was known to contain Henslow's Sparrows throughout the period. A 1991 survey by K. Dodge (unpub. data) found them at several locations in Garrett County; most were at reclaimed surface mines.

Management concern for the Henslow's Sparrow and other grassland species is just developing in Maryland. Although the DNR listed this species as in need of conservation, the designation does not provide habitat protection. Fields in public ownership larger than 20 acres (8.1 ha) should be surveyed, and some should be managed to foster grassland species. Management should provide multiyear

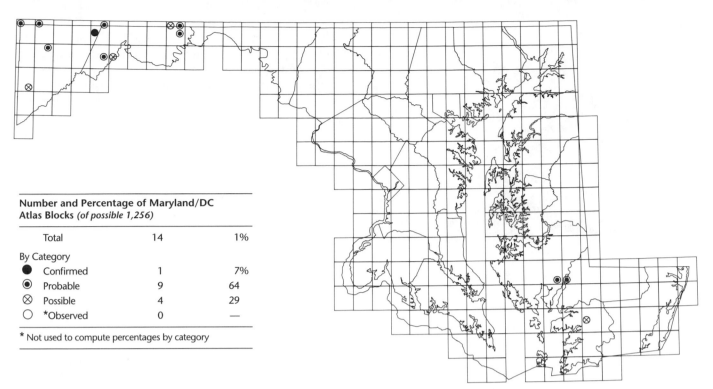

Number and Percentage of Maryland/DC Atlas Blocks *(of possible 1,256)*

Total	14	1%
By Category		
● Confirmed	1	7%
◉ Probable	9	64
⊗ Possible	4	29
○ *Observed	0	—

* Not used to compute percentages by category

Atlas Distribution, 1983–1987

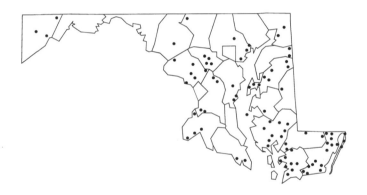

Breeding Distribution, 1958

accumulation of litter (Robins 1971), standing dead vegetation (Zimmermann 1988), and scattered medium and heavy-stemmed forbs or shrubs for singing perches (Hands et al. 1989). Habitat should be managed by periodically setting back succession to retain dense, low vegetation.

Publicly owned fields often are leased for agricultural production, planted with rows of nonnative shrubs, or re-forested. None are currently managed for rare grassland birds. If Maryland is to retain the Henslow's Sparrow as a nesting species, public land management agencies must provide and maintain areas of oldfield succession habitat. Private landowners should be encouraged and assisted in managing for grassland species.

D. Daniel Boone and Barbara A. Dowell

Saltmarsh Sharp-tailed Sparrow

Ammodramus caudacutus

A secretive, skulking bird of salt-marsh meadows, the Saltmarsh Sharp-tailed Sparrow is difficult to see even where it thrives. During the summer months, a male may occasionally be seen flying low across the marsh or singing its high, thin song from among the lush blades of salt-meadow cordgrass. Although a few remain throughout the winter on the lower Eastern Shore (Stewart and Robbins 1958), most move to the southeastern United States for the winter months (AOU 1983). Spring migrants begin returning in April, and the bulk of the fall migration is over by the end of October (Robbins and Bystrak 1977).

The first record of a Saltmarsh Sharp-tailed Sparrow in our area was a specimen taken in DC in September 1862 (Ridgway 1882). Kirkwood (1895) reported the first summer record south of Ocean City in June 1894, and he also reported the first Maryland nest, which contained 3 eggs on 3 June 1896 at Bloodsworth Island, Dorchester County (MNRF). Hampe and Kolb (1947) described the Maryland breeding range as coastal Worcester County and referenced specimens taken in summer at Chesapeake Beach in Calvert County. Stewart and Robbins (1947a) added that these sparrows bred throughout the salt and brackish marshes of the Chesapeake Bay as far north as Queen Anne's County on the Eastern Shore and Sandy Point in Anne Arundel County on the Western Shore. A decade later, Stewart and Robbins (1958) showed the same distribution, adding only that they were found along the Potomac River as far west as Cobb Island in Charles County.

The Saltmarsh Sharp-tailed Sparrow is an uncommon to locally abundant breeding species in the higher reaches of salt and brackish salt-meadow cordgrass marshes that are not flooded by daily tides (Hill 1968). It is also found in marshes of needlerush and, more sparingly, in marshes where salt-marsh cordgrass or seashore salt-grass is prevalent and in marshes dominated by needlerush or seashore salt-grass (Stewart and Robbins 1958; MNRF). Springer and Stewart (1948a) recorded an impressive nesting density of 100 territorial males per 100 acres (40.5 ha) in a salt-meadow cordgrass marsh-meadow in Somerset County. Breeding is promiscuous and distinctly colonial (Hill 1968). Woolfenden (1956) reported that the males are not territorial, and speculated that the male, which does not participate in raising the young, does not even know where the nest is located. Judd (1901), studying the contents of 51 stomachs, determined that 81 percent of the contents comprised animal remains. The chief food items were leafhoppers, sand fleas, bugs, flies and their larvae, and seeds of cordgrass and wild rice (Martin et al. 1951).

Woolfenden (1956) estimated that the female's territory is about 0.5 acre (0.2 ha); she selects the nest site and builds the nest, typically close to the ground. Heights of five Maryland nests (MNRF) range from 0 to 8 in. (0–20 cm), but only one is over 3 in. (8 cm). Egg dates for ten Maryland nests range from 11 May to 21 August; clutch sizes in seven nests range from 1 (probably incomplete) to four. Woolfenden (1956) reported that clutches of 3 and 4 eggs are most common; two broods are frequently attempted (Harrison 1975). The female incubates for 11 days (Hill 1968), and young fledge 10 days after hatching. Dates for young in four Maryland nests range from 4 to 24 June (MNRF), but the season is clearly longer, judging from the egg dates.

The Atlas revealed an apparent contraction of the range of this species in Maryland. Although still locally common in the salt and brackish marshes of the lower Chesapeake Bay and in southern Worcester County, it is not found in much of the range mapped by Stewart and Robbins (1958). The only Atlas record for the Western Shore came from Sandy Point State Park in Anne Arundel County. On the Eastern Shore, where it had previously nested north to Kent Narrows in Queen Anne's County, the only records north of Dorchester County were of birds on territory in two blocks on Tilghman Island in Talbot County. Coastal Worcester County had only one report north of Assateague Island, although Saltmarsh Sharp-tailed Sparrows had ranged north to the Delaware line in the 1950s. BBS data from 1966 through 1989 show stable populations in the Eastern Region; data are too few to estimate a Maryland trend.

Habitat destruction and fragmentation are probably responsible for the range contraction. While the secretive nature of the species suggests that some may have been overlooked, its nearly complete disappearance from the upper Chesapeake Bay and the lower Potomac River cannot be attributed to observer error. Elliott (1962) suggested fragmentation of once-continuous salt marsh was a factor in the species' decline on Long Island, New York. He also noted that patches of salt marsh less than 2 acres (0.8 ha) were too small to support breeding sharp-tailed sparrows. The need for larger, unbroken stretches of marsh may be a result of colonial breeding. Preservation of high, unflooded salt meadows is crucial to this species' future in Maryland.

Michael O'Brien

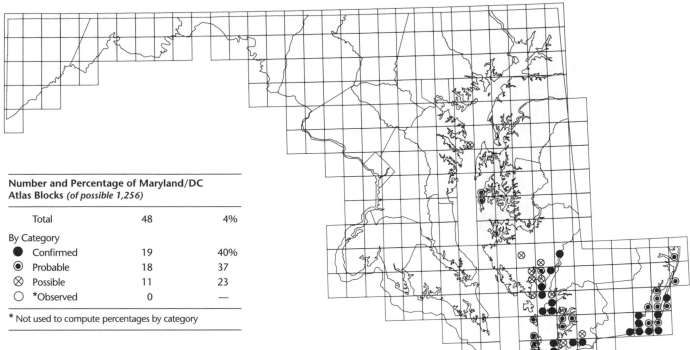

Number and Percentage of Maryland/DC Atlas Blocks *(of possible 1,256)*

Total	48	4%
By Category		
● Confirmed	19	40%
◉ Probable	18	37
⊗ Possible	11	23
○ *Observed	0	—

* Not used to compute percentages by category

Atlas Distribution, 1983–1987

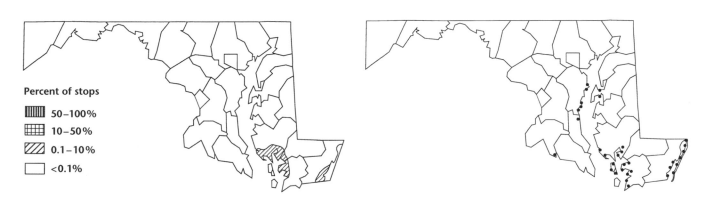

Percent of stops

▥ 50–100%
▦ 10–50%
▨ 0.1–10%
☐ <0.1%

Relative Abundance, 1982–1989

Breeding Distribution, 1958

Saltmarsh Sharp-tailed Sparrows were detected only in the extensive salt and brackish marshes of southern Dorchester, southern Wicomico, and western Somerset counties and in the coastal marshes of southern Worcester County. Miniroutes provide incomplete sampling of marsh habitats; consequently, birds in many breeding areas not close to roads were missed.

Seaside Sparrow

Ammodramus maritimus

Unlike the sharp-tailed sparrows, the Seaside Sparrow is a highly vocal defender of its salt-marsh territory, emitting its odd insectlike song from a perch or during its weak flight. It can be heard day or night during the spring and summer months. The breeding population is present from late April through early October (Stewart and Robbins 1958). This drably colored sparrow is well camouflaged on the blue-gray ooze of tidal mudflats where it feeds. It is primarily insectivorous but also takes small crabs (Martin et al. 1951).

The Seaside Sparrow is a common and conspicuous breeder in wetter portions of salt and brackish marshes just above the high-tide line. Although not a colonial species, it may appear to be so because aggregations tend to occur in prime habitat (Greenlaw 1983). The most favorable nesting habitats are low marsh dominated by smooth cordgrass and high marsh dominated by salt-meadow cordgrass with scattered shrubs of marsh elder and groundsel tree (Stewart and Robbins 1958; Greenlaw 1983). Adjacent feeding areas, such as ponds, creeks, mudflats, or areas with sparse vegetation where mud is exposed at low tide, are equally important in habitat selection (Greenlaw 1983). This species occurs more sparingly in stands of needlerush (Stewart and Robbins 1958) and in vast expanses of smooth cordgrass where shrubs are few and clear access to the mud substrate is limited (Greenlaw 1983). Small numbers are present in mild winters in coastal areas. The highest breeding density published for Maryland is 10 territorial males per 100 acres (40.5 ha) in salt-marsh bulrush–salt-grass marsh in Somerset County (Springer and Stewart 1948a).

Maryland's first specimen was one of a pair shot by Kirkwood (1895) on 27 May 1893 at Start's Point on Langford Creek, Kent County. This is several miles north of the currently known northern breeding range on the Eastern Shore of the Chesapeake Bay. On 6 June 1894 Kirkwood (1895) found the first Maryland nest, with 5 eggs, on Assateague Island, Worcester County.

Maryland nests were located primarily in needlerush, smooth cordgrass, and salt-meadow cordgrass, but three were found in salt grass (MNRF). Nest materials were noted for only one nest, which was made of smooth cordgrass lined with salt-meadow cordgrass. Eight New Jersey nests were constructed of needlerush (Woolfenden 1968). Heights above ground or water of 17 Maryland nests (MNRF) range from 0 to 10 in. (0–25 cm), with most between 3 and 4 in. (8–10 cm). Egg dates from 23 nests range from 16 May to 30 June, with 14 from 6 June to 15 June. Clutch sizes in 10 Maryland nests range from 2 to 5 (mean of 3.4), although Woolfenden (1968) reported 4 or 5 typical for the subspecies that breeds in Maryland (AOU 1957). Incubation, by the female, lasts 11 or 12 days (Harrison 1978). Both parents care for the young, which leave the nest nine days after hatching. Nestlings have been found in Maryland from 2 May to 14 June (MNRF). Brood sizes in nine nests were two (2), three (4), four (2), and five (1). There is normally only one brood (Woolfenden 1968), but occasionally a second will be raised in late June or early July (Harrison 1978). Friedmann (1963) listed the Seaside Sparrow as a rare victim of the Brown-headed Cowbird; he cited only one Massachusetts record. There is no Maryland record of parasitism.

Atlas distribution is similar to that reported by Stewart and Robbins (1958). Western Shore records included a pair in Newport Marsh, Charles County, and an adult carrying food at Miller Island, Baltimore County. The Miller Island birds were at the northern limit of the range on the western edge of the Chesapeake Bay, but this location is no longer in use since construction of the Hart-Miller dike covered most of the island (E. Blom, pers. comm.). Most of the population occurs in the extensive marshes of Dorchester, Somerset, and Worcester counties. Over one-third (42%) of the Atlas records were "confirmed." Adults were frequently seen carrying food, and dependent young were conspicuous as they foraged with adults on tidal flats. BBS data from 1966 through 1989 show a highly significant average annual increase of 4.1 percent in the Eastern Region; there are too few data to estimate a Maryland trend.

Although the Seaside Sparrow thrives where good habitat exists, it leads a fragile existence throughout its range. The entire population occupies a very narrow band of marsh along the Atlantic and Gulf coasts. If this band of marsh continues to be filled, dredged, or flooded, the population will steadily decline. One subspecies, the Dusky Seaside Sparrow, is extinct, and another, the Cape Sable Seaside Sparrow, is endangered. The USFWS has listed the Seaside Sparrow as a migratory nongame bird of management concern in the southeastern United States (USFWS 1987). To ensure that a viable population survives in Maryland, we should protect all salt and brackish marshes, especially the low, regularly flooded marsh dominated by smooth cordgrass and high marsh with scattered shrubs.

Michael O'Brien

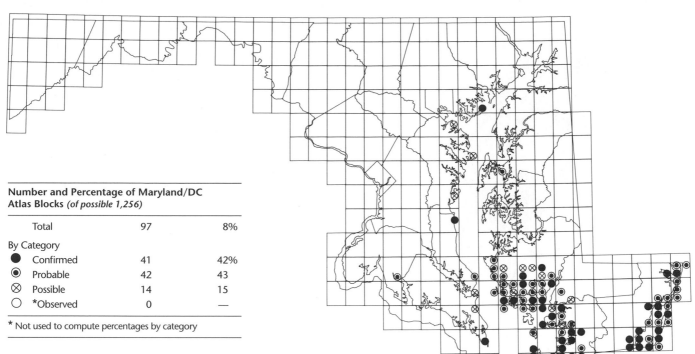

Number and Percentage of Maryland/DC Atlas Blocks *(of possible 1,256)*

	Total	97	8%
By Category			
●	Confirmed	41	42%
◉	Probable	42	43
⊗	Possible	14	15
○	*Observed	0	—

* Not used to compute percentages by category

Atlas Distribution, 1983–1987

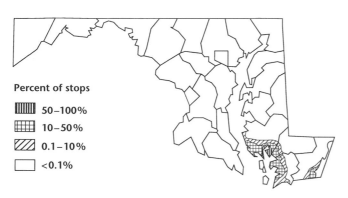

Percent of stops

▥	50–100%
▦	10–50%
▧	0.1–10%
☐	<0.1%

Relative Abundance, 1982–1989

Breeding Distribution, 1958

The Seaside Sparrow was found only in marshlands on the lower Eastern Shore. The highest abundance was recorded in the brackish marshes of the mainland of southern Dorchester County, where there is excellent road access to extensive marshes.

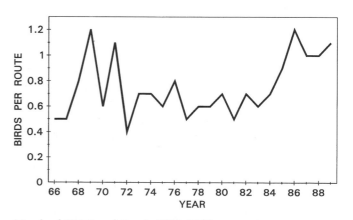

Maryland BBS Trend Graph, 1966–1989

MOB

Song Sparrow

Melospiza melodia

The aptly named Song Sparrow is widely distributed and common in most of Maryland during its breeding season and in migration; it is uncommon to abundant in winter (Stewart and Robbins 1958). Although most parts of the state have a resident population, large numbers of migrants also move through Maryland. Spring birds begin arriving in mid-February in most years and continue through April (Stewart and Robbins 1958). Fall migration spans late September to late November. Brackbill (1953) found that of 101 Song Sparrows banded at Baltimore in summer, 98 were summer residents and only 3 were permanent residents.

The status of Song Sparrows in Maryland has changed little during the past century. All early writers deemed it a common to abundant summer or year-round resident in Maryland and DC (Coues and Prentiss 1862, 1883; Richmond 1888; Kirkwood 1895; Eifrig 1904; Cooke 1929; Hampe and Kolb 1947). Stewart and Robbins (1958) described it as common during the breeding season from the western edge of the state to the tidewater areas of the Chesapeake Bay, becoming less common and more local in the interior of the Eastern and Western Shore sections.

Song Sparrows use many brushy and edge habitats, including residential areas, hedgerows, and the edges of woodlands and marshes (Stewart and Robbins 1958). The highest reported Maryland breeding density is 109 territorial males per 100 acres (40.5 ha) in a shrubby, stream-bordered field in Baltimore County (Cooley 1947). Territory is established principally or entirely by the male (Brackbill 1953) and in a special five-part ceremony that consists mainly of singing but also includes posturing and fighting (Nice 1937). Many

fieldworkers have commented on the variability of males' songs; individual birds have from 6 to 24 unique variations (Nice 1943). Males become strongly territorial in late winter and early spring and continue to be so through the end of the nesting period (Nice 1937). The territory is typically less than 1 acre (0.4 ha) (Nolan 1968).

Song Sparrows are usually monogamous, but polygyny occurs when the male dies during the breeding season or when there are excess females in the breeding population (Smith et al. 1982). Although both sexes influence the choice of nest site (Nice 1943), the female usually builds the nest (Nice 1937), a cup of grasses, weed stems, leaves, and bark fibers (Harrison 1975). Nest heights from the MNRF range from 0 to 10 ft (0–3.0 m), with a mean of 2.8 ft (0.9 m). Of 256 nests, only 10 were higher than 6 ft (1.8 m); 85 were at 1 ft (0.3 m) or less. The earliest Maryland egg date is 12 April; the latest is 21 August (Stewart and Robbins 1958). Clutch sizes in 152 Maryland nest records range from 2 to 6, with a mean of 3.9 (MNRF). Young have been found in the nest in Maryland from 1 May to 23 September, with peaks in late May and late June. Brood sizes in 126 nests (MNRF) range from 1 to 5 (mean of 3.3). Only the female incubates and broods the young (Nice 1937). Eggs hatch in 12 or 13 days, and young fledge in about 10 days, becoming independent at 28 to 30 days. Song Sparrows commonly raise two or, sometimes, three broods (Harrison 1975). Most fledglings are tended by a single parent; males are more likely to care for older offspring (Smith and Merkt 1980). The Song Sparrow is a favorite victim of the Brown-headed Cowbird (Nice 1937). Although only 14 of 253 Maryland nests (5.5%) were parasitized (MNRF), in Ontario 420 of 1,812 (23.2%) contained Brown-headed Cowbird eggs or young (Peck and James 1987).

Plant food dominates the Song Sparrow's diet, ranging in proportion from 54 percent in the spring to 92 percent in the fall (Martin et al. 1951). During spring and summer, insects form more than 40 percent of the diet.

Atlas fieldwork showed no appreciable change in this species' distribution during the past 100 years. It is locally distributed in southern Maryland and the interior of the southern Eastern Shore counties, where it occurs primarily around human habitation. Although absent from some of the more extensive marsh blocks, it was frequently found along marsh edges. "Confirmed" records were fairly frequent, in part because of its relative abundance and in part because of ease of locating fledged young.

BBS data from 1966 through 1989 show a significant average annual decline of 1.1 percent in Eastern Region populations; the Maryland population is stable. The Song Sparrow is found commonly in a wide variety of habitats. It is also reasonably tolerant of human presence and should remain a stable part of the breeding avifauna in Maryland for many years.

David A. Harvey and Joanne K. Solem

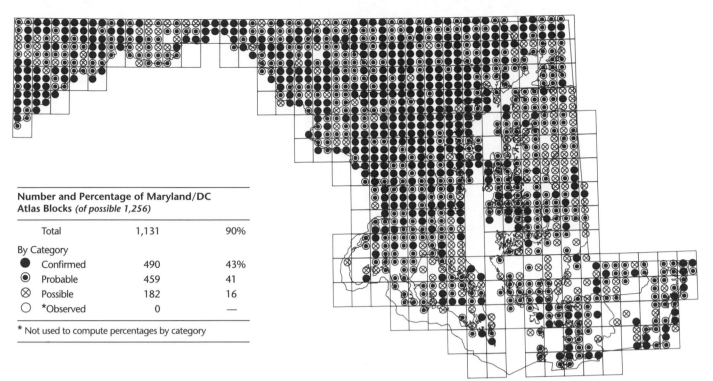

Number and Percentage of Maryland/DC Atlas Blocks *(of possible 1,256)*

	Total	1,131	90%
By Category			
●	Confirmed	490	43%
◉	Probable	459	41
⊗	Possible	182	16
○	*Observed	0	—

* Not used to compute percentages by category

Atlas Distribution, 1983–1987

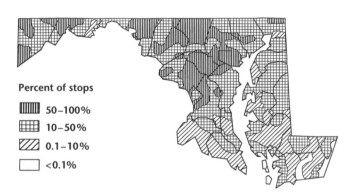

Percent of stops

⦀⦀	50–100%
▦	10–50%
▨	0.1–10%
☐	<0.1%

Relative Abundance, 1982–1989

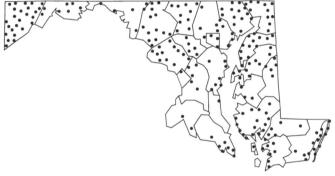

Breeding Distribution, 1958

The Song Sparrow is most abundant in the developed and agricultural areas of the Piedmont and Ridge and Valley sections and in the more open portions of the Allegheny Mountain Section. Numbers decrease to the south on the Coastal Plain, with most birds found in marshes and residential areas.

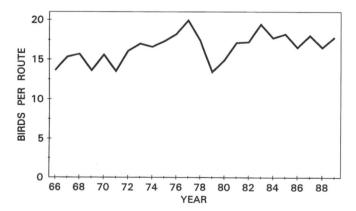

Maryland BBS Trend Graph, 1966–1989

Swamp Sparrow

Melospiza georgiana

Swamp Sparrows have long been known to breed in the mountain bogs of Garrett County (Eifrig 1904) and to winter in the other sections of Maryland (Stewart and Robbins 1958). Bond and Stewart (1951) described a new Coastal Plain subspecies (*M. g. nigrescens*) from the Nanticoke marshes near Vienna, Wicomico County; Stewart and Robbins (1958) reported it as breeding also in the Elkton marshes, Cecil County. This subspecies also breeds in tidal marshes in Delaware and New Jersey (AOU 1957). Spring migrants move through Maryland from mid-March to late May and fall migrants from mid-September to late November (Stewart and Robbins 1958). Greenberg and Droege (1990) found that Coastal Plain birds arrive later, appearing on the breeding grounds in mid- to late May.

Swamp Sparrows nest in wet shrubby and marshy habitat, usually with standing water (Greenberg 1988). In the mountains they are found in open spruce and alder bogs; in coastal areas they inhabit brackish and fresh marshes and wet meadows with scattered shrubs and small trees (Greenberg and Droege 1990). The highest Maryland breeding density in the mountains is 21 territorial males per 100 acres (40.5 ha) in an open spruce-hemlock bog in Garrett County (Robbins 1949c). Although Greenberg and Droege (1990) found most Coastal Plain birds nesting in small colonies or singly, they reported 50 to 70 pairs nesting in Black Marsh, Baltimore County, by far the largest single concentration reported in Maryland.

Clutch sizes in seven Maryland nests range from 3 to 5; brood sizes in three Maryland nest records are 2, 3, and 4 (MNRF). Maryland egg dates for ten clutches from mountain birds extend only from 2 to 22 June; brood dates are from 10 to 15 June. In New York, eggs have been found from 5 May to 22 July (Bull 1974), so the season in Maryland must be much longer than is indicated. Greenberg and Droege (1990) stated Coastal Plain birds from Black Marsh, Baltimore County, nest later than those in New York and Pennsylvania, with completed clutches not found until late May.

Clutch sizes in 23 Black Marsh nests ranged from 2 to 4, with a mean of 3.3 (S. Droege, unpub. data). Nest heights in both populations were always less than 3 ft (0.9 m) above water, although Wetherbee (1968) found nests several feet up in bushes in Massachusetts. There was a highly significant difference in clutch sizes between the populations (Greenberg and Droege 1990). Fifty-two New York and Pennsylvania clutches averaged 4.6 eggs, contrasted with an average 3.5 eggs for 34 Maryland Coastal Plain clutches. Greenberg and Droege (1990) suggest the lower clutch sizes for Coastal Plain nests are an adaptation permitting more successful renesting attempts that follow occasional spring high tides and storms, conditions experienced only by Coastal Plain birds. Nothing is known about the breeding biology of Piedmont and Ridge and Valley birds. The following information from Wetherbee (1968) may apply only to the inland population. Incubation, by the female only, requires 12 to 15 days. The male feeds the female while she is incubating and brooding. The young fledge after 11 to 13 days and are tended by both parents. Two broods are regularly attempted. Although 31 of 236 Ontario nests (13%) were parasitized by Brown-headed Cowbirds (Peck and James 1987), no Maryland parasitism has been reported.

The Swamp Sparrow diet consists equally of insects and plant seeds; animal matter is more important in the spring and early summer (Martin et al. 1951). The chief insect foods are beetles, ants, bees, caterpillars, grasshoppers, and crickets. Seeds of sedges, smartweed, panic grass, and vervain head the list of plant foods identified.

Prior to the Atlas work, the Coastal Plain Swamp Sparrows in Maryland were thought to be limited to a few sites along the Chesapeake Bay. Atlas fieldwork confirmed the distribution in the mountains of Garrett County to be as described by Stewart and Robbins (1958), but the range on the Coastal Plain proved more extensive than suspected. Although numerous only in Black Marsh, Swamp Sparrows are now widely distributed throughout the Maryland portion of the Chesapeake Bay and its tributaries, up the Potomac River into Montgomery County, and at inland locations in Baltimore and Carroll counties. It is still not certain whether birds at inland locations represent an extension of the Coastal Plain population or the mountain population, or whether they are intermediate between the two (Greenberg and Droege 1990).

BBS data from 1966 through 1989 show stable populations in the Eastern Region; there are too few data to estimate a Maryland trend. Much remains to be learned about breeding populations of Swamp Sparrows in Maryland. Protection of alder and spruce bogs in Garrett County is needed to maintain the Garrett County population. In the vicinity of the Chesapeake Bay and its tributaries, tidal brackish and fresh marshes should be preserved. Isolated breeding sites in the Piedmont should be protected. The Piedmont and Coastal Plain birds need further study to determine their relationship to other populations of the Swamp Sparrow.

Sam Droege and Eirik A. T. Blom

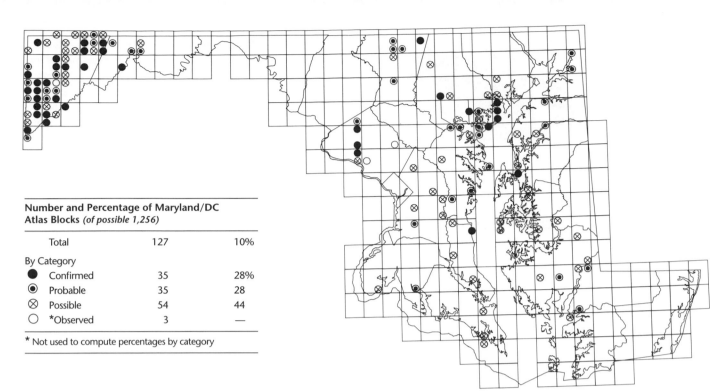

Number and Percentage of Maryland/DC Atlas Blocks *(of possible 1,256)*

Total	127	10%
By Category		
● Confirmed	35	28%
◉ Probable	35	28
⊗ Possible	54	44
○ *Observed	3	—

* Not used to compute percentages by category

Atlas Distribution, 1983–1987

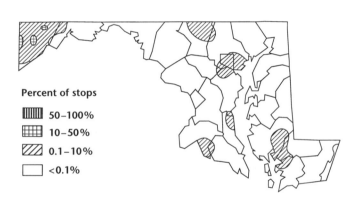

Percent of stops

▥	50–100%
▦	10–50%
▨	0.1–10%
▢	<0.1%

Relative Abundance, 1982–1989

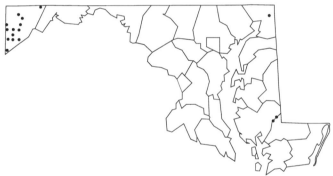

Breeding Distribution, 1958

The Swamp Sparrow is common only in the bogs and glades of Garrett County in the Allegheny Mountain Section. Small numbers were detected in marshes along the Chesapeake Bay and Potomac River and at two inland locations in Carroll County in the Piedmont Section.

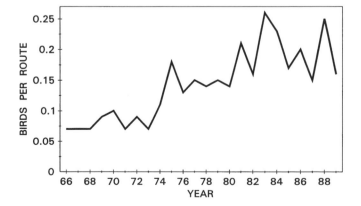

Maryland BBS Trend Graph, 1966–1989

MOB

Dark-eyed Junco

Junco hyemalis

Although it is a familiar winter visitor throughout Maryland, the Dark-eyed Junco nests only in the mountains of Garrett County. Its breeding range extends far to the north across Canada and Alaska, and south through the higher Appalachians to Georgia, and through the Rocky Mountains and along the Pacific Coast in the western U.S. (AOU 1983). The migration peaks in Maryland from mid-March to mid-April and from mid-October to mid-November (Stewart and Robbins 1958). In winter the Dark-eyed Junco is found at lower elevations in a variety of habitats, including woodland edges, thickets, brushy fields, hedgerows, roadsides, parks, gardens, and suburban lawns, where it is often seen foraging on the ground for seeds. In spring, insects and spiders comprise 60 percent of its diet, but by summer 90 percent is grass and weed seeds (Martin et al. 1951).

The four distinct forms of the Dark-eyed Junco (White-winged, Slate-colored, Oregon, and Gray-headed), which were formerly considered separate species, were lumped into one by the AOU (1983). The widespread Slate-colored form is the one that breeds and winters in Maryland. It includes *J. h. carolinensis,* the race that breeds in Maryland, and *J. h. hyemalis,* the race that winters throughout the state (Eaton 1968; Sprunt 1968). Some Dark-eyed Juncos migrate considerable distances. Birds banded in Maryland have been recovered as far north as Vermont, Ontario, and Quebec and as far south as South Carolina (Bird Banding Laboratory, unpub. data). The Appalachian birds, *J. h. carolinensis,* however, are short-distance migrants, retreating primarily to lower elevations for the winter (Hall 1983; Rabenold and Rabenold 1985).

The Dark-eyed Junco has been known as a breeder in the Appalachian Mountains of Maryland since the nineteenth century (Coues and Prentiss 1883). At the beginning of the twentieth century, it was described as breeding in numbers in the highest parts of Garrett County (Eifrig 1904). Stewart

and Robbins (1958) described it as nesting fairly commonly at elevations above 3,000 ft (914 m) on Backbone Mountain and uncommonly elsewhere above 2,500 ft (762 m) in Garrett County. Above 3,000 ft (914 m), it occurs in brushy cutover hardwood forests; below that height it occurs primarily in coniferous or mixed second-growth forest. It appears to have adapted well to humans, probably because it is partial to forest edges and cutover forests and because it benefits from bird feeders during winter. No breeding densities have been recorded in Maryland, but in nearby West Virginia, 92 territorial males per 100 acres (40.5 ha) were recorded in a virgin spruce-northern hardwood forest (Hall 1983).

Dark-eyed Junco nests are usually located on or near the ground, although they sometimes are found as high as 8 ft (2.4 m) or more in trees (Tanner 1958; Hostetter 1961; Sprunt 1968). Observations in Pennsylvania and Maine indicate that upturned tree trunks are favorite nest sites (Harrison 1975). In southwestern Virginia, they seem to prefer gently sloping banks with overhanging vegetation (Hostetter 1961). They occasionally nest in unusual places, such as porch beams (Hostetter 1961), tobacco cans (Eaton 1968), swinging fern baskets, and garage rafters (Sprunt 1968).

The female constructs a compact nest of grasses, rootlets, bark shreds, mosses, and twigs, lining it with finer grasses, rootlets, and hair (Hostetter 1961). Although the males have sometimes been observed carrying nesting material, they do not assist in either nest construction or incubation. They sing from a perch near the nest and actively defend the territory (Tanner 1958; Hostetter 1961). In Virginia, there are typically two broods, the first with 4 or 5 eggs, and the second with 3 (Hostetter 1961). In Garrett County, Maryland, eggs have been observed as early as 18 May and as late as 9 July, and nestlings from 31 May to 5 July (Stewart and Robbins 1958). Fledglings have been seen as early as 5 June (Ringler 1983b). Incubation takes 12 days, and the young fledge in another 12 days (Tanner 1958; Hostetter 1961). Both parents bring food to the young (100% insects) and attend to nest sanitation. Mortality in young birds is high, mainly because of predation. Tanner (1958) estimated a nesting success rate of between 35 percent and 40 percent in the Great Smoky Mountains; Hostetter (1961) estimated a rate of 53 percent in Virginia. In Virginia, chipmunks are among the chief predators, and population fluctuations of chipmunks greatly affect Dark-eyed Junco numbers (C. Ziegenfus, pers. comm.). The average annual survival rate of a winter population at PWRC was 53 percent (Karr et al. 1990). They are infrequent hosts of Brown-headed Cowbird parasitism (Friedmann 1963). Terrill (1961) listed only 8 of 75 Quebec nests (11%) as parasitized; Peck and James (1987) reported that 7 of 153 Ontario nests (4.6%) were parasitized. There are no records of parasitism from Maryland.

During the Atlas fieldwork, breeding was "confirmed" in five blocks in western Garrett County; "possible" or "probable" breeding was reported in an additional ten blocks in the same county. Adjacent areas in Pennsylvania, West Virginia, and western Virginia showed a similar pattern, all in areas with elevations above 2,500 ft (762 m). The Atlas map sug-

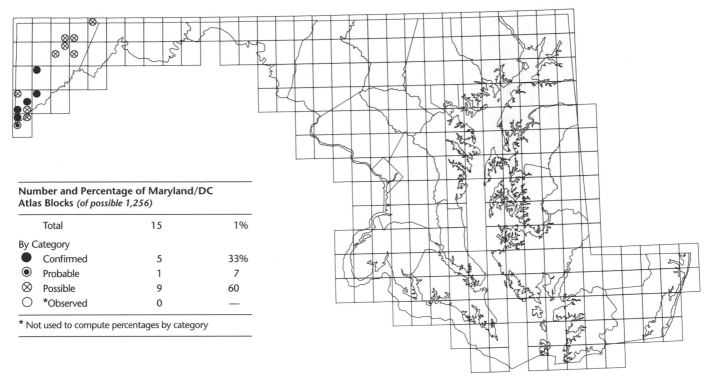

Number and Percentage of Maryland/DC Atlas Blocks *(of possible 1,256)*

Total	15	1%

By Category

●	Confirmed	5	33%
◉	Probable	1	7
⊗	Possible	9	60
○	*Observed	0	—

* Not used to compute percentages by category

Atlas Distribution, 1983–1987

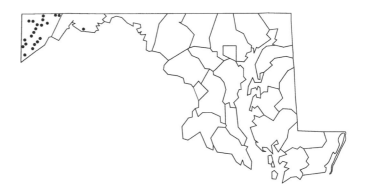

Breeding Distribution, 1958

gests the breeding distribution of the Dark-eyed Junco in Garrett County is more restricted than it was in 1958.

There are too few BBS routes in Maryland to estimate a state trend; however, data from 1966 through 1989 show stable populations in the Eastern Region. Little information was provided on Maryland breeding sites, but at least some were in road cuts, a favored breeding site in western Virginia (J. Simpson, pers. comm.). Further study of the Dark-eyed Junco's Maryland habitat is required to assess its needs.

Ann S. Hobbs

Bobolink

Dolichonyx oryzivorus

The male Bobolink, one of Maryland's showiest black-birds, is the only North American landbird that is white above and black below (Robbins et al. 1966); the sparrow-like female is nondescript and difficult to observe. Bobolinks breed in the northern United States and southern Canada and winter in southern South America from Peru to Argentina (AOU 1983); they are noted for the impressive distances they cover in migration. In Maryland, they announce their spring arrival in late April or early May (Robbins and Bystrak 1977) by their bubbling song that is frequently given in flight; they are most often observed as colorful flocks settling into agricultural fields. They linger in fall until mid-October. Huge fall flocks once gathered in tidal marshes; as many as 20,000 were recorded on 12 September 1899 in Snow's Marsh, Baltimore County (Stewart and Robbins 1958).

Historically, Bobolink populations have fluctuated with rollercoasterlike regularity, similar to, but more dramatically than, other meadow and hayfield birds (Arbib 1988b). Before colonial settlers drastically altered the landscape, the Bobolink was probably confined to river valleys with flood-plain fields and marsh borders (Eaton 1914; Forbush 1929), but it expanded rapidly as the inhospitable forests were cleared for agriculture. The increases continued through the eighteenth century, but in the mid-nineteenth century, a great slaughter of Bobolinks ensued when they seriously depredated southeastern rice fields during fall migration (Bent 1958). Although protected for many years, they have never reached their former numbers.

Kirkwood (1895) knew the Bobolink only as a migrant. Eifrig (1904), describing its status in western Maryland, could only speculate that it bred in some years in the fields of Garrett County. Stewart and Robbins (1958) called it fairly common in the Allegheny Mountain Section at elevations above 2,500 ft (762 m). They also cited isolated records from the Worthington Valley in Baltimore County and near Buckeystown in the Frederick Valley.

Bobolinks use tall grass fields, pastures, and grain fields for breeding (Terres 1980); in Garrett County, they favor hayfields in close association with dairy farms (B. Dowell, pers. obs.). In spring and summer, their diet consists largely of insects, especially caterpillars, grasshoppers, and beetles, but in fall it also includes large quantities of weed seeds, wild rice, and bristlegrass (Martin et al. 1951).

The nest is placed on the ground in a scrape, either natural or created by the female (Terres 1980). Clutch sizes for first broods vary from 4 to 7 and are most commonly 5 or 6 (Bent 1958). Incubation, by both sexes, lasts 10 to 13 days; the young fledge in 10 to 14 days. Bobolinks are regularly polygynous. Gavin (1984) documented renesting when clutches failed. Although one brood is typical (Bent 1958), Gavin (1984) found that second broods were common in some populations; however, clutch sizes dropped from a mean of 5.3 to 3.8 in second broods. In most populations, males are far more attentive to primary broods (Wittenberger 1980). Helpers have been seen feeding nestlings (Beason and Trout 1984).

The first nest reported for Maryland was found near Red House, Garrett County; it had eggs on 20 June 1932 (Brooks 1936). Brooks (1934) also reported a nest with a brood of 4 on 24 June 1932—possibly the same nest. In New York, eggs have been found from 18 May to 20 June, and nestlings from 30 May to 20 July (Bull 1974); Maryland's breeding season is probably similar. Friedmann (1963) considered the Bobolink an uncommon host of the Brown-headed Cowbird. No parasitism has been observed in Maryland; 8 of 136 Ontario nests (5.9%) were parasitized (Peck and James 1987).

Loss of farmland to development continues to reduce Bobolink nesting habitat. Bent (1958), discussing declines in the eastern part of the range, cited improved and earlier harvesting techniques as one cause for concern. There has also been concern about the changing practices of dairy farmers, who now cut hayfields two or three times per season, sometimes as early as late May (Ellison 1985b); this leaves insufficient time for Bobolinks to raise a brood of young between mowings. BBS data from 1966 through 1989 show stable populations in the Eastern Region; Maryland data are too few to estimate a trend.

During the Atlas period, Bobolinks nested throughout Garrett County and were scattered in the Frederick Valley. Because late migrants, even in small flocks, are regularly found into early June (R. Ringler, pers. comm.), it is difficult to establish the true breeding status in Frederick County. Records from Adams and York counties in Pennsylvania, just north of Frederick and Carroll counties, and from the Shenandoah Valley, just to the south in Virginia, suggest that Bobolinks sometimes breed in extensive fields in the Frederick Valley.

Although the Bobolink is well established in Garrett County and may breed in small numbers in the Frederick

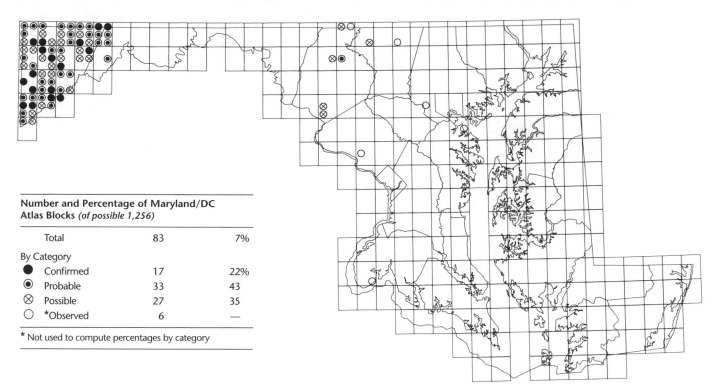

Number and Percentage of Maryland/DC Atlas Blocks *(of possible 1,256)*

Total	83	7%
By Category		
● Confirmed	17	22%
◉ Probable	33	43
⊗ Possible	27	35
○ *Observed	6	—

* Not used to compute percentages by category

Atlas Distribution, 1983–1987

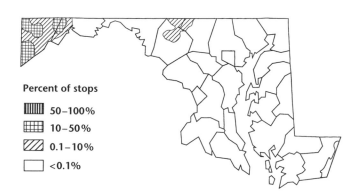

Percent of stops

▥	50–100%
▦	10–50%
▨	0.1–10%
☐	<0.1%

Relative Abundance, 1982–1989

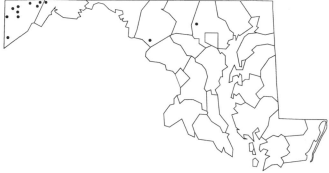

Breeding Distribution, 1958

The Bobolink is most common in open agricultural areas of Garrett County and less common in areas of mixed woods and fields in Garrett County and western Allegany County. A few were reported in agricultural areas of northern Frederick and northwestern Carroll counties in the Frederick Valley.

Valley, it, like all grassland species, is vulnerable to changes in agricultural practices. To ensure that this colorful blackbird remains a breeding species in Maryland, we must identify and preserve grasslands and determine more precisely the status and population trends of local breeding colonies.

Barbara A. Dowell

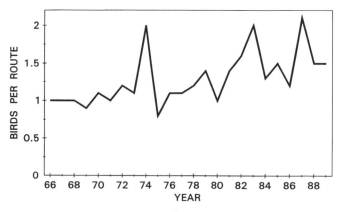

Maryland BBS Trend Graph, 1966–1989

Red-winged Blackbird

Agelaius phoeniceus

The Red-winged Blackbird is an abundant and conspicuous summer resident of marshes, grasslands, agricultural fields, and wet shrubby habitats throughout Maryland. It is common to locally abundant in the counties east of Frederick, Frederick County, and fairly common in the mountains and woodlands in the western part of the state (Stewart and Robbins 1958). The highest breeding density reported for Maryland is 73 territorial males per 100 acres (40.5 ha) in a cattail marsh in Calvert County in 1948 (Springer and Stewart 1948a).

All early writers considered the Red-winged Blackbird a common to abundant nesting bird and year-round resident (Coues and Prentiss 1862, 1883; Kirkwood 1895; Eifrig 1904; Cooke 1929). Many Red-winged Blackbirds are permanent residents in Maryland, but some of the state's breeding birds move south for the winter and are replaced by huge flocks that nest to the north but spend the winter in Maryland. Birds banded in Maryland have been recovered as far north as Vermont and Ontario and as far south as Georgia and Florida (Bird Banding Laboratory, unpub. data). Birds banded as far north as New Hampshire and Ontario, as far south as South Carolina and Louisiana, and as far west as Pennsylvania and Ohio have been encountered in Maryland. The migration peaks occur in March and from mid-October through the first two-thirds of November (Stewart and Robbins 1958). Frank Kirkwood saw "millions" at Carroll Island in Baltimore County on 15 March 1896 (Stewart and Robbins 1958).

In February, before the winter flocks disperse, territorial males are already filling Maryland marshes and cultivated fields with their gurgling *kong-ka-reee* whistle. As they sing, they spread their wings to expose their red, yellow, and white epaulets. Territorial activities begin on the breeding grounds by the end of February if the weather is warm. When the brown females arrive several weeks later, the battle is on to attract mates (Stokes 1979). Red-winged Blackbirds

are polygynous, and males average three mates per season. Those males with the more desirable territories attract the largest numbers of females (Ehrlich et al. 1988). The mates of each male usually begin their breeding cycles at different times (Stokes 1979). Each female defends a subterritory within her mate's territory. She builds the cup-shaped nest on aquatic vegetation in a marsh, among the weeds of a meadow, and, less frequently, in a tree, bush, or even on the ground. Sometimes a female stops feeding her fledglings to start a new nest while her mate continues feeding the young (Stokes 1979; Orians 1985).

In 319 Maryland nests (MNRF), heights range from 1 to 25 ft (0.3–7.6 m), with a mean of 3.6 ft (1.1 m). Maryland egg dates range from 28 April to 14 August (Robbins and Bystrak 1977), with a peak from mid-May through early June (MNRF). Clutch sizes in 300 Maryland nests range from 1 to 5 (mean of 3.2). Incubation, only by the female, lasts 10 to 12 days (Bent 1958). Nests with young have been found in Maryland from 12 May to 9 August (MNRF), with a peak in early to middle June. Brood sizes in 159 Maryland nests (MNRF) range from 1 to 4 (mean of 3.1). Friedmann (1963) called the Red-winged Blackbird a frequent victim of Brown-headed Cowbird parasitism, but only 2 from a random sample of 1,000 Maryland nests (0.2%) (MNRF) and 163 of 6,027 Ontario nests (2.7%) were parasitized (Peck and James 1987). The rate of parasitism varies greatly (0–54%) depending on habitat, density of Red-winged Blackbird nests, and time of year (Freeman et al. 1990). These birds thrive on the insects, such as weevils, other beetles, and caterpillars, that constitute half their diet during the breeding season (Martin et al. 1951).

Atlas results show only a few scattered blocks in which Red-winged Blackbirds were not found; most are largely open water or heavily forested. Fledged young and adults carrying food for young accounted for 56 percent of "confirmed" records.

As abundant and adaptable as this species seems to be, its numbers have been decreasing more than most people realize. BBS data from 1966 through 1989 show Red-winged Blackbird populations declining at a highly significant average annual rate of 1.7 percent in the Eastern Region and 2.1 percent in Maryland; however, the data for the continental population show only an indication of a decline. Maryland data from 1980 through 1989 show a stable population.

Habitat loss is certainly one factor in the decline in Maryland populations. Nesting sites disappear when fields and ponds are replaced by buildings and roads or when fields return to woodlands. Other possible causes of their decline are poisons in the food chain, pollution in the marshes, and changes in agricultural practices. Red-winged Blackbirds are very adaptable, however, and seem certain to remain a significant part of the Maryland avifauna for many years to come.

Claire E. Miller

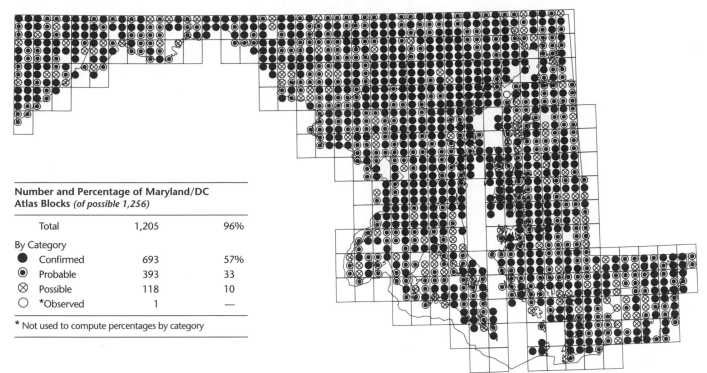

Atlas Distribution, 1983–1987

Number and Percentage of Maryland/DC Atlas Blocks *(of possible 1,256)*

	Total	1,205	96%
By Category			
●	Confirmed	693	57%
◉	Probable	393	33
⊗	Possible	118	10
○	*Observed	1	—

* Not used to compute percentages by category

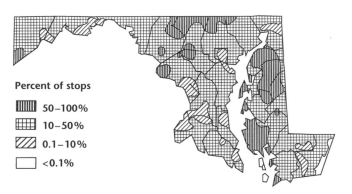

Percent of stops

▦	50–100%
▦	10–50%
▨	0.1–10%
☐	<0.1%

Relative Abundance, 1982–1989

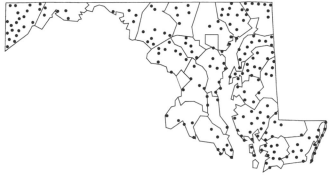

Breeding Distribution, 1958

The Red-winged Blackbird is abundant in marshes in Dorchester County and in agricultural areas in the Frederick Valley, northern Piedmont, and the northern Eastern Shore Section. It is least common in urban areas and the more wooded sections of the Coastal Plain.

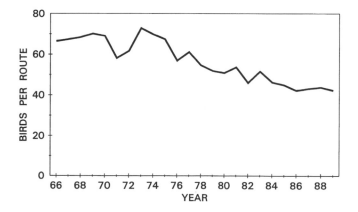

Maryland BBS Trend Graph, 1966–1989

E. Thompson

Eastern Meadowlark

Sturnella magna

The Eastern Meadowlark, with its bright yellow underparts and familiar whistled song, is a resident of grassy habitats. It is a widespread, common species found year-round in Maryland, although most individuals are migratory. Migration peaks occur from late March to mid-April and mid-October to mid-November (Stewart and Robbins 1958). It breeds throughout the state wherever there are extensive meadows or pastures; nests have been found at elevations up to 2,600 ft (793 m) in Garrett County (MNRF).

Early authors considered the Eastern Meadowlark a common permanent resident (Coues and Prentiss 1862, 1883; Kirkwood 1895; Cooke 1929). Stewart and Robbins (1958) described its breeding status as common in all sections. Favorable habitat increased after European settlers cleared the forests but has recently decreased as farms and fields have given way to development, reverted to forests, or shifted from pastures to row crops.

Nests are built on the ground, usually in a field or pasture, but sometimes in vacant lots and salt-meadow cordgrass marshes (MNRF). Of the three BBC plots cited by Stewart and Robbins (1958), this species was as common in one of the two marsh-meadow plots (Springer and Stewart 1948a) as in the mixed hayfield-pasture site, with a density in each of seven territorial males per 100 acres (40.5 ha).

The partly or completely domed cup nest is composed of grasses and, occasionally, of weed stems; it is placed in a hollow or in a clump of grasses or wildflowers (Gross 1958). The earliest Maryland date for nest building is 1 May (Stewart and Robbins 1958), but it surely occurs in late April. Eggs have been found from 4 May to 9 August, with peak periods in mid-May, early June, and late June (MNRF). Clutch sizes of 66 nests range from 1 to 6 (mean of 4.2). Young birds have been found in Maryland from 16 May to 31 July (MNRF). Brood sizes from 19 nests range from 2 to 6 (mean of 3.7). According to Friedmann (1963), the Eastern Meadowlark is an uncommon victim of the Brown-headed Cowbird; no

parasitism has been recorded in Maryland. Only 9 of 370 Ontario nests (2.4%) were parasitized (Peck and James 1987).

An eight-year Illinois study (Roseberry and Klimstra 1970) provided additional nesting information: Almost one-third of nests built were apparently not used for nesting; nest density was highest on ungrazed pasture and other idle and fallow areas. Vegetation cover around the nests ranged from 10 to 20 in. (25–51 cm) high. These authors considered the Eastern Meadowlark double-brooded, although it also laid replacement clutches; the percentage of successful nests increased as the season progressed. Nests in hayfields were less successful than in other habitats, apparently because of mowing schedules. Knapton (1988) found a higher nesting success rate among females mated to polygynous males than among those mated to monogamous males. According to Gross (1958), the female builds the nest and incubates for 13 to 15 days, and young fledge in 11 or 12 days. Eastern Meadowlarks are almost entirely insectivorous in summer; grasshoppers and crickets are the chief foods (Martin et al. 1951).

Atlas fieldworkers found the Eastern Meadowlark from sea level through the Allegheny Plateau. It was absent from large areas in the Baltimore-Washington corridor; this area lacks suitable habitat. As recently as 1929, however, Cooke (1929) still considered it common in the immediate DC area. Its absence from some blocks in the Allegheny Mountain and Ridge and Valley sections can be attributed to the extensive forests there. Near the Chesapeake Bay and the lower Potomac River, its spotty occurrence results from a lack of suitable habitat or the fact that many of these blocks are largely open water. In places such as southern Dorchester County, Eastern Meadowlarks breed in cordgrass dominated tidal marshes. Most "confirmed" records were of recently fledged young (36%) or of adults carrying food (45%).

BBS data from 1966 through 1989 show a highly significant average annual decline of 3.7 percent in the Eastern Region and 5.7 percent in Maryland. This decreased to a significant average annual decline of 3.2 percent in Maryland from 1980 to 1989. All neighboring states show decreases of similar magnitude. Maryland's population has not recovered from the sharp decline that occurred during the severe winters of 1976–77 and 1977–78.

The future of Eastern Meadowlarks depends on the continued presence of field, pasture, and meadow habitat. They are declining in Maryland and adjacent states as habitat is lost and agricultural practices change. Intensive management of hayfields and earlier and more frequent mowing adversely affect nesting success (S. Droege, pers. comm.). Also, the continued use of chemical fertilizers and pesticides disrupts Eastern Meadowlark habitat and food supply. To maintain the Eastern Meadowlark as a breeding bird in Maryland, it is essential to preserve grassland and pastureland habitats, to adjust mowing schedules, and to implement more biological and integrated pest management programs.

Robert Hilton

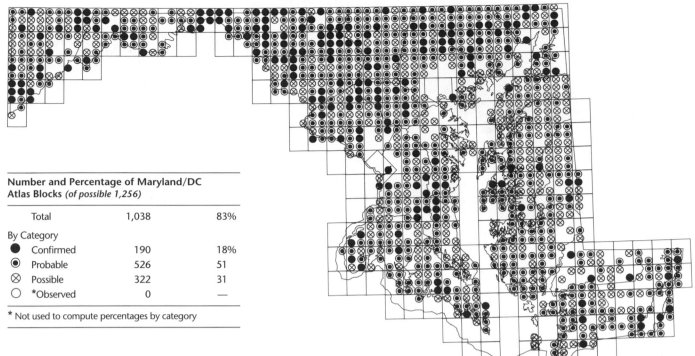

Atlas Distribution, 1983–1987

Number and Percentage of Maryland/DC Atlas Blocks *(of possible 1,256)*

	Total	1,038	83%
By Category			
●	Confirmed	190	18%
◉	Probable	526	51
⊗	Possible	322	31
○	*Observed	0	—

* Not used to compute percentages by category

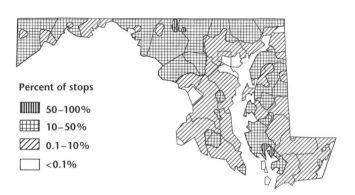

Percent of stops

▓	50–100%
▦	10–50%
▨	0.1–10%
☐	<0.1%

Relative Abundance, 1982–1989

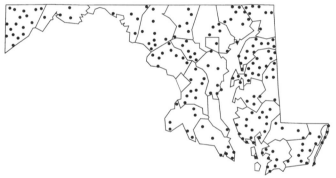

Breeding Distribution, 1958

The Eastern Meadowlark is abundant in scattered agricultural areas of the Piedmont and in marshes on the lower Eastern Shore. It is much less common in the most extensively wooded sections of the state and absent from a few urban areas.

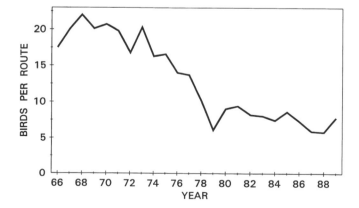

Maryland BBS Trend Graph, 1966–1989

Boat-tailed Grackle

Quiscalus major

Boat-tailed Grackles in Maryland are almost unknown more than a few miles from salt water. Nesting away from salt water north of central Florida is limited to a single instance in South Carolina (Post 1988). They are fairly common residents along the coast of Maryland and in southern portions of the Chesapeake Bay. Although a permanent resident, this species has some seasonal movement. Like other blackbirds, Boat-tailed Grackles gather in large flocks after the breeding season and disperse in April when nesting activity begins. They prefer nesting in brushy areas near salt water. Most Maryland records are for small groups, numbering up to 27 nests, although a few solitary nests have been reported (MNRF).

The first reported, and perhaps the first known, Maryland breeding colony (16 nests) was discovered by W. Wholey north of Ocean City, Worcester County, on 7 July 1892 (MNRF). Bailey (1913) suggested the Boat-tailed Grackle's range extended only as far north as Chincoteague and the Cedar Islands in Virginia, although he also wrote that this species was expanding northward each season (Sprunt 1958). Hampe and Kolb (1947) called it a regular but not common summer resident along the ocean in Worcester County, although they knew of no recent breeding records. Stewart and Robbins (1947a) wrote that in 1945 and 1946, the Boat-tailed Grackle occurred fairly commonly along the coast to the Delaware line and along the eastern shore of the Chesapeake Bay north to Deal Island WMA, Somerset County. In 1958 these authors listed the breeding status as fairly common in coastal Worcester County and in tidewater areas of Somerset County, and as rare, local, and irregular in the remaining tidewater areas of the Eastern and Western Shore sections. Since that time, it has expanded northward to Long Island, New York, where it bred in 1981 (Connor 1988).

Boat-tailed Grackles nest in bushes, shrubs, and small trees near salt marshes or on small brushy islands (MNRF). The female constructs a bulky nest of grasses and mud (Sprunt 1958). More than half of 66 Maryland nests were in groundsel trees; others were in bayberry, loblolly pine,

marsh elder, and eastern red cedar (MNRF). Heights above the ground or water of 70 Maryland nests range from 3 to 15 ft (0.9–4.6 m), most commonly 3.9 to 7.8 ft (1.2–2.4 m), with a mean of 6.2 ft (1.9 m). Maryland egg dates range from 24 April to 7 July (MNRF), peaking in June and early July. Clutch sizes from 85 Maryland nests range from 1 to 6 (mean of 2.7). The typical clutch is 3 eggs; exceptional clutches of 6 eggs may have been laid by more than one female. Although only one brood is raised per year, this may require up to three nesting attempts (Sprunt 1958). The female incubates for 14 days.

Brood sizes in 38 Maryland nests range from 1 to 4, with a mean of 2.3 (MNRF). Young have been found in the nest from 9 May to 26 July. It is unknown whether the Boat-tailed Grackle is promiscuous or polygamous, but Sprunt (1958) stated that it is certain that the male does not confine himself to one mate. Bancroft (1986), in a detailed Florida study, found that females do all the nest building, incubation, and care of nestlings. In large colonies or at sites with less than 0.12 acre (0.05 ha) of available habitat, males were unable to maintain exclusive territories, and nests often were less than 3 ft (0.9 m) apart—occasionally less than 1 ft (0.3 m). In 605 nests in cattails, 60.5 percent of nests with complete clutches fledged young. The greatest source of nest mortality was predators, which took 14.8 percent of 1,605 eggs and 13.1 percent of 1,145 nestlings. There are no records of Brown-headed Cowbird parasitism in this species (Friedmann 1929, 1963, 1971).

Boat-tailed Grackles forage in salt marshes, along sandy beaches, and on mud flats as well as in fields, on lawns, in parking lots, and in a variety of other habitats close to humans. Animal food, especially crustaceans, beetles, and grasshoppers, comprises their principal diet in summer, but corn is the chief food during other seasons (Martin et al. 1951).

Atlas results show that Boat-tailed Grackles are now common breeders in the tidal areas of Worcester and Somerset counties and have expanded their range since 1958 (Stewart and Robbins 1958). They are now locally uncommon to fairly common along the western and southern edges of Dorchester County and southwestern Wicomico County. One "confirmed" record and five "possible" records came from the Western Shore, in southern St. Mary's County. One-third (35%) of Atlas records were "confirmed," most of fledglings or of females carrying food. BBS data from 1966 through 1989 show stable populations in the Eastern Region; there are too few data to estimate a Maryland trend.

Boat-tailed Grackle populations appear to be stable, or even increasing, in Maryland. Nest building was recorded at Tilghman Island in Talbot County in 1991. Year-to-year fluctuations in numbers is normal in colonial nesting species and they frequently shift to different nesting sites. As long as there are plenty of protected bushy areas with adjacent salt marshes, this species should maintain its present population level.

Michael O'Brien

Number and Percentage of Maryland/DC Atlas Blocks *(of possible 1,256)*

	Total	79	6%
By Category			
●	Confirmed	27	34%
◉	Probable	34	43
⊗	Possible	18	23
○	*Observed	0	—

* Not used to compute percentages by category

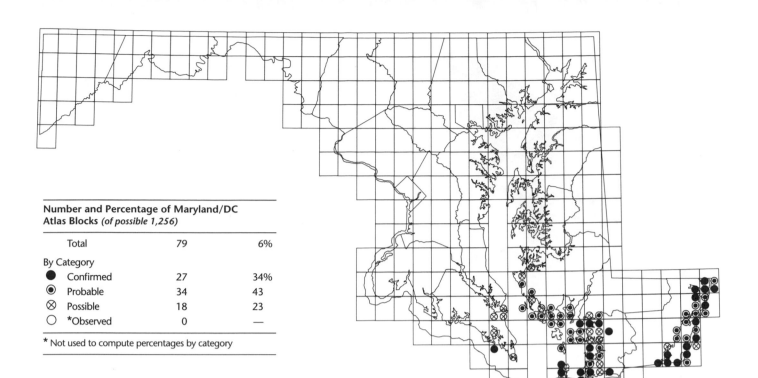

Atlas Distribution, 1983–1987

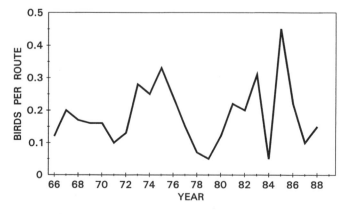

Breeding Distribution, 1958

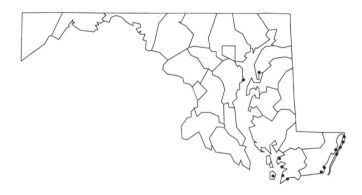

Maryland BBS Trend Graph, 1966–1989

Boat-tailed Grackle 419

Common Grackle

Quiscalus quiscula

The wide range of nest sites used by the Common Grackle helps explain its breeding status as common to abundant throughout Maryland. It nests singly and in colonies, from the Eastern Shore through the Allegheny Mountains, at various elevations, and in diverse habitats (MNRF). Evergreen trees near agricultural land or in residential areas are prime nesting habitat. Millions of grackles spend at least part of the winter on Maryland's Eastern Shore. Peak migration periods are late February to late March and late October to late November (Stewart and Robbins 1958).

Corn, oats, wheat, and acorns constitute the majority of the diet, except in summer, when animal food dominates (Martin et al. 1951). In addition to insects, especially bees, grasshoppers, and crickets, Common Grackles eat earthworms, snails, toads, salamanders, mice, and birds' eggs.

Coues and Prentiss (1862, 1883) reported the Crow Blackbird, as the Common Grackle was then known, to be an abundant summer resident, breeding in smaller numbers than the flocks observed during spring and fall migration. Stewart and Robbins (1958) described its breeding status as abundant in the Eastern Shore and Upper Chesapeake sections and in the southern part of the Western Shore Section; common in the Piedmont and the eastern part of the Ridge and Valley Section; and fairly common but somewhat local in the Allegheny Mountain, western Ridge and Valley, and northern Western Shore sections. BBS data from 1966 through 1989 show a highly significant decline of 1.8 percent in Eastern populations but a stable Maryland population. A Maryland peak in 1970 was followed by a gradual decline through 1989 attributed, in part, to blackbird control operations at winter roosts in the southern United States (Robbins et al. 1986). Despite this decline, the BBS identifies Maryland and its neighboring states of Delaware and Virginia as a region in which the Common Grackle occurs in greatest abundance.

Most Common Grackles in Maryland nest in loose colonies in evergreen trees in residential or farming communities (MNRF). Nest-site selection begins after the female is paired, and nest completion takes about two weeks. During this time, the male defends not only the area close to the nest site but also the female when she is away from the nest (Ficken 1963), following her closely to defend her against other males. The area the Common Grackle defends is so small that Howe (1979) referred to this species as nonterritorial. Maxwell and Putnam (1972) reported variable roles for each parent during the breeding cycle. Howe (1978) stated the species is mainly monogamous, although polygyny is not uncommon.

An analysis of 2,601 nest cards maintained by the Cornell Laboratory of Ornithology showed that 62.5 percent of these nests were located in coniferous trees, 23.4 percent in deciduous trees, 7.8 percent in shrubs, and 6.3 percent in other nest sites, including cavities (Maxwell et al. 1976). This analysis reported the mean nest height as 7.5 ft (2.3 m) in coniferous trees, 10.8 ft (3.3 m) in deciduous trees, and 5.9 ft (1.8 m) in shrubs. Heights of 278 Maryland nests (MNRF) range from 2 to 80 ft (0.6–24 m), with a mean of 14 ft (4.3 m). Bent (1958) stated that nest structure varies less than nesting site. The well-made, bulky nests are typically 3 in. (8 cm) deep, 4 in. (10 cm) in internal diameter, 5 to 8 in. (13–20 cm) in height, and 7 to 9 in. (18–23 cm) in external diameter. At least one Maryland nest was found in a Purple Martin box (K. Klimkiewicz, unpub. data).

Nests with eggs have been reported in Maryland from 27 March to 16 August, with peaks in late April and mid-May (MNRF). Clutch sizes in 164 Maryland nests (MNRF) range from 2 to 7 (mean of 4.4). The female incubates the eggs for 11 days (Bent 1958). Nests with young have been found in Maryland from 13 April to 8 July, with a peak in mid-May (MNRF). Based on the late egg date of 16 August, it is clear that nests with young occasionally occur into late August. Brood sizes of 132 Maryland nests (MNRF) range from 1 to 6 (mean of 3.3). Common Grackles are rarely parasitized by Brown-headed Cowbirds (Friedmann 1963). Peck and James (1987) reported that only 4 of 2,091 Ontario nests (0.2%) were parasitized. Only 1 of a random sample of 1,000 Maryland nests (0.1%) was parasitized (MNRF).

Atlas fieldworkers found the Common Grackle breeding throughout Maryland. It was least widespread in the extensive brackish marshes of the lower Chesapeake Bay and on Assateague Island, Worcester County. Only the Barn Swallow and the Northern Cardinal were found in more Atlas blocks. The high percentage of "confirmed" records (77%) shows the Common Grackle is abundant and conspicuous and has adapted to the presence of humans near its nest sites. Most "confirmed" records were of fledged young (42%) or adults with food for young (38%).

The outlook for the Common Grackle in Maryland is bright. It promises to be one of our more common nesters for years to come.

Jane H. Farrell

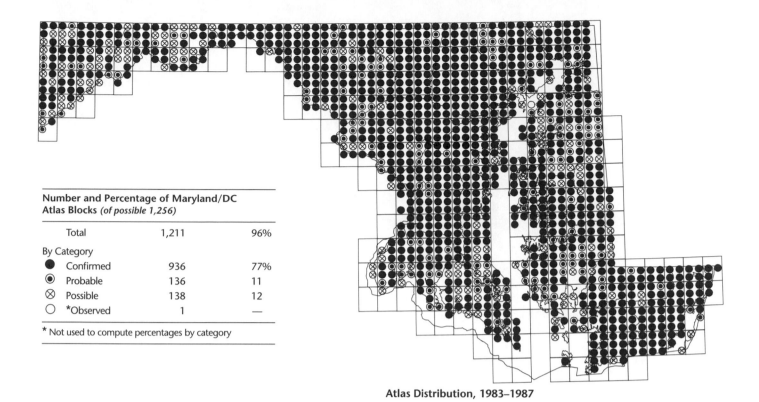

Atlas Distribution, 1983–1987

Number and Percentage of Maryland/DC Atlas Blocks *(of possible 1,256)*		
Total	1,211	96%
By Category		
● Confirmed	936	77%
◉ Probable	136	11
⊗ Possible	138	12
○ *Observed	1	—

* Not used to compute percentages by category

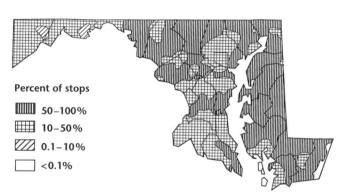

Percent of stops

▥	50–100%
▦	10–50%
▨	0.1–10%
☐	<0.1%

Relative Abundance, 1982–1989

Breeding Distribution, 1958

The Common Grackle is most abundant in the agricultural areas of the Eastern Shore, the Piedmont Section, and the Hagerstown Valley. Lower numbers are found in urban and marsh habitats and in the heavily wooded areas of the Ridge and Valley and Allegheny Mountain sections in western Maryland.

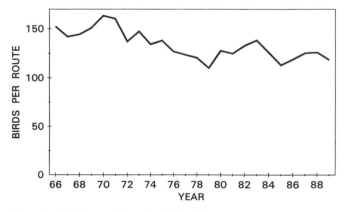

Maryland BBS Trend Graph, 1966–1989

Brown-headed Cowbird

Molothrus ater

Many birdwatchers speak disparagingly about the Brown-headed Cowbird. The generic epithet, *Molothrus,* means "parasite, tramp, or vagabond" (Bent 1958); it is an obligate parasite and lays its eggs in nests of other species, leaving the host to rear its young. Among many colloquial names for this species are Buffalo Bird, Cow Blackbird, Cuckold, and Lazybird; the first two reflect its tendency to feed near domestic or wild cattle (Terres 1980).

Brown-headed Cowbird populations have increased in Maryland and DC during the past 100 years. Coues and Prentiss (1883) called it a not very common summer resident of DC; Kirkwood (1895) implied they were uncommon in summer. Cooke (1929) referred to it as "tolerably" common in summer. By the 1950s it was a fairly common summer resident throughout Maryland except in the Western Shore Section, where it was uncommon (Stewart and Robbins 1958). It is common to uncommon in winter in Maryland, except in the Allegheny Mountain Section, where it is rare. Maryland birds winter from Pennsylvania to Georgia and Alabama (Bird Banding Laboratory, unpub. data). Spring migration begins in early February and is complete by mid-April.

Male Brown-headed Cowbirds are monogamous to totally promiscuous, depending on the density of available host nests (Ehrlich et al. 1988). When more nests are available, they become more monogamous. Males usually establish a small territory with a singing tree; females establish a breeding territory (Bent 1958). Territories are not aggressively defended; two females may lay in the same nest (Stokes and Stokes 1983). To find host nests, females observe quietly from a high perch, move quietly through the shrubs or on the ground, or fly vigorously into bushes to flush nesting birds (Stokes and Stokes 1983). Females usually wait until the host has laid 2 or more eggs before depositing their own. Often they remove a host egg either the day before or the day after they lay their egg (Pettingill 1970).

Heights above the ground for 107 parasitized Maryland nests (MNRF) range from 0 to 29 ft (0.0–8.8 m), with a mean of 5.2 ft (1.6 m). This mean may be low owing to observer inability to examine high nests. Eggs have been found in Maryland as early as 17 April and as late as 28 July, peaking between 14 May and 20 June (MNRF). The female lays up to 25 eggs in a season (Friedmann 1963). One egg per host nest is normal, but as many as 4 have been noted (MNRF). The incubation period is 11 or 12 days; the Brown-headed Cowbird often hatches a day or so before the host eggs, giving it an advantage (Bent 1958). Nests with young have been recorded in Maryland from 4 May to 14 July (MNRF).

Maryland records (MNRF) show 58 host species, including 19 warblers. Half the eggs or young were found with five host species: Red-eyed Vireo (15.7%), Song Sparrow (12.0%), Northern Cardinal (8.5%), Wood Thrush (7.2%), and Field Sparrow (6.6%). These data are consistent with the findings of Friedmann (1929), who noted that most victims were in four families: flycatchers, finches and sparrows, vireos, and warblers. Friedmann et al. (1977) found 216 species that serve as Brown-headed Cowbird hosts in North America, but only 139 of those were true fosterers. Species that eject Brown-headed Cowbird eggs, abandon the nest, or build another nest on top of the first are hosts but not fosterers; they include the American Robin, Gray Catbird, Eastern Kingbird, Blue Jay, Brown Thrasher, and Yellow Warbler. In summer, 50 percent of the Brown-headed Cowbird diet is insects, especially grasshoppers; in winter more than 90 percent is weed seeds and grain (Martin et al. 1951).

Atlas results show Brown-headed Cowbirds widespread throughout the state. Most "confirmed" records (78%) were of host species feeding young Brown-headed Cowbirds. Nearly half the "probable" records (49%) were of pair sightings. The high number of "possible" reports reflects the difficulty of finding specific breeding evidence.

There is no reason for concern about the long-term survival of the Brown-headed Cowbird. Although BBS data from 1966 through 1989 indicate a stable Maryland population, the Eastern Region shows a highly significant average annual decline of 2.3 percent and the continental population indicates an increase. Of greater concern are its effects on the host species. Although one study showed that rearing a young Brown-headed Cowbird reduced the host brood by an average of only one fledgling (Stokes and Stokes 1983), species that abandon a nest rather than tolerate the egg may fail to produce any young during that season (Ehrlich et al. 1988). Conservation efforts on behalf of these host species may be necessary. Increasing fragmentation of Maryland's forests since the 1940s has led to a dramatic increase in Brown-headed Cowbird parasitism (Robbins et al. 1986). More effort must be devoted to protecting the integrity of our forest ecosystems to prevent further fragmentation, which will lead to increases in Brown-headed Cowbird parasitism.

Alfred J. Fletcher and Emily D. Joyce

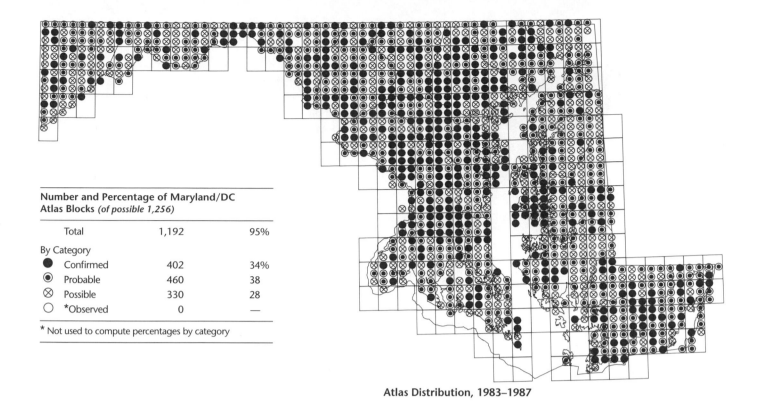

Number and Percentage of Maryland/DC Atlas Blocks *(of possible 1,256)*

	Total	1,192	95%
By Category			
● Confirmed		402	34%
◉ Probable		460	38
⊗ Possible		330	28
○ *Observed		0	—

* Not used to compute percentages by category

Atlas Distribution, 1983–1987

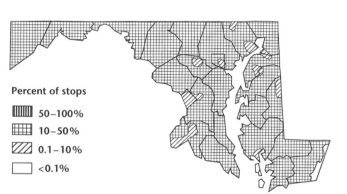

Percent of stops

- ▥ 50–100%
- ▦ 10–50%
- ▨ 0.1–10%
- ☐ <0.1%

Relative Abundance, 1982–1989

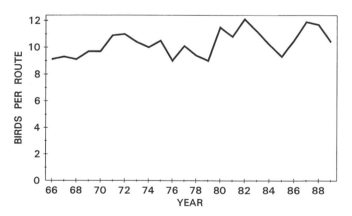

Breeding Distribution, 1958

The Brown-headed Cowbird is common and evenly distributed throughout the state. The scattered lower densities are principally in urbanized and developed areas and in the marsh blocks of southern Dorchester County.

Maryland BBS Trend Graph, 1966–1989

Orchard Oriole

Icterus spurius

The Orchard Oriole is an inconspicuous summer resident of suburban trees and farm orchards. It spends as few as ten weeks in Maryland each year before returning to its Central and South American wintering grounds (AOU 1983). The first spring migrants arrive in late April; fall migrants are on the move in mid-July and leave by early September (Stewart and Robbins 1958).

Coues and Prentiss (1862, 1883) called the Orchard Oriole a not uncommon breeding bird around DC; Kirkwood (1895) stated that it was common in Maryland, although he had only one record from western Maryland. Eifrig (1904) reported it was not common in Garrett and Allegany counties and was apparently absent from the higher elevations. Although Hampe and Kolb (1947) called it a common summer resident in all sections of the state, Stewart and Robbins (1958) described its summer distribution as common in the Eastern and Western Shore sections, fairly common in the Upper Chesapeake and Piedmont sections, uncommon in the Ridge and Valley Section, and rare in the Allegheny Mountain Section.

Judd (1902) counted about a dozen Orchard Oriole pairs nesting on a 230-acre (93-ha) farm along the Potomac River in Charles County. He noted that they preferred trees along the river bank rather than those along the fence lines and that they tended to nest near Eastern Kingbirds. They avoid heavily forested areas but favor street trees and yards of towns and suburbs, farmyards, and orchards (Bent 1958). On the Eastern Shore, they can also be found in loblolly pines along tidal marsh edges (Stewart and Robbins 1958). The highest breeding density recorded in Maryland is 29 territorial males per 100 acres (40.5 ha) in farmyards and small or-

chards in Prince George's County in 1951 (Stewart and Robbins 1958).

The nest is woven from grasses and suspended from a forked terminal twig 10 to 20 ft (3–6.1 m) above the ground, well hidden by surrounding leaves (Bent 1958). Nests in marsh plants such as phragmites have been observed (Bent 1958). Heights above the ground of 133 Maryland nests (MNRF) range from 5 to 65 ft (1.5–20 m), with a mean of 18 ft (5.5 m). Maryland egg dates range from 16 May to 14 July, peaking in late May and early June. Clutch sizes in 53 Maryland nests (MNRF) range from 2 to 6 (mean of 4.20). Incubation, by the female, takes 12 to 14 days (Bent 1958), during which time the male feeds the female. Nests with young have been found in Maryland from 27 May to the very late date of 14 August, with a peak in mid-June (MNRF). Brood sizes in 44 nests range from 1 to 5 (mean of 2.9). The young are fed by both parents and fledge in 11 to 14 days (Bent 1958). Normally there is only one brood, and both parents are very protective of the eggs and the young (Bent 1958).

Orchard Orioles are frequent victims of Brown-headed Cowbirds (Friedmann 1963). Of 24 Ontario nests, 7 (29.2%) were parasitized (Peck and James 1987); of 111 Maryland nests, only 5 (4.5%) contained Brown-headed Cowbird eggs or young. One Maryland nest held 4 eggs of each species (MNRF). Caterpillars are the main food item, followed by bugs, grasshoppers, ants, beetles, and spiders (Martin et al. 1951).

More than half (53%) the "confirmed" records were of fledged young or adults with food for young. Atlas results show Orchard Orioles widely distributed throughout the state; they were found in nearly every block in the Eastern Shore and Upper Chesapeake sections. Elsewhere in Maryland, the map indicates a decline in frequency toward the north and west. They were reported in only a few blocks in Garrett County, with no "confirmed" records. As the Atlas map shows, Orchard Orioles avoid the most heavily urbanized blocks. Pennsylvania Atlas data showed the densest distribution along that state's southern border, particularly in the southeast and southwest corners (Brauning 1992). Populations were low in the mountains and in northern Pennsylvania. In Virginia, the distribution appeared fairly uniform, with the fewest records in the Piedmont and the mountains.

BBS data from 1966 through 1989 show a highly significant average annual increase of 6.3 percent in Maryland. Data from 1966 through 1989 show stable populations in the Eastern Region and a highly significant average annual decline of 1.5 percent for the continent. The future of the Orchard Oriole in Maryland seems bright.

George B. Wilmot

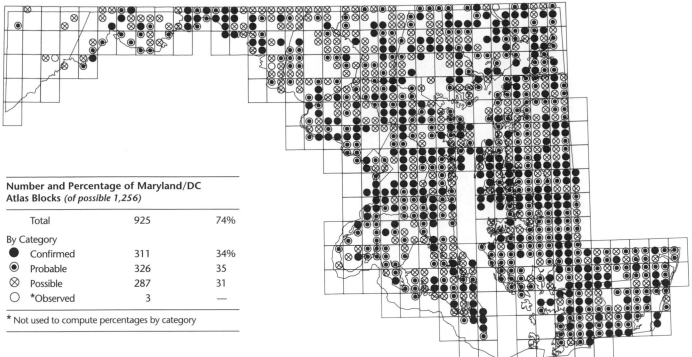

Atlas Distribution, 1983–1987

Number and Percentage of Maryland/DC Atlas Blocks (of possible 1,256)

	Total	925	74%
By Category			
●	Confirmed	311	34%
◉	Probable	326	35
⊗	Possible	287	31
○	*Observed	3	—

* Not used to compute percentages by category

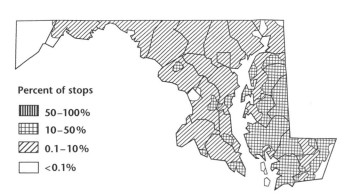

Percent of stops

▦	50–100%
▦	10–50%
▨	0.1–10%
☐	<0.1%

Relative Abundance, 1982–1989

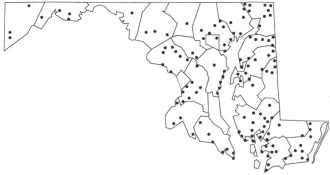

Breeding Distribution, 1958

The Orchard Oriole is most common on the Eastern Shore and in scattered pockets in southern Maryland, with numbers decreasing to the north and west. The band of low abundance on the southern Eastern Shore represents the extensive wet woodlands of the Pocomoke River and its tributaries.

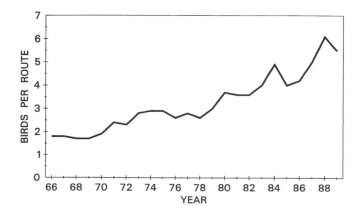

Maryland BBS Trend Graph, 1966–1989

Baltimore Oriole

Icterus galbula

The AOU (1983) combined the eastern Baltimore Oriole and the western Bullock's Oriole into a single species, the Northern Oriole, then separated them thirteen years later (AOU 1995). Whatever its official name, this handsome bird will always be the Baltimore Oriole to birdwatchers and other Maryland residents. It is the state bird, and the Baltimore baseball team is named for it. Legend has it that George Calvert, the first Baron Baltimore, was cheered by its beauty and took its colors for his coat of arms. Later, when Linnaeus saw the skins of the Golden Robin or Fire-hangbird, he named it the Baltimore Oriole, as it wore the colors of Lord Baltimore (Forbush 1927). The appearance of the two males is so distinct that field observers had continued to use the names Baltimore and Bullock's (Robbins et al. 1986) during the brief time these two species were combined.

Coues and Prentiss (1862, 1883) considered the Baltimore Oriole chiefly a spring and autumn migrant, although they noted that many bred. Kirkwood (1895) called it a locally common summer resident. Stewart and Robbins (1958) listed it as a fairly common breeding bird in the Allegheny Mountain, Ridge and Valley, and Piedmont sections; uncommon in the Upper Chesapeake and Eastern Shore sections; and rare, or perhaps absent, in the Western Shore Section. During migration it is fairly common in all sections. Spring migration is from late April to late May, with a peak in mid-May; fall migration is from early August to late September, with a peak between 20 August and 15 September. The winter range extends from Mexico to northern South America (AOU 1983).

The Baltimore Oriole nests in shade trees in residential areas, on farms, and in open stands of floodplain and moist upland forests (Stewart and Robbins 1958). Baltimore County had a high nesting density of 10 territorial males per 100 acres (40.5 ha) in a mixed habitat of tall trees and shrubs at Lake Roland (Cooley 1947). The nest—deeply pendent, like a sock, with a side entrance near the top—hangs by its rim from the tip of a drooping forked branch, usually high in a deciduous tree (Tyler 1958a). It is woven of long fibers, such as string, grapevine bark, and, when available, horsehair. Soft materials like hair, wool, and soft grass line the nest, which takes five to eight days to complete and is about 5 in. (13 cm) long and 2.5 in. (6 cm) wide. The female is the principal nest builder and builds a new nest each year. The Baltimore Oriole is single-brooded.

The nesting period of early May to early July peaks between mid-May and mid-June (MNRF). The earliest recorded nest-building date is 28 April (Ringler 1990b). Heights of 141 Maryland nests (MNRF) range from 5 to 100 ft (1.5–31 m), with a mean of 30 ft (9.1 m); 80 percent are 40 ft (12 m) or lower. Clutch sizes from 12 nests range from 2 to 6 (mean of 4.5). Although the earliest observed egg date is 18 May, an earlier date of about 4 May can be reached by subtracting the 14-day incubation period from the earliest date for young. The latest egg date is 16 June. The female incubates the eggs for 12 to 14 days (Forbush 1927). Brood sizes in 32 Maryland nests range from 1 to 5, with a mean of 2.4 (MNRF). The earliest date of a nest with young is 18 May; the latest is 27 August, with a peak in mid-June (MNRF). Both parents tend the nestlings for 12 to 14 days (Stokes and Stokes 1983). Friedmann (1929, 1963) considered the Baltimore Oriole an uncommon victim of the Brown-headed Cowbird. Peck and James (1987) reported a 6 percent parasitism rate (10 of 168 nests) in Ontario. This rate may be low because the Baltimore Oriole frequently rejects Brown-headed Cowbirds eggs (Rothstein 1975). No Maryland records exist.

Northern Orioles feed heavily on caterpillars, often destroying whole infestations of the forest tent caterpillar. They also eat larvae of the whitemarked tussock moth, gypsy moth, and browntail moth, and even the spiny caterpillar of the mourning cloak butterfly (McAtee 1926).

Atlas data show the Baltimore Oriole is widespread throughout the Allegheny Mountain, Ridge and Valley, and Piedmont sections; spottily distributed in the northern Coastal Plain; and decreasing south into southern Maryland and on the lower Eastern Shore. The major change since the 1950s is expansion into the Western Shore Section. Because of the difficulty of examining its highly placed pendent nests, only 48 "confirmed" records (12%) resulted from the examination of nest contents. Most of these were observations of fledged young (22%), occupied nests (19%), or nest building (16%).

BBS data from 1966 through 1989 show stable populations in the Eastern Region and Maryland; Maryland data from 1980 through 1989, however, indicate a decline. Continental data from 1966 through 1989 indicate an increase in Baltimore Oriole populations. Robbins et al. (1989b) concluded that forest destruction in both the breeding and wintering ranges is contributing to population declines of migratory forest birds, including the Baltimore Oriole. Protection of breeding and wintering habitat is required to maintain healthy Baltimore Oriole populations.

John Cullom

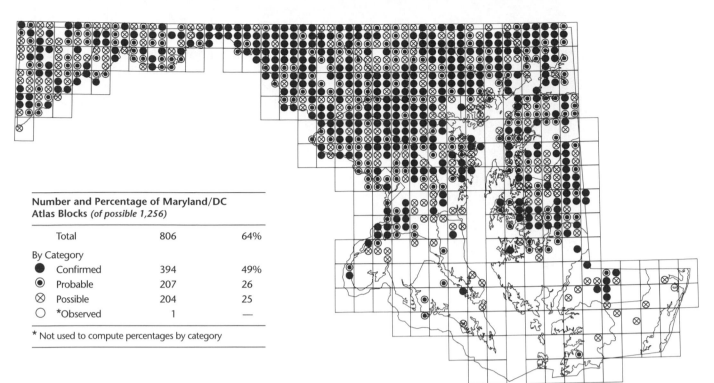

Number and Percentage of Maryland/DC Atlas Blocks *(of possible 1,256)*

Total	806	64%
By Category		
● Confirmed	394	49%
◉ Probable	207	26
⊗ Possible	204	25
○ *Observed	1	—

* Not used to compute percentages by category

Atlas Distribution, 1983–1987

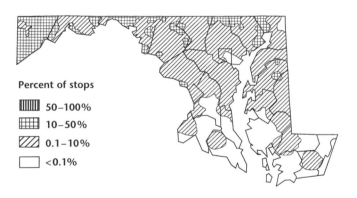

Percent of stops

▦	50–100%
▦	10–50%
▨	0.1–10%
☐	<0.1%

Relative Abundance, 1982–1989

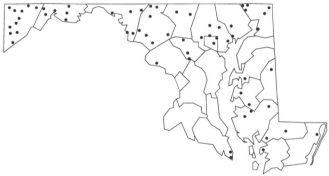

Breeding Distribution, 1958

The Baltimore Oriole is most common in the western and northern parts of the state. It decreases to the south and east and is uncommon to rare and local on most of the Coastal Plain.

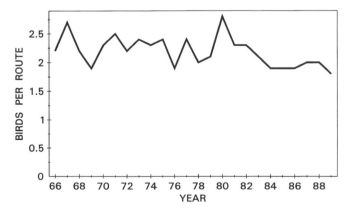

Maryland BBS Trend Graph, 1966–1989

MOB

Purple Finch

Carpodacus purpureus

The Purple Finch breeds in the high mountains of western Maryland, near the southern limit of its eastern breeding range (AOU 1983). All Maryland nesting reports are from Garrett County. Its winter range in the East extends from southern Ontario to the Gulf Coast (AOU 1983). In recent years many observers have commented on declining winter populations and have suggested, as has Shedd (1990), that the cause may be competition with the recently established and expanding House Finch population. Although Purple Finches can be found in Maryland annually during migration and winter, their numbers vary considerably. Kennard (1977) reported that southward movements are biennial and are tied to seed production in conifers. Spring migration spans mid-March to mid-May, and fall migration extends from mid-September to mid-November (Stewart and Robbins 1958).

Scarcity of historical data make it impossible to determine with certainty any trends associated with breeding Purple Finches in Maryland. Except for Eifrig (1904), who collected a summer male near Accident in Garrett County on 27 July 1903, early authors considered the Purple Finch only an irregular migrant and winter visitor (Coues and Prentiss 1883; Kirkwood 1895; Cooke 1929). Brooks (1936) reported nesting at Cranesville Swamp but supplied no details, and Stewart and Robbins (1947b) cited summer records from Cherry Creek Swamp near McHenry. The first confirmed breeding record for the state was on 29 May 1949, when a nest with eggs was found in the Maryland portion of Cranesville Swamp (Robbins 1949c). A decade later Stewart and Robbins (1958) described this finch as an uncommon to occasionally fairly common breeding bird in Garrett County.

In Maryland, the breeding habitat consists primarily of coniferous trees, especially spruce and eastern hemlock, in bogs and along streams. The Purple Finch is usually found at elevations above 2,500 ft (762 m) (Stewart and Robbins 1958). It typically places its nest well away from the trunk in a conifer, 6 to 40 ft (1.8–12 m) above the ground (Bent 1968d). Clutch sizes range from 3 to 6, with 4 and 5 most common. Incubation, by the female, lasts about 13 days. The young fledge approximately 14 days after hatching. One brood is reported in the East, but two are raised in the West. The young remain dependent on their parents for about three weeks after fledging (Middleton 1987).

The breeding season probably spans mid-May to mid-July in Maryland. The only documented Maryland nest had 5 eggs from 25 to 29 May 1949 and 2 young on 12 June (Robbins 1949c). It was 23 ft up in a red spruce. Although some authors (Terres 1980; Ehrlich et al. 1988) consider the Purple Finch to be an uncommon host to the Brown-headed Cowbird, Friedmann et al. (1977) found that parasitism was common in Michigan. Peck and James (1987) reported that 35 of 88 Ontario nests (39.8%) were parasitized; in Grey County, Ontario, 27 of 37 nests (72.9%) were affected.

The Purple Finch diet consists mostly of fruits and seeds, including the buds of many trees and shrubs (Bent 1968d). In the late spring some insects are taken, especially caterpillars and beetles. This species is a regular visitor at winter bird feeders, especially those stocked with sunflower seeds.

Although Atlas results suggest the Purple Finch is widespread in Garrett County, it remains uncommon. Many of the records came from the three-year period prior to the beginning of the statewide effort, and the population may be smaller now. In 1980 and 1981, Atlas workers found Purple Finches nesting in spruce trees around small settlements and individual houses in Garrett County. At the end of the Atlas period, field observers reported that many of those sites had been usurped by House Finches (E. Blom, pers. obs.; C. Jeschke, pers. comm.). Fledged young provided two of the four "confirmed" records; there were single reports of nest building and distraction display.

BBS data from 1966 through 1989 show stable populations in the Eastern Region; there are too few Maryland routes with Purple Finches to estimate a state trend. Despite this species' irregular winter movements, many observers are concerned that its winter numbers have been dropping steadily for the past decade. The winter population of Purple Finches at PWRC in Prince George's County has declined drastically since 1984, compared with a dramatic increase in the House Finch population (K. Klimkiewicz, pers. comm.). Competition with the House Finch has been cited as a cause of the decline in the New England breeding population of Purple Finches (Ehrlich et al. 1988).

More fieldwork is needed to clarify the status of the Purple Finch in Maryland and to determine its specific habitat requirements for breeding. Monitoring of the breeding season relationship between House and Purple Finches should be undertaken. Until these questions are answered, we can do little to ensure that the Purple Finch will remain a part of the breeding avifauna of Maryland except to preserve spruce forests in Garrett County.

Eirik A. T. Blom

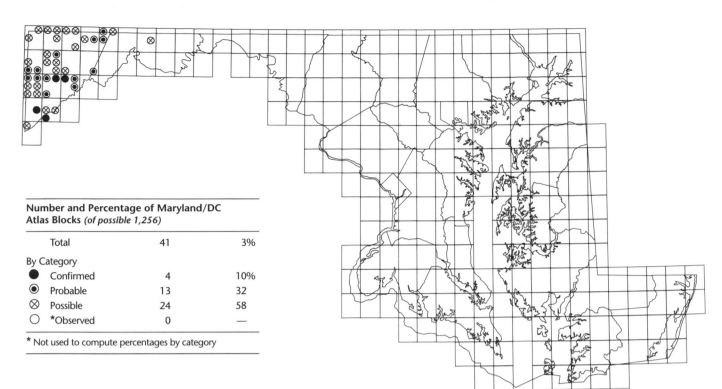

Number and Percentage of Maryland/DC Atlas Blocks *(of possible 1,256)*

Total	41	3%
By Category		
● Confirmed	4	10%
◉ Probable	13	32
⊗ Possible	24	58
○ *Observed	0	—

* Not used to compute percentages by category

Atlas Distribution, 1983–1987

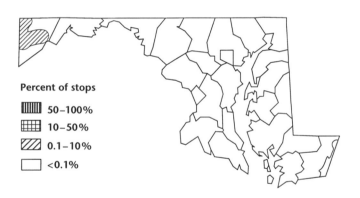

Percent of stops

▥	50–100%
▦	10–50%
▨	0.1–10%
☐	<0.1%

Relative Abundance, 1982–1989

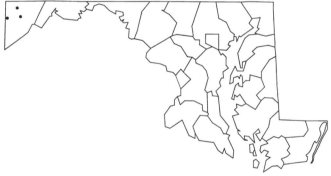

Breeding Distribution, 1958

The Purple Finch was recorded only in small numbers in central and northwestern Garrett County in the Allegheny Mountain Section. Because of low populations it was not detected in some portions of its range.

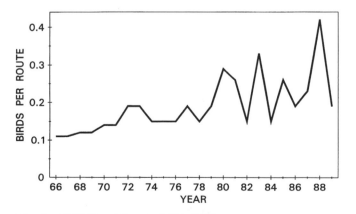

Maryland BBS Trend Graph, 1966–1989

House Finch

Carpodacus mexicanus

Unknown in Maryland until 1958, the House Finch is now one of the most ubiquitous residents of central Maryland and DC. Its cheerful song, which starts as early as late February, serves as one of the first signs of winter's passing.

The explosion of House Finch populations throughout the East followed the release of caged birds in the New York City area subsequent to a Federal ban on its commercial sale (Bock and Lepthien 1976). They were first seen on Long Island, New York, in 1941; these colonies depended on feeding stations, ornamental shrubs, and tree nurseries for food and nest sites. By 1951, a breeding population of about 280 birds had become established in New York. Although western House Finches are sedentary, eastern birds are highly migratory; banded birds that breed in New England have been recovered in Maryland and Maryland birds have been recovered in New England (K. Klimkiewicz, unpub. data).

The first Maryland House Finch was recorded on 6 April 1958 when a bird banded at Ardmore, Pennsylvania, was shot at Havre de Grace, Harford County (Marshall 1958). The first nest was recorded in 1963 at Towson, Baltimore County (Garland 1963). The first DC record was of a bird banded on 10 November 1962 (Pyle 1963); the first summer record was in 1970, when several birds were recorded nesting around University Park, Prince George's County (DuMont and DuMont 1970). Numbers rapidly increased in urban and suburban areas; only seven individuals were recorded during the 1962 Maryland CBC period (Cruickshank 1962), but House Finches were found on more than half the 1966 Maryland CBCs (Cruickshank 1966), with a total of more than 300 individuals. They are now common in urban and suburban environments throughout the state except on the lower Eastern Shore and are one of the few birds commonly found in downtown urban areas. This species is also found in rural areas with suitable habitat.

The House Finch is often associated with human habitation and breeds in cultivated areas and around buildings (Terres 1980). Its nest is typically 5 to 35 ft (1.5–11 m) up in a tree, shrub, or cavity in a wall or building. The nest, built by the female, is made of twigs, grass, debris, or hair. Favored sites are ivy-covered buildings or thick evergreens, but this species may nest in Christmas wreaths, hanging planters, awnings, porch lights, on the ground, or in another bird's nest. Nests may be reused for later broods or in subsequent years. House Finches rarely use nest boxes but have nested in Purple Martin boxes in Pennsylvania (J. Hill, pers. comm.). Although they have shown an interest in boxes at PWRC, no box nesting has occurred there.

Maryland egg dates range from 26 March to 25 June (MNRF). The average House Finch clutch size is 4 in the western United States but is nearer 5 in the East (Harrison 1978; Wootton 1986). Clutch sizes in nine Maryland nests range from 4 to 6; brood sizes in ten nests range from 1 to 5 (mean of 2.6). Incubation, by the female, takes 12 to 14 days; young birds require 11 to 19 days to fledge (Woods 1968). Young have been seen in Maryland nests from 20 April to 25 June (MNRF). Fledglings have been reported as late as September in DC (D. Czaplak, pers. comm.). Three broods a year are possible (Harrison 1978). Friedmann (1963) listed the House Finch as an occasional victim of the Brown-headed Cowbird. Of 21 Maryland nests, 3 (14%) were parasitized (MNRF). Of 64 Ontario nests, 27 (42%) were parasitized, but the Brown-headed Cowbird young died because of the seed diet (Peck and James 1987). In the western United States, animal matter is only 8 percent of the House Finch diet in spring, 4 percent in summer, 0 percent in fall, and 1 percent in winter (Martin et al. 1951). In addition to sunflower seeds, it eats many weed seeds and fruits.

Atlas workers found the House Finch in virtually all central blocks, from Washington County to well south of DC. Populations are denser in the Piedmont than on the Coastal Plain, reflecting the higher human population in the center of the state. It was regularly, but less frequently, encountered in the highlands of Garrett and Allegany counties and was absent from large parts of the Eastern Shore and southern Maryland, where records are centered around the larger towns. The reasons this species has colonized rural western Maryland more successfully than rural southeastern Maryland are unknown. Although the House Finch was originally associated with arid regions in the West (Salt 1952), it uses a wide variety of habitats in the East. The high number of ornamental shrubs and dense conifers in western Maryland may offer better nest sites than are available in southeastern Maryland.

BBS data from 1966 through 1989 show a highly significant average annual increase of 20.2 percent in the Eastern Region. Maryland data indicate a similar increase of 23.5 percent; data from 1980 through 1989 show an even higher increase of 36.7 percent. The future of the House Finch in Maryland is assured.

Byron Swift

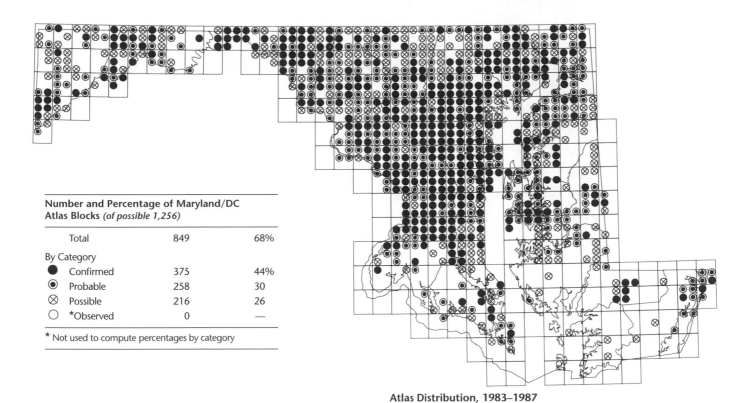

Atlas Distribution, 1983–1987

Number and Percentage of Maryland/DC Atlas Blocks *(of possible 1,256)*

Total	849	68%
By Category		
● Confirmed	375	44%
◉ Probable	258	30
⊗ Possible	216	26
○ *Observed	0	—

* Not used to compute percentages by category

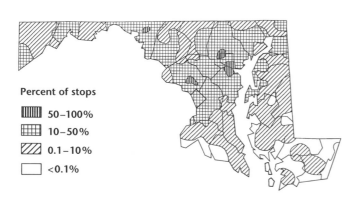

Percent of stops

▥	50–100%
▦	10–50%
▨	0.1–10%
▢	<0.1%

Relative Abundance, 1982–1989

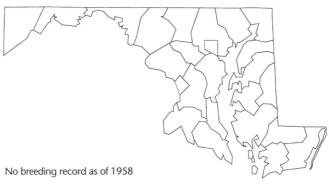

No breeding record as of 1958

Breeding Distribution, 1958

The House Finch is abundant in the Baltimore, Washington, and Hagerstown areas and common throughout the populated center of the state. Its numbers decrease rapidly to the south and east; on the lower Eastern Shore it was reported only from more developed areas.

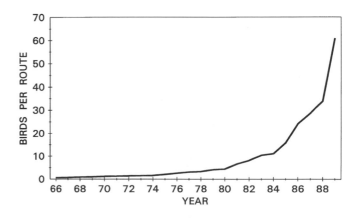

Maryland BBS Trend Graph, 1966–1989

Pine Siskin

Carduelis pinus

The Pine Siskin is an irregular winter visitor from the north. It undulates across the sky in large, compact flocks, feeds on cones at the tops of conifers, and gleans thistle seed from feeders. It was once known as the American Siskin or Pine Linnet (Coues and Prentiss 1883). Kirkwood (1895) called it the Pine Siskin, but Cooke (1908) referred to it as the Pine Finch.

This migratory species is an extremely rare breeder in Maryland. Because the Pine Siskin is nomadic and moves southward primarily in years when its food supply is low in the North, it is an irregular transient and winter resident ranging from common to absent (Kirkwood 1895; Cooke 1929; Fletcher et al. 1956; Stewart and Robbins 1958). It prefers conifer stands, wet deciduous forests, woods edges, and hedgerows. It normally occurs in Maryland from early October to early May, with sightings from across the state (Stewart and Robbins 1958).

The first records of Pine Siskins in the Maryland and DC area were in February 1842 in DC and on 16 November 1859 at Piney Branch in Prince George's County (specimens in National Museum of Natural History). The first suggestion of nesting occurred on 1 July 1937, when Brooks (1937) noted young of the year feeding and calling from eastern hemlocks along the Youghiogheny River in Swallow Falls State Forest, Garrett County. Forty-five years later, J. Sheppard (pers. comm.) watched a pair exhibiting courtship and nesting behavior in Laurel, Anne Arundel County, in May 1982. Kathleen Klimkiewicz (pers. comm.) banded females with active brood patches and eggs in the oviduct at PWRC, Prince George's County, in early May 1987 and two on 1 May 1988 (Ringler 1988c). Because Pine Siskins are very nomadic in their movements, even during the breeding season, these were considered "probable" records. There were unprecedented sightings in mid-June and early July 1988 at Bethesda, Montgomery County; Bowie, Prince George's

County; and Ocean City, Worcester County (Armistead 1989). Pine Siskins have been reported nesting south of their normal range following unusually large winter flights (Weaver and West 1943). Southern nesting attempts may also be influenced by cool spring weather (Swenk 1929). The increased popularity of thistle seed feeders also may encourage Pine Siskins to remain south into the breeding season (Brewer and Merritt 1979).

The breeding habitat of Pine Siskins consists of coniferous and mixed woodlands, alder thickets, and weed patches adjacent to forests (Reilly 1968). They nest almost exclusively in conifers. Nearly all recent nest records from Ohio have been from ornamental conifers within cities (Peterjohn and Rice 1991); Pine Siskins there seem to prefer nesting in residential yards, especially where bird feeders provide a reliable source of food. Pine Siskins do not exhibit nest site fidelity from year to year (Harrison 1975). They may nest singly or, more typically, in loose colonies. Adults defend an area within 3 to 6 ft (0.9–1.8 m) of the nest (Weaver and West 1943). Nesting occurs very early. Most complete sets of fresh eggs recorded from the United States and Canada were from early April to early May (Palmer 1968).

The nest is placed on a horizontal conifer branch, usually well away from the trunk, 3 to 50 ft (0.9–15 m) above the ground (Palmer 1968). Most nest heights reported in Ontario (Peck and James 1987) were 11.5 to 20 ft (3.5–6.1 m). The female chooses the nest site and builds a large shallow cup of twigs, grasses, mosses, lichens, bark strips, and rootlets, lining it with mosses, rootlets, hair, fur, and feathers (Palmer 1968). Clutch sizes range from 2 to 6 eggs, commonly 3 or 4. The female incubates the eggs for 13 days, beginning with the first egg. The male feeds the female throughout incubation and assists in feeding the young (Weaver and West 1943), which fledge at about 15 days (Palmer 1968). Friedmann (1963) considered Pine Siskins to be rare victims of the Brown-headed Cowbird, but Peck and James (1987) stated 3 of 15 Ontario nests (20%) were parasitized.

The Pine Siskin is a vegetarian except during its nesting season, when 80 percent of its diet is insects and spiders (Martin et al. 1951). It eats primarily caterpillars, aphids, spiders, bugs, and fly larvae at this season.

BBS data from 1980 through 1989 show stable populations in the Eastern Region; there are no data for Maryland. Populations may fluctuate with cone crops (DeGraaf and Rudis 1986). The Pine Siskin's breeding range in the eastern United States normally extends only as far south as northwestern Pennsylvania (AOU 1983). Pennsylvania recorded several breeding records in the central and north-central part of the state during that atlas project (Brauning 1992); Virginia had only one breeding record.

During the Maryland Atlas period, there was a single "possible" breeding record in Garrett County and a "probable" report from PWRC, both in 1987. In 1988, the first year after Atlas fieldwork was completed, N. Laitsch found the first Maryland nest, which contained 3 young, at Swallow Falls State Park in Garrett County on 23 April (Ringler

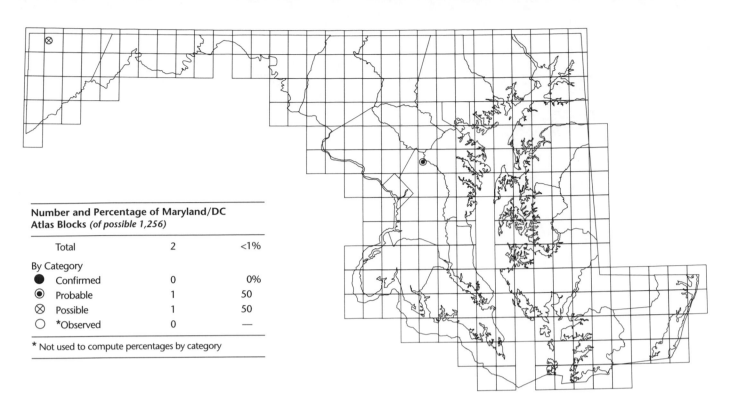

Number and Percentage of Maryland/DC Atlas Blocks *(of possible 1,256)*

Total	2	<1%
By Category		
● Confirmed	0	0%
◉ Probable	1	50
⊗ Possible	1	50
○ *Observed	0	—

* Not used to compute percentages by category

Atlas Distribution, 1983–1987

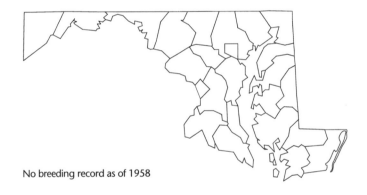

No breeding record as of 1958

Breeding Distribution, 1958

1988c). "Probable" breeding was also reported from PWRC (K. Klimkiewicz, pers. comm.). Perhaps Pine Siskins will become a more regular breeder in Maryland in the future. Management techniques to attract this interesting species should include maintaining stands of conifers and sources of thistle seed.

Nancy J. Stewart

American Goldfinch

Carduelis tristis

At a time when most birds have finished nesting, the American Goldfinch is just beginning. It is a common permanent resident, but local populations are swelled by northern birds in winter.

The American Goldfinch once may have been more abundant in Maryland. Coues and Prentiss (1883) considered it formerly exceedingly abundant but still common. Numbers were reduced, in part, by reclamation of large tracts of brushy habitat and the high population of House Sparrows. Stewart and Robbins (1958) listed its breeding status as fairly common in the Eastern and Western Shore sections, and common elsewhere. BBS data from 1966 through 1989 show a highly significant average annual decline of 1.5 percent in the Eastern Region; Maryland data indicate a decline during the same period, but the population was stable from 1980 through 1989.

The American Goldfinch nests in deciduous shrubs and saplings in hedgerows, wood margins, brushy fields, shrub swamps, and orchards (Stewart and Robbins 1958). The greatest breeding density recorded in Maryland is 40 territorial males per 100 acres (40.5 ha) in an abandoned field in Prince George's County (Klimkiewicz and Holmes 1972).

One Maryland nest was in a conifer; the other 35 were in deciduous trees or shrubs (MNRF). Of these, 21 (60%) were in sweet gum or maple trees; others were in peach, hawthorn, black locust, sycamore, tulip tree, ash, oak, and buttonbush. Heights of 38 Maryland nests range from 2 to 32 ft (0.6–9.8 m), with a mean of 10.3 ft (3.1 m); 62 percent were from 6 to 15 ft (1.8–4.6 m) and only 3 were over 20 ft (6.1 m). Stokes (1950) reported an average territory size 66 ft (20 m) in diameter for 38 American Goldfinch pairs in a dry Wisconsin marsh. The nest, built by the female, is so tightly constructed that it can hold water and often remains in place for several years (Nickell 1951). Walkinshaw (1938) noted that southern Michigan nests were usually placed in the fork of a tree and anchored to three, or occasionally two, branches.

American Goldfinches breed in Maryland from early July

to early September (Robbins and Bystrak 1977). Nickell (1951) believed their nesting is timed to coincide with thistle seed production. Thistle seeds are used for food as well as for nest construction. The earliest record of nest building in Maryland is 6 July; extreme egg dates (MNRF) are 12 July (DC) and 21 September (Maryland). Clutch sizes in 17 nests range from 4 to 6 (mean of 4.9). The female incubates for 12 to 14 days; during this time she is fed by the male (Walkinshaw 1939a). This feeding continues even during the early nestling phase, when the female regurgitates seeds for the young.

Brood sizes in 16 Maryland nests range from 1 to 6, with a mean of 3.4 (MNRF). Young remain in the nest 11 to 15 days (Walkinshaw 1939a). Maryland broods have been recorded from 3 August to 6 October, with a peak from late August to mid-September (MNRF). Despite the late breeding cycle, the American Goldfinch may raise a second brood (Walkinshaw 1939a), although there are no records of second broods in Maryland. The average annual survival rate of a PWRC population was 44 percent (Karr et al. 1990). Animal food, primarily aphids and caterpillars, comprises nearly half the diet in spring but is insignificant at other seasons (Martin et al. 1951). Seeds of thistle, ragweed, and sweet gum rate high among favored plant foods.

Friedmann (1929, 1963) listed the American Goldfinch as a fairly common victim of the Brown-headed Cowbird. Parasitism is uncommon from New York northward because the overlap in the nesting cycle of the two species is very short (Friedmann 1963). Terrill (1961) gave a 2.2 percent parasitism rate (7 of 318 nests) in Quebec; 90 of 1,066 Ontario nests (8.4%) were parasitized (Peck and James 1987). Middleton (1991) found 47 of 802 Ontario nests (6%) to be parasitized, but only 13 eggs hatched. Because of the regurgitated seed diet fed to them, 12 of these nestlings died within four days and the other within 12 days. Although the earliest parasitism record was from Baltimore, Maryland (Wilson 1810), there is no record in the MNRF.

Atlas results show American Goldfinches occurring throughout Maryland and DC. They were absent from several blocks composed largely of water and marshland on the western edge of the Eastern Shore. American Goldfinches were reported as "confirmed" or "probable" over 70 percent of the time. Behaviors betraying their presence included the familiar *perchickory* flight call, acrobatic courtship flight displays, and the presence of noisy chicks begging for food.

The decline in the American Goldfinch population is not well understood, although loss of habitat may be a factor. Open areas and edge habitats are created by housing or industrial development, but brushy, weedy fields usually are not. In fact, they are more often consumed by development. With a continuing demand on lands for suburban development, the amount of "idle" land reverting to forest is bound to decline. The American Goldfinch requires these transitional habitats. To maintain suitable habitat for this species, an active management program may be necessary.

Sue A. Ricciardi

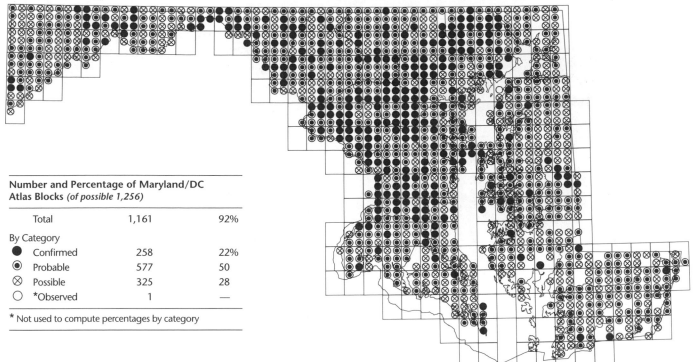

Number and Percentage of Maryland/DC Atlas Blocks *(of possible 1,256)*

Total		1,161	92%
By Category			
●	Confirmed	258	22%
◉	Probable	577	50
⊗	Possible	325	28
○	*Observed	1	—

*Not used to compute percentages by category

Atlas Distribution, 1983–1987

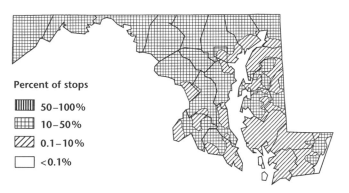

Percent of stops

▥	50–100%
▦	10–50%
▨	0.1–10%
▢	<0.1%

Relative Abundance, 1982–1989

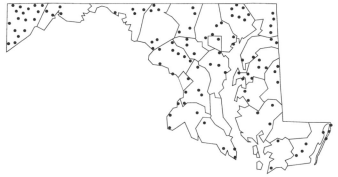

Breeding Distribution, 1958

The American Goldfinch is most common west of the Fall Line, where it is uniformly distributed, and in much of southern Maryland and the central Eastern Shore. Densities on the Coastal Plain are irregular, with the lowest numbers throughout most of the lower Eastern Shore.

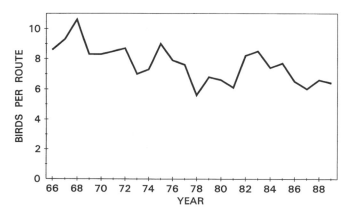

Maryland BBS Trend Graph, 1966–1989

House Sparrow

Passer domesticus

The introduction of the House Sparrow into this country was a serious ecological blunder that has had adverse effects on native cavity-nesting birds. An aggressive competitor for nest sites, it is a common to locally abundant permanent resident throughout Maryland.

The House Sparrow, formerly known as the English or European Sparrow, was introduced into Washington County in 1865 and Baltimore County in 1874. From these areas, it spread across Maryland, occupying the Ridge and Valley Section from 1865 through 1870; the Allegheny Mountain and Piedmont sections from 1872 through 1876; and the Upper Chesapeake, Western Shore, and Eastern Shore sections from 1877 through 1880 (Coues and Prentiss 1883; Kirkwood 1895). Kirkwood (1895) described the House Sparrow as a common resident throughout Maryland. Stewart and Robbins (1958) wrote that it was common and locally abundant in the Upper Chesapeake Section and fairly common and locally abundant elsewhere.

Except for densely wooded areas, swamps, or marshes, House Sparrows have readily adapted to natural habitats and thrive in areas associated with human activity (Kalmbach 1940). Favored sites are in rural areas where animals are raised or grain is harvested. Waste food and gleanings from the fields supply abundant food, and the eaves of farm buildings provide a surplus of nest sites. Seeds found in horse droppings were a major winter food source for House Sparrows; when machines began to replace horses both on the farm and in urban areas, the population began to decline (Forbush 1929). More efficient methods of harvesting crops, better storage of grains, and an overall tendency toward cleanliness have resulted in a continuing decline. Severe winters also have taken their toll. BBS data from 1966 through 1989 show a highly significant average annual decline of 1.6 percent in House Sparrow populations in the Eastern Region; Maryland data show a similar but greater decline of 4.3 percent. Data from 1980 through 1989 show a highly significant decline of 8 percent in Maryland populations. Although the introduction of the House Finch into the eastern states may be contributing to the House Sparrow's reduced numbers (Kricher 1983), BBS data show no direct correlation between the increase of one species and the decline of the other.

Both sexes build the domed nest, which is usually constructed 6 to 18 ft (1.8–5.5 m) above the ground, and sometimes as high as 75 ft (23 m) (Scott 1977; Peck and James 1987). Nest material consists of dried grasses and weeds, interspersed with many feathers, hair, string, pieces of paper, plastic, or other debris (Cink 1976). Nests, sometimes in small groups or colonies, can be found in crevices or holes in artificial structures, in vines growing on walls, in natural tree cavities, or in nest boxes erected for native cavity-nesting species. Even the clay nests of Cliff Swallows and the burrows of Bank Swallows are not safe from House Sparrows. Although females prefer cavities, they occasionally build huge ball nests of grasses, weeds, and trash in the fork of a tree branch (Cink 1976).

Typically, House Sparrows raise two broods; in some years they raise three (Harrison 1975). Incubation, by the female, lasts 12 or 13 days; fledging occurs at 15 days (Harrison 1978). Heights of 146 Maryland nests (MNRF) range from 2 to 35 ft (0.6–11 m), and egg dates extend from 29 March to 17 August, with small peaks at about ten-day intervals from mid-April to late May. After a gap in early June, peaks resume in mid-June, early July, and early August. Clutch sizes in 75 Maryland nests (MNRF) range from 3 to 6 (mean of 4.4). Nestling dates extend from 15 April to 6 September, peaking in mid- to late May. Brood sizes in 59 Maryland nests (MNRF) range from 1 to 5 (mean of 3.7). The House Sparrow diet is 96 percent vegetable matter, mostly agricultural grains such as corn and wheat, as well as the seeds and buds of many trees (Kalmbach 1940). Nestlings are fed mostly insects. There are only five records, one from Maryland, of Brown-headed Cowbird parasitism of the House Sparrow (Friedmann 1929, 1963).

Atlas results demonstrate that the House Sparrow is one of the 15 most widely distributed birds in Maryland. It is missing from extensive marshlands, Chesapeake Bay islands, Assateague National Seashore, and a few heavily wooded blocks in the mountains of western Maryland. Owing to its abundance and conspicuousness, Atlas fieldworkers easily located this species. "Confirmed" records were most frequently of a bird on its nest with contents unknown (33%).

As early as 1883, Coues and Prentiss (1883) described the nuisance to humans and the danger to native birds created when the House Sparrow became established in this country. In their words, "To offset all this what have we done? Nothing, absolutely nothing." After 140 years of doing practically nothing, there must be some way to further reduce the impact of the mistake made in 1851 when the first House Sparrows were introduced in New York City (Forbush 1929).

Delos C. Dupree

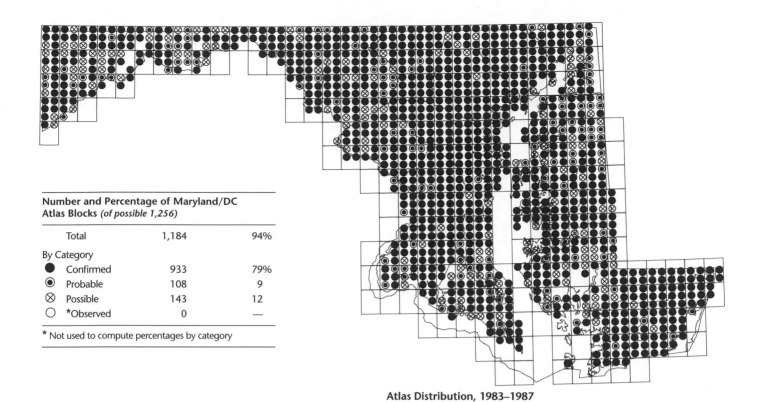

Number and Percentage of Maryland/DC Atlas Blocks *(of possible 1,256)*

Total	1,184	94%
By Category		
● Confirmed	933	79%
◉ Probable	108	9
⊗ Possible	143	12
○ *Observed	0	—

*Not used to compute percentages by category

Atlas Distribution, 1983–1987

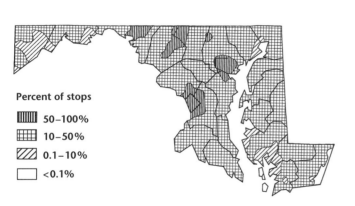

Percent of stops

▥	50–100%
▦	10–50%
▨	0.1–10%
☐	<0.1%

Relative Abundance, 1982–1989

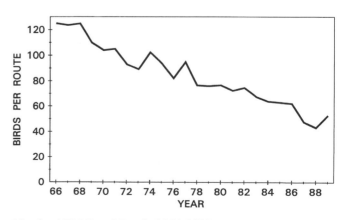

Breeding Distribution, 1958

The House Sparrow is abundant in the urban centers of Baltimore and Washington and in the agricultural areas of the Hagerstown and Frederick valleys. Lowest numbers are in Eastern Shore marshes and in the heavily wooded southeastern section of Garrett County in the Allegheny Mountain Section.

Maryland BBS Trend Graph, 1966–1989

Exotic Species Not Yet Established in Maryland or DC

Ringed Turtle-Dove

Streptopelia risoria

The Ringed Turtle-Dove, also known as the Barbary Dove, has been reared in captivity for so many centuries that its genetic and geographic origins are uncertain. The species designation of *Streptopelia risoria* is tentative; the domestic stock may have been derived from either *S. roseogrisea,* the African Collared Dove (AOU 1983), whose song it closely resembles (C. Robbins, pers. comm.), or *S. decaocto,* the Collared Turtle-Dove from Eurasia (AOU 1983). Some authors consider these two species conspecific; the usage of *S. risoria* is therefore retained. The Ringed Turtle-Dove is widely held in captivity in the United States, but it occasionally escapes. It was first recognized as an established North American species in 1957 (AOU 1957). Isolated populations have become established in Puerto Rico, Florida (Pinellas County), Texas (near Houston), and California (in the vicinity of Los Angeles).

The first report for Maryland, on 31 March 1966, was of a bird that spent the winter in Bethesda, Montgomery County (Robbins 1967a). This bird was quite tame and survived the winter because a man took it into his home on cold nights. Feral birds most likely would not be able to survive a Maryland winter without assistance. About 20 subsequent reports, most from feeders in urban areas, have been published in the season reports in *Maryland Birdlife.* The most recent records were of single birds at feeders in fall and winter 1991 in Talbot (J. Effinger, pers. comm.) and Anne Arundel Counties (H. Wierenga, pers. comm.) and of a bird at a feeder in Talbot County in January 1992 (G. Therres, pers. comm.).

This species is recorded in only two Atlas blocks. The reports from Fort McHenry in Baltimore City (Baltimore East SW), represent the only known breeding site for the state. In October 1980 an immature was seen there on 27 February 1981 when a nest with two eggs was found; during summer 1982, one fledged young was seen (Ringler 1982); on 1 October 1982, two young hatched in a nest near the feeder (Ringler 1983a). There were no subsequent sightings at Fort McHenry. The other record was of a bird calling east of Winfield, Carroll County (Winfield CE), in June 1987.

Monk Parakeet

Myiopsitta monachus

The Monk Parakeet was first recognized as an established North American species in 1983 (AOU 1983). It is resident in South America from central Bolivia, Paraguay, and southern Brazil south to central Argentina. This species has also been kept as a cage bird in the United States. The Monk Parakeet is established locally in Puerto Rico, southern Florida, and at a few localities in Atlantic Coast states north to New York and Connecticut (AOU 1983). Because of its reputation for damaging fruit crops efforts have been made to remove feral populations.

There are approximately 20 reports for Maryland, almost all of single individuals (season reports from *Atlantic Naturalist* and *Maryland Birdlife*). The first report for the state was in July 1972, during the first Montgomery County atlas, when two birds remained in Silver Spring (Kensington quadrangle) into September; they built a typical bulky stick nest but raised no young (Klimkiewicz 1972). In January 1973 two birds were again seen in the same area and nest building was observed, but one bird disappeared later (DuMont and DuMont 1973). The only other Maryland nest record was obtained in July 1973 when two Monk Parakeets constructed a nest on a telephone pole in Beltsville, Prince George's County (Robbins 1973c); no young were raised. Other records prior to the Atlas came from Washington, Howard, Baltimore, Calvert, Talbot, and Worcester counties from 1972 through 1981. Reports during, and subsequent to, the Atlas were from Baltimore, Prince George's, Anne Arundel, St. Mary's, and Worcester counties (season reports from *Maryland Birdlife;* Craig 1989). The last report was on 30 December 1990 near Edgewater, Anne Arundel County.

The only Atlas record was of a single bird at Governor's Bridge, over the Patuxent River in Anne Arundel County (Bowie CW) on 20 July 1986.

Appendixes
Literature Cited
Index

Pied-billed Grebe	15 May–15 July	Common Moorhen	20 May–20 Sept.
American Bittern	20 May–15 Aug.	American Coot	10 June–25 Aug.
Least Bittern	20 May–1 Aug.	Wilson's Plover	1 June–31 July
Great Blue Heron	15 May–15 July	Piping Plover	15 June–20 July
Great Egret	20 May–20 June	Killdeer	20 Apr.–5 July
Snowy Egret	20 May–1 July	American Oystercatcher	1 May–25 July
Little Blue Heron	20 May–20 June	Willet	10 June–10 July
Tricolored Heron	20 May–1 July	Spotted Sandpiper	5 June–25 June
Cattle Egret	20 May–20 June	Upland Sandpiper	20 May–25 June
Green Heron	1 May–15 July	American Woodcock	10 Apr.–20 Sept.
Black-crowned Night-Heron	20 Apr.–1 July	Laughing Gull	5 June–20 July
Yellow-crowned Night-Heron	20 Apr.–1 July	Herring Gull	5 June–20 July
Glossy Ibis	20 May–1 July	Great Black-backed Gull	5 June–20 July
Mute Swan	1 May–1 Sept.	Gull-billed Tern	25 May–5 July
Canada Goose	10 May–20 Aug.	Royal Tern	25 May–5 July
Wood Duck	1 May–15 Aug.	Sandwich Tern	25 May–5 July
Green-winged Teal	20 May–20 Aug.	Roseate Tern	25 May–5 July
American Black Duck	20 May–20 Aug.	Common Tern	5 June–30 June
Mallard	15 May–20 Aug.	Forster's Tern	15 May–25 June
Blue-winged Teal	5 June–10 Aug.	Least Tern	25 May–5 July
Gadwall	15 May–20 Aug.	Black Skimmer	1 June–31 July
Hooded Merganser	1 June–20 Sept.	Rock Dove	1 Jan.–31 Dec.
Ruddy Duck	1 June–20 Sept.	Mourning Dove	1 May–20 July
Black Vulture	1 Apr.–1 Aug.	Black-billed Cuckoo	15 June–20 July
Turkey Vulture	1 May–20 Aug.	Yellow-billed Cuckoo	15 June–31 July
Osprey	1 June–31 Aug.	Barn Owl	1 May–30 Sept.
Bald Eagle	15 Apr.–5 Aug.	Eastern Screech-Owl	1 Apr.–15 Aug.
Northern Harrier	15 May–25 July	Great Horned Owl	15 Dec.–31 Aug.
Sharp-shinned Hawk	1 June–15 Aug.	Barred Owl	15 Jan.–31 Aug.
Cooper's Hawk	20 May–20 Aug.	Long-eared Owl	1 May–30 Sept.
Northern Goshawk	1 Apr.–30 Sept.	Short-eared Owl	1 May–30 Sept.
Red-shouldered Hawk	1 May–31 Aug.	Nothern Saw-whet Owl	5 May–10 Sept.
Broad-winged Hawk	5 June–10 Aug.	Common Nighthawk	5 June–15 July
Red-tailed Hawk	1 May–31 Aug.	Chuck-will's-widow	1 May–10 Aug.
American Kestrel	15 May–31 July	Whip-poor-will	10 May–15 July
Peregrine Falcon	25 May–31 Aug.	Chimney Swift	20 May–15 Aug.
Ring-necked Pheasant	15 Apr.–30 Sept.	Ruby-throated Hummingbird	25 May–31 July
Ruffed Grouse	1 Apr.–31 July	Belted Kingfisher	10 Apr.–20 July
Wild Turkey	15 Apr.–30 Sept.	Red-headed Woodpecker	25 May–20 Aug.
Northern Bobwhite	15 Apr.–30 Sept.	Red-bellied Woodpecker	15 Mar.–31 Aug.
Black Rail	1 May–15 Aug.	Yellow-bellied Sapsucker	20 May–10 Sept.
Clapper Rail	1 May–31 Aug.	Downy Woodpecker	15 Mar.–31 Aug.
King Rail	1 May–31 Aug.	Hairy Woodpecker	15 Mar.–31 Aug.
Virginia Rail	20 May–15 Aug.	Red-cockaded Woodpecker	15 Mar.–31 Aug.
Sora	1 June–1 Aug.	Northern Flicker	10 May–25 Aug.
Purple Gallinule	20 June–31 July	Pileated Woodpecker	15 Mar.–31 Aug.

Olive-sided Flycatcher	15 June–5 Aug.	Magnolia Warbler	5 June–5 Aug.
Eastern Wood-Pewee	1 June–15 Aug.	Black-throated Blue Warbler	5 June–5 Aug.
Acadian Flycatcher	25 May–5 Aug.	Black-throated Green Warbler	10 June–5 Aug.
Alder Flycatcher	10 June–20 July	Blackburnian Warbler	10 June–31 July
Willow Flycatcher	10 June–20 July	Yellow-throated Warbler	1 May–15 July
Least Flycatcher	5 June–20 July	Pine Warbler	20 Apr.–10 Aug.
Eastern Phoebe	1 May–31 Aug.	Prairie Warbler	25 May–20 July
Great Crested Flycatcher	25 May–31 July	Cerulean Warbler	25 May–5 Aug.
Eastern Kingbird	25 May–5 July	Black-and-white Warbler	15 May–25 July
Horned Lark	10 Apr.–5 Sept.	American Redstart	10 June–20 July
Purple Martin	1 June–25 June	Prothonotary Warbler	10 May–20 July
Tree Swallow	25 May–25 June	Worm-eating Warbler	20 May–20 July
Northern Rough-winged Swallow	1 June–25 June	Swainson's Warbler	20 Apr.–31 Aug.
Bank Swallow	25 May–25 June	Ovenbird	20 May–5 Aug.
Cliff Swallow	5 June–25 June	Northern Waterthrush	5 June–15 July
Barn Swallow	25 May–25 June	Louisiana Waterthrush	1 May–10 July
Blue Jay	10 June–5 Sept.	Kentucky Warbler	25 May–15 July
American Crow	15 May–31 Aug.	Mourning Warbler	15 June–10 Aug.
Fish Crow	10 May–31 Aug.	Common Yellowthroat	25 May–10 Aug.
Common Raven	1 May–31 Aug.	Hooded Warbler	25 May–25 July
Black-capped Chickadee	1 May–20 Sept.	Canada Warbler	5 June–31 July
Carolina Chickadee	1 Mar.–31 Aug.	Yellow-breasted Chat	25 May–5 Aug.
Tufted Titmouse	1 Mar.–31 Aug.	Summer Tanager	1 June–10 Aug.
Red-breasted Nuthatch	1 June–5 Aug.	Scarlet Tanager	25 May–10 Aug.
White-breasted Nuthatch	10 May–15 Aug.	Northern Cardinal	15 Mar.–30 Sept.
Brown-headed Nuthatch	20 Mar.–15 Aug.	Rose-breasted Grosbeak	5 June–15 Aug.
Brown Creeper	15 May–31 Aug.	Blue Grosbeak	25 May–15 Aug.
Carolina Wren	1 Mar.–30 Sept.	Indigo Bunting	1 June–15 Aug.
Bewick's Wren	10 May–31 Aug.	Dickcissel	1 June–31 Aug.
House Wren	20 May–15 Aug.	Eastern Towhee	20 May–31 Aug.
Winter Wren	15 May–31 Aug.	Bachman's Sparrow	1 June–31 July
Sedge Wren	10 June–20 Sept.	Chipping Sparrow	1 May–31 Aug.
Marsh Wren	25 May–25 Aug.	Field Sparrow	1 May–31 Aug.
Golden-crowned Kinglet	15 May–10 Sept.	Vesper Sparrow	1 May–31 Aug.
Blue-gray Gnatcatcher	15 May–31 July	Lark Sparrow	1 June–31 July
Eastern Bluebird	15 May–31 Aug.	Savannah Sparrow	1 June–31 Aug.
Veery	10 June–10 Aug.	Grasshopper Sparrow	25 May–31 Aug.
Swainson's Thrush	10 June–10 Aug.	Henslow's Sparrow	15 May–31 Aug.
Hermit Thrush	25 May–15 Sept.	Saltmarsh Sharp-tailed Sparrow	1 June–10 Aug.
Wood Thrush	25 May–20 Aug.	Seaside Sparrow	1 June–10 Aug.
American Robin	1 May–31 Aug.	Song Sparrow	1 May–10 Sept.
Gray Catbird	25 May–31 Aug.	Swamp Sparrow	1 June–31 Aug.
Northern Mockingbird	1 Apr.–10 Sept.	White-throated Sparrow	10 June–31 Aug.
Brown Thrasher	15 May–31 Aug.	Dark-eyed Junco	1 June–31 Aug.
Cedar Waxwing	15 June–31 July	Bobolink	15 June–10 July
Loggerhead Shrike	20 Apr.–20 July	Red-winged Blackbird	1 May–10 July
European Starling	1 Apr.–5 Sept.	Eastern Meadowlark	1 May–10 Sept.
White-eyed Vireo	25 May–15 Aug.	Boat-tailed Grackle	15 Apr.–31 Aug.
Solitary Vireo	5 June–20 Aug.	Common Grackle	15 Apr.–10 July
Yellow-throated Vireo	25 May–15 Aug.	Brown-headed Cowbird	1 May–10 July
Warbling Vireo	10 June–10 Aug.	Orchard Oriole	1 June–5 July
Red-eyed Vireo	1 June–31 July	Baltimore Oriole	1 June–25 July
Blue-winged Warbler	25 May–20 July	Purple Finch	1 June–10 Aug.
Golden-winged Warbler	25 May–20 July	House Finch	1 May–15 July
Nashville Warbler	25 May–15 Aug.	Pine Siskin	15 June–30 Sept.
Northern Parula	1 June–15 Aug.	American Goldfinch	10 June–15 Sept.
Yellow Warbler	1 June–10 July	House Sparrow	1 Feb.–30 Sept.
Chestnut-sided Warbler	1 June–10 Aug.		

Appendix B   *Abundance Definitions*

The terms used to describe the relative abundance of birds are necessarily subjective. Atlas field workers were not asked to record the actual number of each species they encountered in the course of their fieldwork, and miniroute data provide relative rather than actual abundance. In general, we have attempted to follow the guidelines Hall (1983) established for relative abundance terms; however, the decision of which term to use is frequently based on our own experience and perception. Abundance terms cited from publications in the species accounts do not necessarily follow these guidelines. The definitions from Hall (1983) are as follows:

Very abundant: Species for which more than 1,000 individuals can be seen by a single observer in a full day's work in the field in a suitable habitat. A species for which more than 300 individuals can be listed on a 24.5-mile (39-km) BBS.

Abundant: A species for which an observer can see between 201 and 1,000 in a full day's work in a suitable habitat. A species for which 101 to 300 individuals can be listed on a 24.5-mile (39-km) BBS. A species for which a Singing Male Census has a density of more than 100 males per 100 hectares (247 acres).

Very common: A species for which an observer can see between 51 and 100 in a full day's work in a suitable habitat. A species for which between 31 and 100 individuals can be listed on a 24.5-mile (39-km) BBS. A species that has a density of between 51 and 100 males per 100 hectares (247 acres) on a Singing Male Census.

Common: A species for which an observer can see between 21 and 50 a day. A species for which between 11 and 30 can be listed on a 24.5-mile (39-km) BBS. A species that has a density between 26 and 50 males per 100 hectares (247 acres) on a Singing Male Census.

Fairly common: A species for which an observer would list between 7 and 20 in a full day. A species for which between 4 and 10 can be listed on a 24.5-mile (39-km) BBS. A species with a density of between 11 and 25 males per 100 hectares (247 acres) on a Singing Male Census.

Uncommon: A species for which an observer will list between 1 and 6 in a full day's work. A species for which between 1 and 3 individuals will be listed on a 24.5-mile (39-km) BBS. A species with a density of between 6 and 10 males per 100 hectares (247 acres) on a Singing Male Census.

Rare: A species for which an observer can expect to list between 1 and 6 birds per season, but which is found in every appropriate season.

Appendix C Former Breeding Species

Green-winged Teal
Anas crecca

In the East, the Green-winged Teal is a rare breeder south to West Virginia (Hall 1983), Delaware (AOU 1983), and Maryland. There are two breeding records for Maryland: a nest with eggs on 5 June 1971 at Deal Island WMA in Somerset County (Armistead 1971) and an adult with two half-grown young at a dredge spoil impoundment in Cecil County in June 1990 (E. Blom, pers. comm.). Nonbreeding individuals are found in the tidewater areas of Maryland during most summers.

Greater Prairie Chicken
Tympanuchus cupido

The Greater Prairie Chicken, also known as the Heath Hen, formerly occurred as a permanent resident, at least locally, on the Coastal Plain in Maryland (Cuvier 1826; Cabot 1855). It was last observed near Marshall Hall, Prince George's County, in the spring of 1860 (Bent 1932). No actual nest was found, and the eastern subspecies is now extinct.

Purple Gallinule
Porphyrula martinica

The Purple Gallinule breeds from South America north to the Gulf Coast states and irregularly farther north (AOU 1983). It is rare in Maryland in any season. The only breeding record for the state was from a pond near Upper Marlboro, Prince George's County, in 1976 (Patterson 1976). A bird was also present there in the summer of 1978, but there was no evidence of breeding (Ringler 1978b).

Sandwich Tern
Sterna sandvicensis

The Sandwich Tern breeds in coastal areas from northern South America north to Virginia (AOU 1983). It breeds irregularly in coastal Virginia (S. Ridd, pers. comm.). The only breeding record for Maryland was on an island in coastal Worcester County in 1974 (Weske et al. 1977). Since 1985, a few have been reported each year in coastal Worcester County during summer (MCWP). In 1994, after the Atlas fieldwork was completed, two pairs nested near Ocean City but have not been found since (DNR, unpubl. data).

Roseate Tern
Sterna dougallii

The Roseate Tern breeds at scattered locations in coastal areas of the southeastern United States (AOU 1983). It is rare and declining as a breeding bird in eastern North America. Roseate Terns nested commonly in coastal Worcester County from 1933, when adults and eight sets of eggs were collected on 10 June (Court 1936), through 1938 (Poole 1942). These are the only breeding records for the state. A nest reported in 1963 on Cedar Island near the Virginia line was not well documented (Bridge and Bridge 1964).

Passenger Pigeon
Ectopistes migratorius

The Passenger Pigeon was formerly abundant, at least locally. Grant (1951) listed it as formerly nesting in Garrett County. A large roost was reported near Oakland (Eifrig 1904). Although there were summer records of this species, it was most abundant as a migrant. The last birds were recorded on 17 July 1903, when Eifrig (1904) recorded a pair in western Maryland. Stewart and Robbins (1958) give a more detailed account of the former status of this now-extinct species.

Long-eared Owl
Asio otus

The eastern breeding range of the Long-eared Owl extends south to Pennsylvania and, in the mountains, to western Virginia (AOU 1983). There are approximately ten breeding records for Maryland and one for DC, most from the 1890s, but none since 1950 (Stewart and Robbins 1958).

Short-eared Owl
Asio flammeus

The breeding range of the Short-eared Owl in the East extends south into Pennsylvania and New Jersey and, formerly, to coastal Virginia (AOU 1983). The three known breeding records for Maryland occurred in 1923 (Stewart and Robbins 1958), 1958 (Stewart 1958), and 1972 (Klimkiewicz 1972). Since 1871, there have been about five other summer records, some of which may pertain to breeding birds.

Red-cockaded Woodpecker
Picoides borealis

The Red-cockaded Woodpecker is a permanent resident in the southeastern United States north to central Virginia (AOU 1983). There are summer records for Maryland from the area of Golden Hill, Dorchester County, in 1932 and 1933 (Stewart and Robbins 1958), and three to nine individuals were seen near there at Blackwater NWR in spring and summer 1976 (Devlin et al. 1980). Meanley (1943a) observed a young bird on Assateague Island, Worcester County, on 9 June 1939. Fall records were reported from the Golden Hill area in 1955 and 1956 (Stewart and Robbins 1958). In recent years, the population has been declining throughout the range; all sites but one have been abandoned in Virginia (S. Ridd, pers. comm.). During the Atlas period a single bird was observed for several hours on 22 June 1984 at Periwinkle Point, Point Lookout State Park, St. Mary's County, but it could not be located subsequently.

Swainson's Thrush
Catharus ustulatus

The breeding range of the Swainson's Thrush in the East extends south in the mountains to West Virginia and southwestern Virginia (AOU 1983). The last breeding records for Maryland were around 1908 near Jennings, Garrett County (Behr 1914), and on 13 June 1917, near Oakland, Garrett County, when a nest with 3 eggs was found (Stewart and Robbins 1958).

Lark Sparrow
Chondestes grammacus

The Lark Sparrow is a rare and irregular breeding bird in the East (AOU 1983). A colony of about 50 birds, including young, was reported at Accident, Garrett County, on 24 July 1901 (Eifrig 1902a). Lark Sparrows were reported as common in summer near Red House, Garrett County, until about 1926 (Brooks 1936). No subsequent breeding evidence has been found, although recent breeding was confirmed just south of Garrett County in West Virginia.

Bachman's Sparrow
Aimophila aestivalis

The Bachman's Sparrow breeds in the southeastern United States north to North Carolina, Kentucky, and Illinois (AOU 1983).

It is declining and is now endangered in much of its former range in the East. It was formerly an uncommon and local but regular breeding bird along and near the Potomac River in DC and in Prince George's, Montgomery, Allegany, and Garrett counties in Maryland (Stewart and Robbins 1958). The last breeding record was of a young bird seen with adults on 7 July 1962 in Green Ridge State Forest, Allegany County (Robbins 1962).

Red Crossbill
Loxia curvirostra

The Red Crossbill breeds in the East in southern Canada and New England and irregularly at scattered locations south to North Carolina (AOU 1983). Because of this species' erratic movements, summer records are difficult to interpret. It may have bred near Laurel, Prince George's County; a female was collected on 23 May 1884 with "unmistakable evidence of having lately incubated" (Ridgway 1884). A young bird barely able to fly was observed with an adult near DC in 1885 (Smith 1885). Red Crossbills have bred at isolated locations in Virginia and West Virginia.

Appendix D   *Vagrant Species Recorded on the Atlas*

Common Loon *(Gavia immer)*
Horned Grebe *(Podiceps auritus)*
Great Cormorant *(Phalacrocorax carbo)*
Tundra Swan *(Cygnus columbianus)*
Snow Goose *(Chen caerulescens)*
Green-winged Teal *(Anas crecca)*
Northern Pintail *(Anas acuta)*
American Wigeon *(Anas americana)*
Canvasback *(Aythya valisineria)*
Ring-necked Duck *(Aythya collaris)*
Greater Scaup *(Aythya marila)*
Lesser Scaup *(Aythya affinis)*
Oldsquaw *(Clangula hyemalis)*
Black Scoter *(Melanitta nigra)*
Common Goldeneye *(Bucephala clangula)*

Bufflehead *(Bucephala albeola)*
Common Merganser *(Mergus merganser)*
Ruddy Duck *(Oxyura jamaicensis)*
Chukar *(Alectoris chukar)*
American Avocet *(Recurvirostra americana)*
Franklin's Gull *(Larus pipixcan)*
Little Gull *(Larus minutus)*
Bonaparte's Gull *(Larus philadelphia)*
Ring-billed Gull *(Larus delawarensis)*
Lesser Black-backed Gull *(Larus fuscus)*
Caspian Tern *(Sterna caspia)*
Long-eared Owl *(Asio otus)*
Olive-sided Flycatcher *(Contopus borealis)*
Swainson's Thrush *(Catharus ustulatus)*
White-throated Sparrow *(Zonotrichia albicollis)*

Appendix E *Nonavian Fauna Cited**

Invertebrates

ant	Hymenoptera
aphid	Aphididae
Atlantic ribbed mussel	*Modiolus demissus*
bee	Hymenoptera
black-fingered mud crab	*Panopeus* sp.
browntail moth	*Euproctis chrysorrhoea*
caddisfly	Tricoptera
cankerworm	Geometridae
carpenter ant	*Camponotus* sp.
cicada	Cicadidae
clover leaf weevil	*Hypera punctata*
crane fly	*Tipula* sp.
crayfish	Cambaridae
cricket	*Gryllus* sp.
daddy-long-legs	Phalangiidae
damselfly	Odonata
dragonfly	Odonata
earthworm	Oligochaeta
fiddler crab	*Uca* sp.
fly	Diptera
forest tent caterpillar	*Malacosoma disstris*
ghost crab	*Ocypode quadrata*
grasshopper	Orthoptera
gypsy moth	*Lymantria dispar*
Japanese beetle	*Popillia japonica*
katydid	Tettigoniidae
ladybug beetle	Coccinellidae
leaf beetle	Chrysomelidae
leaf chafer	Scarabaeidae
leafhopper	Cicadellidae
leaf-roller	Tortricidae
locust	Orthoptera
mantid	Mantidae
May beetle	*Phyllophaga fervida*
mayfly	Ephemeroptera
mosquito	Culicidae
mourning cloak butterfly	*Nymphalis antiopa*
paper wasp	*Polistes* sp.
sand flea	Amphipoda
sand worm	Polychaeta
sawfly	Hymenoptera
scale insect	Homoptera
spider	Araneae
spruce budworm	*Choristoneura fumiferana*
squash bug	*Anasa tristis*
tent caterpillar	Lasiocampidae
tick	Acarina
wasp	Hymenoptera
white-marked tussock moth	*Orgyia leucostigma*

Fish

American sand lance	*Ammodytes americanus*
bass	*Micropterus* sp.
killifish	Cyprinodontidae
menhaden	*Brevoortia* sp.
northern pipefish	*Syngnathus fuscus*
sand lance	*Ammodytes* sp.

Mammals

beaver	*Castor canadensis*
chipmunk	*Tamias* sp.
eastern chipmunk	*Tamias striatus*
fox	Canidae
fox squirrel	*Sciurus niger*
gray squirrel	*Sciurus carolinensis*
horse	*Equus caballus*
meadow vole	*Microtus pennsylvanicus*
mouse	Muridae
muskrat	*Ondatra zibethicus*
rabbit	Leporidae
raccoon	*Procyon lotor*
red fox	*Vulpes vulpes*
skunk	Mustelidae
squirrel	Sciuridae
Virginia opossum	*Didelphis virginiana*
white-tailed deer	*Odocoileus virginianus*

Reptiles

snapping turtle	*Chelydra serpentina*
toad	*Bufo* sp.
treefrog	*Hyla* sp.

*From Banks et al. 1987; Gosner 1978; Robins et al. 1980; Sutherland 1978.

Appendix F *Plants Cited**

alder	*Alnus* sp.	crabgrass	*Digitaria* sp.
alfalfa	*Medicago sativa*	dogwood	*Cornus* sp.
American bee balm	*Monarda didyma*	duckweed	*Lemna* sp.
American beech	*Fagus grandifolia*	eastern hemlock	*Tsuga canadensis*
American chestnut	*Castanea dentata*	eastern red cedar	*Juniperus virginiana*
American holly	*Ilex opaca*	eelgrass	*Zostera marina*
American hornbeam	*Carpinus caroliniana*	elm	*Ulmus* sp.
American mountain ash	*Pyrus americana*	fir	*Abies* sp.
apple	*Pyrus malus*	flowering dogwood	*Cornus florida*
arrow arum	*Peltandra virginica*	glasswort	*Salicornia* sp.
arrowwood	*Viburnum* sp.	grape	*Vitis* sp.
ash	*Fraxinus* sp.	grass	Gramineae
aspen	*Populus* sp.	greenbrier	*Smilax* sp.
aster	*Aster* sp.	groundsel tree	*Baccharis halimifolia*
Atlantic white cedar	*Chamaecyparis thyoides*	gum	*Nyssa* sp.
bald cypress	*Taxodium distichum*	hackberry	*Celtis* sp.
bayberry	*Myrica pensylvanica*	hair-cap moss	*Polytrichum commune*
beachgrass	*Panicum amarulum*	hawthorn	*Crataegus* sp.
beech	*Fagus* sp.	heartwood decay fungus	*Fomes* sp.
big cordgrass	*Spartina cynosuroides*	hemlock	*Tsuga* sp.
big laurel	*Rhododendron maximum*	hickory	*Carya* sp.
birch	*Betula* sp.	holly	*Ilex* sp.
blackberry	*Rubus* sp.	honeysuckle	*Lonicera* sp.
black birch	*Betula lenta*	horse chestnut	*Aesculus hippocastanum*
black cherry	*Prunus serotina*	hydrilla	*Hydrilla verticillata*
black locust	*Robinia pseudoacacia*	ivy	*Hedera* sp.
blueberry	*Vaccinium* sp.	Japanese honeysuckle	*Lonicera japonica*
bracken fern	*Pteridium aquilinum*	jewelweed	*Impatiens* sp.
bristlegrass	*Setaria* sp.	laurel	*Kalmia* sp.
broad-leaved cattail	*Typha latifolia*	lespedeza	*Lespedeza* sp.
broomsedge	*Andropogon virginicus*	loblolly pine	*Pinus taeda*
bulrush	*Scirpus* sp.	maple	*Acer* sp.
bur-reed	*Sparganium* sp.	marsh elder	*Iva* sp.
buttonbush	*Cephalanthus occidentalis*	milfoil	*Myriophyllum* sp.
cattail	*Typha* sp.	milkweed	*Asclepias* sp.
cedar	*Juniperus* sp.	mimosa	*Albizzia julibrissin*
cherry	*Prunus* sp.	mountain laurel	*Kalmia latifolia*
chestnut	*Castanea* sp.	mulberry	*Morus* sp.
chestnut oak	*Quercus prinus*	multiflora rose	*Rosa multiflora*
clover	*Trifolium* sp.	muskgrass	*Chara* sp.
club moss	*Lycopodium* sp.	narrow-leaved cattail	*Typha angustifolia*
common rush	*Juncus effusus*	needlerush	*Juncus roemerianus*
cordgrass	*Spartina* sp.	northern red oak	*Quercus rubra borealis*
corn	*Zea mays*	Norway spruce	*Picea abies*
crabapple	*Pyrus* sp.	oak	*Quercus* sp.

*From Brown and Brown 1972; Brown and Brown 1984; Fernald 1970; Hurley 1990; Tiner 1988.

oats	*Avena* sp.	sorghum	*Sorgum vulgare*
Olney's bulrush	*Scirpus olneyi*	southern arrowwood	*Viburnum dentatum*
panic grass	*Panicum* sp.	soybean	*Glycine max*
pawpaw	*Asimina triloba*	Spanish moss	*Tillandsia usneoides*
peach	*Prunus* sp.	spruce	*Picea* sp.
persimmon	*Diospyros virginiana*	sugar maple	*Acer saccharum*
phragmites	*Phragmites* sp.	sunflower	*Helianthus* sp.
pickerelweed	*Pontederia cordata*	swamp azalea	*Rhododendron viscosum*
pine	*Pinus* sp.	swamp rosemallow	*Hibiscus moscheutos*
pitch pine	*Pinus rigida*	sweetbay	*Magnolia virginiana*
plum	*Prunus* sp.	sweet gum	*Liquidambar styraciflua*
poison ivy	*Rhus radicans*	sweet pepperbush	*Clethra alnifolia*
pondweed	*Potamogeton* sp.	switchgrass	*Panicum virgatum*
poplar	*Populus* sp.	sycamore	*Platanus occidentalis*
quaking aspen	*Populus tremuloides*	thistle	Compositae
ragweed	*Ambrosia* sp.	three-square	*Scirpus americanus*
red cedar	*Juniperus* sp.	timothy	*Phleum* sp.
red-head pondweed	*Potamogeton richardsonii*	trumpet creeper	*Campsis radicans*
red maple	*Acer rubrum*	tulip tree	*Liriodendron tulipifera*
red oak	*Quercus rubra*	vervain	*Verbena* sp.
red pine	*Pinus resinosa*	viburnum	*Viburnum* sp.
red spruce	*Picea rubens*	Virginia creeper	*Parthenocissus quinquefolia*
reed	*Arundo* sp.	Virginia pine	*Pinus virginiana*
rhododendron	*Rhododendron* sp.	water lily	*Nymphaea* sp.
rush	*Juncus* sp.	wax myrtle	*Myrica cerifera*
sago pondweed	*Potamogeton pectinatus*	wheat	*Triticum* sp.
saltgrass	*Distichlis* sp.	white birch	*Betula alba*
salt-marsh bulrush	*Scirpus maritimus*	white oak	*Quercus alba*
salt-meadow cordgrass	*Spartina patens*	white pine	*Pinus strobus*
sassafras	*Sassafras albidum*	widgeon grass	*Ruppia* sp.
scarlet oak	*Quercus coccinea*	wild celery	*Vallisneria americana*
seashore saltgrass	*Distichlis spicata*	wild rice	*Zizania aquatica*
sedge	*Carex* sp.	willow	*Salix* sp.
shortleaf pine	*Pinus echinata*	winterberry	*Ilex verticillata*
smartweed	*Polygonum* sp.	witch hazel	*Hamamelis virginiana*
smooth cordgrass	*Spartina alterniflora*	yellow birch	*Betula alleghaniensis*

Quad No.	Quad Name	NW(1)	NE(2)	CW(3)	CE(4)	SW(5)	SE(6)
001	Friendsville	69	76	77	70	76	90
002	Accident	97	74	70	62	68	72
003	Grantsville	79	94	69	83	75	108
004	Avilton	75	86	86	87	102	76
005	Frostburg	100	84	110	76	75	83
006	Cumberland	59	68	74	49	47	109
007	Evitts Creek	71	73	80	82	80	65
008	Flintstone	59	77	76	73	82	75
009	Artemas	65	67	75	72	60	64
010	Bellegrove	62	97	83	92	81	97
011	Hancock	91	95	93	91	95	—
012	Cherry Run	97	98	105	92	—	95
013	Clear Spring	78	52	90	69	79	75
014	Mason Dixon	70	77	80	75	81	62
015	Hagerstown	66	60	65	73	61	73
016	Smithsburg	66	88	67	81	75	91
017	Blue Ridge Summit	70	72	73	71	80	67
018	Emmitsburg	78	74	78	74	65	66
019	Taneytown	73	59	71	63	71	64
020	Littlestown	61	55	69	66	60	88
021	Manchester	88	69	65	63	83	66
022	Lineboro	71	72	67	86	57	83
023	New Freedom	68	64	63	68	72	76
024	Norrisville	75	72	61	77	71	87
025	Fawn Grove	62	68	71	69	72	86
026	Delta	69	60	72	89	80	72
027	Conowingo Dam	73	63	82	78	81	81
028	Rising Sun	79	72	68	76	63	68
029	Bay View	82	72	68	68	67	65
030	Newark West	77	—	75	—	66	—
031	Sang Run	62	58	70	82	85	82
032	McHenry	68	107	77	90	75	84
033	Bittinger	75	75	89	77	85	75
034	Barton	87	75	81	63	64	63
035	Lonaconing	43	57	62	80	66	74
036	Cresaptown	58	54	98	—	—	—
037	Patterson Creek	82	75	71	68	—	58
038	Oldtown	72	63	75	82	86	70
039	Paw Paw	67	87	69	52	75	—
040	Big Pool	—	67	—	—	—	—
041	Hedgesville	80	73	—	77	—	—
042	Williamsport	67	63	77	70	72	73
043	Funkstown	72	67	70	70	66	77
044	Myersville	70	89	80	84	80	100
045	Catoctin Furnace	72	92	69	75	72	74
046	Woodsboro	73	79	88	80	70	69
047	Union Bridge	63	62	59	61	61	64
048	New Windsor	56	72	61	67	65	70
049	Westminster	72	67	73	67	76	73
050	Hampstead	61	66	68	77	65	76
051	Hereford	68	72	94	81	71	85
052	Phoenix	82	80	80	70	88	75
053	Jarrettsville	69	85	79	72	76	90
054	Bel Air	66	91	77	72	62	60
055	Aberdeen	73	88	79	71	68	73
056	Havre de Grace	65	70	59	71	69	—
057	North East	64	72	67	71	70	63
058	Elkton	75	—	63	—	60	—
059	Oakland	71	87	87	101	73	96
060	Deer Park	78	83	93	72	79	81
061	Kitzmiller	82	77	68	74	73	61
062	Westernport	58	76	87	—	—	—
063	Keyser	77	64	73	—	—	—
064	Shepherdstown	68	76	—	69	—	—
065	Keedysville	78	85	69	87	83	81
066	Middletown	91	76	93	72	72	66
067	Frederick	76	61	69	61	69	63
068	Walkersville	63	70	65	77	69	68
069	Libertytown	67	66	69	73	74	69
070	Winfield	77	89	86	85	84	80
071	Finksburg	78	89	83	77	89	72
072	Reisterstown	83	76	71	78	79	83
073	Cockeysville	77	68	72	71	82	73
074	Towson	75	72	52	81	58	55
075	White Marsh	78	70	82	67	64	76
076	Edgewood	90	83	37	67	80	53
077	Perryman	66	83	86	—	98	01
078	Spesutie	65	—	54	—	—	60
079	Earleville	78	65	75	60	62	59
080	Cecilton	53	—	58	—	56	—
081	Table Rock	84	83	88	93	78	85
082	Gorman	89	81	84	81	83	—
083	Mount Storm	72	—	—	—	—	—
084	Harpers Ferry	70	86	68	78	—	—
085	Point of Rocks	68	75	65	76	—	68
086	Buckeystown	64	78	79	98	80	88
087	Urbana	74	70	81	77	84	93
088	Damascus	71	87	82	95	83	88
089	Woodbine	86	88	88	85	99	87
090	Sykesville	96	92	81	95	88	89
091	Ellicott City	76	67	86	86	82	89
092	Baltimore West	59	58	76	63	77	47
093	Baltimore East	50	59	40	61	38	31
094	Middle River	61	75	78	56	68	75
095	Gunpowder Neck	74	52	67	55	32	18
096	Hanesville	01	53	01	84	65	73
097	Betterton	80	92	85	78	71	73
098	Galena	73	66	69	60	63	66
099	Millington	72	84	65	84	77	82
100	Davis	86	71	78	—	—	—
101	Waterford	—	—	—	—	—	77

Quad No.	Quad Name	NW(1)	NE(2)	CW(3)	CE(4)	SW(5)	SE(6)
102	Poolesville	80	88	79	78	82	80
103	Germantown	84	83	79	91	78	92
104	Gaithersburg	85	77	73	62	79	71
105	Sandy Spring	83	95	70	76	78	79
106	Clarksville	81	89	89	85	95	97
107	Savage	85	89	85	81	89	82
108	Relay	92	77	83	68	71	63
109	Curtis Bay	55	50	58	74	63	63
110	Sparrows Point	60	83	58	—	76	—
111	Swan Point	—	—	—	69	—	78
112	Rock Hall	84	68	86	82	76	67
113	Chestertown	65	81	91	61	60	56
114	Church Hill	72	78	54	56	62	64
115	Sudlersville	81	55	58	55	58	53
116	Sterling	79	84	67	91	—	—
117	Seneca	85	80	84	84	—	—
118	Rockville	75	93	86	74	83	80
119	Kensington	73	75	66	84	73	62
120	Beltsville	76	88	70	72	63	84
121	Laurel	90	79	101	88	86	88
122	Odenton	77	79	84	71	88	71
123	Round Bay	73	64	81	68	82	75
124	Gibson Island	70	61	64	61	64	99
125	Love Point	—	—	—	—	15	42
126	Langford Creek	61	35	79	64	99	58
127	Centreville	61	61	66	65	65	64
128	Price	41	61	56	53	54	60
129	Goldsboro	67	66	76	69	56	65
130	Falls Church	90	86	—	65	—	34
131	Washington West	52	61	82	76	73	42
132	Washington East	50	69	62	49	65	47
133	Lanham	87	91	85	87	75	87
134	Bowie	78	76	90	73	80	85
135	South River	91	76	77	72	69	81
136	Annapolis	75	65	77	—	78	—
137	Kent Island	71	71	65	63	64	31
138	Queenstown	59	62	70	64	51	68
139	Wye Mills	58	58	76	55	70	54
140	Ridgely	82	84	83	78	84	64
141	Denton	61	69	70	65	73	79
142	Alexandria	21	41	25	67	68	74
143	Anacostia	70	50	52	84	82	93
144	Upper Marlboro	84	86	82	93	87	95
145	Bristol	97	91	94	84	115	89
146	Deale	85	70	72	64	76	63
147	Claiborne	50	67	01	76	76	66
148	St. Michaels	59	75	67	82	70	73
149	Easton	82	67	82	75	79	74
150	Fowling Creek	50	47	69	78	82	79
151	Hobbs	81	79	80	82	60	49
152	Hickman	71	—	83	—	66	—
153	Mount Vernon	—	83	83	90	88	86
154	Piscataway	80	89	87	88	84	82
155	Brandywine	87	93	86	83	101	92
156	Lower Marlboro	98	90	95	93	97	97
157	North Beach	69	73	78	82	86	49
158	Tilghman	75	65	69	01	—	—
159	Oxford	67	76	73	73	—	70
160	Trappe	73	84	76	78	71	70
161	Preston	82	50	81	68	71	62
162	Federalsburg	67	80	69	85	76	63
163	Seaford West	63	—	56	—	46	—
164	Indian Head	—	71	65	77	80	67
165	Port Tobacco	66	77	78	67	64	74
166	La Plata	65	85	91	91	67	61
167	Hughesville	73	79	70	76	73	71
168	Benedict	99	89	86	96	84	86
169	Prince Frederick	72	70	62	44	68	91
170	Hudson	—	49	—	53	01	01
171	Church Creek	06	75	78	79	77	61
172	Cambridge	57	80	63	53	65	70
173	East New Market	57	57	63	60	60	61
174	Rhodesdale	76	60	49	69	58	74
175	Sharptown	57	—	75	—	51	—
176	Widewater	—	68	—	59	—	44
177	Nanjemoy	62	70	79	88	66	76
178	Mathias Point	72	68	68	66	43	01
179	Popes Creek	69	64	63	68	77	69
180	Charlotte Hall	70	27	70	40	—	56
181	Mechanicsville	58	66	38	80	59	84
182	Broomes Island	75	58	53	73	65	69
183	Cove Point	—	—	89	—	67	93
184	Taylors Island	42	70	—	63	—	59
185	Golden Hill	69	78	87	89	83	74
186	Blackwater River	81	72	103	82	58	42
187	Chicamacomico River	65	65	68	71	54	53
188	Mardela Springs	71	78	61	77	55	73
189	Hebron	77	—	69	63	70	63
190	Delmar	—	—	61	72	78	71
191	Pittsville	—	—	64	62	80	67
192	Whaleysville	—	—	87	69	81	58
193	Selbyville	—	—	63	53	60	63
194	Assawoman Bay	—	—	61	37	74	25
195	King George	42	01	—	—	—	—
196	Colonial Beach North	60	67	01	77	—	41
197	Rock Point	02	72	18	67	55	58
198	Leonardtown	64	60	66	83	63	80
199	Hollywood	63	69	76	65	76	85
200	Solomons Island	65	71	57	74	75	84
201	Barren Island	—	07	—	32	—	—
202	Honga	63	72	32	59	20	43
203	Wingate	60	40	73	38	55	42
204	Nanticoke	32	25	46	57	13	51
205	Wetipquin	64	69	72	67	73	74
206	Eden	68	69	64	71	63	72
207	Salisbury	60	69	92	80	73	73
208	Wango	64	67	70	60	69	65
209	Ninepin	65	68	73	69	73	71
210	Berlin	61	74	68	75	82	72
211	Ocean City	67	—	65	—	34	—
212	Stratford Hall	—	52	—	—	—	—
213	St. Clements Island	01	51	—	—	—	—
214	Piney Point	72	61	01	61	—	55
215	St. Marys City	62	69	65	68	62	59
216	Point No Point	—	—	74	—	71	—
217	Richland Point	10	02	—	—	—	—
218	Bloodsworth Island	39	20	05	11	07	—
219	Deal Island	07	61	47	78	58	39
220	Monie	71	87	81	68	53	66
221	Princess Anne	75	70	71	75	71	73
222	Dividing Creek	79	72	77	73	88	71

Quad No.	Quad Name	Species Totals by Block					
		NW(1)	NE(2)	CW(3)	CE(4)	SW(5)	SE(6)
223	Snow Hill	75	70	74	75	79	70
224	Public Landing	73	74	73	85	66	78
225	Tingles Island	51	60	19	53	33	45
226	St. George Island	53	61	—	—	—	—
227	Point Lookout	63	—	77	—	03	—
228	Kedges Straits	07	22	—	01	—	44
229	Terrapin Sand Point	—	—	01	—	01	—
230	Marion	67	79	51	64	70	74
231	Kingston	77	69	70	80	84	80

Quad No.	Quad Name	Species Totals by Block					
		NW(1)	NE(2)	CW(3)	CE(4)	SW(5)	SE(6)
232	Pocomoke City	74	79	74	72	72	74
233	Girdletree	75	69	67	74	67	75
234	Boxiron	78	22	74	19	26	58
235	Whittington Point	64	11	48	—	32	—
236	Ewell	04	49	01	—	—	—
237	Great Fox Island	01	19	—	08	—	—
238	Crisfield	70	73	37	—	—	—
239	Saxis	85	67	—	—	—	—

— = Block not covered

Literature Cited

Adamus, P. R. 1988. Atlas of the breeding birds in Maine, 1978–1983. Maine Dept. Inland Fish. and Wildl., Augusta.

Adkisson, C. S. 1988. Cavity nesting birds of North America: Past history, present status, and future prospects. Pp. 85–100 *in* J. A. Jackson, ed. Bird Conservation 3. Univ. Wisconsin Press, Madison.

Adkisson, C. S., and R. N. Conner. 1978. Interspecific vocal imitation in White-eyed Vireos. Auk 95:602–06.

Advisory and Planning Board. 1982. Maryland & DC breeding bird atlas project handbook, 1983–1987. Maryland Birdlife (Suppl.) Vol. 38, 21–22.

Afton, A. D. 1979. Time budget of breeding Northern Shovelers. Wilson Bull. 91:42–49.

Ake, J. R., R. L. Ake, and W. W. Fogleman. 1976. Savannah Sparrow nest in Highland County first nesting record for Virginia. Raven 47:57–58.

Akers, J. W. 1975. The Least Tern in Virginia: Breeding biology and population distribution. M.A. Thesis. College of William and Mary, Williamsburg, Virginia.

Aldrich, J. W. 1944. Geographic variation of Bewick Wrens in the eastern United States. Louisiana State Univ., Occ. Papers Mus. Zool. 18:305–09.

Allen, A. A., ed. 1930. Rubythroat. Bird-Lore 32:223–31.

Allen, F. H. 1929. The White-breasted and Red-breasted Nuthatches. Bird-Lore 14:316–19.

Alsop, F. J., III. 1978. Savannah Sparrow nesting in upper east Tennessee. Migrant 49:1–4.

———. 1979. Mantids selected as prey by Blue Grosbeaks. Wilson Bull. 91:131–32.

———. 1980. Bewick's Wren. Pp. A47–A48 *in* D. C. Eagar and R. M. Hatcher, eds. 1980. Tennessee's rare wildlife, Vol. 1: The vertebrates. Tennessee Wildl. Resource Agency and Tennessee Conserv. Dept., Nashville.

———. 1981. The Cliff Swallow in Tennessee. Migrant 52:1–11.

Altman, R. L., and R. D. Gano, Jr. 1984. Least Terns nest alongside harrier jet pad. J. Field Ornith. 55:108–09.

Ames, P. L., and C. S. Mersereau. 1964. Some factors in the decline of the Osprey in Connecticut. Auk 81:173–85.

Anderson, D. R., and C. J. Henny. 1972. Population ecology of the Mallard. I. A review of previous studies and the distribution and migration from breeding areas. U.S. Fish Wildl. Serv., Resource Publ. 105, Washington, D.C.

Andrew, J. M., and J. A. Mosher. 1982. Bald Eagle nest site selection and nesting habitat in Maryland. J. Wildl. Manage. 46:382–90.

Andrle, R. F. 1971. Range extension of the Golden-crowned Kinglet in New York. Wilson Bull. 83:313–16.

Andrle, R. F., and J. R. Carroll. 1988. The atlas of breeding birds in New York State. Cornell Univ. Press, Ithaca, N.Y.

Ankney, C. D., and A. D. Afton. 1988. Bioenergetics of breeding Northern Shovelers: diet, nutrient reserves, clutch size, and incubation. Condor 90:459–72.

AOU. 1931. Check-list of North American birds. 4th ed. American Ornithologists' Union, Lancaster, Pa.

———. 1957. Check-list of North American birds. 5th ed. Port City Press, Baltimore, Md.

———. 1983. Check-list of North American birds. 6th ed. Allen Press, Lawrence, Kans.

———. 1993. Thirty-ninth supplement to the American Ornithologists' Union Check-list of North American birds. Auk 110:675–82.

———. 1995. Fortieth supplement to the American Ornithologists' Union Check-list of North American birds. Auk 112:819–30.

Arbib, R. S. 1973. The blue list for 1974. Amer. Birds 27:943–45.

———. 1988a. Double-crested Cormorant. Pp. 30–31 *in* R. F. Andrle and J. R. Carroll, eds. The atlas of breeding birds in New York State. Cornell Univ. Press, Ithaca, N.Y.

———. 1988b. Bobolink. Pp. 466–67 *in* R. F. Andrle and J. R. Carroll, eds. The atlas of breeding birds in New York State. Cornell Univ. Press, Ithaca, N.Y.

Arendt, W. J. 1988. Range expansion of the Cattle Egret (*Bubulcus ibis*) in the greater Caribbean Basin. Colonial Waterbirds 11:252–62.

Armistead, H. T. 1970. The first Maryland breeding of American Coot at Deal Island. Maryland Birdlife 26:79–81.

———. 1971. First Maryland breeding of Green-winged Teal. Maryland Birdlife 27:111–14.

———. 1974. Iceland Gulls, Forster's Tern nests, and breeding herons in Dorchester County, summer 1974. Maryland Birdlife 30:128–32.

———. 1975. Breeding of the Greater Black-backed Gull, Herring Gull, and Gadwall at Smith Island, Maryland. Maryland Birdlife 31:131–34.

———. 1977. American Oystercatcher and Herring Gull breed in Dorchester County. Maryland Birdlife 33:111–12.

———. 1978. Summer birds of lower Chesapeake Bay islands in Maryland. Maryland Birdlife 34:99–151.

———. 1987. The nesting season June 1–July 31, 1987: middle Atlantic coast region. Amer. Birds 41:1418–22.

———. 1989. Middle Atlantic coast region. Amer. Birds 43: 76–80.

———. 1990. Middle Atlantic coast region. Amer. Birds 44:1299–1303.

———. 1991. Middle Atlantic coast region. Amer. Birds 45:426.

Armistead, H. T., and W. C. Russell. 1967. First Black-necked Stilt and fourth Ruff. Maryland Birdlife 23:62–63.

Armstrong, E. R., and D. L. Euler. 1983. Hermit Thrush nesting on rock face. Wilson Bull., 95–160.

Audubon, J. J. 1839. A synopsis of the birds of North America. Adam and Charles Black, Edinburgh, Scotland.

———. 1842. The birds of America. Vol. 4. J. B. Chevalier, Philadelphia, Pa.

Austin, O. L., Jr. 1932. The breeding of the Blue-winged Teal in Maryland. Auk 49:191–98.

Austing, G. R., and J. B. Holt, Jr. 1966. The world of the Great Horned Owl. J. B. Lippincott Co., Philadelphia, Pa.

Bailey, H. H. 1913. The birds of Virginia. J. P. Bell Co., Inc., Lynchburg, Va.

Baird, J. 1968. Eastern Savannah Sparrow. Pp. 678–96 in O. L. Austin, Jr., ed. Life histories of North American cardinals, grosbeaks, buntings, towhees, finches, sparrows, and allies. U.S. Natl. Mus. Bull. 237, Washington, D.C.

Baird, S. F., J. Cassin, and G. N. Lawrence. 1858. Explorations and surveys for a railroad route from the Mississippi River to the Pacific Ocean. A. O. P. Nicholson, Washington, D.C.

Ball, W. H. 1930. Notes for eastern Maryland. Auk 47:94–95.

———. 1932. Notes from the Washington, D.C. region. Auk 49:362.

Ball, W. H., and R. B. Wallace. 1936. Further remarks on birds of Bolling Field, D.C. Auk 53:345–46.

Bancroft, G. T. 1986. Nesting success and mortality of the Boat-tailed Grackle. Auk 103:86–99.

Banks, R. C., R. W. McDiarmid, and A. L. Gardner, eds. 1987. Checklist of vertebrates of the United States, the U.S. territories, and Canada. U.S. Fish and Wildl. Serv., Resource Publ. 166.

Barbour, R. W. 1951. Observations on the breeding habits of the Red-eyed Towhee. Amer. Midl. Nat. 45:672–78.

Barclay, J. S. 1970. Ecological aspects of defensive behavior in breeding Mallards and Black Ducks. Ph.D. diss., Ohio State Univ., Columbus.

Barclay, R. M. R., M. L. Leonard, and G. Friesen. 1985. Nocturnal singing by Marsh Wrens. Condor 87:416–22.

Barrows, W. B., and E. A. Schwarz. 1895. The Common Crow of the United States. U.S. Dept. Agric. Bull. 6, Washington, D.C.

Basore, N. S., L. B. Best, and J. B. Wooley, Jr. 1986. Bird nesting in Iowa no-tillage and tilled croplands. J. Wildl. Manage. 50:19–28.

Batts, H. L., Jr. 1958. The distribution and population of nesting birds on a farm in southern Michigan. Jack-Pine Warbler 36:131–46.

Baynard, O. E. 1913. Home life of the Glossy Ibis (Plegadis autumnalis Linn.). Wilson Bull. 25:103–17.

Beal, F. E. L. 1911. Food of the woodpeckers of the United States. U.S. Dept. Agric. Bull. 37, Washington, D.C.

———. 1912. Food of our more important flycatchers. U.S. Biol. Surv. Bull. 44, Washington, D.C.

———. 1915. Food habits of the thrushes of the United States. U.S. Dept. Agric. Bull. 280, Washington, D.C.

———. 1918. Food habits of the swallows, a family of valuable native birds. U.S. Dept. Agric. Bull. 619, Washington, D.C.

Beal, F. E. L., W. L. McAtee, and E. R. Kalmbach. 1916. Common birds of southeastern United States in relation to agriculture. U.S. Dept. Agric., Farmers Bull. 755, Washington, D.C.

Beason, R. C., and E. C. Franks. 1974. Breeding behavior of the Horned Lark. Auk 91:65–74.

Beason, R. C., and L. L. Trout. 1984. Cooperative breeding of the Bobolink. Wilson Bull. 96:709–10.

Bednarz, J. C., and J. J. Dinsmore. 1982. Nest sites and habitat for Red-shouldered and Red-tailed Hawks in Iowa. Wilson Bull. 94:31–45.

Bednarz, J. C., D. Klem, Jr., L. J. Goodrich, and S. E. Senner. 1990. Migration counts of raptors at Hawk Mountain, Pennsylvania, as indicators of population trends, 1934–1986. Auk 107:96–109.

Behr, H. 1914. Some breeding birds of Garrett Co., Md. Auk 31:548.

Bekhuis, J., R. Bijlsma, A. van Dijk, F. Hustings, R. Lensink, and F. Saris, eds. 1987. Atlas van de Nederlandse Vogels. SOVON, Arnhem, The Netherlands.

Belles-Isles, J. C., and J. Picman. 1986a. House Wren nest-destroying behavior. Condor 88:190–93.

———. 1986b. Nesting losses and nest site preference of House Wrens. Condor 88:483–86.

———. 1986c. Destruction of heterospecific eggs by the Gray Catbird. Wilson Bull. 98:603–05.

Bellrose, F. C. 1943. Two Wood Ducks incubating in the same box. Auk 60:446–47.

———. 1976. Ducks, geese and swans of North America. Stackpole Books, Harrisburg, Pa.

Bellrose, F. C., K. L. Johnson, and T. U. Meyers. 1964. Relative value of natural cavities and nesting houses for Wood Ducks. J. Wildl. Manage. 28:661–76.

Bendel, P. R., and G. D. Therres. 1990. Nesting biology of Barn Owls from Eastern Shore marshes. Maryland Birdlife 46:119–23.

Bendire, C. E. 1892. Life histories of North American birds. U.S. Natl. Mus. Spec. Bull. 1, Washington, D.C.

———. 1895a. Life histories of North American birds. U.S. Natl. Mus. Spec. Bull. 3, Washington, D.C.

———. 1895b. The American Barn Owl breeding in Washington, D.C., in winter. Auk 12:180–81.

Bent, A. C. 1921. Life histories of North American gulls and terns. U.S. Natl. Mus. Bull. 113, Washington, D.C.

——— 1923. Life histories of North American wild fowl. U.S. Natl. Mus. Bull. 126, Washington, D.C.

——— 1926. Life histories of North American marsh birds. U.S. Natl. Mus. Bull. 135, Washington, D.C.

——— 1927. Life histories of North American shore birds. Part 1. U.S. Natl. Mus. Bull. 142, Washington, D.C.

——— 1929. Life histories of North American shore birds. Part 2. U.S. Natl. Mus. Bull. 146, Washington, D.C.

——— 1932. Life histories of North American gallinaceous birds. U.S. Natl. Mus. Bull. 162, Washington D.C.

——— 1937. Life histories of North American birds of prey. Part 1. U.S. Natl. Mus. Bull. 167, Washington, D.C.

——— 1938. Life histories of North American birds of prey. Part 2. U.S. Natl. Mus. Bull. 170, Washington, D.C.

——— 1939. Life histories of North American woodpeckers. U.S. Natl. Mus. Bull. 174, Washington, D.C.

——— 1940. Life histories of North American cuckoos, goatsuckers, hummingbirds and their allies. U.S. Natl. Mus. Bull. 176, Washington, D.C.

——— 1942. Life histories of North American flycatchers, larks, swallows, and their allies. U.S. Natl. Mus. Bull. 179, Washington, D.C.

——— 1946. Life histories of North American jays, crows, and titmice. U.S. Natl. Mus. Bull. 191, Washington, D.C.

——— 1948. Life histories of North American nuthatches, wrens, thrashers, and their allies. U.S. Natl. Mus. Bull. 195, Washington, D.C.

——— 1950. Life histories of North American wagtails, shrikes, vireos, and their allies. U.S. Natl. Mus. Bull. 197, Washington, D.C.

——— 1953. Life histories of North American wood warblers. U.S. Natl. Mus. Bull. 203, Washington, D.C.

——— 1958. Life histories of North American blackbirds, orioles, tanagers, and allies. U.S. Natl. Mus. Bull. 211, Washington, D.C.

——— 1968a. Eastern Cardinal. Pp. 1–15 in O. L. Austin, Jr., ed. Life histories of North American cardinals, grosbeaks, buntings, towhees, finches, sparrows, and allies. U.S. Natl. Mus. Bull. 237, Washington, D.C.

———— 1968b. Rose-breasted Grosbeak. Pp. 36–55 in O. L. Austin, Jr., ed. Life histories of North American cardinals, grosbeaks, buntings, towhees, finches, sparrows, and allies. U.S. Natl. Mus. Bull. 237., Washington, D.C.

———— 1968c. Eastern Blue Grosbeak. Pp. 67–75 in O. L. Austin, Jr., ed. Life histories of North American cardinals, grosbeaks, buntings, towhees, finches, sparrows, and allies. U.S. Natl. Mus. Bull. 237, Washington, D.C.

———— 1968d. Eastern Purple Finch. Pp. 264–78 in O. L. Austin, Jr., ed. Life histories of North American cardinals, grosbeaks, buntings, towhees, finches, sparrows, and allies. U.S. Natl. Mus. Bull. 237, Washington, D.C.

Berger, A. J. 1968. Eastern Vesper Sparrow. Pp. 868–82 in O. L. Austin, Jr., ed. Life histories of North American cardinals, grosbeaks, buntings, towhees, finches, sparrows, and allies. U.S. Natl. Mus. Bull. 237, Washington, D.C.

Bergstrom, P. W. 1986. Daylight incubation sex roles in Wilson's Plover. Condor 88:113–15.

Bergtold, W. H. 1917. A study of the incubation periods of birds. Kendrick-Bellamy, Denver, Colo.

Besley, F. W. 1910. The forests and their products. Pp. 361–79, Part 6 in F. Shreve, M. A. Chrysler, F. H. Blodgett, and F. W. Besley, eds. The plant life of Maryland. Maryland Weather Service, Spec. Publ., Vol. 3.

Best, L. B. 1978. Field Sparrow reproductive success and nesting ecology. Auk 95:9–22.

Best, L. B., and N. L. Rodenhouse. 1984. Territory preference of Vesper Sparrows in cropland. Wilson Bull. 96:72–82.

Best, L. B. 1977. Nestling biology of the Field Sparrow. Auk 94:308–19.

Bevier, L.R., ed. 1994. The atlas of breeding birds of Connecticut. Bull. 113, State Geol. and Nat. Hist. Survey of Connecticut, Hartford.

Blakers, M., S. J. J. Davies, and P. N. Reilly. 1984. The atlas of Australian birds. Melbourne Univ. Press, Melbourne, Australia.

Blem, C. R, and L. B. Blem. 1990. Bank Swallows at Presquile National Wildlife Refuge 1975–1989. Raven 61:3–6.

Blem, C. R., W. H. N. Gutzke, and C. Filemyr. 1980. First breeding record of Double-crested Cormorant in Virginia. Wilson Bull. 92:127–28.

Blodgett, F. H. 1910. The agricultural features of Maryland. Pp. 305–359 in F. Shreve, M. A. Chrysler, F. H. Blodgett, and F. W. Besley, eds. The plant life of Maryland. Maryland Weather Service, Spec. Publ., Vol. 3.

Blodgett, K. D., and R. M. Zammuto. 1979. Chimney Swift nest found in hollow tree. Wilson Bull. 91:154.

Blom, E. A. T. 1986. Atlasing night birds. Pp. 23–24 in S. M. Sutcliffe, R. E. Bonney, and J. D. Lowe, eds. Proc. second northeastern breeding bird atlas conference. Cornell Lab. Ornith., Ithaca, N.Y.

Blumton, A. K., J. D. Fraser, and K. Terwilliger. 1989. Loggerhead Shrike survey and census. Pp. 116–18 in Virginia nongame and endangered wildlife investigations, annual report, July 1, 1988 through June 30, 1989. Virginia Dept. Game and Inland Fish., Richmond.

Blus, L. J., A. A. Belisle, and R. M. Prouty. 1974. Relations of the Brown Pelican to certain environmental pollutants. Pesticides Monitor. J. 7:181–94.

Bock, C. E., and L. W. Lepthien. 1976. Growth in the eastern House Finch population, 1962–71. Amer. Birds 30:791–92.

Bond, G. M., and R. E. Stewart. 1951. A new Swamp Sparrow from the Maryland coastal plain. Wilson Bull. 63:38–40.

Boone, D. D. 1975. 24th annual nest card summary, 1972. Maryland Birdlife 31:17–24.

————. 1978. Breeding bird atlas of Washington County. Maryland Birdlife 34:46.

————. 1981. Nashville Warbler nest in Garrett County. Maryland Birdlife 37:2–4.

————1984. First confirmed nesting of a goshawk in Maryland. Wilson Bull. 96:129.

Boone, J. E. 1982. A Maryland nesting of the Golden-crowned Kinglet. Maryland Birdlife 38:79–85.

Booth, W. M. 1958. The Cliff Swallow in Maryland: Its distribution, ecology, and habits. Maryland Birdlife 14:83–92.

Borden, R., and H. A. Hochbaum. 1966. Gadwall breeding in New England. Trans. N. Amer. Wildl. Nat. Resources Conf. 31:79–87.

Borror, D. J. 1970. Songs of eastern birds. Dover Publ., Inc., N.Y.

————. 1987. Song in the White-eyed Vireo. Wilson Bull. 99:377–97.

Bortner, J. B. 1990. American Woodcock harvest and breeding population status, 1990. U.S. Fish and Wildl. Serv., Laurel, Md.

Boxall, P. C. 1983. Observations suggesting parental division of labor by American Redstarts. Wilson Bull. 95:673–74.

Brackbill, H. 1943. A nesting study of the Wood Thrush. Wilson Bull. 55:72–87.

————. 1944. The Cardinal's period of dependency. Wilson Bull. 56:173–74.

————. 1949. Courtship feeding by the Carolina Chickadee and Tufted Titmouse. Auk 66:290–92

————. 1953. Migratory status of breeding Song Sparrows at Baltimore, Maryland. Bird-Banding 24:68.

————. 1955. Three-brooded Cardinals. Maryland Birdlife 11:29.

————. 1958. Nesting behavior of the Wood Thrush. Wilson Bull. 70:70–89.

————. 1969a. Red-bellied Woodpeckers taking birds' eggs. Bird-Banding 40:323–24.

————. 1969b. Status and behavior of color-banded White-breasted Nuthatches at Baltimore. Maryland Birdlife 25:87–91.

————. 1970. Tufted Titmouse breeding behavior. Auk 87:522–36.

Bradley, R. A. 1980. Vocal and territorial behavior in the White-eyed Vireo. Wilson Bull. 92:302–11.

Brakhage, G. K. 1965. Biology and behavior of tub-nesting Canada Geese. J. Wildl. Manage. 29:751–71.

Braun, E. L. 1950. Deciduous forests of eastern North America. Blackiston Co., Philadelphia, Pa.

Brauning, D. W., ed. 1992. Atlas of breeding birds in Pennsylvania. Univ. of Pittsburgh Press, Pittsburgh.

Breckenridge, J. W. 1956. Measurements of the habitat niche of the Least Flycatcher. Wilson Bull. 68:47–51.

Brewer, R., G. McPeek, and R. Adams. 1991. The atlas of breeding birds of Michigan. Michigan State Univ. Press, East Lansing.

Brewer, R., and P. G. Merritt. 1979. Pine Siskin nesting in Kalamazoo County, Michigan. Jack-Pine Warbler 57:27–28.

Brewster, W. 1906. The birds of the Cambridge region of Massachusetts. Nuttall Ornith. Club Mem. 4.

Bridge, D. 1959. Maryland nest summary for 1959. Maryland Birdlife 15:89–96.

————. 1966. The birds of Big Run, Garrett County. Maryland Birdlife 22:62.

Bridge, D., and M. Bridge. 1964. Maryland nest summary for 1963. Maryland Birdlife 20:40–47.

Bridge, D., and M. Riedel. 1962. Maryland nest summary for 1961. Maryland Birdlife 18:64–70.

Bridge, D., and J. S. Weske. 1961. Breeding birds on Maryland's coastal islands. Maryland Birdlife 17:3–6.

Bridge, M. A. 1963. Maryland nest summary for 1962. Maryland Birdlife 19:55–63.

Briggs, S. A., and J. H. Criswell. 1979. Gradual silencing of spring in Washington. Atlantic Nat. 32:19–26.

Brigham, R. M. 1989. Roost and nest sites of Common Nighthawks: Are gravel roofs important? Condor 91:722–24.

Brinker, D. F., and K. M. Dodge. 1993. Breeding biology of the Northern Saw-whet Owl in Maryland: First nest record and associated observations. Maryland Birdlife 49:3–15.

Briskie, J. V., and S. G. Sealey. 1987. Polygyny and double-brooding in the Least Flycatcher. Wilson Bull. 99:492–94.

———. 1988. Nest re-use and egg burial in the Least Flycatcher, *Empidonax minimus*. Canadian Field-Nat. 102:729–31.

———. 1989. Determination of clutch size in the Least Flycatcher. Auk 106:269–78.

Brittingham, M. C., and S. A. Temple. 1983. Have cowbirds caused forest songbirds to decline? Bioscience 33:31–35.

Brooks, A. B. 1934. Some ornithological contributions by the nature school. Redstart 1:1–3.

Brooks, M. G. 1936. Notes on the land birds of Garrett County, Maryland. Bull. Nat. Hist. Soc. Maryland 7:6–14.

———. 1937. Pine Siskins in western Maryland. Wilson Bull. 49:294.

———. 1938. Shorebirds at a western Maryland lake. Auk 55:126–27.

———. 1944. A check-list of West Virginia birds. West Virginia Univ. Agric. Exp. Sta. Bull. 316.

Broun, M. 1949. Hawks aloft: The story of Hawk Mountain. Dodd Mead, N.Y.

———. 1957. Blue-winged Warbler. Pp. 44–45 *in* L. Griscom and A. Sprunt, Jr., eds. The warblers of America. Devin-Adair Co., N.Y.

Brown, B. W. 1973. The Big Lake Wood Duck: A two-year study of its pre-flight mortality, nest population, growth and migration, 1970–71. Proc. Annual Conf. Southeastern Assoc. Game and Fish Comm. 26:195–292.

Brown, C. R. 1985. The costs and benefits of coloniality in the Cliff Swallow. Ph.D. diss. Princeton Univ., Princeton, N.J.

Brown, C. R., and M. B. Brown. 1988. The costs and benefits of egg destruction by conspecifics in colonial Cliff Swallows. Auk 105:737–48.

Brown, L., and D. Amadon. 1989. Eagles, hawks and falcons of the world. Vol. 1. Wellfleet Press, Secaucus, N.J.

Brown, M. L., and R. G. Brown. 1984. Herbaceous plants of Maryland. Port City Press, Baltimore, Md.

Brown, M. L., J. L. Reveal, C. R. Broome, and G. F. Frick. 1987. Comments on the vegetation of colonial Maryland. Huntia 7:247–83.

Brown, R. G., and M. L. Brown. 1972. Woody plants of Maryland. Port City Press, Baltimore, Md.

Browning, M. 1859. Forty-four years of the life of a hunter. Lippincott Co., Philadelphia, Pa.

Bruch, A., H. Elvers, C. Pohl, D. Westphal, and K. Witt. 1978. Die Vögel in Berlin (West) - eine Übersicht. Ornithologischer Bericht fur Berlin (West).

Brumbaugh, C. S. 1915. Chestnut-sided Warbler nesting near Baltimore. Bird-Lore 17:456–57.

Brunton, D. H. 1988. Sequential polyandry by a female Killdeer. Wilson Bull. 100:670–72.

Brush, G. S., C. Lenk, and J. Smith. 1980. The natural forests of Maryland: An explanation of the vegetation map of Maryland. Ecol. Mongr. 50:77–92.

Buckelew, A. R., Jr., and G. A. Hall. 1994. The West Virginia breeding bird atlas. University of Pittsburgh Press, Pittsburgh, Pa.

Buckley, F. G., and P. A. Buckley. 1972. The breeding ecology of Royal Terns Sterna (Thalasseus) maxima. Ibis 114:344–59.

———. 1980. Habitat selection and marine birds. Pp. 69–112 *in* J. Burger, B. L. Olla, and H. E. Winn, eds. Behavior of marine animals, 4, marine birds. Plenum Press, N.Y.

Buckley, F. G., and C. A. McCaffrey. 1978. Use of dredged material islands by colonial seabirds and wading birds in New Jersey. U.S. Army Eng. Waterways Exp. Sta., Tech. Rep. D-78-1, Vicksburg, Miss.

Buckley, P. A., and F. G. Buckley. 1976. Guidelines for the protection and management of colonial nesting water birds. Natl. Park Serv., Boston.

———. 1984. Seabirds of the north and middle Atlantic coasts of the United States: Their status and conservation. Pp. 101–33 *in* J. P. Croxall, P.G.H. Evans, and R. W. Schreiber, eds. Status and conservation of the world's seabirds. Internatl. Counc. Bird Preserv. Tech. Publ. 2.

Buech, R. R. 1982. Nesting ecology and cowbird parasitism of Clay-colored, Chipping, and Field Sparrows in a Christmas tree plantation. J. Field Ornith. 53:363–63.

Buehler, D. A., T. J. Mersmann, J. D. Fraser, and J.K.D. Seegar. 1991. Differences in distribution of breeding, nonbreeding, and migrant Bald Eagles on the northern Chesapeake Bay. Condor 93:399–08.

Buhnerkempe, J. E., and R. L. Westemeier. 1984. Nest-sites of Turkey Vultures in buildings in southeastern Illinois. Wilson Bull. 96:495–96.

Bull, J. 1974. Birds of New York State. Amer. Mus. Nat. Hist., N.Y.

Bull, J., and J. Farrand, Jr. 1977. The Audubon Society field guide to North American birds (eastern region). A. A. Knopf, N.Y.

Bull, P. C., P. D. Gaze, and C. J. R. Robertson. 1978. Bird distribution in New Zealand, a provisional atlas, 1969–1976. Ornith. Soc. of New Zealand, Wellington North.

Bump, G. 1941. The introduction and transplantation of game birds and mammals in the state of New York. Trans. N. Amer. Wildl. Conf. 5:409–20.

Bump, G., R. W. Darrow, F. C. Edminster, and W. F. Crissey. 1947. The Ruffed Grouse: Life history, propagation, management. N.Y. Conserv. Dept., Albany.

Burger, G. V., and J. P. Linduska. 1967. Habitat management related to Bobwhite populations at Remington Farms. J. Wildl. Manage. 31:1–12.

Burger, J. 1978a. Great Black-backed Gulls breeding in salt marsh in New Jersey. Wilson Bull. 90:304–05.

———. 1978b. Competition between Cattle Egrets and native North American herons, egrets, and ibises. Condor 80:15–23.

———. 1979a. Competition and predation: Herring Gulls versus Laughing Gulls. Condor 81:269–77.

———. 1979b. Resource partitioning: Nest site selection in mixed species colonies of herons, egrets, and ibises. Amer. Midl. Nat. 101:191–210.

Burger, J., and J. Shisler. 1978. Nest site selection and competitive interactions of Herring and Laughing Gulls in New Jersey. Auk 95:252–66.

Burns, F. L. 1915. Comparative periods of deposition and incubation of some North American birds. Wilson Bull. 27:275–86.

Burns, J. T. 1982. Nests, territories, and reproduction of Sedge Wrens (*Cistothorus platensis*). Wilson Bull. 94:338–49.

Burt, W. G., III. 1987. Tales of two rails: Deceiving a feathered mouse. Audubon Mag. (September 1987):78–83.

Bush, M. E., and F. R. Gehlbach. 1978. Broad-winged Hawk nest in central Texas: Geographic record and novel aspects of reproduction. Bull. Texas Ornith. Soc. 11:41–43.

Bushman, E. S., and G. D. Therres. 1988. Habitat management guidelines for forest interior breeding birds of coastal Maryland. Maryland Dept. Nat. Resources, Wildl. Tech. Publ. 88-1, Annapolis.

Buss, I. O., and A. S. Hawkins. 1939. The Upland Plover at Faville Grove, Wisconsin. Wilson Bull. 51:202–20.

Butcher, G. 1989. Bird conservation: Establishing priorities. Birdscope 3:1–5.

Butler, R. W. 1988. Population dynamics and migration routes of Tree Swallows, *Tachycineta bicolor*, in North America. J. Field Ornith. 59:395–402.

Butts, W. K. 1931. A study of the chickadee and White-breasted Nuthatch by means of marked individuals. Bird-Banding 2:59–76.

Bystrak, D. 1970. Maryland nest summary for 1969. Maryland Birdlife 26:30–34.

———. 1971. 22nd annual nest card summary, 1970. Maryland Birdlife 27:173–81.

Cabot. 1855. Proc. Boston Soc. Nat. Hist. 5:154.

Cadman, M. D., P. F. J. Eagles, and F. M. Helleiner. 1987. Atlas of breeding birds of Ontario. Univ. of Waterloo Press, Waterloo, Ontario, Canada.

Cairns, W. E. 1982. Biology and behavior of breeding Piping Plovers. Wilson Bull. 94:531–45.

Cannings, R. J. 1987. The breeding biology of Northern Saw-whet Owls in southern British Columbia. Pp. 193–98 *in* R. W. Nero, R. J. Clark, R. J. Knapton, and R. H. Hamre, eds. Biology and conservation of northern forest owls: Symposium proceedings. U.S. Forest Serv., Rocky Mountain Forest Range Exp. Sta., Gen. Tech. Rep. RM-142, Fort Collins, Colo.

Cantwell, R. 1961. Alexander Wilson, naturalist and pioneer. J. B. Lippincott, Philadelphia, Pa.

Carpenter, N. K. 1918. Observations in a swallow colony. Condor 20:90–91.

Carreker, R. G. 1985. Habitat suitability index models: Least Tern. U.S. Fish and Wildl. Serv., Biol. Rep. 82(10.103), Washington, D.C.

Chapin, E. A. 1925. Food habits of the vireos. U.S. Dept. Agric. Bull. 1355, Washington, D.C.

Chapman, F. M. 1907a. The warblers of North America. D. Appleton, N.Y.

———. 1907b. The Starling in America. Bird-Lore 9:206.

Charbeck, R. H. 1963. Breeding habits of the Pied-billed Grebe in an impounded coastal marsh in Louisiana. Auk 80:447–52.

Choate, E. A. 1973. The dictionary of American bird names. Gambit, Boston, Mass.

Christensen, N. L. 1988. Vegetation of the southeastern coastal plain. Pp. 317–63 *in* M. G. Barbour and W. D. Billings, eds. North American terrestrial vegetation. Cambridge Univ. Press, N.Y.

Christy, B. H. 1939. Northern Pileated Woodpecker. Pp. 171–89 *in* A. C. Bent, ed. Life histories of North American woodpeckers. U.S. Natl. Mus. Bull. 174, Washington, D.C.

———. 1942. Acadian Flycatcher. Pp. 183–97 *in* A. C. Bent, ed. Life histories of North American flycatchers, larks, swallows and their allies. U.S. Natl. Mus. Bull. 179, Washington, D.C.

Cink, C. L. 1976. The influence of early learning on nest site selection in the House Sparrow. Condor 78:103–04.

Clapp, R. B., and P. A. Buckley. 1984. Status and conservation of seabirds in the southeastern United States. Pp. 135–55 *in* J. P. Croxall, P. G. H. Evans, and R. W. Schreiber, eds. Status and conservation of the world's seabirds. Internatl. Counc. Bird Preserv. Tech. Publ. 2.

Clapp, R. B., D. Morgan-Jacobs, and R. C. Banks. 1983. Marine birds of the southeastern United States and Gulf of Mexico. Part 3: Charadriiformes. U.S. Fish and Wildl. Serv., FWS/OBS-83/30.

Clapp, R. B., R. C. Banks, D. Morgan-Jacobs, and W. A. Hoffman. 1982. Marine birds of the southeastern United States and the Gulf of Mexico. Part 1: Gaviiformes through Pelecaniformes. U.S. Fish and Wildl. Serv., FWS/OBS-82/01.

Clark, K. L., and R. J. Robertson. 1981. Cowbird parasitism and evolution of anti-parasite strategies in the Yellow Warbler. Wilson Bull. 93:249–58.

Clark, R. J. 1972. Observations of nesting Marsh Hawks in Manitoba. Blue Jay 30:43–48.

Clark, R. J., D. W. Smith, and L. Kelso. 1987. Distributional status and literature of northern forest owls. Pp. 47–55 *in* R. W. Nero, R. J. Clark, R. J. Knapton, and R. H. Hamre, eds. Biology and conservation of northern forest owls: Symposium proceedings. U.S. Forest Serv., Rocky Mountain Forest Range Exp. Sta., Gen. Tech. Rep. RM-142, Fort Collins, Colo.

Cline, K. W. 1986. Chesapeake Bay Bald Eagle banding project report 1986. Natl. Wildl. Fed., Washington, D.C.

Coleman, J. S., and J. D. Fraser. 1987. Food habits of Black and Turkey Vultures in Pennsylvania and Maryland. J. Wildl. Manage. 51:733–39.

———. 1989. Black and Turkey Vultures. Pp. 15–21 *in* B. G. Pendleton, ed. Proc. of the northeast raptor management symposium and workshop. Natl. Wildl. Fed., Sci. Tech. Ser. 13, Washington, D.C.

Collins, C. T. 1970. The Black-crowned Night Heron as a predator of tern chicks. Auk 87:584–86.

Colvin, B. A. 1984. Barn Owl foraging behavior and secondary poisoning hazard from rodenticide use on farms. Ph.D. diss., Bowling Green Univ., Bowling Green, Ohio.

———. 1985. Common Barn-Owl population decline in Ohio and the relationship to agricultural trends. J. Field Ornith. 56:224–35.

Confer, J. L., and K. Knapp. 1981. Golden-winged Warblers and Blue-winged Warblers: The relative success of a habitat specialist and a habitat generalist. Auk 98:108–114.

Conner, R. N. 1975. Orientation of entrances to woodpecker nest cavities. Auk 92:371–74.

———. 1978. Snag management for cavity nesting birds. Pp. 120–28 *in* R. M. DeGraaf, ed. Proc. workshop management of southern forests for nongame birds. U.S. Forest Serv., Gen. Tech. Rep. SE-14, Asheville, N.C.

Conner, R. N., and C. S. Adkisson. 1977. Principal component analysis of woodpecker nesting habitat. Wilson Bull. 89:122–29.

Connor, P. F. 1988b. Boat-tailed Grackle. Pp. 476–77 *in* R. F. Andrle and J. R. Carroll, eds. The atlas of breeding birds in New York State. Cornell Univ. Press, Ithaca.

Cooke, M. T. 1921. Birds of the Washington region. Proc. Biol. Soc. Wash. 34:1–22.

———. 1929. Birds of the Washington, D.C. region (20-mile radius). Proc. Biol. Soc. Wash. 42:1–80.

Cooke, W. W. 1904. Distribution and migration of North American warblers. U.S. Dept. Agric., Biol. Surv. Bull. 18, Washington, D.C.

———. 1908. Bird migration in the District of Columbia. Proc. Biol. Soc. Wash. 21:107–118.

Cooley, A. P. 1982. A Mourning Dove nest on a Long Island sand dune. Kingbird 32:27.

Cooley, E. G. 1947. Breeding bird census: Shrubby field with stream-bordered trees. Maryland Birdlife 3:59–61.

Cornwell, G. W. 1963. Observations of the breeding biology and nesting populations of Belted Kingfishers. Condor 65:426–31.

Coues, E., and D. W. Prentiss. 1862. List of birds ascertained to inhabit the District of Columbia, with the times of arrival and departure of such as are non-resident, and brief notices of habits, etc. Annual Rep. Board Regents, Smithsonian Institution, Washington, D.C.

———. 1883. Avifauna Columbiana: Being a list of birds ascertained to inhabit the District of Columbia, with the times of arrival and departure of such as are non-resident, and brief notices of habits, etc. 2nd ed. U.S. Natl. Mus. Bull. 26, Washington, D.C.

Court, E. J. 1921. Some records of breeding birds for the vicinity of Washington, D.C. Auk 38:281–82.

———. 1924. Black Vulture (*Coragyps urubu*) nesting in Maryland. Auk 41:475–76.

———. 1936. Four rare nesting records for Maryland. Auk 53:95–96.

Cox, G. W. 1960. A life history of the Mourning Warbler. Wilson Bull. 72:5–28.

Craig, P. A. 1989. Christmas Bird Count: Pt. Lookout, MD. Amer. Birds 43:778.

Cramp, S., ed. 1985. Handbook of the birds of Europe, the Middle East and North Africa. Vol. 4. Oxford Univ. Press, N.Y.

———, ed. 1988. Handbook of the birds of Europe, the Middle East and North Africa. Vol. 5. Oxford Univ. Press, N.Y.

Crawford, R. D. 1977. Polygynous breeding of Short-billed Marsh Wrens. Auk 94:359–62.

Criswell, J. H., and S. A. Briggs. 1965. Wood Thrush and Veery populations in the census area. Atlantic Nat. 20:227–28.

Crocker-Bedford, D. C. 1990. Goshawk reproduction and forest management. Wildl. Soc. Bull. 18:262–69.

Cruickshank, A. D., ed. 1962. Sixty-second Christmas bird count: Maryland. Audubon Field Notes 16:192–205.

———, ed. 1966. Sixty-sixth Christmas bird count: Maryland. Audubon Field Notes 20:227–42.

Curran, H. M. 1902. The forests of Garrett County. Pp. 303–29 *in* Maryland Geological Survey, Garrett County. Johns Hopkins Press, Baltimore, Md.

Custer, T. W., G. L. Hensler, and T. E. Kaiser. 1983. Clutch size, reproductive success, and organochlorine contaminants in Atlantic coast Black-crowned Night Herons. Auk 100:699–710.

Custer, T. W., R. G. Osborn, and W. F. Scott. 1980. Distribution, species abundance, and nesting-site use of Atlantic coast colonies of herons and their allies. Auk 97:591–600.

Cuvier, M. Le Baron. 1826. Oeuvres completes de Buffon. Oiseaux. 21:249–55.

Cyrus, D., and N. Robson. 1980. Bird atlas of Natal. Univ. of Natal Press, Pietermaritzburg, South Africa.

Daniel, J. W., Jr. 1901. Nesting of the Hairy Woodpecker near Washington, D.C. Auk 18:272.

Darley, J. A., D. M. Scott, and N. K. Taylor. 1977. Effects of age, sex, and breeding success on site fidelity of Gray Catbirds. Bird-Banding 48:145–51.

Davidson, L. M. 1988. Loggerhead Shrike nest in Washington County, Md. Maryland Birdlife 44:3–5.

Davie, O. 1898. Nests and eggs of North American birds. 5th ed. D. McKay, Philadelphia, Pa.

Davis, C. M. 1978. A nesting study of the Brown Creeper. Living Bird 17:237–64.

Davis, J. 1960. Nesting behavior of the Rufous-sided Towhee in coastal California. Condor 62:434–56.

Davis, M. 1945. Black-crowned Night Heron in Washington, D.C. Auk 62:458.

DeGarmo, W. R. 1948. Breeding-bird population studies in Pocahontas and Randolph counties, West Virginia. Audubon Field Notes 2:219–22.

DeGeus, D. W. 1991. Brown-headed Cowbirds parasitize Loggerhead Shrikes: First records for family Laniidae. Wilson Bull. 103:504–06.

DeGraaf, R. M., and D. D. Rudis. 1986. New England wildlife: Habitat, natural history, and distribution. U.S. Forest Serv., Gen. Tech. Rep. NE-108, Broomall, Pa.

DeGraaf, R. M., G. M. Witman, J. W. Lanier, B. J. Hill, and J. M. Keniston. 1980. Forest habitat for birds of the northeast. U.S. Dept. Agric., Washington, D.C.

de Juana, E. 1980. Atlas Ornitologico de la Rioja. Instituto de Estudios Riojanos, Logroño, Spain.

Dennis, J. V. 1958. Some aspects of the breeding biology of the Yellow-breasted Chat. Bird-Banding 39:169–83.

Department of Natural Resources. 1983. Maryland wildlife management—a comprehensive plan for the 80's. Maryland Dept. Nat. Resources, Annapolis.

Devereux, J. G., and J. A. Mosher. 1984. Breeding ecology of Barred Owls in the central Appalachians. Raptor Res. 18:49–58.

Devlin, W. J., J. A. Mosher, and G. J. Taylor. 1980. History and present status of the Red-cockaded Woodpecker in Maryland. Amer. Birds 34:314–16.

Dexter, R. W. 1981. Nesting success of Chimney Swifts related to age and number of adults at the nest, and the subsequent fate of the visitors. J. Field Ornith. 52:228–32.

Dickerman, R. W., and K. C. Parkes. 1960. The Savannah Sparrows of Minnesota. Flicker 32:110–113.

Dickinson, J. C., Jr. 1968. Rufous-sided Towhee: Eastern U.S. subspecies. Pp. 562–80 *in* O. L. Austin, Jr., ed. Life histories of North American cardinals, grosbeaks, buntings, towhees, finches, sparrows, and allies. U.S. Natl. Mus. Bull. 237, Washington, D.C.

Dilger, W. C. 1956. Adoptive modifications and ecological isolating mechanisms in the thrush genera *Catharus* and *Hylocichla*. Wilson Bull. 68:171–99.

Dingle, E. von S. 1942. Rough-winged Swallow. Pp. 424–33 *in* A. C. Bent, ed. Life histories of North American flycatchers, larks, swallows, and their allies. U.S. Natl. Mus. Bull. 179, Washington, D.C.

———. 1946. Carolina Chickadee. Pp. 344–55 *in* A. C. Bent, ed. Life histories of North American jays, crows, and titmice. U.S. Natl. Mus. Bull. 191, Washington, D.C.

———. 1953. Swainson's Warbler. Pp. 30–38 *in* A. C. Bent, ed. Life histories of North American wood warblers. U.S. Natl. Mus. Bull. 203, Washington, D.C.

Dixon, C. L. 1978. Breeding biology of the Savannah Sparrow on Kent Island. Auk 95:235–246.

Dolton, D. D. 1991. Mourning Dove breeding population status, 1991. U.S. Fish and Wildl. Serv., Washington, D.C.

Dorsey, C. 1947. Observations on the nesting habits of the Black

Vulture in Anne Arundel County, Maryland. Maryland Conserv. 24:13.

Duebbert, H. F., and J. T. Lokemoen. 1977. Upland nesting of American Bitterns, Marsh Hawks and Short-Eared Owls. Prairie Nat. 9:33–40.

DuMont, P. G. and P. A. DuMont. 1970. Birds of the season—June, July, and August 1970. Atlantic Nat. 25:186.

———. 1973. Birds of the season: December 1972 through February 1973. Atlantic Nat. 28:121–29.

Dutcher, W. 1901. Results of special protection to gulls and terns obtained through the Thayer Fund. Auk 18:76–104.

Dybbro, T. 1976. De Danske Ynglefugles Udbredelse. Dansk Ornithologisk Forening, Copenhagen, Denmark.

Eaton, E. H. 1914. Birds of New York. Part 2. New York State Mus., Albany.

Eaton, S.W. 1957. A life history study of *Seiurus noveboracensis*. St. Bonaventure Univ. Sci. Studies 19:7–36.

———. 1958. A life history of the Louisiana Waterthrush. Wilson Bull. 70:211–36.

———. 1968. Northern Slate-colored Junco. Pp. 1029–43 *in* O. L. Austin, Jr., ed. Life histories of North American cardinals, grosbeaks, buntings, towhees, finches, sparrows, and allies. U.S. Natl. Mus. Bull. 237, Washington, D.C.

———. 1988a. Northern Shoveler. Pp. 74–75 *in* R. F. Andrle and J. R. Carroll, eds. The atlas of breeding birds in New York State. Cornell Univ. Press, Ithaca, N.Y.

———. 1988b. Prothonotary Warbler. Pp. 402–03 *in* R. F. Andrle and J. R. Carroll, eds. The atlas of breeding birds in New York State. Cornell Univ. Press, Ithaca.

Eckert, A. W. 1981. The wading birds of North America (north of Mexico). Doubleday & Co. Inc., Garden City, N.Y.

Eddleman, W. R., K. E. Evans, and W. H. Elder. 1980. Habitat characteristics and management of Swainson's Warbler in southern Illinois. Wildl. Soc. Bull. 8:228–33.

Eddy, G. E. 1988. Yellow-rumped Warbler nesting record in West Virginia. Redstart 55:56–57.

Ehrlich, P. R., D. S. Dobkin, and D. Wheye. 1988. The birder's handbook: A guide to the natural history of North American birds. Simon and Schuster, N.Y.

Eifrig, C. W. G. 1902a. Lark Sparrow and Olive-sided Flycatcher in western Maryland. Auk 19:83–84.

———. 1902b. Northern birds at Cumberland, Md. Auk 19:211–12.

———. 1904. Birds of Allegany and Garrett counties, western Maryland. Auk 21:234–50.

———. 1909. Additions to the list of birds of Allegany and Garrett counties, western Maryland. Auk 26:437–438.

———. 1915. Notes on some birds of the Maryland Alleghenies: An anomaly in the check-list. Auk 32:108–10.

———. 1920a. In the haunts of Cairn's Warbler. Auk 37:551–58.

———. 1920b. Additions to the birds of Allegany and Garrett Counties, Maryland. Auk 37:598–600.

———. 1923. Prairie Horned Lark (*Otocoris alpestris praticola*) in Maryland in summer. Auk 40:126.

———. 1933. In the haunts of Cairn's Warbler—a retrospect and a comparison. Wilson Bull. 45:60–66.

Eisenmann, E. 1973. Thirty-second supplement to the American Ornithologists' Union check-list of North American birds. Auk 90:411–19.

Eisenmann, E. 1976. Thirty-third supplement to the American Ornithologists' Union Check-list of North American Birds. Auk 93:875–79.

Eiserer, L. A. 1976. The American Robin: A backyard institution. Nelson Hall, Chicago.

Elliott, J. J. 1962. Sharp-tailed and Seaside Sparrows on Long Island, New York. Kingbird 12:115–23.

Ellison, W. G. 1985a. Yellow-rumped Warbler. Pp. 294–95 in S. B. Laughlin and D. P. Kibbe, eds. The atlas of breeding birds of Vermont. Univ. Press of New England, Hanover, N.H.

———. 1985. Bobolink. Pp. 358–59 *in* S. B. Laughlin and D. P. Kibbe, eds. The atlas of breeding birds of Vermont. Univ. Press of New England, Hanover, N.H.

Elosegui, A. J. 1985. Navarra Atlas de Aves Nidificantes. Caja de Ahorros de Navarra, Navarra, Spain.

Emlen, J. T., Jr. 1954. Territory, nest building, and pair formation in the Cliff Swallow. Auk 71:16–35.

Enser, R. W. 1992. The atlas of breeding birds in Rhode Island. Rhode Island Dept. of Environmental Manage., Providence.

Erskine, A. J. 1979. Man's influence on potential nesting sites and populations of swallows in Canada. Canadian Field-Nat. 93:371–77.

Erwin, R. M. 1977. Black Skimmer breeding ecology and behavior. Auk 94:709–17.

———. 1979. Coastal waterbird colonies: Cape Elizabeth, Maine to Virginia. U.S. Fish and Wildl. Serv., Biol. Serv. Prog., FWS/OBS-79/10, Washington, D.C.

———. 1983. Feeding habitats of nesting wading birds: Spatial use and social influences. Auk 100:960–70.

———. 1985. Monitoring colonial waterbird populations in the northeast: Historical and future perspectives. Trans. Northeast Fish Wildl. Conf. 41:97–109.

Erwin, R. M., V. P. Anders, and K. Miles-Iverson. 1990. Industrial strength herons. Maryland Mag. (Spring 1990):14.

Erwin, R. M., J. Galli, and J. Burger. 1981. Colony site dynamics and habitat use in Atlantic coast seabirds. Auk 98:550–61.

Erwin, R. M., and C. E. Korschgen. 1979. Coastal waterbird colonies: Maine to Virginia, 1977. An atlas showing colony locations and species composition. U.S. Fish and Wildl. Serv., Biol. Serv. Prog., FWS/OBS-79/08, Washington, D.C.

Evans, E. W. 1978. Nesting responses of Field Sparrows (*Spizella pusilla*) to plant succession on a Michigan old field. Condor 80:34–40.

Ewert, D. N. 1980. Recognition of conspecific song in the Rufous-sided Towhee. Anim. Behav. 28:379–86.

Faanes, C. A. 1980. Breeding biology of Eastern Phoebes in northern Wisconsin. Wilson Bull. 92:107–10.

———. 1981. Birds of the St. Croix River valley: Minnesota and Wisconsin. N. Amer. Fauna 73, Washington, D.C.

Fales, J. H. 1969. Breeding bird census: Mixed hardwood forest. Audubon Field Notes 23:706.

———. 1972. Breeding bird census: Mixed hardwood forest. Amer. Birds 26:945.

———. 1973. Breeding bird census: Mixed hardwood forest. Amer. Birds 27:965.

———. 1974. Breeding bird census: Mixed hardwood forest. Amer. Birds 28:1000.

Farnham, A. B. 1891. Secretary's report, Ornithologists Association. Oologist 8:219–20.

Fasola, M. 1984. Activity rhythm and feeding of nesting night herons *Nycticorax nycticorax*. Ardea 72:217–22.

Feare, C. 1984. The starling. Oxford Univ. Press, N.Y.

Fenneman, N. M. 1938. Physiography of eastern United States. McGraw-Hill, N.Y.

Fenwick, G. H., and D. D. Boone. 1984. The peatlands of western

Maryland. Pp. 139–59 *in* A. W. Norden, D. C. Forester, and G. H. Fenwick, eds. Threatened and endangered plants and animals of Maryland. Maryland Nat. Heritage Prog., Spec. Publ. 84–1, Annapolis.

Fernald, M. L. 1970. Gray's manual of botany. 8th ed. Dioscorides Press, Portland, Oreg.

Ficken, M. S. 1962. Maintenance activities of the American Redstart. Wilson Bull. 74:153–65.

———. 1964. Nest site selection in the American Redstart. Wilson Bull. 76:189–90.

Ficken, M. S., and R. W. Ficken. 1967. Singing behavior of Blue-winged and Golden-winged warblers and their hybrids. Behavior 28:149–81.

———. 1968a. Courtship of Blue-winged Warblers, Golden-winged Warblers, and their hybrids. Wilson Bull. 80:161–172.

———. 1968b. Territorial relationships of Blue-winged Warblers, Golden-winged Warblers, and their hybrids. Wilson Bull. 80:442–451.

———. 1969. Responses of Blue-winged Warblers and Golden-winged Warblers to their own and the other species' song. Wilson Bull. 81:69–74.

Ficken, R. W. 1963. Courtship and agonistic behavior of the Common Grackle, *Quiscalus quiscula*. Auk 80:52–72.

Fischer, R. B. 1958. The breeding biology of the Chimney Swift *Chaetura pelagica* (Linnaeus). New York State Mus. Bull. 368.

Fisher, A. K. 1935. Natural history of Plummers Island, Maryland. Proc. Biol. Soc. Wash. 48:159–167.

Fisher, W. H. 1899. Nesting of the Bald Eagle in Baltimore County, Md. Osprey 4:21.

———. 1903. Nesting of the Red-bellied Woodpecker in Harford County, Maryland. Auk 20:305–06.

Fletcher, A. J., and R. B. Fletcher. 1956. Maryland nest summary for 1955. Maryland Birdlife 12:41–48.

———. 1959. Maryland nest summary for 1958. Maryland Birdlife 15:5–12.

Fletcher, A. J., R. B. Fletcher, M. W. Hewitt, A. O'C. Knotts, and A. M. Thompson. 1956. List of Caroline County birds. Maryland Avifauna 1:1–22.

Follen, D. 1986. Harriers, 1984, a reproductive disaster. Passenger Pigeon 48:17–20.

Follen, D. G., and J. C. Haug. 1981. Saw-whet Owl nest in Wood Duck box. Passenger Pigeon 43:47–48.

Forbush, E. H. 1912. A history of game birds, wildfowl, and shore birds of Massachusetts and adjacent states. Massachusetts State Board Agric., Boston.

———. 1925. Birds of Massachusetts and other New England states. Vol. 1. Massachusetts Dept. Agric., Boston.

———. 1927. Birds of Massachusetts and other New England states. Vol. 2. Massachusetts Dept. Agric., Boston.

———. 1929. Birds of Massachusetts and other New England states. Vol. 3. Massachusetts Dept. Agric., Boston.

Forbush, E. H., and J. B. May. 1939. A natural history of American birds of eastern and central North America. Bramhall House, N.Y.

Foss, C. R., ed.1994. Atlas of breeding birds in New Hampshire. Audubon Soc. of N.H., Concord.

Frederickson, L. H. 1971. Common Gallinule breeding biology and development. Auk 88:914–19.

———. 1977. American Coot. Pp. 123–47 *in* G. C. Sanderson, ed. Management of migratory shore and upland game birds in North America. Internatl. Assn. Fish and Wildl. Agencies, Washington, D.C.

Freeman, S., D. F. Gori, and S. Rohwer. 1990. Red-winged Blackbirds and Brown-headed Cowbirds: Some aspects of a host-parasite relationship. Condor 92:336–40.

Fretwell, S. 1977. Is the Dickcissel a threatened species? Amer. Birds 31:923–32.

Friedmann, H. 1929. The cowbirds: A study in the biology of social parasitism. C. C. Thomas, Springfield, Ill.

———. 1963. Host relations of the parasitic cowbirds. U.S. Natl. Mus. Bull. 233, Washington, D.C.

———. 1971. Further information on the host relations of the parasitic cowbirds. Auk 88:239–55.

Friedmann, H., L. F. Kiff, and S. I. Rothstein. 1977. A further contribution to knowledge of the host relations of the parasitic cowbirds. Smithsonian Contributions to Zoology 235, Washington, D.C.

Frieswyk, T. S., and D. M. DiGiovanni. 1988. Forest statistics for Maryland—1976 and 1986. U.S. Forest Serv., Northeastern Forest Exp. Sta., Res. Bull. NE-107, Broomall, Pa.

Frohling, R. C. 1965. American Oystercatcher and Black Skimmer nesting on salt marsh. Wilson Bull. 77:193–94.

Frost, P. G. H., and W. R. Siegfried. 1977. The cooling rate of eggs of moorhen *Gallinula chloropus* in single and multi-egg clutches. Ibis 119:77–80.

Fuller, M. R. 1979. Spaciotemporal relationships of four sympatric raptor species. Ph.D. diss. Univ. of Minnesota, Minneapolis.

Fuller, R. W., and E. G. Bolen. 1963. Dual Wood Duck occupancy of a nesting box. Wilson Bull. 75:94–95.

Galati, B., and C. B. Galati. 1985. Breeding of the Golden-crowned Kinglet in northern Minnesota. J. Field Ornith. 56:28–40.

Garber, D. P., and J. R. Koplin. 1972. Prolonged and bisexual incubation by California Ospreys. Condor 74:201–02.

Garland, M. 1963. First Maryland nest of House Finch. Maryland Birdlife 19:78.

Garrett, K., and J. Dunn. 1981. Birds of southern California: Status and distribution. Los Angeles Audubon Soc., Los Angeles.

Gates, J. M. 1962. Breeding biology of the Gadwall in northern Utah. Wilson Bull. 74:43–67.

Gates, J. M., and J. B. Hale. 1974. Seasonal movements, winter habitat use, and population distribution of an east central Wisconsin pheasant population. Wisconsin Dept. Nat. Resources, Tech. Bull. 76, Madison.

Gauthreaux, S. A., Jr. 1978. The structure and organization of avian communities in forests. Pp. 17–37 *in* R. M. DeGraaf, ed. Proc. workshop management of southern forests for nongame birds. U.S. Forest Serv., Gen. Tech. Rep. SE-14, Asheville, N.C.

Gavin, T. A. 1984. Broodedness in Bobolinks. Auk 101:179–81.

Geissler, P. H., and B. R. Noon. 1981. Estimates of avian population trends from the North American breeding bird survey. Pp. 42–51 *in* C. J. Ralph and J. M. Scott, eds. Estimating numbers of terrestrial birds. Studies Avian Biol. 6.

Geissler, P. H., and J. R. Sauer. 1990. Topics in route-regression analysis. Pp. 54–57 *in* J. R. Sauer and S. Droege, eds. Survey design and statistical methods for the estimation of avian population trends. U.S. Fish and Wildl. Serv., Biol. Rep. 90(1), Washington, D.C.

Gill, F. B. 1980. Historical aspects of hybridization between Blue-winged and Golden-winged Warblers. Auk 97:1–18.

———. 1985. Birds. Pp. 299–351 *in* H. H. Genoways and F. J. Brenner, eds. Species of special concern in Pennsylvania. Carnegie Mus. Nat. Hist., Spec. Pub. 11, Pittsburgh, Pa.

———. 1987. Allozymes and genetic similarity of Blue-winged and Golden-winged warblers. Auk 104:444–49.

Gill, F. B., and W. E. Lanyon. 1964. Experiments on species discrimination in Blue-winged Warblers. Auk 81:53–64.

Gill, F. B., and B. B. Murray, Jr. 1972. Discrimination behavior and hybridization of Blue-winged and Golden-winged Warblers. Evol. 26:282–93.

Girard, G. L. 1939. Notes on the life history of the Shoveler. Trans. N. Amer. Wildl. Conf. 4:364–71.

Glover, F. A. 1953. Nesting ecology of the Pied-billed Grebe in northwestern Iowa. Wilson Bull. 65:32–39.

———. 1956. Nesting and production of the Blue-winged Teal (*Anas discors* Linnaeus) in northwest Iowa. J. Wildl. Manage. 20:28–46.

Gochfeld, M. 1978. Colony and nest site selection by Black Skimmers. Proc. 1977 Conf. Colonial Waterbird Group 1:78–90.

Gochfeld, M., J. Burger, and F. Lesser. 1989. First Royal Tern nest for New Jersey. Records New Jersey Birds 14:66.

Godfrey, W. E. 1979. The birds of Canada. Natl. Mus. Nat. Sci. Canada., Ottawa, Ontario, Canada.

———. 1986. The birds of Canada. Rev. ed. Natl. Mus. Nat. Sci., Ottawa, Ontario, Canada.

Golden Software, Inc. 1987. Surfer reference manual. Golden, Colo.

Gollop, J. B., and W. H. Marshall. 1954. A guide for ageing duck broods in the field. Mississippi Flyway Counc. Tech. Ser.

Gooders, J. 1986. Ducks of North America and the northern hemisphere. Facts on File Publ., N.Y.

Goodwin, D. 1967. Pigeons and doves of the world. British Mus. Nat. Hist. Publ. 663. London.

———. 1970. Pigeons and doves of the world. 2nd ed. British Mus. Nat. Hist. Publ. 663. London.

———. 1976. Crows of the world. Cornell Univ. Press, Ithaca, N.Y.

Gosner, K. L. 1978. A field guide to the Atlantic seashore. Houghton Mifflin, Boston, Mass.

Graber, J. W. 1968. Western Henslow's Sparrow. Pp. 779–88 *in* O. L. Austin, Jr., ed. Life histories of North American cardinals, grosbeaks, buntings, towhees, finches, sparrows, and allies. U.S. Natl. Mus. Bull. 237, Washington, D.C.

Graber, J. W., R. R. Graber, and E. L. Kirk. 1977. Illinois birds: Picidae. Illinois Nat. Hist. Surv., Biol. Notes 102, Urbana.

Graber, R. R., and J. W. Graber. 1951. Nesting of the Parula Warbler. Wilson Bull. 63:75–83.

Graber, R. R., J. W. Graber, and E. L. Kirk. 1970. Illinois birds: Mimidae. Illinois Nat. Hist. Surv., Biol. Notes 68, Urbana.

———. 1974. Illinois birds: Tyrannidae. Illinois Nat. Hist. Surv., Biol. Notes 86, Urbana.

Grant, E. R. 1951. The last Maryland flight of the Passenger Pigeon. Maryland Birdlife 7:27–29.

Greenberg, R. 1987. Seasonal foraging specialization in the Worm-eating Warbler. Condor 89:158–68.

———. 1988. Water as a habitat cue for breeding Swamp and Song Sparrows. Condor 90:420–27.

Greenberg, R., and S. Droege. 1990. Adaptions to tidal marshes in breeding populations of the Swamp Sparrow. Condor 92:393–404.

Greenlaw, J. S. 1978. The relation of breeding schedule and clutch size to food supply in the Rufous-sided Towhee. Condor 80:24–33.

———. 1983. Microgeographic distribution of breeding Seaside Sparrows in New York salt marshes. Pp. 99–114 *in* T. L. Quay, J. B. Funderburg, Jr., D. S. Lee, E. F. Potter, and C. S. Robbins, eds. The Seaside Sparrow, its biology and management. Occas. Papers North Carolina Biol. Surv. 1983–5, Raleigh.

Greller, A. M. 1988. Deciduous forests. Pp. 288–316 *in* M. G. Barbour and W. D. Billings, eds. North American terrestrial vegetation. Cambridge Univ. Press, N.Y.

Grice, D., and J. P. Rogers. 1965. The Wood Duck in Massachusetts. Massachusetts Div. Fish and Game, Final Fed. Aid. Rep., Proj. W-19-12, Boston.

Grinnell, G. B. 1901. American duck shooting. Forest and Stream Publ. Co., N.Y.

Grinnell, J., and A. H. Miller. 1944. The distribution of the birds of California. Pacific Coast Avifauna 27:1–608.

Griscom, L., and A. Sprunt, Jr. 1957. The warblers of America. Devin-Adair, N.Y.

Gross, A. O. 1923. The Black-crowned Night Heron (*Nycticorax nycticorax naevius*) of Sandy Neck. Auk 40:1–30, 191–214.

———. 1940. Eastern Nighthawk. Pp. 206–34 *in* A. C. Bent, ed. Life histories of North American cuckoos, goatsuckers, hummingbirds and their allies. U.S. Natl. Mus. Bull. 176, Washington, D.C.

———. 1942a. Bank Swallow. Pp. 400–24 *in* A. C. Bent, ed. Life histories of North American flycatchers, larks, swallows, and their allies. U.S. Natl. Mus. Bull. 179, Washington, D.C.

———. 1942b. Northern Cliff Swallow. Pp. 463–84 *in* A. C. Bent, ed. Life histories of North American flycatchers, larks, swallows, and their allies. U.S. Natl. Mus. Bull. 179, Washington, D.C.

———. 1946. Eastern Crow. Pp. 226–59 *in* A. C. Bent, ed. Life histories of North American jays, crows, and titmice. U.S. Natl. Mus. Bull. 191, Washington, D.C.

———. 1948a. Eastern House Wren. Pp. 131–41 *in* A. C. Bent, ed. Life Histories of North American nuthatches, wrens, thrashers, and their allies. U.S. Natl. Mus. Bull. 195, Washington, D.C.

———. 1948b. Catbird. Pp. 320–51 *in* A. C. Bent, ed. Life histories of North American nuthatches, wrens, thrashers, and their allies. U.S. Natl. Mus. Bull. 195, Washington, D.C.

———. 1949. Eastern Hermit Thrush. Pp. 143–62 *in* A. C. Bent, ed. Life histories of North American thrushes, kinglets, and their allies. U.S. Natl. Mus. Bull. 196, Washington, D.C.

———. 1953a. Eastern Ovenbird. Pp. 457–76 *in* A. C. Bent, ed. Life histories of North American wood warblers, U.S. Natl. Mus. Bull. 203, Washington, D.C.

———. 1953b. Northern and Maryland Yellowthroats. Pp. 542–65 *in* A. C. Bent, ed. Life histories of North American wood warblers, U.S. Natl. Mus. Bull. 203, Washington, D.C.

———. 1953c. Southern American Redstart. Pp. 656–81 *in* A. C. Bent, ed. Life histories of North American wood warblers. U.S. Natl. Mus. Bull. 203, Washington, D.C.

———. 1958. Eastern Meadowlark. Pp. 53–80 *in* A. C. Bent, ed. Life histories of North American blackbirds, orioles, tanagers, and allies. U.S. Natl. Mus. Bull. 211, Washington, D.C.

Gullion, G. W. 1954. The reproductive cycle of American Coots in California. Auk 71:366–12.

———. 1977. Forest manipulation for Ruffed Grouse. Trans. N. Amer. Wildl. Nat. Resources Conf. 42:449–58.

Haig, S. M., and L. W. Oring. 1985. Distribution and status of the Piping Plover throughout the annual cycle. J. Field Ornith. 56:334–45.

Hall, C. C. 1910. Narratives of early Maryland, 1633–84. Charles Scribner's and Sons, N.Y.

Hall, G. A. 1969. Breeding range expansion of the Brown Creeper in the middle Atlantic states. Redstart 36:98–103.

———. 1983. West Virginia birds: Distribution and ecology. Carnegie Mus. Nat. Hist. Spec. Publ. 7, Pittsburgh, Pa.

Hall, L. W., Jr., A. E. Pinkney, and L. O. Horseman. 1985. Mortality of striped bass larvae in relation to contamination and water quality in Chesapeake Bay tributaries. Trans. Amer. Fish Soc. 114:861–68.

Halle, L. J. 1948. Veeries breed in Washington. Wood Thrush 4:2.

Hamerstrom, F. 1969. A harrier population study. Pp. 367–83 *in* J. J. Hickey, ed. Peregrine Falcon populations: Their biology and decline. Univ. of Wisconsin Press, Madison.

Hamerstrom, F., F. N. Hamerstrom, and C. J. Burke. 1985. Effect of voles on mating systems in a central Wisconsin population of harriers. Wilson Bull. 97:332–46.

Hamilton, R. B. 1975. Comparative behavior of the American Avocet and Black-necked Stilt (*Recurvirostridae*). Ornith. Monogr. 17, Washington, D.C.

Hampe, I. E., R. M. Bowen, and G. M. Bond. 1947. The breeding bird census and bird watching. Maryland: J. Nat. Hist. 17:67–72.

Hampe, I. E., and H. Kolb. 1947. Preliminary list of the birds of Maryland and the District of Columbia. Nat. Hist. Soc. Maryland, Baltimore.

Hancock, J., and J. Kushlan. 1984. The herons handbook. Harper and Row, N.Y.

Hands, H. M., R. D. Drobney, and M. R. Ryan. 1989. Status of the Henslow's Sparrow in the northcentral United States. Missouri Coop. Fish and Wildl. Res. Unit, Univ. of Missouri, Columbia.

Hann, H. W. 1937. Life history of the Ovenbird in southern Michigan. Wilson Bull. 49:145–237.

Hanson, H. C., and C. W. Kossack. 1963. The Mourning Dove in Illinois. Illinois Dept. Conserv. Tech. Bull. 2, Southern Illinois Univ. Press, Carbondale.

Harding, B. D. 1979. Bedfordshire bird atlas. Beds. Nat. Hist. Soc., Luton, England.

Harlow, R. G. 1922. The breeding habits of the Northern Raven in Pennsylvania. Auk 39:399–410.

Harmeson, J. P. 1974. Breeding ecology of the Dickcissel. Auk 91:348–59.

Haramis, G. M. 1991. Wood Duck. Pp. 15.1–15.11 *in* S. L. Funderburk, J. A. Mihursky, S. J. Jordon, and D. Riley, eds. Habitat requirements for Chesapeake Bay living resources. Living Resources Subcommittee, Chesapeake Bay Program. Annapolis, Md.

Harrison, C. 1978. A field guide to the nests, eggs, and nestlings of North American birds. Wm. Collins Sons, Glasgow, Scotland.

Harrison, H. H. 1975. A field guide to birds' nests in the United States east of the Mississippi River. Houghton Mifflin, Boston, Mass.

———. 1984. Wood warblers' world. Simon and Schuster, N.Y.

Hatfield, J. S., S. A. Ricciardi, G. A. Gough, D. Bystrak, S. Droege, and C. S. Robbins. 1994. Distribution and abundance of birds wintering in Maryland, 1988–1993. Maryland Birdlife 50:3–83.

Hausman, L. A. 1938. The warblers of New Jersey. Part 1. Summer resident warblers. New Jersey Agric. Res. Sta., Bull. 646, New Brunswick.

Hayman, P., J. Marchant, and T. Prater. 1986. Shorebirds: An identification guide to the waders of the world. Houghton Mifflin, Boston, Mass.

Hays, H. 1972. Polyandry in the Spotted Sandpiper. Living Bird 11:43–57.

Heckenroth, H. 1985. Atlas del Brutvögel Niedersachsens 1980. Naturschurz und Landschaftspflege in Niedensachsen,Germany.

Heinzel, H., R. Fitter, and J. Parslow. 1972. The birds of Britain and Europe with north Africa and the Middle East. Wm. Collins Sons, London.

Henny, C. J. 1972. An analysis of the population dynamics of selected avian species with special reference to changes during the modern pesticide era. U.S. Fish and Wildl. Serv., Wildl. Res. Rep. 1, Washington, D.C.

Henny, C. J., and N. E. Holgersen. 1974. Range expansion and population increase of the Gadwall in eastern North America. Wildfowl 25:95–101.

Henny, C. J., F. C. Schmid, E. M. Martin, and L. L. Hood. 1973. Territorial behavior, pesticides, and the population ecology of Red-shouldered Hawks in central Maryland, 1943-1971. Ecology 54:545–54.

Henny, C. J., M. M. Smith, and V. D. Stotts. 1974. The 1973 distribution and abundance of breeding Ospreys in the Chesapeake Bay. Chesapeake Sci. 15:125–33.

Henny, C. J., and W. T. Van Velzen. 1972. Migration patterns and wintering localities of American Ospreys. J. Wildl. Manage. 36:1133–41.

Hepp, G. R., and D. Hair. 1983. Reproductive behavior and pairing chronology in wintering dabbling ducks. Wilson Bull. 95:675–82.

Heusmann, H. W. 1972. Survival of Wood Duck broods from dump nests. J. Wildl. Manage. 36:620–24.

———. 1974. Mallard–Black Duck relationships in the Northeast. Wildl. Soc. Bull. 2:171–77.

Hewitt, O. H., ed. 1967. The Wild Turkey and its management. Wildl. Soc., Washington, D.C.

Hickey, J. J., and D. W. Anderson. 1968. Chlorinated hydrocarbons and eggshell changes in raptorial and fish-eating birds. Sci. 162:271–73.

Hicks, L. E. 1934. A summary of cowbird host species in Ohio. Auk 51:385–86.

Higgins, K. F. 1975. Shorebird and gamebird nests in North Dakota croplands. Wildl. Soc. Bull. 3:176–79.

Hill, J. R., III. 1987. An exceptionally tall Eastern Phoebe nest. Wilson Bull. 99:501–02.

———. 1988. Nest-depth preference in pipe-nesting Northern Rough-winged Swallows. J. Field Ornith. 59:334–36.

Hill, N. P. 1968. Eastern Sharp-tailed Sparrow. Pp. 795–812 *in* O. L. Austin, Jr., ed. Life histories of North American cardinals, grosbeaks, buntings, towhees, finches, sparrows, and allies. U.S. Natl. Mus. Bull. 237, Washington, D.C.

Hindman, L. J., and F. Ferrigno. 1990. Atlantic flyway goose populations: Status and management. Trans. N. Amer. Wildl. Nat. Resour. Conf. 55:293–311.

Hochbaum, H. A. 1944. The Canvasback on a prairie marsh. N. Amer. Wildl. Inst., Washington, D.C.

Hofslund, P. B. 1954. Incubation period of the Mourning Warbler. Wilson Bull. 26:198–205.

———. 1959. A life history study of the Yellow-throat. Proc. Minnesota Acad. Sci. 27:144–74.

Holmes, R. T. 1986. Foraging patterns of forest birds: Male-female differences. Wilson Bull. 98:196–213.

Holmes, R. T., C. P. Black, and T. W. Sherry. 1979. Comparative population bioenergetics of three insectivorous passerines in a deciduous forest. Condor 81:9–20.

Holmes, R. T., and T. W. Sherry. 1986. Bird community dynamics in a temperate deciduous forest: Long-term trends at Hubbard Brook. Ecol. Monogr. 56:201–20.

Holroyd, G. L., and J. G. Woods. 1975. Migration of the Saw-whet Owl in eastern North America. Bird-Banding 46:101–05.

Hooper, D. C. 1951. Waterfowl nesting at Minto Lakes, Alaska. Proc. Alaskan Sci. Conf. 2:318–21.

Hooper, R. G. 1977. Nesting habitat of Common Ravens in Virginia. Wilson Bull. 89:233–42.

Hooper, R. G., H. S. Crawford, D. R. Chamberlain, and R. F. Harlow. 1975. Nesting density of Common Ravens in the Ridge-Valley Region of Virginia. Amer. Birds 29:931–35.

Hooper, R. G., and C. A. Dachelet. 1976. Flocks of nonbreeding Common Ravens in Virginia. Raven 47:23–24.

Horak, G. J. 1970. A comparative study of the foods of the Sora and Virginia Rail. Wilson Bull. 82:206–13.

Hostetter, D. R. 1961. Life history of the Carolina Junco, *Junco hyemalis carolinensis* Brewster. Raven 32:97–170.

Houston, C. S., and M. G. Street. 1959. The birds of the Saskatchewan River, Carlton to Cumberland. Saskatchewan Nat. Hist. Soc., Spec. Publ. 2, Regina, Saskatchewan, Canada.

Howe, H. F. 1978. Initial investment, clutch size, and brood reduction in the Common Grackle (*Quiscalus quiscula* L). Ecology 59:1109–22.

———. 1979. Evolutionary aspects of parental care in the Common Grackle, *Quiscalus quiscula*. Evolution 33:41–51.

Howe, M. A. 1982. Social organization in a nesting population of eastern Willets (*Catoptrophorus semipalmatus*). Auk 99:88–102.

Howell, A. H. 1924. Birds of Alabama. Alabama Dept. Game and Fisheries, Birmingham.

———. 1932. Florida bird life. Florida Dept. Game and Freshwater Fish in cooperation with Bureau Biol. Surv., U.S. Dept. Agric., N.Y.

Howell, T. 1953. Racial and sexual differences in migration in *Sphyrapicus varius*. Auk 70:118–26.

Howes-Jones, D. 1985a. Relationships among song activity, context, and social behavior in the Warbling Vireo. Wilson Bull. 97:4–20.

———. 1985b. Nesting habits and activity patterns of Warbling Vireos, *Vireo gilvus*, in southern Ontario. Canadian Field-Nat. 99:484–89.

Hurley, L. M. 1990. Field guide to the submerged aquatic vegetation of the Chesapeake Bay. U.S. Fish and Wildl. Serv., Annapolis, Md.

Hussell, D. J. T. 1987. Horned Lark. Pp. 270–71 *in* M. D. Cadman, P. F. J. Eagles, and F. M. Helleiner, eds. Atlas of breeding birds of Ontario. Univ. Waterloo Press, Waterloo, Ontario, Canada.

Hyde, A. S. 1939. The life history of the Henslow's Sparrow, *Passerherbulus henslowii* (Audubon). Univ. of Michigan Misc. Publ., Ann Arbor.

Imhof, T. A. 1962. Alabama birds. Univ. of Alabama Press, University.

Ingold, D. J. 1989. Nesting phenology and competition for nest sites among Red-headed and Red-bellied Woodpeckers and European Starlings. Auk 106:209–17.

Jackson, J. A. 1970. A quantitative study of the foraging ecology of Downy Woodpeckers. Ecology 51:318–23.

———. 1976. A comparison of some aspects of the breeding ecology of Red-headed and Red-bellied Woodpeckers in Kansas. Condor 78:67–76.

———. 1983. Nesting phenology, nest site selection, and reproductive success of the Black and Turkey Vulture. Pp. 245–70 *in* S. R. Wilbur and J. A. Jackson, eds. Vulture biology and management. Univ. of California Press, Berkeley.

———. 1988a. American Black Vulture. Pp. 11–24 *in* R. S. Palmer, ed. Handbook of North American birds. Vol. 4. Diurnal raptors (Part 1). Yale Univ. Press, New Haven, Conn.

———. 1988b. Turkey Vulture. Pp. 25–42 *in* R. S. Palmer, ed. Handbook of North American birds. Vol. 4. Diurnal raptors (Part 1). Yale Univ. Press, New Haven, Conn.

———. 1988c. The southeastern pine forest ecosystem and its birds: Past, present, and future. Pp. 119–59 *in* J. A. Jackson, ed. Bird Conservation 3. Univ. Wisconsin Press, Madison.

Jackson, R. W. 1941. Breeding birds of the Cambridge area, Maryland. Bull. Nat. Hist. Soc. Maryland 11:65–74.

James, R. D. 1978. Pairing and nest site selection in Solitary and Yellow-throated Vireos with a description of a ritualized nest building display. Canadian J. Zool. 56:1163–69.

Janik, C. A., and J. A. Mosher. 1982. Breeding biology of raptors in the central Appalachians. Raptor Res. 16:18–24.

John, R. D. 1991. Observations on soil requirements for nesting Bank Swallows, *Riparia riparia*. Canadian Field-Nat. 105:251–54.

Johnsgard, P. A. 1961. Wintering distribution changes in Mallards and Black Ducks. Amer. Midl. Nat. 66:477–84.

———. 1967. Sympatry changes and hybridization incidence in Mallards and Black Ducks. Amer. Midl. Nat. 77:51–63.

Johnson, R. R., and J. J. Dinsmore. 1985. Brood-rearing and post-breeding habitat use by Virginia Rails and Soras. Wilson Bull. 97:551–54.

Johnston, D. W. 1965. Ecology of the Indigo Bunting in Florida. Quarterly J. Florida Acad. Sci. 28:199–211.

———. 1971. Ecological aspects of hybridizing chickadees (*Parus*) in Virginia. Amer. Midl. Nat. 85:124–34.

Jones, R. E., and A. S. Leopold. 1967. Nesting interference in a dense population of Wood Ducks. J. Wildl. Manage. 31:221–28.

Jouy, P. L. 1877. Catalogue of the birds of the District of Columbia. Field and Forest 2:154–56, 178–81.

Judd, S. D. 1901. The relation of sparrows to agriculture. U.S. Dept. Agric., Div. Biol. Surv. Bull. 15, Washington, D.C.

———. 1902. Birds of a Maryland farm. U.S. Dept. Agric. Bull. 17, Washington, D.C.

Kahl, R. B., T. S. Baskett, J. A. Ellis, and J. N. Burroughs. 1985. Characteristics of summer habitats of selected nongame birds in Missouri. Univ. of Missouri—Columbia Agric. Exp. Sta. Res. Bull. 1056.

Kain, T., ed. 1987. Virginia's birdlife: An annotated checklist. Virginia Avifauna 3, Virginia Soc. Ornith., Richmond.

Kalmbach, E. R. 1940. Economic status of the English Sparrow in the United States. U.S. Dept. Agric. Tech. Bull. 711, Washington, D.C.

Karr, J. R., J. D. Nichols, M. K. Klimkiewicz, and J. D. Brawn. 1990. Survival rates of birds of tropical and temperate forests: Will the dogma survive? Amer. Nat. 136:277–91.

Keith, L. B. 1961. A study of waterfowl ecology on small impoundments in southeastern Alberta. Wildl. Monogr. 6.

Kellner, C. J., and G. Ritchison. 1988. Possible functions of singing by female Acadian Flycatchers (*Empidonax virescens*). J. Field Ornith. 59:55–59.

Kendeigh, S. C. 1963. Regulation of nesting time and distribution in the House Wren. Auk 75:418–27.

Kennard, J. H. 1977. Biennial rhythm in Purple Finch migration. Bird-Banding 48:155–56.

Kent, D. M. 1986. Behavior, habitat use and food of three egrets in a marine habitat. Colonial Waterbirds 9:25–30.

Keran, D. 1978. Nest site selection by the Broad-winged Hawk in north central Minnesota and Wisconsin. Raptor Res. 12:15–20.

Kercheval, S. 1833. A history of the Valley of Virginia. Republished in 1902 by W. N. Grabill, Woodstock, Va.

Kibbe, D. P. 1985. Wood Thrush. Pp. 248–49 *in* S. B. Laughlin and D. P. Kibbe, eds. The atlas of breeding birds of Vermont. Univ. Press of New England, Hanover, N.H.

Kilham, L. 1961. Reproductive behavior of Red-bellied Woodpeckers. Wilson Bull. 73:237–54.

———. 1962. Breeding behavior of Yellow-bellied Sapsuckers. Auk 79:31–43.

———. 1971. Roosting habits of White-breasted Nuthatches. Condor 73:113–14.

———. 1972. Reproductive behavior of White-breasted Nuthatches (II. Courtship). Auk 89:115–29.

———. 1973. Reproductive behavior of the Red-breasted Nuthatch, I. Courtship. Auk 90:597–609.

———. 1977. Nesting behavior of Yellow-bellied Sapsuckers. Wilson Bull. 89:310–24.

———. 1985. Behavior of American Crows in the early part of the breeding cycle. Florida Field Nat. 13:25-31.

Kimmel, J. T., and R. H. Yahner. 1990. Status and habitat requirements of Northern Goshawk in Pennsylvania. Final report. Pennsylvania State Univ., University Park.

Kirkwood, F. C. 1895. A list of the birds of Maryland. Trans. Maryland Acad. Sci. 1895:241–81.

———. 1901. The Cerulean Warbler as a summer resident in Baltimore County, Maryland. Auk 18:137.

Kirsch, L. M., and K. F. Higgins. 1976. Upland Sandpiper nesting and management in North Dakota. Wildl. Soc. Bull. 4:16–20.

Klaas, E. E., S. N. Wiemeyer, H. M. Ohlendorf, and D. M. Swineford. 1978. Organochlorine residues, eggshell thickness and nest success in Barn Owls from the Chesapeake Bay. Estuaries 1:46–53.

Kleen, R. L. 1956. A trip to Sharps Island. Maryland Birdlife 12:3–5.

Kleen, V. M. 1965. Banding highlights in Maryland. Maryland Birdlife 21:17–20.

Klimkiewicz, M. K. 1972. Breeding bird atlas of Montgomery County. Maryland Birdlife 28:130–41.

———. 1974a. Breeding bird census: Oak–beech hardwood forest. Amer. Birds 28:1000–01.

———. 1974b. Breeding bird census: Oak gum–mixed hardwood forest. Amer. Birds 28:1001–02.

Klimkiewicz, M. K., and A. G. Futcher. 1987. Longevity of North American birds: *Coerebinae* through *Estrildidae*. J. Field Ornith. 58:318–33.

Klimkiewicz, M. K., and D. W. Holmes. 1972. Breeding bird census: Abandoned fields. Amer. Birds 26:995–96.

Klimkiewicz, M. K., and J. K. Solem. 1978. The breeding bird atlas of Montgomery and Howard counties, Maryland. Maryland Birdlife 34:3–39.

Kline, B. F., Jr. 1976. Tall pines and winding rivers: The history of logging railroads of Maryland. Privately publ.

Knapton, R. W. 1988. Nesting success is higher for polygynously mated females than for monogamously mated females in the Eastern Meadowlark. Auk 105:325–29.

Knight, O. W. 1908. The birds of Maine. C. H. Glass, Bangor, Maine.

Knight, R. L., D. J. Grout, and S. A. Temple. 1987. Nest-defense behavior of the American Crow in urban and rural areas. Condor 89:175–77.

Kolb, C. H., Jr. 1943. Status of *Dendroica cerulea* in eastern Maryland. Auk 60:275–76.

———. 1950. Breeding bird census: Mixed oak forest. Audubon Field Notes 4:300.

Koplin, J. R. 1973. Differential habitat use by sexes of American Kestrels wintering in northern California. Raptor Res. 7:39–42.

Kricher, J. C. 1983. Correlation between House Finch increase and House Sparrow decline. Amer. Birds 37:358–64.

Kroodsma, R. L. 1975. Hybridization in buntings (*Passerina*) in North Dakota and eastern Montana. Auk 92:66–80.

Kuerzi, R. G. 1941. Life history studies of the Tree Swallow. Proc. Linnaean Soc. New York 52–53:1–52.

Kull, R. C., Jr. 1977. Color selection of nesting material by Killdeer. Auk 94:602–04.

Kumlien, L. 1880. The Yellow-rumped Warbler (*Dendroica coronata*) breeding in eastern Maryland. Bull. Nuttall Ornith. Club 5:182–83.

Kushlan, J. A. 1973. Least Bittern nesting colonially. Auk 90:685–86.

———. 1978. Feeding ecology of wading birds. Pp. 249–97 *in* A. Sprunt, Jr., J. C. Ogden, and S. Winckler, eds. Wading birds. Natl. Audubon Soc. Res. Rep. 7, N.Y.

Kwak, R. G. M. and Reyrink. 1984. Unknown Dutch publication.

Lack, P. 1986. The atlas of wintering birds in Britain and Ireland. British Trust for Ornithology, Tring, Hertfordshire.

Landin, M. C. 1978. Wading birds and wetland management. Pp. 135–41 *in* R. M. DeGraaf, ed. Proc. workshop management of southern forests for nongame birds. U.S. Forest Serv., Southeastern Forest Exp. Sta., Gen. Tech. Rep. SE-14, Asheville, N.C.

Lansdowne, J. F., and J. A. Livingston. 1970. Birds of the eastern forest: Vol. 2. Houghton Mifflin, Boston.

Larner, Y. 1979. Virginia's birdlife, an annotated checklist. Virginia Avifauna 2. Virginia Soc. Ornith., Richmond.

Laskey A. R. 1944. A study of the Cardinal in Tennessee. Wilson Bull. 68:111–17.

———. 1957. Some Tufted Titmouse life history. Bird-Banding 28:135–45.

———. 1962. Breeding biology of Mockingbirds. Auk 79:596–606.

Laughlin, S. B., ed. 1982. Proc. northeastern breeding bird atlas conf. Vermont Inst. Nat. Sci., Woodstock.

Laughlin, S. B., and D. P. Kibbe. 1985. Atlas of the breeding birds of Vermont. Univ. Press of New England, Hanover, N.H.

Lawrence, L. de K. 1953. Nesting life and behaviour of the Red-eyed Vireo. Canadian Field-Nat. 67:47–87.

———. 1967. A comparative life history of four species of woodpeckers. Ornithol. Monogr. 5.

Lea, R. B. 1942. A study of the nesting habits of the Cedar Waxwing. Wilson Bull. 54:225–37.

Leatherman, S. P. 1984. Shoreline evolution of north Assateague Island, Maryland. Shore and Beach (July):3–10.

Leck, C. F., and F. C. Cantor. 1979. Seasonality, clutch size, and hatching success in the Cedar Waxwing. Auk 96:196–98.

Lenington, S., and T. Mace. 1975. Mate fidelity and nesting site tenacity in the Killdeer. Auk 92:149–51.

Levine, E. 1988a. Northern Saw-whet Owl. Pp. 212-213 *in* R. F. Andrle and J. R. Carroll. The atlas of breeding birds in New York State. Cornell Univ. Press., Ithaca, N.Y.

———. 1988b. Yellow-bellied Sapsucker. Pp. 230–31 *in* R. F. Andrle and J. R. Carroll, eds. The atlas of breeding birds in New York State. Cornell Univ. Press, Ithaca, N.Y.

Lindmeier, J. P. 1960. Plover, rail, and godwit nesting on a study area in Mahnomen County, Minnesota. Flicker 32:5–9.

Linduska, J. P. 1964. Waterfowl tomorrow. U.S. Fish and Wildl. Serv., Washington, D.C.

Liscinsky, S. A. 1972. The Pennsylvania Woodcock Management Study. Pennsylvania Game Comm. Bull. 171, Harrisburg.

Lombardo, M. P. 1986. Attendants at Tree Swallow nests: 1. Are attendants helpers at the nest? Condor 88:297–303.

Long, J. L. 1981. Introduced birds of the world. Universe Books, N.Y.

Lord, J., and D. J. Munn. 1970. Atlas of breeding birds of the West Midlands. Collins, London.

Loughry, F. D., and T. Wheatley. 1977. First nesting of Hooded Merganser on Maryland's Eastern Shore. Maryland Birdlife 33:55.

Low, G., and W. Mansell. 1983. North American marsh birds. Collins, Don Mills, Ontario, Canada.

Lunk, W. A. 1962. The Rough-winged Swallow *Stelgidopteryx ruficollis* (Vieillot), a study based on its breeding biology in Michigan. Nuttall Ornith. Club Publ. 4.

Luther, D. H. 1974. Observations at a Carolina Wren nest from which Brown-headed Cowbirds fledged. Wilson Bull. 86:51–57.

Lutz, H. J. 1934. Ecological relations in the pitch pine plains of southern New Jersey. Yale Univ. School Forestry Bull. 38.

Luukkonen, D. R., and J. D. Fraser. 1987. Loggerhead Shrike status and breeding biology in Virginia. Virginia Polytech. Inst. and State Univ., Blacksburg.

Lynch, J. F., and D. F. Whigham. 1984. Effects of forest fragmentation on breeding bird communities in Maryland, USA. Biol. Conserv. 28:287–324.

Lyons, D. M., and J. A. Mosher. 1987. Morphological growth, behavioral development, and parental care of Broad-winged Hawks. J. Field Ornith. 58:334–44.

MacClintock, L. 1978. Breeding bird census: Mature tulip-tree–oak forest. Amer. Birds 32:60.

MacInnes, C. D., R. A. Davis, R. N. Jones, B. C. Lieff, and A. J. Pakulak. 1974. Reproductive efficiency of McConnell River small Canada Geese. J. Wildl. Manage. 38:686–707.

MacIvor, L. H. 1990. Population dynamics, breeding ecology, and management of Piping Plovers on outer Cape Cod, Massachusetts. M.S. thesis, Univ. of Massachusetts, Amherst.

Marshall, E. W. 1958. Banding recovery adds House Finch to Maryland list. Maryland Birdlife 14:96.

Martin, A. C., H. S. Zim, and A. L. Nelson. 1951. American wildlife and plants: A guide to wildlife food habits. U.S. Dept. Interior, Washington, D.C.

Martz, G. F. 1967. Effects of nesting cover removal on breeding puddle ducks. J. Wildl. Manage. 31:236–47.

Maryland Department of Agriculture. 1988. Maryland agricultural statistics summary for 1987. Annapolis.

Maryland Department of State Planning. 1974. Forest vegetation in Maryland. Baltimore, Md.

Maryland Office of Planning. 1991. Maryland's land, 1973–1990: A changing resource. Maryland Office of Planning, Publ. 91–8, Baltimore.

Massey, B. W., and J. L. Atwood. 1981. Second-wave nesting of the California Least Tern: Age composition and reproductive success. Auk 98:596–605.

Matray, P. F. 1974. Broad-winged Hawk nesting and ecology. Auk 91:307–24.

Maxwell, G. R., II, J. M. Nocilly, and R. I. Shearer. 1976. Observations at a cavity nest of the Common Grackle and an analysis of grackle nest sites. Wilson Bull. 88:505–07.

Maxwell, G. R., and L. S. Putnam. 1972. Incubation, care of young, and nest success of the Common Grackle (*Quiscalus quiscula*) in northern Ohio. Auk 89:349–59.

Maxwell, H. 1910–11. Use and abuse of forests by the Virginia Indians. William and Mary Quarterly, Ser. 1, No. 19.

May, J. B. 1935. The hawks of North America. Natl. Assoc. Audubon Soc., N.Y.

Mayhew, W. W. 1958. The biology of the Cliff Swallow in California. Condor 60:7–37.

Mayre, W. B. 1955. The great Maryland barrens. Maryland Hist. Mag. 50:11–23, 120–42, 234–53.

McAtee, W. L. 1908. Food habits of the grosbeaks. U.S. Dept. Agric. Biol. Surv. Bull. 32.

———. 1926. The relation of birds to woodlots in New York State. Roosevelt Wild Life Bull. 4:1–152.

McAtee, W. L., and F.E.L. Beal. 1912. Some common game, aquatic and rapacious birds in relation to man. U.S. Dept. Agric. Farmers Bull. 497.

McAuley, D. G., J. R. Longcore, and G. F. Sepik. 1990. Renesting by American Woodcock (*Scolopax minor*) in Maine. Auk 107:407–10.

McCracken, J. D. 1987. Pp. 402–03 *in* M. D. Cadman, P.F.J. Eagles, and F. M. Helleiner, comps. Atlas of the breeding birds of Ontario. Univ. Waterloo Press, Waterloo, Ontario, Canada.

McGill-Harelstad, P. 1981. The effects of interspecific competition on reproductive success of Great Black-backed and Herring-Gulls. Colonial Waterbirds 4:197(Abstr.).

McGilvrey, F. B. 1969. Survival in Wood Duck broods. J. Wildl. Manage. 33:73–76.

McGowan, J. D. 1975. Distribution, density and productivity of Goshawks in interior Alaska. Alaska Dept. Fish Game, Fed. Aid Proj. Rep. W-17-445.

Mead, C., and K. Smith. 1982. The Hertfordshire breeding bird atlas. H.B.B.A., Tring, Hertfordshire.

Meanley, B. 1938. Chestnut-sided Warbler nesting near Baltimore, Maryland. Auk 55:542–43.

———. 1943a. Red-cockaded Woodpeckers breeding in Maryland. Auk 60:105.

———. 1943b. Nesting of the Upland Plover in Baltimore County, Maryland. Auk 60:603.

———. 1950. Swainson's Warbler on the coastal plain of Maryland. Wilson Bull. 62:93–94.

———. 1969. Natural history of the King Rail. N. Amer. Fauna 67, Washington, D.C.

———. 1971. Natural history of the Swainson's Warbler. N. Amer. Fauna 69, Washington, D.C.

———. 1973. February nesting of Mourning Doves near Laurel, Maryland. Maryland Birdlife 29:33.

———. 1981. Nesting of the Fish Crow in the Shenandoah Valley, Virginia. Raven 52:45–46.

———. 1985. The marsh hen—a natural history of the Clapper Rail of the Atlantic coast salt marsh. Tidewater Publ., Centreville, Md.

Melvin, S. 1984. Results of the 1984 census of Piping Plovers, American Oystercatchers, and Willets in Massachusetts. Bird Observer East. Massachusetts 12:325–27.

Mendenhall, V. M., and R. M. Prouty. 1978. Recovery of breeding success in a population of Brown Pelicans. Proc. Colonial Waterbird Group 1978:65–70.

Mengel, R. M. 1965. The birds of Kentucky. Ornith. Monogr. 3.

Merritt, P. G. 1981. Narrowly disjunct allopatry between Black-capped and Carolina Chickadees in northern Indiana. Wilson Bull. 93:54–66.

Meyer, K. D., and H. C. Mueller. 1982. Recent evidence of Sharp-shinned Hawks breeding in North Carolina. Chat 46:78–80.

Meyerrecks, A. J. 1960. Comparative breeding behavior of four species of North American herons. Nuttall Ornithol. Club Bull. 2.

———. 1971. Further observations on use of the feet by foraging herons. Wilson Bull. 83:435–38.

Mickelson, P. G. 1973. Breeding biology of the Cackling Geese (*Branta canadensis minima* Ridgway) and associated species on the Yukon-Kuskokwim Delta, Alaska. Ph.D. diss. Univ. of Michigan, Ann Arbor.

Middleton, A. L. A. 1987. Purple Finch. Pp. 490–91 *in* M. D. Cadman, P. F. J. Eagles, and F. M. Helleiner, eds. Atlas of the breeding birds of Ontario. Univ. of Waterloo Press, Waterloo, Ontario, Canada.

———. 1991. Failure of Brown-headed Cowbird parasitism in nests of the American Goldfinch. J. Field Ornith. 62:200–03.

Middleton, A. L. A., and D. R. C. Prescott. 1989. Polygyny, extra-pair copulations, and nest helpers in the Chipping Sparrow, *Spizella passerina*. Canadian Field-Nat. 103:61–64.

Miller, F. P. 1967. Maryland soils. Univ. Maryland Coop. Ext. Serv., Ext. Bull. 212, College Park.

Miller, G. E. 1958. First nesting of Herring Gulls on the Maryland coast. Maryland Birdlife 14:92–93.

———. 1959. First nesting of the Cattle Egret in Maryland. Maryland Birdlife 15:22.

Miller, L. M., and J. Burger. 1978. Factors affecting nesting success of the Glossy Ibis. Auk 95:353–61.

Mills, G. S. 1976. American Kestrel sex ratios and habitat separation. Auk 93:740–48.

Moeller, A. P. 1983. Breeding habitat selection in the swallow *Hirundo rustica*. Bird Study 30:134–42.

Montier, D. 1977. Atlas of the Breeding Birds of the London Area. London Nat. Hist. Soc.

Monroe, B. L., Sr. 1955. Impressions on changes in urban bird populations. Ky. Warbler 31:39–47.

Morgan, R. P., II, D. W. Meritt, S. B. Block, S. T. Sulkin, and F. B. Lee. 1984. Frequency of Mallard-Black Duck hybrids along the Atlantic coast determined by electrophoresis and plumage analysis. Biochem. Systematics Ecol. 12:125–28.

Morse, T. E., J. L. Jakabosky, and V. P. McCrow. 1969. Some aspects of the breeding biology of Hooded Merganser. J. Wildl. Manage. 33:596–04.

Morse, T. E., and H. M. Wight. 1969. Dump nesting and its effect on production in Wood Ducks. J. Wildl. Manage. 33:284–93.

Morton, E. S. 1982. Grading, discreteness, redundancy, and motivation-structural rules. Pp. 183–12 *in* D. E. Kroodsma and E. H. Miller, eds. Acoustic communication in birds. Vol. 1. Academic Press, N.Y.

Muldal, A., H. L. Gibbs, and R. J. Robertson. 1985. Preferred nest spacing of an obligate cavity-nesting bird, the Tree Swallow. Condor 87:356–63.

Mumford, R. E. 1962. Notes on Least Flycatcher behavior. Wilson Bull. 74:98–99.

———. 1964. The breeding biology of the Acadian Flycatcher. Univ. Michigan, Mus. Zool. Misc. Publ. 125, Ann Arbor.

Murphey, M. T. 1983. Clutch size in the Eastern Kingbird: Factors affecting nestling survival. Auk 100:326–34.

———. 1986. Brood parasitism of Eastern Kingbirds by Brown-headed Cowbirds. Auk 103: 626–28.

———. 1987. The impact of weather on kingbird foraging behavior. Condor 89:721–30.

———. 1988. Comparative reproductive biology of kingbirds (*Tyrannus* spp.) in eastern Kansas. Wilson Bull. 100:357–76.

Murray, B. G., Jr., and F. B. Gill. 1976. Behavioral interactions of Blue-wing and Golden-winged warblers. Wilson Bull. 88:231–54.

Murray, G. A. 1976. Geographic variation in the clutch sizes of seven owl species. Auk 93:602–13.

Murray, J. J. 1949. Nesting habits of the raven in Rockbridge County. Raven 20:40–43.

Nelson, A. L. 1933. Golden-winged Warbler feeding on larvae of *Talponia plummeriana*. Auk 50:440–41.

Nice, M. M. 1937. Studies in the life history of the Song Sparrow, I. Trans. Linn. Soc. 4. N.Y.

———. 1943. Studies in the life history of the Song Sparrow, 2. Trans. Linn. Soc. 6. N.Y.

Nichols, W. 1985. Tufted Titmouse. Pp. 214–15 *in* S. B. Laughlin and D. P. Kibbe, eds. The atlas of breeding birds of Vermont. Univ. Press of New England, Hanover, N.H.

Nicholls, T. H., and D. W. Warner. 1972. Barred Owl habitat use as determined by radiotelemetry. J. Wildl. Manage. 36:213–24.

Nickell, W. F. 1951. Studies of habitats, territories and nests of the Eastern Goldfinch. Auk 68:444–70.

Nickell, W. P. 1966. The nesting of the Black-crowned Night Heron and its associates. Jack Pine Warbler 44:130–39.

Nikolaus, G. 1987. Distribution atlas of Sudan's birds with notes on habitat and status. Bonner Zool. Monographien 25, Bonn, Germany.

Nisbet, I. C. T. 1971. The Laughing Gull in the Northeast. Amer. Birds 25:677–83.

Nol, E., A. J. Baker, and M. D. Cadman. 1984. Clutch initiation dates, clutch size, and egg size of the American Oystercatcher in Virginia. Auk 101:855–67.

Nol, E., and A. Lambert. 1984. Comparison of Killdeers *Charadrius vociferus*, breeding in mainland and peninsular sites in southern Ontario. Canadian Field-Nat. 98:7–11.

Nolan, V., Jr. 1968. Eastern Song Sparrow. Pp. 1492–1512 *in* O. L. Austin, Jr., ed. Life histories of North American cardinals, grosbeaks, buntings, towhees, finches, sparrows, and allies. U.S. Natl. Mus. Bull. 237, Washington, D.C.

———. 1978. The ecology and behavior of the Prairie Warbler *Dendroica discolor*. Ornith. Monogr. 26.

Nolan, V., Jr., and C. F. Thompson. 1975. The occurrence and significance of anomalous reproductive activities in two North American cuckoos *Coccyzus* spp. Ibis 117:496–503.

Norris, R. A. 1958. Comparative biosystematics and life history of the nuthatches *Sitta pygmaea* and *Sitta pusilla*. Univ. of California Publ. Zool. 56:119–300.

Norse, W. J., and D. P. Kibbe. 1985. Least Flycatcher. Pp. 180–81 *in* S. B. Laughlin and D. P. Kibbe, eds. The atlas of breeding birds of Vermont. Univ. Press of New England, Hanover, N.H.

North American Ornithological Atlas Committee. 1990. Handbook for atlasing American breeding birds. Vermont Inst. Nat. Sci., Woodstock.

Oates, E. W. 1902. Catalog birds' eggs. British Mus. 2:135.

Oberholser, H. C. 1920. The season, Dec. 15, 1919 to Feb. 15, 1920. Washington region. Bird-Lore 22:106.

———. The bird life of Texas. Univ. of Texas Press, Austin.

Office of Migratory Bird Management. 1990. Conservation of avian diversity in North America. U.S. Fish Wildl. Serv., Washington, D.C.

Oresman, S., J. Tiffany, and C. S. Robbins. 1948. Breeding bird census: Damp deciduous scrub with numerous standing dead trees. Audubon Field Notes 2:226–27.

Orians, G. H. 1985. Blackbirds of the Americas. Univ. of Washington Press, Seattle.

Oring, L. W. 1968. Growth, molts, and plumages of the Gadwall. Auk 85:355–80.

Oring, L. W., and M. Knudson. 1972. Monogamy and polyandry in the Spotted Sandpiper. Living Bird 11:59–73.

Oring, L. W., D. W. Lank, and S. J. Maxson. 1983. Population studies of the polyandrous Spotted Sandpiper. Auk 100:272–85.

Osborn, R. G., and T. W. Custer. 1978. Herons and their allies: Atlas of Atlantic coast colonies, 1975 and 1976. U.S. Fish and Wildl. Serv., Biol. Serv. Prog., FWS/OBS-77/08.

Owen, R. B., Jr. 1977. American Woodcock. Pp. 149–86 *in* G. C. Sanderson, ed. Management of migratory shore and upland game birds in North America. Internatl. Assn. Fish and Wildl. Agencies, Washington, D.C.

Page, J. 1990. Pushy and brassy, the starling was an ill-advised import. Smithsonian 21(6):77–83.

Palmer, R. S., ed. 1962. Handbook of North American birds. Vol. 1. Loons through flamingos. Yale Univ. Press, New Haven, Conn.

———. 1968. Pine Siskin. Pp. 424–47 *in* O. L. Austin, Jr., ed. Life histories of North American cardinals, grosbeaks, buntings, towhees, finches, sparrows, and allies. U.S. Natl. Mus. Bull. 237, Washington, D.C.

———, ed. 1976a. Handbook of North American birds. Vol. 2. Waterfowl (Part 1). Yale Univ. Press, New Haven, Conn.

———, ed. 1976b. Handbook of North American birds. Vol. 3. Waterfowl (Part 2). Yale Univ. Press, New Haven, Conn.

———, ed. 1988a. Handbook of North American birds. Vol. 4. Diurnal raptors (Part 1). Yale Univ. Press, New Haven, Conn.

———, ed. 1988b. Handbook of North American birds. Vol. 5. Diurnal raptors (Part 2). Yale Univ. Press, New Haven, Conn.

Palmer, T. S. 1909. The black rail in Maryland. Auk 26:427.

———. 1917. In memoriam: Wells Woodbridge Cooke. Auk 34:119–32.

Parkes, K. C. 1951. The genetics of the Golden-winged x Blue-winged Warbler complex. Wilson Bull. 63:5–15.

———. 1987. Sorting out the chickadees in southwestern Pennsylvania. Pennsylvania Birds 1:105–06.

Parnell, J. F., D. G. Ainley, H. Blokpoel, B. Cain, T. W. Custer, J. L. Dusi, S. Kress, J. A. Kushlan, W. E. Southern, L. E. Stenzel, and B. C. Thompson. 1988. Colonial waterbird management in North America. Colonial Waterbirds 11:129–69.

Parnell, J. F., and M. A. Shields. 1990. Management of North Carolina's colonial waterbirds. Univ. of North Carolina, Sea Grant College Prog. UNC-SG-90-03.

Parnell, J. F., and R. F. Soots. 1975. Herring and Great Black-backed Gulls nesting in North Carolina. Auk 92:154–57.

Patterson, M. E., J. D. Fraser, and J. W. Roggenbuck. 1991. Factors affecting Piping Plover productivity on Assateague Island. J. Wildl. Manage. 55:525–31.

Patterson, R. M. 1976. First nesting confirmation of Purple Gallinule in Maryland. Maryland Birdlife 32:110–12.

———. 1978. The Prince George's County breeding bird atlas, 1975–77. Maryland Birdlife 34:43–45.

———. 1981. Range expansion of Cliff Swallow into Maryland coastal plain. Maryland Birdlife 37:43–44.

Paulus, J. 1975. First Cattle Egrets and White-winged Scoters in Allegany County. Maryland Birdlife 31:148.

Pearson, T. G., ed. 1917. Birds of America. Univ. Soc., N.Y.

———. 1926. The Double-crested Cormorant. Bird-Lore 28:303–06.

———. 1936. Birds of America. Garden City Books, Garden City, N.Y.

Peck, G. K., and R. D. James. 1983. Breeding birds of Ontario: Nidiology and distribution. Vol. 1: Nonpasserines. Royal Ontario Mus., Toronto, Ontario, Canada.

———. 1987. Breeding birds of Ontario: Nidiology and distribution. Vol. 2: Passerines. Royal Ontario Mus., Toronto, Ontario, Canada.

Perkins, S. E., III. 1933. Notes from Dorchester Co., Maryland. Auk 50:367–68.

Perkins, S. E., III, and R. P. Allen. 1931. Notes on some winter birds of Maryland. Maryland Conserv. 8:3–5.

Perring, F. H., and S. M. Walters. 1962. Atlas of the British Flora. Botanical Soc. of the British Isles. T. Nelson, London.

Peterjohn, B. G., and D. L. Rice. 1991. The Ohio breeding bird atlas. Ohio Dept. Nat. Resources, Columbus.

Peterson, A. T. 1986. Rock Doves nesting in trees. Wilson Bull. 98:168–69.

Peterson, R. A. 1995. South Dakota breeding bird atlas. South Dakota Ornithologists' Union, Aberdeen.

Peterson, R. T., W. H. Stickel, S. Postupalsky, D. D. Berger, H. C. Mueller, and K. H. Moll. 1969. Brief reports: The status of the Osprey. Pp. 333–43 *in* J. J. Hickey, ed. Peregrine Falcon populations: Their biology and decline. Univ. of Wisconsin Press, Madison.

Petit, L. J., W. J. Fleming, K. E. Petit, and D. R. Petit. 1987. Nest-box use by Prothonotary Warblers (*Protonotaria citrea*) in riverine habitat. Wilson Bull. 99:485–88.

Petrides, G. A. 1938. A life history of the Yellow-breasted Chat. Wilson Bull. 50:184–89.

———. 1942. Nesting of Mallard, Pintail and Black Duck at Washington, D.C. Auk 59:437–38.

Pettingill, O. S., Jr. 1970. Ornithology in laboratory and field. Burgess, Minneapolis, Minn.

Phillips, C. L. 1887. Egg-laying extraordinary in Colaptes auratus. Auk 4:346.

Phillips, J. C., and F. C. Lincoln. 1930. American waterfowl: Their present situation and the outlook for their future. Houghton Mifflin, Boston, Mass.

Phillips, R. E. 1972. Sexual and agonistic behavior in the Killdeer (*Charadrius vociferus*). Anim. Behav. 20:1–9.

Picman, J. 1984. Experimental study on the role of intra- and interspecific competition in the evolution of nest-destroying behavior in Marsh Wrens. Canadian J. Zool. 62:2353–56.

Pilcher, R. W. 1985. Northern Cardinal. Pp. 330–31 *in* S. B. Laughlin and D. P. Kibbe, eds. The atlas of breeding birds of Vermont. Univ. Press of New England, Hanover, N.H.

Pinkowski, B. C. 1974. Prolonged incubation record for an Eastern Bluebird. Inland Bird Banding News 46:15–19.

Pitelka, F. A. 1940. Breeding behavior of the Black-throated Green Warbler. Wilson Bull. 52:3–18.

Pleasants, J. H., Jr. 1893. Rare birds near Baltimore, Maryland. Auk 10:371–72.

Poole, F. G. 1942. Breeding notes eastern shore birds. Nat. Hist. Soc. Maryland Bull. 12:56–58.

Pospichal, L. B., and W. H. Marshall. 1954. A field study of Sora Rail and Virginia Rail in central Minnesota. Flicker 26:2–32.

Post, W. 1988. Boat-tailed Grackles nest in freshwater habitat in interior South Carolina. Wilson Bull. 100:326–27.

Potter, E. F. 1980. Notes on nesting Yellow-billed Cuckoos. J. Field Ornith. 51:17–29.

Potter, E. F., J. F. Parnell, and R. P. Teulings. 1980. Birds of the Carolinas. Univ. of North Carolina Press, Chapel Hill.

Potter, P. E. 1972. Territorial behavior in Savannah Sparrows in southeastern Michigan. Wilson Bull. 84:48–59.

Pough, R. H. 1946. Audubon bird guide: Eastern land birds. Doubleday and Co., Garden City, N.Y.

———. 1951. Audubon water bird guide. Doubleday, Garden City, N.Y.

Powell, D. S., and N. P. Kingsley. 1980. The forest resources of Maryland. U.S. Forest Serv., Northeastern Forest Exp. Sta., Resource Bull. NE–61, Broomall, Pa.

Powell, G.V.N., and H. L. Jones. 1978. An observation of polygyny in the Common Yellowthroat. Wilson Bull. 90:656–57.

Preble, E. A. 1900. List of summer birds in western Maryland. Pp. 294–307 *in* Maryland Geological Survey, Allegany County. Johns Hopkins Press, Baltimore, Md.

Preble, N. A. 1957. Nesting habits of the Yellow-billed Cuckoo. Amer. Midl. Nat. 57:474–82.

Prescott, D.R.C. 1987. Alder Flycatcher. P. 258 *in* M. D. Cadman, P.F.J. Eagles, and F. M. Helleiner, eds. Atlas of the breeding birds of Ontario. Univ. of Waterloo Press, Waterloo, Ontario, Canada.

Prescott, K. W. 1965. Studies in the life history of the Scarlet Tanager. New Jersey State Mus. Investigation 2.

Pyle, R. L. 1963. House Finch reaches District of Columbia and Virginia. Atlantic Nat. 18:32–33.

Pyne, S. J. 1982. Fire in America: A cultural history of wildland and rural fire. Princeton Univ. Press, Princeton, N.J.

Quinney, T. E., and C. D. Ankney. 1985. Prey size selection by Tree Swallows. Auk 102:245–50.

Rabenold, K. N., and P. P. Rabenold. 1985. Variation in altitudinal migration, winter segregation, and site tenacity in two subspecies of Dark-eyed Juncos in the southern Appalachians. Auk 102:805–19.

Rabenold, P. P., and M. D. Decker. 1989. Black and Turkey Vultures expand their ranges northward. Eyas 12:11–15.

Reed, J. M. 1986. Vegetation structure and Vesper Sparrow territory location. Wilson Bull. 98:144–47.

Reese, J. G. 1969a. Mute Swan breeding in Talbot County, Maryland. Maryland Birdlife 25:14–16.

———. 1969b. A Maryland Osprey population 75 years ago and today. Maryland Birdlife 25:116–19.

———. 1970. Reproduction in a Chesapeake Bay Osprey population. Auk 87:747–59.

———. 1972. A Chesapeake Barn Owl population. Auk 89:106–14.

———. 1975a. Osprey nest success in Eastern Bay, Maryland. Chesapeake Sci. 16:56–61.

———. 1975b. Productivity and management of feral Mute Swans in Chesapeake Bay. J. Wildl. Manage. 39:280–86.

———. 1975c. Diurnal vocalization by a wintering Black Rail. Maryland Birdlife 31:13–14.

———. 1977. Reproductive success of Ospreys in central Chesapeake Bay. Auk 94:202–21.

———. 1980. Demography of European Mute Swans in Chesapeake Bay. Auk 97:449–64.

———. 1984. Population ecology of European Mute Swan in Chesapeake Bay. Natl. Geogr. Soc., Res. Rep. 17:745–50.

Reilly, E. M., Jr. 1968. Audubon illustrated handbook of American birds. McGraw-Hill, N.Y.

Rendell, W. B., and R. J. Robertson. 1989. Nest site characteristics, reproductive success and cavity availability for Tree Swallows breeding in natural cavities. Condor 91:875–85.

Renken, R. B., and E. P. Wiggers. 1989. Forest characteristics related to Pileated Woodpecker territory size in Missouri. Condor 91:642–52.

Resler, A. 1890. List of birds resident in summer near the city of Baltimore. Trans. Maryland Acad. Sci. 1:105–38.

Rheinwald, G. 1977. Atlas der Brutverbreitung westdeutscher Vogelarten. Dachverband Deutscher Avifaunisten, Bonn.

Richards, D. G. 1981. Alerting and message components in songs of Rufous-sided Towhees. Behavior 76:223–48.

Richmond, C. W. 1888. An annotated list of birds breeding in the District of Columbia. Auk 5:18–25.

Ridgely, R. S., and G. Tudor. 1989. The birds of South America. Vol. 1. The oscine passerines. Univ. of Texas Press, Austin.

Ridgway, R. 1882. Birds new to or rare in the District of Columbia. Nuttall Ornith. Club Bull. 7:253.

———. 1884. Probable breeding of the Red Crossbill in central Maryland. Auk 1:292.

———. 1889. The ornithology of Illinois. Vol 1. Illinois Nat. Hist. Surv., Reprint 1913, Pantagraph Printing, Bloomington.

Riley, J. H. 1902. Notes on the habits of the Broad-winged Hawk (*Buteo platypterus*) in the vicinity of Washington, D.C. Osprey 1:21–23.

Ringler, R. F. 1977. The season: Spring migration, 1977. Maryland Birdlife 33:116–24.

———. 1978a. The season: Winter season, December 1, 1977–February 28, 1978. Maryland Birdlife 34:78–84.

———. 1978b. The season: Breeding season, June 1–July 31, 1978. Maryland Birdlife 34:178–181.

———. 1979a. The season: Winter season, December 1, 1978–February 28, 1979. Maryland Birdlife 35:55–62.

———. 1979b. The season: Breeding season, June 1–July 31, 1979. Maryland Birdlife 35:98–104.

———. 1980a. The season: Fall migration, August 1–November 30, 1979. Maryland Birdlife 36:18–36.

———. 1980b. The season: Breeding season, June 1–July 31, 1980. Maryland Birdlife 36:140–50.

———. 1981a. The season: Fall migration, August 1–November 30, 1980. Maryland Birdlife 37:17–38.

———. 1981b. The season: Spring migration, March 1–May 31, 1981. Maryland Birdlife 37:105–21.

———. 1981c. The season: Breeding season, June 1–July 31, 1981. Maryland Birdlife 37:133–41.

———. 1982. The season: Summer season, June 1–July 31, 1982. Maryland Birdlife 38:135–43.

———. 1983a. The season: Fall migration, August 1–November 30, 1982. Maryland Birdlife 39:7–24.

———. 1983b. The season: Breeding season, June 1–July 31, 1983. Maryland Birdlife 39:98–105.

———. 1984a. The season: Fall migration, August 1–November 30, 1983. Maryland Birdlife 40:5–28.

———. 1984b. The season: Spring migration, March 1–May 31, 1984. Maryland Birdlife 40:58–73.

———. 1984c. The season: Breeding season, June 1–July 31, 1984. Maryland Birdlife 40:94–100.

———. 1985a. The season: Fall migration, August 1–November 30, 1984. Maryland Birdlife 41:6–20

———. 1985b. The season: Breeding season, June 1–July 31, 1985. Maryland Birdlife 41:109–15.

———. 1986a. The season: Fall migration, August 1–November 30, 1985. Maryland Birdlife 42:5–24.

———. 1986b. The season: Spring migration, March 1–May 31, 1986. Maryland Birdlife 42:60–79.

———. 1986c. The season: Breeding season, June 1–July 31, 1986. Maryland Birdlife 42:108–16.

———. 1987a. The season: Winter season, December 1, 1986–February 28, 1987. Maryland Birdlife 43:50–59.

———. 1987b. The season: Breeding season, June 1–July 31, 1987. Maryland Birdlife 43:95–103.

———. 1988a. The season: Autumn migration, August 1–November 30, 1987. Maryland Birdlife 44:6–29.

———. 1988b. The season: Spring migration, March 1–May 31, 1988. Maryland Birdlife 44:84–106.

———. 1988c. The season: Breeding season, June 1–July 31, 1988. Maryland Birdlife 44:122–30.

———. 1989a. The season: Spring migration, March 1–May 31, 1989. Maryland Birdlife 45:94–117.

———. 1989b. The season: Breeding season, June 1–July 31, 1989. Maryland Birdlife 45:137–47.

———. 1990a. The season: Winter, December 1, 1989–February 28, 1990. Maryland Birdlife 46:50–59.

———. 1990b. The season: Breeding season, June 1–July 31, 1990. Maryland Birdlife 46:86–108.

Ripley, S. D. 1977. Rails of the world. David R. Godine, Boston, Mass.

Ritchison, G. 1988. Responses of Yellow-breasted Chats to the songs of neighboring and non-neighboring conspecifics. J. Field Ornith. 59:37–42.

Robbins, C. S. 1949a. Breeding bird census: Virgin hemlock forest. Audubon Field Notes 3:257–58.

———. 1949b. Breeding bird census: Mature and lumbered oak-maple ridge forest. Audubon Field Notes 3:259–61.

———. 1949c. Breeding bird census: Open hemlock-spruce bog. Audubon Field Notes 3:269.

———. 1950. Ecological distribution of the breeding *Parulidae* of Maryland. M.S. thesis. George Washington Univ., Washington, D.C.

———. 1952. The season: May, June, July, August 1951. Maryland Birdlife 8:20–26.

———. 1961. The season: April, May, June 1961. Maryland Birdlife 17:82–94.

———. 1962. The season: July, August, September 1962. Maryland Birdlife 18:101–08.

———. 1963. The season: April, May, June 1963. Maryland Birdlife 19:68–77.

———. 1965. The season: October, November, December 1964. Maryland Birdlife 21:22–27.

———. 1966. The season: July, August, September 1966. Maryland Birdlife 22:116–23.

———. 1967a. The season: January, February, March 1967. Maryland Birdlife 23:36–40.

———. 1967b. The season: April, May, June 1967. Maryland Birdlife 23:70–79.

———. 1969. The season: April, May, June 1969. Maryland Birdlife 25:92–100.

———. 1970. The season: April, May, June 1970. Maryland Birdlife 26:99–108.

———. 1972. The season: April, May, June 1972. Maryland Birdlife 28:105–117.

———. 1973a. The season: April, May, June 1973. Maryland Birdlife 29:114–124.

———. 1973b. Breeding bird census: Hickory-oak-ash floodplain forest. Amer. Birds 27:963–64.

———. 1973c. The season: July, August, September 1973. Maryland Birdlife 29:153–59.

———. 1974. The season: April, May, June 1974. Maryland Birdlife 30:105–116.

———. 1975a. The season: April, May, June 1975. Maryland Birdlife 31:110–122.

———. 1975b. The season: July, August, September 1975. Maryland Birdlife 31:141–48.

———. 1976. The season: April, May, June 1976. Maryland Birdlife 32:88–101.

———. 1977a. Impact of the severe winter of 1977 on woodland birds in the Maryland piedmont. Maryland Birdlife 33:8–11.

———. 1977b. The season: January, February, March 1977. Maryland Birdlife 33:92–103.

———. 1978. Determining habitat requirements of nongame species. Trans. N. Amer. Wildl. Nat. Resour. Conf. 43:57–68.

———. 1979. Effects of forest fragmentation on bird populations. Pp. 198–212 *in* R. M. DeGraaf and K. E. Evans, eds. Management of north central and northeastern forests for nongame birds. U.S. Forest Serv., N. Central Forest Exp. Sta., Gen. Tech. Rep. NC-51, St. Paul, Minn.

———. 1980. Effect of forest fragmentation on breeding bird populations in the piedmont of the Mid-Atlantic region. Atlantic Nat. 33:31–36.

———. 1989. Breeding bird census: Selectively logged mature tulip tree–oak forest. J. Field Ornith. (Suppl.) 60:71–72.

———. 1990a. Breeding bird census: Isolated moist tulip tree–red maple upland forest. J. Field Ornith. (Suppl.) 61:35–36.

———. 1990b. Use of breeding bird atlases to monitor population change. Pp. 18–22 *in* J. R. Sauer and S. Droege, eds. Survey designs and statistical methods for the estimation of avian population trends. U.S. Fish Wildl. Serv., Bio. Rep. 90(1). Washington, DC.

———. 1991. Breeding bird census: Mature beech–maple–oak bottomland forest. J. Field Ornith. (Suppl.) 62:37–38.

Robbins, C. S., and I. R. Barnes. 1949. Breeding bird census: Red pine plantation. Audubon Field Notes 3:258.

Robbins, C. S., and D. D. Boone. 1984. Threatened breeding birds of Maryland. Pp. 363–89 *in* A. W. Norden, D. C. Forester, and G. H. Fenwick, eds. Threatened and endangered plants and animals of Maryland. Maryland Nat. Heritage Prog., Spec. Publ. 84–1, Annapolis.

Robbins, C. S., B. Bruun, and H. S. Zim. 1966. Birds of North America. Golden Press, N.Y.

Robbins, C. S., and D. Bystrak. 1974. The winter bird survey of central Maryland, USA. Acta Ornith. 14:288–93.

———. 1977. Field list of the birds of Maryland, 2d ed. Maryland Ornith. Soc., Maryland Avifauna 2, Baltimore.

Robbins, C. S., D. Bystrak, and P. H. Geissler. 1986. The breeding bird survey: Its first fifteen years, 1965–1979. U.S. Fish and Wildl. Serv., Resource Publ. 157, Washington, D.C.

Robbins, C. S., D. K. Dawson, and B. A. Dowell. 1989a. Habitat area requirements of breeding forest birds of the middle Atlantic states. Wildl. Monogr. 103.

Robbins, C. S., and B. A. Dowell. 1989. Why supplement an atlas study with an intensive random sample? Ann. Zool. Fennici 26:303–04.

Robbins, C. S., S. Droege, and J. R. Sauer. 1989c. Monitoring bird populations with Breeding Bird Survey and atlas data. Ann. Zool. Fennici 26:297–303.

Robbins, C. S., J. W. Fitzpatrick, and P. B. Hamel. 1992. A warbler in trouble: *Dendroica cerulea*. Pp. 549–62 *in* J. M. Hagan and D. W. Johnston, ed. Ecology and conservation of neotropical migrant land birds. Smithsonian Inst. Press, Washington, D.C.

Robbins, C. S., J. R. Sauer, R. S. Greenberg, and S. Droege. 1989b. Population declines in North American birds that migrate to the neotropics. Proc. Natl. Acad. Sci. 86:7658–62.

Robbins, C. S., and R. E. Stewart. 1951a. Breeding bird census: Mature northern hardwood forest. Audubon Field Notes 5:320–21.

———. 1951b. Breeding bird census: Scrub spruce bog. Audubon Field Notes 5:325.

Robbins, C. S., R. E. Stewart, and M. Karplus. 1947. Breeding bird census: Dry deciduous scrub. Audubon Field Notes 1:200–01.

Robbins, C. S., and W. T. Van Velzen. 1967. The breeding bird survey, 1966. U.S. Fish and Wildl. Serv., Spec. Sci. Rep.—Wildl. 102, Washington, D.C.

Robbins, S. D. 1991. Wisconsin birdlife. Univ. of Wisconsin Press, Madison.

Roberts, T. S. 1936. The birds of Minnesota. Vol. 2. 2d ed. Univ. of Minnesota Mus. Nat. Hist., Minneapolis.

Robins, C. R., R. M. Bailey, C. E. Bond, J. R. Brooker, E. A. Lachner, R. N. Lea, and W. B. Scott, eds. 1980. A list of common and scientific names of fishes from the United States and Canada. Amer. Fish. Soc. Spec. Publ. 12, Bethesda, Md.

Robins, J. D. 1971. Differential niche utilization in a grassland sparrow. Ecol. 52:1065–70.

Robinson, J. C. 1989. A concentration of Bewick's Wrens in Stewart County, Tennessee. Migrant 60:1–3.

Rodenhouse, N. L., and L. B. Best. 1983. Breeding ecology of Vesper Sparrows in corn and soybean fields. Amer. Midl. Nat. 110:265–75.

Roest, A. I. 1957. Notes on the American Sparrow Hawk. Auk 74:1–19.

Rogers, C. M. 1985. Growth rate and determinants of fledgling weight in Michigan-breeding Savannah Sparrows. Condor 87:302–03.

Root, R. B. 1969. The behavior and reproductive success of the Blue-gray Gnatcatcher. Condor 71:16–31.

Root, T. 1970. Changes in redstart breeding territory. Auk 87:359–61.

———. 1988. Atlas of wintering North American birds. Univ. of Chicago Press, Chicago, Ill.

Roseberry, J. L., and W. D. Klimstra. 1970. The nesting ecology and reproductive performance of the Eastern Meadowlark. Wilson Bull. 82:243–67.

———. 1984. Population ecology of the Bobwhite. Southern Illinois Univ. Press, Carbondale.

Rosene, W. 1969. The Bobwhite quail: Its life and management. Rutgers Press, New Brunswick, N.J.

Roth, R., S. E. Kleiner, and C. R. Bartlett. 1991. A case of polygny in the Wood Thrush. Wilson Bull. 103:509–10.

Rothstein, S. I. 1975. An experimental and teleonomic investigation of avian brood parasitism. Condor 77:250–71.

———. 1976a. Cowbird parasitism of the Cedar Waxwing and its evolutionary implications. Auk 93:498–509.

———. 1976b. Experiments on defenses Cedar Waxwings use against cowbird parasitism. Auk 93:675–91.

Rue, L. L., III. 1973. Game birds of North America. Harper & Row, N.Y.

Rummel, L. H. 1979. Canada Geese of the Patuxent Wildlife Research Center: Family relationships, behavior and productivity. M.S. thesis, Univ. of Maryland, College Park.

Rumsey, R. L. 1970. Woodpecker nest failures in creosoted utility poles. Auk 87:367–69.

Runde, D. E., and D. E. Capen. 1987. Characteristics of northern hardwood trees used by cavity-nesting birds. J. Wildl. Manage. 51:217–23.

Runkle, J. R. 1985. Disturbance regimes in temperate forests. Pp. 17–33 in S. T. A. Pickett and P. S. White, eds. The ecology of natural disturbance and patch dynamics. Academic Press, Orlando, Fla.

Ryan, M. R. 1986. Nongame management in grassland and agricultural ecosystems. Pp. 117–36 in J. B. Hale, L. B. Best, and R. L. Clawson, eds. Management of nongame wildlife in the mid-west: A developing art. Proc. Symp. 47th Midwest Fish and Wildl. Conf.

Sabo, S. R. 1980. Niche and habitat relations in subalpine bird communities of the White Mountains of New Hampshire. Biol. Monogr. 50:241–49.

Salt, G. W. 1952. The relation of metabolism to climate and distribution of three finches of the genus *Carpadocus*. Ecol. Monogr. 22:121–52.

Sauer, J. R., and S. Droege. 1990a. Survey designs and statistical methods for the estimation of avian population trends. U.S. Fish and Wildl. Serv., Biol. Rep. 90(1), Washington, D.C.

———. 1990b. Recent population trends of the Eastern Bluebird. Wilson Bull. 102:239–52.

Saunders, A. A. 1938. Studies of breeding birds in the Allegany State Park. New York State Mus. Bull. 318, N.Y.

Schifferli, A., P. Geroudet, and R. Winkler. 1980. Verbreitungsatlas der Brutvogel der Schweiz. Schweizerische Vogelwarte Sempach, Sempach, Switzerland.

Schlosnagle, S., and the Garrett County Bicentennial Committee. 1989. Garrett County, a history of Maryland's tableland. 2d ed. McClain Printing, Parsons, W.V.

Schnell, J. H. 1958. Nesting behavior and food habits of Goshawks in the Sierra Nevada of California. Condor 60:377–403.

Schrantz, F. G. 1943. Nest life of the eastern Yellow Warbler. Auk 60:367–87.

Schreiber, R. W. 1980. Nesting chronology of the Eastern Brown Pelican. Auk 97:491–508.

Schroeder, R. L. 1985. Habitat suitability index models: Northern Bobwhite. U.S. Fish and Wildl. Serv., Biol. Rep. 82 (10.104).

Scott, D. M. 1963. Changes in the reproductive activity of the Brown-headed Cowbird within the breeding season. Wilson Bull. 75:123–29.

Scott, D. M., J. A. Darley, and A. V. Newsome. 1988. Length of the laying season and clutch size of Gray Catbirds at London, Ontario. J. Field Ornith. 59:355–60.

Scott, F. R., and D. A. Cutler. 1966. Middle Atlantic coast region. Audubon Field Notes 20:556–59.

———. 1970. Middle Atlantic coast region. Audubon Field Notes 24:670.

———. 1974. Middle Atlantic coast region. Amer. Birds 38:885–89.

Scott, J. M., B. Csuti, J. E. Estes, and S. Caicco. 1991. Gap analysis of species richness and vegetation cover: An integratedbiodiversity conservation strategy. Pp. 282–97 in K. Kohn, ed. Balancing on the brink of extinction: The endangered species act and lessons for the future. Island Press, Washington, D.C.

Scott, V. E. 1977. Cavity-nesting birds of North American forests. U.S. Dept. Agric., Handbook 511, Washington, D.C.

Sealey, S. G. 1978. Clutch size and nest placement of the Pied-billed Grebe in Manitoba. Wilson Bull. 90:301–02.

Sealey, S. G., and G. C. Bierman. 1983. Timing of breeding and migrations in a population of Least Flycatchers in Manitoba. J. Field Ornith. 54:113–22.

Semenchuk, G. P. 1992. The atlas of breeding birds in Alberta. Fed. Alberta Naturalists, Edmonton.

Sepik, G. F., R. B. Owen, Jr., and M. W. Coulter. 1981. A landowner's guide to woodcock management in the northeast. U.S. Fish and Wildl. Serv., Maine Agric. Exp. Sta., Misc. Rep. 253, Univ. of Maine, Orono.

Serrentino, P. 1987. The breeding ecology and behavior of Northern Harriers in Coos County, New Hampshire. M.S. thesis. Univ. of Rhode Island, Kingston.

Serrentino, P., and M. England. 1989. Northern Harrier. Pp. 37–46 *in* B. G. Pendleton, ed. Proc. Northeast Raptor Management Symposium and Workshop. Natl. Wildl. Fed. Sci. Tech. Ser. 13, Washington, D.C.

Sharp, W. M. 1963. The effects of habitat manipulation and forest succession on Ruffed Grouse. J. Wildl. Manage. 27:664–71.

Sharpe, R. B. 1898. Catalogue of the birds in the British Museum. Vol. 26. *Plataleae* (ibises and spoonbills) and *Herondiones* (herons and storks). British Mus. Nat. Hist., London.

Sharrock, J. T. R. 1976. The atlas of breeding birds in Britain and Ireland. British Trust for Ornithology, Tring, Hertfordshire.

Shaver, N. E. 1918. A nest study of the Maryland Yellow-throat. Univ. of Iowa Studies Nat. Hist. 8:1–12.

Shedd, D. H. 1990. Aggressive interactions in wintering House Finches and Purple Finches. Wilson Bull. 102:178–80.

Sheldon, W. G. 1967. The book of the American Woodcock. Univ. of Massachusetts Press, Amherst.

Sherman, A. R. 1911. Nest life of the Screech Owl. Auk 28:155–68.

Sherwood, G. A. 1965. Canada Geese of the Seney National Wildlife Refuge. U.S. Fish and Wildl. Serv., Compl. Rep. Wildl. Manage. Study 1 and 2, Minneapolis, Minn.

Short, L. L., Jr. 1963. Hybridization in the wood warblers *Vermivora pinus* and *V. chrysoptera*. Proc. Internatl. Ornith. Congress 13:147–60.

Shugars, J. C. 1978. The Wild Turkey in Maryland: History, current status and future management. Maryland Wildl. Admin., Annapolis.

Shugart, H. H., T. M. Smith, J. T. Kitchings, and R. L. Kroodsma. 1978. The relationship of nongame birds to southern forest types and successional stages. Pp. 5–16 *in* R. M. DeGraaf, ed. Proc. Workshop Management of Southern Forests for Nongame Birds. U.S. Forest Serv., Gen. Tech. Rep. SE-14, Asheville, N.C.

Sidle, J. 1984. Piping Plover proposed as an endangered and threatened species. Federal Register 49:44712–15.

———. 1985. Determination of endangered and threatened status for the Piping Plover. Federal Register 50:50726–34.

Simmons, G. F. 1925. Birds of the Austin [Texas] region. Univ. of Texas Press, Austin.

Simmons, R. E. 1984. Do harriers lay replacement clutches? Raptor Res. 18:103–06.

Simpson, M. B., and P. G. Range. 1974. Evidence of breeding of Saw-whet Owls in western North Carolina. Wilson Bull. 86:173–74.

Simpson, R. B. 1909. American Goshawk nesting in Pennsylvania. Oologist 26:85–87.

Sims, A., and W. R. DeGarmo. 1948. A study of Swainson's Warbler in West Virginia. Redstart 16:1–8.

Sisson, R. F. 1974. The heron that fishes with bait. Natl. Geogr. Mag. 145:143–47.

Skead, C. J. 1956. The Cattle Egret in Africa. Audubon Mag. 58:206-209, 221, 224–26.

Slack, R. S., and C. B. Slack. 1987. Spring migration of Long-eared and Northern Saw-whet Owls at Nine Mile Point, New York. Wilson Bull. 99:480–85.

Smallwood, J. A. 1987. Sexual segregation by habitat in American Kestrels wintering in south-central Florida: Vegetative structure and responses to differential prey availability. Condor 89:842–49.

Smith, A. R. 1996. Atlas of Saskatchewan birds. Special Publ. 22, Saskatchewan Nat. Hist. Soc. (Nature Saskatchewan), Regina.

Smith, H. M. 1885. Breeding of *Loxia americana* in the District of Columbia. Auk 2:379–80.

Smith, J. N. M., and J. R. Merkt. 1980. Development and stability of single-parent family units in the Song Sparrow. Canadian J. Zool. 58:1869–75.

Smith, J.N.M., Y. Yom-Tov, and R. Moses. 1982. Polygyny, male parental care, and sex ratios in Song Sparrows: An experimental study. Auk 99:555–64.

Smith, R. 1936. The food and nesting habits of the Bald Eagle. Auk 53:301–05.

Smith, R. L. 1968. Grasshopper Sparrow. Pp. 725–45 *in* O. L. Austin, Jr., ed. Life histories of North American cardinals, grosbeaks, buntings, towhees, finches, sparrows, and allies. U.S. Natl. Mus. Bull. 237, Washington, D.C.

Smith, W. J. 1988. Patterned daytime singing of the Eastern Wood-Pewee, *Contopus virens*. Anim. Behav. 36:1111–23.

Soots, R. F., Jr., and J. F. Parnell. 1975. Ecological succession of breeding birds in relation to plant succession on dredge islands in North Carolina. Sea Grant Publ. UNC-SG-75-27, Univ. of North Carolina, Raleigh.

Southern, W. E. 1958. Nesting of the Red-eyed Vireo in the Douglas Lake region, Michigan. Part 2. Jack-Pine Warbler 36:185–207.

Sowls, L. K. 1955. Prairie ducks: A study of their behavior, ecology, and management. Stackpole, Harrisburg, Pa. and Wildl. Manage. Inst., Washington, D.C.

Speiser, R., and T. Bosakowski. 1987. Nest site selection by Northern Goshawk in northern New Jersey and southeastern New York. Condor 89:387–94.

———. 1988. Nest site preferences of Red-tailed Hawks in the highlands of southeastern New York and northern New Jersey. J. Field Ornith. 59:361–68.

———. 1991. Nesting phenology, site fidelity, and defense behavior of Northern Goshawks in New York and New Jersey. J. Raptor Res. 25:132–35.

Spencer, O. R. 1943. Nesting habits of the Black-billed Cuckoo. Wilson Bull. 55:11–22.

Spendelow, J. A., D. S. Hopkins, F. J. Gallo, and M. G. Bull. 1983. Colonial waterbird banding and species interactions. N. Amer. Bird Bander 8:136–37.

Spendelow, J. A., and S. R. Patton. 1988. National atlas of coastal waterbird colonies in the contiguous United States: 1976–1982. U.S. Fish and Wildl. Serv., Biol. Rep. 88(5), Washington, D.C.

Spitzer, P. 1980. Dynamics of discrete breeding populations of Ospreys in the northeastern United States, 1969–1979. Ph. D. diss. Cornell Univ., Ithaca, N.Y.

Spitzer, P. R., R. W. Risebrough, W. Walker II, R. Hernandez, A. Poole, D. Puleston, and I.C.T. Nisbet. 1978. Productivity of Ospreys in Connecticut–Long Island increases as DDE residues decline. Sci. 202:333–35.

Springer, P. F., and R. E. Stewart. 1948a. Breeding bird census: Tidal marshes. Audubon Field Notes 2:223–26.

———. 1948b. Breeding bird census: Apple orchards. Audubon Field Notes 2:227–29.

———. 1948c. Breeding bird census: Immature loblolly–shortleaf pine stand. Audubon Field Notes 2:239.

———. 1948d. Breeding bird census: Second growth river swamp. Audubon Field Notes 2:240–41.

———. 1950. Gadwall nesting in Maryland. Auk 67:234–35.

Sprunt, A., Jr. 1942. Purple Martin. Pp. 489–509 *in* A. C. Bent, ed. Life histories of North American flycatchers, larks, swallows, and their allies. U.S. Natl. Mus. Bull. 179, Washington, D.C.

————. 1948. Eastern Mockingbird. Pp. 295–315 *in* A. C. Bent, ed. Life histories of North American nuthatches, wrens, thrashers and their allies. U.S. Natl. Mus. Bull. 195, Washington, D.C.

————. 1953. Eastern Yellow-throated Warbler. Pp. 349–59 *in* A. C. Bent, ed. Life histories of North American wood warblers. U.S. Natl. Mus. Bull. 203, Washington, D.C.

————. 1954. Florida bird life. Coward-McCann, N.Y.

————. 1955. North American birds of prey. Harper and Row, N.Y.

————. 1958. Eastern Boat-tailed Grackle. Pp. 365–74 *in* A. C. Bent, ed. Life histories of North American blackbirds, orioles, tanagers, and allies. U.S. Natl. Mus. Bull. 211, Washington, D.C.

————. 1968. Carolina Slate-colored Junco. Pp. 1043–49 *in* O. L. Austin, Jr., ed. Life histories of North American cardinals, grosbeaks, buntings, towhees, finches, sparrows, and allies. U.S. Natl. Mus. Bull. 237, Washington, D.C.

Stabler, H. B. 1891. Nesting of the Sharp-shinned Hawk. Oologist 8:161–62.

Stalmaster, M. V. 1987. The Bald Eagle. Universe Books, N.Y.

Stanwood, C. J. 1910. The Black-throated Green Warbler. Auk 27:289–94.

Stein, R. C. 1958. The behavioral, ecological and morphological characteristics of two populations of the Alder Flycatcher, *Empidonax traillii* (Audubon). New York State Mus. Bull. 371.

————. 1963. Isolating mechanisms between populations of Traill's Flycatchers. Proc. Amer. Phil. Soc. 107:21–50.

Stewart, P. A. 1980. Population trends of Barn Owls in North America. Amer. Birds 34:698–700.

————. 1982. Migration of Blue Jays in eastern North American. N. Amer. Bird Bander 7:107–11.

Stewart, R. E. 1949. Ecology of a nesting Red-shouldered Hawk population. Wilson Bull. 61:26–35.

————. 1951. Clapper Rail populations of the middle Atlantic states. Trans. N. Amer. Wildl. Conf. 16:421–30.

————. 1953. A life history study of the Yellow-throat. Wilson Bull. 65:99–115.

————. 1957. Eastern Glossy Ibis nesting in southeastern Maryland. Auk 74:509.

————. 1962. Waterfowl populations in the upper Chesapeake region. U.S. Fish and Wildl. Serv., Spec. Sci. Rep. Wildl. 65, Washington, D.C.

Stewart, R. E., J. B. Cope, C. S. Robbins, and J. W. Brainerd. 1946. Effects of DDT on birds at the Patuxent Research Refuge. J. Wildl. Manage. 10:195–201.

————. 1952. Seasonal distribution of bird populations at the Patuxent Research Refuge. Amer. Midl. Nat. 47:257–363.

Stewart, R. E., and H. A. Kantrud. 1972. Population estimates of breeding birds in North Dakota. Auk 89:766–88.

Stewart, R. E., M. Karplus, and C. S. Robbins. 1947. Breeding bird census: Damp deciduous scrub with numerous standing dead trees. Audubon Field Notes 1:200.

Stewart, R. E., and B. Meanley. 1960. Clutch size of the Clapper Rail. Auk 77:221–22.

Stewart, R. E., and C. S. Robbins. 1947a. Recent observations on Maryland birds. Auk 64:266–74.

————. 1947b. Breeding bird census: Virgin central hardwood deciduous forest. Audubon Field Notes 1:211–12.

————. 1951a. Breeding bird census: Virgin spruce–hemlock bog forest. Audubon Field Notes 5:317–18.

————. 1951b. Breeding bird census: Scrub spruce bog. Audubon Field Notes 5:325.

————. 1951c. Breeding bird census: Lightly grazed meadow. Audubon Field Notes 5:326–27.

————. 1958. Birds of Maryland and the District of Columbia. N. Amer. Fauna 62, Washington, D.C.

Stickel, L. F., N. J. Chura, P. A. Stewart, C. M. Menzie, R. M. Prouty, and W. L. Reichel. 1966. Bald Eagle pesticide relations. Trans. N. Amer. Wildl. Nat. Resour. Conf. 31:190–200.

Stiehl, R. B. 1985. Brood chronology of the Common Raven. Wilson Bull. 97:78–87.

Stiles, E. W. 1978. Vertebrates of New Jersey. Edmund W. Stiles, Somerset, N.J..

Stoddard, H. L. 1931. The bobwhite quail: Its habits, preservation and increase. Scribner, N.Y.

Stokes, A. W. 1950. Breeding behavior of the goldfinch. Wilson Bull. 62:107–27.

————. 1967. Behavior of the Bobwhite, *Colinus virginianus*. Auk 84:1–33.

Stokes, D. W. 1979. A guide to the behavior of common birds. Vol. 1. Little, Brown, Boston, Mass.

Stokes, D. W., and L. Q. Stokes. 1983. A guide to bird behavior. Vol. 2. Little, Brown, Boston, Mass.

————. 1989. A guide to bird behavior. Vol. 3. Little, Brown, Boston, Mass.

Stoll, R. J., M. W. McClain, R. L. Boston, and G. P. Honchul. 1979. Ruffed Grouse drumming site characteristics in Ohio. J. Wildl. Manage. 43:324–33.

Stone, W. 1937. Bird studies at old Cape May, an ornithology of coastal New Jersey. Vol. 2. Delaware Valley Ornith. Club, Philadelphia, P.A.

Storey, A. 1978. Adaptations in Common Terns and Forster's Terns for nesting in the salt marsh. Ph.D. diss. Rutger's Univ., New Brunswick, N.J.

Stotts, V. D., and D. E. Davis. 1960. The Black Duck in the Chesapeake Bay of Maryland: Breeding behavior and biology. Chesapeake Sci. 1:127–54.

Stotts, V. D., and C. J. Henny. 1975. The age at first flight for young American Ospreys. Wilson Bull. 87:277–78.

Strohmeyer, D. L. 1977. Common Gallinule. Pp. 110–17 *in* G. C. Sanderson, ed. Management of migratory shore and upland game birds in North America. Internatl. Assoc. Fish and Wildl. Agencies, Washington, D.C.

Stull, W. DeM. 1968. Eastern and Canadian Chipping Sparrows. Pp. 1166–84 *in* O. L. Austin, Jr., ed. Life histories of North American cardinals, grosbeaks, buntings, towhees, finches, sparrows, and allies. U.S. Natl. Mus. Bull. 237, Washington, D.C.

Sturm, L. 1945. A study of the nesting activities of the American Redstart. Auk 62:189–206.

Summerour, B. 1986. Nesting records for the Sharp-shinned Hawk (*Accipiter striatus*) in Alabama. Alabama Birdlife 33:11–18.

Sutherland, D. W. S., ed. 1978. Common names of insects and related organisms. Entomol. Soc. of Amer., Spec. Publ. 78-1.

Swales, B. H. 1922. Prairie Horned Lark (*Otocoris alpestris praticola*) in Maryland in summer. Auk 39:568–69.

Swank, W. G. 1955. Nesting and production of the Mourning Dove in Texas. Ecology 36:495–505.

Swengel, S. R., and A. B. Swengel. 1987. Study of a Northern Saw-whet Owl population in Sauk County, Wisconsin. Pp. 199–208 *in* R. W. Nero, R. J. Clark, R. J. Knapton, and R. H. Hamre, eds. Biology and conservation of northern forest owls: Symposium proceedings. U.S. Forest Serv., Rocky Mountain Forest Range Exp. Sta., Gen. Tech. Rep. RM-142, Fort Collins, Colo.

Swenk, M. H. 1929. The Pine Siskin in Nebraska. Wilson Bull. 41:77–92.

Szaro, R., and B. Shapiro. 1990. Conserving our heritage: America's biodiversity. U.S. Dept. Agric., Forest Serv., Washington, D.C.

Taber, W., and D. W. Johnston. 1968. Indigo Bunting. Pp. 80–111 *in* O. L. Austin, Jr., ed. Life histories of North American cardinals, grosbeaks, buntings, towhees, finches, sparrows, and allies. U.S. Natl. Mus. Bull. 237, Washington, D.C.

Tanner, J. T. 1958. Juncos in the Great Smoky Mountains. Migrant 29:61–65.

Tate, J., Jr. 1981. The blue list for 1981: The first decade. Amer. Birds 40:227–36.

———. 1986. The blue list for 1986. Amer. Birds 40:227–36.

Taylor, G. J., and S. A. Dawson. 1981. Brown Pelican in Maryland in winter. Maryland Birdlife 37:4–5.

Taylor, W. K. 1972. Analysis of Ovenbirds killed in central Florida. Bird-Banding 43:15–19.

Taylor, W. K., B. H. Anderson, and H. M. Stevenson. 1989. Breeding range expansions of the Indigo Bunting, Painted Bunting, and Blue Grosbeak in Florida, with new records for Seminole County. Florida Field Nat. 17:1–24.

Teixeira, R. M. 1979. Atlas van de Nederlandse Broedvogels. Vereniging tot Behoud van Natuurmonumenten in Nederland, 's-Graveland, The Netherlands.

Terborgh, J. 1989. Where have all the birds gone? Princeton Univ. Press, Princeton, N.J.

Terres, J. K., 1980. The Audubon Society encyclopedia of North American birds. Alfred A. Knopf, N.Y.

Terrill, L. McI. 1961. Cowbird hosts in southern Quebec. Canadian Field-Nat. 75:2–11.

Terrill, S. B., and R. D. Ohmart. 1984. Facultative extension of fall migration by Yellow-rumped Warblers (*Dendroica coronata*). Auk 101:427–38.

Therres, G. D. 1982. Ruffed Grouse populations and relative predator abundance on a grouse management area in central Pennsylvania. M.S. Thesis. Pennsylvania State Univ., University Park.

———. 1986. Maryland's breeding bird atlas project's data processing system. Pp. 169–72 *in* S. M. Sutcliffe, R. E. Bonney, Jr., and J. D. Lowe, comps., Proc. Second Northeastern Breeding Bird Atlas Conference, Cornell Lab. Ornith., Ithaca, N.Y.

———. 1989. Analysis of pheasant population trends, agricultural practices, and land use in Maryland. Maryland Dept. Nat. Resources, Fed. Aid Final Rep., Proj. WEP-100, Annapolis.

———. 1996. Breeding biology of Peregrine Falcons nesting on Maryland's Coastal Plain. Maryland Birdlife 42:47–51.

Therres, G. D., and P. R. Bendel. 1990. Barn Owls are marsh birds too! Maryland Mag. 23:56–57.

Therres, G. D., S. Dawson, and J. C. Barber. 1993. Peregrine Falcon restoration in Maryland. Maryland Dept. of Nat. Resour., Wildl. Tech. Publ. 93-1, Annapolis.

Therres, G. D., J. S. Weske, and M. A. Byrd. 1978. Breeding status of Royal Tern, Gull-billed Tern, and Black Skimmer in Maryland. Maryland Birdlife 34:75–77.

Tiner, R. W., Jr. 1984. Wetlands of the United States: Current status and recent trends. U.S. Fish and Wildl. Serv., Natl. Wetlands Inventory, Washington, D.C.

———. 1988. Field guide to nontidal wetland identification. Maryland Dept. Nat. Resources, Annapolis, and U.S. Fish and Wildl. Serv., Newton Corner, Mass.

Titus, K., and M. R. Fuller. 1990. Recent trends in counts of migrant hawks from northeastern North America. J. Wildl. Manage. 54:463–70.

Titus, K., and J. A. Mosher. 1981. Nest-site habitat selected by woodland hawks in the central Appalachians. Auk 98:270–81.

———. 1987. Selection of nest tree species by Red-shouldered and Broad-winged Hawks in two temperate forest regions. J. Field Ornith. 58:274–83.

Todd, W.E.C. 1940. Birds of western Pennsylvania. Univ. of Pittsburgh Press, Pittsburgh.

Tomkins, I. R. 1944. Wilson's Plover in its summer home. Auk 61:259–69.

———. 1955. The summer schedule of the eastern Willet in Georgia. Auk 67:291–96.

———. 1959. Life history notes on the Least Tern. Wilson Bull. 71:313–22.

———. 1965. The Willets of Georgia and South Carolina. Wilson Bull. 77:151–67.

Townsend, C. W. 1921. Herring Gull. Pp. 102–20 *in* A. C. Bent, ed. Life histories of North American gulls and terns. U.S. Natl. Mus. Bull. 113, Washington, D.C.

———. 1926. Virginia Rail. Pp. 292–301 *in* A. C. Bent, ed. Life histories of North American marsh birds. U.S. Natl. Mus. Bull. 135, Washington, D.C.

———. 1929. Killdeer. Pp. 202–17 *in* A. C. Bent, ed. Life histories of North American shore birds. U.S. Natl. Mus. Bull. 146, Washington, D.C.

———. 1937. Black Vulture. Pp. 28–44 *in* A. C. Bent, ed. Life histories of North American birds of prey. Part 1. U.S. Natl. Mus. Bull. 167, Washington, D.C.

Trautman, C. G. 1982. History, ecology, and management of the Ring-necked Pheasant in South Dakota. South Dakota Dept. Game, Fish, and Parks, Wildl. Res. Bull. 7, Pierre.

Trautman, M. B. 1940. The birds of Buckeye Lake, Ohio. Univ. of Michigan Misc. Publ. Mus. Zool. 44, Univ. of Michigan, Ann Arbor.

Turnbull, W. P. 1869. The birds of eastern Pennsylvania and New Jersey. Philadelphia.

Turner, A., and C. Rose. 1989. Swallows and martins: An identification guide and handbook. Houghton Mifflin, Boston, Mass.

Tyler, W. M. 1929. Piping Plover. Pp. 236–46 *in* A. C. Bent, ed. Life histories of North American shore birds. Part 2. U.S. Natl. Mus. Bull. 146, Washington, D.C.

———. 1932. Eastern Mourning Dove. Pp. 402–16 *in* A. C. Bent, ed. Life histories of North American gallinaceous birds. U.S. Natl. Mus. Bull. 162, Washington, D.C.

———. 1937. Turkey Vulture. Pp. 12–28 *in* A. C. Bent, ed. Life histories of North American birds of prey. Part 1. U.S. Natl. Mus. Bull. 167. Washington, D.C.

———. 1939. Yellow-bellied Sapsucker. Pp. 126–41 *in* A. C. Bent, ed. Life histories of North American woodpeckers. U.S. Natl. Mus. Bull. 174, Washington, D.C.

———. 1940a. Chimney Swift. Pp. 271–93 *in* A. C. Bent, ed. Life histories of North American cuckoos, goatsuckers, hummingbirds, and their allies. U.S. Natl. Mus. Bull. 176, Washington, D.C.

———. 1940b. Ruby-throated Hummingbird. Pp. 332–52 *in* A. C. Bent, ed. Life histories of North American cuckoos, goatsuckers, hummingbirds, and their allies. U.S. Natl. Mus. Bull. 176, Washington, D.C.

———. 1942a. Eastern Kingbird. Pp. 11–29 *in* A. C. Bent, ed. Life histories of North American flycatchers, larks, swallows, and their allies. U.S. Natl. Mus. Bull. 179, Washington, D.C.

———. 1942b. Eastern Phoebe. Pp. 140–54 *in* A. C. Bent, ed. Life histories of North American flycatchers, larks, swallows, and their allies. U.S. Natl. Mus. Bull. 179, Washington, D.C.

———. 1942c. Eastern Wood Pewee. Pp. 266–79 *in* A. C. Bent, ed.

Life histories of North American flycatchers, larks, swallows, and their allies. U.S. Natl. Mus. Bull. 179, Washington, D.C.

———. 1946a. Northern Blue Jay. Pp. 32–52 *in* A. C. Bent, ed. Life histories of North American jays, crows, and titmice. U.S. Natl. Mus. Bull. 191, Washington, D.C.

———. 1946b. Black-capped Chickadee. Pp. 322–38 *in* A. C. Bent, ed. Life histories of North American jays, crows, and titmice. U.S. Natl. Mus. Bull. 191, Washington, D.C.

———. 1948a. White-breasted Nuthatch. Pp. 1–12 *in* A. C. Bent, ed. 1948. Life histories of North American nuthatches, wrens, thrashers, and their allies. U.S. Natl. Mus. Bull. 195, Washington, D.C.

———. 1948b. Red-breasted Nuthatch. Pp. 22–35 *in* A. C. Bent, ed. 1948. Life histories of North American nuthatches, wrens, thrashers, and their allies. U.S. Natl. Mus. Bull. 195, Washington, D.C.

———. 1948c. Brown Creeper. Pp. 56–70 *in* A. C. Bent, ed. 1948. Life histories of North American nuthatches, wrens, thrashers, and their allies. U.S. Natl. Mus. Bull. 195, Washington, D.C.

———. 1949a. Eastern Robin. Pp. 14–45 *in* A. C. Bent, ed. Life histories of North American thrushes, kinglets, and their allies. U.S. Natl. Mus. Bull. 196, Washington, D.C.

———. 1949b. Veery. Pp. 217–31 *in* A. C. Bent, ed. Life histories of North American thrushes, kinglets, and their allies. U.S. Natl. Mus. Bull. 196, Washington, D.C.

———. 1950a. Cedar Waxwing. Pp. 79–102 *in* A. C. Bent, ed. Life histories of North American wagtails, shrikes, vireos, and their allies. U.S. Natl. Mus. Bull. 197, Washington, D.C.

———. 1950b. Red-eyed Vireo. Pp. 335–48 *in* A. C. Bent, ed. Life histories of North American wagtails, shrikes, vireos, and their allies. U.S. Natl. Mus. Bull. 197, Washington, D.C.

———. 1950c. Eastern Warbling Vireo. Pp. 362–73 *in* A. C. Bent, ed. Life histories of North American wagtails, shrikes, vireos, and their allies. U.S. Natl. Mus. Bull. 197, Washington, D.C.

———. 1953. Golden-winged Warbler. Pp. 47–57 *in* A. C. Bent, ed. Life histories of North American wood warblers. U.S. Natl. Mus. Bull. 203, Washington, D.C.

———. 1958a. Baltimore Oriole. Pp. 247–70 *in* A. C. Bent, ed. Life histories of North American blackbirds, orioles, tanagers, and allies. U.S. Natl. Mus. Bull. 211, Washington, D.C.

———. 1958b. Scarlet Tanager. Pp. 479–91 *in* A. C. Bent, ed. Life histories of North American blackbirds, orioles, tanagers, and allies. U.S. Natl. Mus. Bull. 211, Washington, D.C.

Tyrrell, W. B. 1936. The Ospreys of Smith's Point, Virginia. Auk 53:261–68.

Ulke, T. 1935. Rare birds in the District of Columbia. Auk 52:461.

U.S. Fish and Wildlife Service. 1982. The Chesapeake Bay region Bald Eagle recovery plan. U.S. Fish and Wildl. Serv., Boston.

———. 1987. Migratory nongame birds of management concern in the United States: The 1987 list. U.S. Fish and Wildl. Serv., Washington, D.C.

Urban, E. K., C. H. Fry, and S. Keith. 1986. The birds of Africa, Vol. 2. Academic Press, London.

Valentine, J. M., Jr. 1958. Cattle Egrets nesting in Maryland. Maryland Birdlife 14:49.

Van Camp, L. F., and C. J. Henny. 1975. The Screech Owl: Its life history and population ecology in northern Ohio. N. Amer. Fauna 71, Washington, D.C.

Van Velzen, W. T. 1966. Maryland nest summary for 1965 and 10-year recapitulation. Maryland Birdlife 22:71–76.

———. 1967. First observed Brown Creeper nest in Maryland. Maryland Birdlife 23:68–69.

———. 1968. Nest records of the Brown Thrasher in Maryland. Maryland Birdlife 24:3–9.

Vaughn, C. 1978. Somerset County breeding bird atlas. Maryland Birdlife 34:40–43.

Veit, R. R., and W. R. Petersen. 1993. Birds of Massachusetts. Massachusetts Audubon Soc., Lincoln.

Verbeek, N.A.M. 1967. Breeding biology and ecology of the Horned Lark in alpine tundra. Wilson Bull. 79:208–18.

Verner, J. 1962. Song rates and polygamy in the Long-billed Marsh Wren. Proc. Internatl. Ornith. Congr. 13:299–307.

———. 1965. Breeding biology of the Long-billed Marsh Wren. Condor 67:6–30.

Walbeck, D. E. 1988. Solitary nesting by Great Blue Herons in Maryland. Maryland Birdlife 44:119–21.

———. 1989. Observations of roof-nesting Killdeer and Common Nighthawks in Frostburg, Maryland. Maryland Birdlife 45:3–9.

Walkinshaw, L. H. 1938. Life history studies of the Eastern Goldfinch. Part 1. Jack-Pine Warbler 16:3–11, 14–15.

———. 1939a. Life history studies of the Eastern Goldfinch. Part 2. Jack-Pine Warbler 17:3–12.

———. 1939b. Nesting of the Field Sparrow and survival of the young. Bird-Banding 10:107–14, 149–57.

———. 1944. The eastern Chipping Sparrow in Michigan. Wilson Bull. 56:193–205.

———. 1957. Incubation period of the Sora Rail. Auk 74:496.

———. 1968. Eastern Field Sparrow. Pp. 1217–35 *in* O. L. Austin, Jr., ed. Life histories of North American cardinals, grosbeaks, buntings, towhees, finches, sparrows, and allies. U.S. Natl. Mus. Bull. 237, Washington, D. C.

Walton, R. K., and R. W. Lawson. 1989. Birding by ear: A guide to bird-song identification. Houghton Mifflin, Boston, Mass.

Warbach, O. 1958. Bird populations in relation to changes in land use. J. Wildl. Manage. 22:23–28.

Warren, B. H. 1890. Report on the birds of Pennsylvania, with special reference to the food-habits, based on over four thousand stomach examinations. Commonwealth of Pennsylvania, Harrisburg.

Watts, B. D. 1988. Foraging implications of food usage patterns in Yellow-crowned Night-Herons. Condor 90:860–65.

Wayne, A. T. 1910. Birds of South Carolina. Contributions Charleston Mus. 1, Charleston, S.C.

Weatherhead, P. J., and R. J. Robertson. 1978. Intraspecific nest parasitism in the Savannah Sparrow. Auk 95:744–45.

Weaver, F. G. 1949. Wood Thrush. Pp. 101–23 *in* A. C. Bent, ed. Life histories of North American thrushes, kinglets, and their allies. U.S. Natl. Mus. Bull. 196, Washington, D.C.

Weaver, R. L., and F. H. West. 1943. Notes on the breeding of the Pine Siskin. Auk 60:492–504.

Weber, W. J. 1975. Notes on Cattle Egret breeding. Auk 92:111–17.

Webster, H. L. 1951. Summary of Maryland nest records, 1950. Maryland Birdlife 7:8–16.

Weeks, H. P., Jr. 1978. Clutch size variation in the Eastern Phoebe in southern Indiana. Auk 95:656–66.

Weller, M. W. 1961. Breeding biology of the Least Bittern. Wilson Bull. 73:11–35.

Werschkul, D. F. 1979. Nestling mortality and the adaptive significance of early locomotion in the Little Blue Heron. Auk 96:116–30.

Weske, J. S. 1969. An ecological study of the Black Rail in Dorchester County, Maryland. M.S. thesis, Cornell Univ., Ithaca, N.Y.

Weske, J. S., R. B. Clapp, and J. M. Sheppard. 1977. Breeding records of Sandwich and Caspian Terns in Virginia and Maryland. Raven 48:59–65.

Weske, J. S., and H. Fessenden. 1963. Glossy Ibis nesting in tidewater Maryland away from the ocean. Bird–Banding 34:161.

Westmoreland, D., and L. B. Best. 1987. What limits Mourning Doves to a clutch of two eggs? Condor 89:486–93.

Westmoreland, D., L. B. Best, and D. E. Blockstein. 1986. Multiple brooding as a reproductive strategy: Time-conserving adaptations in Mourning Doves. Auk 103:196–203.

Westneat, D. F. 1988. Male parental care and extrapair copulations in the Indigo Bunting. Auk 105:149–60.

Weston, F. M. 1949. Blue-gray Gnatcatcher. Pp. 344–64 in A. C. Bent, ed. Life histories of North American thrushes, kinglets, and their allies. U.S. Natl. Mus. Bull. 196, Washington, D.C.

Weston, F. M., L. H. Walkinshaw, and L. Griscom. 1957. Pine Warbler. Pp. 174–77 in L. Griscom and A. Sprunt, Jr, eds. The warblers of America. Devin-Adair, N.Y.

Wetherbee, D. K. 1968. Southern Swamp Sparrow. Pp. 1475–90 in O. L. Austin, Jr., ed. Life histories of North American cardinals, grosbeaks, buntings, towhees, finches, sparrows, and allies. U.S. Natl. Mus. Bull. 237, Washington, D.C.

Wetmore, A. 1924. Food and economic relations of North American grebes. U.S. Dept. Agric. Bull. 1196.

———. 1925. Food of American phalaropes, avocets, and stilts. U.S. Dept. Agric. Bull. 1359, Washington, D.C.

———. 1935. The Short-billed Marsh Wren breeding in Maryland. Auk 52:455.

———. 1936. The Chuck-will's-widow in Maryland. Auk 53:333.

———. 1964. Song and garden birds of North America. Natl. Geog. Soc., Washington, D.C.

Wetmore, A., and F. C. Lincoln. 1928. The Dickcissel in Maryland. Auk 45:508–09.

Wetmore, A., and R. H. Manville. 1968. Natural history of Plummers Island: XX. Birds. Wash. Biol. Field Club Spec. Publ.

Whitcomb, B., D. Bystrak, and R. Whitcomb. 1977. Breeding bird census: Selectively logged mature tulip-tree oak forest. Amer. Birds 31:92–93.

Whitcomb, R. F. 1975. Breeding bird census: Upland mixed forest with small creek. Amer. Birds 29:1089–91.

Whitcomb, R. F., C. S. Robbins, J. F. Lynch, B. L. Whitcomb, M. K. Klimkiewicz, and D. Bystrak. 1981. Effects of forest fragmentation on avifauna of the eastern deciduous forest. Pp. 125–206 in R. L. Burgess and D. M. Sharpe, eds., Forest island dynamics in man-dominated landscapes. Ecol. Studies 41, Springer-Verlag, N.Y.

Whitmore, R. C. 1979. Short-term change in vegetation structure and its effect on Grasshopper Sparrows in West Virginia. Auk 96:621–25.

Whitmore, R. C., and G. A. Hall. 1978. The response of passerine species to a new resource: Reclaimed surface mines in West Virginia. Amer. Birds 32:6–9.

Wiemeyer, S. N., P. R. Spitzer, W. C. Krantz, T. G. Lamont, and E. Cromartie. 1975. Effects of environmental pollutants on Connecticut and Maryland Ospreys. J. Wildl. Manage. 39:124–39.

Wiemeyer, S. N., P. R. Spitzer, and P. D. McLain. 1978. Organochlorine residues in New Jersey Osprey eggs. Bull. Environ. Contam. Toxicol. 19:56–63.

Wiens, J. A. 1969. An approach to the study of ecological relationships among grassland birds. Ornith. Monogr. 8.

———. 1973. Interterritorial habitat variation in Grasshopper and Savannah Sparrows. Ecology 54:877–84.

Wilcove, D. S. 1985. Nest predation in forest tracts and the decline of migratory songbirds. Ecology 66:1211–14.

Williams, B. 1989. The first breeding record of the Brown Pelican in Virginia: A chronology. Raven 60:1–3.

Williams, L. E., Jr. 1981. The book of the Wild Turkey. Winchester Press, Tulsa, Okla.

Williams, T. J. C. 1906. A history of Washington County, Maryland, from the earliest settlements to the present time. Runk and Titsworth Publ.

Willoughby, E. J., and T. J. Cade. 1964. Breeding behavior of the American Kestrel (Sparrow Hawk). Living Bird 3:75–96.

Wilmore, S. B. 1974. Swans of the world. Taplinger, N.Y.

Wilson, A. 1810. American ornithology. Vol. 2. Bradford and Inskeep, Philadelphia, Pa.

Wimsatt, W. A. 1939. Black Vulture and Duck Hawk nesting in Maryland. Auk 56:181–82.

———. 1940. Early nesting of the Duck Hawk in Maryland. Auk 57:109.

Witmer, E. 1988. Lancaster County. Pennsylvania Birds 2:107.

Wittenberger, J. F. 1980. Feeding of secondary nestlings by polygynous male Bobolinks in Oregon. Wilson Bull. 92:330–40.

Woods, R. S. 1968. House Finch. Pp. 290–314 in O. L. Austin, Jr., ed. Life Histories of North American cardinals, grosbeaks, buntings, towhees, finches, sparrows, and allies. U.S. Natl. Mus. Bull. 237, Washington, D.C.

Woolfenden, G. E. 1956. Comparative breeding behavior of Ammospiza caudacuta and A. maritima. Univ. of Kansas, Mus. Nat. Hist. Publ. 10:45–76.

———. 1968. Northern Seaside Sparrow. Pp. 819–31 in O. L. Austin, Jr., ed. Life histories of North American cardinals, grosbeaks, buntings, towhees, finches, sparrows, and allies. U.S. Natl. Mus. Bull. 237, Washington, D.C.

Wootten, J. T. 1986. Clutch-size differences in western and introduced eastern populations of House Finches: Patterns and hypotheses. Wilson Bull. 98:459–62.

Wray, T., II, K. A. Straight, and R. C. Whitmore. 1982. Reproductive success of grassland sparrows on a reclaimed surface mine in West Virginia. Auk 99:157–64.

Wray, T., II, and R. C. Whitmore. 1979. Effects of vegetation on nesting success of Vesper Sparrows. Auk 96:802–05.

Wright, A. H. 1912. Early records of the Carolina paroquet. Auk 29:343–63.

Yeatman, L. 1976. Atlas des oiseaux nicheurs de France. Soc. Ornithologique de France, Paris.

Zach, R., and F. B. Falls. 1975. Response of the Ovenbird to an outbreak of the spruce budworm. Canadian J. Zool. 53:1669–72.

Zeleny, L. 1976. The bluebird. Indiana Univ. Press, Bloomington.

Zeranski, J. D., and T. R. Baptist. 1990. Connecticut birds. Univ. Press of New England, Hanover, N.H.

Zicus, M. C. 1990. Nesting biology of Hooded Mergansers using nest boxes. J. Wildl. Manage. 54:637–43.

Zimmerman, J. L. 1966. Polygyny in the Dickcissel. Auk 83:534–46.

———. 1971. The territory and its density dependent effect in Spiza americana. Auk 88:591–612.

———. 1982. Nesting success of Dickcissels in preferred and less preferred habitats. Auk 99:292–98.

———. 1988. Breeding season habitat selection by the Henslow's Sparrow (Ammodramus henslowii) in Kansas. Wilson Bull. 100:17–24.

Author and Species Index

PENNS

79°   78°

ALLEGANY   WASHINGTON

GARRETT

FREDERIC

WEST VIRGINIA

MON

VIRGINIA

DISTRICT O
COLUMBIA